Commentary on
ROMANS

Commentary on
ROMANS

by
ROBERT HALDANE

Foreword by
D. Martyn Lloyd-Jones

kregel
PUBLICATIONS

Grand Rapids, MI 49501

Commentary on Romans by Robert Haldane

Foreword by D. Martyn Lloyd-Jones

Published in 1996 by Kregel Publications, a division of Kregel, Inc., P. O. Box 2607, Grand Rapids, MI 49501. Kregel Publications provides trusted, biblical publications for Christian growth and service. Your comments and suggestions are valued.

The publisher gratefully acknowledges the permission of The Banner of Truth to include the Foreword by D. Martyn Lloyd-Jones.

Cover design: Alan G. Hartman

Library of Congress Cataloging-in-Publication Data
Haldane, Robert, 1764–1842.
  [Exposition of the Epistle to the Romans]
  Commentary on Romans / Robert Haldane. Foreword by D. Martyn Lloyd Jones.
     p. cm.
  Reprint. Originally published: Exposition of the Epistle to the Romans. New York: R. Carter & Brothers, 1853.
  1. Bible. N.T. Romans—Commentaries. I. Title.
BS2665.H13   1988   227'.107—dc19   88-18715
                                           CIP

ISBN 0-8254-2865-3 (pbk.)

2 3 4 5 6 Printing / Year 00 99 98 97 96

Printed in the United States of America

CONTENTS

FOREWORD

IT IS WITH PARTICULAR PLEASURE that I recommend this commentary on the Epistle to the Romans. I do so for many reasons.

First and foremost is the fact that I have derived such profit and pleasure from it myself. I always find it very difficult to decide as to which is the better commentary on this Epistle, whether that of Charles Hodge or this by Haldane. While Hodge excels in accurate scholarship, there is greater warmth of spirit and more practical application in Haldane. In any case, both stand supreme as commentaries on this mighty Epistle.

However, that which gives an unusual and particularly endearing value to this commentary is the history that lies behind it. In 1816, Robert Haldane, being about 50 years of age, went to Switzerland and to Geneva. There, to all outward appearances as if by accident, he came into contact with a number of students who were studying for the ministry. They were all blind to spiritual truth but felt much attracted to Haldane and to what he said. He arranged, therefore, that they should come regularly twice a week to the rooms where he was staying and there he took them through and expounded to them Paul's Epistle to the Romans. One by one they were converted, and their conversion led to a true revival of religion, not only in Switzerland, but also in France. They included such men as Merle D'Aubigne, the writer of the classic *History of the Reformation*; Frédric Monod, who became the chief founder of the Free Churches in France; Bonifas, who became a theologian of great ability; Louis Gaussen, the author of *Theopneustia*,* a book on the inspiration of the Scriptures; and César Malan. There were also others who were greatly used of God in the revival. It was at the request of such men that Robert Haldane decided to put into print what he had been telling them. Hence this volume. And one cannot read it without being conscious of the preacher as well as the expositor.

What a distinguished French minister such as Dr. Reuben Saillens says of what became known as "Haldane's Revival" can be applied with equal truth to this commentary: "The three main characteristics of Haldane's Revival, as it has sometimes been called, were these: (1) it gave a prominent emphasis to the necessity of a personal knowledge and experience of grace; (2) it maintained the absolute authority and divine inspiration of the Bible; and (3) it was a return to Calvinistic doctrine against Pelagianism

---

* Published by Kregel Publications as *Divine Inspiration of the Bible.*

and Arminianism. Haldane was an orthodox of the first water, but his orthodoxy was blended with love and life."

God grant that it may produce that same "love and life" in all who read it.

D. MARTYN LLOYD–JONES*

---

* Used by permission from the edition published previously by The Banner of Truth.

PREFACE

ALL SCRIPTURE is given by inspiration of God. Every page of the sacred volume is stamped with the impress of deity, and contains an inexhaustible treasure of wisdom, knowledge, and consolation. Some portions of the Word of God, like some parts of the material creation, may be more important than others. But all have their proper place, all proclaim the character of their glorious Author, and all ought to be earnestly and reverentially studied. Whatever be their subject, whether it relates to the history of individuals or of nations, whether it contains the words of precept or exhortation, or whether it teaches by example, all is profitable for doctrine, for reproof, for correction, for instruction in righteousness. But while every part of the Word of God demands the most serious attention, it is not to be doubted that certain portions of the sacred volume call for more frequent and deeper meditation. In the Old Testament, the Book of Psalms contains a summary of all Scripture, and an abridgment of its most important instructions and sweetest consolations. In the New Testament, the Epistle to the Romans is entitled in peculiar regard. It is the only part of Scripture which contains a detailed and systematic exhibition of the doctrines of Christianity. The great truths which are embodied and inculcated in every other part of the Bible, are here brought together in a condensed and comprehensive form. More especially, the glorious doctrine of justification by faith is clearly unfolded and exhibited in the strongest light.

The Epistle to the Romans has always attracted the peculiar notice of those whose study has been directed to the interpretation of Scripture. To this portion of the divine record, all who look for salvation by grace have constantly appealed, and here they have a rich mine of evidence alike solid and inexhaustible. No considerable difference of interpretation has ever been given of its contents by those who have renounced their own wisdom, and determined to follow implicitly the obvious meaning of the Word of God. This Epistle has been equally an object of attention to those who admit the authority of Scripture, but follow their own wisdom in forming their system of religious doctrine. Salvation by grace and salvation by works are so incompatible with each other, that it might well be supposed no attempt would ever be made to bring them into harmony. Still the attempt has been made. Human wisdom cannot receive the doctrine of the Epistle to the Romans, and men professing Christianity cannot deny it to be a part of Scripture. What, then, is to be done? A compromise is proclaimed between the wisdom of man and the revelation of God. All the ingenuity of Mr. Locke, one of the most acute and subtle metaphysicians that ever appeared, has been exerted to bring the doctrine of Paul into accordance with human science. Like him, many others have labored to give a view of the Epistle that may reconcile human merit with divine grace.

Nothing is more manifest than the direct opposition between the doctrine of inspiration, as unfolded in the Epistle to the Romans with respect to the state and prospects of mankind, and the doctrine of this world's philosophy. Paul contemplates all men in their natural state as ruined by sin, and utterly unable to restore themselves to the divine favor. Philosophers, on the contrary, survey the aspect of society with real or affected complacency. They perceive, indeed, that imperfection and suffering prevail to a considerable extent; but they discover a vast preponderance of happiness and virtue. They cannot deny that man is of a mixed character; but this is necessary in order that his virtue may be his own, and that in passing onwards to the summit of moral excellence, his strength of principle may be more illustriously displayed, and his happiness promoted by his progress in virtue, as well as by his advancement in knowledge. Nor is this remarkable difference altogether confined to philosophy. Even many professors and expounders of Christianity cannot entirely agree with the Apostle Paul in his representations of human nature. Man, it seems to them, is not so completely lost, but that he may do something to regain the divine favor; and if a sacrifice were necessary for the expiation of sin, its blessing must be equally bestowed on all mankind.

The doctrine of justification in particular so far transcends the powers of our discovery, that men are ever attempting to set it aside, or to mold it into accordance with their own preconceived notions. How wonderful is the contrast between the justification of which this Apostle treats, and the justification which critical ingenuity has often extorted from his epistles! While Paul speaks of the believer as possessing a righteousness perfectly commensurate to all the demands of the law, and standing at the bar of God spotless and blameless, human wisdom has contrived to exhibit his doctrine as representing salvation to be the result of a happy combination of mercy and merit.

The doctrine of salvation by faith without works has ever appeared to the wise of this world not only as a scheme insufficient to secure the interests of morality, but as one which disparages the divine authority. Yet its good effects are fully demonstrated in every age, and while nothing but the doctrine of salvation by grace has ever produced good works, this doctrine has never failed of its designed object. In all the ways of God there is a characteristic wisdom, which stamps them with the impress of divinity. There is here a harmony and consistency in things which are most different in appearance; while the intended result is invariably produced, although in a way which to man would appear most unlikely to secure success.

The mind of every man is by nature disaffected to the doctrine of this Epistle, but it is only in proportion to the audacity of his unbelief, that any one will directly avow his opposition. While some by the wildest suppositions will boldly set aside whatever it declares that opposes their own preconceived opinions, others will receive its statements only with the reserve of certain necessary modifications. Thus, in the deviations from truth, in the exposition of its doctrines, we discover various shades of the same unhallowed disregard for the divine testimony.

The spirit of speculation and of novelty which is now abroad, loudly calls upon Christians to give earnest heed to the truth inculcated in the Epistle to the Romans. There is hardly any doctrine which has not been of late years exposed to the corruptions and perversions of men who profess to be believers of divine revelation. Many, altogether destitute of the Spirit of God and the semblance of true religion, have nevertheless chosen the Word of God, and its solemn and awfully momentous truths, as the arena upon which to exercise their learning and display their ingenuity. In consequence of the Scriptures being written in the dead languages, there is doubtless scope for the diligent employment of critical research. But if it were inquired how much additional light has been thrown upon the sacred volume by the refinements of modern critics, it would be found to bear a very small proportion to the evil influence of unsanctified learning applied to the holy doctrines of revelation. It has become common, even among Christians, to speak of the critical interpretation of Scripture as requiring little or nothing more than mere scholarship, and many seem to suppose that the office of a critical and that of a doctrinal interpreter are so widely different that a man may be a safe and useful critic who has no relish for the grand truths of the Bible. There cannot be a more lamentable delusion or one more calculated to desecrate the character and obscure the majesty of the Word of God. To suppose that a man may rightly interpret the Scriptures, while he is ignorant of the truths of the gospel, or disaffected to some of its grand fundamental doctrines,—to imagine that this can be to him a useful or even an innocent occupation, is to regard these Scriptures as the production of ordinary men, treating of subjects of ordinary importance, instead of containing, as they do, the message of the Most High God, revealing life or death to every soul to whom they come.

If the Scriptures have not testified in vain that the carnal mind is enmity against God; if we are bound to believe that there is no middle state between the Christian and the unbeliever; can we wonder at the manner in which they have been perverted not only by the ignorance but by the inveterate prejudices of men from whom the gospel is hid? Is it reasonable—is it agreeable to the dictates of common sense, to believe that the critical interpretations of such men are not tinged with their own darkened and hostile views of the divine character and the divine revelation? And yet such is the opinion entertained of the labors of some of the most unenlightened commentators, that their works have obtained a celebrity altogether unaccountable on any principle of Christian wisdom.

Christians ought to be particularly on their guard against tampering in any degree with the Word of God. We should never forget, that when we are explaining any expression of Scripture, we are treating of what are the very words of the Holy Ghost, as much as if they had been spoken to us by a voice from heaven. The profane rashness of many critics is much emboldened by the circumstance that men have been employed as the instruments of the Almighty in communicating His revelation. A sort of modified inspiration only is granted to the Scriptures, and they are often treated as the words merely of those who were employed as the penmen. When God is thus kept out of sight, little ceremony is used with the words of the apostles. The profound reverence and awe with which the Scriptures ought to be read and handled, are in many instances too little exemplified. The poor man's Bible is the Word of God, in which he has no suspicion that there is anything but perfection. The Bible of the profoundly erudite scholar is often a book that is not so necessary to instruct him, as one that needs his hand for alteration, or amendment, or confirmation. Learning may be usefully employed, but if learning ever forgets that it must sit at the feet of Jesus, it will be a curse instead of a blessing. It will raise clouds and darkness, instead of communicating light to the world.

The evil of studying the Scriptures, and commenting upon them with as little reverence as a scholar might comment upon the plays of Aristophanes to Terence, has extended itself much farther than might be supposed. This is the spirit in which the German Neologians have written, and indeed it is to be feared that, as the Neologian form of infidelity originated from this profane method of criticizing the Scriptures, so the same cause may produce the same effect in this country. Certain it is that works have been republished or translated here, which are very little calculated to uphold the ancient faith of the church of Christ, or to advance the knowledge of the truth as it is in Jesus.

From present appearances, there is every reason to fear that Britain will be inundated with German Neology. The tide has strongly set in, and unless the Christian public be upon their guard, the whole country will be brought under its influence. It is a solemn thing to be instrumental in ushering into more extended notoriety, publications that have a tendency to lower the character of the Holy Scriptures, to introduce doubt and confusion into the minds of those who are weak in the faith and to embolden others who seek an apology for casting away the fetters of education and authority, and desire to launch out into the ocean of wild and dangerous speculation. While some appearances in Germany of a return to the Scripture doctrine of salvation by Jesus Christ should be gladly hailed by every Christian, yet it must be admitted that those who in that country seem to have made the greatest advances in the knowledge of the gospel, are still far from being entitled to be pointed out as guides to the Christians of Great Britain. Their modifications of divine truth are manifestly under the influence of a criticism too nearly allied to Neology. There is great danger, that in the admiration of German criticism a tincture may be received from continental errors. It would be far preferable if learned Christians at home would pursue truth in a diligent examination of its own sources, rather than spend their time in retailing the criticisms of German scholars. "Their criticisms," it is observed by Dr. Carson, "are arbitrary, forced, and in the highest degree fantastical. Their learning is boundless, yet their criticism is mere trash. The vast extent of their literary acquirements has overawed British theologians, and given an importance to arguments that are self-evidently false."

In these days of boasted liberality, it may appear captious to oppose with zeal the errors of men who have acquired a name in the Christian world. The mantle of charity, it will be said, ought to be thrown over mistakes that have resulted from a free and impartial investigation of truth, and if not wholly overlooked, they should be noticed with a slight expression of disapprobation. Such, however, was not the conduct of the Apostle Paul. He spared neither churches nor individuals when the doctrines they maintained tended to the subversion of the gospel, and the zeal with which he resisted their errors was not inferior to that with which he encountered the open enemies of Christianity. He affirms that the doctrine introduced into the Galatian churches is another gospel, and twice pronounces a curse against all by whom it was promulgated. Instead of complimenting the authors of this corruption of the gospel as only abusing, in a slight degree, the liberty of free examination, he decides that they should be cut off as troublers of the churches. Let not Christians be more courteous in expressing their views of the guilt and danger of corrupting the gospel, than faithful and compassionate to the people of Christ, who may be injured by false doctrine. It is highly sinful to bandy compliments at the expense of truth.

The awful responsibility of being accessory to the propagation of error is strongly expressed by the Apostle John. "If there come any unto you, and bring not this doctrine, receive him not into your house, neither bid him God speed; for he that biddeth him Godspeed is partaker of his evil deeds." If the imputation of Adam's sin and of Christ's righteousness be doctrines contained in the Word of God, commentaries that labor to expel them from that Word must be grossly pestiferous books which no Christian ought to recommend, but which, on the contrary, to the utmost of his power, it is his duty to oppose.

A very dangerous misrepresentation of some of the great doctrines of the Epistle to the Romans has lately come before the public, in a commentary on that Epistle, from the pen of professor Moses Stuart of America. As that work has obtained an extensive circulation in this country,—as it has been strongly recommended, and is likely to produce a considerable effect,—it has appeared proper to make frequent references to his glaring perversions of its important contents. On the same principle, various remarks are introduced on the well-known heterodox commentary of Dr. Macknight; I have also alluded occasionally to the heretical sentiments contained in that of Professor Tholuck.

In the following exposition, I have availed myself of all the assistance I could obtain, from whatever quarter. Especially, I have made use of everything that appeared to be most valuable in the commentary of Claude, which terminates at the beginning of the twenty-first verse of the third chapter. I have also had the advantage of the assistance of Dr. Carson, whose profound knowledge of the original language and well-known critical discernment peculiarly qualify him for rendering effectual aid in such a work. As it is my object to make this exposition as useful as possible to all descriptions of readers, I have not always confined myself simply to an explanation of the text, but have occasionally extended at some length, remarks on such subjects as seemed to demand particular attention, either on account of their own importance, or of mistaken opinions entertained concerning them. As to those which required a fuller discussion than could be conveniently introduced, I have referred to my work on the *Evidence and Authority of Divine Revelation.**

By studying the Epistle to the Romans, an exact and comprehensive knowledge of the distinguishing doctrines of grace, in their various bearings and connections, may, by the blessing of God, be obtained. Here

---

* Published by Kregel Publications as *The Authenticity and Inspiration of the Holy Scriptures.*

they appear in all their native force and clearness, unalloyed with the wisdom of man. The human mind is ever prone to soften the strong features of divine truth, and to bring them more into accordance with its own wishes and preconceived notions. Those lowering and debasing modifications of the doctrines of Scripture, by which, in some popular works, it is endeavored to reconcile error with orthodoxy, are imposing only in theory, and may be easily detected by a close and unprejudiced examination of the language of this Epistle.

INTRODUCTION

THE EPISTLE TO THE ROMANS was written by the Apostle Paul from Corinth, the capital of Achaia, after his second journey to that celebrated city for the purpose of collecting the pecuniary aid destined for the church at Jerusalem. This appears from the fifteenth chapter, where he says that he was going to Jerusalem to minister to the saints. "For," he adds, "it hath pleased them of Macedonia and Achaia, to make a certain contribution for the poor saints which are at Jerusalem." The Epistle appears to have been carried to Rome by Phebe, a deaconess of the church at Cenchrea, which was the port of Corinth, and we learn from the nineteenth and twentieth chapters of the Acts, and from different parts of the two Epistles to the Corinthians, that after having remained about three years at Ephesus, Paul purposed to pass through Macedonia and Achaia, to receive the contributions of the Corinthians, and afterwards proceed to Jerusalem.

As to the period when this Epistle was written, it is certain that it was at a time previous to Paul's arrival at Rome. On this account he begins by declaring to the disciples there, that he had a great desire to see them, and to preach to them the gospel, that he had often purposed this, but had hitherto always been prevented. This statement he repeats in the fifteenth chapter. It appears to be earlier in date than the Epistles to the Ephesians and Philippians, and those to the Hebrews and Philemon, and the second to Timothy, for all of these were written during the Apostle's first or second imprisonment at Rome, but later than the two Epistles to the Corinthians. It is generally supposed that it was written in the year 57 of the Christian era, about 24 years after the resurrection of our Lord.

Notwithstanding that this Epistle was written after some of the rest, it has been placed first in order among them on account of its excellence, and the abundance and sublimity of its contents. It contains, indeed, an abridgment of all that is taught in the Christian religion. It treats of the revelation of God in the works of nature, and in the heart of man, and exhibits the necessity and the strictness of the last judgment. It teaches the doctrine of the fall and corruption of the whole human race, of which it discovers the source and its greatness. It points out the true and right use of the law, and why God gave it to the Israelites, and also shows the vanity of the temporal advantages over other men which that law conferred on them, and which they so criminally abused. It treats of the mission of our Lord Jesus Christ, of justification, of sanctification, of free will, and of grace, of salvation and of condemnation, of election and of reprobation, of the perseverance and assurance of the salvation of believers in the midst of their severest temptations, of the necessity of afflictions, and of the admirable consolations which God gives His people under them, of the calling of the Gentiles, of the rejection of the Jews, and of their final restoration to the communion of God. Paul afterwards lays down the principal rules of Christian morality, containing all that we owe to God, to ourselves, to our neighbors, and to our brethren in Christ, and declares the manner in which we should act in our particular employments; uniformly accompanying His precepts with just and reasonable motives to enforce their practice. The form, too, of this Epistle, is not less admirable than its matter. Its reasoning is powerful and conclusive; the style condensed, lively, and energetic; the arrangement orderly and clear, strikingly exhibiting the leading doctrines as the main branches from which depend all the graces and virtues of the Christian life. The whole is pervaded by a strain of the most exalted piety, true holiness, ardent zeal, and fervent charity.

This Epistle, like the greater part of those written by Paul, is divided into two general parts: the first of which contains the doctrine, and extends to the beginning of the twelfth chapter; and the second, which relates to practice, goes on to the conclusion. The first is to instruct the spirit, and the other to direct the heart; the one teaches what we are to believe, the other what we are to practice. In the first part, he discusses chiefly the two great questions which at the beginning of the gospel were agitated between the Jews and the Christians, namely, that of justification before God, and that of the calling of the Gentiles. For as on the one hand the gospel held forth a method of justification very different from that of the law, the Jews could not relish a doctrine which appeared to them novel, and was contrary to their prejudices; and as, on the other hand, they found themselves in possession of the covenant of God, to the exclusion of other nations, they could not endure that the Apostles should call the Gentiles to the knowledge of the true God, and to the hope of his salvation, nor that it should be supposed that the Jews had lost their exclusive preeminence over the nations. The principal object, then, of the Apostle, was to combat these two prejudices. He directs his attention to the former in the first nine chapters, and treats of the other in the tenth and eleventh. As to what regards the second portion of the Epistle, Paul first enjoins general precepts for the conduct of believers, afterwards in regard to civil life, and finally with regard to church communion.

In the first five chapters, the great doctrine of justification by faith, of which they exclusively treat, is more fully discussed than in any other part of Scripture. The design of the Apostle is to establish two things: the one, that there being only two ways of justification before God, namely, that of works, which the law proposes, and that of grace by Jesus Christ, which the gospel reveals. The first is entirely shut against men, and in order to their being saved, there remains only the last. The other thing that he designs to establish, is that justification by grace through faith in Jesus Christ respects indifferently all men, both Jews and Gentiles, and that it abolishes the distinction which the law had made between them. To arrive at this he first proves that the Gentiles as well as the Jews are subject to the judgment of God, but that being all sinners and guilty, neither the one nor the other can escape condemnation by their works. He humbles them both. He sets before the Gentiles the blind ignorance and unrighteousness both of themselves and of their philosophers of whom they boasted, and he teaches humility to the Jews by showing that they were chargeable with similar vices. He undermines in both the pride of self merit, and teaches all to build their hopes on Jesus Christ alone, proving that their salvation can neither emanate from their philosophy nor from their law, but from the grace of Christ Jesus.

In the first chapter, the Apostle commences by directing our attention to the person of the Son of God in His incarnation in time, and His divine nature from eternity, as the great subject of that gospel which he was commissioned to proclaim. After a most striking introduction, every way calculated to arrest the attention, and conciliate the affection of those whom he addressed, he briefly announces the grand truth which he intends afterwards to establish, that, "the gospel is the power of God unto salvation to every one that believeth," because in it is revealed "THE RIGHTEOUS-NESS OF GOD." Unless such a righteousness had been provided, all men must have suffered the punishment due to sin, seeing God had denounced His high displeasure against all "ungodliness and unrighteousness." These are the great truths which the Apostle immediately proceeds to unfold. And as they stand connected with every part of that salvation which God has prepared, he is led to exhibit a most animating and consolatory view of the whole plan of mercy, which proclaims "glory to God in the highest, and on earth peace, good will towards men."

The first point which the Apostle establishes is the ruined condition of men, who, being entirely divested of righteousness, are by nature all under sin. The charge of "ungodliness" and of consequent "unrighteousness," he proves first against the Gentiles. They had departed from the worship of God, although in the works of the visible creation they had sufficient notification of His power and Godhead. In their conduct they had violated the law written in their hearts, and had sinned in opposition to what they knew to be right, and to the testimony of their conscience in its favor. All of them, therefore, lay under the sentence of condemnation, which will be pronounced upon the workers of iniquity in the day when God shall judge the secrets of men. In the second chapter, a similar charge of transgression and guilt is established against the Jews, notwithstanding the superior advantage of a written revelation, with which they had been favored.

Having proved, in the first two chapters, by an appeal to undeniable facts, that the Gentiles and the Jews were both guilty before God, in the third chapter, after obviating some objections regarding the Jews, Paul takes both Jews and Gentiles together, and exhibits a fearful picture, drawn from the testimony of the Old Testament Scriptures, of the universal guilt and depravity of all mankind, showing that "there is none righteous, no not one," and that all are depraved, wicked, and alienated from God. He thus establishes it as an undeniable truth, that every man in his natural state lies under the just condemnation of God, as a rebel against Him, in all the three ways in which He has been pleased to reveal Himself, whether by the works of creation, the work of the law written on the heart, or by the revelation of grace. From these premises, he then draws the obvious and inevitable conclusion, that by obedience to law no man living shall be justified; that so far from justifying, the law proves every one to be guilty and under condemnation. The way is thus prepared for the grand display of the grace and mercy of God announced in the gospel, by which men are saved consistently with the honor of the law. What the law could not do, not from any deficiency in itself, but owing to the depravity of man, God has fully accomplished. Man has no righteousness of his own which he can plead, but God has provided a righteousness for him. This righteousness, infinitely superior to that which he originally possessed, is provided solely by grace, and received solely by faith. It is placed to the account of the believer for his justification, without the smallest respect either to his previous or subsequent obedience. Yet so far from being contrary to the justice of God, this method of justification, "freely by his grace," strikingly illustrates His justice, and vindicates all His dealings to men. So far from making the law void, it establishes it in all its honor and authority. This way of salvation equally applies to all, both Jews and Gentiles—men of every nation and every character; "there is no difference," for all, without exception, are sinners.

The Apostle, in the fourth chapter, dwells on the faith through which the righteousness of God is received, and in obviating certain objections, further confirms and illustrates his doctrine, by showing that Abraham himself, the progenitor of the Jews, was justified not by works but by faith, and that in this way he was the father of all believers, the pattern and the type of the justification of both Jews and Gentiles. And in order to complete the view of the great subject of his discussion, Paul considers, in the fifth chapter, two principal effects of justification by Jesus Christ, namely peace with God and assurance of salvation, notwithstanding the troubles and afflictions to which believers are exposed. And because Jesus Christ is the author of this divine reconciliation, he compares Him with Adam, who was the source of condemnation, concluding with a striking account of the entrance of sin and of righteousness, both of which he had been exhibiting. He next shows the reason why, between Adam and Jesus Christ, God caused the law of Moses to intervene, by means of which the extent of the evil of sin, and the efficiency of the remedy brought in by righteousness, were both fully exhibited, to the glory of the grace of God. These five chapters disclose a consistent scheme in the divine conduct, and exhibit a plan of reconciling sinners to God, that never could have been discovered by the human understanding. It is the perfection of wisdom, yet in all its features it is opposed to the wisdom of this world.*

As the doctrine of the justification of sinners, by the imputation of the righteousness of Christ, without regard to their works, which manifests, in all their extent, the guilt, the depravity, and the helplessness of man, in order to magnify grace in His pardon, might be charged with leading to licentiousness, Paul does not fail to state this objection, and solidly to refute it. This he does in the sixth and seventh chapters, in which he proves that, so far from setting aside the necessity of obedience to God, the doctrine of justification stands indissolubly connected with the very foundation of holiness and obedience. This foundation is union with the Redeemer, through that faith by which the believer is justified. On the contrary, the law operates by its restraints to stimulate and call into action the corruptions of the human heart, while at the same time it condemns all who are under its dominion. But through their union with Christ, believers are delivered from the law; and being under grace, which produces love, they

---

* The former editions of this Exposition were published in three separate volumes. Of the first volume, including these five chapters, the present is the fifth edition.

are enabled to bring forth fruit acceptable to God. The law, however, is in itself holy, just, and good. As such, it is employed by the Spirit of God to convince His people of sin, to teach them the value of the remedy provided in the gospel, and to lead them to cleave unto the Lord, from a sense of the remaining corruption of their hearts. This corruption, as the Apostle shows, by a striking description of his own experience, will continue to exert its power in believers, so long as they are in the body.

As a general conclusion from all that had gone before, the believer's entire freedom from condemnation through union with his glorious head, and his consequent sanctification, are both asserted in the eighth chapter, neither of which effects could have been accomplished by the law. The opposite results of death to the carnal mind, which actuated man in his natural state; and of life to the spiritual mind, which he receives in his renovation, are clearly pointed out. And as the love of God had been shown in the fifth chapter to be so peculiarly transcendent, from the consideration that Christ died for men, not as friends and worthy objects, but as "without strength," "ungodly," "sinners," "enemies," so here the natural state of those on whom such unspeakable blessings are bestowed is described as "enmity against God." The effects of the inhabitation of the Holy Spirit in those who are regenerated are next disclosed, together with the glorious privileges which it secures. Amidst present sufferings, the highest consolations are presented to the children of God, while their original source and final issue are pointed out.

The contemplation of such ineffable blessings as he had just been describing, reminds the Apostle of the mournful state of the generality of his countrymen, who, though distinguished in the highest degree by their external privileges, still, as he himself had once done, rejected the Messiah. And as the doctrine he had been inculcating seemed to set aside the promises which God had made to the Jewish people, and to take from them the Divine covenant under which they had been placed, Paul states that objection and obviates it in the ninth chapter. He shows that on the one hand the promises of spiritual blessings regarded only believers, who are the real Israelites, the true seed of Abraham, and on the other, that faith itself being an effect of grace, God bestows it according to His sovereign will, so that the difference between believers and unbelievers is a consequence of His free election, of which the sole cause is His good pleasure, which He exercises, both in regard to the Jews and the Gentiles. Nothing, then, had frustrated the purpose of God, and His Word had taken effect so far as He had appointed. The doctrine of God's sovereignty is here fully discussed, and that very objection which is daily made, "why doth he yet find fault?" is stated, and forever put down. Instead of national election, the great subject in this chapter is national rejection, and the personal election of a small remnant, without which the whole nation of Israel would have been destroyed; so devoid of reason is the objection usually made to the doctrine of election, that it is a cruel doctrine. In the end of the ninth chapter, the Apostle is led to the consideration of the fatal error of the great body of the Jews who sought justification by works and not by faith. Mistaking the intent and the end of their law, they stumbled at this doctrine, which is the common stumbling-stone to unregenerate men.

In the tenth chapter Paul resumes the same subject, and by new proofs, drawn from the Old Testament, shows that the righteousness of God which

the Jews, going about to establish their own righteousness for their justification, rejected, is received solely by faith in Jesus Christ, and that the
gospel regards the Gentiles as well as the Jews; and if rejected by the Jews
it is not surprising, since this had been predicted by the prophets. The Jews
thus excluded themselves from salvation, not discerning the true character
of the Messiah of Israel as the end of the law, and the author of righteousness, to every believer. And yet when they reflected on the declaration of
Moses, that to obtain life by the law, the perfect obedience which it
demands must in every case be yielded, they might have been convinced
that on this ground they could not be justified; on the contrary, by the law
they were universally condemned. The Apostle also exhibits the freeness
of salvation through the Redeemer, and the certainty that all who accept it
shall be saved. And since faith comes by hearing, and hearing by the Word
of God, the necessity of preaching the gospel to the Gentiles is inferred and
asserted. The result corresponded with the prediction. The righteousness
which is by faith was received by the Gentiles, although they had not been
inquiring for it; while the Jews, who followed after the law of righteousness, had not attained to righteousness.

The mercies of God, as illustrated by the revelation of the righteousness
which is received by faith, was the grand subject which had occupied Paul,
in the preceding part of this Epistle. He had announced at the beginning
that he was "not ashamed of the gospel of Christ; because it is the power
of God unto salvation to every one that believeth—to the Jew first, and also
to the Greek." This great truth he had undertaken to demonstrate, and he
had done so with all the authority and force of inspiration, by exhibiting,
on the one hand, the state and character of man; and on the other, the depth
of the riches, both of the wisdom and knowledge of God.

In the prosecution of this subject, the Apostle had shown that the wrath
of God is revealed against all ungodliness and unrighteousness of men; and
by arguments the most irresistible, and evidence that could not be gainsaid,
he had brought in both Jews and Gentiles as guilty and condemned sinners,
justly obnoxious to the vengeance of heaven. Had the Almighty been
pleased to abandon the apostate race of Adam, as He did the angels, to
perish in their sins, none could have impeached His justice, or arraigned
the rigor of the Divine procedure. But in the unsearchable riches of the
mercies of God, He was pleased to bring near a righteousness by which His
violated law should be magnified, and a multitude whom no man can
number rescued from destruction. This righteousness is revealed in the
gospel—a righteousness worthy of the source from which it flows a
righteousness which shall forever abase the pride of the creature, and bring
glory to God in the highest. The mercies of God are thus dispensed in such
a way as to cut off all ground for boasting on the part of those who are
justified. They are, on the contrary, calculated to exalt the divine
sovereignty, and to humble those in the dust who are saved before Him
who worketh all things according to the counsel of His own will, and
without giving any account of His matters, either justifies or condemns the
guilty according to His supreme pleasure.

In the eleventh chapter, the Apostle finished his argument, and in a
manner concludes his subject. He here resumes the doctrine of the
personal election of a remnant of Israel, of which he had spoken in the ninth
chapter, and affirms, in the most express terms, that it is wholly of grace,

which consequently excludes as its cause every idea of work, or of merit, on the part of man. He shows that the unbelief of the Jews has not been universal, God having still reserved some of them by His gratuitous election, while as a nation He has allowed them to fall, and that this fall has been appointed in the wise providence of God to open the way for the calling of the Gentiles. But in order that the Gentiles may not triumph over that outcast nation, Paul predicts that God will one day raise it up again, and recall the whole of it to communion with Himself. He vindicates God's dealings both towards Jews and Gentiles, showing that since all were guilty and justly condemned, God was acting on a plan by which both in the choice and partial rejection, as well as in the final restoration of the Jews, the Divine glory would be manifested, while in the result, the sovereign mercies of Jehovah would shine forth conspicuous in all His dealings toward the children of men. A most consolatory view is, accordingly given of the present tendency and final issue of the dispensations of God in bringing in the fulness of the Gentiles, and in the general salvation of Israel. And thus also by the Annunciation of the reception which the gospel should meet with from the Jews, first in rejecting it for a long period, and afterwards in embracing it, the doctrine of the sovereignty of Him who hath mercy on whom He will have mercy, and hardeneth whom He will, is further displayed and established. Lost in admiration of the majesty of God as discovered in the gospel, the Apostle prostrates himself before his Maker, while, in language of adoring wonder, he summons all whom he addresses to unite in ascribing glory to Him who is the first and the last, the beginning and the end, the Almighty.

From this point, Paul turns to survey the practical results which naturally flow from the doctrine he had been illustrating. He was addressing those who were at Rome, "beloved of God called, saints," and by the remembrance of those mercies of which, whether Jews or Gentiles, they were the monuments, he beseeches them to present their bodies a living sacrifice to God, whose glory is the first and the last end of creation. In thus demanding the entire surrender or sacrifice of their bodies, he enforces the duty by designating it their reasonable service. Nothing can be more agreeable to the dictates of tight reason, than to spend and be spent in the service of that God, whose glory is transcendent, whose power is infinite, whose justice is inviolable, and whose tender mercies are over all His works. On this firm foundation, the Apostle establishes the various duties to which men are called, as associated with each other in society, whether in the ordinary relations of life, or as subjects of civil government, or as members of the most exalted. It presents nothing of that incongruous medley, which is discernible in the schemes of philosophy. It exhibits no traces of confusion or disorder. It places everything on its right basis, and in its proper place. It equally enjoins our duty towards God and our duty towards man; and in this it differs from all human systems, which uniformly exclude the former or keep it in the background. It shows how doctrine and practice are inseparably connected,—how the one is the motive, the source or the principle,—how the other is the effect; and how both are so united that, such as is the first, so will be the last. According to our views of the character of God, so will be our conduct. The corruption of morals, which degraded and destroyed the heathen world, was the natural result of what infidels have designated "their elegant mythology."

The abominable characters of the heathen gods and goddesses were at once the transcript and the provocatives of the abominations of their worshippers; but wherever the true God has been known—wherever the character of Jehovah has been proclaimed, there a new standard of morals has been erected; and even those by whom His salvation is rejected are induced to counterfeit the virtues to which they do not attain. True Christianity and sound morals are indissolubly linked together; and just in proportion as men are estranged from the knowledge and service of God, so shall we find their actions stained with the corruptions of sin.

Where in all the boasted moral systems of Socrates, Plato, Aristotle, Cicero, Epictetus, Seneca, or the rest of the Greek and Roman philosophers, shall be found anything comparable to the purity and beauty of the virtues enjoined by Paul in the closing chapters of this Epistle? Even modern writers on ethics, when departing from the only pure standard of virtue, discover the grossest ignorance and inconsistency. But Paul, writing without any of the aids of human wisdom, draws his precepts from the fountain of heavenly truth, and inculcates on the disciples of Jesus a code of duties, which, if habitually practiced by mankind, would change the world from what it is—a scene of strife, jealousy, and division—and make it what it was before the entrance of sin, a paradise fit for the Lord to visit and for man to dwell in.

CHAPTER 1 / PART 1

ROMANS 1:1 – 15

THIS chapter consists of three parts. In the first fifteen verses, which form a general preface to the whole Epistle, Paul, after announcing his office and commission, declares the majesty and power of Him by whom he was appointed, who is at once the Author and Subject of the Gospel. He then characterises those to whom he writes, and states his longing desire to visit them, for the purpose of confirming their faith. The second part of the chapter, comprising only the 16th and 17th verses, embraces the substance of the grand truths which were about to be discussed. In the remainder of the chapter, the Apostle, at once entering on the doctrine thus briefly but strikingly asserted, shows that the Gentiles were immersed in corruption and guilt, and consequently subjected to condemnation.

Ver. 1.—*Paul, a servant of Jesus Christ, called to be an apostle, separated unto the Gospel of God.*

Conformably to the practice of antiquity, Paul commences his Epistle by prefixing his name, title, and designation. He had, as was usual among his countrymen, two names: by the first, as a Jew, he was known in his own land; by the second, among the Gentiles. Formerly his name was SAUL, but after the occurrence related of him, Acts xiii. 9, he was called PAUL.

Paul was of unmingled Jewish descent, a Hebrew of the Hebrews, born at Tarsus in Cilicia, but educated at Jerusalem; a Pharisee by profession, and distinguished among the disciples of Gamaliel, one of the most celebrated teachers of his age and nation. Before his conversion, he was an ardent and bigoted supporter of the traditions of his fathers, violently opposed to the humbling doctrines of Christianity, and a cruel persecutor of the Church. From the period of his miraculous conversion —from the hour when Jesus met him on the road to Damascus—down to the moment when he sealed his testimony with his blood, his eventful life was devoted to the promulgation of the faith which once he destroyed. Throughout the whole of his long and arduous course, he experienced a continual alternation of trials and graces, of afflictions and benedictions; always borne down by the hand of man, always sustained by the hand of God. The multiplied persecutions he endured, furnish a remarkable example of that just retribution which even believers seldom fail to experience in this world. When scourged in the synagogues of the Jews —when persecuted from city to city, or suffering from cold and hunger in the dungeons of Nero—with what feelings must he have remembered the time when, 'breathing out threatenings and slaughter against the disciples of the Lord,' he 'punished them oft in every synagogue,' and, 'being exceedingly mad against them, persecuted them even unto strange cities;' or, when he was stoned at Lystra, and cast out of the city as dead, how must he have reflected on the prominent part he bore in the stoning of Stephen?

A servant of Jesus Christ.—Paul, who once verily thought that he ought to do many things contrary to the name of Jesus of Nazareth, now subscribes himself His servant—literally, slave. This is an expression both of humility and of dignity—of humility, to signify that he was not his own, but belonged to Jesus Christ; of dignity, to show that he was accounted worthy to be His minister, as Moses and Joshua are called the servants of God. In the first sense, it is an appellation common to believers, all of whom are the slaves, or exclusive property of Jesus Christ, who has purchased them for Himself by the right of redemption, and retains them by the power of His word and Holy Spirit. In the second view, it denotes that Jesus Christ had honoured Paul by employing him in His Church, and making use of his services in extending the interests of His kingdom. He assumes this title to distinguish himself from the ministers or servants of men, and in order to command respect for his instructions, since he writes in the name and by the authority of Jesus Christ.

Called to be an Apostle, or a called Apostle.—Paul adds this second title to explain more particularly the first, and to show the rank to which he had been raised, and the employment with which he was intrusted. He was called to it by Jesus Christ Himself; for no man could bestow the office of an Apostle, or receive it from the hand of man, like the other offices in the church. Called, too, not merely externally as Judas, but internally and efficaciously; and called with a vocation which conferred on him all the qualities necessary to discharge the duties of the office he was appointed to; for the Divine calling is in this respect different from that which is merely human, inasmuch as the latter supposes those qualities to exist in the person called, while the former actually confers them. The state of Paul before his calling, and that in which his calling placed him, were directly opposite to each other.

The office to which Paul was called was that of an *Apostle*, which signifies one that is sent by another. The word in the original is some-times translated messenger, but is specially appropriated in Scripture to those who were sent forth by Jesus Christ to preach His Gospel to the ends of the earth; and this appellation was given to the twelve by Himself, Luke vi. 13, and has, as to them, a more specific signification than that of being sent, or being messengers. This office was the highest in the church, distinct from all others, in which, both from its nature and authority, the manner of its appointment, and the qualifications necessary for its discharge, those on whom it was conferred could have no successors. The whole system of the man of sin is built on the false assumption that he occupies the place of one of the Apostles. On this ground he usurps a claim to infallibility, as well as the power of working miracles, and in so far he is more consistent than others who, classing themselves with those first ministers of the word, advance no such pretensions.

As the Apostles were appointed to be the witnesses of the Lord, it was indispensably necessary that they should have seen Him after His resurrection. The keys of the kingdom of heaven were committed to them exclusively. They were to promulgate its laws, which bind in heaven and on earth, proclaiming that word by which all men shall be judged at the last day. When Jesus Christ said to them, ' As My Father hath sent Me, even so send I you,' He pledged Himself for the truth of their doctrine; just as when the voice from the excellent glory proclaimed, 'This is My beloved Son, hear Him,' the Father set His seal to whatever His Son taught. In preaching the Divine word, though not in their personal conduct, the Apostles were fully inspired; and the Holy Scriptures, as indited or sanctioned by them, are not the words of man, but the words of the Holy Ghost. The most awful anathema is accordingly annexed to the prohibition either to add to or take from the sacred record. Thus the Lord, who had appointed the Apostles not to a ministry limited or attached to a particular flock, but to one which extended generally through all places, to preach the Gospel in all the world, and to regulate the churches, endowed them with an infallible Spirit which led them into all truth. They were also invested with the gift of working miracles on every necessary occasion, and of exclusively communicating that gift to others by the laying on of their hands. From all this it followed that they were perfectly qualified to preach the everlasting Gospel, and possessed full authority in the churches to deliver to them those immutable and permanent laws to which thenceforth to the end of time they were to be subject. The names of the twelve Apostles of the Lamb are accordingly inscribed in the twelve foundations of the wall of the New Jerusalem; and all His people are built upon the foundation of the Apostles and Prophets, Jesus Christ Himself being the chief cornerstone.

Every qualification of an Apostle centred in Paul, as he shows in various places. He had seen the Lord after His resurrection, 1 Cor. ix. 1. He had received his commission directly from Jesus Christ and God the Father, Gal. i. 1. He possessed the signs of an Apostle, 2 Cor. xii. 12. He had received the knowledge of the Gospel, not through any man, or by any external means, but by the revelation of Jesus Christ, Gal. i. 11, 12 ; and although he was as one born out of due time, yet, by the grace vouchsafed to him, he laboured more abundantly than all the rest. When he here designates himself a called Apostle, he seems to refer to the insinuations of his enemies, who, from his not having been appointed during the ministry of our Lord, considered him as inferior to the other Apostles. The object of nearly the whole of the Second Epistle to the Corinthians is to establish his apostolic authority ; in the third chapter especially, he exhibits the superiority of the ministration committed to the Apostles, over that entrusted to Moses. Thus the designation of servant, the first of the titles here assumed, denotes his general character ; the second, of Apostle, his particular office ; and the term Apostle being placed at the beginning of this Epistle, impresses the stamp of Divine authority on all that it contains.

Separated unto the Gospel of God.—This may regard either God's eternal purpose concerning Paul, or His pre-ordination of him to be a preacher of the Gospel, to which he was separated from his mother's womb, as it was said to Jeremiah, i. 5, 'Before I formed thee in the belly I knew thee ; and before thou camest forth out of the womb I sanctified thee, and I ordained thee a prophet unto the nations ; ' or rather it refers to the time when God revealed His Son in him, that he might preach Him among the heathen, Gal. i. 16. The term *separated*, here used, appears to allude to his having been a Pharisee before his conversion, which signifies one separated or set apart. Now, however, he was separated in a far different manner ; for then it was by human pride, now it was by Divine grace. Formerly he was set apart to uphold the inventions and traditions of men, but now to preach the Gospel of God.

The Gospel of God, to which Paul was separated, signifies the glad tidings of salvation which God has proclaimed. It is the supernatural revelation which He has given, distinguished from the revelation of the works of nature. It denotes that revelation of mercy and salvation, which excels in glory, as distinguished from the law, which was the revelation of condemnation. It is the Gospel of God, inasmuch as God is its author, its interpreter, its subject: its author, as He has purposed it in His eternal decrees ; its interpreter, as He Himself hath declared it to men ; its subject, because in the Gospel His sovereign perfections and purposes towards men are manifested. For the same reasons it is also called the Gospel of the grace of God, the Gospel of peace, the Gospel of the kingdom, the Gospel of salvation, the everlasting Gospel, the glorious Gospel of the blessed God. This Gospel is the glad tidings from God of the accomplishment of the promise of salvation that had been made to Adam. That promise had been typically represented by the institution of sacrifice, and transmitted by oral tradition. It had been solemnly proclaimed by Enoch and by Noah before the flood ; it had been more particularly announced to Abraham, to Isaac, and to Jacob ; by Moses, it was exhibited in those typical representations contained in the law, which had a shadow of good things to come. Its fulfilment was the spirit and object of the whole prophetic testimony, in the predictions concerning a new covenant, and in all that was foretold respecting the advent of the Messiah.

Ver. 2.—*Which He had promised afore by His prophets in the Holy Scriptures.*

By declaring that the Gospel had been before *promised*, Paul tacitly repels the accusation that it was a novel doctrine. At the same time, he states its Divine origin as a reason why nothing new is to be admitted in religion. He further shows in what respect the Old and New Testaments differ—not as containing two religions essentially dissimilar, but as exhibiting the same grand truth—predicted, prefigured, and fulfilled. The Old Testament is the promise of the New, and the New the accomplishment of the Old. The Gospel had been promised by all the prophecies which foretold a new covenant,—by those which predicted the coming of the Messiah,—by all the observances, under the law, that contained in themselves the promise of the things they prefigured,—by the whole of the legal economy, that preceded the Gospel, in which was displayed the strictness of Divine justice, which in itself would have been a ministration only of condemnation, had it not been accompanied by all the revelations of grace and mercy, which were in substance and embryo the Gospel itself, and consequently foretold and prepared the way for a more perfect development.

By His Prophets.—Paul here also repels another accusation of the Jews, namely, that the Apostles were opposed to Moses and the Prophets; and intimates their complete agreement. He thus endeavours to secure attention and submission to his doctrine, by removing the prejudices entertained against it, and by showing that none could reject it without rejecting the Prophets. In addition to this, he establishes the authority of the Prophets by intimating that it was God Himself who spoke by them, and consequently that their words must be received as a revelation from heaven.

In the Holy Scriptures.—Here he establishes the inspiration of the Scriptures, by pronouncing them *holy*, and asserting that it was God Himself who spoke in them ; and shows whence we are now to take the true word of God and of His Prophets,—not from oral tradition, which must be uncertain and fluctuating, but from the written word, which is certain and permanent. He teaches that we ought always to resort to the Scriptures ; for that, in religion, whatever they do not contain is really novel, although it may have passed current for ages ; while all that is found there is really ancient, although it may have been lost sight of for a long period.

Ver. 3.—*Concerning His Son Jesus Christ our Lord, which was made of the seed of David according to the flesh.*[1]

The Gospel of God *concerns His Son.* The whole of it is comprised in the knowledge of Jesus Christ ; so that whoever departs one step from Him, departs from the Gospel. For as Jesus Christ is the Divine image of the Father, He is set before us as the real object of our faith. It is of Him that the Gospel of God, promised by the Prophets, treats; so that He is not simply a legislator or interpreter of the Divine will, like Moses, and the Prophets, and the Apostles. Had the law and the Gospel been given by others than Moses and the Apostles, the essential characteristics of these two economies would have remained the same. But it is altogether different respecting Jesus Christ, who is exclusively the Alpha and Omega of the Gospel, its proper object, its beginning and its end. For it is He who founded it in His blood, and who has communicated to it all its

---

[1] In the original, the words, ' Jesus Christ our Lord,' stand at the conclusion of verse 4th, and the words between them and ' concerning His Son ' may be read as a parenthesis ; but the sense remains the same.

virtue. On this account He Himself says, 'I am the Way, and the Truth, and the Life; no man cometh unto the Father but by Me.' He is the Son of God, His own Son, the Only-begotten of the Father; which proves that He is truly and exclusively His Son, of the same nature, and equal with the Father, and not figuratively, or in a secondary sense, as angels or men, as Israel or believers.

Jesus Christ.—He was called Jesus, the Greek name of the Hebrew Joshua, signifying Jehovah that saveth; and so called by the angel before He was born. 'Thou shalt call His name Jesus; for He shall save His people from their sins,' Matt. i. 21. The title Christ—that is, Messiah, or 'Anointed'[1]—being so often added in designation of His office, at length came into use as a part of His name. *Our Lord.*—This follows from His being the Son of God. The word translated Lord, comprehends the different names or titles which the Hebrews gave to God, but most usually corresponds with that of Jehovah. Where it is used as the name of God, it designates essentially the three persons of the Godhead; but it is also applied to any one of the Divine persons. In the Acts of the Apostles, and Epistles, it generally refers to Christ; and in these Divine writings this appellation is applied to Him in innumerable instances. He is called 'the Lord of glory;' 'the Lord both of the dead and living;' 'the Lord of all.' The name *Jesus* refers to His saving His people; the designation *Christ*, to His being anointed for that purpose; and that of *Lord*, to His sovereign authority.

On whatever subject Paul treats, he constantly introduces the mystery of Christ. In writing to the Corinthians, he says, 'I determined not to know anything among you, save Jesus Christ and Him crucified.' This is a declaration that the doctrine concerning Christ is the whole of religion, in which all besides is comprehended. In delivering his instructions to the saints at Corinth respecting the incestuous person, he points out to them Jesus Christ as the Lamb that was sacrificed. If his subject respects the promises he has made, or the engagements he has entered into, he draws our attention to the promises of God, which are all yea and amen in Christ Jesus. When he treats of the precepts to be obeyed, he regards them as connected with the knowledge of Christ. All duties are considered in relation to Him, as the only Saviour from whom we can derive power to fulfil them, the only altar on which they can be accepted, that model according to which they are to be performed, and the motive by which those who perform them are to be actuated. He is the head that gives life to the members, the root which renders the branches fruitful. Believers are the workmanship of God, created in Christ Jesus unto

---

[1] Oil was the instituted emblem of the grace of the Holy Spirit, which was given to the Lord Jesus Christ without measure; and anointing oil was the outward visible sign of the Spirit's inward and spiritual graces. We meet with the institution, Ex. xxx. 22, to the end. The holy ointment was to be used in consecrating the tabernacle and all its vessels, and in setting apart certain persons for some great offices. It was unlawful to use it upon any other occasion; whosoever did so was to be cut off from the people. This consecrating unction was used on the tabernacle, which was a type of the body of Christ, and on all the vessels of the tabernacle, to show that Christ, and everything respecting Him, was under the sanctifying influence of the Holy Spirit; and it was used to set apart the prophets, the priests, and the kings, because He was to sustain these offices.

good works. Jesus Christ is the end and object of their obedience, in order that the name of the Father may be glorified in the Son, and that the name of the Son may be glorified in them. Accordingly, the Scriptures speak of the commencement and the continuation of the life of believers as being derived from Christ; of their being planted together with Him; buried and risen with Him; walking in Him; living and dying with Him. The principal motives to holiness, in general, or to any particular duty, are drawn from some special view of the work of redemption, fitted to excite to the fulfilment of such obligations. The love of God in Christ is set before us, in a multitude of passages, as the most powerful motive we can have to love Him with all our heart, with all our soul, and with all our mind. When we are exhorted to look not to our own things only, but also to those of others, it is because we ought to have the same mind in us that was in Christ Jesus, who, being in the form of God, humbled Himself to do such wonderful things for us. The duty of almsgiving is enforced by the consideration that He who was rich for our sakes became poor, that we through His poverty might be rich. Forbearance to weak brethren has for its motive the death of Christ for them. If we are exhorted to forgive the offences of others, it is because God, for Christ's sake, hath forgiven us. The reciprocal duties of husband and wife are enforced by the consideration of the love of Christ, and the relation in which He stands to His Church. The motive to chastity is, that we are members of Christ's body, and temples of the Holy Ghost. In one word, the various exhortations to the particular duties of a holy life, and the motives which correspond to each of them, are all taken from different views of one grand and important object, the mystery of redemption. He 'His own self bare our sins in His own body on the tree, that we, being dead to sins, should live unto righteousness.' 'Ye are bought with a price; therefore glorify God in your body, and in your spirit, which are God's.' Having referred to Jesus Christ under the title of the Son of God, the Apostle immediately subjoins a declaration concerning His person as God and man.

Which was made of the seed of David.—The wisdom of God was displayed in the whole of the dispensation that related to the Messiah, who, in His human nature, was, conformably to many express predictions, to descend from David king of Israel.[1] He was born of a virgin of the family of David; and the first promise, containing His earliest name, *the seed of the woman*, indicated that He was in this supernatural manner to come into the world; as also that He was to be equally related to Jews and to Gentiles. To Abraham it was afterwards promised, that the Messiah should spring from him. 'In thy seed shall all the nations of the earth be blessed.' But as this promise was still very general, it was next limited to the tribe of Judah. 'The sceptre shall not depart from Judah, nor a lawgiver from between his feet, until Shiloh come.' And to David the Lord had sworn, 'Of the fruit of thy body will I set upon thy throne.' Thus, as the period of His birth approached, the promises con-

---

[1] In regard of His Divine subsistence, Jesus Christ was begotten, not made; in regard of His manhood, He was not begotten, but made of the seed of David, John i. 14; Gal. iv. 4.

cerning Him were more particular and more restricted. The wisdom of God was pleased in this manner to designate the family in which the Messiah, as to His human nature, was to be born, that it might be one of the characteristics which should distinguish and make Him known, as well as to confound the unbelief of those who should reject Him, and deny His advent. For, if He has not yet come, it was to no purpose that the prophets foretold that He should descend from a certain family, since all the genealogies of the Jews are now lost. It must therefore be admitted either that these predictions, thus restricted, were given in vain, or that the Messiah must have appeared while the distinction of Jewish families still subsisted, and the royal house of David could still be recognised. This declaration of the Apostle was calculated to have great weight with all, both Jews and Gentiles, who reverenced the Old Testament Scriptures, in convincing them that Jesus Christ was indeed the Messiah, the hope of Israel.

God has also seen it good to exhibit, in the birth of Jesus Christ, that union of majesty and dignity on the one hand, and weakness and abasement on the other, which reigns through the whole of His economy on earth. For what family had there been in the world more glorious than that of David, the great king of Israel, most honoured and beloved of God, both as a prophet and a king? And what family was more reduced or obscure when Jesus Christ was born? This is the reason why He is represented by the prophet Isaiah as the rod out of the stem of Jesse, and a branch growing out of his roots, which marks a family reduced, as if nothing more remained but the roots, which scarcely appeared above ground. And by the same prophet it is also said, 'He shall grow up before him as a tender plant, and as a root out of a dry ground.'

According to the flesh.—The prophets had abundantly testified that the Messiah was to be truly man, as well as truly God, which was necessary in order to accomplish the purpose of His advent. ' Forasmuch then as the children are partakers of flesh and blood, He also Himself likewise took part of the same ; that through death He might destroy him that had the power of death.' The Apostle John declares that Jesus Christ is come in the flesh. This expression could not be employed respecting any mere man, as no one who was only a man could come except in the flesh. Since, then, Jesus Christ might have come in some other manner, these words affirm His humanity, while at the same time they prove His pre-existence.

Ver. 4.—*And declared to be the Son of God with power, according to the Spirit of holiness, by the resurrection from the dead.*

Declared to be the Son of God.—The word here translated ' declared,' imports, according to the sense of the original as well as the connection, defined or proved. The term properly signifies, to point out, or to limit, as when bounds are set to a field to regulate its measurement. Jesus Christ was made or became the Son of David; but He did not become, but was declared, defined, or demonstrated to be *the Son of God*. That Jesus Christ is not called in this place the Son of God with reference to His incarnation or resurrection merely, is evident from the fact that His nature as the Son of God is here distinguished from His descent from

David. This expression, the Son of God, definitely imports Deity, as applied to Jesus Christ. It as properly denotes participation of the Divine nature, as the contrasted expression, Son of Man, denotes participation of the human nature. As Jesus Christ is called the Son of Man in the proper sense to assert His humanity, so, when in contrast with this He is called the Son of God, the phrase must be understood in its proper sense as asserting His Deity. The words, indeed, are capable of a figurative application, of which there are many examples in Scripture. But one part of the contrast is not to be taken as literal, and the other as figurative; and if the fact of a phrase being capable of figurative acceptation incapacitates it from expressing its proper meaning, or renders its meaning inexplicably uncertain, no word or phrase could ever be definite. A word or phrase is never to be taken in a figurative sense, where its proper sense is suitable; for language would be unintelligible if it might be arbitrarily explained away as figurative. This appellation, Son of God, was indeed frequently ascribed to pious men; but if this circumstance disqualified the phrase from bearing a literal and definite meaning, there is not a word or phrase in language that is capable of a definite meaning in its proper signification.

The Apostle John says, ' But these are written, that ye might believe that Jesus is the Christ, the Son of God,' by which he means to say who Christ is. Paul, after his conversion, ' preached Christ in the synagogues.' And what did he preach concerning Him?—' That He was the Son of God.' The great burden of Paul's doctrine was, to prove that Jesus is the *Son of God.* That term, then, must definitely import His Divine nature. It is not only used definitely, but as expressing the most important article in the Christian faith; it is used as an epitome of the whole creed. When the eunuch desired to be baptized, ' Philip said, If thou believest with all thine heart, thou mayest. And He answered and said, I believe that Jesus Christ is the Son of God.' The belief, then, of the import of this term is the substance of Christianity. Faith in Jesus Christ, as the Son of God, overcometh the world. ' Who is he that overcometh the world, but he that believeth that JESUS is the Son of God?' In the confession of Peter, Matt. xvi. 16, this phrase is employed as an epitome of the Christian faith. To the question, ' Whom say ye that I am?' Peter replies, ' Thou art the Christ, the Son of the living God.' We have here the very essence of Christianity. It is asked, Who is Christ? The reply, then, must answer this question; it must inform us *who* Christ is, both as to His person, His office, and nature. *Thou art the Christ*, is the answer to the question, so far as it respects His person and office; Thou art *the Son of the living God*, is the answer as to His nature. The parable in which the king makes a marriage for his son, speaks the same doctrine, Matt. xxii. 2. Christ is there represented to be the *Son of God*, in the same sense in which a royal heir is the son of the king his father. If, then, the king's son partake of the nature of his father, so must Jesus Christ, the Son of God, partake of the nature of His Father; if the king's son be a son in the perfect **sense** of the term, and not a son figuratively, in like manner the Son of God is God's Son in the proper sense.

The question put to the Pharisees by Jesus, Matt. xxii. 42, proves that the phrase *Son of God* means sonship by nature. 'What think ye of Christ? Whose Son is He?' This question evidently refers to proper, not figurative sonship. When we ask whose son such a person is, it is palpably evident that we mean real, not figurative sonship. Though the question might have reference to our Lord's human nature, and the inquiry relate to His father after the flesh, as the Pharisees understood, still it clearly denotes the natural relation; but that Christ did not intend it exclusively of His father as to the flesh, is evident from His next question : 'If David, then, call Him Lord, how is He his Son?' Jesus Christ could not mean to deny that He was the Son of David; but He intimates that, though He was the Son of David as to the flesh, He must be the Son of God in the same sense in which He was David's Son. He asks, Who is the father of the Messiah? and from something affirmed of Him, intimates that there is a sense in which He is not David's Son. The answer He received was true, but not full; the supply of the deficiency is '*the Son of God.*' The question, then, and the proper answer, imports that Jesus was the Son of God in the literal sense of the words. Besides, David could not call Him Lord as to His human nature; nor was He David's Lord in any sense but that in which He was God.

The condemnation, also, of unbelievers rests on the foundation of the Saviour's dignity as *the Son of God.* 'He that believeth not is condemned already; because he hath not believed in the name of the only-begotten Son of God.' They are condemned not merely for rejecting His message, but for not believing in the name of the only-begotten Son of God. Faith, then, respects not His doctrine only, but Himself, especially as exhibited in His doctrine. Such sonship implies Deity.

In this Epistle, ch. viii., Paul argues that God will deny nothing to those for whom He has given His Son. But this argument would be ill founded, if Jesus be only figuratively His Son. 'He that spared not His own Son, but delivered Him up for us all, how shall He not with Him also freely give us all things?' This supposes that the gift of Christ is greater than the gift of all other things besides, and that in such a disproportion as to bear no comparison. If so, can He be anything else than truly Divine? Had He been the highest of created beings, it would not follow as a self-evident consequence that such a gift of Him implied the gift of all things else.

The epithets attached to this phrase, Son of God, show it to import proper sonship. Jesus is called God's *own* Son,—the *beloved*—the *well-beloved* Son,—the *begotten*—the *only-begotten Son of God.* This sonship, then, is a sonship not only in a more eminent degree, but in a sense in which it is not true of any other in the lowest degree. God has other sons, but He has no other son in the sense in which Jesus is His Son. He has no other son who enjoys the community of His nature. Therefore this Son is called His begotten, or His only-begotten Son. A begotten son is a son by nature; and Jesus must be designedly so designated, to distinguish His natural sonship from that which is figurative. The phrase is rendered still more definite by the addition of the word *only.* Jesus is the ONLY-*begotten Son*, because He is the only Son of

God in the proper sense of the term. Other sons are figuratively sons, but He is the begotten Son, and the *only-begotten Son*.

The phrase *own Son* imports the truth of the sonship by another term, and is therefore an additional source of evidence. *Own Son* is a son by nature, in opposition to the *son of another*, to a *son by law*, and to all *figurative sons*. Christ, then, is God's *own Son*, because He is His Son by nature, because He is not His Son by adoption in the view of the law, and because He is His Son in opposition to figurative sonships.

That the words, *I and My Father are one*, John x. 30, mean unity of nature, and not unity of design, is clear from our Lord's account of the charge of the Jews: they charged Him with blasphemy for calling Himself the Son of God. 'Say ye of Him whom the Father hath sanctified, and sent into the world, Thou blasphemest, because I said, I am the Son of God?' Now the words used were not, *I am the Son of God*. The words *I and My Father are one* must therefore be the same in import as I am the Son of God; but if the expression, I and My Father are one, is the same in import as, I am the Son of God, the former cannot mean, I am one in design with My Father. Jesus, in the 36th verse, represents the Jews as charging Him with blasphemy, not for saying that He was God, but for saying that He was the Son of God. This incontrovertibly proves that the Jews understood the phrase, Son of God, as importing Deity. The phrase is blasphemous when applied to a mere creature in no other sense than as importing Deity.[1]

That the Lord Jesus Christ, in his eternal equality with the Father, and not merely as God manifested in the flesh, is called the Son of God, flows directly from the fact that, wherever the first person of the adorable Trinity is personally distinguished in Scripture, it is under the title, the *co-relative* title, of the Father. And what is the objection to this doctrine of our Lord's eternal sonship? It is simply that it differs from all our ordinary notions of the filial relation, to represent the Son as co-eternal with the Father; or that begotten must necessarily mean ' derived,' and that to grant derivation is to surrender Deity. In regard to the last form of the objection, it is only necessary to remark, that the doctrine of Scripture is not to be held chargeable with the vain and unprofitable speculations about derived personality, on which some of its upholders have adventured. And in regard to the first, it is not difficult to see that it is destitute of force, except on the impious assumption that we are not bound to receive any declaration about the Divine nature, about the deepest mysteries which are veiled from our reason, and revealed only to our faith, unless we can fully comprehend it. To demand that the distinction of persons in the undivided essence of the Godhead, and the mode of their eternal subsistence, shall be made plain to us; or to repugn against the doctrine of the eternal filiation of the Son of God, because it overpasses the boundaries of *our*

---

[1] In Dr. Carson's triumphant *Reply to Dr. Drummond's (Arian) Essay on the Doctrine of the Trinity*, published in Dublin, containing a masterly exposition of John x. 30-39, the above subject is fully discussed. He closes a long dissertation on the import of the term, 'the Son of God,' by saying, 'If I have not shown that it definitely expresses Deity, as applied to Jesus Christ, I would despair of proving that the name of Jesus Christ is in the Bible.'

notions of sonship,—what is this but the very summit of unthinking arrogance ?   What is it but to say that we will make our own narrow minds the measure of all things,—that we will accept nothing from pure respect to the authority of God,—that we will give the Faithful One only the credit which we allow to a suspected witness, receiving His evidence where it harmonises with our own apprehensions,—and that, while to our feeble minds every insect is a mystery, there must be no arcana in the nature of Him who dwelleth in the light that is inaccessible ?

With power.—Some explain the meaning of this to be, that by His resurrection Jesus Christ was powerfully declared to be the Son of God. But He was not merely powerfully declared—which would intimate the high degree of the evidence—but, according to the Apostle, He was absolutely declared to be the Son of God.   Some, again, suppose that He was declared to be the Son of God by the power of the Father who raised Him up.   If this had been intended, it would not, it appears, have simply been said, with power, but by the power and glory of the Father, as in Rom. vi. 4, and 2 Cor. xiii. 4.   The expression, with power, is to be construed with that of the Son of God which immediately precedes it, not with the word declared, and signifies *invested with power.*   All power was inherent in Him, as ' God blessed for ever ;' but it was given to Him as Mediator, as He Himself declares, Matt. xxviii. 18, John xvii. 2, and clearly manifested by His resurrection. He then appeared possessed of eternal, sovereign, and universal power, and that in opposition to the semblance of weakness in which He had appeared on earth.   The dignity of His person having remained for some time concealed under the veil of weakness, His resurrection gloriously displayed His ineffable power, as the Conqueror of death, and by His power also evinced His dignity as the Son of God.

The power which was given to our Lord when He rose from the dead, was eminently displayed by His sending out the Holy Spirit, when He returned to the Father.   Before His resurrection, if only the veil of infirmity with which, in His birth, he had been covered, was contemplated, He appeared merely as a man.   But after His resurrection, if we turn our eyes to His sending forth the Holy Spirit, we behold Him as the Son of God invested with all power.   For He who thus sends forth this glorious Spirit must be possessed of sovereign and infinite power, and consequently must be the Son of God.   The Holy Spirit, too, whom Jesus Christ communicates, marks His divinity by other characters besides that of power, namely, by that of holiness, by that of majesty, by that of eternity, and that of infinity, proving that He only who bestows the Holy Spirit can be the eternal God, sovereignly holy, and sovereignly glorious.   The Apostle has, however, chosen the characteristic of *power* for two reasons,—the one is to oppose it to the flesh, denoting weakness ; and the other, because He has overcome the world, which is an act of ineffable power.   To destroy the empire of Satan, to subdue the hearts of men, to change the face of the universe, displays a power which is truly Divine.

According to the Spirit of Holiness.—There are various interpretations of these terms, but the proper antithesis can only be preserved by referring them to Christ's Divine nature. If the words are capable of this application, we need not hesitate to adopt it in this place; and though the phrase is unusual, there can be no doubt that it is capable of this meaning. It is equally unusual in whatever sense it may be applied. This circumstance, then, cannot prevent it from referring to the Deity of Jesus Christ, in direct contrast to His humanity. *Spirit of Holiness* may be used here rather than the phrase *Holy Spirit*, because the latter is usually assigned to the third person of the Trinity. Though the exact expression does not occur elsewhere in the Scriptures, other passages corroborate this meaning, as 'the Lord (that is, Christ) is that Spirit,' 2 Cor. iii. 17. He is called 'a quickening Spirit,' 1 Cor. xv. 45, which character belonged to Him in a particular manner after His resurrection, when He appeared as the spiritual Head of His Church, communicating spirit and life to all His members. The unusual expression, Spirit of Holiness, appears, then, here to denote His Deity, in contrast with His humanity, characterizing Him as God, who is a Spirit essentially holy.

In the verse before us, connected with the preceding, we see that it is upon the foundation of the union of the Divine and human natures, in the person of the Messiah, that Paul proceeds to establish all the great and important truths which he sets forth in this Epistle. In another passage, he afterwards explicitly asserts this union: 'Of whom, as concerning the flesh, Christ came, who is over all, God blessed for ever. Amen.' Rom. ix. 5.

In the same manner Matthew commences his Gospel. He traces the genealogy of the human nature of Jesus Christ, and afterwards declares His Divine nature, Matt. i. 18, 21, 23. Mark begins by proclaiming Him to be the Son of God. 'As it is written in the Prophets, Behold, I send My messenger before Thy face, which shall prepare Thy way before Thee. The voice of one crying in the wilderness, Prepare ye the way of the Lord (of Jehovah), make His paths (for our God) straight,' Isa. xl. 3; Mal. iii. 1. Luke introduces his Gospel by asserting His Divine nature. In speaking of the coming of John the Baptist, he says, 'And many of the children of Israel shall he turn to the Lord their God; and he shall go before Him in the spirit and power of Elias;' and then he declares His genealogy according to His human nature, Luke i. 16, and iii. 23. John commences his Gospel by saying, 'In the beginning was the Word, and the Word was with God, and the Word was God;' and afterwards, 'The Word was made flesh,' John i. 1–14. Nearly in the same terms he commences and closes his first Epistle. The leading truth which the Apostles taught when they preached to the Jews at Jerusalem was, that Jesus is the Christ, the Son of God, the Messiah promised, who had been crucified, and who was raised from the dead, and exalted to the right hand of the Father; and the same great truth was declared to Cornelius, when the Gospel was first preached to the Gentiles. The foundation of all that the Apostle advances in the Epistle to the Hebrews, respecting the superiority of the new over the old covenant, is established upon the union of the Divine and human natures of Jesus Christ. Having announced that He is the Son of God, he determines the import of that title, by quoting a passage which ascribes to Him the name, the throne, the kingdom, the righteousness, and the eternity of God. 'Thy throne, O God, is for ever and ever; a sceptre of righteousness is the sceptre of Thy kingdom.' The Apostle Peter begins his first Epistle by referring to the resurrection of Jesus Christ, and his second, by designating Him as 'our God and Saviour.' And as in the last prophetical book of the Old Testament the Messiah is called Jehovah, so the prophetical book which terminates the New Testament opens with announcing Him to be 'Alpha and Omega, the beginning and the ending, which is, and which was, and which is to come, the Almighty,' and closes in a similar manner, 'I am Alpha and Omega, the beginning and the end, the first and the last,' which signifies the self-existent eternal Jehovah.[1]

By the resurrection from the dead.—His resurrection defined or determined Jesus Christ to be the person spoken of by the Prophets as the Son of God, and was the authentic and solemn judgment of God pronouncing Him to be His Son. As it is also written in the second Psalm, 'Thou art My Son; this day have I begotten Thee,' Acts xiii. 33. In Scripture, things are often said to be done, when they are publicly declared and manifested. When the Son of God was raised from the dead, His eternal dignity, which was before concealed, was brought to light. His Divine power, being infinite and unchangeable, could receive no augmentation of dignity or majesty. But, having chosen to appear among men enveloped as in a cloud of sufferings and apparent weakness, His glorification consisted in His emerging from that cloud, leaving the veil of infirmities in the tomb, without any of them adhering to Him, when, as the sun breaks forth in his splendour, He was gloriously manifested as the Son of God.

By His resurrection, God proclaimed to the universe that Christ was His only-begotten Son. The Apostle having in the foregoing verse called Jesus Christ the Son of God, here adds that He was declared to be the Son of God by the resurrection from the dead. His resurrection, then, did not constitute Him the Son of God; it only evinced that He was truly so. Jesus Christ had declared Himself to be the Son of God; and on this account the Jews charged Him with blasphemy, and asserted that He was a deceiver. By His resurrection, the clear manifestation of the character He had assumed, gloriously and for ever terminated the controversy which had been maintained during the whole of His ministry on earth. In raising Him from the dead, God decided the contest. He declared Him to be His Son, and showed that He had accepted His death in satisfaction for the sins of His people, and consequently that He had suffered not for Himself, but for them, which none could have done but the Son of God. On this great fact of the resurrection of Jesus Christ, Paul rests the truth of the Christian religion, without which the testimony of the Apostles would be false, and the faith of God's people vain.

---

[1] The name *Jehovah*, derived from a root which signifies *to be*, is expressive of the most perfect and independent existence. It represents God as the Author of all being. Where the word LORD is printed in the Old Testament in capitals, in the original it is Jehovah.

' But now is Christ risen from the dead, and become the first-fruits of them that slept.' His resurrection is a sure pledge that they who sleep in Jesus, God at His second appearance will bring with Him. As He triumphed in His resurrection over all His enemies, so His people shall arise to victory and blessedness. Then they shall *know* the power of the resurrection of Jesus, the grandeur of that event, and their interest in it through eternity.

The resurrection of Jesus Christ proved His sonship, because He had claimed that character during His life, and had appealed in proof of it to His rising from the dead, John ii. 19. Had this testimony been untrue, it could not have taken place. And it not only proved His own eternal power and Godhead, but also manifested His oneness and union in all the perfections and distinguishing characters which constitute Godhead, in common with the Father and the Holy Ghost, each of these glorious persons concurring in that act, as we learn from other Scriptures.

Professor Stuart, in his Commentary, asks in this place, ' How could the *resurrection* declare, in any special manner, that Christ was the Son of God? Was not Lazarus raised from the dead? Were not others raised from the dead by Christ, by the Apostles, by Elijah, and by the bones of Elisha? And yet was their resurrection proof that they were the sons of God? God did indeed prepare the way for universal dominion to be given to Christ by raising Him from the dead. To the like purpose is the Apostle's assertion in Acts xvii. 31. But how an event common to Him, to Lazarus, and to many others, could of itself demonstrate Him to be the Son of God, ἐν δυνάμει—remains yet to be shown.' This is feeble reasoning. It shows that Mr. Stuart is entirely mistaken as to the manner in which the resurrection of Christ bears testimony to His character. Jesus Christ came into the world professing to be the Son of God, and was put to death for that profession. His resurrection, then, was God's seal to the truth of this claim. In itself, it did not testify whether He was God or only man, but it fully established the truth of everything He taught ; and as He taught His own Godhead, His resurrection is proof of His Deity. But how could it ever be supposed that the resurrection of Lazarus would prove as much for him as for Christ? Lazarus did not, before his death, profess to be the Son of God, and Mediator. He never predicted his resurrection as an event which was to decide the justice of his pretensions ; and had he done so, he would not have been raised to confirm a falsehood. Professor Stuart's argument concludes as strongly against the proof of sonship, in any sense, from the resurrection of Christ, as against proper sonship. The mere fact of being raised from the dead is not evidence of being even a good man. But in whatever sense Jesus is the Son of God, His resurrection is here stated by the Apostle to be the grand proof.

Before His departure, Jesus Christ told His disciples that when the Comforter came He should convince the world ' of righteousness, because,' said He, ' I go to My Father, and ye see Me no more.' In raising Him from the dead, and receiving Him up into glory, God declared that the everlasting righteousness which the Messiah came to ' bring in ' was accomplished. His honourable reception by His Father

who sent Him, furnished the most complete proof that He had faithfully
fulfilled the purposes of His mission. ' For if,' says Archbishop Usher,
' He had broken prison and made an escape, the payment of the debt
which, as our surety, He took upon Himself, being not yet satisfied, He
should have been seen here again; Heaven would not have held Him
more than Paradise did Adam, after He had fallen into God's debt.' To
the same purpose says Bates, ' If He had remained in the grave, it had
been reasonable to believe Him an ordinary person, and that His death
had been the punishment of His presumption; but His resurrection was
the most illustrious and convincing evidence that He was what He
declared Himself to be. For it is not conceivable that God should put
forth an almighty power to raise Him, and thereby authorize His resurrection, if by robbery He had assumed that glorious title of the Son of
God. If, indeed, a single sin which had been "laid on Him" had been
left unexpiated, He must have remained for ever in the grave : death
would in that case have detained Him as its prisoner; for the wages of
sin is death.'

By His incarnation, Jesus Christ received in His human nature the
fulness of His Spirit; but He received it covered with the veil of His
flesh. By His death He merited the Spirit to sanctify His people; but
still this was only a right which He had acquired, without its execution.
By His resurrection He entered into the full exercise of this right; He
received the full dispensation of the Spirit, to communicate it to them;
and it was then He was declared to be the Son of God with power.

Ver. 5.—*By whom we have received grace and apostleship, for obedience to the faith
among all nations, for His name.*

One of the first acts of the power of Jesus Christ, after His resurrection, was to bestow His Spirit and His grace on those who were chosen
by Him, to qualify them to be His witnesses and the heralds of His
Gospel. Paul was among that number, although appointed at a later
period than the rest. *We have received.*—He here speaks of himself in
the plural number. He does not appear to use this style that he may
include the other Apostles : what is true of him will, however, as to
everything essential, apply to all the others. He distinguishes these two
things, *Grace and Apostleship.* The first, which he had experienced in
his conversion, and in every subsequent part of his course, he had
received from Jesus Christ; and by Him also he was appointed to the
office of an Apostle, to the discharge of which that grace was indispensably
necessary.

To the obedience of faith.—Paul, as an Apostle, was commissioned to
preach the Gospel in order to the obedience of faith. Some understand
this of the obedience which faith produces; but the usual import of the
expression, as well as the connection in this place, determines it to apply
to the belief of the Gospel. Obedience is no doubt an effect produced by
that belief; but the office of an Apostle was, in the first place, to persuade
men to believe the Gospel. This is the grand object, which includes the
other. The Gospel reforms those who believe it; but it would be presenting an imperfect view of the subject to say that it was given to

reform the world. It was given that men might believe and be saved. The obedience, then, here referred to, signifies submission to the doctrine of the Gospel. This is quite in accordance with those passages in which the expression is elsewhere found, as in Acts vi. 7; Rom. vi. 17, xvi. 26; Gal. iii. 1; 2 Thess. i. 8; 1 Pet. i. 22; and in Rom. x. 3; where the Israelites are charged with not *submitting* to the righteousness of God; and especially in the 16th verse of that chapter it is said, ' But they have not all *obeyed* the Gospel; for Esaias saith, Lord, who hath believed *our report?*' 'This is His *commandment*, that we should believe on the name of His Son Jesus Christ, 1 John iii. 23.

The object, then, of faith, is not only a promise, but a promise accompanied with a command to accept it. For since it is God who promises, His majesty and authority accompany His promise. In respect to the promise, that which on our part corresponds to it is called faith; but in regard to the commandment which enjoins us to receive the promise, the act on our part is obedience. On this account, unbelief is rebellion against God. Faith, on the other hand, is an act of submission, or the surrender of ourselves to God, contrary to the natural opposition of our minds, in order that He may possess and conduct us, and make us whatever He pleases. When, therefore, that opposition is overcome by the weapons with which the Apostles were armed, namely, the word of truth, our submission is called the obedience of faith. 'This is the work of God, that ye believe on Him whom He hath sent.' The obedience of faith which His people render to Jesus Christ is an adoration which supposes His Deity; for when reason entirely submits and is swallowed up in His authority, it is a real adoration. 'Faith,' says Calvin on this passage, 'is adorned with the title of obedience, because the Lord calls us by His Gospel, and by faith we answer when He calls us; as, on the contrary, unbelief is the height of all rebellion against God.'

Among all nations.—Paul here assigns the reason why he preaches to Gentiles, namely, that it is the destination of his office or apostleship, and not solely his own choice, Gal. ii. 7. In past ages, God had suffered all nations, with the exception of the Jews, to walk in their own ways, although He had not left Himself without witness in the works of creation and providence. Both in the universal deluge, and also upon other occasions, He had manifested His wrath on account of sin, and His determination to punish it. But after the establishment of the nation of Israel in Canaan, after the institution of His public worship among them, and after He had given to them His written revelation, He did not generally interpose His authority in a visible manner to turn the nations from the ways they had chosen. Although, therefore, the times of this ignorance God winked at, He now commanded all men to repent. For ' thus it is written,' that when Christ suffered and rose from the dead, ' repentence and remission of sins should be preached in His name among all nations,' Luke xxiv. 47. And accordingly Paul closes this Epistle by declaring that it was by the commandment of the everlasting God that the mystery, which had been kept secret from ages and generations, should be made known to all nations, in order to the obedience of faith. This was in conformity to the commission given by the Lord

Himself to His eleven Apostles, to go into all the world and preach the
Gospel to every creature; and likewise to the particular command afterwards received by Paul respecting the Gentiles, 'To open their eyes, and
to turn them from darkness to light, and from the power of Satan unto
God.' Thus the Gospel of the uncircumcision was in a special manner
committed to Paul, to which in the verse before us he refers.

For His name.—The Gospel is preached among all nations for the
obedience of faith, but paramount to this is the glory of the name of
Jesus Christ. The name, the glory, and the authority of God have the
same signification. The world was created for God's glory, and His
glory is the chief end of the restoration of sinners. The acts of His
goodness to His people are declared to be done for His own name's sake;
and for the same end His judgments also are executed on sinners, for
His own name, Rom. ix. 17. Men are very unwilling to admit that God
should have any end with respect to them greater than their happiness.
But His own glory is everywhere in the Scriptures represented as the
chief end of man's existence, and of the existence of all things. It is in the
name of Jesus that His people are taught to pray; and we are baptized
into the name of the Father, of the Son, and of the Holy Ghost, as into
one name. This affords unanswerable proof of the divinity of Christ.
Paul was a chosen vessel to bear His name before the Gentiles, Acts ix. 15.
This verse concludes the general introduction to the Epistle; the easy
transition to the particular address should not pass unnoticed.

Ver. 6.—*Among whom are ye also the called of Jesus Christ.*

Those to whom Paul wrote, were included among the nations to whom
his commission extended. He mentions this, that it might not appear
strange that he addresses them for the purpose of instructing them, but
that, on the contrary, they should receive what he wrote with due confidence and respect. He was unknown to them by sight; he was far
distant from them. They might say, What interest had he in them?
He assures them that his apostleship regarded and comprehended them,
and that he did nothing beyond his calling when he desired to increase
their knowledge, and confirm their faith. They were *the called of Jesus
Christ.* Thus he had a double right, and was laid under a double obligation to address them, both as belonging to the nations to whom his
commission extended, and also as having already become obedient to the
faith. The apostolic commission consisted of two parts: first, to make
disciples, and then to teach them to observe all things that Jesus had
commanded. Thus Paul had a measure that reached even to those to
whom he now wrote, as he had to the Church at Corinth, 2 Cor. x. 13.

Of Jesus Christ.—Not only called to Jesus, but called by Him; for
He is not only that glorious person to whom we ought to go, but who
Himself says, *Come unto Me.* The believers at Rome were called both
with an external calling by the Gospel, and also with an internal calling
by the Holy Spirit. Both these callings are ascribed to the Father, and
also, as in this passage, to Jesus Christ, because the Son, as Mediator,
is the minister of the Father, and executes all things for Him. As the
High Priest of His people, He has done for them all that is required for

establishing the New Covenant; but as the Prophet and King of His Church, He converts them and leads them to the Father. This expression, the called of Jesus Christ, imports that they belonged to Him, as in Isa. xlviii. 12, 'Israel, my called,' that is, who are mine by the right of calling.

Ver. 7.—*To all that be in Rome, beloved of God, called, saints: Grace to you, and peace, from God our Father, and the Lord Jesus Christ.*

To all.—The Apostle here addresses all the saints at Rome without distinction, whether they were Jews or Gentiles, rich or poor, learned or unlearned, bond or free. He does not distinguish the pastors from the people, but addresses himself to them all in common—what he writes being equally intended for their common instruction and edification. He addresses them by three designations, *Beloved of God, Called, Saints.* They were saints because they were called, and they were called because they were beloved of God. Their character as saints, then, was not the cause, but the effect, of their being beloved of God.

Beloved of God.—In opposition to the rest of mankind, whom God hath left in unbelief and the corruption of the world. Here, then, is the electing love of God placed first in order. It is that love wherewith He loved them when they were dead in sins, Eph. ii. 5. It is the greatest love that God can show to man, being everlasting love, which originates with Himself. It is purely gratuitous, and does not spring from the foresight of anything worthy in those who are its objects; but, on the contrary, goes before all that is good in the creature, and brings with it infinite blessings. It has for its primary object Jesus Christ, the beloved of the Father; and those whom He beholds in Christ, although in themselves children of wrath, are beloved for His sake. This love is unvarying from eternity and through eternity, although God's dealings towards His people may vary, as it is declared in the 99th Psalm, 'Thou takest vengeance on their inventions.' He may thus be displeased with them, as it is said, 'The thing that David did displeased the Lord,' but His love to them remains the same, like the love of a father to a child, even when he chastens him for his disobedience.

Called.—The first outward effect of election, or of the love of God to His people, is His calling them, not merely by the word, which is common to *many*, but by the Holy Spirit, which is limited to *few*, Matt. xxii. 14. 'I have loved thee with an everlasting love; therefore with lovingkindness have I drawn thee,' Jer. xxxi. 3. The election, then, of believers is to be traced through their calling, 2 Pet. i. 10, and their calling to the everlasting love of God.

Saints.—The end of the Divine calling is to convert sinners into saints or holy persons. Their sanctification is not an external or figurative consecration, as that of Israel was, but a real consecration by which they are made to give themselves to God. It arises from union with Jesus Christ, which is the source of the sanctification of His people; and it consists in internal purity of heart, for God purifies the heart by faith. It supposes a real change of heart and disposition, a new creation, for 'if any man be in Christ, he is a new creature.' 'That which is born of the flesh is flesh, and that which is born of the Spirit is spirit.' They were not then saints by natural birth, nor did they make themselves saints either in whole or in part; but they were made so altogether by sovereign grace resulting from sovereign love. All believers are saints, and in one sense all of them are equally sanctified. They are equally separated or consecrated to God, and equally justified, but they are not all equally holy. The work of sanctification in them is progressive. There are babes, and young men, and fathers in Christ. Some are weak in faith, and some are strong; but none of them are yet perfect, neither have they attained to that measure of holiness at which it is their duty constantly to aim, Phil. iii. 12. They are therefore to forget those things which are behind, and to reach forth unto those things which are before, and are commanded to 'grow in grace, and in the knowledge of our Lord and Saviour Jesus Christ.' 'The path of the just is as the shining light, that shineth more and more unto the perfect day.' 'Certainly, according to Paul,' says Calvin on this place, 'the praise of our salvation does not depend upon our own power, but is derived entirely from the fountain of God's love to us. What other cause but His own goodness can, moreover, be assigned for His love? On this also depends His calling, by which, in His own time, He seals the adoption in those who were first gratuitously chosen by Him. From these premises the conclusion follows, that none truly associate themselves with the faithful who do not place a certain degree of confidence in the Lord's kindness to them: although undeserving and wretched sinners, being called by His goodness, they aspire to holiness. For He hath not called us to uncleanness, but to holiness.'

Grace to you, and peace.—In this way the Apostles usually commence their Epistles to the churches. In those addressed to individuals, mercy is generally added to grace and peace. Grace is uniformly placed first in order, because it is the source whence peace and all the blessings of salvation flow. Grace is the free unmerited favour of God to sinners in the plan of salvation. Grace and peace are joined together, because they are inseparable. God communicates all blessings to those to whom He gives grace, and to none besides; for whatever does not proceed from grace is not a blessing. It is to the praise of His grace that God exercises mercy, and brings those who were His enemies into a state of peace with Him. Grace differs from mercy, as it regards the unworthiness, while mercy regards the sufferings, of its objects.

Grace or favour is spoken of in Scripture in three points of view: either as the unmerited favour of God towards men, as *existing in Himself;* or as *manifested in the Gospel*, which is called the Gospel of the grace of God; or in its *operation in men*. Every part of redemption proceeds on the footing of grace. It originates in the grace of God, and flows, in its first manifestations and in all its after acts, from the same unceasing fountain, in calling, adopting, regenerating, justifying, sanctifying, strengthening, confirming grace,—in one word, it is all of grace. On this account Peter calls God *the God of all grace*, which teaches that God is in Himself towards His people grace—grace in His very nature, —that He knows what each of them needs, and lays it up for them, and communicates it to them. The whole of the salvation of man, from the counsels of God from eternity, is planned and executed to ‘ the praise of the glory of His grace,’ Eph. i. 6; ‘ who hath saved us and called us with an holy calling, not according to our works, but according to His own purpose and grace, which was given us in Christ Jesus before the world began,’ 2 Tim. i. 9.

In the operation of grace in the soul, men are not simply passive, nor can it be said that God does a part and they do the rest; but God produces all, and they act all. God is the sole author and source of their acts, but they themselves properly are the agents. In some respects they are wholly passive, and in others wholly active. In the Scriptures, the same things are spoken of as coming from God, and as coming from men. It is said that God purifies the hearts of believers, Acts xv. 9, and that they purify themselves, 1 John iii. 3. They are commanded to work out their own salvation with fear and trembling, because it is God who worketh in them both to will and to do of His good pleasure, Phil. ii. 12. It is not the Holy Spirit, but themselves, by virtue of His power, who love God and their neighbour, who fear the Lord, who confide in Him, and trust in His promises. Paul designates as fruits of the Spirit, love, joy, peace, long-suffering, gentleness, goodness, faith, meekness, temperance. The origin of them all is the Holy Spirit—it is from Him they are derived ; but in their exercise or development they properly belong to believers. If any one falsely infers from the doctrine of grace that there remains nothing for man to do, because it is the grace of God that leads him to act, he understands neither what he says, nor whereof he affirms. He might with the same reason conclude that, as God is the Author of our existence, of our souls, and of all our faculties, therefore we can neither think, nor reason, nor love. Grace is in our hearts a living principle, implanted by God, and at His sovereign disposal. To exercise this principle, is as much our duty as to preserve our life and health ; and as the care which these require demand attention and certain acts of the will, in the same manner the exercise of grace in the soul supposes corresponding dispositions and acts. But it is not thus with grace as *manifested,* which is an object of choice, received or rejected, according as grace has operated in us or not. In this manner, grace, as the principle of renovation, by the sole operation of the Holy Spirit, stands in opposition to every notion of independent power in man, by which it might be supposed he could regenerate himself; while, on the other hand, considered in its exercise, it supposes the efforts of man.

Peace includes everything that belongs to the idea of tranquillity in its largest extent. But the foundation of all must be peace with God. Without this, the Christian can have no peace, though he should be on good terms with all mankind; but, possessing this, God will either give him peace with his enemies, or He will give him peace along with their enmity. The Christian may not only have peace, but joy, in the midst of persecution and external affliction. Peace with God is the substance of happiness, because without it there can be no happiness, and with it there is happiness, whatever else is wanting. This salutation, grace to you and peace, may be considered either as a prayer or a benediction. In the latter sense, it bears the character of apostolic authority.

From God our Father, and the Lord Jesus Christ.—God is the Father of our Lord Jesus Christ, and the Father of all who are in Him. Paul here speaks of God as both his Father and the Father of all those whom he addressed, and so constituting one family, whether Jews or Gentiles. God the Father, and the Lord Jesus Christ, are the source of all grace and peace, and can alone communicate these blessings, which are the gracious effects that flow from the covenant of love and favour of the Triune Jehovah. Here again we see an incontrovertible proof of the deity of Jesus Christ; for, if He were not God, He could not without impiety be thus joined with, or invoked along with, the Father to impart blessings, of which God alone is the author.

Ver. 8.—*First, I thank my God through Jesus Christ for you all, that your faith is spoken of throughout the whole world.*

First, I thank my God.—This is a first in order, as if Paul had said, I commence my Epistle by giving thanks to God. It proceeds from that feeling of piety which ought to pervade all our actions; at the same time he bestows on those whom he addresses the praise which they deserved. It is also a first in importance, as if he said, Above all, I render thanks to God for you. He shows that their state was a matter of great joy to him, arising both from his zeal for the glory of God, and from the interest he took in those whom he addressed.

My God.—Paul calls God his God, indicating a lively and ardent feeling of love to Him, of confidence in Him, and of liberty of access, which includes a persuasion that his thanksgivings will be agreeable to God. It is also a confession of his duty, and of the obligations he is under to render thanks to God, because He is his God. It is, besides, an intimation of his own character, as walking in communion with God. This is an example of the working of the Spirit of adoption, and of a believer taking to himself, in particular, the blessing of having God for his God, and of being a partaker of all the blessings of the New Covenant, flowing from that most gracious declaration, 'I will be their God, and they shall be My people.' Of such appropriation there are numerous instances recorded in the Book of Psalms. 'I will love Thee, O Lord, *my* strength. The Lord is *my* rock, and *my* fortress, and *my* deliverer; *my* God, *my* strength, in whom I will trust; *my* buckler, and the horn of *my* salvation, and *my* high tower,' Ps. xviii. 1. Job says, 'I know that *my* Redeemer liveth.' 'I live,' says Paul, 'by the faith of the Son of God, who loved *me*, and gave Himself for *me*.' Such language it is the privilege of every believer to use, and he will do so in proportion as the love of God is shed abroad in his heart by the Holy Ghost, which is given unto him. The Christian can thus address God as *his own* God, and often he should do so even in his public declarations. This displeases the world, because it condemns the world. They affect to consider it as presumption, but it is only a proper expression of our belief of God's testimony with regard to His Son. Studiously to avoid such expressions on proper occasions, is not to show humility, but to be ashamed of the truth.

Paul thanked God, *through Jesus Christ*, who is our Great High Priest, and presents the prayers of all saints upon the golden altar before the

throne. It is through Him alone that all our worship and all our works
in the service of God are acceptable. Thus, not only must our petitions
ascend to the Father through the Son, but our thanksgivings also, according to the precept, 'By Him, therefore, let us offer the sacrifice of praise
to God continually, that is, the fruit of our lips, giving thanks to His
name,' Heb. xiii. 15. We can have no intercourse with God, but through
the one Mediator between God and man, John xiv. 6; and except
through Him, we are not permitted even to return thanksgivings to God.

Paul thanks God for *all* to whom he writes. He had addressed them
all as saints, making no exception. It is to such exclusively that the
apostolic Epistles are written, whether as churches or individuals,—as
being all united to Christ, children of God, heirs of God, and joint heirs
with Jesus Christ,—who should first suffer and afterwards reign with
Him. In the first churches, in which everything was regulated by the
Apostles according to the will of God, there may have been hypocrites or
self-deceivers; but as far as man could judge, they were all believers;
or if any among them appeared not to be such, the churches were told
it was to their shame. If any were discovered who had crept in unawares, or were convicted of unbecoming conduct, or who had a form of
godliness, but denied its power, from such they were commanded to turn
away. They were not to be unequally yoked with unbelievers; wherefore
it is said, 'Come out from among them, and be ye separate.' It was
in the confidence that they obeyed such commands, that the Apostles
addressed them all, as in the passage before us, as the children of God. In
the same manner, in writing to the church at Philippi, Paul, after thank-
ing God for their fellowship in the Gospel, and declaring that he was
confident that He who had begun a good work in them would perform it
unto the day of Jesus Christ, adds, 'Even as it is meet for me to think
this of you *all*, because I have you in my heart; inasmuch as both in
my bonds, and in the defence and confirmation of the Gospel, *ye all* are
partakers with me of grace.' This mode of address runs through the
whole of the apostolic Epistles.

The Apostles generally commence their Epistles with the most encouraging views of the present state and future prospects of those to whom
they write, and on these considerations are founded the succeeding exhortations. They first remind those who are addressed of the rich grace
of God towards them in Jesus Christ, and the spiritual blessings of which
they are made partakers, for their strong consolation, and then they
exhort them to a holy conversation becoming such privileges. Of this
we have a striking example in the First Epistle to the Corinthians, which,
although Paul had so many faults to reprehend in them, he commences
by declaring that they were sanctified in Christ Jesus—that he thanked
God always for the grace given unto them by Jesus Christ, who would
also confirm them to the end, that they might be blameless in the day of
His coming, reminding them that God was faithful, by whom they were
called unto the fellowship of His Son Jesus Christ our Lord. The number of times, no fewer than ten, in which, in the first ten verses of that
Epistle, Paul introduces the name of Jesus Christ, should be remarked.

In these Epistles we find no exhortations to unbelievers. This ought

to be particularly observed, as being a key to them, without which they
cannot be understood.   This is no reason, however, for supposing that
exhortations to believe the Gospel ought not to be addressed to those
who are still in unbelief.   The Gospel is to be preached to every creature,
and all should be enjoined, first to believe it, and then to do all that God
requires.   In the Book of Acts, when the Apostles preached to the unconverted, their subject was repentance toward God, and faith toward
our Lord Jesus Christ.   But in the Epistles, where they address believers,
they also admonish and exhort them to the practice of every duty.
There is no exhortation to the performance of any duty which does not
imply that it is to be performed in faith.   'Without faith it is impossible
to please God.'

Believers are taught to regulate all their conduct according to the
great things which the Gospel reveals, which are freely given to them
of God; to be imitators of God, and to live not to themselves but to Him,
as being not their own, but bought with a price, and therefore bound to
glorify God in their bodies and in their spirits, which are His.   Their
obedience, as described in the Scriptures, is as much distinguished by its
motives and its foundation from the morality of the unbelieving world, as
it is elevated above it in its nature and effects.   It is in all respects a
life of faith, subject to the authority of God, and is practised under the
influence and direction of motives inculcated in the Gospel, of which
the light of nature gives no knowledge.   Those who have not this faith
regard it as a barren speculation; but they who possess it know that it
is the sole and powerful source of all their works that are acceptable to
God, which are opposed to 'dead works,' Heb. ix. 14; and that no works
are really good, however excellent they may appear, and however much
esteemed among men, or useful in society, which do not proceed from faith.

That your faith is spoken of.—It is not the piety of the saints at Rome,
but their faith, that is here noticed.   Without holiness no man shall see
the Lord; but it is faith in Christ that is the distinguishing mark of the
Christian.   Paul thanks God that the faith of those to whom he writes
was spoken of.   He thus acknowledges God as the author of the Gospel,
not only on account of His causing it to be preached to them, but because
He had actually given them grace to believe; for if God is thanked for
the distinguished faith of Christians, then not only their faith is His gift,
but also its measure and advancement.   That faith is the gift of God, is
a truth frequently declared, as in Matt. xvi. 17; Luke xvii. 5; Acts xi.
21, xiii. 48, xvi. 14; Rom. xii. 3; Phil. i. 29.   This is also acknowledged in all the thanksgivings of the Apostles for those to whom they
write, and is according to the whole of the doctrine of the Scriptures.   It
is from God that every good and every perfect gift descendeth, and a
man can receive nothing, except it be given him from heaven.   For 'all
things,' therefore, we are commanded to give thanks.   Paul thanks God
for his own prayers, 2 Tim. i. 3.   Here, as in other places, Paul commences with thanksgiving, thus reminding us that every blessing is from
the kindness of God.   If we should observe this in blessings of small
importance, we ought to do it much more with respect to faith, which is
neither an ordinary nor a common blessing of God.

Throughout the whole world.—That is to say, throughout the whole Roman empire, of which Rome being the capital, all that took place there was circulated throughout the whole civilised world. Their faith was proclaimed by the voice of all believers, who alone could form a proper opinion regarding it; for the reference is evidently to their approbation. Unbelievers, who hated both the people of God and their faith, could give no proper testimony concerning it. The commendation of the servants of God was all that the Apostle valued. Thus the faith of the believers whom God had assembled at Rome was held up as an example ; and the Apostle here declares, not only for their encouragement, but also to excite them more and more to the performance of their duty, that the eyes of all the servants of God throughout the world were upon them. He says, their faith was *spoken of,* not that he rests in this circumstance, or that he wishes them to rest in their reputation, as if he would flatter them. Reputation in itself is nothing. If it be unmerited, it only convinces the conscience of imposture ; and when it is real, it is not our chief joy. Paul regards it with reference to the believers at Rome, as a mark of the reality of their faith ; and it is on this reality that he grounds his thanksgiving. It was a reason for thanksgiving that they were thus letting their light shine before men, and so glorifying their Father in heaven. The glory of all that is good in His people belongs to God, and all comes through Jesus Christ.

Ver. 9.—*For God is my witness, whom I serve with my spirit in the Gospel of His Son, that without ceasing I make mention of you always in my prayers.*

God is my witness.—This is substantially an oath ; and refutes the erroneous and mischievous notion of some who maintain, from a misapprehension of what is said by our Lord and the Apostle James, that all oaths are unlawful. Paul's affection for those to whom he wrote was such, that, in making his appeal to God, he desires to expose it to His judgment in respect to its truth and sincerity.

Whom I serve with my spirit.—All the service of God is of this kind ; but it is here expressed for the sake of energy, and to distinguish the true servants of God, who serve in the Gospel with their heart in the work, from hirelings, whose labours are formal and only external. It expresses the sincerity and ardour of the service that Paul rendered to God, as if he had said, with all his heart and all the faculties of his soul. It also imports the nature of the service in which he was employed, namely, a spiritual service, in opposition to the service of the priests and Levites in the tabernacle, which was in a great measure a bodily service. On this account he adds, *in the Gospel of His Son;* that is to say, in the ministry of the Gospel in which he laboured for the unfolding of the Divine mysteries to make them known. Thus Paul shows, from the character of his ministry, that his obedience was not in pretence only, but in sincerity.

Without ceasing I make mention of you always in my prayers.—Some place these last words, ' always in my prayers,' in the beginning of the next verse, as in the Vulgate and the French versions ; but the difference is not material. This is a striking proof of the frequency of Paul's

prayers, in which he interceded for those whom he was addressing—
'without ceasing'—'always.' In like manner, in writing to the Philippians, he says, 'Always, in every prayer of mine for you all, making
request with joy.' We thus learn the duty of Christians to pray for one
another, and that those who believe the Gospel are as much bound to
pray for its success, and the prosperity of the churches, as to labour in
the work. Both prayer and labour ought to go together. To pray
without labouring is to mock God: to labour without prayer is to rob
God of His glory. Until these are conjoined, the Gospel will not be
extensively successful. From many other parts of Paul's writings, we
learn how assiduous he was in the duty of prayer, which he so earnestly
inculcates on all believers. 'In everything giving thanks; for this is the
will of God in Christ Jesus concerning you,' 1 Thess. v. 18. 'Be careful
for nothing; but in *everything* by prayer and supplication, with thanksgiving, let your requests be made known unto God,' Phil. iv. 6. How
precious is the promise connected with this admonition! 'And the peace
of God, which passeth all understanding, shall keep your hearts and
minds through Christ Jesus.'

But since all events are fixed, even from eternity, in the counsels and
wisdom of God, of what avail, it may be said, are these prayers? Can
they change His eternal counsels, and the settled order of events? Certainly not. But God commands us to pray, and even the prayers of His
people are included in His decrees; and what God has resolved to do, He
often gives to their prayers. Instead, then, of being vain, they are among
the means through which God executes His decrees. If, indeed, all
things happened by a blind chance, or a fatal necessity, prayers in that
case could be of no moral efficacy, and of no use; but since they are
regulated by the direction of Divine wisdom, prayers have a place in the
order of events. After many gracious promises, it is added, Ezek. xxxvi.
37, 'Thus saith the Lord God, I will yet for this be inquired of by the
house of Israel to do it for them.' In this verse Paul shows his zeal for
God and his love for believers, which ought never to be separated. We
should love our brethren because we love God. These two things corresponded in Paul to the two favours he had received, which he marked
in the 5th verse, namely, 'Grace and Apostleship.' 'God,' as if he said,
'has given me grace, and on my part I serve Him with my spirit; He
has given me Apostleship, and I have you continually in remembrance.'

Ver. 10.—*Making request, if by any means now at length I might have a prosperous journey, by the will of God, to come unto you.*

Making request.—Paul's affection for those to whom he wrote impelled
him, not once or twice with a passing wish, but at all times, to desire to
be present with them, notwithstanding the inconveniences of so long and
perilous a journey. He asks of God that by some means now at length
he might be permitted to visit them. Thus Christian love searches out
new objects on which to exercise itself, and extends itself even to those
who are personally unknown.

I might have a prosperous journey, by the will of God.—This teaches us
that God, by His providence, regulates all that takes place. There is

nothing with which Christians should be more habitually impressed, than that God is the disposer of all events. They should look to His will in the smallest concerns of life, as well as in affairs of the greatest moment. Even a prosperous journey is from the Lord. In this way they glorify God by acknowledging His providence in all things, and have the greatest confidence and happiness in walking before Him. Here we also learn that, while the will of God concerning any event is not ascertained, we have liberty to desire and pray for what we wish, provided our prayers and desires are conformed to His holiness. But will our prayers be agreeable to God if they be contrary to His decrees? Yes, provided they be offered in submission to Him, and not opposed to any known command; for it is the revealed, and not the secret will of God that must be the rule of our prayers. We also learn in this place, that since all events depend on the will of God, we ought to acquiesce in them, however contrary they may be to our wishes; and likewise, that in those things in which the will of God is not apparent, we should always accompany our prayers and our desires with this condition, if it be pleasing to God, and be ready to renounce our desires as soon as they appear not to be conformed to His will. ' O how sweet a thing,' as one has well observed, ' were it for us to learn to make our burthens light, by framing our hearts to the burthen, and making our Lord's will a law!'

Ver. 11.—*For I long to see you, that I may impart unto you some spiritual gift, to the end ye may be established.*

Paul greatly desired to see the believers at Rome, to impart to them *some spiritual gift*. The opinion of Augustine, that this means the love of one's neighbour, in which he supposes the church at Rome was deficient, has no foundation. It was not a new degree of the Spirit of sanctification that he desired to communicate, for this Paul had it not in his power to bestow, 1 Cor. iii. 6. He appears to refer to some of the extraordinary gifts conferred by the Apostles, by which they might be more established in their most holy faith.

Ver. 12.—*That is, that I may be comforted together with you, by the mutual faith both of you and me.*

That is.—This does not mean that what follows is intended as an explanation of what he had just said, for to those whom Paul addressed it must have been sufficiently clear; but is a modification of it respecting his purpose, lest he should appear to consider them as not well instructed or established in their faith. For although he always acted faithfully, no one, as is evident from his writings, was ever more cautious to avoid unnecessary offence. He therefore joins himself with those to whom he wrote, and refers to the advantage which he also expected reciprocally to derive from them. It is no valid objection to understanding it to be a miraculous gift which he desired to communicate, that he hoped for mutual advantage and comfort with those whom he was about to visit. This comfort or confirmation which he looked for, was not from a spiritual gift to be bestowed by them, but would be the effect of their confirmation, by the gift they received through him. The gift, too, bestowed by him, would be a new proof of the power of God in him, and of His approbation in enabling him to exert such power. He would be comforted and strengthened in witnessing their faith in respect to his own labours in his ministry, by seeing the kingdom of God advancing more and more, and with respect to his numerous afflictions to which he was on all hands subjected, and also in contrasting the coldness and weakness of many of which he often complains, when he observed the increasing power of Divine grace in the saints at Rome. On the other hand, they would derive from Paul's presence the greatest consolation from his instructions in the mysteries of salvation, from his exhortations, which must contribute much to their edification, as well as from his example, his counsels, and his prayers. It is thus the duty of Christians to confirm each other in the faith ; and their mutual intercourse makes known the faith that each possesses. They see that their experience answers as face answers to face in a glass; and by beholding the strength of faith in their brethren, Christians are edified and confirmed.

Ver. 13.—*Now, I would not have you ignorant, brethren, that oftentimes I purposed to come unto you (but was let hitherto), that I might have some fruit among you also, even as among other Gentiles.*

Paul's zeal and affection for those to whom he wrote, were not of recent origin ; they had long been cherished in his heart. Of this he did not wish them to be ignorant. It is of importance that believers should know the love entertained for them by the servants of God. It is a testimony of the love of God Himself. Paul wished to see *some fruit* of his ministry among them. This was his great desire everywhere in the service of Christ. 'I have chosen you and ordained you,' said Jesus to His Apostles, 'that ye should go and bring forth fruit;' and Paul ardently longed to see the fulfilment of this gracious promise among those to whom he wrote, for believers were his joy and crown.

As among other Gentiles.—The apostleship of Paul had not been unfruitful, ch. xv. 17. He had travelled through a great part of Syria, of Asia, and of Greece, and everywhere he had either been the means of converting sinners or edifying believers. This was a source of much joy to him ; but after so many labours, he did not wish for repose. He desired to go to Rome to obtain fruit there also. He had been *let*, or hindered, hitherto. Our desires are always pleasing to God when their object is to promote His glory ; but sometimes He does not see good to give them effect. It was good that it was in David's heart, although he was not permitted, to build the house of God. The times and the ways of God's providence are often unknown to us, and therefore our desires and designs in His service ought always to be cherished in submission to His Divine wisdom. Paul had been hindered till now from going to Rome. This may have happened in different ways, and through what are called second causes. It may have been occasioned by the services he found it indispensable to perform in other churches before leaving them ; or it may have arisen from the machinations of Satan, the god of this world, exciting disturbances and opposition in these churches, 1 Thess. ii. 18; or he may have been prevented by the Spirit of God, Acts

xvi. 7. His being hindered, by whatever means, from going to Rome, when he intended it, shows that the Apostles were sometimes thwarted in their purposes, and were not always under the guidance of Divine inspiration in their plans. This, however, has nothing to do with the subject of their inspiration as it respects the Scriptures, or as it regards their doctrine. Those who raise any objection to the inspiration of the Scriptures, from the disappointments or misconduct of the Apostles, confound things that entirely and essentially differ.

Ver. 14.—*I am debtor both to the Greeks and to the Barbarians, both to the wise and to the unwise.*

Paul was their debtor, not by any right that either Greeks or Barbarians had acquired over him, but by the destination which God had given to his ministry towards them. He does not, however, hesitate to recognise the debt or obligation, because, when God called him to their service, he was in effect their servant, as he says in another place, ' Ourselves your servants for Jesus' sake.' The foundation of this duty was not in those whom he desired to serve, but in God, and the force of this obligation was so much the stronger as it was Divine ; it was a law imposed by sovereign authority, and consequently an inviolable law. With regard to Paul, it included, on the one hand, all the duties of the apostolic office, and, on the other, the dangers and persecutions to which that office exposed him, without even excepting martyrdom, when he should be called to that last trial. All this is similar to what every Christian owes in the service of God, as far as his abilities, of whatever kind they are, and his opportunities, extend.

As the Greeks—under which term all civilised nations were included—were the source of the arts and sciences, of knowledge and civilisation, it might be said that the Apostle should attach himself solely to them, and that he owed nothing to the Barbarians. On the contrary, it might be alleged that he was debtor only to the Barbarians, as the Greeks were already so enlightened. But in whatever way these distinctions were viewed, he declares that both the one and the other were equal to him : he was debtor to them all,—to the Greeks, because their light was only the darkness of error or of idle speculation—to the Barbarians, for he ought to have compassion on their ignorance. He was debtor to the *wise*, that is to say, the philosophers, as they were called among the Greeks ; and to the *unwise*, or those who made no profession of philosophy. He knew that both stood equally in need of the Gospel, and that for them all it was equally adapted. This is the case with the learned and the unlearned, who are both altogether ignorant of the way of salvation, till it be revealed to them by the Gospel, to which everything, by the command of God, the wisdom as well as the folly of the world,—in one word, all things besides,—must yield subjection.

Ver. 15.—*So, as much as is in me, I am ready to preach the Gospel to you that are at Rome also.*

Paul was always zealous to do his duty ; at the same time, he always acknowledged his dependence on God. This is an example which

Christians ought to imitate on all occasions, never to deviate from the path of duty, but to leave events in the hands of God. The contrary of this is generally the case. Christians are often more anxious and perplexed about their success, than with respect to their duty. They forget what regards themselves, and wish to meddle with what does not belong to them but to God. *To you also.*—He does not inquire or decide whether they ought to be reckoned among the Barbarians or the Greeks, the wise or unwise; he was ready to preach the Gospel to them all.

Here terminates the preface to the Epistle. The first five verses include the general introduction, the last ten embrace the particular address to those to whom it is written. The introduction contains the name, the character, and the office of the writer; his vindication of the Gospel against the cavils of the Jews, proving that it was not a novel doctrine, and that the Apostles were not opposed to the Prophets. It authenticates the whole of the Jewish canon, and attests its inspiration. It undermines the errors of the Jews respecting tradition, and directs them to the Scriptures alone. It next announces the Messiah as the subject of the Gospel,—His glorious person as God and man, His birth and resurrection, His abasement and exaltation, and His almighty power. It finally asserts the communication of grace to the Apostle, his appointment to the office he sustained, the purpose for which it was conferred, along with a commission, of which he states the grounds, to all the nations under heaven. Where else shall be found so much matter compressed in so little space? where so much brevity connected with so much fulness?

In the latter part, in which Paul addresses those to whom his Epistle was directed, he introduces many things well calculated to rivet their attention and engage their affections, while at the same time he conveys very grave and salutary instructions. What must have been the feelings of the Roman converts, when they saw the intense interest with which they were regarded by this great Apostle; when they considered the grandeur and value of the Gospel, to which he was about to call their attention in his Epistle; and when they were cheered by the hope of shortly seeing in the midst of them one whose heart glowed with such love to God, and such benevolence to them! All this must have tended to produce a reciprocal regard and reverential feeling towards the Apostle, an ardent desire to profit by his instructions, together with much gratitude to God, and many prayers to hasten his voyage to come among them. Paul did arrive at Rome, but, in the providence of God, in a very different manner, and in circumstances very different, from what he appears to have expected when he prayed for 'a prosperous journey.' He went there a prisoner in bonds, was shipwrecked on his voyage, and kept in confinement after his arrival. But although he was bound, the word of God was not bound; and all fell out, in the adorable providence of God, for the furtherance of the Gospel. The circumstances, however, in which he was placed were not in the meantime joyous, but grievous. Yet now that he stands before the throne, now that he has received the crown of righteousness, and is numbered among the spirits of just men made perfect, what regret can he experience that, during the few and evil days he spent on earth, he was conducted to Rome through persecutions, imprisonments, storms, and shipwreck, an outcast among men, but approved and accepted of God?

CHAPTER 1 / PART 2
ROMANS 1:16 – 32

HAVING concluded his prefatory address, the Apostle now announces, in brief but comprehensive terms, the grand subject which occupies the first five chapters of this Epistle, namely, the doctrine of justification by faith.

Ver. 16.—*For I am not ashamed of the Gospel of Christ ; for it is the power of God unto salvation to every one that believeth ; to the Jew first, and also to the Greek.*

I am not ashamed.—Paul here follows up what he had just said of his readiness to preach the Gospel at Rome, by declaring that he was not ashamed of it. This would also convey a caution to those whom he addressed against giving way to a strong temptation to which they were exposed, and which was no doubt a means of deterring many from embracing the Gospel, to whom it was preached. He knew from personal experience the opposition which the Gospel everywhere encountered. By the Pagans it was branded as Atheism ; and by the Jews it was abhorred as subverting the law and tending to licentiousness ; while both Jews and Gentiles united in denouncing the Christians as disturbers of the public peace, who, in their pride and presumption, separated themselves from the rest of mankind. Besides, a crucified Saviour was to the one a stumbling-block, and to the other foolishness. This doctrine was everywhere spoken against ; and the Christian fortitude of the Apostle, in acting on the avowal he here makes, was as truly manifested in the calmness with which he viewed the disdain of the philosophers, the contempt of the proud, and the ridicule of the multitude, as in the stedfast resolution with which, for the name of the Lord Jesus, he confronted personal danger, and even death itself. His courage was not more conspicuous when he was ready 'not to be bound only, but also to die at Jerusalem,' than when he was enabled to enter Athens or Rome without being moved by the prospect of all that scorn and derision which in these great cities awaited him.

But the grand reason which induced the Apostle to declare at the outset of this Epistle that he was not ashamed of the Gospel, is a reason which applies to every age as well as to that in which Christ was first preached. His declaration implies that, while in reality there is no just cause to be ashamed of the Gospel, there is in it something which is not acceptable, and that it is generally hated and despised among men. The natural man receiveth not the things of the Spirit of God ; for they are foolishness unto him. They run counter to his most fondly-cherished notions of independence ; they abase in the dust all the pride of his self-reliance, and, stripping him of every ground of boasting, and demanding implicit submission, they awaken all the enmity of the carnal mind. Even they who have tasted of the grace of God, are liable to experience, and often to yield to, the deeply-rooted and sinful feeling of being ashamed of the things of God. So prevalent is this even among Christians the most advanced, that Paul deemed it necessary to warn Timothy respecting it, whose faithfulness he so highly celebrates. 'Be not thou therefore ashamed of the testimony of our Lord.' In connection with this, he makes the same avowal for himself as in the passage before us, declaring at the same time the strong ground on which he rested, and was enabled to resist this temptation. Whereunto, he says, 'I am appointed a preacher, and an Apostle, and a teacher of the Gentiles. For which cause I also suffer these things: nevertheless I am not ashamed; for I know whom I have believed, and am persuaded that He is able to keep that which I have committed unto Him against that day.' At 'the same time he commends Onesiphorus for not being ashamed of his chain, 2 Tim. i. 8, 12, 16. And He who knew what is in man, solemnly and repeatedly guarded His disciples against this criminal shame, enforcing His admonitions by the most awful sanction. 'For whosoever shall be ashamed of Me and of my words, of him shall the Son of Man be ashamed, when He shall come in His own glory, and in His Father's, and of His holy angels.'

That system, in which there is nothing of 'foolishness' in the eyes of this world's wisdom, cannot be the Gospel of which Paul deemed it necessary to affirm that he was not ashamed. No other religion is so offensive to the pride of man; no other system awakens shame in the breasts of its votaries; and yet every false doctrine has in it more or less of what is positively absurd, irrational, and disgraceful. It is also observable that the more the Gospel is corrupted, and the more its peculiar features are obscured by error, the less do we observe of the shame it is calculated to produce. It is, in fact, the fear of opposition and contempt that often leads to the corruption of the Gospel. But this peculiarity affords a strong proof of the truth of the Apostle's doctrine. Had he not been convinced of its truth, would it not have been madness to invent a forgery in a form which excites the natural prejudices of mankind! Why should he forge a doctrine which he was aware would be hateful to the world? In this declaration Paul may also have had reference to the false mysteries of the Pagans, which they carefully concealed, because they contained many things that were infamous, and of which they were justly ashamed. When the Apostle says he is not ashamed of the Gospel, it further implies that he gloried in it, as he says, Gal. vi. 14, 'God forbid that I should glory, save in the cross of our Lord Jesus Christ;' and thus he endeavours to enhance, in the eyes of those to whom he wrote, the value and excellence of the Gospel, in order more fully to arrest their attention before he entered on his subject.

The Gospel of Christ.—A little before he had called it 'the Gospel of God;' he now designates it the Gospel of Christ, who is not only its author, but also its essential subject. The Gospel is therefore called the preaching of Jesus Christ, and of the unsearchable riches of Christ.

This Gospel, then, which Paul was ready to preach, and of which he was not ashamed, was the Gospel of God concerning His Son. The term Gospel, which signifies glad tidings, is taken from Isa. lii. 7, and lxi. 1, where the Messiah is introduced as saying, 'The Lord hath anointed Me to preach *good tidings.*'

For it is the power of God unto salvation.—Here the Apostle gives the reason why he is not ashamed of the Gospel of Christ. The Gospel is the great and admirable mystery, which from the beginning of the world had been hid in God, into which the angels desire to look, whereby His manifold wisdom is made known unto the principalities and powers in heavenly places. It is the efficacious means by which God saves men from sin and misery, and bestows on them eternal life,—the instrument by which He triumphs in their hearts, and destroys in them the dominion of Satan. The Gospel, which is the word of God, is quick and powerful, and sharper than any two-edged sword. By it, as the word of truth, men are begotten by the will of God, Jas. i. 18; 1 Pet. i. 23; and through the faith of the Gospel they are kept by His power unto salvation, 1 Pet. i. 5. The exceeding greatness of the power of God exerted in the Gospel toward those who believe, is compared to His mighty power which He wrought in Christ, when He raised Him from the dead, and set Him at His own right hand, Eph. i. 19. Thus, while the preaching of the cross is to them that perish foolishness, to those who are saved it is the power of God.

The Gospel is *power* in the hand of God, as opposed to our natural impotence and utter inability to obtain salvation by anything we can do, Rom. v. 6; and also in opposition to the law, which cannot save, being 'weak through the flesh,' Rom. viii. 3. It has been observed that the article *the*, before power, is not in the original. The article, however, is not necessary. The Apostle does not mean power as an attribute, for the Gospel is no attribute of God. It is power, as it is the means which God employs to accomplish a certain end. When it is said, the Gospel is God's power unto salvation, all other means of salvation are excluded.

To every one that believeth.—This power of God unto salvation is applied through faith, without which God will neither justify nor save any man, because it is the appointed means of His people's union with Jesus Christ. Faith accepts the promise of God. Faith embraces the satisfaction and merit of Jesus Christ, which are the foundation of salvation; and neither that satisfaction nor that merit would be imputed, were it not rendered ours by faith. Finally, by faith we give ourselves to Jesus Christ, in order that He may possess and conduct us for ever. When God justifies, He gives grace; but it is always in maintaining the rights of His majesty, in making us submit to His law and to the direction of His holiness, that Jesus Christ may reign in our hearts. The Gospel is the power of God unto salvation *to every one*, without any distinction of age, sex, or condition—of birth or of country,—without excepting any one, provided he be a believer in Christ. The expression, 'every one,' respects the extent of the call of the Gospel, in opposition to that of the law, which was addressed to the single family of Abraham.

To the Jew first, and also to the Greek.—This distinction includes all nations; for the Jews were accustomed to comprehend under the name of Greek all the rest of the world, as opposed to their own nation. The Greeks, from the establishment of the Macedonian empire, were better known to the Jews than any other people, not only on account of their power, but likewise of their knowledge and civilisation. Paul frequently avails himself of this distinction.

To the Jew first.—From the days of Abraham, their great progenitor, the Jews had been highly distinguished from all the rest of the world by their many and great privileges. It was their high distinction that of them Christ came, 'who is over all, God blessed for ever.' They were thus, as His kinsmen, the royal family of the human race, in this respect higher than all others, and they inherited Emmanuel's land. While, therefore, the evangelical covenant, and consequently justification and salvation, equally regarded all believers, the Jews held the first rank, as the ancient people of God, while the other nations were strangers from the covenants of promise. The preaching of the Gospel was to be addressed to them first, and, at the beginning, to them alone, Matt. x. 6 ; for, during the abode of Jesus Christ upon earth, He was the minister only of the circumcision, Rom. xv. 8. 'I am not sent,' He says, 'but to the lost sheep of the house of Israel ;' and He commanded that repentance and remission of sins should be preached in His name among all nations, 'beginning at Jerusalem,' Acts iii. 26, xiv. 26. Thus, while Jews and Gentiles were united in the participation of the Gospel, the Jews were not deprived of their rank, since they were the first called.

The preaching of the Gospel to the Jews *first*, served various important ends. It fulfilled Old Testament prophecies, as Isa. ii. 3. It manifested the compassion of the Lord Jesus for those who shed His blood, to whom, after His resurrection, He commanded His Gospel to be first proclaimed. It showed that it was to be preached to the chief of sinners, and proved the sovereign efficacy of His atonement in expatiating the guilt even of His murderers. It was fit, too, that the Gospel should be begun to be preached where the great transactions took place on which it was founded and established ; and this furnished an example of the way in which it is the will of the Lord that His Gospel should be propagated by His disciples, beginning in their own houses and their own country.

Ver. 17.—*For therein is the righteousness of God revealed from faith to faith ; as it is written, The just shall live by faith.*

The righteousness of God.—This phrase may, according to circumstances, mean either the personal attribute of God, or, as in this place, the righteousness which God has provided, which He has effected, and which He imputes for justification to all His elect. It is through this righteousness, revealed in the Gospel, that the Gospel is the power of God unto salvation. Paul reverts to its manifestation, ch. iii. 21, where the signification of this most important expression will be fully considered. At present it is sufficient to remark that the grand object of the Apostle is to show that man, having lost his own righteousness, and thereby fallen under condemnation, God has provided for him a righteousness—the complete fulfilment of the law in all its threatenings and all its precepts—by which, being placed to his account through faith, he is acquitted from guilt, freed from condemnation, and entitled to the reward of eternal life.

Is revealed.—This expression regards the assertion in the second verse of this chapter, that the Gospel had formerly been promised by the Prophets. The righteousness of God must be contemplated at three periods: first, at the period when God purposed it; second, at the period when He promised it; and third, at the period when He revealed it. He purposed it in His eternal decrees, He promised it after the fall, and now it is actually revealed in the Gospel. Paul does not say that it began only under the Gospel to display its efficacy, or that it was not known under the Mosaic dispensation; on the contrary, he was about to show that the Prophet Habakkuk had referred to it, and in the fourth chapter he proves that Abraham was justified by the imputation of this same righteousness; but he here declares that its full and perfect revelation was made by the Gospel, in which it is testified that at length it has been 'brought in,' as had been promised, Dan. ix. 24. Looking forward to the revelation of this righteousness, the Prophet Isaiah, lvi. 1, writes, 'Thus saith the Lord, Keep ye judgment, and do justice; for My salvation is near to come, and *My righteousness* to be *revealed*.' The Prophet thus announced in his time that it was *near to be revealed*, and the Apostle affirms that *it is now revealed*.

From faith to faith.—Various interpretations have been given of this phrase, although there appears to be little difficulty in ascertaining its meaning. Some explain it as signifying from the faith of the Old Testament to the faith of the New; some, from one degree of faith to another; some, from the faith of the Jew to the faith of the Gentile; and others, altogether of faith. The expression is evidently elliptical; and in order to understand it, it is necessary to observe that the literal rendering is not '*from* faith to faith,' but '*by* faith to faith.' The same words in the original are thus translated in the same verse: 'The just shall live *by faith*.' The meaning, then, is, the righteousness which is by faith, namely, which is received by faith, is revealed to faith, or in order to be believed. This is entirely consistent with what the Apostle says in ch. iii. 22, where he reverts to the subject, and announces that the righteousness of God, which is by, or through, faith of Jesus Christ, is unto all and upon all them that believe. There is then no difficulty in this expression, especially since the meaning is placed beyond dispute in this passage, where the same truth is fully expressed.

As it is written.—Here is a reference to the Old Testament Scriptures, as attesting what had just been affirmed, thus proving the correspondence between the Old Testament and the New, as was also shown in the second verse of this chapter, and teaching us to rest our faith on the testimony of the Scriptures, in whatever part of them it is found. *The just shall live by faith*, or rather, following the order of the words in the original, the just, or the righteous, by faith shall live. The doctrine, however, is substantially the same in whichsoever of these ways the phrase is rendered, and the meaning is, they who are righteous by faith, that is, by having the righteousness of God which is received by faith imputed to them, shall live. Paul repeats the same declaration in two other places, namely, in Gal. iii. 11, where he proves that men cannot be justified by the law, and also in Heb. x. 38, where he is exhorting those to whom he writes to continue firm in the faith; and immediately afterwards, explaining the meaning of that expression, he shows at large, in the following chapter, that men were saved by faith before, as well as after, the coming of the Messiah. In both cases the eye of faith was stedfastly fixed on the same glorious object. Before His advent, faith rested on that event, considered in the promise. After the coming of the Messiah, faith rejoices in the accomplishment of the promise. Thus it is only by faith in the testimony of God, as receiving His righteousness wrought by the Messiah, that man can be just or righteous in His sight. The passage itself is quoted from the prophecies of Habakkuk, and is generally supposed to relate, in its primary sense, to the deliverance from the Babylonish captivity, which was a type of the deliverance obtained by the Gospel. Through faith in the Divine promises the first was obtained, and the second in like manner is obtained through faith. But in whatever sense the Prophet used these words, the Apostle, speaking by the same Spirit, assigns to them their just and legitimate extension. They are true in respect to an earthly and temporal deliverance, and are equally true in respect to a spiritual deliverance.

Many, however, understand such quotations, where the Apostle says *it is written*, as mere *accommodation*, not implying prediction of the thing to which they are applied. This is a most unwarrantable and baneful method of handling the word of God. It is in this light that Professors Tholuck and Stuart, in their Commentaries on this Epistle, often view this form of expression. But, on the contrary, it is always used as introducing what is represented as a fulfilment of prediction, or an interpretation of its meaning. If Neologians are to be held guilty for explaining the miracles of Christ on natural principles, are *they* less criminal who explain, as mere accommodation of Scripture language, what is quoted by an Apostle as a fulfilment of prophecy? Several quotations from the Old Testament in this Epistle are explained by both these authors on the above Neological principle. Professor Stuart, on this passage, says, 'It is not necessary to suppose, in all cases of this nature, that the writer who makes such an appeal regards the passage which he quotes as *prediction*. Plainly this is not always the case with the writers of the New Testament, as nearly all commentators now concede.' Professor Tholuck remarks that 'the pious Jew loved to use Bible phrases in speaking of the things of common life, as this seemed to connect, in a manner, his personal observations and the events of his own history with those of holy writ.' He adds, that the Talmud contains numerous quotations introduced by such forms, 'without,' he continues, 'there being understood any real fulfilment of the text in the fact which is spoken of. This practice was also followed by the Apostles.'[1] The

---

[1] In the *Presbyterian Review*, No. xxx. p. 237, it is observed, 'This idea of quotation by accommodation is as old as the time of Aarias Montanus;' and, after remarking that in the above passage it is visited with merited castigation, the

subject of quotation by accommodation is one of such paramount importance, involving so deeply the honour of the Holy Scriptures, and at the same time is so lightly thought of by many, that it challenges the most serious attention.

Nothing can be more dishonourable to the character of Divine revelation, and injurious to the edification of believers, than this method of explaining the quotations in the New Testament from the Old, not as predictions or interpretations, but as mere illustrations by way of accommodation. In this way many of the prophecies referred to in the Epistles are thrust aside from their proper application, and Christians are taught that they do not prove the very things the Apostles adduced them to establish.

The great temptation to this manner of understanding them, is the fact that such prophecies generally, as they lie in the Old Testament, are obviously applied to temporal events, whereas, in the New, they are applied to the affairs of Christ and His kingdom. But this is a difficulty to none who understand the nature of the Old Testament dispensation, while the supposition that it is a difficulty, argues an astonishing want of attention to both covenants. Not only the ceremonies, but the personages, facts, and whole history of the Jewish people, have a letter and a spirit, without the knowledge of which they cannot be understood either in their true sense, or in a sense at all worthy of God. That the Old Testament predictions, then, should primarily refer to temporal events in the Jewish history, and in a secondary but more important view, to the Messiah and the Gospel, is quite in accordance with what is taught us everywhere by the New Testament.[1] Instead of creating a difficulty, this peculiarity is entirely consistent with the prominent features of Christianity, and calls for fresh admiration of the Divine wisdom. It is one of those characteristics which prove the Bible to be God's own book; and, as usual, men's attempts to mend it only serve to mar its beauty and obscure its evidence. In Gal. iii. 10, it is asserted that ' as many as are of the works of the law are under the curse.' Why are they affirmed to be under the curse? Because *it is written*, ' Cursed is every one that continueth not in all things which are written in the book of the law to do them.' The phrase *it is written* is used here to connect an inference or conclusion with the premises on which it is founded. The assertion, that all who are of the works of the law are under the curse, is founded on

reviewer adds, ' Professor Tholuck's authority, indeed, in any matter in which the honour of inspiration is involved, is not very high ; so at least we think all who have escaped the chilling influence of Socinianism must acknowledge respecting any writer, who in one place tells us that " Paul probably used certain words, without attaching to them any definite idea" (p. 156); in another, suggests the supposition that the Apostle " had forgotten what ought to have followed " (p. 157) ; and, in the present verse, informs us that, with the view of better adapting the declaration of the Prophet to his subject, he gave a " violent construction to the translation of the Septuagint ; " and whatever Tholuck's authority may be, Stuart's is no greater ; for water cannot rise higher than its source ; and on this subject of accommodation, with the exception of the very obnoxious sentiment which we have just cited, the American critic is no more than the copyist of the German."

[1] See the author's book *On the Evidences, etc.*, on the primary and secondary senses of prophecy, and its division into three branches, vol. i. p. 445, 3d edition.

the thing said to be written. The phrase, then, is indicative of true fulfilment or interpretation of meaning.

In like manner, what is spoken of, Matt. xiii. 14, and John xii. 39, 40, is, in Rom. xi. 8, introduced with the phrase 'it is written.' By the same phrase also is introduced, Gal. iv. 27, the reference to the prophecy of Isaiah, liv. 1. This must be prediction, because there does not appear to be any reference to a subordinate event in the Jewish history. It is an immediate prophecy of the calling of the Gentiles.

We learn from Gal. iv. 21–26, that even the history of Abraham's family was typical, and the recorded facts of ancient times are explained as predictions of Gospel times. 'Tell me, ye that desire to be under the law, do ye not hear the law?' In what respect could they hear the law on the point referred to? In the events that took place in Abraham's house. These facts are represented as a part of the law, and the spiritual truth at the proper interpretation.

Not only is the phrase 'it is written' always applied to indicate prediction or interpretation, but it was so understood and applied in our Lord's time. When the priests and scribes were asked where Christ should be born, they answered, in Bethlehem, *for thus it is written*, Matt. ii. 5. This phrase, then, they employed to indicate true fulfilment of prediction.

This very reference to Habakkuk is explained, Gal. iii. 11, as prediction. It is asserted in the beginning of the verse, that no man can be justified by the law, because *it is written* by the Prophet. Here the impossibility of justification by the law is founded on the prophecy quoted. But if this prophecy related only to a temporal event in the Jewish history, the fact being so written would not bear out the conclusion. That the prophecy there refers to the justification of sinners before God, as its true and most important meaning, is the necessary sense of the passage. So little foundation have the above-named writers for their bold perversions of the word of God on this point. Their doctrine respecting it manifests great ignorance of Scripture.

The passage in Matt. ii. 15, has been supposed by some to be utterly incapable of interpretation, in the sense of real fulfilment, as prediction. 'Out of Egypt have I called My Son.' The prophecy there referred to is found in Hos. xi. 1, and evidently refers to the calling of the Israelites out of Egypt. How then can it be the fulfilment of the prophecy according to the application in the Evangelist? Nothing is more easy than the solution of this supposed insuperable difficulty. The words of the Prophet have, in the primary or literal sense, a reference to the historical event—the calling of the Israelites, as nationally the typical Son of God, out of the land of Egypt; and, in the secondary or spiritual sense, couched under the figure, they refer to the calling of the true Son of God out of Egypt, where He had gone to sojourn in order to accomplish this prediction. The Son of God is, in Isa. xlix. 3, expressly addressed under the name of Israel. It argues the highest presumption, and even blasphemy, to explain this quotation on the principle of accommodation, when the Evangelist says 'that it might be fulfilled,' and thus intimates that this event was one predetermined in the counsels of

Eternity.   Is mere accommodation fulfilment in any sense?   How must infidels sneer at such violent efforts to explain away a difficulty, which is, after all, imaginary.   The language here used by the Evangelist establishes beyond all contradiction the double reference of many of the prophecies of the Old Testament.

Some commentators refer to Acts xxviii. 25, as an example of a passage which the Apostle quotes as *prediction*, when it is not·prediction. This Scripture is supposed to have reference to the Jews, as neglecting all warnings till they were finally carried into captivity.   It may have such a reference.   But this is not so certain as that it has the secondary reference to the state of the Jews with respect to the rejection of the Gospel.   Instead, then, of being received as applied to the latter by way of accommodation, or as illustrative cf the same principle, there is no absolute certainty of a primary reference; but there can be no doubt that it predicts the unbelief and hardness of heart manifested by the Jews in the time of our Lord, and afterwards.   This is irresistibly evident from Matt. xiii. 14.   Here it is expressly said to be a fulfilling of the prophecy, that 'in them is fulfilled the prophecy of Esaias, which saith,' etc.   The unbelief of the Jews is here, in express words, stated as the fulfilment of this same prophecy.   Is it not wonderful blindness, is it not the most profane temerity, to explain as mere accommodation what the Holy Spirit asserts to be a real fulfilment?   The same prophecy is referred to in John's Gospel as fulfilled in the Jews of our Lord's time, ch. xii. 39, 'Therefore they could not believe, because that Esaias said again.'   What can more strongly express prediction?   Belief was impossible, because of the prediction.   They were the words of God, and, therefore, must be fulfilled.   As this is a subject of so much importance, demanding the serious attention of all who tremble at the word of God, and one which is so frequently, I may say so generally, misrepresented, I shall further repeat the following remarks respecting it, from my *Book of Evidences*, vol. i. p. 450, third edition, on the Old Testament prophecies:—

' It is not as setting aside the literal application of such passages, that the Apostles quote them in their spiritual import; nor in the way of accommodation, as is often erroneously asserted: but in their ultimate and most extensive significations.   Nothing has been more mischievous, more audacious, and more dishonourable to the character of revelation, than the doctrine that represents the New Testament writers as quoting the Old Testament prophecies by way of accommodation.   It is based on the supposed difficulty or impossibility of explaining the agreement in the literal accomplishment.   To this it may be replied, that satisfactory solutions of the cases of difficulty have been given.   But though no satisfactory solution were given, the supposition would be inadmissible. It contradicts most explicitly the Spirit of God, and must be rejected, let the solution be what it may.   The New Testament writers, in quoting the Old Testament prophecies, quote them as being fulfilled in the event which is related.   If it is not truly fulfilled, the assertion of fulfilment is false.   The fulfilment by accommodation is no fulfilment in any real sense of the word.   This interpretation, then, cannot be admitted, as being palpably contradictory to the language of inspiration. To quote the Old Testament prophecies in this way, could not, in any respect, serve the purpose of the writers of the New Testament. What confirmation to their doctrine could they find from the language of a prophecy that did not really refer to the subject to which they applied it, but was merely capable of some fanciful accommodation? It is ascribing to these writers, or rather to the Spirit of God, a puerility of which every writer of sound judgment would be ashamed. The application of the language of inspiration by way of accommodation, is a theory that has sometimes found patrons among a certain class of writers; but a due respect for the inspired writings will ever reject it with abhorrence. It is an idle parade of ingenuity, even when it coincides in its explanations with the truths of the Scriptures; but to call such an accommodation of Scripture language a fulfilment, is completely absurd. There is nothing in Scripture to warrant such a mode of explanation.'

'To say,' observes Mr. Bell, on the *Covenants*, 'that these Scriptures had no relation to these events, what is this but to give the inspired penman the lie? The question is not what the Old Testament writers intended in such and such sayings, but what the Spirit which was in them did signify. The Prophets might often not know the full extent of their own prophecy, but certainly the Spirit, by which they spake, always did. The Spirit in the Old Testament writers was the same who inspired those of the New, 2 Cor. iv. 13; therefore, when the latter quote the words of the former as predictive of, and fulfilled in, certain events, the Holy Spirit is pointing out what He Himself intended. And who dare say but that He may point out more fully under the New Testament what He intended in the Old, than ever could have entered into the heart of man? 1 Cor. ii. 9, 10. Surely the only wise God must be allowed to know the full sense of His own words. When the Evangelists or Apostles tell us that such and such Scriptures were fulfilled in such events, they do not give a new sense to these Scriptures which they never had before, but only show what before was latent with us. To say that any of their quotations from the Old Testament are mere allusions, or only used by way of accommodation to their purpose, beyond the true sense of the words and the intention of the Holy Ghost, effectually cuts the sinews of their argumentation, and, of course, destroys the proofs they adduce,' p. 56. The misunderstanding, or rather denial on this point, of the plain import of Scripture, in representing the New Testament writers as quoting from the Old Testament in the way of accommodation, appears to originate, so far as concerns Professors Tholuck and Stuart, in their want of acquaintance with the nature of the inspiration of the Bible. Were this not the case, they could not have ventured to take such liberties with the Scriptures as appear in their Commentaries.[1]

The declaration in the 16th and 17th verses, that the Gospel is the

---

[1] On the subject of Inspiration, see the author's work on *The Authenticity and Inspiration of the Holy Scriptures,* and Dr. Carson's unanswered and unanswerable treatise on *The Theories of Inspiration by the Rev. Daniel Wilson (now Bishop of Calcutta), the Rev. Dr. Pye Smith, and the Rev. Dr. Dick, proved to be erroneous,* and his *Refutation of Dr. Henderson's Doctrine on Divine Inspiration, with a Critical Discussion on 2 Tim.* iii. 16.

power of God unto salvation to every one that believeth, to the Jew first, and also to the Greek, because therein is the righteousness of God revealed, serves as the text or ground of the whole of the subsequent disquisition in this and the following nine chapters.

Ver. 18.—For the wrath of God is revealed from heaven against all ungodliness and unrighteousness of men, who hold the truth in unrighteousness.

Here commences the third division of this chapter, where the Apostle enters into the discussion, to prove that all men being under the just condemnation of God, there remains for them no way of justification but that by grace, which the Gospel holds out through Jesus Christ.

Mr. Stuart understands this verse and the 17th as co-ordinate, and as supplying—each of them severally—a reason of the statement that Paul was not ashamed of the Gospel; but the subsequent discussion shows the utter inapplicability of verse 18th to the Gospel, inasmuch as the Apostle developes, at great length, the truth that the, wrath of God is declared against those to whom no explicit revelation has been given. It is connected by the particle *for* with the preceding verse, and constitutes an argument in favour of the statement, that nowhere, except in the Gospel, is the righteousness of God revealed for the justification of sinners, and marks the necessity, for this purpose, of that revelation. This argument is evolved at great length, and the exposition of it does not terminate till the 20th verse of the third chapter. In this long section of the Epistle, a foundation is laid for the doctrine of grace in the announcement of the doctrine of wrath : all men are concluded under sin, that the promise by faith of Jesus Christ might be given to them that believe—that it might be shown, beyond question, that if men are to be justified, it cannot be by a righteousness of their own, but by the righteousness provided by God, and revealed in the Gospel. The Apostle begins here by proving that the Gentiles were all guilty, and all subjected to the just judgment of God.

The wrath of God is revealed.—The declaration of the wrath of God is a fit preparation for the announcement of grace,—not only because wrath necessarily precedes grace in the order of nature, but because, to dispose men to resort to grace, they must be affected with the dread of wrath and a sense of their danger. The wrath of God denotes His vengeance, by ascribing, as is usual in Scripture, the passions of men to God. It implies no emotion in God, but has reference to the judgment and feeling of the sinner who is punished. It is the universal voice of nature, and is also revealed in the consciences of men. It was revealed when the sentence of death was first pronounced, the earth cursed, and man driven out of the earthly paradise, and afterwards by such examples of punishment as those of the deluge, and the destruction of the Cities of the Plain by fire from heaven, but especially by the reign of death throughout the world. It was proclaimed in the curse of the law on every transgression, and was intimated in the institution of sacrifice, and in all the services of the Mosaic dispensation. In the eighth chapter of this Epistle, the Apostle calls the attention of believers to the fact that the whole creation has become subject to vanity, and groaneth and travaileth together in pain.

The same creation which declares that there is a God, and publishes His glory, also proves that He is the enemy of sin and the avenger of the crimes of men. So that this revelation of wrath is universal throughout the world, and none can plead ignorance of it. But, above all, the wrath of God was revealed from heaven when the Son of God came down to manifest the Divine character, and when that wrath was displayed in His sufferings and death, in a manner more awful than by all the tokens God had before given of His displeasure against sin. Besides this, the future and eternal punishment of the wicked is now declared in terms more solemn and explicit than formerly. Under the new dispensation, there are two revelations given from heaven, one of wrath, the other of grace.

Against all ungodliness and unrighteousness of men.—Here the Apostle proceeds to describe the awful state of the Gentiles, living under the revelation of nature, but destitute of the knowledge of the grace of God revealed in the Gospel. He begins with accusing the whole heathen world, first of *ungodliness*, and next of *unrighteousness*. He proves that, so far from rendering to their Creator the love and obedience of a grateful heart, they trampled on His authority, and strove to rob Him of His glory. Failing, then, in their duty towards God, and having plunged into the depths of all ungodliness, it was no wonder that their dealings with their fellowmen were characterized by all unrighteousness. The word *all* denotes two things: the one is, that the wrath of God extends to the entire mass of ungodliness and unrighteousness, which reigns among men, without excepting the least part; the other is, that ungodliness and unrighteousness had arrived at their height, and reigned among the Gentiles with such undisturbed supremacy, that there remained no soundness among them.

The first charge brought under the head of ungodliness, is that of *holding the truth in unrighteousness*. The expression, the *truth*, when it stands unconnected in the New Testament, generally denotes the Gospel. Here, however, it is evidently limited to the truth concerning God, which, by the works of creation, and the remains of the law of conscience, and partly from tradition, was notified to the heathens. The word 'hold,' in the original, signifies to hold fast a thing supposed to be valuable, as well as to withhold, as it is rendered 2 Thess. ii. 6, and to restrain or suppress. The latter is the meaning here. The heathens did not hold fast the truth, but they suppressed or restrained what they knew about God. The expression signifies they retained it as in a prison, under the weight and oppression of their iniquities.

But besides this general accusation, the Apostle appears particularly to have had reference to the chief men among the Pagans, whom they called philosophers, and who professed themselves wise. The declaration that the wrath of God is revealed from heaven against all ungodliness and unrighteousness of men, who suppress the truth in unrighteousness, attacked directly the principle which they universally held to be true, namely, that God could not be angry with any man. Almost all of them believed the truth of the Divine unity, which they communicated to those who were initiated into their mysteries. But all of them, at the

same time, held it as a maxim, and enjoined it as a precept on their
disciples, that nothing should be changed in the popular worship of their
country, to which, without a *single* exception, they conformed, although
it consisted of the most absurd and wicked idolatrous rites, in honour of
a multitude of gods of the most odious and abominable character. Thus
they not only resisted and constantly acted in opposition to the force of
the truth in their own minds, but also suppressed what they knew of it,
and prevented it from being told to the people.

Ver. 19.—*Because that which may be known of God is manifest in them; for God
hath showed it unto them.*

The Apostle here assigns the reason of what he had just affirmed
respecting the Gentiles as suppressing the truth in unrighteousness,
namely, that which may be known of God, God hath manifested to them.
They might have said, they did not suppress the truth in unrighteousness, for God had not declared it to them as He had done to the Jews.
He had, however, sufficiently displayed, in the works of creation, His
almighty power, wisdom, and goodness, and other of His Divine attributes, so as to render them without excuse in their ungodliness and
unrighteousness.

That which may be known of God,—that is to say, not absolutely, for
that surpasses the capacity of the creature.—God is incomprehensible
even by angels, and it is by Himself alone that He can be fully and
perfectly comprehended; the finite never can comprehend the infinite,
Job xi. 7. Nor do the words before us mean all that can be known of
Him by a supernatural revelation, as the mystery of redemption, that of
the Trinity, and various other doctrines; for it is only the Spirit of God
who has manifested these things by His word. It is on this account that
David says, ' He showeth His word unto Jacob, His statutes and His
judgments unto Israel. He hath not dealt so with any nation; and as
for His judgments, they have not known them,' Ps. cxlvii. 19. But
what may be known of God by the works of creation, He has not concealed from men.

Is manifest in them, or rather, to them.—This respects the clearness of
the evidence of the object in itself, for it is not an obscure or ambiguous
revelation; it is a manifestation which renders the thing certain. It is
made to them; for the Apostle is referring here only to the external
object, as appears by the following verse, and not to the actual knowledge which men had of it, of which he does not speak till the 21st
verse.

For God hath showed it unto them.—He has presented it before their
eyes. They all see it, though they do not draw the proper conclusion
from it. In like manner He has shown Himself to the world in His Son
Jesus Christ. ' He that hath seen Me hath seen the Father.' Yet many
saw Him who did not recognise the Father in Him. These words, ' hath
showed it unto them,' teach us that in the works of creation God has
manifested Himself to men to be glorified by them; and that, in preserving the world after sin had entered, He has set before their eyes those
great and wonderful works in which He is represented; and they further

show that there is no one who can manifest God to man except Himself, and consequently that all we know of Him must be founded on His own revelation, and not on the authority of any creature.

Ver. 20.—*For the invisible things of Him from the creation of the world are clearly seen, being understood by the things that are made, even His eternal power and Godhead ; so that they are without excuse.*

Invisible things of Him.—God is invisible in Himself, for He is a Spirit, elevated beyond the reach of all our senses. Being a Spirit, He is exempted from all composition of parts, so that when the Apostle here ascribes to Him 'invisible things' in the plural, it must not be imagined that there is not in God a perfect unity. It is only intended to mark the different attributes of Deity, which, although one in principle, are yet distinguished in their objects, so that we conceive of them as if they were many.

From the creation of the world are clearly seen.—By the works of creation, and from those of a general providence, God can be fully recognised as the Creator of heaven and earth, and thence His natural attributes may be inferred. For that which is invisible in itself has, as it were, taken a form or body to render itself visible, and visible in a manner so clear that it is easy to discover it. This visibility of the invisible perfections of God, which began at the creation, has continued ever since, and proves that the Apostle here includes with the works of creation those of providence, in the government of the universe. Both in the one and the other, the Divine perfections very admirably appear.

Being understood by the things that are made.—The works of creation and providence are so many signs or marks, which elevate us to the contemplation of the perfections of Him who made them, and that so directly, that in a manner these works, and these perfections of their Author, are as only one and the same thing. Here the Apostle tacitly refutes the opinion of some of the philosophers respecting the eternity of the world; he establishes the fact of its creation, and at the same time teaches, contrary to the Atheists, that, from the sole contemplation of the world, there are sufficient proofs of the existence of God. Finally, by referring to the works of creation, he indicates the idea that ought to be formed of God, contrary to the false and chimerical notions of the wisest heathens respecting Him.

Even His eternal power and Godhead.—The Apostle here only specifies God's eternal power and Godhead, marking His eternal power as the first object which discovers itself in the works of creation, and in the government of the world ; and afterwards denoting, by His Godhead, the other attributes essential to Him as Creator. His *power* is seen to be eternal, because it is such as could neither begin to exist, nor to be communicated. Its present exertion proves its eternal existence. Such power, it is evident, could have neither a beginning nor an end. In the contemplation of the heavens and the earth, every one must be convinced that the power which called them into existence is eternal. *Godhead.*— This does not refer to all the Divine attributes, for they are not all manifested in the works of creation. It refers to those which manifest

God's deity. The heavens and the earth prove the deity of their Author. In the revelation of the word, the grand truth is the deity of Christ; in the light of nature, the grand truth is the deity of the Creator. By His power may be understood all the attributes called relative, such as those of Creator, Preserver, Judge, Lawgiver, and others that relate to creatures; and by His Godhead, those that are absolute, such as His majesty, His infinity, His immortality.

So that they are without excuse.—The words in the original may either refer to the end intended, or to the actual result—either to those circumstances being designed to leave men without excuse, or to the fact that they are without excuse. The latter is the interpretation adopted by our translators, and appears to be the true meaning. It cannot be said that God manifested Himself in His works, in order to leave men without excuse. This was the result, not the grand end. The revelation of God by the light of nature the heathens neglected or misunderstood, and therefore are justly liable to condemnation. Will not then the world, now under the light of the supernatural revelation of grace, be much more inexcusable? If the perverters of the doctrine taught by the works of creation were without excuse, will God sustain the excuses now made for the corrupters of the doctrine of the Bible?

When the heathens had nothing else than the manifestation of the Divine perfections in the works of creation and providence, there was enough to render them inexcusable, since it was their duty to make a good use of them, and the only cause of their not doing so was their perversity. From this, however, it must not be inferred, that since the entrance of sin, the subsistence of the world, and the providence which governs it, sufficiently furnish man, who is a sinner, with the knowledge of God, and the means of glorifying Him in order to salvation. The Apostle here speaks only of the revelation of the natural attributes of God, which make Him indeed the sovereign good to man in innocence, but the sovereign evil to man when guilty. The purpose of God to show mercy is not revealed but by the Spirit of God, who alone searcheth the deep things of God, 1 Cor. ii. 10. In order to this revelation, it was necessary that the Holy Spirit should have animated the Prophets and Apostles. It is therefore to be particularly observed that, while, in the next chapter, where the Apostle proceeds to prove that the Jews are also without excuse, he urges that the forbearance, and long-suffering, and goodness of God, in the revelation of grace, led them to repentence, he says nothing similar respecting the heathens. He does not assert that God, in His revelation to them, called them to repentance, or that He held out to them the hope of salvation, but affirms that that revelation renders them inexcusable. This clearly shows that in the whole of the dispensation to the heathen, there was no revelation of mercy, and no accompanying Spirit of grace, as there had been to the Jews. The manifestations made by God of Himself in the works of creation, together with what is declared concerning the conduct of His providence, Acts xiv. 17; and what is again said in ch. ii. of this Epistle, ver. 14, 15, respecting the law written in the heart, comprise the whole of the revelation made to the heathen, after they had lost sight of the original

promise to Adam of a deliverer, and the preaching of the righteousness
of God by Noah; but in these ways God had never left Himself without
a witness.   The works of creation and providence spoke to them from
without, and the law written in their heart from *within*.   In conjunction,
they declared the being and sovereign authority of God, and man's
accountableness to his Creator.   This placed all men under a positive
obligation of obedience to God.   But His law, thus made known, admits
not of forgiveness when transgressed, and could not be the cause of justification, but of condemnation.   The whole, therefore, of that revelation
of God's power and Godhead, of which the Apostle speaks in this discourse, he regards as the foundation of the just condemnation of men, in
order afterwards to infer from it the necessity of the revelation of grace.
It must not be supposed, then, that he regards it as containing in itself a
revelation of grace in any manner whatever, for this is an idea opposed
to the whole train of his reflections.   But how, then, it may be said, are
men rendered inexcusable?   They are *inexcusable*, because their natural
corruption is thus discovered; for they are convicted of being sinners,
and consequently alienated from communion with God, and subjected to
condemnation, which is thus shown to be just.

Ver. 21.—*Because that, when they knew God, they glorified Him not as God,
neither were thankful ; but became vain in their imaginations, and their foolish heart
was darkened.*

Knew God.—Besides the manifestation of God in the works of creation,
the heathens had still some internal lights, some principles and natural
notions, which are spoken of, ch. ii. 12, 15, from which they had, in a
measure, the knowledge of the existence and authority of God.   There
may be here, besides, a reference to the knowledge of God which He
communicated in the first promise after the fall, and again after the
flood, but which, not liking to retain God in their knowledge, and being
' haters of God,' mankind had lost.   Elsewhere, Paul says that the
Gentiles were without God in the world, Eph. ii. 12; yet here he says
they knew God.   On this it may be observed, that they had very confused ideas of the Godhead, but that they further corrupted them by an
almost infinite number of errors.   Respecting their general notions of
deity, these represented the true God; but respecting their erroneous
notions, these only represented the phantoms of their imagination.   In
this way they knew God, yet nevertheless they were without God.   They
knew his existence and some of His perfections; but they had so entirely
bewildered their minds, and added so many errors to the truth, that they
were in reality living without God.   They might be said to know God
when they confessed Him as the Creator of the world, and had some
conception of His unity, wisdom, and power.   The Apostle may particularly refer to the wise men among the heathens, but the same truth
applies to all.   They all knew more than they practised, and the most
ignorant might have discovered God in His works, had not enmity
against Him reigned in their hearts.   But when Paul says, Eph. ii. 12,
that they were without God, he has respect to their worship and their
practice.   For all their superstitions were exclusively those of impiety,
which could only serve to alienate them from the love and the communion

of the true God.   They were therefore, in reality, without God in the world, inasmuch as they set up devils, whom, under the name of gods, they served with the most abominable rites.

They glorified Him not as God.—Paul here marks what ought to be the true and just knowledge of God, namely, that knowledge which leads men to serve and worship Him in a manner agreeable to His sovereign will, and worthy of His holy character.   To glorify God signifies to acknowledge and worship Him with ascriptions of praise, because of His glorious attributes.   Now the heathens, though in their speculations they might speak of God in a certain way consistent with some of His attributes, as His unity, spirituality, power, wisdom, and goodness, yet never reduced this to practice.   The objects of their professed worship were either the works of God, or idols.   To these they gave the glory that belonged to God; to these they felt and expressed gratitude for the blessings which God bestowed on them.   God left them not without a witness of His existence and goodness, in that He gave them rain from heaven, and fruitful seasons; but the glory for these things, and for all other blessings, they rendered to the objects of their false worship.   It appears also that the Apostle had in view the fact, that the philosophers in their schools entertained some proper ideas of God, but in their worship conformed to the popular errors.   Men often justify their neglect of God by alleging that He has no need of their service, and that it cannot be profitable to Him ; but we here see that He is to be glorified for His perfections, and thanked for His blessings.

Neither were thankful.—We should constantly remember that God is the source of all that we are, and of all that we possess.   In Him we live, and move, and have our being.   From this it follows that He ought to be our last end.   Consequently, one of the principal parts of our worship is to acknowledge our dependence, and to magnify Him in all things by consecrating ourselves to His service.   The opposite of this is what is meant by the expression, ' neither were thankful ; ' and this is what the heathens were not, for they ascribed one part of what they possessed to the stars, another part to fortune, and another to their own wisdom.

But became vain in their imaginations, or rather in their reasonings, that is, speculations.—Paul calls all their philosophy reasonings, because they related to words and notions, divested of use or efficacy.   Some apply this expression, ' became vain in their reasonings,' to the attempts of the heathen philosophers to explore, in a physical sense, the things which the poets ascribed to the gods.   Dr. Macknight supposes that the object of the wise men was to show that the religion of the vulgar, though untrue, was the fittest for them.   Many explanations, equally fanciful, have been given of these words.   The language itself, in connection with the writings of the wise men to whom the Apostle refers, leaves no good reason to doubt that he speaks of those speculations of the Grecian philosophers in which they have manifested the most profound subtilty and the most extravagant folly.   Their reasonings diverged very far from that truth which they might have discovered by the contemplation of the works of creation ; and, besides, produced nothing for the glory of God, in which they ought to have issued.   In fact, all their reasonings were to no purpose, so far as regarded their sanctification, or the peace of their conscience. The whole of what the Apostle here says aptly describes, and will equally apply to, vain speculations of modern times. It suits not only modern schools of philosophy, but also some of theology; not only the vain interpretations of Neologians, but of all who explain away the distinguishing doctrines of revelation. Without being carried away with the learning and research of such persons, every one who loves the Scriptures and the souls of men, should lift up his voice against such degradations of the oracles of God.

Their foolish heart was darkened.—' Imprudent heart,' as Dr. Macknight translates this, comes not up to the amount of the phrase. It designates the heart, or understanding, as void of spiritual discernment and wisdom —unintelligent in Divine things, though subtle and perspicacious as to the things of the world. Their speculations, instead of leading them to the truth, or nearer to God, were the means of darkening their minds, and blinding them still more than they were naturally. The Apostle here marks two evils : the one, that they were destitute of the knowledge of the truth ; and the other, that they were filled with error, for here their darkness does not simply signify ignorance, but a knowledge false and depraved. These two things are joined together.

Ver. 22.—*Professing themselves to be wise, they became fools.*

It appears that, by the term *wise*, the Apostle intended to point out the philosophers,—that is to say, in general, those who were most esteemed for their knowledge, like those among the Greeks who were celebrated by the titles either of men wise or philosophers. To the two evils remarked in the foregoing verse, of their foolishness and their darkness, Paul here adds a third—that with all this they believed themselves to be wise. This is the greatest unhappiness of man, not only not to feel his malady, but to extract matter of pride from what ought to be his shame. What they esteemed their wisdom was truly their folly. All their knowledge, for which they valued themselves, was of no avail in promoting virtue or happiness. Their superstitions were in themselves absurd; and instead of worshipping God, they actually insulted Him in their professed religious observances. How wonderfully was all this exhibited in the sages of Greece and Rome, who rushed headlong into the boundless extravagances of scepticism, doubting or denying what was evident to common sense ! How strikingly is this also verified in many modern philosophers !

So far were the heathen philosophers from wisdom, that they made no approach towards the discovery of the true character either of the justice or mercy of God ; while with respect to the harmony of these attributes, in relation to man, they had not the remotest conception. The idea of a plan to save *sinners*, which, instead of violating the law of God, and lowering His character as the moral governor of the world, magnifies the law and makes it honourable, giving full satisfaction to His justice, and, commensurate with His holiness, is as far beyond the conception of man, as to create the world was beyond his power. It is an idea that could not have suggested itself to any finite intellect.

Want of knowledge of the justice of God gave occasion to the manifestation of human ignorance. All the ancient philosophers considered that consummate virtue and happiness were attainable by man's own efforts ; and some of them carried this to such an extravagant pitch, that they taught that the wise man's virtue and happiness were independent of God. Such was the insanity of their wisdom, that they boasted that their wise man had in some respects the advantage of Jupiter himself, because his virtue was not only independent, or his own property, but was voluntary, whereas that of the divinity was necessary. Their wise man could maintain his happiness, not only independent of man and in the midst of external evils, but also in defiance of God Himself. No power, either human or divine, could deprive the sage of his virtue or happiness. How well does all this prove and illustrate the declaration of the Apostle, that professing themselves to be wise, they became fools !

Ver. 23.—*And changed the glory of the incorruptible God into an image made like to corruptible man, and to birds, and four-footed beasts, and creeping things.*

Here Paul produces a proof of the excess of the folly of those who professed themselves to be wise. Their ideas of God were embodied in images of men, and even of birds and beasts, and the meanest reptiles. *Changed the glory of the incorruptible God,*—that is, the ideas of His spirituality, His immateriality, His infinity, His eternity, and His majesty, which are His glory, and distinguish Him from all creatures. All these are included in the term *incorruptible ;* and as the Apostle supposes them to be needful to the right conception of God, he teaches that these are all debased and destroyed in the mind of man when the Creator is represented under human or other bodily resemblances ; for these lead to conceptions of God as material, circumscribed, and corruptible, and cause men to attribute to Him the meanness of the creature, thus eclipsing His glory, and changing it into ignominy. The glory of God, then, refers to His attributes, which distinguish Him from the idols which the heathens worshipped. In verse 25 it is called *the truth of God*, because it essentially belongs to the Divine character. Both expressions embrace the same attributes, but under different aspects. In the one expression, these attributes are considered as constituting the Divine glory ; in the other, as essential to His being, and distinguishing Him from the false gods of the heathen.

It is impossible to conceive of anything more deplorably absurd, further removed from every semblance of wisdom, or more degrading in itself and dishonouring to God, than the idolatrous worship of the heathens ; yet among them it was universal. The debasing images to which the Apostle here refers, were worshipped and feared by the whole body of the people, and not even *one* among all their philosophers, orators, magistrates, sages, statesmen, or poets, had discernment sufficient to detect the enormity of this wickedness, or honesty enough to reclaim against it. On the contrary, every one of them conformed to what the Apostle Peter calls ' abominable idolatries.'

It is to no purpose to say that the heathens did not believe that their images which they set up, were gods, but only resemblances; for the Apostle condemns them under the character of resemblances or *likenesses*. Nor is it to any purpose to affirm that those resemblances were only aids to assist the weakness of the human mind; for he also shows that those pretended aids were hurtful and not beneficial, because they cor-- rupted the holy and reverential notions we ought to entertain of the Deity. Neither does it avail to say that they did not serve their images as God, but that the adoration they rendered was to God, since the medium itself derogates from His glory. Nor will it do to profess that by those images they did not intend to express the essence, but only the perfections or attributes of God, and that they were rather emblems than images. The heathens said all this, and the Roman Catholics now say the same; but they are not on this account the less condemned by the Apostle.

Ver. 24.—*Wherefore God also gave them up to uncleanness through the lusts of their own hearts, to dishonour their own bodies between themselves.*

Wherefore God also gave them up.—The impurities into which the Gentiles were plunged, sprung from their own corrupt hearts. We must therefore distinguish between their abandonment by God, and the awful effects of that abandonment. The abandonment proceeded from Divine justice, but the effect from the corruption of man, in which God had no part. The abandonment is a negative act of God, or rather a negation of acting, of which God is absolutely master, since, being under no obligation to confer grace on any man, He is free to withhold it as He sees good; so that in this withholding there is no injustice. But besides this, it is a negation of acting which men have deserved by their previous sins, and consequently it proceeds from His justice, and is in this view to be considered as a punishment. Sin is indeed the conse- quence of this abandonment, but the only cause of it is human perversity. God's *giving them up*, then, does not signify any positive act, but denotes His net holding them in check by those restraints by means of which He usually maintains a certain degree of order and appearance of moral rectitude among sinners. God did not, however, totally withdraw those restraints, by which His providence rules the world in the midst of its corruption; for if He had done so, it would have been impossible that society could have subsisted, or the succession of generations con- tinued. God, for these ends, still preserved among them some common rectitude, and certain bonds of humanity. But in other respects, so far as concerned the impurities to which the Apostle here refers, He relaxed His restraints on the fury of their passions, as a corresponding punish- ment for their idolatries. Thus was His justice manifested in giving up those who had dishonoured Him to dishonour themselves, in a manner the most degrading and revolting.

Ver. 25.—*Who changed the truth of God into a lie, and worshipped and served the creature more than the Creator, who is blessed for ever. Amen.*

By changing the *truth of God*, referring to the attributes essential to His being, is here meant the changing of the just and legitimate notions which ought to be formed of Him, not only in contemplation, but chiefly in practice. The *lie* in the same way principally refers to practice, not consisting only in speculative errors, but in perversity of action in superstitions and idolatries. The heathens changed the truth of God, that is, the true idea of God exhibited in the works of creation, into the false representations made of Him in their superstitious idolatries. Thus departing from the true God, and receiving false gods in His stead, they worshipped the creature more, or rather, than the Creator. They pretended, indeed, that they did not forsake the Creator, while they served numerous divinities. They acknowledged that these were inferior to the sovereign God, whom they called the Father of gods and men. But whenever religious worship is offered to the creature in any manner whatever, it is forsaking God, whose will it is, not only that His creatures should serve Him, but that they should serve Him alone, on which account He calls Himself a jealous God. The idolatry of the Pagans was in reality, according to the view here given by the Apostle, a total abandonment of the worship of God.

Who is blessed for ever. Amen.—This expression is here used by the Apostle for the purpose of inflicting a greater stigma on idolatry, denoting that we ought to honour and adore God alone, and are not permitted to take away from Him even the smallest ray of His glory. It is an expression that was almost in perpetual use among the Jews, and is still frequently found in their writings when they speak of God. It denotes that we should never speak of God but with profound respect, and that this respect ought to be accompanied with praise and thanksgiving. In particular, it condemns idolatry, and signifies that God alone is worthy to be eternally served and adored. The word 'Amen' is here not only an affirmation, or an approval; it is also an aspiration of pious feeling, and a token of regard for the honour of God.

Ver. 26.—*For this cause God gave them up unto vile affections: for even their women did change the natural use into that which is against nature.*

Ver. 27.—*And likewise also the men, leaving the natural use of the woman, burned in their lust one toward another; men with men working that which is unseemly, and receiving in themselves that recompense of their error which was meet.*

The Apostle having awfully depicted the magnitude of Pagan wickedness, and having shown that their ungodliness in abandoning the worship of the true God was the reason why they had been abandoned to their lusts, here descends into particulars, for the purpose of showing to what horrible excesses God had permitted them to proceed. This was necessary, to prove how odious in the sight of God is the crime of idolatry. Its recompense was this fearful abandonment. It was also necessary, in order to give a just idea of human corruption, as evinced in its monstrous enormities when allowed to take its course, and also in order to exhibit to believers a living proof of the depth of the evil from which God had delivered them; and, finally, to prove the falsity of the Pagan religion, since, so far from preventing such excesses, it even incited and conducted men to their commission.

Receiving in themselves that recompense.—As the impiety of the Pagans respecting God reached even to madness, it was also just that God should permit their corruption to recoil upon themselves, and proceed also to madness. It was just that they who had done what they could to cover the Godhead with reproaches, should likewise cover themselves with infamy, and thus receive a proportionate and retributive recompense.

Ver. 28.—*And even as they did not like to retain God in their knowledge, God gave them over to a reprobate mind, to do those things which are not convenient.*

The Apostle shows here how justly the Pagan idolaters were abandoned since they had so far departed from the right knowledge of God. In the 18th verse, he had declared that the wrath of God was revealed against all ungodliness and unrighteousness of men. He had now conclusively established the first charge of *ungodliness* against the Gentiles, adding to it their consequent abandonment to the vilest affections; he next proceeds to demonstrate their *unrighteousness.*

And as they did not like.—This is not quite literal, yet it seems the best phrase that can be used to convey the spirit of the original. The word in the Greek signifies to prove or approve. They did not approve of retaining God in their knowledge. But this cannot mean that their approbation respected their conscience, dark as it was. They did not approve, because, as the common translation well expresses it, they did not like.[1] There is no just ground to conclude, with Dr. Macknight, that there is here a reference to the magistrates and lawgivers, who did not approve of giving the knowledge of God to the people. It applies to them all; neither the lawgivers, nor the people, liked to hold in remembrance a God of holiness and justice.

To retain God in their knowledge.—The common translation has here substantially given the spirit of the original, and is better than ' holding God with acknowledgment,' as rendered by Dr. Macknight. The heathens are thus said to have known God, but, knowing Him, they did not wish to retain that knowledge. This is a crime in the sight of God which subjects men to the most awful judgments of His justice; for it is on this account that the Apostle adds, that God also gave them up to a *reprobate mind.* This pointedly refers to the word applied to them, as not approving the retaining of the knowledge of God. It denotes a mind judicially blinded, so as not to discern the difference between things distinguished even by the light of nature. Thus the dark eclipse of their understanding concerning Divine things, which they had despised and rejected, had been followed by another general eclipse respecting things human, to which they had applied themselves, and in this consisted the proportion which God observed in their punishment. They did not act according to right reason and judgment towards God,—this is their crime; they did not act according to it among themselves in society,— this was the effect of the abandonment of God, and became their punishment. This passage clearly shows that all that remains of moral uprightness among men is from God, who restrains and sets bounds to the force of their perversity.

Not convenient.—This is a very just and literal translation, according to the meaning of the word convenient in an early stage of the history of

---

[1] The words, not to approve, are frequently used in the sense of not liking. It is often said that a person does not approve of, *i.e.* does not like, a person.

our language; but it does not, at present, give the exact idea. The original word signifies what is suitable to the nature of man as a rational and moral being. To do things not convenient, is a figurative expression denoting the doing of things directly contrary and opposite, namely, to the light of reason, the reflections of prudence, and the dictates of conscience.

Ver. 29.—*Being filled with all unrighteousness, fornication, wickedness, covetousness, maliciousness; full of envy, murder, debate, deceit, malignity; whisperers.*

Being filled.—This signifies that the vices here exposed were not tempered with virtues, but were alone and uncontrolled, occupying the mind and heart even to overflowing. *Unrighteousness.*—When this word in the original is taken in a limited sense, it signifies injustice. It is often used for iniquity in general, as in the 18th verse. Some understand it here in the latter sense, as a general word which includes all the different particulars that follow. There is no reason, however, why we should not understand it as one species of the evils which are here enumerated, and confine it to its specific meaning, viz. injustice. This was the public crime of the Romans, who built their empire on usurpation and rapine. *Fornication.*—Cicero speaks of fornication as unblameable, as a thing universally allowed and practised, which he had never heard was condemned, either in ancient or modern times. Here it includes all the violations of the seventh commandment, and is not to be confined to the distinctive idea which the term bears in our language. *Wickedness.*—This refers to the general inclination to evil that reigned among the heathens, and made them practise and take pleasure in vicious and unprofitable actions. *Covetousness.* — The original word strictly signifies taking the advantage, overreaching in a bargain, having more than what is just in any transaction with our neighbour. Of this, covetousness is the motive. This was universal among rich and poor, and was the spring of all their actions. *Maliciousness* denotes a disposition to injury and revenge. *Full of envy.*—Tacitus remarks that this was the usual vice of the villages, towns, and cities. *Murder* was familiar to them, especially with respect to their slaves, whom they caused to be put to death for the slightest offences. *Debate*, strife about words for vainglory, and not truth. *Deceit* was common to them all, and exemplified in their conduct and conversation, as is said, ch. iii. 13. *Malignity.*—Though the word in the original, when resolved into its component parts, literally signifies bad custom or disposition, yet it generally signifies something more specific, and is with sufficient propriety rendered malignity, which is a desire to hurt others without any other reason than that of doing evil to them, and finding pleasure in their sufferings. The definition of the term, as quoted from Aristotle by Dr. Macknight, seems true rather as a specification than as a definition. It ' is a disposition,' he says, ' to take everything in the worst sense.' No doubt malevolence is inclined to this, but this is only one mode of discovering itself. *Whisperers.*—Dr. Macknight errs in saying that the original word signifies ' those who secretly speak evil of persons when they are present.' The word does not import that the speaker whispers lest the person against whom he speaks, being present, should hear. The person spoken against may as well be absent. It refers to that sort of evil-speaking which is communicated in secret, and not spoken in society. It is called whispering, not from the tone of the voice, but from the secrecy. It is common to speak of a thing being whispered, not from being communicated in a low voice, but from being privately spoken to individuals. It refers to sowing divisions. It is one of the most frequent and injurious methods of calumny, because, on the one hand, the whisperer escapes conviction of falsehood, and, on the other, the accused has no means of repelling the secret calumny.

Ver. 30.—*Backbiters, haters of God, despiteful, proud, boasters, inventors of evil things, disobedient to parents.*

Backbiters.—The original word is here improperly translated backbiters. Dr. Macknight equally misses the meaning of this term, which he translates 'revilers,' distinguishing it from whisperers, or 'persons who speak evil of others to their face,' giving them opprobrious language and bad names. The word indeed includes such persons; but it applies to evil-speaking in general,—to those, in short, who take a pleasure in scandalizing their neighbours, without any reference to the presence or absence of those who are spoken against; and it by no means designates, as he says, the giving of 'opprobrious language and bad names.' Such persons are included in it, but not designated by it. Whisperers or tattlers are evil-speakers, without any peculiar distinction. Our translators have erred in rendering it *backbiters*. As Dr. Macknight has no authority to limit the word to what is spoken face to face, it is equally unwarrantable to confine it to what is spoken in the absence of those who are spoken against. The word translated 'whisperers' refers, according to Mr. Tholuck, to a secret, and the word translated 'backbiters,' to an open slander. Secrecy is undoubtedly the characteristic of the first word, but the last is not distinguished from it by contrast, as implying publicity; on the contrary, the former class is included in the latter, though here specifically marked. Besides, though the communication of both the classes referred to may usually be slander, yet it appears that the signification is more extensive. Whisperers, as speakers of evil, may be guilty when they speak nothing but truth. Mr. Stuart has here followed Mr. Tholuck. The former he makes a slander in secret, the latter a slander in public. It is not necessary that all such persons should be slanderers, and the evil-speaking of the latter may be in private as well as in public.

Haters of God.—There is no occasion, with Mr. Tholuck, to seek a reference here to 'those heathens mentioned by Cyprian, who, whenever a calamity befell them, used to cast the blame of it upon God, and denied a providence.' Nor is it necessary to suppose, with him, that the propriety of the charge is to be found in the fact that superstition begets a hatred of the gods. The charge is applicable to the whole heathen world, who hated God, and therefore did not like to keep Him in remembrance. This was manifest throughout the world in the early introduction of Polytheism and idolatry. No other cause can be assigned for the nations losing the knowledge of the true God. They did not like to retain Him in their knowledge. Had men loved God, He would have been known to them in all ages and all countries. Did not mankind receive a sufficient lesson from the flood? Yet such was their natural enmity to God, that they were not restrained even by that awful manifestation of Divine displeasure at forgetfulness of the Almighty. Although no one will acknowledge this charge to be applicable to himself, yet it is one which the Spirit of God, looking deeply into human nature, and penetrating the various disguises it assumes, brings home to all men in their natural state. 'The carnal mind is enmity against God.' They hate His holiness, His justice, His sovereignty, and even His mercy in the way in which it is vouchsafed. The charge here advanced by the Apostle against the heathens was remarkably verified, when Christianity, on its first appearance among them, was so violently opposed by the philosophers and the whole body of the people, rich and poor, learned and unlearned. This melancholy fact is written in the history of the persecutions of the early Christians in characters of blood.[1] *Despiteful.* —This term does not express the meaning of the original. Archbishop Newcome translates it injurious; but though this is one of the ideas contained in the word, it is essentially deficient. It signifies injury accompanied with contumely; insolence, implying insult. It always implies contempt, and usually reproach. Often, treatment violent and insulting. Mr. Stuart translates it '*reproachful,*' *i.e.,* he says, 'lacerating others by slanderous, abusive, passionate declarations.' But this does not come up to the meaning of the original. All this might be done without affecting to despise its object, or in any point of view to assume superiority over him,—an idea always implied in the original word. Besides, the reproachful words may not be slanderous. Mr. Tholuck makes it pride towards a fellow-creature; but this designation is not sufficiently peculiar. A proud man may not insult others. This vice aims at attaching disgrace to its object; even in the injuries it commits on the body, it designs chiefly to wound the mind. It well applies to hootings, hissings, and peltings of a mob, in which, even when the most dignified persons are the objects of attack, there is some mixture of contempt.

Proud.—This word translates the original correctly, as it refers to the feeling generally, and not to any particular mode of it, which is implied in arrogance, insolence, haughtiness, to persons puffed up with a high opinion of themselves, and regarding others with contempt, as if they were unworthy of any intercourse with them. *Boasters.*—The term in the original designates ostentatious persons in general; but as these usually affect more than belongs to them, it generally applies to persons who extend their pretensions to consideration beyond their just claims. *Inventors of evil things.*—Dr. Macknight translates this inventors of unlawful pleasures, and no doubt such inventions are referred to, but there is no reason to restrict it to the invention of pleasures when there are many other evil inventions. In such a case it is proper to give the expression the utmost latitude it will admit, as including all evils. *Dis-*

---

[1] Hatred to God, and not dislike to mysteries, is remarkably verified in infidels. Hatred to God is the origin of Arianism and Socinianism. It is hatred to the sovereignty of God that influences the Arminian. Hatred to God manifests itself by an almost universal neglect of His laws.

obedient to parents.—Obedience to parents is here considered as a duty taught by the light of nature, the breach of which condemns the heathens, who had not the fifth commandment written in words. It is a part of the law originally inscribed on the heart, the traces of which are still to be found in the natural love of children to their parents. When the heathens, then, disregarded this duty, they departed from the original constitution of their nature, and disregarded the voice of God in their hearts.

Ver. 31.—*Without understanding, covenant-breakers, without natural affection, implacable, unmerciful.*

Without understanding.—This well expresses the original; for although the persons so described were not destitute of understanding as to the things of this world, but as to these might be the most intelligent and enlightened, yet, in a moral sense, or as respects the things of God, they were unintelligent and stupid. This agrees with the usual signification of the word, and it perfectly coincides with universal experience. All men are by nature undiscerning as to the things of God, and to this there never was an exception. Dr. Macknight entirely misses the meaning, when he explains it as signifying persons who are 'imprudent in the management of affairs.' The translation of Mr. Stuart, 'inconsiderate,' is equally erroneous. *Covenant-breakers.*—This is a correct translation, if covenant is understood to apply to every agreement or bargain referring to the common business of life, as well as solemn and important contracts between nations and individuals. *Without natural affection.*—There is no occasion to seek for some particular reference in this, which has evidently its verification in many different things. Dr. Macknight supposes that the Apostle has the Stoics in his eye. Beza, and after him Mr. Stuart, supposes that it refers to the exposure of children. Mr. Tholuck, with more propriety, extends the term to filial and parental love. But still the reference is broader; still there are more varieties comprehended in the term. Why limit to one thing what applies to many? Even though one class should be peculiarly prominent in the reference, to confine it to this robs it of its force.

Implacable.—The word in the original signifies as well persons who will not enter into league, as persons who, having entered into league, perfidiously break it. In the former sense it signifies implacable, and designates those who are peculiarly savage. In the latter sense it refers to those who violate the most sacred engagements, entered into with all the solemnities of oaths and religious rites. Our translation affixes to it the first sense. But in this sense it applies to none but the rudest and most uncivilised nations, and was not generally exemplified in the Roman empire. It appears that it should rather be understood in the latter sense, as designating the common practice of nations in every age, who, without hesitation, violate treaties and break oaths sanctioned by every solemn obligation. The word above rendered covenant-breakers, designates the violators of any engagement. The word employed here signifies the breaker of solemn engagements, ratified with all the solemnities of oaths and religious ceremonies.

Unmerciful.—There is no reason, like Dr. Macknight, to confine this

to those who are unmerciful to the poor.   Such, no doubt, are included;
but it extends to all who are without compassion.   Persons need our
compassion who are not in want; they may be suffering in many ways.
It applies to those who do not feel for the distresses of others, whatever
may be the cause of their distresses; and to those who inflict these distresses it peculiarly applies.

Ver. 32.—*Who, knowing the judgment of God, that they which commit such things
are worthy of death, not only do the same, but have pleasure in them that do them.*

Knowing the judgment of God.—Sentence or ordinance of God.   This
the heathens knew, from the work of the law written in their hearts.
Although they had almost entirely stifled in themselves the dictates of
conscience, it did not cease, in some measure, to remonstrate against the
unworthiness of their conduct, and to threaten the wrath of God, which
their sins deserved.   They recognised it by some remains they had of
right notions of the Godhead, and by which they still understood that God
was judge of the world; and this was confirmed to them by examples
of Divine vengeance which sometimes passed before their eyes.   They
knew it even by the false ideas of the superstition in which they were
plunged, which required them to seek for expiations.   That they knew
it in a measure is evident by their laws, which awarded punishments to
some of those vices of which they were guilty.

Worthy of death.—It is difficult to deetrmine with certainty whether
death is here to be understood literally or figuratively.   Mr. Stuart considers it as decided that it cannot mean literal death, because it cannot
be supposed that the heathens judged everything condemned by the
Apostle to deserve capital punishment.   He understands it in its figurative
sense, as referring to future punishment.   But an equal difficulty meets
him here.   Did the heathens know that God had determined to punish the
things thus specified with death, according to its figurative import—everlasting punishment?   He does not take the word, then, in this sense to its
full amount, but as meaning punishment, misery, suffering.   But this is
a sense which the word never bears.   If it refer to future punishment, it
must apply to that punishment in its full sense.   That the heathens
judged many of the sins here enumerated worthy of death, is clear from
their ordaining death as their punishment.   And the Apostle does not
assert that they judged them all worthy of death, but that they judged
the doers of such things worthy of death.   It seems quite enough, then,
that those things, for the commission of which they ordained death,
were such as he mentions.   In this sense Archbishop Newcome understands the word, 'For they themselves,' he says, ' punished some of their
vices with death.'

Not only do the same, but have pleasure in them that do them.—This is
added to mark the depth of their corruption.   For when men are not
entirely abandoned to sin, although they allow of it in their own circumstances and practice, yet they condemn it in their general notions, and in
the practice of others, because then it is not connected with their own
interest and self-love.   But when human corruption has arrived at its
height, men not only commit sins, but approve of them in those who

commit them.   While this was strictly applicable to the whole body of the
people, it was chargeable in the highest degree on the leaders and philosophers, who, having more light than the others, treated in their schools
some of those things as crimes of which they were not only guilty themselves, but the commission of which they encouraged by their connivance,
especially in the abominable rites practised in the worship of their gods.

By these conclusive proofs Paul substantiates his charge, in verse 18,
against the whole Gentile world, first of *ungodliness,* and then of *unrighteousness* as its consequence, against which the wrath of God is revealed.
It should also be observed that as, in another place, Tit. ii. 12, he
divides Christian holiness into three parts, namely, *sobriety, righteousness,*
and *godliness,* in the same way, in this chapter, he classes Pagan depravity
under three heads.   The first is their *ungodliness,* namely, that they have
not glorified God—that they have changed His glory into images made-
like to corruptible creatures—that they have changed His truth into a
lie, which is opposed to godliness.   The second is *intemperance.*   God
had delivered them up to uncleanness and vile affections, which are opposed to sobriety.   The third is *unrighteousness,* and all the other vices
noted in the last verses, which are opposed to righteousness.

It is impossible to add anything to the view here given of the reign of
corruption among the heathens, even the most celebrated and civilised,
which is fully attested by their own historians.   Nothing can be more
horrible than this representation of their state; and as the picture is
drawn by the Spirit of God, who is acquainted not only with the outward
actions, but with the secret motives of men, no Christian can suppose
that it is exaggerated.   The Apostle, then, had good reason to conclude
in the sequel, that justification by works is impossible, and that in no
other way can it be obtained but by grace.   From the whole, we see
how terrible to his posterity have been the consequences of the sin of the
first man; and, on the other hand, how glorious in the plan of redemption is the grace of God by His Son.

CHAPTER 2
ROMANS 2:1 – 29

In the preceding chapter, the Apostle had described the state of the
idolatrous Pagans, whom he had proved to be under the just condemnation of God.   He now passes to that of the Jews, who, while they rejected the *righteousness of God,* to which the law and the prophets bore
witness, looked for salvation from their relation to Abraham, from their
exclusive privileges as a nation, and from their observance of the law.
In this and the two following chapters, Paul combats these deeply-rooted
prejudices, and is thus furnished with an opportunity of clearly unfolding
the doctrine of the Gospel, and of proving that it alone is the power of
God unto salvation.   In the first part of this chapter, to the 24th verse,
he shows that the just judgment of God must be the same against the
Jews as against the Gentiles, since the Jews are equally sinners.   In the

second part, from the beginning of the 25th verse to the end, he proves
that the external advantages which the Jews had enjoyed, were insufficient to ward off this judgment. From his language at the commencement of this chapter, in respect to that judgment which the Jews were
accustomed to pass on the other nations, and to which he reverts in the
17th verse, it is evident that through the whole of it he is addressing the
Jews, and not referring, as many suppose, to the heathen philosophers
or magistrates. It was not the Apostle's object to convince them in particular that they were sinners. Besides, neither the philosophers nor
magistrates, nor any of the heathens, occupied themselves in judging others
respecting their religious worship and ceremonies. Such observances, as
well as their moral effects on those by whom they were practised, appeared to the sages of Greece and Rome a matter of perfect indifference.
The Jews, on the contrary, had learned from their law, to judge, to condemn, and to abhor all other religions; to keep themselves at the greatest
distance from those who profess them; and to regard all idolaters as
under the wrath of God. The man, then, who *judges others*—to whom, by
a figure of speech, Paul addresses his discourse in the first verse—is the
same to whom he continues to speak in the rest of the chapter, and whom
he names in the 17th verse, ' Behold, thou art called a Jew.'

Ver. 1.—*Therefore thou art inexcusable, O man, whosoever thou art that judges:
for wherein thou judgest another, thou condemnest thyself; for thou that judgest doest
the same things.*

Therefore.—This particle introduces a conclusion, not from anything in
the preceding chapter, but to establish a truth from what follows. The
Apostle had proved the guilt of the Gentiles, who, since they had a
revelation vouchsafed to them in the works of God, though they did not
possess His word, were inexcusable. The Jews, who had His word, yet
practised the same things for which the former were condemned, must
therefore also be inexcusable. In the sequel, he specifies and unfolds
the charge thus generally preferred.

O Man.—This is a manner of address betokening his earnestness,
which Paul frequently employs, as in the ninth chapter of this Epistle.
Whosoever thou art that judgest.—The Apostle here refers to the judgment
which the Jews passed on the Gentiles. It is generally explained as if
he was finding fault with those whom he addressed, and declaring they
were inexcusable, because they judged others. But this is erroneous.
What he censures, is not their judging, but their doing the same things
with those whom they condemned. The character of the Jews, which
distinguished them from the Gentiles, was that they judged others. God
had conferred on them this distinction, when He manifested His covenant
to them, to the exclusion of all the other nations of the world. This
character of judging, then, can belong only to the Jews, who, according
to a principle of their religion, condemned the other nations of the earth,
and regarded them as strangers from the covenants of promise, having no
hope, and without God in the world. In this manner the Jews were
seated as on a tribunal, from which they pronounced judgment on all
other men. Paul, then, had good reason for apostrophizing the Jew as
thou that judgest. But as there were also distinctions among the Jews

themselves, and as the priests, the scribes, and chiefly the Pharisees, were regarded as more holy than others, he says, *whosoever thou art,*— thus not excepting even one of them.

Thou art inexcusable.—Paul intended to bring in all men guilty before God, as appears by what he says in the 19th verse of the third chapter, 'that every mouth may be stopped, and all the world may become guilty before God.' He had already proved the inexcusableness of the Gentiles, and he here proceeds to do the same respecting the Jews, whom he addresses directly, and not in a manner only implying that he refers to them, as is supposed by Professors Tholuck and Stuart. Mr. Stuart, especially, endeavours to show that in the first part of this chapter Paul does not proceed at once to address the Jews, 'but first,' he says, 'prepares the way, by illustrating and enforcing the general proposition, that all who have a knowledge of what is right, and approve of it, but yet sin against it, are guilty.' This view of the passage is equally erroneous with that of those who suppose that the Apostle is addressing the philosophers and magistrates. Both these interpretations lead away from the true meaning of the several parts of the chapter, through the whole of which the address to the Jew is direct and exclusive. The Apostle's object was to conduct men to the grace of the Gospel, and so to be justified in the way of pardon and acquittance. Now, in order to this, their conviction of sin and of their ruined condition was absolutely necessary, since they never would have recourse to mercy, if they did not feel compelled to confess themselves condemned. It is with this view that he here proceeds to strip the Jews, as he had done the Gentiles, of all *excuse.*

For wherein thou judgest another, thou condemnest thyself.—*Wherein,* that is, in the thing in which thou condemnest another, thou condemnest thyself. Dr. Macknight translates it *whilst.* But though the words in the original thus translated often in certain situations bear this significa- tion, here this cannot be the case. When there is nothing in the context to fix the reference, the most general substantive must be chosen. There is nothing in the context to suggest the idea of time, and thing is a more general idea. It is indeed true that the self-condemnation of the Jew is contemporaneous with his condemnation of the Gentile. But it is so, because this is implied in the very thing that is alleged, and the thing alleged is more important than the time in which it occurs. Nothing, then, is gained by thus deviating from the common version. The transla- tion, *because that,* which is suggested by Professors Tholuck and Stuart as a possible meaning, is also to be rejected. To suggest a great variety of possible meanings has the worst tendency ; instead of serving the truth, it essentially injures it. Besides, as has been remarked, the cause of the condemnation of the Jew was not his *judging* the Gentiles : the cause of his condemnation was his *doing the things* which he condemned.

The reasoning of the Apostle is clear and convincing. It consists of three particulars, on which the Jew had nothing to object, namely,—1st, Thou judgest another ; 2d, Thou doest the same things ; 3d, Thou con- demnest thyself ; consequently thou art without excuse. *Thou judgest another.*—That is to say, Thou holdest the Gentiles to be criminal and

guilty before God ; thou regardest them as people whom God has abandoned to themselves, and who, therefore, being plunged in vice and sin
of all kinds, are the objects of His just vengeance. This is what the
Jew could not deny. *Thou doest the same things.*—This the Apostle was
to prove in the sequel. *Thou condemnest thyself.*—The consequence is
unavoidable ; for the same evidence that convicts the Gentiles in the
judgment of the Jew, must, if found in him, also bring him in guilty.

Ver. 2.—*But we are sure that the judgment of God is according to truth against
them which commit such things.*

Paul proceeds here to preclude a thought that might present itself,
and to stifle it, as it were, before its birth. It might be suggested that
the judgment of God—that is, the sentence of condemnation with respect
to transgressors—is not uniform ; that He condemns some and acquits
others, as it pleases Him ; and therefore, although the Jew does the same
things as the Gentile, it does not follow that he will be held equally
culpable,—God having extended indulgence to the one, which He has
not vouchsafed to the other. The Jew, then, does not hold himself guilty
when he condemns the Gentile, although he does the same things. This
is the odious and perverse imagination which the Apostle here repels.
We are sure, or more literally, we know. Who knows ? 'Koppe,' says
Mr. Tholuck, 'deems that there is here an allusion to the Jews, who
boasted that they alone possessed the true knowledge.' But this is
palpably erroneous, because the Jews in general did not believe the thing
asserted to be known. The Apostle's object is to correct their error.
Mr. Tholuck himself is still farther astray when he understands it of
' those apprehensions of a Divine judgment which are spread among all
mankind, to which the Apostle had alluded, ch. i. 32.' It was the
Apostle himself, and those taught by the same Spirit, who knew with
unfaltering assurance the thing referred to. *The judgment of God,*—that
is, sentence of condemnation,—not, as Dr. Macknight says, the curse of
the law of Moses. The law of Moses and its curse are different from the
sentence which God pronounces according to them. *According to truth,*
against them which commit such things.—Not *truly.* This would qualify
the assertion that the judgment of God is against such persons, which, as
a general truth, neither the Jew nor the Gentile is supposed to question.
In this sense, truly would express the same as really. Nor does it
signify according to truth, as synonymous with justice, as Mr. Tholuck
supposes. About the justice of the thing there is no question. If the
Gentile is justly condemned for every breach of the law written on the
heart, the justice of the condemnation of the transgressing Jew could not
be a question. Nor, with Mr. Stuart, is it to be understood as meaning,
agreeably to the real state of things,—that is, according to the real
character of the person judged. This is doubtless a truth, but not the
truth asserted in this passage. This meaning applies to the judgment
that examines and distinguishes between the righteous and the wicked.
But the judgment here spoken of, is the sentence of condemnation with
respect to transgressors. Nor, with Dr. Macknight, are we to understand
this phrase as signifying, ' according to the true meaning of God's cove-

nant with the fathers of the Jewish nation.' This is not expressed in the text, nor is it suggested by the context.

The real import of this phrase will be ascertained in considering the chief error of the Jews about this matter. While they admitted that God's law, in general, condemns all its transgressors, yet they hoped that, as the children of Abraham, God would in their case relax the vigour of His requirements. What the Apostle asserts, then, is designed to explode this error. If God should sentence Gentiles to condemnation for transgression of the work of the law written in the heart, and pass a different sentence on Jews transgressing the law of Moses, His judgment or sentence would not be according to truth. If some transgressors escaped, while others were punished, the truth of the threat or penalty was destroyed. The truth of God in His threatening, or in the penalty of the breach of His law, is not affected by the deliverance of those saved by the Gospel. The penalty and the precept are fulfilled in Jesus Christ the surety. While God pardons, He by no means clears the guilty. His people are absolved, because they are righteous; they have fulfilled the law, and suffered its penalty, in the death and obedience of Jesus Christ, with whom they are one. The object of the Apostle, then, was to undeceive the Jews in their vain hope of escape, while they knew themselves to be transgressors. And it equally applies to nominal Christians. It is the most prevalent ground of hope among false professors of Christianity, that God will not be so strict with them as His general threatening declares, because of their relation to Him as His professed people.

Ver. 3.—*And thinkest thou this, O man, that judgest them which do such things, and doest the same, that thou shalt escape the judgment of God?*

Thinkest thou.—This question evidently implies that the Jews did think they would escape, while they committed the very sins for which they believed the heathens would be condemned. This affords a key to the meaning of the foregoing phrase, *according to truth*, which implies the contrary of this, namely, that all will be punished according to the truth of the threatening or penalty. *Escape.*—This expression imports three things: first, that the Jew could not avoid being judged; second, that he could not avoid being condemned; and third, that he could not prevent the execution of the sentence that God will pronounce. We may decline the jurisdiction of men, or even, when condemned by them, escape from their hands, and elude the execution of their sentence; but all must stand before the judgment-seat of Christ; all must be judged according to their works; and all who are not written in the book of life shall be cast into the lake of fire.

We may here observe how prone men are to abuse, to their own destruction, those external advantages which God bestows on them. God had separated the Jews from the Gentiles, to manifest Himself unto them; and, by doing so, He had exalted them above the rest of the world, to whom He had not vouchsafed the same favour. The proper and legitimate use of this superiority would have been to distinguish themselves from the Gentiles by a holy life. But instead of this, owing to a fatal confidence which they placed in this advantage, they committed the same sins as the Gentiles, and plunged into the same excesses. By this means, what they considered as an advantage became a snare to them; for wherein they judged others, they condemned themselves. We may likewise remark how much self-love blinds and betrays men into false judgments. When all the question was respecting the Gentiles, the Jews judged correctly, and conformably to Divine justice; but when the question is respecting themselves, although they were equal in guilt, they would not admit that they were equally the subjects of condemnation.

Ver. 4.—*Or despisest thou the riches of His goodness, and forbearance, and long-suffering; not knowing that the goodness of God leadeth thee to repentance?*

Goodness.—This is the best translation of the word. Mr. Tholuck says that it signifies love in general. But the idea expressed is more general than love. An object of goodness may be very unworthy of being an object of love. A distinction must be made between *goodness, forbearance,* and *long-suffering.* Goodness imports the benefits which God hath bestowed on the Jews. Forbearance denotes God's bearing with them, without immediately executing vengeance—His delaying to punish them. It signifies the toleration which He had exercised towards them after extending to them His goodness; so that this term implies their ingratitude after having received the benefits which God had bestowed, notwithstanding which He had continued the course of His goodness. Long-suffering signifies the extent of that forbearance during many ages, denoting a degree of patience still unexhausted. Their sins were not immediately visited with the Divine displeasure, as would be the case in-the government of men. The term goodness respects their first calling, which was purely gratuitous, Deut. vii. 7. Forbearance respects what had passed after their calling, when, on different occasions, the people having offended God, He had, notwithstanding, restrained His wrath, and had not consumed them. It is this that David celebrates in Ps. ciii. 10, and cvi. Long-suffering adds something more to forbearance; for it respects a long course of ingratitude and sins on the part of that people, and imports an extreme degree of patience on the part of God,—a patience which many ages, and a vast accumulation of offences, had .not exhausted. The Apostle calls all this the *riches* of His goodness, and long-suffering, and forbearance, to mark the greatness of their extent, their value and abundance, and to excite admiration in beholding a God all-powerful, who has no need of any of His creatures, and is infinitely exalted above them, striving for so long a period with an unrighteous, ungrateful, rebellious, and stiff-necked people, but striving with them by His goodness and patience. This language is also introduced to correct the false judgments of men on this patience of God; for they are apt, on this account, to imagine that there is no God. If, say they, God existed, He would not endure the wicked. They suppose that God does not exercise His providence in the government of the world, since He does not immediately punish their sins. To repress these impious thoughts, the Apostle holds forth this manner of God's procedure as the riches of goodness and patience, in order that the impunity which it appears that sinners enjoy, might not be attributed to any wrong principle.

Or despisest thou.—God's goodness is despised when it is not improved as a means to lead men to repentance, but, on the contrary, serves to harden them, from the supposition that God entirely overlooks their sin. The Jews despised that goodness; for the greatest contempt that could be shown to it was to shut the ear against its voice, and to continue in sin. This is acting as if it were imagined that the justice which lingers in its execution has no existence, and that it consists solely in empty threats. The interrogations of the Apostle in this and the preceding verse add much force to his discourse. *Thinkest thou*, says he, that thou canst avoid the judgment of God? By this he marks the erroneousness and folly of such a thought. *Despisest thou* the riches of His goodness? This is added to indicate the greatness of the crime.

Not knowing.—There is no necessity, with Professors Tholuck and Stuart, to translate this ' not acknowledging.' The thing itself the Jews did not know, and the bulk of those called Christians are equally ignorant of it. The whole of the Old Testament was sufficiently clear on this point, but the Jews excluded the light it furnished. They did so by the presumptuous opinion they entertained of their own external righteousness, in which they made the essence of holiness to consist, imagining that by it they would obtain acceptance with God. They likewise did so by the confidence they placed in the promises that God had made to Abraham and his posterity, flattering themselves with the vain thought that these promises acquired for them a right of impunity in their sins. And, finally, they did so by the gross error into which they had fallen, that the sacrifices and other legal expiations were sufficient to procure the pardon of their sins. By reason of these delusive prejudices they remained in their state of corruption, and did not penetrate farther into the design of God, who, by lavishing on them so much goodness, loudly called them to repentance.

Leadeth thee to repentance.—It has been already remarked that the Apostle said nothing like this when speaking in the first chapter respecting the Gentiles. He did not ascribe to God either goodness, or forbearance, or long-suffering in regard to them. He did not say that God invited, or called, or led them to repentance. This shows, as has also been observed, that in the dispensation of providence which regarded them, there was no revelation of mercy. But if there was none for the Gentiles, it was otherwise with the Jews. The Old Testament contained in substance all the promises of the Gospel, as well as the temporal covenant which God had made with the Jews, which was a figure and type of the spiritual covenant made in Christ; and even all the rigours of the law indirectly conducted the Jews to the grace of God, and consequently called them to repentance. This call was all along accompanied among some of them by the spirit of sanctification, as appears by the example of the prophets and others. But with respect to the greater number, it remained unaccompanied with that spirit, and consequently continued to be merely an external calling, without any saving effect. The Apostle, in the following verse, declares that the Jews by their impenitence drew down upon themselves the just anger of God. From this it evidently follows that God externally calls many to whom He has not purposed to give the grace of conversion. It also follows that it cannot be said that when God thus externally calls persons on whom it is not His purpose to bestow grace, His object is only to render them inexcusable. For if that were the case, the Apostle would not have spoken of the riches of His goodness, and forbearance, and long-suffering, —terms which would not be applicable, if, by such a call, it was intended merely to render men inexcusable.

Ver. 5.—But, after thy hardness and impenitent heart, treasurest up unto thyself wrath against the day of wrath and revelation of the righteous judgment of God.

The Apostle here intimates that the contempt which the Jews had evinced of the Divine calling could not remain unpunished. *Thy hardness.*—This is a figurative expression, and strongly expresses the natural obduracy and insensibility of their hearts with respect to God, as impenetrable by the strongest external force. Nothing but the power of the Spirit of God can overcome it. It is the term which Moses often employs to express the obstinacy of Pharaoh. He also employs it to mark the corruption of the Israelites; and, in general, the Prophets use it to signify the inflexible perversity of sinners. It is in this sense that Ezekiel attributes to man a heart of stone,—a heart which does not feel, and which nothing in man himself can soften. These passages, and many similar ones, denote an inclination to wickedness so strong and so rooted, that it has entire possession of the man and of all the powers of the soul, without his being able to undeceive himself, and to turn to God. It is this also which is marked by the expression *impenitent heart;* for it does not refer merely to the act of impenitence, and to the heart being in that state at present, but to the fact of its being so enslaved to sin, that it never would or could repent. Dr. Macknight, while he admits that the word literally signifies 'cannot repent,' most erroneously adds, ' here it signifies, which does not repent.' The greatness of this obduracy was made manifest by the number and force of the external invitations which God had employed to lead the Jews to repentance, and which the Apostle calls His goodness, forbearance, and long-suffering; for these invitations refer to the frequent and earnest exhortations of His word, His temporal favours, the afflictions and the chastisements He had sent, and all His other dispensations towards the Jewish people, respecting which it is said, ' What could have been done more to My vineyard that I have not done in it?' Isa. v. 4; and again, ' I have spread out My hands all the day unto a rebellious people,' Isa. lxv. 2. When men remain inflexible under such calls, it is the indication of an awful obduracy, of a heart steeled and shut up in impenitence. Such was the state of the Jews. This passage is explicit in opposition to all who suppose that God employs nothing for men's conversion but the efficacy of His word, accompanied with other circumstances calculated to make an impression on their minds. Without the immediate operation of the Holy Spirit, these will always prove ineffectual.

Thou treasurest up unto thyself wrath.—This is a strong expression, and a beautiful figure. It proves that sins will be punished according to their accumulation. A man is rich according to his treasures. The wicked will be punished according to the number and aggravation of their sins. Dr. Macknight makes the whole beauty and energy of the expression to evaporate, when he explains it as comprehending the thing referred to by an Hebraistic extension of meaning. There are two treasures, which Paul opposes to each other,—that of goodness, of forbearance, and long-suffering,—and that of wrath; and the one may be compared to the other. The one provides and amasses blessings for the creature, the other punishments; the one invites to heaven, the other precipitates to hell; the one looks on sin to pardon it on repentance, the other regards obstinate continuance to punish it, and avenge favours that are despised. God alone prepares the first, but man himself the second; and on this account the Apostle says, 'Thou treasurest up unto thyself wrath.' He had just before ascribed to the Jew a hard and impenitent heart,—expressions which, as we have seen, signify an entire and settled inclination to evil, a corruption which nothing in man can overcome. He adds, that by this means he treasures up wrath. This is very far, then, from countenancing the opinion of those who say that if men were absolutely and entirely unable to convert themselves, they would be excusable, and that God could not justly require of them repentance. Such is not the doctrine of the Apostle Paul, which, on the contrary, teaches that the more a man is hardened in crime, the more he becomes an object of Divine justice and wrath. The reason is, that this want of power has its seat in the will itself, and in the heart, and that it consists in an extreme degree of wickedness and perversity, for which there can be no excuse.

Against the day of wrath and revelation of the righteous judgment of God. —That is, the day of the last judgment, which is called the day of wrath, because then the wrath of God will display itself upon the wicked without measure. Till that day the judgments of heavenly justice remain, as it were, concealed and covered under the veil of Divine patience; and till then the sins of men are treasured up as in a heap, and punishment is awaiting them. But on that day, the coming of which is plainly declared in the Scriptures, but which will then be actually *revealed*, a deluge of wrath will descend upon the wicked. It is called the day of *the righteous judgment of God*, namely, of the display of His strict justice; for judgment will then be laid to the plummet, and the hail shall sweep away the refuge of lies, and the waters shall overflow the hiding-place. It will therefore be the day of the execution of the justice of God; for it is in its execution that it will be fully made manifest.

When the Apostle speaks here of the day of wrath, and of God's righteous judgment, he refers to the judgment of those who are under the law. There is no judgment of God which is not according to strict justice; there is none that is a judgment of mercy. Mercy and justice are irreconcilable except in Christ, in whom mercy is exercised consistently with justice. There is no judgment that admits repentance and amendment of life as satisfactory to justice. Repentance and amendment are not admitted to stand in the room of righteousness. It is a truth to which there is no exception, either with respect to God or man, that righteous judgment admits no mercy. The acquittal of the believer in

that day will be as just as the condemnation of the sinner. It will be
the day in which God, by Jesus Christ, will judge the world in *righteousness*, according to the strict rules of justice, Acts xvii. 31, in which none
will be acquitted except those whom the Lord, in His representation of
the judgment, calls the ' righteous,' Matt. xxv. 37–46 ; and He calls them
righteous because they are really so in Christ Jesus. But the judgment
to which the Apostle here refers, which he characterizes as the day of
wrath and revelation of the righteous judgment of God, is that of the
execution of unmingled wrath upon the wicked. He is not speaking of
believers who are in Christ, but of those who are *under the law*, before
which nothing but perfect and personal conformity to all its demands can
subsist ; ' for as many as are of the works of the law are under the curse :
for it is written, Cursed is every one that continueth not in all things
which are written in the book of the law to do them.' All the sins of
such persons will be punished, but especially those of obstinacy and contempt which shall have been shown towards the goodness and patience of
God ; for what the Apostle is here aiming at, is to convince the Jews
that it is to that judgment those will be remitted who reject the grace
manifested to them.

Ver. 6.— *Who will render to every man according to his deeds.*

God, as the sovereign judge of men, receives from them their good and
evil actions. These He takes from their hands, so to speak, such as they
are, and places them to their account, whether they are to His glory or
dishonour. Sinners do not calculate upon this righteous procedure.
They commit sin without thinking of God, and without considering that
He remembers all their actions. There is, however, an invisible hand
which is treasuring up all that a man thinks, all that he says, and all
that he does ; not the least part is lost ; all is laid up in the treasury of
justice. Then, after God has thus received all, He will also restore all,—
He will cause to descend again upon men what they have made to ascend
to Him. *To every man.*—The judgment will be particular to every
individual ; every one will have to answer for himself. This judgment
of those who are under the law will not receive either an imputation of
good or of bad works of one to another, as the judgment of those who
are under grace receives for them the merits of Jesus Christ ; but every
one of the former shall answer for his own proper works.

According to his deeds.—That is to say, either according to his righteousness, if any were found in himself righteous, which will not be the
case, for all men are sinners, but it will be according to the judgment to
require righteousness,—or it will be according to his sins,—in one word,
according as every one shall be found either righteous or unrighteous.
This signifies also that there will be a diversity of punishment, according
to the number or greatness of the sins of each individual, not only as to
the nature, but also the degree, of their works, good or bad ; for the
punishment of all will not be equal, Matt. xi. 22, 24 ; Luke xii. 47, 48.
There will not, however, as the Pharisees imagined, and as many nominal
Christians suppose, be two accounts for each person, the one of his good
works, the other of his sins,—the judgment being favourable or unfavour-

able to him according as the one or the other predominates; for there will be no balancing of this sort.[1] 'According to his deeds,' means that, in the judgment, God will have no regard either to descent or to birth, either to the dignity or quality of the person,—or whether he were Jew or Gentile, as to the privileges he enjoyed, or any such thing, which might counteract justice, or turn it from its course; but that it will regard solely the works of each individual, and that their deeds will comprehend everything that is either obedience or disobedience to the law of God. The judgment of the great day will be to all men according to their works. The works of those who shall be condemned will be the evidence that they are wicked. The works of believers will not be appealed to as the *cause* of their acquittal, but as the *evidence* of their union with Christ, on account of which they will be pronounced *righteous*, for in them the law has been fulfilled in their Divine surety.

Ver. 7.—*To them who, by patient continuance in well-doing, seek for glory, and honour, and immortality, eternal life.*

Patient continuance in well-doing.—This well expresses the sense of the original. It signifies perseverance in something arduous. It is not mere continuance, but continuance in doing or suffering something that tries patience. The word is used to signify perseverance, patience, endurance,—a perseverance with resistance to all that opposes, namely, to all temptations, all snares, all persecutions, and, in general, to all that could discourage or divert from it, in however small a degree. It is not meant that any man can produce such a perseverance in good works, for there is only one, Jesus Christ, who can glory in having wrought out a perfect righteousness. He alone is holy, harmless, undefiled, and separate from sinners. But here the Apostle only declares what the Divine judgment will demand according to the law, to which the Jews were adhering for justification before God, and rejecting that righteousness which He has provided in the Gospel. He marks what the law will require for the justification of man, in order to conclude from it, as he does in the sequel, that none can be justified in this way, because all are guilty. This shows how ignorantly the Church of Rome seeks to draw from this passage a proof of the merit of works, and of justification by works, since it teaches a doctrine the very contrary; for all that the Apostle says in this chapter is intended to show the necessity of another mode of justification than that of the law, namely, by grace, which the Gospel sets before us through faith in Jesus Christ, according to which God pardons sins, as the Apostle afterwards shows in the third chapter. To pretend, then, to establish justification by works, and the merit of works, by what is said here, is directly to oppose the meaning and reasoning of the Apostle.

Seek for glory, and honour, and immortality.—Glory signifies a state brilliant and illustrious, and honour the approbation and praise of God, which, with immortality, designate the blessings of eternal life. These

---

[1] This most erroneous sentiment, in direct opposition to the word of God, is maintained by Dr. Macknight. See his note on verse 3d of chapter iv. afterwards quoted.

God would, without doubt, confer in consequence of perseverance in good works, but which cannot be obtained by the law. Here we see a condemnation of that opinion which teaches that a man should have no motive in what he does in the service of God but the love of God. The love of God, indeed, must be the predominant motive, and without it no action is morally good. But it is not the only motive. The Scriptures everywhere address men's hopes and fears, and avail themselves of every motive that has a tendency to influence the human heart. The principles of human nature have God for their author, and are all originally right. Sin has given them a wrong direction. Of the expressions, glory and honour, Dr. Macknight gives the following explanations:—' Glory is the good fame which commonly attends virtuous actions, but honour is the respect paid to the virtuous person himself by those who have intercourse with him.' According to this interpretation, those who are seeking for immortality and eternal life are seeking for the favour and respect of men !

Eternal life.—The Apostle does not say that God will render salvation, but ' eternal life.' The truth declared in this verse, and in those that follow, is the same as that exhibited by our Lord when the rich young man asked Him, ' What good thing shall I do that I may inherit eternal life ? ' His reply was, ' If thou wilt enter into life, keep the commandments,' Matt. xix. 16 ; and when the lawyer, tempting Him, said, ' Master, what shall I do to inherit eternal life ? ' Jesus answered, ' Thous halt love the Lord thy God with all thy heart, and with all thy soul, and with all thy strength, and with all thy mind, and thy neighbour as thyself,' Luke x. 25. The verse before us, then, which declares that eternal life shall be awarded to those who seek it by *patient continuance in well-doing,* and who, according to the 10th verse, *work good,* both of which announce the full demand of the law, are of the same import with the 13th verse, which affirms that *the doers of the law shall be justified.* In all these verses the Apostle is referring to the law, and not, as it is generally understood, to the Gospel. It would have been obviously calculated to mislead the Jews, with whom Paul was reasoning, to set before them in this place personal obedience as the way to eternal life, which, in connection with what he had said on repentance, would tend directly to lead them to mistake his meaning on that subject. But besides this, if these verses refer to the Gospel, they break in upon and disturb the whole train of his reasoning, from the 18th verse of the first chapter to the 20th of the third, where he arrives at his conclusion, that by the deeds of the law there shall no flesh be justified in the sight of God. Paul was afterwards to declare the way of justification, as he does, ch. iii. 21, 26, immediately after he drew the above conclusion ; but till then, his object was to exhibit, both to Jews and Gentiles, the impossibility of obtaining justification by any works of their own, and, by convincing them of this, to lead them to the grace of the Gospel. In conversing with the late Mr. Robert Hall at Leicester, respecting the Epistle to the Romans, he remarked to me that this passage had always greatly perplexed him, as it seemed to be not only aside from, but even opposed to what appeared, from the whole context, to be the drift of the Apostle ; and I believe

that every one who supposes that the Apostle is here referring to the
Gospel will experience a similar difficulty.

I know that the view here given of these verses is contrary to that of
almost all the English commentaries on this Epistle. I have consulted a
great number of them, besides those of Calvin, and Beza, and Maretz,
and the Dutch annotations, and that of Quesnel, all of which, with one
voice, explain the 7th and 10th verses of this chapter as referring to the
Gospel. The only exception that I am aware of among the English
commentaries is that of Mr. Fry, who, in his exposition of the 16th verse,
remarks as follows :—' He (the Apostle) introduces this statement of the
certainty of a judgment to come, of the universal guilt and inevitable
condemnation of mankind in the course of justice, in order to show the
universal necessity of a Saviour, and of that righteousness which was of
God by faith. And it seems altogether extraordinary that some exposi
tors should conceive the above account of the last judgment to include a
description of the Redeemer's bestowing the reward of the inheritance
upon His people, and that of such the Apostle speaks when he says,
" To them that, by patient continuance in well-doing, seek glory, honour,
and immortality, eternal life ; " " Glory, honour, and peace, to every one
that doeth good." For most assuredly this is not the language of
the righteousness of faith, but the exact manner of speaking which the
Apostle ascribes to the righteousness of the law.' To the same purpose
Mr. Marshall, in his work on *The Gospel Mystery of Sanctification*,
14th edit., p. 94, observes, 'They grossly pervert these words of Paul,
" Who will render to every man according to his deeds; to them who,
by patient continuance in well-doing, seek for glory, and honour, and
immortality, eternal life," where they will have Paul to be declaring
the terms of the Gospel, when he is evidently declaring the terms of the
law, to prove that both Jews and Gentiles are all under sin, and that no
flesh can be justified by the works of the law, as appeareth by the
tenor of the following discourse.'

I have noticed that from this passage the Church of Rome endeavours
to establish the merit of works, and of justification by means of works.
Accordingly, Quesnel, a Roman Catholic, in expounding the 6th verse,
exclaims, ' *Merites veritables ; necessité des bonnes œuvres. Ce sont nos
actions bonnes ou mauvaises qui rendent doux ou severe le jugement de Dieu !*'
' Real merits; necessity of good works. They are our good or bad
actions which render the judgment of God mild or severe !' And
indeed, were the usual interpretation of this and the three following
verses the just one, it must be confessed that this Romanist would have
some ground for his triumph. But if we take the words in their plain and
obvious import, and understand the Apostle in this place as announcing
the terms of the law, in order to prove to the Jews the necessity of
having recourse to grace, and of yielding to the goodness and forbearance of God, leading them to repentance, while he assures them that
' not the hearers of the law are just before God, but the doers of the
law shall be justified,' then the whole train of his discourse is clear and
consistent. On the other supposition, it appears confused and self-
contradictory, and calculated not merely to perplex, but positively to

mislead, and to strengthen the prejudices of those who were going about to establish their own righteousness.   For in whatever way these expressions may with certain explanations and qualifications be interpreted in an evangelical sense, yet unquestionably, as taken by themselves, and especially in the connection in which they stand in this place, they present the same meaning as is announced in the 13th verse, where the Apostle declares that *the doers of the law* shall be justified.

Ver. 8.—*But unto them that are contentious, and do not obey the truth, but obey unrighteousness, indignation and wrath.*

Paul here describes the wicked by three characteristics.   Their first characteristic is, that they are *contentious;* that is, rebellious, and murmurers against the Divine laws, quarrellers with God, and indicating their natural enmity against God by disapproving of His government or authority.   The second is, *rebels against the truth;* that is to say, in revolt and at open war against what is true and right concerning God and His will as made known to them, and as opposed to unrighteousness, which God abhors.   Ths third is, *obedient to unrighteousness;* that is, revolting against what is good, and becoming slaves to what is evil. Here a striking contrast is indicated between that contentious spirit which disobeys the truth, and yet obeys unrighteousness.   The one denotes an extraordinary haughtiness, and an exceeding boldness; and the other, extreme meanness and servility of soul.   They who do not choose to serve God as their legitimate sovereign, become the slaves of a master who is both a tyrant and usurper.

Indignation and wrath.—These two terms united, mark the greatness of the wrath of God, proportioned to the dignity of the sovereign Judge of the world, to the authority of those eternal laws which have been violated, to the majesty of the legislator by whom they have been promulgated, to the favours which sinners have received from Him, and proportioned also to the unworthiness and meanness of the creature compared with God.   Although, when human passions are ascribed to God, we must not suppose that He is affected as we are, yet the expressions employed here show that God will certainly punish the wicked. The Scriptures represent God in the character of a just judge, as well as of a merciful father.   The flattering doctrine which insinuates the hope of the final universal happiness of transgressors, both of devils and men, is altogether without countenance from Scripture.   The word of God contains the most awful denunciations of the Divine wrath.   It is a fearful thing to fall into the hands of the living God.   Yet some writers lead sinners to hope that the character of God will secure them from punishment.

Ver. 9.—*Tribulation and anguish, upon every soul of man that doeth evil, of the Jew first, and also of the Gentile.*

Tribulation and anguish.—These two terms denote the punishment, as the indignation and wrath designate the principle on which the condemnation proceeds..   They also designate the greatness of the punishment.   *Upon every soul of man.*—This universality is intended to point to the vain expectations of the Jews, that they would be exempt from that punishment, and assists in determining the import of the phrase 'according to truth' in verse 2, meaning what is just. It signifies, too, the whole man, for it must not be imagined that the wicked do not also suffer in their body. Jesus Christ says expressly that they shall come forth unto the resurrection of damnation. This refutes the opinion of Socinian heretics and others, who insist that the punishment of the wicked will consist in an entire annihilation both of body and soul. The terms 'tribulation and anguish' signify a pain of sensation, and consequently suppose the subsistence of the subject.

That doeth evil.—The word in the original designates evil workers, as persons who practise wickedness habitually. The connection of punishment with sin is according to the order of Divine justice; for it is just that those who have offended infinite Majesty should receive the retribution of their wickedness. It is likewise according to the denunciation of the law, whether it is viewed as given externally by the word, or as engraven internally in the conscience of every man, for it threatens punishment to transgressors. *Of the Jew first, and also of the Gentile* (literally Greek).—In this place, 'the Jew first' must mean the Jew principally, and implies that the Jew is more accountable than the Gentile, and will be punished according to his superior light; for as the Jew will have received more than the Gentile, he will also be held more culpable before the Divine tribunal, and will consequently be more severely punished. His privileges will aggravate his culpability, and increase his punishment. 'You only have I known of all the families of the earth; therefore I will punish you for all your iniquities,' Amos iii. 2; Matt. xi. 22; Luke xii. 47. But although the judgment will begin with the Jew, and on him be more heavily executed, it will not terminate with him, but will be also extended to the Gentile, who will be found guilty, though not with the same aggravation.

Ver. 10.—*But glory, honour, and peace, to every man that worketh good; to the Jew first, and also to the Gentile.*

Glory, honour, and peace.—Glory, as has already been observed, refers to the state of blessedness to which those who shall inherit eternal life will be admitted; honour, to the praise and approbation of God, to which is here added *peace*. Peace is a state of confirmed joy and prosperity. As added to glory and honour, it may appear feeble as a climax, but in reality it has all the value that is here ascribed to it. No blessing can be enjoyed without it. What would glory and honour be without peace? What would they be if there was a possibility of falling from the high dignity, or of being afterwards miserable?

To every man that worketh good.—Happiness, by the established order of things, is here asserted to be the inseparable consequence of righteousness, so that virtue should never be unfruitful; and he who had performed what is his duty, if any such could be found, should enjoy rest and satisfaction. This is also according to the declaration of the Divine law; for if, on the one hand, it threatens transgressors, on the other, it promises good to those who observe it. 'The man that doeth them shall live in them,' Gal. iii. 12. Since, then, no righteous man could be disappointed of the fruit of his righteousness, it may, in consequence, be asked if any creature who had performed his duty exactly would merit anything from God? To this it is replied, that the infinite majesty of God, which admits of no proportion between Himself and the creature, absolutely excludes all idea of merit. For God can never be laid under any obligation to His creature; and the creature, who is nothing in comparison of Him, and who, besides, has nothing but what God has given him, can never acquire any claim on his Creator. Whenever God makes a covenant with man, and promises anything, that promise, indeed, engages God on His part, on the ground of His truth and faithfulness; but it does not so engage Him as to give us any claim of merit upon Him. 'Who hath first given to Him, and it shall be recompensed unto him again?' Rom. xi. 35. Thus, in whatever manner we view it, there can be before God no merit in men; whence it follows that happiness would not be conferred as a matter of right on a man who should be found innocent. It must be said, however, that it would be given by a right of judgment, by which the order and proportion of things is preserved, the majesty of the law of God maintained, and the Divine promises accomplished. But, in awarding life and salvation to him who has the righteousness of Christ imputed to him, God is both faithful and just, on account of the infinite merit of His Son. *To the Jew first, and* also *to the Greek.*—When glory and honour are promised to the Jew first, it implies that he had walked according to his superior advantages, and of course would be rewarded in proportion; while the Gentile, in his degree, would not be excluded.

Ver. 11.—*For there is no respect of persons with God.*

Whatever difference of order there may be between the Jew and the Gentile, that difference does not change the foundation and substance of the judgment. To have respect to the appearance of persons, or to accept of persons, is the vice of an iniquitous judge, who in some way violates justice; but the Divine judgment cannot commit such a fault. Besides, we must never lose sight of the train of the Apostle's reasoning. His design is to show that the Jews, being, as they really are, sinners equally with the Gentiles, are involved with them in the same condemnation. This is what he proves by the nature of the Divine judgment, *which is according to truth,* that is, which is perfectly just, ver. 2; which *renders to every man according to his deeds,* ver. 6; and which *has no respect of persons,* ver. 11; and consequently it will be equal to the Jew and the Gentile, so that neither the one nor the other can defend himself against its sentence.

The declaration that God has no respect of persons is frequently quoted as militating against the doctrine of election; but it has no bearing on the subject. It relates to men's character, and God's judgment according to character. Every man will be judged according to his works. This, however, does not say that God may not choose some eternally to life, and give them faith, and create them unto good works, according to which, as evidences that they belong to Christ, they shall

be judged.   God's sovereign love to the elect is manifested in a way that
not only shows Him to be just in their justification, but also true to His
declaration with respect to the future judgment.   The assertion of the
Apostle in this place is a truth of great importance, not only with respect to the Jews, but also with respect to the professors of Christianity,
many of whom fancy that there is a sort of favouritism in the judgment of God, that will overlook in some what is in others accounted
condemnatory.

Ver. 12.—*For as many as have sinned without law shall also perish without law:
and as many as have sinned in (or under) law shall be judged by law.*

Here Paul explains the equality of the judgment, both with respect to
the Gentiles and the Jews.   *Without law*, that is, a written law; for
none are without law, as the Apostle immediately afterwards shows.
The Gentiles had not received the written law; they had, however,
sinned, and they shall perish—that is to say, be condemned—without
that law.   The Jews had received the written law; they had also sinned,
they will be judged—that is to say condemned—by that law; for in the
next verse Paul declares that only the *doers* of the law shall be justified;
and consequently, as condemnation stands opposed to justification, they
who are not doers of it will be condemned.   In one word, the Divine
justice will only regard the sins of men; and wherever these are found,
it will condemn the sinner.   The Gentiles shall perish without law.
They will perish, though they are not to be judged by the written law.
It is alleged by some, that although the Apostle's language shows that
all the Gentiles are guilty before God, yet it does not imply that they
will be condemned; for that they may be guilty, yet be saved by mercy
through Jesus Christ.   But the language of the Apostle entirely precludes
the possibility of such a supposition.   It is not said that they who have
sinned without law are guilty without law, but that they shall '*perish
without law.*'   The language, then, does not merely assert their guilt,
but clearly asserts their condemnation.   They shall *perish*.   No criticism
can make this expression consistent with the salvation of the Gentiles
who know not God.   They will be condemned by the work of the law
written in their hearts.   Many are inclined to think that the condemnation of the heathen is peculiarly hard; but it is equally just, and not
more severe, than the punishment of those who have sinned against
revelation.   They will not be judged by the light which they had not,
nor punished so severely as they who resisted that light.

Ver. 13.—*(For not the hearers of the law are just before God, but the doers of the
law shall be justified.*

This verse, with the two following, forms a parenthesis between the
12th and 16th, explanatory of the two propositions contained in the 12th.
Some also include the 11th and 12th in the parenthesis.   If this mode of
punctuation were adopted, the 13th, 14th, and 15th verses would be a
parenthesis within a parenthesis ; but for this there is no occasion, as
the 11th and 12th verses connect with the 10th, and also with the 16th.
For not the hearers of the law.—Against what the Apostle had just said

concerning the equality of the judgment, two objections might be urged,—the one in favour of the Gentiles, the other in favour of the Jews. The first is, that since God has not given His law to the Gentiles, there can be no place for their condemnation,—for how can they be condemned as transgressors if they have not received a law? The second objection, which is contrary to the first, supposes that the Jews ought to be more leniently treated, since God, who has given them His law, has, by doing so, declared in their favour, and made them His people: He will therefore, without doubt, have a regard for them which He has not for the others, whom he has abandoned. The Apostle obviates both these objections in this and the two following verses, and thus defends his position respecting the equality of the judgment. As for the last of them, which he answers first in this 13th verse, he says that it is not sufficient for justification before God to have received the law, and simply to be hearers of it; but that it must be observed and reduced to practice. This is an incontestible truth. For the law has not been given as a matter of curiosity or contemplation as a philosophical science, but to be obeyed; and the greatest outrage against the law and the Legislator, is to hear it and not to take heed to practise it. It will be in vain, therefore, for the Jew to say, I am a hearer of the law, I attend on its services, I belong to the covenant of God, who has given me His testimonies. On all these accounts, being a transgressor, as he is, he must be condemned. The presence of the article before the word law in both the clauses of this verse, which is wanting in the preceding verse, shows that the reference is here to the Jews under the written law.

The doers of the law shall be justified.—By this we must understand an exact obedience to the law to be intended, which can defend itself against that declaration, ' Cursed is every one that continueth not in all things which are written in the book of the law to do them.' For it is not the same with the judgment of the law as with that of grace. The Gospel indeed requires of us a perfect obedience to its commands, yet it not only provides for believers' pardon of the sins committed before their calling, but of those also which they afterwards commit. But the judgment of the law admits of no indulgence to those who are under it; it demands a full and perfect personal observance of all its requirements—a patient continuance in well-doing, without the least deviation, or the smallest speck of sin; and when it does not find this state of perfection, condemns the man. But did not the law itself contain expiations for sin? and consequently, shall not the judgment which will be passed according to the law, be accompanied with grace and indulgence through the benefit of these expiations? The legal expiations had no virtue in themselves; but inasmuch as they were figures of the expiation made by Jesus Christ, they directed men to His sacrifice. But as they belonged to the temporal or carnal covenant, they neither expiated nor could expiate any but typical sins, that is to say, uncleanness of the flesh, Heb. ix. 13, which were not real sins, but only external pollutions. Thus, as far as regarded the legal sacrifices, all real sins remained on the conscience, Heb. x. 1, for from these the law did not in the smallest degree discharge; whence it follows that the judgment, according to the law, to those who are under it, will be a strict judgment according to law, which pardons nothing. The word *justified* occurs here for the first time in this Epistle, and being introduced in connection with the general judgment, means being declared just or righteous by a judicial sentence.

Ver. 14.—*For when the Gentiles, which have not a law, do by nature the things contained in the law, these, having not a law, are a law unto themselves.*

For.—This is the proper translation of the Greek particle, and not *therefore*, according to Dr. Macknight, who entirely misunderstands both the meaning of the passage itself, and the connection in which it stands, and founds upon it a doctrine opposed to all that is contained on the subject, both in the Old Testament and the New. This verse has no connection with, or dependence whatever on, the foregoing, as is generally supposed, but connects with the first clause of verse 12, which it explains. Together with the following verse, it supplies the answer to the objection that might be made to what is contained in the beginning of that verse, namely, that God cannot justly condemn the Gentiles, since He has not given them a law. To this the Apostle here replies, that though they have not an external and written law, as that which God gave to the Israelites, they have, however, the law of the conscience, which is sufficient to establish the justice of their condemnation. This is the meaning of that proposition, *having not a law, are a law unto themselves;* and of that other, *which show the work of the law written in their hearts;* by which he also establishes the justice of what he had said in the 12th verse, that *as many as have sinned without law shall also perish without law.* He proves it in two ways : 1st, Because they do naturally the things that the law requires, which shows that they have a law in themselves, since they sometimes act according to its rule ; 2d, He proves it by their not being devoid of a conscience, since, according to its decisions, they accuse or excuse one another. This evidently shows that they have a law, the work of which is written in their hearts, by which they discern the difference between right and wrong—what is just, and what is unjust.

They who *have not a law,*—that is, an externally written law,—*do by nature the things contained in the law.* It could not be the Apostle's intention to assert that the heathens in general, or that any one of them, kept the law written in the heart, when the contrary had been proved in the preceding chapter ; but they did certain things, though imperfectly, commanded by the law, which proved that they had, by their original constitution, a discernment of the difference between right and wrong. They did nothing, however, in the *manner* which the law required, that is, from the only motive that makes an action good, namely, a spirit of obedience, and of love to God. God governs the world in this way. He rules the actions of men and beasts by the instincts and affections which He has implanted in them. Every good action that men perform by nature, they do by their constitution, not from respect to the authority of God. That the Pagans do many things that, as to the outward act, are agreeable to the law of God, is obviously true, and should not be denied. That they do anything acceptable to God is not true, and is not here asserted.

Ver. 15.—*Which show the work of the law written in their hearts, their conscience also bearing witness, and their thoughts the meanwhile accusing or else excusing one another.*

The work of the law.—We have here a distinction between the *law* itself, and the *work* of the law. The work of the law is the thing that the law doeth,—that is, what it teaches about actions, as good or bad. This work, or business, or office of the law, is to teach what is right or wrong. This, in some measure, is taught by the light of nature in the heart of every man. There remains, then, in all men, to a certain degree, a discernment of what the law requires, designated here the ' work' of the law; the performance or neglect of which is followed by the approbation or disapprobation of the conscience. It has no relation to the authority of the lawgiver, as the principle of the law itself; but solely to the distinction between actions, as right or wrong in themselves, and the hope of escaping future punishment, or of obtaining future reward. The love and the reverential fear of God, which are the true principles of obedience, have been effaced from the mind; but a degree of knowledge of His justice, and the consciousness that the violations of His law deserve and will be followed by punishment, have been retained.

Written in their hearts.—This is an allusion to the law written by the finger of God upon tables of stone, and afterwards recorded in the Scriptures. The great principles of this law were communicated to man in his creation, and much of it remains with him in his fallen state. This natural light of the understanding is called the law written in the heart, because it is imprinted on the mind by the Author of creation, and is God's work as much as the writing on the tables of stone. *Conscience witnessing together,*—together with the law written in the heart. But it may be asked, Are not these two things the same? They are not. They are different principles. Light, or knowledge of duty, is one thing, and conscience is another. Knowledge shows what is right,—the conscience approves of it, and condemns the contrary. We might suppose a being to have the knowledge of duty, without the principle that approves of it, and blames the transgression.

Their thoughts the meanwhile accusing, or else excusing between one another.—Not alternately, nor in turn. Their reasonings (not thoughts) between one another, condemning, or else defending. What is the object of their condemnation or defence? Not themselves, but one another; that is, those between whom the reasonings take place. The reference evidently is to the fact that, in all places, in all ages, men are continually, in their mutual intercourse, blaming or excusing human conduct. This supposes a standard of reference,—a knowledge of right and wrong. No man could accuse and condemn another, if there were not some standard of right and wrong; and no man could defend an action without a similar standard. This is obviously the meaning of the Apostle. To these ideas of right and wrong are naturally joined the idea of God, who is the sovereign Judge of the world, and that of rewards and punishments, which will follow either good or bad actions. These ideas do not fail to present themselves to the sinner, and inspire fear and inquietude. But as, on the other hand, self-love and corruption reign in the heart,

these come to his support, and strive, by vain reasonings, to defend or
to extenuate the sin. The Gentiles, then, however depraved, lost, and
abandoned, and however destitute of the aid of the written law, are, notwithstanding, a law to themselves, having the law written in their hearts.
They have still sufficient light to discern between good and evil, virtue
and vice, honesty and dishonesty; and their conscience enables them
sufficiently to make that distinction, whether before committing sin, or
in the commission of it, or after they have committed it. Besides this,
remorse on account of their crimes reminds them that there is a God, a
Judge before whom they must appear to render account to Him of their
actions. They are, then, a law to themselves; they have the work of
the law written in their hearts.

That the knowledge of the revealed law of God has not been preserved
in every nation, is, however, entirely to be attributed to human depravity;
and if it was restored to one nation for the benefit of others, it must be
ascribed to the goodness of God. The law of God, and the revelation
respecting the Messiah, had been delivered to all men after the flood by
Noah, who was a preacher of the everlasting righteousness, 2 Pet. ii. 5,
which was to be brought in, to answer the demands of that law. But all
the nations of the earth had lost the remembrance of it, not liking to
retain God in their knowledge. God again discovered it to the Jews in
that written revelation with which they were favoured. If it be asked,
Why was the law vouchsafed in this manner to that nation and not also
to the Gentiles? Paul explains this mystery, ch. xi. It is sufficient
then to say that God has willed to make known, by this abandonment,
how great and dreadful was the fall of the human race, and by that
means one day to magnify the glory of the grace which He purposed to
bestow on men by Jesus Christ. He willed to leave a great part of men
a prey to Satan, to show how great is His abhorrence of sin, and how
great was the wrath which our disobedience had kindled against the
world. But why did He not also abandon the Jews? Because He chose
to leave some ray of hope in the world, and it pleased Him to lay the
foundation of redemption by His Son. But why was the greater part
abandoned? Because then was the time of Divine wrath and justice,
and sin must be allowed to abound that grace might superabound. Why,
in fine, choose the nation of the Jews rather than any other nation?
Because, without any further reason, it was the sovereign good pleasure
of God.

Ver. 16.—*In the day when God shall judge the secrets of men by Jesus Christ,
according to my Gospel.*

This verse is to be construed in connection with the 12th, to the contents of which the three intermediate verses had given, in a parenthesis,
the explanatory answers. *In the day when God shall judge.*—It is here
assumed by the Apostle that God is the Judge of the world. This is a
truth which nature and right reason teach. Since intelligent creatures
are capable of obedience to law, it necessarily follows that they have a
judge, for the law would be null and void if it were left as a dead letter,
without a judge to put it in execution. And as there is a law common
to the whole human race, it must also be admitted that there is a common

Judge. Now this Judge of all can only be God, for it is only God who possesses all the qualifications for such an office. The Apostle likewise assumes that there will be a *day* when God will hold this judgment. This is also a truth conformable to right reason, for there must be a fixed time for rendering public the decrees of justice, otherwise it would not be duly honoured, since its honour consists in being recognised to be what it is before all creatures. If, then, there were only individual judgments, either in this life or at death, justice would not be manifested as it ought to be. Hence it follows that there must be a public and solemn day in which God will execute judgment before the assembled universe. Besides, the Apostle here intimates that there will be an end to the duration of the world, and the succession of generations; for if there be a day appointed for a universal judgment, it follows that all men must there appear. And if such be the case, their number must also be determined, while, without a single exception, the time of their calling and of their life must terminate, so that the succession of generations must come to an end.

The secrets of men.—It is not here meant that God will judge only their secrets, so that their public and known actions should pass without being judged; for there is nothing that God does not judge. But it is intended to show with what exactness the judgment will proceed, since it takes account of things the most secret and the most concealed. It will not resemble the judgment of men, which cannot fathom the hearts and thoughts. God will not only take cognisance of external, but also of internal actions, and will discover even the inmost thoughts of men. All actions, then, whether open or secret, will come into judgment; but secrets or hidden things are here said to be judged, because they are reached by no other judgment. If men can conceal their evil deeds, they are safe from human judgment. Not so with respect to the Judge at the great day. The most secret sins will then be manifested and punished.

By Jesus Christ.—God will carry into effect that judgment by Jesus Christ. 'He hath appointed a day, in the which He will judge the world in righteousness by that man whom He hath ordained,' Acts xvii. 31. Jesus Christ will conduct the judgment, not only as it respects believers, but also the wicked. If the secrets of men are to be brought into judgment, and if Jesus Christ is to be the Judge, He must be the Searcher of hearts, Acts i. 24; Rev. ii. 23. He must then be truly God.

In the economy of Jesus Christ there are two extreme degrees, one of abasement, the other of exaltation. The lowest degree of His abasement was His death and burial. The opposite degree of His exaltation will be the last judgment. In the former He received the sentence which condemned Him, and which included in His condemnation the absolution of His people. In the latter He will pronounce the condemnation or absolution of all creatures. In the one, covered over with reproaches, and pierced with the arrows of Divine justice, He was exposed on the cross as a spectacle to the whole city of Jerusalem, when He cried, 'My God, My God, why hast Thou forsaken Me?' In the other, arrayed in glory and majesty, He will appear before the whole universe, in the glory of His Father, who commands all the angels to worship Him.

According to my Gospel.—Paul calls the Gospel his Gospel, not that he
is the author of it, for it is solely from God; but to say that of it he is
the minister and herald,—that it is the Gospel which he preached. The
Gospel, in a large sense, includes everything revealed by Jesus Christ.
The judgment then shall take place according to the declarations therein
contained.

Ver. 17.—*Behold, thou art called a Jew, and restest in the law, and makest thy
boast of God.*

Here commences the second part of this chapter, where Paul purposes
to show that all the external advantages of the Jews over the Gentiles
were unavailing for their protection from the just condemnation of God.
In the first place, he enumerates all their privileges, on account of which
the Jews could exalt themselves above the Gentiles. Afterwards he lays
it to their charge that, notwithstanding all these privileges, they were
sinners, equally guilty as others. Finally, he shows that, being sinners,
as they all were, their advantages would avail them nothing, and would
only aggravate their condemnation.

Behold, thou art called a Jew.—The Apostle here continues his discourse to the same persons whom, from the commencement of the
chapter, he had addressed, and now calls on the Jew by name. In this
verse, and the three following, Paul classes the advantages of the Jews
under six particulars: 1. Their bearing the name of Jew. 2. Having
received the law. 3. Having the true God as their God. 4. Knowing
His will. 5. Discerning what is evil. 6. Their ability to teach and
guide other men.

As to the first of these, the name *Jew* embraces three significations:
—confession, praise, and thanksgiving; and by these three things that
people was distinguished from all other nations. The Jew alone had
been chosen as the confessor of God, while all the rest of the world had
abjured His service. The Jew alone was appointed to celebrate His
praises, while by others He was blasphemed. The Jew alone was
appointed to render thanksgiving to God for multiplied benefits received,
while others were passed by. In that name, then, in which the Jews
gloried, and which distinguished them from all other nations, and implied
all the privileges they enjoyed, they possessed already a signal advantage
over the Gentiles.[1] Dr. Macknight and Mr. Stuart prefer surnamed to
called; but the name was not exactly what is called a surname. It was
the name of a whole people. The word *called*, or *denominated*, is more
appropriate, for it answers both to their name as a people and to their
religion, both of which are comprised in the name Jew.

And restest in the law.—That is to say, thou hast no occasion to study
any other wisdom or philosophy than the law. It is thy *wisdom* and thy
understanding, Deut. iv. 6. The term *restest* signifies two things: the one,
that the labour was spared the Jews of employing many years and great

---

[1] The name of Jew was in use before the return from the captivity, for we find it
in the 32d chapter of Jeremiah. It appears, then, that it took its rise even from the
time of the separation of the ten tribes, for the ten tribes retained that of Israel, and
the others that of Judah; the country was called Judea, Ps. lxxvi., and the language
Jewish, 2 Kings xviii. 26, and Isa. xxxvi. 11-13; and afterwards the inhabitants
Jews, for this name is also found in Dan. iii. 8.

endeavours, and travelling to distant countries, as was the case with other nations, in acquiring some knowledge and certain rules of direction. The law which God had given them rendered this unnecessary, and furnished abundantly all that was required for the regulation of their conduct. The other idea which this term conveys is, that they had an entire confidence in the law as a heavenly and Divine rule which could not mislead them, while the Gentiles could have no reliance on their deceitful philosophy.

And makest thy boast of God.—Namely, in having Him for their God, and being His people, while the Gentiles, having only false gods, were ' without God in the world,' Eph. ii. 12. The Jews had the true God, the Creator and Lord of heaven and earth, the Lord who had performed glorious miracles in their favour, who had even spoken to them from the midst of fire, for the Author of their calling, for their Deliverer, for their Legislator, for the Founder of their government, and for their King and Protector. His earthly palace was in the midst of them; He had regulated their worship, and caused them to hear His voice. The other nations possessed nothing similar. They had therefore great reason to glory in Him, and on this account David said that in God was his strength and his refuge, Ps. xviii., lxii. 7, and cxliv.

Ver. 18.—*And knowest His will, and approvest the things that are more excellent, being instructed out of the law.*

And knowest His will.—That is, what is agreeable to Him, what He requires them to do, what He commands, what He prohibits, what He approves, and what He rewards. The term *knowest* signifies not a confused knowledge, such as the Gentiles had by the revelation of nature, but a distinct knowledge by the revelation of the word, which the Gentiles did not possess. ' He showeth His word unto Jacob, His statutes and His judgments unto Israel. He hath not dealt so with any nation: and as for His judgments, they have not known them,' Ps. cxlvii. 19, 20. At the same time, the Apostle does not mean to say that the Jews had a practical knowledge of the will of God, for he immediately accuses them of the contrary.

And approvest things that are excellent.—This is the fifth advantage, which follows from the preceding. They knew the will of God, and, knowing that will, they consequently knew what was contrary to it; that is to say, those things which God does not approve, and which He condemns. For the declaration of what God approves includes, in the way of opposition and negation, those things which He does not approve. From this we learn the perfection of the written law, in opposition to unwritten traditions; for nothing more is needed in order to know the will of God, and to discern what contradicts it. *Being instructed out of the law.*—This refers to the two preceding articles—to the knowledge of the will of God, and to the discernment of the things that are contrary to it. From their infancy the Jews were instructed in the law.

Ver. 19.—*And art confident that thou thyself art a guide of the blind, a light of them which are in darkness:*

This is the sixth advantage, depending on those preceding. The law

not only instructed the Jews for themselves, but also for others, and in
this they held that they enjoyed a great superiority over the other
nations. *A guide to the blind.*—The Gentiles are here called blind, for
with all the lights of their philosophy, of their laws and their arts, they
were after all blind, since, with the exception of those of true religion,
which they did not possess, there is no true saving light in the world.
A light of them which are in darkness.—The Rabbis called themselves the
light of the world, to which our Lord appears to refer when He gives
this title to His Apostles.

Ver. 20.—*An instructor of the foolish, a teacher of babes, which hast the form of
knowledge and of the truth in the law.*

An instructor of the foolish, a teacher of babes.—These titles explain
clearly what the others indicate in metaphorical terms, and further
exalt the privileges of the Jews. Here we may remark that, although
to the Gentiles God had given abundance of temporal good things, all
this was still as nothing in comparison of the blessings vouchsafed to the
Jews. *Which hast the form of knowledge, and of the truth in the law.*—
This does not signify semblance in contradistinction to substance, for it
was the thing of which the Jews boasted. It means the representation
or exhibition of truth and summary of knowledge which was contained
in the law. The meaning is the same as when we speak of a body of
divinity. The Jews considered that they had a body of truth and
knowledge in the law. In these expressions, then, truth and knowledge
are represented as embodied in a visible form. The Jews had that
form in the law, that is to say, the law was to them a form and model,
whence they were to take all the true notions of God, of His religion,
and of the duty of man, and a rule to which they ought to be referred.
In general, from all these advantages which God had so liberally bestowed
on the Jews, we may collect that His goodness had been great in not entirely abandoning the human race, but in having still lighted up for it, in
a corner of the earth, the lamp of His law, to serve as His witness. His
wisdom has not been less conspicuous in having thus prepared the way
for the mission of His Son, and the establishment of His Gospel throughout the whole world. For the law was a schoolmaster until the coming
of Christ. We also learn that when God does not accompany His
external favours with the internal grace of His Holy Spirit, the depravity
of man is such, that, instead of turning to God, he multiplies his transgressions, as the Apostle immediately proceeds to show by the example
of the Jews. We see, too, how aggravated was their ingratitude in the
midst of such distinguished benefits.

Ver. 21.—*Thou, therefore, which teachest another, teachest thou not thyself? thou
that preachest a man should not steal, dost thou steal?*

This and the two following verses are in the Vulgate without interrogation, but the ancient interpreters read them with the interrogation. The
meaning, in either case, remains the same. After having exalted the
advantages of the Jews above the Gentiles with as much force as they
could have done themselves, Paul unveils their hypocrisy, and exhibits

the vices which were concealed under so fair an exterior. He afterwards confirms the whole of his charges by the testimony of Scripture. In this manner he establishes more fully what he had said in the beginning of the chapter, that they condemned themselves, and that they could not hope to escape the just judgment of God, but were accumulating a treasure of wrath. *Teachest thou not thyself.*—This implies that the Jews did not practise the precepts of their law. It implies that they were practically ignorant of it. *Preachest,* or proclaimest.—There is no reason to suppose, with Dr. Macknight, that the learned Jews are here the persons addressed. The whole of the Jews are addressed as one person. What is said applies to them as a body, and does not exclusively relate to the scribes and teachers. *Should not steal.*—The sins here specified were evidently such as were practised among the Jews. They are not merely supposed cases, or specifications for illustration. It is taken for granted that, as a body, the sins mentioned were very generally chargeable on them. Would the Apostle, addressing the Jews as one man, have asked why they were guilty of such a sin, if they were not very generally guilty of it? Mr. Tholuck, then, has no ground to suppose the contrary.

Ver. 22.—*Thou that sayest a man should not commit adultery, dost thou commit adultery? thou that abhorrest idols, dost thou commit sacrilege?*

Oppression of the poor, and adultery, are the crimes with which the Jews were chiefly charged by our Lord. *Abhorrest idols.*—The Jews now generally abhorred the idolatry to which in the former ages of their history they were so prone, even in its grossest forms. The word in the original signifies to abominate, alluding to things most disagreeable to the senses. This is according to God's account of the sin of idolatry. According to human standards of morality, idolatry appears a very innocent thing, or at least not very sinful; but in Scripture it is classed among the works of the flesh, Gal. v. 20, and is called ' abominable,' 1 Pet. iv. 3. It robs God of His glory, transferring it to the creature. *Commit sacrilege.*—The word here used literally applies to the robbery of temples, for which the Jews had many opportunities, as well as of appropriating to themselves what was devoted to religion, as is complained of, Neh. xiii. 10 ; and of robbing God in tithes and offerings, Mal. iii. 8 ; also of violating and profaning things sacred.

Ver. 23.—*Thou that makest thy boast of the law, through breaking the law, dishonourest thou God?*

The Jews gloried in the law as their great national distinction, yet they were egregiously guilty of breaking it, which was highly inconsistent and dishonourable to God, not merely ' as God was the author of the law,' which is the explanation of Mr. Stuart, but because they professed to be God's people and to glory in His law. In any other light, the breach of the law by the Gentiles, when they knew it to be God's law, would have been equally dishonourable to God. But God is dishonoured by the transgressions of His people, in a manner in which He is not dishonoured by the same transgressions in the wicked, who make no profession of being His. It is a great aggravation of the sins of God's

people, if they are the occasion of bringing reproach on His religion.
The world is ready to throw the blame on that religion which He has
given them; and it is for this that the Apostle, in the following verse,
reproaches the Jews in regard to the heathen.   Sinners also are thus
emboldened to sin with the hope of impunity, and opposers make it a
handle to impede the progress of Divine truth.

It appears that in the above three verses the Apostle alludes to what
is said, Ps. l. 16–21.   'But unto the wicked God saith, What hast thou
to do to declare My statutes, or that thou shouldest take My covenant in
thy mouth?   Seeing thou hatest instruction, and castest My words
behind thee.   When thou sawest a thief, then thou consentedst with him,
and hast been partaker with adulterers.   Thou givest thy mouth to evil,
and thy tongue frameth deceit.   Thou sittest and speakest against thy
brother; thou slanderest thine own mother's son.   These things hast
thou done, and I kept silence; thou thoughtest that I was altogether
such an one as thyself: but I will reprove thee, and set them in order
before thine eyes.'   On this it may be remarked, that the 50th Psalm
predicts the change which God was to make in His covenant at the coming
of the Messiah, and likewise His rejection of His ancient people.   As to
the change of the covenant, it was declared that the sacrifices of the law
were not acceptable to Him, and that henceforth He will not require
from men any other than those of praises, thanksgivings, and prayers,
which are the only acceptable worship.   Respecting the rejection of
His ancient people, God reproaches them with their crimes, and more
especially with hypocrisy, which are precisely the charges made against
them in this place by the Apostle.   The conclusion from the whole is,
that the pretended justification of the Jews by the external advantages
of the law was a vain pretence; and that, as they had so vilely abused
the law of which they boasted, according to the prediction of the
Psalmist, it must follow that the accusation now brought against them
was established.

The Apostle, in these verses, exhibits the most lively image of
hypocrisy.   Was there ever a more beautiful veil than that under which
the Jew presents himself?   He is a man of confession, of praise, of
thanksgiving; a man whose trust is in the law, whose boast is of God,
who knows His will, who approves of things that are excellent; a man
who calls himself a conductor of the blind, a light of those who are in
darkness, an instructor of the ignorant, a teacher of babes; a man who
directs others, who preaches against theft, against adultery, against
idolatry; and, to sum up the whole, a man who glories in the commandments of the Lord.   Who would not say that this is an angel arrayed in
human form—a star detached from the firmament, and brought nearer
to enlighten the earth?   But observe what is concealed under this mask.
It is a man who is himself untaught; it is a thief, an adulterer, a
sacrilegious person,—in one word, a wicked man, who continually
dishonours God by the transgression of His law.   Is it possible to imagine
a contrast more monstrous than between these fair appearances and
this awful reality?

Doubtless Paul might have presented a greater assemblage of particular vices prevalent among the Jews, for there were few to which that nation was not addicted. But he deems it sufficient to generalize them all under these charges,—that they did not teach themselves that they dishonoured God by their transgressions of the law; and of these vices he has only particularized three, namely, theft, adultery, and sacrilege: and this for two reasons,—first, because it was of these three that God had showed the greatest abhorrence in His law; and, secondly, because these three sins, in spite of all their professions to the contrary, were usual and common among the Jews. There was no people on earth more avaricious and self-interested than they. It is only necessary to read the narrations of their prophets and historians, to be convinced how much they were addicted to robbery, to usury, and to injustice. They were no less obnoxious to the charge of fornication and adultery, as appears from the many charges preferred against them in the writings of the Prophets. They converted the offerings to the purposes of their avarice, they profaned the holy places by vile and criminal actions; and as the Lord Himself, after Jeremiah, upbraided them, they turned God's house of prayer into a den of thieves.

These three capital vices, which the Apostle stigmatizes in the Jews, like those which he had preferred against the Gentiles, stand opposed, on the one hand, to the three principal virtues which he elsewhere enumerates as comprehending the whole system of sanctity, namely, to live *soberly, righteously, and godly;* and, on the other hand, they are conformable to the three odious vices which he had noted among the Gentiles, namely, *ungodliness, intemperance, unrighteousness.* For theft includes, in general, every notion of unrighteousness; adultery includes that of intemperance; and the guilt of sacrilege, that of ungodliness. Hence it is easy to conclude that, whatever advantages the Jews possessed above the Gentiles, they were, notwithstanding, in the same condition before the tribunal of God,—like them unrighteous, like them intemperate, like them ungodly, and, consequently, like them subjected to the same condemnation.

Ver. 24.—*For the name of God is blasphemed among the Gentiles through you, as it is written.*

The charge alleged here against the Jews, is not that they themselves blasphemed the name of God, as some understand it, but that they gave occasion to the heathen to blaspheme. The Apostle is not charging the Jews with speaking evil of God, or with one particular sin, but with the breach of their law in general. He here confirms what he had just said to this purpose in the foregoing verse, by the authority of Scripture. Many suppose that he refers to a passage of Isaiah, lii. 5, where the Prophet says, 'And my name continually every day is blasphemed.' But there the Prophet does not charge the Jews as having, by their bad conduct, occasioned the injury which the name of God received. He ascribes it, on the contrary, to the Assyrians, by whom they had been subjected. In the passage before us, the reference is to Ezek. xxxvi. 17–20, where it is evident that the Jews, by the greatness and the number of their sins, had given occasion to the Gentiles to insult and blaspheme the holy name of God, which is precisely the meaning of the Apostle.

The Gentiles, as the Prophet there relates, seized on two pretexts to insult the name of God,—the one drawn from the afflictions which the sins of His people had brought upon them, and the other from the contemplation of the sins themselves. According to the first, they accused the God of Israel of weakness and want of power, since He had not saved His people from so miserable a dispersion. According to the second, they imputed to the religion and the God of the Israelites all the crimes which they saw that people commit, as if it had been by the influence of God Himself that they were committed. It is on account of these two arrogant and malignant accusations that God reproaches His people for having profaned His name among the nations; and adds (not for the sake of His people, who had rendered themselves altogether unworthy, but for that of His own name) two promises opposed to those two accusations,—the one of deliverance, the other of sanctification:— 'For I will take you from among the heathen, and gather you out of all countries, and will bring you unto your own land. Then will I sprinkle clean water upon you, and ye shall be clean,' Ezek. xxxvi. 24, 25. I will deliver you, in order to repel their insult on Me, in accusing Me of want of power. I will cleanse you, in order to vindicate Myself from the accusation of being the author of your crimes. God had no need of either of these ways of justifying Himself. He had shown, on numerous occasions, the irresistible power of His arm in favour of the Israelites; and the sanctity of His law was self-evident. Yet He promises to do these things for His own glory, inasmuch as the Gentiles and His people had dishonoured His name.

No accusation against the Jews could be more forcible than that which, in the verse before us, was preferred from the testimony of their own Scriptures. It proved that not only were they chargeable before God with their own sins, but that they were likewise chargeable with the sins which the Gentiles committed in blaspheming His name. This showed clearly that they were no more prepared to sustain the judgment of the strict justice of God than were the Gentiles, whom they were as ready to condemn as the Apostle himself was.

Ver. 25.—*For circumcision verily profiteth, if thou keep the law: but if thou be a breaker of the law, thy circumcision is made uncircumcision.*

Paul here pursues the Jew into his last retreat, in which he imagined himself most secure. He presses him on the subject of circumcision, which the Jews viewed as their stronghold—that rite even more ancient than Moses, and by which they were distinguished from the other nations. The sum of this, and the following verses to the end of the chapter, is, that the Jews being such as the Apostle had represented them, all their advantages, including circumcision, could only enhance their condemnation before the tribunal of God, and that, on the contrary, if the Gentiles, who have not received the law, observed its precepts, they would be justified without circumcision. Two things are here to be observed, namely, what is asserted of the Jews and Gentiles, and the proof that follows. The assertions are, that circumcision serves only as a ground of condemnation to transgressors of the law; and, on the other hand, that the want of it would be no detriment to those who fulfilled the law. The proof is, that before God the true Jew and the true circumcision consist not in external qualities, but in internal and real holiness. The reason why circumcision was not included in the enumeration before given of the advantages of the Jews is, that in itself it is not an advantage, but only a sign of other advantages; and it is mentioned here, because, in the character of a sign, it includes them: to name circumcision, then, is to refer to them all. In this verse the Apostle does not speak of circumcision according to its real and most important signification as he does in the two concluding verses, but in that view in which the Jews themselves considered it, as the initiatory and distinctive rite of their religion, without the observance of which they believed they could not be saved.

Circumcision verily profiteth, if thou keep the law.—It is not meant that circumcision will come into the account before the tribunal of God, as the fulfilling of the law, but that it would be an aid and motive to the observance of the law, and viewed in the light of an obligation to keep the law ; if the Jew had kept it, he could refer to his circumcision as an obligation which he had fulfilled. Circumcision may be viewed in two lights, either as given to Abraham, or as enjoined by Moses. 1. It was the token of the covenant that Abraham should be the father of the promised Saviour, and, moreover, a seal or pledge of the introduction and reality of the righteousness imputed to him through faith, while uncircumcised, in order that he might be the father of all believers, whether circumcised or not, to whom that righteousness should also be imputed. 2. Circumcision, as enjoined by Moses, was a part of his law, John vii. 22, 23. In the first view, it was connected with all the privileges of Israel, Phil. iii. 4, 5 ; in the second, it was a part of the law, whose righteousness is described, Rom. x. 5.[1] The Jews entirely mistook the object of the law, Rom. v. 20, Gal. iii. 19, which shut up all under sin, Gal. iii. 22, by cursing every one who continued not in all things written in the book of the law to do them; and in this view, as a part of the law of Moses, circumcision could only profit those who kept the whole law. But instead of this, the name of God was blasphemed among the Gentiles, through the wickedness of the Jews, and hence their having the form of knowledge and of the truth in the law would only aggravate their condemnation. When, therefore, the Apostle says, *if thou keep the law,* he supposes a case, not implying that it was ever verified ; but if it should exist, the result would be what is stated. If, on the other hand, the Jew was a *breaker of the law,* his circumcision was made uncircumcision, Jer.

---

[1] It is in this second view of circumcision being a part of the law, that the Apostle tells the Galatians that if they were circumcised, they were debtors to do the whole law. They had professed to receive Christ, who is the end of the law for righteousness to every one that believeth ; but their want of confidence in Christ's righteousness, in which they professed to rest, was evident by their adding to it the observance of circumcision. 'Thus they returned to the law, and were debtors to fulfil it,' Gal. v. 3, 4. The righteousness of the law and Christ's righteousness cannot, even in the least degree, be united.

ix. 26 ; it would be of no more avail than if he had not received it, and would give him no advantage over the uncircumcised Gentile. This declaration is similar to the way in which our Lord answers the rich young man. If the law is perfectly kept, eternal life will be the reward, as the Apostle had also said in verses 7 and 10 ; but if there be any breach of it, circumcision is of no value for salvation.

Ver. 26.—*Therefore, if the uncircumcision keep the righteousness of the law, shall not his uncircumcision be counted for circumcision ?*

The Apostle does not mean to affirm that an uncircumcised Gentile can fulfil the righteousness of the law, nor does he here retract what he had said in the first chapter respecting the corruption and guilt of the Gentiles, but he supposes a case in regard to them like that concerning the Jews in the preceding verse. This hypothetical mode of reasoning is common with Paul, of which we have an example in this same chapter, where he says that *the doers of the law shall be justified;* of whom, however, in the conclusion of his argument, ch. iii. 19, he affirms that none can be found. The supposition, then, as to the obedience of the Gentile, though in itself impossible, is made in order to prove that, before the judgment-seat of God, neither circumcision nor uncircumcision enters at all into consideration for justification or condemnation. If an uncircumcised Gentile kept the law, his uncircumcision would avail as much as the circumcision of the Jew. The reason of this is, that the judgment of God regards only the observance or the violation of the law, and not extraneous advantages or disadvantages, and, as is said above, with God there is no respect of persons. In reality, then, the Jews and Gentiles were on a level as to the impossibility of salvation by the law ; in confirmation of which truth, the inquiry here introduced is for the conviction of the Jew on this important point. But what is true upon a supposition never realized, is actually true with respect to all who believe in Jesus. In Him they have this righteousness which the law demands, and without circumcision have salvation. Dr. Macknight egregiously errs when he supposes that the law here referred to is the law of faith, which heathens may keep and be saved: this is a complication of errors.

Ver. 27.—*And shall not uncircumcision which is by nature, if it fulfil the law, judge thee, who by the letter and circumcision dost transgress the law ?*

Paul continues in this verse to reason on the same supposition as in the one preceding, and draws from it another consequence, which is, that if the Gentile who is uncircumcised fulfilled the law, he would not only be justified, notwithstanding his uncircumcision, but would judge and condemn the circumcised Jew who did not fulfil it. The reason of this conclusion is, that in the comparison between the one and the other, the case of the circumcised transgressor would appear much worse, because of the superior advantages he enjoyed. In the same way it is said, Matt. xii. 41, that the Ninevites shall condemn the Jews. *The uncircumcision which is by nature.*—That is to say, the Gentiles in their natural uncircumcised state, in opposition to the Jews, who had been distinguished and set apart by a particular calling of God. Dr. Macknight commits great violence when he joins the words 'by nature' with the words 'fulfil the law,' as if it implied that some Gentiles did fulfil the law by the light of nature. *Who by the letter and circumcision dost transgress the law.*—Dr. Macknight affirms that the common translation here 'is not sense.' But it contains a very important meaning. The Jews transgressed the law by means of their covenant and circumcision being misunderstood by them. This fact is notoriously true: they were hardened in their sin from a false confidence in their relation to God. Instead of being led to the Saviour by the law, according to its true end, they transgressed it, through their views of the letter of the law and of circumcision; of both of which, especially of circumcision, they made a saviour. The fulfilling of the law and its transgression are here to be taken in their fullest import, namely, for an entire and complete fulfilment, and for the slightest transgression of the law; for the Apostle is speaking of the strict judgment of justice by the law, before which nothing can subsist but a perfect and uninterrupted fulfilment of all the commandments of God. But it may be asked how the uncircumcised Gentiles could fulfil the law which they had never received. They could not indeed fulfil it as written on tables of stone and in the books of Moses, for it had never been given to them in that way; but as the work of the law, or the doctrine it teaches, was written in their hearts, it was their bounden duty to obey it. From this it is evident that in all this discussion respecting the condemnation of both Gentiles and Jews, the Apostle understands by the law, not the ceremonial law, as some imagine, but the moral law; for it is the work of it only which the Gentiles have by nature written in their hearts. Besides, it is clear that he speaks here of that same law of which he says the Jews were transgressors when they stole, committed adultery, and were guilty of sacrilege.

Ver. 28.—*For he is not a Jew, which is one outwardly ; neither is that circumcision, which is outward in the flesh :*
Ver. 29.—*But he is a Jew, which is one inwardly ; and circumcision is that of the heart, in the spirit, and not in the letter ; whose praise is not of men, but of God.*

The Apostle now passes to what is reality, not supposition, and gives here the proof of what he had affirmed, namely, that circumcision effects nothing for transgressors of the law, except to cause their deeper condemnation, and that the want of circumcision would be no loss to those who should have fulfilled the law. The reason of this is, that when the Jew shall appear before the tribunal of God, to be there judged, and when he shall produce his title as a Jew, as possessing it by birth, and his circumcision, as having received it as a sign of the covenant of God, God will not be satisfied with such appearances, but will demand of him what is essential and real. Now the essence and reality of things do not consist in names or in external signs; and when nothing more is produced, God will not consider a man who possesses them as a true Jew, nor his circumcision as true circumcision. He is only a Jew in shadow and appearance, and his is only a figurative circumcision void of its truth.

But he is a Jew, who is one inwardly ; that is to say, that in judging, God will only acknowledge as a true Jew, and a true confessor of His name, him who has the reality,—namely, him who is indeed holy and righteous, and who shall have fulfilled the law; for it is in this fulfilment that confession, and praise, and giving of thanks consist, which are the things signified by the name Jew. It is thus we are to understand the contrast which Paul makes between 'outwardly' and 'inwardly.' What is outward is the name, what is inward is the thing itself represented by the name.

And circumcision is that of the heart, in the spirit, and not in the letter.— It is essential to keep in view that here, and in all that precedes, from the beginning of the 18th verse of the first chapter, Paul is referring not to the Gospel, but exclusively to the law, and clearing the ground for the establishment of his conclusion in the following chapter, verses 19th and 20th, concerning the universal guilt of mankind, and the consequent impossibility of their being justified by the law. The whole is intended to prepare the way for the demonstration of the grand truth announced, ch. i. 17, and resumed, ch. iii. 21, of the revelation of a righteousness adequate to the demands of the law, and provided for all who believe. From a misapprehension in this respect, very erroneous explanations have been given by many of this verse and the context, as well as of the 7th, 8th, 9th, and 10th of the second chapter, representing these passages as referring to the Gospel, and not exclusively to the law. This introduces confusion into the whole train of the Apostle's reasoning, and their explanations are entirely at variance with his meaning and object.

And circumcision.—This passage is often considered as parallel to that in the Epistle to the Colossians, ch. ii. 11. 'In whom also ye are circumcised with the circumcision made without hands, in putting off the body of the sins of the flesh, by the circumcision of Christ.' But the purpose of the Apostle in the one place and the other is altogether different. Many passages, in different connections, which are similar in their expressions, are not so at all in their meanings. For the illustration of this, it is necessary to remember that the Apostle, as has just been observed, is here referring solely to the law, and likewise that circumcision in one view respected the legal covenant, of which it was a ceremonial obligation, and in another, the evangelical covenant, of which it was a type. In the character of a ceremonial obligation of the legal covenant, it represented the entire and perfect fulfilling of the law, which consisted not merely in external holiness, but in perfect purity of soul; and in this sense it represented what no man possessed, but which every man must have in order to be justified by the law. In the character of a type, it represented regeneration and evangelical holiness, which consists in repentance and amendment of life by the Spirit of Christ, and in that sense shadowed forth what really takes place in those who believe in Jesus Christ. In Colossians, ii. 11, the Apostle views it in this last aspect; for he means to say that what the Jew had in type and figure under the law, the believer has in reality and truth under the Gospel.

But in the passage before us Paul views it in its first aspect; for he is treating of the judgment of strict justice by the law, which admits of no repentance or amendment of life. The meaning, then, here is, that if the Jew will satisfy himself with bringing before the judgment of the law what is only external and merely a ceremonial observance, without his possessing that perfect righteousness which this observance denotes, and which the Judge will demand, it will serve for no purpose but his condemnation.

That of the heart in the spirit.—That is to say, what penetrates to the bottom of the soul; in one word, that which is real and effective. The term spirit does not here mean the Holy Spirit, nor has it a mystical or evangelical signification; but it signifies what is internal, solid, and real, in opposition to that which was ceremonial and figurative. *And not in the letter.*—Not that which takes place only in the flesh, according to the literal commandment, and in all the prescribed forms. In one word, it is to the spiritual circumcision that the Apostle refers, which is real in the heart and spirit. *Whose praise is not of men, but of God.*—Here Paul alludes to the name of Jew, which signifies praise, which may be taken either in an active sense, as signifying praising, or in a passive sense, as praised. Moses has taken it in this second meaning; when relating the blessing of Jacob, he says, 'Judah, thou art he whom thy brethren shall praise.' The Apostle here takes it in the same way; but he does not mean that this praise is of men, but of God. The meaning is, that in order to be a true Jew, it is not sufficient to possess external advantages, which attract human praise, but it is necessary to be in a condition to obtain the praise of God.

The object of the whole of this chapter is to show that the Jews are sinners, violators of the law as well as the Gentiles, and consequently that they cannot be justified before God by their works; but that, on the contrary, however superior their advantages are to those of the Gentiles, they can only expect from His strict justice, condemnation. The Jews esteemed it the highest honour to belong to their nation, and they gloried over all other nations. An uncircumcised person was by them regarded with abhorrence. They did not look to character, but to circumcision or uncircumcision. Nothing, then, could be more cogent, or more calculated to arrest the attention of the Jews, than this argument respecting the name in which they gloried, and circumcision, their distinguishing national rite, with which Paul here follows up what he had said concerning the demands of the law, and of their outward transgressions of its precepts. He had dwelt, in the preceding part of this chapter, on their more glaring and atrocious outward violations of the law, as theft, adultery, and sacrilege, by which they openly dishonoured God. Now he enters into the recesses of the heart, of which, even if their outward conduct had been blameless, and the subject of the praise of men, its want of inward conformity to that law, which was manifest in the sight of God, could not obtain his praise.

CHAPTER 3 / PART 1
ROMANS 3:1 – 20

THIS chapter consists of three parts. The first part extends to the 8th verse inclusively, and is designed to answer and remove some objections to the doctrine previously advanced by the Apostle. In the second part, from the 9th to the 20th verses, it is proved, by the testimonies of various scriptures, that the Jews, as well as the Gentiles, are involved in sin and guilt, and consequently that none can be justified by the law. The third part commences at verse 21, where the Apostle reverts to the declaration, ch. i. 17, with which his discussion commenced, and exhibits the true and only way of justification for all men, by the righteousness of God imputed through faith in Jesus Christ.

Ver. 1.—*What advantage then hath the Jew? or what profit is there of circumcision?*

If the preceding doctrine be true, it may be asked, What advantage hath the Jew over the Gentile; and what profit is there in circumcision, if it does not save from sin? If, on the contrary, the Jews, on account of their superior privileges, will be held more culpable before the tribunal of Divine justice, as the Apostle had just shown, it appears obviously improper to allege that God has favoured them more than the Gentiles. This objection it was necessary to obviate, not only because it is specious, but because it is important, and might, in regard to the Jews, arrest the course of the Gospel. It is specious; for if, in truth, the advantages of the Jews, so far from justifying them, contribute nothing to cause the balance of Divine judgment to preponderate in their favour—if their advantages rather enhance their condemnation—does it not appear that they are not only useless, but positively pernicious? In these advantages, then, it is impossible to repose confidence. But the objection is also important; for it would be difficult to imagine that all God had done for the Jews—His care of them so peculiar, and His love of them so great,—in short, all the privileges which Moses exalts so highly—were lavished on them in vain, or turned to their disadvantage. The previous statement of the Apostle might then be injurious to the doctrine of the Gospel, by rendering him more odious in the eyes of his countrymen, and therefore he had good reasons for fully encountering and answering this objection. In a similar way, it is still asked by carnal professors of Christianity, Of what use is obedience to the law of God or the observance of His ordinances, if they do not save the soul, or contribute somewhat to this end?

Ver. 2.—*Much every way; chiefly, because that unto them were committed the oracles of God.*

Paul here repels the foregoing objection as false and unfounded. Although the privileges of the Jews cannot come into consideration for their justification before the judgment-seat of God, it does not follow that they were as nothing, or of no advantage; on the contrary, they were marks of the peculiar care of God for that people, while He had, as it were, abandoned all the other nations. They were as aids, too, which God had given to deliver them from the impiety and depravity of the Gentiles; and, by the accompanying influences of His Spirit, they were made effectual to the salvation of many of them. Finally, the revelation made to the Jews contained not only figures and shadows of the Gospel, but also preparations for the new covenant. God had bestowed nothing similar on the Gentiles: the advantage, then, of the Jews was great. *Much every way.*—This does not mean, in every sense; for the Apostle does not retract what he had said in the preceding chapter, namely, that their advantages were of no avail for justification to the Jews continuing to be sinners,—for, on the contrary, in that case they only enhanced their condemnation; but this expression signifies that their advantages were very great, and very considerable.

Chiefly, because that unto them were committed the oracles of God.—The original denotes *primarily*, which is not a priority of order, but a priority in dignity and advantage; that is to say, that of all the advantages God had vouchsafed to them, the most estimable and most excellent was that of having entrusted to them His oracles. The word here used for *oracles* signifies the responses or answers given by an oracle; and when the Scriptures are so designated, it implies that they are altogether, in *word*, as well as in sense, the communications of God. By these oracles we must understand, in general, all the Scriptures of the Old Testament, especially as they regarded the Messiah; and, in particular, the prophecies which predicted His advent. They were oracles, inasmuch as they were the words from the mouth of God Himself, in opposition to the revelation of nature, which was common to Jews and Gentiles; and they were promises in respect to their matter, because they contained the great promise of sending Jesus Christ into the world. God had entrusted these oracles to the Jews, who had been constituted their guardians and depositaries till the time of their fulfilment, when they were to be communicated to all, Isa. ii. 3; and through them possessed the high character of the witnesses of God, Isa. xliii. 10, xliv. 8, even till the time of their execution, when they were commanded to be communicated to the whole world, according to what Isaiah, ii. 3, had said,—' For out of Sion shall go forth the law, and the word of the Lord from Jerusalem.' These oracles had not, however, been entrusted to the Jews simply as good things for the benefit of others, but also for their own advantage, that they might themselves make use of them; for in these oracles the Messiah—who was to be born among them, and among them to accomplish the work of redemption—was declared to be the proper object of their confidence, and through them they had the means of becoming acquainted with the way of salvation.

But why were these oracles given so long before the coming of the Messiah? It was for three principal reasons:—*First*, To serve as a testimony that, notwithstanding man's apostasy, God had not abandoned the earth, but had always reserved for Himself a people; and it was by these great and Divine promises that He had preserved His elect in all

ages. *Secondly,* These oracles were to characterize and designate the
Messiah when He should come, in order that He might be known and
distinguished ; for they pointed Him out in such a manner that He could
be certainly recognised when He appeared. On this account Philip said
to Nathanael, John i. 45, ' We have found Him of whom Moses in the
law, and the Prophets, did write, Jesus of Nazareth, the son of Joseph.'
Thirdly, They were to serve as a proof of the Divine origin of the Christian
religion ; for the admirable correspondence between the Old Testament
and the New is a clear and palpable demonstration of its divinity. It is,
moreover, to be observed that this favour of having been constituted the
depositaries of the sacred oracles was peculiar to the Jews, and one in
which the Gentiles did not at all participate. This is what the Apostle
here expressly teaches, since he considers it as an illustrious distinction
conferred upon his nation, a pre-eminence over all the kingdoms of the
world.

But why, again, does the Apostle account the possession of these oracles
their greatest advantage? Might not other privileges have been considered as equal, or even preferable, such as the glorious miracles which
God had wrought for the deliverance of the Israelites ; His causing them
to pass through the Red Sea, in the face of all the pride and power of
their haughty oppressor ; His guiding them through the sandy desert
by a pillar of fire by night, and of cloud by day ; His causing them to
hear His voice out of the fire, when He descended in awful majesty upon
Sinai ; or, finally, His giving them His law, written with His own finger,
on tables of stone ? It is replied, the promises respecting the Messiah,
and His coming to redeem men, were much greater than all the others.
Apart from these, all the other advantages would not only have been
useless, but fatal to the Jews ; for, being sinners, they could only have
served to overwhelm them with despair, in discovering, on the one hand,
their corruption, unmitigated by the kindness of Jehovah, and, on the
other, the avenging justice of God. In these circumstances, they would
have been left under the awful impossibility of finding any expiation for
their sins. If, then, God had not added the promises concerning the
Messiah, all the rest would have been death to them, and therefore the
oracles which contained these promises were the first and chief of their
privileges.

Ver. 3.—*For what if some did not believe ? shall their unbelief make the faith of
God without effect ?*

This is not the objection of a Jew, but, as it might readily occur, is
supposed by the Apostle. It is not ' *But what,*' as Dr. Macknight translates the first words, it is '*For what.*' The Apostle answers the objection in stating it. ' For what if some have not believed ; ' that is, ' the
unbelief of some is no objection to my doctrine.' ' Will their unbelief
destroy the faithfulness of God ? ' This repels, and does not, as Dr.
Macknight understands it, assert the supposition. The meaning is, that
the unbelief of the Jews did not make void God's faithfulness with
respect to the covenant with Abraham. Though the mass of his descendants were unbelievers at this time, yet many of them, both then,
as the Apostle asserts, ch. xi. 2, and at all other times, were saved in

virtue of that covenant. Paul, then, here anticipates and meets an objection which might be urged against his assertion of the pre-eminence of the Jews over the Gentiles, testified by the fact that to them God had confided His oracles. The objection is this, that since they had not believed in the Messiah, whom these oracles promised, this advantage must not only be reckoned of little value, but, on the contrary, prejudicial.

In reply to this objection, the Apostle, in the first place, intimates that their unbelief had not been universal, which is tacitly understood in his only attributing unbelief to *some ;* for when it is said that some have not believed, it is plainly intimated that some have believed. It does not, indeed, appear that it would have been worthy of the Divine wisdom to have given to one nation, in preference to all others, so excellent and glorious an economy as that of the Old Testament, to have chosen them above all others of His free love and good pleasure, and to have revealed to them the mysteries respecting the Messiah, while, at the same time, none of them should have responded to all this by a true faith. There is too much glory and too much majesty in the person of Jesus Christ, and in His work of redemption, to allow it to be supposed that He should be revealed only externally by the word, without profit to some, Isa. lv. 10, 11. In all ages, before as well as since the coming of the Messiah, although in a different measure, the Gospel has been the ministration of the Spirit. It was fitting, then, that the ancient promises, which were in substance the Gospel, should be accompanied with a measure of that Divine Spirit who imprints them in the hearts of men, and that, as the Spirit was to be poured out on all flesh, the nation of the Jews should not be absolutely deprived of this blessing. This was the first answer, namely, that unbelief had not been so general, but that many had profited by the Divine oracles ; and consequently, in respect to them at least, the advantage to the Jews had been great. But the Apostle goes farther; for, in the second place, he admits that many had fallen in incredulity, but denies that their incredulity impeached the faithfulness of God. Here it may be asked whether the Apostle refers to the Jews under the legal economy who did not believe the Scriptures, or to those only who, at the appearing of the Messiah, rejected the Gospel? The reference, it may be answered, is both to the one and the other.

But it may be said, How could unbelief respecting these oracles be ascribed to the Jews, when they had only rejected the person of Jesus Christ? For they did not doubt the truth of the oracles; on the contrary, they expected with confidence their accomplishment; they only denied that Jesus was the predicted Messiah. It is replied, that to reject, as they did, the person of Jesus Christ, was the same as if they had formally rejected the oracles themselves, since all that was contained in them could only unite and be accomplished in His person. The Jews, therefore, in reality rejected the oracles ; and so much the more was their guilt aggravated, inasmuch as it was their prejudices, and their carnal and unauthorized anticipations of a temporal Messiah, which caused their rejection of Jesus Christ. Thus it was a real disbelief of the oracles themselves ; for all who reject the true meaning of the Scriptures, and attach to them another sense, do in reality disbelieve them, and set up in their stead a phantom of their own imagination, even while they profess to believe the truth of what the Scriptures contain. The Apostle, then, had good reason to attribute unbelief to the Jews respecting the oracles, but he denies that their unbelief can make void the faith, or rather destroy the faithfulness, of God.

By the *faithfulness of God* some understand the constancy and faithfulness of His love to the Jews ; and they suppose that the meaning is, that while the Jews have at present fallen into unbelief, God will not, however, fail to recall them, as is fully taught in the eleventh chapter. But the question here is not respecting the recall of the Jews, or the constancy of God's love to them, but respecting their condemnation before His tribunal of strict justice, which they attempted to elude by producing these advantages, and in maintaining that if these advantages only led to their condemnation, as the Apostle had said, it was not in sincerity that God had conferred them. This objection alone the Apostle here refutes. The term, then, *faith of God*, signifies His sincerity or faithfulness, according to which He had given to the Jews these oracles ; and the Apostle's meaning is, that the incredulity of the Jews did not impeach that sincerity and faithfulness, whence it followed that it drew down on them a more just condemnation, as he had shown in the preceding chapter.

Ver. 4.—*God forbid : yea, let God be true, but every man a liar ; as it is written, That Thou mightest be justified in Thy sayings, and mightest overcome when Thou art judged.*

God forbid.—Literally, let it not be, or far be it, a denial frequently made by the Apostle in the same way in this Epistle. It intimates two things, namely, the rejecting of that which the objection would infer, not only as what is false, but even impious ; for it is an affront to God to make His faithfulness dependent on the depravity of man, and His favour on our corruption. Though the privileges of the Jew, and the good which God had done for him, terminated only in his condemnation, by reason of his unbelief, it would be derogatory to the Almighty to question His faithfulness, because of the fault of the unprincipled objects of these privileges. The Apostle also wished to clear his doctrine from this calumny, that God was unfaithful in His promises, and insincere in His proceedings. *Let God be true, but every man a liar.*—The calling of men, inasmuch as it is of God, is faithful and sincere ; but the fact that it produces a result contrary to its nature and tendency, is to be attributed to man, who is always deceitful and vain. If the Jews had not been corrupted by their perversity, their calling would have issued in salvation ; if it has turned to their condemnation, this is to be attributed to their own unbelief. We must therefore always distinguish between what comes from God and what proceeds from man : that which is from God is good, and right, and true ; that which is from man is evil, and false, and deceitful. Mr. Tholuck grievously errs in his Neological supposition, that this inspired Apostle ' utters, in the warmth of his discourse, the wish that all mankind might prove covenant-breakers, as this would only tend to glorify God the more, by being the occasion of manifesting how great is His fidelity.' This would be a bad wish ; it would be desiring evil that good might come. It is not a wish. Paul states a truth. God in every instance is to be believed, although this should imply that every man on earth is to be condemned as a liar.

As it is written, That Thou mightest be justified in Thy sayings, and mightest overcome when Thou art judged.—This passage may be taken either in a passive signification, *when Thou shalt be judged*, or in an active signification, *when Thou shalt judge*. In this latter sense, according to the translation in Ps. li. 4, the meaning will be clear, if we have recourse to the history referred to in the Second Book of Samuel, ch. xii. 7, 11, where it is said that Nathan was sent from God to David. In that address, God assumed two characters, the one, of the party complaining and accusing David as an ungrateful man, who had abused the favours he had received, and who had offended his benefactor; the other, of the judge who pronounces in his own cause, according to his own accusation. It is to this David answers, in the 4th verse of the Psalm:—' *Against Thee, Thee only have I sinned, and done this evil in Thy sight, that Thou mightest be justified when Thou speakest.*' As if he had said, Thou hast good cause to decide against me; I have offended Thee; I am ungrateful; Thou hast reason to complain and to accuse me; Thou hast truth and justice in the words which Thy prophet has spoken from Thee. He adds, *that Thou mightest be clear when Thou judgest;* that is to say, as my accuser Thou wilt obtain the victory over me, before Thy tribunal, when Thou pronouncest Thy sentence. In one word, it signifies that whether in regard to the ground of that sentence or its form, David had nothing to allege against the judgment which God had pronounced in His own cause, and that he fully acknowledged the truth and justice of God. Hence it clearly follows that when God pleads against us, and sets before us His goodness to us, and, on the other hand, the evil return we have made, it is always found that God is sincere and true towards us, but that we have been deceivers and unbelieving in regard to Him, and therefore that our condemnation is just. This is precisely what the Apostle proposed to conclude against the Jews. God had extended to them His favours, and they had requited them only by their sins, and by a base incredulity. When, therefore, He shall bring them to answer before His judgment-seat, God will decide that He had been sincere in respect to them, and that they, on the contrary, had been wicked, whence will follow their awful but just condemnation. Paul could not have adduced anything more to the purpose than the example and words of David on a subject altogether similar, nor more solidly have replied to the objection supposed.

The answer of the Apostle will lead to the same conclusion, if the passive sense be taken, Thou shalt be judged. Though so eminent a servant of God, David had been permitted to fall into his foul transgressions, that God might be justified in the declarations of His word, which assert that all men are evil, guilty, and polluted by nature, and that in themselves there is no difference. Had all the eminent saints, whose lives are recorded in Scripture, been preserved blameless, the world would have supposed that such men were an exception to the character given of man in the word of God. They would have concluded that

human nature is better than it is. But when Abraham and Jacob, David
and Solomon, and Peter and many others, were permitted to manifest
what is in human nature, God's word is justified in its description of
man. God 'overcomes when He is judged;' that is, such examples as
that of the fall of David prove that man is what God declares him to be.
Wicked men are not afraid to bring God to their bar, and impeach His
veracity, by denying that man is as bad as He declares. But by such
examples God is justified. The passive sense, then, of the word 'judge'
is a good and appropriate meaning; and the phrase acquitting, or clearing, or overcoming, may be applicable, not to the person who judges God,
but to God who is judged. This meaning is also entirely to the Apostle's
purpose. Let all men be accounted liars, rather than impugn the veracity
of God, because, in reality, all men are in themselves such. Whenever,
then, the Divine testimony is contradicted by human testimony, let man
be accounted a liar.

Ver. 5.—*But if our unrighteousness commend the righteousness of God, what shall
we say? Is God unrighteous who taketh vengeance? (I speak as a man.)*

Out of the answer to the question in the first verse of this chapter,
another objection might arise, which is here supposed. It is such as a
Jew would make, but is proposed by the Apostle classing himself with
the Jews, as is intimated when he says, I speak as a man, just as any
writer is in the habit of stating objections in order to obviate them.
The objection is this: if, then, it be so that the righteousness of God,—
that righteousness which is revealed in the Gospel, ch. i. 17, by the
imputation of which men are justified,—if that righteousness which God
has provided is more illustriously manifested by our sin, showing how
suitable and efficacious it is to us as sinners, shall it not be said that God
is unjust in punishing the sin that has this effect? *What shall we say?*
or what answer can be made to such an objection? Is God, or rather,
is not God unjust, who in this case taketh vengeance? This is a sort
of insult against the doctrine of the Gospel, as if the objection was so
strong and well founded that no reply could be made to it. *I speak as a
man.*—That is to say, in the way that the impiety of men, and their want
of reverence for God, leads them to speak. The above was, in effect, a
manner of reasoning common among the Jews and other enemies of the
Gospel. It is, indeed, such language as is often heard, that if such
doctrines as those of election and special grace be true, men are not to
be blamed who reject the Gospel.

Ver. 6.—*God forbid; for then how shall God judge the world?*

Far be it.—Paul thus at once rejects such a consequence, and so
perverse a manner of reasoning, as altogether inadmissible, and proceeds
to answer it by showing to what it would lead, if admitted. *For then
how shall God judge the world?*—If the objection were well founded, it
would entirely divest God of the character of judge of the world. The
reason of this is manifest, for there is no sin that any man can commit
which does not exalt some perfection of God, in the way of contrast.
If, then, it be concluded that because unrighteousness in man illustrates
the righteousness of God, God is unrighteous when He taketh vengeance,

it must be further said, that there is no sin that God can justly punish; whence it follows that God can no longer be judge of the world. But this would subvert all order and all religion. The objection, then, is such that, were it admitted, all the religion in the world would at once be annihilated. For those sins, for which men will be everlastingly punished, will no doubt be made to manifest God's glory. Such is the force of the Apostle's reply.

Ver. 7.—*For if the truth of God hath more abounded through my lie unto His glory ; why yet am I also judged as a sinner ?*

This verse is generally supposed to contain the objection here reiterated, which was before stated in the 5th verse. It would appear strange, however, that the Apostle should in this manner repeat an objection—in a way, too, in which it is not strengthened—which he had effectually removed, and that after proposing it a second time he should add nothing to his preceding reply, further than denouncing it. It is not, then, a repetition of the same objection, but a second way in which Paul replies to what had been advanced in the 5th verse. In the preceding verse he had, in his usual brief but energetic manner, first repudiated the consequence alleged in the 5th verse, and had next replied to it by a particular reference, which proved that it was inadmissible. Here, by the word *for*, he introduces another consideration, and proceeds to set aside the objection, by exposing the inconsistency of those by whom it was preferred. The expression (καγω) I also, shows that Paul speaks here in his own person, and not in that of an opponent, for otherwise he would not have said, *I also*, which marks an application to a particular individual. His reply, then, here to the objection is this: If, according to those by whom it is supposed and brought forward, it would be unrighteous in God to punish any action which redounds to His own glory, Paul would in like manner say that if his lie—his false doctrine, as his adversaries stigmatized it—commended the truth of God, they, according to their own principle, were unjust, because on this account they persecuted him as a sinner. In this manner he makes their objection recoil upon those by whom it was advanced, and refutes them by referring to their own conduct towards him, so that they could have nothing to reply. For it could not be denied that the doctrine which Paul taught respecting the justification of sinners solely by the righteousness of God, whether true or false, ascribed all the glory of their salvation to God.

Ver. 8.—*And not rather, (as we be slanderously reported, and as some affirm that we say,) Let us do evil that good may come ; whose damnation is just.*

This is the third thing which the Apostle advances against the objection of his adversaries, and is in substance, that they established as a good and just principle what they ascribed to him as a crime, namely, that men might do evil that good may come. They calumniously imputed to Paul and his fellow-labourers this impious maxim, in order to render them odious, while it was they themselves who maintained it. For if, according to them, God was unrighteous in punishing the unrighteousness of men when their unrighteousness redounded to His glory, it followed that the Apostles might without blame do evil, provided that out of it good should arise. Their own objection, then, proved them guilty of maintaining that same hateful doctrine which they so falsely laid to his. charge.

As we be slanderously reported.—Here Paul satisfies himself with stigmatizing as a slanderous imputation this vile calumny, from which the doctrine he taught was altogether clear. *Whose damnation is just.*— This indignant manner of cutting short the matter by simply affirming the righteous condemnation of his adversaries, was the more proper, not only as they were calumniators, but also because the principle of doing evil that good might come, was avowed by them in extenuation of sin and unbelief. It was fitting, then, that an expression of abhorrence, containing a solemn denunciation of the vengeance of God, on account of such a complication of perversity and falsehood, should for ever close the subject. On these verses we may observe, that men often adduce specious reasonings to contradict the decisions of the Divine word; but Christians ought upon every subject implicitly to credit the testimony of God, though many subtle and plausible objections should present themselves, which they are unable to answer.

Ver. 9.—*What then? are we better than they? No, in no wise: for we have before proved both Jews and Gentiles, that they are all under sin.*

Here commences the second part of the chapter, in which, having proposed and replied to the above objections to his doctrine, Paul now resumes the thread of his discourse. In the two preceding chapters he had asserted the guilt of the Gentiles and of the Jews separately; in what follows he takes them together, and proves by express testimonies from Scripture that all men are sinners, and that there is none righteous, no, not one. In this manner he follows up and completes his argument to support the conclusion at which he is about to arrive in the 20th verse, which all along he had in view, namely, that by works of law no man can be justified, and with the purpose of fully unfolding, in verses 21, 22, 23, and 24, the means that God has provided for our justification, which he had briefly announced, ch. i. 17. In the verse before us he shows that, although he has admitted that the advantages of the Jews over the Gentiles are great, it must not thence be concluded that the Jews are better than they. When he says 'are *we* better,' he classes himself with the Jews, to whom he was evidently referring; but when, in the last clause of the verse, he employs the same term '*we*,' he evidently speaks in his own person, although, as in some other places, in the plural number.

What then? are we better than they?—The common translation here is juster than Mr. Stuart's, which is, 'have we any preference?' The Jews had a preference. The Apostle allows that they had many advantages, and that they had a preference over the Gentiles; but he denies that they were better. *Not at all.*—By no means. This is a strong denial of what is the subject of the question. Then he gives the reason of the denial, namely, that he had before proved both Jews and Gentiles *that they are all under sin.* *All* not only signifies that there were sinners among both Jews and Gentiles, for the Jews did not deny this; on this point there was no difference between them and the Apostle; but he includes them all singly, without one exception. It is in this sense of universality that what he has hitherto said, both of Jews and Gentiles, must be taken. Of all that multitude of men there was not found one who had not wandered from the right way. One alone, Jesus Christ, was without sin, and it is on this account that the Scriptures call Him the 'Just or Righteous One,' to distinguish Him by this singular character from the rest of men.

Under sin.—That is to say, guilty; for it is in relation to the tribunal of Divine justice that the Apostle here considers sin, in the same way as he says, Gal. iii. 22, 'The Scripture hath concluded (shut up) all under sin, that the promise by faith of Jesus Christ might be given to them that believe.' That it is in this sense we must understand the expression *under sin*, and not, as Roman Catholic commentators explain it, as under the dominion of sin, evidently appears,—1st, Because in this discussion, to be *under sin* is opposed to being *under grace*. Now, to be under grace, Rom. vi. 14, 15, signifies to be in a state of justification before God, our sins being pardoned. To be under sin, then, signifies to be guilty in the eye of justice. 2d, It is in reference to the tribunal of Divine justice, and in the view of condemnation, that Paul has all along been considering sin, both in respect to Jews and Gentiles. To be under sin, then, can only signify to be guilty, since he here repeats in summary all that he had before advanced. Finally, he explains his meaning clearly when he says, in verse 19, 'that every mouth may be stopped, and all the world may become guilty before God.'

Ver. 10.—*As it is written, There is none righteous, no, not one.*

After having proceeded in his discussion, appealing to the natural sentiments of conscience and undeniable fact, Paul now employs the authority of Scripture, and alleges several passages drawn from the books of the Old Testament, written at different times, more clearly to establish the universal guilt both of Jews and Gentiles, in order that he might prove them all under condemnation before the tribunal of God. *There is none righteous.*—This passage may be regarded as the leading proposition, the truth of which the Apostle is about to establish by the following quotations. None could be more appropriate or better adapted to his purpose, which was to show that every man is in himself entirely divested of righteousness. There is none righteous, no, not one. Not one possessed of a righteousness that can meet the demands of God's holy law. The words in this verse, and those contained in verses 11 and 12, are taken from Ps. xiv. and liii., which are the same as to the sense, although they do not follow the exact expressions. But does it seem proper that Paul should draw a consequence in relation to all, from what David has only said of the wicked of his time? The answer is, That the terms which David employs are too strong not to contemplate the universal sinfulness of the human race. 'The Lord looked down from heaven upon the children of men, to see if there were any that did understand, and seek God. They are all gone aside; they are altogether become filthy; there is none that doeth good, no, not one.' This notifies universal depravity, so that, according to the Prophet, the application is just. It is not that David denies that God had sanctified some men by His Spirit; for, on the contrary, in the same Psalm, he speaks of the afflicted, of whom God is the refuge; but the intention is to say that, in their natural condition, without the grace of regeneration, which God vouchsafes only to His people, who are a small number, the whole human race is in a state of universal guilt and condemnation. This is also what is meant by Paul, and it is the use, as is clear from the context, that he designed to make of this passage of David, according to which none are excepted in such a way as that, if God examined them by their obedience to the law, they could stand before Him; and, besides this, whatever holiness is found in any man, it is not by the efficacy of the law, but by that of the Gospel, and if they are now sanctified, they were formerly under sin as well as others; so that it remains a truth, that all who are under the law, to which the Apostle is exclusively referring, are *under sin*, that is, guilty before God. Through the whole of this discussion, it is to be observed that the Apostle makes no reference to the doctrine of sanctification. It is to the law exclusively that he refers, and here, without qualification, he asserts it as a universal truth that there is *none righteous*—not one who possesses righteousness, that is, in perfect conformity to the law; and his sole object is to prove the necessity of receiving the righteousness of God in order to be delivered from condemnation. The passage, then, here adduced by Paul, is strictly applicable to his design.

Dr. Macknight supposes that this expression, 'There is none righteous,' applies to the Jewish common people, and is an Eastern expression, which means that comparatively very few are excepted. There is not the shadow of ground for such a supposition. It is evident that both the passages quoted, and the Apostle's argument, require that every individual of the human race be included. And on what pretence can it be restricted to 'the Jewish common people'? Whether were they or their leaders the objects of the severest reprehensions of our Lord during His ministry? Did not Jesus pronounce the heaviest woes on the scribes and Pharisees? Matt. xxiii. 15. Did He not tell the chief priests and elders that the publicans and the harlots go into the kingdom of heaven before them? Matt. xxi. 31.

Mr. Stuart also supposes that the charge is not unlimited, and justifies this by alleging that the believing Jews must be excepted. But it is clear that the believing Jews are not excepted. For though they are now delivered, yet they were by nature under sin as well as others; and that all men are so, is what Paul is teaching, without having the smallest reference to the Gospel or its effects. In this manner Dr. Macknight and Mr. Stuart, entirely mistaking the meaning of the Apostle and the whole drift of his argument, remove the foundation of the proofs he adduces that all men are sinners. Mr. Stuart also appears to limit the charges to the Jews, and in support of this refers to the 9th and 19th verses. The 9th verse speaks of both Jews and Gentiles; and the purpose of the 19th evidently is to prove that the Jews are not excepted; while the 20th clearly shows that the whole race of mankind are included, it being the general conclusion which the Apostle draws from all he had said, from the 18th verse of the first chapter, respecting both Jews and Gentiles, of whom he affirms in the 9th verse that they were all under sin.   And is it not strictly true, in the fullest import of the term, that there is none righteous in himself, no, not one? Is not righteousness the fulfilling of the law? And do not the Scriptures testify and everywhere show that 'there is no man that sinneth not'? 1 Kings viii. 46. 'Who can say, I have made my heart clean, I am pure from my sin?' Prov. xx. 9. 'For there is not a just man upon earth, that doeth good and sinneth not,' Eccles. vii. 20. And the Apostle James, including himself as well as his brethren to whom he wrote, declares, 'In many things we all offend.'[1]

Like Mr. Stuart, Taylor of Norwich, in his Commentary, supposes that in this and the following verses to the 19th, the Apostle means no universality at all, but only the far greater part, and that they refer to bodies of people, of Jews and Gentiles in a collective sense, and not to particular persons. To this President Edwards, in his treatise *On Original Sin*, p. 245, replies, ' If the words which the Apostle uses do not most fully and determinately signify a universality, no words ever used in the Bible are sufficient to do it. I might challenge any man to produce any one paragraph in the Scripture, from the beginning to the end, where there is such a repetition and accumulation of terms, so strongly and emphatically, and carefully, to express the most perfect and absolute universality, or any place to be compared to it. What instance is there in the Scripture, or indeed any other writing, when the meaning is only the much greater part, where this meaning is signified in such a manner by repeating such expressions, *They are all—they are all—they are all— together—every one—all the world*, joined to multiplied negative terms, to show the universality to be without exception, saying, *There is no*

---

[1] ' Here a question,' it is observed in the *Presbyterian Review*, ' arises, which materially affects the interpretation of the next two verses,—" whether Paul continues to devote himself to the inculpation of the Jews only, or of all mankind." It is natural, of course, to refer the quotations from the Old Testament to the sentiment which is nearest them, that *all*, whether Jews or Gentiles, are under sin ; and it is right to do so, unless some strong reason can be shown to the contrary. Mr. Stuart imagines he has discovered such a reason, in the alleged fact that " in the Old Testament, in the connection in which they stand, some of the passages have not an unlimited signification." But this argument, if of any weight at all, proves a great deal too much. For, if their original meaning was so specific as not to comprehend all the world, it was likewise so specific as not to comprehend all the Jews. On Mr. Stuart's supposition, most of them refer primarily to the "*impious part* of the Jewish nation." Would, then, those who made their boast of God submit to be marked as of this fraternity ? No, not one of them would identify himself with the impious ; and the arrows which the Apostle designed to pierce their hearts, would prove either pointless or misdirected. If, therefore, we *must* restrict the signification of these verses, according to our previous views of their force in the passages whence they have been transplanted, let us do so consistently, and affirm at once that the Apostle, wishing to bring home guilt to the Jewish people (for we go on Mr. Stuart's own supposition), adduced authorities which bear only upon part of them, and were of no efficacy for the conviction of the whole. But if this is too appalling for our acceptance, let us renounce the argument which involves it ; let us learn from Paul himself the object of his own citations, connect them (as is most natural) with the nearest context, and understand them as expressive of the most perfect and absolute universality.'

flesh—there is none—there is none—there is none—there is none, four times over, besides the addition of *no, not one—no, not one,* once and again! When the Apostle says, *That every mouth may be stopped,* must we suppose that he speaks only of those two great collective bodies, figuratively ascribing to each of them a mouth, and means that those two mouths are stopped?' Again, p. 241, 'Here the thing which I would prove, viz., that mankind, in their first state, before they are interested in the benefits of Christ's redemption, are universally wicked, is declared with the utmost possible fulness and precision. So that, if here this matter be not set forth plainly, expressly, and fully, it must be because no words can do it; and it is not in the power of language, or any manner of terms or phrases, however contrived and heaped one upon another, determinately to signify any such thing.'

Ver. 11.—*There is none that understandeth, there is none that seeketh after God.*

Paul here applies equally to Jews and Gentiles that which he charges upon the Gentiles, Eph. iv. 18, ' *Having the understanding darkened, being alienated from the life of God through the ignorance that is in them, because of the blindness (or hardness) of their hearts.*' This is true of every individual of the human race naturally. ' The natural man receiveth not the things of the Spirit of God ; for they are foolishness unto him.' In the parable of the sower, the radical distinction between those who finally reject, and those who receive the word and bring forth fruit, is, that they who were fruitful ' understood ' the word, while the others understood it not, Matt. xiii. 19–23, and the *new man,* he who is born again, is said to be renewed in knowledge, after the image of Him that created him. The assertion, then, in this passage, requires no limitation with respect to those who are now believers, for they were originally like others. All men are naturally ignorant of God, and by neglecting the one thing needful, show no understanding. They act more irrationally than the beasts.

None that seeketh after God.—To seek God is an expression frequently used in Scripture to denote the acts of religion and piety. It supposes the need all men have to go out of themselves to seek elsewhere their support, their life, and happiness, and the distance at which naturally we are from God, and God from us,—we by our perversity, and He by His just wrath. It teaches how great is the blindness of those who seek anything else but God, in order to be happy, since true wisdom consists in seeking God for this, for He alone is the sovereign good to man. It also teaches us that during the whole course of our life God proposes Himself as the object that men are to seek, Isa. lv. 6, for the present is the time of His calling them, and if they do not find Him, it is owing to their perversity, which causes them to flee from Him, or to seek Him in a wrong way. To seek God is, in general, to answer to all His relative perfections; that is to say, to respect and adore His sovereign majesty, to instruct ourselves in His word as the primary truth, to obey His commandments as the commandments of the sovereign Legislator of men, to have recourse to Him by prayer as the origin of all things. In particular, it is to have recourse to His mercy by repentance; it is to place our confidence in Him ; it is to ask for his Holy Spirit to support us, and to implore His protection and blessing ; and all this through Him who is the way to the Father, and who declares that no man cometh to the Father but by Him.

Ver. 12.—*They are all gone out of the way, they are together become unprofitable ; there is none that doeth good, no, not one.*

Sin is a wandering or departure from the right way ; that is to say, out of the way of duty and obligation, out of the way of the means which conduct to felicity. These are the ways open before the eyes of men to walk in them ; he who turns from them wanders out of the way. The Prophet here teaches what is the nature of sin ; he also shows us what are its consequences ; for as the man who loses his way cannot have any rest in his mind, nor any security, it is the same with the sinner ; and as a wanderer cannot restore himself to the right way without the help of a guide, in the same manner the sinner cannot restore himself, if the Holy Spirit comes not to his aid. *They are together become unprofitable.*—They have become corrupted, or have rendered themselves useless ; for everything that is corrupted loses its use. They are become unfit for that for which God made them ; unprofitable to God, to themselves, and to their neighbour. *There is none that doeth good, no, not one*—not one who cometh up to the requirements of the law of God. This is the same as is said above, *there is none righteous,* and both the Prophet and the Apostle make use of this repetition to enhance the greatness and the extent of human corruption.

Ver. 13.—*Their throat is an open sepulchre ; with their tongues they have used deceit ; the poison of asps is under their lips.*

What the Apostle had said in the preceding verses was general ; he now descends to something more particular, both respecting words and actions, and in this manner follows up his assertion, that there is none that doeth good, by showing that all men are engaged in doing evil. As to their words, he marks in this and the following verse, all the organs of speech, the *throat,* the *tongue,* the *lips,* the *mouth.* All this tends to aggravate the depravity of which he speaks. The first part of this verse is taken from Ps. v. 9, and the last from Ps. cxl. 3. *Open sepulchre.*— This figure graphically portrays the filthy conversation of the wicked. Nothing can be more abominable to the senses than an open sepulchre, where a dead body beginning to putrify steams forth its tainted exhalations. What proceeds out of their mouth is infected and putrid ; and as the exhalation from a sepulchre proves the corruption within, so it is with the corrupt conversation of sinners. *With their tongues they have used deceit*—used them to deceive their neighbour, or they have flattered with the tongue, and this flattery is joined with the intention to deceive. This also characterizes in a striking manner the way in which men employ speech to deceive each other, in bargains, and in everything in which their interest is concerned. *The poison of asps is under their lips.*—This denotes the mortal poison, such as that of vipers or asps, that lies concealed under the lips, and is emitted in poisoned words. As these venomous creatures kill with their poisonous sting, so slanderers and evil-minded persons destroy the characters of their neighbours. 'Death and life,' it is said in the Book of Proverbs, 'are in the power of the tongue.'

Ver. 14.—*Whose mouth is full of cursing and bitterness.*

This is taken from Ps. x. 7. Paul describes in this and the foregoing verse the four principal vices of the tongue,—filthy and infected discourse; deceitful flatteries; subtle and piercing evil-speaking; finally, outrageous and open malediction. This last relates to the extraordinary propensity of men to utter imprecations against one another, proceeding from their being hateful and hating one another. *Bitterness* applies to the bitterness of spirit to which men give vent by bitter words. All deceit and fraud is bitter in the end,—that is to say, desolating and afflicting. 'They bend their bows to shoot their arrows, even bitter words.' 'Their teeth are spears and arrows, and their tongue a sharp sword,' Ps. lxiv. 3, lvii. 4. 'The tongue,' says the Apostle James, 'is set on fire of hell.'

Ver. 15.—*Their feet are swift to shed blood.*

After having spoken of men's sinfulness, as shown by their words, the Apostle comes to that of actions, which he describes in this and the two following verses. This passage is taken from Isa. lix. 7, and from Prov. i. 16, which describe the general sinfulness of men, the injustice and violence committed among them, and how ready they are to shed blood when not restrained either by the consideration of the good of society, or by fear of the laws. Every page of history attests the truth of this awful charge.

Ver. 16.—*Destruction and misery are in their ways.*

This declaration, taken also from Isa. lix. 7, must be understood in an active sense,—that is to say, men labour to destroy and to ruin one another; proceeding in their perverse ways, they cause destruction and misery.

Ver. 17.—*And the way of peace have they not known.*

They have not known peace to follow and approve of it; and are not acquainted with its ways, in which they do not walk in order to procure the good of their neighbour,—for peace imports prosperity, or the way to maintain concord and friendship. Such is a just description of man's ferocity, which fills the world with animosities, quarrels, hatred in the private connections of families and neighbourhoods; and with revolutions, and wars, and murders, among nations. The most savage animals do not destroy so many of their own species to appease their hunger, as man destroys of his fellows; to satiate his ambition, his revenge, or cupidity.

Ver. 18.—*There is no fear of God before their eyes.*

This is taken from Ps. xxxvi. 1. After having followed up the general charge, that there is 'none righteous, no, not one,' by producing the preceding awful descriptions of human depravity, and having begun with the declaration of man's want of understanding and his alienation from God, the Apostle here refers to the primary source of all these evils, with which he sums them up. There is 'no fear of God before their eyes.'

They have not that reverential fear of Him which is the beginning of wisdom, which is connected with departing from evil, and honouring and obeying Him, and is often spoken of in Scripture as the sum of all practical religion; on the contrary, they are regardless of His majesty and authority, His precepts and His threatenings. It is astonishing that men, while they acknowledge that there is a God, should act without any fear of His displeasure. Yet this is their character. They fear a worm of the dust like themselves, but disregard the Most·High, Isa. li. 12, 13. They are more afraid of man than of God—of his anger, his contempt, or ridicule. The fear of man prevents them from doing many things from which they are not restrained by the fear of God. That God will put His fear in the hearts of His people, is one of the distinguishing promises of the new covenant, which shows that prior to this it is not found there.

The Apostle could have collected a much greater number of passages from the law and the Prophets to prove what he intended, for there is nothing more frequent in the Old Testament than the reproaches of God against the Israelites, and all men, on account of their abandoning themselves to sin; but these form a very complete description of the reign of sin among men. The first of them, ver. 10, prefers the general charge of unrighteousness; the second, vers. 11, 12, marks the internal character or disorders of the *heart*; the third, vers. 13, 14, those of the *words*; the fourth, vers. 15, 16, 17, those of the *actions*; and the last, ver. 18, declares the *cause* of the whole. In the first and second, we see the greatness of the corruption, and its universality: its greatness, in the extinction of all righteousness, of all wisdom, of all religion, of all rectitude, of all that is proper, and, in one word, of all that is good; its universality, in that it has seized upon the whole man, without leaving anything that is sound or entire. In the third, we observe the four vices of the tongue, which have been already pointed out,—namely corrupt conversation, flattery and deceit, envenomed slander, outrageous malediction. In the fourth, justice violated in what is most sacred—the life of man; charity subverted, in doing the evil which it prohibits; and that which is most fundamental and most necessary—peace—destroyed. And in the last, what is most essential entirely cast off, which is the fear of God. In this manner, having commenced his enumeration of the evils to which men are addicted, by pointing out their want of understanding and desire to seek God, the Apostle terminates his description by exposing the source from whence they all flow, which is, that men are destitute of the fear of God; His fear is not before their eyes to restrain them from evil. They love not His character, not rendering to it that veneration which is due; they respect not His authority. Such is the state of human nature while the heart is unchanged. From all this a faint idea may be formed of what will be the future state of those who shall perish, from whom the Gospel has been hid,—of those whose minds the god of this world has blinded, lest the light of the glorious Gospel of Christ, who is the image of God, should shine into them. Then the various restraints which in this life operate so powerfully, so extensively, and so constantly, will be taken off, and the natural depravity of fallen man will burst forth in all its unbridled and horrible wickedness.

Ver. 19.—*Now we know that whatsoever thing the law saith, it saith to them who are under the law ; that every mouth may be stopped, and all the world may become guilty before God.*

The article is in this verse prefixed to the term law, while it is wanting in the following verse. This shows that here the reference is to the legal dispensation, and applies in the first clause specially to the Jews ; while, in the last clause, the expression 'all the world,' and, in the following verse, the term 'law,' without the article, refers to all mankind.

Paul here anticipates two general answers which might be made to those passages which he had just quoted, to convict the Jews, as well as all other men, of sin. First, that they are applicable not to the Jews but to the Gentiles, and that, therefore, it is improper to employ them against the Jews. Second, that even if they referred to the Jews, they could only be applied to some wicked persons among them, and not to the whole nation ; so that what he intended to prove could not thence be concluded, namely, that no man can be justified before God by the law. In opposition to these two objections, he says, that *when the law speaks, it speaks to those who are under it*,—to the Jews therefore ; and that it does so in order that the mouths of *all*, without distinction, may be stopped. If God should try the Jews according to the law, they could not stand before His strict justice, as David said, 'If Thou, Lord, shouldst mark iniquity, O Lord, who shall stand?' Ps. cxxx. 3. And, in addition to this, whatever there was of piety and holiness in some, it was not by the efficacy of the law, but by that of the Gospel—not by the spirit of bondage, but by the spirit of adoption ; so that it remains true that all those who are under the law are under sin.

That, or in order that.—This must be taken in three senses. 1st, The law brought against the Jews those accusations and reproaches of which Paul had produced a specimen in the passages quoted, in order that every mouth may be stopped ; this is the end which the law proposed. 2d, This was also the object of God, when He gave the law, for He purposed to make manifest the iniquity of man, and the rights of justice, Rom. v. 20. 3d, It was likewise the result of the legal economy. *Every mouth may be stopped.*—This expression should be carefully remarked. For if a man had fulfilled the law, he would have something to allege before the Divine tribunal, to answer to the demands of justice ; but when convicted as a sinner, he can only be silent—he can have nothing to answer to the accusations against him ; he must remain convicted. This silence, then, is a silence of confession, of astonishment, and of conviction. This is what is elsewhere expressed by confusion of face. 'O Lord, righteousness belongeth unto Thee ; but unto us, confusion of faces,' Dan. ix. 7.

And all the world.—That is to say, both Jews and Gentiles. The first clause of this verse, though specially applicable to the Jews, proves that since they, who enjoyed such peculiar privileges, were chargeable with those things of which the law accused them, the rest of mankind, whom the Apostle here includes under the term 'all the world,' must also be under the same condemnation. The law of nature, written on their consciences, sufficiently convicts the Gentiles ; and as to the Jews, who try to stifle the conviction of their consciences by abusing the advantages of the law, that law itself, while it accuses, convicts them also. This expression, then, must include the whole human race. It applies to all men, of every age and every nation. None of all the children of Adam are excepted. Words cannot more clearly include, in one general condemnation, the whole human race. Who can be excepted? Not the Gentiles, since they have all been destitute of the knowledge of the true God. Not the Jews, for them the law itself accuses. Not believers, for they are only such through their acknowledgment of their sins, since grace is the remedy to which they have resorted to be freed from condemnation. All the world, then, signifies all men universally.

May become guilty.—That is, be compelled to acknowledge themselves guilty. The term guilty signifies subject to condemnation, and respects the Divine judgment. It denotes the state of a man justly charged with a crime, and is used both in the sense of legal responsibility and of blameworthiness. This manifestly proves that in all this discussion the Apostle considers sin in relation to the condemnation which it deserves. *Before God.*—When the question respects appearing before men, people find many ways of escape, either by concealing their actions, by disguising facts, or by disputing what is right. And even when men pass in review before themselves, self-love finds excuses, and various shifts are resorted to, and false reasonings, which deceive. But nothing of this sort can have place before God. For although the Jews flattered themselves in the confidence of their own righteousness, and on this point all men try to deceive themselves, it will be entirely different in the day when they shall appear before the tribunal of God; for then there will be no more illusions of conscience, no more excuses, no way to escape condemnation. His knowledge is infinite, His hand is omnipotent, His justice is incorruptible, and from Him nothing can be concealed. Before Him, therefore, every mouth will be stopped, and all the world must confess themselves guilty.

Ver. 20.—*Therefore by the deeds of law there shall no flesh be justified in His sight ; for by law is the knowledge of sin.*

This is the final conclusion drawn from the whole of the preceding discussion, beginning at verse 18th of chapter first. The Apostle had shown that both the Gentiles and the Jews are under sin ; that is, they have brought down upon themselves the just condemnation of God. He had proved the same thing in the preceding verse, according to the scriptures before quoted. *Therefore.*—The conclusion, then, from the whole, as contained in this verse, is evident. *By the deeds of the law*, or, as in the original, *of law.*—The reference here is to every law that God has given to man, whether expressed in words, or imprinted in the heart. It is that law which the Gentiles have transgressed, which they have naturally inscribed in their hearts. It is that law which the Jews have violated, when they committed theft, adulteries, and sacrileges, and which convicted them of impiety, of evil-speaking, of calumny, of murder, of injustice. In one word, it is that law which shuts the mouth of the whole world, as had been said in the preceding verse, and brings in all men guilty before God.

The deeds, or works of law.—When it is said, by works of law no flesh shall be justified, it is not meant that the law, whether natural or written, was not capable of justifying. Neither is it meant that the righteousness thus resulting from man's fulfilment of all its demands would not be a true righteousness, but that no man being able to plead this fulfilment of the law before the tribunal of God—that perfect obedience which it requires—no man can receive by the law a sentence pronouncing him to be righteous. To say that the works of the law, if performed, are not good and acceptable, and would not form a true righteousness, would contradict what had been affirmed in the preceding chapter, verse 13, that *the doers of the law shall be justified.* The Apostle, then, does not propose here to show either the want of power of the law in itself, or of the insufficiency of its works for justification, but solely to prove that no man fulfils the law, that both Gentiles and Jews are under sin, and that all the world is guilty before God. *No flesh.*—This reference appears to be to Ps. cxliii. David there says, ' *no man living.*' Paul says, ' *no flesh.*' The one is a term which marks a certain dignity, the other denotes meanness. The one imports that whatever excellence there might be supposed to be in man, he could not be justified before God; and the other, that being only flesh,—that is to say, corruption and weakness, —he ought not to pretend to justification by himself. Thus, on whatever side man regards himself, he is far from being able to stand before the strict judgment of God.

Shall be justified in His sight.—The meaning of the term justified, as used by the Apostle in the whole of this discussion, is evident by the different expressions in this verse. It appears by the *therefore*, with which the verse begins, that it is a conclusion which the Apostle draws from the whole of the foregoing discussion. Now, all this discussion has been intended to show that neither Gentiles nor Jews could elude the con-demnation of the Divine judgment. The conclusion, then, that no flesh shall be justified in the sight of God by the works of law, can only signify that no man can be regarded as righteous, or obtain by means of his works a favourable sentence from Divine justice. It is in this sense that David has taken the term *justify* in Ps. cxliii., to which the Apostle had reference, *Enter not into judgment with Thy servant; for in Thy sight shall no man living be justified.* The terms *in His sight* testify the same thing, for they accommodate themselves to the idea of a tribunal, before which men must appear to be judged. It is the same with regard to the other terms, *by the deeds of law;* for if we understand a justification of judgment, the sense is plain: no one can plead before the tribunal of God a perfect and complete fulfilment of the law, such as strict and exact justice demands; no one, therefore, can in that way obtain justification. In justifying men, God does all, and men receiving justification, contribute nothing towards it. This is in opposition to the justification proposed by the law by means of obedience, in which way a man would be justified by his own righteousness, and not by the righteousness which God has provided and bestows.

For by law is the knowledge of sin.—Paul does not here intend simply to say that the law makes known in general the nature of sin, inasmuch as it discovers what is acceptable or displeasing to God, what He commands, and what He forbids ; but he means to affirm that the law convicts men of being sinners. For his words refer to what he had just before said in the preceding verse, that *all that the law saith, it saith to them who are under the law ; that every mouth may be stopped, and all the world may become guilty before God,* which marks a conviction of sin. But how, it may be said, does the law give that knowledge or that conviction of sin ? It does so in two ways. By the application of its commandments, and its prohibitions in the present state in which man is placed, for it excites and awakens the conscience, and gives birth to accusing thoughts. This is common both to the written law and the law of nature. It does this, secondly, by the declaration of punishments and rewards which it sets before its transgressors and observers, and as it excites the conscience, and gives rise to fear and agitation, thus bringing before the eyes of men the dreadful evil of sin. This also is alike common to the law of nature and the written law.

Here it is important to remark that God, having purposed to establish but one way of justification for all men, has permitted, in His providence, that all should be guilty. For if there had been any excepted, there would have been two different methods of justification, and consequently two true religions, and two true churches, and believers would not have had that oneness of communion which grace produces. It was necessary, then, that all should become guilty. *The Scripture hath concluded all under sin, that the promise by faith of Jesus Christ might be given to them that believe,* Gal. iii. 22 ; Rom. xi. 32.

CHAPTER 3 / PART 2
ROMANS 3:21 – 31

AT the opening of his discussion, ch. i. 16, 17, Paul had announced that the Gospel is the power of God unto salvation to every one that believeth, *because therein is the righteousness of God revealed.* He had said that the righteous by faith shall live, intimating that there is no other way of obtaining life. In proof of this, he had declared that the wrath of God is revealed from heaven against all ungodliness and unrighteousness of men, and had shown at large that both Jews and Gentiles are all under sin, and that, therefore, by obedience to law no flesh shall be justified. He now proceeds to speak more particularly of the righteousness of God provided for man's justification, describing the manner in which it is conferred, and the character of those by whom it is received. To this subject, therefore, he here reverts.

Ver. 21.—*But now the righteousness of God without law is manifested, being witnessed by the law and the prophets.*

Now,—that is to say, under the preaching of the Gospel—in the period of the revelation of the Messiah ; for it denotes the time present, in opposition to that time when God appeared not to take notice of the state of the Gentile nations, as it is said, Acts xvii. 30, 'The times of this ignorance God winked at, but *now* commandeth all men everywhere to repent.' And also in opposition to the legal economy respecting the Jews, as again it is said, John i. 17, 'The law was given by Moses, but grace and truth came by Jesus Christ.' This is what the Scriptures call 'the fulness of times,' Eph. i. 10; Gal. iv. 4. 'The last days,' Isa. ii. 2; Heb. i. 2; Acts ii. 17; 1 John ii. 18. 'The acceptable year of the Lord,' Isa. lxi. 2. '*Now* is the accepted time; behold, *now* is the day of salvation,' 2 Cor. vi. 2. The day of the Saviour that Abraham saw, John viii. 56.

The righteousness of God.—This is one of the most important expressions in the Scriptures. It frequently occurs both in the Old Testament and the New; it stands connected with the argument of the whole of the first five chapters of this Epistle, and signifies that fulfilment of the law which God has provided, by the imputation of which sinners are saved. Although perfectly clear in itself, its meaning has been involved in much obscurity by the learned labours of some who know not the truth, and by the perversions of others by whom it has been greatly corrupted. By many it has been misunderstood, and has in general been very slightly noticed even by those whose views on the subject are correct and scriptural. To consider its real signification is the more necessary, as it does not appear always to receive that attention from Christians which its importance demands. When the question is put, why is the Gospel the power of God unto salvation? how few give the clear and unfaltering answer of the Apostle, *Because therein is* THE RIGHTEOUSNESS OF GOD *revealed.* Before attending to the true import of this phrase, it is proper to advert to some of the significations erroneously attached to it. Of these I shall select only a few examples from many that might be furnished.

Origen understood by this righteousness God's attribute of justice, while Chrysostom explained it as Divine clemency.

According to Dr. Campbell of Aberdeen, *the righteousness of God* consists in man's conformity to the declared will of God. In his note on Matt. vi. 33, he says, '*The righteousness of God*, in our idiom, can mean only the justice or moral rectitude of the Divine nature, which it were absurd in us to seek, it being, as all God's attributes are, inseparable from His essence. But in the Hebrew idiom, that righteousness, which consists in a conformity to the declared will of God, is called *His righteousness*. In this way the phrase is used by Paul, Rom. iii. 21, 22, x. 3, where the *righteousness of God* is opposed by the Apostle to that of the unconverted Jews; and *their own righteousness*, which he tells us they went about to establish, does not appear to signify their personal righteousness, any more than the righteousness of God signifies His personal righteousness. The word *righteousness*, as I conceive, denotes there what we should call a system of morality or righteousness, which he denominates their own, because fabricated by themselves, founded partly on the letter of the law, partly on tradition, and consisting mostly in ceremonies and mere externals. This creature of their own imaginations they had cherished, to the neglect of that purer scheme of morality which was truly of God, which they might have learned even formerly from the law and the Prophets, properly understood, but now more explicitly from the doctrine of Christ.'

Such is the explanation by this learned critic of that leading phrase, 'the righteousness of God,' according to which, the reason why the Gospel is the power of God unto salvation, is, *because therein a pure scheme of morality is revealed.* Were this explanation just, so far from being the reason why the Gospel should be the means of salvation to sinners, it would be the cause of their universal and hopeless condemnation.

Dr. Macknight supposes that *the righteousness of God* signifies a righteousness belonging to faith itself, and not the righteousness conveyed and received by faith. '*Righteousness by faith,*' he says, on Rom. iii. 22, 'is called *the righteousness of God,*—1st, Because God hath enjoined faith as the righteousness which He will count to sinners, and hath declared that He will accept and reward it as righteousness ; 2d, Because it stands in opposition to *the righteousness of men*, which consists in a sinless obedience to the law of God.' Thus, while Dr. Macknight differs from Dr. Campbell in the meaning of the expression, *the righteousness of God*, he so far coincides with him in his radical error as to suppose that it does not signify the righteousness which God *provides* for the salvation of sinners, but the righteousness which He *requires* them to perform. The explanations of both of these writers are destructive of the Scripture doctrine of justification, opposed to the justice of God, subversive of the plan of salvation, and render the whole train of the Apostle's reasoning, from Rom. i. 16 to the end of the fifth chapter, inconclusive and self-contradictory.

Archbishop Newcombe, whose translations are so much eulogized by Socinians, together with many who have followed him, translates this phrase, 'God's *method* of justification.' What the Apostle has declared in precise terms, is thus converted into a general and indefinite annunciation, pointing to a different sense. In the Socinian version, as might be anticipated, it is also translated, ' God's *method* of justification.'

'The righteousness of God' cannot mean *God's method of justification, nor the justification which God bestows*, because the word translated *righteousness* does not signify *justification*. Righteousness and justification are two things quite different. God's righteousness is revealed in the Gospel, just as God Himself is said to be revealed. To reveal God is not to reveal a method of God's acting, and to reveal God's righteousness is not to reveal a method of God's making sinners righteous, but to reveal the righteousness itself. This righteousness is also said to be of God *by faith*, that is, sinners become partakers of it by faith. The righteousness of God, then, is not a method of justification, but the thing itself which God has provided, and which He confers through faith. Nor can the expression, ' the righteousness of God,' in the tenth chapter, signify God's method of justification. It is true the Jews were ignorant of God's method of justification, but that is not the thing which is there asserted. They were ignorant of the righteousness which God had provided for the guilty, and, in consequence, went about to establish their own righteousness. What is there meant by God's righteousness,

is seen by the contrast.   It is opposed to their own righteousness.   Now,
it was not a method of justification that the Jews went about to establish,
but it was *their own righteousness* which they endeavoured to establish—
a righteousness in which they trusted, of their own working.   If so, the
righteousness of God contrasted with this must be, not a method of
justification, but the righteousness which God confers on His people
through faith.   To establish a man's righteousness is not to establish a
method with respect to this, but to establish the thing itself.

To say that the Gospel is the power of God unto salvation, because
*that in it is revealed a Divine method of justification, or the justification
which God bestows,* leaves the great question which immediately presents
itself utterly without an answer.   It gives no light to the reader as to
what the Gospel reveals.   It is only in general a Divine scheme of
justification.   But the language itself, Rom. i. 17, leaves no such
uncertainty.   It shows that the Gospel is the power of God unto salvation, because it reveals God's righteousness,—that righteousness which
fulfils the demands of His law, which His justice will accept, and which
is upon all them that believe.

Mr. Tholuck explains the phrase, the righteousness of God, thus:—
'The Gospel makes known a way to that perfect fulfilment of the law
which is required by God.'   What is the meaning of this exposition?
It does not give the true meaning, and may have a most erroneous
import.   The best that can be said for it is, that it is so dark, and vague,
and equivocal, that it may elude condemnation on the principle of its not
having any one definite meaning.   It is more ambiguous than the answer
of an oracle that has only two meanings, for it may have several.   Does
it mean that the Gospel reveals a way by which man may himself fulfil
the law, so as to be perfectly righteous?   If Mr. Tholuck does not mean
this, the expression might mean it.   Does it mean that the law is not
yet fulfilled, but that the Gospel reveals a way in which it may be
fulfilled?   This is the most obvious sense.   Does it mean that the Gospel
reveals a way in which men perfectly fulfil the law by faith?   This is
evidently false, even according to Mr. Tholuck's sentiments; for though
faith were, as held forth by him, 'the most excellent of virtues,' he could
not affirm that it fulfils the law.   After this dark and vague account
of the term *righteousness*, we need not wonder at that most erroneous
meaning which he affixes to it in chapter iv. 3.[1]

Mr. Stuart, in his translation of the Epistle, renders this phrase, in

---

[1] Not only has Mr. Tholuck failed in giving any distinct explanation of the
term 'the righteousness of God,' he has, besides, entirely mistaken the meaning of
that other great leading expression, ch. vi. 2, 'dead to sin.'   The former of these
terms is laid as the foundation of the doctrine of justification, the latter of that
of sanctification.   After such interpretations as Mr. Tholuck has given of these
declarations which form the groundwork of the grand subjects of discussion in this
Epistle, is it surprising that he should so often mistake the meaning of the Apostle,
and the train of his argument, or in points of high importance directly contradict
him?   What has been affirmed of the Commentary of Professor Stuart on this Epistle,
applies with equal truth to that of Professor Tholuck.   'The technicalities of his
discussions are a very inadequate compensation for the errors he has broached ; and
the truth he has elicited may be put in a nutshell.   The useful illustrations in his
work on the Romans bear no proportion to his pernicious errors.'

Rom. i. 17, and iii. 21, 'The justification which is of God;' and in his explanation of it, '*the justification which God bestows*, or *the justification of which God is the author*.' He observes that this 'is a phrase among the most important which the New Testament contains, and fundamental in the right interpretation of the Epistle before us.' This is true; and the effect of his misunderstanding the proper signification of the original word in these passages, and rendering it *justification* instead of *righteousness*, appears most prominently in several of his subsequent interpretations, especially as shall afterwards be pointed out in the beginning of the fourth chapter, where, like Mr. Tholuck, he entirely misrepresents the doctrine of justification. His translation he endeavours to defend at some length; but none of his allegations support his conclusion. The proper meaning of the original word in ch. i. 17, and iii. 21, which he makes justification, is righteousness; and this meaning will apply in the other passages where it is found. In the New Testament it occurs ninety-two times, and, in the common version, is uniformly rendered *righteousness*. It occurs thirty-six times in the Epistle to the Romans, in which Mr. Stuart has sixteen times translated it righteousness. But he appears to have been led to adopt the translation he has given in the above verses from the supposed necessity of the case; and, indeed, this was necessary for Mr. Stuart, who not only denies expressly the imputation of Adam's sin to his posterity, but also the imputation of Christ's *righteousness* to believers. This should put Christians on their guard against a translation founded on the denial that Christ's righteousness is placed to their account for salvation, a doctrine which Dr. Macknight most ignorantly maintains is not to be found in the Bible.

Mr. Stuart observes that there are three expressions, viz., ' δικαιοσύνη, δικαίωμα, and δικαίωσις, all employed occasionally in the very same sense, viz., that of justification, *i.e.*, acquittal, pardon, freeing from condemnation, accepting and treating as righteous.' There may be situations in which the one might supply the place of the other, but they have a clear characteristic difference. The difference appears to be this: δικαιοσύνη, the original word in the verse before us, is not justification; it signifies justice or righteousness in the abstract; that is, the quality of righteousness. It signifies also complete conformity or obedience to the law; for if there be any breach of the law, there is no righteousness. Δικαίωμα, as distinguished from this, signifies an act of righteousness, or some righteous deed. It is accordingly used for the ordinances of God, because they are His righteous appointments, and perhaps because they typically refer to the true 'righteousness of God.' In a few places it may be an equivalent to δικαιοσύνη. Δικαίωσις is neither the one nor the other of the above. It is the act of being justified by this righteousness when on trial. Obedience to law is a different thing from being cleared, or acquitted, or justified, when tried by law. A man is justified on the ground of righteousness. There is the same difference between δικαιοσύνη and δικαίωσις, that there is in English between righteousness and justification.

In support of his explanation of the phrase, 'the righteousness of God,' namely, that it is the justification which God bestows, Mr. Stuart, in the following observations, shows a wonderful misapprehension of the doctrine of those who oppose the view of it which he adopts. On verse 22 he says, 'What that δικαιοσύνη Θεου (righteousness of God) is, which is χωρις νόμου (without law), the Apostle next proceeds explicitly to develope. Δικαιοσύνη δε . . . 'Ιησου Χριστου, *the justification which is of God by faith in Jesus Christ.* This explanation makes it clear as the noonday sun that δικαιοσύνη Θεου (righteousness of God), in this connection, does not mean righteousness, or the love of justice, as an *attribute* of God. For in what possible sense can it be said that God's righteousness or justice (as an essential attribute) is by faith in Christ? Does He possess or exercise this attribute, or reveal it, by faith in Christ? The answer is so plain that it cannot be mistaken,' p. 157. Why does Mr. Stuart labour to prove that the phrase in question cannot here mean the justice of God, or a Divine attribute? Does any man suppose that it has here such a sense? We do not understand it of a Divine attribute, but of conformity to law by a Divine work. This righteousness is God's righteousness, not because it is an attribute of His nature, but because it is the righteousness which God has provided and effected for His people, through the obedience unto death of His own Son. The word δικαιοσύνη, indeed, always signifies righteousness; but it may mean either a personal attribute, or conformity to law. Does not Mr. Stuart himself afterwards explain the phrase in this latter sense? Why, then, does he take it for granted that if it does not signify justification, as he makes it here, it must signify a personal attribute of God? In ch. iv. 3, 6, and elsewhere, he admits that the word δικαιοσύνη (righteousness) cannot signify *justification,* but must be understood as denoting *righteousness.* 'To say,' he observes (p. 177), ' *was counted for justification,* would make no tolerable sense.' But nothing can be more obvious than that the Apostle is in the fourth chapter treating of the same thing of which he is treating in this chapter, from the 21st verse. In all this connection he is still speaking of this δικαιοσύνη (righteousness) in the same view. Having here spoken of God's righteousness, he goes on to show that it was through this very righteousness that Abraham was justified. The justification of Abraham, instead of being an exception to what he had been teaching, as if it had been on the ground of Abraham's own obedience to law, is appealed to by the Apostle as a proof, as well as an illustration and example, of justification by God's righteousness received by faith.

It makes nothing in favour of Mr. Stuart that there may be instances in which the word δικαιοσύνη (righteousness) may be interpreted by the word justification, so as to make sense. There is no signification that may not be ascribed to any word upon this principle. A word may make sense in a passage, when it is explained in a meaning directly the opposite of its true meaning. This principle the reader may see fully established in the writings of Dr. Carson. Several instances have been alleged from the Septuagint, in which it is asserted that δικαιοσύνη has the meaning of goodness, etc.; but there is no instance there in which the word may not have its true meaning, and it is only ignorance of the import of the phrase, 'righteousness of God,' that has induced writers to give the term a different meaning. For instance, nothing at first sight appears more to countenance the idea that δικαιοσύνη (righteousness) expresses mercy than Ps. li. 14. How could David speak of righteousness, if God would deliver him from blood-guiltiness? He might well speak of goodness or compassion, but would not righteousness in God prevent him from being acquitted? Not so. The righteousness of God was what David looked to,—the same righteousness that is more clearly revealed by Paul in this Epistle. And well might David speak of that righteousness, when by it he was cleared from all the guilt of his enormous wickedness.

The word rendered 'righteousness,' Rom. i. 17, and in the verse before us, signifies both justice and righteousness; that is to say, conformity to the law. But while both of these expressions denote this conformity, there is an essential difference between them. Justice imports conformity to the law in executing its sentence; righteousness, conformity in obeying its precepts, and this is the meaning of the word here. If these ideas be interchanged or confounded, as they often are, the whole scope of the Apostle's reasoning will be misunderstood.

In various parts of Scripture this phrase, ' the righteousness of God,' signifies either that holiness and rectitude of character which is the attribute of God, or that distributive justice by which He maintains the authority of His law; but where it refers to man's salvation, and is not merely a personal attribute of Deity, it signifies, as in the passage before us, ver. 21, that fulfilment of the law, or perfect conformity to it in all its demands, which, consistently with His justice, God has appointed and provided for the salvation of sinners. This implies that the infinite justice of His character requires what is provided, and also that it is approved and accepted; for if it be God's righteousness, it must be required, and must be accepted by the justice of God. The righteousness of God, which is received by faith, denotes something that becomes the property of the believer. It cannot, then, be here the Divine attribute of justice, but the Divine work which God has wrought through His Son. This, therefore, determines the phrase in this place as referring immediately not to the Divine attribute, but to the Divine work. The former never can become ours. This also is decisive against explaining the phrase as signifying a Divine method of justification. The righteousness of God is contrasted with the righteousness of man ; and as Israel's own righteousness, which they went about to establish, was the righteousness of their works, not their method of justification, so God's righteousness, as opposed to this, Rom. x. 3, must be a righteousness wrought by Jehovah. As in 2 Cor. v. 21, the imputation of sin to Christ is contrasted with our becoming the righteousness of God in Him, the latter cannot be a method of justification, but must intimate our becoming perfectly righteous by possessing Christ's righteousness, which is provided by God for us, and is perfectly commensurate with the Divine justice.

No explanation of the expression, 'the righteousness of God,' will at once suit the phrase and the situation in which it is found in the passage before us, but that which makes it that righteousness, or obedience to the law, both in its penalty and requirements, which has been yielded to it by our Lord Jesus Christ. This is indeed the righteousness of God, for it has been provided by God, and from first to last has been effected by His Son Jesus Christ, who is the mighty God and the Father of eternity. Everything that draws it off from this signification tends to darken the Scriptures, to cloud the apprehension of the truth in the children of God, and to corrupt the simplicity that is in Christ. To that righteousness is the eye of the believer ever to be directed; on that righteousness must he rest; on that righteousness must he live; on that righteousness must he die; in that righteousness must he appear before the judgment-seat; in that righteousness must he stand for ever in the presence of a righteous God. 'I will greatly rejoice in the Lord; my soul shall be joyful in my God: for He hath clothed me with the garments of salvation, He hath covered me with the robe of righteousness,' Isa. lxi. 10.

The righteousness of God provided for the salvation of sinners, like that salvation itself, differs essentially from all other righteousness that ever was or can ever be performed. It differs entirely from the righteousness of men and angels in its AUTHOR, for it is the righteousness not of creatures but of the Creator. '*I the Lord have created it,*' Isa. xlv. 8. It is a Divine and infinitely perfect righteousness, wrought out by Jehovah Himself, which in the salvation of man preserves all His attributes inviolate. It is the righteousness of God, as of the Godhead, without respect to distinction of personality, and strictly so in that sense in which the world is the work of God. The Father created it by the Son, in the same way as by the Son He created the world: and if the Father effected this righteousness because His Son effected it, then His Son must be one with Himself. Peter, in his Second Epistle, ch. i. 1, according to the literal rendering of the passage, calls this righteousness the righteousness of Jesus Christ. 'Simon Peter, a servant and an Apostle of Jesus Christ, to them that have obtained like precious faith with us, in the righteousness of our God and Saviour Jesus Christ.' Most of the places in which the righteousness of God is spoken of, refer to it as the righteousness of the Father, as in 2 Cor. v. 21, where the Father is distinguished from the Son; but in this passage of Peter it is explicitly declared to be the righteousness of the Son, where He is expressly called God. As it would be a palpable contradiction to assert that the work of creation could be executed by any creature, for He that built all things must be God, so the righteousness of God could not be ascribed to Jesus Christ unless He had been in the beginning, 'God,' 'with God,' and 'over all, God blessed for ever.'

It was during His incarnation that the Son of God wrought out this righteousness. Before He came into the world, He was not a member or subject of the kingdom of heaven,—He was its Head. He then acted in the form of God,—that is to say, as the Creator and Sovereign of the world,—but afterwards in the form of a servant. Before that period He was perfectly holy, but that holiness could not be called obedience. It might rather be said that the law was conformed to Him, than that He was conformed to the law. His holiness was exercised in making the law, and by it governing the world. But in His latter condition it was that law by which He Himself was governed. His righteousness or obedience, then, was that of infinitely the most glorious person that could

be subjected to the law. It was the righteousness of Emmanuel, God
with us; and this obedience of the Son of God in our nature conferred
more honour on the law than the obedience of all intelligent creatures.
He gave to every commandment of the law, and to every duty it enjoined,
more honour that it had received of dishonour from all the transgressors
that have been in the world. When others obey the law, they derive from
that obedience honour to themselves; but on the occasion now referred
to, it was the law that was honoured by the obedience of its Sovereign.
'The Lord,' says the Prophet, 'is well pleased for His righteousness' sake;
He will magnify the law, and make it honourable,' Isa. xlii. 21.

The obedience of Jesus Christ magnified the law, because it was
rendered by Divine appointment. He was chosen of God, and anointed
for this end. He was Jehovah, whom Jehovah sent. 'Lo, I come, and
I will dwell in the midst of thee, saith Jehovah;' 'and thou shalt know
that Jehovah of Hosts hath sent Me unto thee,' Zech. ii. 10, 11. And
when it is considered that the most astonishing work of God which can
be conceived is the incarnation of His Son, and His sojourning in the
world, and that these wonders were performed in order to magnify the
law, it necessarily follows that it is impossible to entertain too exalted an
idea of the regard which God has for the character of His holy law. In
its AUTHOR, then, this righteousness is immeasurably distinguished from
any other righteousness. And not only does it differ in its AUTHOR, it
differs also in its NATURE, in its EXTENT, in its DURATION, and in its INFLUENCE,
from all other righteousness that ever was or ever can be performed.

In its NATURE, this righteousness is twofold, fulfilling both the precept
of the law and its penalty. This, by any creature the most exalted, is
absolutely impossible. The fulfilment of the law, in its precepts, is all
that could be required of creatures in their original sinless condition.
Such was at the beginning the state of all the angels, and of the first man.
But the state of the Second Man, the Lord from heaven, when He came
into the world, was essentially different. Christ was made under the law,
but it was a BROKEN LAW; and consequently He was made under its
curse. This is not only implied when it is said, He was 'made of a
woman,' who was a transgressor, but it is also expressly asserted that He
was 'made a curse for us,' Gal. iii. 13. Justice therefore required that
He should fulfil not only the *precept*, but also the *penalty* of the law,—
all that it threatens, as well as all that it commands.

A mere creature may obey the precept of the law, or suffer the
penalty it denounces, but he cannot do both. If he be a transgressor, he
may be punished with everlasting destruction from the presence of the
Lord; and God, whose vengeance he is suffering, being to him an object
of unmingled hatred and abhorrence, there can be no place for his repentance, his love, or obedience. But Jesus Christ was capable at the same
moment of suffering at the hand of God and of obeying the precept to
love God. This was made manifest during the whole period of His incarnation, as well as by the memorable words which He uttered on the
cross, 'My God, My God, why hast Thou forsaken Me?' We are here
taught that the prediction by the Prophet, 'Awake, O sword, against the
man that is My fellow,' was at that moment receiving its accomplish-

ment. The sword of Divine justice, according to the prophetic declarations contained in the 22d Psalm, was then piercing His inmost soul, but still He addressed God as His God. From this it is evident that, while suffering under the full weight of His Father's wrath against the sins of His people, which He had taken upon Him, all the feelings both of love and confidence also expressed in the same Psalm were at that moment in full exercise. His righteousness, therefore, or conformity to the law, was at once a conformity in two respects, which could not have been exemplified but by Himself throughout the whole universe.

By the sufferings of Jesus Christ, the execution of the law was complete; while no punishment which creatures could suffer can be thus designated. The law was fully executed when all the threatenings it contained were carried into effect. Those who are consigned to everlasting punishment will never be able to say, as our blessed Lord said on the cross, 'It is finished.' It is He only who could *put away sin* by the sacrifice of Himself. By enduring the threatened punishment, He fully satisfied justice. In token of having received a full discharge, He came forth from the grave; and when He shall appear the second time, it shall be without sin,—the sin which He had taken upon Him, and all its effects, being for ever done away.

This fulfilment of the law, in its penalty, by the Son of God, is an end which cannot otherwise than through eternity be attained by the punishment of mere creatures. Sin, as committed against God, is an infinite evil, and requires an infinite punishment, which cannot be borne in any limited time by those who are not capable of suffering punishment in an infinite degree. But the sufferings, as well as the obedience, in time, of Him who is infinite, are equivalent to the eternal obedience and sufferings of those who are finite.

The doctrine that sin is an infinite evil, and requires an infinite punishment, is objected to by the Socinians. They say that if each sin we commit merits eternal death—in other words, an infinite punishment—and since there are almost an infinite number of sins committed by men, then it must be said that they merit an almost infinite number of punishments, and consequently that they cannot be expiated but by a like number of infinite satisfactions. It is replied, that the infinite value of the death of the Redeemer equals an infinite number of infinite punishments. For such is the nature of infinitude, that it admits of no degrees; it knows nothing of more or less; it cannot be measured; it cannot be augmented; so that ten thousand infinites are still only one infinite. And if Jesus Christ had suffered death as many times as the number of the sins of the redeemed, His satisfaction would not have been greater or more complete than by the one death which He suffered.

The death of the Son of God serves to magnify the law, by demonstrating the certainty of that eternal punishment, which, if broken, it denounces as its penalty. There are no limits to eternity; but when the Son of God bore what was equivalent to the eternal punishment of those who had sinned, He furnished a visible demonstration of the eternal punishment of sin.

But if nothing beyond the suffering of the penalty of the law had taken place, men would only have been released from the punishment due to sin. If they were to obtain the reward of obedience, its precepts must also be obeyed ; and this was accomplished to the utmost by Jesus Christ. Every command it enjoins, as well as every prohibition it contains, were in all respects fully honoured by Him. In this manner, and by His sufferings, He fulfilled all righteousness. The righteousness, therefore, of our God and Saviour Jesus Christ is infinitely glorious. It is the righteousness of the Lawgiver ; and, being in its character twofold, it differs entirely in its NATURE from all other righteousness, and is of an order infinitely higher than ever was or can be exemplified by any or all of the orders of intelligent creatures.

This righteousness differs also from all other righteousness in its EX-TENT. Every creature is bound for himself to *all* that obedience to his Creator of which he is capable. He is under the obligation to love God with all his heart, with all his soul, and with all his strength, and beyond this he cannot advance. It is evident, therefore, that he can have no *superabounding* righteousness to be placed in the way of merit to the account of another. And, besides this, if he has sinned, he is bound to suffer for himself the *whole* penalty annexed to disobedience, no part of which, consequently, can be borne by him to satisfy for the transgression of others. He is not in possession of a life at his own disposal to lay down for them ; and if he had laid it down, it being in that case forfeited for ever, he could not take it again. But the obedience of Jesus Christ, who is Himself infinite, as well as the punishment He suffered, being in themselves of infinite value, are capable of being transferred in their effects without any diminution in their respective values. His life, too, was His own ; and as He suffered voluntarily, His obedience and sufferings, which were infinitely meritorious, might, with the most perfect regard to justice, be imputed to as many of those of whose nature He partook, as to the Supreme Ruler shall seem good.

This righteousness likewise differs from all other righteousness in its DURATION. The righteousness of Adam or of angels could only be available while it continued to be performed. The law was binding on them in every instant of their existence. The moment, therefore, in which they transgressed, the advantages derived from all their previous obedience ceased. But the righteousness of God, brought in by His Son, is an ' *everlasting* righteousness,' Dan. ix. 24. It was performed within a limited period of time, but in its effects it can never terminate. ' Lift up your eyes to heaven, and look upon the earth beneath ; for the heavens shall vanish away like smoke, and the earth shall wax old like a garment, and they that dwell therein shall die in like manner : but My salvation shall be *for ever*, and My righteousness shall *not be abolished*— My righteousness shall be *for ever*,' Isa. li. 6, 8. ' Thy righteousness is an *everlasting* righteousness,' Ps. cxix. 142. ' By *one* offering He hath perfected *for ever* them that are sanctified,' Heb. x. .14. ' By His own blood He entered in *once* into the holy place, having obtained *eternal* redemption,' Heb. ix. 12. In respect to its duration, then, this righteousness reaches back to the period of man's fall, and forward through the endless ages of eternity.

The paramount INFLUENCE of this righteousness is also gloriously conspicuous. It is the sole ground of the reconciliation of sinners with God, and of their justification before Him, and also of intercession with Him before the throne. 'If any man sin, we have an Advocate with the Father, Jesus Christ *the righteous*,' 1 John ii. 1. It is the price paid for those new heavens and that new earth, wherein dwelleth righteousness ; for that kingdom prepared for those who are clothed with righteousness —a kingdom commensurate with the dignity of Him by whom it was provided. The paradise in which Adam was placed at his creation was a paradise on *earth*. It might be *corrupted*, it might be *defiled*, and it might *fade away*, all of which accordingly took place. But the paradise which, in virtue of the righteousness of God, is provided, and to the hope of which, by the resurrection of Jesus Christ from the dead, His people are begotten, is an inheritance which is *incorruptible* and *undefiled*, and that *fadeth not away*, reserved in *heaven*. This righteousness, then, is the ransom by which men are delivered from going down to the pit of everlasting destruction, and the price of heavenly and eternal glory. It is the fine linen, clean and white, in which the bride, the Lamb's wife, shall be arrayed, 'for the fine linen is the righteousness of saints.' Man was made lower than the angels, but this righteousness exalts him above them. The redeemed people of God stand nearest to the throne, while the angels stand 'round about' them. They enter heaven clothed with a righteousness infinitely better than that which angels possess, or in which Adam was created.

The idea which some entertain, that the loss incurred by the fall is only compensated by what is obtained through the redemption that is in Christ Jesus, is so far from being just, that the superabounding of the gain is unspeakable and immense. By the disobedience of the first Adam, the righteousness with which he was originally invested was lost for himself and all his posterity, and the sin which he had committed was laid to their charge. By the obedience of the second Adam, not only the guilt of that one offence is removed, but pardon also is procured for all the personal transgressions of the children of God ; while the righteousness, infinitely glorious, which He wrought, is placed to their account. By the entrance of sin and death, the inheritance on earth was forfeited. By the gift of the everlasting righteousness, their title to eternal glory in heaven is secured. *And not as it was by one that sinned, so is the gift: for the judgment was by one to condemnation, but the free gift is of many offences unto justification. For if by one man's offence death reigned by one; much more they which receive abundance of grace and of the gift of righteousness shall reign in life by one, Jesus Christ*, ch. v. 16, 17.

The evidence of the truth of Christianity might be rested on this one point—THE RIGHTEOUSNESS OF GOD provided for the salvation of sinners. How could such an idea as that of a vicarious everlasting righteousness, to meet all the demands of a BROKEN LAW, have ever entered into the conception of men and angels ? If it could have suggested itself to the highest created intelligence, and had the question been asked of all the host of heaven standing around the throne of God, 'on His right hand and His left,' Who shall work this righteousness ? what answer could have been given? what expedient for its accomplishment could have been proposed by one or all of them together? All must have stood silent before their Maker. As no one in heaven, nor on earth, neither under the earth, was able to open the book with the seven seals, neither to look thereon,—which was a subject of such bitter lamentation to the beloved disciple,—so no one, neither man nor angel, nor all the elect angels together, could have wrought the righteousness necessary for the justification of a sinner. He alone who is Emmanuel, God with us, who alone could open that book and loose the seals thereof, could 'bring in this everlasting righteousness,' of which it may be truly said that eye had not seen it, nor ear heard it, neither had it entered into the heart of man, till God revealed it by His Spirit.

Without law.—This righteousness is 'the righteousness of God,' and altogether independent of any obedience of man to law, more or less. As the righteousness of God is the perfect *fulfilment* which the law demands, it is evidently impossible that any other righteousness or obedience can be added to it or mixed with it. On the cross, Jesus Christ said, *It is finished,*—that is, it is perfected. To exhibit this PERFECTION, this fulfilment of the law, this grand consummation, is the great object of the Apostle in the Epistle to the Hebrews, ch. vi. 1. And Christ, it is said, Rom. x. 4, is the end of the law for righteousness to every one that believeth. In each of these passages the word used for 'perfection,'[1] or ' end,' is, in the original, the same as the word 'finished,' used on the cross. And those persons are described as ignorant of God's righteousness who go about to establish their own righteousness, and have not submitted themselves to the righteousness of God. ' Without law,' then, signifies, not without perfect obedience, but without any regard whatever to the obedience of man to the law. The obedience which the believer is enabled to render to the law has no part in his justification, nor could it justify, being always imperfect. The Apostle had, in the foregoing verse, affirmed that by his obedience to the law no man could be justified. He establishes the same truth in the 28th verse of this chapter, and in the fifth verse of the fourth chapter, in a manner so explicit, as to place his meaning beyond all question. In the same sense he declares, Gal. iii. 21, that ' if there had been a law given which could have given life, verily righteousness should have been by the law.' And again, he affirms, Gal. ii. 21, ' If righteousness come by the law, then Christ is dead in vain.' It is needless here to dispute, as many do, about what law the Apostle alludes to, whether moral or ceremonial. It is to the law of God, whether written or unwritten,—whatever is sanctioned by His authority, whether ceremonial or moral,—all of which have been fulfilled by the righteousness of God, Matt. iii. 15.

The righteousness of God is now *manifested*,—that is, clearly discovered,

---

[1] The import of this word *perfection* (Heb. vi. 1), which is the leading expression in the Epistle to the Hebrews, and the key to the whole of it, Mr. Stuart has entirely misunderstood in his Commentary on that Epistle, as he has misunderstood the meaning of the phrase, *the righteousness of God*, the leading expression in this Epistle to the Romans. For the signification of the word perfection, which so often occurs in the Epistle to the Hebrews, and is also misunderstood by the other commentators, I refer to my *Evidences*, vol. i. p. 438, third edition.

or made fully evident. It was darkly revealed in the shadows of the law, and more clearly in the writings of the Prophets; but now it is revealed in its accomplishment. It was manifested in the life and death of Jesus Christ, and was, by His resurrection from the dead, openly declared on the part of God. By Him, who was God manifest in the flesh, it was wrought out while He was on earth. He fulfilled all righteousness; not one jot of the law, either in its precepts or threatenings, passed from it, but all was accomplished; and of this righteousness the Holy Spirit, when He came, was to convince the world, John xvi. 8.

This righteousness is *manifested* in the doctrine of the Apostles. Besides being introduced so frequently in this Epistle to the Romans, it is often referred to and exhibited in the other apostolical Epistles. To the Apostles was committed the ministration of the new dispensation characterized as the 'ministration of *righteousness*,' 2 Cor. iii. 9. By that dispensation, and not by the law, *righteousness* is come, Gal. ii. 21. In writing to the Philippians, Paul calls it 'the *righteousness which is of God by faith*,' and contrasts it with his own righteousness, which is of the law, Phil. iii. 9. Peter addresses his Second Epistle to those who had obtained precious faith *in the righteousness of our God and Saviour Jesus Christ*, 2 Pet. i. 1. In one word, besides expressly naming it in many places under the designation of righteousness, the grand theme of the writings of the Apostles, as well as of their preaching, was the obedience and sufferings even unto death of the Lord Jesus Christ. Him they declared to be 'the end of the law for righteousness to every one that believeth;' while they exposed the error of such as went about to establish their own righteousness, and did not submit themselves to *the righteousness of God.*

Being witnessed by the law.—In the first part of this verse, 'without law,' where the article is wanting, signifies law indefinitely,—whatever has been delivered to man by God as His law, and in whatever way; but here, with the article, it refers to the five books of Moses, thus distinguished from the writings of the Prophets, according to the usual division of the Old Testament Scriptures, and adopted by our Lord, Luke xxiv. 44. This righteousness was obscurely testified in the first promise respecting the bruising of the serpent's head. It was expressly named in the declaration of the manner of Abraham's justification, where it is recorded that he believed in the Lord, and He counted it to him for *righteousness*, Gen. xv. 6; as also in the covenant which God made with him, of which the sign—that is, circumcision—was a seal or pledge of the righteousness which is by faith; and when it was promised that the blessing of Abraham, which is this righteousness, was to come on all nations, Gen. xii. 3. It was intimated in the writings of Moses, in every declaration of the forgiveness of sin, and every call to repentance. All the declarations of mercy that are to be found in the law of Moses belong to the Gospel. They are all founded on the Messiah and His *righteousness*, and are made in consequence of God's purpose to send His Son in the fulness of time into the world, and of the first promise respecting the seed of the woman.

The righteousness of God was witnessed not only in all the declarations of mercy and calls to repentance, but also by the whole economy of the law of which Moses was the mediator. Abraham was chosen, his posterity collected into a nation, and a country appropriated to them, that from the midst of them, according to His promise, God might raise up a Prophet, who, like unto Moses, was to be a Lawgiver and Mediator, to whom, turning from Moses, they should listen so soon as He appeared, Deut. xviii. 15, 19. The law of everlasting obligation was given to that nation, and renewed after it had been broken by them, and then solemnly deposited in the ark of the testimony, in token that it should be preserved entire, and in due time fulfilled by Him of whom the ark was a type.

The sacrifices offered by the patriarchs, and the whole of the ceremonial law in all its typical ordinances and observances, bear their direct though shadowy testimony to the righteousness of God, of which Noah was alike a preacher and an heir, 2 Pet. ii. 5 ; Heb. xi. 7.

The righteousness of God *was witnessed by the Prophets.* Of their testimonies to it the following are a few examples from the Psalms:— ' Deliver me from blood-guiltiness, O God, Thou God of my salvation ; and my tongue shall sing aloud of *Thy righteousness,*' Ps. li. 14. ' My mouth shall show forth *Thy righteousness* and Thy salvation all the day ; for I know not the numbers thereof. I will go in the strength of the Lord God ; I will make mention of *Thy righteousness,* even of Thine only. *Thy righteousness,* also, O God, is very high. My tongue also shall talk of *Thy righteousness* all the day long,' Ps. lxxi. 15, 16, 19, 24. ' Mercy and truth are met together ; *righteousness* and peace have kissed each other. Truth shall spring out of the earth ; and righteousness shall look down from heaven. *Righteousness* shall go before Him, and shall set us in the way of His steps,' Ps. lxxxv. 10, 13. ' In Thy name shall they rejoice all the day ; and in *Thy righteousness* shall they be exalted,' Ps. lxxxix. 16. ' *Thy righteousness* is an everlasting righteousness,' Ps. cxix. 142. ' They shall abundantly utter the memory of Thy great goodness, and shall sing of *Thy righteousness,*' Ps. cxlv. 7.

The *righteousness* of the Messiah, as connected with *salvation,* is the constant theme of the Prophets, especially of Isaiah. ' The Lord is well pleased for His *righteousness*' sake ; He will magnify the law, and make it honourable,' Isa. xlii. 21. ' Drop down, ye heavens, from above, and let the skies pour down *righteousness;* let the earth open, and let them bring forth salvation, and let *righteousness* spring up together ; I the Lord have created it,' Isa. xlv. 8. The heavens were to drop down this righteousness, and the skies were to pour it down, while men's hearts, barren like the earth without rain, were to be opened to receive it by faith, having no part in doing anything to procure the gift. ' Surely, shall one say, In the Lord have I *righteousness* and strength : In the Lord shall all the seed of Israel be justified, and shall glory,' Isa. xlv. 24, 25. ' I bring near *My righteousness;* it shall not be far off, and My salvation shall not tarry ; and I will place salvation in Zion for Israel My glory,' Isa. xlvi. 13. ' *My righteousness* is near ; My salvation is gone forth—My salvation shall be for ever, and *My righteousness* shall not be abolished. Hearken unto Me, ye that know *righteousness,*' Isa. li. 5, 7. ' By His knowledge shall My *righteous* servant justify many,' Isa. liii. 11.

'This is the heritage of the servants of the Lord, and their *righteousness* is of Me, saith the Lord,' Isa. liv. 17. 'Thus saith the Lord, Keep ye judgment, and do justice: for My salvation is near to come, and *My righteousness* to be revealed,' Isa. lvi. 1. 'For as the earth bringeth forth her bud, and as the garden causeth the things that are sown in it to spring forth; so the Lord God will cause *righteousness* and praise to spring forth before all the nations,' Isa. lxi. 11. 'For Zion's sake will I not hold my peace, and for Jerusalem's sake I will not rest, until the *righteousness* thereof go forth as brightness, and the salvation thereof as a lamp that burneth. And the Gentiles shall see *Thy righteousness*, and all kings Thy glory,' Isa. lxii. 1, 2.

'Behold the days come, saith the Lord, that I will raise unto David a *righteous Branch*, and a King shall reign and prosper, and shall execute judgment and justice in the earth. In His days Judah shall be saved, and Israel shall dwell safely; and this is His name whereby He shall be called, JEHOVAH OUR RIGHTEOUSNESS,' Jer. xxiii. 5. 'Seventy weeks are determined upon thy people, and upon thy holy city, to finish the transgression, and to make an end of sins, and to make reconciliation for iniquity, and to bring in *everlasting righteousness*,' Dan. ix. 24. 'It is time to seek the Lord, till He come and rain *righteousness* upon you,' Hos. x. 12. 'But unto you that fear My name shall the *Sun of righteousness* arise with healing in His wings,' Mal. iv. 2. To Balaam, who beheld the Saviour at a distance, He appeared as a *star;* 'There shall come a Star out of Jacob,' Num. xxiv. 17; while to Malachi, the last of the Prophets, on His nearer approach, He appeared as the *sun*.

Ver. 22.—*Even the righteousness of God, which is by faith of Jesus Christ unto all and upon all them that believe.*

This righteousness of God, to which the law and the Prophets render their testimony, and which is now manifested in the Gospel, whereby man is justified, is not imputed to him on account of any work of his own in obedience to the law, but is received, as the Apostle had already declared in the 17th verse of chapter first, by faith alone. Faith is no part of that righteousness; but it is through faith that it is received, and becomes available for salvation. Faith is the belief of the Divine testimony concerning that righteousness, and trust in Him who is its Author. Faith perceives and acknowledges the excellency and suitableness of God's righteousness, and cordially embraces it. 'Faith is the substance of things hoped for, the evidence of things not seen;' because, though we do not yet possess what God has promised, and do not yet see it accomplished in ourselves, we see it accomplished in Jesus Christ, in whom what we hope for really exists. In respect to the promises not yet fulfilled, believers are now in the same situation as the fathers were of old respecting the unaccomplished promises in their day. Like them, they see these promises afar off, are persuaded of them, and embrace them. Believers thus flee to Christ and His righteousness as the refuge set before them in the Gospel. By faith they receive Him as their surety, and place their trust in Him, as representing them on the cross, in His death, and in His resurrection.

Before we can have a right to anything in Christ, we must be *one* with Him ; we must be joined with Him as our head, being dead to the law and married to Him ; and as this union is accomplished through faith, His righteousness, which we receive, and which becomes ours in this way, is therefore called the righteousness which is *by faith of Jesus Christ*, Rom. iii. 22 ; *the righteousness of faith*, Rom. iv. 11, 13 ; and *the righteousness which is through the faith of Christ, the righteousness which is of God by faith*, Phil. iii. 9. It is called the righteousness of faith, because faith is the only instrument which God is pleased to employ in applying His righteousness. It is not called the righteousness of any other grace but of faith ; we never read of the righteousness of repent- ance, of humility, of meekness, or of charity. These are of great price in the sight of God, but they have no office in justifying a sinner. This belongs solely to faith ; for to him that worketh not, but believeth, is righteousness imputed ; and faith is the gift of God.

This righteousness is *unto all.*—It is set before all, and proclaimed to all, according to the commandment of our blessed Lord,—' Go ye into all the world, and preach the Gospel to every creature.' *Upon all,* is con- nected with the words that follow, viz., them that believe. While it is proclaimed *to* all men, it is actually *upon* believers. It is not put *into* them, as their sanctification is wrought in the soul by the Holy Spirit ; but it is placed *upon* them as a robe :—' He hath covered me with the robe of *righteousness,*' Isa. lxi. 10. It is the white raiment given by Jesus Christ to them who hear His voice, that they may be clothed, and that the shame of their nakedness may not appear, Rev. iii. 18. It is the fine linen, clean and white, with which the bride, the Lamb's wife, is arrayed ; for the fine linen is the *righteousness* of saints, Rev. xix. 8. Thus Jesus Christ is made of *God,* to them that are in Him, *righteousness,* 1 Cor. i. 30.

Righteousness.—' This, doubtless, is meant,' says Archbishop Leighton, in his sermon on 1 Cor. i. 30, ' of the righteousness by which we are justified before God ; and He is *made this to us,* applied by faith : *His righteousness becomes ours.* That exchange made, our sins are laid over upon Him, and His obedience put upon us. This, the great glad tidings, that we are made righteous by Christ: It is not a righteousness wrought by us, but given to us, and put upon us. This, carnal reason cannot apprehend, and, being proud, therefore rejects and argues against it, and says, how can this thing be ? But faith closes with it, and rejoices in it ; without either doing or suffering, the sinner is acquitted and justified, and stands as guiltless of breach, yea, as having fulfilled the whole law. And happy they that thus fasten upon this righteousness— they may lift up their faces with gladness and boldness before God : whereas the most industrious self-saving justiciary, though in other men's eyes, and his own, possibly, for the present, he makes a glistering show, yet when he shall come to be examined of God, and tried according to the law, he shall be covered with shame, and confounded in his folly and guiltiness. But faith triumphs over self-unworthiness, and sin, and death, and the law ; shrouding the soul under the mantle of Jesus Christ ; and there it is safe. All accusations fall off, having nowhere to fasten, unless some blemish could be found in that righteousness in which faith hath wrapt itself. This is the very spring of solid peace, and fills the soul with peace and joy. But still men would have something within themselves to make out the matter, as if this robe needed any such piecing, and not finding what they desire, thence disquiet and unsettlement of mind arise! True it is that faith purifies the heart and works holiness, and all graces flow from it: But in this work of justifying the sinner it is alone, and cannot admit of any mixture.'

Ver. 23.—(*For there is no difference; for all have sinned, and come short of the glory of God.*)

The Apostle introduces this parenthesis to preclude the supposition that the receiving of the righteousness of God is not indispensably necessary to *every individual* of the human race in order to his salvation, and lest it should be imagined that there is any difference in the way in which, or on account of which, it is received. As there is no difference between Jews and Gentiles with respect to their character as sinners, so there is no difference with respect to them as to the receiving of God's righteousness—no difference either as to sin or salvation—all of them are guilty, and salvation through faith is published to them all. ' For there is no difference between the Jew and the Greek ; for the same Lord over all is rich unto all that call upon Him,' Rom. x. 12. Before men receive this righteousness, they are all under the curse of the broken law, and in a state of condemnation. Whatever distinction there may be among them otherwise, whether moral in their conduct, good and useful members of society, discharging respectably and decently the external duties of that situation in which they are placed, or having a zeal of God, but not according to knowledge, and going about to establish their own righteousness,—or whether they be immoral in their lives, entirely abandoned to every vice,—they all stand equally in need of this righteousness—it is equally preached to them all—it is in the same manner bestowed upon all who believe. The reason of this is, that *all have sinned* —all, without one exception, as had been proved, are ' under sin.'

The Apostle adds, as a consequence of this, that they *have come short of the glory of God.* They have come short, as in running a race, having now lost all strength (Rom. v. 6) and ability in themselves to glorify God, and attain to the possession and enjoyment of His glory. In the second chapter, the Apostle, in announcing the terms of the law, had declared that the way to obtain eternal life was in seeking for glory by patient continuance in well-doing, and that to those who work good, honour and peace would be awarded. In other words, ' if thou wilt enter into life, keep the commandments ; ' but he had afterwards proved that in this way it was altogether unattainable, since by the deeds of the law no flesh shall be justified. In this place he more briefly repeats the same truth, that all men, without exception, being sinners, have come short of this glory, while he is pointing out the way in which, through the atonement of the Saviour, and faith in that atonement, believers may now ' rejoice in hope of the glory of God.' All men, on the ground of their obedience to law, come short of glorifying God, for to glorify

God is the whole of the law,—even the second table is to be obeyed to glorify God, who requires it. If they come short of obeying the law, they have, as sinners, come-short of that glory, and honour, and immortality, in His presence, which can only be obtained through the 'salvation which is in Christ Jesus, with eternal glory,' 2 Tim. ii. 10.

Ver. 24.—*Being justified freely by His grace, through the redemption that is in Christ Jesus.*

Justified.—Justification stands opposed both to accusation and condemnation. 'Who shall lay anything to the charge of God's elect? It is God that justifieth; who is he that condemneth?' 'Them whom God effectually calleth, He also freely justifieth; not by infusing righteousness into them,' as is well expressed in the Westminster Confession of Faith, 'but by pardoning their sins, and by accounting and accepting their persons as righteous,—not for anything wrought in them, or done by them, but for Christ's sake alone; not by imputing faith itself, the act of believing, or any other evangelical obedience, to them as their righteousness; but by imputing the obedience and satisfaction of Christ unto them, they receiving and resting on Him and His righteousness by faith; which faith they have not of themselves, it is the gift of God.' Or, according to Dr. Owen *On Justification,* 'This imputation is an act of God, *ex mera gratia,* of His mere love and grace, whereby, on the consideration of the mediation of Christ, He makes an effectual grant and donation of a true, real, perfect righteousness—even that of Christ Himself—unto all that do believe, and accounting it as theirs, on His own gracious act, both absolves them from sin, and granteth them right and title unto eternal life.' The Helvetic Confession of Faith, adopted by the church at Geneva in 1536, and by all the evangelical churches in Switzerland thirty years afterwards, explains justification as follows :—'The word, to justify, signifies, in the writings of the Apostle St. Paul, when he speaks of justification, to pardon sins, to absolve from guilt and punishment, to receive into grace, and to declare righteous. *The righteousness of Jesus Christ is imputed to believers.*—Our Saviour is then charged with the sins of the world, He has taken them away, He has satisfied Divine justice. It is, then, only on account of Jesus Christ, dead and risen, that God, pacified towards us, does not impute to us our sins, but that He imputes to us the righteousness of his Son, as if it were ours; so that, thenceforward, we are not only cleansed from our sins, but, besides, clothed with the righteousness of Christ, and by it absolved from the punishment of sins, from death, or from condemnation, accounted righteous, and heirs of eternal life. Thus, to speak properly, it is God only who justifies us, and He justifies us solely for the sake of Jesus Christ, not imputing to us our sins, but imputing to us the righteousness of Christ.'

In the Homily of the Church of England, on 'justification,' it is said —'Justification is not the office of man, but of God; for man cannot make himself righteous by his own works, neither in part nor in whole; for that were the greatest arrogancy and presumption of man that Antichrist could set up against God, to affirm that a man might, by his own works, take away and purge his own sins, and so justify himself.

But justification is the office of God only, and is not a thing which we render unto Him, but which we receive of Him; not which we give to Him, but which we take of Him by His free mercy, and by the only merits of His most dearly beloved Son, our only Redeemer, Saviour, and Justifier, Jesus Christ: So that the true understanding of this doctrine, we be justified freely by faith without works, or that we be justified by Christ only, is not that this our own act to believe in Christ, or this our faith in Christ which is within us doth justify us, and deserve our justification unto us (for that were to count ourselves to be justified by some act or virtue that is within ourselves), but the true understanding and meaning thereof is, that although we hear God's word, and believe it, although we have faith, hope, charity, repentance, dread, and fear of God within us, do never so many works thereunto; yet we must renounce the merit of all our said virtues, of faith, hope, charity, and all other virtues, which we either have done, shall do, or can do, as things that must be far too weak, and insufficient, and imperfect to deserve remission of our sins and our justification; and therefore we must trust only in God's mercy, and that sacrifice which our High Priest and Saviour Jesus Christ, the Son of God, once offered for us on the cross.'   Again, ' This doctrine all old and ancient authors of Christ's Church do approve. This doctrine adorneth and setteth forth the glory of Christ, and beateth down the glory of man ; this whosoever denieth, *is not to be accounted for a Christian man*, nor for a setter forth of Christ's glory, but for an adversary of Christ and His Gospel, and for a setter forth of man's vain glory.' The above quotations are not given in the way of authority, but as expressing the truth, and evincing the unanimity of believers of different communions on this all-important point.   The sum of them is, that believers are absolved from condemnation, and entitled to eternal life, by the free and sovereign favour of God as its original first moving cause, without any desert in themselves, but solely in virtue of the righteousness of Christ, which includes an infinitely valuable price of redemption, a price that was paid for them by His obedience and sufferings to death.

There is no ' condemnation to them which are in Christ Jesus.'   The moment a sinner is united to Him, the sentence of condemnation under which he formerly lay, is remitted, and a sentence of justification is pronounced by God.   Justification, then, is at once complete—in the imputation of a perfect righteousness, the actual pardon of all past sins, the virtual pardon of future sins, and the grant and title to the heavenly inheritance.   The believer is found in Christ *having* the righteousness which is of God, Phil. iii. 9.   ' Surely, shall one say, in the Lord *have I righteousness*,' Isa. xlv. 24.   He is *complete* in Christ, Col. ii. 10, who, by one offering, hath for ever *perfected* him, Heb. x. 14.   In Him the law has been fulfilled, Rom. viii. 4 ; his sin has been made Christ's, and the righteousness which God requireth by the law has been made his.   ' He hath made Him to be sin for us, who knew no sin ; that we might be made the righteousness of God in Him,' 2 Cor. v. 21.   On this passage Chrysostom remarks, ' What word, what speech is this ? what mind can comprehend or express it ?   For He saith, He made Him who was righteous to be made a sinner, that He might make sinners righteous. Nor yet doth He say so neither, but that which is far more sublime and excellent. For He speaks not of an inclination or affection, but expresseth the quality itself. For He says not, He made him a sinner, but sin, that we might be made not merely righteous, but righteousness—and that the righteousness of God.'[1] When we are here said to be made the righteousness of God in Him, the meaning is, that we are made righteous in such a degree as admits of no addition. We could not be more righteous if our whole nature and constitution were made up of this one attribute, and there were nothing in us or about us but righteousness.

After the Lord Jesus Christ condescended to take on Him our sins, it would not have been just for Him not to account for them ; His responsibility for them was then the same as if He had Himself sinned. On this proceeded God's treatment of Him in hiding His face from Him, till the debt was paid. Christ hath redeemed us from the curse of the law, being made a curse for us ; that is, being *cursed*, as the Apostle explains it. As the sins of Israel were all laid on the head of the scapegoat, so 'the Lord hath laid on Him the iniquity of us all.' ' How could He die,' says Charnock, ' if He was not a reputed sinner ? Had He not first had a relation to our sin, He could not in justice have undergone our punishment. He must, in the order of justice, be supposed a sinner really, or by imputation. Really He was not ; by imputation, then, He was.' On the whole, believers are accounted and pronounced righteous by God ; and if so accounted by Him, it is and must be true in fact that they are *righteous*, for righteousness is imputed to them ; that is, it is placed to their account—made over to them, because really theirs—and, therefore, without the smallest deviation from truth or fact—which is impossible in the great Judge—he will, from His throne of judgment in the last day, pronounce them ' *righteous*,' Matt. xxv. 37, 46.

The plan of salvation through the righteousness of Jesus Christ is so deep and astonishing an instance of Divine wisdom, that while it is not at all perceived by the wisdom of the world, it even in some measure lies hid from those who are savingly enlightened by it. Many Christians are afraid to give the scriptural language on this subject the full extent of its meaning ; and instead of representing themselves as being made righteous, perfectly righteous, by the righteousness of the Son of God, they look on their justification as merely an accounting of them as

---

[1] To explain Christ's being made *sin* in this passage, with Dr. Macknight, Mr. Stuart, and others, as signifying His being made *a sin-offering*, ought to be most strenuously rejected. It entirely perverts the meaning of the passage, which asserts the transference of the sin of the believer to Christ, and of Christ's righteousness to the believer. He submitted not only to be treated as a sin-offering, but to be made sin for His people. It takes away the contrast, and obscures one of the strongest expressions of the vicarious nature of Christ's sufferings that is to be found in the Bible. In the same way, when it is said (Heb. ix. 28), He shall 'appear the second time without sin unto salvation,' the true meaning of the passage is lost by changing the phrase, 'without sin,' as in the common version, to 'without a sin-offering,' according to Dr. Macknight and Mr. Stuart. When Jesus Christ first appeared, He came covered over with the sin which was imputed to Him ; but when He shall come the second time, not the smallest remainder of it shall be found either upon Him or His people.

righteous while they are not so in reality. They think that God mercifully looks on them in a light which is more favourable than the strictness of truth will warrant. But the Scriptures represent believers as truly righteous, possessing a righteousness fully answerable to all the demands of the law. By their union with Christ they are ' dead to sin,' and the righteousness of the law is fulfilled in them, ch. viii. 4. They have paid its penalty and fulfilled its utmost demands, and are ' made the righteousness of God in Him.' God never accounts any one to be what he is not in reality ; and as Christ's righteousness is reckoned ours as well as Adam's sin, believers ought to consider themselves as truly righteous in Christ as they are truly guilty in Adam. These two facts mutually reflect light on each other. Adam was the figure of Christ, and our sin in Adam is perfectly analogous to our righteousness in Christ, ' For as by one man's disobedience many were made sinners, so by the obedience of one shall many be made righteous,' ch. v. 19.

Freely by His grace.—The expression is redoubled, to show that all is of God, and that nothing in this act of justification belongs to, or proceeds from man. It is perfectly gratuitous on the part of God, both as to the mode of conveyance and the motive on which it is vouchsafed. Nothing being required of man in order to his justification, in the way of price or satisfaction, and there being no prerequisite or preparatory dispositions to merit it at the hand of God, believers are therefore said to be justified by His *grace*, which excludes on their part both price and merit. And lest it should be imagined that grace does not proceed in its *operation*, as well as in the *choice* of its objects, consistently with its character of sovereign and unmerited goodness, the Apostle adds the word *freely;* that is, without cause or motive on the part of man. The word here rendered ' freely ' is the same as that used by our Lord when He says, they hated *Me without a cause*, John xv. 25. ' Freely ' (gratuitously) ye have received, freely give,' Matt. x. 8 ; 2 Cor. xi. 7 ; 2 Thess. iii. 8 ; ' For nought ' (gratis), Rev. xxi. 6, and xxii. 17 ; or without price, as Isa. lv. 1. This term ' freely ' in the most absolute manner excludes all consideration of anything in man as the cause or condition of his justification. The means by which it is received is faith ; and, in the commencement of the next chapter, faith is placed in opposition to all works whatever, and in verse 16th of that chapter it is said, ' Therefore it is of faith, that it might be by grace.' Faith is the constituted medium through which man receives ' the gift of righteousness ;' because, as Paul there affirms, it interferes not with the gratuitous nature of the gift. It is impossible to express more strongly than in this place, that justification is bestowed without the smallest regard to anything done by man. It cannot be pretended that it comes in consequence of repentance, or anything good either existing or foreseen in him. God ' justifieth the *ungodly*,' Rom. iv. 5. It comes, then, solely by grace— free, unmerited favour. ' And if by grace, then it is no more of works ; otherwise grace is no more grace,' Rom. xi. 6. This is said respecting the election of believers to eternal life, and equally holds, according to the passage before us, in respect to their justification. Speaking of the advocates of human merit, ' What can they say,' observes Luther, in answer to Erasmus, ' to the declaration of St. Paul? Being justified freely by His grace. Freely, what does that word mean? How are good endeavours and merit consistent with a gratuitous donation? Perhaps you do not insist on a merit of condignity, but only of congruity. Empty distinctions. How does Paul in one word confound in one mass all the assertors of every species and of every degree of merit? All are justified freely, and without the works of the law. He who affirms the justification of all men who are justified to be perfectly free and gratuitous, leaves no place for works, merits, or preparations of any kind—no place for works either of condignity or congruity; and thus, at one blow, he demolishes both the Pelagians with their complete merits, and our sophists with their petty performances.'

Through the redemption that is in Christ Jesus.—The great blessing of justification is described above as proceeding from the free grace of God, which is the fountain from whence flow pardon, righteousness, and salvation, excluding all works, whether before or after faith. Here it is referred to the meritorious price provided by God, and that is the redemption which is in Christ Jesus. For though it comes freely to man, yet it is through the redemption or purchase of the Son of God.

The word *redemption* signifies a buying back, and necessarily supposes an alienation of what is redeemed. In general, it imports a deliverance effected by a *price*, and sometimes a deliverance by *power*. In this last sense it is said, 'Now these are Thy servants, and Thy people, whom Thou hast redeemed by Thy great power,' Neh. i. 10. 'I will redeem you with a stretched out arm,' Ex. vi. 6; Ps. lxxvii. 15. The resurrection of the body by an act of Divine power is called a redemption, Ps. xlix. 15; Rom. viii. 23. But, more generally, redemption signifies, in Scripture, deliverance by *price*, as that of slaves, or prisoners, or persons condemned, when they are delivered from slavery, captivity, or death, by means of a ransom. The word is here used in this last acceptation. Man had rebelled against God, and incurred the just condemnation of His law; but God, by His free grace, and of infinite compassion, hath substituted His own Son in the place of the guilty, and transferred from them to Him the obligation of their punishment. He hath made Him to suffer and die for their sins, the just for the unjust, that He might bring them to Himself. 'His own self bare our sins in His own body on the tree,' 1 Pet. iii. 18, ii. 24. In this manner the Scriptures represent the blood or death of Jesus Christ as the ransom price. He came to give His life a ransom for many, Matt. xx. 28; 1 Cor. vi. 20. 'Ye were not *redeemed* with corruptible things, as silver and gold, from your vain conversation, received by tradition from your fathers, but with the precious blood of Christ,' 1 Pet. i. 18. 'Thou wast slain, and hast *redeemed* us to God by Thy blood,' Rev. v. 9. 'Having predestinated us unto the adoption of children by Jesus Christ to Himself, according to the good pleasure of His will, to the praise of the glory of His grace, wherein He hath made us accepted in the Beloved; in whom we have *redemption* through His blood, the forgiveness of sins, according to the riches of His grace, wherein He hath abounded toward us in all wisdom and prudence,' Eph. i. 5-8; Col. i. 14. If, then, we are accounted righteous before God, because redeemed with a price paid by another, we receive what is not in ourselves, or in any measure from ourselves.

In every place in Scripture where our redemption in Christ is mentioned, there is an allusion to the law of redemption among the Jews. This law is contained in the Book of Leviticus, ch. xxv., where we find regulations laid down for a twofold redemption, a redemption of persons and a redemption of possessions. The redemption of possessions or inheritances is regulated, verses 23–28, and that of persons, from verse 47 to the end of the chapter. In both these cases, none had a right to redeem but either the person himself who had made the alienation, or some other that was near of kin to him. But none of Adam's family ever was, or ever will be, able to redeem himself or others. 'None of them can by any means redeem his brother, nor give to God a ransom for him; for the redemption of their soul is precious,' Ps. xlix. 7. It is too precious to be accomplished by such means; and had there been no other, it would have 'ceased for ever.' All mankind had been engaged in a warfare against God, and, as rebels, were condemned to death. Satan had taken the whole human race captive, and employed them in the drudgery of sin. From the sentence of death and the slavery of sin, it was impossible for any of them ever to have been set free, if Christ had not paid the ransom of His blood. But He, the Son of God, having from all eternity undertaken the work of redemption of those whom God gave Him, and being substituted by the everlasting covenant which God made with Him in their place, the right of redemption was vested in Him, by virtue of His covenant relation to them. And that nothing might be wanting either to constitute Him their legal kinsman-Redeemer, or to evidence Him to be so, He took on Him their nature, and in that nature paid their ransom to the last mite. Thus He performs the part of the Redeemer of His people, redeeming them from slavery and from death, and redeeming for them that inheritance which they had forfeited, and which they could not redeem for themselves. In some cases both these sorts of redemption were conjoined, and the person redeemed was espoused to him who redeemed her; and in this manner our Lord Jesus Christ has redeemed His Church. Having redeemed the heavenly inheritance for her, He has at the same time redeemed her from her state of bondage, and has betrothed her to Himself. 'I will betroth thee unto Me for ever; yea, I will betroth thee unto Me in righteousness, and in judgment, and in loving-kindness, and in mercies. I will even betroth thee unto Me in faithfulness; and thou shalt know the Lord,' Hos. ii. 19, 20.

The Socinian talks of redemption as an act merely of God's power, and of Christ as offering His sacrifice by presenting Himself in heaven after His death. But this is not redemption. There is not only a price paid, but that price is expressly stated. 'In whom we have redemption *through His blood.*' His blood, then, is the price by which we have redemption, 'even the forgiveness of sins,' Col. i. 14. The same thing that is redemption, is in another point of view forgiveness; yet these two things in human transactions are incompatible. Where there is forgiveness, there is no price or redemption; where there is redemption, there is no forgiveness. But in the salvation of the Gospel there are both. There is a price; but as God Himself has paid the price, it is forgiveness with respect to man, as much as if there had been no price. How wonderful is the wisdom of God manifested in the Gospel! Grace and justice, mercy and punishment, are blended together in the most perfect harmony.

Many seem to think that nothing can be essentially wrong in the views of those who speak of gratuitous salvation. Yet this may be most explicitly confessed, and the distinguishing features of the Gospel overlooked or even denied. Arians do not deny a gratuitous salvation. They contend that salvation is gratuitous, and boast that they are the only persons who consistently hold this doctrine. Calvinists, they say, have not a God of mercy: He gives nothing without a price. Their God, they boast, is a God of mercy; for He pardons without any ransom. Now the glory of the Gospel is, that *grace reigns through righteousness.* Salvation is of grace; but this grace comes to us in a way of RIGHTEOUSNESS. It is grace to us; but it was brought about in such a way that all our debt was paid. This exhibits God as just, as well as merciful. Just, in requiring full compensation to justice; and merciful, because it was He, and not the sinner, who provided the ransom. He who is saved, is saved without an injury to justice. Salvation is in one point of view forgiveness, but in another it is redemption.

Still, however, it is urged, that though it is here said that God justifies man freely by His grace, yet, as a price has been paid for it, this takes away from the freeness of the gift. But He who pays the ransom is one and the same, as has just been observed, with Him who justifies; so that the freeness of the blessing on the part of God is not in the smallest degree diminished. This proves that the doctrine of a free justification, through an atonement, rests entirely on the doctrine of the deity of Jesus Christ; on which also rests the transfer of His righteousness to the guilty; for, as has already been shown, no mere creature can have the least particle of *merit* to transfer to another. Every creature is bound for himself to fulfil the whole law. After doing all that is possible for him in the way of obedience, he must confess himself to be an unprofitable servant, Luke xvii. 10.

This redemption is *in*, or *by*, *Christ Jesus.*—It is wholly in Him, and solely accomplished by Him. Through the period of His ministry on earth, His disciples who followed Him were not aware of the work He was accomplishing. During His agony in the garden they were asleep. When seized by His persecutors to be put to death, they all forsook Him and fled. 'Behold,' says He, 'the hour cometh, yea, is now come, that ye shall be scattered every man to his own, and shall leave Me alone.' No one participated or bore any share with Him in that great work, which, according to His appeal to His Father, on which He founded the petitions He offered for Himself and His people, He alone had consummated: 'I have glorified Thee on the earth: I have finished the work which Thou gavest Me to do.'

Ver. 25.—*Whom God hath set forth to be a propitiation through faith in His blood, to declare His righteousness for the remission of sins that are past, through the forbearance of God.*

In the end of the preceding verse, the Apostle had said that believers are justified freely by the grace of God, through the redemption that is in Christ Jesus. This redemption he here further explains. God hath set forth His Son to be a propitiatory sacrifice to make satisfaction to His justice. The expression, *set forth*, means to exhibit to public view —to place before the eyes of men—to manifest,—according as it is said, ' Who verily was fore-ordained before the foundation of the world, but was manifested in these last times for you,' 1 Pet. i. 20. *To be a propitiation.*—Some understand this as meaning a propitiatory, signifying the mercy-seat, as the same word is translated, Heb. ix. 5 ; some as a propitiatory sacrifice, which is to be preferred. But it comes to the same thing, if, according to our translation, it be rendered propitiation, considering the word to be the adjective taken substantively. And this is countenanced by 1 John ii. 2, and iv. 10, though a different word is employed, but of the same derivation. By a propitiation is meant that which appeaseth the wrath of God for sins and obtains His favour, as it is said, Heb. ii. 17, where the corresponding verb is used, to make reconciliation for (to propitiate) the sins of the people; and ' God be merciful to me a sinner.' He was thus pacified towards believers in Jesus Christ, and made favourable to them, the demands of His law and justice being satisfied, and every obstruction to the exercise of His mercy towards them removed. This propitiation of Christ was typified by the propitiatory sacrifices whose blood was shed, and by the mercy-seat, which was called the propitiatory, that illustrious type of Christ and His work, covering the ark in which the law to be fulfilled by Him was deposited, and on it, and before it, the blood of the sacrifices was sprinkled by the high priest. *Through faith in His blood.*—This propitiation was made by blood, by which is to be understood all the sufferings of Christ, and, above all, His death, by which they were consummated. And this becomes a propitiation to us through faith in His blood,—that is, when we believe that His death is a sacrifice which makes atonement for us, and when we rest on it as a sufficient answer to all accusations against us of the law of God, which in the punishment of death it demanded for sin, for ' without shedding of blood is no remission.' The expression, ' through faith in His blood,' limits to believers the effect of this propitiation.[1]

God hath not only set forth His Son to be a propitiatory sacrifice, to be available through faith in His blood, but also hath done this to declare or manifest His righteousness. *Righteousness.*—Some here translate this word *faithfulness*, or the righteousness of the character of God, or *veracity;* some *goodness;* some *holiness;* some pardoning *mercy.*

---

[1] This passage makes clear the meaning of 1 John ii. 2 :—' He is the propitiation for our sins ; and not for ours only, but also for the sins of the whole world,'—for all, both Jews and Gentiles, *who have faith in His blood.* In the end of that Epistle, ch. v. 19, the expression ' the whole world ' is also used in a restricted sense, being distinguished from those who are ' of God.' 'And we know that we are of God, and the whole world lieth in wickedness.'

But all are wrong, and such translations are opposed to the sense of the passage. It is righteousness, namely, the righteousness of God, on account of which the Gospel is the power of God unto salvation, ch. i. 17, to which the Apostle had recurred in the 21st and 22d verses of this chapter, declaring that it is now manifested. 'Righteousness' in the above passages is the same as in the one before us, and in the following verse. In the 21st and 22d verses, the expression employed is the 'righteousness of God;' and in this and the following verse, 'His righteousness.' Is it then to be supposed that, in repeating the same expression four times in the same breath, and with a view to establish the same truth, the Apostle used it in various senses,—first, as that righteousness which fulfils the law which God has provided for sinners; and then as the faithfulness, or goodness, or holiness, or mercy, or justice of God, or the righteousness of His character?—ideas entirely different from the former. That the meaning of the expression, 'His righteousness,' is the same in this and the following verse as that of the 'righteousness of God' in verses 21, 22, appears unquestionable, from the reason given in this 25th verse for setting forth Jesus Christ to be a propitiation for sin. This, as is twice repeated, first here, and then in the following verse, was for the purpose of declaring or manifesting God's righteousness. In the 21st verse it is asserted that the righteousness of God is now manifested; and in the 25th verse it is shown in what way it is now manifested, namely, by setting forth Christ as a propitiation for sin; and in the following verse the reason is given, namely, for what purpose it is now manifested. On the whole, then, notwithstanding that a different sense is generally affixed to it by commentators, it appears clear that the signification of the expression 'righteousness' is the same in each of these four verses, which stand in so close a connection. This signification being the same in all the above instances, and generally in the various other places in the Epistle, in which it so often occurs, entirely corresponds with the whole tenor of the Apostle's discourse, which is to prove that a perfect righteousness is provided by God for man, who has lost his own righteousness, and on which he had so forcibly dwelt throughout the first and second chapters, and down to the 21st verse of the chapter before us.

For the remission of sins that are past;—rather, as to, or with regard to, the passing by of sins before committed. Jesus Christ hath been set forth by God to be a propitiatory sacrifice, by which He brought in 'everlasting righteousness,' and by which it is now publicly manifested. On account, then, of this righteousness, even before it was introduced, God pardoned or remitted the sins of His people under the Old Testament dispensation. These, having received the promises, although their accomplishment was yet afar off, were persuaded of them and embraced them; thus exercising faith in the blood of that great propitiatory sacrifice which was typified by the legal sacrifices, and through this faith they received the remission of their sins.

Through the forbearance of God.—It was owing to God's forbearance that He passed by the sins of His people before the death of Christ, till which time His law was not honoured, and His justice had received no satisfaction. No sufficient atonement previous to that event was made for their sins, yet, through the forbearance of God, He did not immediately proceed to punish them, but had respect to the everlasting righteousness to be brought in, in the fulness of time, Dan. ix. 24, by the propitiatory sacrifice of His Son, by which their sins were to be expiated. This verse beautifully indicates the ground on which Old Testament saints were admitted into heaven before the death of Christ.

The same truth is declared in the Epistle to the Hebrews, ix. 15, where the Apostle refers to the inefficacy of the legal sacrifices to take away sins, and speaks of the blood of Jesus, by which He entered into the holy place, and obtained eternal redemption for His people. 'And for this cause He is the Mediator of the New Testament, that by means of death, for the redemption of the transgressions that were under the first testament, they which are called (literally the called) might receive the promise of eternal inheritance.' All the people on whom the blood of the sacrifices was sprinkled, were sanctified to the purifying of the flesh, but those of them who were efficaciously called, and offered the sacrifices in faith of the promise of God, received a real remission of their sins. They were, like Noah, heirs of the righteousness which is by faith, and consequently partakers in its benefits. To the same purpose the Apostle speaks towards the end of that Epistle, of 'the spirits of just men made *perfect*,' Heb. xii. 23. They had entered heaven on the pledge of that righteousness which was afterwards to be wrought; but until that took place, their title to heavenly glory had not been completed or perfected.[1] Hence the declaration at the end of the eleventh chapter of that Epistle, 'that they without us should not be made perfect,' that is, without the introduction of that righteousness in the days of the Gospel, the ministry of which was committed to the Apostles, 2 Cor. iii. 3.

Ver. 26.—*To declare, I say, at this time His righteousness ; that He might be just, and the justifier of him which believeth in Jesus.*

God hath at this time also set forth His Son as a propitiatory sacrifice, in order to make manifest His righteousness, on account of which now, under the Gospel dispensation, He remits the sins of His people. He was always just in forgiving sin, but now the ground on which He forgives it is manifested, which vindicates His justice in doing so. The word here rendered *just*, is variously translated by those who do not understand God's plan of salvation. Some make it to signify benevolent, kind, merciful, etc.; but it has here its own proper meaning, which it never deserts. God is *just;* He acts according to strict justice, as becometh His character, while He justifies, accounts, and treats as perfectly righteous, all who believe in Jesus, who are thus one with Him, and consequently have His righteousness imputed to them. In all this we see the accomplishment of that prediction, 'Mercy and truth are met together, righteousness and peace have kissed each other. Truth shall spring out of the earth; and righteousness shall look down from heaven.

---

[1] Mr. Stuart's explanation is, 'exalted to a state of final reward.' This is not the truth here declared. The other commentators equally mistake the meaning, explaining it to signify exalted to a state of holiness and felicity.

Yea, the Lord shall give that which is good; and our land shall yield her increase. Righteousness shall go before Him, and shall set us in the way of His steps,' Ps. lxxxv. 10.

From the last two verses we learn that, in the continuance of the legal dispensation, notwithstanding the sins of men, and also in the preservation of the nations, God had suspended the immediate effects of His justice. For if He had not acted in this manner, He would at once have put an end to that dispensation and to the economy of His providence with respect to the other nations, in destroying both them and the people of Israel. During all that time which preceded the coming of His Son, He appeared to have forgotten the merited punishment of men's sins, and all the world remained under the shadow of His forbearance. But when Jesus Christ came, God did two things: the first was to continue no longer an economy of patience, or of an apparent forgetfulness of sin, but to bring in everlasting righteousness, by which He bestowed a true justification, which the law, whether written or natural, could not do, as it left men under guilt; but Jesus Christ has brought the true grace of God. The second thing which God has done, is to manifest, in the revelation of His righteousness, His avenging justice, by the shedding of the blood of His Son upon the cross. And thus he now appears to be just in Himself as the real avenger of sins, and, at the same time, the justifier of men, granting them a real remission of their sins by the imputation of His righteousness, which answers every demand of law and justice; whereas in the period of the forbearance of God, which continued to the time of Jesus Christ, God neither appeared just nor justifying. He did not appear just, for He suspended the effects of His justice. He did not appear the justifier, for He seemed only to suspend for a time the punishment of sins, and to leave men under the obligation of that punishment. But in the economy of Jesus Christ He manifests Himself both as just and as the justifier, for He displays the awful effects of His justice in the person of His Son in the work of propitiation, in the shedding of His blood; and, at the same time, He justifies His people, granting to them a true remission of their sins. And when the greatness of Him by whom this expiation was made is considered, the glory of the Divine justice, as exhibited in His death, is elevated in the highest possible degree.

In the propitiation, then, of Jesus Christ, the justice of God in the salvation of sinners shines conspicuously. No man hath seen God at any time; the only-begotten Son hath in His own person revealed Him. Jesus Christ was set forth to display every attribute of Godhead. The wisdom and power of God are seen in the constitution and person of Christ and His work, incomparably more fully than in the creation of the heavens and the earth. Perfect justice, mercy, and love to sinners, are beheld nowhere else. Here God is revealed as infinite in *mercy;* not so the God of man's imagination, whose mercy is a mixture of injustice and weak compassion, and extends only to those who are supposed to deserve it. But in the incarnate God infinite mercy is extended to the chief of sinners. Here is pure mercy without merit on the part of man. And where do we find the perfection of Divine *justice?* Not in the God of man's imagination, where justice is tempered with mercy, and limited in a thousand ways. Not even in the eternal punishment of the wicked shall we find justice so fully displayed as in the propitiation of Jesus Christ. He gave justice all it could demand, so that it is now shown to have secured the salvation of the redeemed in every age of the world as much as mercy itself. God is shown not only to be merciful to forgive, but He is *faithful and just* to forgive the sinner his sins. Justice, instead of being reduced to the necessity of taking a part from the bankrupt, has received full payment, and guarantees his deliverance. Even the chief of sinners are shown, in the propitiatory sacrifice of their Surety, to be perfectly worthy of Divine love, because they are not only perfectly innocent, but have *the righteousness of God.* He hath made Him to be sin for us who knew no sin, that we might be made the righteousness of God in Him.

Ver. 27.—*Where is boasting then ? It is excluded. By what law ? of works ? Nay ; but by the law of faith.*

Where is boasting then ?—That is, according to the doctrine which the Apostle, by the Spirit of God, is teaching. There is no ground for it, or for ascribing salvation in any part or degree to the works of men. This shows that salvation was appointed to come to the redeemed through faith, for the very purpose of excluding all pretences to allege that human merit has any share in it. This applies to all works, moral as well as ceremonial. If ceremonial works only were here meant, as many contend, and if moral works have some influence in procuring salvation, or in justification, then the Apostle could not have asked this question. Boasting would not have been excluded.

Paul had declared the only way in which a man can be 'just with God.' He had proved that it is not by His own righteousness, which is of the law, but by that righteousness which is received by faith. This is clear from what had been advanced in the preceding verse, from which this is an inference. If, then—as if he had said—God had purposed that men should have any ground of boasting, He would not have set forth Christ to be a propitiation through faith in His blood, that thereby a way might be opened for justifying sinners, so that His justice might suffer no prejudice. But now He has taken this course ; and therefore the only way of justification precludes all boasting.

'Paul is not here,' says Calvin, 'disputing merely concerning ceremonies, or any external works, but comprehends all works of every kind and degree. Boasting is excluded without all doubt, since we can produce nothing of our own that merits the approbation or commendation of God. And here he is not speaking of limitation or diminution of merit, since he does not allow the least particle of it. Thus, if boasting of works be removed by faith, so that it takes away from man all praise, while all power and glory are ascribed to God, it follows that no works whatever contribute to the attainment of righteousness.'

By what law is boasting excluded ?—It is not by that of works ; for if works were admitted, in the smallest degree, to advance or aid man's justification, he might in that proportion have ground of boasting. It is, then, by the law of faith ; not by a law requiring faith, or as if the

Gospel was a law, a new law, or, as it has been termed, a remedial or mitigated law ; but the word law is here used in allusion to the law of works, according to a figure usual in the Scriptures. By the same figure Jesus says, 'This is the work of God, that ye believe in Him whom He hath sent.' Here faith is called a work, for a similar reason. Faith in the righteousness of Christ is, by the appointment of God, the medium of a sinner's justification, without any consideration of works. This way of justification clearly shows that a man has no righteousness of his own, and that he can obtain nothing by means of conformity to the law, which can have no place, since he must admit that he is a transgressor. It impels him to flee out of himself, and to lay hold of the righteousness of another, and so leaves no room for glorying or boasting in himself, or in his own performances more or less. His justification is solely by faith ; and it is clear that to believe a testimony, and rely on what has been done by another, furnish no ground for boasting. 'Therefore it is by faith, that it might be by grace.' The whole plan of salvation proceeds on this principle, 'that no flesh should glory in His presence,' but 'that, according as it is written, he that glorieth, let him glory in the Lord.' No ingenuity can ever make salvation by human merit consistent with the passage before us.

Ver. 28.—*Therefore we conclude, that a man is justified by faith without the deeds of the law.*

Therefore we conclude.—In the 20th verse the Apostle had arrived at the conclusion, from all he had said before, that by works of law no man shall be justified in the sight of God. He had next pointed out the way of justification by faith in the atonement; and here He comes to His second grand and final conclusion, as the sum of all He had taught in the preceding part of the Epistle. *Justified by faith.*—Faith does not justify as an act of righteousness, but as the instrument by which we receive Christ and His righteousness. Believers are said to be justified *by faith* and *of faith*, and *through faith*, but never *on account of faith*. The declaration of James, that a man is justified by works, and not by faith only, is not in any respect opposed to the affirmation in the passage before us. The question with him is not how men may obtain righteousness for themselves in the presence of God, but how they are proved to be righteous; for he is refuting those who make a vain boast of having faith, when they have only what he calls a dead faith,—that is, faith only in profession, which he illustrates by a man's having the appearance of compassion without the reality, and by referring to the body without the spirit or breath.[1]

Without the deeds of the law, literally *without works of law*, for here, as in verse 31st, the article is wanting.—This does not signify, as Dr. Macknight understands it, that 'perfect obedience' to law is not necessary ; it signifies that no degree of obedience to law is necessary. Good works are necessary for the believer, and are the things which accompany salvation, but they are not in any respect necessary to his justification. They have nothing to do with it. This passage asserts not merely that

---

[1] See on this subject the author's work on *Evidences*, etc., vol. ii. p. 385, third edition.

men are justified by faith without *perfect* obedience to any law, but without *any* obedience of their own. It may likewise be remarked, that believers will not be acquitted at the last day on account of their works, but will be judged according to their works. But God does not justify any according to their works, but freely by His grace; and not by works, or according to the works of righteousness which they have done, Tit. iii. 5.

Ver. 29.—*Is He the God of the Jews only ? is He not also of the Gentiles ? Yes, of the Gentiles also.*

Rather, Is He the God of Jews only? Is He not also of Gentiles? The article before Jews and Gentiles, which is not in the original, makes the assertion respect Jews and Gentiles in general. In the sense of the passage, God is not the God either of the Jews or of the Gentiles in general; but He is the God of Jews and Gentiles indifferently, when they believe in His Son.

Ver. 30.—*Seeing it is one God which shall justify the circumcision by faith, and uncircumcision through faith.*

Seeing it is one God.—This assigns the reason why God must be the God of Gentiles as well as of Jews. If He justifies both in the same way, He must be equally the God of both. In the previous part of the discussion, Paul had shown that by works of law no flesh shall be justified, proving it first respecting Gentiles, and afterwards respecting Jews. Now he affirms that God's method of justifying man applies equally to Jews and Gentiles. This confirms his doctrine respecting the ruin of all men by sin, and of there being only one way of recovery by the righteousness of God received through faith. To urge this was likewise of great importance, with a view to establish the kingdom of Christ in all the earth, Rom. x. 11, 13. Having thus reduced the whole human race to the same level, it follows that all distinction among them must be from God, and not from themselves,—all standing on the same footing with respect to their works. There is but one God, and so but one way of becoming His people, which is by faith.

By faith, and through faith.—It is difficult to see why the prepositions here are varied. Similar variations, however, occur in other places, where there appears to be no difference of meaning, as in Gal. ii. 16, where justification, as applied to the same persons, is spoken of in the same sense, ‘Knowing that a man is not justified *by* works of law, but *through* the faith of Jesus Christ, even we have believed in Jesus Christ that we might be justified *by* the faith of Christ.’

Ver. 31.—*Do we then make void law through faith? God forbid: yea, we establish law.*

From the doctrine of justification by faith alone, which the Apostle had been declaring, it might be supposed that the law of God was made void. This consequence might be drawn from the conclusion that a man is justified by faith without any respect to his obedience to law. This the Apostle denies, and, on the contrary, asserts that by his doctrine the law is established. The article is here wanting before law, indicating that the reference is not to the legal dispensation, or to the books of

Moses, as in the last clause of verse 21, but to the general law of God, whether written or unwritten. *Make void law.*—'Bring it to nought,' as the same word in the original is rendered, 1 Cor. i. 28; or 'destroy,' 1 Cor. vi. 13, and xv. 26; 'done away,' 2 Cor. iii. 7–14; 'abolished,' Eph. ii. 15; 2 Tim. i. 10. Professors Tholuck and Stuart, not perceiving how the doctrine of the Apostle establishes the authority of the law, understand law in this place as signifying the Old Testament. This entirely destroys the meaning and use of the passage. That the Old Testament teaches the same way of justification as that taught by the Apostles, is indeed a truth, an important truth, but not the truth here asserted. Mr. Stuart says, 'How gratuitous justification can be said to confirm or establish the *moral* law (as this text has been often explained), it seems difficult to make out.' There is not here the smallest difficulty. It is quite obvious in what way gratuitous justification by Christ *establishes law.* Can there be any greater respect shown to the law, than that when God determines to save men from its curse, He makes His own Son sustain its curse in their stead, and fulfil for them all its demands? When a surety pays all that is due by a debtor, the debtor receives a gratuitous discharge: but has the debt, or the law that enforces the debt, been on that account made void? Here, as well as in so many other parts of his exposition of this Epistle, we discover the unhappy effect of this commentator's misunderstanding the meaning of the expression at its commencement, *the righteousness of God.* That he should feel the difficulty he states above, is not surprising, for, according to the view he gives of justification, the law of God is completely made void.

Dr. Macknight explains establishing law to be making it 'necessary in many respects.' 'The Gospel,' he says, in his view and illustration of ch. i. 16, 17, 'teaches, that because all have sinned, and are incapable of perfect obedience, God hath appointed, for their salvation, *a righteousness without law;* that is, a righteousness which does not consist in perfect obedience to any law whatever, even *the righteousness of faith,*[1] that being the only righteousness attainable by sinners; and at the same time declares that God will accept and reward that kind of righteousness through Christ, as if it were a perfect righteousness.'[2] Accordingly, in his interpretation of the 21st verse of chapter iii., he says: 'But *now,* under the Gospel, *a righteousness appointed by God,* as the means of the justification of sinners, *without* perfect obedience to *law* of any kind, *is made known.'* In this manner, mistaking, like Professors Tholuck and Stuart, although in a different way, the import of the expression, 'the righteousness of God,' *he misunderstands the whole train of the Apostle's reasoning,* from the 17th verse of the first chapter to the end of the fifth chapter, as well as its object, in this discussion on justification, and by his explanation, *altogether makes void the law.* Instead of making it 'necessary in many respects,' Dr. Macknight, as well as Mr. Stuart and Mr. Tholuck, by representing it as satisfied with an imperfect obedience, which does

---

[1] Here, as elsewhere, he misunderstands the meaning of the expression, *the righteousness of faith,* imagining that it signifies the righteousness that belongs to faith, and not the righteousness which is received by faith.

[2] 'These inferences, indeed,' he adds, 'the Apostle hath not drawn in this part of his letter.' The Apostle never could draw such inferences.

not meet the demands of any law, either human or Divine, makes it void *in every respect*. Such is the entire consistency among themselves of the doctrines of Scripture, that whenever any one of them is misunderstood, it invariably leads to the misunderstanding of the rest.

Many commentators, with more or less clearness, refer to the doctrine of sanctification, either in whole or in part, the Apostle's denial that he makes void the law. According to them, it is not made void for this reason, because it convinces men of sin, and does not release from personal obedience to its precepts. That the doctrine of justification, by the imputation of Christ's righteousness, does not release believers from obedience to the law, is a most important truth, which Paul fully establishes in the sixth chapter of this Epistle. On the contrary, it lays them under additional obligations to obey it, by furnishing additional motives to the love of God. But since their sanctification is always in this life imperfect, were there nothing else to meet the demands of the law, it would be made void—it would remain unfulfilled, both in its precept and penalty. In addition to this, the whole of the previous discussion regards the doctrine of justification, while not a word is said respecting sanctification. And it is evident that this verse is introduced to obviate an objection which might naturally present itself, namely, if man's obedience, in order to his justification, be set aside, the law, which requires obedience, is made void.

But Paul appeals to his doctrine, and, according to his usual manner, strongly rejects such an inference. In the preceding verses, from the 20th, he had been announcing that the righteousness of God, which is the complete fulfilment of the law, is placed to the account of him who believes for his justification, whereby God, in thus justifying the sinner solely on the ground of a perfect obedience, shows Himself to be *just*. Do we *then*, he says, make void the law? This doctrine not only maintains the authority of the law of God, but also exhibits the fulfilment of all its demands. The connecting particle shows that Paul rests his proof on what had gone before, to which he appeals, and not on the ground of sanctification, to which he had been making no reference, and which, if he had referred to it, would not have borne out his assertion.

'Think not,' said our blessed Lord, 'that I am come to destroy the law and the Prophets: I am not come to destroy, but to fulfil. For verily I say unto you, till heaven and earth pass, one jot or one tittle shall in nowise pass from the law, till all be fulfilled.' It is to this fulfilment—to the *righteousness of God*, which in the context the Apostle had been illustrating, and which Jesus Christ brought in—that he here appeals. Do we make law void when we conclude that a man is justified by faith without doing the works of law, since we show that through his faith he receives a perfect righteousness, by which, in all its demands and all its sanction, it is *fulfilled?* No; it is in this very way we establish it. In this glorious establishment of the law of God, Paul, in another place, exults, when he counts all things but loss for the excellency of Christ, and desires to be found in Him, not having his own righteousness, which is of the law, but that which is through the faith of Christ, the righteousness which is of God by faith. While he thus tramples on his own righteousness, by which the law never could be established, he confidently appeals to the righteousness of God, now made his by faith. This is precisely in accordance with his conclusion in the 28th verse, that a man is justified by faith without the deeds of law; and afterwards, at the termination of his mortal career, in the immediate prospect of death, he triumphs in the consideration that there is laid up for him a crown of *righteousness*—a crown, the reward of that perfect obedience by which *the law is magnified and made honourable.*

CHAPTER 4
ROMANS 4:1 – 25

THIS chapter beautifully connects with all that precedes it. In the first chapter the Apostle had announced that ' the righteousness of God ' was revealed in the Gospel, which is on that account the power of God unto salvation to every one that believeth. He had shown at great length that this way of salvation was necessary for man, proving by an appeal to fact, and then to Scripture, that both Jews and Gentiles were guilty before God, and that, consequently, no one could be justified by his own obedience. He had afterwards reverted to this righteousness which God had provided in His Son. In this fourth chapter he strikingly illustrates these truths, by first obviating the objection that might be offered by the Jews respecting their great progenitor Abraham, whose character they held in such veneration. This would lead them to suppose that he must be an exception to the Apostle's doctrine, by furnishing an example of one justified by works. Having refuted this objection in the particular case of Abraham, and confirmed the truth of what he had advanced by the testimony of David, Paul makes use of the history of Abraham himself to prove what he had previously asserted, and to show that in the matter of justification before God there was no exception, and no difference between Jews and Gentiles.

The chapter consists of four parts. In the first, the Apostle, by referring, as has just been observed, to the history of Abraham and the authority of David, illustrates his doctrine of justification by faith. Nothing could be so well calculated to convince both Jewish and Gentile believers, especially the former, how vain is the expectation of those who look for justification by their own works. Abraham was a patriarch eminently holy, the head of the nation of Israel, the friend of God, the father of all who believe, in whose seed all the nations of the world were to be blessed. David was a man according to God's own heart, the progenitor of the Messiah, His great personal type, and a chosen and anointed king of Israel. If, then, Abraham had not been justified by his works, but by the righteousness of God imputed to him through faith, and David, speaking by the Spirit of God, had declared that the only way in which a man can receive justification is by his sin being covered by the imputation of that righteousness, who could suppose that it was to be obtained by any other means? By these two references, the Apostle likewise shows that the way of justification was the same from the beginning, both under the old and the new dispensation. This he had before intimated, in saying that both the law and the Prophets bore witness to the righteousness of God, which is now manifested, and which is upon all them that believe.

In the other three parts of this chapter, Paul shows, first, that circumcision, to which the Jews ascribed so much efficacy, contributed nothing to Abraham's justification, and that the righteousness imputed to him was bestowed before his circumcision, with the express intention of proving that righteousness should be imputed to all who believe though they be not circumcised. In the next place, he proves that the promise of the inheritance made to Abraham was not through obedience to law, but through that righteousness which is received by faith; and that the whole plan of justification was arranged in this manner, in order that the blessing conveyed through faith by the free favour of God might be made sure to all the seed of Abraham,—that is, to ' the children of the promise,' Rom. ix. 8, whether Jews or Gentiles. And, lastly, Paul describes Abraham's faith, and states the benefit resulting from its exhibition to believers, for whose sake chiefly his faith was recorded. It is particularly to be noticed that not a word is said respecting Abraham's sanctification, although his whole history, after leaving his own country, furnishes so remarkable an example of a holy walk and conversation. All that is brought into view is his faith. It is thus shown that neither moral nor ceremonial, neither evangelical nor legal works, are of any account whatever in the act of justification, or contribute in any degree to procure that blessing. The whole of this chapter is particularly calculated to make a deep impression on the Jews; and no doubt the day is approaching, and propably near at hand, when they will read it with much interest, and derive from it signal benefit.

Ver. 1.—*What shall we then say that Abraham, our father as pertaining to the flesh, hath found?*

In the third chapter the Apostle had replied to the objections which might be offered to what he had before advanced respecting the Jews. First, it might be inquired if, as appeared from his doctrine, the Jews could not be saved by their distinguished privileges connected with the law, or by observing the rite of circumcision, what *advantage* did they possess over others, and what *profit* had they from circumcision? Second, on the supposition of their being transgressors, it was asked, if their sin was the means of *commending* the righteousness of God, was it not unjust to punish them as sinners? Lastly, if all that had been said was true, what were they *better* than others? After obviating all these objections, and proving from the character of the Jews, and of all other men, as delineated in the Scriptures, the impossibility of their justification by the works of law, Paul had exhibited the only way in which sinners could be justified before God, and had shown that it was effected in such a way that all boasting on the part of man is excluded. Another objection might now naturally present itself to the Jews in connection with the case of Abraham, who had received the ordinance of circumcision from God Himself, and whose eminent piety they held in such veneration. It might be asked what, according to the Apostle's doctrine, could be said regarding him: what had he found, or obtained? Did not he obtain justification in these ways? Such is the objection which the Apostle introduces in this and the following verse, and answers fully in both its parts.

Abraham our father.—In the course of this chapter Abraham is again and again denominated, in a spiritual sense, the father of all believers; but in this place, in which the argument from his circumcision and holy character refers chiefly to the Jews, to whom much of what is said in the preceding chapter relates, it appears that he is here spoken of as the natural progenitor of the Jewish nation. The expression *our* is therefore to be considered as referring to the Jews, with whom, as being a Jew, the Apostle here classes himself, and not to believers generally, whether Jews or Gentiles, as in other verses of this chapter. That it is thus to be understood does not appear, however, from the expression *pertaining to the flesh*, since it is not joined with that of *father* in the original. The order there is, ' Abraham our father hath found as pertaining to the flesh.'

As pertaining to the flesh.—That is, by circumcision, of which the Apostle had spoken, ch. ii. ; or by any work or privilege, Phil. iii. 4. The expression, to the flesh, should rather be translated *by* the flesh, as the word here translated as pertaining to, is rendered, ch. ii. 7, and in many other passages. *Circumcision* especially was the token of the covenant which contained all the promises that God had made to Abraham, saying, ' My covenant shall be in your flesh for an everlasting covenant.' Could it be supposed that this rite, so solemnly enjoined and connected with such privileges, and his other good works, had no procuring influence in Abraham's justification? Such is the objection which it is supposed in this first verse would occur to the Jews, and is therefore stated by the Apostle, which he fully answers.in the sequel.

Ver. 2.—*For if Abraham were justified by works, he hath whereof to glory; but not before God.*

The term ' works' is here explanatory of the word flesh in the first verse, signifying any works, whether moral or ceremonial. If Abraham were justified on account of his works, as the Jews believed, it must be admitted that he had something to boast of, contrary to what the Apostle had just before declared, that all boasting on such grounds is excluded, whose doctrine, consequently, must be set aside. Than this, no objection that could be offered would appear to the Jews more forcible; it was therefore important to advert to it. Being, however, entirely groundless, the Apostle at once repels it, and replies to the question previously proposed, respecting circumcision, or any work or privilege, in that prompt and brief manner of which we see an example at the end of the 8th verse of the former chapter. He answers, *But not before God.* Abraham had no ground of boasting before God, not having been justified either by the observance of the rite of circumcision, or by any other work of obedience which he had performed; and this Paul fully proves in the sequel.

Ver. 3.—*For what saith the Scripture? Abraham believed God, and it was counted unto him for righteousness.*

Having denied in the foregoing verse that Abraham was justified, or had any ground of boasting, either on account of his circumcision or his obedience, Paul next supports his denial by an appeal to Scripture, which was calculated to carry stronger conviction to the Jews than all things else he could have alleged. His proof is drawn from the historical records of the Old Testament, and thus he sets his seal to its complete verbal inspiration, quoting what is there recorded as the decision of God; yet some who profess to receive the Bible as the word of God, deny that portion of it to be inspired! His meaning, then, by the question, *What saith the Scripture?* is, that God Himself, by His own word, has decided this matter; for the fact is there declared that *Abraham believed God, and it was counted unto him for righteousness.* This quotation is taken from Gen. xv. 6, where the promise to Abraham is recorded that his seed should be innumerable as the stars of heaven, being the renewal of the promise, Gen. xii. 2, when he was called out of his own country. It thus comprehended the truth announced to him at different times, that all the nations of the world should be blessed in his *seed*, that is, in the Messiah, Gal. iii. 16. That promise referred to the one made to our first parents after the fall, in which was included the hope of redemption to be accomplished by the Deliverer of mankind, who was to spring from him, as God declared to Abraham. The above passage, then, according to Paul, proves that the *righteousness of God* is received by faith, and is an example of the testimony that is rendered to it by the law. It refutes the opinion of those who, misunderstanding the manner in which the Apostle James expresses himself, affirm that a man is first justified only by faith, but afterwards by works which flow from faith.

And it was counted to him for righteousness, rather, *unto righteousness.* —It is not instead of righteousness, as this translation *for righteousness* has led many to suppose. By faith a man becomes truly righteous. Faith is the recipient of that righteousness by which we are justified. *Unto* righteousness is the literal rendering, as the same word in the original is so often translated in this discussion, as where it is said, ch. i. 16, the Gospel is the power of God *unto* salvation; and ch. iii. 22, even the righteousness of God which is *unto* all; and so in innumerable other places, but especially in a passage precisely parallel to the one before us, ch. x. 10, 'For with the heart man believeth *unto* righteousness.' This is the signification of the phrase in the verse before us, which ought to have been translated in the same way. The expression ' unto righteousness' is elliptical, and signifies unto the receiving of righteousness. In the different French translations, the meaning of the original is properly expressed *à justice;*' that is, to, or *unto* righteousness; and in the same way in the Vulgate, ' *ad justitiam*,' to righteousness; and in this meaning is fixed down definitely by the verses immediately succeeding, where the Apostle introduces a passage from the Psalms in illustration of the manner in which Abraham and his spiritual seed are justified.

That faith is not itself the justifying righteousness, is demonstrably evident from the phraseology of many passages that speak of faith and righteousness in the same place. 'Even the *righteousness of God*, which is *by faith* of Jesus Christ unto all, and upon all them that believe.' Here righteousness is supposed to be one thing, and faith to be another. Can language more expressly show that righteousness and faith are two different things, for two different purposes, though always found united in the same persons, and both equally necessary? Righteousness is what we want in order to justification; faith in the Lord Jesus Christ, as testified in the Gospel, is the means through which we receive this righteousness. Believing, then, is not the righteousness, but it is the means through which we become righteous. In like manner, in Rom. x. 10, above quoted, the Apostle says, 'For with the heart man believeth unto righteousness.' Here it is necessarily implied that faith is not righteousness, but that it is the means through which we receive righteousness. Nothing, then, can be a greater corruption of the truth than to represent faith itself as accepted instead of righteousness, or to be the righteousness that saves the sinner. Faith is not righteousness. Righteousness is the fulfilling of the law.

This verse, connected with the following, proves, like the 28th verse of the foregoing chapter, that faith is opposed to works, and not considered as a work in the matter of justification. Yet many speak of the excellence of Abraham's faith in such a way as to represent the patriarch to be saved by faith as a work—as the most excellent of all works. Mr. Tholuck advances many observations on this subject that are altogether unscriptural, discovering most erroneous views of the Gospel. He quotes various passages from Philo, which he calls 'beautiful,' in which Philo extols faith as 'the queen of virtues,' 'the price of every blessing;' and adds, 'and well is it said that faith was counted to him (Abraham) for righteousness.' Here Philo exhibits faith as the righteousness by which Abraham was justified—the *price* of that blessing. Mr. Tholuck says, ' Δικαιοσύνη (righteousness) denotes here *subjective holiness*. God looked upon Abraham's childlike submission as if it were *real holiness*, and attached value to it alone.' A greater perversion of Scripture, or a sentiment more directly opposed to the meaning of the passage and to all the Apostle is proving in the context, and has been labouring to prove throughout the whole of his previous discussion from the 16th verse of the first chapter, as well as subversive of the grand doctrine of justification, cannot be imagined. If Abraham was justified by faith as a '*price*,' or ' *as* righteousness,'—an expression which Mr. Tholuck employs again and again,—then he was justified by faith as a work, 'as if it were real holiness,' and God is thus represented as attaching a value to faith which does not belong to it! In opposition to such unscriptural and fallacious statements, which at once make void the law and the Gospel, we are here taught that Abraham was not justified by faith, either as a price, or as a virtue, or as if it were really righteousness, but as the appointed medium of receiving righteousness, even the righteousness of God. This fundamental error of Mr. Tholuck and Mr. Stuart, and long ago of Socinus, that faith, although it is really not righteousness, is reckoned by

God *as righteousness*, is most dishonourable to the character of God, and derogatory to His holy law. That law, which is a transcript of His own unchangeable nature, can acknowledge nothing as its fulfilment but perfect conformity to all its requirements. Nor did the Gospel come to pour dishonour upon it by modifying its demands, or to substitute another law for it, making faith meritorious. And besides, the nature of faith will not admit of this, for it excludes boasting. It implies a fleeing out of one's self, and our own performances,—it consists in looking to another as the bestower of eternal salvation.

Dr. Macknight has a long note on this verse, which is also directly opposed to the Apostle's doctrine of justification. ' In judging Abraham,' he says, ' God will place on the one side of the account his *duties*, and on the other his *performances*. And on the side of his performances he will place his faith, and by mere favour will value it as equal to a complete performance of his duties, and reward him as if he were a righteous person. But neither here, nor in Gal. iii. 6, is it said that *Christ's righteousness was counted to Abraham*. In both passages the expression is, *Abraham believed God, and it*, viz., his believing God, *was counted to him for righteousness*. Further, as it is nowhere said in Scripture that Christ's righteousness was imputed to Abraham, so neither is it said anywhere that Christ's righteousness is imputed to believers.' These statements, affirming that God, in judging Abraham, will place on the one side of the account his duties, and on the other his performances, and by mere favour will value faith as equal to a complete performance of his duties, argue most deplorable ignorance of the whole plan of salvation. The assertion, that it is nowhere said in Scripture that Christ's righteousness is imputed to believers, is directly contrary to fact. It is contradicted by the whole strain of Scripture relating to the subject, and expressly by the Apostle Peter, in his address to them that have obtained like precious faith with us, in the righteousness of our God and Saviour Jesus Christ, 2 Pet. i. 1. (This is the literal rendering.) And also by the Prophet Jeremiah, xxiii. 6, by whom Jesus Christ is called *the Lord our righteousness*. But by such groundless assertions does Dr. Macknight misrepresent the character of God, and labours to banish from the Bible the doctrine of the imputation of Christ's righteousness, without which, consistently with the perfections of God and the demands of the law, there could be no salvation. He misunderstands, too, the meaning of the expression, *for* righteousness.

Ver. 4.—*Now to him that worketh is the reward not reckoned of grace, but of debt.*

Some understand this as implying *working perfectly*—doing all that a man is bound to do. But this is contrary to the meaning: it applies to work of any kind, and excludes all working of every kind or degree. No reward can be said to be of grace that is given for work of any description. Abraham did not obtain righteousness by faith as a good disposition, or by counting that disposition above its value. Had Abraham been justified by faith as an act or disposition worthy of approbation, or by anything whatsoever that he had done, he would have been justified by works, and might have boasted.

Ver. 5.—*But to him that worketh not, but believeth on Him that justifieth the ungodly, his faith is counted for righteousness.*

But to him that worketh not.—This is entirely misunderstood by Dr. Macknight and Mr. Stuart, as if it meant, according to Dr. Macknight, 'one who does not work all that he is bound to do;' or, according to Mr. Stuart, 'the sinner who has not exhibited perfect obedience.' It means, however, what it literally expresses, namely, that the person who is justified does not *work at all* for his justification. It is not that he does not perform all the works that he ought, but that for justification he does nothing. It is true that he works, but not for justification. Mr. Tholuck, who likewise misunderstands in this place the whole of the Apostle's argument, seems to think that the case of Abraham is only an analogy, and not an example of justification by faith. But Abraham's faith respected the Messiah, whose day he saw afar off, and by His righteousness he was justified.

Justifieth the ungodly.—If the expression, 'to him that worketh not,' needed any explanation, this term—the ungodly—would place its meaning beyond all doubt. The term ungodly is applied throughout the Scriptures to wicked men, Rom. v. 6; 1 Tim. i. 9; 1 Pet. iv. 18; 2 Pet. ii. 5, iii. 7; Jude 4, 15. Men are ungodly in themselves, though, as soon as they are justified, they cease to be ungodly. They are ungodly till *they believe;* but in the moment that they receive the gift of faith, they are thereby united to the Saviour, and are instantly invested with the robe of righteousness, and also partake, according to the measure of their faith, of all those other graces that are received out of His fulness. They then pass from *death* to *life,*—a transition in which there is no medium; they are turned from darkness to light, and from the power of Satan unto God; for till then, being without Christ, they are the children of the devil. They cannot at the same time be both dead and alive —under the power of God, and under the power of the devil; they must in every instant of their existence be either under the one or the other. In that moment, then, in which they believe, they are justified; and to justify, signifies not to treat men as if they were just or righteous, though they are not so, but because they are in truth righteous by imputation, really righteous, the law having been fulfilled in them, ch. viii. 4. In this Professors Tholuck and Stuart most grossly err. To justify, with them, is not to acquit as being perfectly righteous, but to hold men to be righteous when they are not righteous. The expression, justifieth the ungodly, Dr. Macknight says, 'does not imply that Abraham was an ungodly person when he was justified; the Apostle's meaning is, *justifieth him who had been ungodly.*' This is making, not explaining Scripture. It entirely sets aside the Apostle's declaration.

It is much to be regretted that it should be necessary to introduce the name of Mr. Scott in connection with such writers as Macknight, Stuart, and Tholuck. As an expositor of Scripture, he deserves to be spoken of in terms very different from any of them; but an impartial regard for the interest of truth requires that his very erroneous remarks on the passage last referred to should not pass unnoticed. Mr. Scott's note, in his Commentary on this expression, 'justifieth the ungodly,' is incorrect, and his ideas on the subject are confused. Contrary to the Apostle, he asserts that a man is not 'absolutely ungodly at the time of his justification.' It is true, as has been observed, that the moment a man is justified, he is godly; but the question is, if he be godly or ungodly in the moment which precedes his justification? If he be godly before, then the words of the Apostle are false ; and the contrary, that God justifies the *godly*, would be true. But Mr. Scott's views on this point are very erroneous, as appears from his remarks on Cornelius, in his note preceding the verse before us. He says, ' Even the proposition, Good works are the fruits of faith, and follow after faith, in Christ, though a general truth, may admit of some exception, in such cases as that of Cornelius.' This contradicts the 12th and 13th articles of his church, to which he appears to refer; but what is of more consequence, his statement explicitly contradicts the whole tenor of the Holy Scriptures, and of the plan of redemption. The case of Cornelius forms no exception, nor does it contain even the shadow of an exception to the truth declared in the verse we are considering. Mr. Scott closes his note on Acts x. 1, 2, by remarking, ' Perhaps these observations may assist the reader in understanding this instructing chapter, which cannot easily be made to accord with the exactness of systematical writers on these subjects.' Now there is not the smallest difficulty in showing that all which that chapter contains is in exact accordance with every other part of Scripture.

Mr. Scott, after some further remarks on the justification of the ungodly, says, ' Nay, the justified believer, whatever his holiness or diligence may be, never works *for this purpose*, and he still comes before God as *ungodly in this respect*.' This is incorrect. He always comes as a sinner ; that is, as one who is daily, hourly, and every moment sinning. And when he comes so, he comes as he is ; for this is truth. But he is not *ungodly* after he believes, which is a character belonging only to the enemies of God. The Christian, then, cannot in any respect come in such a character, for he cannot come in a character that is no longer his. There is an essential difference between coming to God as a sinner, and coming to Him as ungodly. 'Abraham,' Mr. Scott subjoins, ' several years before, by faith obeyed the call and command of God, and therefore could not be, strictly speaking, altogether *ungodly*, when it was said, " He believed God, and it was counted to him for righteousness ;" so that the example of Abraham alone is a full and clear refutation of the construction by some put upon this text, that men are altogether and in every sense ungodly and unregenerate at the time when God justifies them,—a sentiment of most dangerous tendency.' The assertion of the Apostle is, that God justifies the ungodly, which can have no other meaning than that men are ungodly in the moment that precedes their justification. It is truly astonishing that the example of Abraham should be referred to as a full and clear refutation of the plain and obvious construction of this assertion of the Apostle, which it never can be of dangerous tendency implicitly to believe. The danger lies in not receiving it, and in raising difficulties and objections which obscure and neutralize a declaration, the meaning of which is so clear and manifest. This must always have the effect, as in the case before us, of leading into most palpable error, inconsistency, and misrepresentation of the Divine testimony. If Abraham was godly before the time when it was recorded that he believed God, and it was counted to him for righteousness, he was also a believer before that time, and justified before that time, although his justification was then first recorded. The limitations, therefore, ' strictly speaking,' and ' altogether *ungodly*,' which Mr. Scott introduces, are entirely misplaced. He was not ungodly at all. To intimate, as Mr. Scott does, that Abraham was not a justified believer till the period when it is recorded that his faith was counted to him for righteousness, is to say that a man may exercise strong faith, and obey God, and walk in communion with Him, long before he is justified, which is to overturn the doctrine of justification. But no such confusion and discrepancies are to be found in the Scriptures. When, in the eleventh chapter of the Hebrews, the Apostle illustrates his declaration in the end of the tenth chapter, that *the just shall live by faith*, he affirms that ' *By faith*, Abraham, when he was called to go out into a place, which he should after receive for an inheritance, obeyed.' If, then, faith justifies, as the Apostle is there showing, Abraham was justified by faith when he ' departed as the Lord had spoken to him,' Gen. xii. 4, many years before the time of the declaration recorded in Gen. xv. 6. On the whole, there is not a spark of godliness in any man before he is united to Christ; and the moment he is united to Him, he is for ever justified.

In the 4th and 5th verses before us, the distinction between receiving a reward for works, and receiving it through faith, is clearly established. In the first case, a man receives what is due to him as his wages ; in the second, all comes in the way of favour. Here also faith and works are directly opposed to each other. To preserve the doctrine of these verses from abuse, it is only necessary to recollect that works are denied as having anything to do in justification, but that they are absolutely necessary in the life of the believer. ' Works,' says Luther, ' are not taken into consideration when the question respects justification. But true faith will no more fail to produce them than the sun can cease to give light. But it is not on account of works that God justifies us.' ' We offer nothing to God,' says Calvin ; ' but we are prevented by His grace altogether free, without His having any respect to our works.'

Men are prone to magnify one part of the Divine counsel, by disparaging or denying another, which to their wisdom appears to stand in opposition to it. Some speak of faith in such a manner as to disparage works ; others are so zealous for works as to disparage faith ; while some, in order to honour both, confound them together. The Apostle Paul gives every truth its proper value and its proper place. In this Epistle he establishes the doctrine of justification by faith alone, and speaks not of the fruits of faith till the fifth chapter. But these fruits he shows to be the necessary result of that faith which justifies.

Ver. 6. — *Even as David also describeth the blessedness of the man, unto whom God imputeth righteousness without works.*

As the blessing of the pardon of sin cannot be separated from our being viewed as perfectly righteous in the sight of God, Paul further confirms his doctrine by a reference to the 32d Psalm, which gives the meaning of David's words. In this manner one part of Scripture is employed to open and explain what is said in another part. *Imputeth.*—The same word in the original, which in verses 3, 4, 5, is rendered *counted* or *reckoned,* is here rendered imputed. All of them bear the same meaning, of placing to the believer's account the righteousness of Jesus Christ, called in ch. v. 19 His ' obedience.' ' Here we see,' says Calvin, ' the mere cavil of those who limit the works of the law within ceremonial rites, since what before were denominated works of the law are now called *works* simply, and without an adjunct. The simple and unrestricted language occurring in this passage, which all readers must understand as applying indifferently to every kind of work, must for ever conclude the whole of this dispute. For nothing is more inconsistent than to deprive ceremonies alone of the power of justifying, when Paul excludes works indefinitely.'

The expression ' imputeth righteousness without works,' is important, as it clearly ascertains that the phrase ' for righteousness,' literally *unto righteousness,* signifies unto the receiving of righteousness. It signifies receiving righteousness itself, not a substitute for righteousness, nor a thing of less value than righteousness, which is accounted or accepted as righteousness. In Dr. Macknight's note, however, on verse 3d, already quoted, where he is labouring to prove that faith is counted FOR righteousness, or, according to Mr. Stuart and Mr. Tholuck, AS righteousness, he affirms, as has been observed, that God values faith as equal to complete performance of duty, and that it is nowhere said in Scripture that Christ's righteousness is imputed to believers. The verse before us contains an explicit refutation of these unscriptural statements, which subvert not only the whole of the Apostle's reasoning on the doctrine of justification, but the whole doctrine of salvation. The righteousness here said to be imputed is that righteousness to which Paul had all along been referring, even *the righteousness of God* on account of the revelation of which the Gospel is the power of God unto salvation, and which, as has been noticed above, is by the Apostle Peter called *the righteousness of our God and Saviour Jesus Christ,* in which believers have obtained precious faith. That the Apostle refers in the verse before us to this righteousness *which fulfils the law,* is evident, if we look back to what he says in the 21st verse of the preceding chapter, and to what he continues to say respecting it ònwards to this 6th verse, and *to the effect he here ascribes to it.* If any one can·suppose that all this is insufficient to settle the question, I shall produce an argument which is unanswerable, and which all the ingenuity of man is unable to gainsay. *It must be the righteousness of God (or the righteousness of Christ, which is the same) that is here spoken of,* BECAUSE THERE IS NO OTHER RIGHTEOUSNESS ON EARTH.

To say with the above writers, that the God of truth values anything ' as equal to the complete performance of duty,' which is not so in reality, is to give a most unworthy, not to say a blasphemous, representation of His character. Far different are the following sentiments of Dr. Owen in his treatise *On Justification.* ' The sinner is not accepted *as if* he were righteous, but *because* in Christ Jesus he is so. The majesty of the law is not sacrificed; its requirements are fulfilled in their exceeding breadth; its penalty is endured in all its awfulness. And thus, from the meeting of mercy and loving-kindness with justice and judgment, there shines a most excellent glory, of which the full demonstration to men, and angels, and all the rational creatures of God, shall fill up the cycles of eternity.'

Mr. Stuart comes far short of the truth when he represents the Apostle as here confirming his doctrine by the case of David, as a second example or single instance. David is appealed to by Paul, not in respect to his own justification, but as to the doctrine which he taught with respect to this subject in one of his Psalms, where he speaks as he was moved by the Holy Ghost. He is here teaching how all are justified, who ever were, or ever shall be justified. It is, then, much more than a second example. It is the declaration of God Himself, who spoke *by the mouth of His servant David*, Acts iv. 25. The effect of Mr. Stuart's mis-understanding the expression, ' the righteousness of God,' ch. i. 17, and iii. 21, and ascribing to it the signification of ' the justification which God bestows,' is, in his explanation of the verse before us, as in so many other places, abundantly evident. Although compelled here to attach to the original word its proper meaning of *righteousness*, instead of ' justi-fication,' the vagueness of the meaning he had, as above, so erroneously ascribed to it, leaves an opening for explaining it to be a fictitious righteousness belonging to faith itself, instead of a real righteousness, namely, the righteousness of Christ received by faith. ' Here,' he says, ' and elsewhere in this chapter, where the same phraseology occurs, it is evident that the word is not to be understood in the sense of justification, which is the most common meaning of it in our Epistle.' So far from this being its most common meaning, it is not even once its meaning out of no fewer than thirty-six times in which it occurs in this Epistle.

Mr. Stuart's views on the all-important subject of justification, are not only completely erroneous and unscriptural, but such as they are, he holds them in a manner so confused and indistinct, that he alternately asserts and contradicts what he has advanced. He one while speaks of faith as ' not of itself such an act of obedience to the Divine *law*, as that it will supply the place of perfect obedience.' ' Nor has it,' he adds, ' any efficacy in itself, as a *meritum ex condigno* to save men; it is merely *the instrument of union to Christ, in order that they may receive a gratuitous salvation*,' p. 176. At other times, he speaks as if faith were accepted at a rate much above its value, and that the justification of a sinner is gratuitous because of such acceptance. ' Their faith,' he says, ' was *gratuitously* reckoned as equivalent to the δικαιοσύνη (righteousness) demanded by the law.' Here faith itself is made the ground of justi-fication, and taken at a value far above its intrinsic worth. But faith is in no point of view equivalent to the obedience the law requires. It is Christ's obedience that is taken as an equivalent to an obedience to the law; and for the best of all reasons, because it is an equivalent. The value of faith is, that by the Divine appointment it is the medium of union with Christ. If it be true that faith is ' merely ' an instrument of union to Christ, in order that we may receive a gratuitous salvation, as, in one of these passages, Mr. Stuart asserts, how is it that faith was gratuitously reckoned as equivalent to the righteousness demanded by the law ? If faith be accepted as an equivalent to righteousness, then it cannot be merely the medium of connecting us with Christ. He observes, p. 177, 'To say, *was counted* (namely, their faith) *for justification*, would make no tolerable sense ; but to say, *was counted as complete obedience*, would be saying just what the Apostle means to say, viz., that the believer is gratuitously justified.' And again, he affirms that faith ' is counted *as* righteousness,' p. 172. Here and in other places the imputation of Christ's righteousness for the justification of a sinner is excluded by Mr. Stuart, as it is by Dr. Macknight. Mr. Stuart's self-contradictions, contained in his Commentary, are noticed in the following term sin the American theological magazine, called *The Biblical Repertory*, of July 1833, where it is reviewed. ' Respected sir, you admit what you deny, and deny what you admit, in such rapid succession, your readers are bewildered.'

According, then, to these statements, righteousness, that is, the righteousness of Christ, which does indeed fulfil the demands of the law, is not imputed to the believer for justification—although this is explicitly asserted in the text, when it is said, ' God imputeth righteousness,' for on earth, as has been observed, there is no other righteousness—while faith, which does not fulfil so much as one of its demands, is reckoned as equivalent to all its demands; and besides, righteousness is thus counted to a man as belonging to him, which ' in reality does not belong to him.' And this, we are told by Mr. Stuart, is 'just what the Apostle means to say.' Paul affirms that God is just when He justifies him that believeth. But, according to Mr. Stuart, in thus representing God as counting for a reality what is a mere figment, and counting ' something' to a man ' which does not belong to him,' not a trace of anything that has even the semblance of justice in a sinner's justification is left. And on *these grounds*, salvation is asserted by him to be ' gratuitous !'

Mr. Stuart considers that the mercy of God, for Christ's sake, accepts believers as just, while they are not so in reality. This overturns the Gospel and the justice of the Divine character. It destroys both law and Gospel. If a man is not truly just, God cannot account him just, nor treat him as just. Why cannot Mr. Stuart see believers perfectly just in Jesus Christ, their head and substitute? But this is what might be expected from one who cannot see the human race guilty in Adam. It is quite natural, then, that he should not see believers righteous in Christ. According to Mr. Stuart, God is not a just God in saving sinners, for He acquits as just those whom He knows to be unjust. He represents God as an unjust God in punishing the innocent, for He visits with suffering and death infants, who are supposed innocent of Adam's sin.

According to the doctrine of the Apostle, when a sinner is justified, it is by the imputation of righteousness—not a fictitious, but a real righteousness. The believer, in his union with Christ, is viewed as perfectly righteous, because in truth he is so, for the righteousness of God is 'upon him,' ch. iii. 22; Jehovah is his righteousness, Jer. xxiii. 6. God is therefore *just* in justifying him; and in the day of judgment the Great Judge will pronounce him 'righteous,' Matt. xxv. 37–46, and award to him 'a crown of righteousness,' according to the strictest justice. The gift of this righteousness, with the justification it brings along with it, is indeed perfectly gratuitous, and the manner of bestowing it is gratuitous—freely by grace; but 'grace reigns *through righteousness*,' Rom. v. 21,—in that way which meets every demand of law and justice. This last is a most important declaration, with which the Apostle closes his discussion on the doctrine of justification; but important as it is, Mr. Stuart has altogether mistaken its meaning, and misrepresented it in the same way as he has misrepresented the corresponding expression at the opening of this discussion, ch. i. 17. Had he understood it, he would not have perverted the Apostle's reasoning as he has done, and propounded sentiments respecting the all-important doctrine of justification which annihilate the glory of that redemption in which righteousness and peace have kissed each other,—sentiments which compromise the justice, and dishonour the character of God.

'Faith,' says Mr. Bell, in his *View of the Covenants*, p. 226, 'rests upon Christ alone. It in effect excludes itself as a work in the matter of justification. It is not a thing upon which a sinner rests; it is his resting on the Surety. Therefore, that man who would bring in his faith as a part of his justifying righteousness before God, thereby proves that he has no faith in Jesus Christ. He comes as with a lie in his right hand; for such is the absurdity, that he trusts in the act of faith, not in its object,—*i.e.*, he believes in his faith, not in Jesus Christ. Having taken Christ, as he pretends, he would have that very act whereby he received Him sustained at the Divine tribunal as his righteousness. Thus Christ is bid to stand at a distance, and the sinner's own act is by himself bid to come near in the case of justification. This is nothing else but works under another name. It is not faith, for that necessarily establishes grace.'

Ver. 7.—Saying, Blessed are they whose iniquities are forgiven, and whose sins are covered.

This verse, in connection with the preceding, shows that sins are not forgiven, except in a way in which righteousness is imputed. Anciently, the high priest was appointed to bless the people, Num. vi. 24, as the type of Jesus Christ, who, as the Great High Priest, imparts a real blessedness. 'Blessed be the God and Father of our Lord Jesus Christ, who hath blessed us with all spiritual blessings in heavenly places in Christ.' In Him it was promised that all nations should be blessed. When about to ascend into heaven, He lifted up His hands and blessed His disciples; and at the last day He will, from the throne of His glory, pronounce all His people the *blessed* of His Father. On that day, and not till then, shall any of them be able fully to comprehend all that is implied in this term in the verse before us.

Blessed are they.—'Blessed is he' (the man), says David, 'whose transgression is forgiven.' David speaks of one person, but Paul speaks of many. This alteration which the Apostle makes should not be overlooked. The work of redemption being now finished, the Apostle is commissioned by the Holy Ghost, who dictated the words, thus to include for their encouragement the whole mystical body of Christ,—all that are His, whether Jews or Gentiles. *Covered.*—This appears to be in allusion to the mercy-seat, which covered the law: Sins must be covered before they can be forgiven. There must be a way in which this is done according to justice. This way is by the blood of Christ; and he that is dead with Him is justified from sin, Rom. vi. 7. His sins are for ever covered, as being cast into the depths of the sea, Micah vii. 19. They are blotted out with the Saviour's blood. 'I, even I, am He that blotteth out thy transgressions for Mine own sake, and will not remember thy sins,' Isa. xliii. 25. He is saved from the guilt of sin immediately on his believing. The righteousness of the Saviour being imputed to the sinner, none of his own unrighteousness can attach to him; the imputation of both cannot take place. There is a full remission of his past sins, and none which he shall afterwards commit shall be judicially laid to his charge, Rom. viii. 33. Being stripped of the filthy garments, and clothed with a change of raiment, Zech. iii. 4, as certain as God is unchangeable, it shall never be taken off him. 'He hath clothed me with the garments of salvation; He hath covered me with the robe of righteousness,' Isa. lxi. 10. 'I will forgive their iniquity, and I will remember their sin no more,' Jer. xxxi. 34. 'As far as the east is from the west, so far hath He removed our transgressions from us, Ps. ciii. 12. 'Wearied at length,' says Luther, 'with your own righteousness, rejoice and confide in the righteousness of Christ. Learn, my dear brother, to know Christ, and Christ crucified, and learn to despair of thyself, and to sing to the Lord this song:—Lord Jesus! Thou art my righteousness, but I am Thy sin. Thou hast taken what belonged to me; Thou hast given me what was Thine. Thou becamest what Thou wert not, in order that I might become what I was not myself.'

Ver. 8.—*Blessed is the man to whom the Lord will not impute sin.*

Righteousness is imputed when sin is not imputed, for we here see that the man to whom sin is not imputed is *blessed.* As Jesus was *accursed*, Gal. iii. 13, when the sins of His people were imputed to Him, so they are *blessed* when His righteousness is imputed to them. Justification, or the judgment of God by which He renders us 'blessed,' consists of two acts, by one of which He pardons our sins, by the other He gives us the kingdom. This appears in the sequel of this chapter, where we see that the justification of Abraham includes the promise of making him heir of the world, ver. 13; and this truth the Apostle establishes not only in the person of Abraham, but also extends it to all the people of God, ver. 16. In the eighth chapter of this Epistle, where Paul joins together the Divine calling and justification, he also connects justification and glorification. Afterwards he adds, 'What shall we then say to these things? If God be for us, who can be against us? He that spared not His own Son, but delivered Him up for us all, how shall He not with

Him also freely give us all things?' The expression, *God is for us,* marks the effect of justification. It is not said, God is not against us, as should be said if justification was only the pardon of sin; but God is for us,—which signifies that He not only pardons but blesses us, giving us a right to the kingdom. He not only delivers us from being children of wrath, but adopts us into His family, and makes us His own children. When He discharges us from the pains of the second death, He destines us to the glory of heaven. The words that follow, respecting the delivering up of His Son, and freely giving us all things, clearly import these two great acts of pardon and blessing. The same is also declared by the Prophet Malachi, iii. 17, 'And they shall be Mine, saith the Lord of Hosts, in that day when I make up My jewels; and I will spare them, as a man spareth his own son.' Justification, then, corresponds to the righteousness of God, by the imputation of which it is received. By that righteousness the penalty of the law is fulfilled, which secures the pardon of sin, and also the precept on account of which the inheritance is awarded.

Ver. 9.—*Cometh this blessedness then upon the circumcision only, or upon the uncircumcision also? for we say that faith was reckoned to Abraham for righteousness.*

The Apostle having fully established the truth, that a man is justified by faith without works, now reverts to the allusion made to circumcision at the beginning of this chapter, in demanding what Abraham had obtained as pertaining to the flesh. He now shows, in the most decisive manner, that Abraham had not obtained justification by means of circumcision, since he was justified before he was circumcised. And, proceeding to prove what he had affirmed, ch. iii. 30, that justification is not confined to the Jews, he asks if the blessedness he had spoken of comes only to those who are circumcised, or to the uncircumcised also. It was the more necessary to decide this question, because the Jews not only believed that justification depended, at least in part, on their works, but that the privileges of the people of God were inseparably connected with circumcision. In the sequel Paul shows that justification has no necessary connection with, or dependence on, circumcision. *For we say.* —This is not the language of an objector, as Mr. Stuart supposes; it is the position which the Apostle lays down for the purpose of establishing his conclusion. The fact that faith was counted to Abraham unto righteousness, is the groundwork on which he builds.

Ver. 10.—*How was it then reckoned? when he was in circumcision, or in uncircumcision? Not in circumcision, but in uncircumcision.*

How was it? or in what circumstances was righteousness counted to him?—This question, with the affirmation which follows, determines that Abraham's justification by faith was previous to circumcision, and therefore circumcision could not be its cause. If righteousness was imputed to him before he was circumcised, then circumcision is not necessary to justification. It may come on Gentiles as well as on Jews. This is founded on the history of Abraham, recorded in the Old Testament, who **was** in a state of justification before Ishmael's birth, many years antecedent to the appointment of circumcision.

Ver. 11.—*And he received the sign of circumcision, a seal of the righteousness of the faith which he had yet being uncircumcised : that he might be the father of all them that believe, though they be not circumcised ; that righteousness might be imputed unto them also.*[1]

If, then, Abraham was justified in uncircumcision, for what purpose, it might be asked, was he circumcised? It is replied, that he received circumcision, which was appointed as a figure or sign of his paternity, literally with respect to a numerous seed, and spiritually of all believers. It intimated that He in whom all the families of the earth should be blessed, was to spring from Abraham. This blessedness is described by David as consisting in the imputation of righteousness without works. But this was not all: circumcision was not only a sign, but a seal of that righteousness which was imputed to Abraham through faith while he was uncircumcised. This does not mean, as is generally understood, that it was a seal of Abraham's faith. This is not said. It is said that it was a seal of the 'righteousness' of the faith which he had; that is, a seal of that righteousness itself, namely, the righteousness of God, which he had received by his faith. It was a seal, assurance, or pledge that the *righteousness*, by the imputation of which, through his faith, he was justified, *although not then in existence, should in its appointed period be brought in.* Circumcision, then, being such a seal or pledge, and as the appointment of Abraham as the father of Christ, by whom this righteousness was to be introduced, included his being the father of the line from which Christ was to spring, it was to be affixed to his posterity, and not to cease to be so till the thing signified was accomplished. Here, it would appear, we learn the reason why this seal was to be affixed on the *eighth* day after birth. On the eighth day, the first day of the week, when Jesus, the seed of Abraham, arose from the dead, that righteousness, of which circumcision was a seal or pledge, was accomplished. In reference to this, and to the change respecting the Sabbath from the seventh to the *eighth* day, in consequence of His resurrection, when our Lord brought in the everlasting righteousness, and entered into His rest, the eighth day is in many ways distinguished throughout the Old Testament. *That he might be the father,* etc.—In order to his being the *father.* This, mark, then, was a sign of Abraham's being the father of all believers, both Jews and Gentiles, to all of whom this righteousness was to be imputed. As it was a seal of the righteousness which he had received by the faith which he had in a state of uncircumcision, it implied that righteousness would be imputed to believers in the same state.

Ver. 12.—*And the father of circumcision to them who are not of the circumcision only, but who also walk in the steps of that faith of our father Abraham, which he had, being yet uncircumcised.*

This implies that there is a sense in which Abraham is a father of some of his descendants, in which he is not a father to others. To those

---

[1] Some read the first part of this verse ending with the words 'yet being uncircumcised,' as a parenthesis, connecting the remaining part of it with the verse preceding. For this there is no occasion.

of them who walk in the steps of his faith, he is a spiritual father. While all Abraham's children were circumcised, he was not equally the father of them all. It was only to such of them as had his faith that he was a father in what is spiritually represented by circumcision. As it is said, ' They are not all Israel which are of Israel; neither, because they are the seed of Abraham, are they all children; but in Isaac shall thy seed be called; that is, they which are the children of the flesh, these are not the children of God: but the children of the promise are counted for the seed,' Rom. ix. 6. This is also established by our Lord Himself, who denied that the unbelieving Jews were the children of Abraham, John viii. 39. He was, however, not only the father of his believing children, who were circumcised, but of all, in every nation, who walk in the steps of his faith. Believing Gentiles are therefore said to be grafted, contrary to nature, into a good olive-tree, Rom. xi. 24; and to be Abraham's seed, Gal. iii. 29.

Ver. 13.—*For the promise, that he should be the heir of the world, was not to Abraham, or to his seed, through law, but through the righteousness of faith.*

Paul here continues to prove that the blessing of justification is received through faith, and not in any other way. *Heir of the world.*—The promise to Abraham included three things,—1. That the promised seed of the woman should descend from him; 2. That all nations should be blessed in that seed; 3. That, as a pledge of all this, he and his seed should inherit the land of Canaan. ' And I will give unto thee, and to thy seed after thee, the land wherein thou art a stranger, all the land of Canaan, for an everlasting possession.' Canaan, however, was but an emblem of the heavenly country, of which last only Abraham could have an everlasting possession; for he was a stranger on the earth, and Canaan was to him ' a strange country,' Heb. xi. 9. This he understood it to be, and accordingly to the former he looked forward as what was substantially promised, Heb. xi. 13, 16. This was ' that world,' as it is designated by our Lord, Luke xx. 35,—a possession so often called an inheritance, Heb. ix. 15; 1 Pet. i. 4, of which not only Abraham, but also his spiritual posterity, were constituted heirs. They were to inherit all things, Rev. xxi. 7; and although the whole creation groaneth and travaileth in pain, yet all things are theirs, 1 Cor. iii. 21–23. Abraham, however, being the father or first heir according to that promise, he might properly, by way of distinction, be called ' the heir,' and on the same ground, the father of many nations, being the father of all God's people; as is likewise promised in the covenant, which is so often referred to in this chapter.

The expression ' heir ' has a manifest relation to the title of children, which is given to the people of God in their adoption. It is on this account that Paul joins them together,—' If children, then heirs, heirs of God, and joint heirs with Christ,' Rom. viii. 17; by which he teaches that they have not only a right to the good things that God confers, but that they have right in virtue of their adoption, and not of their works. The birthright of a child, which gives him a right to the good things of his father, and distinguishes him from those who may gain them by their

services, resembles the privilege conferred by the free and gratuitous
adoption of God of His children. In conferring the right in this way,
every pretension to merit is excluded; and as God, in the law, had
rendered inheritances inalienable, such also is the inviolable stability of
the inheritance which God confers. The grandeur of this inheritance is
represented in Scripture by the appellations of a *kingdom*, Luke xii. 32;
of a *crown*, 2 Tim. iv. 8; and of a *throne*, Rev. iii. 21.

Or to his seed.—The covenant, in all its promises, and in its fullest
extent, in reference to spiritual blessings, was established in Christ, who
was emphatically and eminently Abraham's seed, Gal. iii. 16; and in Him,
with all His members, who are the spiritual seed of Abraham, of whom
the natural seed were typical, as the land of Canaan was typical of the
heavenly inheritance. The promise to the *seed* was, that all nations
should be blessed in Him, and this promise was made to Abraham also,
as it implied that the Messiah was to be Abraham's seed. The promise
to Christ included all the children that God had given Him, who are in
Him, and one with Him. These are all 'joint heirs with Jesus Christ,'
Rom. viii. 17.

Many are spoken of before Abraham as the children of God; but we
do not read that the first promise respecting the seed, Gen. iii. 15, was
repeated to any of them. Though, in the time of Enos, men began to
call themselves by the name of the Lord; though Enoch walked with
God; though Noah was an heir of the righteousness which is by faith;
though Jehovah was the God of Shem—it is not said that the promise of
the seed was renewed to them. But to Abraham it was expressly renewed; and hence we see the reason why he is so frequently alluded to in
the New Testament, and spoken of as the father of believers.

Through the law.—Literally *through law*, without the article. The
Apostle had shown above that the blessing of righteousness came upon
Abraham before he was circumcised, and here he shows that the promise
that he should be the heir of the world was not made to him on account
of any works of law, but through the righteousness received by faith.
In this way Paul follows out his argument in proof that justification and
the blessings connected with it were not the consequence either of circumcision or of personal obedience, but were received through faith.

But through the righteousness of faith.—The righteousness of faith is an
elliptical expression, meaning the righteousness which is received by
faith. This is the only way in which the promise, in order to prove
effectual, could be given. 'If there had been a law given which could
have given life, verily righteousnes should have been by the law; but
the Scripture hath concluded all under sin, that the promise by faith
of Jesus Christ might be given to them that believe.' It was therefore
to receive its accomplishment only by virtue of, and through the
communication of, the righteousness received by faith. This is that
righteousness which was counted or imputed to Abraham, when, upon
the promise being made to him of a numerous seed, he believed in the
Lord, Gen. xv. 6. The inheritance comes solely in virtue of this
righteousness to those who by it are '*made righteous*.' 'They shall be
called *trees of righteousness*, the planting of the Lord, that He may be

glorified,' Isa. lxi. 3. 'Thy people *shall be all righteous,* they shall *inherit* the land for ever,' Isa. lx. 21.

Ver. 14, 15.—*For if they which are of law be heirs, faith is made void, and the promise made of none effect: for the law worketh wrath: for where no law is, there is no transgression.*

When it is said, 'If they which are of law,' that is, who by obeying the law of God be heirs, the case is supposed, as in ch. ii. 13, 26, 27, though not admitted, which would be contrary to the whole train of the Apostle's argument. If, however, possession of the inheritance come by obedience to law, then the obtaining it by faith is set aside, and consequently, as by works of law no man can be justified, the promise is made of none effect. This is entirely consistent with all the Apostle had said before respecting the manner in which the blessedness of Abraham had come upon him, solely by the imputation of righteousness received by faith, irrespective of any works of his. *For the law worketh wrath.*—It is indeed the nature of every law to afford opportunity of transgression. But this does not make it work wrath. It is law which is transgressed that works wrath. The Apostle had shown that by obedience to law no man can be justified, since all men are transgressors, and that the wrath of God is revealed against all unrighteousness ; and this is what here he again declares. Such is the state of human nature, that the law of God, which all men transgress, so far from justifying them, can only work wrath, or punishment ; for no law makes provision for the exercise of mercy, but requires perfect obedience to all its commands, and when this is not yielded, denounces wrath on every transgressor. *For where no law is, there is no trangression.*—This is the reason why the law works wrath. It gives occasion to transgress, and transgression brings wrath. And this, the Apostle asserts, is the nature of law in general. Where there is law, there is occasion or room for transgression. Where there is no law, there can be no breach of law. If a man could be placed in a situation without law, he would not be exposed to wrath as guilty ; for as sin is the transgression of the law, so no transgression could be charged on him. This assertion, then, is equivalent to affirming that, considering the character of man, where law is there must be transgression, and only where there is no law there is no transgression, as it is said, ch. v. 13, 'Sin is not imputed where there is no law.' From all this it follows, that if the fulfilment of the promise was dependent on man's obedience to the law, the obtaining of the inheritance by faith would be made void, and so the promise would become of no effect ; thus the possibility of obtaining the inheritance would be destroyed altogether.

Ver. 16.—*Therefore it is of faith, that it might be by grace; to the end the promise might be sure to all the seed, not to that only which is of the law, but to that also which is of the faith of Abraham, who is the father of us all,*

Having affirmed, in the end of the 13th verse, that the promise of the inheritance was not through obedience to law, but through the righteousness received by faith, and having in the 14th and 15th verses shown that it could not be obtained through obedience to law, Paul here proceeds to state why faith was appointed to be the way through which it should be carried into effect.

Therefore it is of faith, that it might be by grace.—Since, then, the promise of the inheritance, that is, of eternal salvation, could not be fulfilled through obedience to law, it was appointed that it should be fulfilled through faith, because in this way it is effected by grace. A reward must be reckoned either of grace, or of debt, on account of works performed; and these cannot be combined. For 'if by grace, then it is no more of works; otherwise grace is no more grace; but if it be of works, then is it no more grace; otherwise work is no more work,' Rom. xi. 6. As the reward, then, could not be bestowed through the works of the law, of which every man is a transgressor, and which, therefore, could only work wrath to him, it must be conferred by grace through faith, which can in nowise be considered as meritorious, but is the gift of God, and simply receives His righteousness, opposed through the whole of this discussion to the works of man of every description. In this way, then, the promise is bestowed by grace. This accords with the whole plan of salvation, that regards man as a sinner, and according to which, as had been shown, ch. iii. 27, boasting is excluded, and he is saved, not of works, but by grace through faith, Eph. ii. 8. In no other way, then, but through faith, could salvation have been by grace. Had it been bestowed in part or in whole as the reward of one good thought, it would not have been by grace. Paul had before declared that they who have obtained the righteousness of God by faith are justified *freely by His grace;* and now he affirms that salvation is through faith, for this very purpose, that it might be by grace.

To the end that the promise might be sure to all the seed.—The fulfilment of the promise to Abraham and to his seed not being grounded on obedience to law, which, in the case of every man, would have made it void, and as its fulfilment was determined by God, He has rested its accomplishment wholly on grace—His own gratuitous favour, which cannot be frustrated. Grace selects its objects, and its only motive is in God Himself. The way, then, in which the promise was to be accomplished, depending on the sovereign will of God, who hath said, 'My counsel shall stand, and I will do all My pleasure,' Isa. xlvi. 10, and whose gifts and calling are without repentance, was rendered secure, and the promise could not be made void by the unworthiness or mutability of man.

Not to that only which is of the law, but to that also which is of the faith of Abraham.—The promise, then, was made sure by the grace of God, through faith, to all Abraham's spiritual seed, not only to such as were 'of the law,' namely, his natural offspring under the legal dispensation, denominated in verses 9 and 12 the circumcision, but also to all of every nation who, though uncircumcised, possess his faith. To himself and to all of them it is accomplished through the righteousness of faith. Here it is worthy of observation, that none are supposed to be Abraham's spiritual seed, or heirs as his seed, except believers, whether they be his descendants or Gentiles. *Who is the father of us all.*—That is, the spiritual father both of Jewish and Gentile believers. He is equally in this sense the father of all believers. It is only by faith that he is the spiritual father of any.

Ver. 17.—(*As it is written, I have made thee a father of many nations,*) *before Him whom he believed, even God, who quickeneth the dead, and calleth those things which be not as though they were.*

As it is written, I have made thee a father of many nations.—According to the Apostle's interpretation of this promise, it imports a numerous spiritual offspring, as well as a numerous natural posterity. It is not by way of what is called accommodation that this is said; it is the real interpretation of the promise, whether Abraham himself understood it so or not. This interpretation of the Apostle is a key to all that is said on this subject. It shows that Abraham had a double seed, that the promise had a double meaning, and both are distinctly verified. Thus, each of the three promises made to Abraham had a double fulfilment :—Of a numerous posterity; of God being a God to his seed; and of the earthly and heavenly country. *Before Him.*—At that moment, when he stood in the presence of God whom he believed, Gen. xvii. 4, he was made the father of all his natural and spiritual posterity ; and though he was not then actually a father, yet, being so in the purpose of God, it was made as sure to him as if it had already taken place. God now willed it, and the result would follow as surely as creation followed His word. *Quickeneth the dead.*—Does this refer to the literal general fact of bringing the dead to life, or to Abraham's body now dead, and Sarah's incapacity of having children at her advanced age, or to the raising of Isaac had he been sacrificed ? The first appears to be the meaning, and includes the others ; and the belief of it is the ground on which the others rest. Faith in God's power, as raising the dead, is a proper ground of believing any other work of power which God engages to perform, or which is necessary to be performed, in order to fulfil His word. If God raises the dead, why should Abraham look with distrust on his own body, or consider Sarah's natural incapacity to bear children? Why should he doubt that God will fulfil His promise as to his numerous seed by Isaac, even though Isaac shall be slain ? God could raise him from the dead. *Calleth those things' which be not as though they were.*— This does not say that God calls into existence the things that exist not, as He calls into existence the things that are. But God speaks of the things that exist not, in the same way as He speaks of the things that exist ; that is, He speaks of them as existing, though they do not then actually exist. And this is the way He spoke of Abraham as the father of many nations. *I have made thee.*—God calls him now a father, though he was not actually a father of many nations, because, before God, or in God's counsel, he was such a father.

Ver. 18.—*Who against hope believed in hope,*[1] *that he might become the father of many nations, according to that which was spoken, So shall thy seed be.*

Against hope, or beyond hope.—The thing was utterly beyond all that could be expected according to natural principles. *In hope,* or upon hope ; that is, he believed the thing that was an object of hope. He

---

[1] Some place the point after believed. Who against hope believed, in hope that he might become, etc. That is, he believed the thing that was an object of hope. He believed the promise, and hoped for its accomplishment.

believed the promise.   Belief respects anything that is testified, whether desirable or otherwise.   But the thing testified to Abraham was an object of hope, therefore he is said beyond hope to believe in hope. *That he might become.*—This is explained by some as importing that Abraham believed that he should become, etc. ; that is, his becoming *the father of many nations* was the object of his belief.   Others explain it, that he believed the promise in order that he might become ; that is, his faith was the means through which the promise was to be made good to him. Both of these are true, but the last appears to be most agreeable to the expression, and is the more important sense.   He was made such a father through faith.   Had he not believed the promise, he would not have been made such a father.   *According to that which was spoken.*—This shows that Abraham's expectation rested solely on the Divine promise.   He had no ground to hope for so numerous a posterity, or any posterity at all, except on the warrant of the promise of God.   This he received in its true and obvious meaning, and did not, like many, explain away, modify, or fritter it down into something less wonderful.   He hoped for the very thing which the words of the promise intimated, and to the very utmost extent of the meaning of these words, *So shall thy seed be.*

Ver. 19.—*And being not weak in faith, he considered not his own body now dead, when he was about an hundred years old, neither yet the deadness of Sarah's womb.*

Not weak in faith.—This is a usual way of expressing the opposite, implying that his faith was peculiarly strong.   Faith is the substance of things hoped for, inasmuch as we believe that we shall in due time be put in possession of them.   It is the evidence of things not seen, as thereby we are persuaded of the truth of all the unseen things declared in Scripture.   Faith thus makes future things present, and unseen things evident.   *He considered not his own body.*—This is an example which ought ever to direct our faith.   There are always obstacles and difficulties in the way of faith.   We should give them no more weight than if they did not exist, reflecting that it is God who has to remove them. Nothing can be a difficulty in the way of the fulfilment of God's own word.   This ought to encourage us, not only with respect to ourselves, but with respect to the cause of God in the world.   The government rests on the shoulders of Emmanuel.   *His own body now dead*, etc.—Had Abraham looked on any natural means, he would have staggered ; but he looked only to the power of Him who promised.

Ver. 20.—*He staggered not at the promise of God through unbelief ; but was strong in faith, giving glory to God.*

He staggered not.—This well expresses the meaning, the word signifying to doubt or hesitate.   Dr. Macknight's translation is bad,—'He did not dispute.'   He might have hesitated or doubted, though he did not dispute.   *At the promise*, or with respect to the promise, Abraham was not staggered by the difficulties or seeming impossibilities that stood in the way, but believed the promise of God, and trusted that it would be fulfilled.   He would not listen to the suggestions of carnal reasonings ; they were all set aside ; he rested entirely on the fidelity of the promise.   And all are bound to imitate this ; for the Apostle says that the history of

Abraham's faith stands on record in Scripture, not for his sake only, but for us also, that we, after his example, may be encouraged to believe in Him that raised up Jesus our Lord from the dead.

But was strong in faith.—In the foregoing verse, Abraham is said not to have been weak in faith; here it is affirmed that he was strong in faith. This imports that there are degrees in faith,—a doctrine which some deny, but a doctrine which Scripture, in many places, most clearly establishes. Our Lord charges His disciples in general, and at another time Peter particularly, Matt. vi. 30, xiv. 31, as having little faith : they had faith ; but, unlike to Abraham's, it was deficient in strength. Our Lord, too, speaks of the comparatively strong faith of the centurion, Matt. viii. 10. He had not found so great faith in Israel. The Apostles, also, addressing Jesus, pray, 'Lord, increase our faith,' Luke xvii. 5. In the same manner, the Apostle Paul speaks of the 'measure of faith,' Rom. xii. 3, importing that believers were endowed with different degrees of this gift. With such a profusion of instruction as the Scriptures afford on this point, it is strange that the love of theory should induce any to assert that faith is equal in all Christians. *Giving glory to God.*—How did he give glory to God? By believing that He would do what He promised, although nothing less than almighty power could effect what was promised. This is an important thought, that we glorify God by ascribing to Him His attributes, and believing that He will act according to them, notwithstanding many present appearances to the contrary. But how often is the opposite of this exemplified among many who profess to have the faith of Abraham, who, when unable to trace Divine wisdom, are apt to hesitate in yielding submission to Divine authority. Nothing, however, to countenance this is found in Scripture. On the contrary, no human action is more applauded than that of Abraham offering up Isaac in obedience to the command of God, in which he certainly could not then discover either the reason or the wisdom from which it proceeded. Without disregarding it for a moment, he yielded to the Divine authority. He was strong in faith, giving glory to God ; that is, he gave full credit for the propriety of what was enjoined, and a ready acknowledgment of that implicit submission which on his part was due.

Vers. 21, 22.—*And being fully persuaded that what He had promised He was able also to perform. And therefore it was imputed to him for righteousness.*

Fully persuaded, or fully assured, being strongly convinced.—This is the explanation of the way in which he gave glory to God. We might suppose that every one who professes to believe in the attributes of God, would judge as Abraham did ; yet experience shows the contrary. Even Christians do not act up to their principles on this point. The Israelites believed in God's power and favour to them ; but in time of trial they failed in giving Him glory by confiding in Him. In like manner, Christians, in their own individual cases, do not generally manifest that confidence in God which their principles would lead to expect. *Also,* that is, He was as able to perform as to promise. *And therefore.*— Because he believed God, notwithstanding all contrary appearances, his faith was imputed to him unto righteousness.

Ver. 23.—*Now it was not written for his sake alone, that it was imputed to him.*

This history of the way in which Abraham received righteousness is not recorded for his sake alone, or applicable to himself only, but is equally applicable to all believers. The Apostle here guards us against supposing that this method of justification was peculiar to Abraham, and teaches that it is the pattern of the justification of all who shall ever find acceptance with God. The first recorded testimony respecting the justification of any sinner, as has been already observed, is that of Abraham. Others had been justified from the fall down to his time; but it was reserved for him to possess the high privilege and distinction of being thus the first man singled out and constituted the progenitor of the Messiah. In him all the nations of the earth were to be blessed, and consequently he was to be the father of all believers, who are all the children of Christ, Heb. ii. 13, and the heir of that inheritance on earth that typified the inheritance in heaven, which belongs to Jesus Christ, who is 'appointed heir of all things,' with whom all believers are joint heirs. And in Abraham we see that, in the first declaration of the nature of justification, it is held out as being conferred by the imputation of righteousness through faith only. This passage, then, which refers to what is *written*, as well as those preceding it in this chapter, it must again be remarked, exhibit the character of the historical parts of Scripture as all divinely inspired, and all divinely arranged, in the wisdom of God, to apply to events the most important in the future dispensation. Every fact and every circumstance which they announce, as well as the whole narrative, was ordered and dictated by Him, to whom all His works are known from the beginning of the world, Acts xv. 18.

Ver. 24.—*But for us also, to whom it shall be imputed, if we believe on Him that raised up Jesus our Lord from the dead.*

Righteousness shall be imputed to us, as well as to Abraham, if we have his faith. *If we believe on Him that raised,* etc.—Here God is characterized by the fact that He raised up Christ. This, then, is not a mere circumstance, but it is in this very character that our faith must view God. To believe for salvation, we must believe not in God absolutely, but in God as the raiser up of Jesus Christ. This faith in God, as raising up our Lord, must also include a right view of Him. It must imply a belief of the Gospel, not only as to the fact of a resurrection, but also as to the person and work of Christ.

Ver. 25.— *Who was delivered for our offences, and was raised again for our justification.*

Delivered.—The Father gave over the Son to death, delivering Him into the hands of wicked men. Here we must look to a higher tribunal than that of Pilate, who delivered Him into the hands of the Jews. He was delivered by the determinate counsel and foreknowledge of God. When Herod, Pilate, and the Gentiles, with the people of Israel, were gathered together against Him, it was to do whatsoever God's word and counsel had determined before to be done, Acts iv. 28. The crucifixion of Christ being the greatest of all crimes, was hateful and highly provoking in the sight of God; yet it was the will of God that it should take place, in order to bring to pass the greatest good. God decreed this event; He willed that it should come to pass, and ordered circumstances, in His providence, in such a way as gave men an opportunity to carry into effect their wicked intentions. In their sin God had no part; and His determination that the deed should be done, formed no excuse for its perpetrators, nor did it in any degree extenuate their wickedness, which the Scriptures charge upon them in the fullest manner. 'Him, being delivered by the determinate counsel and foreknowledge of God, ye have taken, and by wicked hands have crucified and slain,' Acts ii. 23. This was an example of the same truth declared by Joseph to his brethren, 'As for you, ye thought evil against me; but God meant it unto good,' Gen. l. 20. *For our offences*, or on account of our offences. —This shows the need of Christ's death. It was not for an example, or for a witness merely, but for our offences. *Raised again for our justification.*—That is, He was raised that He might enter the holy place not made with hands, and present His own blood, that we might be made righteous through His death for us. As the death of Christ, according to the determinate counsel of a holy and righteous God, was a demonstration of the guilt of His people, so His resurrection was their acquittal from every charge.

It is of importance to distinguish the persons to whom the Apostle refers in this and the following verses, where he says, if *we* believe, and speaks of righteousness being imputed to *us*, and of *our* offences, and *our* justification. In the beginning of the chapter he uses the expression, 'Abraham *our* father;' but there he is introducing an objection that might be offered by the Jews, and appears to speak of Abraham as his own and their progenitor. But when, in the 12th verse, he says, ' *Our* father Abraham,' and, in the 16th, 'the father of *us* all,' he applies these expressions not to the Jews, or the natural descendants of Abraham, but to himself and those to whom he is writing, that is, to believers, to all of whom, whether Jews or Gentiles, in every age, as walking in the same steps of Abraham's faith, they are applicable. And of the same persons he here speaks in the 24th and 25th verses, for whose offences Jesus was delivered, and for whose justification He was raised again. They are those whom the Father had given Him, John vi. 37, xvii. 2; Heb. ii. 13; for the effect of His death was not to depend on the contingent will of man, but was fixed by the eternal purpose of God. They are those of whom it was promised to the Redeemer, that when He should make Himself an offering for sin, He should see of the travail of His soul and be satisfied,—those who are or shall be saved, and called with an holy calling, not according to their works, but according to God's purpose and grace which was given them in Christ Jesus before the world began, 2 Tim. i. 9,—those who have the faith of God's elect, who are brought by Him to the acknowledgment of the truth which is after godliness, who have the hope of eternal life, which God, that cannot lie, promised from eternity to their Head and Surety, Tit. i. 1, 2. No one, then, is entitled to consider himself among the number of those to whom the Apostle's words are here applicable, unless he has obtained precious faith in the righteousness of our God and Saviour Jesus Christ. Yet the expression, *our Saviour*, is often used by persons who reject God's testimony concerning Him, and consequently have neither part nor lot in His salvation.

Having substituted Himself in the place of sinners, Jesus Christ suffered in His own person the punishment of sin, conformably to that declaration, ' In the day that thou eatest thereof thou shalt surely die.' He came forth from among the dead, in testimony that the threatening of God was accomplished, and as a pledge of the acceptance of His sacrifice, and that by His obedience unto death Divine justice was satisfied, the law honoured and magnified, and eternal life awarded to those for whom He died, whose sins He had borne in His own body on the tree, 1 Pet. ii. 24. He was quickened by the Spirit, 1 Pet. iii. 18; by whom He was also justified, 1 Tim. iii. 16, from every charge that could be alleged against Him as the Surety and Covenant-head of those whose iniquities He bore. The justification, therefore, of His people, which includes not only the pardon of their sins, but also their title to the eternal inheritance, was begun in His death, and perfected by His resurrection. He wrought their justification by His death, but its efficacy depended on His resurrection. By His death He paid their debt; in His resurrection He received their acquittance. He arose to assure to them their right to eternal life, by fully discovering and establishing it in His own person, for all who are the members of His body.

CHAPTER 5
ROMANS 5:1 – 21

THE Apostle describes in this chapter the blessed accompaniments, the security, and the foundation of justification. This last branch of the subject is interwoven with an account of the entrance of sin and death into the world; while a parallel is drawn between the first and the second Adam in their opposite tendencies and influences. By the first came sin, condemnation, and death; by the second, righteousness, justification, and life. From this comparison, occasion is taken to show why God had made the promulgation of the written law to intervene betwixt the author of condemnation and the author of justification. On the one hand, the extent, the evil, and the demerit of sin, and the obstructions raised up by law and justice to man's recovery, were thus made fully manifest; while, on the other hand, the superabundant riches of Divine grace, in its complete ascendancy and victory over them in the way of righteousness, were displayed to the greatest advantage, and with the fullest effect.

Ver. 1.—*Therefore, being justified by faith, we have peace with God, through our Lord Jesus Christ.*

Therefore.—This particle of inference draws its conclusion from the whole foregoing discussion concerning justification by faith, though it may have a more immediate reference to the nearest preceding context. The Apostle having fully proved that salvation is by grace, and that it is by faith, now shows the consequences of this doctrine.

Justified by faith.—This expression is elliptical; faith must be understood as inclusive of its object. This is very usual in all cases where the thing elliptically expressed is frequently spoken of, and therefore sufficiently explained by the elliptical expression. It is not by faith, abstractly considered, that we are justified, nor even by faith in everything that God reveals. It is by faith in the Lord Jesus Christ. Even this phrase itself, namely, faith in the Lord Jesus Christ, is still elliptical, and supposes the knowledge of what is to be believed with respect to Christ. It is not believing in His existence, but believing on Him as revealed in the Scriptures, in His person and work. In the same manner as we have the phrase, 'justified by faith,' we have the phrase, justified by the blood of Christ. As, in the former case, faith implies its object, so, in the latter, it is implied that we are justified by faith in the blood of Christ. The blood of Christ justifies by being the object of belief and of trust.

We have peace with God.—This shows that all men, till they are justified, are at war with God, and that He is at war with them. But when they are justified by faith, the wrath of God, which *abideth* on those who believe not on His Son, John iii. 36, is turned away, and they cease to be enemies to God. Thus peace, succeeding hostility, brings with it every blessing; for there is no middle place for the creature between the love and the wrath of God. This peace, then, arises from righteousness, —the imputation of the righteousness of God by which the believer is justified,—and is followed by a sense of peace obtained. While guilt remains in the conscience, enmity will also rankle in the heart; for so long as men look upon their sins as unpardoned, and on God as the avenger of their transgressions, they must regard Him as being to them a consuming fire. But when they view God in Christ reconciling them to Himself, not imputing their iniquities to them, peace, according to the measure of faith, is established in the conscience. This never can be experienced by going about to establish our own righteousness. If any man have peace in his conscience, it must flow from Christ's righteousness—it must be the effect of that righteousness which God has 'created,' Isa. xlv. 8; and of which the Spirit, when He comes, brings with Him the conviction, John xvi. 8. Resting on this righteousness, the believer beholds God at peace with him, perfectly reconciled. The belief of this satisfies his conscience, which, being purged by blood, Heb. ix. 14, he is freed from guilty fears, and reconciled to God. Through this sense of the pardon of sin, and of friendship with God, the peace of God, which passeth all understanding, keeps his heart and mind through Christ Jesus. The maintenance of this peace, by preserving the conscience free from guilt by continual application to the blood of Christ, is the main point in the believer's walk with God. and the powerful spring of His obedience. In the New Testament God is frequently denominated 'the God of peace.' The Apostle prays that the Lord Himself may give His people peace by all means, and enjoins that the peace of God should rule in the hearts of

believers, to which they are also called in one body, and that they should
be thankful.   Peace is the fruit of the Spirit; and the kingdom of God
is righteousness, and peace, and joy in the Holy Ghost.

Through our Lord Jesus Christ.—Peace comes through the death of
Jesus Christ.   The faith, therefore, by which it is obtained, must refer
to Him who made peace through the blood of His cross.   He alone, as
the one Mediator, can make peace between God, who is holy, and man,
who is sinful.   God has established three covenants, or three ways of
communication with man.   The first was the covenant of nature; the
second, the covenant of the law; the third, the covenant of the Gospel.
Under the first covenant, man, being in a state of innocence, needed no
mediator.   Under the second, there was a mediator simply of communication, and not of reconciliation,—a mediator as to the exterior, or a
messenger who goes between two parties, a simple depository of words
spoken on the one side or the other, without having any part in the
interior or essence of the covenant, of which he was neither the founder
nor the bond.   Under the third covenant, Jesus Christ is a true mediator
of reconciliation, who has produced a real peace between God and man,
and is the founder of their mutual communion.   ' He is our peace.'   It
is established by the new covenant in His hands, and is everlasting, being
made through the blood of that everlasting covenant.   ' The Lord is
well pleased for His righteousness' sake,' Isa. xlii. 21.   ' The work of
righteousness shall be *peace,* and the effect of righteousness, quietness and
assurance for ever,' Isa. xxxii. 17.   This peace, then, is through Jesus
Christ and His righteousness, which brings this quietness and assurance.
He is the King of righteousness and Prince of Peace.   In parting from
His disciples before His death, He said, ' These things have I spoken unto
you, that in Me ye might have peace;' and this peace He bequeathed to
them.   ' Peace I leave with you, My peace I give unto you.'   When He
met them again after His resurrection, His first salutation to them was,
' Peace be unto you.'

Ver. 2.—*By whom also we have access by faith into this grace wherein we stand,
and rejoice in hope of the glory of God.*

Believers have *access into grace* as well as peace.—The one is distinguished from the other.   In what, then, do they differ?   Peace denotes
a particular blessing; access into grace, or a state of favour, implies
general blessings, among which peace and all other privileges are included.
And as they are justified by means of faith, and have peace with God
through the Lord Jesus Christ, so likewise it is through Him that they
enter into this state of grace; for it is through Him they have access by
one Spirit unto the Father, by that new and living way which He hath
consecrated for them through the vail; that is to say, His flesh.   They
have access to a mercy-seat, to which they are invited to come freely;
and boldness and access with confidence by the faith of Jesus—boldness
to come to the throne of grace, and enter into the holiest by His blood.
And as it is by Him they enter into this state of grace, so by Him they
stand in it, accepted before God, 1 Pet. v. 12; secured, according to His
everlasting covenant, that they shall not be cast down; but that they are
fixed in this state of perfect acceptance, conferred by sovereign grace,

brought into it by unchangeable love, and kept in it by the power of a faithful God. 'They shall be My people, and I will be their God.' 'I will not turn away from them to do them good; but I will put My fear in their hearts, that they shall not depart from Me,' Jer. xxxii. 38, 40.

And rejoice.—This is an additional blessing. The word here translated rejoice signifies to glory or exult, and is the same that in the following verse is rendered ' to glory.' It may designate not only the excess of joy possessed by the soul in the contemplation of the future inheritance, but the language of triumph expressing this joy, which is properly meant by glorying. The Christian should speak nothing boastingly, so far as concerns himself; but he has no reason to conceal his sense of his high destination as a son of God, and an heir of glory. In this he ought to exult, in this he ought to glory,—and, in obedience to His Lord's command, to rejoice, because his name is written in heaven. The hope of eternal salvation through the grace of our Lord Jesus Christ cannot but produce joy; for as there can be no true joy without such a hope, so it carries with it the very essence of joy. Joy springing from faith is called the joy of faith, Phil. i. 25, and is made a distinguishing characteristic of the Christian, Phil. iii. 3.

' Where Christ is truly seen,' says Luther, *On the Galatians*, p. 85, ' there must needs be full and perfect joy in the Lord, with peace of conscience, which most certainly thus thinketh:—Although I am a sinner, by the law, and under condemnation of the law, yet I despair not, I die not, because Christ liveth, who is both my righteousness and my everlasting life. In that righteousness and life I have no sin, no fear, no sting of conscience, no care of death. I am indeed a sinner, as touching this present life, and the righteousness thereof, as the child of Adam; where the law accuseth me, death reigneth over me, and at length would devour me. But I have another righteousness and life above this life, which is Christ, the Son of God, who knoweth no sin nor death, but righteousness and life eternal; by whom this, my body, being dead, and brought into dust, shall be raised up again, and delivered from the bondage of the law, and sin, and shall be sanctified together with the Spirit.'

In the hope of the glory of God.—This form of expression will equally apply to the glory that God bestows on His people, and to His own glory. The view and enjoyment of God's glory is the hope of believers. It is the glory that shall be revealed in them when they shall be glorified together in Christ—when they shall behold the glory which the Father hath given to the Son, and which the Son gives to them, John xvii. 22–24. Thus faith relies on the truth of what God has promised, and hope expects the enjoyment of it. This hope is full of rejoicing, because everything it looks for depends on the truth and faithfulness of a covenant God. There can be no failure on His part, and consequently on the believer's no disappointment.

Here it should be particularly observed, that before saying one word of the fruits produced by the believer, the Apostle describes him as rejoicing in the hope of the glory of God. He represents him as drawing no motive of consolation but from a view of God in Christ, whom he has received as his Saviour by faith; and this is the true source of his hope and joy. The disciples, after the day of Pentecost, as soon as they heard the word that Peter preached, gladly embraced it, and did eat their meat with gladness and singleness of heart. In the same way, when Christ was preached to them, the eunuch and the jailor rejoiced the moment they believed. This hope is indeed capable of confirmation; but if it has not its origin in Jesus Christ and His sacrifice alone, it is a false hope. As soon as a man believes the Gospel of Christ, he ought to imitate the faith of Abraham, and give glory to God, resting securely on the sure foundation which is the basis of the hope; and he never can acquire a different title to glory, than that of which he is in possession in the moment when he believes, although, as he grows in grace, he perceives it more distinctly. Paul, while he urges the brethren at Colosse to a higher degree of conformity, in many particulars, to the will of God, yet gives thanks to the Father, who had already made them meet for the inheritance of the saints in light, Col. i. 12. This was the state of the thief on the cross, and is so of every converted sinner, in the moment when he is united to Christ; for then he is justified by faith, and has peace with God. Christians are characterized as holding fast the beginning of their confidence, and the rejoicing of their hope, firm unto the end, Heb. iii. 6–15. The beginning of their confidence and hope of salvation rested wholly on the person and righteousness of Jesus Christ, the Surety of the new covenant. It is true that at the commencement of their new life, faith is often weak, and its object seen indistinctly. Love, and joy, and hope, cannot transcend the faith from which they flow. Hence the propriety of that prayer by all the disciples of Jesus, 'Lord, increase our faith;' hence also the necessity of using diligence in the work and labour of love, to the full assurance of hope unto the end, Heb. vi. 11.

Ver. 3.—*And not only so, but we glory in tribulations also; knowing that tribulation worketh patience.*

Not only does the believer rejoice in hope of future glory, but he rejoices even in tribulations. This rejoicing, however, is not in tribulations considered in themselves, but in their effects. It is only the knowledge of the effects of afflictions, and of their being appointed by his heavenly Father, that enables the Christian to rejoice in them. Being in themselves an evil, and not joyous but grievous, they would not otherwise be a matter of rejoicing, but of sorrow. But viewed as proceeding from his heavenly Father's love, Heb. xii. 6; Rev. iii. 19, they are so far from depriving him of his joy, that they tend to increase it. The way to the cross was to his Saviour the way to the crown, and he knows that through much tribulation he must enter into the kingdom of God, Acts xiv. 22. The greatest tribulations are among those things that work together for his good. God comforts him in the midst of his sorrows, 2 Cor. i. 4. Tribulation, even death itself, which is numbered among his privileges, 1 Cor. iii. 22, shall not separate him from the love of God, which is in Christ Jesus our Lord. The Apostle Peter addresses believers as greatly rejoicing in the hope of salvation, though now, if need be, they are in heaviness through manifold trials.

Tribulation worketh or effecteth *patience.*—Christians should be well instructed on this point, and should have it continually in their eye : their happiness is greatly concerned in it. If they forget the end and tendency of afflictions, they will murmur like the Israelites. Patience is a habit of endurance; and Christian patience implies submission to the will of God. Paul says here that affliction worketh patience, and James, i. 3, says that the trying of faith worketh patience. This proves that the afflictions of a Christian are intended as a trial of his faith. What by the one Apostle is called tribulation, is by the other called trial of faith. The effect of affliction is patience, a grace which is so necessary, as we are all naturally impatient and unwilling to submit unreservedly to the dispensations of God. Patience gives occasion to the exercise of the graces of the Spirit, and of submission under afflictions to the will of God.

Ver. 4.—*And patience, experience ; and experience, hope.*

Experience.—The Greek word translated experience signifies trial or proof. Here it means proof; for trial may detect a hypocrite as well as a manifest saint. But proof implies that the trial has proved the genuineness of the tried person, and also of the faithfulness and support of God, which will enable us to overcome every difficulty. And proof worketh *hope.* That is, when the genuineness of our profession is manifested by being proved, our hope of enjoying the glory promised to the genuine people of God is confirmed. Hope is here introduced a second time. This should be carefully noticed. At first, as we have seen, it springs solely from a view of the mediation and work of our Lord Jesus Christ. Here it acquires a new force, from the proof the believer has of the reality of his union with the Saviour, by his being filled with the fruits of righteousness which are by Jesus Christ. Thus the ' good hope through grace ' must be produced solely by faith, and confirmed, not produced, by the fruits of faith.

Ver. 5.—*And hope maketh not ashamed ; because the love of God is shed abroad in our hearts by the Holy Ghost, which is given unto us.*

Hope maketh not ashamed.—This may import, either that hope will not be disappointed, or that hope will not allow us to be ashamed of its object. Various passages speak of the believer as not being put to shame in the day of retribution ; and the expression here is generally interpreted to signify that hope will not be disappointed, but will receive the object of its anticipation. This is an important truth ; yet the Apostle may rather be understood as speaking of the usual effect of hope as exemplified in the life of a Christian ; and that it is not the future effect of hope in believers, but its present effect, as it is the present effect of the other particulars mentioned, to which he refers. Besides, the primary signification of the word in the original is, not to disappoint, but to shame, put to shame, or make ashamed. Paul here evidently speaks of hope as a general principle, which, in every instance, and on all subjects, has this effect ascribed to it. It is its nature, with regard to everything which is its object, to destroy shame, and excite to an open avowal, and even glorying in it, though it may be a thing of which others may be ashamed, and which is ridiculed in the world. The experience of every

Christian confirms this view. When is he inclined to be ashamed of the Gospel? Not when his hopes are high, his faith unwavering, and his impressions of future glory strong. It is when His hopes fade and grow weak. Just in proportion as his hope is strong, will he make an open and a bold profession of the truth. Here, then, by a well-known figure, the assertion before us appears to import that, so far from being ashamed, believers glory and exult. Hope causes Christians, instead of being ashamed of Christ and His word (which without hope they would be), to glory and proclaim their prospects before the world, Gal. vi. 14; 1 Pet. i. 6–8, v. 1; 1 John iii. 2. They glory in the cross of Christ through hope. This shows the great importance of keeping our hope unclouded. If we suffer it to flag or grow faint, we shall be ashamed of it before men, to which, from the enmity of the world against the Gospel, there is much temptation. Accordingly, our blessed Lord, who knew what was in man, has in the most solemn and awful manner warned His disciples against it; and the Apostle Peter enjoins on believers to add to their faith *virtue*—courage to profess it.

Because.—This casual particle may be understood to intimate the reason why hope makes not ashamed, or to give an additional reason why Christians are not ashamed. Agreeably to the latter interpretation, hope is one reason, and then another is subjoined; and certainly the love of God is a strong reason to prevent us from being ashamed of the Gospel. *Love of God.*—This phrase in itself is ambiguous, and, according to the connection or other circumstances, it may be understood, in its different occurrences, to refer either to God's love to us, or to our love to God,—two things which are entirely distinct. God's love to us is in Himself; but the love He pours into our hearts may signify either a sense of His love to us, or, as Augustine explains it, our love to Him. The use of language admits of the first of these meanings, which appears to be the true one; and it is certain that it contributes more to our consolation to have our minds fixed upon God's love to us, than upon our love to God; while our hope does not depend on our love to God, but on our sense of His love to us. The connection, too, leads us to understand the phrase in the sense of God's love to us.[1] It connects with what follows, where the Apostle proceeds to prove God's love to His people from the wonderful manner in which, as is said in the 8th verse, He commendeth His love towards us in the way He has acted in the gift of His Son, notwithstanding our unworthiness and enmity against Him. In the same way it is said, John iii. 16, ' God so loved the world, that He gave His only-begotten Son, that whosoever believeth in Him should not perish, but have everlasting life.' It coincides, too, with such declarations as, ' In this was manifested the love of God towards us, because that God sent His only-begotten Son into the world, that we might live through Him.' ' We have known and believed the love of God to

---

[1] Some prefer explaining this expression, the love of God, as God's love to us rather than our love to God, because, they observe, while our love is variable, and liable to fail, God's love is unchangeable. But as our love to God is produced and maintained in us by the Holy Spirit, and is the effect of God's love to us, it can no more fail than God's love to us.

us,' 1 John iv. 9, 16. We cannot be beforehand with God in love, and we must perceive His love to make us love Him. The first feeling of love springs up in the heart from a view of His grace and mercy to us in Jesus Christ. His love to us is the foundation of our love to God ; and it is a view of His love that not only produces, but maintains and increases, our love to Him. ' Thy love is better than wine.'

Poured out.—This refers to the abundant measure of the sense of the love of God to us, which is communicated to His people, and poured into their hearts, through all the faculties of their souls, moving and captivating their affections. *By the Holy Ghost.*—It is the Holy Ghost who pours out into the heart of the believer a sense of the love of God to him, fully convincing him of it, and witnessing this love to his spirit, Rom. viii. 16. This sense of the love of God never exists in the human heart till communicated by the Holy Ghost. All men naturally hate God, Rom. viii. 7 ; and it is only when they have a view of His love thus given by the promised Comforter, and behold His love in the gift of His Son, that they repent and love God. *Given unto us.*—The gift of the Holy Ghost, in His operation in the heart in His sanctifying influences, was not confined to Apostles and Evangelists, but is enjoyed in common by all the saints, in all of whom the Holy Spirit dwells, and who are habitations of God through the Spirit, 1 Cor. iii. 16 ; Eph. ii. 22 ; Rom. viii. 9. Here we see that everything in us that is good is the effect of the Spirit of God. Man possesses by nature no holy disposition. The lowest degree of true humility, and godly sorrow for sin, and a sense of the love of God, and consequently our love to God, are not to be found in any of the children of Adam till they are enlightened by the Spirit through the knowledge of the Gospel, nor can they be maintained for one moment in the soul without His sacred influence. Though sinners should hear ten thousand times of the love of God in the gift of His Son, they are never properly affected by it, till the Holy Spirit enters into their hearts, and till love to Him is produced by the truth through the Spirit. Here also we may see the distinct work of the Holy Spirit in the economy of redemption. Each of the persons of the Godhead sustains a peculiar office in the salvation of sinners, and it is the office of the Spirit to convert and sanctify those for whom Christ died.

What fulness and variety of instruction and consolation are contained in the first five verses of this chapter ! The work of the Father, of the Son, and of the Holy Ghost is exhibited, all severally acting, as God alone can act, in the various parts of man's salvation. The righteousness of God is imputed to the believer, who is therefore justified, and pronounced by the Judge of all the earth righteous. As righteous, he has peace with God, and free access to Him through Jesus Christ ; and being thus introduced into the favour of God, he stands in a justified state, rejoicing in hope of future glory. Being justified, he is also sanctified, and enabled to glory even in present afflictions. He enjoys the indwelling of the Holy Ghost, through whose Divine influence the love of God is infused into his soul. Here, then, are the peace, the joy, the triumph of the Christian. Here are faith, hope, and love, the three regulators of the Christian's life. Faith is the great and only means of obtaining every privilege, because it unites the soul to Christ, and receives all out of His fulness. Hope cheers the believer in his passage through this world, with the expectation of promised blessings to be accomplished in future glory, and is thus the anchor of the soul, both sure and stedfast, which holds it firm, and enables it to ride out all the storms and troubles of life. Love is the renewal of the image of God in the soul, and the true principle of obedience. 'The end of the commandment is love, out of a pure heart, and of a good conscience, and of faith unfeigned.' Faith is thus the root of the whole. Faith in the resurrection of Christ produces a good conscience, 1 Pet. iii. 21; the conscience being discharged from guilt, the heart is purified; and from the heart when purified proceeds love. Thus faith purifies the heart, Acts xv. 9; faith works by love, Gal. v. 6. Faith overcomes the world, 1 John v. 4.

Ver. 6.—*For when we were yet without strength, in due time Christ died for the ungodly.*

For.—This introduces the proof of the love of God to us, not a reason why the hope of the Christian will not disappoint him. Having spoken of the love of God shed abroad in our hearts, the Apostle here declares the evidence of this love. Though the Holy Ghost inspires our love to God, yet in doing so He shows us the grounds on which it rests, or the reasons why it should exist. In making us love God, He makes us perceive the grounds on which we ought to love Him. This also shows us another important fact, namely, that the Holy Spirit works in His people according to their constitution or the nature that He has given them; and, in endowing us with proper feelings and affections, He discovers to us the proper objects towards which they ought to be excited. The word of God through the Spirit, both in conversion and growth of grace, acts according to the original constitution that God has been pleased to bestow on the Christian.

Without strength.—Christ died for us while we were unable to obey Him, and without ability to save ourselves. This weakness or inability is no doubt sinful; but it is our inability, not our guilt, that the Apostle here designates. When we were unable to keep the law of God, or do anything towards our deliverance from Divine wrath, Christ interposed, and died for those whom He came to redeem.

In due time.—At the time appointed of the Father, Gal. iv. 2, 4. The fruits of the earth are gathered in their season; so in His season, that is, at the time appointed, Christ died for us, 1 Tim. ii. 6. *For the ungodly.* —Christ died for us, considered as ungodly, and without His gift of Himself we must have for ever continued to be so. It was not then for those who were in some degree godly, or disposed in some measure to do the will of God, that Christ died. There are none of this character by nature. It is by faith in His death that any are made godly.

Ver. 7.—*For scarcely for a righteous man will one die: yet peradventure for a good man some would even dare to die.*

For.—This brings into view a fact that heightens and illustrates the love of God to sinners. *A righteous* or just *man.*—A just man is distinguished here from a good or benevolent man. They are quite distinct

characters among men.   A just man is approved—a benevolent man is
loved.   Scarcely, however, would any one give his life for the former,
yet perhaps some one might do so for the latter.   *Scarcely.*—This furnishes the reason why the Apostle uses the word righteous or just, when
he denies that any one would die in his stead, because he does not mean
to make the denial universal.   ' *Even.*'—This is designed to qualify the
verb *to die*, not the verb *to dare*, though it stands immediately before it.
It is not even dare, but *dare even to die.*   This intimates that to die is a
thing to which men are of all things most averse.   It is the greatest trial
of love, John xv. 13.   ' Hereby perceive we the love of God, because
He laid His life down for us,' 1 John iii. 16.

Ver. 8.—*But God commendeth His love toward us, in that, while we were yet
sinners, Christ died for us.*

His love.—Here God's love to us is distinguished in the original as
His own love, which in this place takes away all ambiguity from the
expression.   *Yet sinners.*—This is literally true with respect to all who
are saved since Christ's death, and is substantially true of all who were
saved before it.   This may be said of Abel as well as of Paul.   Christ
died for him as a sinner.   It was Christ's death through which Abel was
accepted.   *For us.*—Not for us as including all men, but for those believers and himself whom the Apostle was addressing; and this equally
applies to all believers,—to all who are or shall be in Christ.   Christ's
death for us as sinners, in an astonishing manner, *commends*, *manifests*, or
exhibits God's love to us.

Ver. 9.—*Much more then, being now justified by His blood, we shall be saved from
wrath through Him.*

If God's love to us were such that Christ died for us when we were
sinners, *much more*, when we are perfectly righteous through that death,
He will save us from future punishment.   The meaning of the expression
much more in this verse, which is repeated in the 10th, 15th, and 17th
verses, is not at first sight obvious in these different occurrences, since
the things, which are compared to what follows, are complete in themselves.   The sense appears to be, that in using these expressions, the
Apostle, though inspired, reasons on the common principles that commend
themselves to the mind of man.   Having stated one thing, he proceeds
to state another as still more clear to our perception.   *Justified by His
blood.*—This shows that when we are said to be justified by *faith*, faith
includes its object, and imports that we are not saved by faith as a virtue.
It shows also that Christ's death was not that of a mere witness to the
truth which He declared, but that it was for sin, and in order that we
should be *saved from wrath through Him.*   All men are by nature the
children of wrath; and without the death of Christ, and faith in Him,
we must have continued in that awful condition.   ' He that believeth
not the Son, shall not see life ; but the wrath of God abideth on him.'
Dr. Macknight's explanation of this verse is as follows :—' *Much more then
being now allowed to live* under the new covenant, *through* the shedding of
His blood, we shall be saved from future punishment through Him, if we
behave well under that covenant.'   In his note he adds :—' Here *justified*

by His blood means, that, in the view of Christ's shedding His blood,
Adam and Eve were respited from death, and, being allowed to live, he
and they were placed under a new covenant, by which they might regain
immortality. This is what is called *justification of life*,' v. 18. And this
explanation follows naturally from what he gives as the meaning of the
foregoing verse :—' *His own love to men, God hath raised* above all human
love, *because we being still sinners, Christ died for us*, to procure us a
temporary life on earth, under a better covenant than the first.' On
such interpretations it is unnecessary to remark. They contain statements the most unscriptural and heretical, exhibiting most deplorable
ignorance.[1] He supposes, too, that it is here implied that some are said
to be justified who are not saved from wrath. But this is not the fact.
Justification is spoken of as having taken place, and salvation as future,—
not because any shall be punished who have been justified, but because
the wrath spoken of is future. The salvation of the Christian from
wrath is said to be future, in reference to the time of the general execution of wrath in the day of judgment. It is evidently implied in the
expression, that they who are justified shall never be punished. This
expression, justified *by His blood*, gives a most awful view of the infinite
evil of sin, of the strict justice of God, and of His faithfulness in carrying
into execution the first sentence, ' In the day that thou eatest thereof,
thou shalt surely die.' Without the shedding of His blood, and entering
with it into the holy place, Christ could not have obtained eternal
salvation for those who had sinned. On the other hand, what an
astonishing view is thus presented of the love of God, who spared not
His own Son, but delivered Him up for His people, and who with Him
will freely give them all things.

The Divine wisdom is admirable in the manner in which the Scriptures are written. It is not without design that inspiration varies the
phraseology respecting justification. Each variety is calculated to meet
a different abuse of the doctrine. The human heart is so prone to self-
righteousness, that the very doctrine of faith has been made to assume
a legal sense. Faith is represented as a work; and the office assigned
to it is not merely that of the medium of communicating righteousness,
but it is made to stand itself for a certain value, either real or supposed.
Had inspiration never varied the expressions, and always used the phrase
justified by faith, though there would have been no real ground to conclude
that faith is in itself the ground of justification, yet evidence to the
contrary would not have been exhibited in the manner in which it is
held forth by varying the diction. Instead of 'justified by faith,' we
here read *justified by the blood of Christ*. This shows that when we are
said to be justified by faith, it is not by faith as a work of the law, but
by faith as a medium,—that is, faith in the blood of Christ. To the
same purpose, also, is the expression in the following verse, *reconciled
to God by the death of His Son*. On the other hand, there are some who,
strongly impressed with the great evil of making faith a work, have
plunged into a contrary extreme, and are unwilling to look at the subject

---

[1] *The Presbyterian Review*, referring to Dr. Macknight, charges him with the
most ' audacious heterodoxy.'

in any light but that in which it is represented in the phrase, 'justified by His blood,' as if justification were independent of faith, or as if faith were merely an accidental or unimportant thing in justification. This also is a great error. Faith is as necessary in justification as the sacrifice of Christ itself, but necessary for a different purpose. The blood of Christ is the price that has value in itself. Faith, which unites the soul to Christ, is the necessary medium, through the Divine appointment. Again, we have *justified freely by grace*, Rom. iii. 24. Self-righteousness is fruitful in expedients. It is difficult to put it to silence. It will admit that justification is by faith in its own legal sense, and that it is through Christ's blood, as a general price for the sins of all men ; but it holds that every man must do something to entitle him to the benefits of Christ's sacrifice. Here, then, the phrase *justification by grace* comes in to cut off every evasion.

Another variety of phraseology on this subject we have in the expression *justified by Christ*, Gal. ii. 17. This points to the ground of our justification, or our union with Christ. We are accounted perfectly righteous, having paid the debt of sin, and having fulfilled the whole law, by our union or oneness with Christ, as we were sinners by our natural connection with Adam. It is of immense importance to the satisfaction of the mind of the believer, constantly and stedfastly to consider himself as a member of Christ—as truly a part of Him. He rose for our justification. When He was justified from the sins which He took on Him by having suffered for them, and when He had fulfilled the law, we were justified in His justification. We are therefore said not merely to be pardoned, but to be justified, by Christ. We have suffered all the punishment due to our sins, and have kept every precept of the law, because He with whom we are *one* has done so. It is also worthy of remark that, while the Apostle speaks of being justified by Christ, he had in the preceding verse spoken of being justified by the faith of Christ. This shows that faith is the way in which our union with Christ is effected.

Ver. 10.—*For if, when we were enemies, we were reconciled to God by the death of His Son ; much more, being reconciled, we shall we saved by His life.*

Enemies.—It greatly enhances the love of God that He gave His Son for us while we were yet His *enemies*. Had we discovered any symptoms of willingness to obey Him, or any degree of love to Him, His love to us would not have been so astonishing. But it is in this light only that the proud heart of man is willing to view his obligations to redeeming love. He will not look upon himself as totally depraved and helpless. He desires to do something on his part to induce God to begin His work in him by His Spirit. But Christ died for His people when they were the enemies of God, and He calls them to the knowledge of Himself when they are His enemies. Here, then, is the love of God. At the time when Christ died for us, we were not His friends, but His enemies. ' The carnal mind is enmity against God.'

Reconciled to God by the death of His Son.—The word rendered 'reconciled,' signifies to change the state of matters between persons at variance, by removing their grounds of difference. The Divine word and declara-

tions, as well as the Divine perfections, forbid us to imagine that God
will clear the guilty. In order, then, to reconciliation with God, satisfaction must be made to His justice. What is meant here, is not our
laying aside our enmity to God, but God's laying aside His enmity to
us, on account of the death of His Son. It is true that we lay aside our
enmity to God when we see that He has laid aside His enmity to us, and
never till then will we do so; but what is here meant is, that God is
reconciled to us. In Scripture this is spoken of as our being reconciled
to God. We are reconciled to God, when He is pacified towards us
through His Son, in whom we believe. This is quite agreeable to the
use of the term in Scripture with respect to other cases, 1 Sam. xxix. 4;
Matt. v. 23, 24. Socinians, however, maintain that reconciliation between God and man consists only in bending and pacifying the heart of
man towards God, and not in averting His just anger. This error,
arising from their denial of the satisfaction made by Jesus Christ, is refuted
by the consideration that God pardons our sins: whence it follows that
He was angry with us; and the redemption of Jesus Christ is declared
to be made by a propitiatory sacrifice, which clearly proves that God
was angry. To this the idea of a sacrifice necessarily leads; for a sacrifice is offered to pacify God towards men, and not to reconcile men to
God. Aaron was commanded to make an atonement for the congregation, for there was wrath gone out from the Lord. 'And he stood
between the living and the dead, and the plague was stayed,' Num. xvi..
46. God's anger was thus turned away by making this atonement. In
David's time, by offering burnt-offerings and peace-offerings, the Lord
was entreated for the land, and the plague was stayed from Israel. By
this it is clear that the primary intention of such sacrifices, and consequently of the priest who offered them, immediately respected the reconciliation of God. The same is evident from the following passages:—
'Thou hast forgiven the iniquity of Thy people; Thou hast covered all
their sin. Selah. Thou hast taken away all Thy wrath; Thou hast
turned from the fierceness of Thine anger,' Ps. lxxxv. 2, 3. 'Though
Thou wast angry with me, Thine anger is turned away, and Thou com-
fortedst me,' Isa. xii. 1. 'I will establish My covenant with thee; and
thou shalt know that I am the Lord: that thou mayest remember, and be
confounded, and never open thy mouth any more because of thy shame,
when I am pacified (reconciled, Lev. viii. 15 xvi. 20; 2 Chron. xxix.
24) toward thee for all that thou hast done, saith the Lord God,' Ezek.
xvi. 63.

All men being sinners, are in themselves, while in unbelief, under the
displeasure of God, who cannot look upon iniquity, Hab. i. 13, and are
by nature children of wrath, or of the judgment of God; but as viewed
in Christ, and in relation to His death, the elect are the objects of God's
everlasting love, and this love in His good time takes effect. He sends
His Son to be a propitiatory sacrifice for them,—thus making satisfaction
to His justice, and removing every obstacle to His being reconciled. He
unites them to the Son of His love; and in Him, clothed with His righteousness, they become the children of God, and then in themselves the
proper objects of His love. The ministry committed to the Apostles is

called the ministry of reconciliation. Men are besought to be reconciled to God from the consideration of His having made Him to be sin for His people who knew no sin. Here is a double reconciliation, namely, of God to men, and of men to God. The latter is urged from the consideration of the former, and this consideration is effectual for all for whom the reconciliation was made. The whole of this reconciliation is through the death of His Son. Thus does God call His people with a holy calling. He invites them to friendship with Himself, through an all-sufficient atonement; and they lay aside their enmity to Him when they see that God has laid aside His anger against them. They are reconciled to Him through the death of His Son.

What, in the preceding verse, is spoken of as the *blood* of Christ, is here spoken of as His *death*. These varied terms are useful to express the idea in such a manner that it cannot be innocently evaded. Christ's blood was an *atonement*, as it was His *death*. This shows that no degree of suffering would have been sufficient as an atonement for our sins without the actual death of the sacrifice, according to the original sentence against man. Jesus Christ might have suffered all that He did suffer without a total extinction of life; but He must not only suffer, —He must also die. This phraseology, then, is calculated to meet the error of those Christians who, from a desire of magnifying the efficacy of the blood of Christ, have said that one drop of it would have been sufficient to save. Had one drop been sufficient, two drops would never have been shed.

Much more, being reconciled, we shall be saved by His life.—If we were reconciled by His death, much more clear is it that we shall be saved by His life. Some find a difficulty in this, as if it implied that the atonement and price of redemption were not complete at the death of Christ. But the Apostle is not speaking on that point. He is speaking of the security of the believer from any danger, by Christ as alive. The meaning is, we shall be saved by Him as existing alive, or as living, Heb. vii. 25. We need Christ raised from the dead to intercede for our daily transgressions, and to save us from wrath. The efficacy of the death and the intercession of Jesus Christ have the same objects and the same extent, John xvii. 9. He intercedes for all those for whom He died. 'It is Christ that died, yea, rather that is risen again, who is even at the right hand of God, who also maketh intercession for us,' Rom. viii. 34. *For us*, that is, for those whom the Apostle is addressing as *beloved* of God, and *called*, and *saints*, ch. i. 7, and all that are such.

Two comparisons are made in this passage, one between the past and the present state of believers: they were once the enemies, they are now the friends, of God. The other is between the past and the present condition of Christ: He was once dead, He is now alive. And the proposition that unites these two is, that reconciliation with God is entirely owing to the death of Christ as its meritorious cause. Since, then, the death of the Redeemer could produce so great an effect as the reconciliation to Himself of those who were the enemies of the Most High, what room can there be to doubt that the life of Christ is sufficient to accomplish what is less difficult; that is to say, to obtain the continuation

of the Divine friendship and benevolence for those whose reconciliation has been already purchased at a price of such infinite cost? By
the death which He suffered in their place, they are freed from condemnation, the rigour of the law having run its course, and received its
execution by the punishment of their sins in Him; and thus they are
saved from the effects of wrath. By His resurrection, His life, and His
entrance into eternal glory, the reward reserved for His work as Mediator,
they become partakers of that glory. 'In My Father's house are many
mansions. I go to prepare a place for you.' 'Because I live, ye shall live
also.' 'Father, I will that they also whom Thou hast given Me be with
Me where I am, that they may behold My glory which Thou hast given
Me.' Thus Jesus Christ, who was delivered for the offences of His people,
was raised again for their justification; and this unparalleled love of God,
who has not spared His well-beloved Son, is the surest foundation for the
absolute and unlimited confidence in Him of every man who, renouncing
his own righteousness, submits to His righteousness. At the same time,
the necessity of the shedding of blood infinitely precious, in order to the
justification of believers, is the strongest proof of the infinite evil of sin,
and of the infinite holiness and awful justice of God. It shows the extreme difficulty there was in reconciling God to man, as it could only be
done by a satisfaction to His justice, which could not be accomplished
but by the death of His only-begotten Son.

Ver. 11.—*And not only so, but we also joy in God, through our Lord Jesus Christ,*
by whom we have now received the atonement.

This verse exhibits the last of those fruits which proceed from being
brought into a state of justification. The first of them is peace with God,
involving the communication and enjoyment of every blessing which the
creature is capable of receiving; for if God be with us, who can be
against us? and when this peace is known to be permanently established,
immediately the cheering hope of future glory springs up in the mind.
This hope, transporting the believer beyond this world, and looking forward to unbounded blessedness, enables him to bear up under those
tribulations that are inseparable from his present state. In them, though
not in themselves joyous but grievous, he even glories; and, experiencing
their salutary effects, they confirm his hope of future and eternal enjoyment. The Holy Ghost, too, sheds abroad the love of God in his heart;
while his attention is directed to what God has done in giving for him
His Son to the death, even while he was in the most determined state of
hostility towards God. From the whole, the Apostle argues how much
more it is evident that, being reconciled, he shall be saved from all the
fearful effects of the wrath and displeasure of God against sin. The view
of all of these unspeakable blessings conducts to that feeling of exultation
and joy, with the declaration of which the enumeration is here terminated,
of the effects which the knowledge of his justification in the sight of God,
by the death and resurrection of Jesus Christ, produces in the heart of
the believer.

Not only so.—That is, we shall not only escape the wrath to come, by
the death of Christ, but attain to glory by His life. The measure of
excess is future glory above mere exemption from misery. These two

things are entirely distinct, and afford distinct grounds of thanksgiving. *Joy in God.*—The word here translated joy, is the same which in verse 2 is rendered rejoice, and in verse 3, glory. It was before declared that believers have peace with God, that they have access to Him, and that they rejoice in the hope of His glory. Now, the Apostle represents them as arrived at the fountain-head, looking through all the blessings conferred on them, and rejoicing, boasting, or glorying in God Himself as the source of them all. The Christian's joy is all in God. He exults in his prospects; but all are ascribed to God, and not to anything in Himself. God, even His own covenant-God, is the great and ultimate object of his joy. 'My soul shall make her boast in the Lord.' ' O magnify the Lord with me, and let us exalt His name together.' ' I will rejoice in the Lord, I will joy in the God of my salvation.' ' The Lord is the portion of mine inheritance, my portion for ever. I will go unto the altar of God, unto God my exceeding joy.' The sentiment of the love of God, in so great a salvation, and of joy in Him, is more deeply impressed upon the believer, by considering the rock from which he has been hewn, and the hole of the pit from which he has been dug. In the above verses, the former situation of those who are saved is declared in the strongest language. They were WITHOUT STRENGTH, UNGODLY, SINNERS, UNDER WRATH, ENEMIES TO GOD. If such, then, was their original condition, what reason have they not only to rejoice in the hope of glory, but, above all, in the goodness and mercy of God, who has now reconciled them to Himself! Phil. iii. 1, iv. 4.

Through our Lord Jesus Christ.—Joy in God, with all those unspeakable blessings above enumerated, are again and again declared to come by Him, through whom God manifests His love, and is reconciled to His people. The name of Jesus Christ being here introduced so often, should be especially remarked. The Christian joys and glories in God only through Christ; without Christ, God could not be viewed as a friend. He must be an object of hatred. Our friendly relation to God is all through Christ. *By whom we have now received the atonement,* or reconciliation, according to the translation of the same word in the preceding verse. Atonement has been made through the death of Christ. The Apostle, and they whom he addressed, being believers, had received the atonement, which Christ has not only accomplished, but makes His people receive it. Among the various errors that have discovered themselves in modern times, few are more lamentable or dangerous than the views of the atonement that have been adopted by many. Instead of considering the atonement of Christ as a real compensation to the Divine justice for the sins of those who are saved, so that God may remain just, while He is merciful to the chief of sinners, many look on it as nothing but a mere exhibition of the displeasure of God against sin, intended for the honour and maintenance of His government of the universe. This altogether destroys the Gospel, and in reality leaves men exposed to the Divine justice.

It is alleged by those who represent the atonement as only an expedient, subservient to the interests of morality, that sins are called debts merely in a figurative sense. But nothing can be more clear than that the Scriptures, which speak of sin as a debt, speak quite literally. The word debt extends to everything that justly demands an equivalent. We are said to be bought with the blood of Christ, as the price paid for our sins, which certainly implies that the blood of Christ is that which has given an equivalent to the justice of God, and made an atonement for those who, according to justice, must otherwise have suffered the penalty of sin, which is death. In the remission, then, of the sins of those who have received the atonement, God is at once the just God and the Saviour, which He could not be without this atonement.

In reference to the sacrifice of Christ, by which He made the atonement, it is said, ' Thou wast slain, and hast redeemed us to God by Thy blood,' Rev. v. 9. ' Without shedding of blood is no remission, for it is the blood that maketh an atonement for the soul,' Heb. ix. 22 ; Lev. xvii. 11. The blood is the life, Deut. xii. 23. It was the shedding, then, of the blood of Christ, which signifies His death, that procured this remission of sin. This was the ransom that God declared He had found, by which He saved His people from going down to destruction, Job xxxiii. 24. It was their redemption. Redemption signifies a purchasing back, and supposes an alienation of what is redeemed ; and thus Christ redeemed them with His blood, which was the price He paid, and they are ' His purchased possession.' His blood was the ransom paid to the justice of God, without which it was impossible they should have been released from the bondage of Satan and the sentence of death. He died for the ungodly, who, being justified by His blood, shall be saved from wrath. The ransom, then, which Christ paid, was the price that Divine justice demanded ; and, having made His soul an offering for sin, God has declared Himself ' well pleased for His righteousness' sake,' He having ' magnified the law, and made it honourable.' It was necessary that He should yield obedience to its precepts, and suffer the penalty annexed to its violation. The law condemned sinners to eternal death. In order, then, to redeem them, it behoved Him to suffer, and He did actually suffer, the full equivalent of that death by which He made atonement for sin, and through faith His people receive that atonement. His blood is put, by a usual figure of speech, for His death, in which His sufferings and His obedience terminated, and which was their consummation, containing a full answer to all the demands on His people, of law and justice. God, then, is now ' faithful and just to forgive them their sins, and to cleanse them from all unrighteousness,' 1 John i. 9. Believers have redemption through His blood, even the forgiveness of sins, Eph. i. 7 ; Col. i. 14. Ye are bought with a price, 1 Cor. vii. 20–23. ' Ye were not redeemed with corruptible things, such as silver and gold, from your vain conversation, received by tradition from your fathers ; but with the precious blood of Christ,' 1 Pet. i. 18.

Many who look on atonement as something real, yet overturn it by making it universal. This is an error which at once opposes the Scriptures, and could be of no service, even were it true. Where is the difference, as respects the Divine character, whether a man does not obtain pardon, from his sins not being atoned for by the blood of Christ, or because he has not been elected to eternal life ? If Christ's death pays the price of the sins of all men, all men must be saved. If His redemption be universal, then all are redeemed from the captivity of Satan and the guilt of sin, and delivered from wrath. For what can they be punished, if atonement has been made for their sins? If a man's debts are paid, how can he afterwards be imprisoned for those debts? A just God cannot punish a second time for the same offence. If Christ has paid the debt of all sinners, there is nothing remaining to pay in the case of any man. Would it be just that any should be punished in hell for the sins for which Christ was punished on earth? If Christ bore the sins of all men in His own body on the tree, shall any man bear them a second time? Had the sins of all men been imputed to Christ, in that case His sacrifice did not answer its end. It left the greater part of them for whom it was offered under the curse of the broken law. But God, in appointing Christ to make atonement for sin, and Christ Himself, in undertaking to perform it, had in view from all eternity a certain select number of mankind, who were and still are known to God. For their salvation only was that atonement made, and for them it will be ultimately effectual. A Saviour being provided for any of the lost children of Adam was an act of pure grace; and therefore the extent of this salvation depends solely on Him who worketh all things according to the counsel of His own will.

As Christ prayed not, John xvii. 9,[1] so He died 'not, for the world,' but for those whom God had given Him out of the world. And all that the Father giveth Him shall come to Him. For those for whom He is the propitiation He is the Advocate, and for whom He died He makes intercession, and for no others. In Israel there were sacrifices accompanied with the burning of incense, but these were not for the world but for Israel. The sin-offering, on the great day of atonement, was for Israel only. It was for Israel, whose sins were laid upon the scape-goat, that intercession was made; and when, after offering his sacrifice, the high priest came out from the holiest of all, it was Israel who received the blessing. Of whose redemption was the deliverance of Israel from Egypt a figure? For whose healing was the serpent lifted up in the wilderness? In one word, of whom was Israel a type? Not of all mankind, but only of the people of God. As, then, the high priest under the law offered sacrifice only for Israel, interceded only for them, and blessed them only, so Christ, the High Priest of our profession, has offered His *sacrifice* only for His people, for whom He *intercedes* on the ground of that sacrifice, and whom, in consequence of His sacrifice and intercession, He will at last come out of the heavenly sanctuary to *bless*, Matt. xxv. 34; thus discharging for them, and for them only, the three functions

---

[1] It is objected that in these words the Lord refers specially to His Apostles; but He clearly excludes the world, which also He does afterwards, when He prays for none but for those who should believe in Him. 'Neither pray I for these alone, but for them also which shall believe on Me through their word.' The whole of this sublime prayer is exclusively offered up by the Lord, first for Himself, next for the Apostles, and, lastly, for all believers; and for this purpose He says He received power over all flesh, that He might give eternal life to *as many as the Father had given Him*, and all that the Father giveth Him shall come to Him, John vi. 37. No fewer than eight times does He refer to those who were *given* to Him, for whom alone He prays that they might be with Him to behold His glory.

of the priestly office. His sacrifice and intercession, then, which are inseparable, are of the same extent, and for all for whom He offered His sacrifice He presents His intercession, which is founded upon it. Could it be supposed that He never intercedes for those for whom He gave the highest proof of His love in laying down His life? Did He *bear in His own body on the tree* the sins of those to whom at last He will profess, 'I never knew you,' and will leave them under the curse, saying, 'Depart from Me, ye cursed,' whose sins, as the Lamb of God, He had taken away, on account of which, notwithstanding, He will consign them to punishment everlasting? Far different is His language respecting those whom He calls His sheep, for whom He says He lays down His life. Them He professes to know, and declares that they know Him. 'I am the Good Shepherd, and know My sheep, and am known of Mine. As the Father knoweth Me, so know I the Father, and I lay down My life for the sheep. My sheep hear My voice, and I know them, and they follow Me, and I give unto them eternal life.'

Witsius, in his *Economy of the Covenants*, observes:—'That fictitious satisfaction for the reprobate and those who perish is altogether a vain and useless thing. For whom does it profit? Not certainly God, who by no act can be rendered happier than He is. Not Christ Himself, who, as He never seeks them, so He never receives them, for His peculiar property, and neither is He enriched by possessing them, though supposed to have purchased them at a dear rate. Not believers, who, content with their portion in God and in Christ, and fully redeemed by Christ, enjoy a happiness in every respect complete. In fine, not those that perish, who are constrained to satisfy in their own persons for their sins, to the uttermost farthing. The blood of Christ, says Remigius, formerly Bishop of Lyons, is a great price; such a price can in no respect be in vain and ineffectual, but rather is filled with the superabundant advantage arising from those blessings for which it is paid. Nay, the satisfaction of Christ for the reprobate had not only been useless, but highly unworthy both of God and of Christ. Unworthy of the wisdom, goodness, and justice of God, to exact and receive satisfaction from His most beloved Son for those whom He neither gave nor wanted to give His Son, and whom He decreed to consign to everlasting confinement to suffer in their own persons, according to the demerit of their crimes. Unworthy of Christ, to give His blood a price of redemption for those whom He had not in charge to redeem.'

'In respect of its intrinsic worth,' says Brown of Haddington, 'as the obedience and sufferings of a Divine person, Christ's satisfaction is sufficient for the ransom of all mankind, and, being fulfilled in human nature, is equally suited to all their necessities. But in respect of His and His Father's intention, it was paid and accepted instead of the elect, and to purchase their eternal happiness. Christ died for those only for whom He undertook, as Surety, in the covenant of grace, in order to obtain their eternal salvation.' Brown of Wamphray, in his *Arguments against Universal Redemption*, says:—'All that Christ died for must certainly be saved. But all men shall not be saved. Christ's death was a redemption, and we are said to be redeemed thereby. And therefore all such as He laid down this redemption or redemption-money for, must of necessity be redeemed and saved; and consequently He did not die for all, seeing all are not redeemed and saved. That all such for whom this redemption-money was paid, and this ransom was given, must be saved, is clear, otherwise it were no redemption; a ransom given for captives doth say that these captives, in law and justice, ought to be set at liberty. Christ's intercession is really a presenting unto God the oblation made. Therefore, says the Apostle, Heb. ix. 24, that Christ is entered into heaven itself, to appear in the presence of God for us; and so, by appearing, He intercedeth, and His appearing in His own blood, whereby He obtained eternal redemption, Heb. ix. 12; and so His intercession must be for all for whom the oblation was made, and the eternal redemption was obtained.'

Many suppose that in preaching the Gospel it is necessary to tell every man that Christ died for him, and that if Christ did not actually atone for the sins of every individual, the Gospel cannot be preached at all. But this is very erroneous. The Gospel declares that Christ died for the guilty, and that the most guilty who believe it shall be saved. ' It is a faithful saying, and worthy of all acceptation, that Christ Jesus came into the world to save sinners,' even the chief of sinners. The Gospel does not tell every individual to whom it is addressed, that Christ died for him, but that if he believes he shall be saved. This is a warrant to preach the Gospel unto all men; and it is only as he is a believer that it is known to any man that Christ died for him individually. To preach the Gospel then to every man, and call on every one to believe and be saved, is quite consistent, as it is a truth that whoever believes shall be saved. If the most guilty of the human race believe in Jesus, there is the most perfect certainty that he shall be saved. If any man is straitened in preaching the Gospel, and finds a difficulty in calling on all men to believe, except he can at the same time tell them that Christ died for every individual of the human race, he does not clearly understand what the Gospel is. It is the good news that Christ died for the most guilty that believe, not that He died for every individual, whether he believe or not. To the truth that every man shall be saved who believes, there is no exception. If there are any sins that will never be pardoned, they imply that the individuals guilty of them will never believe; for if they believe, they will be saved. Whatever, then, the sin against the Holy Ghost may be supposed to be, it implies final unbelief; and the best way to relieve those persons who may think they are guilty of this sin, is not to labour to make them understand what the sin against the Holy Ghost is, but to make them see that, if they now believe, they cannot have ever committed the unpardonable sin. To suppose that any believe who will not be saved, is to suppose a contradiction in the word of God.

The difficulty of those who feel themselves restrained in exhorting sinners to believe the Gospel, on the ground that the atonement of Christ was not made for all, is the same as that which is experienced by some who, believing the doctrine of election, suppose it inconsistent to exhort all indiscriminately to believe the Gospel, since it is certain that they who are not chosen to eternal life will never be saved. In this they err. The Gospel, according to the commandment of the everlasting God, is to be made known to all nations for the obedience of faith. It is certain, however, that they for whom Christ did not die, and who do not belong to the election of grace, will not believe. These are secret things which belong to God, to be revealed in their proper time. But the Gospel is the fan in Christ's hand, who, by means of it, will thoroughly purge His floor, separating those who are His sheep from the rest of the world lying in the wicked one. He has therefore commanded it to be preached to all men ; and by it those will be discovered for whom His atonement was made, and whom God hath chosen from the foundation of the world, and predestinated unto the adoption of children by Jesus Christ unto Himself. We are not, then, to inquire first, either for ourselves or others, for whom Christ died, and who are chosen to eternal life, before we determine to whom the Gospel is to be preached ; but to preach it to all, with the assurance that whoever believes it shall receive the remission of sins. In believing it, we ascertain for ourselves that Christ bare our sins in His own body on the tree, and that God from the beginning hath chosen us to salvation, through sanctification of the Spirit and belief of the truth.

The atonement of Christ is of infinite value ; and the reason why all men are not saved by it, is not for want of its being of sufficient value, but because it was not made for all. In itself, it was sufficient to make atonement for the sins of all mankind, had it been so intended. His sacrifice could not have been sufficient for any, if it had not been sufficient for all. An atonement of infinite value was necessary for every individual that shall be saved, and more could not be necessary for all the world. This intrinsic sufficiency of Christ's sacrifice was doubtless in view in the Divine appointment concerning it. God made provision of such a sacrifice as was not only sufficient effectually to take away the sins of all the elect, but also sufficient to be laid before all mankind, in the dispensation of the Gospel. In the Gospel it was to be declared to all men, that in their nature the Son of God had made an atonement of infinite value, and brought in everlasting righteousness, which shall be upon all that believe. This atonement, then, being all-sufficient in itself, is proclaimed to all who hear the Gospel. All are invited to rely upon it for pardon and acceptance, as freely and fully as if they knew that God designed it for them from all eternity ; and all who thus rely upon it shall experience the blessing of its efficacy and infinite value. In the proclamation of the Gospel, no restriction is held forth respecting election or reprobation. No difference is announced between one sinner and another. Without any distinction the call is addressed, and a gracious welcome proclaimed, to all the children of Adam. ' Unto you, O men, I call, and my voice is to the sons of men.' And well might the Apostle say in his own name, and that of the believers whom he addresses in the passage before us, ' *We joy in God through our Lord Jesus Christ, by whom we have now received the atonement.*'

We come now to the second division of this chapter, from verse 12 to 19. Having spoken of justification by faith, and having called our attention to several points connected with it, the Apostle now speaks of it as it was figuratively exhibited in the condemnation of the human race in Adam. He first directs attention to the one man by whom sin was brought into the world, and declares that death came by sin. This necessarily imports that death is the lot of all that sin, and of none but such as are sinners. If death entered because of sin, it could affect none who were not guilty. But the Apostle does not leave this to be inferred, although this inference is both necessary and obvious. He draws it himself. ' So death passed upon all men, for that all have sinned ; ' thus plainly asserting that all are sinners upon whom death passes. Every step in this process is natural and obvious. We may trace the very train in the Apostle's mind. We may see the reason of every subjoined expression. Having said that all are sinners who die, it immediately occurs to him that to some this would appear strange ; he proceeds, therefore, to show how all have sinned. This he does by observing that sin was in the world before the law of Moses, and that it had existed from Adam until the law was given. But this, as he observes, could not have been the case, had not law existed ; ' for sin is not imputed where there is no law.' What, then, is the evidence that sin existed before the law of Moses ? The evidence is, that death reigned. And what is the evidence that sin existed in infants ? The evidence is, that death reigned over them. If death came upon man by sin, it could have no dominion over any of the human race who were not sinners. Adam is called the figure of Him that was to come ; and this must not be confined to one or two particulars, but must extend to everything in which Christ's seed are one with Him, as contrasted with everything in which Adam's seed are one with him. If Christ's seed are one with Him in any characteristic point in which Adam's seed are not one with him, then the ' figure,' or type, would fail. Having shown the similarity, the Apostle proceeds to show the dissimilarity, or the abounding of grace over what was lost in Adam. This he continues to the end of verse 19, summing up in the 18th and 19th verses what he had referred to in the 12th, from which he was led by the considerations above specified.

In proceeding to analyse what is taught in verses 12–19, Mr. Stuart professes to feel great difficulty. Considering the lamentable manner in which he has perverted and misrepresented the whole passage, this is not at all surprising. In his *Synopsis*, he says, ' As the consequences of Adam's sin were extended to all men, so the consequences of Christ's obedience (viz., unto death) are extended to *all ; i.e.*, Jews and Gentiles, all come on an equal footing into the kingdom of Christ,' p. 196. And again he says, that verses 12–19 ' are designed at once to confirm the statement made in ch. iii. 23–30, and iv. 10–19 ; *i.e.*, to confirm the sentiment that Gentiles as well as Jews may rejoice in the reconciliation effected by Christ ; while, at the same time, the whole representation serves very much to enhance the greatness of the blessings which Christ has procured for sinners by the *contrast* in which these blessings are placed,' p. 198. There is here no reference at all to the distinction between Jews and Gentiles. The design is evidently to show the likeness between the way in which righteousness and life came, and the way in which condemnation and death came, the former by Christ, the latter by Adam. He adds,

' I cannot perceive the particular design of introducing such a contrast in this place, unless it be to show the propriety and justice of extending the blessings of reconciliation to the Gentiles as well as to the Jews, and to set off to the best advantage the greatness of these blessings.' But the extension of these blessings to the Gentiles, however important a truth, and however much dwelt on in other places, has nothing to do in this place, or with this contrast. The contrast here introduced is the same, whether the blessings are supposed to be confined to the Jews, or also extended to the Gentiles. The contrast is not between Jew and Gentile, but between Adam and Christ, between the way of condemnation and the way of justification. How does Mr. Stuart bring in the distinction between Jews and Gentiles ? He might as well introduce it into the history of the creation. But the common view of the passage is quite in accordance with the preceding context. The difficulty he feels is a difficulty to reconcile it with his own unscriptural views of this part of the word of God.

The following observations of President Edwards on the connection of this passage, in reference to the Commentary of Dr. Taylor, are equally applicable to the difficulties experienced respecting it by Mr. Stuart:—
' No wonder, when the Apostle is treating so fully and largely of our restoration, righteousness, and life by Christ, that he is led by it to consider our fall, sin, death, and ruin by Adam ; and to observe wherein these two opposite heads of mankind agree, and wherein they differ, in the manner of conveyance of opposite influences and communications from each. Thus, if this place be understood, as it is used to be understood by orthodox divines, the whole stands in a natural, easy, and clear connection with the preceding part of the chapter, and all the former part of the Epistle ; and in a plain agreement with the express design of all that the Apostle had been saying ; and also in connection with the words last before spoken, as introduced by the two immediately preceding verses where he is speaking of our justification, reconciliation, and salvation by Christ ; which leads the Apostle directly to observe how, on the contrary, we have sin and death by Adam. Taking this discourse of the Apostle in its true and plain sense, there is no need of great extent of learning, or depth of criticism, to find out the connection; but if it be understood in Dr. Taylor's sense, the plain scope and connection are wholly lost, and there was truly need of a skill in criticism, and art of discerning, beyond, or at least different from, that of former divines, and a faculty of seeing something afar off, which other men's sight could not reach, in order to find out the connection.'—*Orig. Sin*, p. 312. It would be well if those who will not receive the kingdom of God as little children, would employ their ' skill in criticism, and art of discerning,' on any other book than the Bible.

Ver. 12.—*Wherefore, as by one man sin entered into the world, and death by sin ; and so death passed upon all men, for that all have sinned.*

The general object of the Apostle in this place it is not at all difficult to perceive. He had treated largely of the doctrine of justification by faith, evinced its necessity, shown its accordance with the Old Testament Scriptures, and unfolded some of the privileges of a justified state ; and now he illustrates and displays the Gospel salvation, by contrasting it with the misery and ruin introduced by the fall, and manifesting, in the plan of mercy, a superabounding of grace over transgression, and thus, as has been already remarked, exhibits the foundation both of condemnation and of justification.

In the preceding verse, Paul had stated that he himself, and those to whom he wrote, had been brought into a state of reconciliation with God. Reconciliation, as has been noticed, implies two things,—first, that the parties referred to had been in a state of alienation and hostility; and, secondly, that this hostility has ceased, and their discord been amicably terminated. Occasion is here given to the development and illustration of both these points,—first, the ground of the hostility and its effects, with which the Apostle commences in the verse before us; and next, the manner, with its consequences, in which this hostility has been terminated. This last he unfolds in the 15th and following verses, to the end of the 18th verse, and then in the 19th sums up the whole discussion which properly follows from the declaration in the 11th verse of the reconciliation.

Wherefore.—This introduces the conclusion which the Apostle draws in the 18th verse, but which is for a few moments interrupted by the explanatory parenthesis interposed from verse 13th to 17th inclusive. It connects with what goes before from the beginning of the 10th verse, especially with the one preceding, in which it is declared that through our Lord Jesus Christ believers have now received the reconciliation. It also connects with what follows, as an inference drawn from what is still to be mentioned, of which we have several examples in the apostolic writings. Wherefore, or for this reason, namely, that as by one man sin entered, so by one Man came righteousness. *As* introduces a comparison or contrast, of which, however, only one branch is here stated, as the Apostle is immediately led off into the explanatory parenthesis already noticed, which terminates with the 17th verse. In the 18th verse he reverts to the comparison, not directly, however, but with reference to the intermediate verses and on account of the interruption, not only states it in substance, but repeats it in both its parts.

By one man sin entered into the world.—Mr. Stuart interprets this as equivalent to sin *commenced* with one man. Sin did indeed commence with one man; but this is not the Apostle's meaning. If ever sin commenced among the human race, it must have commenced by one. But the Apostle means to tell us not merely that sin commenced by one, but that it came upon all the world from one. This is the only point of view in which the sin of Adam causing death can be contrasted with the righteousness of Christ giving life.

Death by sin.—If death came through sin, then all who die are sinners. This proves, contrary to Mr. Stuart's view, that infants are sinners in Adam. Death is the wages of sin. It is the dark badge of man's alienation from God, the standing evidence that he is by nature separated from the Fountain of Life, and allied to corruption. If infants did not participate in the guilt of Adam's sin, they would not experience death, disease, or misery, until they become themselves actual transgressors. 'Who ever perished, being innocent? or where were the righteous cut off?' Job iv. 7. *And so*, that is, *consequently*, or *in this manner*, and not, as Mr. Stuart interprets it, *in like manner.*—This shows the consequence of what is said in the former clauses, namely, that death comes upon all because all have sinned, being participators in the one man's offence. *Death passed*, literally passed through; that is, passed through from father to son. *All men*—that is, all of the human race, and not all merely who actually sin. As a matter of fact, we see that death does pass upon all without exception. *For that*—or inasmuch as. Augustine, Beza, and others, translate this 'in whom,' and this interpretation most conclusively supports the doctrine of imputed sin.[1] But the ordinary rendering, as adopted by our translators, as well as by Calvin and others, seems on the whole to be preferable; nor does the doctrine in question require for its support any other than the common translation. The meaning is, that death passes on all men *because* all men are sinners. Mr. Stuart makes this to refer to those who are actually sinners. But there is no warrant for this. Besides, all have not actually sinned. And this would not serve his purpose, because, at all events, it is here implied that death comes on men on account of sin. Since, then, infants die, it proves that they are sinners. If the assertion be, that death passes on adults because they are sinners, it may be asked why death, which is 'the wages of sin,' passes upon children, on the supposition that they are not sinners? And further, where is the *likeness*, if the expression '*and so*' be interpreted *in like manner?* Is there any likeness between sin entering the world through one offence, and a man dying by his own actual sin? Is there not rather the strongest contrast? Still less would this illustrate the way of justification through Christ, which is the Apostle's object in this place. It is quite obvious that the Apostle designs to assert that all die because all are sinners.

All have sinned.—That is, all have really sinned, though not in their own persons. This does not mean, as some explain it, that infants become involved in the consequences of Adam's sin without his guilt. Adam stood as the head, the forefather and representative of all his posterity. They were all created in him; and in the guilt of his sin, as well as its consequence, they became partakers.[2] These truths, that sin, death, and condemnation come upon all by one man, are clearly expressed in the following verses, 15, 16, 17, 18, 19. *Through the offence of one, many are dead. The judgment was by the one that sinned to condemnation. By one man's offence death reigned by one. By the offence of one, judgment came upon all men to condemnation. By one man's disobedience many were made sinners.* Mr. Stuart labours to restrict the declaration in the first to an assertion of individual and actual transgression. If he

---

[1] We may observe that *ἐφ' ᾧ*, which our translators have rendered 'for that,' has been by many, both of the fathers and of the moderns, rendered 'in whom.' Any one who wishes to see how much may be said for this meaning may consult Maresii *Defensio Fidei Catholicæ*, Dis. 2, sec. 6, p. 382, etc. It is not correct to say, as Mr. Stuart does, that Augustine's view of original sin was founded on this exegesis of *ἐφ' ᾧ*. That venerable writer took a much more enlarged view of the subject than such an insinuation suggests.

[2] No man will allege that it is by a separate act of creative power that each of Adam's descendants come into this world. They were in the loins of Adam when he was created, Heb. vii. 10.

could have succeeded,[1] the doctrine of the sin of Adam being counted to us would have remained unshaken, because it no more depends only on this verse, than the doctrine of our Lord's divinity solely upon those individual texts against which Socinians direct all the force of their unhallowed criticisms. But the doctrine of imputed sin is evidently contained in the verse under consideration. Adam's sin was as truly the sin of every one of his posterity, as if it had been personally committed by him. It is only in this way that all could be involved in its consequences. Besides, it is only in this light that it is illustrative of justification by Christ. Believers truly die with Christ, and pay the debt in Him by their union or oneness with Him. It belongs not to us to inquire how these things can be. We receive them on the testimony of God. Secret things belong to the Lord our God; but those things which are revealed belong unto us and our children.

Ver. 13.—(*For until the law sin was in the world: but sin is not imputed where there is no law.*

This verse and the following are obviously interposed in vindication of the assertion that 'all have sinned.' It might be argued by opponents of the Gospel, that if there was no law, and therefore no transgression, anterior to Moses, the Apostle's declaration would not hold good in respect to that long period which elapsed before the promulgation of the written commandments at Mount Sinai. In reply, Paul reasons backward from death to sin, and from sin to law. Admitting, in the last clause of the verse, that sin could not be imputed without law, he proves that sin was in the world by the undeniable fact that there was death; and if this proves that there was sin, then it inevitably follows that there must have been law: and thus he evinces the fallacy of the assumption on which the objection is founded. Death, he had shown, was, *in all*, the consequence of sin. But before the Mosaic law, as well as afterward, death reigned in the world universally, and with supreme dominion.

Until the law.—That is, from the entrance of sin and death by Adam until the law of Moses. It is hardly needful to remark that the use of the word 'until' does not imply a cessation of sin on the introduction of the Mosaic economy. *Was,*—that is, really was, or truly existed,—not, according to Dr. Macknight, 'was counted,' as if Adam's posterity had his first sin counted to them, though it was not really theirs. It was their sin as truly as it was that of Adam, otherwise the justice of God would never have required that they should suffer for it. But it is not our business to try to account for this on principles level to the capacity

---

[1] If verse 12th, as Mr. Stuart would have it, means simply, as by one man sin entered into the world, and death by sin, and so death passed upon all men, for that all have *actually* sinned; then the other member of the comparison may be expressed (strongly, indeed, but on this principle amply) in the words of the Socinian Curcel-loeus :—'So life passed upon all men who have been spiritually born again of Christ by faith, since they all, after their conversion, have kept the commands of God.' But will Mr. Stuart accept this completion of the parallel ?—a completion by which Christ is dishonoured, and the glory of justifying sinners (for that is the opposite of condemnation) is parcelled out between the perfect righteousness of the Son of God, and the poor performances of those whom He came to save. In the words of Maresius, 'Certainly that is the sin of all on account of which death passed through upon all : Therefore Adam's sin is the sin of all.'

of man, but to receive it as little children, on the authority of God. *But sin is not imputed.*—Many are greatly in error in the interpretation of this expression, understanding it as if before the giving of the law sin existed, but was not imputed; but if sin exists, it must be reckoned sin. It means that sin does not exist where there is no law. The conclusion, therefore, is, that as sin is not reckoned where there is no law, and as sin was reckoned, or as it existed, before the law of Moses, therefore there was law before the law of Moses. The passage may be thus paraphrased: —'For sin existed among men from Adam to Moses, as well as afterwards. Yet there is no sin where there is no law. There were, then, both sin and law before the giving of the law of Moses.' The law before Moses is that which God had promulgated, besides the law written in the heart, which makes all men accountable.

Ver. 14.—*Nevertheless death reigned from Adam to Moses, even over them that had not sinned after the similitude of Adam's transgression, who is the figure of Him that was to come.*

Nevertheless, or *but.*—That is, though it is a truth that there is no sin where there is no law, and that where there is no law transgressed there is no death, yet we see that death reigned from Adam to Moses, as well as from Moses to the present time. The conclusion from this is self-evident, and therefore the Apostle leaves his readers to draw it,—namely, that the human race have always been under law, and have universally been transgressors. *Even over them that had not sinned after the similitude of Adam's transgression.*—Some suppose that the persons referred to are those who did not, like Adam, break a revealed or a positive law. But this is objected to on the following grounds:—1st, There is no strong or striking difference, and therefore no contrast, between the different methods of promulgating a law. Whether a law is made known by being written on the heart or on tables, is to the persons to whom it comes a matter with which they have no concern. A contrast might as well be made between those who know a law by reading it themselves, and those who hear it read, or between those who hear it immediately from the lawgiver, and those who hear it through the medium of others. 2d, The reason of introducing the persons referred to by the word *even,* implies that they are such persons as apparently ought to be excluded from the reign of sin and death. This cannot designate those who in any way know the law. But it evidently applies to infants. No one will cordially receive this except the man who, like a little child, submits to the testimony of God. Indeed, no man can understand the grounds of this imputation, so as to be able perfectly to justify it on principles applicable to human life. It must always stand, not on our ability to see its justice, but on our belief that God speaks true, and that it is just, as the Judge of all the earth in all things does justly, whether we are able to see it or not. 3d, The word *even* supposes that the persons referred to are but a portion of those generally included in the declaration of the preceding clauses. These cannot be such as received not a *positive law,* for all, from Adam to Moses, are such; but it will apply to infants. Death reigned from Adam to Moses, over all the human race, *even over infants,* who did not actually sin, but sinned in Adam. 4th, *Who is the image, figure, or type.*—This appears to have been suggested from the immediately preceding clause, and to imply that the persons referred to were *sinners*, or transgressors of law, just as the saved are righteous—the former sinners in Adam, although they had not actually sinned as he did, just as the others are righteous in Christ, although not actually righteous like Him. Those who are saved fulfil the law just as the others break the law, namely, in their great head or representative. But, 5th, Even if the persons here referred to were those who did not break a positive or a revealed law, yet it will come to the same thing. If the reign of death proves the reign of sin in such persons, must not the reign of death over infants equally prove the reign of sin? If the death of adults before the time of Moses was a proof of their being sinners, then of necessity the death of infants must prove the same thing. If death does not prove sin in infants, it cannot prove sin in any. If infants may die though they are not sinners, then may adults die without being sinners.

In alluding to the second and third reasons given above, it is observed in the *Presbyterian Review*, 'Such reasons as the two which we have copied above from Mr. Haldane, no advocate of the other explanation, so far as we have observed, has ever attempted to touch. They are clear and unembarrassed, and the last of them, especially, possesses all the power of a *reductio ad absurdum*. It places in a strange light the somewhat inelegant and feeble iteration, to say the least, which Turretine and Stuart would ascribe to the Apostle,—nevertheless sin reigned where there was no law, *even* over those who sinned without a law. The general import of verses 13 and 14 is given with great precision and beauty by Cornelius à Lapide. " You will object, that where there is no law, there can be no sin. As the men, however, in the interval between Adam and Moses died, it is obvious that they must necessarily have been sinners. And in case you may perchance insinuate that this is merely a proof of their actual sins, and not of original guilt, I appeal to children, who, although they had not offended against any (positive) Divine law, were also, during that period, subject to death. If infants, then, are included in the Apostle's declaration, we may infer from it directly the imputation to them of Adam's sin, as they have no actual transgression of their own which could render them obnoxious to the threatened punishment; and indeed, whether they are directly included or not, the simple fact that they die cannot be set aside, nor can the inference be evaded, that they are sinners by imputation." We are not ignorant that Mr. Stuart, in one of his *Excursus*, demurs to this conclusion, considering " temporal evils and death as discipline, probation, *sui generis*,"—p. 521. We started, we confess, to find so glaring a revival of the miserable sophistry of Taylor of Norwich, and felt disposed just to repeat the words " *sui generis*," and leave to his own power of refutation a sentiment which would have made even Heraclitus smile. But, seriously, if death is discipline, it is of the nature of chastisement; and is it the custom of a most tender parent to chastise a child that never offended him? Is it the practice of men who wish to be understood, to speak of mere discipline in such language as this,—" *Cursed* is the ground for thy

sake ; "—" the last *enemy* that shall be destroyed is death ? " Is it quite
consistent to deny, under every variety of form, and with all possible
intensity of asseveration, the moral agency of infants, and then to represent them as the subjects of a discipline from which, on this hypothesis,
they can derive no benefit, or to resolve death, in one place, into a kind
of *sui generis* probation, and in another to admit that the facts of the
evils of this life turning to a good account in respect to those who love
God, " does not show that they are not evils in themselves, nor that
they are not a part of the curse ? " In fine, does not the fantasy that
death is a sort of discipline, go to overturn the doctrine of the Saviour's
sacrifice ? If death is discipline generally, how can you show that it was
anything else in the case of Christ ? Yet unless in His case it was puni-
tive, the salvation of sinners must cease for ever,—it is not true that by
His stripes we can be healed.'

Figure of Him that was to come.—Efforts are made by some to involve
in uncertainty and obscurity a very clear subject, making it a matter of
difficulty. What are the aspects in which this likeness consists ? Mr.
Stuart instances a number of particulars, in which he makes the likeness
on the part of Christ to extend to certain benefits, which His death has
conferred on all mankind. But this is neither contained in this place,
nor in any other passage of Scripture. This fanciful and most unscriptural commentator wishes to evade the conclusion that Adam's sin
condemned all his posterity, and attempts to establish that it only
indirectly led to that result. But it is evident, from the connection,
that Adam must here be represented as a figure of Christ in that transgression which is spoken of, and in its consequences. His transgression,
and the ruin it brought on all mankind, as being one with him, was a
figure of the obedience to the law, and the suffering of the penalty, and
the recovery from its condemnation, by our being one with Christ as
our covenant-head.

The resemblance, on account of which Adam is regarded as the type
of Christ, consists in this, that Adam communicated to those whom he
represented what belonged to him, and that Christ also communicated
to those whom He represents what belonged to Him. There is, however, a great dissimilarity between what the one and the other communicates. By his disobedience Adam has communicated sin and
death, and by His obedience Christ has communicated righteousness
and life ; and as Adam was the author of the natural life of his posterity,
so Christ is the author of the spiritual life which His people now possess,
and which they shall enjoy at their resurrection, so that, in accordance
with these analogies, He is called the *last Adam.* If, then, the actual
obedience of Christ is thus imputed to all those of whom He is the
head, and is counted to them for their justification as their own
obedience ; in the same way, the actual sin of Adam, who is the type
of Christ, is imputed to all those of whom he is the head, and is counted
for their condemnation, as their own sin. In writing to those at
Corinth, who were ' sanctified in Christ Jesus,' the Apostle says, ' The
first man is of the earth, earthy; the second man is the Lord from
heaven. As is the earthy, such are they also that are earthy ; and as

is the heavenly, such are they also that are heavenly. And as we have borne the image of the earthy, we shall also bear the image of the heavenly.'

The information which the Scriptures give us of the sin of the first man, show that it was a complete subversion of nature, and the establishment of the kingdom of Satan in the world; they also show us that the purpose of sending Jesus Christ into the world was to destroy the empire of Satan, sin, and death. ' We read, says Mr. Bell *On the Covenants*, ' of two Adams, 1 Cor. xv. 45–49. As the one is called the first man, the other is called the second, even the Lord from heaven. Now, as there were innumerable multitudes of men between the first man and Him, it is plain that He is called the second man for some very peculiar reason. And what else can that be, but because He is the representative and father of all His spiritual seed, as the first man was of all his natural seed ? The one is the head, the federal head of the earthly men, the other of the heavenly. Since the one is called the second man, not because He was the second in the order of creation, but because He was the second public head, it follows that the other is called the first man not because he was first created, or in opposition to his descendants, but because he was the first public head in opposition to Christ the second. Thus the two Adams are the heads of the two covenants. The one the representative of all who are under the covenant of works, communicating his image unto them ; the other the representative of all who are under the covenant of grace, and communicating His image unto them. By the one man's disobedience many were made sinners, and by the obedience of the other many shall be made righteous.'

Ver. 15.—*But not as the offence, so also is the free gift. For if through the offence of one many be dead ; much more the grace of God, and the gift by grace, which is by one man, Jesus Christ, hath abounded unto many.*

Not as the offence, so also is the free gift.—There is a likeness between the sin of Adam and the gift of righteousness by Christ. But, as in most instances with regard to types, the antitype surpasses the type ; and while in some respects the type furnishes a likeness, in others it may be very dissimilar. The sin of Adam involved all his posterity in guilt and ruin, as they were all created in him as their head, and consequently in him are *guilty* by his disobedience. This was a shadow of the gift of righteousness by grace. All Christ's seed were created in Him, Eph. ii. 10, and are *righteous* by His obedience. But while the one was a type of the other in this respect, there is a great dissimilarity both as to the degree of the evil and of the blessing. The evil brought death, but the blessing not only recovered from ruin, but abounded to unspeakable happiness. *If through the offence of one many be dead,* or *died.*—Here it is taken for granted that ' the many ' who die, die through Adam's offence. Infants, then, die through Adam's offence, for they are a part of ' the many.' But we have before seen that death comes only by sin,—that is, none die who are not sinners, and there is no sin where there is no law, —consequently infants are sinners, and must be included in the law under which Adam sinned. If infants die by Adam's offence, they must be guilty by Adam's offence; for God does not visit with the punishment of sin where there is no sin. *Grace of God, and gift by grace.*—These differ, as the one is the spring and fountain of the other. The gift, namely, the gift of *righteousness* (ver. 17), is a gift which results purely from grace. Some explain this phrase as if by a figure one thing is made into two. But they are really two things. *By one man, Jesus Christ.*—The gift comes only by Jesus Christ. Without His atonement for sin, the gift could not have been made. Grace could not operate till justice was satisfied.

Much more hath abounded unto many.—The greater abounding cannot possibly be with respect to the greater number of individuals benefited. None are benefited by Christ but those who were ruined in Adam; and only a part of those who were ruined are benefited. In this respect, then, instead of an abounding, there is a shortcoming. The abounding is evidently in the gift extending, not only to the recovery of what Adam lost, but to blessings which Adam did not possess, and had no reason to expect. The redeemed are raised in the scale of being above all creatures, whereas they were created lower than the angels. Some are of opinion that the Apostle here rests the *abounding* of the gift on a supposition, which in the following verses he proves. Thus, as so much evil has come by Adam, it may well be supposed that much more good will come by Christ. But this is evidently mistaking the meaning altogether. The Apostle does not rest on supposition derived from the nature of the case; he asserts a fact. He does not say that it may well be supposed that a greater good comes by Christ than the evil that came by Adam; but he says that the good that comes by Christ does more than repair the evil that came by Adam.

Ver. 16.—*And not as it was by one that sinned, so is the gift: for the judgment was by one to condemnation, but the free gift is of many offences unto justification.*

By one that sinned.—Many read *by one sin;* but the common reading is preferable. The meaning is, in the case of the *one that sinned,* namely, Adam, condemnation came by *one offence;* but the free gift of righteousness extends to many offences, and to life eternal. This is another particular in which the gift exceeds the evil. It not only, as is stated in the last verse, confers more than Adam lost, but it pardons many sins; whereas condemnation came by one sin on the part of Adam. The gift by grace, then, not only procures to him who receives it the pardon of that one offence on account of which he fell under condemnation, but it brings to him the pardon of his many personal offences, although these offences deepen and aggravate the condemnation, and bear witness that he allows the deeds of his first father. *Judgment,* or sentence.—The original word here often itself signifies condemnation, or a condemning sentence; but as it here issues in condemnation, it must denote simply sentence, a judgment, without involving the nature of that sentence. *Condemnation.*—Here it is expressly asserted that condemnation has come by the one sin of the one man. If, then, all are condemned by that sin, all must be guilty by it, for the righteous Judge would not condemn the innocent. To say that any are condemned or punished for Adam's sin, who are not guilty by it, is to accuse the righteous God of injustice. Can God impute to any man anything that is not true? If Adam's sin is not ours as truly as it was Adam's sin, could God impute it to us? Does God deal with men as sinners, while they are not truly such? If God deals with men as sinners on account of Adam's sin, then it is self-evident that they are sinners on that account. The just God could not deal with men as sinners on any account which did not make them truly sinners. The assertion, however, that Adam's sin is as truly ours as it was his, does not imply that it is his and ours in the same sense. It was his personally; it is ours because we were in him. Adam's sin, then, is as truly ours as it was his sin, though not in the same way. *By one.*—Some make the substantive understood to be man. But though this would be a truth, yet, from the nature of the sentence, it is evident that the substantive understood is not *man*, but *sin;* for it is opposed to the *many offences.* It is, then, the one offence opposed to many offences. *Unto justification.*— The free gift confers the pardon of the many offences in such a way that the person becomes righteous; he is, of course, justified.

Ver. 17.—*For if by one man's offence death reigned by one; much more they which receive abundance of grace, and of the gift of righteousness, shall reign in life by one, Jesus Christ.*)

By one man's offence—rather, by *the* offence of *the* one man. The margin has 'by one offence,' for which there is no foundation. *Death reigned.*—It is here said that death reigned by *the* offence of *the* one man; consequently every one over whom death reigns is involved in that one offence of that one man. The empire of death, then, extends over infants and all men, on account of the one man. Instead of dying for their actual sins, death is to all men the penalty of the first sin. *Reigned.*— Those who die are here supposed to be the subjects of death, and death is considered as their king. If infants were not guilty in Adam, they could not be under the dominion of death. If they are not worthy of condemnation till they sin actually, they would not die till they sin actually. *Much more.*—Here the abounding of the gift over the evil is specified. Those redeemed by the death of Christ are not merely recovered from the fall, but made to reign through Jesus Christ, to which they had no title in Adam's communion. The saved are described as receiving abundance of grace, or the superabundance,—that is, the grace that abounds over the loss. This applies to all the redeemed. They all receive the superabundance of grace; they all receive more than was lost. They are also said to receive the superabounding of the gift of righteousness. This refers to the superior righteousness possessed by the redeemed, which is better than that which in innocence was possessed by Adam; for theirs is the righteousness of Christ, the righteousness of Him who is God. To this the righteousness of Adam and of angels cannot be compared. *Shall reign in life.*—Believers are to be kings as well as priests. All this they are to be through the one Jesus Christ; for as they were one with Adam in his fall, so they are one with Christ in His victory and triumph. If He be a king, they also are kings; for they are one with Him as they were one with Adam. They shall not be re-established in the terrestrial paradise in which man was first placed, subject to the danger of falling, but shall be conducted to honour, and glory, and immortality, in the heavenly world, before the throne of God, without the smallest danger of ever losing that blessing. They shall eat of the tree of life, which, says Christ, 'I will give' them, not on earth, but in the *midst* of the *paradise of God*. Speaking of His sheep, in the character of a Shepherd, Jesus Christ Himself says, 'I am come that they might have life, and that they might have it more abundantly.' 'I give unto them eternal life, and they shall never perish, neither shall any pluck them out of My hand. My Father, which gave them Me, is greater than all, and none is able to pluck them out of My Father's hand.' 'Your life is hid with Christ in God,' Col. iii. 3. By all this we learn the excellence of that life in which believers shall reign, by whom it is conferred, its absolute security, and eternal duration.

Ver. 18.—*Therefore, as by the offence of one judgment came upon all men to condemnation; even so by the righteousness of one the free gift came upon all men unto justification of life.*

Therefore, or wherefore, then.—There are two words in the original: the one word signifies wherefore, the other signifies then, or consequently. It states the result of what was said. *By the offence of one, or by one offence.*—Both of these are equally true, but the latter appears to be the design of the Apostle, as the word *one* wants the article. There is nothing in the original corresponding to the terms judgment and free gift, but they are rightly supplied by an ellipsis from verse 16. *Condemnation.*—Here it is expressly asserted that all men are condemned in the first offence. Infants, then, are included. If they are condemned, they cannot be innocent—they must be sinners; for condemnation would not have come upon them for a sin that is not theirs. The whole human race came under the condemnation of death in all its extent—spiritual, temporal, and eternal. *Even so,*—that is, in the same manner. *By the righteousness of one,* or rather, by one righteousness. Mr. Stuart prefers the former, because of the antithesis, δι' ἑνὸς δικαιώατος, which, he says, 'naturally cannot mean anything but the *righteousness of one* (not *one righteousness*).' But the phrase alluded to can very naturally and properly signify one righteousness, as the obedience of Christ is summed up in His act of obedience to death. Righteousness here, Mr. Stuart renders obedience, holiness, righteousness. But it is *righteousness* in its proper sense. By the one act of giving Himself for our sins, Christ brought in everlasting righteousness. *The free gift came upon all men.*—How did the free gift of the righteousness of God come upon all men, seeing all are not saved? Mr. Stuart explains it as signifying that righteousness is provided for all. But this is not the Apostle's statement. The coming of the free gift upon all is contrasted with the coming of condemnation on all, and therefore it cannot mean that condemnation actually came upon all, while the free gift was only provided for all. Besides, it is added, *unto justification of life.*—This is the issue of the coming of the free gift. It ends in the justification of life. *Upon all men.*—The persons here referred to must be those, and those only, who are partakers of justification, and who shall be finally saved. What then? Are all men to be justified? No; but the 'all men' here said to be justified, are evidently the 'all' of every nation, tribe, and kindred, whether Jews or Gentiles, represented by Christ. All who have been one with Adam were involved in his condemnation, and all who are one with Christ shall be justified by His righteousness.

No violence is necessary in order to restrict the universality of the terms 'all men' as they appear in this verse. General expressions must ever be construed with reference to their connection, and the context sufficiently defines their meaning. There is here an obvious and specific reference to the two heads of the human race, the first and the second man; and the 'all men,' twice spoken of in this verse, are placed in contrast to each other, as denoting the two families into which the world is divided.[1] The *all men*, then, must be limited to their respective heads. When this is understood, the meaning is alike clear and consistent, but without this all is dark and incongruous. If the 'all men' in the latter clause of the verse are made to apply to mankind without exception, then it follows that all men are justified, and all are made partakers of eternal life. But as this would contradict truth and Scripture, so the whole tenor of the Apostle's argument proves that the interpretation already stated is the true one. On account of the offence of Adam, sentence of death was pronounced upon *all* whom he represented. On account of the righteousness of Jesus Christ, sentence of justification unto life was pronounced in favour of *all* whom He represented.

'That the two multitudes,' it is observed in the *Presbyterian Review*, 'are co-extensive, that the point of the similitude is in some effect common to the *whole human race*, Mr. Stuart infers, quite as a matter of course, from this 18th verse, "As by the offence of one judgment came upon *all men* to condemnation, even so by the righteousness of one the free gift came upon *all men* to justification of life." And were we to confine our view to that verse, the inference might appear sufficiently probable. But we must attend to the scope of the whole section, and take care that we do not affix to one clause a signification which would make it a downright contradiction of another, of which the meaning is written as with a sunbeam. Now the sacred penman is throughout comparing Adam and Christ in their influence on two great bodies of human beings, and illustrating, by the comparison, the doctrine of justification. He states the likeness at first broadly, but lest his readers should be disposed to extend it too far, he accompanies it, in verses 15–17, with some explanations and restrictions. In these verses, therefore, the two contrasted multitudes must be the same as those mentioned in the general statement of verses 18 and 19, unless we wish to make the Apostle guilty of the deception of changing his terms upon us in the course of his argument, and while he is developing a similarity between A and B, interposing some limitations which have no reference to the connection of these terms, but which bear upon the relative positions of A and C. Now the multitude mentioned in the latter member of the

---

[1] This division was announced by God in pronouncing sentence on the serpent, ' I will put enmity between thee and the woman, and between thy seed and her seed, Gen. iii. 15.

contrast, which verses 15–17 express, is not the whole of mankind. It will not be pretended that *all men* obtain justification (ver. 16), or that all " shall reign in life through Jesus Christ" (ver. 17). In these verses the second member *cannot* be understood as comprising the entire human race ; and as, confessedly, the phrase " all men" (see John xii. 32 ; 2 Cor. iii. 2) *may* be used in a limited signification, there is no obvious reason why, in verse 18, it *must* be so used.

' There is just one objection to this exegesis which it is worth while to notice. Mr. Stuart thus states it :—" If we say that sentence of eternal perdition, in its highest sense, comes upon all men by the offence of Adam, and this without any act on their part, or even any voluntary concurrence in their present state and condition of existence, then, in order to make grace *superabound* over all this, how can we avoid the conclusion that justification, in its highest sense, comes upon all men without their concurrence ? " It is always a great convenience to a reviewer when an author refutes himself. This is the case in the present instance. " In regard to the *superabounding* of the grace of the Gospel," says Mr. Stuart in the very same page, " it must be noted, in order to avoid mistake, that I do not construe it as appertaining to the *number of the subjects*, but to the *number of offences* forgiven by it." Now, on this principle, our view of the diversity of the two multitudes does not abolish the superabundance of grace. To the elect, not merely the penal consequences of Adam's sin are remitted, but those of all their own innumerable transgressions, and thus grace still maintains its due pre-eminence.

' This objection vanishing so easily by a wave of the same wand which conjured it up, we are enabled fully to conclude, that although the whole of mankind are comprehended in the first number of the comparison, only the elect are included in the second; that the notion of placing *extent* of influence—the *number* of persons to whom the condemning or saving energy reaches—among the points of resemblance, obtains no countenance from Paul ; and that the opinion resting upon it, that sentence of condemnation can be passed upon none except for actual transgression, has no foundation.'[1]

Ver. 19.—*For as by one man's disobedience many were made sinners, so by the obedience of one shall many be made righteous.*

For.—This assigns a reason for what the Apostle has said in the preceding verses. *By one man's disobedience many were made sinners.*—Here it is expressly asserted that *the many* (not many ; it includes all who were in Adam, that is, all the human race) were made sinners by Adam's disobedience. Mr. Stuart attempts to evade this, by supposing that they are led into sin by the occasion of Adam's sin. This is a great perversion. Adam's disobedience is said not merely to be the occasion of leading his posterity into sin, but to have made them sinners. Mr. Stuart rests much on the absurdity of supposing that one man is punished for another's offence. But Adam's offence is the offence of all his posterity. It made

---

[1] Here it may be observed, that if all men had been saved, it would have given countenance to the supposition that fallen men had some claim upon God, that there was some hardship connected with their being brought under condemnation, not by their individual transgression, but by that of Adam, and thus the riches of grace would have been tarnished.

them sinners. That sin must be theirs by which they were made sinners. If there is any self-evident truth, this is one of the clearest. We must, like little children, receive God's testimony upon this as well as every other subject. We must not rest our acquiescence in God's testimony upon our ability to fathom the depth of His unsearchable counsels. Mr. Stuart makes Adam's sin merely what he calls the instrumental or occasional cause. But with no propriety can Adam's sin be called the instrument by which his posterity sinned. This is altogether absurd. And an occasional cause is no cause. Every person knows the difference between a *cause* and an *occasion*. Besides, to suppose that Christ's own obedience is the real cause of our justification, and that Adam's sin is only the *occasion*, not properly the cause, of our condemnation, is to destroy the contrast between Adam and Christ, on which the Apostle here insists. If Christ's obedience is the ground of our justification, Adam's disobedience must, by the contrast, be the ground of our condemnation.

So by the obedience of one shall the many be made righteous.—Only a part of mankind are included in that covenant of which Christ is the surety. In consequence of Adam being the covenant-head of all mankind, all are involved in his condemnation; but Christ is not the head of all mankind, but of the Church, and to all but the Church He will say, ' I never knew you.' *So,*—that is, in *this way*, not *in like manner.*—It is not in a manner that has merely some likeness, but it is in the very same manner. For although there is a contrast in the things, the one being disobedience, and the other obedience, yet there is a perfect *identity* in the manner. This is important, as by the turn given to the word translated *so*, Mr. Stuart perverts the passage. *The many* shall be constituted righteous. The many here applies to all in Christ. It is argued that the phrase, ' the many,' must be equally extensive in its application in both cases. So it is as to the respective representatives. *The many*, with reference to Adam, includes all his race. *The many*, with respect to Christ, implies all His seed. Again, if it is said that Adam's posterity became sinners merely by the example, influence, or occasion of his sin, it may with equal propriety be said that Christ's posterity became righteous by the example or occasion of His righteousness. This makes the Gospel altogether void.

The passage before us is of the highest importance. It forms a striking conclusion to all that goes before, from the beginning of the 12th verse, and asserts, in plain terms, two grand truths, on which the Gospel in all its parts proceeds, though by many they are strenuously opposed, and by others only partially admitted. In the 12th verse, the Apostle had said that death passed upon all men, *for that all have sinned.* In the 13th and 14th verses, he had shown that to this there is no exception; and had further declared that Adam was the figure of Christ who was to come. In the following verses, to the end of the 17th, he had asserted the opposite effects that follow from the sin of the one and the righteousness of the other. In the 18th verse, he had given a summary of what he had said in the preceding verses. Condemnation, he had there affirmed, had come by the offence of one, and justification by the righteousness of one.

But as it would not be readily admitted that either a curse or a blessing should come on men on account of the sin or righteousness of another, he here explicitly affirms this truth, which was indeed included in his preceding statements, but being of so great importance, it was proper that it should be declared in the plainest terms. It is grounded on the constituted unity of all men with their covenant-heads. By the disobedience of Adam, those who were one with him in the first creation were made *sinners*. In the same way, by the obedience of Jesus Christ, they who are one with Him in the new creation are made *righteous*. This 19th verse contains the explicit declaration of these two facts, and the appellations 'sinners' and 'righteous' must be understood in the full extent of these terms.' Here, then, these two doctrines of the imputation of sin and of righteousness, which is taught throughout the whole of the Scriptures, is exhibited in a manner so clear, that, without opposing the obvious meaning of the words, they cannot be contested. It is impossible to conceive how men could be made sinners by the disobedience of Adam, or righteous by the obedience of Jesus Christ, in any degree whatever, if the truth of the doctrine of the imputation of the sin of the former, and of the righteousness of the latter, be not admitted.

In order to remove every pretext for the supposition that the sin of Adam is not asserted in this 19th verse to be truly our sin, it is essential to observe that when it is here said that by one man's disobedience many were made 'sinners,' there is no reference to the *commission* of sin, or to our proneness to it from our innate corruption. The reference is exclusively to its *guilt*. It was formerly shown, in the exposition of the third chapter, that it was in reference to the Divine tribunal, and respecting condemnation, that Paul had all along been considering sin both in regard to Jews and Gentiles, and that his assertion that they are *under sin* can only signify that they are guilty, since he there repeats in summary what he had before advanced. And he fully establishes this meaning when he afterwards says, in the 19th verse of that chapter, 'that every mouth may be stopped, and all the world may become *guilty* before God.' Now these remarks equally apply to every part of his discussion, from the beginning of the Epistle to the end of this fifth chapter. In the whole course of it, all he says of the commission of sin is solely with a view to establish the *guilt* of those of whom he speaks, on account of which they are under condemnation, in order that, in contrast, he might exhibit that righteousness by which men, being justified, are freed from guilt and condemnation. In the same manner, it is evident from all the preceding context that by the term *sinners* in the verse before us, Paul does not mean that through the disobedience of one many were rendered depraved and addicted to the commission of sin, but that they become guilty of sin. In the 15th and 17th verses, he says that through the offence of one many are 'dead,' and that death reigned; and in verse 16, that the judgment was by one to 'condemnation;' and this he repeats in the 18th verse, where he says that as by the offence of one or by one offence judgment came upon all men to 'condemnation,' so by the righteousness of one, or by one righteousness, the free gift came upon all men unto 'justification' of life. He is speaking, then, all along of sin only in reference to condemnation, and of righteousness only in reference to justification. In the same way, in this 19th verse, where he repeats or sums up all that he had asserted in the preceding verses, when he says that by the disobedience of one many were made 'sinners,' the reference is exclusively to the guilt of sin, which occasions condemnation. When, on the other hand, he says that by the obedience of one many were made righteous, the reference is exclusively to justification. And as it is evident that the expression righteousness has here no reference to inherent righteousness or sanctification, so the term sinners has no reference to the pollution, indwelling, or actual commission of sin, or the transmission of a corrupt nature; otherwise the contrast would be destroyed, and, without any notification, a new idea would be introduced entirely at variance with the whole of the previous discussion from the beginning of the Epistle, and of that in the immediate connection of this verse with its preceding context. It is then in the *guilt* of Adam's sin that the Apostle here asserts we partake; and therefore that sin must be truly our sin, otherwise its guilt could not attach to us.

But although men are here expressly declared to be sinners by the disobedience of Adam, just as they are righteous by the obedience of Christ, this is rejected by multitudes, and by every man in his natural state, to whom the things of God are foolishness. If such an one attends to it at all, it must undergo certain modifications, which, changing its aspect, makes it altogether void. On the other hand, that men are righteous in the way here declared, though not so repulsive to the natural prepossessions of the human mind, meets also with much opposition. But why should there be such reluctance to receive these truths, which by every means possible are attempted to be avoided? To him that submits to them nothing can be more consolatory. He is compelled to acknowledge that he sinned in Adam, and fell under condemnation; but at the same time he is called to rejoice in the heart-cheering declaration, that the righteousness of Christ is his righteousness, because he has been 'created in Christ Jesus,' Eph. ii. 10, with whom he is one, Gal. iii. 28; and that, being thus righteous in Him, he shall reign with Him in life.

While, however, it is solely of the imputation of Adam's sin, and the imputation of Christ's righteousness, that the Apostle is treating, showing that by our oneness with these our respective covenant-heads the sin of the first and the righteousness of the last Adam are really ours, it is proper to remark that, though it is not touched upon in the verse before us, there is a further beautiful analogy between the effect of our union with the first man, who is of the earth earthy, and of our union with the second man, who is the Lord from heaven. We not only partake of the guilt of the personal sin of Adam, and consequently of condemnation, but also of a corrupt nature transmitted from him. In the same way we are partakers not only of the righteousness of Jesus Christ, and consequently of justification, but also of sanctification, by a new nature derived from Him.

Mr. Stuart seems to understand that, according to the doctrine of imputation, sins are accounted to Adam's race that are not their sins, or, in other words, that God accounts a thing to be fact which is not fact; just as he had before affirmed that faith is imputed *as* righteousness. But Adam's sin is imputed to his posterity because it is their sin in reality, though we may not be able to see the way in which it is so. Indeed, we should not pretend to explain this, because it is to be believed on the foundation of the Divine testimony, and not on human speculation, or on our ability to account for it. 1. If God testifies that Adam's first sin is also that of all his posterity, is He not to be credited? If there be no such Divine testimony, we do not plead for the doctrine. It is on the Divine testimony the doctrine must rest. 2. Mr. Stuart speaks of imputation in its strict sense, or in a rigid sense. This too much resembles an artifice designed to deceive the simple into the belief that he admits the doctrine, if not substantially, at least in some sense. This, however, is not the fact. He cannot admit imputation in any sense. He does not admit Adam's sin to be our sin in the lowest degree. 3. If, in reality, he does admit imputation in the lowest degree, then it is not impossible in the highest. If it is essentially unjust, it cannot exist in the lowest degree. Why then does he speak in this uncandid manner? Does this language betoken a man writing under the full conviction that he is contending for the truth of God? He professes to determine this question by an appeal to the natural sentiments of men. But if this tribunal is sufficient to decide this point, is it not equally so with respect to innumerable others, in which deists and heretics have made a like appeal? On this ground, may not a man say, I cannot admit the eternity of future punishment, for it is contrary to my natural sentiments; I cannot admit that a good Being is the Creator of the world, for He would not have permitted evil to enter it, had He been able to keep it out? He says, p. 233, ' We never did, and never can, feel guilty of another's act, which was done without any knowledge or concurrence of our own.' But if God has testified that there is a sense in which that act is our own, shall we not be able to admit and feel it? It altogether depends on the Divine testimony. Now, such is the testimony of the verse before us in its obvious sense. How this is, or in what sense this is the case, we may not be able to comprehend. This is no part of our business; this is no part of the Divine testimony. We are to believe God on His word, not from our capacity to understand the manner in which the thing testified is true. Mr. Stuart himself asserts, p. 235, that the sufferings of infants may conduce to their eternal good, yet he says, ' in what way I pretend not to determine.' And are we to determine in what way Adam's sin is ours, before we admit the fact on the Divine testimony? He says, p. 233, ' We may just as well say that we can appropriate to ourselves and make our own the righteousness of another, as his unrighteousness.' Here he denies the imputation of the righteousness of Christ. If the Divine testimony assures us that by a Divine constitution we are made one with Christ, is not His righteousness ours? If it be declared that God ' hath made Him to be sin for us, who knew no sin, that we might be made the righteousness of God in Him,' shall we not believe it? In opposition to all such infidel reasonings, it is becoming in the believer to say, I fully acknowledge, and I humbly confess, on the testimony of my God, that I am guilty of Adam's sin; but by the same testimony, and by the same Divine constitution, I believe that I am a partaker of God's righteousness—the righteousness of my God and Saviour Jesus Christ—of the free gift of that righteousness, which not only removes the guilt and all the fatal consequences of that first sin, but of the many offences which I have myself committed. Regarding the difficulties that in both these respects present themselves, I hear my Saviour say, ' What is that to thee ? follow thou Me.' In the meantime, it is sufficient for me to know that the Judge of all the earth will do right. What I know not now, I shall know hereafter.

The summary argument commonly used against the imputation of Adam's sin, namely, that it is ' contrary to reason,' proceeds on a mere assumption—an assumption as unwarrantable as that of the Socinian, who denies the Trinity in unity because it is above his comprehension. Most persons are in the habit of considering many things which they cannot fathom, and which they cannot relish, as being contrary to reason. But this is not just. A thing may be very disagreeable, and far beyond the ken of human penetration, which is not contrary to reason. We are not entitled to pronounce anything contrary to reason which does not imply a contradiction. A contradiction cannot be true, but all other things may be true, and, on sufficient evidence, ought to be received as true. That Adam's sin may, in a certain view, be our sin, and that Christ's righteousness may, in a certain view, be our righteousness, no man is entitled to deny on the ground of self-evident truth. Whether it is true or not must depend on evidence. Now the testimony of God in the Scriptures leaves no doubt on the subject. Adam's sin is our sin. Christ's righteousness is the righteousness of all His people.

If it be contrary to reason to have the sin of Adam counted as our own, it is still worse to suppose that we suffer, as is generally admitted, for a sin which is not ours. If there is injustice in the one, there is much more injustice in the other. This surely is the language of reason, and, as such, has been insisted on by orthodox writers both of our own and of other countries. Of this I shall give the following examples :—' If that sin of Adam,' says Brown of Wamphray, in his *Life of Justification Opened*, p. 179, ' If that sin of Adam be imputed in its curse and punishment, the sin itself must be imputed as to its guilt ; else we must say that God curseth and punisheth the posterity that is noways guilty, which to do suiteth not the justice of God, the righteous Governor of the world.'

' Certainly,' says B. Pictet, in his *Christian Theology*, vol. i. p. 368, ' if the sin of Adam had not been imputed to his descendants, we could not give a reason why God has permitted that the corruption which was in Adam, the consequence of his first sin, should have passed to his posterity. That this reasoning may appear just, we must consider that the corruption which we bring from the womb of our mothers is a very great evil, for it is the source of all sins. To permit, then, that this corruption should pass from fathers to their children, is to inflict a punishment. But how is it that God should punish men, if they had not sinned, and if they were not guilty ? Now it is certain that, when this corruption communicates itself from fathers to children, the children themselves have not sinned. It must then be the fact that the sin of Adam is imputed to them, and that God considers them as having part in the sin of their first father.'

'It cannot be explained, consistent with Divine justice,' says Witsius in his *Economy*, vol. i. p. 153, 'how, without a crime, death should have passed upon Adam's posterity. Prosper reasoned solidly and elegantly as follows:—" Unless, perhaps, it can be said that the punishment, and not the guilt, passed on the posterity of Adam; but to say this is in every respect false, for it is too impious to judge so of the justice of God, as if He would, contrary to His own law, condemn the innocent with the guilty. The guilt, therefore, is evident where the punishment is so; and a partaking in punishment shows a partaking in guilt,—that human misery is not the appointment of the Creator, but the retribution of the Judge." If, therefore,' continues Witsius, 'through Adam all are obnoxious to punishment, all, too, must have sinned in Adam.'

A considerable part of the resistance to the imputation of Adam's sin is owing to the ground on which the evidence of the fact is often rested. It is not simply placed on the authority of the testimony of God, but is attempted to be justified by human procedure. The difficulty that some persons feel on this subject, arises from the supposition that though the sin of the first man is charged upon his posterity, yet it is not theirs. But the Scriptures hold it forth as ours in as true a sense as it was Adam's. We may be asked to explain how it can be ours, and here we may find ourselves at a loss for an answer. But we ought to consider that we are not obliged to give an answer on this point either to our-selves or others. We are to receive it on the Divine testimony, assured that what God declares must be true, however unable we may be to comprehend it. We ought not to perplex ourselves by endeavouring to ascertain the grounds of the Divine testimony on this subject. Our duty is to understand the import of what is testified, and to receive it on that authority—not to inquire into the justice of the constitution from which our guilt results. This is not revealed, and it is utterly beyond our province and beyond our depth. Did Abraham understand why he was commanded to offer up his son? No. But he was strong in faith, and his faith in obeying in that instance is held forth in Scripture for our imitation. Like Abraham, let us give glory to God, by believing implicitly what we have no means of knowing to be true, but simply on the testimony of God.

The defenders of scriptural truth take wrong ground when they rest it on anything but the testimony of Scripture. It is highly dishonourable to God to refuse to submit to His decisions till we can demonstrate their justice. Those who have endeavoured to vindicate the Divine justice in accounting Adam's sin to be ours, and to reconcile the mind of man to that procedure, have not only laboured in vain, but actually injured the cause they meant to uphold. The connection according to which we suffer with our first father, is not such as is to be vindicated or illustrated by human transactions. The union of Adam and his posterity is a Divine constitution. The grounds of this constitution are not to be found in any of the justifiable transactions of men; and all attempts to make us submit by convincing us of its propriety, from what we are able to understand upon a comparison with the affairs of men, are only calculated to impose on credulity, and to produce unbelief. We receive it because God says it, not because we see it to be just. We know it to be just because it is part of the ways of the just God. But how it is just we may not be able to see. We receive it like little children who believe the testimony of their father, though they do not understand the grounds or reasons of the thing testified.

Nothing is more common than to vindicate the equity of our implication in the ruin of Adam's fall, by alleging that had he stood, we should have been partakers in all his blessings. Had he stood, it is said, you would have reaped the benefit of his standing; is it not therefore just that you should also suffer the loss of his failure? Here the matter is rested, not on God's testimony, but on our sense of justice in the affairs of men. To this it will be replied, that if the transaction is not entered into with our consent, there is no apparent equity in our being punished with the loss. Adam's sin, then, we acknowledge to be ours, not because a similar thing would be just among men, but because God, the just God, testifies that it is so; and we know that the righteous God will do righteously. To submit in this way is rational; to submit on the ground of understanding the justice of the thing, is to pretend to understand what is incomprehensible, and to rest faith on a fallacy, namely, that the ground of the imputation of Adam's sin is of the same nature with human transactions. The method of vindicating Divine truth here censured, has also the most unhappy tendency in encouraging Christians to think that they must always be able to give a reason for their believing God's testimony, from their ability to comprehend the thing testified. It accustoms them to think that they should believe God, not simply on His testimony, but on seeing with their own eyes that the thing is true independently of His testimony. On the contrary, the Christian ought to be accustomed to submit to God's testimony without question, and without reluctance, even in things the farthest beyond the reach of the human mind. ' Speak, Lord, for Thy servant heareth,' ought to be the motto of every Christian. Yet how few follow out to their full extent the plain statements of the word of God on these subjects; and while many utterly deny and abhor every representation of the imputation of sin and righteousness, others hide its genuine features by an attempt to enable men to understand the reasons of it, and to justify the Divine procedure. This is altogether improper. The ways of God are too deep for our feeble minds to fathom them, and it is impious as well as arrogant to make the attempt. Against nothing ought Christians to be more constantly and earnestly guarded, than the opinion that they ought to be able to comprehend and justify what they believe on the authority of God.

The true ground on which to vindicate it is the explicit testimony of God in the Scripture. This is so clear, that no man can set it aside, we need not say, without wresting the Scriptures, but, we may assert, without being conscious of violence of interpretation. Our defence of this doctrine, then, should ever be, ' Thus saith the Lord.' This method of defence, which we are taught in this same Epistle, ch. ix. 20, is not merely the only scriptural one, but it is the one that will have the greatest success. As long as a reason is alleged by the wisdom of man in support of the doctrine, so long, from the same source, an argument will be produced on the other side. But when the word of God is appealed to, and upon it all the stress of evidence rested, the Christian must submit. The writer knows from personal experience the effect of this method of teaching this doctrine.

' You cannot comprehend,' says Luther, ' how a just God can condemn those who are born in sin, and cannot help themselves, but must, by a necessity of their natural constitution, continue in sin, and remain children of wrath. The answer is, God is incomprehensible throughout ; and therefore His justice, as well as His other attributes, must be incomprehensible. It is on this very ground that St. Paul exclaims, " O the depth of the riches and the knowledge of God ! How unsearchable are His judgments, and His ways past finding out ! " Now His judgments would not be past finding out, if we could always perceive them to be just.'

The imputation and consequences of Adam's sin are well expressed in the Westminster Confession of Faith, in which it is said, 'These (our first parents) being the root of all mankind, the guilt of this sin was imputed, and the same death in sin and corrupt nature conveyed to all their posterity, descending from them by ordinary generation.' And again, ' The covenant being made with Adam as a public person, not for himself only, but for his posterity, all mankind descending from him by ordinary generation, *sinned in him* and fell with him in the first transgression. . . . The sinfulness of that estate whereinto man fell consisteth in the guilt of Adam's first sin.'

Ver. 20.—*Moreover, the law entered, that the offence might abound ; but where sin abounded, grace did much more abound.*

The Apostle had now arrived at the conclusion of the discussion, commencing at the 17th verse of the first chapter, in the course of which, after having briefly announced the remedy which God had provided for the salvation of man, he had proceeded to show the need there is for the application of this remedy by proving the sinful state of all, both Jews and Gentiles, whatever had been their various means of instruction. He had next fully exhibited that remedy for their deliverance, and also the manner in which it is applied. In the beginning of this fifth chapter he had unfolded the blessed effects that follow from its reception, in the experience of all believers, and had extolled the love of God in its appointment. Having next proved, from the universality of the reign of death, that the law and sin existed from the beginning, and so before the public promulgation of the law at Mount Sinai, he had taken occasion to point out the entrance both of sin and righteousness, and of the imputation first of the one and next of the other. And as it might now be asked, ' Wherefore, then, serveth the law ? ' Gal. iii. 19, if man's personal obedience to it enters in no respect into his justification, it therefore formed a proper conclusion to the whole to recur, as in the verse before us, to that law at which, in passing, Paul had glanced in the 13th verse, and to show that it had been introduced in order that on the one hand the abounding of sin might be made manifest, and on the other the superabounding of grace, on both of which he had been insisting in proof of the reality and fatal effects of the former, and the necessity, the glory, and the blessedness of the latter.

The law entered, ' privily entered,' says Dr. Macknight, referring to the law of nature, which, he says, privily entered after the fall of our first parents. But no new law entered after the fall. What is called the law of nature, is only the remains of the law written in creation on the heart of man. The law here is evidently the law of Moses, and the word in the original signifies that the law entered *in addition* to the law which Adam transgressed, and to the law written in the heart. This is the effect of παρα in this place. *That the offence might abound.*—The word translated offence, here and in several of the verses above, literally signifies ' fall,' and is applied in these verses to the first sin of Adam. In verse 16, however, in the plural, it refers to sins in general, and in some other places is rendered trespasses. In that before us it may refer particularly, as in those preceding, to the first sin, which, as the root and cause of all other sins, has abounded in its baneful effects, and; like a noxious plant, shot up and spread in all directions; so that, as God had testified before the flood, ' the wickedness of man is great on the earth,' Gen. vi. 5. This was fully discovered by the entrance of the law. The law then entered, not that sinners might be justified by it, for no law could give life to fallen man, Gal. iii. 21. Sinners, in order to be saved, must be redeemed from the curse of the law, and created again in Christ Jesus. But it entered that the offence might abound, and that every mouth may be stopped, and all the world may become guilty before God, ch. iii. 19 ; that we might learn that the righteous God loveth righteousness, that His law is exceeding broad, that it is spiritual, extending to all the imaginations of the thoughts, that He will not abate one jot or tittle of this perfect standard, which is a transcript of His character. The law is a perfect standard, by which men are taught to measure themselves, that they may see their guilt and condemnation, and be led to look to Him who is the end of the law for righteousness to every one that believeth. Some translate this clause, which is rendered, that the offence might abound, ' so as the offence eventually abounds.' This is not the Apostle's meaning. They say that the intention of the law was not to make sin abound, but to restrain sin, and make fewer sins. If this was the intention of giving the law, the Lawgiver has been disappointed, for sins have been multiplied a thousandfold by the entrance of the law. This their view of the matter admits ; for they acknowledge that this was the *event*, though not the *intention*. But if this was the event, it must also have been the intention of the Lawgiver, though not of the law. God cannot be disappointed of His intentions. But it is self-evidently clear that the intention of the promulgation of the law of Moses could not be to lessen the number of sins, when almost the whole ceremonial part of it makes things to be sin which were not sin before the giving of the law, and which are not sinful in their own nature. Besides, sin is greatly increased as to the guilt of the breach of the moral law, by the promulgation of the law of Moses. While the law of God is holy, and just, and good, it was evidently God's intention, in the giving of it, that offences might abound. In this way the wickedness of the human heart was manifested. It showed men that they were sinners. Had not the law been repeated in its extent and purity at Sinai, such was the darkness in men's minds, that they would not have thought themselves transgressors of its precepts, or obnoxious to its curse; and not seeing themselves sinners, they would not have seen the necessity of a surety. The 'commandment is a lamp, and the law is light,' Prov. vi. 23. It discovers the real state of human nature, and manifests not only the evil and aggravation, but also the vast accumulation and extent, of the wickedness of man. The entrance, then, of the law between the author of condemnation and the author of justification, in order that sin might abound, was of the highest importance. 'By the law is the knowledge of sin.' The law did not put sin into the heart, but it was an instrument to display the depravity already existing in the heart. But vain man will be wise, and he will compel the word of God to submit to his own views. It may be justly said that such displays of the deep things of God as are made in His word, are intended to manifest the blindness of the human mind, and the deep depravity of human nature.

Where sin abounded grace did much more abound.—This was another effect of the entrance of the law, that as, by the clear light it imparts, sin would abound in all its extent and enormity, so grace might be exhibited as abounding above sin. The grace of God, dispensed from His throne, not only pardons the most numerous and most heinous sins, but also confers eternal life upon him who has sinned. It restores him to communion with God, which by transgression he had forfeited, re-establishing it not only in a far higher degree, but in a manner so permanent as never again to be interrupted. 'When sin,' says Calvin, ' had held men plunged under its power, grace came to their relief. For Paul teaches us that the more sin is known, the grandeur and magnificence of grace is the more evident; and is poured out in so copious a manner as not only to overcome, but even to overwhelm the overflowing deluge of iniquity.'

Ver. 21.—*That as sin hath reigned unto death, even so might grace reign through righteousness unto eternal life by Jesus Christ our Lord.*

As sin hath reigned unto death.—Death here, and throughout this chapter, as well as in many other places, signifies not temporal death merely, but the whole punishment of sin, of which temporal death is perhaps the smallest part. Eternal misery is included in it, but the word 'death' does not literally denote eternal misery. This is called the '*second death*,' and this expression gives us the key to understand the full extent of the meaning of the word. The punishment of hell is the *second death*, according to Scripture explanation, Rev. xx. 14, xxi. 8, and therefore it is no fancy to understand future eternal punishment as included in the term. But though the expression includes this, it is not proved from the literal meaning of the word death. As death is the greatest of all temporal evils, it was not only a part of the punishment of the first sin, but it was the symbol of the second death. It is another proof that death includes the whole punishment of sin, that, in Rom. vi. 23, death is called the wages of sin. If death be the wages of sin, then death must include everything that is the wages or punishment of sin. But the Scriptures point out future misery, as well as temporal death, as the wages of sin. This proof is incontrovertible. The Scriptures show that the punishment of sin is eternal misery; if so, death includes eternal misery. While this lays no stress on the necessary literal meaning of the word death, it comes to the same conclusion. Another proof that death here signifies the whole punishment of sin, and consequently that it includes eternal misery, is, that the gift of God is said to be 'eternal life.' Now life literally is as limited as death. Yet life here signifies not merely existence in a state of consciousness, but of *happiness*. Life, indeed, even without the word eternal, is in Scripture taken to signify all the happiness of the future state of the blessed. What objection, then, can there be to a like extended signification of the term death? That it includes spiritual death is beyond a question, as the Scriptures expressly use this term in this sense, Eph. ii. 1; Col. ii. 13. That they are all included in the threatening against the eating of the forbidden fruit, is most certain. It is no objection that it was not explained to Adam in this sense. If any part of Scripture explains it in this sense, it is sufficient. It may be said that it would be unjust to punish Adam in any extent that he did not understand as included in the threatening. He understood by it destruction, or at least we have no ground to say that he did not. Returning to the dust is not the explanation of the threatening, it being God's appointment in connection with the promise of Christ. But it is perfectly sufficient that he knew the law that was given him. To make him guilty, there was no necessity for any threatening. Is not a child guilty when he breaks the command of a father, even though the command be unaccompanied with threatening? With regard to Christ's suffering for us, it was not necessary that He should suffer eternally. It answers all the ends of justice if He has suffered a perfect equivalent. That He has done so, we have the clear testimony of the Scriptures, and we have no need to show how He has done so by metaphysical explanations and calculations of our own.

Even so might grace reign through righteousness.—Mr. Stuart having subverted, by his interpretations and reasonings, every idea of the imputation of sin, as he had formerly altogether set aside the imputation of righteousness, is only consistent in misrepresenting the meaning of this passage. As he has mistaken the import of the expression *righteousness* at the commencement of this discussion, so he also misunderstands it here. His explanation is, that 'grace might reign or have an influence widely extended, in the bestowment of justification or pardoning mercy.' The passage informs us that grace reigns unto eternal life, which does indeed include the bestowment of justification. But it informs us of something more, and that of the last importance, which Mr. Stuart's mistaking righteousness for justification leads him entirely to omit. Grace reigns THROUGH RIGHTEOUSNESS, *even the righteousness of God*, which *fulfils His law*, and *satisfies His justice*, and *displays His holiness;* whereas, did grace bestow a justification in such a way as Mr. Stuart describes, it would do so at the expense of law and justice, and dishonour the whole Divine administration.

Unto eternal life by Jesus Christ our Lord.—This is that life of which Jesus Christ, who is risen from the dead, is the author, as the death here spoken of is that which *He* came to destroy. The source of our natural life is Adam, but he is dead, and in his communion we all die. But a new source of life is provided in the second Adam, that He may deliver from death all that are in His communion. 'The first Adam was made a living soul,' that he might communicate natural life to those who had not received it. 'The last Adam was made a quickening spirit,' that He might impart spiritual life to those who had lost it. The first communicated an earthly and perishable life, the second a life that is celestial and immortal. Jesus Christ is that eternal life which was with the Father, and was manifested unto us; and the Father hath given Him power over all flesh, to give eternal life to as many as He hath given Him. 'My sheep hear My voice, and I know them, and they follow Me, and I give unto them eternal life.' The termination, then, of the reign of death over those whom He represents, and the establishment of the reign of grace through the everlasting righteousness which He has brought in, are all by Jesus Christ. He hath abolished death. By Him came grace and truth; He brought life and immortality to light. He 'is the true God, and eternal life.' And 'to this end Christ both died, and rose, and revived, that He might be the Lord both of the dead and the living.' The similarity of the Apostle's commencement in unfolding the doctrine of justification, and of his conclusion, is very striking. He begins, ch. i. 17, by declaring that the *Gospel of Christ* is the power of God *unto salvation*, because therein is the *righteousness* of God revealed; and he here ends by affirming that *grace* reigns through *righteousness* unto *eternal life* by *Jesus Christ* our Lord.

In this 21st verse the doctrine of the whole preceding context, of the salvation of believers, is summed up in a manner most beautiful and striking. Having exhibited in a strong light the righteousness of God, ch. iii. 21, 22, the Apostle returns to it in this chapter; and, having contrasted Christ and Adam, he brings out his conclusion in this verse with a contrast of the reign of sin and grace. Sin had an absolute sway over all the descendants of Adam. There was nothing good among them, or in any of them. Sin existed and predominated in every human soul. Therefore it is said to *reign*. The absolute and universal influence of sin is figured by the empire of a monarch exercising authority in uncontrolled sovereignty. Grace also *reigns*. There was nothing in men to merit salvation, or to recommend them in any measure to God. Grace therefore *reigns* in their salvation, which is wholly and entirely of free favour. Sin is said to reign unto, or in, death. This shows that death was, in every human being, the effect of his sin. The way in which death manifested its universal reign over the human race, was in causing their death. This most fully proves that infants are sinners. If sin ruled in causing death to its subjects, then all who died are the subjects of sin. Death to the human race is in every instance the effect of the dominion of sin. *Sin reigns unto death.*—But if sin has reigned, grace reigns. If the former has reigned in death, the latter reigns in life; yea, it reigns unto eternal life. How, then, does it reign unto life?

Is it by a gratuitous pardon? Doubtless it is. But it is not by forgiving the sinner in an arbitrary way, with respect to the punishment due to sin. Forgiveness is indeed entirely gratuitous; but if it cost believers nothing, it has cost much to their Surety. *Grace reigns through righteousness.*— How beautifully is thus fulfilled the prophetic declaration of Ps. lxxxv. 10–13. Grace did not, could not, deliver the lawful captives without paying the ransom. It did not trample on justice, or evade its demands. It reigns by providing a Saviour to suffer in the room of the guilty. By the death of Jesus Christ, full compensation was made to the law and justice of God.

The Apostle, in the end of this chapter, brings his argument to a close. Every individual of the human race is proved to be guilty before God, and on the ground of his own righteousness no man can be saved. The state of the Gentile world is exhibited in the most degrading view, while history and experience fully concur in the condemnation. Man is represented as vile, as degraded below the condition of the brutes; and the facts on which the charge is grounded were so notorious that they could not be denied. Nor could the most uncultivated Pagans offer any apology for their conduct. Their sins were against nature, and their ignorance of God was in spite of the revelation of His character in the works of creation. They are condemned by the standard they themselves recognise, and their own mutual recriminations and defences prove that they were fully aware of sin and responsibility.

But are not the Jews excepted from this black catalogue of crimes? Are they not righteous through that holy, just, and good law which they received from the God of Israel? By no means. By the testimony of that revelation which they received, all men are guilty, and this testimony directly implies those to whom the revelation was given. With this experience also coincides. The Apostle charges them as actually doing the same things which they condemned in the heathens. Both, then, are guilty; and, from their superior light, the Jews must be the most guilty.

Nor was it ever in contemplation of the law of Moses to give the Jews a righteousness by their own obedience. The law was designed rather to manifest their guilt. By the law there was to no individual a righteousness unto life; by the law was the 'knowledge of sin.' All men, then, without exception, were shut up unto condemnation.

But this law veiled the truth which the Apostle now unfolds and exhibits in the strongest light. He proclaims a righteousness so perfect, as to answer all the demands of law, both as to penalty and obedience— a righteousness so free, as to extend to the very chief of sinners. This righteousness is in Jesus Christ. He has borne the curse of the law, and perfectly obeyed all its precepts. All His obedience becomes ours by believing the testimony of the Father concerning His Son, and trusting in Him. The most guilty child of Adam, whether he be Jew or Gentile, becomes perfectly righteous the moment he believes in the work of Christ. This glorious plan of salvation vindicates the law, exalts the character of God, and reconciles mercy with justice. In the Gospel grace appears; in the Gospel grace reigns; but it reigns not on the ruins of law and justice, but in the more glorious establishment of both; it reigns through righteousness unto eternal life by Jesus Christ our Lord. In the salvation of men by the Son of God, the law is not made void. It is magnified and made honourable. In this salvation sin is not represented as harmless. It is here seen in a more awful light than in the future punishment of the wicked. The Gospel is the only manifestation of God in the full glory of His character as the just God, yet the Saviour— punishing sin to the utmost extent of its demerit, at the same time that His mercy reaches to the most guilty of the children of men.

The doctrine contained in this chapter is so important, and often so ill understood, that it appears proper to subjoin the following valuable remarks from the *Presbyterian Magazine*, contained in the conclusion of the review[1] which has again and again been quoted above. They are introduced by observing that Mr. Stuart's denial of *a federal theology* bears a most impressive witness respecting the evil of surrendering any part of the truth of Scriptures.

'The rejection of Adam's covenant headship has led Mr. Stuart to an abandonment of the doctrine of Christ's representative character. The indissoluble connection between these was, indeed, long ago remarked, and the progress of error, as exemplified in this author, verifies with surprising accuracy the anticipation of the doctors of the Theological Faculty of Leyden, in a testimony on the subject of original sin, borne by them on the 15th November 1645. "We have learned," say they, "with great pain, that the doctrine which has been, by common consent, received as scriptural, respecting the imputation of Adam's sin, is now disturbed; although, when it is denied, the original corruption of human nature cannot be just, and a transition is easy to a denial of the imputation of the second Adam's righteousness."

'We need not enter into any lengthened refutation of the perilous and unsupported assertion that the federal "form of theology" is not essential "to the Christian doctrine of redemption." The marvel is, how any man who had studied the Epistle to the Hebrews could evade the force of such declarations as that Christ is "the Mediator of the new covenant," or escape the conviction that He represented the elect as their head in a federal arrangement. To such a relationship between Him and His people, likewise, the whole legal dispensation pointed. The impressive ceremony of the scape-goat represented, by the plainest symbols, a transfer—an imputation of guilt; and prophecy intimated it in the unambiguous announcement, that "the Lord *laid on Him* the iniquity of us all." The Scripture is so pervaded by federal language and allusions, that he who would remove from it the doctrine of Christ's covenant headship, would need either to write it anew, or to expound it on some unheard-of principle.

'But is a covenant relation necessary "to the Christian doctrine of

---

[1] From a memoir of the life of Mr. James Halley, which has lately been published, it appears that he was the author of the above review. His learning and accomplishments as a scholar, but, above all, his solidity and spirituality of mind, promised, had his life been spared, to have made him a workman eminently fitted rightly to divide the word of God.

depravity"? So at least it appears to us; and the reader who will consult the dissertation of Rivetus, from which the above opinion of the divines of Leyden has been extracted, will find that it has appeared so to almost all the fathers of the Reformation, and to a host of eminent reformed divines, a mere catalogue of whose names would occupy several of our pages. But we are very far from resting this sentiment on human authority; we appeal to the law and to the testimony of God.

' First, then, that God treated with Adam not merely by way of commandment, but by way of covenant, we regard as manifest from the train of events as recorded in the commencement of Genesis. There were two contracting parties. There was something to be done by the one, which on the part of the other was to meet with a certain recompense ; for the threatening of death, in case of eating the forbidden fruit, bears with it the counterpart assurance that, if the creature continued in obedience, his state of happiness would be indefinitely prolonged ; the existence of a promise is implied in the words of the Apostle (Gal. iii. 12), "the man that doeth them shall live in them," and similar expressions elsewhere ; and the very thought that a menace was uttered, unmingled with any more cheering intimation, accuses the God of all grace of being more ready to punish than to crown. There was, in fine, on the part of Adam, an acceptance of the offered terms; for to suppose it otherwise is to embrace the contradiction that a creature could be holy, and yet his will at war with his Creator's. It is of no consequence to object that the covenant is not fully developed ; for the early part of the Mosaic narrative is remarkable for its rapidity ; and neither is the covenant of grace evolved into any amplitude of detail in the record of its first announcement in paradise.

' Secondly, that Adam in the covenant was the head of all his offspring, appears from a variety of considerations. For example, the train of events as recorded in Genesis, to which we may here renew our reference, intimates, not obscurely, that Adam was dealt with in all things as the representative of humanity. The blessing of increase was not designed for him alone ; nor the donation of empire over the creatures ; nor the institution of the sabbatic rest; nor the curse that was launched forth against the ground ; nor the sentence which consigned him over to the grave. It is in vain to object that not one word is *said* of posterity in the recital of these promises, and injunctions, and threatenings, and maledictions; for experience proves their universal application, and proves it antecedently to all individual guilt, for the infant is affected by that curse wherewith the earth is stricken. And if any one is included in the sentence, he must first have been comprehended in the threatening ; which lands us in the doctrine of the federal headship of Adam. Again, why, in 1 Cor. xv., is Christ called the second man—the second Adam ? The only assignable reason in His covenant headship ; for never could His resurrection have been viewed, not only as demonstrative of the possibility of the reviviscence of others, but as betokening and implying the final disruption, by all believers, of the bands of death, except on some principle, amounting to the admission of the fundamental truth that He was their great federal representative.

242   Commentary on Romans

'From this view, which rests on such clear grounds, of the constituted connection between our first progenitor and his offspring, the imputation of his guilt to them directly follows. If they were one with him in receiving the law, in possessing ability to observe it, and in coming under an obligation to obedience, they were one with him also in his breach of the condition of the covenant. He broke the first link of the golden chain which primarily united all mankind to their Maker, and the dependent parts of it necessarily partook of the separation. But imputation might be established by independent processes of reasoning; and thus, from two different directions, a flood of light might be poured upon the doctrines, if we had space to pursue the inquiry.

'1. We might refer, for a strong presumptive proof, to the analogy and correspondence between the economy of condemnation and the economy of redemption—the ministration of death and the ministration of life. In the latter we find an imputed righteousness and an inherent holiness, the one constituting the matter of the believer's justification, and the other preparing him for glory; and so, in the former, we might expect to find an imputed guilt and an inherent sinfulness, the one being the antecedent ground of the sentence of death, and the other carrying the criminal downwards in an augmented fitness for the society of the lost. Thus imputed guilt occupies, in the one part of the scheme, a place co-ordinate to that which imputed righteousness holds in the other; inborn depravity corresponds to the implanted principles of sanctification, and an exact harmony is maintained between the Divine dispensations.

'2. We might prosecute, in the next place, an argument, at which we have already hinted, from the sufferings and mortality of sucklings. Not only do "the cries of infants, who are only eloquent to grief, but dumb to all things else, discover the miseries that attend them," and "the tears which are born with their eyes, signify they are come into a state of sorrow," but a very large proportion of the human race is swept away into the grave at the very dawn of their being. Like Jonah's gourd, they spring up and wither in a night. Now, on Mr. Stuart's principle, that nothing but actual transgression deserves the name, we have here a punishment without a crime—the wages apart from the deed which earns them. But this cannot be under the government of Him who is righteous in all His ways. Assuredly infants would not die if they were not guilty—a sinless soul would not be lodged in a mortal habitation. It is no valid objection to this, that Christ's body was mortal; for "He was made sin for us." Death, then, follows sin like its shadow; and, like the shadow, demonstrates the real presence of the substance. It follows that infants are sinners; and since actual offence is impossible, they are sinners in the ancient transgression of their first father.

'3. We might, in fine, argue backwards from the fact, acknowledged even by Mr. Stuart, that we "are born destitute of holiness." This original destitution, in virtue of which we are "by nature children of wrath," must proceed from God, either as a Creator, or as the Sovereign Lord, or as a Judge. But it does not come from Him as Creator simply, for in this respect we hold the same relation to Him as Adam did, who was formed in righteousness and true holiness; nor as Lord over all, for it were blasphemy to imagine that He would employ His supreme dominion in promoting the ruin of a rational creature. It is resolved, therefore, into a judicial infliction—an infliction on account of some sin committed before we had a being; and as this infliction has passed upon every man since our first progenitor, to *his* grand offence, which the Apostle throughout this passage represents as so pregnant with evil, it must of consequence be referred. Hence, as punishment infers guilt, the stain of his iniquity is ours—his guilt is ours by imputation.

'Mr. Stuart admits that, "in consequence of Adam's fall, and without any act or concurrence of their own," all his posterity are subject to "sufferings in the present state;" that their nature is brought under a "*moral degradation*,"—"an imperfect condition, in which it is *certain* that the sensual passions will get the victory and lead them to sin, and certain that they will never have any holiness without being born again,"—and in which "the second death will certainly come upon them, without the interposition of mercy through Christ." This is stated, doubtless, in milder phrases than the other,—in the language of a man giving forth an opinion which he receives, not denouncing one which he rejects; but it possesses all the substantial features of the other scheme, and involves all its principles, with the exception of that principle, the principle of imputation, which, so far as man's feeble intellect can penetrate, supplies the only key to the whole, and vindicates the Creator from the charge of cruelty. The question is simply,—shall we regard the deprivation of original righteousness as judicially connected with Adam's first transgression, or as linked to it by some bond of arbitrary and mysterious severity? The reader expects, no doubt, to find all "the elements" of Mr. Stuart's "moral nature spontaneously in array" against the letter of these suppositions. But no; it is his own opinion,—an opinion of which the native hideousness can only be veiled by the novel expedient of transforming into a peculiar species of discipline all the evils which originate in the fall.

'But it is urged, again, that such an imputation of guilt is at variance with the general principles of the Divine administration, of which it is a fundamental law that "the son shall not bear the iniquity of the father," Ezek. xviii. 20. We had always understood that the fundamental laws of God's moral government were embodied in the Decalogue. And there we read (Ex. xx. 5) that the Lord is a "jealous God, visiting the iniquity of the fathers upon the children." But is there indeed an inconsistency in the word of inspiration? Are contradictory principles announced as alike fundamental? No, truly. God's general right to punish the offspring for their parent's guilt was declared from Sinai; and the course of Providence, in such cases as that of Dathan and Abiram, as well as in the indiscriminate destruction wrought by the flood, which spared not a single infant because of its imagined innocency, has impressively repeated the intimation. Ezekiel was only commissioned to declare, in a special instance, a forbearing to insist on this right. Besides, were the Prophet's message taken as the promulgation of a fundamental statute, it would be impossible to escape from the imputation of contravening it, even although we were to prune and pare down our theological system till it was reduced to the most meagre Pelagianism. By having the evil example of our parents set before us—to take no higher ground—we are, in consequence of Adam's transgression, placed in less favourable circumstances than those in which he was situated; and in this way we bear the iniquity of our father. On Mr. Stuart's system, this becomes more obvious still; so that, with his view of the announcement of Ezekiel, his own scheme is at irreconcilable variance. The view of that announcement, which we have presented above removes *this* difficulty from his scheme; but it also removes it from ours.

'But there is one consequence of Mr. Stuart's views of original sin, which, at the risk of being blamed for prolixity, we cannot omit to notice. This opinion, as already stated, is, that no one can be sentenced to the extreme punishment of sin, except for actual transgression—that we are not born in a state of condemnation—that, in the highest and most awful sense of the words, we are not " by nature the children of wrath." Now, from this it irresistibly follows that infants, not having sinned actually, and so (according to him) not being under the curse, do not need salvation. The whole have no need of a physician, but they that are sick. Mr. Stuart evidently feels this difficulty, and labours to escape from it. He urges that, since infants are born destitute of holiness, and since " without holiness no man shall see the Lord," Christ has much to do for them by His Spirit, in removing the imperfection of their nature, and in imparting to them a positive taste for the sacred exercises and joys of heaven. On this ground, and to this extent, he thinks that the Lord Jesus may properly enough be called their Saviour. But this falls far short of the scriptural representations of the great salvation of the Gospel. In that salvation, deliverance from wrath is a principal element. But, according to Mr. Stuart's scheme, this has no place in the case of infants. They are not saved from wrath; they are not saved from sin; no positive evil is removed from them; they are only made partakers of certain good dispositions to which they were primarily strangers. Their first state is a pure negative; Christ bestows some positive gifts upon them, and so becomes their Saviour. In short, He sanctifies them by His Spirit. But He does not procure their justification; they obtain it for themselves; although not holy, they are harmless and undefiled. And hence *ipso facto* they are accepted as righteous. They are directly, and without Emmanuel's intervention, embraced in the provisions of that eternal law which annexes immortality to innocence; of redemption, therefore, properly so called, they have no necessity. This system involves some strange anomalies—enough to destroy the authority of any scheme of doctrine. Christ is in it *called* a Saviour; but the first step in the mighty process is taken, and one important part of it is fully accomplished, not in consequence of His work, but because of the very condition of nature in those whom He came to save. These objects of His love are promoted and perfected, but not redeemed; and although in a certain sense He saved them, their lips must be sealed, when, among the ranks of the glorified, there reverberates the everlasting song,—" Thou wast slain, and hast redeemed us to God by Thy blood."

'In dismissing the subject of original sin, we cannot permit it to escape without a passing remark,—Mr. Stuart's repeated affirmation that the received doctrine on that topic originated with Augustine. As he gives no proof of this, we shall be excused for meeting his authority with that (certainly not inferior) of Gerard John Vossius, from whose history of Pelagianism we extract the following thesis, which he supports by appropriate quotations from the fathers. "The Church universal has ALWAYS thus judged, that that first sin is imputed to all," etc. And again, "Augustine proves this dogma from the writings of the earlier fathers, from whom he produces testimonies so plain (and scarcely less remarkable are many which he has omitted), that it is altogether marvellous that there were any of old, or are any of this day, who themselves believe, and would persuade others, that this doctrine is an invention of Augustine."

' No truth revealed in the Divine word stirs up against itself more than the doctrine of original sin the enmity of the human heart; and none, accordingly, has met, in different ages, with more determined and persevering opposition; yet a right understanding of it is absolutely necessary to any satisfactory knowledge of the plan of mercy. In the Church's earlier days, all the ingenuity of Pelagius was exerted in attempts to explain it away from the page of inspiration. Shortly after the Reformation, the Remonstrants and Socinians revived his heresy, the former veiling it under many cautious restrictions, and the latter far overstepping even the errors of their master; more recently still, Taylor of Norwich proposed a new and unheard-of system, rivalling Socinianism in audacity of interpretation; and, in our own days, Professor Stuart has assailed the faith of the Reformed Churches, and, as we firmly believe, of that scripture on which they are built, with a calmness, indeed, which honourably distinguishes him from the mass of its enemies, but we feel bound to say, with a want of logic, and a straining of criticism, which would do no dishonour to the most accomplished disciple of the school of Taylor. Our readers must have gathered ere now that we do not estimate Mr. Stuart's scholarship so highly as it has generally been valued, and that we regard his theology as most unsound. We coincide entirely in Mr. Haldane's impressions of the responsibility resting upon those who have recommended his Commentary.'

CHAPTER 6
ROMANS 6:1 – 23

IN the preceding part of the Epistle the universal depravity and guilt of man, and the free salvation through the blood of the Lord Jesus Christ, had been fully exhibited. Paul now proceeds to prove the intimate connection between the justification of believers and their sanctification. He commences by stating an objection which has in all ages been advanced as an unanswerable argument against salvation by grace. He asks, What is the consequence of the doctrine he has been inculcating? If justification be bestowed through faith, without works, and if, where sin abounded, grace has much more abounded, may we not continue in sin that grace may abound? No objection could be more plausible. It is such as will forcibly strike every natural man, and is as common now as it was in the days of the Apostle.

Paul repels this charge by declaring the union of believers with Jesus Christ, by whom, as is represented in baptism, His people are dead to sin, and risen with Him to walk in newness of life. Having established these important truths, he urges (ver. 11) on those whom he addresses the duty of being convinced that such is their actual state. In verses 12 and 13, he warns them not to abuse this conviction; and for their encouragement in fighting the good fight of faith, to which they are called, assures them, in the 14th verse, that sin shall not have dominion over them, because they are not under the law but under grace. Thus the Apostle proves that, by the gracious provision of the covenant of God, ratified by the blood of Him with whom they are inseparably united, they who are justified cannot continue to live in sin; but though sin shall not have dominion over them, still, as their sanctification is not yet perfect, he goes on to address them as liable to temptation. What he had said, therefore, concerning their state as being in Christ, did not preclude the duty of watchfulness; nor, since they had formerly been the servants of sin, of now proving that they were the servants of God, by walking in holiness of life. Paul concludes by an animated appeal to their own experience of the past, and to their prospects for the future. He asks, what fruit had they in their former ways, which could only conduct to shame and death? On the other hand, he exhorts them to press onwards in the course of holiness, at the end of which they would receive the crown of everlasting life. But, along with this assurance, he reminds them of the important truth, that while the just *recompense* of sin is death, eternal life is the *gift* of God, through Jesus Christ our Lord.

Ver. 1.—*What shall we say then? Shall we continue in sin, that grace may abound?*

What shall we say then?—That is, what conclusion are we to draw from the doctrine previously taught? The question is first asked generally. In the following words it is asked particularly,—*Shall we continue in sin, that grace may abound?* Many expound this objection as coming from a Jew, and imagine a sort of dialogue between him and the Apostle. For this there is no ground. The supposition of a dialogue in different parts of this Epistle, has been said to give life and interest to the argument; but instead of this, it is only cumbersome and entangling. There is no necessity for the introduction of an objector. It is quite sufficient for the writer to state the substance of the objection in his own words. It was essential for the Apostle to vindicate his doctrine, not only from such objections as he knew would be made by the enemies of the cross of Christ, to whom he has an eye throughout the whole of the Epistle, but also to Christians themselves, whom he was directly addressing. We see in his answer in the following verses, to the questions thus proposed, what an ample field it opened for demonstrating the beautiful harmony of the plan of salvation, and of proving how every part of it bears upon and supports the rest.

Ver. 2.—*God forbid. How shall we, that are dead to sin, live any longer therein ?*

Paul, in his usual manner on similar occasions, strongly rejects such a consequence as the question in the first verse supposes, and asks another, which implies the absolute incongruity of the assumption that Christians will be emboldened to continue in sin, by the knowledge of their being freely justified. On the very ground on which the objection rests, he shows that this is impossible.

We that are dead to sin.—The meaning of this expression is very generally misunderstood, and extended to include death to the *power* of sin, to which it has not the smallest reference. It exclusively indicates the justification of believers, and their freedom from the *guilt* of sin, having no allusion to their sanctification, which, however, as the Apostle immediately proceeds to prove, necessarily follows. It was indispensable, in the view of obviating the objection proposed, distinctly to characterize both the persons, and their state of justification, to whom the answer he was about to give applied. Accordingly, by using the term *we*, he shows that he speaks of the same persons of whose justification he had been treating in the conclusion of the fourth, and in the first part of the foregoing chapter, to whom, in this way, he there refers more than twenty times. Their justification he expresses by the term *dead to sin*, which, though only a part of justification, implies all that it includes. No other designation could have been so well adapted to introduce the development of their state, and its inseparable consequences, as contained in the following verses. This term, then, is most appropriately employed. Formerly, the persons spoken of were dead in sin, but now they were dead to it, as it is said in the 7th verse, they are justified from it. In the seventh chapter, it is affirmed that believers are dead to the law. They are therefore dead to sin, for the strength of sin is the law ; and consequently sin has lost its power to condemn them, their connection with it, in respect to its guilt, being for ever broken. In the 10th verse, it is said that Christ died unto sin, and liveth to God ; and in the same way believers have died to sin, and are alive to God, to serve Him in newness of life.

It has indeed been argued, that if the expression dead to sin does not comprehend death to the *power* of sin, it does not contain an answer to the objection urged in the preceding verse. Even, however, though the power of sin were included, it could not be considered as an answer by which the objection was removed, but simply a denial of its validity. But it is not intended as an answer, though it clearly infers that union with Jesus Christ which is immediately after exhibited as the complete answer. Without this union we cannot be dead to sin ; but, being united to Him, believers are not only dead to it, but also, by necessary consequence, risen with Him *to walk in newness of life.* Nothing could be more conclusive than in this manner to show that, so far from the doctrine of justification leading to the evil supposed, on the contrary, it provides full security against it. Paul accordingly presents that very aspect of this doctrine, namely, death to sin, which peculiarly bears on the point, and this for the purpose of introducing that union by which it takes place, which is at once the cause both of justification and sanctification. So far, therefore, from these being contrary the one to the other, or of the first being in the smallest degree opposed to the last, they are inseparable; and thus the possibility of those who are justified continuing in sin, that grace may abound, is absolutely precluded.

Dr. Macknight translates the phrase, ' dead to sin,' ' have died by sin.' This does not convey the Apostle's meaning, but an idea altogether different, and entirely misrepresents the import of the passage. All men have died by sin, but believers only are dead to the guilt of sin; and it is of its guilt exclusively that the Apostle here speaks. Unbelievers will not, through all eternity, be dead to sin. Dr. Macknight says that the common translation ' is absurd, for a person's living in sin who is dead to it, is evidently a contradiction in terms.' But had he understood the meaning of the expression ' dead to sin,' he would have seen that there is nothing in this translation either contradictory or absurd. He ought also to have observed that the phraseology to which he objects is not an assertion that they who are dead to sin live in it, but is a question that supposes the incompatibility of the thing referred to.

Mr. Stuart also totally misunderstands the signification of the expression ' dead to sin,' which, he says, ' means to renounce sin; to become, as it were, insensible to its exciting power and influence, as a dead person is incapable of sensibility.' The clause that follows—Shall we that are dead to sin, live any longer therein?—he interprets thus : ' How shall we, who have renounced sin, and profess to be insensible to its influence, any more continue to practise it, or to be influenced by it?' On this it is remarked, in the *Presbyterian Review*, that ' the objection stated by the Apostle is, that the tendency of his doctrine of justification by faith was bad, leading to licentiousness; and what sort of refutation is it to reply, whatever its tendency may be, nevertheless *it should* not produce such effects, because we have professed otherwise? Professions might be multiplied a thousandfold, and yet the tendency of the doctrine would remain the same, and the objection consequently would remain in all its force. Nay, it is plain that such a reply as this takes for granted that the tendency of the doctrine by itself is to licentiousness; and that, in order to prevent these its natural effects from being developed, the person who receives it must be hemmed around with innumerable professions and obligations to renounce those sins into which he might naturally be led by such a doctrine standing alone.' Mr. Stuart's explanation of becoming insensible to the exciting power or influence of sin, as a dead person is incapable of sensibility, perfectly coincides with the popish interpretation of the passage:—' The spirit, the heart, the judgment, have no more life for sin than those of a dead man for the world.' But the Roman Catholic Quesnel, perceiving that his interpretation is contradicted by experience, immediately adds: ' Ah, who is it that is dead and insensible to the praises, to the pleasures, to the advantages of the world?' Mr. Stuart, however, disregarding both fact and experience, adheres to his interpretation, and announces the third time, ' *To become dead to sin*, or *to die to sin*, plainly means, then, to become insensible to its influence, to be unmoved by it; in other words, to renounce it, and refrain from the practice of it.' This is justly chargeable with the absurdity unjustly charged by Dr. Macknight on the common translation of the passage. The assertion, then, would be, as we refrain from the practice of sin, we cannot continue to practise it. According to Mr. Stuart's interpretation, when it is enjoined on believers, verse 11, to reckon themselves dead to sin, the meaning would be, that they should reckon themselves perfect.

In order to understand the manner in which the Apostle meets and obviates the objection that the doctrine of justification by grace tends to encourage Christians to continue in sin, the ground on which he founds his denial of its validity must be particularly attended to. He does not rest it, according to Dr. Macknight, on the impossibility of believers ' hoping to live eternally by continuing in sin,' if they have died by it. This would not only be no adequate security against such an effect, but, owing to the strength of human depravity, no security at all. Neither does he rest it on their having ceased, according to Mr. Stuart, to feel the influence of sin, which is alike contrary to Scripture and experience. Nor, according to Mr. Tholuck, because ' they obey it in nothing more,' which is not only repugnant to truth, but would be simply a denial of the allegation without the shadow of proof. He rests it in no degree either on any motive presented to them, or on any change produced in themselves, as these writers suppose. It should also be observed that, when the Apostle characterizes believers as dead to sin, he is not introducing something new, as would be the case were either Dr. Macknight's, or Mr. Stuart's, or Mr. Tholuck's explanation of the term correct. He is indicating the state of those to whom the objection applies, in order to its refutation. That it does not lead them to continue in sin, he had in effect shown already, in verses 3d and 4th of the foregoing chapter, where he had declared the accompaniments of their justification. But as this objection is constantly insisted on, and is so congenial to human nature, and, besides, might appear plausible from the fact that they are the *ungodly* who are justified, ch. iv. 5, he still considered it proper to meet it fully and directly. Paul therefore proceeds formally to repel such a calumny against his doctrine, by exhibiting in further detail, in the following verses, the grounds of justification to which he had referred, ch. iv. 24, 25,—namely, the interest of believers both in the death and resurrection of our Lord Jesus Christ. The expression, then, dead to sin, does not in any degree relate to their *character* or *conduct*, but exclusively to their *state* before God. Their character or conduct with regard to abstinence from the commission of sin, is referred to in the question that follows, demanding, How those who are dead to sin shall ' *live any longer therein*'? But to explain the expression, ' dead to sin,' as meaning dead to the influence and love of sin, is entirely erroneous, and what the Apostle by no means asserts. Death to the influence and love of sin must involve their annihilation in the person of whom this could be affirmed; for death annihilates to its subject all things whatsoever; and in this case it might well be said, with Mr. Stuart, that a man who is dead to sin has ' become insensible to its exciting power or influence, as a dead person is incapable of sensibility.' How Mr. Stuart could make such statements, thrice repeated, yet totally unfounded, and flatly contradicted by every man's experience, is indeed astonishing.

Utterly erroneous, too, is the explanation of other commentators, who say that the meaning is, dead to 'the guilt and power' of sin,—thus joining death to the *power*, to death to the *guilt*, of sin. This indicates a condition with respect to sin which was never realized in any of the children of Adam while in this world. No believer is dead to the power of sin, as Paul has abundantly shown in the seventh chapter of this Epistle. On the contrary, he there affirms that there was a law in his members which warred against the law of his mind; that he did the things he would not; and that when he would do good, evil (and what is this but the power of sin?) was present with him. The same truth is clearly exhibited in all the other Epistles, in which believers are so often reproved for giving way to the power of sin, and earnestly exhorted and warned against doing so. But when the expression is understood as exclusively signifying dead to the GUILT of sin, it may and must be taken in the full sense of what death imparts, being nothing less than absolute, total, and final deliverance from its guilt. To suppose, then, that in these words there is the smallest reference to the character or conduct of believers—to their freedom from the love or power of sin—to conjoin these in any respect or in any degree with their freedom from its *guilt*, —in other words, with their justified state,—is not merely to misapprehend the meaning of the Apostle, but to represent him as stating that to be a fact which has no existence; while it deprives the passage of the consolation to believers which, when properly understood, it is so eminently calculated to impart.

In proof of the correctness of this view of the subject, let it be remembered that the Apostle's refutation, in the following verses, of the supposed objection, does not rest on the supposition that sin is mortified in himself and those whom he is addressing, or that they are released from any propensity to it, but on the fact of their being one with Jesus Christ. They are united to Him in His death, and consequently in His life, which was communicated to them by Him who is a 'quickening Spirit;' and thus their walking with Him in newness of life, as well as their resurrection with Him, are secured. These ideas are exhibited in the 3d, 4th, 5th, and 6th verses. In the 7th verse, the reason of the whole is summed up,—'For he who is dead (with Christ) is justified from sin;' and in the 8th verse, that which will afterwards follow our being justified from sin is stated,—'If we be dead with Christ, we believe that we shall also live with Him.' Finally, in the 9th and 10th verses, the Apostle declares the consequence of Christ's dying to sin to be, that He liveth unto God. The same effect in respect to the members must follow as to the Head with whom believers are one; and therefore he immediately proceeds to assure them, in the 14th verse, that sin shall not have dominion over them. The result, then, of the doctrine of justification by grace is the very reverse of giving not merely licence, but even place, to continue in sin. On the contrary, according to that doctrine, *the power of God is engaged to secure to those who are dead to sin*

—*i.e.*, justified—a life of holiness, corresponding with that state into which, by their union with His Son, He has brought them.

The full import and consequence of being dead to sin will be found, ch. iv. 7, 8:—'Blessed are they whose iniquities are forgiven, and whose sins are covered. Blessed is the man to whom the Lord will not impute sin.' They who are dead to sin, are those from whom, in its guilt or condemning power, it is in Christ Jesus entirely removed. Such persons, whose sins are thus covered, are pronounced 'blessed.' They enjoy the favour and blessing of God. The necessary effect of this blessing is declared in the new covenant, according to which, when God is merciful to the unrighteousness of His people, and remembers their sins and iniquities no more, He puts His laws into their mind, and writes them in their hearts, and promises that He will be to them a God, and they shall be to Him a people. In one word, they who are dead to sin are united to Him who is the Fountain of life and holiness, and are thus delivered from the curse pronounced upon those who, being under the law, continue not in all things that are written in the book of the law to do them. The guilt of their sins, which separated between them and God, having now been cancelled, they enjoy His favour, and all its blessed effects. It is upon these great truths that the Apostle rests his absolute denial that the doctrine of justification by grace, which he had been unfolding, is compatible with continuing to live in sin.

Live any longer therein.—To continue in sin, and to live any longer therein, are equivalent expressions, implying that, before their death to sin, the Apostle himself, and all those whom he now addressed, were enslaved by sin, and lived in it. In the same way, in writing to the saints at Ephesus, he says that formerly he and all of them had their conversation among the children of disobedience, fulfilling the desires of the flesh and of the mind. By denying, then, that believers continue in sin, he does not mean to say that they never commit sin, or fall into it, or, according to Mr. Stuart, have become insensible to its influence, or to Mr. Tholuck, that they 'obey it in nothing any more;' for, as has been observed, it is abundantly shown in the seventh chapter, where he gives an account of his own experience (which is also the experience of every Christian), that this is very far from being a fact; but he denies that they continue to live as formerly in sin and ungodliness, which he had shown was impossible. Here it may, however, be remarked, that the full answer which in the following verses is given to the objection brought against the tendency of the doctrine of justification, cannot be understood by the natural man, to whom it must appear foolishness. Hence the same calumny is repeated to the present day against this part of Divine truth.

Ver. 3.—*Know ye not, that so many of us as were baptized into Jesus Christ, were baptized into His death?*

In this and the following verses, Paul proceeds to give his full answer to the objection he had supposed, by showing that *the sanctification of believers rests on the same foundation, and springs from the same source, as their justification, namely, their union with Jesus Christ, and therefore, so far from their being contrary to each other, they are not merely in perfect harmony, but absolutely inseparable ; and not only so, but the one cannot exist without the other.* In the conclusion of the preceding chapter, he had declared that sin had reigned unto death. It reigned unto the death of Jesus Christ, the surety of His people, who, as is said in the 10th verse of the chapter before us, ' died unto sin.' But as in His death its reign as to Him terminated, so its reign also terminated as to all His people, who with Him are ' dead to sin.' The effect, then, of His death being the termination of the reign of sin, it was at the same time to them the commencement of the reign of grace, which took place '·through righteousness,—the everlasting righteousness brought in by His death.' Instead, therefore, of being under the reign of sin, Christians are under grace, whereby they ' serve God acceptably with reverence and godly fear,' Heb. xii. 28. It may, however, be remarked, that although their union with Christ is the ground of the Apostle's denial, that believers will be induced to continue in sin that grace may abound, and of their absolute security that this shall not be its effect, yet he does not fail to present, as in the concluding part of this chapter, such motives to abstain from sin as are calculated powerfully to influence their conduct. The consideration, too, that they died with Christ, and are risen with Him to newness of life, connected with the certainty that they shall live with Him in future glory, announced in the 5th and 8th verses, furnishes the strongest motives to the love of God, which is the grand spring of obedience, for we love Him when we know that He has first loved us. That this view of the death of Christ, and of our death with Him, operates as a powerful motive to the love of God, is shown, 2 Cor. v. 14, where it is said, ' The love of Christ constraineth us ; because we thus judge, that if one died for all, then were all dead (or all died). And that he died for all, that they which live should not henceforth live unto themselves, but unto Him which died for them, and rose again.' Although, then, the solid ground and absolute security that believers shall not live in sin, is shown to consist in their union with Christ, yet motives are not excluded.

In the verse before us, the Apostle proves that Christians are dead to sin, because they died with Christ. The rite of baptism exhibits Christians as dying, as buried, and as risen with Christ. *Know ye not.—* He refers to what he is now declaring as a thing well known to those whom he addresses. *Baptized into Jesus Christ.*—By faith believers are made one with Christ : they become members of His body. This oneness is represented emblematically by baptism. *Baptized into His death.*—In baptism, they are also represented as dying with Christ. This rite, then, proceeds on the fact that they have died with Him who bore their sins. Thus the satisfaction rendered to the justice of God by Him, is a satisfaction from them, as they are constituent parts of His body. The believer is one with Christ as truly as he was one with Adam—he dies with Christ as truly as he died with Adam. Christ's righteousness is his as truly as Adam's sin was his. By a Divine constitution, all Adam's posterity are one with him, and so his first sin is really and truly theirs. By a similar Divine constitution, all Christ's people are one with Him, and His obedience is as truly theirs as if they had yielded it, and His death as if they had suffered it. When it is said that Christians have died with Christ, there is no more figure than when it is said that they have died in Adam.

The figure of baptism was very early mistaken for a reality, and accordingly some of the fathers speak of the baptized person as truly born again in the water. They supposed him to go into the water with all his sins upon him, and to come out of it without them. This indeed is the case with baptism figuratively. But the carnal mind soon turned the figure into a reality. It appears to the impatience of man too tedious and ineffectual a way to wait on God's method of converting sinners by His Holy Spirit through the truth, and therefore they have effected this much more extensively by the performance of external rites. When, according to many, the rite is observed, it cannot be doubted that the truth denoted by it has been accomplished. The same disposition has been the origin of Transubstantiation. The bread and wine in the Lord's Supper are figuratively the body and blood of Christ; but they have been turned into the real body, blood, soul, and divinity of the Lord, and the external rite has become salvation.

So many of us.—This does not imply that any of those to whom the Apostle wrote were not baptized, for there could be no room for such a possibility. It applies to the whole of them, as well as to himself, and not merely to a part. It amounts to the same thing as if it had been said, ' We who were baptized;' as in Acts iii. 24, 'As many as have spoken,' that is, all who have spoken, for all the Prophets spoke.

Ver. 4.—*Therefore we are buried with Him by baptism into death: that like as Christ was raised up from the dead by the glory of the Father, even so we also should walk in newness of life.*

The death of Christ was the means by which sin was destroyed, and His burial the proof of the reality of His death. Christians are therefore represented as buried with Him by baptism into His death, in token that they really died with Him; and if buried with Him, it is not that they shall remain in the grave, but that, as Christ arose from the dead, they should also rise. Their baptism, then, is the figure of their complete deliverance from the guilt of sin, signifying that God places to their account the death of Christ as their own death: it is also a figure of their purification and resurrection for the service of God.

By the glory of the Father.—The exercise of that almighty power of God, by which, in various passages, it is asserted that Christ was made alive again, was most glorious to God who raised Him up. Christ's resurrection is also ascribed to Himself, because He was a partaker with the Father of that power by which He was raised. 'I lay down my life, that I might take it again.' 'Destroy this temple, and in three days I will raise it up.' To reconcile these and similar passages with those that ascribe His resurrection to the Father, it must be observed, that if the principle be regarded by which our Lord was raised up, it is to be referred to that Divine power which belongs in common to the Father and the Son. The Son was raised equally by His own power as by that of His Father, because He possessed the Divine as well as the human nature. But as in the work of redemption the Father acts as the sovereign ruler, it is He who has received the satisfaction, and who, having received it, has given to the Son its just recompense in raising Him from the dead. His resurrection, then, in this view, took place by the decree of the Eternal Father, pronounced from His judgment throne.

Even so we also should walk in newness of life.—It is the purpose of our rising with Christ, that we also, by the glory or power of the Father, 2 Cor. xiii. 4, should walk in newness of life. The resurrection of Christ was the effect of the power of God, not in the ordinary way of nature, but of a supernatural exertion of power. In the same manner, believers are raised to walk in newness of life. It is thus that, when Paul, Eph. i. 20, exalts.the supernatural virtue of grace by which we are converted, he compares it to the exceeding greatness of that power by which Christ was raised from the dead. This shows the force of the Apostle's answer to the objection he is combating. Believers are dead to the guilt of sin, and if so, the ground of their separation from God being removed, His almighty power is engaged and exerted to cause them to walk with their risen Lord in that new life which they derive from Him. It was, then, the purpose of Christ's death that His people should become dead to sin, and alive unto righteousness. 'Who His own self bare our sins in His own body on the tree, that we being dead to sins, should live unto righteousness,' 1 Pet. ii. 24. On this same ground, when viewing it simply as a motive, Paul reminds believers that since they are dead with Christ, they should set their affections on things above, and not on things on the earth, assuring them that when He who is their life shall appear, then shall they also appear with Him in glory, Col. iii. 4. And again he declares, 'If we be dead with Him, we shall also live with Him,' 2 Tim. ii. 11.

Dr. Macknight is greatly mistaken when he applies what is said in this verse to the new life, which does not take place till after the resurrection of the body. This destroys the whole force of the Apostle's reasoning, who is showing that believers cannot continue in sin, not only as they are dead to sin, but as they are risen with Christ, thus receiving a new and supernatural life, for the purpose of walking in obedience to God.

Ver. 5.—*For if we have been planted together in the likeness of His death, we shall be also in the likeness of His resurrection :*

For if.—The conditional statement is here evidently founded on what is premised. The Apostle does not pass to a new argument to prove that we are dead with Christ; but, having asserted the burial of the Christian with Christ in baptism, he goes on to show that his resurrection with Him is equally implied. If we have been buried with Christ, so we shall rise with Him. *Planted together.*—The word in the original, when it refers to trees, designates planting them in the same place or bed. It signifies the closest union of any kind, as being incorporated, growing together, joined with, united. The meaning, then, is, that as in baptism we have been exhibited as one with Christ in His death, so in due time we shall be conformed to Him in the likeness of His resurrection.

We shall be.—The use here of the future tense has caused much perplexity respecting the connection of this verse with the preceding, and, contrary to its obvious meaning, the present time has been substituted. But, while the proper force of the future time is preserved, the two verses stand closely connected. Both a spiritual and a literal resurrection are referred to in the emblem of baptism; but, in the preceding verse, the former only is brought into view, as being that which served the Apostle's immediate purpose. In this verse, in employing the future tense, he refers to the literal resurrection hereafter, as being inseparably connected with what he had just advanced concerning walking in newness of life; and thus he unfolds the whole mystery included in dying and rising with Christ, both in this world and the world to come. Believers have already been raised spiritually with Christ to walk with Him on earth in newness of life, and with equal certainty they shall be raised to live with Him in heaven. This meaning is confirmed by what is said afterwards in the 8th and 9th verses. How powerful is this consideration, if viewed as a motive to the believer to walk in this world with his risen Lord in newness of life! 'Every man that hath this hope in him purifieth himself, even as He is pure,' 1 John iii. 3.

Ver. 6.—*Knowing this, that our old man is crucified with Him, that the body of sin might be destroyed, that henceforth we should not serve sin.*

Knowing this.—That is, assuming it as a thing with which they were already well acquainted, or a thing which they should know. *That our old man was crucified with Him.*—Paul draws here the same conclusion from the believer's crucifixion with Christ that he had previously drawn from his baptism into Christ's death. All believers died with Christ on the cross, as they were all one in Him, and represented by Him. Their old man, Eph. iv. 22 ; Col. iii. 9, or sinful nature, was crucified together with Christ. If, then, their old man has been crucified with Him, it cannot be that they will for the future live according to their old nature. *That the body of sin might be destroyed.*—Body of sin, that is, sin embodied, meaning the whole combination and strength of corruption, as having all its members joined into a perfect body. The purpose of His people's crucifixion with Christ was, that this body of sin should finally perish and be annihilated. It is called a body, as consisting of various members, like a complete and entire body—a mass of sin ; not one sin, but all sin. The term body is used, because it is of a body only that there can be a literal crucifixion ; and this body is called the body of sin, that it may not be supposed that it is the natural body which is meant.

That henceforth we should not serve sin.—The design of the believer's crucifixion with Christ is, that he may not henceforth be a slave to sin. This implies that all men who do not believe in Christ are slaves to sin, as wholly and as absolutely under its power as a slave is to his master. But the end of our crucifixion with Christ, by faith in His death, is, that we may be delivered from this slavery. Believers, then, should resist sin as they would avoid the most cruel slavery. If this be the end of crucifixion with Christ, those cannot be considered as crucified with Christ who are the slaves of sin. Christians, then, may be known by their lives, as the tree is known by its fruits. It was the result of Paul's crucifixion with Christ, that Christ lived in him. 'I am crucified with Christ : nevertheless I live ; yet not I, but Christ liveth in me,' Gal. ii. 20.

Ver. 7.—*For he that is dead is freed from sin.*

For he that is dead ; that is, dead with Christ, as is said in the following verse.—This does not mean natural death, but death in all its extent,
signifying 'the second death,' the penalty of which Christ suffered, and
therefore all His members have suffered it with Him. *Freed from sin.*—
The original word, which is here translated *freed,* different from that
rendered *free* in verses 18, 20, 22, is literally *justified.* It occurs fifteen
times in this Epistle, and twenty-five times in other parts of the New
Testament ; and, except in this verse, and one other where it is translated
righteous, is uniformly rendered by the word justified. In this verse,
as in all the other passages, its proper rendering ought to be retained,
instead of being exchanged for the term '*freed,*' which has evidently been
selected to convey a different sense. To retain its proper translation in
this place is absolutely necessary, in order clearly to perceive the great
and cheering truth here announced, as well as to apprehend the full
force of the Apostle's answer to the objection stated in the first verse.
As to the phrase, 'justified from sin,' we find the Apostle expressing
himself in the same manner (Acts xiii. 39), 'By Him all that believe are
justified from all things, from which ye could not be justified by the law
of Moses.'

No objection can be made to the use of the expression 'justified,'
since the Apostle is speaking of the *state* of believers, to which it is
strictly applicable. In justification, which is a judicial and irrevocable
sentence pronounced by God, there are two parts : the one includes
absolution from the guilt of the breach of the law ; the other, the
possession of that obedience to its precepts which the law demands.
These being inseparable, they are both included in the expression *justified from sin.* If a man be dead with Christ, he possesses, as has been
observed, all the blessings which, according to the tenor of the new
covenant, are included in, and connected with, the state of justification
by grace. Instead, then, of encouraging him to continue in sin, it
furnishes absolute security against such a result, and ensures the certainty
that he shall walk in newness of life until he attains the possession of
eternal glory. The Apostle, therefore, is so far from admitting that,
according to the supposed objection which he is combating, gratuitous
justification is opposed to sanctification, that, after having shown in the
preceding verses that sanctification springs from union with Christ, he
here asserts, as he had formerly proved, that on the very same ground
the doctrine of justification is established. The one cannot, therefore,
be hostile to the interests of the other.

The bond by which sinners are kept under the power of sin, is the
curse of the law. This curse, which is the penalty of disobedience,
consists in man being cut off from all communion with God. By throwing off his allegiance to his Creator, he has become the subject of the
devil, and is led captive by him at his will. The curse consists in being
given up to sin, which is represented as reigning over the human race,
and exercising an absolute dominion. So long as the sinner is under the
guilt of sin, God can have no friendly intercourse with him ; for what
communion hath light with darkness ? But Christ having cancelled His

people's guilt, having redeemed them from the curse of the law, and invested them with the robe of His righteousness, there is no longer any obstacle to their communion with God, or any barrier to the free ingress of sanctifying grace. As the sin of the first man divested of holiness every one of his descendants, causing each individual to enter the world dead in trespasses and sins, in like manner the obedience of the second Adam imparts holiness to all His members, so that they can no longer remain under the thraldom of sin. Were a sinner, when he is redeemed, not also sanctified, it would argue that he was still under the curse, and not restored to the favour of God. Besides, what is the state of the believer? He is now united to Him who has the inexhaustible fulness of the Spirit, and he cannot fail to participate in the spirit of holiness which dwells without measure in his glorious Head. It is impossible that the streams can be dried up when the fountain continues to flow; and it is equally impossible for the members not to share in the same holiness which dwells so abundantly in the Head. As the branch, when united to the living vine, necessarily partakes of its life and fatness, so the sinner, when united to Christ, must receive an abundant supply of sanctifying grace out of His immeasurable fulness. The moment, therefore, that he is by faith brought into union with the second Adam—the grand truth on which the Apostle had been insisting in the preceding part of this chapter, by means of which believers are dead to sin—in that moment the source of sanctification is opened up, and streams of purifying grace flow into his soul. He is delivered from the law whereby sin had dominion over him. He is one with Him who is the fountain of holiness.

These are the grounds on which justification and sanctification are inseparably connected, and the reasons why those who are dead to sin, or, as it is here expressed, justified from sin, can no longer live therein. From all this we see the necessity of retaining the Apostle's expression in the verse before us, *justified* from sin. That it has been exchanged for the term *freed* in the English, as well as in most of the French versions, and that commentators are so generally undecided as to the proper rendering, arises from not clearly perceiving the ground on which the Apostle exclusively rests his denial of the consequence charged on his doctrine of justification, as leading to licentiousness. But on no other ground than that, as above explained, on which he has triumphantly vindicated it from this supposed pernicious consequence, can it be proved not to have such a tendency, and not to lead to such a result. On this ground his vindication must for ever stand unshaken. Had his answer to the question in the first verse ultimately rested, according to the reason given by Dr. Macknight, on the force of a *motive* presented to believers, however strong in itself, such as their having experienced the dreadful effects of sin in having died by it, or on the fallacious idea, according to Mr. Stuart, that they were insensible to its influence, how weak, as has been remarked, insufficient, and delusive, considering the state of human nature, would such reasons have been, on which to have rested his confident denial that they could continue to live in sin? But when the Apostle exhibits, as the cause of the believer's not continuing in sin, his union with Christ, and the power of God in Christ Jesus, as he does in the preceding verses, he rests it on a foundation as stable as the throne of God. He had taught, in the foregoing part of the Epistle, that Jesus Christ is made to His people righteousness : he here teaches that He is also made to them sanctification. Throughout the whole of the discussion, it is material to keep in mind that they to whom, along with himself, the Apostle is referring, are those whom he had addressed (ch. i. 7) as ' beloved of God,' as ' called,' as ' saints.'

The same great truths are fully developed in the 29th and 30th verses of the eighth chapter, where it is shown that the persons who are conformed to the image of Christ were those who are justified, and who shall be glorified, the whole of which Paul there traces up to the sovereign appointment of God. There, in like manner, he shows that the people of God, being conformed to Christ in His death, are also conformed to Him in their walking in newness of life, as the prelude of their resurrection with Him to glory. To the same purpose he writes to the saints at Colosse, where he assures them that they are ' complete in Christ, being buried with Him in baptism, wherein also they are risen with Him, through the faith of the operation of God, who hath raised Him from the dead.'

Ver. 8.—*Now, if we be dead with Christ, we believe that we shall also live with Him :*

Now—rather, *since, then*—believers are one with Christ in His death, they have the certain prospect of for ever living with Him. That the life here mentioned is the life after the resurrection, as in verse 5th, appears from the phraseology. The Apostle speaks of it as a future life, which it is unnatural to interpret as signifying the believer's spiritual life here, or as importing the continuation of it to the end of his course. There is no need of such straining, when the obvious meaning is true and most important. Besides, the point is decided by the assertion, ' we believe.' It is a matter of faith, and not of present experience.

' *We believe.*'—Upon this it is useful to remark, that though the Apostle reasons and deduces from principles, yet we are to be cautious not to consider his doctrine as needing any other support but his own assertion. His statement, or expression of belief, is demonstration to a Christian. It was a truth believed by those whom he addressed, because taught by Paul and the other Apostles.

Ver. 9.—*Knowing that Christ, being raised from the dead, dieth no more ; death hath no more dominion over Him.*

Knowing that.—The Apostle states the assumption that, as Christ, having been raised from the dead, will not die again, so neither will those die again who have died and risen with Him. This obviously refers to the resurrection life, and not to the present spiritual life. It is a fact of inconceivable consolation, that after the resurrection the believer will never again die. All the glory of heaven could not make us happy without this truth.

Death hath no more dominion over Him.—This implies that death had once dominion over Christ Himself. He was its lawful captive, as He took our place, and bore our sins. It is far from being true, according to Mr. Tholuck, that the word here used ' seems to involve the idea of a usurped power, for properly, as Christ was an innocent being, there was no reason why He should die.' Christ was lawfully under the power of death for a time ; and the word which signifies this applies to a lawful lord as well as to a usurper. Jesus Christ being declared by His resurrection to be the Son of God with power, His people are engaged to put their trust in Him as the Creator and Ruler of the universe. In His resurrection they receive the assurance of the effect of His death, in satisfying Divine justice while making full atonement for their sins ; and in His rising from the dead to an immortal life, as their Lord and Head, they have a certain pledge of their own resurrection to life and immortality.

Ver. 10.—*For in that He died, He died unto sin once ; but in that He liveth, He liveth unto God.*

In that—or with respect to that—*He died, He died unto sin.*—Here we have the same declaration concerning our Lord and Saviour as in the 2d verse concerning believers, of whom the Apostle says that they are *dead to sin.* Whatever, then, the expression signifies in the one case, it must also be understood to signify in the other. But those who attach a wrong interpretation to the phrase in the first occurrence, are necessitated to attribute to it a different one in the second. Accordingly Calvin remarks on this 10th verse,—' The very form of expression, as applied to Christ, shows that He did not, like us, die to sin for the purpose of ceasing to commit it.' Here are two misinterpretations,—first, of the 2d verse, and next, as a natural consequence, of this 10th. A similar difference of interpretation will be found in the other commentators. Having mistaken the meaning of the one, they are compelled to vary it in the other. In the first, they introduce the idea of death to the *power* of sin, but in the last this is impossible. Our Lord never felt the power of sin, and therefore could not die to it. But He died to the *guilt* of sin—to the guilt of His people's sins, which He had taken upon Him ; and they, dying with Him, as is above declared, die to sin precisely in the same sense in which He died to it. This declaration, then, that Christ *died to sin*, explains in the clearest manner the meaning of the expression ' dead to sin,' verse 2d, proving that it signifies exclusively dying to the guilt of sin ; for in no other sense could our Lord Jesus Christ die to sin.

The effect of the death of believers to sin, the Apostle, after concluding his argument, shows to be, that sin shall not have dominion over them, verse 14th, for they are not under the law but under grace. His argument is, that the doctrine of a free justification, which he had asserted in the fifth chapter, according to which believers are dead to, or justified from sin, by their oneness with Christ in His death, brings them into an entirely different state from that in which they formerly were in respect to their relation to God. Having been delivered from its guilt, —dead to it, or justified from it, verse 7th,—they are in consequence delivered from its power. But to include the idea of power in the expression, ' dead to sin,' verse 2d, entirely confuses and misrepresents his meaning.

Jesus Christ suffered the penalty of sin, and ceased to bear it. Till His death He had sin upon Him; and therefore, though it was not committed by Him personally, yet it was His own, inasmuch as He had taken it upon Him. When He took it on Him, so as to free His people from its guilt, it became His own debt as truly as if it had been contracted by Him. When, therefore, He died on account of sin, He died to it, as He was now for ever justified from it. He was not justified from it till His resurrection; but from that moment He was dead to it. When He shall appear the second time, it will be 'without sin,' Heb. ix. 28.

Once.—He died to sin once, and but *once*, because He fully atoned for it by His death. On this circumstance the Apostle, in the Epistle to the Hebrews, lays much stress, and, in proving the excellence of His sacrifice beyond the legal sacrifices, often repeats it, Heb. ix. 12, 26, 28, x. 10, 12, 14. *He liveth unto God.*—It need not excite any surprise that Christ is said henceforth to live unto God. The glory of God must be the great end of all life. Christ's eternal life in human nature will, no doubt, more than all things else, be for the glory of God.

Ver. 11.—*Likewise reckon ye also yourselves to be dead indeed unto sin, but alive unto God through Jesus Christ our Lord.*

Believers are here commanded to reckon themselves to be really and effectually dead to sin—dead to its guilt—and alive unto God *in* Jesus Christ, as it ought to be rendered. The obligation thus enjoined follows from all that the Apostle had been inculcating respecting their blessed state as partakers with Christ, both in His death and in His life. As this is their real condition, he here commands them to maintain a full sense and conviction of it. The duties of the Christian life, flowing from their union with Jesus Christ and acceptance with God, he immediately proceeds to enforce. But here it is the obligation to maintain the conviction of their state that he exclusively presses upon them. To note this is of the greatest importance. Unless we keep in mind that we are dead to sin, and alive unto God in Jesus Christ our Lord, we cannot serve Him as we ought: we shall otherwise be serving in the oldness of the letter, and not in newness of spirit. But when the believer's state of reconciliation with God, and his death to sin, from which he is delivered, is steadily kept in view, then he cultivates the spirit of adoption—then he strives to walk worthy of his calling, and, in the consideration of the mercies of God, presents his body a living sacrifice, holy and acceptable unto God, Rom. xii. 1; he rejoices in the Lord, and abounds in hope through the power of the Holy Ghost; he has peace in his conscience, his heart is enlarged, and he runs the way of God's commandments.

Of their high privileges and state of acceptance with God, believers are ever reminded in Scripture; and it is not till a man has the answer of a good conscience toward God by the resurrection of Jesus Christ, 1 Pet. iii. 21, and a sense of being justified from sin, *having his conscience purged from dead works* by the blood of Christ, that he can serve the living God, Heb. ix. 14. How important, then, is this admonition of the Apostle, *Reckon ye also yourselves to be dead indeed unto sin,* though often much obscured by false glosses turning it away from its true and appropriate meaning! By many it would be accounted presumptuous in Christians to take it home to themselves. Hence they are not aware of the obligations they are under to labour to maintain the *assurance* of their union with Christ, and of their participation with Him in His death and resurrection. But we see that the Apostle, after he had fully developed the blessed state of believers, and declared the foundation on which it rests, with which their continuing to live in sin is incompatible, *expressly enjoins this* as a positive duty on those whom he addresses, and consequently on all Christians, thus reminding them that what he had said was not to be viewed in the light of abstract truth, but ought to be practically and individually brought home to their own bosoms. How seldom is this use made of the text before us! How seldom, if ever, is the duty it enforces urged upon Christians![1] How little is it considered as binding on their consciences! Yet, without attending to this duty, which, in connection with a right understanding of the Gospel, is consistent with the deepest humility, how can they possibly bring forth those precious fruits of the Spirit which lie at the foundation of all the rest, *love*, and *joy*, and *peace?* How, in a word, can they walk with God?

There was no part of the Exposition in which I felt so much difficulty as in the commencement of this chapter. In consulting a multitude of commentators, I found no satisfactory solution. Most of them explain the expression 'dead to sin,' in the 2d verse, as importing death not only to the guilt, but also, as has been remarked, to the power of sin,—a proof that the assertion of the Apostle is misunderstood. But when it is perceived that the guilt of sin only is included, a clear light is thrown on this highly important part of the Epistle. This is the way in which it appears to have been viewed by Mr. Romaine, of which, till lately, I was not aware, and I do not recollect ever meeting with it in the works of any other writer. I subjoin the following interesting passage from his treatise *On the Walk of Faith.*

'True spiritual mortification does not consist in sin not being in thee, nor in its being put upon the cross daily, nor yet in its being kept upon it. There must be something more to establish perfect peace in thy conscience; and that is the testimony of God concerning the body of sin. He has provided for thy perfect deliverance from it in Christ. Everything needful for this purpose was finished by Him upon the cross. He was thy Surety. He suffered for thee. Thy sins were crucified with Him, and nailed to His cross. They were put to death when He died: for He was thy covenant-head, and thou wast legally represented by Him, and art indeed dead to sin by His dying to sin once. The law has now no more right to condemn thee, a believer, than it has to condemn Him. Justice is bound to deal with thee, as it has with thy risen and ascended Saviour. If thou dost not thus see thy complete mortification in Him, sin will reign in thee. No sin can be crucified either in heart or life, unless it be first pardoned in conscience; because there will be want of

---

[1] I do not recollect that I ever heard any one preach on this text, Rom. vi. 11, although it contains so important an injunction, and is of such practical importance.

faith to receive the strength of Jesus, by whom alone it can be crucified. If it be not mortified in its guilt, it cannot be subdued in its power. If the believer does not see his perfect deadness to sin in Jesus, he will open a wide door to unbelief; and if he be not persuaded of his completeness in Christ, he gives room for the attacks of self-righteous and legal tempers. If Christ be not all in all, self must still be looked upon as something great, and there will be food left for the pride of self-importance and self-sufficiency; so that he cannot grow into the death of Christ in sensible experience, further than he believes himself to be dead to sin in Christ. The more clearly and stedfastly he believes this, as the Apostle did—*I am crucified with Christ*—in proportion will he cleave to Christ, and receive from Him greater power to crucify sin. This believing view of his absolute mortification in Christ, is the true Gospel method of mortifying sin in our own persons. Read the sixth of the Romans, and pray for the Spirit of revelation to open it to thee. There thou wilt discover the true way to mortify sin. It is by believing that thou art planted together with Christ in His death; from thence only thy pardon flows, from thence thy daily victory is received, and from thence thy eternal victory will be perfected.'

Ver. 12.—*Let not sin therefore reign in your mortal body, that ye should obey it in the lusts thereof.*

Having proved how unfounded is the objection that the doctrine of justification leads to the indulgence of sin, the Apostle now exhorts those whom he addresses to live agreeably to the holy nature and design of the Gospel. With this object he presents, throughout the rest of the chapter, various considerations adapted to induce them to walk in that newness of life to which they are risen with Christ. It should here be remarked, that although the Apostle had expressly taught that they who are justified are likewise sanctified, yet as God is pleased to cause His people to act with Him in their sanctification—so that they shall both will and do, because He worketh in them to will and to do of His good pleasure—the earnest exhortations to obedience, and the motives held forth in the conclusion of the chapter, are entirely consistent with what had been declared as to the certainty of their sanctification resting on the power of God, and to be viewed as outward means which God employs to effect this purpose.

Therefore.—The exhortation in this verse is founded on the preceding. Here, then, we have an example of the manner in which the Apostle urges believers to the performance of their duty to God. Because being united to Christ they were dead to sin, the conviction of which he had just before enjoined them to maintain, he exhorts them in this and the following verse to abstain from sin. Unless they possessed that conviction, the motive on which he here rests his exhortation would be inapplicable. This is his manner in all his Epistles, in common with the other Apostles, of enforcing the obligation of Christians to the performance of their duty. ' Be ye kind one to another, forgiving one another, *even as God for Christ's sake hath forgiven you.*' He proceeds on the fact of their knowledge that their sins were forgiven.

It is difficult to see what precise idea the Apostle intends to communicate by the addition of the epithet *mortal;* yet it is certain that he uses no unmeaning appendages, and that this word must add to the sense. The propriety of the epithet, as ascribed to the body, is evident; but still, why is this epithet added here? Paul had just charged believers to reckon themselves dead to sin, but alive to God. When, therefore, he here urges them not to allow sin to reign in their bodies, and designates their bodies as mortal, it may be that he means to intimate either that their struggle with sin, which will only continue while they are in the body, will be short, or to contrast the present state of the body with its future spiritual state. As in its future glorified state it is to live entirely to God, and to be without sin, so it follows that, even in its present mortal state, sin should not have it in subjection. Calvin is undoubtedly mistaken in saying that the word body here 'is not taken in the sense of flesh, skin, and bones; but means, if I may be allowed the expression, the whole mass of the man;' that is, man as soul and body in its present earthly state. This would import that the soul is now mortal.

Sin reign.—Sin is here personified and viewed as a king. Such a ruler is sin over all the world, except those who believe in the Lord Jesus Christ, 1 John v. 19. This is the reason why men will spend their substance and their labour in the works of the flesh. Sin rules in them as a sovereign; and they of their own accord with eagerness pursue every ungodly course to which their corrupt nature impels them; and in the service of sin they will often ruin their health as well as their fortune. *That ye should obey it,* or, so as to obey it.—Sin is still a law in the members of believers, but it is not to be allowed to reign. It must be constantly resisted. *Obey it in the lusts thereof.*—That is, to obey sin in the lusts of the body. Sin is obeyed in gratifying the lusts or corrupt appetites of the body. The term lusts imports the inward corrupt inclination to sin from whence the acts of sin proceed, and of which the Apostle speaks particularly in the following chapter, where he shows that till after the commandment came to him in power, he had not known that corrupt inclination to be sin. Augustine here remarks that the Apostle does not say that in believers there is no sin, but that it should not reign, because while they live there must be sin in their members.

Ver. 13.—*Neither yield ye your members as instruments of unrighteousness unto sin ; but yield yourselves unto God, as those that are alive from the dead, and your members as instruments of righteousness unto God.*

Neither yield.—That is, do not present, afford, or make a donation of your members. *Instruments*—or weapons, or organs, to be employed in works of unrighteousness. *Unto sin.*—This surrender, against which the believer is cautioned, is to sin. They who employ the members of their bodies in doing the works of the flesh, present their bodies to sin as their sovereign. *Members.*—There is no occasion, with Dr. Macknight and others, to suppose that the word members here includes the faculties of the mind as well as the members of the body. It is of the body that the Apostle is speaking. It follows, indeed, as a consequence, that if sin is not to be practised through the members of the body, neither is it to be indulged in the thoughts of the mind, for it is the latter that leads to the former. The word instruments evidently limits the expression to the members of the body.

But yield yourselves unto God.—Yield yourselves soul and body. The exhortation, as it respected the service of sin, mentions only the members of the body which are the instruments of gratifying the corruptions of the mind. But this, as was observed, sufficiently implies that we are forbidden to employ the faculties of the soul in the service of sin, as well as the members of the body. There can be no doubt that all we are commanded to give to God, we are prohibited from giving to sin. If we are commanded to present ourselves unto God, then we are forbidden to present either the faculties of the mind or the members of the body to sin. The believer is to give himself up to God without any reservation. He is to employ both body and mind in every work required of him by God. He must decline no labour which the Lord sets before him, no trial to which He calls him, no cross which He lays upon him. He is not to count even his life dear if God demands its sacrifice.

As those that are alive from the dead.—Here again Christians are addressed as those who know their state. They are already in one sense raised from the dead. They have a spiritual life, of which they were by nature entirely destitute, and of which unbelievers are not only altogether destitute, but which they cannot even comprehend. *Your members as instruments of righteousness.*—The members of the body are not only to be used in the direct worship of God, and in doing those things in which their instrumentality is required, but in every action they ought to be employed in this manner, even in the common business of life, in which the glory of God should be constantly kept in view. The labourer who toils in the field, if he acts with an eye to the glory of God, ought to console himself with the consideration that when he has finished his day to man, he has wrought a day to God. This view of the matter is a great relief under his daily toils. *Unto God.*—That is, yield your members unto God. As the natural man presents his members to sin, so the believer is to present his members to God.

Ver. 14.—*For sin shall not have dominion over you : for ye are not under the law, but under grace.*

For sin shall not have dominion over you.—Such is the unqualified affirmation with which Paul in this place shuts up his triumphant reply to the objection to his doctrine urged in the first verse. No truth is more certain than that sin shall not have dominion over believers. God's veracity and glory are pledged to prevent it. They are dead to the guilt of sin, and therefore its power shall no more predominate in them. They have put on the new man, and the warfare with the old man shall finally terminate in his destruction. The first *for* in this verse gives a reason why believers should exert themselves to give their members to the service of God. They shall not fail in their attempt, for sin shall not have dominion over them. The next *for* gives the reason why sin shall not have dominion over them.

For ye are not under the law—literally, under law.—A great variety of interpretations are given of this declaration. But the meaning cannot be a matter of doubt to those who are well instructed in the nature of salvation by grace. It is quite obvious that the law which believers are here said not to be under, is the moral law, as a covenant of works, and not the legal dispensation,—to distinguish it from which may be the reason why the article is here omitted. To affirm that law here is the legal dispensation, is to say that all who lived under the law of Moses were under the dominion of sin. In the sense in which law is here understood, the Old Testament saints were not under it. They had the Gospel in figure. They trusted in the promised Saviour, and sought not to justify themselves by their obedience to the law. Besides, all unbelievers, both Jews and Gentiles, are under the law, in the sense in which believers are here said not to be under it. Believers are not under the law as a covenant, because they have endured its curse and obeyed its precept in the person of their great Head, by whom the righteousness of the law has been fulfilled in them, ch. viii. 4. But every man, till he is united to Christ, is under the law, which condemns him. When united to Him, the believer is no longer under the law either to be condemned or to be justified. When Mr. Stuart says that it is from the law, 'as inadequate to effect the sanctification and secure the obedience of sinners,' that the Apostle here declares us to be free, he proves that he entirely misunderstands what is meant. The circumstance that the law cannot sanctify the sinner, and secure his obedience, confers no emancipation from its demands. The believer is free from the law, because another has taken his place, and fulfilled it in his stead. This implies that all who are under the law are also under the dominion of sin, and under the curse, Gal. iii. 10. The self-righteous who trust in their works, and boast of their natural ability to serve God, are under the dominion of sin; and the very works in which they trust are sinful, or 'dead works,' Heb. ix. 14. They are such works as men perform before their consciences are purged by the blood of Christ.

But under grace.—Believers are not under the covenant of works, but under the covenant of grace, by which they enjoy all the blessings of that gracious covenant in which all that is required of them is promised to them. They are in a state of reconciliation with God. They know the Lord. According to the tenor of that gracious covenant, His law is written in their hearts, and His fear is put within them. He has promised not to depart from them, and that they shall not depart from Him, Jer. xxxii. 40 ; and their sins and iniquities, which separated them from God, are no more remembered by Him. Being made partakers of the favour of God through Jesus Christ, in whom grace was given them before the world began, 2 Tim. i. 9, they have every spiritual supply through Him who is full of grace. His grace is sufficient for them, 2 Cor. xii. 9. The grace of God, which bringeth salvation, that hath appeared to all men, teacheth them to deny ungodliness and worldly lusts, and to live soberly, righteously, and godly, Tit. ii. 11. Not only is this grace manifested to them, but it operates within them. God works in them what is well pleasing in His sight, both to will and to do of His good pleasure. They who are under the law have nothing but their own strength in order to their obedience : sin, therefore, must have the dominion over them. But they who are under grace are by God Himself thoroughly furnished unto all good works: sin, therefore, shall not have dominion over them.

The great principle of evangelical obedience is taught in this passage. Holiness is not the result of the law, but of the liberty wherewith Christ has made His people free. He sends forth the Spirit of grace into the hearts of all who belong to the election of grace, whom God hath from the beginning chosen to salvation through sanctification of the Spirit and belief of the truth ; and the word of God worketh effectually in all who believe, 1 Thess. ii. 13. Jesus Christ is the absolute master of the hearts of His people, of which He has taken possession, and in whom He reigns by the invincible power of the Spirit of grace. The new covenant made with Him, for those whom He has redeemed, and which is ratified with His blood, is immutable and irreversible.

Here, again, it should be observed that the assurance thus given to believers, that sin shall not have dominion over them, could not be duly appreciated except on the ground that they *knew* that they were dead to sin and alive to God. Just in proportion as Christians are convinced of this, they will feel encouragement from this promise to persevere in their course. The assurance given to them that sin shall not have the dominion over them, is then very far from furnishing a pretext or inducement to a life of sin. On the contrary, they are thereby bound by every consideration of love and gratitude to serve God, while, by the certain prospect of final victory, they are encouraged to persevere, in spite of all difficulties and opposition, either from within or from without.

Ver. 15.—*What then ? shall we sin, because we are not under law, but under grace? God forbid.*

The Apostle had been proving that his doctrine of a free justification by faith without works furnishes no licence to believers to continue in sin, but, on the contrary, that the death of Jesus Christ for the sins of His people, and His resurrection for their justification, secures their walking in holiness of life. On this ground, in verses 12 and 13, he had urged on them the duty of obedience to God ; and having finally declared, in the 14th verse, that, by the blessing of God, they should be enabled to perform it, he now proceeds to caution them against the abuse of this gracious declaration. If a man voluntarily sins, on the pretext that he is not under the law, but under grace, it is a proof that the grace of God is not in him. ' Whosoever is born of God doth not commit sin, for his seed remaineth in him ; and he cannot sin, because he is born of God.'

What then ?—What is the inference which should be deduced from the preceding declaration? *Shall we sin, because we are not under law, but under grace?*—This question, proposed by the Apostle as an objection likely to be urged against his doctrine, plainly shows in what sense we are to understand the term *law* in the 14th verse. Were it not understood of the moral law, it would not be liable to the supposed objection. The fact of not being under the ceremonial law, or of a change of dispensation from that of Moses to that of Christ, would never lead to such an objection. No one could suppose that the abolition of certain external rites would authorize men to break moral precepts. No view of the law could give occasion to the objection but that which includes freedom from the moral law. This would at once appear to furnish a licence to sin with impunity; and it would be justly liable to this objection if freedom from the moral law meant, as some have argued, a freedom from it in every point of view. The freedom from the moral law which the believer enjoys, is a freedom from an obligation to fulfil it in his own person for his justification—a freedom from its condemnation on account of imperfection of obedience. But this is quite consistent with the eternal obligation of the moral law as a rule of life to the Christian. Nothing can be more self-evidently certain than that, if the moral law is not a rule of life to believers, they are at liberty to disregard its precepts. But the very thought of this is abominable. The Apostle therefore rejects it in the strongest terms, in the way in which he usually expresses his disapprobation of what is most egregiously wrong.

Ver. 16.—*Know ye not, that to whom ye yield yourselves servants to obey, his servants ye are to whom ye obey; whether of sin unto death, or of obedience unto righteousness?*

Know ye not?—That is, the thing by which I am now going to illustrate the subject, is a fact of which you cannot be ignorant. All of them well knew the truth of what Paul was about to say, and by this similitude they would be able to comprehend the doctrine he was teaching. The ground, however, of the use of this phraseology has no resemblance, as Mr. Stuart supposes, to that used in verses 6 and 9. Here the Apostle speaks of a thing which all men know, and which belongs to the common relations of society. There he speaks of what they know only as Christians by revelation.

Yield yourselves, or, present yourselves.—Not, as Mr. Stuart translates it, 'proffer yourselves.' It is possible among men that proffered service may be rejected, or that, at least, something may occur to prevent performance of the actual service; and it is of transactions among men that the Apostle is speaking; but, in the Apostle's view, the presented service is accepted. Mr. Stuart's translation in his Commentary is better. 'Where you have once given up yourselves to any one as servants.' This, however, is quite a different idea from what he expresses in the text.

Servants to obey, literally, unto obedience.—Mr. Stuart's translation is not to be approved of here, 'ready to obey,' or 'bound to obey.' The idea is not that they were bound by this presentation of themselves to continue in obedience to the master. The servants unto obedience are not servants who are bound to obey, but servants who actually obey— whose servitude is proved and perfected in their works. Mr. Stuart entirely mistakes the sentiment expressed by the Apostle when he paraphrases thus:—'When you have once given up yourselves to any one as δούλους εἰς ὑπακοήν, you are no longer your own masters, or at your own disposal; you have put yourselves within the power and at the disposal of another master.' The language of the Apostle is not designed to prove that, by presenting themselves to a master, they are bound to his service, but to state the obvious fact that they are the servants of him whose work they do. If we see a number of labourers in a field, we know they are the servants of the proprietor of the field—of the person in whose work they are employed. The application of this fact to the Apostle's purpose is obvious and important. If men are doing the work of Satan, must they not be Satan's servants? If they are doing God's work, must they not be the servants of God? Mr. Stuart's exposition leads entirely away from the Apostle's meaning.

Of sin.—Sin is here personified, and sinners are its servants. *Unto death.*—That is, which ends in death. This is the wages with which sin rewards its servants. *Obedience unto righteousness.*—Obedience is also personified, and the work performed to obedience is righteousness; that is, the works of the believer are righteous works. Nothing can be more false as a translation, or more erroneous in sentiment, than the version of Mr. Stuart. ' Obedience unto justification.' In his paraphrase he says, ' But if you are the servants of that *obedience which is unto justification—i.e.*, which is connected with justification, which ends in it—then you may expect eternal life.' Δικαιοσύνη, which he here translates justification, is righteousness, and never justification. In verses 18, 19, and 20, that follow, he himself translates it righteousness. And what can be more completely subversive of the doctrine of justification, and of the Gospel itself, than the assertion that obedience ' ends in,' or, as he says afterwards, *will lead to justification?* This is the translation of the English Socinian version, and of that adopted in their different editions of the New Testament by the Socinian pastors of the church of Geneva. ' De l'obeissance qui *conduit* à la justification.' Of obedience which leads to justification. They have, however, printed the word ' conduit ' (leads to) in italics, to show that it is a supplement.

Mr. Stuart says that his view seems to him quite clear, from justification being the antithesis unto death. But justification is not an exact antithesis to death. It is life that is the antithesis to death. There is no need, however, that there should be such an exact correspondence in the parts of the antithesis as is supposed. And there is a most obvious reason why it could not be so. Death is the wages of sin, but life is not the wages of obedience. Mr. Stuart asks, ' How can δικαιοσύνην here mean *holiness, uprightness,* when ὑπακοή itself necessarily designates this very idea? What is an obedience which *leads* to righteousness? Or how does it differ from righteousness itself, inasmuch as it is the very act of obedience which constitutes righteousness in the sense now contemplated?' It is replied that obedience is here personified, and therefore righteous actions are properly represented as performed to it. Mr. Stuart might as well ask why are obedience to sin, and the lusts of sin, supposed to be different things in verse 12. In like manner we have righteousness and holiness in verse 19, and fruit and holiness in verse 22. Besides, obedience and righteousness are not ideas perfectly coincident. Righteousness refers to works as to their nature; obedience refers to the same works as to their principle. Mr. Stuart's remark is both false in criticism, and heretical in doctrine.

Ver. 17.—*But God be thanked, that ye were the servants of sin; but ye have obeyed from the heart that form of doctrine which was delivered you.*

The Apostle here expresses his thankfulness to God that they who had formerly been the servants of sin were now the servants of righteousness. To suppose, as some do, that sin itself could be a matter of thankfulness, is a most palpable error, than which nothing can be more remote from the meaning of this passage. *Obeyed from the heart.*—Christian obedience is obedience from the heart, in opposition to an obedience which is by constraint. Any attempt at obedience by an unconverted man, is an obedience produced by some motive of fear, self-interest, or constraint, and not from the heart. Nothing can be more convincing evidence of the truth of the Gospel than the change which, in this respect, it produces on the mind of the believer. Nothing but almighty power could at once transform a man from the love of sin to the love of holiness.

That form of doctrine which was delivered you.—There are various solutions of this expression, all substantially agreeing in meaning, but differing in the manner of bringing out that meaning. The most usual way is to suppose that there is a reference to melted metals transferred to a mould, which obey or exactly conform to the mould. It is perhaps as probable that the reference is to wax or clay, or any soft matter that takes the form of the stamp or seal. There is another method of explaining the phraseology not unworthy of consideration—Ye have obeyed from the heart that form or model of doctrine unto which you have been committed. In this way the form of doctrine or the Gospel is considered as a teacher, and believers are committed to its instructions. The word translated delivered, will admit of this interpretation, and it is sufficiently agreeable to the general meaning of the expression. The substance of the phrase, however, is obvious, and let it be translated as it may, there is no essential difference in the meaning. It proves the holy tendency of the doctrine of grace which believers have received, the blessed effects of which they have felt, and manifested in its fruits, Tit. ii. 11, 12.

Ver. 18.—*Being then made free from sin, ye became the servants of righteousness.*

Being then made free from sin.—The original word here rendered *free*, as also in verses 20 and 22, is different, as has been observed, from that improperly rendered *freed* in verse 7th, and has no respect to the justified state of the believer, as is clear from the context, but relates to his freedom from the dominion of sin assured to him in the 14th verse. There is here a reference to the emancipation of slaves from their masters. Formerly they were slaves to sin; now they have been emancipated by the Gospel. This deliverance is called their freedom. It does not, however, by any means import what has been called sinless perfection, or an entire freedom from the influence of sin. *Ye became servants of righteousness.*—Here we see the proper meaning of the word δικαιοσύνη. The servants of righteousness are men obedient to righteousness, being devoted to the practice of such works as are *righteous*, or, as is said in other words, in verse 22, 'servants of God.' What meaning could we attach to servants of justification? The idea is, that the believer ought to be as entirely devoted to God as a servant or slave is to his master. Mr. Stuart is here of necessity compelled to allow the true meaning of the same word, which, in the 16th verse, in consistency with his unscriptural system, he had mistranslated, by rendering it justification.

Ver. 19.—*I speak after the manner of men, because of the infirmity of your flesh : for as ye have yielded your members servants to uncleanness, and to iniquity unto iniquity ; even so now yield your members servants to righteousness unto holiness.*

I speak after the manner of men.—This refers to the illustration of the subject by the customs of men as to slavery. Mr. Stuart has either missed the idea here, or expressed it too generally. He translates, ' in language usual to men,' and expounds, ' I speak as men are accustomed to speak, viz., I use such language as they usually employ in regard to the affairs of common life.' This makes the reference merely to the words used ; whereas the reference is to the illustration drawn from human customs. In what way could the Apostle speak but as men are accustomed to speak ? Could he speak in any other language than that which was usual to men ? This is a thing in which there is no choice. If he speaks at all, he must use human language. But to illustrate spiritual subjects by the customs of men is a matter of choice, because it might have been avoided. This establishes the propriety of teaching Divine truth through illustrations taken from all subjects with which those addressed are acquainted. This method not only facilitates the right perception or apprehension of the subject, but also assists the memory in retaining the information received. Accordingly, it was much used by our Lord and His Apostles.

Calvin has not caught the spirit of this passage: 'Paul,' he says, 'means that he speaks after the manner of men with respect to forms, not the subject-matter, as Christ (John iii. 12) says, " If I have told you earthly things," when He is, however, discoursing on heavenly mysteries, but not with so much majesty as the dignity of the subject demanded, because He accommodated Himself to the capacity of a rude, dull, and slow people.' Here Calvin also makes the reference apply not to human customs, but to human language and style. It may also be asked, why the Lord did not express Himself with so much majesty as the dignity of the subject demanded ? It cannot be admitted that His language, or the language of inspiration, ever falls short of the *dignity demanded* by the subject.

Because of the infirmity of your flesh.—That is, the weakness of their spiritual discernment through the corruption of human nature. This does not refer, as Mr. Stuart supposes, to ' the feeble or infantile state of spiritual knowledge among the Romans,' but is applicable to mankind in general. Men in all places, and in all ages, and in every period of their lives, are weak through the flesh, both in spiritual discernment, and in the practice of holiness. Men of the most powerful mental capacity are naturally dull in apprehending the things of the Spirit. Accordingly errors abound with them as much as with the most illiterate, and often in a far greater degree. Besides, such a peculiar application to those in the church at Rome is inconsistent with chapter xv. 14, where the Apostle says that they were 'filled with all knowledge, able also to admonish one another.'

For as ye have yielded your members servants to uncleanness.—This shows the state of men by nature, and especially the state of the heathen world at the period of the highest refinement. *Uncleanness* means all impurity, but especially the vice opposed to chastity. *Iniquity,* as distinguished from this, refers to conduct opposed to laws human and Divine. The one refers principally to the pollution, the other to the guilt of sin.

Unto iniquity.—Some understand this as signifying from one iniquity to another, or from one degree of iniquity to another, which is not its meaning. Neither can it signify, as it is sometimes understood, for the purpose of iniquity, for men often sin when it cannot be justly said that they do so *for the purpose of sinning.* They often sin from the love of the sin, when they wish it was not a sin. Their object is selfish gratification. It is evident that the phrase is to be understood on a principle already mentioned, namely, that iniquity is in the first occurrence personified, and in the second, it is the conduct produced by obedience to this sovereign. They surrender their members unto the slavery of iniquity as a king, and the result is, that iniquity is practised. This corresponds with the sense, and suits the antithesis. *Righteousness unto holiness.*—Righteousness is here personified as iniquity was before, and obedience to this sovereign produces holiness.

Ver. 20.—*For when ye were the servants of sin, ye were free from righteousness.* Mr. Tholuck misunderstands this verse, which, in connection with the 21st, he paraphrases thus : ' While engaged in the service of sin, you possessed, it is true, the advantage of standing entirely out of all subjection to righteousness ; but let us look to what is to be the final result.' The Apostle is not speaking of freedom from righteousness as an advantage either real or supposed, nor could he thus speak of it. He is speaking of it as a fact ; and from that fact he argues that, as when they were the servants of sin they were free from righteousness—yielding no obedience to it, and acting as if they had nothing to do with, and had no relation to it—so now, as they are the servants of righteousness, they ought to hold themselves free from the slavery of sin. The consequence, indeed, is not drawn, but is so plain that it is left to the reader. The sentiment is just and obvious. When they were the subjects of their former sovereign, they were free from the service of their present sovereign. So now, as they are subjects to righteousness, they ought to be free from sin.

Mr. Stuart also misunderstands this verse. He explains it thus : ' When you served sin, you deemed yourselves free from all obligation to righteousness.' This the Apostle neither says, nor could say. For it is not true that natural men, whether Pagans or under a profession of Christianity, regard themselves as bound by no obligations to righteousness. The law of nature teaches the contrary. But whatever is their light on this subject, it is a fact that they are free from righteousness. This, we learn, is the state of all natural men.

Ver. 21.—*What fruit had ye then in those things whereof ye are now ashamed ? for the end of those things is death.*

What fruit had ye then in those things ?—Besides the exhortations to holiness which he had already employed, the Apostle here sets before believers the nature and consequences of sin. Unprofitable and shameful in it character, its end is death. He asks what advantage had they derived from their former conduct. Fruit here signifies advantage, and not pleasure. Many interpret this verse as if the Apostle denied that they had any pleasure in their sins at the time of committing them. This the Apostle could not do ; for it is a fact that men have pleasure in sin. To say that sinful pleasure is no pleasure, but is imaginary, is to abuse terms. All pleasure is a matter of feeling, and a man is no less happy than he feels himself to be ; if he imagines that he enjoys pleasure, he actually enjoys pleasure. But what advantage is there in such pleasure ? This is the question which the Apostle asks.

Whereof ye are now ashamed.—It is a remarkable fact that men in a state of alienation from God will commit sin not only without shame, but will glory in many things of which they are ashamed the moment they are changed by the Gospel. They now see their conduct in another light. They see that it was not only sinful but shameful. *For the end of those things is death.*—Here is the answer to the question with respect to the fruit of unrighteous conduct. Whatever pleasure they might have found in it, the end of it is ruin. *Death.*—This cannot be confined to natural death, for that is equally the end with respect to the righteous as well as the wicked. It includes the whole penalty of sin—eternal punishment.

Ver. 22.—*But now, being made free from sin, and become servants to God, ye have your fruit unto holiness, and the end everlasting life.*

Having concluded his triumphant reply to the objection, that his doctrine concerning justification leads to indulgence in sin, the Apostle here assures those to whom he wrote of the blessed effects of becoming servants to God. In the eighth chapter these are fully developed. *But now, being made free from sin,*—that is, emancipated from a state of slavery to sin. *Fruit unto holiness.*—Fruit, in this verse, denotes conduct, and holiness its specific character or quality. When conduct or works are called fruit, their nature is not expressed ; they are merely considered as the production of the man. Fruit unto holiness is conduct that is holy. *And·the end everlasting life.*—Fruit unto holiness, or holy conduct, is the present result of freedom from sin, and of becoming servants to God ; eternal life is the final result. Eternal life is the issue of the service of God, but it is not the reward of its merit. Hence the Apostle here uses the phrase eternal life when he is speaking of the issue of the service of God. But in verse 16 he says, ' obedience unto righteousness,' and not ' obedience unto eternal life,' because he had, in the preceding member of the sentence, spoken of death as the punishment of sin. Had he used the word eternal life in connection with obedience in this antithesis, it would have too much resembled an assertion that eternal life is the reward of our obedience.

Ver. 23.--*For the wages of sin is death ; but the gift of God is eternal life, through Jesus Christ our Lord.*

The wages of sin is death.—Here, as in the conclusion of the preceding chapter, death is contrasted with eternal life. Sin is a service or slavery, and its reward is death, or eternal misery. As death is the greatest evil in this world, so the future punishment of the wicked is called death figuratively, or the second death. In this sense death is frequently spoken of in Scripture ; as when our Lord says, ' Whosoever believeth on Me shall never die.' Death is the just recompense of sin. The Apostle does not add, But the wages of obedience is eternal life. This is not the doctrine of Scripture. He adds, *But the gift of God is eternal life.* The gift that God bestows is eternal life. He bestows no less upon any of His people ; and it is the greatest gift that can be bestowed.

Dr. Gill on this passage remarks, ' These words, at first sight, look as if the sense of them was, that eternal life is the gift of God through Christ, which is a great and glorious truth of the Gospel ; but their standing in opposition to the preceding words require another sense, namely, that God's gift of grace issues in eternal life, through Christ : Wherefore, by *the gift of God* is not meant eternal life, but either the gift of a justifying righteousness or the grace of God in regeneration and sanctification, or both, which issue in eternal life.' This remark does not appear to be well founded. The wages of sin do not issue in death, or lead to it, but the wages of sin is death. Death is asserted to be the wages of sin, and not to be another issue to which the wages of sin lead ; and the gift of God is not said to issue in eternal life, but to be eternal life. Eternal life is the gift here spoken of. It is not, as Dr. Gill represents, ' eternal life is the gift of God,' but ' the gift of God is eternal life.' The meaning of these two propositions, though nearly alike, are not entirely coincident. The common version is perfectly correct. Both of the propositions might with truth be rendered convertible, but as they are expressed by the Apostle they are not convertible ; and we should receive the expression as it stands. No doubt the gift of righteousness issues in eternal life ; but it is of the gift of eternal life itself, and not of the gift of righteousness, that the Apostle is here speaking ; and the Apostle's language should not be pressed into a meaning which is foreign to his design.

Life and death are set before us in the Scriptures. On the one hand, indignation and wrath, tribulation and anguish ; on the other, glory, and honour, and peace. To one or other of these states every child of Adam will finally be consigned. To both of them, in the concluding verse of this chapter, our attention is directed ; and the grounds on which never-ending misery or everlasting blessedness will be awarded, are expressly declared. ' The wages of sin is *death ;* but the gift of God is *eternal life,* through *Jesus Christ our Lord.*'

The punishment of that *death* which was the threatened penalty of the first transgression, will, according to Scripture, consist in the pains both of privation and suffering. Its subjects will not only be bereaved of all that is good, they will also be overwhelmed with all that is terrible. As the chief good of the creature is the enjoyment of the love of God, how great must be the punishment of being deprived of the sense of His love, and oppressed with the consciousness of His hatred! The condemned will be entirely divested of every token of the protection and blessing of God, and visited with every proof of His wrath and indignation. According to the awful declaration of the Apostle, they shall be punished with everlasting destruction from the presence of the Lord, and from the glory of His power, in that day ' when the Lord Jesus shall be revealed from heaven with His mighty angels, in flaming fire, taking vengeance on them that know not God, and that obey not the Gospel of our Lord Jesus Christ.'

This punishment will be adapted to both the component parts of man's nature—to the soul as well as to the body. It will connect all the ideas of the past, the present, and the future. As to the past, it will bring to the recollection of the wicked the sins they committed, the good they abused, and the false pleasures by which they were deluded. As to the present, their misery will be aggravated by their knowledge of the glory of the righteous, from which they themselves are for ever separated, and by the direful company of the devil and his angels, to the endurance of whose cruel slavery they are for ever doomed. As to the future, the horrors of their irreversible condition will be rendered more insupportable by the overwhelming conviction of its eternity. To the whole must be added that rage against God, whom they will hate as their enemy, without any abatement or diminution.

It is not to be questioned that there will be degrees in the punishment of the wicked. This is established by our Lord Himself, when He declares that it shall be more tolerable for Tyre and Sidon in the day of judgment than for the Jews. This punishment being the effect of Divine justice, the necessary proportion between crime and suffering will be observed; and as some crimes are greater and more aggravated than others, there will be a difference in the punishment inflicted. In one view, indeed, all sins are equal, because equally offences against God, and transgressions of His law ; but, in another view, they differ from each other. Sin is in degree proportioned not only to the want of love to God and man which it displays, but likewise to the manner in which it is perpetrated. Murder is more aggravated than theft, and the sins against the second table of the law are less heinous than those committed against the first. Sins likewise vary in degree, according to the knowledge of him who commits them, and inasmuch as one is carried into full execution, and another remains but in thought or purpose. The difference in the degree of punishment will not consist, however, in what belongs to privation—for in this it must be equal to all—but in those sufferings which will be positively inflicted by God.

Our Lord three times in one discourse repeats that awful declaration, 'Their worm dieth not, and the fire is not quenched.' The term fire presents the idea of the intensity of the wrath or vengeance of God. It denotes that the sufferings of the condemned sinner are such as the body experiences from material fire, and that entire desolation which accompanies its devouring flames. Fire, however, consumes the matter on which it acts, and is thus itself extinguished. But it is not so with those who shall be delivered over to that fire which is not quenched. They will be upheld in existence by Divine justice, as the subjects on which it will be ever displayed. The expression, 'their worm dieth not,' indicates a continuance of pain and putrefaction such as the gnawing of worms would produce. As fire is extinguished when its fuel is consumed, in the same way the worm dies when the subject on which it subsists is destroyed. But here it is represented as never dying, because the persons of the wicked are supported for the endurance of this punishment. In employing these figures, the Lord seems to refer to the two methods in which the bodies of the dead were in former times consigned to darkness and oblivion, either by incremation or interment. In the first, they were consumed by fire; in the second, devoured by worms. The final punishment of the enemies of God is likewise represented by their being cast into the lake which burneth with fire and brimstone. This imports the multitude of griefs with which the wicked will be overwhelmed. What emblem can more strikingly portray the place of torment than the tossing waves, not merely of a flood of waters, but of liquid fire? And what can describe more awfully the intensity of the sufferings of those who are condemned, than the image of that brimstone by which the fierceness of fire is augmented?

These expressions, their worm dieth not, and the fire is not quenched, to which it is added, 'for every one shall be salted with fire,' preclude every idea either of annihilation or of a future restoration to happiness. Under the law, the victims offered in sacrifice were appointed to be salted with salt, called 'the salt of the covenant,' Lev. ii. 13. Salt is an emblem of incorruptibility, and its employment announced the perpetuity of the covenant of God with His people. In the same manner, all the sacrifices to His justice will be salted with fire. Every sinner will be preserved by the fire itself, becoming thereby incorruptible, and fitted to endure those torments to which he is destined. The just vengeance of God will render incorruptible the children of wrath, whose misery, any more than the blessedness of the righteous, will never come to an end.

'The Son of Man,' said Jesus, 'goeth, as it is written of Him; but woe unto that man by whom the Son of Man is betrayed! it had been good for that man if he had not been born.' If the punishment of the wicked in the future state were to terminate in a period, however remote, and were it to be followed with eternal happiness, what is here affirmed of Judas would not be true. A great gulf is fixed between the abodes of blessedness and misery, and every passage from the one to the other is for ever barred.

The punishment, then, of the wicked will be eternal, according to the figures employed, as well as to the express declarations of Scripture. Sin being committed against the infinity of God, merits an infinite punishment. In the natural order of justice, this punishment ought to be infinitely great; but as that is impossible, since the creature is incapable of suffering pain in an infinite degree, infinity in greatness is compensated by infinity in duration. The punishment, then, is finite in itself, and on this account it is capable of being inflicted in a greater or less degree; but as it is eternal, it bears the same proportion to the greatness of Him who is offended.

The metaphors and comparisons employed in Scripture to describe the intensity of the punishment of the wicked, are calculated deeply to impress the sentiment of the awful nature of that final retribution. 'Tophet is ordained of old; yea, for the king it is prepared; he hath made it deep and large; the pile thereof is fire and much wood; the breath of the Lord, like a stream of brimstone, doth kindle it,' Isa. xxx. 33.

While the doctrine of eternal happiness is generally admitted, the eternity of future punishment is doubted by many. The declarations, however, of the Holy Scriptures respecting both are equally explicit. Concerning each of them the very same expressions are used. 'These shall go away into everlasting (literally, eternal) punishment: but the righteous unto life eternal,' Matt. xxv. 46. Owing to the hardness of their hearts, men are insensible to the great evil of sin. Hence the threatenings of future punishment, according to the word of God, shock all their prejudices, and seem to them unjust, and such as never can be realized. The tempter said to the woman, ' *Ye shall not surely die,*' although God had declared it. In the same way that malignant deceiver now suggests that the doctrine of eternal punishment, although written as with a sunbeam in the book of God, although expressly affirmed by the Saviour in the description of the last judgment, and so often repeated by Him during His abode on earth, is contrary to every idea that men ought to entertain of the goodness and mercy of God. He conceals from his votaries the fact that if God is merciful He is also just; and that, while forgiving iniquity, and transgression, and sin, He will by no means clear the guilty. Some who act as His servants in promoting this delusion, have admitted that the Scriptures do indeed threaten everlasting punishment to transgressors; but they say that God employs such threatenings as a veil to deter men from sin, while He by no means intends their execution. The veil, then, which God has provided, is, according to them, too transparent to answer the purpose He designs, and they, in their superior wisdom, have been able to penetrate it. And this is one of their *apologies* for the Bible, with the design of making its doctrines more palatable to the world. On their own principles, then, they are chargeable with doing all in their power to frustrate what they affirm to be a provision of mercy. Shall men, however eminent in the world, be for a moment listened to, who stand confessedly guilty of conduct so impious?

Infinitely great are the obligations of believers to that grace by which they have been made to differ from others, to flee to the refuge set before them in the Gospel, and to wait for the Son of God from heaven, whom He raised from the dead, even Jesus, which delivered us from the wrath to come.

Eternal life.—Of the nature of that glory of which the people of God shall be put in possession in the day of their redemption, we cannot form a clear and distinct idea. ' It doth not yet appear what we shall be; but we know that, when He shall appear, we shall be like Him, for we shall see Him as He is.' In the present state, believers, beholding as in a glass the glory of the Lord, are changed into the same image from glory to glory, as by the Spirit of the Lord. This transformation, while they see only through a glass darkly, is gradually proceeding; but when they see face to face, and shall know even as they are known, this image shall be perfected. Their blessedness will consist in a knowledge of God and His mysteries, a full and exquisite sense of His love, ineffable consolation, profound tranquillity of soul, a perfect concord and harmony of the soul with the body, and with all the powers of the soul among themselves; in one word, in an assemblage of all sorts of blessings. These blessings will not be measured in the proportion of the creatures who receive them, but of God who confers them; and of the dignity of the person of Jesus Christ, and of His merit: of His person, for they shall obtain that felicity only in virtue of the communion which they have with Him; of His merit, for He has purchased it with the price of His blood. So far, then, as we can conceive of majesty, excellency, and glory, in the person of the Redeemer, so far, keeping always in view the proportion of the creature to the Creator, ought we to conceive of the value, the excellence, and the abundance of the eternal blessings which He will bestow upon His people. The Scriptures call it a fulness of satisfaction, not a fulness of satiety, but a fulness of joy, at the right hand of God, where there are pleasures for evermore. It will be a crown of righteousness; they shall sit down with Christ in His throne, as He is set down with His Father in His throne. 'Blessed are they which are called unto the marriage-supper of the Lamb.'

As to the duration of this blessedness, it shall be eternal. But why eternal? Because God will bestow it upon a supernatural principle, and consequently upon a principle free from changes to which nature is exposed, in opposition to the happiness of Adam, which was natural. Because God will give it, not as to hirelings, but as to His children in title of inheritance. 'The servant,' or the hireling, says Jesus Christ, 'abideth not in the house for ever, but the son abideth ever.' Because God will confer it as a donation, that is to say, irrevocably. On this account Paul declares that 'the gift of God is eternal life.' None of the causes which produce changes will have place in heaven;—not the inequality of nature, for it shall be swallowed up in glory—not sin, for it will be entirely abolished—not the temptations of Satan, for Satan will have no entrance there—not the mutability of the creature, for God will possess His people fully and perfectly.

Through Jesus Christ.—Eternal life comes to the people of God as a free gift, yet it is through Jesus Christ. By His mediation alone reconciliation between God and man is effected, peace established, communion restored, and every blessing conferred. The smallest as well as the greatest gift is bestowed through Him; and they are not the less free gifts from God, because Christ our Lord has paid the price of redemption. He Himself was given for this end by the Father, and He and the Father are one. He, then, who pays the ransom is one and the same who justifies, so that the freeness of the gift is not in the smallest degree diminished.

This gift of eternal life is bestowed through Jesus Christ, and by Him it is dispensed,—'Glorify Thy Son, that Thy Son may also glorify Thee: as Thou hast given Him power over all flesh, to give eternal life to as

many as Thou hast given Him.' 'My sheep hear My voice, and I know
them, and they follow Me, and I give unto them eternal life.' *Our Lord.*
—His people are constantly to keep in mind that Jesus Christ is their
Lord, whose authority they are ever to regard, and whom, as their Lord
and Master, they are implicitly to obey. He is the Lord both of the dead
and the living, to whom every knee shall bow, and before whose judgment-seat we shall all stand.

There is a striking similarity between the manner in which the Apostle
winds up his discussion on the free justification of sinners, in the close
of the preceding chapter, and that in which he now concludes the doctrine of their sanctification. 'Grace,' he there says, reigns 'through
righteousness, unto eternal life, by Jesus Christ our Lord;' and through
Him, it is here said, 'the gift of God is eternal life.' All is of grace, all
is a free gift, all is vouchsafed through and in Him who was delivered for
our offences, and raised again for our justification, from whom neither
death nor life shall separate us. 'Thanks be unto God for His unspeakable gift.'

The doctrine of free justification by faith without works, on which the
Apostle had been insisting in the preceding part of the Epistle, is vindicated in this chapter from the charge of producing those consequences
which are ascribed to it by the wisdom of the world, and by all who are
opposed to the Gospel. Far from conducting to licentiousness, as many
venture to affirm, it stands inseparably connected with the sanctification
of the children of God.

In the conclusion of the preceding chapter, Paul had asserted that, as
the reign of sin had been terminated by the death of the Redeemer, so
the reign of grace, through righteousness, unto eternal life, by Jesus
Christ our Lord, has succeeded. He had shown in the third and fourth
chapters that this righteousness is upon all them that believe, who are
thus justified freely by grace. In the fifth chapter, he had exhibited the
effects and accompaniments of their justification. The objection which
he had seen it proper to introduce in the beginning of this sixth chapter,
had led to a further development of the way in which these blessed
effects are produced. In order to this, he says nothing, as has been
observed, of the character or attainments of believers, but simply
describes their state before God, in consequence of their union with
Christ. The sanctification of believers, he thus shows, proceeds from the
sovereign determination, the eternal purpose, and the irresistible power
of God, which are exerted according to His everlasting covenant, through
the mediation of His beloved Son, and in consistency with every part
of the plan of salvation. While this, however, is the truth—truth so
consolatory to every Christian—it is an incumbent duty to consider, and
to seek to give effect to those motives to holiness, presented by the Spirit
of God in His own word, as the means which He employs to carry on
this great work in the soul—presented, too, in those very doctrines
which the wisdom of the world has always supposed will lead to
licentiousness. Every view of the character of God, and every part of
the plan of salvation, tends to promote holiness in His people; and on

every doctrine contained in the Scriptures, holiness is conspicuously inscribed.

The doctrine of justification without works, so far from leading to licentiousness, furnishes the most powerful motive to obedience to God. They who receive the doctrine of justification by the righteousness of God, have the fullest and most awful sense of the obligation which the holy law of God enforces on His creatures, and of the extent and purity of that law connected with the most profound sentiment of the evil of sin. Every new view that believers take of the Gospel of their salvation is calculated to impress on their minds a hatred of sin, and a desire to flee from it. In the doctrine of Christ crucified, they perceive that God, who is holy and just, pardons nothing without an atonement, and manifests His hatred of sin by the plan which He adopts for the salvation of sinners. The extent of the evil of sin is exhibited in the dignity and glory of Him by whom it has been expiated, the depth of His humiliation, and the greatness of His sufferings. The obligation of the law of God also derives unutterable force from the purity of its precepts as well as from the awfulness of its sanction.

If the principal object, or one of the essential characteristics, of the doctrine of justification by faith was to represent God as easily pacified towards the guilty, as taking a superficial cognizance of the breach of His holy law, and punishing it lightly, it might with reason be concluded that it relaxes the bonds of moral obligation. But far from this, that doctrine maintains in the highest degree the holiness of God, and discovers the danger of continuing in sin. It teaches that, even when the Almighty is determined to show compassion to the sinner, He cannot deny Himself, and therefore His justice must be satisfied. That Jesus Christ should have purchased, at the price of His own blood, a licence to sin against God, would be utterly incompatible with the wisdom and uniformity of the Divine government. God cannot hate sin before its expiation by His Son, and love it after the sufferings inflicted on account of it. If it behoved Him to punish sin so severely in the Divine Surety of His people, it can never be pleasing to Him in those for whom the Surety has made satisfaction. His holiness is further displayed by this doctrine, which teaches that it is only through a righteous advocate and intercessor that they who are justified have access to God.

The Gospel method of justification by the blood of Christ discovers sin and its fatal consequences in the most hideous aspect, while at the same time it displays the mercy of God in the most attractive form. Believers are punished with death in the person of their Divine Surety, according to the original and irrevocable sentence pronounced against man on account of his transgression. But as Jesus Christ has been raised from the dead by the power of the Father, they also have been raised with Him to walk in newness of life. They are therefore bound by every consideration of love and fear, of gratitude and joyful hope, to regulate the actions of that life which has thus been granted to them in a new and holy way. Being baptized into the death of Christ, in whom they are ' complete,' they ought to be conformed to Him, and to separate themselves from sin by its entire destruction. Their baptism, which is the instituted sign of their forfeiture by sin of Adam's life, and their regeneration and fellowship with Christ in His death and resurrection, exhibit to them in the clearest manner the necessity of purity and holiness, the way by which these are attained conformably to the Gospel, and their obligation to renounce everything incompatible with the service of God. 'I am crucified,' says the Apostle Paul, 'with Christ; nevertheless I live; yet not I, but Christ liveth in me; and the life which I now live in the flesh, I live by the faith of the Son of God, who loved me, and gave Himself for me.' And, addressing the believers to whom he wrote, he says, 'As many of you as have been baptized into Christ, have put on Christ.' Ye are 'buried with Him in baptism, wherein also ye have risen with Him through the faith of the operation of God, who hath raised Him from the dead,' Col. ii. 12. These blessings believers enjoy by that faith which unites them to Christ, and which is wrought in their hearts by the same power that raised up Jesus from the dead, and that will raise them up at the last day.

The inducements, then, to love and gratitude to God, held out and enforced by the doctrine of justification by faith, are the strongest that can be conceived. The inexpressible magnitude of the blessings which they who are justified have received; their deliverance from everlasting destruction; the right they have obtained to eternal blessedness, and their meetness for its enjoyment; the infinite condescension of the great Author of these gifts, extending mercy to those who, so far from serving Him, have provoked His wrath; the astonishing means employed in the execution of His purpose of saving them, and the conviction which believers entertain of their own unworthiness,—all impose the strongest obligations, and furnish the most powerful motives, to walk in obedience to God. 'We have known and believed,' says the Apostle John, 'the love that God hath to us.' As long as the sinner continues to live under the burden of unpardoned guilt, so long as he sees Divine justice and holiness armed against him, he can only be actuated, in any attempt towards obedience, by servile fear; but when he believes the precious promises of pardon flowing from the love of God, when he knows the just foundation on which this pardon is established, he cleaves with reciprocal love to God. He rests his confidence solely on the merits of the Lord Jesus Christ, and ascribes to his Heavenly Father all the glory of his salvation. Being justified by faith, he has peace with God, which he no longer labours to acquire by his own works. His obedience is a constant expression of love and thankfulness for the free gift of that righteousness which the Son of God was sent to introduce, which He finished on the cross, and which confers a title to Divine favour sufficient for the most guilty of mankind. If any man professes to believe in Jesus Christ, to love His name, and to enjoy communion with God, yet obeys not His commandments, he 'is a liar, and 'the truth is not in Him. But whoso keepeth His word, in Him verily is the love of God perfected.' That which does not produce obedience is not love; and what does not proceed from love is unworthy of the name of obedience. The pretence of love without obedience is hypocrisy; and obedience without love is a real slavery.

The sanctification of the people of God depends on the death of Christ in the way of its meritorious cause : for through His death they receive the Holy Spirit, by whom they are sanctified. Jesus Christ has also sanctified Himself, that He might sanctify them.—He had, indeed, no corruption from which He needed sanctification ; but when He took on Him the sins of His people, they were His sins as truly as if He had been personally guilty. This is in accordance with what is declared, 2 Cor. v. 21, ' He hath made Him to be sin for us, who knew no sin : that we might be made the righteousness of God in Him.' In this light, then, He must be sanctified from sin, and this was effected by His suffering death. He was sanctified from the sin He had taken upon Him by His own blood shed upon the cross, and in Him they are sanctified.

The sanctification of believers depends, too, on the death of Jesus Christ in the way of obligation ; for, having redeemed His people to Himself, He has laid them under an inviolable obligation to be holy.' ' Ye were not redeemed with corruptible things, as silver and gold, from your vain conversation received by tradition from your fathers, but with the precious blood of Christ, as of a lamb without blemish and without spot.' ' Ye are bought with a price, therefore glorify God in your body and in your spirit, which are God's.' Their sanctification arises also from the example of Jesus Christ ; for, in His death, as well as in His life, all Christian virtues were exhibited and exercised in a manner the most admirable, and set before us for our imitation. ' Christ also suffered for us, leaving us an example that we should follow His steps.'

The sanctification of believers likewise depends on the death of Christ in the way of motive ; for it furnishes an almost infinite number of motives to holiness of life. In His death, believers discover the profound misery in which they were plunged in the slavery of sin and Satan—as children of rebellion and wrath separated from the communion of God. To procure their deliverance, it was necessary not only that the Son of God should come into the world, but that He should suffer on the cross ; whence they ought to regard their former condition with holy terror and abhorrence. In His death they perceive how hateful sin is in the sight of God, since it was necessary that the blood of an infinite and Divine person should be shed in order to its expiation. In that death they discover the ineffable love of God, which has even led to the delivering up of His only-begotten Son for their salvation. They discover the love and compassion of the Son Himself, which induced Him to come down from heaven to save them, which should beget reciprocal love, and an ardent zeal for His service. They perceive the hope of their calling, and realize the blessings of the eternal inheritance of God, which have been acquired by that death. They contemplate the honour and dignity of their adoption, for Jesus Christ has died that they might become the children of God. They have been born of His blood, which binds them never to lose sight of this heavenly dignity, but to conduct themselves in a manner suitable to their high vocation.

In the death of Jesus Christ the eyes of believers are directed to the Spirit of sanctification, whom God hath sent forth ; for in dying Jesus Christ has obtained for His people the inexhaustible graces of the Holy

Spirit. This leads them to renounce the spirit of the world, and submit to the direction and guidance of the Spirit from on high. They feel the honour of their communion with Jesus Christ, being His brethren and joint heirs, the members of His body, those for whom He shed His blood, and whom He hath redeemed at so astonishing a price. They behold the peace which He has made between God and them, which imposes on them the duty of never disturbing that blessed reconciliation, but, on the contrary, of rendering the most profound obedience to the Divine law. They discover the most powerful motives to humility; for the death of Jesus Christ is a mirror, in which they behold the vileness and indignity of their natural corruption, and perceive that they have nothing in themselves wherewith to satisfy Divine justice for their sins. His death, placing before their eyes their original condition, leads them to cry out before God, 'O Lord, righteousness belongeth unto Thee; but unto us confusion of face.' Our justification is a blessing which proceeds from Thy grace: Thou hast conferred on us the righteousness of Thy Son; but to ourselves belongeth nothing but misery and ruin. The death of Jesus Christ presents the strongest motives to repentance; for if, after the redemption He has wrought, they should still continue in their sins, it would be making Him, as the Apostle says, 'the minister of sin.' And, finally, the death of Jesus Christ teaches them not to dread their own death; for He hath sanctified the tomb, and rendered death itself innoxious to His people, since for them He has condescended to suffer it Himself. Their death is the last part of their fellowship on earth with their suffering Redeemer; and as His death was the gate through which He entered into His glory, so the earthly house of their tabernacle must be dissolved, that they may be also glorified together with Him. 'O death, where is thy sting? O grave, where is thy victory? Thanks be to God which giveth us the victory through our Lord Jesus Christ.'

The resurrection of Jesus Christ, as well as His death, presents the strongest motives for the encouragement and sanctification of believers. His resurrection establishes their faith, as being the heavenly seal with which God has been pleased to confirm the truth of the Gospel. Having been declared to be the Son of God with power by His resurrection from the dead, they regard Him as the Creator of the world, and the eternal Son of the Father. It assures them of the effect of His death in expiating their sins, and obliges them to embrace the blood of His cross as the price of their redemption. His resurrection being the victory which He obtained over the enemies of His Church, they are bound to place all their confidence in Him, and to resign themselves for ever to His guidance. It presents the most powerful motive to have constant recourse to the mercy of the Father, for having Himself raised up the Head and Surety of His people; it is an evident pledge of His eternal purpose to love them, and of their freedom of access to God by His Son.

In the resurrection and exaltation of Jesus Christ, believers are taught the certainty of their immortality and future blessedness. Lazarus, and others who were raised up, received their life in the same state as they possessed it before; and after they arose they died a second time; but Jesus Christ, in His resurrection, obtained a life entirely different. In

his birth a life was communicated to Him which was soon to terminate
on the cross. His resurrection communicated a life imperishable and
immortal. Jesus Christ being raised from the dead, death hath no more
dominion over him. Of this new life the Apostle speaks as being already
enjoyed by His people. 'He hath raised us up together, and made us sit
together in heavenly places in Christ Jesus.' Elsewhere he calls that
heavenly life which Jesus Christ now possesses, their life. 'Your life is
hid with Christ in God.' 'When Christ, who is our life, shall appear,
ye also shall appear with Him in glory.' 'Whosoever liveth and believeth in Me,' He Himself hath said, 'shall never die.' All this should
inspire His people with courage to finish their course here, in order to
go to take possession of the heavenly inheritance which He has gone
before to prepare for them, and from whence He will come again to
receive them to Himself. It should inspire them with fortitude, that
they may not sink under the afflictions and trials which they experience
on earth. The Apostle counted all things but loss and dung that he
might win Christ—that he might know Him, and the power of His
resurrection. On the resurrection of Jesus Christ he rests the whole
value and evidence of the truth of the Gospel. 'If Christ be not risen,
then is our preaching vain, and your faith is vain.' 'But now is Christ
risen from the dead, and become the first fruits of them that slept.'

The resurrection of Jesus Christ, on which believers rest their hope, is
intimately connected with every part of the Christian religion. The
perfections of the Father—His power, His justice, His faithfulness—were
all engaged in raising up His Son from the grave. The constitution of
the person of Jesus Christ Himself also required it. He was the Son of
God, the Prince of Life, holy, and without spot,—consequently, having
nothing in common with death. His body was joined with His deity, of
which it was the temple, so that it could not always remain under the
power of the grave. His resurrection was also necessary on account of
His office as Mediator, and of the general purposes of His coming into
the world to destroy the works of the devil, to subvert the empire of
death, to make peace between God and man, and to bring life and
immortality to light. It was necessary, too, in consideration of His
office as a Prophet, in order to confirm by His resurrection the word
which He had spoken; and of His office as a Priest, for, after having
presented His sacrifice, He must live to intercede for His people and to
bless them. And to reign as a King, He must first triumph personally
Himself over all His enemies, in order to cause His people to triumph.

Upon the whole, as in the preceding part of the Epistle, the Apostle
had rested the justification of believers on their union with Jesus Christ,
so upon the same union he rests in this chapter their sanctification. It
is in virtue of this union between Him as the Head, and the Church as
His body, that the elect of God are the subjects of His regenerating
grace, enjoy the indwelling of His Spirit, and bring forth fruit unto God.
'As the branch cannot bear fruit of itself, except it abide in the vine;
no more can ye, except ye abide in Me. I am the vine, ye are the
branches. He that abideth in Me, and I in him, the same bringeth forth
much fruit; for without Me ye can do nothing.'

This union of believers with Jesus Christ is represented in Scripture in various expressions, and by different images. The Scriptures declare that we are one with Him, that He dwells in our hearts, that He lives in us and we in Him, that we are changed into His image, and that He is formed in us. This union is spoken of as resembling the union of the head with the other parts of the body, and the foundation with the superstructure. This union does not result solely from Jesus Christ having taken upon Him, by His incarnation, the human nature. For if in this alone our union with Him consisted, unbelievers would be as much united with Him as believers. The union of believers with Jesus Christ is a spiritual and mystical union; and, as one with Him, by Him they are represented. He represents them in the act of making satisfaction to the Father, taking their sins upon Him, and enduring the punishment they deserved; for it was in their place, as their Head and Mediator, that He presented to God that great and solemn sacrifice which has obtained for them heavenly glory. He represents them in the act of His resurrection; for, as the Head, He has received for them of His Father life and immortality. He represents them in His intercession in their name, and also in His exaltation on His throne. The spiritual life which they derive from Him consists in present grace and future glory. In grace there are three degrees. The first is peace with God; the second is holiness, comprehending all that constitutes their duty; and the third is hope, which, like an anchor of the soul, enters into that within the veil. In glory there are also three degrees: the resurrection of the bodies of believers; their elevation to heaven; and the eternal enjoyment of the kingdom prepared for them from the foundation of the world.

Paul enjoins on Titus to affirm constantly the great truths he had been declaring, in order that they which have believed in God might be careful to maintain good works. Those doctrines alone, which, in the opinion of many, make void the law, and give a licence to sin—against which, since the days of the Apostle, the same objections have been repeated which in this chapter Paul combats—those doctrines are the means which the Holy Spirit employs for the conversion of sinners, and for producing effects entirely the opposite in their hearts. The Bible teaches us that the plan of salvation, which delivers man from sin and from death by the death of the Son of God, which had its origin in eternity in the counsels of God, both as to the choice of its objects, and the manner in which they are justified and sanctified, and as to its consummation in glory, is founded wholly in grace. 'By the grace of God,' says Paul, 'I am what I am.' 'Now unto Him that is able to do exceeding abundantly above all that we ask or think, according to the power that worketh in us, unto Him be glory in the Church by Christ Jesus, throughout all ages, world without end. Amen.'

CHAPTER 7
ROMANS 7:1 – 25

In the preceding chapter the Apostle had answered the chief objection against the doctrine of justification by faith without works. He had proved that, by union with Christ in His death and resurrection, believers who are thereby justified are also sanctified ; he had exhibited and enforced the motives to holiness furnished by the consideration of that union ; he had, moreover, affirmed that sin shall not have dominion over them, for this specific reason, that they are not under the law, but under grace. To the import of this declaration he now reverts, both to explain its meaning, and to state the ground of deliverance from the law. This, again, rendered it proper to vindicate the holiness of the law, as well as to demonstrate its use in convincing of sin ; while at the same time he proves that all its light and all its authority, so far from being sufficient to subdue sin, on the contrary, only tend, by the strictness of its precepts and the awful nature of its sanctions, the more to excite and bring into action the corruptions of the human heart.

Paul next proceeds plainly to show what might be inferred from the preceding chapter. Although he had there described believers as dead to the guilt of sin, he had, notwithstanding, by his earnest exhortations to watchfulness and holiness, clearly intimated that they were still exposed to its seductions. He now exhibits this fact, by relating his own experience since he became dead to the law and was united to Christ. By thus describing his inward conflict with sin, and showing how far short he came of the demands of the law, he proves the necessity of being dead to the law as a covenant, since, in the highest attainments of grace during this mortal life, the old nature, which he calls flesh, still remains in believers. At the same time he represents himself as delighting in the law of God, as hating sin, and looking forward with confidence to future deliverance from its power. In this manner he illustrates not only the believer's real character, but the important fact that the obedience of the most eminent Christian, which is always imperfect, cannot have the smallest influence in procuring his justification. He had proved that men cannot be justified by their works in their natural state. He now shows, by a reference to himself, that as little can they be justified by their works in their regenerated state. And thus he confirms his assertion in the 3d chapter, that by the deeds of the law there shall no flesh be justified. He might have described more generally the incessant combat between the old and new natures in the believer ; but he does this more practically, as well as more efficiently, by laying open the secrets of his own heart, and exhibiting it in his own person.

Ver. 1.—*Know ye not, brethren (for I speak to them that know law), how that the law hath dominion over a man as long as he liveth ?*

Brethren.—Some have erroneously supposed that, by employing the term brethren, the Apostle was now addressing himself exclusively to the Jews who belonged to the church at Rome. He is here, as in other parts of the Epistle, addressing the whole Church,—all its members, whether Jews or Gentiles, being equally concerned in the doctrine he was inculcating. It is evident, besides, that he continues in the following chapters to address the same persons to whom he had been writing from the commencement of the Epistle. They are the same of whom he had affirmed in the preceding chapter, verse 14th, that they were not under the law, which is the proposition he here illustrates. Brethren is an appellation whereby Paul designates all Christians, Gentiles as well as Jews, and by which, in the tenth chapter, he distinguishes them from the unbelieving Jews.

Know ye not.—There is much force in this interrogation, and it is one usual with Paul when he is affirming what is in itself sufficiently clear, as in ch. vi. 16; 1 Cor. iii. 16, vi. 19. He here appeals to the personal knowledge of those to whom he wrote. *For I speak to them that know law.*—This parenthesis appears to imply that, as they were acquainted with the nature of law, they must in the sequel be convinced of the truth of the explanations he was about to bring under their notice; and in this manner he bespeaks their particular attention.

The law hath dominion over a man.—Man here is not man as distinguished from woman, but man including both men and women, denoting the species. This first assertion is not confined to the law of marriage, by which the Apostle afterwards illustrates his subject, but extends to the whole law, namely, the law of God in all its parts. *As long as he liveth.*—The words in the original, as far as respects the phraseology, are capable of being rendered, either as long as *he* liveth, or as long as *it* liveth. It appears, however, that the meaning is, as long as the man liveth; for to say that the law hath dominion as long as it liveth, would be saying it is in force as long as it is in force.

Ver. 2.—*For the woman which hath an husband is bound by law to her husband so long as he liveth ; but if the husband be dead, she is loosed from the law of her husband.*

Ver. 3.—*So then if, while her husband liveth, she be married to another man, she shall be called an adulteress ; but if her husband be dead, she is free from that law ; so that she is no adulteress, though she be married to another man.*

The Apostle here proves his assertion by a particular reference to the law of marriage. And no doubt this law of marriage was purposely adapted by God to illustrate and shadow forth the subject to which it is here applied. Had it not been so, it might have been unlawful to become a second time a wife or a husband. But the Author of human nature and of the law by which man is to be governed, has ordained the lawfulness of second marriages, for the purpose of shadowing forth the truth referred to, as marriage itself was from the first a shadow of the relation between Christ and His Church. Some apply the term law in this place to the Roman law, with which those addressed must have been acquainted; but it is well known that it was usual both for husbands and wives among the Romans to be married to other husbands and wives during the life of their former consorts, without being considered guilty of adultery. The reference is to the general law of marriage, as instituted at the beginning.

Ver. 4.—*Wherefore, my brethren, ye also are become dead to the law by the body of Christ ; that ye should be married to another, even to Him who is raised from the dead, that we should bring forth fruit unto God.*

In the illustration it was the husband that died, and the wife remained alive to be married to another. Here it is the wife who dies ; but this does not make the smallest difference in the argument ; for whether it is the husband or wife that dies, the union is equally dissolved.

Dead to the law.—By the term the law, in this place, is intended that law which is obligatory both on Jews and Gentiles. It is the law, the work of which is written in the hearts of all men ; and that law which was given to the Jews in which they rested, ch. ii. 17. It is the law, taken in the largest extent of the word, including the whole will of God in any way manifested to all mankind, whether Jew or Gentile. All those whom the Apostle was addressing had been under this law in their unconverted state. Under the ceremonial law, those among them who were Gentiles had never been placed. It was therefore to the moral law only that they had been married. Those who were Jews had been under the law in every form in which it was delivered to them, of the whole of which the moral law was the grand basis and sum. To the moral law exclusively, here and throughout the rest of the chapter, the Apostle refers. The ordinances of the ceremonial law, now that their purpose was accomplished, he elsewhere characterizes as 'weak and beggarly elements,' but in the law of which he here speaks he declares, in verse 22 of this chapter, that he delights.

Mr. Stuart understands the term 'dead to the law' as importing to renounce it 'as an adequate means of sanctification.' But renouncing it in this sense is no freedom from the law. A man does not become free from the law of his creditor when he becomes sensible of his insolvency. The most perfect conviction of our inability to keep the law, and of its want of power to do us effectual service, would not have the smallest tendency to dissolve our marriage with the law. Mr. Stuart entirely misapprehends this matter. Dead to the law means freedom from the power of the law, as having endured its curse and satisfied its demands. It has ceased to have a claim on the obedience of believers in order to life, although it still remains their rule of duty. All men are by nature placed under the law, as the covenant of works made with the first man, who, as the Apostle had been teaching in the fifth chapter, was the federal or covenant-head of all his posterity ; and it is only when they are united to Christ that they are freed from this covenant.

What is simply a law implies no more than a direction and obligation authoritatively enforcing obedience. A covenant implies promises made on certain conditions, with threatenings added, if such conditions be not fulfilled. The language, accordingly, of the law, as the covenant of works, is, 'Do and live ;' or, 'If thou wilt enter into life, keep the commandments ;' and 'Cursed is every one that continueth not in all things that are written in the book of the law to do them.' It thus requires perfect obedience as the condition of life, and pronounces a curse on the smallest failure. This law is here represented as being man's original or first husband. But it is now a broken law, and therefore all men are

by nature under its curse. Its curse must be executed on every one of
the human race, either personally on all who remain under it, or in
Christ, who was made under the law, and who, according also to the
fifth chapter of this Epistle, is the covenant-head or representative of all
believers who are united to Him and born of God. For them He has
borne its curse, under which He died, and fulfilled all its demands, and
they are consequently dead to it, that is, no longer under it as a covenant.

By the body of Christ.—That is, by 'the offering of the body of Jesus
Christ,' Heb. x. 10. Although the body is only mentioned in this place,
as it is said on His coming into the world, 'A body hast Thou prepared
Me,' yet His whole human nature, composed of soul and body, is intended. Elsewhere His soul, without mentioning His body, is spoken of
as being offered. 'When Thou shalt make His soul an offering for sin,'
Isa. liii. 10. Dead to the law by the body of Christ, means dead to it
by dying in Christ's death. As believers are one body with Christ, so
when His body died, they also died, Rom. vi. 3, 4. They are therefore,
by the sacrifice of His body, or by His death, dead to the law. They
are freed from it, and done with it, as it respects either their justification
or condemnation, its curse or its reward. They cannot be justified by
it, having failed to render to it perfect obedience, Rom. iii. 20 ; and
they cannot be condemned by it, being redeemed from its curse by Him
who was made a curse for them. As, then, the covenant relation of a
wife to her husband is dissolved by death, so believers are released from
their covenant relation to the law by the death of Christ, with whom
they died ; for He died to sin, ch. vi. 10, and to the law having fulfilled
it by His obedience and death, so that it hath no further demand upon
Him.

Married to another, even to Him who is raised from the dead.—Being
dead to the law, their first husband, by their union with Christ in His
death, believers are married to Him, and are one with Him in His resurrection. Christ is now their lawful husband, according to the clear
illustration employed by the Apostle respecting the institution of marriage,
so that, though now married to Him, no fault can be found in respect to
their original connection with their first husband, which has been dissolved by death. To believers this is a most consoling truth. They are
as completely and as blamelessly free from the covenant of the law as if
they had never been under it. Thus the Apostle fully explains here
what he had briefly announced in the 14th verse of the preceding
chapter, 'Ye are not under the law, but under grace.' From the covenant
of Adam or of works, believers have been transferred to the covenant of
Christ or of grace. I will ' give thee for a covenant of the people'—all
the redeemed people of God.

Before the coming of Christ, those who relied on the promise concerning Him, likewise partook of all the blessings of the marriage union with
Him, and were therefore admitted to heavenly glory, though, as to their
title to it, not ' made perfect' (Heb. xii. 23) till He died under the law,
and put away sin by the sacrifice of Himself. Till that period there was
in the Jewish ceremonial law a perpetual recognition of sin, and of a
future expiation, which had not been made while that economy subsisted.

It was, so to speak, the bond of acknowledgment for the debt yet unpaid —the handwriting of ordinances which Jesus Christ, in paying the debt, cancelled and tore asunder, 'nailing it to His cross,' Col. ii. 14, as a trophy of the victory He had accomplished.

Christ, then, is the husband of the Church; and, under this figure, His marriage relation to His people is very frequently referred to in Scripture. Thus it was exhibited in the marriage of our first parents. In the same way it is represented in the Book of Psalms, and the Song of Solomon, and in the New Testament, where Christ is so often spoken of under the character of 'the Bridegroom,' and where the Church is called 'the bride, the Lamb's wife.' What ignorance, then, does it argue in some to deny the inspiration and authenticity of the Song of Solomon, because of the use of this figure![1]

But though believers, in virtue of their marriage with Christ, are no longer under the law in respect to its power to award life or death, they are, as the Apostle says, 1 Cor. ix. 21, 'not without law to God, but under law to Christ.' They receive it from His hand as the rule of their duty, and are taught by His grace to love and delight in it; and, being delivered from its curse, they are engaged, by the strongest additional motives, to yield to it obedience. He hath made it the inviolable law of His kingdom. When Luther discovered the distinction between the law as a covenant and as a rule, it gave such relief to his mind, that he considered himself as at the gate of paradise.

That we should bring forth fruit unto God.—One of the great ends of marriage was to people the world, and the end of the marriage of believers to Christ is, that they may bring forth fruit to God, John xv. 4-8. From this it is evident that no work is recognised as fruit unto God before union with Christ. All works that appear to be good previous to this union with Christ are 'dead works,' proceeding from self-love, self-gratification, pride, self-righteousness, or other such motives. 'They that are in the flesh cannot please God.' 'The carnal mind is enmity against God; for it is not subject to the law of God, neither indeed can be.' We can never look upon the law with a friendly eye till we see it disarmed of the sting of death; and never can bear fruit unto God, nor delight in the law as a rule, till we are freed from it as a covenant, and are thus dead unto sin. How important, then, is the injunction, 'Likewise reckon ye also yourselves to be dead indeed unto sin,'—and this applies equally to the law,—' but alive unto God through Jesus Christ our Lord,' Rom. vi. 11.

'It is impossible,' says Luther, 'for a man to be a Christian without having Christ; and if he has Christ, he has at the same time all that is in Christ. What gives peace to the conscience is, that by faith our sins are no more ours, but Christ's, upon whom God has laid them all; and that, on the other hand, all Christ's righteousness is ours, to whom God hath given it. Christ lays His hand upon us, and we are healed. He casts

---

[1] On the genuineness and authenticity of the Song of Solomon, see the author's work on *The Books of the Old and New Testament proved to be canonical, and their Verbal Inspiration maintained and established; with an Account of the Introduction and Character of the Apocrypha.* Fifth edition, enlarged. And also his *Work of Evidences*, etc., vol. i. p. 164. Fourth edition.

His mantle upon us, and we are clothed ; for He is the glorious Saviour, blessed for ever. Many wish to do good works before their sins are forgiven them, whilst it is indispensable that our sins be pardoned before good works can be done ; for good works must be done with a joyful heart, and a good conscience toward God, that is, with remission of sins.'

Ver. 5.—*For when we were in the flesh, the motions of sins, which were by the law, did work in our members to bring forth fruit unto death.*

When we were in the flesh, that is, in our natural state.—The flesh here means the corrupt state of nature, not 'the subjects of God's temporal kingdom,' as paraphrased by Dr. Macknight, to which many of those whom the Apostle was addressing never belonged. Flesh is often opposed to spirit, which indicates that new and holy nature communicated by the Spirit of God in the new birth. 'That which is born of the flesh is flesh, and that which is born of the Spirit is spirit,' John iii. 6. In these words our Lord points out the necessity of regeneration, in order to our becoming subjects of His spiritual kingdom. The nature of man since the fall, when left to itself, possesses no renovating principle of holiness, but is essentially corrupt and entirely depraved. On this account, the word flesh here signifies man in his ruined condition, or that state of total corruption in which all the children of Adam are born. On the other hand, the word spirit has acquired the meaning of a holy and Divine principle, or a new nature, because it comes not from man but from God, who communicates it by the living and permanent influence of His Holy Spirit. Hence the Apostle Peter, in addressing believers, speaks of them as 'partakers of the Divine nature.'

The motions of sins, or affections or feelings of sins. When the Apostle and the believers at Rome were *in the flesh,* the desires or affections forbidden by the law forcibly operated in all the faculties of their depraved nature, subjecting them to death by its sentence. Dr. Macknight and Mr. Stuart translate this our 'sinful passions.' But this has the appearance of asserting that the evil passions of our nature have their origin in the law. The Apostle does not mean what, in English, is understood by the passions, but the working of the passions. *Which were by the law,* rather, through the law.—Dr. Macknight translates the original thus, 'which we had under the law.' But the meaning is, not which we had under the law, but that were through the law. The motions of sin, or those sinful thoughts or desires, on our knowing that the things desired are forbidden, are called into action through the law. That it is thus natural to the corrupt mind to desire what is forbidden, is a fact attested by experience, and is here the clear testimony of Scripture. With the philosophy of the question we have nothing to do. Why or how this should be, is a question we are not called to resolve. Thus the law as a covenant of works not only cannot produce fruits of righteousness in those who are under it, but excites in them the motions of sin, bringing forth fruit unto death. *Did work in our members.*—The sinful desires of the mind actuate the members of the body to gratify them, in a manner adapted to different occasions and constitutions. Members appear to be mentioned here rather than body, to denote that sin, by the impulse of their various evil desires, employs as its slaves all the different members of the body. *To bring forth fruit unto death.*—In the same way as bringing forth fruit unto God is spoken of in the 4th verse, so here the Apostle speaks of bringing forth fruit unto death, that is, doing works which issue in death. Death is not viewed as the parent of the works. It is the desires that are the parents of the works. This is contrasted with fruit unto God, which does not mean that God is the parent of the fruit, but that the fruit is produced on God's account.

Ver. 6.—*But now we are delivered from the law, that being dead wherein we were held ; that we should serve in newness of spirit, and not in the oldness of the letter.*

But now we are delivered from the law.—This does not import merely that the Jews were, according to Dr. Macknight, delivered from the law of Moses, but that believers are delivered from the moral law, in that sense in which they were bound by it when in unbelief. Christ hath fulfil'ed the law, and suffered its penalty for them, and they in consequence are free from its demands for the purpose of obtaining life, or that, on account of the breach of it, they should suffer death. Mr. Stuart paraphrases thus : ' No longer placing our reliance on it as a means of subduing and sanctifying our sinful natures.' But ceasing to rely on the law for such a purpose was not, in any sense, to be delivered from the law. The law never proposed such a thing, and therefore ceasing to look for such an effect is not a deliverance from the law.

That being dead wherein we were held.—By death, whether it be considered of the law to believers, or of believers to the law, the connection in which they stood to it, and in which they were held, in bondage under its curse, is dissolved. All men, Jews and Gentiles, are by nature bound to the moral law, under its condemning power and curse, from which nothing but Christ can to all eternity deliver them. Dr. Macknight translates the passage, ' having died in that by which we were tied,' and paraphrases thus : ' But now we Jews are loosed from the law of Moses, having died with Christ by its curse, in that fleshly nature by which, as descendants of Abraham, we were tied to the law.' But this most erroneously confines the declaration of the Apostle to the Jews and the legal dispensation.

That we should serve in newness of spirit, and not in the oldness of the letter.—This is the effect of being delivered from the law. The Apostle here refers to the difference in practice between those who were married to Christ, and those who were still under the law. A believer serves God from such principles, dispositions, and views, as the Spirit of God implants in hearts which He renews. Serving in the spirit is a service of filial obedience to Him who gave Himself for us, as constrained by His love, and in the enjoyment of all the privileges of the grace of the new covenant. Believers have thus, under the influence of the Holy Spirit, become capable of serving God with that new and Divine nature of which they partake, according to the spiritual meaning of the law, as His children, with cordial affection and gratitude. It is the service not of the hireling but of the son, not of the slave but of the friend, not with the view of being saved by the keeping of the law, but of rendering grateful obedience to their almighty Deliverer.

Serving in the oldness of the letter, respects such service as the law, by its light, authority, and terror, can procure from one who is under it, and seeking life by it, without the Spirit of God, and His sanctifying grace and influence. Much outward conformity to the law may in this way be attained from the pride of self-righteousness, without any principle better than that of a selfish, slavish, mercenary, carnal disposition, influenced only by fear of punishment and hope of reward. Serving, then, in the oldness of the letter, is serving in a cold, constrained, and wholly external manner. Such service is essentially defective, proceeding from a carnal, unrenewed heart, destitute of holiness. In this way Paul describes himself, Phil. iii., as having formerly served, when he had confidence in the 'flesh,' as he there designates such outward service. Serving in newness of spirit and in oldness of the letter, are here contrasted as not only different, but as incompatible the one with the other.

Ver. 7.—*What shall we say then? Is the law sin? God forbid. Nay, I had not known sin, but by the law: for I had not known lust, except the law had said, Thou shalt not covet.*

What shall we say then? Is the law sin?—In the 5th verse Paul had described the effect of the law on himself and those whom he addressed before conversion, while he and they were under its dominion. In the 6th verse he had spoken of their deliverance and his own from the law; here and in the four following verses he illustrates what were the effects of the law on himself. While he peremptorily rejects the supposition that there was anything evil in the law, he shows that, by the strictness of its precepts exciting the corruptions of his heart, it was the means of convincing him that he was a sinner, and under its condemnation, and was thus the instrument to him of much good, for he would not have known sin to be sin but by the law.

Mr. Stuart says this is the language of an objector against the Apostle. For this there is no foundation whatever. It is a mere figment to suppose that there is here a kind of discussion between the Apostle and a Jewish objector. It is an objection stated by the Apostle in his own name, an objection that will occur to the carnal mind in every age and country, and is therefore properly introduced by the Apostle. If the law occasions more sin, is it not itself sinful? *God forbid*—literally, let it not be, by no means.—It is the expression, as formerly noticed, by which the Apostle usually intimates his abhorrence of whatever is peculiarly unworthy of God. Paul now begins to describe his own experience respecting the operation of the law.

Nay.—Mr. Stuart says that this expression intimates that the Apostle had some exception to the universal sense of the words translated God forbid. But this is not the effect here of the word rendered 'Nay.' There could be no exception to the denial of the consequence in the sense in which the thing is denied. Is it possible that there can be any exception to the denial that the law is sinful? It is not possible. That the law is the occasion of sin, or, as Mr. Stuart expresses it, though 'not the sinful or efficient cause of sin,' is no exception to the universal denial in any point of view. An occasion of sin and a cause of sin are two things essentially different. It is no exception to the assertion that the law is not the cause of sin, to say that it is the occasion of sin. The word here translated *nay*, intimates opposition. So far from the law being sinful, I had not known sin, says the Apostle, but by the law.

Known sin but by the law.—Paul does not say that he would not have been a sinner without the law, but that he would not have known sin as now he knew it, or have seen himself to be a sinner. Now, though no man is without sin, yet a proud Pharisee might think himself free from sin by his keeping the law, when he did not look to it as extending to the thoughts of the heart. Paul, referring to his state before his conversion, says that, touching the righteousness of the law he was blameless, Phil. iii. 6 ; and it was only when he understood the law in its full extent, that he became self-condemned.

For I had not known lust.—The original word for lust signifies strong desire, whether good or bad. Here it is used in a bad sense. It is that disposition by which we are inclined to evil,—the habit and inclination to sin, and not merely the acts which proceed from it. It is evident that the Apostle here speaks of this habit, that is to say, of our inclination to sin, and habitual corruption ; for he distinguishes this inclination from its acts in verse 8th, saying, sin, taking occasion by the commandment, wrought in me all manner of concupiscence, or lust.

Except the law had said, Thou shalt not covet.—Without the law he would not have known that the desire of what is forbidden is sinful ; that the very thought of sin is sin, is known only by the word of God. Indeed, many who hear that word will not receive this doctrine. The Roman Catholics hold that such desires are not criminal, if the mind do not acquiesce in them. *Thou shalt not covet.*—This implies lusting against the will of God, and extends to the first rise and lowest degree of every evil thought. It is not to be confined to what are called inordinate desires, or desires carried to excess, but comprehends every desire contrary to the commandment.

Ver. 8.—*But sin, taking occasion by the commandment, wrought in me all manner of concupiscence. For without the law sin was dead.*

The same word rendered lust in the foregoing verse is here rendered concupiscence, which is not so proper a translation, having a more limited meaning generally attached to it. In both verses the original word indicates our natural inclination to sin, and not voluntary sinful acts—not sins produced, which are the acts proceeding from lust, but our innate and vicious propensity to sin producing those acts. In the preceding verse Paul had shown that the law does not cause sin, but discovers it, stripping it of its disguise, and bringing it to light. Here he asserts that the commandment discovered to him the sinful nature of evil desires. It laid on him the most solemn obligations to resist them ; and the natural corruption of his heart took occasion, from the restraints of the law, to struggle against it, and break out with more violence. Sin, he says, wrought in him all manner of lust. It excited and discovered in him those corruptions of which he had been unconscious, until they were encountered and provoked by the restraints of the law. It does not appear that it is by feeling the curse and condemnation of the law that sin takes occasion by the law to work in us all manner of concupiscence. By feeling the curse and condemnation of the law, the impenitent sinner is excited to hate the law and to hate God. But the thing to which we are here said to be excited is not this, but we are excited to desire things forbidden by the law. It is quite true that the feeling of the condemnation of the law aggravates the evil of our hearts, but it is lust or concupiscence that is here said to be inflamed by the prohibitions of the law. Nothing can more clearly discover the depravity of human nature than the holy law of God, the unerring standard of right and wrong becoming an occasion of sin; yet so it is. Whatever is prohibited is only the more eagerly desired. So far, then, was the law from subduing the love of sin, that its prohibitions increased the desire of what is prohibited. It may restrain from the outward act, but it excites the evil inclinations of the mind.

Without the law sin was dead.—Some understand this as meaning the same with the declaration, that ' where there is no law there is no transgression;' but the connection requires that we understand it of the sleeping or dormant state of sin. The Apostle would not have been without sin, but he would not have felt the action of his unlawful desires, if the strictness of the commandment had not become the occasion of exciting and making them manifest; for without the law, sin, or the workings of his corrupt nature, encountering no opposition, their operation would not have been perceived.

Every Christian knows by experience the truth of all the Apostle declares in this verse. He knows that, as soon as his eyes were opened to discover the spirituality of the law, he discerned in himself the fearful working of that corruption in his heart, which, not being perceived before, had given him no uneasiness. He knows that this corruption was even increased in violence by the discovery of the strictness of the law, which makes not the smallest allowance for sin, but condemns it in its root, and in its every motion. ' The wicked nature,' says Luther, ' cannot bear either the good, or the demands of the law; as a sick man is indignant when he is desired to do all that a man in health can do.' Such is the effect of the law when the eyes of the understanding are first opened by the Spirit of God. A power, formerly latent and inefficacious, then appears on a sudden to have gathered strength, and to stand up in order to oppose and defeat the purposes of the man, who hitherto was altogether unconscious of the existence in himself of such evils as those which he now perceives.

Ver. 9.—*For I was alive without the law once; but when the commandment came, sin revived, and I died.*

Paul was alive without the law when he thought proudly of his good life; but when the commandment came with the power of the Spirit, then it slew him, and destroyed all his legal hopes. *I was alive.*—That is, in my own opinion. Mr. Stuart finds fault with this sense, as given by Augustine, Calvin, and many others. But his reasons are without weight. After exhibiting the meaning of the whole connection in this view, he asks, 'Is this, then, the way in which the law of God proves *fatal* to the sinner, viz., by convincing him of the true and deadly nature of sin?' Not fatal to the sinner, but fatal to his view of salvation by the law. Nothing can be clearer than this passage, and nothing more consistent than this meaning with the whole context. *Without the law once.*—Was Paul ever without the law? He was in ignorance of it till his conversion; and this he here calls being without the law. He was ignorant of its spirituality, and consequently had no true discernment of his innate corruption. Mr. Stuart asks, 'But when did the *commandment* come?' and answers, 'We may suppose it to be in childhood, or in riper years.' It cannot have been in childhood, or in riper years, at any time previous to his seeing Christ. For if he had had such a view of the law previously, he would not, in his own opinion, have been blameless concerning its righteousness. It is obvious that Paul had his proper view of the law only in the cross of Christ.

When the commandment came.—That is, when he understood the true import of the commandment as forbidding the desire of anything prohibited by the law. He had heard and studied it before in its letter; but never till then did it come in its full extent and power to his conscience. All men know that, to a certain extent, they are sinners; but from this passage and its context, in which the Apostle gives an account of his own experience both in his unconverted and renewed state, we learn that unconverted men do not perceive the sin that is in them in its root, called, in the 7th and 8th verses, 'lust' or 'concupiscence.' This is only felt and known when, by the Holy Spirit, a man is *convinced of sin*—when, as it is here said, the commandment comes—when it comes to him with power, so that he perceives its real extent and spiritual import. He then discerns sin, not only in its various ramifications and actings, both internal and external, but also sees that it is inherent in him, and that in his flesh dwells no good thing; that he is not only by nature a sinner and an enemy to God, but that he is *without strength*, Rom. v. 6, entirely unable to deliver himself from the power of sin, and that this can only be effected by the Spirit of God, by whom he is at the same time convinced of the righteousness of God—that righteousness which has been provided for those who are destitute in themselves of all righteousness.

Sin revived.—It was, in a manner, dead before, dormant, and unobserved. Now that the law was understood, it was raised to new life, and came to be perceived as living and moving. The contrast is with sin as dead, without the understanding of the law. It is true, as Mr. Stuart observes, that sin gathers additional strength in such circumstances; but this is not the idea held forth in the context. *I died.*—That is, I saw myself dead by the law, as far as my own observance of the law was concerned. All Paul's hopes, founded on what he was in himself, were destroyed, and he discovered that he was a sinner condemned by the law; so that the law which promised life to those who observed it, to which he had looked for justification, he now saw subjected him to death. The expression by no means imports, as Mr. Stuart understands it, that Paul at the period referred to was really under the sentence of death as a sinner who had not fled to Jesus. 'I fell under the sentence of death,' is the explanation that Mr. Stuart gives; which he confirms by 'The soul that sinneth shall die.' 'The wages of sin is death.' At the period when Paul *died*, in the sense of this passage, he was really brought to spiritual life. It was then that he, through the law, became dead to the law, that he might live unto God, Gal. ii. 19.

Thus Paul was without the law during all that time when he profited in the Jews' religion above many of his equals, when, according to the straitest sect of their religion, he lived a Pharisee, and when, as touching the law, according to the common estimation, he was blameless. He was without the true knowledge of it and its spiritual application to his heart; but, in his own esteem, he was *alive*. He was confident of the Divine favour. Sin lay as dead in his heart. He could therefore go about to establish his own righteousness. He had not found the law to be a 'killing letter,' working wrath; so far from it, he could make his boast of the law, and assume it as the ground of his rejoicing before God. But when the commandment came, sin revived, and he died. Such is the account which Paul now gives of himself, who declared, Acts xxii. 3, that formerly he had been, and, as he affirms in the beginning of the tenth chapter of this Epistle, that the unconverted Jews still were, 'zealous towards God.'

Ver. 10.—*And the commandment, which was ordained to life, I found to be unto death.*

And the commandment, which was ordained to life.—Literally, the commandment which was unto life. That is, which was appointed to give continuance of life to those who obeyed, and which, therefore, it would have been life to obey, as it is said, 'The man that doeth them shall live in them.' By the commandment here referred to, the law, in all its parts, appears to be meant, with a special allusion to the tenth commandment, which shows that the desire of what is forbidden is sin. This commandment might well be put for the whole law; for it could not be obeyed without the whole law being kept. As the law held out the promise of life to those who obeyed it, on this ground Paul had sought, and imagined he had attained, a title to eternal life. *Unto death.*—The law was ordained to life, but, through sin, it was found to be unto death. As soon, then, as it came home to his conscience, Paul found himself condemned by that law from which he had expected life, for, though it could not justify a sinner, it was powerful to condemn him. It then destroyed all the hope he had founded on it, and showed him that he was obnoxious to the curse which it pronounces on all transgressors. The law, however, which was ordained to life, will at last be proved to have attained this object in all in whom it has been fulfilled, Rom. viii. 4, by Him who is the end of the law for righteousness to every one that believeth. All such shall, according to its original appointment, enjoy everlasting life.

Ver. 11.—*For sin, taking occasion by the commandment, deceived me, and by it slew me.*

Sin, by blinding his mind as to the extent of the demands of the law, had led Paul to believe that he could fulfil it, and so obtain justification and life, and had thus by the law taken occasion to deceive him. Till the commandment came home to him in its spiritual application, sin was never brought to such a test as to make a discovery to Paul of its real power. But when he was enlightened to perceive this, sin by the law slew him. It showed him that he was a transgressor of the law, and therefore condemned by that very law from which he had before expected life. Thus sin, as he had said, revived, and he died. All his high thoughts of himself, and self-confidence, from supposing that he had kept the law, were swept away and destroyed.

Ver. 12.—*Wherefore the law is holy, and the commandment holy, and just, and good.*

Having now shown that the law is not the cause, but only the occasion of sin, Paul here draws the conclusion as to its character and excellence. *Wherefore.*—In the 7th verse he had strongly denied that there was anything sinful in the law; and, in the intermediate verses, had shown, by its effects, that, so far from being the cause of sin, it had been the means of enlightening his mind, in giving him to discover the evil nature of sin, and its deceitful workings in himself. From these effects he now draws the conclusion here stated, which fully illustrates the above assertion, proving how far the law is removed from sin, namely, that it is holy, and just, and good. The two words, law and commandment, appear to be used to give the greater force to his declaration,—thus meaning the law and every precept it enjoins. It is *holy*, in opposition to whatever is sinful,—holy, as embodying the perfect rule of what is right and conformable to the character of God, and a transcript of His perfections. It is *just.* Can anything be more just than that we should abstain from all that God prohibits? It is highly just that we should not only abstain from all that God forbids, but that we should not even desire what is forbidden. The law demands what is equitable, and due to God, and nothing more,—and what is just and equitable in regard to man; and a just law could demand no less. *And good.*—It is not only just, it is also good. It is good in itself, and its whole tendency is adapted to maintain perfect order, and to establish in the highest degree the happiness of all who are under its authority. Every commandment of the Decalogue tends to promote human happiness. This is the glory of the law, and shows that it proceeds from the Giver of every good and perfect gift—from Him who alone is good. But this is not the ground of obedience; and those who have endeavoured to place the foundation of morals on the principle of utility, or of the happiness of the many, have only proved their shortsighted ignorance, and verified the declaration of Scripture, 'professing themselves to be wise, they become fools.'

From the nature of the Apostle's description of the glory and excellence of the law, it is clear that he is speaking of the Decalogue, and not of the ceremonial law or the Mosaic institutions. These had a figurative excellence 'for the time present,' but 'made nothing perfect,' as he himself declares in the Epistle to the Hebrews, but consisted only in 'carnal ordinances' intended to continue 'until the time of reformation.' But the law, as embodied in the ten commandments, is in itself eternal

and immutable, while the words of the Apostle in this verse beautifully
accord with those of the Psalmist in the nineteenth Psalm:—'The law
of the Lord is perfect, converting the soul: the testimony of the Lord is
sure, making wise the simple. The statutes of the Lord are right, rejoicing the heart: the commandment of the Lord is pure, enlightening the
eyes. The fear of the Lord is clean, enduring for ever: the judgments
of the Lord are true and righteous altogether. More to be desired are
they than gold, yea, than much fine gold; sweeter also than honey and
the honey-comb.' If God had left men free from the law, it would still
be for the happiness of society that they should strictly obey its precepts.

Ver. 13.—*Was then that which is good made death unto me? God forbid. But
sin, that it might appear sin, working death in me by that which is good ; that sin by
the commandment might become exceeding sinful.*

Was that then which is good made death unto me?—This is not, as Dr.
Macknight supposes, an objection in the person of a Jew, but an objection
put by the Apostle himself, which was likely to occur to every carnal
man in every age. It might require an answer even with respect to
Christians themselves. If the law is holy, and just, and good, how could
it be found by the Apostle to be unto death? Could a good law be the
cause of death? By no means. It was not the good law that was the
cause of death. *But sin.*—That is, it is sin, which is the transgression of
the law, that causeth death.
   That it might appear sin.—Dr. Macknight translates, 'That sin might
appear working out death.' But the construction evidently is, 'But sin
has caused death, that it might appear sin,'—that is, that it might
manifest itself in its own proper character. *Working death in me by that
which is good.*—It was not the good law that wrought death in him, but
sin by means of the good law. Hence the manifestation of the exceeding
vileness and hatefulness of sin. How evil must that thing be which
works the greatest evil through that which is the perfection of righteousness! *That sin by the commandment might become exceeding sinful.*—This,
again, is another form of expression designed to aggravate the evil character of sin. There is nothing worse than sin itself. The Apostle, then,
does not resolve it into supposed first principles that would exhibit its
guilt. The worst that can be said of it is, that it is *sin*, and is so in
excess. Here, and in the preceding verses from the 7th, Paul does not
speak merely of outward sin, or sinful acts, but also, and chiefly, of the
sinful and disordered lusts of the mind, or the depraved inclination to
commit sin; and this naturally conducts him, in what follows to the end
of the chapter, to describe and dwell on the workings of that inward evil
disposition which he calls the law of sin in his members. It was by
having his attention turned to this inward working of sin, when, as he
says, 'the commandment came,' that he was convinced he was a sinner.

Ver. 14.—*For we know that the law is spiritual ; but I am carnal, sold under sin.*

In the foregoing part of the chapter, the Apostle had illustrated the
truth that believers are dead to the law by the sacrifice of Christ. He
had next shown the effects of the law on Himself before his conversion,

when he was under it, and after his conversion, when delivered from it. During the former period, he was ignorant of its true nature, and consequently of himself, supposing that he was righteous. ' I was alive without the law.' But when he understood its real character, he discovered the deceitfulness and sinfulness of sin closely cleaving to him, and inherent in him. 'When the commandment came, sin revived, and I died.' He had remarked that sin, taking occasion by the commandment, had wrought in him all manner of evil desires, and had deceived him. He affirms, nevertheless, that the law is holy, and just, and good ; and, lastly, he now further asserts that it is *spiritual*. This last characteristic of the holy law, proving that it takes cognizance not only of the outward conduct, but also of the thoughts and intents of the heart, leads him, as has just been observed, to show how far sin still continued to adhere to and afflict him. The view, however, which he gives, through the remainder of the chapter, of this working of sin in his members, in no respect contradicts his assertion in the preceding chapter, that believers are 'dead to sin ; ' for there he refers exclusively to its *guilt*, but here to its *power*. Nor does it contradict his affirmation that sin should ' not have dominion ' over them ; for, notwithstanding the struggle he describes, proving the power of the law of sin in his flesh, he asserts that with his mind he serves the law of God ; while he expresses his conviction that even from that power of indwelling sin God would finally deliver him. From all this we see how naturally the Apostle was conducted to detail in what follows his own personal and internal experience, both past and present, which formed also so full an illustration of his leading argument throughout the whole of the previous part of the Epistle, of the impossibility of a just law justifying those by whom it is not perfectly obeyed.

For we know.—This assertion, ' we know,' is the usual form under which Paul states what needs no proof. This fundamental and important truth, that *the law is spiritual*, although, while in his unconverted state, he was ignorant of it, he now affirms that both he and they to whom he wrote knew it. It is a thing of which no Christian is ignorant. All Christians know it experimentally. They know it when the *commandment comes* to them, not in word only, but also in power, and in the Holy Ghost; when, according to the promise of the new covenant, God puts His law in their inward parts, and writes it in their hearts ; when they receive it, written not with ink, but with the Spirit of the living God, —not outwardly in tables of stone, but in the fleshly tables of the heart.

The law is spiritual.—The law which proceeds from the Holy Spirit of God, demands not only the obedience of external conduct, but the internal obedience of the heart. If Paul had still regarded the law as a rule extending merely to his outward conduct, he might, as formerly, when he strictly adhered to its letter, have continued to suppose himself just and good. But when he now understood that it was also spiritual, extending to the most secret desires of his heart, he discovered in himself so much opposition to its penetrating and discerning power, that, as he had said, *sin revived, and he died.* Perceiving, then, that it requires truth in the inward parts, piercing even to the dividing asunder of soul and spirit, not only prohibiting the smallest outward deviation from holiness, but detecting every hidden ambush of the deceitful heart, Paul the Apostle, a man of like passions with ourselves, exclaims, *I am carnal, sold under sin.* He here begins to declare his present experience, and changes the past time for the present, in which he continues afterwards to speak to the end of the chapter.

Having so fully declared the nature and extent of the law, the Apostle now, applying the whole to his own case, proceeds to exhibit in its light the inward state of his own mind. And all he here says is entirely conformable to every description in the word of God of man in his present fallen condition; for 'if we say that we have no sin, we deceive ourselves, and the truth is not in us.' Thus, in the most forcible and impressive manner, Paul, in declaring his own experience, exhibits the light which the law in its spiritual aspect also sheds on the character of all other believers, in whom, notwithstanding that they are renewed in the spirit of their minds, the old man is not yet dead, nor the body of sin altogether destroyed. For if such was the state of mind of Paul the Apostle in regard to the remainder within him of indwelling sin, and the working of the old man, where is the Christian that can suppose that he is exempted from that inherent corruption, and that internal spiritual warfare, which, in the following context, the Apostle so feelingly describes?

I am carnal.—This respects what the Apostle was in himself. It does not imply that he was not regenerated, but shows what he was even in his renewed state, so far as concerned anything that was natural to him. Every Christian in this sense is carnal: in himself he is corrupt. Paul applies the epithet carnal to the Corinthians, although they were sanctified in Christ Jesus, and even in the same sentence in which he denominates them *carnal* he calls them *babes in Christ.* The word carnal, however, has not here exactly the same meaning that it has in 1 Cor. iii. 3. The Corinthians were comparatively carnal. Their disputes and envyings showed their attainments in the Divine life to be low. But, in the sense of the word in this place, all Christians—the best on earth not excepted —are always carnal. They are so when compared with the spiritual law of God. They have an evil principle in their hearts or nature. While in this world, Adam lives in them, called the old man, which is corrupt, according to the deceitful lusts.

Sold under sin.—Dr. Macknight and Mr. Stuart suppose that this expression decidedly proves that this account of carnality belongs not to the regenerate, but only to the unregenerate. It has, however, no such import. All men have been sold under sin by the fall, and as long as any of the evil of their nature, introduced by the fall, remains in them, so long do they remain sold under sin, to whatever extent and in whatever respect it exists. The Christian, it is true, receives a new nature, and the old nature is mortified; but it still lives, and, so far as it lives, the individual is properly said to be sold under sin. The old nature is not made holy, but a new nature is communicated. As far, then, as the old man manifests himself, and acts, so far even the Christian is *sold under sin.* It is not to be admitted, as these writers take it for granted, that the phrase imports the height of wickedness.   Let it be remarked, also, that, as signifying the greatest wickedness, the expression is nct more suitable to their own view, than it is to that of those whom they oppose.   If the Apostle speaks of unregenerate men, it must be in a character that will suit all unregenerate men.   But all unregenerate men are not excessively abandoned to wickedness.   Many of them are moral in their lives.

Looking to the external form of the law, the Apostle declares (Phil. iii. 6) that he was, in his unconverted state, blameless ; and in respect to his conduct afterwards as before men, he could appeal to them (1 Thess. ii. 10) how holily, and justly, and unblameably he had behaved himself among them.   But in referring, also, as he does here, to what is internal, and therefore speaking as before God, who alone searcheth the heart, and measuring himself by the holy law in all its extent, he confesses himself to be carnal and sold under sin.   His nature, or old man, was entirely opposed to the spirituality of the law.   He felt a law or power within him against which he struggled, from which he desired to be free, but which still asserted its tyrannical authority.   Notwithstanding the grace he had obtained, he found himself far from perfection, and in all respects unable, though ardently desiring, to attain that much wished for object. When he says he is carnal—sold under sin—he expresses the same senti- ment as in the 18th verse, where, distinguishing between his old and new nature, he says, ' in me (that is, in my flesh) dwelleth no good thing;' or, as he speaks elsewhere concerning the old man in believers, ' which is corrupt according to the deceitful lusts,' which he exhorts them to put off.   It ought to be noted that, when the Apostle says, I am carnal, sold under sin, it is the language of bitter complaint, as appears from the sequel, and especially from the 24th verse, which ex- presses a feeling respecting sin that does not belong to any unregenerate man.

It is, then, in comparing himself with the holy, just, good, and spiritual law, now come home in its power to his conscience, that the Apostle here declares himself to be *carnal, sold under sin.*   The law requires us to love God with all our heart, and with all our soul, and with all our mind, and with all our strength ; and our neighbour as ourselves.   Of this, every man in his best state, and in his very best thought or action, falls con- tinually short.   He proceeds a certain length in his obedience, but be- yond that he cannot go.   And why is it that into the region beyond this he does not advance ?   Because he is carnal, sold under sin.   The sin that remains in him binds him so that he cannot proceed.   Sin, however, does not reign over him ; otherwise, as it is directly opposed to every degree of obedience to the law, it would not suffer him to do anything, even the least, in conformity to the will of God.   Yet it so far prevails as to hinder him, as is here immediately added, from doing the good that he would ; and in so far he is sold under it.   It therefore prevents him from attaining to that perfection of obedience to the law of God which is the most earnest desire of every Christian, and to which the believer shall attain when he sees his blessed Lord as He is, 1 John iii. 2.   That Paul had not attained to this state of perfection, he in another place assures us, Phil. iii. 12. 'Not as though I had already attained, either were already perfect.' How, then, are these expressions, carnal, sold under sin, inapplicable to the Apostle?

If Paul had said he had no sin, he would have deceived himself, and the truth would not have been in him, 1 John i. 8. And if he had sin, and was unable to free himself from its power, was he not carnal, sold under it? There was spirit in him, but there was also flesh, and in his flesh he tells us dwelt no good thing: it was still sin or corrupt nature, and nothing but sin. In one point of view, then, Paul the Apostle could truly say that he was spiritual; in another, with equal truth, that he was *carnal*: literally and truly both spiritual and carnal. 'The flesh lusted against the spirit, and the spirit against the flesh, and these were contrary the one to the other.' He was sold under sin as a child of the first Adam, and he delighted in the law of God as a child of the second Adam. Accordingly, through the whole of this passage to the end of the chapter, Paul describes himself as a twofold person, and points to two distinct natures operating within him. This is a universal truth respecting all believers. As Paul declares to the churches of Galatia, and, as in the passage before us, he affirms of himself, they cannot do the things that they would, Gal. v. 17. In the end of this chapter he asserts the same truth. *So then with the mind*—what he before called the inward man— *I myself serve the law of God, but with the flesh*—what remained of his corrupt nature, in which dwelt no good thing—*the law of sin.*—Sin was displaced from its dominion, but not from its indwelling. There was, then, in the Apostle Paul, as in every Christian, 'as it were the company of two armies,' Song of Solomon, vi. 13. From this warfare, and these opposing principles within, no Christian in this world is ever exempt; and of this every one who knows the plague of his own heart is fully convinced.

Ver. 15.—*For that which I do I allow not: for what I would, that do I not; but what I hate, that do I.*

For.—This verse explains and confirms the preceding. *That which I do, I allow not.*—Literally, I know not. The English word *know*, as well as the word in the original, is often used as implying recognition or acknowledgment. We are said not to know a person whom we do not choose to recognise. Paul committed sin, but he did not recognise or approve it. He disclaimed all friendly acquaintance with it. *For what I would, that do I not; but what I hate, that do I.*—Every man, regenerate or unregenerate, must be sensible of the truth of this, so far as it imports that he does what he knows to be wrong. As there is no regenerate man in whom this is not verified, it cannot be confined to the unregenerate. But as it is of the regenerate the Apostle is here speaking, —that is, as he is speaking of himself at the time of writing,—it is necessary to apply it here peculiarly to the regenerate. Besides, as it is said that he did what he hated, it must be here applied exclusively to the regenerate. Though an unregenerate man disapproves of evil, he cannot be said to *hate sin*. This is characteristic of the regenerate, and of such only: 'Ye that love the Lord, hate evil,' Ps. xcvii. 10. It is characteristic of the Redeemer Himself: 'Thou hast loved righteousness and hated iniquity,' Heb. i. 9. The following words are decisive on the subject:—'The fear of the Lord is to hate evil,' Prov. viii. 13. Some suppose that what the Apostle says in this verse is to the same purpose with the noted heathen confession, ' *Video meliora proboque, deteriora sequor.*'— ' I see what is better and approve of it; I follow what is worse.' But these propositions are not at all identical. The heathen confesses that he practises what he knows to be wrong, but his inconsistency arises from the love of the evil. Paul confesses that he does what is wrong, but declares that instead of loving the evil, he regards it with hatred and abhorrence.

Ver. 16.—*If then I do that which I would not, I consent unto the law that it is good.*

If then I do that which I would not.—Dr. Macknight translates, ' *which I incline not.*' But this is not according to fact. A man may do what his conscience disapproves, but in acting thus he does not thwart his *inclination.* Inclination is a tendency or bent in a particular direction, and the bent of every man is naturally to sin. Mr. Stuart translates the word ' desire,' but neither is this correct. Sin may be contrary to reason and conscience, but it is agreeable to desire. *I consent unto the law that it is good.*—When a regenerate man does what he hates, his own mind testifies his approval of the law that prohibits the sin which he has practised.

Ver. 17.—*Now then, it is no more I that do it, but sin that dwelleth in me.*

By the *I* here, Dr. Macknight and Mr. Stuart understand reason and conscience. But reason and conscience can in no sense be called a man's *self.* In this way a murderer might affirm that it was not he who committed the crime, for no doubt his reason and conscience disapproved of the action. It is quite obvious that the reason why Paul says that it was not *he* but *sin* in him, is because, as he had just stated, that which he did he allowed not, for he did that which he would not. This implies more than reason and conscience. It was therefore *sin that dwelt in him*—the old man, his carnal nature, which not only existed and wrought in him, but had its abode in him, as it has in all those who are regenerated, and will have so long as they are in the body. It is not, then, to extenuate the evil of sin, or to furnish an excuse for it, that Paul says, It is no more I, but sin that dwelleth in me; but to show that, notwithstanding his seeing it to be evil, and hating it, the root still subsisted in him, and was chargeable upon him. It is not necessary to be able to point out metaphysically the way in which the truth that all sin is voluntary, harmonises with Paul's declaration, *the good that I would I do not.* Things may be consistent which the human mind cannot penetrate. We are to receive God's testimony from the Apostle, and believe it on God's authority; and every Christian knows, by painful experience, the truth of all that the Apostle asserts.

' What here would strike any mind free of bias,' says Mr. Frazer in his excellent exposition of this chapter, in his work *On Sanctification,* ' is, that this (I) on the side of holiness against sin is the most prevailing, and what represents the true character of the man ; and that *sin* which

he distinguishes from this (I) is not the prevailing reigning power in the
man here represented; as it is, however, in every unregenerate man.'[1]
On this verse Calvin also has remarked,—'This passage clearly proves
Paul is disputing concerning none but the pious, who are now regenerated. For man, while he continues like himself, whatever his character
may be, is justly considered to be vicious.' No one can disclaim sin, as
in this verse it is disclaimed, except the converted man; for who besides
can conscientiously and intelligibly affirm, 'Now then it is no more I that
do it, but sin that dwelleth in me?'

Ver. 18.—*For I know that in me (that is, in my flesh) dwelleth no good thing: for
to will is present with me; but how to perform that which is good I find not.*

I know.—This is a thing which Paul knew as an Apostle of the Lord
Jesus Christ, and that he must have known by experience also. Whoever has a proper knowledge of himself will be convinced that naturally
there is nothing good in him. What Paul knew was, that in him dwelt
no good thing. This goes beyond what he had asserted in the end of the
preceding verse. There he asserts that the evil which he did was caused
by sin dwelling in him. Here he asserts not only that sin dwelt in him,
but that *no good thing dwelt in him.* But how could he say so, if he was
a regenerated man? If there was something in him which he calls himself, and which he would not allow to have any share in his sin, how can
he say that there is in him no good thing? Is not this principle that
hates the sin which he commits a good principle? Certainly it is. And
to prevent such an inference from his words, he explains by a parenthesis
the sense in which he asserts that no good thing dwelt in him. *That is,
in my flesh.*—He confines the assertion to his carnal nature. Nothing
can more clearly and expressly show that this description is a description
of the regenerate man. What has an unrenewed man but flesh? His
very reason and conscience are defiled, Tit. i. 15.

*To will is present with me; but how to perform that which is good I find
not.*—'That is,' says Mr. Frazer, 'to will what is good and holy: and
thus it is with him habitually and ready with him.' Mr. Stuart, in his
Commentary, renders this, 'For to will that which is good, is in my
power; but to do it, I do not find (in my power).' Yet in the text he
translates it, 'For to desire what is good, is easy for me; but to do it, I
find difficult,' which is an entirely different and contradictory idea. A
thing that is very difficult may yet be performed. Dr. Macknight renders
it, 'Indeed, to incline lies near me; but to work out what is excellent, I
do not find NEAR ME,'—giving no distinct sense, from an affectation of
rendering literally. Calvin says, 'He (Paul) does not mean that he has
nothing but an ineffectual volition and desire, but he asserts the efficacy
of the work does not correspond to the will, because the flesh hinders
him from exactly performing what he is engaged in executing.'

---

[1] A man of God so deeply acquainted with the human heart, and so advanced in
the Divine life as this writer evidently was, is a much better judge of the import of
this chapter than a mere critic, however distinguished for talents and learning. To
eminent godliness, Mr. Frazer added profound penetration and remarkable discrimination,—qualities in which many critics, who attempt to expound the Scripture,
are greatly deficient.

Ver. 19.—*For the good that I would I do not : but the evil which I would not, that I do.*

For the good that I would I do not.—This does not imply that he did not attempt, or in some sense perform, what he purposed, but that in all he came short. Calvin, in continuation of the last quotation from him, says, ' What follows—*to do the evil which he would not*—must also be taken in the same sense, because the faithful are not only hindered from running speedily by their own flesh, but it also opposes many obstacles against which they stumble ; and they do not, therefore, perform their duty, because they do not engage in it with becoming alacrity. The *will*, therefore, here mentioned, is the readiness of faith, while the Holy Spirit forces the pious to be prepared and zealous in employing their time to perform obedience to God. But Paul, because his power is unequal to the task, asserts that he does not find what he was wishing to attain—the accomplishment of his good desires.' *But the evil which I would not do, that I do.*—So far from being unsuitable to the real character of a regenerate man, every regenerate man must be sensible from his own experience that this charge is true.

Ver. 20.—*Now, if I do that I would not, it is no more I that do it, but sin that dwelleth in me.*

This is a confirmation of what was asserted, verse 17, by alleging the reason on which the assertion is founded. It is not reason and conscience that Paul here declares to have no share in the evil ; it is the will which he expressly mentions, and, whatever metaphysical difficulties it may involve, of the will it must be understood. The conclusion we ought to draw, is not to contradict the Apostle by denying that he speaks of the will, but that in one sense it is true that no sin is involuntary, and that, in another sense, what the Apostle here asserts is also an undoubted truth.

Ver. 21.—*I find then a law, that, when I would do good, evil is present with me.*

The evil propensity of our nature the Apostle calls a law, because of its strength and permanence. It has the force of a law in corrupt nature. This proves that it is of himself, as to his present state, that the Apostle speaks. None but the regenerate man is properly sensible of this law. It does not refer to conscience, which in an unregenerate man will smite him when he does that which he knows to be wrong. It refers to the evil principle which counteracts him when he would do that which is right. This law is the greatest grievance to every Christian. It disturbs his happiness and peace more than any other cause. It constantly besets him, and, from its influence, his very prayers, instead of being in themselves worthy of God, need forgiveness, and can be accepted only through the mediation of Christ. It is strange that any Christian should even hesitate as to the character in which the Apostle uses this language. It entirely suits the Christian, and not in one solitary feature does it wear the feeblest semblance of any other character.

Ver. 22.—*For I delight in the law of God after the inward man.*

In the preceding verse Paul had said, I would do good ; here he more fully expresses the same desire after conformity to the holy law. *For I delight in the law of God.*—This is decisive of the character in which the Apostle speaks. None but the regenerate delight in the law of God. Mr. Stuart, after the Arminian Whitby, and the Arian Taylor, has referred to a number of passages, in order to lower the import of this term. But they have no similarity to the present case. They are too numerous to be introduced and discussed in this place. Whoever wishes to examine them may consult Mr. Frazer's work *On Sanctification,* in which they are most satisfactorily proved to be misapplied, and wrested to the perversion of the truth.

To delight in the law of the Lord is characteristic of the regenerate man. The unregenerate man hates that law as far as he sees the extent of its demands to transcend his power of fulfilment. He is enmity against God, and is not subject to the law of God, neither indeed can be, ch. viii. 7. How, then, can he delight in it? *After the inward man.*— The inward man is a term used only by Paul, and in reference to those who are regenerated. It is the new or spiritual nature, not merely the reason and conscience. Than this nothing can be more obviously characteristic of the Christian. Notwithstanding the evil of his corrupt nature, he is conscious of delighting in the law of God in its full extent.

Ver. 23.—*But I see another law in my members warring against the law of my mind, and bringing me into captivity to the law of sin which is in my members.*

In the preceding verse the Apostle had spoken of the law of God in the inward man; here he speaks of *another law in his members, warring against the law of his mind.* Thus he denominates his new and spiritual nature his 'inward man' and his 'mind,' and his old and carnal nature his 'members.' The bent of the Apostle's mind, according to his renewed nature, inclined him to delight in the law of God. But he found an opposite bent in his corrupt nature, which he calls a law in his members. This he represents as warring against the other. Is not this the experience of every Christian? Is there not a constant struggle of the corruptions of the heart against the principle of holiness implanted by the Spirit of God in the new birth?

And bringing me into captivity to the law of sin and death.—Mr. Stuart endeavours to aggravate this description in such a manner as to render it unsuitable to the regenerate man. He supposes that this represents the person as brought entirely and completely into captivity, which cannot be supposed of the regenerate. He refers to captives taken in war, who are entirely in the power of their conquerors, and are reduced to the most abject slavery. This is feeble reasoning. How far this captivity extends cannot be known from the figure. And, as a matter of fact, if the evil principle of our nature prevails in exciting one evil thought, it has taken us captive. So far it has conquered, and so far we are defeated and made prisoners. But this is quite consistent with the supposition that, on the whole, we may have the victory over sin.

Ver. 24.—*O wretched man that I am! who shall deliver me from the body of this death?*

O wretched man that I am!—This language is suitable only to the regenerate. An unregenerate man is indeed wretched, but he does not feel the wretchedness here expressed. He may be sensible of misery, and he may be filled with anxious fears and dreadful forebodings; but the person here described is wretched only from a sense of the evil principle which is in his members. Such a feeling no unregenerate man ever possessed. An unregenerate man may wish to be delivered from danger and punishment; but instead of wishing to be delivered from the law of his nature, he delights in that law. He has so much pleasure in indulging that law, that for its sake he risks all consequences.

The body of this death.—Some understand this of his natural body, and suppose the exclamation to be a wish to die. But this would be a sentiment totally at variance with the principles of the Apostle, and unsuitable to the scope of the passage. It is evidently an expression of a wish to be free from that corrupt principle which caused him so much affliction. This he calls a body, as before he had called it his members. And he calls it *a body of death,* because its demerit is death. It causes death and everlasting ruin to the world; and had it not been for the coming of the Lord Jesus Christ, it must have had the same consequences with respect to all.

Ver. 25.—*I thank God, through Jesus Christ our Lord. So then with the mind I myself serve the law of God, but with the flesh the law of sin.*

I thank God.—Some suppose that this expresses thanks for the victory as already obtained. But this cannot be the meaning, as, in the same breath, the Apostle speaks of his wretchedness because of the existence of the evil. Some, again, supposing that it refers to present deliverance, explain it to be the freedom from the law spoken of in the preceding part of the chapter. But this would make the Apostle speak entirely away from the purpose. He is discoursing of that corruption which he still experiences. Besides, the form of the expression requires that the deliverance should be supposed future,—*who* SHALL *deliver me.* I thank God, *through Jesus Christ.*—The natural supplement is, *He will deliver me.* At death Paul was to be entirely freed from the evil of his nature. The consolation of the Christian against the corruption of his nature is, that although he shall not get free from it in this world, he shall hereafter be entirely delivered.

So then.—This is the consequence which Paul draws, and the sum of all that he had said from the 14th verse. In one point of view he served the law of God, and in another the law of sin. Happy is the man who can thus, like Paul, with conscious sincerity say of himself,— ' *With the mind I myself serve the law of God; but with the flesh the law of sin.*' Here he divides himself, as it were, into two parts,—*the mind,* by which he means his inward man, his renewed self; and the flesh, by which he designs his carnal nature, or the old man, that was sold under sin; and thus he accounts for his serving two different laws—*the law of God* written on his mind, and in the service of which he delighted as a regenerate man; and *the law of sin,* by which he was sometimes carried captive. Beyond this no child of God can go while in this world; it will ever remain the character of the regenerate man. But this fully ascertains that Paul himself, in his predominant disposition and fixed purpose, serves God, although he is compelled to acknowledge that the power of the old man within him still subsists, and exerts itself; while it is his earnest desire daily to put him off, Eph. iv. 22, and to be transformed by the renewing of his mind.

In every believer, and in no one else, there are these two principles,—sin and grace, flesh and spirit, the law of the members and the law of the mind. This may be perverted by the opposer of Divine truth into a handle against the Gospel, and by the hypocrite to excuse his sin. But it gives ground to neither. It is the truth of God, and the experience of every Christian. If any man will pervert it to a wicked purpose, he shall bear his sin. We are not at liberty to pervert the word of God in order to preserve it from a contrary perversion. Many, no doubt, wrest the Scriptures to their own destruction. *I serve.*—Employing, as he does, through the whole of this passage, the present tense, Paul does not say, I have served, as referring to his state of unregeneracy, but 'I serve,' as respecting his present state as a believer in Christ, composed of flesh and spirit, which, as they are different principles, regard two different laws. It is further to be observed, that this last account which he gives of himself, and which agrees with all he had said before, and confirms the whole, is delivered by him, after he had, with so much faith and fervency, given thanks to God in view of his future and complete deliverance from sin. This, as Gill well remarks, is a conclusive argument and proof that he speaks of himself, in this whole discourse concerning indwelling sin, as a regenerated person.

As if to render it altogether impossible to imagine that the Apostle was personating another man, he here, in conclusion, uses the expression *I myself,* which cannot, if language has a meaning, be applied to another person. It is a phrase which again and again he employs,—Rom. ix. 3; 2 Cor. x. 1, and xii. 13.

On the whole, then, we here learn that the Apostle Paul, notwithstanding all the grace with which he was favoured, found a principle of evil operating so strongly in his heart, that he denominates it a law always present and always active to retard him in his course. He was not, however, under its dominion. He was in Christ Jesus a new creature, born of God, renewed in the spirit of his mind. He delighted in the holy law of God in all its extent and spirituality, while at the same time he felt the influence of the other hateful principle—that tendency to evil which characterizes the old man,—which waged perpetual war against the work of grace in his soul, impelling him to the commission of sin, and constantly striving to bring him under its power. Nothing can more clearly demonstrate the fallen state of man, and the entire corruption of his nature, than the perpetual and irreconcilable warfare which that corruption maintains in the hearts of all believers against 'the Divine nature' of which they are made partakers; and nothing can more forcibly enhance the value of the Gospel, and prove its necessity in order to salvation, or more fully illustrate the great truth which Paul had been illustrating, that by the deeds of the law no flesh shall be justified in the sight of God.

When, in the hour and power of darkness, the prince of this world came to assault the Redeemer, he found nothing in Him—nothing on which his temptations could fix or make an impression; but how different was it when he assailed the Apostle Peter! Him he overcame, and to such an extent as to prevail on him to deny his Lord and Master, notwithstanding all the firmness and sincerity of his previous resolutions. Had not the Lord interposed to prevent his faith from entirely failing, Satan would have taken full possession of him, as he did of Judas. In the same way, it was only by grace that the Apostle Paul was what he was, 1 Cor. xv. 10; and by that grace he was enabled to maintain the struggle against his old corrupt nature, until he could exclaim, in the triumphant language of victory, 'I have fought a good fight, I have finished my course, I have kept the faith.' 'My grace,' said Jesus to him, 'is sufficient for thee; for My strength is made perfect in weakness.'

The whole concluding part of this chapter is most violently perverted by Dr. Macknight, and Mr. Stuart, and Mr. Tholuck. In his explanation of this last verse, Dr. Macknight, by first converting the assertion it contains into a question, and then boldly adding to it, makes the Apostle say precisely the reverse of what he actually affirms. '*Do I myself, then, as a slave, serve with the mind* the law of God, but with the flesh the law of sin?* BY NO MEANS.'

Mr. Tholuck, after denying all along that the Apostle, in the conclusion of this chapter, describes his own experience, and affirming that he is speaking in the name of a legalist, arrives at the 25th verse, in the first clause of which, though not in the last, he judges that the Apostle must be speaking in his own person.

'After the struggle of the legalist,' he says, 'with the wretchedness arising from his sense of inward schism has in this description been wrought up to the highest pitch, Paul comes forward of a sudden in his own person, and breaks forth in thankfulness to God for having delivered him by the redemption from that miserable condition.' A more unfounded interpretation cannot be imagined.

Mr. Tholuck considers the position in which, according to his view, Paul has thus placed himself to be so awkward, that he does not allow it to pass unnoticed. 'As this sally of gratitude, however, interrupts,' he adds, 'the course of the argument, and is quite involuntary, inasmuch as Paul meant still to draw his inference from all that he had previously said, he finds himself compelled, in a way not the most appropriate, after the expression of his gratitude, still to append the conclusion, which is intended briefly and distinctly to show the state of the legalist.' Can any Christian be satisfied with this manner of treating the Scriptures? Can any sober-minded man acquiesce in such an interpretation? This is a 'sally of gratitude,' and worse, it is *involuntary!* Did Paul utter things incoherently? *He finds himself compelled, in a way* NOT THE MOST APPROPRIATE, to append the conclusion. Is this a reverent manner of speaking of the dictate of the Holy Ghost? In the proper and obvious sense of the expression, as employed by the Apostle, it is most appropriate; yet Mr. Tholuck affixes to it a ludicrous import![1]

---

[1] The above explanation of the passage is not only false and irreverent, but absurd. It is worthy, however, of Mr. Tholuck's Neological views of the inspiration of the Scriptures, of which I have given so full a specimen in a pamphlet entitled, *Further*

The warfare between the flesh and the spirit, described in this chapter, has greatly exercised the ingenuity of men not practically acquainted with its truth. Few are willing to believe that all mankind are naturally so bad as they are here represented, and it is fondly imagined that the best of men are much better than this description would prove them to be. Every effort of ingenuity has accordingly been resorted to, to divert the Apostle's statements from the obvious conclusion to which they lead, and so to modify his doctrine as to make it worthy of acceptance by human wisdom. But they have laboured in vain. Their theories not only contradict the Apostle's doctrine, but are generally self-contradictory. Every Christian has in his own breast a commentary on the Apostle's language. If there be anything of which he is fully assured, it is that Paul has in this passage described his experience; and the more the believer advances in knowledge and holiness, the more does he loathe himself, as by nature a child of that corruption which still so closely cleaves to him. So far is the feeling of the power of indwelling sin from being inconsistent with regeneration, that it must be experienced in proportion to the progress of sanctification. The more sensitive we are, the more do we feel pain ; and the more our hearts are purified, the more painful to us will sin be. Men perceive themselves to be sinners in proportion as they have previously discovered the holiness of God and of His law.

The conflict here described by Paul, his deep conviction of sin consisting with delight in the law of God, and this agreement of heart with its holy precepts, are peculiar to those only who are regenerated by the Spirit of God. They who know the excellence of that law, and earnestly desire to obey it, will feel the force of the Apostle's language. It results from the degree of sanctification to which he had attained, from his hatred of sin and profound humility. This conflict was the most painful of his trials, compelling him in bitterness to exclaim, 'O wretched man that I am ! '—an exclamation never wrung from him by all his multiplied persecutions and outward sufferings. The proof that from the 14th verse to the end of the chapter he relates his own experience at the time when he wrote this Epistle, is full and complete.

Throughout the whole of this passage, instead of employing the past time, as he does from the 7th to the 14th verse, Paul uniformly adopts the present, while he speaks in the first person about forty times, without the smallest intimation that he is referring to any one else, or to himself at any former period. His professed object, all along, is to show that the law can effect nothing for the salvation of a sinner, which he had proved to be the character of all men ; and, by speaking in his own name, he shows that of this every one who is a partaker of His grace is in his best state convinced. In the end he triumphantly affirms that Christ will deliver him, while in the meantime he experiences this painful and unremitting warfare ; and closes the whole by saying, ' So then with the mind I myself serve the law of God ; but with the flesh the law of sin.'

Considerations for the Ministers of the Church of Scotland, occasioned by D.˙. Tholuck's Perversions of the Word of God, and his Attack on some of the most important Scriptural Doctrines.

Can it be supposed that in saying, 'I myself,' the Apostle meant another man; or that, in using the present time, he refers to a former period? Of what value is language, if it can be so tortured as to admit of an interpretation at direct variance with its obvious meaning? To suppose that another, and not the Apostle himself, is here designed, is contrary to every principle of sound interpretation.

Paul, in this chapter, contrasts his former with his present state. Formerly, when ignorant of the true import of the law, he entertained a high opinion of himself. 'I was alive without the law once.' Accordingly he speaks in other parts of his writings of his sincerity, his religious zeal, and his irreproachable moral conduct before his conversion. Afterwards, when the veil of self-delusion was removed, he discovered that he had been a blasphemer, a persecutor, injurious, and in unbelief; so that, when he was an Apostle, he calls himself the chief of sinners. If he was convinced that he had been a sinner, condemned by the law, it was when the Lord Jesus was revealed to him; for till then he was righteous in his own esteem. Before that time he was dead in trespasses and sins, having nothing but his original corrupted nature, which he calls sin. He had no conviction that he was radically and practically a sinner, of which the passage before us proves he was now fully conscious. From this period, the flesh, or sin, which he elsewhere calls 'the old man,' remained in him. Though it harassed him much, he did not walk according to it; but, being now in the spirit, the new nature which he had received predominated. He therefore clearly establishes, in this chapter, the opposition between the old man and the working of the new nature. This is according to the uniform language of his Epistles, as well as of the whole of Scripture, both in its doctrinal and historical parts. In consistency with this, he exhorts the 'saints' at Ephesus to 'put off the old man, which is corrupt according to the deceitful lusts;' and calls on the 'faithful brethren' at Colosse to mortify their members which are upon the earth. All his instructions to 'them that are sanctified in Christ Jesus' proceed on the same principle. And why were they cautioned by him even against the grossest sins, but because there was still in them a principle disposed to every sin?

There are three circumstances in this passage which are of themselves decisive of the fact that Paul here recounts his own present experience. The first is, that the Apostle hates sin. He hates it, because it is rebellion against God, and the violation of His law. This no unconverted man does, or can do. He may dislike the evil effects of sin, and consequently wish that he had not committed it; but he does not, as the Apostle here declares of himself, hate *sin*. Hating sin is the counterpart of loving the law of God.

The second circumstance in proof that the Apostle is here referring to the present time, is, that he delights in the law of God after the inward man. Now it is only when sin is dethroned, and grace reigns in the heart, that this can be a truth. 'I delight,' says the Psalmist, 'to do Thy will, O my God; yea, Thy law is in my heart.' 'I will delight myself in Thy commandments, which I love,' Ps. xl. 8, cxix. 16, 24, 35, 47, 92, 97, 174. Delight in His law and the fear of God cannot be separated. The Holy Spirit pronounces such persons blessed. 'Blessed is the man that feareth the Lord, that delighteth greatly in His commandments,' Ps. cxii. 1. 'Blessed is the man that walketh not in the counsel of the ungodly, nor standeth in the way of sinners, nor sitteth in the seat of the scornful; but his *delight is in the law of the Lord*,' Ps. i. 1. Thus the man that delights in the law of the Lord is blessed; and who will affirm that an unconverted man is blessed? Far from delighting in the law of God, which the first commandment enjoins,— 'Thou shalt love the Lord thy God with all thy heart,'—'the carnal mind is enmity against God; for it is not subject to the law of God, neither indeed can be.' Such is the state of every unconverted man. And if, as all Scripture testifies, enmity against God be the characteristic of the wicked, and delight in God and His law be the characteristic of a regenerate man, by what perversion of language, by what species of sophistry, can it be affirmed that the Apostle, while describing his inward delight in God, is to be regarded as portraying himself in his original unconverted state? So far was he, while in that state, from delighting in God, either inwardly or outwardly, that his carnal mind was enmity against Jehovah, and his zeal was manifested in persecuting the Lord of glory.

The third circumstance which incontestibly proves that Paul is here relating his present personal experience, is his declaration that he expects his deliverance from Jesus Christ.' Is this the language of a man dead in trespasses and sins—of one who is a stranger to the truth as it is in Jesus, and to whom the things revealed by the Spirit of God are foolishness? 1 Cor. ii. 14. 'No man,' says Jesus, 'can come to Me, except the Father, which hath sent Me, draw him,' John vi. 44. 'No man can say that Jesus is the Lord, but by the Holy Ghost,' 1 Cor. xii. 3. How, then, shall an unconverted man look to Him for deliverance?

In another place already referred to, the Apostle describes the internal warfare experienced by Christians between the flesh and the spirit, or the old and new man, in language precisely similar to what he here employs concerning himself; 'The flesh lusteth against the spirit, and the spirit against the flesh, and these are contrary the one to the other: so that ye cannot do the things that ye would,' Gal. v. 17.

In the midst of his apostolic labours, where he is endeavouring to animate those to whom he wrote, Paul represents himself engaged as here in the same arduous struggle. 'I keep under my body, and bring it into subjection, lest that by any means, when I have preached to others, I myself should be a castaway,' 1 Cor. ix. 27. Having there a different object in view, he refers to his success in the struggle; while, in the chapter before us, his design is to exhibit the power of the enemy with whom he has to contend. But in both cases he speaks of a severe contest with an enemy within, striving to bring him into captivity to sin and death. In another place, addressing those at Ephesus, whom he describes as 'quickened together with Christ,' and including himself, whilst speaking in the character of 'an Apostle of Jesus Christ by the will of God,' he uses the following unequivocal and energetic language—'For we wrestle not against flesh and blood, but against principalities, against powers, against the rulers of the darkness of this world, against spiritual wickedness in high places.' He therefore calls on those to whom he wrote to 'take the whole armour of God, that they may be able to withstand and to quench the fiery darts of the wicked one,' Eph. vi. 12. Does not this describe a conflict equally severe as that in which, in the passage before us, he represents himself to be engaged? Does not this imply that evil existed in himself, as well as in those to whom he wrote, without which the fiery darts of the devil could have taken no more effect than on Him in whom the prince of this world when he came found 'nothing'? And what is the purpose of the Christian armour, but to fit us to fight with flesh and blood, namely, our corruptions, as well as other enemies, against which Paul says, *we* wrestle?

Was the Apostle Peter chargeable with the sin of dissimulation, and did the Apostle Paul experience no internal struggle with the old man which caused the fall of his fellow Apostle? Did Paul call upon other saints to put off the old man, and was there not in him an old man? Did he admonish all his brethren, without exception, to mortify their members which were upon the earth, and had he no sins to mortify? And why was it necessary for the Lord to send him a thorn in the flesh, the messenger of Satan to buffet him, to curb the pride of his nature and prevent him from being exalted above measure, had it not been for the remaining corruption of his nature working powerfully in his heart, which from this it appears all his other severe trials and afflictions were insufficient to subdue? This alone determines the question. Was it not incumbent, too, on Paul, as on all other believers, to pray daily for the forgiveness of his sins? Was it not necessary for him, like David, to pray that his heart might be enlarged, that he might run the way of God's commandments? Ps. cxix. 32.

All that Paul says in this chapter concerning himself and his inward corruption, entirely corresponds with what we are taught both in the Old Testament and the New respecting the people of God. The piety and devotedness to God of the holiest men did not prevent the evil that was in them from appearing in many parts of their conduct; while at the same time we are informed of the horror they expressed on account of their transgressions. God declares that there was no man like Job on the earth, a perfect and an upright man, one that feared God and eschewed evil; and by God Himself Job is classed with two others of His most eminent saints, Ezek. xiv. 14. Yet Job exclaims, 'Behold, I am vile; what shall I answer Thee? I will lay mine hand upon my mouth.' 'I have heard of Thee by the hearing of the ear; but now mine eye seeth Thee: wherefore I abhor myself in dust and ashes,' Job xl. 4, xlii. 5, 6. 'My soul,' says the Psalmist, in the same Psalm in which he so often asserts that he delights in the law of God,—'my soul cleaveth unto the dust;' while in the preceding sentence he had declared, 'Thy testimonies also are my delight:' and again, 'I will delight myself in Thy commandments, which I have loved;' 'O how I love Thy law! it is my meditation all the day;' 'My soul hath kept Thy testimonies; and I love them exceedingly;' yet he says, 'Mine iniquities are gone over my head as an heavy burden; they are too heavy for me. My wounds stink and are corrupt, because of my foolishness;' 'My loins are filled with a loathsome disease, and there is no soundness in my flesh;' 'My groaning is not hid from Thee;' 'I will declare mine iniquity.' Yet in the same Psalm David says, 'In Thee, O Lord, do I hope.' 'They also that render evil for good are mine adversaries, because I follow the thing that is good. Make haste to help me, O Lord, my salvation.' 'Iniquities,' he says, 'prevail against me,' while he rejoices in the forgiveness of his sins. 'Pardon mine iniquity, for it is great.'

'Woe is me,' exclaims the Prophet Isaiah, 'for I am a man of unclean lips,' Isa. vi. 5. 'Who can say, I have made my heart clean, I am pure from my sin?' Prov. xx. 9. God promised to establish an everlasting covenant with Israel, Ezek. xvi. 63; and the consequence was to be, that they should loathe themselves and be confounded when God was pacified towards them. The complaints of the servants of God all proceeded from the same source, namely, their humiliating experience of indwelling sin, at the same time that, after the inward man, they *delighted* in the law of God. And could it be otherwise in men who, by the Spirit of God, were convinced of sin? John xvi. 8. There is not a man on earth that *delights* in the law of God who does not know that his soul *cleaveth unto the dust*.

Comparing himself with the law of God, Paul might well lament his remaining corruption, as the Apostle Peter, experiencing the same consciousness of his sinfulness, exclaims, 'Depart from me, for I am a sinful man, O Lord;' or as the Apostle James confesses, 'In many things we all offend.' Both Peter and James here declare that they themselves, although Apostles of Christ, had sin in them. Was then Paul an exception to this? and if he had sin, is it not a just account of it, when he says that there was a law within him warring against the law of his mind; in short, a contest between what he elsewhere calls the new and the old man? If, on the other hand, on account of anything done either by him or in him, of any zeal, excellency, or attainment, Paul, or any man, should fancy himself in a state of sinless perfection, the Holy Ghost, by the mouth of the Apostle John, charges him with self-deception. 'If we' (Apostle or others) 'say that we have no sin, we deceive ourselves, and the truth is not in us,' 1 John i. 8. Whence, then, is there any difficulty in admitting that in the account of the internal struggle in the passage before us, Paul described his own warfare with indwelling sin, or that it portrays a state of mind incompatible with that of an Apostle? Did Paul's sanctification differ in kind from that of other believers, so as to render this incredible, or, in as far as it may have exceeded that of most other believers, did it differ only in degree? There is then no ground whatever for denying that he here related his own personal experience, according to the plain, literal, and obvious import of the expressions he employs. Were Paul, when judged at the tribunal of God, to take his stand on the best action he ever performed in the midst of his apostolic labours, he would be condemned for ever. Imperfection would be found to cleave to the very best of his services; and imperfection, even in the least possible degree, as it respects the law of God, is sin. 'Cursed is every one that *continueth* not in *all things* that are written in the book of the law to do them.' And who is the mere man that, since the fall, came up for one moment to the standard of this holy law, which says, 'Thou shalt love the Lord with *all* thy heart?'

It was on a ground very different from that of his own obedience, that Paul, when about to depart from the world, joyfully exclaimed, 'Henceforth there is laid up for me a crown of righteousness, which the Lord the righteous Judge shall give me at that day.' Yes, it will be a crown of *righteousness*, because Christ, having been made of God unto him 'wisdom,' Paul had renounced his own righteousness, that so being found in Him he might possess 'the righteousness which is of God by faith.' He was therefore covered with the robe of righteousness, even the righteousness of our Lord and Saviour Jesus Christ,—Jehovah our righteousness,—who is the end of the law for righteousness to every one that believeth. And thus, in the judgment of *strict justice*, Paul, with all believers, notwithstanding all his and their sins and shortcomings, shall be pronounced 'righteous,'—a character twice given to those who shall appear on the right hand of the throne, Matt. xxv. 37–46,—in that day when the 'righteous servant' of Jehovah shall judge the world in righteousness. Thus, too, when the great multitude of those who have washed their robes in the *blood* of the Lamb shall stand before the throne, the full import of the words of Paul, with which in the fifth chapter of this Epistle he closes the account of the entrance of sin and death, and of righteousness and life, will be made gloriously manifest. 'That as sin hath reigned unto death, even so might grace reign through *righteousness* unto eternal life by Jesus Christ our Lord.' That great truth, which Paul has also declared will then be fully verified, that the Gospel is the power of God unto salvation, because *therein is the righteousness of God revealed.*

With carnality, then—the corruption of his nature—Paul the Apostle was chargeable ; and of this, at all times after his conversion, he was fully sensible. Conscious that he had never for one moment attained to the perfection of obedience to the law of God, and knowing, by the teaching of the Spirit of God, that there was a depth of wickedness in his heart which he never could fathom,—for who but God can *know* the heart, which 'is deceitful above all things, and desperately wicked'? Jer. xvii. 9,—well might he designate himself a 'wretched man,' and turn with more earnestness than ever to his blessed Lord to be delivered from such a body of death. With what holy indignation would he have spurned from him such perverse glosses as are put upon his words to explain away their obvious import, by men who profess to believe the doctrines, and to understand the principles, which form the basis of all he was commissioned by his Divine Master to proclaim to the fallen children of Adam. He would have warned them not to think of him above that which is written, 1 Cor. iv. 6. And most assuredly they who cannot persuade themselves that the confessions and lamentations in the passage before us, strong as they undoubtedly are, could possibly be applicable to the Apostle Paul, do think of him above what is declared in every part of the word of God to be the character of every renewed man while he remains in this world.

In Mr. Toplady's works it is stated that some of Dr. Doddridge's last words were, ' The best prayer I ever offered up in my life deserves damnation.' In this sentiment Dr. Doddridge did not in the smallest degree exceed the truth. And with equal truth Mr. Toplady says of himself, ' Oh that ever such a wretch as I should be tempted to think highly of himself ! I that am of myself nothing but sin and weakness. In whose flesh naturally dwells no good thing ; I who deserve damnation for the best work I ever performed,' vol. iv. 171, and 1–41. These are the matured opinions concerning themselves of men who had been taught by the same Spirit as the Apostle Paul.

Every man who knows ' the plague of his own heart,' whatever may be the view he has taken of this passage, *knows for certain* that even if the Apostle Paul has not given here an account of his own experience at the time when he wrote this Epistle, *such was actually the Apostle's experience day by day*. He also knows that the man who is not daily constrained to cry out to himself, ' O wretched man that I am,' from a sense of his indwelling corruption and his shortcomings, *is not a Christian.* He has not been convinced of sin by the Spirit of God ; he is not one of those who, like the Apostle Paul, are forced to confess, ' We that are in this tabernacle do groan,' 2 Cor. v. 2, 4 ; or to say, ' We ourselves also which have the first fruits of the Spirit, even *we ourselves,* groan within ourselves,' Rom. viii. 23. The Apostle's exclamation in the passage before us, ' O wretched man that I am,' is no other than this *groaning.* And every regenerate man, the more he is convinced of sin, which in his natural state never disturbed his thoughts, the more he advances in the course of holiness, and the more nearly he approaches to the image of his Divine Master, the more deeply will he groan under the more vivid conception and the stronger abhorrence of the malignity of his indwelling sin.

It is easy to see how suitable it was that the author of this Epistle should detail his own experience, and thus describe the internal workings of his heart, and not merely refer to his external conduct. He speaks of himself, that it might not be supposed that the miserable condition he described did not concern believers ; and to prove that the most holy ought to humble themselves before God, since God would find in them a body of sin and death ; guilty, as in themselves, of eternal death. Nothing, then, could serve more fully to illustrate his doctrine in the preceding part of it, respecting human depravity and guilt, and the universality of the inveterate malady of sin, than to show that it was capable, even in himself, with all the grace of which he was so distinguished a subject, of opposing with such force the principles of the new life in his soul. In this view, the passage before us perfectly accords with the Apostle's design in this chapter, in which, for the comfort of believers, he is testifying that by their marriage with Christ they are *dead to the law,* as he had taught in the preceding chapter that by union with Him in His death and resurrection they are *dead to sin,* which amounts to the same thing. As, in the concluding part of that chapter, he had shown by his exhortations to duty, that, by affirming that they were dead to sin he did not mean that they were exempt from its commission, so, in the concluding part of this chapter, he shows, by detailing his own experience, that he did not mean that by their being dead to the law they were exempt from its violation. In one word, while, by both of these expressions, dead to sin, and dead to the law, he intended to teach that their justification was complete, he proves, by what he says in the concluding parts of both chapters, that their sanctification was incomplete. And as, referring to himself personally, he proves the incompleteness of the *sanctification* of believers, by looking forward to a *future* period of deliverance, saying, 'Who *shall* deliver me?' so, referring to himself personally in the beginning of the 2d verse of the next chapter, he proves the completeness of their *justification*, by speaking of his deliverance in respect to it as *past*, saying, 'The law of the Spirit of life in Christ Jesus *hath* made me free from the law of sin and death.'

The view which the Apostle here gives of his own experience clearly demonstrates that the pain experienced by believers in their internal conflicts is quite compatible with the blessed and consolatory assurance of eternal life. This he also proves in those passages above quoted, 2 Cor. v. 1, ' We *know* that if our earthly house of this tabernacle were dissolved, we have a building of God, an house not made with hands, eternal in the heavens. For in this (tabernacle) we *groan*, earnestly desiring to be clothed upon with our house, which is from heaven.' And in chapter viii. 23, where he says, 'Ourselves also which have the first fruits of the Spirit; even we ourselves groan within ourselves.'

It was, then, to confirm the faith of the disciples, and furnish a living exhibition of their spiritual conflict, that Paul here lays open his own heart, and discloses the working of those two warring principles, which to a greater or less extent contend for the mastery in the bosom of every child of God. Every perversion, then, of this highly important part of the Divine testimony ought to be most strenuously opposed. It is not an insulated passage; it contains the clear development of a great general principle which belongs to the whole of Divine revelation, and is essential to its truth,—a principle of the utmost importance in Christian experience. 'Blessed be God,' says Mr. Romaine, 'for the seventh chapter of the Romans.'

The wisdom discovered in making the present experience of Paul the object of contemplation, ought to awaken in our hearts feelings of the liveliest gratitude. Had we been presented with a spectacle of the internal feelings of one less eminently holy, the effect would have been greatly weakened. But when this Apostle, whose life was spent in labouring for the glory of God ; when he, whose blameless conduct was such as to confound his enemies who sought occasion against him ; when he, who finished his course with joy, having fought a good fight, and kept the faith ; when he, whose conscience enabled him to look back with satisfaction on the past, and forward with joy to the future ; when he, who stood ready to receive the crown of righteousness which, by the eye of faith, he beheld laid up for him in heaven,—when one so favoured, so distinguished, as the great Apostle of the Gentiles, is himself constrained, in turning his eye inward upon the rebellious strivings of his old nature, to cry out, 'O wretched man that I am!'—what a wonderful exhibition do we behold of the malignity of that sin, which has so deeply poisoned and corrupted our original nature, that death itself is needful in order to sever its chains and destroy its power in the soul!

This passage, then, is peculiarly fitted to comfort those who are oppressed with a sense of indwelling sin in the midst of their spiritual conflicts, unknown to all except themselves and the Searcher of hearts. There may be some believers, who, not having examined it with sufficient care, or being misled by false interpretations, mistake its natural and obvious meaning, and fear to apply the words which it contains to Paul as an Apostle. When these shall have viewed this portion of the Divine word in its true light, they will bless God for the instruction and consolation it is calculated to afford; while the whole of the representation, under this aspect, will appear foolishness to all who are Christians only in name, and who never experienced in themselves that internal conflict which the Apostle here describes. It is a conflict from which not one of the people of God, since the fall of the first man, was ever exempted,—a conflict which He alone never experienced who is called 'the Son of the Highest,' of whom, notwithstanding, it has of late been impiously affirmed that He also was subjected to it.

CHAPTER 8
ROMANS 8:1 – 39

THIS chapter presents a glorious display of the power of Divine grace, and of the provision which God has made for the consolation of His people. While the Apostle had proved, in the sixth, that his previous doctrine gave no licence to believers to continue in sin, he had still kept in view his main purpose of establishing their free justification. In the seventh he had prosecuted the same object, declaring that by their marriage with Christ they were delivered from the law as a covenant of life or death, while he vindicated its character, use, and authority. In this chapter, he continues the subject of justification, and resumes that of the believer's assurance of his salvation, of which he had spoken in the fifth, establishing it on new grounds; and from the whole train of his argument from the commencement of the Epistle, he now draws the general conclusion, that to them who are in Christ Jesus there is no condemnation. While this could not have been accomplished by the law, he shows that it had been effected by the incarnation of the Son of God, by whom the law has been fulfilled for all who are one with Him as members of His body. Paul next points out the difference of character between those who, being in their natural state under the law and under sin, are carnally-minded; and those who, being renewed by grace, in whom the law has been fulfilled, are spiritually-minded. The condition of the former is death, that of the latter life and peace. Of these last he proceeds, through the remainder of the chapter, to assert the high privileges and absolute security.

Those who are spiritually-minded have the Spirit of Christ, and possess spiritual life. Although their bodies must return to the dust, they shall be raised up again. They are led by the Spirit; they are the sons of God, and in His service are delivered from a spirit of bondage. They look to Him as their Father; are heirs of God, and joint-heirs with Jesus Christ. To encourage believers to sustain the sufferings to which, while in this world, they are exposed, the most varied and abundant consolations are exhibited. Their salvation is declared to have taken its rise in the eternal counsels of God, by whom, through all its steps, it is carried into effect. Their condemnation, then, is impossible; for who shall condemn those whom God justifieth,—for whom Christ died, and rose, and intercedes? The Apostle concludes by defying the whole universe to separate believers from the love of God in Christ Jesus our Lord. In this manner he follows out, in this chapter, what had been his grand object through all the preceding part of the Epistle.

Ver. 1.—*There is therefore now no condemnation to them which are in Christ Jesus, who walk not after the flesh, but after the Spirit.*

Therefore.—This is an inference from the general strain of the doctrine which the Apostle had been teaching in the preceding part of the Epistle; especially it follows from what he had asserted, in the sixth and seventh chapters, with respect to believers dying with Christ, and consequently being dead to sin and to the law.

Now no condemnation.—This implies that there would have been condemnation to those to whom he wrote, had they remained under the law; but *now*, since they have died with Christ, and thereby given complete satisfaction to the law, both in its penalty and precept, it is not possible that by it they can be condemned. And, to mark the completeness of this exemption, he says, there is now *no* condemnation to them; the reason of which he fully explains in the 2d, 3d, and 4th verses. This *now*, then, distinguishes two conditions of a man, namely, his condition under the law, and his condition under grace,—that is, his natural and his supernatural conditions. For by nature we are children of wrath, but now God has rendered us accepted in the Beloved. Being now in Christ, we are not under the curse of the law, because He has borne it for us. In the moment in which we believed in Him, we were redeemed from its curse; we entered into another covenant, in which there is nothing but grace and pardon. That there is now no condemnation to them that are in Him is according to our Lord's declaration, ' Verily, verily, I say unto you, he that heareth My word, and believeth on Him that sent Me, hath everlasting life, and shall not come into condemnation.' It is often remarked that the Apostle does not say that there is in them which are in Christ Jesus neither matter of accusation nor cause of condemnation; and yet this is all included in what he does say. In themselves there is much indeed for both, but here they are viewed exclusively in Jesus Christ. Afterwards, in express terms, he denies that they can be either accused or condemned—which they might be, were there any ground for either. All that was condemnable in them, which was sin, has been condemned in their Surety, as is shown in the 3d verse.

To them.—The Apostle, discoursing in the preceding chapter of the remainder of sin in believers, speaks of himself in his own person, in

order to show that the highest advances in grace do not exempt from the
internal warfare which he there describes. But in this verse he changes
the number, and does not say, there is no condemnation to *me*, but to
them, who are in Christ Jesus. This was proper, lest believers, who are
often disposed to deprive themselves of those consolations which the
Scriptures present, and prone either to despair or to presume on account
of their own righteousness, should say that such a declaration was right
and suitable in an Apostle, who enjoyed peculiar privileges, but it did
not follow that they could say of themselves, ' There is for us no condemnation.' Paul therefore here changes the expression, and speaks
in general terms, to show that he ascribes nothing peculiar to himself,
but that he refers to the general condition of believers, in order that
each of them might apply to himself the fruit of this consideration. In
the seventh chapter he had spoken of himself to prove that the holiest
among men have reason to humble themselves before God, and to
acknowledge that, if God should view them in themselves, they would be
found to be a body of death,—that is to say, guilty of eternal death. But
here he does not speak in his own person, in order that we may not
doubt that he refers to the condition of believers in general. Again, in
the 4th verse, he speaks of the righteousness of the law being fulfilled in
us ; thus showing that the unspeakable blessing of deliverance from condemnation equally belongs to all the people of God. In the 2d verse,
for an obvious and important reason, as we shall presently see, he reverts
again to the singular number, and says, ' hath made *me* free.' This
manner of expressing himself ought tó be particularly noted ; for we
are certain that, in the word of God, nothing of this kind occurs without a purpose.

Which are in Christ Jesus.—To be in Christ Jesus is to be one with
Him, as united to Him by faith. Those and those only who are thus
one with Him are the persons to whom there is no condemnation. All
who are not in Christ Jesus are under the law and its curse. It is not
here said that Christ is with His people, or at their right hand, but that
they are *in* Him, in order that they may know that, being in Him, they
have nothing to fear ; for what evil can reach those who are one with
the Son of God? This union is represented in Scripture by various
terms and by many similitudes ; its efficacy and power are shown, when
it is said, ' He that is joined to the Lord is one Spirit.' It is in virtue of
this union that the sufferings and obedience of Christ are imputed to His
people, they being one with Him who fulfilled the law, and satisfied the
justice of God. Their union with Him is the source of that spiritual life
by which they are quickened together with Christ, and from which they
derive their justification, their sanctification, and consolation. ' It is
impossible,' Luther remarks, ' for a man to be a Christian without having
Christ, and if he has Christ, he has at the same time all that is in Christ.
What gives peace to the conscience is, that by faith our sins are no more
ours, but Christ's, upon whom God hath laid them all ; and that, on the
other hand, all Christ's righteousness is ours, to whom God hath given it.
Christ lays His hand upon us, and we are healed. He casts His mantle
upon us, and we are clothed ; for He is the glorious Saviour, blessed for

ever.' This union was typified under the law in the person of the high
priest, who carried on his breast the twelve stones, on which were engraven the names of the twelve tribes of the children of Israel; so that,
when he appeared before God, all the people appeared in him, thus
showing that all believers are before God *in* Jesus Christ, their great
High Priest. They are all delivered from condemnation, as being one
body with Christ. As the debts of a wife must be discharged by her
husband, and as, by her marriage, all her previous obligations are at once
transferred to him, so the believer, being married to Christ, is no longer
exposed to the curse of the law. All its demands have been met and
satisfied by His covenant Head, with whom, as the wife is one with the
husband, so he is one.

It is by the human nature of Jesus Christ that we enjoy union with
His Divine nature, and that He is Emmanuel, God with us. His humanity
is the medium by which His divinity communicates itself with all its
graces. Under the former dispensation, God communicated with His
people through the ark of the covenant, which was a type of the human
nature of Jesus Christ, in order to show us that by it we have union with
the whole of His person. And by union with the person of Jesus Christ
we obtain communion with the Father. ' At that day ye shall know that
I am in My Father, and you in Me, and I in you.'

It is not by nature that we enjoy this union, since by nature we are
'children of wrath' and 'without Christ.' The means by which we are
united to Christ are on His part by His Spirit, and on our part by faith.
He communicates His Spirit to us, which is as the soul that unites all the
members of the body with the head, so that 'he who is joined unto the
Lord is one Spirit.' On our part we receive Jesus Christ by faith produced in us by His Spirit, in order that we may reciprocally receive Him
in our hearts. He dwells in our hearts by faith; and thus we learn what
is meant when it is said we are justified by faith, not as being a work, or
anything meritorious, but as the medium through which His righteousness, and all the graces and blessings that are in Jesus Christ, are communicated to our souls.

' Faith,' says Luther, ' unites the soul with Christ as a spouse with her
husband. Everything which Christ has, becomes the property of the
believing soul: everything which the soul has, becomes the property of
Christ. Christ possesses all blessings and eternal life: they are thenceforward the property of the soul. The soul has all its iniquities and
sins: they become thenceforward the property of Christ. It is then that
a blessed exchange commences: Christ who is both God and man, Christ
who has never sinned, and whose holiness is perfect, Christ the Almighty
and Eternal, taking to Himself, by His nuptial ring of *faith*, all the sins of
the believer, those sins are lost and abolished in Him; for no sins dwell
before His infinite righteousness. Thus, by faith, the believer's soul is
delivered from sins, and clothed with the eternal righteousness of her
bridegroom Christ. O happy union! The rich, the noble, the holy Bridegroom takes in marriage his poor, guilty, and despised spouse, delivers
her from every evil, and enriches her with the most precious blessings.
Christ, a King and a Priest, shares this honour and glory with all

Christians. The Christian is a king, and consequently possesses all things; he is a priest, and consequently possesses God; and it is faith, not works, which brings him all this honour. A Christian is free from all things, above all things, faith giving him richly all things.'

On account of this union, all believers bear the name of Christ, being that of their Head. 'For as the body is one, and hath many members, and all the members of that one body being many, are one body; so also is Christ. For by one Spirit are we all baptized into one body,' 1 Cor. xii. 13. 'We are members of His body, of His flesh, and of His bones,' Eph. v. 30. And in this Epistle to the Ephesians, the Apostle denominates the Church not only the body of Jesus Christ, but even His fulness. God 'gave Him to be the Head over all things to the Church, which is His body, the fulness of Him that filleth all in all,' Eph. i. 22. He thus shows that this union with Jesus Christ is such that He who filleth all things would consider Himself without His people to be imperfect and incomplete.

Who walk not after (according to) *the flesh, but after* (according to) *the Spirit.*—These words not being found in all the manuscripts, are considered by some as spurious. But they connect perfectly well with the preceding clause of the verse, as characterizing those who are in Christ Jesus. In no respect, however, do they assign the cause of exemption from condemnation to them who are in Christ. The Apostle does not say, *because* they do not walk, but *who* walk, not after the flesh, but after the Spirit. There is an essential difference between asserting the character of those who are freed from condemnation, and declaring the cause of their being delivered from it. These words refer to the proof of our justification, which proceeds from the efficacy of the Holy Spirit in our hearts, who applies the merit of the blood of Jesus, and imparts a new and eternal life, opposed to sin and corruption, which the Scriptures call death in sin, for the minding of the flesh is death, but the minding of the Spirit is life. In this way, then, we may be assured that we are in Christ Jesus, and that there is no condemnation to us, if we experience the effects of His Spirit in our hearts causing us to walk in holiness. For the life which Jesus Christ has merited for us on the cross, consists not only in the remission of sins, which is a removal of what is evil, but also in the communication of what is good, namely, in our bearing the image of God. The same words as in the clause before us occur again in verse 4th, in which their genuineness is not disputed, where their full import shall be considered.

Ver. 2.—*For the law of the Spirit of life in Christ Jesus hath made me free from the law of sin and death.*

This verse, as is evident by the particle *for*, is connected with the preceding. It connects, however, with the first part of that verse, where the great truth of which it is explanatory is announced, assigning the reason why there is no condemnation to them who are in Christ Jesus; which is continued to the middle of the 4th verse, in the latter part of which the last clause of the first is repeated. On the supposition of that clause being genuine, the Apostle follows here the same method as in the second chapter of this Epistle, where the 14th verse connects with the first part of the 12th. Many, by the phrase 'law of the Spirit of life,' understand the commanding influence of the Holy Spirit in the *sanctification* of the believers to be intended, and by 'the law of sin and death,' the corrupt principle, or power of sin in them, as in chapter vii. 23 and 25. But these explanations do not suit the context. The main proposition contained in the preceding verse is, that to them who are in Christ Jesus there is no *condemnation*. But why is there no condemnation? Is it because they are sanctified? No; but because by their union with Christ they have been freed from the law and its curse, as the Apostle had shown in the preceding chapter, verse 4th. Besides, it is not true that believers are delivered from the law of sin that is in them as respects their sanctification, which would contradict what Paul had just before said of the Christian's internal warfare with sin, as exhibited in his own experience, to which deliverance he looked forward, but which he had not yet obtained. It is further to be observed, that the above explanations do not accord with the two following verses, which point out the ground of that freedom from condemnation which is here asserted, being explanatory of the verse before us, declaring that sin has been punished in Christ, and that the righteousness which the law demands has been fulfilled by Him in those who belong to Him.

Law of the Spirit.—Various significations belong to the term law, according to the connection in which it stands, and to which it is applied. In the conclusion of the preceding chapter, and in the verse before us, where it occurs twice, it is employed in three different senses. In the first of these it is denominated the 'law of sin,' namely, the strength of corruption acting with the force of a law. In the end of the verse before us, where the term 'death' is added to that of sin, it imports the moral law, the transgression of which is sin, and the consequence death, and is employed in the same sense in the two following verses. To the law of the spirit of life belongs a different meaning, signifying the power of the Holy Spirit, by which He unites the soul to Christ, in whose righteousness, as being thus one with Him, it therefore partakes, and is consequently justified. This law is the Gospel, whereof the Holy Ghost is the author, being the authoritative rule and the instrument by which He acts in the plan of salvation. It is the medium through which He promulgates Divine testimony, and His commands to receive that testimony, and exerts His power to produce this effect; by which, also, He quickens and enlightens those in whom He dwells, convinces them of their sin and of the righteousness of Christ, and testifies of the almighty Saviour, whom God hath set forth to be a propitiation through faith in His blood. The Gospel may thus be properly denominated the *law*, or power of the Holy Spirit, because, as a law has authority and binds to obedience, so the Gospel bears the stamp of Divine authority to which, in all that it reveals, we are bound to 'submit,' ch. x. 3. It requires the obedience of faith, and for this end is to be made known to all nations, ch. i. 5, xvi. 26; and when men refuse this submission, it is said that they have not 'obeyed the Gospel,' ch. x. 16. Although, therefore, the Gospel is proclaimed as a grace, it is a grace accompanied with authority, which God commands to be received. Accordingly it is expressly called a 'law,' Isa. ii. 3; Mic. iv. 2. 'Out of Zion shall go forth the law, and the word of the Lord from Jerusalem.' In the Book of Psalms it is again and again called 'the law;' and in Psalm cx. 2, referring to the power exerted by its means, it is said, 'The Lord shall send the rod of thy strength out of Zion,' that is, the Gospel. 'Rule Thou in the midst of Thine enemies,' namely, by Thine almighty power. The Gospel, then, is the law of the Spirit by which He rules, and the rod of His strength, or His power, by which He effects our salvation, just as, in chapter i. 16, it is denominated 'the *power of God* unto salvation.' The Gospel is itself called 'the Spirit,' as being ministered by the Holy Spirit, 2 Cor. iii. 8.

The Gospel is the law of the Spirit *of life*, the ministration of which, being committed to the Apostles, 'giveth life,' in opposition to the 'letter,' or old covenant that *killeth*, 2 Cor. iii. 6. 'It is the Spirit that quickeneth,' John vi. 63, as it is said, 'I shall put My Spirit in you, and ye shall live,' Ezek. xxxvii. 14. In the First Epistle to the Corinthians, xv. 45, the Apostle speaks of two sources of life. He says, 'The first man Adam was made a living soul, the last Adam was made a quickening spirit.' By the living soul is meant the principle of natural life which we derive from Adam by natural generation. The quickening spirit refers to the heavenly and supernatural life communicated by the Holy Spirit from Jesus Christ. The reason of the comparison is, that as Adam, receiving a living soul, his body was made alive; in like manner, believers, receiving in their souls the Spirit of Christ, receive a new life. It is not meant that the Spirit of Christ is not also the author of natural life, Job xxxiii. 4. Jesus Christ is the life itself, and the source of life to all creatures. But here the life referred to is that life which we receive through the Gospel, as the law or power of the Spirit of life in Christ Jesus, which the Apostle calls 'the life of God,' Eph. iv. 18.

The law of the Spirit of life *in Christ Jesus.*—Jesus Christ is set before us in two aspects, namely, as God, and as Mediator. As God, the Spirit of life resides essentially in Him; but as Mediator, and having in that character satisfied the justice of God by His death, the Spirit of life has been given to Him to be communicated to all who are one with Him. On this account the Spirit was not given in His fulness, John vii. 39, till Jesus Christ as Mediator had entered into heaven, to appear in the heavenly sanctuary with His blood, when the Father, solemnly receiving His satisfaction, gave this testimony of His acceptance, in pouring out the abundance of the Spirit on His people. Jesus Christ accordingly says, 'It is expedient for you that I go away, for if I go not away, the Comforter will not come unto you; but if I depart, I will send Him unto you,' John xvi. 7. And the Apostle declares that 'God hath blessed us with all spiritual blessings in heavenly places in Christ,' Eph. i. 3. He says, 'spiritual blessings,' because he speaks of the graces of the Holy Spirit. He says, 'in Christ,' because it is through the Mediator, and in His communion, that our spiritual life and those graces are bestowed on us. He adds, 'in heavenly places,' because, as anciently the high priest entered the sanctuary with the blood of the sacrifice, in order that God, in accepting that blood, might bestow His blessing on the people; in like manner, Jesus Christ, our great High Priest, has entered the heavenly sanctuary, that, being accepted, He should, as Mediator, and so receiving the Holy Spirit, be the source of life, even of that spiritual and eternal life to which He rose from the dead, and of all grace, to communicate it to His Church. This is what His forerunner John teaches when he says that 'God giveth not the Spirit by measure unto Him,' and is the reason why it is said that He was 'full of grace and truth,' and that 'of His fulness we have all received, and grace for grace.' The Apostle John, too, speaks of the anointing which believers have received from Jesus Christ; for as the oil was poured on the head of the high priest, and ran down to the skirts of his garments, in like manner Jesus Christ has been anointed with the Holy Spirit, as He says, 'The Spirit of the Lord is upon me, because He hath anointed Me;' and this anointing was to be poured out on all His body, which is the Church.

That the Spirit of life, then, is in Jesus Christ, not only as God, but also as Mediator, is a ground of the most unspeakable consolation. It might be in Him as God, without being communicated to men; but, as the Head of His people, it must be diffused through them as His members, who are thus complete in Him. Dost thou feel in thyself the sentence of death?—listen, then, to the testimony of the Scriptures concerning Him. 'This is the record, that God hath given to us eternal life; and this life is in His Son.' 'I am come that they might have life.' He that believeth in Me, though he were dead, yet shall he live; and whosoever liveth and believeth in Me, shall never die.' 'Because I live, ye shall live also.' 'I am that bread of life; he that eateth of this bread shall never die.' 'I am the resurrection and the life.' 'This life, then, is in Jesus Christ, and is communicated to believers by the Holy Spirit, by whom they are united to Christ, and from whom it is derived to all who through the law of the Spirit of life are in Him. It is on this account that, in the passage above quoted, 1 Cor. xv. 45, Jesus Christ, as Mediator, is said to be made a quickening spirit. In obtaining this life, the believer receives his justification, the opposite of condemnation, which without this life cannot subsist, and from which it cannot be separated.

Law of sin and death.—In the preceding chapter, verses 23 and 25, 'the law of sin,' which the Apostle says he served with the flesh, signifies, as has been observed, the powerful corrupt principle in the heart, operating with the force of a law. But in the former part of the same chapter, the word 'law' is employed to denote the moral law. It is there spoken of as the law of God, which, though holy, and just, and good, is to fallen man the occasion both of sin and death; and, accordingly, in the point of view in which the Apostle is here regarding it, it is called 'the law of sin and death.' It may be called the law of *sin*, since without it sin could not exist; for 'sin is the transgression of the law,' 1 John iii. 4; but 'where no law is, there is no transgression,' and 'sin is not imputed when there is no law,' Rom. v. 13. 'The motions of sin are by the law,' Rom. vii. 5; and 'the strength of sin is the law,' 1 Cor. xv. 56. 'By the commandment sin becomes exceeding sinful,' Rom. vii. 13. 'The law entered that the offence might abound,' Rom. v. 20. As, therefore, sin could have no existence but by the law, and as the law is the strength of sin, and makes it to abound, the law may, as here, be properly denominated 'the law of sin.'

The holy law may also be called the law of *death*. It threatens with death in case of disobedience, and on account of transgression adjudges to death. 'The commandment,' says the Apostle, 'which was ordained to life, I found to be unto death.' It brings the sinner under the penalty of death. 'In the day thou eatest thereof thou shalt surely die.' The law 'killeth;' and the ministration of the law, written and engraved on stones, was death, 2 Cor. iii. 6, 7. By the law 'death reigned from Adam to Moses,' Rom. v. 14; and the wages of sin, which is the transgression of the law, is death. Since, then, the law of God, which, though it commands holiness, gives the knowledge of sin, and the breach of it is death, and since, without the law, there could neither be sin nor death, it may, without arguing the smallest disrespect or disparagement to the holy law, be called *the law of sin and death*. That it is so denominated in the verse before us, appears from the repetition of the term law in the beginning of the following verse, evidently in connection with that in the end of this verse, where the reference is clearly to the moral law, namely, the law which had been spoken of from the 4th to the 13th verse of the foregoing chapter, which the Apostle had there shown, as he asserts in verse 3 of this chapter, could not set free from sin and death. Besides, that by the law of sin and death is here meant the moral law, appears unquestionable, when it is considered that if the same meaning be attached to it as belongs to the phrase 'the law of sin' in the conclusion of the preceding chapter, the Apostle must be held to have contradicted himself. For in that case he bitterly laments his being under the power of the law of sin, and speaks only of his hope of future deliverance; and here, in the same breath, he unqualifiedly asserts his freedom from it. Notwithstanding, then, the similarity of these two expressions, and their juxtaposition, it is impossible, without charging a contradiction on the Apostle, to assert that he attached the same meaning in both places to the word law, which in different connections is capable of significations quite distinct.

Hath made me free.—The reason why there is no condemnation to them which are in Christ Jesus is, that being in Him they have been made free from the law of sin and death, all its requirements having been fulfilled by Him in them, as is affirmed in verse 4. This freedom is likewise declared in 2 Cor. iii. 17, in which passage it is said, 'Where the Spirit of the Lord is, there is liberty.' 'If the Son therefore shall make you free, ye shall be free indeed.'

Me free.—Here it is to be observed that the Apostle, instead of speaking generally of believers, as he does in the first and fourth verses, saying 'them' and 'us,' changes, as has been above remarked, the mode of expression, and refers to himself personally—'hath made *me* free.' A very striking contrast is thus pointed out between his declaration in the 24th verse of the preceding chapter, and that contained in the verse before us. There, he is speaking of the *power* of sin, which operates in believers as long as they are in this world. Here, in reference to condemnation, he is speaking of the *guilt* of sin, from which they are perfectly freed the moment they are united to the Saviour. In the former case, therefore, where he speaks respecting sanctification, he refers in verse 24th to his deliverance as future, and exclaims, 'Who *shall* deliver me?' In reference to the latter, in which he is treating of justification, he speaks of his deliverance as already obtained, and affirms, He '*hath* made me free.'

The following explanation of the verse before us is given in the Westminster Confession of Faith. 'Albeit the Apostle himself (brought in here for example's cause), and all other true believers in Christ, be by nature under the law of sin and death, or under the covenant of works (called the law of sin and death, because it bindeth sin and death upon us, till Christ set us free); yet the law of the Spirit of Christ Jesus, or the covenant of grace (so called because it doth enable and quicken a man to a spiritual life through Christ), doth set the Apostle, and all true believers, free from the covenant of works, or the law of sin and death; so that every man may say with him, 'The law of the Spirit of life,' or the covenant of grace, hath made me free from the law of sin and death, or covenant of works,' ed. 1773, p. 434.

Every believer should take to himself all the consolation which this verse contains, and with Paul he may with confidence say, 'The law of the Spirit of life in Christ Jesus hath made *me* free from the law of sin and death.' Many, however, will say, We should be happy indeed if we could, with Paul, adopt this language; but what assurance can we have of being free from condemnation, and of being in Christ Jesus, since the flesh is so strong in us and the spirit so weak,—since we are still prone to so many sins, and subject to so many defects? Assuredly if a man is satisfied in sinning and following carnal desires, and is not desirous to turn from these ways, he has no ground to conclude that he is freed from condemnation, for such is not the state of any believer. But if, on the other hand, he groans on account of his sins, crying out with the Apostle, 'O wretched man that I am;' if they displease him, if he have a godly sadness on account of having committed them, and earnestly prays to God to be delivered from them, he may be assured of his salvation. For the Christian is not one who is without sin and evil inclinations, as is abundantly shown in the preceding chapters; but one who resists and combats against them, and returns to God by repentance. His groans on account of his sins, and his meditating on the word of God,—his earnest endeavours to be holy and to grow in grace, although not with all the success he desires,—are proofs of his regeneration. For if he were dead in his sins, he would not be affected on account of them, nor would he resist them. And whoever resists the flesh by the Spirit of God, will in the end obtain the victory, for the Holy Spirit in us is greater in goodness and power than all that is against us,—Satan, and the world, and the flesh. All this should inspire the believer with courage to fight the good fight of faith, and to follow the movements of the blessed Spirit, and the Lord will say to his soul, 'I am thy salvation,' Ps. xxxv. 3; 'My grace is sufficient for thee, for My strength is made perfect in weakness,' 2 Cor. xii. 9; and he, on the other hand, may say with confidence, 'O my soul, thou hast said unto the Lord, Thou art my Lord,' Ps. xvi. 2.

Ver. 3.—*For what the law could not do, in that it was weak through the flesh, God sending His own Son in the likeness of sinful flesh, and for sin condemned sin in the flesh:*

This verse confirms the interpretation that has been given of the preceding, with which it stands connected. It is introduced to explain what is said in the two preceding verses. Both this and the following verse are illustrations of that great truth, that to the believer in Christ there is no condemnation. There are here three principal considerations: namely, the misery of our natural condition; the mercy of God in the incarnation of His Son; and the effect of sending Him into the world, which is our redemption. Under these three heads, the Apostle removes the difficulties that might present themselves from the supposition that, on account of some imperfection in the law, it could not justify. In answer to this, it is here shown that the imperfection is not in the law, but in us. The law could justify those who fulfilled it, as it is said, 'The man that doeth them shall live in them;' but the corruption of human nature renders this impossible. And as it might be objected that the law, which subjects every transgressor to death, is violated by the freedom from it which we obtain by the death of Jesus Christ, the Apostle shows that the punishment it demands was inflicted upon Him. Hence the first proposition, that there is no condemnation to them which are in Christ Jesus, is established; and in the following verse it is added, that the law, which we were required to fulfil, has by Him been fulfilled in us. In this view, the justice of God, which naturally terrifies man, inspires us with confidence. For if God is just, will He exact double payment and satisfaction? Will He condemn those for whom the Surety has borne the condemnation? No; 'He is faithful and just to forgive us our sins,' for 'the blood of Jesus Christ His Son cleanseth us from all sin.'

For what the law could not do, in that it was weak through the flesh.— The law here meant is the same as that spoken of in the end of the preceding verse, namely, the moral law, under which our first parents in the state of innocence were placed, and which was afterwards promulgated by the ministry of Moses. This law was ordained to life, ch. vii. 10,—that is, to justify man, if he had remained in innocence; but by his sinning it condemns him, as the Apostle adds, 'I found it to be unto death;' so that the law, the breach of which constitutes sin, and which on account of this awards death, is now unable to justify, but powerful to condemn.

This verse proves that the method which God takes to justify the sinner is entirely consistent with law and justice. First, the Apostle shows the necessity of this method. *For what the law could not do, in that it was weak through the flesh.*—What is it that the law could not do? It could not justify. Mr. Frazer, however, says that the reason of this alleged weakness of the law forbids this interpretation. 'That,' says he, ' is not the reason why the law cannot justify.' But surely it is the very reason why the law cannot justify. Were it not for the weakness of the flesh, or the corruption and sinfulness of man, the law could justify. 'But,' he continues, ' to turn the disability of the law to justify the sinner upon the corruption of his nature, as the text would do, according to the interpretation I am considering, would imply something by no means consistent with the Apostle's clear doctrine, viz., that after a person had transgressed he might be justified, even by the law, for returning to his duty, and for his subsequent righteousness, if the weakness and poverty of his nature, called the *flesh*, did not disable him from doing his duty; which how contrary to Scripture doctrine I need not stay to prove, the thing is so clear.' But did this acute and worthy author overlook what our Lord says to the rich young man, ' If thou wilt enter into life, keep the commandments ' ? In fact, however, the commandments could not be kept unless every commandment that respects man is obeyed ; therefore the commandment in the garden of Eden is included; because, being guilty of breaking it, no man can be said to have obeyed God as he ought. The weakness of the flesh includes everything that befell us by the fall. Every man is as truly accountable for that first sin of Adam as he is for his own personal sins ; and therefore, as long as he is under condemnation for that sin, he cannot be said to keep the commandments. ' By the law is the knowledge of sin.' It is the test of men being sinners. If it were kept, this would prove that we were not sinners. It entered, that the offence might abound ; and the Lord applied this test for the young man's conviction. Yet what he said was truth : if the young man had kept the commandments, he would, as a holy creature, have enjoyed life ; he would not have been a sinner. But he was so ignorant as to say he had kept them all. The Lord replied, ' One thing thou lackest,' and said, 'Follow Me.' If he had really kept the commandments, he would have had no need of a Saviour; but he was a sinner, and Christ informed him of the only way of salvation. The law could not give life to one by whom it was forfeited.

The weakness of the law through the flesh Mr. Stuart explains thus: ' Because, through the strength of our carnal inclinations and desires, it was unable to regulate our lives, so that we should be perfect or actually free from sin.' But as Christ is said to do what the law through this weakness could not do, this interpretation supposes that Christ has enabled us to regulate our lives so as to be entirely free from sin. Nothing can be more obvious than that the weakness of the law through the flesh is its inability to justify, as it would have done, had not sin entered. The weakness of the law for justification is no disparagement to it. It was never designed to save a *sinner*. How could it be supposed that a creature who had apostatized, and was a rebel against God, could re-establish himself in the Divine favour ? Yet such re-establishment, in order to the enjoyment of the favour of God, was necessary. A creature in such circumstances could only be re-established by God Himself, and that by an act of free and sovereign mercy, compatible with His justice and truth, as well as with the essential glory of His character. It is also impossible that mercy could be extended in any other way than that which the Gospel reveals. How could the justice of God be satisfied but by an atonement of infinite value, to meet the infinite evil of sin ? And how could such an atonement be made for man, but by one who was at the same time both God and man—the infinite God manifest in human nature ? This was the remedy which God provided ; therefore it was the best remedy. It was the highest possible remedy ; therefore there could be no other. It would be inconsistent with infinite wisdom to employ means greater than are necessary in order to accomplish an end. The law was strong to perform its own office,—that is, to justify all by whom it was perfectly obeyed. Its weakness was through the flesh,—that is, the guilt and corruption of our nature. The weakness is not in the law ; it is in man.

God sending His own Son.—God sent His Son to do that which the law could not do. He sent Him in consequence of His great love to His people, 1 John iv. 9 ; and as the accomplishment of His Divine purpose, Acts iv. 28. The object, then, of Christ's mission was not merely that of a messenger or witness ; it was to effect the salvation of guilty sinners in the way of righteousness. He did what the law could not do. The law could justify those only by whom it was observed ; but it could not justify or save those who should violate even the least of its commands. But Christ Jesus both justifies and saves the ungodly.

His own Son.—Christ was God's own Son in the literal sense. It is on this supposition only that the sending of Him is a manifestation of infinite love to men. There is no more appearance of any figurative meaning in the use of this appellation, when ascribed to Jesus Christ, than there is when Isaac is called the son of Abraham. He is here emphatically called not only the Son of God, but the Son of Himself, or His own Son—His very Son. Whether Christ's sonship is a relation in Godhead, or a figurative sonship, has been much disputed. Many who hold the Godhead of Christ explain the passages that assert His sonship as referring to His incarnation. That the phrase *Son of God* imports the Divine nature of Jesus Christ, there can be no doubt, John v. 18 (see pp. 21–25) ; and that it relates not merely to His incarnation, but to His eternal relation to the Father, appears the obvious testimony of Scripture. No reasoning from the import of the relation among men can form a valid objection to this view.

Adam is called the son of God because he was created by the immediate exercise of Divine power. The angels are called the sons of God on account of their creation, and the greatness of their condition ; believers, by the right of their adoption and regeneration ; but none except the Messiah is called the Only-begotten of the Father. These words, ' I have begotten Thee,' are indeed applied to Jesus Christ, Acts xiii. 33, not with respect to His eternal generation, but to His resurrection and establishment in the priesthood ; and import that He was thus made known to be the Son of God, as it is said, Rom. i. 4, that He was declared to be the Son of God with power, by His resurrection from the dead. The exaltation of Jesus Christ, whether in His office of Mediator or in sovereign glory, is the authoritative declaration of the Father that He was His Son, His only-begotten Son ; and this is signified in the second Psalm. There, the elevation of Jesus Christ to the sovereign dominion of the world is spoken of. ' I have set My King upon My holy hill of Zion.' It is as to the act of His elevation that this declaration is made. ' I will declare the decree : The Lord hath said unto Me, Thou art My Son ; this day have I begotten Thee.' Thus, according to the usual style of Scripture, things are said to be done when they are declared or publicly manifested. When it is said, 'This day have I begotten Thee, the eternal dignity of the Saviour, which had been before concealed, was brought to light and fully discovered.

In the likeness of sinful flesh.—Jesus Christ was sent, not in the likeness of flesh, but in the flesh. He was sent, however, not in sinful flesh, but in the *likeness* of sinful flesh. Nothing can more clearly prove that the Lord Jesus Christ, though He assumed our nature, took it without taint of sin or corruption. To His perfect holiness the Scriptures bear the fullest testimony. 'He knew no sin.' 'The prince of this world cometh and hath nothing in Me.' He was 'holy, harmless, undefiled, separate from sinners.' His absolute freedom from sin was indispensable. As God becoming manifest in the flesh, He could not unite Himself to a nature tainted with the smallest impurity. He was conceived by the power of the Holy Ghost, and did not spring from Adam by ordinary generation; and, not belonging to his covenant, had no part in his sin. His freedom from sin, original and actual, was necessary, in order that He should be offered as 'a Lamb without blemish and without spot,' so that He might be the truth of His types, the legal sacrifices, which it was expressly provided should be free from all blemish; thus distinctly indicating this transcendent characteristic of Him who was to be the one great sacrifice.

If the flesh of Jesus Christ was the likeness of sinful flesh, there must be a difference between the appearance of sinful flesh and our nature, or flesh in its original state when Adam was created. Christ, then, was not made in the likeness of the flesh of man before sin entered the world, but in the likeness of his fallen flesh. Though He had no corruption in His nature, yet He had all the sinless infirmities of our flesh. The person of man, in his present state, may be greatly different from what it was when Adam came from the hand of his Creator. Our bodies, as they are at present, are called 'the bodies of our humiliation,' Phil. iii. 21. Jesus Christ was made in man's present likeness. Tradition speaks of the beauty of His person when on earth; but this is the wisdom of man. The Scriptures nowhere represent Christ in His manhood as distinguished by personal beauty. No observation of this kind, proceeding either from His friends or enemies, is recorded in the Gospels.

And for sin.—The reason of the mission of our Lord Jesus Christ into the world—of His incarnation and humiliation—was the abolition of sin, its destruction, both as to its guilt and power. The same expression occurs, 1 Pet. iii. 18, 'Christ also hath once suffered *for sins*, the just for the unjust, that He might bring us to God.' It is sin that is the cause of separation from God; and by its removal reconciliation is made, and peace restored.

Condemned sin in the flesh.—Here, by the flesh is meant, not the body of Jesus Christ only, but His human nature. In this sense the word flesh is used where it is said, 'the Word was made flesh,'—that is to say, was made man, and took our nature, composed of body and soul. The nature and the person who suffered must also be distinguished. Respecting the person, it is Jesus Christ, God and man; as to the nature in which He suffered, it is in the flesh. Of the person we can say that it is

God, as the Apostle says that God hath purchased the Church with His own blood, and consequently that His suffering was of infinite value, since it is that of an infinite person ; and this is the more evident, since Jesus Christ is Mediator in both His natures, and not in His human nature only. For if this were so, His suffering would be finite, since His human nature, in which alone He could suffer, by which He offered His sacrifice, was in itself only finite ; and if He had been Mediator only as to His human nature—which, however, could not be, as He represents both God and man—He could not have been the Mediator of the Old Testament, when He had not taken the human nature. And as it is necessary that, in regard to His person, we should consider Jesus Christ suffering, it is also necessary that we consider that it was in the flesh that He suffered,—that is to say, in our nature, which He took and joined personally to the Divine nature. In this we may admire the wisdom of God, who caused sin to be punished and destroyed in the human nature, in which it had been committed.

Condemned sin.—Condemnation is here taken for the punishment of sin. God punished sin in Christ's human nature. This is the method that God took to justify sinners. It was God who, by His determinate counsel and foreknowledge, Acts ii. 23, punished sin by inflicting those sufferings on Christ of which men were only the instruments. Sin had corrupted the flesh of man, and in that very flesh it was condemned. The guilt and punishment of sin are eminently seen in the death of Christ. Nowhere else is sin so completely judged and condemned. Not even in hell are its guilt and demerits so fully manifested. What must be its demerit, if it could be atoned for by nothing but the death of the Son of God? and what can afford clearer evidence of God's determination to punish sin to the utmost extent of its demerit, than that He thus punished it even when laid on the head of His only-begotten Son.

In all this we see the Father assuming the place of judge against His Son, in order to become the Father of those who were His enemies. The Father condemns the Son of His love, that He may absolve the children of wrath. If we inquire into the cause that moved God to save us by such means, what can we say, but that it proceeded from His incomprehensible wisdom, His ineffable goodness, and the unfathomable depth of His mercies? For what was there in man that could induce the Creator to act in this manner, since He saw nothing in him, after his rebellion by sin, but what was hateful and offensive? And what was it but His love that passeth knowledge which induced the only-begotten Son of God to take the form of a servant, to humble Himself even to the death of the cross, and to submit to be despised and rejected of men? These are the things into which the angels desire to look.

But besides the love of God, we see the wonderful display of His justice in condemning sin in His Son, rather than allowing it to go unpunished. In this assuredly the work of redemption surpasses that of creation. In creation God had made nothing that was not good, and nothing especially on which He could exercise the rigour of His justice ; but here He punishes our sins to the utmost in Jesus Christ. It may be inquired if, when God condemned sin in His Son, we are to understand this of God the Father, so as to exclude the Son; or if we can say that God the Son also condemned sin in Himself. This can undoubtedly be affirmed; for in the Father and the Son there is only one will and one regard for justice; so that, as it was the will of the Father to require satisfaction for sin from the Son, it was also the will of the Son to humble Himself, and to condemn sin in Himself. We must, however, distinguish between Jesus Christ considered as God, and as our Surety and Mediator. As God, He condemns and punishes sin; as Mediator, He is Himself condemned and punished for sin.

When sin was condemned or punished in the Son of God, to suppose that He felt nothing more than bodily pain, would be to conclude that He had less confidence in God than many martyrs who have gone to death cheerfully, and without fear. The extremity of the pain He suffered when He said in the garden, 'My soul is sorrowful even unto death,' was the sentiment of the wrath of God against sin, from which martyrs felt themselves delivered. For the curse of the law is principally spiritual, namely, privation of communion with God in the sense of His wrath. Jesus Christ, therefore, was made a curse for us, as the Apostle says, Gal. iii. 13, proving it by the declaration, 'Cursed is every one that hangeth on a tree.' For this punishment of the cross was the figure and symbol of the spiritual curse of God. As in His body, then, He suffered this most accursed punishment, so likewise in His soul He suffered those pains that are most insupportable, such as are suffered by those finally condemned. But that was only for a short time, the infinity of His person rendering that suffering equivalent to that of an infinity of time. Such, then, was the grief which He experienced when on the cross He cried, 'My God, My God, why hast Thou forsaken Me?' What forsaking was this, unless that for a time God left Him to feel the weight of His indignation against sin? This feeling is the sovereign evil of the soul, in which consists the griefs of eternal death; as, on the other hand, the sovereign good of the soul, and that in which the happiness of eternal life consists, is to enjoy gracious communion with God.

In this verse we see the ground of the Apostle's declaration, that there is now no condemnation to them which are in Christ Jesus, because their sin was punished in Him. This is according to numerous other passages in Scripture, as, Isa. liii. 4–6; Gal. iii. 13; 1 Pet. ii. 24; Rev. v. 9; and, as it is said in 1 Tim. ii. 6, 'who gave Himself a ransom for all.' For our sins are debts of which the payment and the satisfaction for them is their punishment—a payment without which we were held captives under the wrath and by the justice of God. All this shows that sin was really punished in Jesus Christ; and it is evident that, according to the justice and truth of God, such a punishment was necessary in order to our redemption.

Ver. 4.— *That the righteousness of the law might be fulfilled in us, who walk not after the flesh, but after the Spirit.*

That the righteousness of the law might be fulfilled in us.—God not only sent His Son in the likeness of sinful flesh, that He might punish sin in that nature in which it had been committed, but that all which the law demands might by Him be fulfilled in those who are united to Him; for which purpose He obeyed its precepts as well as fulfilled its penalty. The original word here translated *righteousness* is the same as is rendered judgment or sentence, Rom. i. 32, where, and also in the verse before us, it is in some of the French versions, and in the Dutch annotations, rendered 'right.' It is properly here the right of the law. The right of the law is twofold, being that which belongs to it at all times, or what only belongs to it in the event of sin. The first is obedience to its precepts; the second, subjection to its penalty. The first, or what may be called the proper right of the law, corresponds with its proper end, according to which it was ordained unto life to all who obey it. What it demands beyond its proper or first end, is the fulfilment of its penalty, as cursing all who disobey it. For it is not the first end of the law to curse men, but only what it demands since the entrance of sin. Such is the right of the law. The Gospel does not take away this right; for it does not make void the law, Rom. iii. 31, but establishes it. In those, therefore, who are saved by the Gospel, they being all sinners, both the one and the other of the rights of the law are fulfilled in Christ, who is the end or fulfilling of the law for righteousness to every one that believeth, Rom. x. 4. His people having sinned, He fulfils its right as to them, in suffering the punishment of sin,—namely, the curse of the law, to save them from punishment. And to introduce them into life. He accomplishes its proper or original right, according to which, as it is said, 'the man that doeth them shall live in them.' For if the Gospel establishes the law, it must do so as to its first end, and it must also do so as to its end since the entrance of sin, otherwise the law would, as to those who are saved, rather be abolished than fulfilled by the Gospel. In this way Christ has fully satisfied the law, having fulfilled its righteousness,— all that conformity to it which is its right in every respect, and under every aspect, and as to every state of those who are its subjects. And as His people are in Him, so the law is thus, in all its extent, fulfilled *in them*, which is the very circumstance in which their justification consists. For if they are one body, or one with Him, as the Apostle had been showing, His fulfilment of the law is their fulfilment of it. Such being their communion with Him, that they sit with Him in heavenly places, Eph. ii. 6; and by the same communion His righteousness is their righteousness, 2 Cor. v. 21.

The end, then, of Christ's mission was, that the right of the law might be fulfilled in His people. Here we see the ground on which believers are saved. It is in a way consistent with the law, a way in which all that it has a right to demand is fulfilled in them. The mercy, then, which saves sinners does not interfere with justice. They who are saved by mercy have that very righteousness which the law demands. In Christ they have paid the penalty of their disobedience, and in Christ they have yielded obedience to every precept of the law. This fulfilment of the law cannot signify, as some commentators erroneously explain it, that obedience which believers are enabled to yield by the Holy Spirit in their regenerate state; for it is obvious that this is not the righteousness of the law. The very best of all their actions and thoughts come short of the perfection which the law demands; besides, its penalty would in this way be unfulfilled.

They are indeed sanctified, but their sanctification is far from being com-- mensurate with the claims of the holy law, either as to its penalty or its precept.

Here, then, is solid consolation for the believer in Jesus. For, divested as he is of righteousness in himself, he enjoys the blessedness of having the righteousness of God—the righteousness of his Lord and Saviour— imputed to Him, so that the law which had been broken is fulfilled in him in all its precepts, and in its full penalty.

Hitherto, from the beginning of the 2d verse, the Apostle had been illustrating the truth contained in the first clause of the first verse, namely, that there is no condemnation to them which are in Christ Jesus. He now repeats the last clause of that verse, which he goes on to illustrate to the end of the 8th verse.

Who walk not after (according to) *the flesh, but after* (according to) *the Spirit.*—These words characterize those in whom the righteousness of the law is fulfilled and serve the double purpose of showing that they who are walking according to the principles of the renewed spiritual nature, and according to that covenant of which the Lord Jesus is the spirit, are one with Him, and that none are united to Him who are living after the principles of their corrupt nature, and seeking justification and acceptance with God, by cleaving to the covenant of works. The ex- pression, to 'walk,' is frequently employed in Scripture regarding any particular line of conduct, as when it is said, Acts xxi. 21, 'that they ought not to circumcise their children, neither to walk after the customs;' or it denotes the course of life in which we are proceeding, as in Eph. ii. 2, 'Ye walked according to the course of this world.' In this way, com- paring our life to a journey, in the usual style of Scripture, the Apostle comprehends all our actions under the figure of walking. To walk, then, according to the flesh, is to act agreeably to the principles of corrupt nature. To walk according to the Spirit, means to regulate the conduct according to the influence and dictates of the Holy Spirit, who has given us a new nature, serving God in newness of spirit.

The terms *flesh* and *spirit* have various significations, and are employed in different senses in this chapter. The word flesh is used in a sense either bad or indifferent. Sometimes it means simply human nature, and some- times corrupt human nature, or man in his natural state without the Holy Spirit, and frequently wicked works. At other times it denotes outward services in adherence to the law for justification, Phil. iii. 4. To the word spirit various meanings are likewise attached. It imports either the angelic nature, or the soul of man, or the Holy Spirit, or the renewed image of the Son of God in the soul. In both of these last senses it is employed by our Lord, when, declaring the necessity of regeneration, He says, 'That which is born of the Spirit is spirit.' Sometimes, when opposed to flesh or to *letter*, it is used as equivalent to the new covenant, —'who also hath made us able ministers of the New Testament, not of the letter, but of the *spirit.*'

The expression, walking not according to the flesh, but according to the Spirit, in the verse before us, is generally interpreted as referring ex- clusively to the practice of good or of wicked works. It is supposed that the Apostle is here guarding his doctrine of gratuitous justification from abuse, by excluding all claim to union with Christ, and to exemption from condemnation, where there is not purity of conduct, under the influence of the Holy Spirit. This is undoubtedly a highly important truth, which is to be constantly affirmed and insisted on. Holiness of life and conversation is an inseparable concomitant of union with Christ; for to whom He is made righteousness He is also made sanctification, and they that are Christ's have crucified the flesh with the affections and lusts. Of this the Apostle never loses sight, not indeed in any point of view as the cause of that union, but as its never-failing consequence and concomitant, as he has abundantly proved in the sixth chapter. There are, however, many different paths in the broad way ; that is, many ways of walking after the flesh, all of which lead to destruction. Among these, that of seeking acceptance with God by works of righteousness, either moral or ceremonial, is equally incompatible with union to Christ and freedom from condemnation, as living in the grosser indulgence of wicked works; and this way of going about to establish their own righteousness, by those who profess to have received the Gospel, and who have even a zeal of God, ch. x. 2, is probably that by which the greater number of them are deceived. There is the greatest danger lest the fleshly wisdom, under the notion of a zeal for God and of regard for the interests of virtue, should set men on the painful endeavour of working out their salvation, in part at least, by keeping the law as a covenant, thus attending to its requirements for justification, serving in the oldness of the letter, and not in the newness of spirit. In this way, multitudes who profess to have received the Gospel, are walking after the flesh, seeking to satisfy their conscience, and saying peace when there is no peace.

While, therefore, the other ways of walking according to the flesh may all be comprehended under the term as here employed by the Apostle, for they are all involved in each other, it would appear (especially as in the 5th verse, *minding* the things of the flesh, which certainly denotes immoral conduct, is distinguished from *walking* after the flesh) that it is to the above import of the word, rather than to immoral conduct, that he is referring in this place. In this way Paul himself walked before his conversion, when he thought that he ought to do many things contrary to the name of Jesus of Nazareth ; and it was this same way of walking according to the flesh which he so strenuously opposes in his Epistle to the churches of Galatia. We see, too, how suitable to his purpose it would be in confirming the doctrine he had been teaching, particularly to direct to this point the attention of those to whom he was writing. Paul, then, appears to be here prosecuting his main design, which is to prove that believers are to be justified, not by works of righteousness which they have done, of whatever description, but solely by faith in Jesus Christ, in whom their reconciliation with God is complete. It is this grand truth which, from the beginning of the Epistle, he had been exhibiting, for the conviction and establishment in the faith of those whom he addressed. It is indeed a truth in which Christians need to be fully instructed, which they are all apt to let slip out of their minds, but by which they are saved, if they keep it in memory. There is

nothing which so much retards them in their course as their proneness
to walk according to the flesh, in seeking to establish their own righteousness; and nothing more powerfully tends, when giving way to it in any
degree, to bring them into bondage, to lead them to serve in the oldness
of the letter, and not in newness of spirit, and to mar their joy and peace
in believing.   In the sense here ascribed to it, the word flesh is employed
in the beginning of the fourth chapter of this Epistle.   Flesh, in that place,
cannot, it is evident, signify immoral conduct; for that Abraham was justified by wicked works could never be supposed.   It must there signify
works, moral or ceremonial, as is proved by the rest of that chapter.

In the Epistle to the Galatians, the terms flesh and spirit are likewise
used in this acceptation. 'Are ye so foolish? having begun in the
Spirit, are ye now made perfect by the flesh?' Gal. iii. 3.   'Having
begun your Christian course by receiving the doctrine of the new
covenant, namely, justification by the righteousness of Christ, are ye
seeking to be made perfect by legal observances, or works of any kind?'
In this passage the word flesh cannot be taken for wicked works, any
more than in the fourth chapter of the Romans, just quoted.   It must be
understood in the sense of working for life, or self-justification, in opposition to the way of salvation according to the Gospel.   The Apostle's main
object, in the whole of that Epistle, is to reclaim the Galatian churches
from the error of mixing ceremonial observances, or any works of law,
with the faith of Christ, and thus walking according to the flesh, and not
according to the Spirit.   'Behold, I Paul say unto you, that if ye be
circumcised, Christ shall profit you nothing.   For I testify again to every
man that is circumcised, that he is a debtor to do the whole law.   Christ
is become of no effect unto you, whosoever of you are justified by the
law; ye are fallen from (the doctrine of) grace.   For we, through the
Spirit, wait for the hope of righteousness by faith.'   This reasoning
applies to all works of law, of whatever description, as clearly appears by
the third chapter of that Epistle.

In the same manner, the terms flesh and Spirit are employed, Phil. iii.
3, 'For we are the circumcision, which worship God in the Spirit, and
rejoice in Christ Jesus, and have no confidence in the flesh.'   Here the
word flesh, opposed to Spirit, just as in the passage before us, cannot
signify immoral conduct, in which it would be absurd to suppose that the
Apostle placed confidence.   In the sequel, Paul furnishes a practical
commentary on these words, by referring to his own conduct, as having
formerly walked according to the flesh, resting in external privileges, and
observances, and his obedience to the law; but afterwards as renouncing
them all, and relying solely on 'the righteousness which is of God by
faith.'

According, then, to the above signification of the word flesh, as employed in the fourth chapter of this Epistle, and of the word Spirit,
denoting the new covenant, 2 Cor. iii. 6, this clause, 'who walk not
according to the flesh, but according to the Spirit,' indicates the course
of those who are not walking according to the old covenant, in seeking
justification by the works of law, but who attain it by faith in Him who
is the Lord the Spirit, 2 Cor. iii. 17.   The same idea appears to be ex-

pressed here as in the preceding chapter, where the Apostle reminds believers that they are delivered from the law under which, while in the flesh, they were held, that they should *serve in newness of spirit, and not in the oldness of the letter.* This is consistent with the whole of the previous train of the Apostle's reasoning, in which, as was already noticed, he has been asserting the freedom of believers from the law, and their justification by the righteousness of Christ through faith, in opposition to all self-justifying efforts or obedience of their own. They, then, who walk not according to the flesh, but according to the Spirit, are no longer seeking justification by works of law, but are brought to act on Gospel and spiritual principles. They live in the Spirit, and they also walk in the Spirit.

All men who profess to worship God in any form, walk by nature according to the flesh. As man was originally placed under the law to live by his obedience to it, so, ever since it has been broken, he naturally seeks acceptance with God, and justification by the works of law. This is fully verified at all times, and in all nations, by those who are not in Christ. All men, without exception, have the work of the law[1] written in their hearts, and if ignorant of the only Saviour of sinners, they attempt to satisfy their conscience by means of some religious observances or moral works,—the idolater, by his sacrifices; the Mohammedan, by his lustrations; the Brahmin, by his austerities; the Roman Catholic, by his masses and penances; the Socinian, by his vaunted philanthropy; the nominal Christian, by his assiduous attendance at the Lord's Supper and other religious services: and all, in some way or other, by the merit of their works, moral or ceremonial, seek to obtain their acquittal from sin before God, and a favourable sentence at His tribunal. All of them are going about to establish their own righteousness, being ignorant of the righteousness of God. In this way Saul of Tarsus, as has been noticed, describes himself as having walked, when he had 'confidence in the flesh.' To wait, through the Spirit, for the hope of righteousness by faith, Gal. v. 5, is peculiar to those to whom, being in Christ Jesus, there is no condemnation, and in whom the righteousness of the law is by Him fulfilled.

The verse before us, and the three preceding, contain a summary of the whole that Paul had advanced in the foregoing part of the Epistle, both respecting the justification and the sanctification of believers, and open the way for illustrating the difference between those who are carnal —remaining in their natural state—and those who are spiritual, as renewed by grace. This afterwards leads to a particular and most interesting description, through the remainder of the chapter, of the various trials of believers, as also of their unspeakably glorious privileges, and of the gracious operations and influences of the Holy Spirit in the great work of their sanctification, and to the Apostle's concluding the whole by the most sublime view of the eternal source and absolute

[1] *The work of the law*, Rom. ii. 15. Here let us admire the accuracy with which the Scriptures are written. Speaking of the Gentiles, the Apostle does not say, 'who have the law written in their hearts.' This is the promise of the new covenant, and peculiar to those who belong to it; but he says, 'the work of the law.' For the import of this term, see p..91.

security of the state of dignity and blessedness to which, through Divine favour, they have been elevated.

Ver. 5.—*For they that are after the flesh do mind the things of the flesh ; but they that are after the Spirit the things of the Spirit.*

This appears to confirm the explanation that has been given of the last clause of the first verse and of that of the fourth; for the Apostle here distinguishes between *walking* after the flesh, and *minding* the things of the flesh, and between *walking* after the Spirit, and *minding* the things of the Spirit. As he had proved that union with Christ was necessary to justification, he here shows that its certain consequence is also sanctification ; while they who do not enjoy this union are still under the dominion of sin.

For they that are after the flesh do mind the things of the flesh.—This verse connects with the preceding, and contrasts the opposite effects that follow from walking according to the flesh, or according to the Spirit. The word here translated ' mind,' includes both the understanding and the affections, and signifies the strong bent of the mind regarding the object desired. The minding of the flesh comprehends all the faculties of man in his unregenerate state, there being no power of the mind exempt from sin. If, then, a man walks according to the flesh, seeking acceptance with God by his own works, moral or ceremonial, however earnest or sincere he may be in his endeavours, he will remain under the prevalence and dominion of sinful appetites. Such persons have their minds intent on the things that gratify their corrupt nature. They have no relish for spiritual things ; whatever they may be induced to do from dread of punishment, or hope of reward in a future world, their desires are, in reality, centred in the things of this world. Whatever may be their profession of religion, their hearts are supremely engrossed with earthly things ; and for these, if they could obtain their wish through eternity, they would gladly barter all the glories of heaven. In one word, they *mind the things of the flesh*, they love the world, and all that is in the world. ' If any man love the world, the love of the Father is not in him. For all that is in the world, the lust of the flesh, and the lust of the eyes, and the pride of life, is not of the Father, but is of the world.'

But they that are after the Spirit the things of the Spirit.—They who act according to the principles of the renewed spiritual nature, and seek acceptance with God by faith in Him who is ' the Lord the Spirit,' 2 Cor. iii. 17, *mind spiritual things.* Jesus Christ is the source of every blessing, and they who are in Him are not only justified, and consequently freed from condemnation, but also walk in newness of life. They employ their thoughts and efforts about the things of God. To these they attend, and on these their affections are fixed. None will seek the things which are above, but those who serve God in newness of spirit. All others will ' mind earthly things,' Phil. iii. 19.

On the verse before us Mr. Adam of Wintringham remarks, ' For they that are after the flesh, that is, according to the common interpretation, not led and governed by the Spirit in practice, " still under the direction of the flesh and its sinful appetites," says Mr. Lock, do mind the things of the flesh : very true ; but then this is only affirming a thing of itself, or saying it twice over. And therefore, to clear St. Paul of this absurdity, we suppose that by " they that are after the flesh," he means those who are destitute of faith, or not in Christ: and of them he affirms that, let them pretend to do what they will, they are still under the prevalence of flesh and its appetites, and cannot act from a higher principle, or a nature which they have not. And it must be observed that he is now advancing a step farther in the doctrine of faith, and, besides the necessity of it in order to justification, showing its happy effects as a principle of holiness : but they that are after the Spirit—in the Spirit's dispensation of grace, through faith—and say that Jesus is the Lord by the Holy Ghost, by whom only they can say it, mind the things of the Spirit, now possessing and ruling them.'

Ver. 6.—*For to be carnally minded is death ; but to be spiritually minded is life and peace.*

In the preceding verse the Apostle contrasts the dispositions and practices of believers and unbelievers; here he contrasts their opposite states and conditions. These two states of carnal and spiritual minded-ness include and divide the whole world. All men belong either to the one or the other. They are either in the flesh or in the Spirit ; in a state of nature or in a state of grace. *For to be carnally minded is death.*—This is the awful state of the carnal mind—the mind of the flesh without faith in Christ, and renovation of the Spirit of God. It is death spiritual and eternal. All the works of those who are in this state are ' dead works,' Heb. ix. 14. ' The sacrifice of the wicked is an abomination to the Lord,' although the Lord commanded to offer sacrifices, which therefore was in itself a good work. ' She that liveth in pleasure is dead while she liveth.' All by nature being in this carnal state, are ' dead in trespasses and sins.' Let those whose minds are set on the things of the world consider this fearful saying, that to be carnally minded is death, and let them look to Jesus the Saviour of the guilty, through whom alone they can escape condemnation.

But to be spiritually minded is life and peace.—These are the effects of being enlightened and guided by the Spirit of God, and so having the mind turned from earthly things to the things of the Spirit. To be spiritually minded is *life*, even eternal life. This life is already enjoyed by the believer. ' Whoso eateth My flesh, and drinketh My blood, hath eternal life ;' and with his Redeemer he has risen from the death of sin to walk in this new life. It is also *peace*, both here and hereafter. This peace is the harmony of all the faculties of the soul with God, and with His will, and is altogether the opposite of that enmity against God, which in the following verse is affirmed concerning the carnal mind. While there is nothing so miserable for man as war with his Creator, there is nothing so blessed as peace and communion with God. It is peace in the conscience, in opposition to doubt, for which the Church of Rome contends, as if the effect of being spiritually minded, instead of peace and confidence in God, was servile fear and harassing distrust. That church maintains that the man who is regenerated should doubt of his salvation, and be uncertain of God's love to him. What, then, becomes of this peace that flows from being spiritually minded—which passeth all understanding, keeping the heart and mind through Christ Jesus—this peace, which is one of the fruits of the Spirit, and a characteristic of the kingdom of God? Rom. xiv. 17. The peace here spoken of is opposed to the terrors of conscience which the unregenerate experience, and to the opposition in their hearts to God, as well as to every species of false peace by which they may be deluded. 'There is no peace, saith my God, to the wicked.' And again it is said, 'Thou wilt keep him in perfect peace, whose mind is stayed on Thee, because he trusteth in Thee.'

Ver. 7.—*Because the carnal mind is enmity against God ; for it is not subject to the law of God, neither indeed can be.*

Because the carnal mind is enmity against God.—The word rendered *carnal mind*—or, as it may be rendered, minding of the flesh—comprehends the acts both of the understanding and of the will. Some render it the prudence, or wisdom, of the flesh—or the wise thoughts. The carnal mind in its wisest thoughts is rooted enmity against God. This is the reason why the carnal mind is punished with death. The mind of the flesh, or of man in his unconverted state, walking according to the flesh, in its best as well as in its worst character—however moral in conduct— whether seeking acceptance with God by its own services, or following altogether the course of this world in its sinful practices—is not merely an enemy, but *enmity* itself against God in the understanding, will, and affections. Every man whose heart is set on this world hates God, 1 John ii. 15. 'If any man love the world, the love of the Father is not in him ;' and the heart of every one who has not been renewed in his mind by the Spirit of God is set on this world. Such men hate the holiness of God, His justice, His sovereignty, and even His mercy in the way in which it is exercised. Men of this character, however, have no notion that they hate God. Nay, many of them profess to love Him. But God's testimony is, that they are His enemies ; and His testimony is to be taken against the testimony of all men. This, however, does not suppose that men may not imagine that they love God. But is it not the true God whom they are regarding, but a God of their own imagination —a God all mercy, and therefore a God unjust; while they abhor the just God, and the Saviour, who is the God of the Scriptures. 'He that cometh to God must believe that He is,' Heb. xi. 6. He must believe that He is what He is.

For it is not subject to the law of God.—The carnal mind is not under subjection to the law of God. Whatever it may do to obtain salvation or avoid wrath, it does it not from subjection to the law. It has a rooted aversion to the spiritual law of God, and admits not its claim to perfect and unceasing obedience. All its performances in the way of religion spring from selfish motives, and a hope that, on account of these doings, it will be accepted ; whereas the holy law of God utterly rejects all such service. So far from giving the law all its demands, the carnal mind gives it nothing. Nothing which it does constitutes obedience to the law. The law does not in any degree, or in any instance, recognise the works of the carnal mind as obedience to its requirements.

Neither indeed can be.—Not only is it a matter of fact that the carnal mind is not subject to the law of God, but such subjection is impossible. Sin cannot be in subjection to the law. This would be a contradiction in terms. For, so far as it would be subject to the law of God, it would be holy. If, then, sin is essentially, and in direct terms, contrary to holiness, the sinful nature can never yield subjection to the holy law. Men may speculate about metaphysical possibilities; but whatever explanation may be given of the matter, the decision of the inspired Apostle determines that the thing is impossible.

That an unconverted man cannot be subject to the law of God, appears to many a hard saying; but it is the uniform doctrine of the word of God. All men in their natural state, though they boast that they are free, are the slaves of sin. When Jesus, addressing the Jews who professed to believe in Him, but who understood not His doctrine, said to them, ' Ye shall know the truth, and the truth shall make you free,' they answered, ' We were never in bondage to any man; how sayest Thou, Ye shall be made free?' In the same manner the unconverted boast of their freedom. They affirm that their will is free; and that, as they can choose the evil, so they can choose the good. If, by this freedom, they intend that they can choose without any external force constraining or preventing them, it is true that, in this sense, they are free. But a moral agent chooses according to his inclinations or dispositions. It should always be recollected that the will is the will of the mind, and the judgment the judgment of the mind. It is the mind that judges and that wills. A fool judges foolishly; a wicked man judges wickedly; a good man wills that which is good. In Scripture, it is said that God *cannot* deny Himself; that He *cannot* lie. His nature being perfectly holy, it is impossible that He *can* do what is wrong. On the other hand, the wicked and condemned spirits *cannot* choose what is holy. When the devil ' speaketh a lie, he speaketh of his own; for he is a liar, and the father of it.' Man, therefore, in his carnal state, chooses what is evil; but he *cannot* choose what is good, not indeed because of any external obstruction, for in that case he would not be criminal, but by reason of the opposition of his perverse dispositions. He is inclined to do evil, and evil he will do. ' *Can* the Ethiopian change his skin, or the leopard his spots? then may ye also do good, that are accustomed to do evil.' His language is, ' I have loved strangers, and after them will I go.' ' As for the word that thou hast spoken to us in the name of the Lord, we will not hearken unto thee.' ' My people would not hearken to My voice, and Israel would have none of Me.' They say ' unto God, Depart from us.' ' Depart from us; for we desire not the knowledge of Thy ways.' ' We will not have this man to reign over us.' ' Let us break their bands asunder, and cast their cords from us.'

It is thus that ' wickedness proceedeth from the wicked.' ' Neither can a corrupt tree bring forth good fruit.' ' Except a man be born again, he *cannot* see the kingdom of God.' ' Except a man be born of water, and of the Spirit, he *cannot* enter into the kingdom of God.' ' How *can* ye believe, which receive honour one of another, and seek not the honour that cometh from God only?' ' No man *can* come to Me except the

Father which hath sent Me, draw him.' 'Therefore said I unto you, that no man *can* come unto Me except it were given unto him of My Father.' 'The natural man receiveth not the things of the Spirit of God; for they are foolishness unto him; neither *can* he know them, because they are spiritually discerned.' 'Their ear is uncircumcised, and they *cannot* hearken.' 'How *can* ye, being evil, speak good things? for out of the abundance of the heart the mouth speaketh.' 'The Spirit of truth whom the world *cannot* receive.' 'Why do ye not understand My speech? even because ye *cannot* hear My word.' 'No man *can* say that Jesus is the Lord, but by the Holy Ghost.'

According, then, to Scripture, the natural man is entirely incapable of choosing what is good, although it is his duty, and therefore fit that it should be enjoined on him. He is 'ungodly,' a 'sinner,' an 'enemy to God,' and 'without strength,' Rom. v. 6, 10. Men in this state are represented as walking according to the prince of the power of the air, the spirit that now worketh in the children of disobedience; as being under 'the power of Satan,' and 'taken captive by him at his will.' They are his lawful captives, because they are so voluntarily. From this slavery they cannot be freed but by means of the word of God, the sword of the Spirit, which the Lord employs; granting to those to whom it seemeth good to Him the blessing of regeneration; 'distributing His gifts, and dividing to every man severally as He will.' It is God 'who hath delivered us,' says the Apostle, 'from the power of darkness, and hath translated us into the kingdom of His dear Son.' 'Who worketh in you both to will and to do of His good pleasure.' 'If the Son shall make you *free*, ye shall be *free* indeed.'

When God purposes to do good to men, He fulfils to them this gracious promise, 'I will give them a heart to know Me.' It was this preparation of heart that David prayed to God to grant to his son Solomon. At the same time, he acknowledged with gratitude that his own willingness to offer to God, of which he was conscious, and that of his people, were from Him. After celebrating the praises of Jehovah, David says, 'But who am I, and what is my people, that we should be able to offer so willingly after this sort? for all things come of Thee, and of Thine own have we given Thee. O Lord God of Abraham, Isaac, and of Israel, our fathers, keep this for ever in the imagination of the thoughts of the heart of Thy people, and prepare their hearts unto Thee,' 1 Chron. xxix. 10-18.

There is nothing to prevent men from obeying the will of God but their own depraved dispositions, and aversion to the things of God. The natural faculties of men would be sufficient to enable them to do what He commands, if they employ them properly. If they employ them otherwise, the fault rests exclusively with themselves. And as the corruption of our nature does not deprive a man of any of his natural faculties, or of perfect liberty to act conformably to the decision of his own mind, the obligation under which he lies to do right continues in full force. From this we see, first, how justly God punishes men for their crimes, who, unless inclined and enabled by His grace, cannot liberate themselves from the slavery of sin; and further, that the inability of men to obey God, not being natural but moral inability, cannot deprive

God of the right to command obedience, under the pain of His most awful displeasure.

On this subject, the distinction between natural and moral inability should always be kept in view. Natural inability consists in a defect in the mind or body, which deprives a man of the power of knowing or doing anything, however desirous he may be of knowing or doing it. Natural inability, then, can never render a man criminal. Moral inability consists in an aversion to anything, so great that the mind, even when acting freely—that is, without any external impulse or constraint—cannot overcome it. When this aversion exists as to what is good, it is inseparable from blame; and the greater this aversion is, the greater is the criminality. All men are daily accustomed to make these distinctions, and according to this rule they constantly form their opinion of the conduct of others.

In the nature of things, it is impossible that the justice of God can ever demand of reasonable creatures less than perfect obedience. To say that the moral inability of man to obey the law of God destroys or weakens, in the smallest degree, his obligation to obey that law, is to add insult to rebellion. For what is that moral inability? It is, as has been observed, no other than aversion to God, the depraved inclination of the carnal mind, which not only entertains and cherishes enmity against God, but is itself that enmity. And let it not be said that the view the Scriptures give of the natural depravity of men, and of the sovereign and efficacious grace of God, reduces them to the condition of machines. Between men and machines there is this essential difference, and it is enough for us to know that man is a voluntary agent both in the state of nature and of grace. He wills and acts according to his own dispositions, while machines have neither thought nor will. As long, then, as a man's will is depraved and opposed to God, his conduct will be bad,—he will fulfil the desires of the flesh and of the mind; and, on the other hand, when God gives the sinner a new disposition, and a new spirit, his conduct will undergo a corresponding change. 'The liberty of a moral agent consists in the power of acting conformably to his choice. Every action performed without external constraint, and in pursuance of the determination of the soul itself, is a free action. The soul is determined by motives; but we constantly see the same motives acting diversely on different minds. Many do not act conformably to the motives of which they yet acknowledge all the force. This failure of the motive proceeds from obstacles opposed by the corruption of the heart and understanding. But God, in giving a new heart and a new spirit, takes away these obstacles; and, in removing them, far from depriving a man of liberty, He removes that which hindered him from acting freely, and from following the light of his conscience, and thus, as the Scriptures express it, makes him free. The will of man, without Divine grace, is not free but enslaved, and willing to be so.'

Is it objected, that if a man be so entirely corrupt that he cannot do what is right, he should not be blamed for doing evil? To this it is sufficient to reply, that if there be any force in the objection, the more a voluntary agent is diabolically wicked, the more innocent he should be considered. A creature is not subject to blame if he is not a voluntary agent; but if he be so, and if his dispositions and his will were absolutely wicked, he would certainly be incapable of doing good, and, according to the above argument, he could not be blamed for doing evil. On this ground the devil must be excused, nay, held perfectly innocent, in his desperate and irreconcilable enmity against God. A consequence so monstrous totally destroys the force of the objection whence it is deduced. But if the objection be still pressed—if any one shall proudly demand, who hath resisted His will? Why hath He made me thus?—the only proper answer is that of the Apostle, 'Nay but, O man, who art thou that repliest against God?'

Some, indeed, taking a different and the most common view of this matter, deny the innate depravity of their nature, and, in spite of all that the Scriptures declare on this subject, persist in maintaining that they have not an inclination to evil, and are under no moral incapacity to do what is right. To such persons the same reply should be made as that of our Lord to the ignorant young man who asked Him what he should do to inherit eternal life. 'If thou wilt enter into life, keep the commandments.' You cannot refuse to admit that this is your duty. You ought to love God with all your heart, and soul, and strength, and in all things constantly to obey Him. Have you done so? No! Then, on your own principles, you are justly condemned, for you say that you can do what is right, and yet you have not done it. If, then, you will not submit unconditionally, and without reserve, to be saved in the way which the Gospel points out, in which you learn at once your malady and the remedy of which you stand in need, your blood will be upon your own head. 'Now, you say, We see; therefore your sin remaineth.' The whole, then, resolves itself into this, that all is according to the good pleasure of God. 'Either make the tree good and his fruit good, or else make the tree corrupt and his fruit corrupt; for the tree is known by his fruit. Every good tree bringeth forth good fruit, but a corrupt tree bringeth forth evil fruit. A good tree *cannot* bring forth evil fruit, neither *can* a corrupt tree bring forth good fruit. Ye shall know them by their fruits.' Every man, then, being by nature bad, must be made good before he can do good. In this and the two preceding verses we observe the strong, and expressive, and accumulated terms in which the Apostle describes the alienation of the natural man from God. 1st, He declares that they who walk after the flesh, mind the things of the flesh; 2d, That the minding of the flesh is death; 3d, That the carnal mind is enmity against God; 4th, That it is not subject to the law of God; 5th, That so great is the corruption of the carnal mind, that this is impossible.

From the passage before us, we learn how miserable the state of man is by nature, since even his wisdom and intelligence, in his unconverted state, is enmity against God, so that he cannot submit himself to His law. We learn, too, that the ability both to will and to do anything good must be from God. We should adore His compassion and mercy to us, if our natural enmity against Him has been subdued, and we have been reconciled to God by the death of His Son. In proportion to the greatness of this compassion, we should place our entire confidence in

Him as our covenant God.   For if, when we were enmity against Him,
He loved us, how much more now that we are reconciled and His
children? Rom. v. 10.   And, since there are still remains of the flesh and
enmity against God and His holy law in our minds, we ought to deny
ourselves daily, and flee to Him who can and will entirely deliver us
from the body of this death.

Ver. 8.—*So then they that are in the flesh cannot please God.*

This is the result of what has been said.   A man must be born of the
Spirit before he can even begin to serve God.   How unscriptural and
pernicious, then, is that system which teaches men to seek to please God
by commencing a religious life, that God may be induced to co-operate
with them in their further exertions.   If the man who is not born again
cannot please God, every act of the sinner before faith must be displeasing
to God.   An action may be materially good in itself, but unless it proceed
from a right motive—the love of God—and be directed to a right end—His
glory—it cannot be acknowledged by God.   Before a man's services can
be acceptable, his person must be accepted, as it is said, 'The Lord had
respect unto *Abel*, and to his *offering*.'   'Without faith it is impossible to
please God.'   It is by faith we are united to Christ, and so reconciled to
God ; and till this union and reconciliation take place, there can be no
communion with Him.   If, then, no man who is in the flesh—that is, in
his natural or unconverted state—can please God, how dreadful is the
situation of those who do not even profess to be renewed in the spirit of
their mind!   How many are there who discard the idea of regeneration!
However specious may be the works of such persons in the eyes of men,
they cannot please God ; and not pleasing God, they must abide the condemnation that awaits all His enemies.

Ver. 9.—*But ye are not in the flesh, but in the spirit, if so be that the Spirit of God
dwell in you.   Now, if any man have not the Spirit of Christ, he is none of His.*

In the preceding verses the Apostle had given a description of carnal and
spiritual mindedness.   Here he applies what he had said to those whom he
was addressing.   *Ye are not in the flesh, but in the spirit.*—As the flesh is
here taken for the nature of man corrupted by sin, so to be in the flesh
signifies to be in a state of natural corruption.   On the other hand, to be
in the spirit signifies to be in a state of grace or regeneration, John iii.
6.   Flesh is a principle that attaches to the earth, and the things of the
earth ; but the spirit of regeneration is as a light, which, coming from
heaven, elevates the mind to those things that are celestial.   As to the
understanding, the man in the flesh, or the carnal man, receiveth not the
things of the Spirit of God, for they are foolishness unto him ; but he
who is in the spirit, or spiritual, knows and approves the will of God,
having ' the spirit of wisdom and revelation in the knowledge of God,'
'the eyes of his understanding being enlightened.'   The *will* of the carnal
man is such that the imagination of his thoughts are only evil continually;
but he who is spiritual has his conscience purged from dead works to
serve the living God.   The *affections* of him who is carnal are enmity
against God, and in rebellion against His law ; but the spiritual man

delights in the law of God, and loves His commandments. The former considers the things of the world as his sovereign good; the latter seeks the things that are above at the right hand of God.

Not being in the flesh, but in the spirit, was the state of all in the church at Rome. All belonging to it were, as far as man could judge, 'saints,' ch. i. 7, the regenerated children of God. The Apostle was persuaded that they were all 'his brethren' in Christ, 'full of goodness,' ch. xv. 14. It was meet for him to think this of them all, Phil. i. 7. They were not then in the corrupt state of nature, but in the Spirit, walking in the Spirit, renewed by the Spirit of God. How different at that period was the church at Rome from that apostate body which now usurps its name! Nor only are natural or carnal men recognised as its members, but, like the temples of heathenism, it is filled with abominations and filthiness.

If so be that the Spirit of God dwell in you.—The Apostle, in order to confirm those to whom he wrote in the assurance of their happy condition, now calls their attention to the evidence of being in a converted state, namely, the indwelling of the Holy Spirit. 'Hereby we know that we dwell in Him, and He in us, because He hath given us of His Spirit,' 1 John iv. 13. This indwelling of the Spirit is a sure evidence of a renewed state; and believers should be careful not to grieve the Spirit, and should labour to enjoy a constant sense of His presence in their hearts.

In this verse the word spirit in the first occurrence imports the gift and grace of regeneration. In the 2d and 3d it denotes the Author of that gift, namely, the Holy Spirit, who is Jehovah, a person in the self-existent Godhead, equal with the Father and the Son in every attribute. He is called the Spirit, as being the breather or inspirer of spiritual life. Everything done by Him in this character tends to holiness, and therefore He is so often called the Holy Spirit. It is His Divine office to apply the salvation of Jesus, and to make it effectual. He does all in the heirs of promise. The Father gave them to the Son, the Son redeemed them, but they are in the common mass of corruption, dead in trespasses and sins, till the Spirit of life opens their hearts to receive Him, enters into them, unites them by faith to the Saviour, and makes them the subjects of a new birth. Of the Holy Spirit it is said, 1 Cor. iii. 16, 'Know ye not that ye are the temple of God, and that the Spirit of God dwelleth in you?' If it be asked how the Holy Spirit, who is co-essential with the Father and the Son, and consequently infinite, can dwell in believers, the answer is, that though everywhere present, He is said neverthless to dwell in them on account of His operation and the grace of regeneration, which He produces. It is the Holy Spirit who unites them to Christ the Lord. It is He who quickens and regenerates them, on account of which regeneration is called the 'renewing of the Holy Ghost.' He it is who leads, rules, and governs them, as it is said in the 14th verse, that as many as are led by the Spirit of God are the sons of God. What this expression, 'dwell in you,' imports is, that being united to Jesus Christ and regenerated, the Holy Spirit dwells in His people not as inactive, but operates in them continually, and leads and governs them. In the indwelling, then, of the Holy Spirit, is included

His gracious and continuing presence, and His operations in the soul. The effects of these are illumination, sanctification, supplication, and consolation. Of the Holy Spirit, one of the early Christian writers says, 'He is the author of regeneration, the pledge of the promised inheritance, and, as it were, the handwriting of eternal salvation; who makes us the temple of God and His house, who intercedes for us with groanings which cannot be uttered, acting as our advocate and defender, dwelling in our bodies, and sanctifying them for immortality. He it is who fights against the flesh, hence the flesh fights against the Spirit.'

It is Jesus Christ who gives to His people the Holy Spirit. 'It is expedient for you,' He says, 'that I go away; for if I go not away, the Comforter will not come unto you; but if I depart, I will send Him unto you.' At the ancient Pentecost, God gave the law to the people of Israel fifty days after the institution of the Passover. Jesus Christ, as being the body and truth of the typical ordinances, having chosen to suffer at the feast of the Passover, was pleased also to send forth the Holy Spirit on the day of Pentecost, who by His power accomplishes in the hearts of believers what the law outwardly required; for the law was a letter written in stone, and therefore in itself without efficacy; but the Holy Spirit is that internal power which He puts within them and writes on their hearts. As, then, in the ancient Pentecost, God had given the law inscribed in tables of stone, so on the Christian Pentecost, Jesus Christ, by the power of His Spirit, writes it in their hearts. 'Ye,' says the Apostle, 'are manifestly declared to be the epistle of Christ, ministered by us, written not with ink, but with the Spirit of the living God, not in tables of stone, but in fleshly tables of the heart.' And why do we so often read in the New Testament of the contrast between the spirit and the letter, but to teach us that we have in the Christian Pentecost, by the Spirit of Christ, the truth and effect which the law in vain required from sinners.

Now, or rather, *But, if any man have not the Spirit of Christ, he is none of His.*—Here is a necessary reservation. If the Spirit of God did not really dwell in any of those whom the Apostle addressed, they were still in the flesh, notwithstanding all their profession, and all their present appearances, and his persuasion respecting them. And no doubt some will be found to have escaped for a time the pollutions of the world, who may afterwards show that they were never renewed in heart. Many ridicule the pretensions of those who speak of the Holy Spirit as dwelling in believers; yet if the Spirit of God dwell not in any, they are still in the flesh; that is, they are enemies to God.

The same Spirit that is called the Spirit of God in the preceding part of the sentence, is in this latter part called the Spirit of Christ, because Christ having, by virtue of His sacrifice, obtained the Spirit for His people, sends Him into their hearts, John xvi. 7. Christ, then, who sends the Holy Spirit, must be God. Every Christian has the Spirit of Christ dwelling in him. When Christ takes possession of any man as His, He puts His Holy Spirit within him. Without the presence of His Spirit, we can have no interest in Christ.

Ver. 10.—*And if Christ be in you, the body is dead because of sin ; but the Spirit is life because of righteousness.*

The Apostle having affirmed in the 2d verse that the law of the Spirit of life had made him free from the law of sin and death, and having declared in the 3d and 4th verses in what manner we are freed from the law as the law of *sin*, it remained for him to show how we are freed from it as the law of *death*. This he accordingly does here, and in the following verse. In the 7th and 8th verses, he had confirmed his declaration in the 6th, that to be carnally minded is death. He now illustrates the opposite declaration, that to be spiritually minded is life. He admits, however, that notwithstanding the believer's communion with Christ, the body is dead ; but to this he opposes the double consolation of the eternal life of our souls on account of the righteousness of Christ, and, in the next verse, the resurrection of our bodies through the indwelling of the Holy Spirit.

There is in this verse a triple opposition: first, of the body to the soul; second, of a state of death to a state of life; third, of sin to righteousness. It was necessary to remove the objection replied to in this verse, especially as the Apostle had said that to those who are in Christ Jesus there is no condemnation. Whence, then, it might be asked, does it happen that we who are in Him are still subject to death like other men ? He answers, If Jesus Christ be in you, the body indeed is dead because of sin, but the spirit is life because of righteousness. In what follows, he abundantly shows that the temporary sufferings of believers, among which is the death of the body, are not worthy to be compared with the glory that shall be revealed in them ; and that in the meantime all things that happen to them are working for their good. The term body is, in this verse, to be taken, as is evident from the following verse, in its literal signification ; and by the spirit, as opposed to it, is meant the soul, as in the 16th verse, where our spirit is distinguished from the Holy Spirit.

And, or rather, *But, if Christ be in you.*—The Apostle had just affirmed that if any man have not the Spirit of Christ, he is none of His ; but if He be *in* us, then the consequences here stated follow. Jesus Christ, in regard to His Divine nature, is everywhere present ; but He is in a special manner in believers, as it is said, Eph. iii. 17, ' That Christ may dwell in your hearts by faith.' This indwelling of Christ signifies two things, namely, the close and intimate union we have with Him, and His operation in us. As the Scriptures declare that Jesus Christ is in us, so they also assure us that we are in Him, ch. viii. 1 ; 1 Cor. i. 30 ; 2 Cor. v. 17 ; Col. i. 27. And thus we dwell in Him and He in us, John vi. 56. This union with Jesus Christ is necessary, in order that He should work in us. For He works only in His members ; so that, for this purpose, we must be first incorporated in Him, John xv. 4. By this union we participate in His grace ; because, as we are in Him and He in us, we have all things with Him in common. Our sins are reputed His sins, and His righteousness ours. He that persecutes His people persecutes Him ; he that touches them touches the apple of His eye. And as in this life they partake of His grace, so in the life to come they shall participate in His glory.

The body is dead.—Notwithstanding our union with Jesus Christ, our bodies are dead. The Scriptures speak of three kinds of death : one is in this life, the other at the end of this life, and the third after this life. The first is spiritual death, Eph. ii. 1 ; Col. ii. 13. Natural death takes place at the separation of the soul from the body ; and after this life is the second, or eternal death, which consists in everlasting destruction from the presence of the Lord. It is only of the second or natural death that the Apostle here speaks, for believers are delivered from the first and the third. He says the body is dead, to show that it is the lowest part of man that for a time is affected by death, as it is said, ' Then shall the dust return to the earth as it was,' Eccles. xii. 7.

Because of sin.—Men die for the sin of Adam. ' By one man sin entered into the world, and death by sin ; ' and God said, ' In the day that thou eatest thereof thou shalt surely die.' But why do believers die, since death is the punishment of sin, and as to them God hath remitted this punishment ? for the Apostle shows, chapter iv., that their sins are not imputed to them ; in chapter vi., that they are dead to sin ; and in the beginning of the chapter before us, that there is no condemnation to them which are in Christ Jesus. Jesus Christ, too, has made complete satisfaction for the punishment of their sins, sin having been condemned in His flesh. The Apostle also says, ' Christ has redeemed us from the curse of the law, being made a curse for us ; ' but death is among the curses of the law. We must then distinguish between death considered in itself, and in its nature, and as having changed its nature in Jesus Christ our Lord. In itself, death is the punishment of sin and the curse of the law, and it is such to the wicked and unbelievers. But, by the work of Christ, it is to His people no more a punishment of sin, but the destruction of sin. It is no more the curse of the law, but is changed into a blessing, and has become the passage to eternal life, and the entrance into the heavenly paradise.

The death of believers does not, then, in the least degree derogate from the complete satisfaction of Jesus Christ, and the perfect redemption from the curse of the law, since their death is not a punishment of sin in vindictive justice, as all the afflictions of this life as well as death are to the enemies of God. But by Jesus Christ, in respect to those whom the Father hath given to Him, and who are united to Him, God acts in mercy, and afflictions and death are only chastisements from His fatherly hand,—trials of their faith, and salutary discipline, as the Apostle in this chapter declares that all things work together for their good ; and in the First Epistle to the Corinthians, iii. 22, that all things are theirs, whether life or death. Without, then, making void the first sentence awarding death, God has established another covenant, which is that of grace, according to which those who partake in the death of Christ, by which that sentence was, as to them, carried into full execution, must indeed die ; but death to them is swallowed up in victory ; and instead of the day of their death being a day of punishment of sin, it is a day of triumph over death. The death of the body is as to them the preparation for its immortality and incorruption, as the seed deposited in the earth passes in such a way through death as to overcome it, and revives and fructifies, so that when in the earth it is not lost. In like manner the bodies of believers do not perish by death, but derive from the grave what is contrary to its natural character. They are sown in corruption, but they are to rise in incorruption. They are sown in weakness, but they are to rise in power. They are sown in dishonour, but they are to rise in glory. They are sown natural bodies, but they are to rise spiritual bodies. And as to the soul, death indeed separates it from the body, but transmits it to God. It is evident, then, that such a death is not a punishment of sin, or a curse of the law. Its end and use to the regenerate, as to their bodies, is to extirpate and destroy the sin that remains in them : they must die in order to be purified. The infusion of that moral poison has so corrupted our bodies, that, like the leprous house, they must be taken down and renewed, to be purified from sin. As the grain is not quickened except it die, in the same way our bodies die and moulder in the dust, to be revived and reconstructed in holiness.

If it be said that God, without dooming His people to die, could have changed them in a moment, in the twinkling of an eye, as He will do with respect to those who shall survive to the day of His coming, it should be considered that the wisdom of God hath judged it proper that the believer should be subjected to the death of the body. This tends to lead him to hold sin in abhorrence whence death proceeds. He also sees in death the goodness·and the severity of God, and by it and his other afflictions he may judge what will be the end of those whom God punishes in His anger. He may observe in it the goodness of God to him in depriving it of its sting, and ordering it so that he may more fully taste the sweetness of a lasting and immortal life. Such discipline, too, tends to humble the believer, by which also his graces, given to him by God, are increased, and the power of the Lord made manifest in his weakness. Finally, believers die, that in their death they may be conformed to Jesus Christ ; for if He died, shall they, who are His members, be exempt from this lot ? and if He must in that way enter into His glory, shall they, who are His members, enter by any other way ? And this assuredly is a great consolation, that in dying we follow Jesus Christ, our Head, who hath gone before us.

The eye of nature, which loves its preservation, regards death with fear, in which it sees its destruction. The eye of the flesh, which is enmity against God, regards it with still greater dread, perceiving in it the summons to stand before the tribunal of God. But the believer, by the eye of faith, discovers in death what dissipates the fears of nature, and repels the despair of the flesh. To nature, which apprehends its destruction, faith opposes the weakness of death, which cannot prevent the resurrection ; and to the condemnation which the flesh apprehends, opposes that life which it discovers under the mask of death. It sees that, though its appearance be terrific, yet in Christ it has lost its sting. It is like the phantom walking on the sea which approached to the terrified disciples, but it was Jesus Christ their Lord and Saviour. If unknown evils that may happen in death be apprehended, the believer remembers that the very hairs of his head are all numbered. Jesus, who is with him, he knows will not abandon him. He will not permit him to be tempted above what he is able to bear, for 'precious in the sight of the Lord is the death of His saints.'

The nature, then, of death, is changed to believers by Jesus Christ, so that 'the day of their death is better than the day of their birth.' Death to them is no more a curse, but a blessing, which puts an end to their sins and troubles, causing them to pass to perfect holiness and happiness, and from being absent from the Lord to carry them into His presence in paradise. From being strangers on the earth, it introduces them into their heavenly inheritance. From their wanderings and agitations here below, it brings them into the haven of everlasting rest. If the children of Israel, when they arrived at the river Jordan, were dismayed at the overflowings of its waters, had they not reason to rejoice when they beheld on the other side that fertile land which God had promised them, and into which they were about to enter to enjoy its fruits? But, above all, had they not cause of encouragement when they saw that the ark of the covenant was in the midst of Jordan? Death is the passage of Jordan by which believers enter the heavenly Canaan. In order that its waves may not overwhelm them in passing, Jesus Christ arrests them, since He is in His people, and consequently with them. This was David's support, 'Though I walk through the valley of the shadow of death, I will fear no evil; for Thou art with me.' When the devouring lion roars around His people, ready to destroy them, Jesus Himself is still nearer to defend them; and He commands His angels to encamp about them, who have in charge to bear their spirits to the paradise of God.

But the spirit is life.—To the fact that the body is *dead*, the Apostle here opposes, as a ground of comfort, the consideration that our souls are *life*. The life here spoken of is the life of God in the soul; it is the new and eternal life which His Spirit communicates in regeneration. The souls of believers are possessed of this spiritual life, of which the Scriptures inform us when they say that God hath 'quickened us together with Christ.' 'Whoso eateth My flesh and drinketh My blood *hath* eternal life.' It is life, and eternal life, already possessed, and the commencement of that glorious life which shall be enjoyed in heaven. It is the blessing which the Lord commands, 'even life for evermore.' This life, which, being borne down by so many encumbrances here, is still feeble, and but imperfectly enjoyed, shall, in the world to come, flourish in full vigour, and without any abatement. It is the life of our Lord and Saviour, subsisting in Him, and derived from Him. In Him, His people shall rise and live, and live for ever. He Himself hath said, 'I am the resurrection and the life: he that believeth in Me, though he were dead, yet shall he live; and whosoever liveth, and believeth in Me, shall never die.'

In the verse before us we have a remarkable example of the accuracy with which the Scriptures are written. The Apostle does not say that the body is *dead*, and the spirit alive or *living*; or that the body is *death*, and the spirit *life*. Either of these would have formed the natural contrast; but neither would have conveyed the important sense of this passage, but, on the contrary, a false one. He says the body is *dead*, and the spirit is *life*. The body is not *death*, that is, in a state of everlasting death; it is only dead, and shall live again. On the other hand, the spirit is not merely said to be alive, which it might be although under sentence of death, afterwards to be inflicted; but it is *life* in the sense of that declaration of our Lord, 'He that hath the Son hath life.' The body is dead on account of sin; that is, the body is not only mortal, but may, in some sense, be said to be already dead, being under sentence of death, and in constant progress towards dissolution. It remains with its infirmities unaltered. There is no difference between the body of the wicked man and the body of the believer. Every one may perceive a difference in their minds. The believer's body is *dead* because of sin, according to the original sentence, 'Dust thou art, and unto dust shalt thou return.' But the spirit is *life*—possessed of life eternal, in virtue of its union with Him who is 'the life.'

Because of righteousness.—Here a great difficulty is removed; for it may be said, If our bodies are, dead *because of sin,* how is it that our souls are life, since they are stained with sin, and that it is on account of their sinfulness that our bodies are infected with the same malady? The Apostle, in answer, brings into view the *righteousness* of Him who is in us, and shows that it is on account of His righteousness that our souls are life. And this necessarily follows; for if we have such union with our Lord and Saviour, that we are flesh of His flesh and bone of His bones, that we are His members, and if He and we are one, His righteousness must be ours; for where there is one body, there is one righteousness. On the other hand, through the same union our sins have been transferred to Him, as is said by the Prophet Isaiah, 'The Lord hath laid on Him the iniquities of us all.' And the Apostle Peter says that He 'bore our sins in His own body on the tree;' He bore their punishment. 'He was made sin for us who knew no sin, that we might be made the righteousness of God in Him.' An exchange, then, of sin and righteousness has taken place. By imputation He has been made sin, and by imputation we also are made righteousness. Jesus Christ, as being the surety of the new covenant, has appeared before God for us, and consequently His righteousness is ours.

In the verse before us we have an undeniable proof of the imputation to us of righteousness, for otherwise it would be a manifest contradiction to say that we die on account of our sins, and that we have life on account of our righteousness; for what is sin but the opposite of righteousness? Whoever, then, dies on account of the sin that is in him, cannot obtain life by his own righteousness. Now, if all men die on account of sin, as the Apostle here teaches, then no man can have life by his own righteousness.

Ver. 11.—*But if the Spirit of Him that raised up Jesus from the dead dwell in you, He that raised up Christ from the dead shall also quicken your mortal bodies by His Spirit that dwelleth in you.*

The Apostle here obviates a difficulty which might present itself from what he had said in the preceding verse, of the bodies of believers being dead though their souls have life. He now assures them that, if the Spirit of God who raised Jesus from the dead dwells in them, God will also raise up their bodies, though at present mortal. Thus he sets before them, first, the resurrection of Jesus Christ, and next their own resurrection, as being His members; for he deduces their resurrection from His resurrection.   Their Head has conquered death and the grave, and with Him they shall overcome.   Their freedom, then, from death he rests on the same foundation on which he had already shown that their freedom from sin was secured—on Jesus Christ, the surety of God's gracious covenant.

The Apostle elsewhere proves the resurrection of the bodies of believers, by comparing Jesus Christ with Adam, saying, 'As in Adam all die, even so in Christ shall all be made alive,' 1 Cor. xv. 22 ; showing that if we do not rise by virtue of Jesus Christ our Lord, Christ would be inferior to Adam.   For could the sin and death of Adam have more power to subject those who were in Him to death, than the righteousness and resurrection of Jesus Christ to deliver those who are in Him from death? The Apostle also declares that Jesus Christ, having risen from the dead, has become the first fruits of them that slept, and adds, 'Every man in his own order; Christ the first fruits, afterwards they that are Christ's at His coming.'   This he does for the purpose of showing that, as the first fruits of the ground precede the harvest, so the first fruits of the resurrection of Christ will be followed by that great harvest, in which the bodies of believers sown in the earth, after having died like grain cast into it, shall be revived and raised up.   The life which has been communicated to our souls will, at the glorious resurrection, be also communicated to our bodies.   All men will then arise, but not in glory, as all will not arise in virtue of the resurrection of our Lord.   The wicked shall arise by the power of their Judge, to receive in their body the punishment of their sins, and to suffer 'the second death;' but believers, in virtue of the resurrection, and by the Spirit of Jesus Christ as their Head.   For that Spirit which has been communicated to them from Jesus Christ, as from the head to the members, and who hath made their bodies His temples on earth, will raise them from the dust, and will perfect His work in them.   Believers, then, may defy the grave, and glory over death, being assured of this resurrection.   From the guilt of sin they have been delivered, it being 'condemned' in Christ—punished in His death ; from the power of death they are released by His resurrection.   On Jesus Christ, then, the sure foundation, is the whole of our salvation built.   In Him God is well pleased ; through Him the Holy Spirit is vouchsafed.   Christ is the Alpha and the Omega ; He is the 'All in All.'

Quicken your mortal bodies.—From this it appears that, as to their substance, the bodies of believers will in their resurrection be the same as those that died.   'Though after my skin worms destroy this body, yet in my flesh shall I see God,' Job xix. 26.   'Thy dead men shall live, together with my dead body shall they arise.   Awake and sing, ye that dwell in the dust: for thy dew is as the dew of herbs, and the earth shall cast out the dead,' Isa. xxvi. 19.   The soul of each man will be reunited to his own body in which he has done good or evil.   For as the body is the organ of the soul in this world, so it must participate in the felicity or punishment that shall follow, whether the whole man has remained under the law, or has been received into the covenant of grace. But as to the qualities of the bodies of believers, these will be different from what they were here, as the Apostle teaches, 1 Cor. xv. 50. For as in this world they have borne the image of the first man, who was of the earth earthy; so, in the resurrection, when this corruptible shall put on incorruption, they shalt bear the image of the second man, who is heavenly; the bodies of their humiliation being fashioned like unto the glorious body of the Son of God, Phil. iii. 21, not only in having a perfect beauty, exempt from all maladies, but as being spiritual, adapted to their spiritual and heavenly state. And as, when Jesus was transfigured, His face did shine as the sun, and His raiment was white as light, so the righteous shall shine forth as the sun in the kingdom of their Father. From all this we may judge what will be the condition of the soul, and what its glory conformable to so glorious a body. We see also what is the death of believers, which is only a sleep, since it is to be followed by such a resurrection. Inasmuch as this mystery of the resurrection exceeds our reason, so is it clearly represented to us in Scripture.[1]

By His Spirit that dwelleth in you.—The indwelling of the Holy Spirit, who communicates life to those who are habitations of God through Him, is here set before believers as a pledge that their bodies shall not remain under the power of death. This indwelling, which renders their resurrection, certain, imports His love, His government, the operation of His grace, and His care to adorn and to beautify the temple in which He resides; and the end of it is to confer everlasting life, everlasting purity, and everlasting communion with Himself. It would be derogatory to the majesty and glory of the blessed Spirit to allow those bodies, in which He dwelt as His temple, to lie for ever in ruins in the dust. And God, who raised up Jesus Christ from the dead, that great Shepherd of the sheep, through the blood of the everlasting covenant, will raise up the bodies of His people in virtue of that blood, which purchased not only the redemption of their souls, but also of their bodies, verse 23. The power and efficacy of the three glorious persons of the Godhead are thus brought into view as securing the complete re-establishment of the bodies of believers, which, though at present mortal, shall hereafter partake in all the glories and blessedness of eternal life.

This concurrence of the power of the Godhead in the plan of redemption, in which the Father provides for our salvation, the Son merits it, and the Holy Spirit applies it, is established in a multitude of passages of the Holy Scriptures. In this economy the Father occupies the place of

---

[1] Mr. Stuart explains the quickening of our mortal bodies as signifying—'will make them active instruments.' But we do not see any alteration made in this world on the bodies of believers. They are, indeed, made active instruments ; but this is not by any change on their bodies, but in the mind which governs them. Besides, any change that in this respect might be supposed to take place on the members of the body, would take place at the renewing of the mind. But the change here spoken of contemplates something future which has not yet taken place. Dr. Macknight paraphrases the words thus, ' *Will make even* your dead bodies, *your* animal passions, together with the members of your *mortal bodies, alive,*—that is, subservient to the spiritual life.' But animal passions, under the figure of *dead bodies,* must mean the animal passions as they are sinful, and sin is never turned into holiness. The flesh is not subject to the law of God, and never will be.

the founder of the Church, the sovereign of the world, the protector and avenger of His laws, and the first director of the work of our salvation. The Son has become the Mediator between God and man, to do everything necessary for our redemption, while the Holy Spirit has assumed the office of the comforter and sanctifier of the Church. The first preparation for our salvation is found in what the Father has done, namely, in the plan which He has formed, in the election of His people, and His giving them to His Son; in the appointment of the sacrifice, in the transfer of our sins to Him who has suffered, and in respect to the satisfaction He has received. The second step is seen in what the Son has merited and effected in coming into the world, by His obedience, His death, and resurrection. The third discovers the Holy Spirit making actual application of the whole, uniting us to the Saviour, producing in us faith and sanctification, diffusing in our hearts the sentiment of our peace with God in our justification, causing us to persevere to the end, and raising us up again, as He will do, at the last day. In this Divine economy the Son has received His mission from the Father to come into the world. On this account He so often refers His first advent to His being sent by the Father to take on Himself the office of the Prophet, the Priest, and the King of His Church. To this inequality of office such passages as the following ought to be referred:—'My Father is greater than I,' John xiv. 28; and that in 1 Cor. xv. 28, where it is said, 'Then shall the Son also Himself be subject unto Him;' thus terminating His mediatorial office in delivering up the kingdom by an act of humiliation, in the same way as He had entered upon it. For in neither of these texts is any personal inequality spoken of between the Father and Son, but an inequality of office, according to which the Father is greater than the Son, and the Son inferior to the Father.

The resurrection of Christ, in the passage before us, is ascribed to the Father and the Holy Spirit; but in other places this is also ascribed to the Son Himself. The Father, and the Holy Spirit, and the Son, then, must be one God. It is only those in whom the Spirit of God that raised Jesus from the dead dwells, who shall have their mortal bodies thus quickened, so as to rise again in glory. Christ, indeed, will also raise His enemies, but His own people will be made alive—which is never said of the wicked—to live with Him in glory for ever.

Ver. 12.—*Therefore, brethren, we are debtors, not to the flesh, to live after the flesh.*

This is a consequence drawn from what the Apostle had said with reference to the state of enmity against God, and of the death of those who are in the flesh; and likewise from what He had been showing to be the great privilege of believers, as being not in the flesh but in the Spirit; as having the Spirit of God dwelling in them; and not only giving life to their souls, but securing the future quickening and raising of their bodies. From all this he infers their obligation to live a holy life, in walking according to the Spirit in the character which he had shown belonged to them. They were not then debtors to the flesh—the state in which they had been by nature, which is a state of corruption, guilt, and weakness—to live after the flesh, either to expect life from its best efforts, or to obey it in its lusts. The ways of the flesh promise happiness, but misery is their reward. On the contrary, it is implied that they were debtors to God, to whom they were under so great obligations as being redeemed from the law of sin and death, to serve and obey Him, in walking according to the Spirit, in that new and Divine nature which He has graciously imparted to them.

Ver. 13.—*For if ye live after the flesh, ye shall die : but if ye through the Spirit do mortify the deeds of the body, ye shall live.*

For if ye live after the flesh, ye shall die.—The reason in the former verse why those to whom the Apostle wrote were not debtors to live after the flesh—under any obligation to obey its dictates—was taken from their obligations to God in respect of their privileges ; here it is taken from the doom of those who thus live. If ye live agreeably to your carnal nature, without Christ and faith in Him, and according to the corrupt principles that belong to man in the state in which he is born, *ye shall die.* Ye shall suffer all the misery that throughout eternity shall be the portion of the wicked, which is called death, as death is the greatest evil in this world. Thus the wrath of God is denounced against all who do not live to God, in obedience to His commands, but serve the lusts of the flesh, and do not seek salvation in the way He has appointed, however harmless and even useful they may be in society. At the same time, this proves that nothing done by the natural man, in his best efforts and highest attainments, will lead to God and to life. The Apostle thus repeats what he had affirmed in the sixth verse, that to be carnally minded is death.

But if ye through the Spirit do mortify the deeds of the body.—The deeds of the body are the works which corrupt nature produces. The believer neither indulges nor walks according to them, but mortifies and puts them to death. Those to whom the Apostle wrote had mortified the deeds of the body, yet they are here called to a further mortification of them, which imports that this is both a gradual work, and to be continued and persevered in while we are in the world. This shows that the sanctification of the believer is progressive.

Some have objected to the doctrine of progressive sanctification, and have conceived that to assert it is a great error. They hold that there is no more progress in sanctification than there is in justification, and that both are complete at once on believing the truth. There is just so much truth in this as serves to make the error plausible. It is true that there is a sense in which believers are perfectly sanctified from the moment they believe. That sanctification, however, is not in themselves ; it is in Christ, as much as their justification. The moment they believe, they are justified in Christ, and perfectly righteous ; and the moment they believe, they are sanctified in Him, and in Him are perfectly holy. Viewed in Christ, they are 'complete.' But there is a personal sanctification, which commences with the new birth on believing the truth, and which is not perfected till death. Many passages of Scripture import this doctrine. The following prayer of the Apostle is explicit and decisive :—' And the very God of peace sanctify you wholly,' 1 Thess. v. 23. The Apostle Peter enjoins on believers to desire the pure milk of the word, that they may *grow* thereby, and begins his second Epistle by praying that grace might be multiplied to those to whom he wrote, and concludes it by enjoining on them to *grow in grace.* 'The path of the just is as the shining light, that shineth more and more unto the perfect day.'

Believers obtain sanctification by the Spirit through the truth. Their sanctification, then, must be in proportion as the truth is understood and believed. It is through faith in Christ, Acts xxvi. 18; if so, according to the degree of faith will be the degree of sanctification. But all Christians are not equal in faith, neither, then, are they equal in sanctification; and as a Christian advances in faith, he advances in sanctification. If he may say, 'Lord, increase my faith,' he may likewise say, 'Lord, increase my sanctification.' He receives the Holy Spirit only in a measure. He may and ought, therefore, to pray for a larger measure of influence and grace from Him who gives grace in that measure which pleases Him. We should pray that God would grant unto us according to the riches of His glory, that we may be strengthened with might by His Spirit in the inner man. They who have already put on Christ as their sanctifier, are still exhorted to put Him on, ch. xiii. 14—that is, more and more. There are babes in Christ, 1 Cor. iii. 1; there are little children, and young men, and fathers, 1 John ii. 12.

Through the Spirit.—It is through the power of the Holy Spirit, who testifies of Christ and His salvation, and according to the new nature which He communicates, that the believer mortifies his sinful propensities. It is not then of himself, of his own power or will, that he is able to do this. 'Not that we are sufficient of ourselves to think anything as of ourselves; but our sufficiency is of God.' No man overcomes the corruptions of his heart but by the influence of the Spirit of God. Though it is the Spirit of God who enables us to mortify the deeds of the body, yet it is also said to be our own act. We do this through the Spirit. The Holy Spirit works in men according to the constitution that God has given them. The same work is, in one point of view, the work of God, and in another the work of man.

Ye shall live.—Here eternal life is promised to all who, through the Spirit, mortify the deeds of the body. The promise of life by the Gospel is not made to the work, but to the worker; and to the worker, not for or on *account* of his work, but *according* to his work, for the sake of Christ's work. The promise, then, of life is not made to the work of mortification, but to him that mortifies his flesh; and that not for his mortification, but because he is in Christ, of which this mortification is the effect and the evidence. That they who mortify the flesh shall live, is quite consistent with the truth that the gift of God is eternal life, Rom. vi. 23; and in this gift there is no respect to the merit of the receiver. This describes the character of all who shall receive eternal life; and it is of great importance. It takes away every ground of hope from those who profess to know God, and in works deny Him; for they that are Christ's have crucified the flesh with the affections and lusts.

In all this we are reminded that, while we cannot in this life attain to the fulfilling of the law in our own persons, we must seek to be conformed to that law, and so mortify the old man in our members, otherwise it is a proof that we have no part in the righteousness of Christ. For can it be supposed that by Him we are absolved from sin in order to obtain a licence to continue in sin ourselves? On the contrary, our justification and our sanctification, as is shown in the sixth chapter, are inseparable. Jesus Christ came by water and blood; not by water only, but by water and blood,—signifying by the *blood* the expiation of the guilt of our sins by His death, and by *water* the virtue of His Spirit for our sanctification in washing our souls from the pollution of sin. In like manner, under the law, there were not only sacrifices of animals whose blood was shed, but various washings, to teach us that these two benefits are inseparable in the Gospel. Accordingly, when David describes the blessedness of the man whose transgression is forgiven, whose sin is covered, unto whom the Lord imputeth not iniquity, he immediately adds, in *whose spirit there is no guile.* For ought we to wish to receive the remission of sin, and to continue to walk in guile? Ought we thus to seek to divide Christ, receiving only the efficacy of His blood and not that of His Spirit; desiring that He should be made to us *righteousness* and not also *sanctification?* We are to seek in Him the cause of our justification, and observe in ourselves its proofs and effects. We should see that, as we are pilgrims in this world, we have for our guide the Spirit of sanctification.

Ver. 14.—*For as many as are led by the Spirit of God, they are the sons of God.*

Here is a proof of what had just been said, namely, that if, through the Spirit, those whom the Apostle addressed mortified the deeds of the body, they should live; for all who do so are led by the Spirit. In spiritual things we are as little children, who, on account of their weakness, have need to be led by the hand that they may not fall. It is necessary, then, that believers be led by the Spirit of God. The manner in which the Spirit leads them is not by violence against their inclination, but by bending and changing their will, in a manner consistent with its nature. When Jesus Christ says, 'No man can come to Me except the Father which hath sent Me, draw Him,' it is not meant that God forces against their will those whom He draws, but it shows us that we are naturally so indisposed to go to Jesus Christ, that it is necessary that God, by His Spirit, draw us to Him, and that by His secret but powerful influence He changes our resistance into consent. This is what is meant by the Church in the Song of Solomon, when she says, 'Draw me, we will run after Thee;' for this shows that she is drawn in such a way that she runs, that is, that her will being changed, and her perversity removed, she with alacrity follows the Lord. God gives His people to will and to do of His good pleasure, making them willing in the day of His power, and by His Spirit changes their hearts of stone into hearts of flesh. This leading of the Spirit consists, too, in enlightening our understandings, as Jesus Christ says, ' When He the Spirit of truth is come, He will guide you into all truth.' It consists also in the sanctification of our will and affections; so that he who is led by the Spirit is transformed by the renewing of his mind, proving what is that good, and acceptable, and perfect will of God. He has the eyes of his understanding en-

lightened to know what is the hope of the calling of God, and the riches
of the glory of His inheritance in the saints. The Apostle shows what
the Spirit leads to, when he says that the fruit of the Spirit is 'love, joy,
peace, long-suffering, gentleness, goodness, faith, meekness, temperance.'
It must, however, be remarked that this leading of the Spirit is not such
in this world as to exclude all imperfection. For notwithstanding that
we are thus led, 'in many things we all offend,' Jas. iii. 2. We have
still within us a principle opposing the Spirit, as it is said, 'The flesh
lusteth against the Spirit, and the Spirit against the flesh : and these are
contrary the one to the other ; so that ye cannot do the things that ye
would,' Gal. v. 17. But he is led by the Spirit, who, though enticed by
the flesh to walk in a contrary direction, yet resists and contends against
it, and mortifies the deeds of the body.

The Holy Spirit thus leads those in whom He dwells to the mortification of sin. He takes of the glory of the person of Jesus, as God manifest
in the flesh, and of His office, as the one Mediator between God and
man, and discovers it to His people. Convincing them of their sinful
condition, and of Christ's righteousness, He leads them to renounce
everything of their own, in the hope of acceptance with God. He
teaches them as the Spirit of truth shining upon His own word, striving with them by it externally, and internally by His grace conducting,
guiding, and bringing them onwards in the way of duty, and, as the
promised Comforter, filling them with Divine consolation. Thus He leads
them to Christ, to prayer as the spirit of grace and of supplication, to
holiness, and to happiness. This shows us the cause why the children of
God, notwithstanding their remaining ignorance and depravity, and the
many temptations with which they are assailed, hold on in the way of
the Lord. 'Lead me in Thy truth, and teach me, for Thou art the God
of my salvation ; on Thee do I wait all the day.' 'Thy Spirit is good,
lead me into the land of uprightness.' This leading is enjoyed by none
but Christians ; for 'as many as are led by the Spirit of God, they are the
sons of God.'

The sons of God.—The Scriptures give this character of sons of God
differently, according as it is ascribed either by nature or by grace. By
nature it belongs to Jesus Christ alone, and that in respect to His Divine
nature, so that He is called the only-begotten Son of God. By grace
there are others who are called the sons of God. The grace of the conception by the Holy Spirit, and of the personal union of the Divine nature
which belongs to Jesus Christ as man, is a particular grace, He having
been conceived by the Holy Ghost, and His human nature has been joined
to His Divine nature, forming one person ; and it is of this grace that
the angel speaks in announcing His birth, Luke i. 35. There is also a
grace more general, which is that of creation, by which the angels are
called the sons of God, and from this grace those of them who sinned
have fallen. Finally, there is the grace of redemption, according to
which men are called, as in this place, the sons of God.

As among men there are two ways of becoming children, the one by
birth, the other by adoption, so God hath also appointed that in these
two ways His people should become His children. Adoption supplied

among men the want of children by birth, and no one could be a son except by one of these titles; but God has been pleased that we should be His sons by both of them together. Here and in the following verses the Apostle exhibits four proofs of our being the sons of God. The first is our being led by the Spirit of God; the second is the Spirit of adoption which we receive, crying, 'Abba, Father,' verse 15; the third is the witness of the Spirit with our spirits, verse 16; the fourth is our sufferings in the communion of Jesus Christ; to which is joined the fruit of our sonship, the Apostle saying that if children we are heirs of God, and joint heirs with Christ; if so be that we suffer with Him, that we may be also glorified together.

By this title of the sons of God, the doubts and servile fears of the Church of Rome are condemned, which teaches that believers should be uncertain respecting their salvation and the love of God. But ought they to doubt of the love of their Heavenly Father? The Scriptures teach them to call God their Father, but, according to that apostate church, they ought to be uncertain whether they are the children of God or the children of the devil. This error the Apostle combats in the following verse. The title, then, of sons of God is full of consolation; for we thus approach to God as our Father, and have access with boldness to His throne of grace. Even in our afflictions we lift up our eyes to Him, not as a severe master, but a gracious Father; and we know that our afflictions are only chastisements and trials from His paternal love, which He employs for our profit, that we may be partakers of His holiness.

Ver. 15.—*For ye have not received the spirit of bondage again to fear ; but ye have received the Spirit of adoption, whereby we cry, Abba, Father.*

It is of the greatest importance to believers to be assured that they are indeed the sons of God. Without a measure of this assurance, they cannot serve Him with love in newness of spirit. The Apostle therefore enlarges here on his preceding declaration, that as many as are led by the Spirit of God are the sons of God. In confirmation of this, he reminds those whom he addresses that they had not received the spirit of bondage again to fear, but the Spirit of adoption, leading them to call on God as their Father.

The word spirit occurs twice in this verse. In this chapter, as has already been remarked, it is used in various senses. Sometimes it is taken in Scripture in a bad sense, as when it is said, Isa. xix. 14, 'The Lord hath mingled a perverse spirit in the midst thereof;' and again, Isa. xxix. 10, 'For the Lord hath poured out upon you the spirit of deep sleep.' In the verse before us it is taken both in a bad sense, signifying a sinful affection of the mind, namely, the spirit of bondage, and in a good sense, signifying by the Spirit of adoption the Holy Spirit, as in the parallel passage, Gal. iv. 6, 'And because ye are sons, God hath sent forth the Spirit of His Son into your hearts, crying, Abba, Father.'

The spirit of bondage.—All who are not dead to the law, and know no way to escape Divine wrath but by obeying it, must be under the spirit of bondage; serving in the oldness of the letter, and not in newness of spirit. For so far from fulfilling the demands of the law, they fail in

satisfying themselves. A spirit of bondage, then, must belong to all who
are not acquainted with God's method of salvation.

The spirit of bondage is the effect of the law, which, manifesting his
sinfulness to man, and the fearful wrath of God, makes him tremble
under the apprehension of its curse. The Apostle, comparing the two
covenants, namely the law from Mount Sinai, and the Gospel from Mount
Zion, says that the one from Mount Sinai gendereth to bondage, which
is Hagar, but Jerusalem which is above is free, which is the mother of all
believers; because, like Isaac, they are the children of the promise. Now
this promise is the promise of grace. For as man has sinned, the law,
which demands perfect obedience, and pronounces a curse against him
who continues not in all things which it commands, must condemn and
reduce him to the condition of a slave, who, after he transgresses, expects
nothing but punishment. On this account, when God promulgated His
law amidst thunderings and lightnings, the mountain trembled, and the
people feared and stood afar off. This showed that man could only
tremble under the law, as he could not be justified by it; but that he
must have recourse to another covenant, namely, the covenant of grace,
in which God manifests His mercy and His love, in which He presents
to sinners the remission of their sins, and the righteousness of His well-
beloved Son; for in this covenant He justifies the ungodly, Rom. iv. 5,
and imputes to them righteousness without works. He adopts as His own
children those who were formerly children of wrath, and gives the Spirit
of adoption to them who had before a spirit of bondage and servile fear.

Again to fear.—Paul uses the word *again* to indicate a double opposition,—the one of the state of a man before and after his regeneration,
the other of the New Testament and the Old. Before regeneration, a
man, sensible that he is a sinner, must be apprehensive of punishment,
not having embraced the only remedy provided for the remission of his
sins by Jesus Christ. Not that it should be supposed that this is the
case with all unregenerate men, or at all times, but only when their
consciences are awakened, summoning them before the judgment-seat of
God. For the greater part of them live in profane security, with
hardened consciences, and without any apprehension of their ruined
state. God, however, often impresses that fear on those whom He
purposes to lead to the knowledge of His salvation. But when they are
born of the Spirit, this servile fear gives place to a filial fear which
proceeds from love, as the proper effect of the Spirit of adoption.
'Herein is our love made perfect, that we may have boldness in the day
of judgment; because as He is, so are we in this world. There is no
fear in love: but perfect love casteth out fear; because fear hath torment. He that feareth is not made perfect in love.'

The other opposition which the Apostle marks in saying *again*, is between
the Churches of the Old and of the New Testament. Not that the believers under the Old Testament had not the Spirit of adoption; for they
were sanctified by the Spirit of God, and had fellowship with Jesus
Christ the promised Messiah, being justified by faith, as is declared in the
eleventh chapter of the Hebrews, and called God their Father, Isa. lxiii.
16. But the Church under the Old Testament, being still in its infancy,

did not enjoy the Spirit of adoption in that abundance, nor had it so clear a revelation of grace, as that of the New. Believers only saw Christ at a distance under shadows and figures, while the law and its curses were strongly exhibited. Thus, in comparison of the New Testament and its freedom, they were, in a measure, held under bondage, Gal. iv. 1–3. The believers at Rome, then, whether originally Jews or Gentiles, had not received the spirit of bondage again to fear. They were not come unto the mount that might be touched, and that burned with fire, or to the law, the work of which is written in the hearts of all men, which speaks nothing of mercy; but they were come to Mount Zion. It was the design of Christ's advent that believers in Him might serve God 'without fear,' Luke i. 74. Jesus Christ came that through death He might destroy death, and him that had the power of death, that is, the devil, and to deliver them who, through fear of death, were all their life-time subject to bondage, Heb. ii. 14. All the movements excited by the spirit of bondage are only those of a slave,—selfish and mercenary motives of desire, hope of what will give them happiness, and fear of evil, but no movement of love either of God or holiness, or of hatred of sin.

The passage before us, and many others, as that of 2 Tim. i. 7,—' God hath not given us the spirit of fear, but of power, and of love, and of a sound mind,'—teaches us that servile fear ought to be banished from the minds of believers. This fear is a fear of distrust, and not that fear to which we are enjoined in various parts of Scripture, namely, a reverential fear of God impressed by a sense of His majesty, which is the beginning of wisdom, and which His children should at all times cherish. This fear is connected with the consolations of the Holy Ghost. ' Then had the churches rest throughout all Judea, and Galilee, and Samaria, and were edified ; and walking in the fear of the Lord, and in the comfort of the Holy Ghost, were multiplied.' There is also a salutary fear which ought always to be maintained in the hearts of Christians; for the assurance of his salvation, which a believer ought to cherish, is not a profane assurance which prompts him to disregard the authority of God, but leads to a diligent carefulness to conform to His word, and make use of the means for edification of His appointment. This is what the Apostle intends when he says, ' Work out your own salvation with fear and trembling;' for God designs to banish from our hearts a carnal security, as appears when it is added, ' for it is God which worketh in you, both to will and to do of His good pleasure,' showing that it is God who produces in His people both the will and the performance. This fear is required from the consideration of our weakness, our propensity to evil, and the many spiritual enemies with whom we are surrounded ; and for the purpose of making us careful that we do not fall ; while we ought not to doubt of the love of our Heavenly Father, but, considering the infallible promises of our God, and the intercession of our Lord Jesus Christ, we should hold fast the assurance of our salvation. The Apostle Peter enjoins on those whom he addressed as elect unto obedience, through the foreknowledge of God, as loving Jesus Christ, and as rejoicing in Him with joy unspeakable and full of glory, to pass the time of their sojourning here in fear, because they had been redeemed with the precious blood of Christ. This consideration shows how horrible and dangerous is the nature of sin which works in our members. This fear implanted in the hearts of the children of God tends to their preservation in the midst of dangers, as that instinctive fear which exists in all men operates to the preservation of natural life, and is entirely consistent with the fullest confidence in God, with love, and the joyful hope of eternal glory. If, however, the fear of man, or of any evil from the world, deter believers from doing their duty to God, it arises from the remains of carnal and unmortified fear. But nothing is more unworthy of the Gospel, or more contrary to its spirit, which, in proportion as it is believed, begets love, and communicates joy, peace, and consolation, in every situation in which we are placed.

But ye have received the Spirit of adoption.—The Holy Spirit is called the Spirit of adoption, either as the cause by which God makes us His children, or as the earnest and seal of our adoption. Contrary to the spirit of bondage, the Spirit of adoption produces in the heart a sense of reconciliation with God, love to Him, a regard to holiness, hatred of sin, and peace of conscience through the knowledge of the love of God in Jesus Christ. It begets a desire to glorify God here on earth, and to enjoy the glory of heaven hereafter. Formerly, in their unregenerate state, those to whom Paul wrote had the spirit of slaves, now they had the spirit of sons.

Adoption is not a work of grace in us, but an act of God's grace without us. According to the original word, it signifies putting among children. It is taking those who were by nature children of wrath from the family of Satan, to which they originally belonged, into the family of God. By union with Jesus Christ, being joined with Him, we are one body, and we enter into the communion of His righteousness, and of His title as the Son of God, so that, as we are righteous in Him, we are also in Him, as His members, the sons of God, who, in the moment that the Holy Spirit unites us to Jesus Christ, receives us as His children. All this shows us how great is the benefit which we obtain when we receive the Spirit of adoption and communion with the Son of God. We are thus made children of God, the sons of the Father of lights—a title permanent, and a nature immortal and Divine.

Our adoption reminds us of our original state as children of wrath and rebellion, and strangers to the covenant of God. It discovers to us the honour to which God has called us, in becoming our Father and making us His children,—including so many advantages, rights, and privileges, and at the same time imposing on us so many duties. These may be comprised under four heads. The first regards the privilege and glory of having God for our Father, and being His children. The second includes the rights which this adoption confers, as of free access to God, the knowledge of His ways, and the assurance of His protection. The third implies God's love for us, His jealousy for our interest, and His care to defend us. The fourth, all the duties which the title or relation of children engages us to perform towards our Father and our God.

The term adoption is borrowed from the ancient custom, especially prevalent among the Romans, of a man who had no children of his own adopting into his family the child of another. The father and the adopted child appeared before the prætor, when the adopting father said to the child, *Wilt thou be my son?* and the child answered, *I will.* The allusion to this custom reminds believers that they are not the children of God otherwise than by His free and voluntary election; and that thus they are under far more powerful obligations to serve Him than are their own children to obey them, since it is entirely by His love and free good pleasure that they have been elevated to this dignity. We should also remark the difference between the adoption of man and the adoption of God. In choosing a son by adoption, the adopting party has regard to certain real or supposed qualities which appear meritorious or agreeable; but God, in adopting His people, Himself produces the qualities in those whom He thus chooses. Man can impart his goods and give his name to those whom he adopts, but he cannot change their descent, nor transfer them into his own image; but God renders those whom He adopts not only partakers of His name and of His blessings, but of His nature itself, changing and transforming them into His own blessed resemblance.

This adoption, then, is accompanied with a real change, and so great a change, that it bears the name of that which is the real ground of sonship, and is called *regeneration.* And these are inseparable. There are no sons of God by adoption, but such as are also His sons by regeneration. There is a new life breathed into them by God. He is not only the Father of their spirits by their first infusion into the body, enlivening it by them, but by this new infusion of grace into their souls, which were dead without it; and the Spirit of God renewing them is the Spirit of adoption, by which they cry, 'Abba, Father.' He gives them a supernatural life by His Spirit sent into their hearts; and the Spirit by that regeneration which He works, ascertains to them that adoption which is in Christ Jesus; and in the persuasion of both they call God their Father.

In this manner, after adoption comes our sonship by regeneration, not in the order of time, but of nature; for, being united to Christ, God forms in us His image, and this is the second way in which we are made the children of God. Regeneration, or this new birth, is not a figurative but a real change. 'If any man be in Christ he is a new creature,' or a new creation, 2 Cor. v. 17; for when we are regenerated, we are created in Christ Jesus, Eph. ii. 10. Nor is it a reformation of character, but the renewal of the image of God in the soul, which had been totally effaced. They who are born again, are begotten in Christ Jesus through the Gospel, being born not of corruptible seed, but of incorruptible, by the word of God, which liveth and abideth for ever. Thus they are 'born not of blood, nor of the will of the flesh, nor of the will of man, but of God.' For this new birth the man can do nothing to prepare himself. Neither after he is renewed can he effect anything to ensure his perseverance in his new state. The Spirit of God alone both renews and preserves those who are renewed.

By this regeneration we obtain qualities which are analogous to the nature of God. He enlightens our understanding, sanctifies our will, purifies our affections, and, by the communication of those qualities which have a relation to His Divine nature, begets us in His image and likeness,

which is the new man of which Paul speaks, Eph. iv. 23, 24 ; Col. iii.
10 ; and, as the Apostle Peter declares, we are made 'partakers of the
Divine nature.' The fall of Adam has not deprived man of his subsistence or of his faculties, but has introduced into his understanding
the darkness of ignorance, with malice and evil into his will, and disorder
in his affections ; so that, before his adoption and regeneration, he is by
these vicious qualities the child of Satan, whose image he bears. The
opposite of all this is that spiritual regeneration by means of which he is
the child of God, consisting in the re-establishment of the uprightness of
his faculties, and the abolition of those vicious qualities which have been
introduced by sin. God begets us by His Spirit and by His word,
Jas. i. 18 ; and on His sons, thus formed, He bestows two graces,—
the one is their justification, and the other their sanctification. By the
first, they are invested with the righteousness of Jesus Christ, which is
imputed to them ; and this is the principal part of their spiritual and
supernatural life, which is hid in Jesus Christ, Col. iii. 3. By the
second, the Holy Spirit operates in them, to quicken and make them
walk in newness of life. And as this last grace is not perfect in this
world, but still leaves many faults and imperfections, although they are
the children of God, there are still in them remains of the old man,
and of the image of Satan. In this sense they have more or less
the character of children of God, as they advance more or less in sanctification ; and to this advancement they are continually urged by the
exhortations of the word of God. The adoption of God's people, and
their regeneration, are both declared, John i. 12, 13. Adoption confers
the *name* of sons, and a *title* to the inheritance ; regeneration confers the
nature of sons, and a *meetness* for the inheritance.

Abba, Father.—The interpretation which is generally given of this
expression is, that Paul employs these two words—Syriac and Greek,
the one taken from the language in use among the Jews, the other from
that of the Gentiles—to show that there is no longer any distinction
between the Jew and the Greek, and that all believers, in every nation,
may address God as their Father in their own language. It would rather
appear that the Apostle alludes to the fact that among the Jews slaves
were not allowed to call a free man Abba, which signified a real father.
'I cannot help remarking' (says Claude in his Essay on the Composition
of a Sermon) 'the ignorance of Messieurs of Port-Royal, who have
translated this passage, *My Father*, instead of *Abba, Father*, under
pretence that the Syriac word *Abba* signifies *Father*. They did not
know that St. Paul alluded to a law among the Jews which forbade slaves
to call a free man *Abba*, or a free woman *Imma*. The Apostle meant
that we were no more slaves, but freed by Jesus Christ ; and consequently that we might call God *Abba*, as we call the Church *Imma*. In
translating the passage, then, the word *Abba*, although it be a Syriac
word, and unknown in our tongue, must always be preserved, for in this
term consists the force of the Apostle's reasoning.'

God is indeed our Father, as the Author of our being, beyond all
visible creatures, as it is said, 'We are also His offspring,' Acts xvii. 28.
But the privilege of this our natural relation, the sin of our nature hath

made fruitless to us, till we be restored by grace, and made partakers of a new sonship. We are indeed the workmanship of God ; but, it being defaced by sin, our true name, as considered in that state, is ' children of wrath.' But the sonship that emboldens us to draw near unto God as our Father is derived from His only-begotten Son. He became the Son of man to make us anew the sons of God. Being thus restored, we may indeed look back upon our creation, and remember in prayer that we are His creatures, the workmanship of His hands, and He in that sense *our Father ;* but by reason of our rebellion this argument is not strong enough alone, but must be supported with this other, as the main ground of our comfort, and that wherein the strength of our confidence lies, that He *is our Father in His Son Jesus Christ ;* that by faith we are introduced into a new sonship, and by virtue of that may call Him Father, and move Him by that name to help and answer us. ' To as many as received Him, He gave power to become the sons of God,' John i. 12. But adoption holds in Jesus Christ, as the Head of this fraternity ; therefore He says, ' I go to My Father, and your Father ; to My God, and your God.' He does not say, 'to our Father and our God,' but severally *mine* and *yours ;* teaching us the order of the new covenant, that the sonship of Jesus Christ is not only more eminent in nature, but in order is the spring and cause of ours. So, then, He that puts this word in our mouths, to call God ' Father,' He it is by whom we have this dignity and comfort that we call Him so.

Whereby we cry.—The Spirit of adoption, which, enabling those who receive this Spirit to address God as their Father, gives filial dispositions and filial confidence. ' Because ye are sons, God hath sent forth the Spirit of His Son into your hearts, crying, Abba, Father,' Gal. iv. 6. It is by the Spirit of God that we cry unto Him, according to what is said afterwards, that the Spirit ' helpeth our infirmities, for we know not what we should pray for as we ought ; but the Spirit itself maketh intercession for us with groanings which cannot be uttered.' This teaches us that it is not our own disposition that excites us to prayer, but the Spirit of God. Accordingly we are commanded to pray ' always with all prayer and supplication in the Spirit,' Eph. vi. 18 ; and to build up ' ourselves on our most holy faith, praying in the Holy Ghost,' Jude 20. He is called ' the Spirit of grace and of supplications,' Zech. xii. 10, to teach us that prayer, being His work, and not an effort of our own strength, we are to ask of God His Spirit to enable us to pray. This is the source of our consolation, that since our prayers are effects of His own Spirit within us, they are pleasing to God. ' He that searcheth the hearts knoweth what is the mind of the Spirit, because He maketh intercession for the saints according to the will of God.'

The Holy Spirit, as the Spirit of adoption, also influences the prayers of believers as to their manner and earnestness, for by Him they not only say, but *cry,* ' Abba, Father.' They not only speak, but *groan,* for they cry not so much with the mouth as with the heart. By the term ' we cry ' is also intimated the assurance of faith with which we ought to draw near to God. This expression signifies that we address God with earnestness and confidence ; and that, having full reliance on His promises, which He hath confirmed even with an oath, we should ' come boldly unto the throne of grace, that we may obtain mercy, and find grace to help in time of need.' We are also commanded to ask in faith, nothing wavering, for we come before the throne of God by His beloved Son. We appear as His members, in virtue of His blood, by which our sins, which would hinder our prayers from being heard, are expiated, so that God has no more remembrance of them. It is on this ground that we pray with assurance, for, as we cannot pray to God as our Father, but by His Son, so we cannot cry, 'Abba, Father,' but by Him; and on this account Jesus says, 'I am the Way, and the Truth, and the Life; no man cometh unto the Father but by Me.' Thus the consideration that we invoke God as our Father forms in believers a holy assurance, for, as a father pitieth his children, so the Lord pitieth them that fear Him. Since, then, we call God our Father, as our Lord teaches us to address Him, we should do it with the assurance of His love, and of His readiness to hear us. 'Thou shalt call Me, My Father; and shalt not turn away from Me,' Jer. iii. 19.

The word Father also indicates the substance of our prayers; for when we can say no more to God than 'O God, Thou art our Father,' we say all, and comprehend in this all that we can ask; as the Church said in its captivity, 'Doubtless Thou art our Father, though Abraham be ignorant of us.' Thus, in whatever situation the believer finds himself, the crying, 'Abba, Father,' contains an appeal sufficient to move the compassion of God. Is he in want? he says, 'Abba, Father,' as if he said, 'O Lord, Thou feedest the ravens, provide for Thy son.' Is he in danger? it is as if he said, 'Have the same care of me as a father has for his child, and let not Thy compassion and Thy providence abandon me.' Is he on the bed of death? it is as if he said, 'Since thou art my Father, into Thy hands I commend my spirit.' All acceptable prayer must proceed from the Spirit of adoption; and the cry of the Spirit of adoption is no other than *Abba, Father*.

The crying 'Abba, Father,' then, denotes the earnestness and importunity in prayer to God, which is the effect of the Spirit of adoption in the hearts of the children of God, as well as that holy familiarity, to the exercise of which, as viewing God sitting on a throne of grace, they are encouraged. They call upon God as their Father, after the example of our Lord, who at all times addressed God in this manner during His ministry on earth, with that one memorable exception, when, under the pressure of the sins of His people, and the withdrawing of the light of His countenance, He addressed Him not as His Father but His God, Matt. xxvii. 46. After His resurrection, in like manner, He comforted His disciples with the consolatory assurance that He was about to ascend to His Father and their Father.

The different expressions which the Scriptures employ to denote the filial relation of His people to God, are calculated to aid their conceptions, and to elevate their thoughts to that great and ineffable blessing. One mode of expression serves to supply what is wanting in another. The origin of the spiritual life, and the re-establishment of the image of God in the soul, are expressed by these words—*born of God*. But that they may not forget the state of their natural alienation from God, and in order to indicate their title to the heavenly inheritance, it is said that they are *adopted* by God. And lest they should suppose that this adoption is to be attributed to anything meritorious in them, they are informed that God has *predestinated* them unto the adoption of children, by Jesus Christ, to Himself, *according to the good pleasure of His will, to the praise of the glory of His grace*, Eph. i. 5.

The passage before us is conclusive against the doctrine of the Church of Rome, which maintains that the believer ought to be always in fear of condemnation, always in doubt of the love of God, and of his salvation. But is not this expressly to contradict the words of the Apostle? It should be remarked that they cannot plead here the exception that it was a prerogative peculiar to the Apostle, to be assured of his salvation, by a special revelation that had been made to him. For he speaks expressly to believers, 'Ye have received the Spirit of adoption,' and next he speaks of them with himself, when he says, 'whereby we cry, Abba, Father.' This assurance of the believer is clearly taught in many other places. The Apostle, after saying, Rom. v. 1, 'Being justified by faith, we have peace with God, through our Lord Jesus Christ,' adds, 'By whom also we have access by faith into this grace wherein we stand, and rejoice in hope of the glory of God,'—expressing by the word rejoice (literally boast) a full assurance; for it would be rashness to boast or glory (as the same word is translated in the following verse) in what was not a real certainty. He also declares that hope maketh not ashamed; and that we even glory in tribulations, as assured that they cannot deprive us of the love of God. 'We have boldness, too, and access with confidence,' by the faith we have in Jesus Christ, Eph. iii. 12. 'Let us,' *therefore*' (seeing that we have a great High Priest, that is passed into the heavens), 'come boldly unto the throne of grace,' Heb. iv. 14–16. And why is the Spirit which is given to believers called the seal and earnest of their inheritance, if it is not to give them this assurance? Why, also, are the declarations so express, that there is no condemnation to them which are in Christ Jesus, and that whosoever believes in Him shall not perish, but have eternal life? The Apostle John says, 'These things have I written unto you that believe on the name of the Son of God, that ye may know that ye have eternal life,'—thus showing that he desires that all who believe should *know* that they have eternal life. The reply of the Roman Catholics, that we cannot know assuredly if we have faith, is altogether vain. Paul proves the contrary, when he says, 'Examine yourselves whether ye be in the faith; prove your own selves; know ye not your own selves how that Jesus Christ is in you, except ye be reprobates?' 2 Cor. xiii. 5. This proves that believers may recognise their own faith. Faith combats doubts, as the Apostle James shows when he says, 'Let him ask in faith, nothing wavering; for he that wavereth is like a wave of the sea driven with the wind and tossed.' And, speaking of Abraham, Paul says, 'He staggered not at the promise of God through unbelief; but was strong in faith, giving glory to God.' Believing, then, His promises, and drawing near in the full assurance of faith, gives glory to God.

But does faith, then, exclude all uncertainty of salvation, and has the believer no misgivings after he has received the Spirit of adoption? It

is replied, that as faith is more or less perfect, there is more or less uncertainty or doubt connected with it, for doubts are owing to the weakness or to the want of faith. Faith, as viewed in itself, is one thing, and
another as viewed in an imperfect subject. Faith in itself excludes all
doubts and misgivings; but, because our sanctification is incomplete in
this world, and as there is always in us the remains of the old man and
of the flesh, which is the source of doubts, faith has always to combat
within us, and to resist the servile fear of distrust, arising from the
remains of our corruption. The believer, therefore, need not wonder
though he should sometimes find himself agitated and troubled with
doubts; on which account he should, indeed, be humbled, but not dis-
couraged, for in the end faith will again raise up itself from under the
burden of temptation, and comfort him. The Spirit of adoption is sometimes as if it was extinguished in us; but in the end it exerts its force
in our hearts, so that we cry, 'Abba, Father,' and say with David, 'Make
me to have joy and gladness, that the bones which Thou hast broken may
rejoice.' The language of the Spirit of adoption is, 'Lord, Thou art my
Father, make the light of Thy countenance to shine upon me; cause Thy
peace to reign in my conscience; expel all doubts, scatter the clouds
which prevent me from seeing clearly the light of Thy face, and which
hinder the Sun of Righteousness from shining in my heart.' 'Say Thou
unto my soul, I am Thy salvation,' Ps. xxxv. 3. 'O my soul, thou hast
said unto the Lord, Thou art my Lord,' Ps. xvi. 2. And God says, Hos.
ii. 23, 'I will say to them which were not My people, Thou art My
people; and they shall say, Thou art my God.' That is, 'I will speak
within the believer by My Spirit; I will assure him of My grace, and of
My love; and he also shall lift up his heart to Me, and call Me his Father
and his God.' All this teaches us that the conscience, sprinkled with the
blood of the Son of God, does not accuse or condemn, but consoles and
comforts; for we have, by means of the Spirit that is given us, the earnest
of our final deliverance. This proves how precious the promise of the
Spirit should be to us, in order that we may not grieve Him by giving
way to sin.

Ver. 16.—*The Spirit itself beareth witness with our spirit, that we are the children
of God.*

In the preceding verse it is said, 'Ye have received the Spirit of adoption;' here it is added, 'The Spirit itself'—the same Spirit—'beareth
witness with our spirit that we are the sons of God.' In this verse the
Apostle shows that the sons of God may be assured of their adoption,
because it is witnessed by the Spirit of God. The Holy Spirit, in the
heart of a believer, joins His testimony with his spirit, in confirmation of
this truth, that he is a son of God. It is not merely the fruits of the
Holy Spirit in the lives of believers which afford this testimony, but the
Spirit Himself, by imparting filial confidence, inspires it in the heart.
This is a testimony which is designed for the satisfaction of believers
themselves, and cannot be submitted to the scrutiny of others.

The witnesses here spoken of are two,—our spirit, and the Spirit of
God together with our spirit. We have the testimony of our spirit when
we are convinced of our sinfulness, misery, and ruin, and of our utter

inability to relieve ourselves from the curse of the broken law, and are at the same time convinced of the righteousness of Christ, and of our dependence upon Him for acceptance with God. We have this testimony when we possess the consciousness of cordially acquiescing in God's plan of salvation, and of putting our trust in Christ ; and when we are convinced that His blood is sufficient to cleanse us from all sin, and know that we are willing to rest on it ; and when in this way, and in this way alone, we draw near to God with a true heart, sprinkled from an evil conscience in the discernment of the efficacy of His atonement, thus having the answer of a good conscience towards God. And we have the above testimony confirmed to us when we experience and observe the effects of the renovation of our souls in the work of sanctification begun and carrying on in us; and that not with fleshly wisdom, but by the grace of God, we have our conversation in the world.

In all this the Holy Spirit enables us to ascertain our sonship, from being conscious of, and discovering in ourselves, the true marks of a renewed state. But to say that this is all that is signified by the Holy Spirit's testimony, would be falling short of what is affirmed in this text ; for in that case the Holy Spirit would only help the conscience to be a witness, but could not be said to be a witness Himself, even another witness besides the conscience, which the text asserts. What we learn, therefore, from it is, that the Holy Spirit testifies to our spirit in a distinct and immediate testimony, and also with our spirit in a concurrent testimony. This testimony, although it cannot be explained, is nevertheless felt by the believer ; it is felt by him, too, in its variations, as sometimes stronger and more palpable, and at other times more feeble and less discernible. As the heart knoweth its own bitterness, in like manner a stranger intermeddles not with the joy communicated by this secret testimony to our spirit. Its reality is indicated in Scripture by such expressions as those of the Father and the Son *coming* unto us, and making their *abode* with us,—Christ *manifesting* Himself to us, and *supping* with us,—His giving us the *hidden manna,* and the *white stone,* denoting the communication to us of the knowledge of an acquittal from guilt, and a *new name* written, which no man knoweth saving he that receiveth it. ' The love of God is shed abroad in our hearts by the Holy Ghost, which is given unto us.' ' He that believeth on the Son of God hath the witness in himself,' 1 John v. 10. This witnessing of the Spirit to the believer's spirit, communicating consolation, is never His first work, but is consequent on His other work of renovation. He first gives faith, and then seals. ' After that ye believed ye were sealed with that Holy Spirit of promise.' He also witnesseth with our spirit, graciously shining on His own promises, making them clear, assuring us of their truth, enabling our spirit to embrace them and to discover our interest in them. He witnesseth with our spirit in all the blessedness of His gracious fruits, diffusing through the soul love, and joy, and peace. In the first method of His witnessing with our spirit we are passive ; but in the last method there is a concurrence on our part with His testimony. The testimony of the Spirit, then, is attended with the testimony of conscience, and is thus a co-witness with our spirit. It may also be observed, that where this exists, it brings with it a disposition and promptitude for prayer. It is the testimony of the Spirit of adoption whereby we cry, ' Abba, Father ; ' it disposes the soul to holiness.

The important truth here affirmed, that the Holy Spirit beareth witness with our spirit, does not seduce believers from the written word, or expose them to delusions, mistaken for internal revelations, differing from the revelations of Scripture. This internal revelation must be agreeable to Scripture revelation, and is no revelation of a new article of faith unknown to Scripture. It is the revelation of a truth consonant to the word of God, and made to a believer in that blessed book for his comfort. The Spirit testifies to our sonship by an external revelation in the Scriptures that believers are the sons of God. He concurs with this testimony by illuminating the mind and understanding, and persuading it of the truth of this external revelation. He unites with this testimony by reason of His gracious sanctifying presence in us, and is therefore called the earnest of our inheritance, and God's seal, marking us as His own.

Ver. 17.—*And if children, then heirs ; heirs of God, and joint heirs with Christ : if so be that we suffer with Him, that we may be also glorified together.*

If children, then heirs.—The Apostle, having proved the adoption of believers from the confirmation of the double and concurrent testimony of their own spirit and of the Spirit of God, here infers from it the certainty of their possessing the eternal inheritance. The fact of their being heirs he deduces from their being children. In this world children are, in all nations, heirs of their parents' possessions. This is the law of nature. As such, it not only illustrates but confirms the fact that believers are heirs as being children. By the declaration that they are heirs, we are reminded that it is not by purchase, or by any work of their own, that they obtain the inheritance to which they are predestinated, Eph. i. 11, and begotten, 1 Pet. i. 3. It is solely in virtue of their sonship. The inheritance, which is a kingdom, was provided for them from the foundation of the world, Matt. xxv. 34, before they existed; and as inheritances were under the law inalienable, so this inheritance is eternal. They are heirs according to the promise, Gal. iii. 29 ; heirs of promise, Heb. vi. 17,—that is, of all the blessings contained in the promise of God, which He confirmed by an oath ; heirs of salvation, Heb. i. 14 ; heirs of the grace of life, 1 Pet. iii. 7 ; heirs according to the hope of eternal life, Tit. iii. 7 ; heirs of righteousness, Heb. xi. 7 ; heirs of the kingdom which God hath promised, Jas. ii. 5. All things are theirs : for they are Christ's and Christ is God's, 1 Cor. iii. 23.

Heirs of God.—Here, in one word, the Apostle states what is the inheritance of those who are the children of God. It is God Himself. ' If a son, then an heir of God through Christ,' Gal. iv. 7. This expression, ' heirs of God,' has a manifest relation to the title of ' son,' which is acquired by adoption, on which account the Apostle here joins them together. This teaches that believers have not only a right to the good things of God, but that they have this right by their adoption, and not by merit. As the birthright of a child confers a title to the property of its father, and so distinguishes such property from what the child may acquire by industry and labour, so also is the case with adoption. Here we see the difference between the law and the Gospel. The law treats men as mercenaries, and says, Do, and live; the Gospel treats them as children, and says, Live, and do. God is the portion of His people; and in Him, who is 'the possessor of heaven and earth,' they are heirs of all things. 'He that overcometh shall inherit all things : and I will be his God, and he shall be My son,' Rev. xxi. 7. God is all-sufficient; and this is an all-sufficient inheritance. God is eternal and unchangeable ; and therefore it is an eternal inheritance,— an inheritance incorruptible, undefiled, and that fadeth not away. They cannot be dispossessed of it, for the omnipotence of God secures against all opposition. It is reserved for them in heaven, which is the throne of God, and where He manifests His glory. It is God Himself, then, who is the inheritance of His children. This shows that He communicates Himself to them by His grace, His light, His holiness, His life. They possess God as their inheritance in two degrees, namely, in possessing in this life His grace, and in the life to come His glory. 'Thou shalt guide me with Thy counsel, and afterward receive me to glory. Whom have I in heaven but Thee ? and there is none upon earth that I desire besides Thee ! ' Ps. lxxiii. 24. And what is the inheritance in glory, if it be not God, who is all in all ! Here we have the life of grace,—'The grace of the Lord Jesus Christ, and the love of God, and the communion of the Holy Ghost, be with you all.' In the life to come, it is the enjoyment or the vision of God which, in the seventeenth Psalm, the Prophet opposes to the inheritance of the men of this world,—'Deliver me, O Lord, from men of the world, which have their portion in this life. As for me, I will behold Thy face in righteousness; I shall be satisfied when I awake with Thy likeness.' Into this inheritance Moses—that is to say, the law—cannot introduce us. He alone can do it who is the great Joshua—Jesus Christ, the Mediator of a better covenant.

Joint heirs with Christ.—This, with the expression 'heirs of God,' shows the glorious nature of the inheritance of the children of God. What must this honour be when they are heirs of God, and joint heirs with Christ? Adam was a son of God ; the lordship of paradise was given him, but he lost it. Satan and his angels were also sons of God by creation, and they fell. But the joint heirs of Christ can never fall. They have their inheritance secured by their union with Christ, and hold it by a title which is indefeasible, and a right which never can be revoked. Christ is the heir, as being the Son of God. All things that the Father hath are His; and, as Mediator, He is appointed 'heir of all things,' and they are joint heirs with Him. The inheritance to be possessed by them is the same in its nature as that possessed by the man Christ Jesus ; and the glory that the Father gives to Him, He gives to them, John xvii. 22. They participate of the same Spirit with Him ; for they that have not the Spirit of Christ are none of His. That same life that He has is conferred on them ; and because He lives, they live also. He is the fountain of their life, Ps. xxxvi. 9. The glory of their bodies will be of the same kind with His, Phil. iii. 21. The glory that the Father gave to Him, He has given to them, John xvii. 22. They shall be admitted to the same

glorious place with Him, and shall behold His glory, John xvii. 24.
There must be a conformity between the head and the members, but as
to the degree, He who is the first-born among many brethren must in all
things have the pre-eminence.

If so be that ye suffer with Him.—The Apostle had shown that believers
are the adopted children of God, heirs of God, and joint heirs with Jesus
Christ. He now refers to a possible objection, namely, that notwithstanding this they are often full of trouble and afflictions in this life,
which appears not to be suitable to so near a relationship with God. This
he obviates by reminding them that they suffer with Christ, and that
their sufferings, which result from their bearing them with Him, will
issue in future glory.

The sufferings of Jesus Christ are to be regarded in two points of
view. On the one hand, He suffered as the propitiation for the sins of
His people. On the other hand, His sufferings are to be viewed as the
road conducting Him to glory. In the first of these His people have no
part; He alone was the sacrifice offered for their salvation; He alone
made satisfaction to the justice of God; and He alone merited the reward
for them. But in the second point of view, He is the pattern of their
condition; in this they must follow His steps,· and be made conformable
to Him. Suffering, then, is a peculiarity in the earthly lot of all the
heirs of heaven; they are all called to suffer with Christ. The man professing Christ's religion, who meets with no persecution or opposition from
the world for Christ's sake, may well doubt the sincerity of his profession.
' All that will live godly in Christ Jesus shall suffer persecution.' All the
heirs will come to the enjoyment of their inheritance through tribulation;
most of them through much tribulation. But so far from this being an
argument against the sure prospect of that inheritance, it tends to confirm
it. The expression ' if so be,' or since, does not intimate that this is
doubtful, but establishes its certainty. God causes His children to suffer
in different ways, and for different reasons, for their good, as for the trial
of their faith, the exercise of patience, the mortification of sin, and in
order to wean them from this world and prepare them for heaven.
Their sufferings are effects of His Fatherly love; and the great object of
them is, that they may be conformed to Christ. Sufferings are appointed
for them in order that they should not be condemned with the world,
and to work out for them a far more exceeding and eternal weight of
glory.

That we may be also glorified together.—This ought to support Christians
under their sufferings. What a consolation in the midst of afflictions for
Christ's sake, that they shall also be glorified together with Him! In
His sufferings He is set forth as their pattern, and the issue of them is
their encouragement. They have the honour of suffering with Him, and
they shall have the honour of being glorified with Him. They not only
accompany him in His sufferings, but He also accompanies them in theirs;
not only to sympathize with them, but to be their surety and defender.

This community in suffering with Jesus Christ is sufficient to impart to
His people the highest consolation. What an honour is it to bear, here
below, His cross, on the way to where one day they shall have a place

upon His throne ! Having the same enemies with Him, they must have the some combats, the same victories, and the same triumphs. Since the Lord has been pleased to suffer for them before reigning over them in heaven, it is proper that they should suffer also for His sake and in the prospect of reigning with Him. For suffering with Him, they shall overcome with Him; and overcoming with Him, they shall obtain the crown of life and eternal glory.

Ver. 18.—*For I reckon that the sufferings of this present time are not worthy to be compared with the glory which shall be revealed in us.*

The Apostle had been reminding those to whom he wrote, that their sufferings with Christ is the way appointed by God to bring them to glory. Here he encourages them to endure affliction, because there is no comparison between their present sufferings and their future glory. In order to encourage the Israelites to sustain the difficulties that presented themselves to their entry into Canaan, God sent them of the fruits of the land while they were still in the desert. Our blessed Lord, too, permitted some of His disciples to witness His transfiguration, when His face did shine as the sun, and His raiment was white as light. This was calculated to inspire them with an ardent desire to behold that heavenly glory, of which, on that occasion, they had a transient glimpse, and to render them more patient in sustaining the troubles they were about to encounter. In the same manner God acts towards His people when they suffer in this world. He sends them of the fruits of the heavenly Canaan, and allowing them to enjoy a measure of that peace which passeth all understanding, He favours them with some foretastes of the glory to be revealed.

The first testimony to the truth that the, Apostle is here declaring is his own. *I reckon.*—Paul was better qualified to judge in this matter than any other man, both as having endured the greatest sufferings, and as having been favoured with a sight of the glory of heaven. His sufferings, 1 Cor. iv. 9 ; 2 Cor. xi. 23, appear not to have been inferior to those that exercised the patience of Job, while his being caught up into the third heaven was peculiar to himself. But, independently of this, we have here the testimony of an inspired Apostle, which must be according to truth, as being immediately communicated by the Holy Ghost. Paul makes use of a word which refers to the casting up of an account, marking accurately the calculation, by comparing one thing with another, so as to arrive at the true result.

The sufferings of the present time.—By this we are reminded that the present is a time of suffering, and that this world is to believers as a field of battle. The shortness, too, of the period of suffering is indicated. It is limited to the *present* life, respecting which man is compared to a flower which cometh forth and is cut down ; to a shadow that fleeth and continueth not. ' His days are swifter than a post ; and as the flight of the eagle hastening after its prey.' It is in the present time exclusively that sufferings are to be endured by the children of God. But if they promise to themselves the enjoyment of ease and carnal prosperity, they miscalculate the times, and confound the present with the future. They forget the many assurances of their Heavenly Father that this is not their rest.

They overlook the example of those who by faith obtained a good report. Moses refused to be called the son of Pharaoh's daughter, choosing rather to suffer affliction with the people of God, than to enjoy the pleasures of sin for a season. David, envying for a moment the prosperity of the wicked, having entered the sanctuary and considered their end, views it in a different light. 'Nevertheless I am continually with Thee; Thou hast holden me by Thy right hand; Thou shalt guide me with Thy counsel, and afterwards receive me to glory.' 'In Thy presence is fulness of joy; at Thy right hand there are pleasures for evermore.' 'Thou hast put gladness in my heart more than in the time that their corn and their wine increased. I will both lay me down in peace and sleep, for Thou, Lord, only makest me to dwell in safety.'

Christians often dwell upon their own sufferings, while they overlook the sufferings of their Lord, to whom they must be conformed. They forget their sins, on account of which they receive chastisement that they may not be condemned with the world, and for which they must also partake of their bitter fruits. But as there is no proportion between what is finite, however great it may be, and what is infinite, so their afflictions here, even were their lives prolonged to any period, and although they had no respite, would bear no proportion to their future glory either in intensity or duration. The felicity of that glory is unspeakable, but their afflictions here are not insupportable. They are always accompanied with the compassion and the consolations of God. 'As the sufferings of Christ abound in us, so our consolation also aboundeth by Christ.' The patriarch Jacob, a fugitive from his father's house, constrained to pass the night without a covering, with stones only for his pillow, enjoyed a vision excelling all with which he had been before favoured. This is recorded to show that the believer, in his tribulation, often experiences more joy and peace than in his prosperity. 'Thus saith the Lord God, although I have cast them far off among the heathen, and although I have scattered them among the countries, yet will I be to them as a little sanctuary in the countries where they shall come.' God never permits the sufferings of His people to be extreme.

The glory that shall be revealed.—While the sufferings of believers here are only temporary, the glory which is to be revealed is eternal. Though yet concealed, it is already in existence, its discovery only is future. Now it is veiled from us in heaven, but ere long it shall be revealed. God is a source of ineffable light, joy, knowledge, power, and goodness. He is the sovereign good, and will communicate Himself to them that behold Him, in a way that is incomprehensible.

In us.—The glory here spoken of is that to which the Apostle John refers, when he says that we shall see the Lord as He is, and that we shall be made like Him. If the rays of the sun illuminate the darkness on which they shine, what will be that light which the Sun of Righteousness will produce in the children of Him who is the Father of Lights! If the face of Moses shone, when, amidst the terrors of the law, he talked with God, what shall their condition be who shall behold Him, not on the mountain that might be touched, and that burned with fire, but in the heaven of heavens; not amidst thunderings and lightnings, but amidst the express testimonies of His favour and blessing! They shall appear in the sanctuary of the Lord, and discern plainly the mysteries of the wisdom of God. They shall behold not the ark and the propitiatory, but the things in the heavens which these were made to represent. They shall see as they are seen, and know as they are known. To the enjoyment of this glory after the persecutions and troubles of this life, the Bridegroom is represented as calling His Church. ' Lo, the winter is past, the rain is over and gone, the flowers appear on the earth ; the time of the singing of birds is come. Arise, my love, my fair one, and come away.' As there is no proportion between finite and infinite, so no comparison can be made between the things that are seen and temporal, and the things that are unseen and eternal—between our light afflictions which are but for a moment, and that far more exceeding and eternal weight of glory that shall be revealed in us. Such is the consolation which the Apostle here presents to the children of God.

Ver. 19–22.—*For the earnest expectation of the creature waiteth for the manifesta-tion of the sons of God (for the creature was made subject to vanity, not willingly, but by reason of him who hath subjected the same), in hope that the creature itself also shall be delivered from the bondage of corruption into the glorious liberty of the children of God. For we know that the whole creation groaneth and travaileth in pain together until now.*

In the 18th verse, the Apostle, for the comfort of believers, had declared that there is reserved for them a weight of glory to which their sufferings while in this world bear no comparison. To the same purpose he now refers to the existing state and future destination of the visible creation. In thus appealing to a double testimony—the one the voice of grace uttered by himself, the other the voice of universal nature, which speaks the same language—he encourages the children of God to endure with patience their present trials.

In the verses before us, Paul, by an example of personification common in the Scriptures,[1] which consists in attributing human affections to things inanimate or unintelligent, calls the attention of believers to the fact that the whole creation is in a state of suffering and degradation ; and that, wearied with the vanity to which it has been reduced, it is earnestly looking for deliverance.

That interpretation which, according to Dr. Macknight and Mr. Stuart, applies this expectation to mankind in general, is contrary to fact. Men in general are not looking for a glorious deliverance, nor is it a fact that they will obtain it ; but it is a fact that there will be new heavens and a new earth, wherein dwelleth righteousness. All that Mr. Stuart alleges against this is easily obviated. Most of it applies to passages that have been injudiciously appealed to on the subject, which do not bear the conclusion. But if the earth, after being burnt up, shall be restored in glory, there is a just foundation for the figurative expectation. In order to understand these verses, it is necessary to ascertain the import,—1*st*, of the term *creation*, or creature ; 2*d*, of that of the *vanity* to which it is subjected ; 3*d*, of that *deliverance* which it shall experience.

Creature.—The word in the original, which is translated in the 19th,

[1] Ps. xcvi. 11, 12, cviii. 8, cxlviii. 3, 10 ; Isa. lv. 12 ; Hab. iii. 10.

20th, and 21st verses, creature, and in the 22d, creation, can have no reference to the fallen angels, for they do not desire the manifestation of the children of God ; this they dread, and, looking forward to it, tremble. Neither can it refer to the elect angels, of whom it cannot be said that they shall be delivered from the bondage of corruption, for to this they were never subjected. It does not apply to men, all of whom are either the children of God or of the wicked one. It cannot refer to the children of God, for they are here expressly distinguished from the creation of which the Apostle speaks ; nor can it apply to wicked men, for they have no wish for the manifestation of the sons of God, whom they hate, nor will they ever be delivered from the bondage of corruption, but cast into the lake of fire. It remains, then, that the creatures destitute of intelligence, animate and inanimate, the heavens and the earth, the elements, the plants and animals, are here referred to. The Apostle means to say that the creation, which, on account of sin, has, by the sentence of God, been subjected to vanity, shall be rescued from the present degradation under which it groans, and that, according to the hope held out to it, is longing to participate with the sons of God in that freedom from vanity into which it shall at length be introduced, partaking with them in their future and glorious deliverance from all evil. This indeed cannot mean that the plants and animals, as they at present exist, shall be restored ; but that the condition of those things which shall belong to the new heavens and the new earth, prepared for the sons of God, shall be delivered from the curse, and restored to a perfect state, as when all things that God had created were pronounced by Him very good, and when, as at the beginning, before sin entered, they shall be fully adapted to the use of man.

As men earnestly desire what is good, and, on the contrary, groan and sigh in their sufferings, the like emotions of joy and sorrow are here ascribed to the inanimate and unintelligent creation. In this way the prophets introduce the earth as groaning, and the animals as crying to God, in sympathy with the condition of man. ' The land mourneth, for the corn is wasted; the new wine is dried up ; the oil languisheth, because joy is withered away from the sons of men ! How do the beasts groan ! the beasts of the field cry also unto Thee !' Joel i. 10-20. ' How long shall the land mourn and the herbs of every field wither, for the wickedness of them that dwell therein ? ' Jer. xii. 4. ' The earth mourneth and fadeth away ; the world languishes and fadeth away ; the haughty people of the earth do languish. The earth also is defiled, under the inhabitants thereof; because they have transgressed the laws, changed the ordinance, broken the everlasting covenant. Therefore hath the curse devoured the earth. The new wine mourneth ; the wine languisheth !' Isa. xxiv. 4-7. To the same purpose, Isa. xiii. 13, xxxiii. 9, xxxiv. 4. On the other hand, the Prophet Isaiah, xlix. 13, predicting a better state of things, exclaims, ' Sing, O heavens; and be joyful, O earth ; and break forth into singing, O mountains; for the Lord hath comforted His people, and will have mercy upon His afflicted !' And in Ps. xcviii. 4-6, ' Make a joyful noise unto the Lord, all the earth ; make a loud noise, and rejoice, and sing praises ! Let the sea roar, and the fulness thereof ! Let the floods clap their hands: let the hills be joyful together!' Thus, in the language of Scripture, the sins of men cause the creation to mourn; but the mercy of God, withdrawing His rebukes, causeth it to rejoice.

Vanity.—What is called vanity in the 20th verse, is in the 21st denominated *bondage of corruption.* When the creation was brought into existence, God bestowed on it His blessing, and pronounced everything that He had made very good. Viewing that admirable palace which He had provided, He appointed man to reign in it, commanding all creation to be subject to him whom He had made in His own image. But when sin entered, then, in a certain sense, it may be said that all things had become evil, and were diverted from their proper end. The creatures by their nature were appointed for the service of the friends of their Creator; but since the entrance of sin they had become subservient to His enemies. Instead of the sun and the heavens being honoured to give light to those who obey God, and the earth to support the righteous, they now minister to rebels. The sun shines upon the wicked, the earth nourishes those who blaspheme their Maker; while its various productions, instead of being employed for the glory of God, are used as instruments of ambition, of avarice, of intemperance, of cruelty, of idolatry, and are often employed for the destruction of His children. All these are subjected to vanity when applied by men for vain purposes. This degradation is a grievance to the works of God, which in themselves have remained in allegiance. They groan under it, but, keeping within their proper limits, hold on their course. Had it been the will of the Creator, after the entrance of sin, the creature might have refused to serve the vices, or even the necessities of man. This is sometimes threatened. In reproving the idolatry of the children of Israel, God speaks as if He intended to withdraw His creatures from their service, in taking them entirely away. 'Therefore will I return and take away My corn in the time thereof, and My wine in the season thereof, and will recover My wool and My flax given to cover her nakedness,' Hos. ii. 9. And sometimes the creature is represented as reclaiming against the covetousness and wickedness of men. 'The stone shall cry out of the wall, and the beam out of the timber shall answer it,' Hab. ii. 11.

The whole creation, then, groaneth together, and is under bondage on account of the sin of man, and has suffered by it immensely. As to the inanimate creation, in many ways it shows its figurative groaning, and the vanity to which it has been reduced. 'Cursed is the ground for thy sake; thorns also and thistles shall it bring forth to thee.' It produces all noxious weeds, and in many places is entirely barren. It is subject to earthquakes, floods, and storms destructive to human life, and in various respects labours under the curse pronounced upon it. The lower animals have largely shared in the sufferings of man. They are made 'to be taken and destroyed,' 2 Pet. ii. 12, and to devour one another. They have become subservient to the criminal pleasures of man, and are the victims of his oppressive cruelty. Some partake in the labours to which he is subjected; and all of them terminate their short existence by death, the effect of sin. All that belongs to the creation is fading and transitory, and death reigns universally. The heavens and the earth shall wax old like a garment. The earth once perished by water, and now it is reserved unto fire. 'The heavens shall pass away with a great noise, and the elements shall melt with fervent heat; the earth also and the works that are therein shall be burnt up. The heavens being on fire shall be dissolved.' The cause of this subjection to vanity is not from their original tendencies, or from any fault in the creatures. They have been so subjected, not willingly, not owing to any natural defect or improper disposition in themselves, but by reason of the sin of man, and in order to his greater punishment. The houses of those who were guilty of rebellion were destroyed, Ezra vi. 11; Dan. ii. 5, not that there was guilt in the stones or the wood, but in order to inflict the severer punishment on their criminal possessors, and also to testify the greater abhorrence of their crime, in thus visiting them in the things that belonged to them. In the same manner, man, having been constituted the lord of the creatures, his punishment has been extended to them. This in a very striking manner demonstrates the hatred of God against sin. For as the leprosy not only defiled the man who was infected with it, but also the house he inhabited, in the same way, sin, which is the spiritual leprosy of man, has not only defiled our bodies and our souls, but, by the just judgment of God, has infected all creation.

In whatever way it may be attempted to be accounted for, it is a fact that the world and all around us is in a suffering and degraded condition. This state of things bears the appearance of being inconsistent with the government of God, all-powerful, wise, and good. The proud sceptic is here completely at a stand. He cannot even conjecture why such a state of things should have had place. With Mr. Hume, the language of every reflecting unbeliever must be, 'The whole is a riddle, an enigma, an inexplicable mystery. Doubt, uncertainty, suspense of judgment, appear the only result of our most accurate scrutiny concerning this subject.' The Book of God alone dispels the darkness, and unveils the mystery.

Here, then, we learn how great is the evil of sin. It has polluted the heavens and the earth, and has subjected the whole to vanity and corruption. Evil and misery prevail, and creation itself is compelled to witness the dishonour done to its Author. It would be derogatory to the glory of God to suppose that His works are now in the same condition in which they were at first formed, or that they will always continue as at present. In the meantime, all the creatures are groaning under their degradation, until the moment when God shall remove those obstacles which prevent them from answering their proper ends, and render them incapable of suitably glorifying Him. But the righteous Judge, who subjected them to vanity in consequence of the disobedience of man, has made provision for their final restoration.

The creation, then, is not in that state in which it was originally constituted. A fearful change and disorganization, even in the frame of the natural world, has taken place. The introduction of sin has brought along with it this subjection to vanity and the bondage of corruption, and all that ruin under which nature groans. How miserable is the condition of those who have their portion in this world! Of them it may be truly said, 'Surely they have inherited lies, vanity, and things wherein there is no profit.' Of those 'who mind earthly things,' it is written, their 'end is destruction.' 'The heavens and the earth which are now, by the same word are kept in store, reserved unto fire against the day of judgment and perdition of ungodly men.'

Delivered.—Some suppose that the word delivered signifies an entire annihilation, and in support of this opinion allege such passages as 2 Pet. iii. 10; Rev. xx. 11. But as a tendency of all things in nature is to their own preservation, how could the creation be represented as earnestly expecting the manifestation of the sons of God, if that manifestation were to be accompanied with its final ruin and destruction? Besides, the Apostle promises not merely a future deliverance, but also a glorious future existence. The Scriptures, too, in various places, predict the continued subsistence of the heavens and the earth, as 2 Pet. iii. 13; Rev. xxi. 1. Respecting the passages quoted above, as importing their annihilation, it ought to be observed that the destruction of the substance of things differs from a change in their qualities. When metal of a certain shape is subjected to fire, it is destroyed as to its figure, but not as to its substance. Thus the heavens and the earth will pass through the fire, but only that they may be purified and come forth anew, more excellent than before. In Psalm cii. 26, it is said, 'They shall perish, but Thou shalt endure; yea, all of them shall wax old like a garment; as a vesture shalt Thou change them, and they shall be *changed.*' That the Apostle Peter, when he says that the heavens shall be dissolved, and the elements shall melt with fervent heat, does not refer to the destruction of their substance, but to their purification, is evident from what he immediately adds,—'Nevertheless we, according to His promise, look for new heavens and a new earth, wherein dwelleth righteousness.' A little before he had said, 'The world that then was, being overflowed with water, perished,' although its substance remains as at the beginning. If, then, the punishment of sin has extended to the creatures, in bringing them under the bondage of corruption, so, according to the passage before us, that grace which reigns above sin, will also be extended to their deliverance. And, as the punishment of the sins of men is so much the greater as their effects extend to the creatures, in like manner so much the greater will be the glory that shall be revealed in them, that the creatures which were formed for their use shall be made to participate with them in the day of the restitution of all things. Through the goodness of God they shall follow the deliverance and final destination of the children of God, and not that of His enemies.

When God created the world, He 'saw everything that He had made, and, behold, it was very good.' When man transgressed, God viewed it a second time, and said, 'Cursed is the ground for thy sake.' When the promise that the Deliverer should come into the world to re-establish peace between God and man was given, the effect of this blessed reconciliation was to extend even to the inanimate and unintelligent creation; and God, it may be said, then viewed His work a third time, and held out the hope of a glorious restoration.

The creature, then, has been subjected to the indignity which it now suffers, *in hope*[1] that it will one day be delivered from the bondage of corruption, and partake of the glorious freedom of the children of God. This hope was held out in the sentence pronounced on man, for, in the doom of our first parents, the Divine purpose of providing a deliverer was revealed. We know not the circumstances of this change, how it will be effected, or in what form the creation—those new heavens and that new earth, wherein dwelleth righteousness, suited for the abode of the sons of God—shall then exist; but we are sure that it shall be worthy of the Divine wisdom, although at present beyond our comprehension.

Manifestation of the sons of God.—Believers are even now the sons of God, but the world knows them not, 1 John iii. 1. In this respect they are not seen. Their bodies, as well as their spirits, have been purchased by Christ, and they are become His members. Their bodies have, however, no marks of this Divine relation, but, like those of other men, are subject to disease, to death, and corruption. And although they have been regenerated by the Spirit of God, there is still a law in their members warring against the law of their mind. But the period approaches when their souls shall be freed from every remainder of corruption, and their bodies shall be made like unto the glorious body of the Son of God. Then this corruptible shall put on incorruption, and then shall they shine forth as the sun in the kingdom of their Father. It is then that they shall be manifested in their true character, illustrious as the sons of God, seated upon thrones, and conspicuous in robes of light and glory.

Ver. 23.—*And not only they, but ourselves also, which have the first fruits of the Spirit, even we ourselves groan within ourselves, waiting for the adoption, to wit, the redemption of our body.*

In the four preceding verses, the Apostle had appealed to the state of nature, which, by a striking and beautiful figure, is personified and represented as groaning under the oppression of suffering, through the entrance of sin, and looking forward with ardent expectation, as with outstretched neck, to a future and better dispensation. He now proceeds to call the attention of believers to their own feelings and experience, meaning to say that if the unintelligent creation is longing for the manifestation of the sons of God, how much more earnestly must they themselves long for that glorious event.

Christians who have received the foretastes of everlasting felicity, sympathize with the groans of nature. They enjoy, indeed, even at present, a blessed freedom. They are delivered from the guilt and dominion of sin, the curse of the law, and a servile spirit in their obedience to God. Still, however, they have much to suffer while in the world; but they wait for the redemption of their bodies, and the full manifestation of their character as the children of God. Their bodies, as well as their spirits, have been given to Christ. They are equally the fruit of His purchase, and are become His members. But it is not till

---

[1] The 20th verse should be read in a parenthesis, except the two last words, which should be transferred to the 21st verse, and *that* substituted for *because*. *In hope that the creature itself also shall be delivered.*

His people shall have arisen from the grave that they will enjoy all the privileges consequent on His redemption.

The first fruits of the Spirit.—These are love and joy in the Holy Ghost, peace of conscience, and communion with God. They are the graces of the Spirit conferred on believers, called first fruits, because, as the first fruits of the fields were offered to God under the law, so these graces redound to God's glory. And as the first ears of corn were a pledge of an abundant harvest, so these graces are a pledge to believers of their complete felicity, because they are given to them of God for the confirmation of their hope. They are a pledge, because the same love and grace that moved their Heavenly Father to impart these beginnings of their salvation will move Him to perfect the good work. These first fruits, then, are the foretastes of heaven, or the earnest of the inheritance. This is the most invaluable privilege of the children of God in the present life. It is a joy the world cannot give and cannot take away. The error which would represent these privileges as peculiar to the Apostles and the first Christians, and restrict the fruits of the Spirit to miraculous gifts, ought not for one moment to be admitted. The Apostle is speaking of all the children of God to the end of the world, without excepting even the weakest.

As the first fruits of the harvest were consecrated to God, so we should be careful not to abuse the gifts of the Spirit of God in us. As the first fruits were to be carried to the house of God, so, as God has communicated to us His grace, we should also go to His house making a public profession of His name. The children of Israel, in offering the first fruits, were commanded to confess their miserable original state, and to recount their experience of the goodness of God, Deut. xxvi. 5. In the same way we should consider the graces of the Holy Spirit in us as the first fruits of the heavenly Canaan which God hath given us, and confess that we were by nature children of wrath, dead in trespasses and sins, and that the Lord, having had compassion on us, has delivered us from the servitude of sin, and the power of darkness, and translated us into the kingdom of His dear Son.

Groan within ourselves.—Not only they—the whole creation or every creature—but also believers themselves, with all their advantages, groan. Even they find it difficult to bear up under the pressure which in their present state weighs them down, while carrying about with them a body of sin and death. Of this groaning the Apostle, as we have seen, ch. vii. 24, presents himself as an example,—'O wretched man that I am;' and again when he says, 'We that are in this tabernacle do groan, being burdened,' 2 Cor. v. 4. In the same manner David groaned, when he complained that his iniquities were a burden too heavy for him. Believers groan on account of indwelling sin, of the temptations of Satan and the world, and of the evils that afflict their bodies and souls. They feel that something is always wanting to them in this world. There is nothing but that sovereign good, which can only be found in God, fully able to satisfy their desires. Believers groan *within themselves.* Their groanings are not such as those of hypocrites, which are only outward; they are from within. They do not always meet the ear of man, but they reach the throne of God. 'All my desire,' says David, 'is before

Thee, and my groaning is not hid from Thee,' Ps. xxxviii. 9. These groanings are sighs and prayers to God, which are spoken of in the 26th verse of this chapter, where we learn their efficient cause, which is not flesh and blood. They are fruits of the Spirit, so that by them believers observe in themselves the spirit of regeneration.

Waiting for the adoption.—Believers have already been adopted into the family of God, and are His children ; but they have not yet been openly declared to be so,[1] nor made in all respects suitable to this character. If they are the sons of God, they must be made glorious, both in soul and body ; but till they arrive in heaven, their adoption will not be fully manifested. Adoption may be viewed at three periods. It may be considered in the election of His people, when God decrees their adoption before they are called or united to Jesus Christ; yet they are even then denominated the children of God. In the eleventh chapter of John, where Caiaphas, prophesying of the death of Jesus, says that he should die, not for that nation only, but for all the children of God that were scattered abroad. Under the term children of God were comprehended those who had not yet been called, Acts xviii. 10. In their calling and regeneration they are adopted into God's family, being then united to Christ; but as their bodies do not partake in that regeneration, and are not yet conformed to the glorious body of Jesus Christ, they still wait for the entire accomplishment of their adoption, when, at the resurrection, they shall enter on the full possession of the inheritance. Accordingly Jesus denominates that blessed resurrection ' the regeneration,' because then not only the souls of believers, but also their bodies, shall bear the heavenly image of the second Adam. Then they shall enter fully into the possession of their inheritance ; for in that day Jesus Christ will say to His elect, ' Come, ye blessed of My Father, inherit the kingdom pre-pared for you from the foundation of the world.' Heaven, into which they will then enter, is an inheritance suitable to the dignity of the sons of God, and for this they are waiting.

The children of God wait for the accomplishment of all that their adoption imports. They wait for it as Jacob did. ' I have waited for Thy salvation, O Lord!' Gen. xlix. 18. They wait as the believers at Corinth were waiting for the coming of our Lord Jesus Christ, 1 Cor. i. 7 ; and as all believers who through the Spirit wait for the hope of righteousness by faith, Gal. v. 5. ' Looking for the blessed hope, and the glorious appearing of the great God, even our Saviour Jesus Christ,' Tit. ii. 13. And as the Thessalonians, who, having been turned from idols to serve the living and true God, waited for His Son from heaven, 1 Thess. i. 10; also as is re-corded in Heb. ix. 28 ; Jas. v. 7, 8 ; 2 Pet. iii. 12. In this manner Paul waited for his crown, 2 Tim. iv. 8. It was this waiting for, or ex-pectation of, deliverance from the Lord, that encouraged Noah to build the ark, and Abraham to leave his country, and Moses to esteem the reproach of Christ greater riches than the treasures in Egypt, and the elders who obtained a good report through faith, to seek a better, that is, an heavenly country. It was the expectation of eternal life that sustained those who shed their blood for the testimony of Jesus.

---

[1] Among the Romans there was a twofold adoption,—the one private, the other public.

The redemption of our body.—That there might be no mistake respecting the meaning of the adoption in this unusual application, the Apostle himself subjoins an explanation—even the redemption of our body, because the body will then be delivered from the grave, as a prisoner when redeemed is delivered from his prison.

But why, it may be asked, does the Apostle here employ the term redemption rather than that of resurrection, which is so common in the New Testament? To this it may be replied, that the Holy Scriptures often make use of this expression to represent a great deliverance, as in Ps. cvii. 2: 'Let the redeemed of the Lord say so, whom He hath redeemed from the hand of the enemy!' And as in Isa. lxiii., where those are spoken of who are redeemed of the Lord from the hand of the enemy. It is evident that Paul employs this expression forcibly to designate the greatest of all deliverances, the highest object of our desires, which is to be the subject of our eternal gratitude. When this term is so used, it commonly denotes two things,—the one, that the deliverance spoken of is effected in a manner glorious and conspicuous, exhibiting the greatest effort of power; the other, that it is a complete deliverance, placing us beyond all danger. On this ground, then, it is evident that no work is better entitled to the appellation of redemption than that of the re-establishment of our bodies, which will be an illustrious effect of the infinite power of God. It is the work of the Lord of nature—of Him who holds in His hands the keys of life and death. His light alone can dispel the darkness of the tomb. It is only His hand that can break its seal and its silence. On this account the Apostle appeals, with an accumulation of terms, to the exceeding greatness of the power of God to us-ward who believe, according to the working of His mighty power, which He wrought in Christ when He raised Him from the dead, Eph. i. 19, 20.

This last deliverance will be so perfect, that nothing can be more complete, since 'the children of the resurrection' shall be restored not to their first life, but to a state which will be one of surpassing glory and never-ending immortality. Death will be swallowed up in victory. Earthly warriors may obtain two sorts of victories over their enemies. One may be called a temporary or partial victory, which causes the enemy to fly, which deprives him of part of his force, but does not prevent him from re-establishing himself, returning to the field of battle, and placing the conqueror in the hazard of losing what he has gained. The other may be termed a complete and decisive victory, which so effectually subdues the hostile power, that it can never regain what it has lost. There are also two sorts of resurrections, one like that of Lazarus, in which death was overcome but not destroyed, since Lazarus died a second time; the other is, that of believers at the last day, when death will not only be overcome, but cast out and for ever exterminated. Both of these may be properly called a resurrection; but to speak with greater force, the second is here called a *redemption*. Besides, the Apostle, in employing this term, has reference to the redemption which Jesus Christ has effected at the infinite price of His blood. It is true this price was fully paid on the day of His death; yet two things are certain: the one is, that our resurrection will only take place in virtue of the value and imperishable efficacy of that blood, which has acquired for us life and happiness; the other, that the redemption accomplished on the cross and the resurrection are not two different works. They are but one work, viewed under different aspects, and at different periods; the redemption on the cross being our redemption by price, and the resurrection our redemption by power—a perfect and undivided salvation begun and terminated.

The day, then, of the redemption of our bodies will be the day of the entire accomplishment of our adoption, as then only we shall enter on the complete possession of the children of God. In Jesus Christ our redemption was fully accomplished when He said on the cross, 'It is finished.' In us it is accomplished by different degrees. The first degree is in this life; the second, at death; the third, at the resurrection. In this life, the degree of redemption which we obtain is the remission of our sins, our sanctification, and freedom from the law and the slavery of sin. At death, our souls are delivered from all sin, and their sanctification is complete; for the soul, at its departure from the body, is received into the heavenly sanctuary, into which nothing can enter that defileth; and as to the body, death prepares it for incorruption and immortality, for that which we sow is not quickened except it die. It must therefore return to dust, there to leave its corruption, its weakness, its dishonour. Hence it follows that believers should not fear death, since death obtains for them the second degree of their redemption. But as our bodies remain in the dust till the day of our blessed resurrection, that day is called the day of the redemption of our body, as being the last and highest degree of our redemption. Then the body being reunited to the soul, death will be swallowed up in victory; for the last enemy that shall be destroyed is death, for till then death will reign over our bodies. But then the children of God shall sing that triumphant song, 'O death, where is thy sting? O grave, where is thy victory?' 'I will ransom them from the power of the grave; I will redeem them from death; O death, I will be thy plague; O grave, I will be thy destruction.'

The elevation of His people to glory on the day of their redemption, will be the last act in the economy of Jesus Christ as Mediator. He will then terminate His reign and the whole work of their salvation. For then He will present the whole Church to the Father, saying, 'Behold I and the children whom Thou hast given Me.' Then He will deliver up the kingdom, having nothing further to do in the work of redemption. This will be the rendering of the account by the Son to the Father of the charge committed to Him; and for this reason the Apostle says, 'When all things shall be subdued unto Him, then shall the Son also Himself be subject unto Him that put all things under Him, that God may be all in all;' because, as His economy commenced by an act of submission of the Son to the Father, when in entering into the world He said, 'Lo, I come to do Thy will, O God,' it will also terminate by a similar act, as the Son will then deliver up the kingdom to Him from whom He received it.

Believers are here said to have received the first fruits of the Spirit, and to be waiting for the redemption of their bodies. In the fourth

chapter of the Epistle to the Ephesians, the Apostle says, ' Grieve not
the Holy Spirit of God, whereby ye are sealed unto the day of redemption.' As this last passage has so much similarity to the one before us,
and as they are calculated to throw light on each other, it may be proper
in this place to consider its meaning.

The sealing of believers implies that God has marked them by His
Spirit to distinguish them from the rest of mankind. Marking His
people in this manner as His peculiar property, imports that He loves
them as His own ; that they are His 'jewels,' or peculiar treasure, Mal.
iii. 17. But the Apostle does not say that believers have been merely
marked, but that they have been sealed, which implies much more ; for
although every seal is a mark, every mark is not a seal. Seals are marks
which bear the arms of those to whom they belong, and often their image
or resemblance, as the seals of princes. Thus the principal effect of the
Holy Spirit is to impress on the hearts of His people the image of the Son
of God. As the matter to which the seal is applied contributes nothing
to the formation of the character it receives, and only yields to the impression made on it, so the heart is not active, but passive, under the
application of this Divine seal, by which we receive the image of God, the
characters of which are traced by the Holy Spirit, and depend for their
formation entirely on His efficiency. As seals confirm the covenants or
promises to which they are affixed, in the same manner this heavenly
signet firmly establishes the declaration of the Divine mercy, and makes it
irreversible. It confirms to our faith the mysteries of the Gospel, and
renders certain to our hope the promises of the covenant. The seal
of man, although it alters the form, makes no change on the substance
of the matter to which it is applied, and possesses no virtue to render it
proper for receiving the impression. But the seal of· God changes the
matter on which it is impressed, and although naturally hard, renders it
impressible, converting a heart of stone into a heart of flesh. The seal of
man is speedily withdrawn from the matter it impresses, and the impression gradually becomes faint, till it is at length effaced. But the seal of
the Holy Spirit remains in the heart, so that the image it forms can never
be obliterated.

The Apostle not only affirms that we are sealed by the Holy Spirit of
God, but says that we are sealed *unto the day of redemption ;* that is, this
seal is given us in respect of our blessed resurrection, as the pledge of
our complete transformation into the likeness of Christ. This Divine
seal is that by which the Lord our great Judge will distinguish the
righteous from the wicked, raising the one to the resurrection of life, and
the other to the resurrection of damnation. It is also the Holy Spirit
which forms in us the hope of that future redemption, our souls having
no good desire whatever of which He is not the author. These things
are certain ; but it does not appear to be the principal design of the
Apostle to enforce them here. It seems rather to be to teach that the
Holy Spirit is to us a seal or assured pledge of the reality of our resurrection, or, as is said, 'the earnest of our inheritance until the redemption
of the purchased possession.' Besides this, the Holy Spirit confirms in
our souls everything on which the hope of our resurrection depends.

That hope depends on the belief that Jesus Christ has died for our sins, of which the Holy Spirit bears record in our hearts by giving us the answer of a good conscience. It depends on knowing that Jesus Christ has in dying overcome death, and has gloriously risen again to restore to us life which we had forfeited. This is a truth which the Holy Spirit certifies to us, since He is the Spirit of Christ given in virtue of His resurrection. It depends on knowing that Jesus Christ is in heaven, reigning at the right hand of the Father, and that all power is given unto Him, that He may give eternal life to all His people. The Holy Spirit testifies to us this glory, since His coming is its fruit and effect. ' The Holy Spirit was not yet given, because that Jesus was not yet glorified ; ' and the Saviour Himself says that He will send the Comforter, ' even the Spirit of truth, which proceedeth from the Father,' concerning which the Apostle Peter declares, ' Being by the right hand of God exalted, and having received of the Father the promise of the Holy Ghost, He hath shed forth this which ye now see and hear.' As if he had said that this marvellous effusion of the Holy Spirit is an effect, and consequently an assured proof, of the heavenly glory of Jesus Christ. Since God gives His Holy Spirit to His children to seal them to the day of redemption, it is evident that His care of them must extend to the blessed consummation to which He purposes to conduct them. He will not withdraw His gracious hand from them, but will bring them to the possession and enjoyment of His glory. ' The Lord will perfect that which concerneth me.' ' Being confident of this very thing, that He which hath begun a good work in you will perfect it until the day of Jesus Christ.'

It may be remarked that the Apostle says ' unto the *day* of redemption,' and not simply, to the redemption. This expression, the day of redemption, leads us to consider the advantage that grace has over nature, and the future world over that which we now inhabit. When God created the universe, He made light and darkness, day and night; and our time consists of their alternate successions. But it will not be so in the second creation, for ' there shall be no night there.' It will be one perpetual *day* of life without death, of holiness without sin, and of joy without grief.

The day here referred to may be viewed in contrast with two other solemn days, both of which are celebrated in the Scriptures. One is the day of Sinai, the other of Pentecost: this is the day of redemption. In the economy of the *Father*, the first was a day of public and extraordinary grandeur, appointed to display in the most remarkable manner His glory, when God descended with awful majesty amidst blackness, and darkness, and tempest. In the economy of the *Holy Ghost*, the second was the day when He came as a sound from heaven as of a rushing mighty wind, when the Apostles were assembled, and, under the symbol of cloven tongues of fire, rested upon them. In the economy of the *Son*, there will also be a day of public magnificence, and that will be the day of judgment, when, seated on the throne of His glory, Jesus Christ will come with His mighty angels to judge the quick and the dead. Then calling His elect from the four winds, with the voice of the archangel, He will raise them from the dust, and elevate them to the glory of His kingdom. The first of these days was the day of the publication of the *law*; the second was the day of the publication of *grace*; and the third will be the day of the publication of *glory*. This will be the day of the complete redemption of the children of God, unto which they have been sealed, and of their manifestation in their proper character. It will be the day when their bodies shall come forth from the grave, made like unto the glorious body of the Son of God, by the sovereign efficacy of the application of His blood, and by His infinite power. Then shall the righteous shine forth as the sun in the kingdom of their Father. Then they shall inherit the new heavens and the new earth, wherein dwelleth righteousness, which they now expect according to the promise, for God will make all things new. Then they shall be with Jesus where He is, and shall behold His glory which God hath given Him.

Let those rejoice who are waiting for the Divine Redeemer. Their bodies indeed must be dissolved, and it doth not yet appear what they shall be. But at that great day they shall be raised up incorruptible, they shall be rendered immortal, and shall dwell in heavenly mansions. And that they may not doubt this, God has already marked them with His Divine seal. They have been sealed by the Holy Spirit of God unto the day of the redemption.

Ver. 24.—*For we are saved by hope : but hope that is seen is not hope ; for what a man seeth, why doth he yet hope for ?*

For we are saved by hope.—According to the original, this phrase may either be translated *by* hope, or *in* hope; but from the connection it appears that it ought to be translated, as in the French versions, *in hope*. The word salvation, or *saved*, signifies all the benefits of our redemption, —namely, remission of sins, sanctification, and glorification.' The Son of Man is come to save that which was lost.' In this sense Jesus Christ is called the Saviour, because it is by Him that we are justified, and sanctified, and glorified. This word has in Scripture sometimes a more limited, and sometimes a more extended, meaning. In particular places salvation is spoken of as already possessed, as where it is said, God has 'saved us by the washing of regeneration, and renewing of the Holy Ghost.' Generally it signifies all the benefits of our redemption, when fully possessed by our final admission to glory, as when it is said, 'He that endureth to the end shall be saved.' In this verse it is regarded as enjoyed only in hope,—that is to say, in expectancy, since we have not yet been put in possession of the glory of the kingdom of heaven.

In order to distinguish the measure of salvation which believers have in possession, and what they have of it in hope, we must consider its gradations. The first of these is their eternal election, of which the Apostle speaks, Eph. i. 3, 4, according to which their names were written in heaven before the creation of the world. The second gradation is their effectual calling, by which God has called them from darkness into the kingdom of His beloved Son, so that their souls are already partakers of grace, and their bodies habitations of God through the Spirit, and members of Jesus Christ. Of these gradations of their salvation they are already in possession. But the third gradation, in which sin shall be entirely eradicated from their souls, and their bodies shall be made like to the glorious body of the Lord Jesus Christ, is as yet enjoyed by them only in hope.

The term *hope* is used in two different senses,—the one proper, and the other figurative.   Properly, it means the mixture of expectation and desire of that to which we look forward, so that we are kept stedfast to one object, as where it is said, ' Hope is the anchor of the soul.'   Figuratively, it signifies that which we hope for, as when God is called our hope —' Thou art my hope, O Lord God,' Ps. lxxi. 5 ; or, ' Jesus Christ, which is our hope,' 1 Tim. i. 1 ; and as when it is said, we give thanks to God ' for the hope which is laid up for you in heaven,' Col. i. 5.   The word hope, then, either denotes, as in the verse before us, the grace of hope, in reference to the person hoping, or the object of hope, in reference to the thing hoped for.

Hope is so closely allied to faith, that sometimes in Scripture it is taken for faith itself.   They are, however, distinct the one from the other. By faith we believe the promises made to us by God ; by hope we expect to receive the good things which God has promised ; so that faith hath properly for its object the promise, and hope for its object the thing promised, and the execution of the promise.   Faith regards its object as present, but hope regards it as future.   Faith precedes hope, and is its foundation.   We hope for life eternal, because we believe the promises which God has made respecting it ; and if we believe these promises, we must expect their effect.   Hope looks to eternal life as that which is future in regard to its remoteness ; but in regard to its certainty, faith looks to it as a thing that is present.   ' Hope,' says the Apostle, ' maketh not ashamed ; ' and he declares that ' we rejoice in hope of the glory of God.'   Thus he ascribes to it the same certainty as to faith ; and in the Epistle to the Hebrews he speaks of ' the full assurance of hope.'   Faith and hope are virtues of this life, which will have no place in the life that is to come.   ' Now abideth faith, hope, and love.'   Faith and hope will cease ; and in this respect love is the greatest, as love will abide for ever.

The objects of the believer's hope are spiritual and heavenly blessings. They are different from earthly blessings.   The men of the world hope for riches and the perishable things of this life ; the believer hopes for an inheritance in heaven, that fadeth not away.   For this hope Moses gave up the riches and treasures of Egypt.   By this hope David distinguishes himself from the ungodly.   ' Deliver me from men of the world, which have their portion in this life, and whose belly Thou fillest with Thy hid treasure ; they are full of children, and leave the rest of their substance to their babes.   As for me, I will behold Thy face in righteousness ; I shall be satisfied when I awake with Thy likeness,' Ps. xvii. 13–15.   And, contrasting his condition with that of the children of this world, he says, Ps. lxxiii. 7, ' Their eyes stand out with fatness : they have more than heart could wish ; ' but as to himself, he had been plagued all the day long, and chastened every morning ; yet he adds, ' Nevertheless I am continually with Thee ; Thou hast holden me by my right hand.   Thou shalt guide me with Thy counsel, and afterward receive me to glory.' If it should be said by believers, May not we also hope for perishable and temporal blessings ? the answer is, that Christian hope is founded on the promises of God, and on them it is rested. The hope which exceeds these promises is carnal and worldly. To know, therefore, what is the object of Christian hope, we must observe what are the promises of God. It is true that godliness has the promise of the life that now is, and of that which is to come; but respecting this life God's promises are conditional, and to be fulfilled only as He sees their accomplishment to be subservient to His glory and our good; while as to the life that is to come, they are absolute. Are we, then, to expect only ease and happiness in this world, to whom it has been declared that 'we must through much tribulation enter into the kingdom of God;' and to whom the Lord Himself says, 'If any man will come after Me, let him deny himself, and take up his cross and follow Me?' The people of God should therefore rest their hope on the absolute promises of God, which cannot fail, of blessings that are unperishable, and of a real and permanent felicity.

The foundations and support of Christian hope are firm and certain. First, the word and immutable promise of God; for heaven and earth shall pass away, but His word shall remain for ever. God has promised heaven as the eternal inheritance of His people. Shall they doubt His fidelity? He has said, 'The mountains shall depart, and the hills be removed; but My kindness shall not depart from thee, neither shall the covenant of My peace be removed,' Isa. liv. 10. He has accompanied His promise with His oath. 'Willing more abundantly to show unto the heirs of promise the immutability of His counsel; that by two immutable things, in which it was impossible for God to lie, we might have strong consolation, who have fled for refuge to lay hold upon the hope set before us,' Heb. vi. 17. We have, besides, the blood of the Son of God, with which His promise has been sealed; and His obedience even unto death, which He has rendered to His Father, for the foundation of this hope. We have also the intercession of our great High Priest, of whom the Apostle, in establishing the grounds of the assurance of faith and hope, says not only that He is dead, but that He is risen, and at the right hand of God; who also maketh intercession for us. He declares, too, that our hope enters into heaven, where Jesus our forerunner has entered for us. To these foundations of our hope may be added, that it is said, 'Ye were sealed with that Holy Spirit of promise, which is the earnest of our inheritance, until the redemption of the purchased possession.' The Apostle calls this hope an anchor of the soul,—representing the believer, in the temptations and assaults to which he is exposed, under the similitude of a ship tossed by the sea, but which has an anchor fixed in the ground, firm and stedfast, which prevents its being driven away by the waves. This hope is not only necessary in adversity, but also in prosperity, in raising our affections to things above, and disengaging them from the world. The good hope through grace tranquillizes the soul. 'Why art thou cast down, O my soul? and why art thou disquieted within me? hope in God; for I shall yet praise Him, who is the health of my countenance, and my God,' Ps. xliii. 5. This hope consoles us in life and in death. It softens the bitterness of affliction, supports the soul in adversity, and in prosperity raises the affections to heavenly objects. It promotes our sanctification; for he who hath this hope of beholding Jesus as He is, purifieth himself even as He is pure, 1 John iii. 3. It assures us that, if Jesus died and rose again, them also who sleep in Jesus will God bring with Him. Let believers renounce their vain hopes of happiness in this world. Here they are strangers and pilgrims, and absent from the Lord. Let them hope for His presence, and communion with Him in glory. 'Now,' says the Apostle, 'the God of hope fill you with all joy and peace in believing, that ye may abound in hope, through the power of the Holy Ghost.'

Christian hope is a virtue produced by the Holy Spirit, in which, through His power, we should abound, and by which, resting on the promises of God in Jesus Christ, we expect our complete salvation. This hope is a part of our spiritual armour against principalities and powers, and spiritual wickedness, with which we have to wrestle. We are commanded to put on 'for an helmet the hope of salvation,' 1 Thess. v. 8.

In the preceding verse the Apostle had said, 'We wait for the adoption, to wit, the redemption of our body.' Here he gives it as a reason of our waiting, that as yet we are saved only in hope. As far as the price of redemption is concerned, we are already saved; but in respect to the power by which we shall be put in possession of that for which the price has been paid, namely, our deliverance from the remainder of sin under which we groan, the resurrection of our bodies, and the enjoyment of the eternal inheritance, we are saved only in hope. The hope of all this is present with us, but the enjoyment is future. *Hope that is seen is not hope.*—That is, hope cannot respect anything which we already enjoy. For it is impossible, as the Apostle subjoins, for a man to hope for that which he possesses. Hope and possession are ideas altogether incongruous and contradictory.

Believers, then, are as yet saved only in hope. They have received but the earnest and foretaste of their salvation. They groan under the weight which is borne by them, and their bodies are subject to the sentence of temporal death. If they were in the full possession of their salvation, faith would no longer be the conviction of things hoped for, as things hoped for are not things enjoyed. This corresponds with what the Apostle says elsewhere, when he exhorts believers to work out their salvation, and when he remarks that our salvation is nearer than when we first believed. When it is said we are saved in hope, as it supposes our felicity to be future, so it implies that all the good we can for the present enjoy of that distant and future felicity is obtained by hoping for it; and, therefore, if we could not hope for it, we should lose all the encouragement we have in the prospect.

Ver. 25.—*But if we hope for that we see not, then do we with patience wait for it.*

Hope produces *patience* with respect to all the trials, and labours, and difficulties that must be encountered before we obtain its object. Since we hope for what we see not,—that is, for what we possess not,—there must consequently be a virtue by which, being held firm, we wait for it, and that is patience. For between hope and enjoyment of the thing hoped for a delay intervenes, and there are many temptations within, and afflictions from without, by which hope would be turned into despair, if it were not supported by patience. As long as hope prevails, the combat will not be given up. In the 23d verse, believers are said to be waiting for the adoption; here the inducement to their waiting, and patiently waiting, is stated,—it is their hope supported by patience. Patiently bearing their present burden, and waiting for heaven, implies their expectation that it is reserved for them. They have been begotten again to a lively hope of possessing it by the resurrection of Jesus Christ from the dead, which is a sure pledge of the redemption of their bodies from the grave. This verse and the preceding teach the importance of hope to believers, and of their obeying the exhortation to give all diligence to the full assurance of hope. The hope of beholding Jesus as He is, and of obtaining 'a better resurrection,' is calculated to enable them patiently to sustain the sufferings of the present time. This hope is represented as encouraging the Lord Himself, 'who for the joy that was set before Him endured the cross, despising the shame,' Heb. xii. 2.

Ver. 26.—*Likewise the Spirit also helpeth our infirmities ; for we know not what we should pray for as we ought ; but the Spirit itself maketh intercession for us with groanings which cannot be uttered.*

Believers have need of patience, that, after they have done the will of God, they may receive the promise; but their patience is not perfect as it ought to be, and they are often ready to cast away their confidence, although it hath great recompense of reward. For their support, then, in their warfare, which is attended with so much difficulty, the Apostle presents a variety of considerations. He had reminded them, in the 17th verse, of their communion with Jesus Christ, and that, if they suffer with Him, they shall with Him also be glorified. In the 18th verse, he had told them that their sufferings bear no proportion to that glory of which they shall be made partakers. He had next drawn an argument, from the present state of creation, suffering, but waiting for and expecting its deliverance, and the manifestation of the sons of God ; and reminding them of the pledges they had already received of that glorious manifestation, he had spoken of its certainty, although still future, and therefore as yet enjoyed only in hope. But as they might still object, How, even admitting the force of these encouragements, can we, who are so weak in ourselves, and so inferior in power to the enemies we have to encounter, bear up under so many trials? the Apostle, in the verse before us, points out an additional and internal source of encouragement of the highest consideration, namely, that the Holy Spirit helps their infirmities, and also prays for them, which is sufficient to allay every desponding fear, and to communicate the strongest consolation.

At the close of the sacred canon, the Church is represented as saying, 'Come, Lord Jesus.' Being a stranger on earth, and her felicity consisting in communion with her glorious Lord, she groans on account of His absence, and ardently desires His holy and blessed presence. In the meantime, however, He vouchsafes to His people great consolation to compensate for His absence. He assures them that He has ascended to His Father and their Father, to His God and their God; that in His Father's house are many mansions; that He is gone to prepare a place for them; and that, when He has prepared a place, He will return and receive them to Himself, that where He is they may be also. They also know the way, He Himself being the way and their guide. How encouraging is this doctrine, and how well calculated for the support of hope and patience in expecting the return of the Bridegroom! If He is gone to their common Father, communion in His glory will not long be delayed. If there be many mansions in the house of their Heavenly Father, these are prepared to receive not only the elder Brother, but all His brethren; for were there only one abode, it would be for Him alone. If He is gone to prepare a place, and if He is soon to come again to receive them to Himself, is it not calculated to fill them with joy in the midst of troubles and afflictions? But all these consolations would be insufficient unless Jesus had added, that He would not leave them orphans, but would give them another Comforter to abide with them for ever, even the Spirit of truth. Without such support they would be overwhelmed by the weight of their afflictions, and overcome by their manifold temptations. But since they have not only an almighty Surety, but also an almighty Comforter, even the Holy Spirit, who dwells in them, and abides with them, this is sufficient to confirm their joy, to establish their hope, and to give them the assurance that nothing shall separate them from the love of Christ. Such is the consolation, in addition to all the others which, in the passage before us, the Apostle presents.

Likewise the Spirit also helpeth our infirmities.—Likewise, or in like manner, as we are supported by hope, so the Spirit also helps our infirmities. The expression *helpeth* our infirmities, is very significant. The Apostle intends to say that the Holy Spirit carries, or bears with us, our afflictions. If it be inquired why this help which we receive from the Holy Spirit is distinguished from the support we have from hope and patience, the answer is, that the Holy Spirit supports us, as being the efficient principle and first cause; and hope and patience support us as His instruments. On this account the Apostle, after having referred to the two former, speaks of this support of the Spirit. And here we find the most abundant consolation in Him who is the promised Comforter, for the all-powerful God Himself comes to help our infirmities.

Paul does not say infirmity, but *infirmities*, that we may remember how numerous they are, and may humble ourselves before God, renouncing our pride and presumption, and imploring His support. He also says, *our* infirmities, thus recognising them as also his own, and reminding the strongest of their weakness. The burdens of believers are of two kinds: the one is sin, the other is suffering. Under both of these they are supported. As to sin, Jesus has charged Himself with it. ' He bore our sins in His own body on the tree;' and as to sufferings, they are helped by the Holy Spirit, but only in part, by imparting strength to bear them; for all Christians must bear their cross in following Jesus. But in the kingdom of heaven, where every tear shall be wiped from their eyes, they shall be for ever delivered from all suffering.

Christians have at present many infirmities; they are in themselves altogether weakness; but the Holy Spirit dwells in their hearts, and is their strong consolation. Without Him they could not bear their trials, or perform what they are called to endure. But as He dwells in them,

He gives them that aid of which they stand in need. Are we weak, and our troubles great? here the almighty God comes to support us. Are we bowed down under the weight of our afflictions? behold, He who is all-powerful bears them with us! The care of shepherds over their flocks, and the care of mothers who carry their infants in their bosoms, are but feeble images of the love of God and the care He exercises over His people. A mother may forsake her sucking child, but the Lord will not forsake His children. ' When my father and my mother forsake me, then the Lord will take me up.'

For we know not what we should pray for as we ought ; but the Spirit itself maketh intercession for us with groanings which cannot be uttered.—There are two things in prayer : namely, the matter of prayer, that is, the things we ask for, and the act of prayer, by which we address God respecting our desires and necessities. But so great is the infirmity and ignorance of the believer, that he does not even know what he ought to ask. He is not thoroughly acquainted either with his dangers or his wants. He needs not only to be supplied from on high, but also Divine guidance to show him what he wants. When he knows not what to ask, the office of the Holy Spirit in the heart is to assist him in praying. Though, in a peculiar sense, Jesus is the believer's intercessor in heaven, yet the Holy Spirit intercedes in him on earth, teaching him what to ask, and exciting in him groanings expressive of his wants, though they cannot be uttered ; that is, they cannot be expressed in words. Yet these wants are uttered in groans, and in this manner most emphatically express what is meant, while they indicate the energy of the operation of the Spirit. Here the Apostle goes farther than in the former clause of the verse, and shows that the Spirit helpeth our infirmities, by referring to a particular example of this aid. In order to prove the extent of our weakness, the importance of the help of the Holy Spirit, and the greatness of the assistance He gives, Paul declares that *we know not what we should pray for as we ought.* Our blindness and natural ignorance are such, that we know not how to make a proper choice of the things for which we ought to pray. Sometimes we are ready to ask what is not suitable, as when Moses prayed to be allowed to enter Canaan, although, as being a type of Christ, he must die before the people, for whom he was the mediator, could enter the promised land ; and as Paul, when He prayed to be delivered from the thorn in his flesh, not understanding that it was proper that he should be thus afflicted, that he might not be exalted above measure. Sometimes, too, we ask even for things that would be hurtful were we to receive them ; of which there are many examples in Scripture, as Jas. iv. 3.

The people of God are often so much oppressed, and experience such anguish of mind, that their agitated spirits, borne down by affliction, can neither perfectly conceive nor properly express their complaints and requests to God. Shall they then remain without prayer? No; the Holy Spirit acts in their hearts, exciting in them sighs and groans. Such appear to have been the groanings of Hezekiah, when he said, ' Like a crane or a swallow, so did I chatter ; I did mourn as a dove ; mine eyes fail with looking upward ; O Lord, I am oppressed, undertake for me.' Such also was the experience of David in the seventy-seventh Psalm, when he says, 'I am so troubled that I cannot speak.' Thus, too, Hannah 'spake in her heart ; only her lips moved, but her voice was not heard.' No words of Peter in his repentance are recorded; his groanings are represented by his weeping bitterly ; and in the same way we read of the woman who was a sinner as only washing the feet of Jesus with her tears, which expressed the inward groanings of her heart.

Although these sighings or groanings of the children of God are here ascribed to the Holy Spirit, it is not to be supposed that the Divine Spirit can be subject to such emotions or perturbations of mind; but it is so represented, because He draws forth these groans from our hearts and excites them there. Thus it is *our* hearts that groan, but the operation and emotion is from the Holy Spirit; for the subject of these, and He who produces them, must not be confounded. In this way the Apostle speaks in the fourth chapter to the Galatians. 'Because ye are sons, God hath sent forth the Spirit of His Son into your hearts, crying, Abba, Father.' And in the 15th verse of the chapter before us, he shows that it is we who cry 'Abba, Father,' in order that we may observe that it is not the Spirit who cries, who prays, who groans, but that He causes us to cry, and pray, and groan. Such, then, is the work of the Holy Spirit here spoken of in the heart of believers, from which we learn that if there be any force in us to resist evil, and to overcome temptation, it is not of ourselves, but of our God. And hence it follows that if we have borne up under any affliction or temptation, we ought to render thanks to God, seeing that by His power He has supported us, and to pray, as David did, 'Uphold me with Thy free Spirit.'

The Holy Spirit often, in a peculiar manner, helpeth the infirmities of the children of God in the article of death, enabling them to sustain the pains and weaknesses of their bodies, and supporting their souls by His consolations in that trying hour. The body is then borne down with trouble, but the mind is sustained by the consolations of God. The eye of the body is dim, but the eye of faith is often at that season most unclouded. The outward man perisheth, but the inward man is renewed. Then, when Satan makes his last and greatest effort to subvert the soul, and comes in like a flood, the Spirit of the Lord lifts up a standard against him, exciting in the believer a more ardent faith, and consoling him, though unable to express it, with a strong conviction of the Divine love and faithfulness. It is by this means that so many martyrs have triumphantly died, surmounting, by the power of the Spirit within them, the apprehension of the most excruciating bodily torture, and rejoicing in the midst of their sufferings.

Ver. 27.—*And He that searcheth the hearts knoweth what is the mind of the Spirit, because He maketh intercession for the saints according to the will of God.*

It might be objected, To what purpose are those groanings which we cannot understand? To this the Apostle very fully replies in this verse, —1. God knows what these prayers mean, for ' He searcheth the hearts' of men, of which he hath perfect knowledge. The believer sighs and groans, while, owing to his perplexity and distress, he cannot utter a word before God; nevertheless these sighs and groanings are full of meaning. 2. God knoweth what is ' the mind of the Spirit,' or what He is dictating in the heart, and therefore He must approve of it; for the Father and Spirit are one. 3. Because, or rather, 'that He maketh intercession.' We are not to understand His intercession as the reason why God knows the mind of the Spirit, but as the reason why He will hear and answer the groans which the Holy Spirit excites. A further reason is, that this intercession is made for the saints; that is, for the children of God, of whom He hath said, 'Gather My saints together unto Me, those that have made a covenant with Me by sacrifice,' Ps. i. 5. Finally, it is added, that it is 'according to God,' or to the will of God. These prayers, then, will be heard, because the Spirit intercedes for those who are the children of God, and because He excites no desires but what are agreeable to the will of God. From all this we see how certain it is that these groanings which cannot be uttered must be heard, and consequently answered. For 'this is the confidence that we have in Him, that if we ask anything according to His will He heareth us.' The best prayers are not those of human eloquence, but which spring from earnest desires of the heart.

This verse is replete with instruction as well as consolation. We are here reminded that the Lord is the searcher of hearts. 'Hell and destruction are before the Lord; how much more then the hearts of the children of men.' The reasons of the perfect knowledge that God has of our hearts, are declared in the 139th Psalm :—1. The infinity, the omnipresence, and omniscience of God. 2. He forms the heart, and knows His own work. 3. He preserves and maintains the heart in all its operations. 4. He conducts and leads it, and therefore knows and sees it. The prayer of the heart, then, is attended to by God, as well as the prayer of the lips. Yet this does not prove that oral prayer is unnecessary—not even in our secret devotions. This passage teaches us to look to God for an answer to the secret groanings of our heart; but it does not teach us to neglect communing with God with our lips, when we can express our thoughts. This is abundantly taught in the word of God, both by precept and example. Searching the heart is here given as a characteristic peculiar to God. As, then, it is ascribed in other passages to our Lord Jesus Christ, He must be God. This passage clearly establishes the personal distinction between the Father and the Holy Spirit.

The persons to whom the benefit of this intercession of the Spirit extends are said to be *saints.* This proves that none can pray truly and effectually except the saints. It is only in the saints that the Spirit dwells, and of whose prayers He is the Author; and it is they only who are sanctified by Him. It is the saints, then, emphatically, and the saints exclusively, for whom the Spirit makes intercession. Such only are accepted of God, and fit subjects for the operation of the Spirit; but this is not the first work of the Spirit in them. He first sanctifies and then intercedes. First, He puts into us gracious dispositions, and then stirs up holy desires; and the latter supposes the former. In those in whom the Spirit is a Spirit of intercession, in them He is a Spirit of regeneration. These are therefore joined together in Zech. xii. 10, 'The Spirit of grace and of supplications.' None but saints have an

interest in the blood of Christ, as applied unto them, and in His intercession. None are able to pray for themselves, for whom Christ does not
likewise pray. We can only approach God by the Spirit. 'We have
access by one Spirit to the Father,' Eph. ii. 18. We can only pray under
the influence of the Holy Spirit with groanings which cannot be uttered;
while the wicked may groan without prayer. 'They have not cried unto
Me with their heart, when they howled upon their beds,' Hos. vii. 14.

The other reason which renders acceptable to God the prayers and
sighs excited in the saints by the Holy Spirit, is, that they are *according
to the will of God.* The Spirit Himself being God, these requests must
be agreeable to God. The carnal mind, it is said in verse 7, is enmity
against God; but the mind (the same word here employed) of the Spirit
is agreeable to God. The intercession made by the Holy Spirit is
according to the command and the revealed will of God, and in the name
and in dependence on Christ the Mediator. The Holy Spirit, then,
teaches the saints how to pray, and what to pray for. What He teaches
them to ask on earth, is in exact correspondence with that for which
Jesus, their great High Priest, is interceding for them in heaven. The
intercession of Jesus before the throne is an echo to the prayer taught
by the Holy Spirit in their hearts. It is therefore not only in perfect
unison with the intercession of Christ, and the inditing of the Holy
Spirit, but it is in exact conformity to the will of God. Such, then, is
the security to the saints that their prayers, although only expressed in
groans, shall be heard by their Father in heaven. 'The prayer of the
upright is His delight,' Prov. xv. 8. 'He will fulfil the desire of them
that fear Him,' Ps. cxlv. 19.

Ver. 28.—*And we know that all things work together for good to them that love
God, to them who are the called according to His purpose.*

Nothing is more necessary for Christians than to be well persuaded of
the happiness and privileges of their condition, that they may be able to
serve God with cheerfulness and freedom of spirit, and to pass through
the troubles and difficulties of the world. Here, then, is further consolation: Christians are often in sorrows, sufferings, and trials. This is
not in itself joyous, but grievous; but in another point of view it is a
matter of joy. Though afflictions in themselves are evil, yet in their
effects as overruled and directed by God, they are useful. Yea, all
things, of every kind, that happen to the Christian, are overruled by God
for his good!

Having previously spoken of the various sources of consolation, and,
in the two preceding verses, of the Spirit helping our infirmities, and
dictating those prayers which are heard of God, the Apostle now
obviates another objection. If God hears our sighs and groanings, why
are we not delivered from our afflictions and troubles? In answer, it is
here shown that afflictions are salutary and profitable; so that, although
they are not removed, God changes their natural tendency, and makes
them work for our good. But in order that none should hereby be led
into carnal security, the Apostle adds, that those for whom all things
work together for good are such as *love* God, and are the *called* according

to His purpose. This is not only true in itself, but it is here asserted to be a truth known to believers.

The Apostle had proposed various considerations, to which he now says *we know* this is to be added. This does not mean that believers know it merely in a speculative manner, but that it is a knowledge which enters into their heart and affections, producing in them confidence in its truth. It is a knowledge of faith which implies certainty and self-application, by which the believer not only knows but applies the promises of God, and is able to say, This promise is mine, it belongs to me. For otherwise, what advantage would there be in a general knowledge of this fact? where would be its consolation, and where its practical use? 'The secret of the Lord is with them that fear Him, and He will show them His covenant.' The experience, too, of the believer brings home to his mind the conviction of this encouraging truth. The Church of Rome accuses of presumption those who make such an application to themselves. They allow that the Christian should believe, in general, the promises of God, but that, as to a particular self-application or appropriation of them, he should hold this in doubt, and be always uncertain as to his own salvation. This is to destroy the nature of those consolations, and to render them useless. For if, in order to console one who is afflicted, it be said to him, 'All things work together for good to them that love God,' he will answer, True, but I must doubt whether this belongs to me; and thus the consolation is made of no effect. But if this error be not imbibed, and the duty of such appropriation be not denied, why is it that so many believers experience so little of this consolation in their afflictions? Is it not because they have little of that knowledge of which the Apostle speaks when he says, 'We know that all things work together for good to them that love God?' Carnal affections, the love of the world, and indulgence of the flesh, prevent this consideration from being deeply impressed on their minds; they also darken their understandings, so as not to allow the light of the consolations of God to enter their hearts. But in proportion as their hearts are purified from these affections, in the same degree it is confirmed in their minds. The objection, why sufferings are not removed, should be answered by reminding believers that all things work together for their good.

All things work together for good to them that love God.—All things, whatever they be—all things indefinitely—are here intended. The extent of this expression is by many limited to afflictions. 'Paul, it must be remembered,' says Calvin on this text, 'is speaking only of adversity;' and he adds, 'Paul is here speaking of the cross; and on this account the observation of Augustine, though true, does not bear on this passage—that even the sins of believers are so ordered by the providence of God as to serve rather to the advancement of their salvation than to their injury.' It is true that the Apostle had been referring to the present sufferings of believers, and enumerating various special topics of consolation; but, approaching to the conclusion of his enumeration, it might be expected that the last of them would be no longer of a special but of a most comprehensive description. That it is so, the terms he employs warrant us to conclude. *All things*, he says. If the context necessarily limited this expression, its universality ought not to be contended for; but it does not. If it be, as Calvin admits, that what is here said is true even of the sins of believers (and if applicable to sins, what else can be excepted?), why should the sense be limited to sufferings? It is much more consolatory, and consequently more to the Apostle's purpose, if literally all things be comprehended; and in this view it would form the most complete summing up of his subject. He had been pointing out to believers their high privileges as heirs of God, and partakers of glory with Christ. He had said that their sufferings in the present time are not worthy to be compared with that glory. He had suggested various topics to induce them to wait for it with patience; and had given them the highest encouragement, from the fact of the working of the Spirit of all grace within them, and of the acceptance of that work by God. Is it then more than was to be expected, that he should conclude the whole by saying that all things, without exception, were concurring for their good? Is it too much to suppose that it must be so to them whom he had addressed as heirs of God, and joint heirs with Jesus Christ, who are therefore under the guidance of the Good Shepherd, and honoured by the indwelling of the Holy Ghost? Is it more than the Apostle says on another occasion, when he uses the very same expression, *all things*, and, so far from intimating any exception, adds a most comprehensive catalogue? 'All things are yours; whether Paul, or Apollos, or Cephas, or the world, or life, or death, or things present, or things to come; all are yours, for ye are Christ's and Christ is God's,' 1 Cor. iii. 21. And again, '*All things* are for your sakes,' 2 Cor. iv. 15. Finally, ought the expression here to be restricted, when it is impossible to believe that the same expression, occurring a few sentences afterwards, verse 32, can be restricted? That all things work together for the good of them that love God, is a truth affording the highest consolation. These words teach believers that whatever may be the number and overwhelming character of adverse circumstances, they are all contributing to conduct them into the possession of the inheritance provided for them in heaven. That they are thus working for the good of the children of God, is manifest from the consideration that God governs the world. The first cause of all is God; second causes are all His creatures, whether angels, good or bad men, animals, or the inanimate creation. Second causes move only under His direction; and when God withdraws His hand, they cannot move at all, as it is written, 'In Him we live, and move, and have our being.' As God, then, the first cause, moves all second causes against His enemies, so, when He is favourable to us, He employs all to move and work for our good, as it is said, 'In that day will I make a covenant for them with the beasts of the field, and with the fowls of heaven, and with the creeping things of the ground; and will break the bow, and the sword, and the battle out of the earth, and will make them to lie down safely,' Hos. ii. 18. And as of men it is said, 'When a man's ways please the Lord, He maketh even his enemies to be at peace with him,' Prov. xvi. 7.

If all things work together for good, there is nothing within the compass of being that is not, in one way or other, advantageous to the children of God. All the attributes of God, all the offices of Christ, all the gifts and graces of the Holy Spirit, are combined for their good. The creation of the world, the fall and the redemption of man, all the dispensations of Providence, whether prosperous or adverse, all occurrences and events—all things, whatsoever they be—work for their good. They work *together* in their efficacy, in their unity, and in their connection. They do not work thus of themselves : it is God that turns all things to the good of His children. The afflictions of believers, in a peculiar manner, contribute to this end. 'Before I was afflicted I went astray; but now have I kept Thy word. It is good for me that I have been afflicted, that I might learn Thy statutes.' 'Tribulation worketh patience.' 'No chastening for the present seemeth to be joyous, but grievous; nevertheless afterward it yieldeth the peaceable fruit of righteousness unto them which are exercised thereby.' And believers are chastened by God for their profit, that they may be partakers of His holiness. The Apostle himself was an example of this, when a thorn in his flesh was sent to him to prevent his being exalted above measure. We see how much the sufferings of those spoken of in the eleventh chapter of the Hebrews were calculated to detach their affections from this present world, and lead them to seek a better, even a heavenly country. There is often a need-be for their being in heaviness through manifold temptations.

Even the sins of believers work for their good, not from the nature of sin, but by the goodness and power of Him who brings light out of darkness. Everywhere in Scripture we read of the great evil of sin. Everywhere we receive the most solemn warning against its commission; and everywhere we hear also of the chastisements it brings, even upon those who are rescued from its finally condemning power. It is not sin, then, in itself that works the good, but God who overrules its effects to His children,—shows them, by means of it, what is in their hearts, as well as their entire dependence on Himself, and the necessity of walking with Him more closely. Their falls lead them to humiliation, to the acknowledgment of their weakness and depravity, to prayer for the guidance and overpowering influence of the Holy Spirit, to vigilance and caution against all carnal security, and to reliance on that righteousness provided for their appearance before God. It is evident that the sin of Adam, which is the source of all their sins, has wrought for their good in raising them to a higher degree of glory. Believers fall into sin, and on account of this God hides His face from them, and they are troubled; and, like Hezekiah, they go softly. God left Hezekiah to himself, but it was to do him good at his latter end.

But if our sins work together for our good, shall we sin that grace may abound? Far be the thought. This would be entirely to misunderstand the grace of God, and to· turn it into an occasion of offending Him. Against such an abuse of the doctrine of grace, the Apostle contends in the 6th chapter of this Epistle. Sin should be considered in its nature, not as to what it is adventitiously, or in respect to what is foreign to it. Sin as committed by us is only sin, and rebellion against God and the holiness of His nature. It ought therefore to be regarded with abhorrence, and merits eternal punishment. That it is turned to good, is the work of God, and not ours. We ought no more to conclude that on this account we may sin, than that wicked men do what is right when they persecute the people of God, because persecutions are overruled by Him for good. That all things work together for good to them who love God, establishes the doctrine of the perseverance of the saints; for if all things work together for their good, what or where is that which God will permit to lead them into condemnation?

That all things happen for the best is a common saying among people of the world. This is a fact as to the final issue of the Divine administration, by which all things shall be made to contribute to the glory of God. But as to sinners individually, the reverse is true. All things are indeed working together in one complex plan in the providence of God for the good of those who love Him; but so far from working for good, or for the best to His enemies, everything is working to their final ruin. Both of these effects are remarkably exemplified in the lives of Saul and David. Even the aggravated sin of David led him to deep humiliation and godly sorrow, to a greater knowledge of his natural and original depravity, of the deceitfulness of his heart, and to his singing aloud of God's righteousness. The sins of Saul, as well as everything that befell him in God's providence, led to his becoming more hardened in his impiety, and at last conducted him to despair and suicide. The histories of many others, both believers and sinners, recorded in the Old Testament, abundantly confirm the words of the Psalmist, ' The Lord preserveth all them that love Him, but all the wicked will be destroyed.' ' The way of the wicked He turneth upside down.'

There are two scriptures which should fill the people of God with joy and consolation. The one is, ' The Lord God is a sun and shield; the Lord will give grace and glory; no good thing will He withhold from them that love Him,' Ps. lxxxiv. 11. The other is the passage before us, ' All things work together for good to them that love God, to them who are the called according to His purpose.' If, then, God will withhold nothing that is good for us, and will order and dispose of all things for good to us, what can be wanting to our absolute and complete security? How admirable is the providence of God, not only as all things are ordered by Him, but as He overrules whatever is most disordered, and turns to good things that in themselves are most pernicious. We admire His providence in the regularity of the seasons, of the course of the sun and stars; but this is not so wonderful as His bringing good out of evil in all the complicated acts and occurrences in the lives of men, and making even the power and malice of Satan, with the naturally destructive tendency of his works, to minister to the good of His children.

That love God.—What is said of all things working together for good is here limited to those who love God. This is given as a peculiar characteristic of a Christian. It imports that all believers love God, and that none but believers love Him. Philosophers, falsely so called, and men of various descriptions, may boast of loving God; but the decision of God Himself is, that to love Him is the peculiar characteristic of a Christian. No man can love God till He hath shined into his heart to give him the light of the knowledge of His glory in the face of Jesus Christ. It is therefore only through faith in the blood of Christ that we can love God. Until our faith gives us some assurance of reconciliation with God, we cannot have the confidence which is essential to loving God. Till then we dread God as our enemy, and fear that He will punish us for our sins. In loving God, the affections of the believer terminate in God as their last and highest end; and this they can do in God only. In everything else, there being only a finite goodness, we cannot absolutely rest in it. This is the rest that David had when he said, 'Whom have I in heaven but Thee? and there is none upon earth that I desire besides Thee; God is the strength of my heart and my portion for ever,' Ps. lxxiii. 25. This is what satisfies the believer in his need and poverty, and in every situation in which he may be placed, for it suffices him to have God for his heritage and his possession, since God is his all; and as this Divine love expels the love of the world, so it overcomes the immoderate love of himself. He is led to love what God loves, and to hate what God hates, and thus he walks in communion with God, loving God, and more and more desiring to comprehend what is the breadth and length, and depth and height, and to know the love of Christ which passeth knowledge.

To those who are the called according to His purpose.—This is a further description or characteristic of God's people. They are called not merely outwardly by the preaching of the Gospel, for this is common to them with unbelievers, but called also by the Spirit, with an internal and effectual calling, and made willing in the day of God's power. They are called according to God's eternal purpose, according to which He knew them, and purposed their calling before they were in existence; for all God's purposes are eternal. It imports that their calling is solely the effect of grace; for when it is said to be a calling according to God's purpose, it is distinguished from a calling according to works. 'Who hath saved us, and called us with an holy calling, not according to our works but according to His own purpose and grace, which was given us in Christ Jesus before the world began,' 2 Tim. i. 9. It imports that it is an effectual and permanent calling; for God's purposes cannot be defeated. 'The counsel of the Lord, that shall stand.' Their calling is according to the purpose of Him who worketh all things according to the counsel of His own will,' Eph. i. 11.

Ver. 29.—*For whom He did foreknow, He also did predestinate to be conformed to the image of His Son, that He might be the firstborn among many brethren.*

The Apostle having exhibited to believers many grounds of consolation, to induce them patiently to endure the sufferings of this present time, now points to the source of their future glory, in order to assure them of its certainty. The easy and natural transition to this branch of his subject should be particularly noticed. He had declared in the foregoing verse that *all things* work together for good to them who love God; but as it is always necessary to keep in mind that our love to God is not the cause of His love to us, nor, consequently, of the privileges with which we are favoured, but the effects of His loving us, Deut. vii. 6-8; Jer. i. 5, the Apostle adds, 'Who are the called according to His purpose.' This declaration leads at once to a full and most encouraging view of the progress of the Divine procedure originating with God, and carried, through all its connecting links, forward to the full possession of that glory which shall be revealed in us.

For whom He did foreknow.—The word foreknow has three significations. One is general, importing simply a knowledge of things before they come into existence. In this general sense it is evident that it is not employed in this passage, since it is limited to those whom God predestinated to be comformed to the image of His Son. He foreknows all things before they come to pass; but here foreknowledge refers only to particular individuals. A second signification is a knowledge accompanied by a decree. In this sense it signifies ordinance and providence, as it is said, Acts ii. 23, 'Him being delivered by the determinate counsel and foreknowledge of God;' that is to say, by the ordinance and providence of God. The reason why this word is used to denote the Divine determination, is because the foreknowledge of God necessarily implies His purpose or decree with respect to the thing foreknown. For God foreknows what will be, by determinating what shall be. God's foreknowledge cannot in itself be the cause of any event; but events must be produced by His decree and ordination. It is not because God foresees a thing that it is decreed; but He foresees it because it is ordained by Him to happen in the order of His providence. Therefore His foreknowledge and decrees cannot be separated; for the one implies the other. When He decrees that a thing *shall* be, He foresees that it *will* be. There is nothing known as what will be, which is not certainly to be; and there is nothing certainly to be, unless it is ordained that it shall be. All the foreknowledge of future events, then, is founded on the decree of God; consequently He determined with Himself from eternity everything He executes in time, Acts xv. 18. Nothing is contingent in the mind of God, who foresees and orders all events according to His own eternal and unchangeable will. Jesus Christ was not delivered by God foreknowing it before it took place, but by His fixed counsel and ordination, or His providence. Thus believers are called elect according to the foreknowledge of God the Father, 1 Pet. i. 2; and in the same chapter, ver. 19, 20, the Apostle Peter says that Jesus Christ was foreknown before the foundation of the world. Here foreknown signifies, as it is rendered, fore-ordained.

The third signification of this word consists in a knowledge of love and approbation; and in this sense it signifies to choose and recognise as His own, as it is said, Rom. xi. 2, 'God hath not cast away His people whom He foreknew,'—that is, whom He had before loved and chosen; for the Apostle alleges this foreknowledge as the reason why God had not rejected His people. In this manner the word 'know' is often taken in Scripture in the sense of knowing with affection, loving, approving; as in the first Psalm, 'The Lord knoweth the way of the righteous; but the way of the ungodly shall perish.' To know the way of the just, is to love, to approve, as appears by the antithesis. Paul says to the Corinthians, 'If any man love God, the same is know of Him,' 1 Cor. viii. 3; and to the Galatians, ' But now after ye have known God or rather are known of Him.' In the same way, God said by His Prophet to Israel, 'You only have I known of all the families of the earth,' Amos iii. 2.

At the day of judgment Jesus Christ will say to hypocrites, 'I never knew you,' Matt. vii. 23 ; that is to say, He never loved or acknowledged them, although He perfectly knew their characters and actions. In this last sense the word foreknow is employed in the passage before us. Those whom God foreknew—those whom He before loved, chose, acknowledged as His own—He predestinated to be conformed to the image of His Son. It is not a general anticipated knowledge that is here intended. The Apostle does not speak of all, but of some, whom in verse 33 he calls 'God's elect;' and not of anything in their persons, or belonging to them, but of the persons themselves, whom it is said God foreknew. And He adds, that those whom He foreknew He also did predestinate to be conformed to the image of His Son ; and whom he predestinated He also called, and justified, and glorified.

By foreknowledge, then, is not here meant a foreknowledge of faith or good works, or of concurrence with the external call. Faith cannot be the cause of foreknowledge, because foreknowledge is before predestination, and faith is the effect of predestination. ' As many as were ordained to eternal life believed,' Acts xiii. 48. Neither can it be meant of the foreknowledge of good works, because these are the effects of predestination. ' We are His workmanship, created in Christ Jesus unto good works ; which God hath before ordained (or before prepared) that we should walk in them,' Eph. ii. 10. Neither can it be meant of foreknowledge of our concurrence with the external call, because our effectual calling depends not upon that concurrence, but upon God's purpose and grace, given us in Christ Jesus before the world began, 2 Tim. i. 9. By this foreknowledge, then, is meant, as has been observed, the love of God towards those whom He predestinates to be saved through Jesus Christ. All the called of God are foreknown by Him,—that is, they are the objects of His eternal love, and their calling comes from this free love. ' I have loved thee with an everlasting love ; therefore with loving-kindness I have drawn thee,' Jer. xxxi. 3.

He also did predestinate.—Foreknowledge and predestination are distinguished. The one is the choice of persons, the other the destination of those persons to the blessings for which they are designed. To predestinate signifies to appoint beforehand to some particular end.' In Scripture it is taken sometimes generally for any decree of God, as in Acts iv. 28, where the Apostles say that the Jews were assembled to do whatsoever the hand and the counsel of God had determined (predestinated) before to be done. And Paul says, 1 Cor. ii. 7, 'We speak the wisdom of God in a mystery, even the hidden wisdom which God ordained (predestinated) before the world unto our glory.' Sometimes this word is taken specially for the decree of the salvation of man, as Eph. i. 5, ' Having predestinated us unto the adoption of children by Jesus Christ to Himself, according to the good pleasure of His will, to the praise of the glory of His grace.' In whom also we have obtained an inheritance, being predestinated according to the purpose of Him who worketh all things after the counsel of His own will.' In the same way, in the passage before us, ' Whom He did foreknow, He also did predestinate to be conformed to the image of His Son.' As the term is here used, it respects not all men, but only those on whom God has placed His love from eternity, and on whom He purposes to bestow life through Jesus Christ. As, then, it is absolute and complete, so it is definite; and the number who are thus predestinated can neither be increased nor diminished. It is not that God had foreseen us as being in Christ Jesus by faith, and on that account had elected us, but that Jesus Christ, being the Mediator between God and man, God had predestinated us to salvation only in Him. For as the union which we have with Him is the foundation of all the good which we receive from God, so we must be elected in Him; that is to say, that God gives us to Him to be His members, and to partake in the good things to which God predestinates us. So that Jesus Christ has been the first predestinated and appointed to be the Mediator, in order that God should bless us with all spiritual blessings in Him.

In the passage above quoted, Eph. i. 5, the cause of predestination is traced solely to God. After saying that God had predestinated us unto the adoption of children by Jesus Christ, it is added, ' to Himself,' to show that God has no cause out of Himself moving Him to this grace. In order to enforce this, it is further added, ' according to the good pleasure of His will;' and, in the third place, it is subjoined, ' to the praise of the glory of His grace;' from all which it follows that it must necessarily be by grace,—that is, free, unmerited favour. Love to God, or conformity to the image of Christ, cannot in any respect have its origin in fallen man. ' Herein is love, not that we loved God, but that He loved us.' ' We love Him, because He first loved us.' ' It is a foolish inference,' says Calvin, ' of these disputants, who say that God has elected such only as He foresaw would be worthy of grace. For Peter does not flatter believers, as if they were elected for their own individual merits, but refers their election to the eternal counsel of God, and strips them of all worthiness. In this passage, also, Paul repeats in another word what he had lately intimated concerning God's eternal purpose; and it hence follows that this knowledge depends on the good pleasure of His will, because, by adopting whom He would, God did not extend His foreknowledge to anything out of Himself, but only marked out those whom He intended to elect.'

The *foundation* of predestination is Jesus Christ, by whom we receive the adoption of children. Its *object* is man, not invested with any quality which moves God to predestinate him, but as corrupted and guilty in Adam—dead in trespasses and sins until quickened by God. The *blessing* to which God had predestinated those whom He foreknew is salvation, as it is said, ' God hath not appointed us to wrath, but to obtain salvation by our Lord Jesus Christ;' or, as it is expressed in the verse before us, ' to be conformed to the image of His Son.' The *means* to all this are our calling and justification. The *final end* of predestination is the glory of God,—' to the glory of His grace;' ' and that He might make known the riches of His glory on the vessels of mercy, which He had afore prepared unto glory.' On the consideration of their election, the Apostles urge believers to walk in holiness. ' Put on, therefore, as the elect of God, holy and beloved, bowels of mercies, kindness, humbleness of mind, meekness, long-suffering,' Col. iii. 12. ' Ye are a chosen (elected) generation, a royal priesthood, an holy nation, a peculiar people ; that ye should show forth the praises of Him who hath called you out of darkness into His marvellous light,' 1 Pet. ii. 9.

In the election of some, and the passing by of others, the wisdom of God is manifest ; for by this means He displays both His justice and mercy,—otherwise one of these perfections would not have appeared. If all had been withdrawn from their state of corruption, the justice of God would not have manifested itself in their punishment. If none had been chosen, His mercy would not have been seen. In the salvation of these, God has displayed His grace ; and in the punishment of sin in the others, He has discovered His justice and hatred of iniquity. This doctrine of election is full of consolation, and is the true source of Christian assurance. For who can shake this foundation, which is more firm than that of the heavens and the earth, and can no more be shaken than God Himself? The sheep whom God hath given to His Son by His predestination no one can pluck out of His hands.

But although this doctrine of election of the people of God to eternal life is a doctrine so consoling to them, and must have necessarily entered into the plan of salvation to render it consistent with itself, yet there are many who, in preaching the Gospel, deem it improper, notwithstanding they have the express example of our Lord, John vi. 37, 44, 65, to declare it before promiscuous multitudes, or even generally to believers, although so frequently introduced by the Apostles in their Epistles to the churches. Against this practice, prompted by worldly wisdom, Luther has forcibly remonstrated in the following appeal to Erasmus:—' If, my Erasmus, you consider these parodoxes (as you term them) to be no more than the inventions of men, why are you so extraordinarily heated on the occasion? In that case your arguments affect not me ; for there is no person now living in the world who is a more avowed enemy to the doctrines of men than myself. But if you believe the doctrines in debate between us to be (as indeed they are) the doctrines of God, you must here bid adieu to all sense of shame and decency thus to oppose them. I will not ask, whither is the *modesty* of Erasmus fled? but, which is much more important, where, alas ! are your fear and reverence of the Deity, when you roundly declare that this branch of truth, which He has revealed from heaven, is at best *useless* and unnecessary to know? What! shall the glorious Creator be taught by you, His creature, what is fit to be preached, and what to be suppressed? Is the adorable God so very defective in wisdom and prudence, as not to know, till you instruct Him, what would be *useful* and what pernicious? Or, could not He, whose understanding is infinite, foresee, previous to His revelation of this doctrine, what would be the consequences of His revealing it, till these consequences were pointed out by *you?* You cannot, you dare not, say this. If, then, it was the Divine pleasure to make known these things in His word, and to bid His messengers publish them abroad, and to leave the consequences of their so doing to the wisdom and providence of Him in whose name they speak, and whose message they declare, who art thou, O Erasmus, that thou shouldst reply against God?'

To be conformed to the image of His Son.—This implies that the children of God must all be made to resemble Christ, their head and elder brother. This likeness respects character and sufferings, as well as all things in which such similarity is found to exist. The Lord Jesus Christ, the first elect of God, is the model after which all the elect of God must be formed. Man was created in the image of God ; but when sin entered, he lost this image; and Adam ' begat a son in his own likeness after his image,' Gen. v. 3 ; thus communicating to his posterity his corrupted nature. But as God had determined to save a part of the fallen race, it was ' according to His good pleasure' to renew His image in those whom He had chosen to this salvation. This was to be accomplished by the incarnation of His Son, ' who is the brightness of His glory, and the express image of His person,' to whose image they were predestinated to be conformed.

This image of the Son of God, consisting in supernatural, spiritual, and celestial qualities, is stamped upon all the children of God when they are adopted into His family. Imparting to them spiritual life, He renders them partakers of the Divine nature ; that is to say, of His image, being the new man, which after God is created in righteousness and true holiness. They are the workmanship of God, created in Christ Jesus, being born of the Spirit, and the Spirit of Christ dwelling in them ; and he that is joined to the Lord is one Spirit. Thus the souls of believers are conformed to the image of Christ, as their bodies will be also at His second coming, when they shall be ' fashioned like unto His glorious body.' To this conformity to the image of His Son, all those whom God foreknew are predestinated. For as they have borne the image of the earthy, they shall also bear the image of the heavenly Adam.

Believers are conformed to the image of the Son of God in holiness and suffering in this life, and in glory in the life to come. They are conformed to Him in holiness, for Christ is made unto them sanctification. Beholding as in a glass the glory of the Lord, they are changed into the same image. They put on the new man, which is renewed in knowledge after the image of Him that created him. In suffering they are conformed to Him who was ' a man of sorrows and acquainted with grief.' They must endure tribulation, and fill up what is behind of His afflictions. As the Captain of their salvation was made perfect through sufferings, and through sufferings entered into His glory, so the sufferings of His people, while they promote their conformity to Him in holiness, constitute the path in which they follow Him to that glory. ' Ye are they who have continued with Me in My temptations, and I appoint unto you a kingdom.' What the Apostle hath said in the 17th verse, that if believers suffer with Christ they shall also be glorified together, is here confirmed by his declaration that they are predestinated to be conformed to His image. This image, of which the outlines are in this world traced in them, is only perfected in heaven.

That He might be the firstborn among many brethren.—Here is a reason for those whom God foreknew being conformed to the image of His Son ; and a limitation of that conformity which they shall have to Him. The reason is, that He might have many brethren. Next to the glory of God, the object of His incarnation was the salvation of a multitude which no man can number of those whose nature He assumed, and this was accomplished by His death. Referring to this, He Himself says, 'Except a corn of wheat fall into the ground and die, it abideth alone; but if it die, it bringeth forth much fruit.' Accordingly, in the everlasting covenant between the Father and the Son, when grace was given to His people in Him before the world began, 2 Tim. i. 9, and when God promised to Him for them eternal life also before the world began, Tit. i. 2, it was determined that when He should make His soul an offering for sin, He should see of the travail of His soul and be satisfied, and that by the knowledge of Him *many* should be justified. He was to bear the sins of *many.* 'Glorify Thy Son, that Thy Son also may glorify Thee; as Thou hast given Him power over all flesh, that He might give eternal life to as *many* as Thou hast given Him.' By His obedience *many* were to be made righteous. As the Captain of their salvation, He was to bring *many* sons unto glory. To Him *many* shall come from the east and west, and shall sit down with Abraham, and Isaac, and Jacob in the kingdom of heaven. 'The gift by grace which is by one man Jesus Christ hath abounded unto *many.*' And as He that sanctifieth and they who are sanctified are all of one, He is not ashamed to call them *brethren.* But as in all things He must have the pre-eminence, so this limitation is introduced, that among them all He must be the 'firstborn;' that is to say, the first, the principal, the most excellent, the Governor, the Lord.

Under the law, the firstborn had authority over their brethren, and to them belonged a double portion, as well as the honour of acting as priests,—the firstborn in Israel being holy, that is to say, consecrated to the Lord. Reuben, forfeiting his right of primogeniture by his sin, its privileges were divided, so that the dominion belonging to it was transferred to Judah, and the double portion to Joseph, who had two tribes and two portions in Canaan, by Ephraim and Manasseh; while the priesthood and right of sacrifice was transferred to Levi. The word firstborn also signifies what surpasses anything else of the same kind, as 'the firstborn of the poor,' Isa. xiv. 30, that is to say, the most miserable of all; and the firstborn of death, Job xviii. 13, signifying a very terrible death, surpassing in grief and violence. The term firstborn is also applied to those who were most beloved, as Ephraim is called the firstborn of the Lord, Jer. xxxi. 9, that is, His 'dear son.' In all these respects the appellation of firstborn belongs to Jesus Christ, both as to the superiority of His nature, of His office, and of His glory.

Regarding His *nature*, He was as to His divinity truly the firstborn, since He alone is the only-begotten—the eternal Son of the Father. In this respect He is the Son of God by nature, while His brethren are sons of God by grace. In His humanity He was conceived without sin, beloved of God; instead of which they are conceived in sin, and are by nature children of wrath. In that nature He possessed the Spirit without measure; while they receive out of His fulness according to the measure of the gift of Christ. Regarding his *office*, He is their King, their Head, their Lord, their Priest, their Prophet, their Surety, their Advocate with the Father,—in one word, their Saviour. It is He who of God is made unto them wisdom, and righteousness, and sanctification, and redemption. They are all His subjects, whom He leads and governs by His Spirit, for whose sins He has made atonement by His sufferings. They are His disciples, whom He has called from darkness into His marvellous light. Concerning His *glory*, 'God hath highly exalted Him, and given Him a name which is above every name, that at the name of Jesus every knee should bow, of things in heaven, and things in earth, and things under the earth.' 'He is the head of the body, the Church; who is the beginning, the firstborn from the dead, that in all things He might have the pre-eminence.' He is the firstborn from the dead, as being raised the first, and being made the first-fruits of them that slept; and by His power they shall be raised to a life glorious and eternal.

Ver. 30.—*Moreover, whom He did predestinate, them He also called ; and whom He called, them He also justified ; and whom He justified, them He also glorified.*

Moreover, whom He did predestinate, them He also called.—Here the Apostle connects our calling, which is known, with God's decree, which is concealed, to teach us that we may judge of our election by our calling, 2 Pet. i. 10. For Paul says, they whom God hath predestinated He hath also called and justified; so we may say, those whom He hath called and justified He hath elected and predestinated. If God hath called us, then He hath elected us. Paul had spoken of God's predestinating His people to be conformed to the image of His Son: He now shows us how this is effected. They are to be moulded into this likeness to their elder Brother by being *called* both by the word and Spirit of God. God calls them by His grace, Gal. i. 15,—that is, without regard to anything in themselves. Effectual calling is the first internal operation of grace on those who are elected. They are not merely called externally, as many who are not elected. The Scriptures speak of the universal call of the Gospel, addressed to all men; but this is not inseparably connected with salvation; for in this sense the Lord has said that 'many are called, but few are chosen.' At three periods, all mankind were called. They were called through Adam; they were called by Noah; and, finally, by the Apostles, Col. i. 23; yet how soon in each period was the external call forgotten by the great body of the human race! 'They did not like to retain God in their knowledge.'

In the passage before us, and in various other places, as in verse 28, it is effectual calling that is spoken of. This calling, then, signifies more than the external calling of the word. It is accompanied with more than the partial and temporary effects which the word produces on some, and is always ascribed to the operation of God by the influence of the Holy Spirit. Even when the external means are employed to most advantage, it is God only who gives the increase, 1 Cor. iii. 6. It is He who opens the heart to receive the word, Acts xvi. 14,—who gives a new heart, Ezek. xxxvi. 26,—who writes His law in it,—and who saves His people, not by works of righteousness which they have done, but by the washing of regeneration, and renewing of the Holy Ghost, Tit. iii. 5.

That which is meant, then, by the word *called* in this passage, and in many others, is the outward calling by the word accompanied with the operation of God, by His Spirit, in the regeneration and conversion of sinners. When Jesus Christ thus calls, men instantly believe, Matt.

iv. 19. Grace—the operation of the favour of God in the heart—is communicated, and the sinner becomes a new creature. Regeneration is not a work which is accomplished gradually; it is effected instantaneously. At first, indeed, faith is often weak; but as the new-born infant is as much in possession of life as the full-grown man, so the spiritual life is possessed as completely in the moment of regeneration as ever it is afterwards, and previous to that moment it had no existence. There is no medium between life and death: a man is either dead in sin, or quickened by receiving the Holy Spirit; he is either in Christ, or out of Christ; God has either begun a good work in him, or he is in a state of spiritual death and corruption. By means of the word, accompanied by His Spirit, God enlightens the understanding with a heavenly light, moves the will and the affections to receive and embrace Christ, and forms in the heart His image and the new man, of which the Apostle says that it is created in righteousness and true holiness. God says, 'Awake, thou that sleepest, and arise from the dead, and Christ shall give thee light.' He prophesies upon the dry bones, and the Spirit enters into them. Thus the same grace that operates in the election of the saints is exercised in their calling and regeneration, without which they would remain dead in trespasses and sins. 'No man,' says Jesus, ' can come to Me, except the Father which hath sent Me, draw him.'

All who are elected are in due time effectually called, and all who are effectually called have been from all eternity elected and ordained to eternal salvation. Effectual calling, then, is the proper and necessary consequence and effect of election, and the means to glorification. As those whom God hath predestinated He hath called, so He hath effectually called none besides. These words before us, therefore, are to be taken not only as emphatical, but as exclusive. Consistently with this, we read of the faith of God's elect, Tit. i. 1, as that which is peculiar to them. With this calling sanctification is inseparably connected. It is denominated a holy calling. 'Who hath saved us and called us with an holy calling, 2 Tim. i. 9. The Author of it is holy, and it is a call to holiness. 'As He which hath called you is holy, so be ye holy in all manner of conversation,' 1 Pet. i. 15. 'Ye are a chosen generation, a royal priesthood, an holy nation, a peculiar people; that ye should show forth the praises of Him who hath called you out of darkness into His marvellous light,' 1 Pet. ii. 9. It is a calling into the grace of Christ, Gal. i. 6. In this effectual calling the final perseverance of the saints is also secured, since it stands connected on the one hand with election and predestination, and on the other hand with sanctification and glorification. 'The gifts and calling of God are without repentance.' Calling, as the effect of predestination, must be irresistible, or rather invincible, and also irreversible.

The Church of Rome perverts the meaning of this calling; for, instead of considering it as accompanied with the communication of life to the soul, they view it merely as an act which excites and calls into action some concealed qualities in man, and awakens some feelings of holiness that are in him, and some virtues which he possesses, to receive the grace that is proclaimed to him. In this way it must not be said, with the

Scripture, that God communicates life to those who are dead in trespasses and sins, and regenerates them, but that He only aids their weakness, and calls forth their own exertions.

If it be inquired whether God calls all men with a calling sufficient for their salvation, that is to say, if He gives to all grace sufficient to save them, it is replied, that this calling may be considered as sufficient or insufficient in different points of view; for the sufficiency of grace may be considered either on the part of God or of man. On the part of God, it must be said that His general calling is sufficient, for God having created man upright, with a disposition to obey Him, if we consider this general calling connected with that original perfection, there can be no doubt that it is sufficient. But, on the part of man, viewed in his natural state of corruption, assuredly the outward call is not sufficient, unless accompanied with the internal operation of the Holy Spirit, to enlighten the eyes of the understanding, and to open the heart to receive the calling of God, any more than if Jesus Christ had spoken to a deaf or dead man, without removing his deafness, or imparting to him life. If the voice of Jesus calling Lazarus had been unaccompanied with His power, it would not have been sufficient to raise him from the grave. The calling, then, which is not accompanied with the power of the Spirit of God, is not sufficient in regard to man, while man is inexcusable, and has no just ground of complaint, for he resists that call which, unless he was a sinful creature and an enemy to God, would be sufficient. He is, as the Psalmist says, 'like the deaf adder that stoppeth her ear ; which will not hearken to the voice of the charmers, charm they never so wisely.'

If, again, it be inquired whether men can resist the calling of God, it is evident that, when the calling is only external, and unaccompanied with the internal operation of the Spirit, they can, and always will, resist it, Gen. vi. 3 ; Acts vii. 51. But when the calling is, at the same time, internal,—when God regenerates men, and makes them new creatures,— the question, if they can resist this, is altogether nugatory ; for it is as if it were inquired if a man could resist his creation, or a dead man his being brought to life. God here acts by His almighty power, without, however, forcing our will ; for communicating to us spiritual qualities, He gives us to will and to do of His good pleasure. It is therefore absurd to say that a man can resist this influence by the hardness of his heart, since it removes that hardness, and is the converting of hearts of stone into hearts of flesh. In opposition to this, the saying of our Lord is stated as an objection : 'Woe unto thee, Chorazin ! Woe unto thee, Bethsaida ! for if the mighty works which were done in you, had been done in Tyre and Sidon, they would have repented long ago in sackcloth and ashes.' On this it is to be remarked, that the reference here is to Christ's miracles, not to His preaching ; and what is said of Tyre and Sidon is by comparison, what is meant being, as it seems, that the hardness of heart of those of Chorazin and Bethsaida surpassed that of Tyre and Sidon, and that if such miracles had been performed in Tyre and Sidon, they would not have had so little effect as upon the former, although it is not said that the latter would have repented unto life, or that they could have been convérted to God except by the operation of His Spirit. Here the declaration of our Lord in the same context is decisive: ' At that time Jesus answered and said, I thank Thee, O Father, Lord of heaven and earth, because Thou hast hid these things (the truths of God which He proclaimed) from the wise and prudent, and hast revealed them unto babes.' And this He resolves, not into the difference found in man, but into the sovereignty of God. ' Even so, Father ; for so it seemed good in Thy sight.' And He immediately adds, ' Neither knoweth any man the Father save the Son, and he to whomsoever the Son will reveal Him.' This must refer to an internal revelation ; for as to that which was solely external, Jesus was declaring it to all. Jesus Christ knew from the beginning who they were that would believe and who would not believe, because He knew who they were whom the Father had given Him and would draw unto Him. And it is this eternal decree which He here shows is the rule of God's calling, according to which the Son is or is not revealed : ' Ye believe not, because ye are not of My sheep, as I said unto you.'

And whom He called, them He also justified.—They whom the Holy Spirit effectually calls by the Gospel to the knowledge of God are also justified. They are ' ungodly,' Rom. iv. 5, till the moment when they are called ; but, being then united to Christ, they are in that moment justified. They are instantly absolved from guilt, and made righteous, as having perfectly answered all the demands of the law, for by Him it has been fulfilled in them, verse 4. To justify signifies to pronounce and account righteous such as have transgressed, and forfeited the favour of God, as well as incurred a penalty, conveying to them deliverance from the pénalty, and restoration to that favour. And they who are thus accounted righteous by God, must be righteous, for God looks upon things as they really are; as, being one with Christ, they are perfectly righteous. ' Justification,' says Luther, ' takes place when, in the just judgment of God, our sins, and the eternal punishment due to them, are remitted, and when clothed with the righteousness of Christ, which is freely imputed to us, and reconciled to God, we are made His beloved children, and heirs of eternal life.' The connection between calling and justification is manifest, for we must be united to Christ to enjoy the good derived from Him. We must be members of Christ that His obedience may be ours, that in Him we may have righteousness. Now, it is by our calling that we are brought into His communion, and by communion with Him to the participation of His grace and blessing, which cannot fail to belong to them who are with Him one body, one flesh, and one spirit. Those who are called must therefore be justified. They who are the members of Jesus Christ must be partakers in His righteousness, and of the Spirit of life that is in Him. Whom He calls He justifies. This proves that there are none justified till they are called. We are justified by faith, which we receive when we are effectually called.

Whom He justified, them He also glorified.—A man is justified the moment He believes in Christ ; and here being glorified is connected with justification. No believer, then, finally comes short of salvation. If he is justified, he must in due time be glorified. To be glorified is to be completely conformed to the glorious image of Jesus Christ; when we shall see Him as He is, and be made like unto Him, enjoying that felicity which the Psalmist anticipated: 'Thou wilt show me the path of life; in Thy presence is fulness of joy; at Thy right hand there are pleasures for evermore.' The glorifying of the saints will have its consummation in the day of the blessed resurrection, when their bodies shall be made like unto the glorious body of Jesus Christ; when that natural body, which was sown in corruption, in dishonour, in weakness, shall be raised a spiritual body in incorruption, in glory, in power. Then death will be swallowed up in victory, all tears shall be wiped away, the Lamb will lead and feed them, and God shall be all in all.

In this verse glorification is spoken of as having already taken place, because what God has determined to do may be said to be already done. 'He calls those things that be not as though they were.' The Apostle does not say that those whom God predestinates He calls, and that those whom He justifies He glorifies; but, speaking in the past time, he says that those whom God did predestinate, them He hath also called, and justified, and glorified. By this he expresses the certainty of the counsel of God. In the same way, in the Old Testament, things future were spoken of as already accomplished, on account of the infallibility of the promises of God; so that, before Jesus Christ came into the world, it was said, 'Unto us a child is born, unto us a son is given.' And He Himself speaks of what is future as already accomplished. 'I have finished the work which Thou gavest Me to do.' 'Now I am no more in the world,' John xvii. 4, 11. In like manner the Apostle speaks here of glory as already come, to show how certain it is that those who are called and justified shall be glorified. And this is in accordance with the object he has in view, which is to console the believer amidst his afflictions. For when he thus suffers, and all things appear to conspire for his ruin, and to be opposed to his eternal salvation, he is represented as already glorified by God, and during the combat as having already received the crown of life.

The plan of salvation is here set before us in its commencement, in the intermediate steps of its progress, and in its consummation. Its commencement is laid in the eternal purpose of God, and its consummation in the eternal glory of the elect. He calls those whom He hath predestinated to faith in Christ, to repentance and to a new life. He justifies by the imputation of the righteousness of Christ those whom He hath called; and, finally, He will glorify those whom He hath justified. The opponents of the doctrine contained in this passage distort the whole plan of salvation. They deny that there is any indissoluble connection between those successive steps of grace, which are here united by the Apostle, and that these different expressions relate to the same individuals. They suppose that God may have foreknown and predestinated to life some whom He does not call, that He effectually calls some whom He does not justify, and that He justifies others whom He does not glorify. This contradicts the express language of this passage, which declares that *those* whom He foreknew He predestinated, that *those* whom he predestinated *them* He also called, that *those* whom He called *them* He also justified, and that *those* whom He justified *them* He also glorified. It is impossible to find words which could more forcibly and precisely express the indissoluble connection that subsists between all the parts of this series, or show that they are the same individuals that are spoken of throughout.

The same doctrine is in other places explicitly taught: ' *Of Him*' (by God, according to His sovereign election) ' *are ye in Christ Jesus, who of God*' (by the appointment of God) ' is made *unto us wisdom*' (in our calling), ' *righteousness*' (by the imputation of His righteousness), ' *sanctification*' (in making us conformed to His image), and ' *redemption*' (in giving us eternal glory). These truths are also declared in 2 Thess. ii. 13. ' God hath from the beginning *chosen* you to salvation, through sanctification of the Spirit, and belief of the truth whereunto He *called* you by our Gospel to the obtaining of the *glory* of our Lord Jesus Christ.'

It is, indeed, often objected to the doctrine of grace, that, according to it, men may live as they list; if they are certainly to be saved, they may indulge in sin with impunity. But, according to Paul's statements in this chapter, all the doctrines respecting the salvation of the elect are indissolubly connected, and a single link in the chain is never wanting. He who has ordained the end, has ordained the means. He who has chosen them in Christ, from before the foundation of the world, has chosen them through sanctification of the Spirit and belief of the truth, 2 Thess. ii. 13. If they are predestinated to be conformed to the image of the Son, they are in due time called by the word and Spirit of God. If they are called, they are justified, so that there is no unrighteousness to stand in the way of their acceptance. If they are justified, they will also be glorified in the appointed season. How fatally erroneous, then, is the opinion of those who say that, if we are predestinated, we shall obtain eternal glory in whatever way we live! Such a conclusion breaks this heavenly chain. It is vain for human ingenuity to attempt to find an imperfection in the plans of Divine wisdom in ordering the steps in the salvation of His people: 'the word of God effectually worketh in them that believe,' 1 Thess. ii. 13.

In the passage before us, we see that all the links of that chain by which man is drawn up to heaven, are inseparable. In the whole of it there is *nothing but grace*, whether we contemplate its beginning, its middle, or its end. Each of its parts furnishes the most important instruction. If we are elected, let us feel and experience in ourselves the effects of our election. If we are called, let us walk worthy of our vocation. If we are justified, let us, like Abraham, show our faith and prove our justification by our works. If we shall be glorified, let us live as fellow-citizens of the saints, and of the household of God. Let our conversation be in heaven, and let us confess that we are pilgrims and strangers on the earth.

In looking back on this passage, we should observe that, in all that is stated, man acts no part, but is passive, and all is done by God. He is elected, and predestinated, and called, and justified, and glorified by God. The Apostle was here concluding all that he had said before in enumerating topics of consolation to believers, and is now going on to show that God is 'for us,' or on the part of His people. Could anything, then, be more consolatory to those who love God, than to be in this manner assured that the great concern of their salvation is not left in their own keeping? God, even their covenant God, hath taken the whole upon Himself. He hath undertaken for them. There is no room, then, for chance or change : He will perfect that which concerneth them.

The same great truths are held forth in every part of the new covenant which God makes with His people, Jer. xxxi. 31-34; Heb. viii. 8-12. It consists exclusively of absolute promises on the part of God, and from beginning to end is grace and only grace. But does the doctrine of grace encourage licentiousness? To assert this directly contradicts the Scriptures, which show that grace has the very opposite tendency. ' The grace of God that bringeth salvation hath appeared to all men, *teaching us* that, denying ungodliness and worldly lusts, we should live *soberly, righteously,* and *godly* in this present world,' Tit. ii. 11, 12. Such is the testimony of God. The grace of God manifests His love, and produces love in us, which is the first-fruit of the Spirit, and the foundation of all acceptable obedience.

Let every believer glory in this grace of God by which he is predestinated, and called, and justified, and glorified. This is all his consolation and all his joy, for it is an indissoluble chain, which neither the world nor the powers of hell can break. Does he feel a holy sadness for having offended God, a holy desire to struggle against the corruptions of his heart, and to advance in the work of sanctification? does he hunger and thirst after righteousness, and is he seeking to put on the new man, and to possess more of the image of Christ ? Let him conclude, from these certain marks of his calling, that he is justified, the righteousness of Christ being imputed to him, and that his happiness is as certain as if he was already glorified. But, on the other hand, let none abuse these doctrines. No one shall be glorified who does not previously partake of this holy calling. Let no one attempt to take away any of the parts of this chain, and to pass from election without the intermediate steps to glory. Without holiness no man shall see the Lord.

Ver. 31.—*What shall we then say to these things ? If God be for us, who can be against us ?*

Here the Apostle makes a sudden and solemn pause, while he emphatically demands, *What shall we then say to these things ?* What can be said against them ? Is it possible to value them too highly ? What use shall we make of such consoling truths ? What comfort shall we draw from them ? Can anything detract from the peace they afford ? On the foundation that God is for him, the eternal interest of the Christian is secured, and though he wrestles not only against flesh and blood, but against principalities and powers, and against the rulers of the darkness of this world ; though of himself he can do nothing, yet, through Christ strengthening him, he can do all things. But what shall they say to these things who reject the doctrine of the perseverance of the saints ; who maintain that God allows some to perish whom He hath justified ; and that many things, instead of working for their good, contribute to their ruin? A conclusion entirely the reverse is to be deduced from all the consolations previously set forth by the Apostle, in reference to which he now exclaims, *If God be for us, who can be against us?*.

The expression *if,* which Paul here uses, does not denote doubt, but is a conclusion, or consequence, or affirmation, signifying *since;* as if he had said, Since we see by all these things that God is for us, who shall be against us? For is it not evident that God is for us, since He hath sent forth the Spirit of His Son into our hearts, crying, 'Abba, Father;' since the Spirit helps our infirmities; since all things work together for our good; since we are predestinated to be conformed to the image of His Son? When we were alienated from Him, He called us; when we were sinners, He justified us; and, finally, translating us from a scene of trouble and afflictions, He will confer on us a crown of immortal glory. Since, then, God thus favours us, who can be against us?

Many, however, in every age, speak of these things very blasphemously. They are far from being pleasing to man's wisdom. But they excite a different feeling in the breast of every Christian. They give a security to God's people which supports them under a sense of their own weakness. If they had no strength but their own, if there were no security for their perseverance but their own resolutions, they might indeed despond; for how could they ever arrive at heaven? But as this passage shows that all things are secured by God, and that in His almighty hands all the links of the chain that connects them with heaven are indissolubly united, they have no language in which they can adequately express their wonder, gratitude, and joy. No truth can be more evident than this—that although we have innumerable enemies, and are ourselves utter weakness, yet, if God be for us, nothing can be so against us as finally to do us injury. As the angel said to Gideon, 'The Lord is with thee,' so the same is said in this passage to every Christian. 'No weapon that is formed against thee shall prosper.' 'All men forsook me,' said Paul, 'but the Lord stood by me.' As God had said to Israel, and Moses, and Joshua, so He said, 'Fear not, Paul, for I am with thee.' When Christians, surrounded with difficulties and enemies, are disposed to say, with the servant of Elisha, 'Alas, what shall we do?' the passage before us speaks the same language as did the Prophet, 'Fear not, for they that be with us, are more than they that be with them,' and likewise that of Hezekiah, 'There be more with us than with them. With them is an arm of flesh; but with us is the Lord our God to help us, and to fight our battles.' It is added, 'And the people rested themselves upon the words of Hezekiah, King of Judah.'

In the verse before us we have two propositions. One is, that God is for us; the other, that nothing can be—that is, can prevail—against us. From this we may consider who are against, and who is for believers. There is arrayed against them a formidable host composed of many powerful enemies. There are Satan and all wicked spirits; there are the world, and indwelling sin; there are all sufferings, and death itself. How could believers themselves withstand the power of such antagonists? But, on the other hand, the Apostle shows in one word who is for them. God, says he, is for us! God is the shield of His people: He holds them in

His hand, and none can pluck them out of it. 'The eternal God is thy refuge, and underneath are the everlasting arms!'

Ver. 32.—*He that spared not His own Son, but delivered Him up for us all, how shall He not with Him also freely give us all things?*

In the preceding verse, the Apostle had comforted believers from the consideration that, if God, with all His glorious attributes, were engaged for their defence, they might look without dismay upon an opposing universe. Here, in order to confirm their confidence in God, he presents an argument to prove that God is with them of a truth, and also to assure them that they shall receive from Him every blessing.

There are two circumstances calculated to inspire distrust in the mind of the believer. The one is the afflictions which press upon him in this world; and these of two kinds, namely, such as are common to all men, and such as are peculiar to the followers of Christ. The other circumstance calculated to cloud the hopes of the Christian, is the sins of which he is guilty. When suffering so many troubles, he has difficulty in persuading himself that he is favoured by God, and is ready, with Gideon, to exclaim to the angel, 'Oh my Lord, if the LORD be with us, why then is all this befallen us?' And, on the other hand, as he is by nature a child of wrath, and sins daily, how can he be sure that God is with him, and not rather against him? To these objections the Apostle here opposes the declaration that God hath not spared His own Son, but delivered Him up to the death for His people. No stronger argument could be offered in proof of His favour to them than the gift of His own Son. Him He has given to redeem them from all their sins and all their troubles; while such is the dignity and excellency of Christ, that the Apostle, arguing from the greater to the less, further proves that after such a gift as that of His own Son, nothing can be refused which is consistent with the glory of God and the salvation of their souls. He thus assures them of freedom from the evils they might dread from sin and suffering.

Paul does not say that the *Father* has given His Son, but that *God* has given Him. This is calculated to establish the confidence of believers more firmly, since, by referring to God, He brings into view all His perfections as infinitely good, powerful, wise, and able to render them supremely blessed in holiness and eternal glory. Another effect is to draw their attention to the greatness of the love of God; for one to whom we are in some respects equal may confer upon us His favours, but here we are reminded that the bestower is infinitely above us, being the Creator to whom we are indebted even for our existence. His goodness, then, is so much the more wonderful, that though He is the infinite Jehovah, dwelling in light which is inaccessible, of whom it is said 'that He humbleth Himself to behold the things that are in heaven,' Ps. cxiii. 6, still He draws near to us, and condescends to raise us up, who are as nothing before Him, and who, being the Creator of all things, has set His love on those who are sinful, and poor, and miserable.

What God has given is His *own Son.*—This imports that He is His Son in the sense of that relation among men. It is sonship in this sense only that shows the immensity of the love of God in this gift. This proves that it was greater than if He had given the whole creation. If His Son were related to Him in merely a figurative sonship, it could not be a proof of His ineffable love. God *did not spare Him.*—Not sparing Him may either mean that He spared Him not in a way of justice, 2 Pet. ii. 4, that is, exacted the utmost farthing of debt He had taken upon Him; or that He spared Him not in a way of bounty, that is, withheld Him not. God spared Abraham's son, but He spared not His own Son. This passage shows that Christ was given over by the Father to the sufferings which He bore, and that these sufferings were all necessary for the salvation of His people. Had they not been necessary, He would not have exposed His Son to them. 'It became Him, for whom are all things, and by whom are all things, in bringing many sons unto glory, to make the Captain of their salvation perfect through sufferings.' From all this it appears that God, who cannot deny Himself, 2 Tim. ii. 13, could not show mercy to us without satisfying the demands of His justice, vindicating the authority of His law, and magnifying and honouring all the perfections of His nature.

Delivered Him up for us all.—When the Jews seized and crucified our Lord Jesus Christ, He was delivered up by the Father's decree, and by the direction of His providence, though it was through the guilty criminality of the Jews that He was put to death. It took place when His appointed hour arrived, for till then they could not accomplish their purpose. 'Him, being delivered by the determinate counsel and foreknowledge of God, ye have taken, and by wicked hands have crucified and slain.' As the Father delivered Him up, the great end of His suffering was satisfaction of the justice of God; and as He bore the whole curse of the broken law, His people are never, on that account, to bear any portion of vindictive wrath. 'It was exacted, and He answered,' Isa. liii. 7. 'Then,' says the Son Himself, 'I restored that which I took not away,' Ps. lxix. 4. Thus the Father delivered up His Son to humiliation, involving an assumption of our nature and our transgressions. He delivered Him up to sorrows unparalleled, and even to death itself,—to death, not merely involving the dissolution of the soul and body, but the weight of the sins of men, and the wrath of God against sin. God thus delivered up His Son, that He might rescue us from that misery which He might have justly inflicted upon us, and might take us, who were children of wrath, into His heavenly presence, and there rejoice over us for ever, as the trophies of His redeeming love.

For us all.—That is, for all to whom the Apostle is writing, whom he had addressed as beloved of God, called, saints, Rom. i. 7, among whom he ranks himself. But as these epistles to the churches equally apply to all believers to the end of time, so this expression includes all the elect of God—all who have been given to Jesus—all in whose behalf He addressed the Father in His intercessory prayer. 'I pray for them. I pray not for the world, but for them which Thou hast given Me,' John xvii. 9, 20. That those to whom Paul here refers when he says, 'for *us* all,' applies to none but believers, is evident,—1st, because in the preceding and following verses the Apostle speaks of those who love God, and who are the called according to His purpose; 2d, he says in express terms that He will with Him freely give *us* all things, which implies that we have faith, by which we receive Jesus Christ. This absolute gift, then, con‑ cerns only those who, being elected by God, believe in Him.

How shall He not also with Him freely give us all things?—This is the most conclusive reasoning. If He has given us the greatest gift, He will not refuse the lesser. His Son is the greatest gift that could be given, —plainly, then, nothing will be withheld from those for whom He has given His Son. This also assumes the fact as granted, that Jesus is the Son of God in the literal sense; for in no other sense is the inference just. If Jesus were only figuratively a son, there is no room to infer, from the gift of Him to us, that the Father will give ' us all things.' These ' all things ' are what eye hath not seen, nor ear heard. He will give His Spirit and eternal life. His children are heirs of God and joint heirs with Jesus Christ, whom He hath appointed heir of all things. The Apostle does not here speak of himself alone, as if this were a privilege peculiar to himself, to receive freely all things with Christ, but of all believers,— He will freely give *us*. And the expression, *How*, with which he com‑ mences, imports the absolute certainty that on all such they shall be bestowed.

When it is here said that God will *give* us all things, we are reminded that all the good things that we obtain or hope for are from God, who is the Author of every good and perfect gift; for a man can receive nothing except it be given him from heaven; and all that God gives us He gives *freely*, without money and without price. Here it may be remarked that the Apostle's manner of reasoning, who concludes that, since God has not spared His own Son, but delivered Him up for us all, He will with Him also freely give us all things, teaches us that the believer ought to reason out of the Scriptures, and draw the necessary consequence from what is said in them.

Ver. 33.—*Who shall lay anything to the charge of God's elect? It is God that justifieth.*

Among the temptations to which the believer is exposed in this life, some are from without, others are from within. Within are the alarms of conscience, fearing the wrath of God; without are adversity and tribulations. Unless he overcomes the first, he cannot prevail against the last. It is impossible that he can possess true patience and confidence in God in his afflictions, if his conscience labours under the apprehension of the wrath of God. On this account, the Apostle, in the fifth chapter of this Epistle, in setting forth the accompaniments of justification by faith, first speaks of peace with God, and afterwards of glorying in tribula‑ tions. In the chapter before us he observes the same order; for, in this last part of it, in which he speaks of the triumph of the believer, he first fortifies the conscience against its fears from guilt, and next secures it against external temptations from afflictions. As to the first, he says, ' Who shall lay anything to the charge of God's elect? It is God that justifieth; it is Christ that died, who is even at the right hand of God, who also maketh intercession for us.' And as to the last, ' Who shall separate us from the love of Christ? shall tribulation, or distress, or per‑

secution, or famine, or sword? Nay, in all these things we are more than conquerors.' He does not mean to say that nothing shall occur to trouble believers, but that nothing shall prevail against them. In assuring them of this, he ascends to their election as the source of all their blessings.

Who shall lay anything to the charge of God's elect?—The Apostle speaks here of God's elect. This reminds believers that their election is not to be ascribed to anything in themselves, but is to be traced solely to the grace and mercy of God, by whom they were chosen in Christ before the foundation of the world, Eph. i. 4. Their election demonstrates the vanity of all accusations that can be brought against them, either by their own conscience, by the world, or by Satan. Thus, while the Apostle removes every ground of boasting and vainglory, and all presumptuous thoughts of themselves, of their freewill and self-righteousness, he lays the sure foundation of joy and peace in believing. He leads us to the election of God as the source of all the good we enjoy or hope for, in order to set aside every ground for vainglory, and all presumption as to any worthiness in ourselves of our own will or righteousness, so that we may fully recognise the grace and mercy of God to us, who, even when we did not exist, chose us for Himself, according to His own good pleasure, Eph. i. 4, 5. He likewise does so that we may have a sure foundation to rest on, even God's eternal and unchangeable purpose, instead of any fallacious hope from reliance on anything in ourselves. When it is said here, 'Who shall lay anything to the charge of God's elect?' it does not refer to men generally, but to believers as the elect of God. The word *elect* must be taken in this place in its connection with *called*, as in the preceding verses, since it is here found connected with justification. For a man might be elected, and yet not be for the present justified, as Paul, when he persecuted the Church, who was not justified till he actually believed, though even then elected, and, according to God's purpose and counsel, ordained to salvation.

It is God that justifieth.—This is the first thing which the Apostle opposes to the accusations that might be brought against the elect of God: God justifies them. There is none that justifies besides God. None can absolve and acquit a sinner from guilt, and constitute and pronounce him righteous, but God alone. 'I, even I, am He that blotteth out thy transgressions for Mine own sake,' Isa. xliii. 25; for it is God alone against whom sin is committed, in reference to future condemnation. 'Against Thee, Thee only, have I sinned,' Ps. li. 4. It is God alone that condemns, and therefore it is God alone that justifies. If, then, God has made believers just or righteous, who is he that will bring them in guilty? There are here two grounds upon which the Apostle founds the justification of believers. One is taken from its Author—it is God that justifies; the other is taken from the subjects of this privilege—they are the elect. And thus the freeness of justification, and its permanency, are both certified.

It is here established that the elect are saved in such a way that nothing can be laid to their charge. All their debt, then, must be paid, and all their sins must be atoned for. If full compensation has not been made, something might be laid to their charge. This shows that salvation is by justice, as well as by mercy, and gives a view of salvation that never would have entered into the heart of man. Nay, it is so far from human view, that even after it is revealed, it still lies hid from all the world, except from those who are taught of God. And some, even of them, being slow of heart to believe, are but partially enlightened in this glorious view of the salvation of the guilty.

Ver. 34.—*Who is he that condemneth?* *It is Christ that died, yea rather, that is risen again, who is even at the right hand of God, who also maketh intercession for us.*

Who is he that condemneth?—In the preceding verse it is asked, Who shall lay anything to the charge of God's elect? here it is demanded, Who shall condemn them? They who cannot be accused cannot be condemned. God Himself is pleased to justify the elect, to deliver them from condemnation, and views them as possessing perfect righteousness; and being in this justified state by the judicial sentence of God, who shall dare to condemn them? None can discover a single sin of which to accuse them as still subjecting them to the curse of the law, and to bring them into that condemnation, from which they have been delivered by what God Himself hath done for them. It is here supposed that their condemnation is impossible, because it would be unjust. In similar language, the Lord Jesus Christ, the first elect of God, speaking by the Prophet Isaiah, l. 8, says, 'He is near that justifieth Me; who will contend with Me?' These words relate to His confidence in His Heavenly Father, who would uphold Him as His righteous servant; and it is on His righteousness and work that the acquittal of all those whom the Father hath given Him, and who are elected in Him, is rested. The Apostle having said that it is God that justifieth them, next proceeds to give the reasons of their freedom from condemnation. Four grounds are here stated:—1st, Christ's death; 2d, His resurrection; 3d, His enthronement at the right hand of God; and, 4th, His intercession.

It is Christ that died.—By His death, the penalty of the holy law, on account of its violation by His people, was executed, and satisfaction made to Divine justice. In answer to the question, Who is he that condemneth? the Apostle replies that Christ died. By this he intimates the impossibility of our being absolved from sin, without satisfaction for the injury done to the rights of God's justice and the sacred majesty of His eternal laws which had been violated; for the just God could not set aside His justice by His mercy, and justify sinners without an atonement. It is on this account that God had instituted sacrifices under the law, to hold forth the necessity of a satisfaction, and to prove that without shedding of blood there could be no remission of sin. There is, then, a manifest necessity of repairing the outrage against the perfections of God, which are the original and fundamental rule of the duty of the creature. This reparation could only be made by a satisfaction that should correspond with the august majesty of the holiness of God; and consequently it must be of infinite value, which could only be found in a person of infinite dignity.

To the death of Jesus Christ as the atonement for sin, our eyes are constantly directed throughout the Scriptures, whether by types, by prophecies, or by historical descriptions of the event. Death was the punishment threatened in the covenant of works against sin. But Jesus Christ had neither transgressed that covenant, nor could participate in the imputation of the sin of Adam, because He sprang not from him by the way of natural generation. Being, therefore, without sin, either actual or imputed, the penalty of death could not be incurred on His own account. Death, then, which is the wages of sin, must have been suffered by Him for sinners. Their iniquities were laid on Him, and by His stripes they are healed. His death, therefore, utterly forbids the condemnation of the elect of God, who were given to Him, and are one with Him, of whom only the context speaks. It must be a just and full compensation for their sins. It is evidently implied that none for whom He died can be condemned. For if condemnation be forbidden by His death, then that condemnation must be prohibited with respect to all for whom He died. His death made satisfaction to justice for them, and therefore, in their case, both accusation and condemnation are rendered impossible.

Yea rather, that is risen again.—This is the second ground affirmed by the Apostle against the possibility of the condemnation of God's elect. What purpose would the death of Christ have served, if He had been overcome and swallowed up by it ? ' If Christ be not raised, your faith is vain ; ye are yet in your sins.' If He be not risen, it must be because He had not expiated those sins for which He died, and was therefore retained a prisoner by death. But since the Surety has been released from the grave, complete satisfaction must have been made ; for if but one sin which had been laid upon Him had continued unatoned for, He would have remained for ever in the grave, death being the wages of sin. But now, since He has risen from the grave, the obligation against His people must be effaced and entirely abolished, His resurrection being their resurrection, Col. ii. 12. It is on this account that the Apostle here opposes to condemnation not only the death of Christ, but also His resurrection, as something higher, and as being our full absolution. And, by the commandment of Jesus Christ, the Gospel was not announced to the Gentiles, nor spread through the world, till after His resurrection, as He Himself said, Luke xxiv. 46 : ' It behoved Christ to suffer, and to rise from the dead the third day, that repentance and remission of sins should be preached in His name among all nations.'

The resurrection, then, of Christ, is the proof of His victory, and of the entire expiation of His people's sins. It is therefore opposed to their condemnation, as being the evidence and completion of their absolution and acquittal ; for as the death of Jesus Christ was His condemnation, and that of all united to Him, so His resurrection is His absolution and also theirs. As the Father, by delivering Him to death, condemned their sins in Him, so, in raising Him from the dead, he pronounced their acquittal from all the sins that had been laid upon Him. This is what the Apostle teaches respecting the justification of Jesus Christ. He was justified by the Spirit, 1 Tim. iii. 16 ; that is, declared and recognised to be righteous ; and with regard to His people's justification in Him, that as He had died for their sins, so He was raised for their justification. The resurrection of Jesus Christ was a manifestation of His Godhead and Divine power. He was declared to be the Son of God, and consequently possessing over all things absolute power and dominion. ' For to this end Christ both died and rose, and revived, that He might be Lord both of the dead and living.'

Who is even at the right hand of God.—This is the third ground on which the security of God's elect is rested. Jesus Christ sits at God's right hand. This is a figurative expression, taken from the custom of earthly monarchs, to express special favour, and denotes, with respect to Christ, both dignity and power. ' When He had by Himself purged our sins, He sat down on the right hand of the Majesty on high.' Having finished the work of redemption, this was the result of His labours, and the testimony of its consummation. His thus *sitting down* indicates an essential difference between our Lord Jesus Christ and the Levitical priests. ' Every priest standeth daily ministering, and offering oftentimes the same sacrifices, which can never take away sins. But this Man, after He had offered one sacrifice for sin, for ever sat down on the right hand of God.' The Levitical priests had never finished their work : it was still imperfect. They *stood*, therefore, ministering daily, in token of continued service. But Christ having offered one sacrifice for sins, by which He hath perfected for ever them that are sanctified, for ever *sat down* on the right hand of God, Heb. x. 12.

Jesus Christ, then, is not only raised from the dead, but has also ascended into heaven, and is possessed of all power and glory, and is there to defend His people. His seat at the right hand of God signifies His permanent exaltation as Mediator, and His communion with God in sovereign power and authority, reigning as the Head and King of His Church. The amount of the Apostle's reasoning is, that such being the condition of Him who was dead and is risen again, possessed of the keys of hell and of death, who shall dare to appear before Him to bring an accusation against His members or to condemn the elect of God ?

Who also maketh intercession for us.—This is the fourth and last ground of the security of God's elect. The *intercession* of Jesus Christ is the second act of His priesthood, and is a necessary consequence of His *sacrifice*, which is the first act, and precedes the third, namely, His coming forth from the heavenly sanctuary to *bless* those whom He has redeemed to God by His blood. His intercession consists in that perpetual application which He makes to His Father, in the name of His Church, of the blood which He shed on the cross for the salvation of His people, in order to obtain for them the fruits of that oblation. It was necessary that His sacrifice should be offered upon earth, because it was an act of His humiliation ; but His intercession which supposes the establishment of righteousness and peace, is made in heaven, being an act of His exaltation. This intercession was figuratively represented by the high priest in Israel, when, after having offered in his linen garments the sacrifice, without the precincts of the holy place, he took the blood of the victim, and, clothed in his sacerdotal golden robes, entered alone into the most holy place, and sprinkled the blood on and before the mercy-seat.

Jesus Christ, then, who suffered without the gate, Heb. xiii. 12, in accomplishing the truth of this figure, first offered upon earth His sacrifice, and afterwards entered in His glory into heaven, to present to His Father the infinite price of His oblation by the mystical sprinkling of His blood. This is not to be understood as being any bodily humiliation, as bowing the knee before God, but it is the presenting of His blood of perpetual efficacy. It is the voice of that blood which speaketh better things that the blood of Abel. The blood of Jesus Christ being the blood of the everlasting covenant—that blood which was to reunite God with men, and men with God—it was necessary, after its being shed on the cross, that it should be thus sprinkled in heaven. 'I go,' says He to His disciples, 'to prepare a place for you.' It was necessary that this blood should be sprinkled there, and also upon them, before they could be admitted. But by its means they were prepared to enter into heaven, and heaven itself was prepared for their reception, which without that sprinkling would have been defiled by their presence. 'Neither by the blood of goats and calves, but by His own blood, He entered in once into the holy place, having obtained eternal redemption.' Jesus Christ is not only seated at the right hand of God, but He is there for the very purpose of interceding for His people. By the perpetual efficacy of His blood their sins are removed, and consequently every ground of their condemnation. This never-ceasing intercession of Him who ever liveth to advocate their cause, not only procures the remission of their sins, but also all the graces of the Holy Spirit; and by the efficacy of the Holy Spirit an internal aspersion is made upon their hearts when they are actually converted to God, and when by faith they receive the sprinkling of the blood of their Redeemer. For them He died, He rose, He ascended to heaven, and there intercedes. How, then, can they be condemned? How can they come short of eternal glory?

Ver. 35.—*Who shall separate us from the love of Christ? shall tribulation, or distress, or persecution, or famine, or nakedness, or peril, or sword?*

In the contemplation of those glorious truths and Divine consolations which the Apostle had been unfolding, he had demanded, Who shall *accuse*, who shall *condemn*, the elect of God? he here triumphantly asks, Who shall *separate* them from the love of Christ? Having pointed out the grounds on which the fears of believers from within are relieved, he now fortifies them against fears from without. This order is the more proper, since their internal fears and misgivings are more formidable than their outward trials, and the hatred and opposition of the world; and until the believer, as has been observed, has overcome the former by having the answer of a good conscience towards God, he is not prepared to withstand the latter. Although the people of God are exposed to all the evils here enumerated, these shall not prevail to separate him from the love of Christ.

The term *the love of Christ*, in itself, may signify either our love to Christ, or Christ's love to us; but that it is Christ's love to us in this place there can be no question. A person could not be said to be separated from his own feelings. Besides, the object of the Apostle is to assure

us not so immediately of our love to God, as of His love to us, by directing our attention to His predestinating, calling, justifying, and glorifying
us, and not sparing His own Son, but delivering Him up for us. In
addition to this, it contributes more to our consolation to have our minds
fixed upon God's love to us than upon our love to God ; for, as our love
is subject to many failings and infirmities, and as we are liable to change,
to endeavour to impart consolation from the firmness of our love, would
be less efficacious than holding forth to us the love of God, in whom
there is no variableness, neither shadow of change. The language, too,
employed, favours this sense ; for the Apostle does not say, 'Who shall
separate Christ from our love ? ' but, 'Who shall separate us from the
love of Christ ? ' and, in the 37th verse, the meaning is determined by
the expression, 'We are more than conquerors *through Him that loved us.*'
God, however, in loving His children, makes them love Him ; and believers are enabled to love Christ because He loves them. It is He who
first loved us, and in loving us has changed our hearts, and produced
in them love to Him. Paul prays that believers, 'being rooted and
grounded in love, may be able to comprehend with all saints what is the
breadth, and length, and depth, and height ; and to know the love of
Christ, which passeth knowledge, that they may be filled with all the
fulness of God.'

To have a just idea of the love of Christ, we must contemplate its duration. It was from before the foundation of the world—from all eternity.
We must consider that He who has loved us is the high and lofty One
who inhabiteth eternity, who dwelleth in light that is inaccessible ; before
whom the angels veil their faces, crying, 'Holy, holy, holy is the Lord of
Hosts;' and before whom the inhabitants of the earth are as grasshoppers,
and the nations as a drop of a bucket. We must remember, too, who
we are, who are the objects of His love,—not only creatures who are but
dust and ashes, dwelling in houses of clay, but who were His enemies,
and by nature children of wrath. We must also reflect on the greatness
of His love, that it is His will we should be one with Him, and that
He guards us as the apple of His eye. He loves His people as His
members, of whom He is the Head, and sympathizes with them when they
suffer. He calls their sufferings His sufferings, and their persecutions
His persecutions, as He said to Saul persecuting His members, 'Saul,
Saul, why persecutest thou Me ? ' He will also say to those on His right
hand in the day of judgment, that He hungered, and thirsted, and was
naked, and that they gave Him to eat and drink, and clothed Him, when
these things were done to the least of His members. He loves His people,
too, as being their Husband, by that spiritual marriage He has contracted
with them, as it is said, 'Husbands, love your wives, even as Christ also
loved the Church, and gave Himself for it.'

The love here spoken of as the security of believers being the love of
Christ, Christ must be God. Were Christ not God, we might come short
of heaven without being separated from His love. He might love, and
yet not be able to save the objects of His love.

It is likewise to be remarked, that the confidence of believers that they
shall not be separated from the love of Christ, is not founded on their

high opinion of themselves, or on their own ability to remain firm against temptations, but is grounded on Christ's love, and His ability to preserve and uphold them. As nothing can be laid to their charge—as none can condemn them—as all things that happen to them, instead of proving injurious, work together for their good,—it is impossible that they can be finally lost. If Christ so love them, what shall separate them from that love?

In specifying those evils which in appearance are calculated to separate the believer from the love of Christ, the Apostle points out the sufferings of the people of God, the *time* of these sufferings—all the day long; the *manner*—as sheep for the slaughter; the *cause*—for Thy sake. He distinguishes the seven evils that follow:—1st, *Tribulation.*—This is placed first, as being a general term, comprehending all the particulars which he afterwards enumerates. It means affliction in general. It refers not only to the general state of suffering which, when man had sinned, it was pronounced should be his lot—' In sorrow shalt thou eat of it (of the produce of the ground) all the days of thy life'—but also more particularly to the tribulation which the disciples of Christ shall all more or less experience. 'In the world ye shall have tribulation,' John xvi. 33. The tribulation of unbelievers is the effect of the wrath of God; but the afflictions of His people are salutary corrections, which, so far from separating them from His love, yield the peaceable fruits of righteousness, and are for their profit, that they might not be condemned with the world, but be partakers of His holiness. ' As many as I love, I rebuke and chasten.'

To tribulation is added, 2d, *Distress*, which signifies straits, difficulties, critical situations. It means the perplexity in which we are, when, under pressure or trouble, we see no way of deliverance, and no way to escape presents itself. The word denotes a narrow place, in which we are so much pressed or straitened that we know not where to go or turn; which expresses the condition of the believer when he is not only oppressed, but reduced to extremity. ' Thou hast enlarged me when I was in distress,' Ps. iv. 1.

3d, *Persecution* is affliction for the profession of the Gospel. The persecuted have often been pursued and constrained to flee from place to place, as the Lord Jesus was carried into Egypt when Herod sought to kill Him. ' If they have persecuted Me, they will also persecute you.' But so far is persecution from separating believers from the love of Christ, that ' Blessed are they which are persecuted for righteousness' sake.'

4th, *Famine.*—To this the persecuted are frequently subjected, though they may have been rich and powerful.

5th, *Nakedness.*—The disciples have often been reduced to indigence and poverty, stripped by their enemies, and obliged to wander naked in deserts, and to hide themselves, like wild beasts, in caves of the earth, Heb. xi. 38. Paul himself was frequently exercised with hunger, and thirst, and fastings, and cold, and nakedness.

6th, *Peril.*—This refers to the dangers to which the Lord's people are exposed. These, at some times, and in some countries, are exceedingly many and great; and at all times, and in all countries, are more or less numerous and trying. If God were not their protector, even in this land of freedom, the followers of the Lamb would be cut off or injured. It is the Lord's providence that averts such injuries, or overrules events for the protection of His people. This is too little considered even by themselves, and would be thought a most unfounded calumny or fanatical idea by the world. But let the Christian habitually consider his safety and protection as secured by the Lord, rather than by the liberality of the times. That time never yet was when the Lord's people could be safe, if circumstances removed restraint from the wicked. Those who boast of their unbounded liberality would, if in situations calculated to develope their natural hatred of the truth, prove, after all, bitter persecutors.[1]

7th, *Sword.*—This means violence carried to the utmost extremity. It is persecution which stops not with smaller injuries, but inflicts even death.

Ver. 36.—*As it is written, For Thy sake we are killed all the day long ; we are accounted as sheep for the slaughter.*

As it is written.—To the enumeration of evils presented in the foregoing verse, the Apostle here adds the testimony of the Scriptures, by which he verifies what is declared in the fifteenth chapter. 'For whatever things were written afore time, were written for our learning, that we through patience and comfort of the Scriptures might have hope.' And to what purpose would it be to appeal to the afflictions of the Church under the former dispensation, were it not to lead us to patience under the Gospel ? For if believers in that period bore their trials with patience, how much more should we do so when God now clearly reveals His saving grace, and not as formerly in figures and shadows! In this manner the Lord and His Apostles frequently appeal to the Old Testament Scriptures, by which they testify to them as the word of God, and also show the agreement between the Old Testament and the New. The reference, then, is not intended to state a similar fact in similar language, by way of what is called accommodation, according to the interpretation of Mr. Stuart, Mr. Tholuck, and others. A greater indignity to the Scriptures, and the Spirit of God, by whom they were dictated, cannot be offered, than to assert that passages of the Old Testament, which are quoted by the Apostles as predictions, are only an accommodation of words. This would not merely be silly, but heinously criminal. It is not only irreverent to suppose that the Apostles, in order to enforce the truth of what they were teaching, would quote the language of the Spirit in a meaning which the Holy Spirit did not intend to convey, but it is a charge of palpable falsehood and dishonesty against the writers of the New Testament, as calling that a fulfilment which is not a fulfilment, and appealing to the Old Testament declarations as confirmatory of their own doctrine, when they were aware that it was merely a fanciful accommodation of words, and that they were deluding their readers. Are practices to be admitted, in explanation of the word of God, which are never

---

[1] This was signally demonstrated during the French Revolution, and more recently evidenced by some of the small republics in Switzerland.

tolerated on other subjects, and which, if detected, would cover their authors with disgrace?

The quotation here shows that this passage in the Psalms, to which the reference is made, was in its fullest sense a prediction, and this regards the fulfilment. It was indeed a historical fact, and verified with respect to the Jews. But this fact, instead of proving it not to be prophetical and typical, is the very circumstance that fits it for that purpose. ' The quotation here,' says Professor Stuart, ' comes from Ps. xliv. 22 [Sept., xliii. 22], and is applied to the state of Christians in the Apostle's times, as it was originally to those whom the Psalmist describes; in other words, the Apostle describes the state of suffering Christians, by the terms which were employed in ancient days to describe the suffering people of God.' What could be more degrading to the book of God than the supposition that the Apostles ever quoted the Scriptures in this manner, by way of accommodation? How does this hide the glory of the perfection of the Old Testament, as in figure it exhibits Christ and His Church!

For Thy sake.—It was for God's sake that the Jews were hated and persecuted by the other nations, because, according to the commandment of God, they separated themselves from them in all their worship. They could have not religious fellowship with them, and on that account they were regarded as enemies to the rest of mankind. In like manner, when Christianity appeared, preferring a solemn charge of falsehood against all other religions in the world, Christians were accused of hating all mankind. This was the grand accusation against them in primitive times by the heathens, and even by such historians as the so-called philosophic Tacitus. Christians, in the same way, are still hated by the world, because they profess that salvation is only through the blood of Christ. As this implies that all who do not hold that doctrine are in error and ignorance, and under condemnation, it excites in the strongest manner the enmity of the world. But the cause of this hatred must be traced to a principle still deeper, even the enmity of the carnal mind against God, and against His image in man, wherever it is seen. It is the working of that enmity which God put at the beginning between the seed of the serpent and the seed of the woman, Gen. iii. 15

The afflictions and trials of the people of God are here referred to, to induce believers to exercise patience, to teach them not to promise themselves exemption from the treatment experienced by those who formerly lived under the covenant of God, but rather to remember that, if sometimes spared, it is owing to the forbearance and mercy of God. They are appealed to in order to lead them to consider the goodness of God in former times, as exhibited in the issues of the afflictions with which He visited His people, not to separate them from His love, but to do them good in the latter end. ' Ye have heard of the patience of Job, and have seen the end of the Lord; that the Lord is very pitiful, and of tender mercy.' How much consolation and joy should Christians experience in suffering affliction of any description whatever, when they can appeal to their Lord and Saviour, and say, It is for ' Thy sake,' Matt. v. 11. So far from being separated from the love of Christ by such sufferings, they are by them made more conformable to His image. In suffering for evil, men are conformable to the image of the first Adam.

We are killed.—In speaking of those sufferings, which shall not separate believers from God, the Apostle here refers to death, the highest point to which they can be carried. As to the time, he speaks of it as '*all the day long;*' that is, they are constantly exposed to the greatest measure of suffering in this life, and are frequently exercised with it. As to the manner, he says, *We are accounted as sheep for the slaughter.*—The enemies of the people of God have often given them up to death with as little reluctance as sheep are driven to the slaughter. There is pity even for the murderer on the scaffold, but for Christ and His people there is none. The cry still is against the servants, as it was against the Master, 'Crucify, crucify.' Even in death they find no sympathy. This is attested by history in every age and country; witness the repeated and dreadful persecutions of Christians during the first three centuries, when they were treated not like men but as wild beasts, and the cry of the multitude was, 'The Christians to the lions.' When there is a respite from persecution, it is through the kind providence of God, when He restrains the malice of him who was a murderer from the beginning, and the evil passions of men, who are the willing instruments of Satan.

Ver. 37.—*Nay, in all these things we are more than conquerors, through Him that loved us.*

The sufferings of believers above enumerated, which, as the Apostle had just shown, verify the truth of the ancient predictions of the word of God, shall not separate them from the love of Christ, but, on the contrary, are to them the sources of the greatest benefits. Through them they are *more than conquerors.*—This is a strong expression, but in its fullest import it is strictly true. The Christian not only overcomes in the worst of his trials, but more than overcomes his adversaries, and all those things which seem to be against him. It is possible to overcome, and yet obtain no advantage from the contest, nay, to find the victory a loss. But the Christian not only vanquishes, he is also a gainer by the assault of his enemy. It is better for him than if he had not been called to suffer. He is a gainer and a conqueror, both in the immediate fruits of his sufferings, as God overrules them for his good, bringing him forth from the furnace as gold refined, and also in their final issue; for 'our light affliction, which is but for a moment, worketh for us a far more exceeding and eternal weight of glory.' The term conquerors reminds us that the life of a believer is a warfare, in which he is called to combat, both within and without. We may remark, too, the difference between the judgment of God, and the judgment of men, respecting the victory of believers. In the world, persecutors and oppressors are judged as the conquerors; but here, those are pronounced to be such, who are oppressed and persecuted. They are the servants of Him whom the world put to death, but who said to His disciples, 'Be of good cheer, I have overcome the world.'

Through Him that loved us.—The Apostle says that we are more than conquerors, not through Him that loves us, but through Him that *loved* us,—using the past time, thus directing our attention to Christ dying for us. His love to us is the character by which Christ is often described, as if it were that by which He should be best known to us, and as if, in comparison, there was none but He alone who loved us. ' Who loved me,' says the Apostle, 'and gave Himself for me.' ' Who loved us, and washed us from our sins in His own blood.' ' Christ also loved the Church, and gave Himself for it.' This expression shows that the confidence spoken of in this place is a confidence wholly grounded on Christ's love and power, and not on our own firmness. It is not by our own loyalty and resolution, but through Him that loved us, that we are more than conquerors. In the Apostle Peter we see the weakness of all human affection and resolutions. All the glory, then, of this victory which we obtain is to be ascribed solely to God; for it is He who is at our right hand, and who supports us in all our afflictions. In the seventeenth chapter of the Book of Revelation, the Lamb, who is Jesus Christ, is represented as combating against the enemies of His Church. He is our shield, our rock, and our refuge. It is declared that we are ' kept (as in a garrison) by the power of God,' 1 Pet. i. 5, in order that we may not presume on our own strength, or attribute to ourselves the glory of our preservation; but that we may keep our eyes fixed upon Him who, with His outstretched arm, conducts us to the heavenly Canaan.

Ver. 38.—*For I am persuaded that neither death, nor life, nor angels, nor principalities, nor powers, nor things present, nor things to come.*

In the preceding verses Paul had proclaimed the triumph of believers over everything within and without them, that seemed to endanger their security. He had spoken of tribulation, and distress, and persecutions, and famine, and nakedness, and peril, and sword, over all of which he had pronounced them more than conquerors. He now proceeds, in the same triumphant language, to defy enemies still more formidable; asserting that all the conceivable powers of the universe shall not be able to separate them from the love of God which is in Jesus Christ.

For I am persuaded.—Here Paul introduces his own persuasion of the love of God to His people, that in so doing others may imitate him. This appears more fully in the next verse, by his making the constancy of God's love a privilege not peculiar to himself, but common to all His people. He sets before believers this persuasion, to confirm them in the conviction that they need not fear the want of God's support to enable them to overcome all trials, and surmount all dangers. For this persuasion is not conjectural, but an assured confidence, such as he expresses when he says, ' I know whom I have believed, and am persuaded that He is able to keep that which I have committed unto Him against that day,' 2 Tim. i. 12.

Here we see the nature and quality of faith as opposed to the doctrine of the Church of Rome, which holds it to be merely a general belief of all that God has said, without confidence in His promises, or assurance of His grace. But the object of the Gospel, which is called ' the Gospel of peace,' is, that those who have fled for refuge to the hope set before them, should have strong consolation, Heb. vi. 18, and peace in their conscience. The words, 'I am persuaded,' used by the Apostle, show that faith is a persuasion, and a union and conformity of heart to the word which we believe. Our reception of the promises, then, is a special application of them, when we take home to ourselves the grace and love of God, as the Apostle does when he says, verse 39, that nothing shall be able to separate us, to prove that he speaks in the name of all believers, and that, in this triumph of faith, he employs language common to them all. The objection that the language he used was appropriate only to Apostles, would set aside his intention and object altogether. The Church of Rome, however, objects, that in order to this application of faith, the Gospel should speak to each individual by his name, and say, 'Thou art saved, thou art pardoned.' But if, as they admit, the law, by its general propositions, obliges every one to obey it, while it names no person individually, and in saying, 'Cursed is every one who continueth not in all things which are written in the book of the law to do them,' condemns every man who does not yield obedience to its commands, why should they deny that the propositions of the Gospel comprise every believer in particular, or affirm that in saying, 'He that believeth in Jesus hath eternal life,' it does not speak to all who believe in Jesus, and declare that each one of them hath eternal life? When the law says, 'Thou shalt not kill,' 'Thou shalt not steal,' ought any one to doubt that these commandments are addressed to him? But, in the Gospel, we find the same manner of speaking. 'If thou shalt confess with thy mouth the Lord Jesus, and shalt believe in thy heart that God hath raised Him from the dead, thou shalt be saved.' Every believer, then, should rejoice in the declarations and promises of the Gospel, as if they were addressed to him by name.

That neither death.—Death itself shall not separate believers from the love of God, nor should they question His love because He has appointed that they should die once. Death, with all its accompaniments, which are always solemn; and sometimes terrible, may wear the semblance of God's displeasure. But, notwithstanding the pains and sufferings by which it is usually preceded, especially when inflicted by persecution, to which there may be here a particular allusion,—notwithstanding the humiliating dissolution of the body into dust,—yet God is with His children when they walk through this dark valley, and 'precious in the sight of the Lord is the death of His saints.' In their death they have fellowship with Him who has disarmed it of its sting, and destroyed him that had the power of death. So far from separating them from God, it is His messenger to bring them home to Himself. If its aspect be terrible, it is still like the brazen serpent in the wilderness, which had but the form of a serpent, without its deadly poison. It dissolves the earthly house of their tabernacle, but introduces them into their house not made with hands, eternal in the heavens. It discharges the soul from the burden of sin, that it may be clothed with perfect holiness; for death, although the effect of sin, is the occasion of slaying and destroying it in the believer.

Nor life.—This is the next thing that the Apostle enumerates as threatening to separate believers from the love of God. It includes all the dangers and difficulties they have to encounter while passing through this world, and carrying about with them a body of sin and death amidst the various temptations from prosperity or adversity to which they are exposed. Yet Christ is their shepherd, and the Holy Spirit their leader. So far from separating them from the love of God, life as well as death are included among the privileges which belong to the children of God, 1 Cor. iii. 22.

Nor angels.—Some restrict this to good angels, and some to evil angels. There is no reason why it should not include both. Mr. Stuart asks, How can the *good angels,* ' who are sent forth to minister to such as are heirs of salvation (Heb. i. 14), be well supposed to be *opposers* and *enemies* of Christians?' But how could Mr. Stuart pronounce such a judgment in the face of the Apostle himself on another occasion? If ' an angel from heaven preach any other Gospel unto you than that which we have preached unto you, let him be accursed.' Could an angel from heaven be supposed a false preacher rather than a persecutor? But such suppositions are common in Scripture. They do not imply the possibility of the things supposed; and it fully justifies them, if the consequence would follow from the supposition, were it realized. By the expression, ' nor height, nor depth,' Mr. Stuart understands is meant neither heaven nor hell. Did he not.observe, then, that this is inconsistent with his objection to explaining the term principalities and powers as referring to heavenly angels? If height means heaven, surely it is the inhabitants of the place who are meant, not the place itself.

Nor principalities, nor powers.—This is also variously interpreted. Some confine it to angels, and some to civil rulers. There is no reason that it should not extend to the words in their widest meaning. It is true of civil powers; it is equally true of all angelic powers. It is as true with respect to principalities in heaven, as it is with respect to those in hell. Were all the principalities, through all creation, to use their power against Christians, it would not succeed. They have Christ on their side ; who, then, can prevail against them? This justifies strong expressions in the exhibition of Divine truth. We are warranted by this to illustrate Scripture doctrine from the supposition of things impossible, in order the more deeply to impress the human mind with the truth inculcated. This fact is of great importance as to the explanation of Scripture.

Nor things present, nor things to come.—Neither the trials nor afflictions in which the children of God are at any time involved, nor with which they may at any future period be exercised, will avail to separate them from Christ. There is nothing that can happen against which the providence of God does not secure them. What dangers should they dread when He says, ' Fear not, thou worm Jacob, and ye men of Israel; I will help thee, saith the Lord, and thy Redeemer, the Holy One of Israel.' ' When thou passest through the waters, I will be with thee ; and through the rivers, they shall not overflow thee : when thou walkest through the fire, thou shalt not be burnt ; neither shall the flame kindle upon thee. For I am the Lord thy God, the Holy One of Israel, thy Saviour.' Nothing does happen, nothing can happen, which, from eternity, He hath not appointed and foreseen, and over which He hath not complete control.

Ver. 39.—*Nor height, nor depth, nor any other creature, shall be able to separate us from the love of God, which is in Christ Jesus our Lord.*

Nor height, nor depth.—These expressions appear to comprise all that had been said of angels, principalities, and powers, including them altogether to give greater force to the declaration concerning them. Wherever they were, or whatever other power might inhabit heaven above, or hell beneath, if either a part of them, or the whole in combination, were to assail those whom Jesus loves, it would be of no avail. A reference may also be made to the highest state of prosperity to which a man may be elevated, or the lowest degree of adversity to which he may be depressed —of honour or of reproach. Neither the situation of Solomon the king, amidst the splendours of royalty, nor that of Lazarus the beggar, clothed in rags and covered with sores, although both are dangerous in the extreme, shall separate the believer from the love of God.

Nor any other creature.—The Apostle here, in conclusion of his discourse, after his long enumeration, intending to accumulate into one word all possible created existence in the whole universe, adds this expression, which completes the climax. Any other creature, that is, any creature which at present or hereafter should exist, all being created by and for Jesus Christ, and subordinate to His power,—no such creature shall be able to *separate us* from the love of God which is in Him. From all the evils above enumerated God has delivered His people, not that they should not suffer them, but that they should not be overcome by them.

The love of God.—Here what was before called the love of Christ is called the love of God. Could such a variety of expressions be used if Christ were not God as well as the Father? Among all the uncertainties of this life, that which is certain and can never fail, is the love of God to His children. On this ground, Job, when deprived of all his earthly possessions, exclaims, 'Though He slay me, yet will I trust in Him,' Job xiii. 15. 'My flesh and my heart faileth, but God is the strength of my heart and my portion for ever,' Ps. lxxiii. 26.

In Christ Jesus our Lord.—The love of God is here declared to be in Christ Jesus, to show that it is not God's love in general that is here referred to, but that covenant love with which God loves us as His children, His heirs, and joint heirs with His only-begotten and well-beloved Son. If it were simply said that God loves us, we might say, in reflecting on our sins, how can God love such sinful creatures as we are; and how can we assure ourselves of the continuance of His love, since we are daily sinning, and provoking Him to anger? The Apostle, therefore, sets forth to us Jesus Christ, who is the same yesterday, and to-day, and for ever, as the medium of this love, in order that while we see that we are sinners and worthy of condemnation, we may regard ourselves as in Jesus Christ, in whom we are reconciled, and washed from our sins in His blood. It is this medium to which the Apostle refers when he says, 'He hath made us accepted in the Beloved,' and God 'hath blessed us with all spiritual blessings in heavenly places in Christ;' 'He hath chosen us in Him before the foundation of the world,' Eph. i. 4. As, then, Jesus Christ is the true object of the love of the Father, as He testified by the voice from heaven, so in Him He loves His people with an everlasting love.

To Him He had given them from eternity, and has united them to Him in time, that He might love them in Him, and by Him. Thus the Father loves no man out of the Son. As the sins of men had rendered them enemies to God, His justice could never have permitted them to be the objects of His love, if He had not expiated their sins, and washed them in the blood of His Son. Whoever, then, is not or shall not be in Christ, is not loved by the Father, but the wrath of God abideth on him.· As the Apostle John testifies that God hath given us life, and this life is in His Son, so the Apostle Paul here declares that God hath given us His love, but that this love is in Jesus Christ. Consequently, we should not look for its cause in our works, or in anything in ourselves, but in Jesus Christ alone. Its incomprehensible extent and eternal duration are seen in His own words, when, addressing His Father, He says, ' And hast loved them, as Thou hast loved Me ; ' and again, ' Thou lovedst Me before the foundation of the world,' John xvii. 23.

The love of God, then, to His people, flows entirely through Jesus Christ. Men in general are fond of contemplating God as a God of benevolence. They attempt to flatter Him by praising His beneficence. But God's love to man is exercised only through the atonement made to His justice by the sacrifice of His Son. Those, therefore, who reject Christ and hope to partake of God's love through any other means than Christ's all-powerful mediation, must fail of success. There is no other name under heaven given among men whereby a sinner can be saved. As there was no protection in Egypt from death by the destroying angel except in those houses that were sprinkled with the blood of the paschal lamb, so none will be saved in the day of wrath and revelation of the righteous judgment of God, except those who are sprinkled with the blood of atonement.

The order followed by the Apostle in all this discourse is very remarkable. First, he challenges our enemies in general, and defies them all, saying, ' If God be for us, who can be against us ? ' Next, he shows, in detail, that neither the want of anything good, nor the occurrence of any evil, ought to trouble us. Not the want of any good, for ' God hath not spared His own Son, but delivered Him up for us all ; how, then, shall He not with Him also freely give us all things ? ' Not the occurrence of any evil, for that would be either within us or without us. Not within us, for the evil that is within us is sin, and as to sin, ' It is God that justifieth, who is he that condemneth ? It is Christ that died, yea rather, that is risen again, who is even at the right hand of God, who also maketh intercession for us.' Not anything without us, for it would be either in the creatures, or in God. Not in the creatures, for that would be ' tribulation, or distress, or persecution, or famine, or nakedness, or peril, or sword.' But ' in all these things we are more than conquerors, through Him that loved us.' Not in God, for then there must be variableness and change in His love. ' Now,' says the Apostle, ' I am persuaded that neither death, nor life, nor angels, nor principalities, nor powers, nor things present, nor things to come, nor height, nor depth, nor any other creature, shall be able to separate us from the love of God, which is in Christ Jesus our Lord.' On this he rests the believer's peace and assurance, and with these

words he concludes his animated and most consolatory description of
the victory and triumph of faith.

Well, indeed, may the Gospel be called the wisdom of God. It
harmonizes things in themselves the most opposite. Is it not astonishing
to find the man, who before had declared that there was no good thing in
him, here challenging the whole universe to bring a charge against any of
the elect of God? With respect to every Christian, in one point of view,
it may be asserted that there is nothing good in him; and in another,
it may be as confidently asserted that there is in him nothing evil. How
could Paul say of himself, after he was a partaker of the holiness of the
Spirit of truth, that there was nothing good in him? It was as concerned his own corrupt human nature. On what principle could he say,
Who shall lay anything to the charge of God's elect? It was as they are
in Christ Jesus. This is beautifully exhibited, 1 Cor. i. 30. God hath
united us to Christ Jesus in such an intimate manner, that His obedience
is our obedience; His sufferings are our sufferings; His righteousness
is our righteousness, for He is made unto us righteousness. This fully
explains the ground on which we stand righteous before God: we stand
in Christ. He has taken away all our sins. He who knew no sin was
made sin for us, that we might be made the righteousness of God in
Him. It is of the highest importance fully to understand our oneness
with Christ. This will give the utmost confidence before God, while we
entertain of ourselves the lowest opinion.

Besides all the other strong grounds of consolation contained in this
chapter, it incontrovertibly establishes the doctrine of the perseverance
of the saints, which, though clearly exhibited in so many other parts of
Scripture, is opposed by the Church of Rome, which teaches that
believers may finally fall from the love of God, thus representing that
love as variable and inconstant. They make the grace of God to depend
on the will of man for its effect; and as the will of man is mutable, so
they believe that the grace of God is likewise mutable; and, having
ascribed to their free will the glory of perseverance, they have, like
many who call themselves Protestants, lost altogether the doctrine of the
perseverance of believers unto eternal life. Closely connected with this
doctrine of perseverance, is the believer's knowledge of his acceptance
with God, without which that of final perseverance, or, more properly
speaking, the certainty of preservation by God, could impart to him no
comfort. When one of these doctrines is mentioned in Scriptures, the
other is generally referred to. Both of them are intimately connected
with the Christian's love to God, his joy and peace, and with his being
filled with the fruits of righteousness, which are by Jesus Christ to the
praise and glory of God. The enemies of this doctrine insist that it sets
aside the necessity of attending to good works. On the contrary, it
establishes them, and obliges us to perform them, not from servile fear,
but from gratitude, and filial love to our Heavenly Father. God combats
for us against principalities, and powers, and all our enemies; we ought,
therefore, to fight under His banner. The believer combats along with
God, while the issue of the combat and all the victory is from God, and
not from the believer.

It was one great object of the Apostles to hold out strong consolation to all who had fled for refuge, to lay hold of the hope set before them, and to urge them to give all diligence to the full assurance of hope. In exhorting to the duties of the Christian life, they proceeded on the ground that those to whom they wrote had the knowledge of their interest in the mediation of Christ, of the forgiveness of their sins through His love, and of the enjoyment of the love of God, to whom, by that Spirit of adoption which they had received, they cried, 'Abba, Father' and from all their Epistles it appears that those whom they addressed enjoyed this assurance. Paul accordingly exhorts the believers at Ephesus not to grieve the Holy Spirit of God, whereby *they were sealed unto the day of redemption*, and immediately after enjoins on them the duty of forgiving one another, even as God, *for Christ's sake, had forgiven them.* 'Ye were sometimes darkness, but *now are ye light in the Lord;* walk as children of light.' When Christ, who is our life, shall appear, then *shall ye also appear with Him in glory;* mortify, *therefore,* your members which are upon the earth,' Col. iii. 4. The Apostle Peter exhorts those to whom he wrote to love one another fervently, *seeing they had purified their souls in obeying the truth through the Spirit.* And the Apostle John enjoins on the little children, the young men, and the fathers, not to love the world, because their sins were forgiven ; because they had known Him that is from the beginning, and because *they had known the Father.* The exhortations of the Apostles are in this manner grounded on the knowledge that those to whom they were directed were supposed to have of their interest in the Saviour. Without this, the motives on which they are pressed to obedience would be unavailing.

The whole strain of the apostolic Epistles is calculated to confirm this knowledge, which is referred to as the spring of that joy unspeakable and full of glory with which those who were addressed rejoiced, 1 Pet. i. 8. Their faith, then, must have been an appropriating faith, taking home to themselves individually, according to its measure, the promises of mercy, and enabling them to say each for himself, with the Apostle, 'I am crucified with Christ, nevertheless I live ; yet not I, but Christ liveth in me ; and the life which I now live in the flesh I live by the faith of the Son of God, who loved me, and gave Himself for me.' No believer, without this persuasion that Christ gave Himself for him, and that he is 'dead unto sin,' and 'alive unto God,' should rest satisfied. If, in opposition to this, it be said that assurance of our interest in Christ is a gift of God, which He bestows as He sees good, it should be recollected that so also are all spiritual blessings ; and if of these it is our duty diligently to seek for a continual supply and increase, it is our duty to seek for this personal assurance among the rest. It is glorifying to Christ our Saviour, and highly important to ourselves. This assurance is what we are commanded to aim at, and to give all diligence to attain ; and full provision is made for it in the Gospel, Heb. vi. 11–20 ; 2 Pet. i. 10. We enjoy this assurance of our salvation, when we are walking with God, and in proportion as we walk with Him.

The full assurance of faith, in which believers are commanded to draw near to God, stands inseparably connected with having their hearts sprinkled from an evil conscience. An evil conscience accuses a man as guilty, as deserving and liable to punishment, and keeps him at a distance from God. It causes him to regard the Almighty as an enemy and avenger, so that the natural enmity of the mind against God is excited and strengthened. On the contrary, a good conscience is a conscience discharged from guilt, by the blood of Christ. Conscience tells a man that the wages of sin is death, and that he has incurred the penalty; but when the atonement made by Christ is believed in, it is seen that our sins are no more ours, but Christ's, upon whom God hath laid them all, and that the punishment due for sin, which is death, has been inflicted upon Him; the demands of the law have been fulfilled, and its penalty suffered. On this the believer rests, and his conscience is satisfied. It is thus purged from dead works, and this is what is called the answer of a good conscience toward God, 1 Pet. iii. 21. This answer of a good conscience cannot be disjoined from assurance of our acceptance with Him to whom we draw near; and the degree in which both this assurance, and a good conscience, are enjoyed, will be equal. As far, then, as the duty of a Christian's possessing this assurance is denied, so far the duty of having the answer of a good conscience is not admitted. The same also is true respecting the grace of hope. Hope is the anchor of the soul, to the attainment of the full assurance of which believers are commanded to give all diligence, and they are encouraged to hold fast the rejoicing of the hope firm unto the end. It is when they have the hope of beholding Jesus as He is that they purify themselves even as He is pure, 1 John iii. 3. The 'hope of salvation' covers their heads in the combat in which they are engaged, which they are therefore commanded to put on, and wear as an helmet, 1 Thess. v. 8. In writing to the Thessalonians, the Apostle ascribes to God and the Lord Jesus Christ the everlasting consolation, and good hope through grace, which had been given to them. And he prays for the believers at Rome that the God of hope may fill them with all joy and peace in believing, and that they might abound in hope through the power of the Holy Ghost.

This good hope through grace, then, as well as a conscience purged from dead works—the duty of possessing which no Christian will deny—stand inseparably connected with the personal assurance of an interest in the Saviour, and all of them lie at the foundation of love to God, and consequently of acceptable obedience to Him. We love Him when we see that He hath loved us, and that His Son is the propitiation for our sins. 'Thy loving-kindness is before mine eyes, and I have walked in Thy truth,' Ps. xxvi. 3. 'Lord, I have hoped for Thy salvation, and done Thy commandments,' Ps. cxix. 166. In this manner was David led to serve God. When, according to the precious promise of our blessed Lord, the Spirit takes of the things that are His—the glory of His person, and the perfection of His work—and discovers them to us, we then know whom we have believed, the conscience is discharged from guilt; and thus, hoping in God, and having our hearts enlarged, we run the way of His commandments, Ps. cxix. 32, and bring forth the fruits of the Spirit, love, joy, and peace. But how can there be love without a sense of reconciliation with God; and how can the fruits of joy and peace be brought forth till the conscience is discharged from guilt? It is earnestly and repeatedly enjoined on believers to *rejoice in the Lord;* but how can they rejoice in Him unless they have the persuasion that they belong to Him? '*The joy of the Lord is your strength,*' Neh. viii. 10. '*The end of the commandment is charity, out of a pure heart, and a good conscience, and of faith unfeigned,*' 1 Tim. i. 5. *Love* flows from *a pure heart, a pure heart* from *a good conscience,* and *a good conscience* from *true faith.* The necessity of a good conscience, in order to acceptable obedience to God, is forcibly pointed out, Heb. ix. 14. 'How much more shall the blood of Christ, who through the eternal Spirit offered Himself without spot to God, purge your conscience from dead works to serve the living God?' Till this takes place, all a man's doings are *dead works,* or, as the Apostle expresses it in the seventh chapter of this Epistle, ' fruit unto death.' An evil or guilty conscience leads a man to keep at a distance from God, like Adam, who, conscious of his guilt, hid himself among the trees of the garden. But when the conscience is made good,—that is, is at peace,—the heart is purified, and love is produced. Then, and not till then, when ascribing praise to the Lamb who has washed us from our sins in His own blood, and having a sense of reconciliation with God, and of the enjoyment of His favour, we serve Him in newness of spirit, and not in the oldness of the letter—not from servile fear, but with gratitude and filial affection. Thus, having boldness to enter into the holiest by the blood of Jesus, by a new and living way, which He hath consecrated for us through the vail, that is to say, His flesh; and having an High Priest over the house of God, we draw near with a true heart, in the full assurance of faith, having our hearts sprinkled from an evil conscience, and our bodies washed with pure water. We enjoy the persuasion that by His mercy we are saved by the washing of regeneration and renewing of the Holy Ghost. 'Come unto Me, and I will give you rest.' What is this rest but that peace and repose of the soul which can never be found but in God? Then we can adopt the language of the Psalmist, ' I will go unto God, my exceeding joy.'

The Spirit of God being holy, will not produce Christian assurance without at the same time producing sanctification, and by this sanctification the persuasion is confirmed of our communion with God; for although our sanctification be imperfect, it is a certain mark of our election. When we feel a holy sadness for having offended God, we enjoy the blessedness of those who mourn, and are assured that we shall be comforted. When we hunger and thirst after righteousness, we have the promise that we shall be filled. This mourning for sin, and thirsting after righteousness, on which the Saviour pronounces His blessing, can only proceed from the Spirit of God, and not from the desire of the carnal mind, which is enmity against God. The fruits of the Spirit are first produced by believing in Christ, trusting in Him, and regarding what He has done without us, and are increased and confirmed by what He is doing within us. Abounding in the fruits of righteousness, we make our calling and election sure. Keeping his commandments, we prove our love to our Saviour, and He manifests Himself to us as He doeth not unto the world.

Personal application, or the appropriation of faith, is often signalized
in Scripture. Moses says, 'The Lord is my strength and my song, and
He is become my salvation: He is my God,' Ex. xv. 2. Job says, 'I
know that my Redeemer liveth, and that He shall stand at the latter day
upon the earth ; and though after my skin worms destroy this body, yet
in my flesh shall I see God,' Job xix. 25. ' I know,' says David, ' that
God is for me,' Ps. lvi. 9. 'The Lord is my Shepherd, I shall not want,'
Ps. xxiii. 1. 'The Lord is the portion of mine inheritance and of my
cup,' Ps. xvi. 5. ' I will love thee, O Lord, my strength. The Lord is
my rock, and my fortress, and my deliverer ; my God, my strength, in
whom I will trust ; my buckler, and the horn of my salvation, and my high
tower,' Ps. xviii. 1. ' I know,' says Paul, ' whom I have believed.' John
says, 'We have known and believed the love that God hath to us.' Peter,
classing himself with those to whom he wrote, blesses God that he and
they were begotten again to a lively hope of an inheritance reserved in
heaven ; and, referring to their final perseverance, he adds, that they
were ' kept by the power of God, through faith, unto salvation.' In the
hope of that salvation, those who received the doctrine of the Apostles
rejoiced as soon as it was announced to them, Acts ii. 41, viii. 39, xvi.
34. Their joy, then, had not its source in reflection on, or consciousness
of, their faith, or its effects, although afterwards so confirmed, but arose,
in the first instance, from the view they had of the glory and all-sufficiency
of the Saviour, and His perfect righteousness made theirs by faith, resting on the Divine warrant and promise, ' In whom we have boldness
and access with confidence by the faith of Him,' Eph. iii. 12.

Although the assurance of sense be confirmatory of the assurance of
faith, it is not so strong as the latter. ' Sanctification,' says Rutherford,
' does not evidence justification as faith doth evidence it, with such a sort
of clearness as light evidences colours, though it be no sign or evident
mark of them ; but as smoke evidences fire, and as the morning star in
the east evidenceth the sun will shortly rise; or as the streams prove
there is a head-spring whence they issue; though none of these make
what they evidence visible to the eye; so doth sanctification give evidence
of justification, only as marks, signs, effects, give evidence of the cause.
But the light of faith, the testimony of the Spirit by the operation of free
grace, will cause us, as it were, with our eyes, see justification and faith,
not by report, but as we see the sun's light.'

If it be objected that a man cannot know that he has faith without
seeing its effects, it is replied that this is contrary to fact. When a thing
is testified, or a promise is made to us, we know whether or not we believe it, or trust in it. According to this objection, when Philip said, 'If
thou believest with all thine heart thou mayest,' the eunuch should have
replied, ' You ask me to tell you a thing I cannot know ; ' but instead of
this, he answers, ' I believe.' When the Lord asked the blind man,
' Believest thou in the Son of God ? ' he did not ask a question which it
was impossible to answer. Does the Spirit of God cry in the hearts of
believers, ' Abba, Father,' and witness with their spirits that they are the
children of God, without their being able to know it? If, however, the
flesh raises doubts in the believer, from the weakness of his faith, he

should consider that the weakness of his faith does not prevent it from being true faith; that God accepts not the perfection but the reality of faith; that Jesus Christ recognised the faith of him who said, 'Lord, I believe; help Thou my unbelief;' and that these doubts are not in his faith, but opposed to it. They are in the flesh, which the believer resists, and says, with Paul, 'Now, if I do what I would not, it is no more I that do it, but sin that dwelleth in me.'

'In the first act of believing,' says Mr. Bell in his work *On the Covenants*, 'sinners have no evidence of grace in themselves: they feel nothing within but sin; they see a word without them as the sole foundation of faith, and on that alone they build for eternity. This is a point of no small importance to saints and sinners. Many of the modern builders are at great pains to keep their hearers from all confidence till they first discern the evidences of grace in their hearts; and, having got evidence, then, and not till then, can they have any just, lawful, or well-grounded confidence,—nay, they seem pretty plainly to intimate that a sinner's right to Christ turns on something wrought in him, or done by him, and till he have evidence of this, he can claim no interest in Christ, nor assure himself of salvation by Him. According to this, Christ, the Tree of Life, is forbidden fruit, which the sinner must not touch till he has seen inward evidence. I confess I have not so learned Christ. The sinner's right to Christ turns not at all upon any inward gracious qualifications, but purely on the Divine warrant revealed in the word. Faith is not a qualification in order to come to Christ, but the coming itself; it is not our right to Christ, but our taking and receiving Him to ourselves on the footing of the right conveyed by the Gospel offer.'

''Tis a thing of huge difficulty,' says Archbishop Leighton, 'to bring men to a sense of their natural misery, to see that they have need of a Saviour, and to look out for one. But then, being brought to that, 'tis no less, if not more difficult, to persuade them that Christ is He; that as they have need of Him, so they need no more, He being able and sufficient for them. All the waverings and fears of misbelieving minds do spring from dark and narrow apprehensions of Jesus Christ. All the doubt is not of their interest, as they imagine; they who say so, and think it is so, do not perceive the bottom and root of their own malady. They say they do no whit doubt but that He is able enough, and His righteousness large enough, but all the doubt is, *if He belong to me.* Now, I say this doubt arises from a defect and doubt of the former, wherein you suspect it not. Why doubtest thou that He belongs to thee? Dost thou fly to Him, as lost and undone in thyself? Dost thou renounce all that can be called thine, and seek thy life in Him? Then He is *thine. He came to seek and to save that which was lost.* Oh! but I find so much not only former but still daily renewed and increasing guiltiness. Why? Is He a sufficient Saviour, or is He not? If thou dost say He is not, then it is manifest that here lies the defect and mistake. If thou sayest He is, then hast thou answered all thy objections of that kind: much guiltiness much or little, old or new, neither helps nor hinders, as to thy interest in Him, and salvation by Him. And for dispelling of these mists, nothing can be more effectual than the letting in of those Gospel beams, the clear

expressions of His riches and fulness in the Scriptures, and eminently this
—*made of God wisdom and righteousness.*'

The religion of the Church of Rome leaves a man nothing but doubts
respecting his salvation. It teaches, as has been formerly remarked, that
a Christian should believe in general the promises of God, while personal
application of these promises, and assurance of God's love, it calls presumption. This subject was one of the grand points of discussion between that church and the Reformers. But how many Protestants have
forsaken the ground which their predecessors here occupied, and have
gone over to that of their opponents! The doctrine of the duty of our
personal assurance of salvation, and the persuasion of our interest in
Christ, is denied by many, and doubts concerning this are even converted
into evidences of faith, although they are directly opposed to it. Doubts
of a personal interest in Christ, are evidences either of little faith or of
no faith. ' O thou of little faith, wherefore didst thou doubt?' If this
assurance were built on anything except on the foundation that God
Himself hath laid, it would indeed be eminently presumptuous. But, in
opposition to such opinions, the Apostle John has written a whole Epistle
to lead Christians to this assurance. ' He that believeth on the Son of
God hath the witness in himself. He that believeth not God hath made
Him a liar: because He believeth not the witness which God hath witnessed concerning His Son. And this is the witness, that God hath given
to us eternal life; and this life is in His Son. He that hath the Son hath
life; and he that hath not the Son of God hath not life. These things have
I written unto you that believe on the name of the Son of God, that ye may
know that ye have eternal life, and that ye may believe on the name of the
Son of God.' ' This assurance,' says Archbishop Leighton, ' is no enemy to
holy diligence, nor friend to *carnal* security; on the contrary, it is the only
thing that doth eminently enable and embolden the soul for all adventures
and services. Base fears and doubtings, wherein some place much of religion, and many weak Christians seem to be in that mistake, to think it
a kind of holy spiritual temper to be questioning and doubting. I say,
then, base fears can never produce anything truly generous, no height of
obedience,—they do nothing but entangle and disable the soul for every
good work; *perfect love casts out this fear,* and works a sweet unperplex-
ing fear, a holy wariness, not to offend, which fears nothing else. And
this confidence of love is the great secret of comfort, and of ability to do
God service. Nothing makes so strong and healthful a constitution of
soul as pure love: it dare submit to God and resign itself to Him; it dare
venture itself in His hand, and seeks no more but how to please Him.
A heart thus composed goes readily and cheerfully unto all services, to
do, to suffer, to live, to die, at His pleasure; and firmly stands to this,
that nothing can separate from that which is sufficient to it, what is all
its happiness, the love of God in Christ Jesus.' ' It is true that all
Christians have not alike clear and firm apprehension of their happy and
true state, and scarce any of them are alike at all times; yet they have
all and always the same right to this state, and to the comfort of it;
and where they stand in a right light to view it, they do see it so, and rejoice in it. Many Christians do prejudice their own comfort, and darken

their spirits, by not giving freedom to faith to act according to its nature and proper principles; they will not believe till they find some evidence or assurance, which is quite to invert the order of the thing, and to look for fruit without settling a root for it to grow from. Would you take Christ upon the absolute word of promise tendering Him to you, and rest on Him, this would ingraft you into life itself, for that He is; and so those fruits of the Holy Ghost would bud and flourish in your hearts. From that very believing on Him would arise this persuasion, yea, even to a gloriation, and an humble boasting in His love,—who *shall accuse?* who *shall condemn?* who *shall separate?*'

In opposition to the believer's personal assurance of salvation, Satan will represent to him the number and enormity of his sins, and the strictness of God's justice, which has often fallen on those whom He hardens. But believers will answer, ' We know that to God belongeth righteousness, and unto us confusion of faces, but mercy and pardon belong to the Lord our God. If our sins ascend to heaven, His mercy is above the heavens. It is true that sin abounds in us; but where sin abounded grace and mercy have much more abounded; and the greater our misery, the greater towards us is the glory of the mercy of God. In entering into paradise, our Lord Jesus Christ has not taken with Him angels, but the spirit of a malefactor, that we might know that the greatest sinners are objects of His compassion. He came into the world to save sinners, and He calls to Himself those who are heavy laden with sin. He came to proclaim liberty to the captives, and the opening of the prison to them that are bound. The more, then, that we feel the power of sin, the closer we cleave to Him. If Peter, affrighted, exclaimed, "Depart from me, for I am a sinful man, O Lord," let us, on the contrary, say, Lord Jesus, we come to Thee, and the more so because we are sinners; for Thou hast been made sin for us who knew no sin, that we might be made the righteousness of God in Thee. We have sinned seventy times, and seventy times have fallen again into sin; but God, who commands us to forgive offences even seventy times seven, will many more times pardon! In comparison of His love, the love of man is not as a drop to the ocean.'

The foundation on which believers repel doubts concerning their salvation rests on the excellence of their Mediator, His love and compassion for them, the merit of His obedience, and their communion with Him. As to the excellence of their Mediator, He is the eternal Son of God, the Beloved of the Father, for whom they are beloved in Him, and His intercession for them is acceptable to God and efficacious. ' We have a great High Priest that is passed into the heavens, Jesus the Son of God.' ' He is able to save them to the uttermost that come unto God by Him, seeing He ever liveth to make intercession for them.' It rests on the love and compassion of Jesus. ' For we have not an High Priest which cannot be touched with the feeling of our infirmities, but was in all points tempted like as we are, yet without sin.' His love to us has been stronger than death; and He Himself saith, ' Greater love hath no man than this, that a man lay down his life for his friends.' Having thus given Himself for us, will He reject us? Having ascended to heaven, will He forget us, for whom He descended to earth, and for whom, as the forerunner, He hath again entered heaven to intercede for us, to prepare a place, and to receive us to Himself?

Believers rest their assurance of salvation on the merit of their Redeemer's obedience; for when their sins are red as crimson, they shall be made white as snow. Our robes have been washed in the blood of the Lamb, whose blood cleanseth us from all sin. It is impossible that sin can be more powerful to destroy us, than the grace of God and the merit of Jesus Christ to save us. We are condemned by the law; but, in answer to the law, we plead the blood of Jesus Christ, who hath borne the curse of the law, and who is the end of the law for righteousness to every one that believeth. We have been condemned by the justice of God; but to this justice we present the righteousness of Christ, who is 'Jehovah our righteousness.' God hath been angry with us; but in Jesus Christ He hath not beheld iniquity in Jacob, neither hath He seen perverseness in Israel.

To the temptations of Satan, believers also oppose their union with Jesus Christ; for Jesus Christ and they are one. We are His members, bone of His bones, and flesh of His flesh; His obedience is our obedience; for as we are one body with Him, we appear before our God in Him. We are found in Him, not having our own righteousness, which is of the law, but that which is through the faith of Christ, the righteousness which is of God by faith. By union with Him we are already seated together in heavenly places in Christ. As Jesus Christ has risen to die no more, but to live eternally, it follows that the righteousness which He has wrought is an everlasting righteousness, and that, being united to Him as His members, we derive from Him a life which cannot fail, so that we shall never die; for as the risen Head dies no more, and His life is an everlasting life, in like manner, whoever receives spiritual life from Him, receives a life which can never terminate. Hence it follows that the resurrection of Jesus Christ, assuring us of our justification and eternal life, is a source of the greatest joy and consolation. The Psalmist, accordingly, prophesying of the resurrection of Christ, says 'that his heart is glad, and his glory rejoiceth.' The first words of Jesus Christ to Mary, after His resurrection, were, 'Woman, why weepest thou?' and to the other women, 'Be not afraid;' and to the disciples, 'Why are ye troubled?' His resurrection ought to wipe away the tears of His people, to tranquillize their minds, and dissipate their fears, by the assurance it gives of their acquittal from condemnation before God, and of the destruction of him who had the power of death.

'The words of Jesus, above referred to,' says an eloquent writer, 'are generally applicable to the life of a Christian. He can look upon that rich field of privilege and of promise placed before him in the Bible, and can say that it is all his own. And where is the want that the blessed fruits of that field cannot supply, the distress which they cannot relieve, the wound that they cannot heal, the fear that they cannot quiet, or the sorrow for which they do not furnish abundant consolation? Where, then, is the cause of depression? Friend of Jesus, why weepest thou? If you have an Advocate with the Father, through whom your

sins are all forgiven, and you are made a child of God,—and the Holy
Ghost is given you as your Sanctifier and Comforter,—and you are assured
of having almighty power for your support, and unerring wisdom for
your guide, and heaven for your eternal home,—what can overbalance
or suppress the joy which naturally results from such privileges as these?
Trials we may, we must, meet with ; but can these depress us, when we
know that our light affliction, which is but for a moment, worketh for us
a far more exceeding, even an eternal weight of glory? If tried by
bodily pain, we feel more keenly the happiness of the hope which
anticipates the time when we shall have a building of God, a house not
made with hands, eternal in the heavens! Worldly losses will not overwhelm us, if we know that we are undoubted heirs of an inheritance
that is incorruptible, undefiled, and that fadeth not away. Friends may
change, but we will be comforted by the assurance that in Christ we
have a brother born for adversity,—nay, a friend that sticketh closer
than a brother. There rolls between us and our Father's house the deep
and restless tide of this world's corruption, through which we must of
necessity pass, and the deeper and still more dangerous tide of the
corruption of our hearts, and we are surrounded by enemies on every
side ; and when we feel our own weakness, we may be ready to fear lest
we should one day fall by the hand of some of them. But every
distressing fear is removed, when we recollect that we shall not be
tempted beyond what we are able to bear, and that, in point of fact,
there is no limit to our power, for we can do all things through Christ
strengthening us, and that the life that is in us is the life of Christ, a life
which no power can extinguish in any one of Christ's members, any
more than it can extinguish it in our glorious Head.'

From the 28th verse to the conclusion of the chapter, the greatest
encouragement is held out to repose all our confidence on the love of
God in Christ Jesus, with the assured conviction that, receiving Him,
we shall be enabled to persevere unto the end. The impossibility of
plucking His people out of the Saviour's hand is here established in the
most triumphant manner. Whatever objection is raised against it, is
contrary to the power of Jesus Christ, contrary to His love, to the virtue
of His sacrifice, and to the prevalence of His intercession,—contrary to
the operation of the whole Godhead, Father, Son, and Holy Ghost, in
every part of the plan of salvation. If we look upwards or downwards,
—to heaven above, or the earth or hell beneath,—to all places, to all
creatures,—neither any nor all of them together shall prevail against us.
Were heaven and earth to combine, and all the powers of hell to rise up,
they would avail nothing against the outstretched arm of Him who
makes us more than conquerors. The power of Jesus, who is our Head,
ascends above the heavens, and descends beneath the depths; and in
His love there is a breadth, and length, and depth, and height, which
passeth knowledge. ' Thy mercy, O Lord, is in the heavens, and Thy
faithfulness reacheth unto the clouds. Thy righteousness is like the
great mountains ; Thy judgments are a great deep,' Ps. xxxvi. 5. Can
anything prevail to pluck out of the hands of Jesus Christ those who
have fled to Him as their surety,—those who are members of His body,

of His flesh, and of His bones,—those whom He hath purchased with His precious blood ?

The feelings of the believer, viewed in Christ, as described in the close of this chapter, form a striking contrast with what is said in the end of the former chapter, where he is viewed in himself. In the contemplation of himself as a sinner, he mournfully exclaims, ' O wretched man that I am ! ' In the contemplation of himself as justified in Christ, he boldly demands, Who shall lay anything to my charge ? Who is he that condemneth ? Well may the man who loves God defy the universe to separate him from the love of God which is in Christ Jesus his Lord. Although at present the whole creation groaneth and travaileth in pain together, although even he himself groaneth within himself, yet all things are working together for his good. The Holy Spirit is interceding for him in his heart; Jesus Christ is interceding for him before the throne ; God the Father hath chosen him from eternity, hath called him, hath justified him, and will finally crown him with glory. The Apostle had begun this chapter by declaring that there is no *condemnation* to them who are in Christ Jesus : he concludes it with the triumphant assurance that there is no *separation* from His love. The salvation of believers is complete in Christ, and their union with Him indissoluble.

CHAPTER 9
ROMANS 9:1 – 33

THROUGH the whole of the doctrinal part of this Epistle, Paul has an eye to the state and character of the Jewish nation, and the aspect which the Gospel bears towards them. In the preceding chapters, he had exhibited that righteousness which God has provided for men, all of whom are entirely divested of any righteousness of their own, ' none being righteous, no, not one.' He had discoursed largely on the justification and sanctification of believers, and now he proceeds to treat particularly of the doctrine of predestination, and to exhibit the sovereignty of God in His dealings both towards Jews and Gentiles. The way in which, in the ninth, tenth, and eleventh chapters, he so particularly adverts to the present state and future destination of the Jews, in connection with what regards the Gentiles, furnishes the most ample opportunity for the illustration of this highly important subject.

In the eighth chapter, the Apostle had declared the glorious and exalted privileges of the people of God. But it was impossible for one so ardently attached to his own nation, and so zealously concerned for the welfare of his countrymen, not to be touched with the melancholy contrast which naturally arose to his mind, as he turned from these lofty and cheering contemplations to consider the deplorable state of apostate Israel. If there was a people upon earth to whom, more than to another, the blessings of the Gospel belonged as a birthright, it was assuredly to the descendants, according to the flesh, of Abraham, of Isaac, and of Jacob. But they had wilfully rebelled against their God ; they had rejected the Messiah, and consequently forfeited the rights and immunities secured to their forefathers by covenant. Their condition was therefore itself well calculated to awaken the sympathies of Paul ; while at the same time it was necessary to vindicate the faithfulness of God, and to prove that the rejection of the Jews was by no means opposed to the absolute security of God's elect, on which he had been so largely expatiating. This subject is therefore discussed in the three following chapters ; and as it is one of the greatest importance, so also it is introduced in a manner the most appropriate and the most affecting.

Scarcely has his sublime conclusion to the eighth chapter terminated, when, at the beginning of the ninth, the triumphant language of victory is exchanged by the Apostle for the voice of commiseration, in which he bewails the apostasy of his countrymen. He does not dwell so much upon the magnitude of their guilt, as he does upon the memory of their ancestral glory and ancient privileges. He strongly affirms the ardour of his affection for them as his brethren, and feelingly deplores the misery of their rejected condition. Finally, he turns from this scene of ruin and degradation, to declare that their apostasy, though general, was not universal, and to predict the dawn of a brighter day, which shall yet make manifest the truth and faithfulness of their covenant God, whose purposes concerning Israel had evidently alike included their present rejection and future restoration.

The rejection of Israel, Paul proves to have been from the earliest periods of their history prefigured by God's dealing towards them as a nation. For, after declaring that ' they are not all Israel which are of Israel,' he adduces various and conclusive testimonies in confirmation of this truth, and thus forcibly illustrates the conduct of God towards the natural descendants of Abraham. In following this course of argument, he draws a solemn and most impressive picture of the sovereignty of God in the general administration of His government, and asserts the distinction which God makes between vessels of wrath and vessels of mercy, in order ' that He might make known the riches of His glory on the vessels of mercy, which He had afore prepared unto glory.' He further affirms the calling of a portion both of Jews and Gentiles, with whom in combination he classes himself as one of those ' called of God,' concerning whom he had, in the preceding chapter, so largely discoursed. The introduction of the Gentiles into the Church of Christ, as well as of a remnant or portion of the Jews, being thus clearly intimated, he shows that both of these events had been expressly foretold by the Prophets, who had also affirmed that except the Lord of Sabaoth had left them a seed, the national ruin of Israel would have been as complete as that of Sodom and Gomorrah.

The Apostle had thus two great objects in view. In the first place, he illustrates the sovereignty of God as exhibited in the infallible accomplishment of the Divine purposes predicted by the Prophets, which led to the national rejection of the Jews, with the exception of a remnant who were saved by grace. In the second place, he proves that the purposes of God were equally fulfilled in bringing in the Gentiles; and this he does in such a way as to cut off, on their part, all pretensions to everything like merit, desert, or worthiness, since, without seeking for it, they attained to the righteousness which is of faith.

Having established these two important truths with great force and clearness, Paul accounts for the fact of the Jews having stumbled at and rejected the Messiah. He shows that the Messiah had been characterized by the Prophets as ' that stumbling stone ' which God had laid in Zion; and that the Jews stumbled in consequence of their ignorance of the righteousness which God had provided in the fulfilment of His violated law, and of their vain attempt to establish a righteousness of their own. His discussion of this topic is thus most appropriately introduced. It is also in the last degree important, as furnishing additional confirmation of the sovereignty of God, which is here exhibited in the certainty of the accomplishment of His purposes; while it is testified how well merited was that punishment of rejecting and casting off the great body of the Jews. Paul sums up the whole, by appealing, at the end of the tenth chapter, to the testimonies of Moses and Isaiah, in confirmation of what he had advanced. But still, as the apostasy was so general, it might be concluded that God had for ever cast off the Jewish nation, and had thus made void the promises made to the fathers. This error he once more encounters and largely confutes in the eleventh chapter, where he shows most conclusively that, in whatever form it presents itself, it cannot abide the test of truth. So far is this from being the case, that, in the infallible dispensations of God, a period will arrive when the Redeemer shall come out of Zion, and turn away ungodliness from Jacob; when the whole of Israel shall, as one people, be brought within the bond of that new covenant established with the house of Israel, and with the house of Judah, of the blessings of which they shall all partake. The three following chapters thus hold a very distinguished place in this most instructive Epistle, and exhibit in a manner the most comprehensive, as well as conspicuous and edifying, the sovereignty of God in the government of the world, and the character of His dealings towards men in the whole of the Divine administration.

As the nation of Israel were types of the true Israel, and as their rejection might seem, as has been observed, to militate against the security of the people of God, it was necessary in this ninth chapter to enter fully upon the subject. It was, however, one sure to be highly offensive to the Jews; and therefore Paul introduces it in a manner calculated, as far as possible, to allay their prejudices against him, while at the same time he does not in this matter shun to declare the whole counsel of God, for the instruction of those to whom he wrote.

After expressing the grief with which he contemplated his countrymen, without specifying its cause, he enumerates their distinguished privileges as a nation. He then adverts to their being rejected of God, though not directly mentioning it; and begins with observing that it could not be said that among them the word of God had taken none effect. God had promised to be a God to Abraham and to his seed; and although the greater part of Israel were now cast off, that promise had not failed. When God said to Abraham, ' In Isaac shall thy seed be called,' He intimated that the promise did not refer to all his children, but to a select number. Isaac was given to Abraham by the special promise of Jehovah; and further, in the case of Rebecca, one of her children was a child of promise, the other was not, and this was intimated before they were born. In order to silence all objections against this proceeding, as if the Almighty could be charged with injustice, Paul at once appeals to the sovereignty of God, who disposes of His creatures as to Him seems good. Especially he refers to what God had said to Moses, as recorded in the Scriptures, when He made all His goodness to pass before him, that He will have mercy on whom He will have mercy,—thus intimating that His favours were His own, and that in bestowing or withholding them there was no room for injustice. Against this view of God's sovereignty, the pride of man, until subdued by grace, rises with rebellious violence ; but such is its importance—such its tendency to abase the sinner and exalt the Saviour—that Paul dwells on it in both its aspects, not only as exhibited in the exercise of mercy on whom He will, but also in hardening whom He will. In acting both in the one way and the other, he declares that God contemplates His own glory. This leads the Apostle immediately to the election of those whom God had prepared to be vessels of mercy, both from among the Jews and the Gentiles. These in reality were the only children of promise of whom Isaac was a type, Gal. iv. 28. On the other hand, the rejection of the great body of Israel, so far from being contrary to the Divine purpose, had been distinctly predicted by their own Prophets. He closes the chapter by showing that, while this rejection had taken place according to the counsel of God, its immediate occasion was the culpable ignorance and prejudice of the Jews themselves in seeking acceptance with God by their own righteousness, instead of submitting to the righteousness of God brought in by the Messiah.

The manner in which Paul has treated the subject of this chapter, furnishes an opportunity of illustrating the doctrine of election to eternal life, to which, in the one preceding, he had traced up, as to their origin, all the privileges of believers in Christ. It likewise gives occasion to exhibit the sovereignty of God, as all along displayed respecting the nation of Israel. In this manner the astonishing fact is at the same time accounted for, that so great a portion of the Jews had rejected the promised Messiah, while a remnant among them at that time, as in every preceding age, acknowledged Him as their Lord. Mr. Stuart says that ' with the eighth chapter concludes what may appropriately be termed the *doctrinal* part of our Epistle.' But if the sovereignty of God be a doctrine of Divine revelation, this assertion is evidently erroneous. Without the development of this important doctrine, which accounts for the fact of the election of some, and the rejection of others, the Epistle would not be complete.

Ver. 1.—*I say the truth in Christ, I lie not, my conscience also bearing me witness in the Holy Ghost.*

I say the truth.—The Jews regarded the Apostle Paul as their most determined enemy. What, therefore, he was about to declare concerning his great sorrow on account of the present state of his countrymen, would not easily procure from them credit. Yet it was a truth which he could affirm without hypocrisy, and with the greatest sincerity. *In Christ.* —Paul was speaking as one united to, and belonging to, Christ—acting as in His service. This is a most solemn asseveration, and implies that what he was affirming was as true as if Christ Himself had spoken it. A reference to Christ would have no weight with the Jews. It appears, therefore, that the Apostle adopted this solemn language chiefly with a view of impressing those whom he addresses with a conviction of his sincerity, and also to prove that what he was about to say respecting the rejection of the Jewish nation did not arise, as might be supposed, from any prejudice or dislike to his countrymen. *I lie not.*—This is a repetition, but not properly tautology. In certain situations an assertion may be frequently in substance repeated, as indicating the earnestness of the speaker. The Apostle dwells on the statement, and is not willing to leave it without producing the effect. *My conscience also bearing me witness.*—For the sincerity of his love for the Jewish nation, the Apostle appeals to his conscience. His countrymen and others might deem him their enemy: they might consider all his conduct towards them as influenced by hatred; but he had the testimony of his conscience to the contrary. *In the Holy Ghost.*—He not only had the testimony of his conscience, but what precluded the possibility of his deceiving, he spoke in the Holy Ghost— he spoke by inspiration.

Ver. 2, 3.—*That I have great heaviness and continual sorrow in my heart (for I could wish that myself were accursed from Christ) for my brethren, my kinsmen according to the flesh.*

Many interpretations have been given of this passage. Calvin supposes that Paul, actually in 'a state of ecstasy,' wished himself condemned in the place of his countrymen. 'The additional sentence,' he says, 'proves the Apostle to be speaking not of temporal, but eternal death; and when he says *from Christ*, an allusion is made to the Greek word *anathema*, which means *a separation from anything.* Does not separation from Christ mean, being excluded from all hopes of salvation?' Such a thing is impossible, and would be highly improper. This would do more than fulfil the demands of the law,—it would utterly go beyond the law, and would therefore be sinful; for all our affections ought to be regulated by the law of God. Some understand it of excommunication. But the Apostle could not be excommunicated by Christ, except for a cause which would exclude him from heaven, as well as from the church on earth. He could not be excommunicated without being guilty of some sin that manifested him to be an unbeliever. It is not possible that one speaking in the Holy Ghost could wish to be in such a state. Paul's affection for his countrymen is here indeed expressed in very strong terms, but the meaning often ascribed to it is not for a moment to be admitted. That any one should desire to be eternally separated from Christ, and consequently punished with everlasting destruction from the presence of the Lord, is impossible. The law commands us to love our neighbour as ourselves, but not *more* than ourselves, which would be the case, if to promote his temporal or spiritual benefit we desired to be eternally miserable. It should also be recollected, that it is not only everlasting misery, but desperate and final enmity against God, that is comprised in Paul's wish as it is generally understood. It represents him as loving the creature more than the Creator. But who could ever imagine that the desire of being eternally wicked, and of indulging everlasting hatred to God, could proceed from love to Christ, and be a proper manner of expressing zeal for His glory? It would be strange indeed if Paul, who had just been affirming, in a tone so triumphant, the impossibility of the combined efforts of creation to separate him from the love of Christ, should, the moment after, solemnly desire that this separation should take place, for the sake of any creature, however beloved.

To understand the meaning of this passage, there are three observations to which it is of importance to attend. In the first place, it is the *past*, and not the present tense, which is employed in the original. What is rendered ' I could wish,' should be read in the past tense, ' I was wishing, or did wish,' referring to the Apostle's state before his conversion. The second observation is, that the verb which in our version is translated ' wish,' would have been more correctly rendered in this place *boast ;* ' for I myself boasted, or made it my boast, to be separated from Christ.' For this translation, which makes the Apostle's meaning far more explicit, there is the most unquestionable authority.[1] The third observation is, that the first part of the 3d verse should be read in a parenthesis, as follows: ' I have great heaviness and continual sorrow in my heart (for I myself made it my boast to be separated from Christ) for my brethren, my kinsmen according to the flesh.' By the usual interpretation, the Apostle is understood to say, ' I have great heaviness and continual sorrow in my heart,' and without stating for whom or for what, to add, ' I could wish that myself were accursed from Christ for my brethren.' But it appears evident that these words, *for my brethren,* form the conclusion of the above expression, *I have great heaviness and continual sorrow in my heart.* Paul had himself formerly made it his boast to be separated from Christ, rejecting Him as the Messiah ; and to prove how much he sympathized with the situation of his countrymen, in the bosom of his lamentation over their fallen state, he appeals to his former experience, when, before his conversion, he had been in the same unbelief, and personally knew their deplorable condition. He also intimates his sorrow in such a manner as to show that he is far from glorying over them, having been himself as deeply guilty as they were; while, according to the doctrine he was inculcating, it was in no respect to be ascribed to his own merits that he was happily delivered from that awful condemnation in which, with grief, he beheld them now standing.

Paul's sorrow was for those whom he calls his *brethren.* This does not respect a spiritual relationship, as the term brethren so generally denotes in the New Testament, but natural relationship, as Paul here explains it, when he adds, *my kinsmen according to the flesh.* His sorrow for them is

[1] See, for example, the Sixth Book of the *Iliad*, where the same word occurs, in the dialogue between Diomed and Glaucus, and could not be rendered otherwise.

the subject of his testimony, which, in a manner so solemn, he had confirmed in the preceding verse. Instead of glorying over their calamities and rejection, he forgot his own wrongs, and their cruel persecutions, in the inexpressible affliction with . which he contemplated their obstinate unbelief with all its fatal consequences. In this we may discern a characteristic of a Christian. He who has no sorrow for the perishing state of sinners, and especially of his kindred, is not a Christian. No man can be a Christian who is unconcerned for the salvation of others.

Ver. 4.—*Who are Israelites; to whom pertaineth the adoption, and the glory, and the covenants, and the giving of the law, and the service of God, and the promises.*

Paul here recognises and enumerates the great external privileges belonging to the Jews, which aggravated his profound sorrow, on account of their rejection of the Messiah, and their consequent deplorable condition. *Who are Israelites.*—That is, the most honourable people on earth; the descendants of him who, as a prince, had power with God. They had the name, because that of Israel was given to Jacob their father by God, when vouchsafing so striking a pre-intimation of His future manifestation in the flesh. *Adoption.*—That is, the nation of Israel was a nation adopted by God as a type of the adoption of His children in Christ Jesus; and in that typical sense, in which they were the children of God as no other nation ever was, they are frequently spoken of in Scripture, Ex. iv. 22; Jer. xxxi. 9–20. In this way our Lord Himself recognises them, when anticipating their rejection, He says, ' The children of the kingdom shall be cast out,' Matt. viii. 12. *Glory.*—This most probably refers to the manifestation of the glory of God over the mercy-seat in the sanctuary. God, too, set His tabernacle among the Israelites, and walked among them, which was . their peculiar glory, by which they were distinguished from all other nations, Deut. iv. 32–36. The glory of the Lord appeared in the cloud that went before them in the wilderness. It often filled the tabernacle and the temple. His house was the place of His glory. *Covenants.*—The covenant with Abraham, and the covenant at Sinai, in both of which they were interested, and all the solemn engagements which God had entered into with mankind, were lodged in their hands and committed to their custody. *Giving of the law.*—To them the law was given at Mount Sinai; and they were the only people on earth so distinguished by God. *The service of God.* —This refers to the tabernacle and temple service, or Mosaic institutions of worship. All other nations were left to their own superstitious inventions; the Jews alone had ordinances of worship from God. *Promises.*—The Jews had received the promises, both temporal and spiritual, especially those that related to the Messiah, Acts ii. 39.

Ver. 5.—*Whose are the fathers, and of whom, as concerning the flesh, Christ came, who is over all, God blessed for ever. Amen.*

Whose are the fathers.—The Jews numbered among their illustrious progenitors, Abraham, Isaac, and Jacob, with others to whom God had been pleased to manifest Himself in a manner so remarkable. *Of whom, as concerning the flesh, Christ came.*—This was the completion of all the privileges which the Apostle here enumerates. It was a signal honour to the Jewish nation, that the Messiah was by descent an Israelite. *Concerning the flesh.*—This declares that He was really a man having truly the human nature, and as a man of Jewish origin. At the same time it imports that He had another nature. *Who is over all, God blessed for ever.*—This is a most clear and unequivocal attestation of the Divine nature of our Lord Jesus Christ. Every engine of false criticism has been employed by those who are desirous to evade the obvious meaning of this decisive testimony to the Godhead of our Lord Jesus Christ; but they have never even plausibly succeeded.

The awful blindness and obstinacy of Arians and Socinians in their explanations, or rather perversions, of the word of God, are in nothing more obvious than in their attempts to evade the meaning of this celebrated testimony to the Godhead of our Lord Jesus Christ. They often shelter themselves under various readings ; but here they have no tenable ground for an evasion of this kind. Yet, strange to say, some of them have, without the authority of manuscripts, altered the original, in order that it may suit their purpose. There is no difficulty in the words —no intricacy in the construction ; yet, by a forced construction and an unnatural punctuation, they have endeavoured to turn away this testimony from its obvious import. Contrary to the genius and idiom of the Greek—contrary to all the usual rules of interpreting language, as has often been incontrovertibly shown—they substitute ' God be blessed,' for ' God be blessed for ever;' or, ' God, who is over all, be blessed,' instead of, ' who is over all, God blessed for ever.' Such tortuous explanations are not only rejected by a sound interpretation of the original, but manifest themselves to be unnatural, even to the most illiterate who exercise an unprejudiced judgment. The Scriptures have many real difficulties, which are calculated to try or to increase the faith and patience of the Christian, and are evidently designed to enlarge his acquaintance with the word of God, by obliging him more diligently to search into them, and place his dependence on the Spirit of all truth. But when language so clear as in the present passage is perverted, to avoid recognising the obvious truth contained in the Divine testimony, it more fully manifests the depravity of human nature, and the rooted enmity of the carnal mind against God, than the grossest works of the flesh.

After speaking of the Messiah's coming through the nation of Israel, in respect to His human nature, the Apostle, in order to enhance the greatness of this extraordinary distinction conferred upon it, here refers to His Divine nature, to union with which, in one person, His human nature was exalted. The declaration of His coming in the flesh clearly imports, as has been remarked, that Christ had another nature. When it is said, 1 John iv. 3, that Jesus Christ is come in the flesh—which could not be said of a mere man, who could come in no other way—it shows that He might have come in another way, and therefore implies His pre-existence, which is asserted in a variety of passages of Scripture. Of such passages there are four orders. The first order consists of those where His incarnation is ascribed to Himself. ' Behold, I will send My messenger, and he shall prepare the way before Me; and the Lord whom ye seek shall suddenly come to His temple,' Mal. iii. 1. These words manifestly prove that His incarnation, and the preparation for it, such as the mission of John the Baptist, was a work of the Messiah Himself, and consequently that He existed before His incarnation. The same truth is declared, when it is said, 'Forasmuch, then, as the children are partakers of flesh and blood, He also Himself took part of the same; for verily He took not on Him the nature of angels; but He took on Him the seed of Abraham,' Heb. ii. 14, 16. Here His taking upon Him flesh and blood is represented to be by an act of His own will. The same truth is taught where He is introduced as addressing the Father in these terms. 'Sacrifice and offering Thou wouldst not, but a body hast Thou prepared me: in burnt-offerings and sacrifices for sin Thou hast had no pleasure: then said I, Lo, I come (in the volume of the book it is written of me) to do Thy will, O God,' Heb. x. 5, 7; and again, 'Jesus Christ, being in the form of God, thought it not robbery to be equal with God; but made Himself of no reputation, and took upon Him the form of a servant,' Phil. ii. 6. Here we are taught that Jesus Christ Himself took this form, and consequently existed before He took it.

The second order of passages, asserting the pre-existence of our Lord, are those which expressly declare that Jesus Christ was in heaven before He came into the world. 'No man hath ascended up to heaven, but He that came down from heaven, even the Son of Man, which is in heaven.' And a little after, 'He that cometh from above is above all: he that is of the earth is earthly, and speaketh of the earth: He that cometh from heaven is above all,' John iii. 13-31. 'The bread of God is He which cometh down from heaven,' John vi. 33, 41, 50, 51, 58. 'For I came down from heaven, not to do Mine own will, but the will of Him that sent Me,' John vi. 38. 'What and if ye shall see the Son of Man ascend up where He was before?' John vi. 62. 'And now, O Father, glorify Thou me with Thine own self with the glory which I had with Thee before the world was,' John xvii. 5.

A third order of passages ascribes actions to Jesus Christ before His birth. 'By whom,' says the Apostle, God 'made the worlds,' Heb. i. 2, which signifies the creation of the universe; and verse 3, 'upholding all things by the word of His power,' which signifies His providence; and verse 10, 'And Thou, Lord, in the beginning hast laid the foundation of the earth; and the heavens are the works of Thine hands.' This is part of the response of the Father in the 25th verse of the 102d Psalm to His Son, complaining that He had weakened His strength in the way, and praying not to be taken away in the midst of His days; to which the Father immediately answers, 'Thy years are throughout all generations,' and continues His reply to the end of the Psalm. 'One Lord Jesus Christ, by whom are all things,' 1 Cor. viii. 6, which implies both creation and preservation. 'Who is the image of the invisible God, the firstborn of every creature; for by Him were all things created that are in heaven, and that are in earth, visible and invisible, whether they be thrones, or dominions, or principalities, or powers; all things were created by Him, and for Him; and He is before all things, and by Him all things consist,'

Col. i. 15, 16. Here Jesus Christ is declared to be the Creator of all things. This is also affirmed concerning Him before His incarnation, John i. 3. 'Being put to death in the flesh, but quickened by the Spirit; by which also He went and preached unto the spirits in prison,' 1 Pet. iii. 19. The Son of God preached by His Spirit to the inhabitants of the earth before the flood, who are now in the prison of hell, which supposes His existence before He was born.

A fourth order of passages clearly proves the pre-existence of our Lord Jesus Christ. 'This is He of whom I said, After me cometh a man, which is preferred before me; for He was before me,' John i. 15, 30. He could not be before John unless He had existed prior to his birth, since John was born before Him. 'Verily, verily, I say unto you, Before Abraham was, I am,' John viii. 58. 'But thou, Bethlehem–Ephratah, though thou be little among the thousands 'of Judah, yet out of thee shall He come forth unto me that is to be Ruler in Israel; whose goings forth have been from of old, from everlasting,' Mic. v. 2. 'I am Alpha and Omega, the beginning and the ending, saith the Lord, which is, and which was, and which is to come, the Almighty.' 'I am Alpha and Omega, the first and the last.' 'I am Alpha and Omega, the beginning and the end, the first and the last,' Rev. i. 8–11, xxii. 13.

To all these passages must be added that of Prov. viii. (compared with 1 Cor. i. 24), where Wisdom is declared to have existed when God formed the universe; and also John i. 1, 'In the beginning was the Word, and the Word was with God, and the Word was God.' Than this last passage nothing could more explicitly declare the pre-existence and Godhead of our Lord Jesus Christ.

There are few of the predictions concerning the Messiah in which His two natures are not marked. In the first of them, 'the seed of the woman' denotes His humanity; while the words, 'He shall bruise thy head,' declare His divinity. In the promise to Abraham, His humanity is marked by the words, 'in thy seed;' while in what follows, 'shall all the nations of the earth be blessed,' we read His divinity. 'I know that my Redeemer liveth, and that He shall stand at the latter day upon the earth'—this is His divinity. 'Whom I shall see for myself, and mine eyes shall behold'—this is His humanity. 'Behold, a virgin shall conceive, and bear a son'—this is His humanity; 'and shall call His name Immanuel'—this is His divinity. 'Unto us a child is born, unto us a son is given'—this marks His humanity. 'The government shall be upon His shoulder; and His name shall be called Wonderful, Counsellor, The Mighty God, the Everlasting Father'—these words denote His Godhead. There are multitudes of other passages in the Prophets to the same purpose.

In the same way the two natures of Jesus Christ are spoken of in numerous passages in the New Testament. 'The Word was God,' and 'The Word was made flesh, and dwelt among us.' 'Made of the seed of David according to the flesh, and declared to be the Son of God with power, according to the Spirit of holiness.' 'God was manifest in the flesh.' The same distinction appeared in His actions, and almost all His miracles. Finally, this truth discovers itself in all the most remarkable parts of His economy. In His birth He is laid in a manger as a man, but it is announced by the hallelujahs of angels, and the 'wise men,' led by a star, come to adore Him as God. At the commencement of His public ministry He is baptized in water, but the heavens open to Him, and the Father proclaims from heaven, 'This is My beloved Son, in whom I am well pleased.' In His temptation in the desert He suffers hunger and thirst, but angels come and minister to their Lord. In the garden of Gethsemane He seems as if he were ready to sink under the agonies He endures; but more than twelve legions of the angelic host stand ready to fulfil His mandates, and prostrate His enemies in the dust. In His death He hangs like a malefactor upon the cross, but as Jehovah He bestows paradise upon the dying robber.

In completing the enumeration of the signal honours conferred on the nation of Israel, after having declared that of them the Messiah, as concerning the flesh, came, the reason is obvious why the Apostle immediately referred to our Lord's Divine nature. Had he spoken only of Christ's coming in the flesh, it would not have enhanced as he intended the high and unparalleled privileges by which his countrymen had been distinguished. It was necessary, both for this end, and in order fully to portray the character of Him of whom he spoke, to subjoin, 'who is over all, God blessed for ever.' This addition, then, is not superfluous, or that might have been omitted. It is indispensable, being essential to the Apostle's argument.

To this great truth respecting the coming of God manifest in the flesh, as the foundation on which the whole work of redemption rests, the Apostle subjoins, Amen. In the same way he adds Amen to the expression, 'who is blessed for ever,' Rom. i. 25, applying it to the Creator. Amen signifies truth, stability, or is an affirmation, or expresses consent. In the New Testament Jesus Christ alone makes use of this term at the beginning of sentences, as a word of affirmation. In this sense it appears to be employed at the end of each of the four Gospels. In the Gospel of John only have we any record of the Lord using this word more than once in the same sentence, Amen, amen, or Verily, verily. The Lord employs it again and again in His Sermon on the Mount, the purpose of which, it would seem, was to impress on the minds of His hearers both the truth of what He said, and its importance. Luke, who records this term less frequently than the other evangelists, sometimes substitutes in place of it a simple affirmation, Luke ix. 27; Matt. xvi. 28. Jesus, in addressing the seven churches of Asia, after dividing His glorious attributes and names amongst them, finally denominates Himself 'the Amen,' Rev. iii. 14; and God is called the God Amen, Isa. lxv. 16. The Apostle John, in his ascription of praise to the Redeemer, adds Amen, as he does in the contemplation of His second coming in glory to judge the world, Rev. i. 6, 7; and also in closing the canon of Scripture, when he repeats the declaration of Jesus, that He will come quickly, and after his prayer that the grace of our Lord Jesus Christ may be with all the churches to which he writes, Rev. xxii. 20, 21. The Lord Himself makes use of this term when He declares that He liveth, and was dead, and is alive for evermore, Rev. i. 18.

Ver. 6.—*Not as though the word of God hath taken none effect. For they are not all Israel which are of Israel.*

Not as though.—That is, my grief for the state of the Jewish nation, and their rejection by God, does not imply that with regard to them anything said in the word of God has failed. *For they are not all Israel which are of Israel.*—Here is the explanation of the mystery that the Jews, as a nation, had rejected the Messiah: they are not all true Israelites in the spiritual sense of the promise, who are Israelites after the flesh. The Jews might object, and say that if they were cast off and rejected, then God is unfaithful, and His promises are ineffectual. To this Paul answers by making a distinction among Israelites. Some are Israelites only in respect of their carnal descent, and others are children of the promise. 'The proposition of the Apostle,' says Calvin, 'is that the promise was given in such a manner to Abraham and his seed, that the inheritance has no particular regard to every one of his descendants; and it hence follows, as a consequence, that the revolt of certain individuals from the Lord, who derive their birth from the father of the faithful, has no effect in preventing the stability, permanence, and stedfastness of the Divine covenant. The common election of the Israelitish nation does not prevent the Sovereign of infinite holiness from choosing for Himself, according to His secret counsel, whatever portion of that people He has determined to save. When Paul says they are not all Israel which are of Israel, and afterwards, neither, because they are the seed of Abraham, are they all children, he includes all the descendants of the father of believers under one member of the sentence, and points out by the other those only who are true and genuine sons of the friend of God, and not a degenerate race.' Through the remaining part of this chapter, the Apostle shows that the rejection of the Messiah by the great body of the Jewish nation was neither contrary to the promises nor the purpose of God, but had been predetermined and also typified in His dealings towards individuals among their progenitors, as recorded in the Scriptures, and also there predicted. This furnishes an opportunity of more fully illustrating the doctrine of God's sovereignty in choosing some to everlasting life, which had been spoken of in the 29th and 30th verses of the preceding chapter, and of His rejection of others.

Ver. 7.—*Neither, because they are the seed of Abraham, are they all children: but, In Isaac shall thy seed be called.*

Neither, because they are the seed of Abraham, are they all children.—In the preceding verse the Apostle had shown that there was a difference among Israelites; now he refers to a difference in the seed of Abraham. The error of the Jews was, that they thought they were the children of God by being the children of Abraham. But in this, as the Apostle declares, they were in error. The promise to Abraham and his seed was not made to him and all his descendants in general, but to him and a particular seed. As the children of Abraham, they were all, indeed, in one sense the children of God. God says to Pharaoh with respect to them, ' Let my son go.' But the natural sonship was only a figure of the spiritual sonship of all believers of every nation. None but such are the spiritual seed of Abraham, whether among Jews or Gentiles.

But in Isaac shall thy seed be called.—Reckoned, chosen, or called into
existence, as it is said respecting the birth of Isaac in the fourth chapter,
'God, who quickeneth the dead, and calleth those things which be not
as though they were.' The Messiah, who was emphatically the seed of
Abraham, says, 'The Lord hath called Me from the womb, Isa. xlix. 1.
He was called into existence in His human nature, and to His office of
Mediator, in the line of Isaac. And Israel was called or chosen as God's
people, Isa. xlviii. 12. 'Hearken unto Me, O Jacob, and Israel, My
called.' In this sense the expression called is used in the end of the
11th verse. By thus appealing to the declaration of God to Abraham,
that in Isaac his seed should be called—and reckoned more especially
the seed of Abraham—the Apostle showed that, notwithstanding the
defection of the great body of the nation of Israel which he so much
deplored, it was by no means the case that the word of God had taken
none effect; for from the beginning a distinction had been made among
the descendants of Abraham, indicating that they are not all Israel which
are of Israel. Only a part of that nation, which he calls a remnant,
verse 27, and afterwards ' a remnant according to the election of grace,'
ch. xi. 5, was to participate in the spiritual blessings to be conveyed by
promise. 'When,' says Calvin, 'we see in the two first sons of the
patriarch, the younger chosen by a recent promise (Gen. xxi. 12 ; Heb.
xi. 18), while the older was yet living, how much more might this take
place in a long line of descendants! This prediction is taken from Gen.
xvii. 20, where the Lord answers Abraham, *As for Ishmael, I have heard
thy prayers*, but the blessing shall be granted to the son of Sarah, and the
covenant established with Isaac. It hence follows as a consequence that
certain individuals are, by a singular privilege, chosen from the elect people
of the Jews, in whom the common adoption is ratified and rendered
efficacious.' It may be further remarked that when it is said, ' In Isaac
shall thy seed be called,' it did not imply that all the descendants of
Isaac were to be the spiritual seed of Abraham. Only such were to be
so who belonged to that seed to which the word, being used in the
singular, emphatically and exclusively applied, as the Apostle declares,
Gal. iii. 16, 'Now to Abraham and his seed were the promises made.
He saith not, And to seeds, as of many, but as of one, And to thy seed,
which is Christ.' The meaning, then, of the declaration, ' In Isaac shall
thy seed be called,' is, that as all Abraham's posterity were not to be the
peculiar people whom God was nationally to adopt as His children, but
only such as should descend from Isaac, so not all the Jews are the true
sons of God, but only such as, like Isaac, are children of the promise.
Here it is evident, as also from Gal. iv. 28, that Isaac the child of promise
was typical of all believers.

Ver. 8.—*That is, They which are the children of the flesh, these are not the children
of God ; but the children of the promise are counted for the seed.*

That is, or this explains, the declaration, ' In Isaac shall thy seed be
called.' It is intended to show that not carnal descent, but being included in the promise, constituted the true spiritual seed. This clearly
establishes the difference between the sonship of Israel after the flesh,

and the sonship of Israel after the Spirit. The nation of Israel stood in a relation to God in which no other nation was ever placed; but only a part of them enjoyed a spiritual relation. Hence the distinction here noted, that the children of the flesh are not the children of God, but the children of the promise are counted for the seed—a distinction which the Apostle also makes, ch. ii. 28, between being a Jew outwardly, and a Jew inwardly. These distinctions are explanatory of the declaration, ' In Isaac shall thy seed be called,' and of the rejection of the other children, though the seed of Abraham. In the Epistle to the Galatians, iv. 22, it is said that ' Abraham had two sons, the one by a bond maid, the other by a free woman.' This appears in the original history to be a merely accidental and unimportant matter; but in that place we are taught that it was a shadow of futurity. Ishmael, who was of the bond woman, it is said, was ' born after the flesh.' This denoted that though he was descended from Abraham according to the laws of nature, he was not a son of Abraham's faith. Isaac was also in a certain sense born like Ishmael after the flesh, because he was naturally descended from Abraham; but not of the flesh merely, nor of the flesh naturally,—for according to the course of nature he never would have been born,—but at the same time he was more. He was not only a son of Abraham's flesh, but his son as born after the Spirit, because he was given to Abraham, after, by the course of nature, he could not hope for children. All this indicated the distinction that existed in the nation of Israel, between those who, notwithstanding their being born in the line of Isaac, were the seed of Abraham merely by carnal descent, and not the children of God by a spiritual regeneration. Only these last were the children of the promise, as Isaac was, who were all one in Christ Jesus, and therefore in the highest sense Abraham's seed, and ' heirs according to the promise,' Gal. iii. 29—heirs of all the spiritual blessings secured to Abraham by promise. ' Paul,' says Calvin, ' now deduces from the prophecy a proposition containing his whole meaning, intent, and aim. For if the seed is called in Isaac, not in Ishmael, and this latter is no less a son of the patriarch Abraham than the former, all his children by lineal descent cannot be reckoned as his seed; but the promise is in an especial and peculiar manner fulfilled by some, but has not a common and equal regard to all. Children by lineal descent mean such as are not distinguished by a more excellent privilege than their being offspring by blood; *children of the promise* are those who are peculiarly marked out and sealed by their Heavenly Father.'

Ver. 9.—*For this is the word of promise, At this time will I come, and Sarah shall have a son.*

The birth of Isaac was by promise, and without a miracle it would never have taken place. But the birth of Ishmael was not by promise, but in the ordinary course of nature. Thus the children of God specially promised to Abraham were those who, according to the election of God (who had chosen Isaac in preference to Ishmael), were to come into a spiritual relation with Christ, who is emphatically the promised seed in the line of Isaac, Gal. iii. 16. To them the spiritual blessings were restricted, while only the temporal advantages of the national covenant belonged to the whole of Israel. This was intimated in God's dealings with Abraham.

Ver. 10.—*And not only this ; but when Rebecca also had conceived by one, even by our father Isaac ;*

Not only in the case of Isaac was the election limited to him as the son of promise, but also in a still more remarkable instance was this truth indicated in the case of the two sons of Isaac. They were conceived by Rebecca of the same husband, yet God chose the one and rejected the other. An original difference between Isaac and Ishmael might be alleged, since the one was born of the lawful wife of Abraham, the free woman, and the other was the son of the bond woman ; but in the case now brought forward there existed no original difference. Both were sons of the same father and mother, and both were born at the same time. The great distinction, then, made between the two brothers could only be traced to the sovereign will of God, who thus visibly notified, long before the event, the difference of the Divine purpose, according to election, towards the people of Israel.

Ver. 11.—*(For the children being not yet born, neither having done any good or evil, that the purpose of God according to election might stand, not of works, but of Him that calleth ;)*

In the case of Isaac and Ishmael, it might still be said, that as the latter, as soon as he came to years, gave evidence of a wicked disposition, this was a sufficient reason for preferring Isaac. But here, in a parenthesis, the Apostle shows that the preference was given to Jacob independently of all ground of merit, because it was made before the children were capable of doing either good or evil. This was done for the very purpose of taking away all pretence for merit as a ground of preference. Had the preference been given to Jacob when he had grown up to maturity, there would have been no more real ground for ascribing it to anything good in him ; yet that use would have been made of it by the perverse ingenuity of man. But God made the preference before the children were born.

That the purpose of God according to election might stand.—This was the very end and intention of the early indication of the will of God to Rebecca, the mother of the two children. It was hereby clearly established that, in choosing Jacob and rejecting Esau, God had respect to nothing but His own purpose. Than this what can more strongly declare His own eternal purpose to be the ground of all His favour to man ?

Not of works, but of Him that calleth.—Expressions indicating God's sovereignty in this matter are heaped upon one another, because it is a thing so offensive to the human mind. Yet, after all the Apostle's precaution, the perverseness of men still finds ground of boasting on account of works. Though the children had done neither good nor evil, yet God, it is supposed, might foresee that Jacob would be a godly man, and Esau wicked. But had not God made a difference between Jacob and Esau, Jacob would have been no better than his brother. Were not men blinded by opposition to this part of the will of God, would they not perceive that a preference on account of foreseen good works is *a preference on account of works*, and therefore expressly contrary to the assertion of the Apostle—*Not of works, but of Him that calleth?* The whole ground of preference is in Him that calleth, or chooseth, not in him that is called.

' Paul,' says Calvin, ' had hitherto merely observed, in a few words, the difference between the carnal sons of Abraham ; namely, though all by circumcision were made partakers of the covenant, yet the grace of God was not equally efficacious in all, and the sons of the promise enjoy the blessings of the Most High.   He now plainly refers the whole cause to the gratuitous election of God, which in no respects depends on men, so that nothing can be traced in the salvation of believers higher than the goodness of God ; nothing in the destruction of the reprobate can be discovered higher than the just severity of the Sovereign of the world.   The first proposition of the Apostle is the following :—As the blessing of the covenant separates the nation of the Israelites from all other people, so the election of God separates the men of that nation, while He predestinates some to salvation, others to eternal damnation. The second proposition is, that there is no other foundation of election than the mere goodness and mercy of God, which embrace whom He chooses, without paying the least regard to works, even after the fall of Adam.   Third, the Lord in His gratuitous election is free and un-restrained by the necessity of bestowing the same grace equally on all ; He passes by such as He wills, and chooses for His own according to His will.   Paul briefly comprehends all these propositions in one clause, and will afterwards consider other points.   The following words, *when they were not yet born, neither had done any good or evil,* show that God, in making the difference between them, could have paid no regard to their works, which did not yet exist.   Sophists, who state that God may elect from among mankind by a respect to their works, since He foresees from their future conduct who may be worthy or deserving of grace, attack a principle of theology which no Christian ought to be ignorant of ; namely, that God can regard nothing in the corrupt nature of man, such as that of Jacob and Esau was, by which He may be induced to do them kindness.   When, therefore, Paul says that neither of the children had done any good or evil, we must add also the opinion which he had already formed in his mind, of their both being children of Adam, sinners by nature, not possessed of a single particle of righteousness.   Besides, although the vicious and depraved nature, which is diffused through the whole human race, be of itself sufficient to cause damnation before it has shown its unholiness by any act or deed, and Esau therefore deserved to be rejected, because he was by nature a child of wrath, yet to prevent the least difficulty, as if the state of the elder was worse with respect to the perpetration of any offence or vice than that of the younger, it was necessary for the Apostle to exclude the consideration both of transgres-sions and of virtues.   I confess, indeed, that it is true that the near cause of reprobation is our being all cursed in Adam ; but Paul with-draws us in the meantime from this consideration, that we may learn to rest in the naked and simple good pleasure of God, until he shall have established this doctrine, that the infinite Sovereign las a sufficiently just cause for election and reprobation, in His own will.   He here urges, in almost every word, the gratuitous election of God ; for had he considered works to have any place in our election, he would have stated the re-muneration due to their performance. But he opposes to works the purpose of God, which consists in the good pleasure of His will. And to remove all doubts and controversy concerning the subject, he adds, *according to election*, and closes in a striking manner,—*not of works, but of Him that calleth.* The opinion, therefore, that God elects or reprobates every one according as He foresees good or evil in us, is false, and contrary to the word of eternal truth.'

Ver. 12.—*It was said unto her, The elder shall serve the younger.*

This was a figure of the spiritual election, for in no other point of view is it here to the Apostle's purpose. Not only did God choose one of these sons, who were equal as to their parentage, but chose that one who was inferior in priority of birth, the only point in which there was a difference. He chose the younger son, contrary to the usual custom of mankind, and contrary to the law of primogeniture established by God Himself respecting inheritances in the family of Jacob. The dominion of the younger, then, over the elder, flowed, as is shown in the next verse, from God's love to the one and hatred to the other ; thus proving the election of the one and the reprobation of the other. This strikingly exemplified the manner of God's dealings towards the nation of Israel, in discriminating between those who were the children of the flesh, and the others who were the children of God. How much instruction do these words, ' The elder shall serve the younger,' contain, as standing in the connection in which they are here placed, as well as in that part of Scrip-ture from which they are quoted! They practically teach the great fundamental doctrines of the PRESCIENCE, the PROVIDENCE, the SOVEREIGNTY of God ; His PREDESTINATION, ELECTION, and REPROBATION.

Ver. 13.—*As it is written, Jacob have I loved, but Esau have I hated.*

As it is written.—Here and elsewhere it is remarkable that the writers of the New Testament, and our Lord Himself, generally, or at least very often, simply say, *It is written.* This is on the principle that the word Scripture signifies the word of God. Scripture literally signifies writ-ing, and may refer to any writing ; but in the appropriated sense, it signi-fies the written word of God. *It is written,* then, signifies, it is written in the word of God. When the Apostles refer in this manner to the Scriptures, they do it as adducing authority which is conclusive and not to be questioned.

The words here quoted from Malachi expressly relate to Jacob and Esau. The Prophet likewise declares the dealing of God towards their posterity, but the part here referred to applies to the progenitors them-selves. God is there reproving the people of Israel for their ingratitude, and manifesting His great goodness to them in loving their father Jacob, while He hated his brother Esau, and gave him a mountainous, barren country, as a sign of His hatred.[1] Thus God preferred Jacob before Esau

---

[1] The distinguishing goodness and mercy of God to Israel is in a similar way illus-trated in the 136th Psalm, by contrasting them with the severity of His dispensations as exercised towards others.

without respect to the goodness or wickedness of either, attaching good things to the one, and evil to the other, before they were born. And this quotation by the Apostle is intended to prove that the purpose of God, in choosing who shall be His children according to election, might stand, not by works, but of Him that calleth, verse 11, which shows that all along the reference is to spiritual and eternal blessings, shadowed forth, as is usual in the Prophets, by things that are temporal and carnal. In the same place God likewise declares His dealings towards the posterity of Esau ; but the words here quoted expressly refer to Jacob and Esau personally. The Apostle is speaking of heads of nations ; and in God's dealings towards them is found the reason of the difference of the treatment of their posterities. The introduction of Jacob and Esau personally, presents an emblem of this, while the design is to show that some among the Israelites were the children of God, and not others. That the Apostle quotes these words in reference to Jacob and Esau personally, is clear, since he speaks of them before they were born, and declares their conception by one mother, of one father, which could not be said of their posterity.

Jacob have I loved, but Esau have I hated.—Jacob was loved before he was born, consequently before he was capable of doing good ; and Esau was hated before he was born, consequently before he was capable of doing evil. It may be asked why God hated him before he sinned personally; and human wisdom has proved its folly, by endeavouring to soften the word hated into something less than hatred: but the man who submits like a little child to the word of God, will find no difficulty in seeing in what sense Esau was worthy of the hatred of God before he was born. He sinned in Adam, and was therefore properly an object of God's hatred as well as fallen Adam. There is no other view that will ever account for this language and this treatment of Esau. By nature, too, he was a wicked creature, conceived in sin, although his faculties were not expanded, or his innate depravity developed, which God, who hath mercy on whom He will have mercy, and hardeneth whom He will, and who giveth no account of His matters, did not see good to counteract by His grace, as in the case of Jacob, who originally was equally wicked, and by nature, like Esau, a child of wrath and a fit object of hatred.

It is not unusual to take part with Esau who was rejected, against Jacob who was the object of Divine favour. Everything that can be made to appear either amiable or virtuous in the character of Esau is eagerly grasped at, and exhibited in the most advantageous light. We are told of his disinterestedness, frankness, and generosity ; while we are reminded that Jacob was a cool, selfish, designing man, who was always watching to take advantage of his brother's simplicity, and who ungenerously and unjustly robbed his elder brother of the blessing and the birthright.

This way of reasoning shows more zeal for the interest of a cause than discretion in its support. Instead of invalidating, it only serves to confirm the truth it opposes. While it is evident that Jacob possessed the fear of God, which was not the case with respect to Esau,—and therefore that the one was born of God, and the other remained a child of nature,—

yet there is so much palpable imperfection and evil in Jacob, as to manifest that God did not choose him for the excellence of his foreseen works. In maintaining, then, the doctrine of the sovereignty of God, it is by no means necessary to vindicate the conduct of Jacob towards his brother. Both he and his mother were undoubtedly to blame, much to blame, as to the way in which he obtained his father's blessing, to the prejudice of Esau, while the revealed purpose of God formed no apology for their conduct. That sin is an evil thing and a bitter, Jacob fully experienced. His conduct in that transaction led him into a maze of troubles, from which through life he was never disentangled. While Jacob was a man of God, and Esau a man of the world, there is enough to show that the inheritance was bestowed on the former not of works but of grace.

Nothing can more clearly manifest the strong opposition of the human mind to the doctrine of the Divine sovereignty, than the violence which human ingenuity has employed to wrest the expression, *Jacob have I loved, but Esau have I hated.* By many this has been explained, ' Esau have I loved less.' But Esau was not the object of any degree of the Divine love, and the word *hate* never signifies *to love less.* The occurrence of the word in that expression, ' hate father and mother,' Luke xiv. 26, has been alleged in vindication of this explanation; but the word in this last phrase is used figuratively, and in a manner that cannot be mistaken. Although hatred is not meant to be asserted, yet hatred is the thing that is literally expressed. By a strong figure of speech, *that* is called hatred which resembles it in its effects. We will not obey those whom we hate, if we can avoid it. Just so, if our parents command us to disobey Jesus Christ, we must not obey them; and this is called hatred, figuratively, from the resemblance of its effects. But in this passage, in which the expression, ' Esau have I hated,' occurs, everything is literal. The Apostle is reasoning from premises to a conclusion. Besides, the contrast of loving Jacob with hating Esau, shows that the last phrase is literal and proper hatred. If God's love to Jacob was real literal love, God's hatred to Esau must be real literal hatred. It might as well be said that the phrase, ' Jacob have I loved,' does not signify that God really loved Jacob, but that to love here signifies only to hate less, and that all that is meant by the expression, is that God hated Jacob less than he hated Esau. If every man's own mind is a sufficient security against concluding the meaning to be, ' Jacob have I hated less,' his judgment ought to be a security against the equally unwarrantable meaning, 'Esau have I loved less.'

But why, it may be asked of those who object to the plain meaning of the words, *Jacob have I loved, but Esau have I hated,* and insist that their import is that God loved Esau less than Jacob—why should God love Esau *less* than Jacob, and that, too, before the children were born, or had done good or evil? Can they explain this? Would it not involve a difficulty which, even on their own principles, they are unable to remove? Why then refuse to admit the natural and obvious signification of the passage? If God says that He hated Esau, are we to avoid receiving God's testimony, or justified in employing a mode of torture in expounding His words? If, again, Esau, as some insist, were the better character, why was Jacob preferred to him?

Others translate the word in the original by the term *slighted*. But if God had no just ground to hate Esau, He could have as little ground for slighting him. Why should Esau be unjustly slighted before he was born, more than unjustly hated? However, those who entertain a proper sense of man's guilt by nature, will be at no loss to discern the ground of God's hatred of Esau. Both Jacob and Esau were, like David, shapen in iniquity and conceived in sin, and were in themselves sinners. Esau was justly the object of hatred before he was born, because he was viewed in Adam as a sinner. Jacob was justly the object of God's love before he was born, because he was viewed in Christ as righteous. That the terms love and hatred are here to be understood in their full and proper import, is evident from the question put in the 14th verse, and answered in the 15th, 16th, and 17th verses, with the conclusion drawn in the 18th. ' Therefore hath He mercy on whom He will have mercy, and whom He will He hardeneth.' Compassion is a sign of love, and hardening a proof of hatred. And, besides this, the expression, 'Esau have I hatred,' is not stronger than what the Apostle applies to all men when he says that by nature they are the *children of wrath, dead in trespasses and sins,* and consequently objects of the hatred of the holy and just God. All of them are so in their natural state, as considered in themselves, and all of them continue to be so, unless delivered from that state by the distinguishing grace of God. To be hated on account of Adam's sin and of their own corrupt nature, is common to all men with Esau who are not of the elect of God; and in Esau's case this is exhibited in one instance. Nothing, then, is said of Esau here that might not be said of every man who shall finally perish.

There are few commentators, however, who have not wavered more or less in their explanation of this passage. Mr. Hodge, Professor of Biblical Literature in the Theological Seminary at Princeton, America, gives here the following most erroneous interpretation: ' It is evident that in this case the word *hate* means *to love less, to regard and treat with less favour.*' This false gloss completely destroys the import of the passage, on which no one who understands the doctrine of the fall, and consequent condemnation of all men in Adam, ought to feel the smallest difficulty. In its obvious and literal meaning, what is said of Jacob and Esau must be true of all the individuals of the human race before they are born. Each one of them must either be loved or hated of God.

The opinion held by some, that it may be questioned whether God be ever said to hate any man, is contrary to the revealed character of God. This sentiment appears to be near akin to that of the heathen philosophers, who held it as a maxim that God could not be angry with any one. Like many other unfounded dogmas, it stands in direct opposition to the whole tenor of the Scriptures, which represent God as angry with the wicked every day, and *hating* all workers of iniquity, Ps. v. 5. Does not the passage above quoted, which declares that men are *by nature children of wrath,* express this hatred of sin in the strongest manner; and especially of Adam's sin, on account of which all men are children of wrath by nature? And does not this wrath *abide* on all them that believe not on the Son? John iii. 36. ' The Lord will take vengeance on His adversaries, and He reserveth wrath for His enemies,' Nah. i. 2.

In innumerable passages of Scripture, God ascribes to Himself hatred. Men, however, are averse to this. What, then, can be done? The Scriptures must be explained in a forced manner; and while they say that God hates sinners, they are made to say that He does not hate them. Nothing can be more unjustifiable than this method of tampering with and perverting the word of God, and nothing can be more uncalled for. Hatred in itself is not sinful. That which is sinful ought to be hated; and though there is a mixture of evil in man's hatred of evil, yet there is the same mixture of evil in his love of good. In God's hatred of sinners, as in all His attributes, there is nothing of sinful feeling. We are not able to comprehend this attribute of the Divine mind; but every other attribute has also its difficulties. We must in this, and in all things, submit to God's word, and believe it as it speaks, and not as we would have it to speak.

Respecting God's hatred of sin, and the punishment of transgressors, the late Dr. Thomson refers in his sermons to the following passages:— ' Cursed is every one that continueth not in all things that are written in the book of the law to do them. The wrath of God has been revealed from heaven against *all* unrighteousness and ungodliness of men. Indignation and wrath, tribulation and anguish, will be rendered to every soul of man that doeth evil, of the Jew first, and also of the Gentile. God is love; but it is also said, that God hates all workers of iniquity;—that the Lord revengeth, and is furious;—that His wrath cometh on the children of disobedience. The assertion that God is angry with the wicked every day, is just as level to our apprehension, as the assertion that God loves them that fear Him. We know that His anger is expressed in rebuking, chastening, punishing those who have provoked it, as we know that pity helps, relieves, comforts those who stand in need of its interposition. God is as certainly holy to hate sin, and just to inflict merited punishment on the sinner, as He is good and merciful, and compassionate to the guilty and the miserable for whom He interposed.'

' I cannot help reverting to what I formerly observed respecting the necessity of attributing love to God no further than His own word has warranted, and no further than is consistent with that revelation of His character which He Himself has given us. A greater snare cannot be laid for your piety and your judgment, than that which consists in making love His paramount or His only perfection. For whenever there is a consciousness of guilt, and a dread of responsibility, it must be comfortable to have a God who is divested of all that is frowning and indignant towards transgressors, and clothed with all that is compassionate and kind. And whenever there is a soft or a sentimental temperament at work, that representation of the Divine nature must be peculiarly pleasing and acceptable. And whenever men wish to have a religion which will be without any rigorous exactions of self-denial and of duty, and without any tendency to excite apprehension and alarm, the same predilection must exist for a supreme Ruler in whose benevolence all other qualities are absorbed and lost. And, accordingly, not only is this partial and unscriptural view of the character of God adopted as the leading principle of certain systems of theology, but it is held and cherished and acted upon by multitudes, whose sole concern in matters of faith is to have not what is true, but what is agreeable, and who find in the tenet we are speaking of, the most soothing and satisfying of all persuasions,—that God loves every one of His creatures with such an affection as is depicted in the Gospel. I warn you against the delusion—so dishonourable to the Holy One, the Everlasting Father—so ruinous to all who have surrendered themselves to its influence—so inconsistent with what you read in the book of inspiration—so destructive of that mystery of godliness and of grace which has been made known to us in Jesus Christ.'

The Scriptures teach us that judgment has passed upon all men in Adam, and that it is altogether of grace that any of the human race are saved. Mr. Tholuck, in his exposition of this chapter, may speak most irreverently of God as destroying His hapless creatures, and quote the Apocrypha, which asserts that God does not abhor anything which He has made, from which it would follow that He does not abhor devils for whom everlasting fire is prepared; but the uniform doctrine of Scripture is, that man is self-destroyed, and that it was God's eternal purpose to make known His manifold wisdom by the redemption of the Church, chosen in Christ before the foundation of the world. When the Saviour was first announced, Gen. iii. 15, mankind were divided into two classes, the one to be saved, the other to be lost. To the latter God did no wrong. He left them under condemnation, as is here exemplified in the case of Esau, while He plucked the former, like Jacob, as brands from the burning; and we are expressly told that in this case of Jacob and Esau the reception of the younger, and the rejection of the elder, which were declared previously to their birth, was in order that the purpose of God according to election might stand. This doctrine of the election of some and the rejection of others was also illustrated in Abraham, an idolater, and in the nation of Israél, to whom God showed His word, while He left all other nations to walk in their own ways. Had the whole of Adam's race perished, God would only have dealt with them as He did with the fallen angels. Why then, it may be said, preach the Gospel to all men? Because it is the appointed means of the salvation of sinners; and while all naturally reject it, God makes His people willing in the day of His power, and produces in them faith by what they hear. Paul endured all things for the elect's sake. He used the means, knowing that God would give the increase. The election thus obtain life, and the rest are blinded by the god of this world. Ishmael was rejected, and Isaac was chosen before he was born; and in the same way Jacob the younger was preferred to Esau his elder brother—Jacob was loved, but Esau was hated.

The passage in Malachi, from which these words, 'Esau have I hated,' are quoted by the Apostle, proves what is meant by the expression in the verse before us. ' I have loved you, saith the Lord: yet ye say, Wherein hast Thou loved us? Was not Esau Jacob's brother? saith the Lord: yet I loved Jacob, and I hated Esau, and laid his mountains and his heritage waste for the dragons of the wilderness. Whereas Edom saith, We are impoverished, but we will return and build the desolate places; thus saith the Lord of hosts, They shall build, but I will throw down ; and they shall call them, The border of wickedness, and, The people against whom the Lord hath indignation for ever.' Here the Prophet first speaks of Esau personally as Jacob's brother, which clearly indicates the meaning attached by the Apostle to the quotation. It implies, too, that Jacob had no claim to be preferred to his brother. Afterwards, in the denunciation, Esau's descendants are spoken of under the name of Edom, when the singular is changed for the plural, and the past time for the future and the present. The denunciation of *indignation for ever* upon the Edomites, and the call of God to Israel to observe the difference of His dealings towards them, shows what is meant by God's love of Jacob, and His hatred of Esau.

The declarations of God by the Prophet in the above quoted passage are fully substantiated throughout the Scriptures, both in regard to His loving Jacob and hating Esau personally ; and likewise in regard to the indignation which He manifested against Esau's descendants. Jacob is everywhere spoken of as the servant of God, highly honoured by many Divine communications. Jacob wrestled with God, and had power over Him, and prevailed, Hos. xii. 4, 5. With his dying breath, when he declared that he had waited for the salvation of the Lord, he was honoured to announce as a prophet the future destinies of his sons, and, above all, to utter a most remarkable prediction concerning the advent of the Messiah. Jacob during his life was the object of many special blessings. He died in faith, Heb. xi. 13, 21 ; and of him the Redeemer Himself has testified that, with Abraham and Isaac, he is now in the kingdom of heaven, Matt. viii. 11. Concerning Jacob, such is the decisive testimony of the Scriptures, which cannot be broken.

In the life of Esau, nothing is recorded indicating that he had the fear of God before his eyes, but everything to prove the reverse. The most important transaction recorded concerning him is his profane contempt for God's blessing in selling his birthright, manifesting his unbelief and indifference respecting the promise to Abraham. We see him also taking women of Canaan as his wives, although he had the example before him of Abraham's concern that Isaac should not marry any of the daughters of that country. In this we observe that he held as lightly the curse denounced against Canaan as he did the blessing promised to Abraham. We next see him deliberately resolving to murder his brother. ' The days of mourning for my father are at hand, then will I slay my brother Jacob.' Long after, although restrained from violence, he goes out to meet him with an armed force. At last he turns his back on the habitation of his fathers, and departs for ever from the land of promise. Towards the conclusion of the Epistle to the Hebrews, where the sale of his birthright is referred to, and where Jacob is numbered among those who both lived and died in faith, Esau is characterized as 'a profane person,' Heb. xii. 16. The same word, translated profane, is employed by Paul in his enumeration to Timothy of the most horrible vices, when speaking of the ' ungodly, of sinners, and of unholy persons,' 1 Tim. i. 9. The selling of his birthright proved Esau to be an unbelieving, profane, and ungodly man, and the Apostle warns believers not to act according to his example. The birthright conferred a double inheritance among the Hebrew patriarchs, and likewise pre-eminence, because it was connected with the descent of the Messiah; and they to whom this right belonged were also types of the firstborn, whose names are written in heaven. Despising the birthright proved that he despised the high distinction respecting the coming of the Messiah, and also the eternal inheritance of which the land of Canaan and the double portion of the firstborn were typical. Here the question of Esau's character as an ungodly man is decided by the pen of inspiration long after his death. And is this 'profane person,' who not only despised the birthright fraught with such unspeakable privileges, but who had deliberately made up his mind revengefully to murder his brother in cold blood, to be viewed as he has been represented, as amiable, disinterested, and virtuous, in defiance of every moral principle, and in direct opposition to the testimony of the word of God?

Such is the account which the Scriptures give of Esau personally; and how fully the denunciations above quoted from the Prophet respecting his descendants were accomplished, we learn from numerous passages throughout the Scriptures, as Ezek. xxv. 12, 14; Joel iii. 19; Amos i. 11, and elsewhere; and from the whole of the prophecy of Obadiah, where the destruction of Edom, and the victories of the house of Jacob, are contrasted. 'But upon Mount Zion shall be deliverance, and there shall be holiness; and the house of Jacob shall possess their possessions. And the house of Jacob shall be a fire, and the house of Joseph a flame, and the house of Esau for stubble, and they shall kindle in them, and devour them; and there shall not be any remaining of the house of Esau: for the Lord hath spoken it.' Is it then in the unambiguous testimony of Scripture respecting Esau personally, as a profane person, and respecting his descendants, 'the people against whom the Lord hath indignation for ever,'—is it among the many indications of God's goodness to Jacob, —that we find any countenance given to the imagination that God loved Esau only in a less degree than He loved Jacob? When men, by such methods as are resorted to on this subject, pervert the obvious meaning of the word of God, in order to maintain their preconceived systems, it manifests deplorable disaffection to the truth of God, and most culpable inattention to His plainest declarations.

It is evident that the quotation from the Old Testament of these words, 'Jacob have I loved, but Esau have I hated,' is here made by the Apostle with the design of illustrating the great truth which he is labouring through the whole of this chapter to substantiate; namely, that in the rejection of the great body of the Jewish nation, as being 'vessels of wrath,' while He reserved for Himself a remnant among them as 'vessels of mercy,' verses 22, 23, neither the purpose nor the promises of God had failed. In proof of this, Paul asserts that all the seed of Abraham were not the children of God, and that God had plainly exhibited this truth in distinguishing and choosing Isaac, that in his line, in preference to that of Abraham's other children, the Redeemer should come; and in further proof, he adduces the still stronger example of God's loving Jacob and hating Esau, choosing the one and rejecting the other. And as the manner of God's procedure is so contrary to the opinion which men naturally form of the way in which He should act, the Apostle immediately after affirms that in this there is no unrighteousness in God, and fully proves in what follows, that so far from being contrary to His usual mode of procedure, it is strictly in accordance with it, both in showing mercy on the one hand, according to His sovereign pleasure, and, on the other, in displaying His hatred of those whom He hardens. Having thus asserted that such is God's manner of acting towards men, which, being established, ought to stop every mouth, the Apostle at once shuts the door against all impious reasonings on the subject, and indignantly demands of any one who should dare to controvert this view of the subject,—*Nay but, O man, who art thou that repliest against God?* Such persons, then, as deny that the expression, 'Jacob have I loved, but Esau have I hated,' imports literal love of the one and literal hatred of the other, viewing it as an isolated declaration, detached from its connection, and judging of it from their preconceived opinions, as if such a manner of acting were unworthy of God, not only disregard the usual legitimate rules of interpreting language, and employ a most unwarrantable mode of torture in expounding these words, but prove that they misapprehend the whole drift of the Apostle's argument, and have no discernment of his purpose in introducing this example. For how would God's rejection of a part of the nation of Israel as 'vessels of *wrath*,' and His reserving a remnant among them as 'vessels of *mercy*,' be illustrated by His loving Esau only less than Jacob? Does the idea of *loving less* consist with the idea held forth in the expression *vessels of* WRATH?

Several commentators deny that the declaration, 'Jacob have I loved, but Esau have I hated,' has any reference to their personal, spiritual, and eternal state. 'It is certain,' says Dr. Doddridge, 'the Apostle does not here speak of the eternal state of Jacob and Esau, nor does he indeed so much speak of their persons as of their posterity, since it is plainly to that posterity that both the prophecies which he quotes in support of his argument refer.' On this Mr. Fry remarks, 'If so, the force and pertinency of the Apostle's reasonings are lost. In attending, however, to the Apostle's argument in the passage before us, it will appear plain to every inquirer, who is not biassed by the apprehension of certain consequences, supposed to result from this interpretation, that St. Paul does certainly consider Jacob and Esau to be personally referred to, and concerned in these prophecies which he quotes; and that with them personally, and not altogether with their respective seeds, has his argument to do. The Apostle is showing that the rejection of the natural descendants of the patriarchs does not argue a breach of that word of God, which promises eternal mercies to Abraham and his seed, because by that seed was not intended all the seed born to Abraham after the flesh, but a seed of true believers, of whom Abraham, in the view of God, was the constituted father. In confirmation of this, he refers to the case of Ishmael, who was rejected, and of all the other children of Abraham being passed over in silence, Isaac remaining the only seed to inherit and to entail the promise. Again, as a still more striking proof that the word of promise discriminated a particular seed, and addressed not the children of the flesh universally, the Apostle instances the cases of Jacob and Esau. The first of these is chosen of God, and invested with the promised blessing; the other is rejected, and that in circumstances, as he points out to us, which plainly show that of the descendants of the patriarchs, God, according to His will and pleasure, would make some, and not others, to be counted to Abraham for a " seed" in a spiritual sense, to be of the children of God. It is evident, therefore, that the Apostle means to assert that Jacob was counted for one of "the" spiritual "seed," was " a child of God," and that Esau, though one of "the children" of Abraham " according to the flesh," was "not a child of God," nor " counted for the seed;" and, moreover, that it was the election of God, and no merit or demerit of the parties, which made this difference between them. It follows that whatever these prophecies may refer to *besides*, if we admit that the Apostle understood them, they do refer most certainly to Jacob and Esau personally; nay more, are quoted by the Apostle with this reference alone. For though in these prophecies, as they stand in the Scriptures of the Old Testament, a doom was certainly pronounced, which affected very materially the posterity of Jacob and Esau, and the children of the former were elected to privileges, from the inheritance of which the children of the latter were excluded, yet the Apostle does not quote the prophecies in this sense. That were in fact to overturn his own argument. Because, if what was prognosticated of the respective posterities of the persons mentioned in the prophecies were the object in view, it would prove that the children of the flesh, as far, at least, as the children of Israel were concerned, were counted for the seed. But the Apostle's argument goes to prove that the reverse is the case,—that they are not all Israel who are of Israel. With respect to the natural privileges and the pre-eminence which was given to Jacob and denied to Esau, as the representatives of their respective seeds, it would not stand true that they were not all *Israel who were of Israel.* The privileges in question had been enjoyed by the children of the flesh, and have just been enumerated as possessed by those very Israelites whose rejection from being the children of God the Apostle is now deploring, while, at the same time, he proves that rejection not contrary to the promises made to the fathers. We may therefore safely conclude that the Apostle does not so much speak of the posterity, as of the persons of Jacob and Esau; and that he knew the prophecies he quotes in support of his argument not to refer alone to that posterity; and consequently that it is certain he does speak of the eternal state of Jacob and Esau.'

The whole of the context throughout this ninth chapter, as well as the concluding part of the eighth, proves that respecting Jacob and Esau the reference is to their spiritual and eternal state. At the 29th verse of the preceding chapter, the Apostle, after exhibiting to believers various topics of the richest consolation, had traced up all their high privileges to the eternal purpose of God, and had dwelt in the sequel on their perfect security as His elect. In the beginning of this chapter, he had turned his eye, with deep lamentation, to the very different state of his countrymen, who, notwithstanding all their distinguished advantages, had rejected the Messiah. This gave occasion for enlarging on the sovereignty of God in the opposite aspect to that in which he had treated it in respect to believers. In reference to believers, he had spoken of God's sovereignty as displaying itself in their election, and now, in reference to the great body of the Jews, as manifested in their rejection. By this arrangement, an opportunity was afforded most strikingly to exhibit that doctrine, by personal application in both cases.

It is evident that Paul, throughout this chapter, refers not to the external condition of the Jews, which was indeed involved in their rejection of Christ, but to their spiritual state, as rejecting the righteousness which is of faith, and stumbling at that stumbling-stone, verse 32. He observes that not only at that time, but in former ages, according to the testimony of their own Prophets, a remnant only should be saved. And, besides, while the whole tenor of his discourse makes it obvious that he is treating of their spiritual and eternal condition, this is conclusively evident from what he says in the 22d and 23d verses above referred to, where he speaks, on the one hand, of the vessels of wrath, fitted to destruction, and, on the other, of the vessels of mercy, prepared unto glory. These two verses, were there no other proof, evince beyond all doubt what is his object. His lamentation for his countrymen was not called forth on account of the loss of their external privileges, the destruction of Jerusalem, and their expulsion from their own land. Had it been so, he must have included himself, and also those Jews whom, in the 24th verse, he says God had called. But so far is he from representing these to be in a lamentable state, that he describes them, along with himself, as vessels on whom the riches of the glory of God was made known; while, by the contrast, it is evident that by the wrath and destruction of which the others were vessels, he means something very different from temporal calamities. The vessels of the one description were the 'remnant' which should be saved, the 'seed' which the Lord of Sabaoth had left, verses 27, 29. The vessels of the other description were these who were as ' Sodoma, and had been made like unto Gomorrha,' which suffered the vengeance of eternal fire. What trifling, then, what wresting of this important portion of the word of God, what turning of it entirely away from its true meaning, to represent this chapter, as so many do, as treating of the outward state of the Jews, or to deny, with others, that the spiritual and everlasting condition of Jacob and Esau are here referred to! If the eternal condition of Abraham and of Judas be determined in the Scriptures, so also is that of Jacob and Esau; and no meaning, which, from whatever motive, any man may affix to the whole tenor of Scripture respecting them, will alter their condition. It is better to submit to the word of God on this and every other subject, taking it in its obvious import, than to be deterred from doing so on account of consequences from the admission of which we may shrink back. All Scripture will thus be profitable to us for doctrine, for reproof, for correction, for instruction in righteousness, while we are sure that the Judge of all the earth will do right.

On the whole, we see with what propriety the Apostle here introduces the different states of Jacob and Esau, the one beloved of God, the other hated. Besides elucidating the subject in question respecting God's dealings with the nation of Israel, and of the word which He had spoken taking effect, they illustrate by particular examples both sides of the important doctrine of God's sovereignty in the election, and of His justice in the reprobation of fallen men. For, by acting in this manner, God has clearly shown that He is the Sovereign Master in their calling and election, and of their rejection—that He chooses and rejects as seems good to Him any of the sinful race of Adam, all of whom are justly objects of His displeasure, without regarding natural qualities which distinguish them from one another.

What is said of Jacob and Esau in the Old Testament, in the place to which Paul refers, is both historical and typical. It relates, in the first view, to themselves personally, the elder being made subservient to the younger by selling his birthright. In consequence of that act, the declaration, *The elder shall serve the younger*, was verified from the time when it took place. All the rights of the firstborn were thus transferred to Jacob, and the inheritance of Canaan devolved on him by the surrender of his ungodly brother. At length Esau was compelled to leave that land, and to yield to Jacob. When the riches of both of them were ' more than that they might dwell together,' ' Esau,' it is said, ' took his wives, and his sons, and his daughters, and all the persons of his house, and his cattle, and all his beasts, and all his substance which he had got in the land of Canaan, and went into the country from the face of his brother Jacob,' Gen. xxxvi. 6. Whatever, therefore, might have previously been the opposition of their interests, in this the most important act of his life relating to Jacob, Esau was finally made subservient to his younger brother. And this subserviency, in yielding up the inheritance which naturally belonged to him, continued during the remainder of their lives; so that the declaration, 'The elder shall serve the younger,' was, after various struggles between them, personally and literally fulfilled. In the second view, as being typical, what is said of them relates, on the one hand, to the state of Israel after the flesh, trampling on and forfeiting their high privileges, hated of God, and vessels of wrath fitted to destruction; and, on the other hand, to the vessels of mercy which God had afore prepared unto glory.

In loving Jacob, God showed him unmerited favour, and acted towards him in mercy; and in hating Esau, He showed him no favour who was entitled to none, and acted according to justice. Had God acted also in justice without mercy towards Jacob, He would have hated both; for both were in their origin guilty in Adam, wicked and deserving of hatred. The Apostle unveils the reason why this was not the case, when he afterwards says that God has mercy on whom He will have mercy. The justice of God in hating Esau was made fully manifest in the sequel by his abuse of the high privileges in the course of providence bestowed upon him. Notwithstanding all the advantages of instruction and example with which, beyond all others of the human race (with the exception of the rest of his family), he was distinguished, Esau despised his birthright, fraught with so many blessings, the natural right to which had been conferred on him in preference to his brother Jacob, and lived an ungodly life. If Jacob, who was placed in the same situation, proved himself to be a godly man, it was entirely owing to the distinguishing grace of God. If it be objected, why was not this grace also vouchsafed to Esau? it may as well be asked, why are not the whole of mankind saved? That this will not be the case, even they who oppose the sovereignty of God in the election of grace cannot deny. Besides, will they, who affirm that God chooses men to eternal life because He foresees that they will do good works, deny that, at least, God foresaw the wickedness of Esau's life? Even on their own principles, then, it was just to hate Esau before he was born; and, on the same ground of foreseeing his good works, it would have been just to love Jacob. Or will they say that this hatred should not have taken place till after Esau had acted such a part? This would prove that there is variableness with God, and that He does not hate to-day what He will hate to-morrow. Where, then, is the necessity for any one, whatever may be his sentiments, to resort to the vain attempt to show that, when it is said God loved Jacob and hated Esau, it only means that He loved Esau less than Jacob? As well may it be affirmed that, when, in the prophecy of Amos, v. 15, it is said, 'Hate the evil, and love the good,' the meaning is, that we ought to love evil only in a less degree than good. But the truth is, that all opposition to the plain and obvious meaning of this passage proceeds from ignorance of, or inattention to, the state of death and ruin in which all men by nature lie, and from which no man can be recovered by any outward means alone, however powerful in themselves. This cannot be effected by anything short of the unmerited and invincibly efficacious grace of God, operating in the heart of those on whom He will have mercy according to His sovereign good pleasure. Undoubtedly God was under no more obligation to save any of the human race than He was to save the fallen angels. If He save any man, it is because He hath mercy on whom He will have mercy, or as seemeth good to Him. According to those who oppose this manner of acting, God was under an obligation to send His Son into the world to save sinners.

From the 7th to the end of this 13th verse, we have an incontestible proof of the typical nature of the historical facts of the Old Testament, by which God was pleased to exhibit a picture or representation of spiritual things, and of His dealings respecting the people of Israel, as well as what related to His Church in the future economy. This typical import is fully recognised in various places in the New Testament, showing, as the Apostle declares in the 15th chapter of this Epistle, that 'whatsoever things were written aforetime, were written for our learning,' and also when he speaks of what took place respecting Israel in their journey from Egypt, which is equally applicable to so many other events. 'Now all these things happened to them for examples,' literally, types, 1 Cor. x. 6–11. This proves that these occurrences were expressly ordained by Divine wisdom to be 'a shadow of things to come.' All this, too, we may collect from those types and figures of the Old Testament, which would have been wholly inconclusive, unless, by a particular destination of the providence of God, they had been really instituted to prefigure future events. By many it is indeed affirmed that such historical facts as the Apostle in these verses refers to, are only *accommodated* to the allegorical meaning. This unfounded allegation, so derogatory to the Holy Scriptures, and utterly repugnant to their character as a revelation from God, I have exposed in various parts of this work. I have adverted to it more fully, because, as formerly observed, it brings a palpable charge of falsehood and dishonesty against the inspired writers, representing them as quoting the language of the Holy Spirit in a meaning which He did not intend to convey, and as confirmatory of their own doctrine, when they knew that what they advanced was merely a fanciful accommodation of words. Although this degrading opinion is so much countenanced by such writers as Tholuck and Stuart, and by many others, I am not aware that it has hitherto attracted all that attention, and been marked with that abhorrence, which it so justly merits. Nothing is more clear than that such historical facts and occurrences as those to which Paul in the foregoing passages appeals, were divinely ordered and adapted to represent spiritual things ; and it is of great importance in the present day, when interpreters are so much inclined to overlook the types of the Old Testament, to take every proper opportunity of placing them in their true light, and pointing out the important purpose which they were intended to serve in the future economy, and for which they are referred to as in the passages before us.[1]

Ver. 14.—*What shall we say then ? Is there unrighteousness with God ? God forbid.*

The Apostle anticipated the objection of the carnal mind to his doctrine. Does not loving Jacob and hating Esau before they had done any good or evil, imply that there is injustice in God ? This objection clearly proves that the view taken of the preceding passage is correct. For it is this view which suggests the objection. Is it just in God to love one who has done no good, and to hate one who has done no evil ? If the assertion respecting loving Jacob and hating Esau admitted of being explained away in the manner that so many do, there could be no place for such an objection. And what is the Apostle's reply ? Nothing but a decided rejection of the supposition that God's treatment of Jacob and Esau implied injustice. By asking the question if there be unrighteousness with God, he strongly denies that in God there is here any injustice ; and this denial is sufficient. According to the doctrine which he everywhere inculcates, consistently with that of the whole of Scripture, God is represented as infinitely just, as well as wise, holy, good, and faithful. In the exercise of His sovereignty, therefore, all that God wills to do must be in strict conformity with the perfection of His character. He cannot deny Himself ; He cannot act inconsistently with any of His Divine attributes.

Ver. 15.—*For He saith to Moses, I will have mercy on whom I will have mercy, and I will have compassion on whom I will have compassion.*

What is the ground on which the Apostle here rests his denial that there is unrighteousness with God ? He makes no defence or apology for God, attempts no metaphysical distinctions, but rests solely on the authority of Scripture. He produces the testimony of God to Moses, declaring the same truth that he himself affirms. This is quite enough

---

[1] On ' the types of the Old Testament,' see the chapter on that subject in the Author's work entitled *Evidence and Authority of Divine Revelation,* vol. i., 3d edition.

for Christians. It is not wise in them, as is often the case, to adopt a mode of vindicating God's procedure, so very different from what He Himself employs. How many go about to justify God, and thereby bring God to the bar of man! From the defences of Scripture doctrine, often resorted to, it might be supposed that God was on His trial before men, rather than that all shall stand before Him, and that the will of God is supreme justice. *I will have mercy on whom I will have mercy, and I will have compassion on whom I will have compassion.*—That is, I will have mercy on whom I please—I will bestow My favours, or withhold them, as seemeth to Me good. God by this declaration proves that He is a debtor to none; that every blessing bestowed upon the elect flows from gratuitous love, and is freely granted to whom He pleases. The answer, then, of the Apostle amounts to this, that what is recorded concerning God's loving Jacob and hating Esau is in nothing different from His usual mode of procedure towards men, but is entirely consistent with the whole plan of His government. All men are lost and guilty in Adam; it is of mercy that any are saved; and God declares that He will have mercy or not upon men according to His own good pleasure. It is only of this attribute that such language as is contained in this passage can be employed. The exercise of every other attribute is at all times indispensable, and never can be suspended.

Ver. 16.—*So then it is not of him that willeth, nor of him that runneth, but of God that showeth mercy.*

This is the conclusion from the whole. Salvation is not from the will of man, nor from his efforts in striving for it, but is entirely of God's mercy vouchsafed to whom He pleases. What foundation, then, can be discovered in the word of God for those schemes of self-righteousness, which, in a greater or less degree, make salvation depend on man's own exertions? There may be here an allusion to Jacob's desiring the blessing of the birthright, and his running to provide the venison by which he deceived his father; but his obtaining the blessing was solely the consequence of God's good pleasure, for the means he employed for the purpose merited punishment rather than success. In like manner, the salvation of any man is not to be ascribed to his own good will and diligent endeavours to arrive at it, but solely to the purpose of God according to election, which is 'not of works, but of Him that calleth.' It is true, indeed, that believers both will and run, but this is the *effect*, not the *cause*, of the grace of God being vouchsafed to them. 'Work out your own salvation with fear and trembling.' To whom is this addressed? To 'the saints in Christ Jesus,' in whom *God had begun* a good work, which *He will perform* until the day of Jesus Christ—to them who had *always obeyed*, Phil. i. 1, 6, 29, ii. 12. But besides this, what is the motive or encouragement to work out their salvation? 'For it is God which worketh in you both to will and to do of His good pleasure.' Here all the willing and doing of men in the service of God is ascribed to His operation in causing them to will and to do. The whole of the new covenant is a promise of God that He Himself will act efficaciously for the salvation of those whom He will save. 'I will put my law in their inward parts, and write it in their hearts.' 'I will give them one heart, and one way, that they may fear Me for ever.' 'I will put My fear in their hearts, that they shall not depart from Me.' 'A new heart also will I give you, and a new spirit will I put within you, and I will take away the stony heart out of your flesh, and I will give you a heart of flesh. And I will put My Spirit within you, and cause you to walk in My statutes, and ye shall keep my judgments and do them,' Jer. xxxi., xxxii.; Ezek. xxxvi. In this way the means by which God's elect are brought to Him, their calling, their justification, their sanctification, their perseverance, and their glorification, are all of God, as was shown in the preceding chapter, and not of themselves. 'There is great folly,' say Calvin, 'in the argument that we are possessed of a certain energy in our zeal, but of such a kind as can effect nothing of itself, unless aided by the mercy of Jehovah, since the Apostle shows that we possess nothing of our own, by excluding all our efforts. To infer that we have the power either of running or willing, is a mere cavil, which Paul denies, and plainly asserts that our will or ardour in the race has not the smallest influence in procuring our election. On the other hand, those merit the severest reproof who continue to indulge in sloth, that they may afford room and opportunity for the grace of God to act; since, although their own industry can accomplish nothing, yet the heavenly zeal inspired by the Father of Lights is endued with active efficacy.'

If any shall oppose the declaration of the Apostle, that it is not of him that willeth or of him that runneth, but of God that showeth mercy, and assert that the salvation of man depends on conditions which he is obliged to fulfil, then it may be asked, what is the condition? Is it faith? Faith is the *gift* of God. Is it repentance? Christ is exalted a Prince and a Saviour to *give* repentance. Is it love? God promises to circumcise the heart in order to *love* Him. Are they good works? His people are the workmanship of God created unto *good works*. Is it perseverance to the end? They are *kept* by the power of God through faith unto salvation. It is true that all these things are commanded and enforced by the most powerful motives, consequently they are duties which require the exercise of our faculties. But they are assured by the decree of election, and are granted to the elect of God in the proper season; so that, in this view, they are the objects of promise, and the effects of supernatural and Divine influence. 'Thy people,' saith Jehovah to the Messiah, 'shall be willing in the day of Thy power.' Thus the believer, in running his race, and working out his salvation, is actuated by God, and animated by the consideration of His all-powerful operation in the beginning of his course; of the continuation of His support during its progress; and by the assurance that it shall be effectual in enabling him to overcome all obstacles, and to arrive in safety at its termination.

Ver. 17.—*For the Scripture saith unto Pharaoh, Even for this same purpose have I raised thee up, that I might show My power in thee, and that My name might be declared throughout all the earth.*

This verse stands connected, not with the 15th and 16th, which immediately precede it, but with the 13th and 14th. In the 13th verse, God's love to Jacob and His hatred to Esau are declared. In respect to both, it is demanded in the 14th verse, if there be injustice with God.   In the 15th and 16th verses following, the answer is given regarding the preference and love of God to Jacob.   In this 17th verse, the Apostle replies to the question as it refers to God's hatred of Esau.   And the answer here is precisely similar to that given respecting Jacob.   God's love to Jacob before he had done any good was according to His usual plan of procedure ; and on the same ground, His hatred of Esau before he had done any evil is also vindicated.   Paul here proves his doctrine from the example of one to whom, in Divine sovereignty, God acted according to justice without mercy.   The Scripture saith that God raised up Pharaoh for the very purpose of manifesting His own glory in his punishment.

For the Scripture saith.—By the manner in which the Apostle begins this verse, we are taught that whatever the Scriptures declare on any subject is to be considered as decisive on the point.   ' What saith the Scripture ? '   This is the proof to which the Apostle appeals.   It should further be observed, that Paul ascribes to the Scriptures what was said by God Himself, Ex. ix. 16.   This expressly teaches us that the words of Scripture are the words of God.   In the same manner, in the Epistle to the Galatians, it is said, the Scripture, ' foreseeing that God would justify the heathen ; ' and, ' the Scripture hath concluded all under sin,' Gal. iii. 8, 22.   Here the word of God is so much identified with Himself, that the Scripture is represented as possessing and exercising the peculiar prerogatives of God.   What is done by God, and what belongs only to Him, is ascribed to the Scriptures,—proving that they contain the very words of God.   ' All Scripture is given by inspiration of God, 2 Tim. iii. 16.[1]   The word Scripture is here taken in its appropriated meaning—being confined to the book of God.   All that is written in it is divinely inspired ; and what does writing consist of but of words ?   If any of these are not inspired, then all Scripture is not inspired.   Every word, then, in the book referred to, is the word of God, dictated by Him of whom the writers were the instruments He employed, who spoke or wrote as they were moved by the Holy Ghost.   Why are so many unwilling to admit this view of the inspiration of Scripture so much insisted on in the Scriptures themselves ?   Is it on account of the difficulty of conceiving how words should thus be communicated ?   But is it easier to understand how ideas could be communicated ?   Do they believe that the Lord ' opened the mouth of the ass ' of Balaam, and communicated the words which she spake ?   Is it then more difficult to communicate words to men than to a dumb animal ?   To speak of difficulties where Omnipotence is concerned, is palpably absurd.   Besides, all allow that in the parts of Scripture to which (making vain distinctions respecting inspiration, without the least foundation from any expression the Scriptures contain) they ascribe the inspiration of ' suggestion,' the very words were communicated to the writers.   Those who deny the plenary verbal inspiration of the Scriptures,—who introduce various modifications of the manner in which they have been written,—neither can nor ought to entertain the same profound veneration for them as

[1] See a very full and critical discussion on 2 Tim. iii. 16, appended to Dr. Carson's *Refutation of Dr. Henderson's Doctrine in his late Work on Divine Inspiration.*

those who believe that, without any exception, from beginning to end, they are dictated by God Himself.

The Scripture saith unto Pharaoh,—that is, the Scripture showeth how Moses was commanded to say unto Pharaoh, Ex. ix. 16,—*Even for this same purpose have I raised thee up.*—Here is the destination of Pharaoh to his destruction. *That I might show My power in thee, and that My name might be declared throughout all the earth.*—This is the end and design intended by it. It was not, then, by any concurrence of fortuitous circumstances that Pharaoh was seated on the throne of Egypt, and invested with the power he possessed when Moses was appointed to conduct Israel out of Egypt. He was raised up, or made to stand in that place, in order that, by his opposition, from the perversity of his heart, in him God might show His own power and exalt His own name. It is not merely alleged that God had not shown mercy to this king of Egypt, or that He had suffered him to go on in his wicked ways; but, in language which the unrenewed heart of man will never relish, it is declared, ' Even for this same purpose have I raised thee up, that I might show My power in thee, and that My name might be declared throughout all the earth.' For this very end, the birth, the life, and the situation of Pharaoh were all of Divine appointment. This is language so clear that it cannot be guiltlessly misinterpreted. The unbelieving heart of man will revolt, and his ingenuity may invent expedients to soften this explicit declaration; but it never can be successfully evaded. All the shifts of sophistry will never be able fairly, or even plausibly, to explain this language in a sense that will not testify the sovereignty of God.

The above truth respecting Pharaoh is what the Scriptures declare; and we ought never to pretend to go further into the deep things of God than they go before us, but submissively to bow to every Divine declaration. We know that all sin will be found with man; but here we are taught that even the sin of man will turn out for the glory of God, and for this very purpose the wicked are raised up. If we cannot fathom this depth in the Divine counsels, still let us be certain that what God says is true, and must be received by us. We are assured that the Judge of all the earth will in all things act righteously, although we may not be able to comprehend His ways. Nor are we required to comprehend them. We are required to believe His word, and to believe that it is consistent with the eternal righteousness of His character. ' Let us treasure,' says Calvin, ' the following observation in our minds,—never to feel the least desire to attain any other knowledge concerning this doctrine save what is taught us in Scripture. When the Lord shuts His sacred mouth, let us also stop our thoughts from advancing one step further in our inquiries.' Consistently with the vain attempts that have been made to reconcile the truth above affirmed with philosophy falsely so called, the whole subject of this chapter might be rejected, equally with that of the verbal inspiration of the Scriptures. It has accordingly been perverted by many who have explained it in such a way as to remove all the difficulties which it presents. Our Lord in one short sentence has declared the true reason of their finding it so hard to

understand this chapter. 'Why do ye not understand My speech?—
even because ye cannot hear My word.' It is also written for our
warning. 'Many, therefore, of His disciples, when they had heard this,
said, This is an hard saying; who can hear it?' There is no part of
Scripture, the meaning of which is more obvious than that of this
chapter. But if men will yield to the natural opposition of their minds
to the truth it declares, and, wresting the plainest expressions, affirm that
hatred signifies love, is it surprising that they are bewildered in following
their own devices? [1]

Ver. 18.—*Therefore hath He mercy on whom He will have mercy, and whom He
will He hardeneth.*

Here the general conclusion is drawn from all the Apostle had said
in the three preceding verses, in denying that God was unrighteous
in loving Jacob and hating Esau. It exhibits the ground of God's
dealings both with the elect and the reprobate. It concludes that His
own sovereign pleasure is the rule both with respect to those whom He
receives, and those whom He rejects. He pardons one and hardens
another, without reference to anything but His own sovereign will, in
accordance with His infinite wisdom, holiness, and justice. 'Even so,
Father,' said our blessed Lord, 'for so it seemed good in Thy sight.'
God is not chargeable with any injustice in electing some and not others;
for this is an act of mere mercy and compassion, and that can be no
violation of justice.

Therefore hath He mercy on whom He will have mercy.—Paul here
repeats for the third time, that God has mercy on whom He will have
mercy, without intimating the least regard to anything in man as
deserving mercy. The smallest degree of right in the creature would
furnish reason for displaying justice, not mercy. Mercy is that adorable
perfection of God by which He pities and relieves the miserable. Under
the good and righteous government of God, no one is miserable who
does not deserve to be so. The objects of mercy are persons who are
miserable, because they are guilty, and therefore justly deserving of
punishment. The exercise of mercy is a particular display of the grace
or free favour of God. In no case can it be due to a guilty creature;
it necessarily implies the absence of all right. A man can never have a
right to mercy; and to talk of *deserving* mercy is a contradiction in terms.
God, it is said, 'delighteth in mercy,' Mic. vii. 18; and in the proclamation of His name to Moses, this attribute is particularly signalized.
'The Lord, the Lord God, merciful and gracious,' Ex. xxxiv. 6. He is
'rich' and 'plenteous' in mercy, and 'His tender mercies are over all
His works.'

Mercy, however, is an attribute, the constant exercise of which is not
essential to God, like that of justice, which can never, as has been remarked, for a moment be suspended. Mercy is dispensed according to
His sovereign pleasure in regard to persons or times, as to Him seemeth
good. Towards the fallen children of men it was gloriously displayed

[1] Mr. Tholuck, in his *Exposition of the Epistle to the Romans*, has most fearfully
perverted the meaning of this ninth chapter, as well as many other parts of the
Epistle.

when God sent His Son into the world, which was purely a work of mercy, and not demanded by justice. But to the fallen angels mercy was not vouchsafed. And is this any impeachment of the mercy of God? If not, is it a just ground for complaint, that in order to manifest His hatred of sin, His mercy is not extended to a certain portion of the human race, who we know for certain shall perish? Thus God has mercy on whom He will have mercy. It is one of the fundamental errors of Socinians, and of many besides, to hold that the mercy of God must be necessarily and constantly exercised; while, reversing the order of Scripture, and all its representations of the character of God, they deny this necessity regarding His justice. The same act, however, may be both an act of justice and an act of mercy in reference to different objects. The punishment of the enemies of God, the slaying of the firstborn in Egypt, the overthrow of Pharaoh and his host, the discomfiture of kings, and the transfer of their lands for an heritage to Israel, while they were acts of justice towards the enemies of His people, are all ascribed to the mercy of God to them, Ps. cxxxvi. ' To him that smote Egypt in their first-born : for His mercy endureth for ever: But overthrew Pharaoh and his host in the Red Sea : for His mercy endureth for ever : To Him which smote great kings : for His mercy endureth for ever : And slew famous kings : for His mercy endureth for ever : And gave their land for an heritage : for His mercy endureth for ever : Even an heritage to Israel His servant : for His mercy endureth for ever.'

Mercy, then, which is a particular kind of Divine goodness, is sovereign; and to confer favours freely, consistently with Divine wisdom, does injury to no one. If God was only just, there would be no place for mercy ; if He never acted as a sovereign benefactor, there could be no place for the plan of redemption. God may be considered under two different aspects, either as judging with equity, or as disposing at His will of His benefits ; in other words, as a judge, or as a sovereign. Under either of these aspects, in whatever manner He acts, having nothing higher than Himself, He is the supreme God. Sovereignty, when this word is applied to God, signifies the arbitrary will of a *benefactor*, because that under the other aspects there is no place for the exercise of arbitrary will. In the exercise of His justice, God is sovereign in His judgments and His punishments, but not arbitrary, because He does not judge without demerit in the objects of His judgment. When, therefore, He acts as Judge and Supreme Ruler, His acts are founded upon equity ; but when He acts as Sovereign, His acts are founded upon His free favour, and dispensed with wisdom.

Whatever offence the human mind may take at the attribute of Divine justice, and its exercise in punishing the guilty, we should think that all men would eagerly embrace the view given in Scripture of the Divine mercy. Yet, in reality, the peculiar character of the mercy of God is as disagreeable to men as is His justice itself. The Divine mercy is not only sovereign, but, respecting its object, *it is unlimited.* Neither of these peculiarities is agreeable to the mind of man. Human wisdom views God as merciful, but that mercy it makes to extend equally to all, and unlimitedly to none. For persons not guilty of glaring sins, God's mercy is not only expected by the world, but even claimed and demanded. To deny it to those who are sober and regular in their lives, would be looked on as both cruel and unjust. In the passage before us, however, we see that God's mercy is sovereign, that it extends to one and not to another, while no man can give a reason for the preference of one and the rejection of the other. The only reason God condescends to give is His own pleasure: 'I will have mercy on whom I will have mercy.' The unlimited character of the Divine mercy is a thing that ought to be most agreeable to every man. Even should any be so blind as not to perceive that they need such mercy for themselves, yet, if they loved mankind, they should rejoice that the Divine mercy is such as to extend to the chief of sinners. Constant experience, however, as well as the history of our Lord's life, shows us that this is not the case. Instead of rejoicing in the extent of the Divine mercy, the heart of the self-righteous man will swell with indignation when he hears that mercy is extended to the vile and the profligate. Nothing in the conduct of our Lord gave such offence to the scribes and Pharisees as this peculiarity in His conduct of receiving sinners. In the most prominent manner He exhibited this feature of mercy, and publicans and sinners heard Him, and received His doctrine, and turned from their sins unto God; while the proud, self-righteous Pharisees burned with indignation at the conduct of Christ in this instance. He was constantly upbraided as receiving sinners and eating with them.

Of the mercy of God, Dr. Thomson observes, 'It cannot be that His mercy should be exerted at the expense or to the disparagement, in any the least degree, of one excellence which beautifies His nature, or upholds His government, or speaks His praise. His mercy is sovereign and gratuitous; and therefore it can only be displayed when every other quality that belongs to Him is fully maintained, and there is no sacrifice of the honour that is due to each, and of the consistency which pervades the whole. Whenever His mercy cannot be exercised without refusing the demands of His justice, or without bringing into question the immutability of His faithfulness, or without denying the irresistible energy of His power, or without impeaching the infallibility of His wisdom, or without throwing suspicion on the absolute purity of His nature—in these cases His mercy cannot be exercised at all, for the exercise of it would involve some shortcoming in His perfection, which is necessarily unqualified and unlimited. It is only of this attribute that it can be said, 'He will have mercy on whom He will have mercy.' Of every other attribute it is requisite that we predicate positive and peremptory operation. He *must* be holy; He *must* be wise; He *must* be powerful; He *must* be just; He *must* be true; He *must* be each and all of these, whatever betide His universe; and if we, His apostate creatures, cannot be the objects of His mercy except by some surrender of the homage due to them, or some violation of the harmony that reigns among them, His mercy cannot save, and cannot reach us.'

And whom He will He hardeneth.—If God hath mercy on whom He will, He hardeneth whom He will. In hardening men, God does no injustice, nor does He act in any degree contrary to the perfection of

His character. He does not communicate hardness or perversity to the hearts of men by any positive internal act, as when He communicates His grace. 'Let no man say when he is tempted, I am tempted of God, for God cannot be tempted with evil, neither tempteth He any man.' Wicked men are not restrained by the holy influences of grace, but by the different restraints under which they are placed by Providence. They are hardened when these restraints are removed, and when they are left free to act according to the depraved inclinations of their own hearts, to which the Lord gives them up, Ps. lxxxi. 12; Acts vii. 42; Rom. i. 24, 26, 28. Or they are hardened by the communication of qualities which are neither good nor bad in themselves, but which may become either good or bad according to the use made of them, such as courage, perseverance, or other dispositions which may be employed for bad purposes. Men are also hardened when they are abandoned to the suggestions of Satan, of whom they are the willing slaves. Thus Judas was hardened by Satan, who had taken possession of him, and to whom he submitted himself, although most solemnly warned of his danger. When a man is entirely left to himself, the commands, the warnings, the judgments, the deliverances, and all the truths of Scripture become causes of hardness, of insensibility, of pride, and presumption. Even the delay of merited punishment, and the deliverances from the plagues that fell on his country, were, in respect to Pharaoh, the occasion of hardening his heart. 'Because sentence against an evil work is not executed speedily, therefore the heart of the sons of men is fully set in them to do evil' In these ways men's hearts are hardened, through means that in themselves are calculated to produce the opposite effect.

But by whatever means the heart of men is hardened, they are regulated by God, who also determines that they shall succeed. We see this remarkably verified in the case of Ahab. 'And the Lord said, Thou shalt entice him, and thou shalt also prevail. Go out and do even so. Now, therefore, behold the Lord hath put a lying spirit in the mouth of these thy prophets, and the Lord hath spoken evil against thee,' 2 Chron. xviii. 21. 'If the prophet be deceived when he hath spoken a thing, I the Lord have deceived that prophet; and I will stretch out My hand upon him, and will destroy him from the midst of My people Israel,' Ezek. xiv. 9. 'Truly the Son of Man goeth, as it was determined; but woe unto that man by whom He is betrayed,' Luke xxii. 22. 'Him, being delivered by the determinate counsel and foreknowledge of God, ye have taken, and by wicked hands have crucified and slain,' Acts ii. 23. 'Of a truth against Thy holy child Jesus, whom Thou hast anointed, both Herod and Pontius Pilate, with the Gentiles, and the people of Israel, were gathered together, for to do whatsoever Thy hand and Thy counsel determined before to be done,' Acts iv. 27. 'A stone of stumbling, and a rock of offence, even to them which stumble at the word, being disobedient; whereunto also they were appointed,' 1 Pet. ii. 8. This shows an ordination of God to the thing referred to, which thing was sinful. 'There are certain men crept in unawares, who were before of old ordained to this condemnation.' The persons here spoken of are said to be ordained to condemnation, which, whatever it may be supposed to be, implies pre-appointment to it by God, Jude 4. 'Therefore, they could not believe, because Esaias said again, He hath blinded their eyes, and hardened their heart; that they should not see with their eyes, nor understand with their heart, and I should heal them,' John xii. 39. 'According as it is written, God hath given them a spirit of slumber, eyes that they should not see, and ears that they should not hear, unto this day,' Rom. xi. 8. 'And for this cause God shall send them strong delusion, that they should believe a lie; that they all might be damned who believe not the truth, but had pleasure in unrighteousness,' 2 Thess. ii. 11. It is nothing to the purpose to allege that this was in judgment for not receiving the love of the truth; whatever was the cause, God sent them strong delusion, so that they should believe a lie. In the same way it is said, Rev. xvii. 17, 'God hath put in their hearts to fulfil His will, and to agree and give their kingdom to the beast.' 'Babylon,' says Dr. Carson, in his *History of Providence,* 'was employed by Providence for the chastisement of His people, and commissioned to carry the Jews into captivity. Babylon was guilty in executing the will of the Lord, and was providentially destroyed by Him with an unexampled destruction. The Medes and Persians are sent by God to execute His vengeance on Babylon. He calls out their hosts and gives them victory, yet the Medes and Persians were excited by their own passions. Besides, says God, I will bring up the Medes against them, which shall not regard silver; and as for gold, they shall not delight in it. Their bows also shall dash the young men to pieces; and they shall have no pity on the fruit of the womb; their eye shall not spare children. How awful does Providence appear here! Even when savage idolaters violate every dictate of humanity, they are the executors of the judgments of the Almighty. While their conduct is most horridly guilty, in the Divine sovereignty it fulfils God's will. Who can fathom this depth? In God's dealings with Assyria and Babylon we ought to find a key to His providence in His dealings with the western nations of Europe. Does not Jehovah govern the world? Is there evil in the city, and the Lord hath not done it?'

In all the above acts relating to men, God proceeds in conformity to His justice. He is infinitely just in hating, hardening, and condemning sinners, in adjudging them to punishment for their wickedness, and in placing them in situations in which, in the free exercise of their evil dispositions, they will do what the Lord has appointed for His own glory. Thus God orders events in such a manner, that, as in the passages above quoted, the sin will, through the wickedness of men, certainly be committed, while He is not the author of evil, but, on the contrary, of good. He displays His holiness in the events and in their consequences. Men may employ all their art in wresting the above and similar passages, but they are recorded in the Scriptures, which are the word of God, and which cannot be broken. 'The Lord hath made all things for Himself; yea, even the wicked for the day of evil,' Prov. xvi. 4.[1] 'Why dost

---

[1] These words imply that the existence of sin, and the eternal punishment of it in wicked men, was in the Divine contemplation in the creation of the world, and that God will be glorified in the punishment of the wicked, as well as in the happiness of the righteous. This is a depth which we ought not to pretend to fathom. We receive it on God's testimony.

thou strive against Him? for He giveth not account of His matters,'—or answereth not, Job xxxiii. 13. That God does not harden any man in such a way as to be the author of sin, is most certain. But there must be a sense in which He hardens sinners, or the thing would not be asserted. From His conduct with respect to Pharaoh, it is obvious that sinners are hardened by the providence of God bringing them into situations that manifest and excite their corruptions.

In the history of Pharaoh in the Book of Exodus, it is repeated *ten times*, that God hardened Pharaoh's heart. Pharaoh is also said to have hardened his own heart. This shows that there is a certain connection between God's hardening the hearts of men and their voluntarily hardening their own hearts, so that when the one takes place the other does so likewise. It does not follow from this that God's hardening the heart of Pharaoh, and Pharaoh's hardening his own heart, are one and the same thing. This supposition, although adopted by many, is contrary to the representations and the express words of Scripture. The just inference is, that there is one view in which Pharaoh hardened his heart, and another in which God is said to have hardened it. We should believe both; but to attempt to show the philosophy of their reconciliation, is to attempt to fathom infinity. In Ps. cv. 25, it is said with respect to the people of Egypt, that God 'turned their heart to hate His people.' Can anything be stronger or more clear than this passage? No doubt it was their own sin, but there is also a sense in which the thing was of God. Are we to deny this because we cannot explain the way in which God did this? On the same ground we might reject the doctrine of the Trinity, or any other of the incomprehensible doctrines of Christianity.

On this subject, Dr. Carson, in his book lately published, entitled, *Examination of the Principles of Biblical Interpretation of Ernesti, Ammon, Stuart, and other Philologists*, observes, 'It is said that God hardened the heart of Pharaoh; it is said also that Pharaoh hardened his own heart. What, then, is the lawful way to reconcile these two statements? The statements must both be true. There must be a sense in which God hardened Pharaoh's heart, for this is as expressly asserted as that Pharaoh hardened his own heart. That this is not a sense implying that God is the author of Pharaoh's sin, there cannot be a moment's question. I may be asked how God could in any sense harden a man's heart without being the author of sin? But the most assured belief of the fact does not require that an answer should be given to the question. A thing may be true, yet utterly inexplicable. God's declaration is perfectly sufficient for the belief of anything which He testifies. Our reception of it does not imply that we know the grounds or nature of its truth. We receive it, not because we can explain *how* it is true, but because we know that God cannot lie. The Scriptures testify the fact; the fact, then, must be received as truth. The Scriptures do not testify the *manner* in which the thing is true of God; the *manner*, then, is not a thing to be believed, and consequently not a thing to be explained by man. . . . Many tell us that such assertions mean merely that God *permits* the thing which He is said to do. But is permission sufficient to secure accomplishment? God sent Joseph to Egypt; that is, it is said, *He permitted his brethren to sell him.* Nay, but it was God's will, purpose, and plan, that Joseph should go down to Egypt, and His providence secured the event. "Now, therefore," says Joseph, "be not grieved nor angry with yourselves, that ye sold me hither! for God did send me before you to preserve life." His brethren did it wickedly; God did it in mercy and in wisdom. We know that he did it entirely in consistency with man's accountability; but the *manner of this consistency* is not a matter of revelation, and therefore it is impossible to attempt explanation. "Rom. ix. 18," says Ammon, "appears to be an obscure passage relating to the absolute decrees of God. Light may be thrown upon this by 1 Sam. vi. 6, where Pharaoh is said to have hardened his own heart." How does 1 Sam. vi. 6 throw light upon Rom. ix. 18? We might have expected rather that Ammon would have found a contradiction, as the one passage ascribes to God what the other ascribes to man. The passages indeed are consistent; but their consistency must be made out, not by obliging one of them to silence the other, but by the principle that they assert the same thing in a different view. Ammon's plan, I presume, is to make Rom. ix. 18 recant, in order to harmonize with 1 Sam. vi. 6. But the honour of Scripture, and of God's character, require that they should be reconciled in a way that renders both true.'

Calvin, in his commentary on Exodus, represents those as perverting the Scriptures who insist that no more is meant than a bare permission when God is said to harden the hearts of men. He speaks of such as *frigidi speculatores, diluti moderatores,* to whose delicate ears such Scripture expressions seem harsh and offensive. They therefore, he observes, ' soften them down by turning an action into a permission, as if there were no difference between acting and suffering, *i.e.,* suffering others to act.' Such, he says, who will admit of permission only, suspend this counsel and determination of God, wholly on the will of man; but that he is not ashamed or afraid to speak as the Holy Spirit does, and does not hesitate to approve and embrace what the Scriptures so often declares, viz., that God blinds the minds of wicked men, and hardens their hearts. In his commentary on the passage before us, Rom. ix. 18, to the same purpose he observes, 'The word *hardening,* when attributed to God in Scripture, not only means permission (as some trifling theologians determine), but the action of Divine wrath; for all external circumstances, which contribute to blind the reprobates, are instruments of the Divine indignation. Satan also himself, the internal efficacious agent, is so completely the servant of the Most High, as to act only by His command. The frivolous attempt of the schoolmen to avoid the difficulty by foreknowledge, is completely subverted; for Paul does not say that the ruin of the wicked is foreseen by the Lord, but ordained by His counsel, decree, and will. Solomon also teaches that the destruction of the wicked was not only foreknown, but they were made on purpose for the day of evil' (Prov. xvi. 4).[1]

That ordination, with respect to evil, is merely permission, is an opinion

---

[1] Many call themselves *moderate Calvinists,* a denomination to which it is not easy to affix a precise idea. To the system called Calvinism, there may be nearer or more distant approaches, but those who deny any of the peculiar doctrines of that system cannot in any sense be called Calvinists. To affix the term Calvinism to any

which cannot be maintained.   Permission is not ordination in any sense
of the term, and ordination is quite a different idea from permission.   We
may permit what we do not ordain, and when we ordain anything, we do
more than permit it.   But it will be replied, Does not this make God the
author of sin?   It is answered, that the sense in which God ordains sin
is above our comprehension.   It must be a sense in which He is not the
author of sin—a sense, too, in which responsibility entirely rests with
man.   But the way in which this is true, we cannot explain.   It is enough
to know that God hath declared it.   We are to believe Him on His own
testimony, and to honour Him by submitting to whatever He declares.
God tells us that He doth such things, He tells us also that men do these
things.   We should believe both assertions, though we cannot reconcile
them.   Does not God say in His word—'As the heavens are higher than
the earth, so are My ways higher than your ways, and My thoughts than
your thoughts?'   Does He not say that His ways are past finding out?
If we could fathom all the ways of God, the Scriptures could not be His
word.   What God reveals, let us know: what He conceals, let us not attempt to discover.   God is from eternity; but we are of yesterday, and
know nothing.

God hardened Pharaoh's heart, as He declared from the beginning of
the history He would do; but did not put evil into his mind.   There
was no need for this, for he was previously wicked like all mankind.   God
has no occasion to put evil into the heart of any, in order to their destruction, for in consequence of the curse of the broken law (from which God's
people alone are delivered), there is in no natural man anything good
towards God, Rom. viii. 7.   While He thus punished Pharaoh's wickedness no more than his iniquity deserved, God, in doing so, displayed to
His people Israel their security under His protection.

system, from which the doctrine of predestination is excluded, or in which it is even
modified, is entirely a misnomer.

Some profess Calvinism, but affect to hold it in a more unexceptionable manner
than it is held in the system in general.   They seem to think that in the defence
of that system, Calvin was extravagant, and that he gave unnecessary offence by
exaggerated statements, and by language not warranted by the Scriptures.   Such
persons, it is presumed, are strangers to the writings of Calvin.   Calvin himself is
remarkable for keeping on Scripture ground, and avoiding anything that may justly
be termed extravagant.   No writer has ever indulged less in metaphysical speculation
on the deep things of God than this writer.   To support his system, it was necessary
only to exhibit Scripture testimony; and he seems quite contented to rest the matter
on this foundation.

What is called moderate Calvinism is in reality refined Arminianism.   It is impossible to modify the former without sliding into the latter.   If the doctrine of
God's sovereignty and of unconditional election be denied, regeneration and redemption must undergo a corresponding modification, and all the doctrines of grace will
be more or less affected.   While it is admitted that many of the people of God,
through imperfect views of Divine truth, falter on the subject of election, it is a truth
essential to the plan of salvation, and a truth most explicitly revealed.   No truth in
the Scriptures is more easily defended.   The reason why many find it difficult to defend this doctrine is, that they suppose it necessary to account for it by human
wisdom, and to justify the conduct of God.   We have nothing to do with the grounds
of the Divine procedure, we have to do only with the Divine testimony, that testimony
which Mr. Tholuck so fearfully perverts.   There are many who in words fully admit
the doctrine of predestination, and at the same time neutralize it by dwelling exclusively upon God's being love, and laying the blame of the whole world not being
saved on the sloth of Christians.

Ver. 19.—*Thou wilt say then unto me, Why doth He yet find fault? For who hath resisted His will?*

Here the Apostle obviates a third objection or cavil. The first was, that God is unfaithful, verse 6. The second, that God is unjust, verse 14. This third is, that God is severe and cruel. If God thus shows mercy, or hardens according to His sovereign pleasure, why, then, it may be asked, does He yet find fault with transgressors? This is the only objection that can be made to what the Apostle was stating. *Thou wilt say, then, who hath resisted His will?* If God wills sin, and if He is all-powerful, must He not be the author of sin? Mr. Fry here remarks,—'The thought will frequently start in the mind of the inquirer: If Divine grace is bestowed on some, and withheld from others; especially if the sins and transgressions of men are so under the control of the Almighty, that they but serve His purposes, how is it that such blame and censure attaches to the sinner, and that such dreadful judgments are denounced against him? If our unrighteousness commend the righteousness of God, what shall we say then, is God unrighteous who taketh vengeance? This, it will be perceived, is no other than the difficulty so generally felt in attempting to reconcile the responsibility of man as a moral agent, with a pre-ordination of all events, after the determinate counsel and foreknowledge of God. This pre-ordination the Apostle had asserted and proved from the Scriptures. From the Scriptures, at the same time, is evinced the complete responsibility of man as a moral agent:—God's finding fault; His remonstrances with transgressors; the declaration of their amenableness to a just judgment, the manner in which the Gospel addresses them, and bewails their hardness and their impenetrable heart, unquestionably establishes this point. The proud wisdom of rebellious man, indeed, almost dares to charge the oracles of God with inconsistency on this head; or, what is nearly as bad, takes upon itself either to explain away or to invalidate one part of the Scripture truth in order to establish the other, and, in apologising for Him before His creatures, to make God consistent with Himself! Such is the wicked presumption of man; such, we may lament to add, is the officious folly of some who mean to be the advocates of revelation; and the weak and imprudent defence of a friend is as dishonourable often as the open accusation of an enemy.'

The objection stated in the verse before us is in substance the same as is urged to this day, and it never can be put more strongly than here by the Apostle. What, then, does he answer? This we learn in the subsequent verses, in which he charges upon those who prefer it, their great impiety in presuming to arraign the ways of God, and to take up an argument against their Maker.

Ver. 20.—*Nay but, O man, who art thou that repliest against God? Shall the thing formed say to Him that formed it, Why hast thou made me thus?*

To the preceding objection, the Apostle, in this and the two following verses, gives three distinct answers. His first answer in this verse, similar to Isa. xlv. 9, is directed against the proud reasonings of man, who, though he be born like a wild ass's colt, and being of yesterday, knows nothing, Job xi. 12, presumes to scan the deep things of God,

and to find fault with the plan of His government and providence, into
which angels desire to look, while they find it incomprehensible. We
are here taught that it is perfectly sufficient to silence all objections, to
prove that anything is the will of God. No man, after this is done, has
a right to hesitate or to doubt. The rectitude of God's will is not to be
questioned. What men have to do is to learn what God says, and then
to receive it as unquestionably true and right. *Nay but, O man, who
art thou?*—And what is man that he should take upon him to object to
anything that God says? The reason and discernment between right
and wrong which he possesses is the gift of God; it must, then, be the
greatest abuse of these faculties to employ them to question the conduct
of Him who gave them. The question of the Apostle imports that it is
a thing most preposterous for such a creature as man to question the
procedure of God.

*Shall the thing formed say to Him that formed it, Why hast Thou formed
me thus?*—Can anything be more presumptuous than for the creature to
pretend to greater wisdom than the Creator? Any wisdom the creature
possesses must have been received from the Creator; and if the Creator
has the power of forming rational beings, must He not Himself be infinite
in wisdom? And does it not insult the Creator to pretend to find imperfection in His proceedings? Why, as Thou art all-powerful, hast
Thou formed me in such a manner that I am capable of sin and misery?
The rebellious heart of man is never satisfied with the Apostle's answer,
and still the question is, Why did He make men to be condemned? Let
the Lord's people be satisfied with the Apostle's answer, and let it be
sufficient for them to know that God has willed both the salvation of
the elect, and the destruction of the wicked, although they are not able
to fathom the depths of the ways of God. The Apostle tells us the fact,
and shows us that it must be received on God's testimony, and not on
our ability to justify it. That God does all things right there is no
question, but the grounds of His conduct He does not now explain to
His people. Much less is it to be supposed that He would justify His
conduct by explaining the grounds of it to His enemies. No man has a
right to bring God to trial. What He tells us of Himself, or of ourselves,
let us receive as unquestionably right. ' Paul,' says Calvin, ' doth not
busily labour to excuse God with a lying defence. He would not have
neglected refuting the objection, that God reprobates or elects, according
to His own will, those whom He does not honour with His favour, or
love gratuitously, had he considered it to be false. The impious object,
that men are exempted from guilt if the will of God has the chief part
in the salvation of the elect, or destruction of the reprobate. Does Paul
deny it? Nay; his answer confirms this truth—that God determines to
do with mankind what He pleases, and that men rise up with unavailing
fury to contest it, since the Maker of the world assigns to His creatures,
by His own right, whatever lot He chooses. If we cannot declare a
reason why He vouchsafeth to grant mercy to them that are His, but
because it pleaseth Him, neither also shall we have any other cause in
rejecting of others than His own will; for when it is said that God
hardeneth or showeth mercy to whom He will, men are thereby warned

to seek no cause elsewhere than in His own will.' 'Mere human reason,' says Luther to Erasmus, 'can never comprehend how God is good and merciful; and therefore you make to yourself a god of your own fancy, who hardens nobody, condemns nobody, pities everybody. You cannot comprehend how a just God can condemn those who are born in sin, and cannot help themselves, but must, by a necessity of their natural constitution, continue in sin, and remain children of wrath. The answer is, God is incomprehensible throughout, and therefore His justice, as well as His other attributes, must be incomprehensible. It is on this very ground that St. Paul exclaims, "O the depth of the riches of the knowledge of God! How unsearchable are His judgments, and His ways past finding out!" Now, His judgments would not be past finding out, if we could always perceive them to be just.'

Ver. 21.—*Hath not the potter power over the clay, of the same lump to make one vessel unto honour, and another unto dishonour?*

This is the Apostle's second answer to the objection contained in the 19th verse, in which, by another reference to Scripture, he asserts that the thing formed ought not to contend with Him that formed it, who has a right to dispose of it as He pleases. The words in the original, translated 'power' in this verse and the following, are different. The word here employed is variously applied as signifying authority, licence, liberty, right; but in its application to God there can be no question that it denotes *power justly exercised*. The mere power or ability of doing what God pleases, cannot be the meaning, for this is not the thing questioned. It is the justice of the procedure that is disputed, and it is consequently the justice of this exercise of power that must be asserted. With respect to all other beings, the licence, liberty, or right referred to, may be, as it is, derived from a superior; but in this sense it cannot refer to God. When, therefore, it is said here that God has 'power,' it must mean that He may, in the instance referred to, use His power in conformity to justice. The right has not a reference to a superior as conferring it, but a reference to His own character, to which all the actions of this sovereignty must be conformable.

Power, then, in this place, signifies right or power which is consistent with justice. It is this right or power according to justice that is here asserted. When the potter moulds the clay into what form he pleases, he does nothing contrary to justice; neither does God do injustice in the exercise of absolute power over His creatures. Out of the *same* original lump or mass He forms, in His holy sovereignty, one man unto honour, and another unto dishonour, without in any respect violating justice. Here it is implied that as there is no difference between the matter or lump out of which the potter forms diversity of vessels, so there is no difference in mankind, Rom. iii. 22; all men—both those who are elected, and those who are rejected, that are made vessels of mercy, or vessels of wrath—are alike by nature in the same condemnation in which God might in justice have left the whole, but out of which in His holy sovereignty He saves some, while He exercises His justice in pouring out His wrath.

That we are all in the hand of God, as the clay in the potter's hand, is humbling to the pride of man, yet nothing can be more self-evidently true. If so, God has the same right over us that a potter has over the clay of which he forms his vessels for his own purposes and interest. The same figure as is employed by the Prophet Isaiah, in declaring the right that God had over him and all the people of Israel, God likewise employs, Jer. xviii. 6 : ' O house of Israel, cannot I do with you as this potter? saith the Lord. Behold, as the clay is in the potter's hand, so are ye in Mine hand, O house of Israel.' A potter forms his vessels for himself, and not for his vessels. This determines the question with respect to God's end in the creation of man. Philosophers can discern no higher end in creating man than that of making him happy. But the chief end of the potter in moulding his vessels has a reference to himself, and God's chief end in making man is His own glory. This is plainly held forth in a multitude of passages in Scripture. Let man strive with his Maker as he will, still he is nothing but the clay in the hand of the potter. There cannot, indeed, be a question but that God will act justly with all His creatures; but the security for this is in His own character, and we can have no greater security against God's power than His own attributes. God will do His creatures no injustice ; but this is because justice is a part of His own character. Our security for being treated justly by God is in Himself.

One vessel unto honour, and another unto dishonour.—Some endeavour to explain this as implying that certain vessels may be made for a less honourable use, while they are still vessels for the Master's service. But it is not said that they are made for a less honourable use, but that they are made to *dishonour*, is the Apostle's assertion. It is true, indeed, that even vessels employed for dishonourable purposes are useful, and it is equally true that the destruction of the wicked will be for the glory of God. If any are condemned at all, and on any ground whatever, it is certain that it must be for the glory of God, else He would not appoint it to take place.

On the verse before us, and the preceding, it is to be observed that the Apostle does not say that his meaning in what he had previously affirmed had been mistaken, and that he had not said that it was agreeable to the will of God that the hardness of men's hearts should take place as it does; he implicitly grants this as truth, and that he had asserted it. And so far from palliating or softening down the expression to which the objection is made, if possible, he heightens and strengthens it. All mankind are here represented as originally lying in the same lump or mass; a great difference afterwards appears among them. Whence does this difference arise? The Apostle explicitly answers, It is God who makes the difference. As the potter makes one vessel as readily as he makes another, and each vessel takes its form from his hand, so God makes one man to honour and another to dishonour. And God's sovereign right to do this is here asserted ; and he who objects to this, the Apostle says, speaks against God. Shall the thing *formed* say to Him that *formed* it, Why hast Thou *made* me thus ? This representation is entirely consistent with all that the Scriptures elsewhere teach. In the fundamental doctrine of regeneration, and the new creation in Christ

Jesus, it is expressly inculcated, and is entirely coincident with the
question, 'Who maketh thee to differ from another?' 1 Cor. iv. 7.

Ver. 22.—*What if God, willing to show His wrath, and to make His power known,
endured with much long-suffering the vessels of wrath fitted to destruction ;*

In this and the following verse, in which the substance of the doctrine
of predestination is contained in a few words, the Apostle gives his third
and final answer to the objection stated in the 19th verse, subjoining the
reasons of God's different proceedings with one man and with another.
Hereby God manifests His great displeasure against sin, and His power
to take vengeance on sinners; He exercises great patience towards them,
seeing they are vessels of wrath fitted to destruction by their own wickedness, to which God shuts them up in His judgment. On the other hand,
what can be said against it, if He proceed in mercy with others, thereby
manifesting the riches of His glory, or His glorious grace, since they are
vessels of mercy, whom, by His sovereign election from eternity, and the
sanctification of His Spirit in time, He had afore prepared unto glory? The
sum of the Apostle's answer here is, that the grand object of God, both in
the election and the reprobation of men, is that which is paramount to all
things else in the creation of the universe, namely, His own glory. With
the assertion of this doctrine, however offensive to the natural man, which
must always appear to him foolishness, Paul winds up, in the last verse
of the eleventh chapter, the whole of his previous discussion in this
Epistle.

What if God, willing to show His wrath.—Here the purpose of God, in
enduring the wicked in this world, is expressly stated to arise from His
willingness to show His wrath against sin. We see, then, that the entrance
of sin into the world was necessary to manifest the Divine character in
His justice and hatred of sin. Had sin never entered into the creation
of God, His character would never have been fully developed. Let
wicked men hear what God says in this place. They flatter themselves
that in some way, through mercy, or because great severity, they suppose,
would not be just, they will finally escape. But God here declares by
the Apostle, that He has endured sin in the world for the very purpose
of glorifying Himself in its punishment. How, then, shall they escape?
And to make His power known.—The entrance of sin was also an occasion
of manifesting God's power and wisdom in overruling it for His glory.
The power or ability of God, according to the original word used here, is
different from the power (another word in the original) in the preceding
verse, as is strikingly seen in this place. The 21st verse asserts the
right of God to act in the manner supposed; this verse shows that His
doing so was to manifest His wrath against sin, and His power to make
even sin to glorify His name. Sin is in its own nature to God's dishonour. He has overruled it so that He has turned it to His glory.
This is the most wonderful display of power.

Endured with much long-suffering.—How often do men wonder that
God endures so much sin as appears in the world. Why does not God
immediately cut off transgressors? Why does He not make an end of
them at once? The answer is, He endures them for His own glory, and

in their comdemnation He will be glorified. To short-sighted mortals, it would appear preferable if God would cut off in childhood all whom He foresaw should continue in wickedness. But God endures them to old age, and to the utmost bounds of wickedness, for the glory of His own name. *Vessels of wrath,*—vessels 'full of the fury of the Lord,' Isa. li. 20. Here Paul calls the wicked vessels, in allusion to the figure which he had just before used. *Fitted to destruction.*—They are vessels, indeed, but they are vessels of wrath, and by their sins they are fitted for destruction ; and it is in the counsel of Jehovah that this shall be so.

Ver. 23.—*And that He might make known the riches of His glory on the vessels of mercy, which He had afore prepared unto glory.*

In the preceding verse, Paul had declared that God exercised much long-suffering towards *the vessels of wrath*—that part of Israel which were not of Israel ;[1] and here he shows that it was the will of God to make known the riches of His glory on the vessels of mercy whom He had afore prepared unto glory. In men's rejection of the salvation of Christ, the exceeding sinfulness of sin is manifested ; and we learn that no external means, in truth, nothing short of almighty power, could save a guilty and lost creature. Those, therefore, who are called and saved are saved by a new creation ; not effected by a word, as the old creation was, but by the power and calling of the Holy Spirit through the incarnation and death of the Son of God for the sins of His people, and His resurrection for their justification, made known in the everlasting Gospel.

In this verse it is implied that the awful ruin of the wicked is necessary for the full display of the riches of Divine mercy in saving the elect. Both the righteous and the wicked are by nature equally exposed to wrath ; and the deliverance of the elect from that situation to be made heirs of glory, wonderfully illustrates the infinitude of mercy. The salvation of the elect is mercy, pure mercy ; and it is wonderful mercy, when we consider what was the doom they deserved, and would have experienced, had they not been delivered by God through Jesus Christ. These vessels of mercy were previously prepared for their happy lot by God Himself. *Which He had afore prepared unto glory.*— In the preceding verse it is said that the vessels of wrath are *fitted* for destruction, and in this verse, that the vessels of mercy are *prepared* unto glory. The wicked are fitted for destruction by their sins, and the elect prepared before by God unto glory. No particular stress is to be laid on the word *fitted,* as if it could not apply to the righteous, for they also are fitted for glory. It is usual to say that the wicked were fitted by Satan and their own folly for destruction. No doubt Satan is concerned in it, but as no agent is asserted, it is not necessary to determine this. They also may be said to fit themselves ; yet it appears that it is not the agent, but the means that the Apostle has in view. It is their sins

---

[1] The whole tenor and purport of this chapter, and every declaration it contains, prove how greatly they err who interpret the expression, *Esau have I hated,* as signifying that he was only less loved than Jacob. This altogether neutralizes the purpose for which the quotation is made, and leaves it without any meaning or object whatever ; while it proves that they who thus explain it entirely misunderstand the whole scope of the Apostle's reasoning throughout the chapter.

which fit them for destruction.   On the other hand, the elect are *afore prepared* unto glory.   This cannot be by themselves, but must be by God as the agent.   This is expressly stated: ' Whom He hath prepared.' The elect are not only afore prepared unto glory, but it is God who prepares them.

It is suggested, by what is said in this and the preceding verse, that God does not harden sinners or punish them for the sake of hardening or making them miserable, or because He has any delight or pleasure in their sin or punishment considered in themselves, and unconnected with the end to be answered by them, but He does this to answer a wise and important end.   This great end is the manifestation and display of His own perfections ; to show His wrath, and to make His power known, and to make known the riches of His glory.   That is, He does it for Himself —for His own glory.   It is also suggested that what God does in hardening sinners, and making them vessels unto dishonour, and enduring with much long-suffering those vessels of wrath fitted for destruction, is consistent with their being blameable for their hardness, and for every-thing which renders them dishonourable.   Consequently it is also consistent with His high displeasure at their conduct, and proves that He may justly destroy them for ever for their hardness and obstinacy in sin.   This is supposed and asserted in the words, otherwise sinners could not be vessels of wrath fitted to destruction.   To allege that these scriptures import no more than that God *permits* sin, and orders every-thing respecting the event, so that if God permits, it will certainly take place, does not obviate any difficulty which has been supposed here to present itself.   For this is still representing God as willing that sin should take place, or, on the whole, choosing that it should exist rather than not.

Many who admit the doctrine of predestination object to the use of the term reprobation, so often employed by the first Reformers, and the old and most esteemed Christian writers.   In its place they would sub-stitute the word rejection.   But that word does not always convey the full import of what is intended by the term reprobation ; and whether this term be used or not, all that is comprehended under it is strictly according to Scripture.   Reprobation includes two acts : the one is negative, which consists in what is called preterition, or the passing by of those who are not elected,—that is, leaving them in their natural state of alienation or enmity against God ; the other is positive, and is called condemnation,—the act of condemning on account of sin those who have been passed by.   That first act consists in God's simply withholding His grace, to which no man can have any claim.   For this, accordingly, the Scriptures give no reason but the sovereign pleasure of God, who has mercy on whom He will have mercy, and who might justly have left all men to perish in their sins.   In the second act, God considers man as guilty, and a child of wrath ; and as on this account He punishes him in time, so from all eternity He has ordained to punish him.   In electing sinners, then, or in passing them by, God acts as a sovereign dispensing or withholding His favours, which are His own, as to Him seemeth good. In condemning, He exercises His justice in the punishment of the guilty.

He may impart His grace to whomsoever He pleases, without any one having a right to find fault, since in regard to those whom He destines to salvation He has provided means to satisfy His justice. On the other hand, those who are guilty have no right to complain if He hath appointed them to wrath, 1 Thess. v. 9; 1 Pet. ii. 8; Jude 4; for God was under no obligation to exercise mercy towards sinners. Both these doctrines of election and reprobation are exemplified in the case of Jacob and Esau, in which there is nothing peculiar. Jacob was loved and chosen before he was born, and Esau before he was born was an object of hatred and reprobation. Under one or other of these descriptions, all who receive the above doctrines must be convinced that every individual of the human race is included. Whence comes it, then, that so many venture to set aside the obvious import of these words, '*Jacob have I loved, but Esau have I hated?*'

The term reprobation has been used, then, because it expresses the idea intended, which the term rejection does not; if any are offended at it, it is to be feared that the offence taken is not at the word, but at its import. Unless men reject the Bible, they must admit that all were condemned in Adam; and if they were justly condemned, there can be no injustice in leaving them in that state of condemnation, and punishing them as sinners. It is only from the sovereign good pleasure and love of God that any of the human race are saved. He had no such love to the fallen angels, and they all perished; nor has He such love to those of the human race that shall perish, for He says, 'Depart from Me, ye cursed, *I never knew you.*' Men had no more claim upon God for mercy than the angels. Whatever may be thought of these things at present, God informs us that there is a day coming when His righteous judgment shall be revealed. Then He will be clear when He speaketh, and just when He is judged. No one shall then feel that he has been treated unjustly. Happy they whose high imaginations are cast down by the proclamation of mercy in the Gospel, and who receive the kingdom as little children, becoming fools that they may be wise. The high imaginations of all will be cast down at last, but with very many it will be too late, except to make them feel their condemnation to be just.

In strict conformity with the truths contained in the above verses, it is said in the Westminster Confession of Faith, which contains so scriptural a summary of Christian doctrine:—'The almighty power, unsearchable wisdom, and infinite goodness of God, so far manifest themselves in His providence, that it extendeth itself even to the first fall, and all other sins of angels and men, and that not by a bare permission, but such as hath joined with it a most wise and powerful bounding, and otherwise ordering, and governing of them, in a manifold dispensation, to His own holy ends; yet so, as the sinfulness thereof proceedeth only from the creature, and not from God, who, being most holy and righteous, neither is nor can be the author or approver of sin.' 'The decrees of God are His eternal purpose, according to the counsel of His will, whereby, for His own glory, He hath fore-ordained whatsoever comes to pass. God executeth His decrees in the works of creation and providence. God's works of providence are, His most holy, wise, and powerful preserving and governing all His creatures and all their actions.' And again, ' God, the great Creator of all things, doth uphold, direct, dispose, and govern all creatures, actions, and things, from the greatest even to the least, by His most wise and holy providence, according to His infallible foreknowledge, and the free and immutable counsel of His own will, to the praise of the glory of His wisdom, power, justice, goodness, and mercy.' ' By the decree of God, for the manifestation of His glory, some men and angels are predestinated unto everlasting life, and others fore-ordained to everlasting death.' In these articles it is asserted that God fore-ordained, decreed, and willed the existence of all the evil which ' *comes to pass.*' It is also said that God brings His decrees or His will into effect by creation and His governing providence, by which, in the exercise of His wisdom and holiness, He powerfully governs His creatures, and superintends and directs, disposes and orders, all their actions.

According to the above truths, so well expressed in the Westminster Confession of Faith, to which so many profess to adhere as containing their creed, everything without exception, great and small, that has ever taken place, or shall ever take place in heaven, or on earth, or in hell, has from all eternity been ordained by God, and yet so that the accountableness of the creature is not in the smallest degree removed. This is declared in the clearest manner respecting the greatest sin that ever was committed, even the crucifying of the Lord of glory. It took place according to the express ordination of God, yet the wickedness of those by whom it was perpetrated is explicitly asserted. ' Truly the Son of man goeth, as it was determined; but woe unto that man by whom He is betrayed!' Luke xxii. 22. ' Him, being delivered by the determinate counsel and foreknowledge of God, ye have taken, and by wicked hands have crucified and slain.' ' Who by the mouth of Thy servant David hast said, Why did the heathen rage, and the people imagine vain things? The kings of the earth stood up, and the rulers were gathered together against the Lord, and against His Christ. For of a truth against Thy holy child Jesus, whom Thou hast anointed, both Herod and Pontius Pilate, with the Gentiles and the people of Israel, were gathered together, for to do whatsoever Thy hand and Thy counsel determined before to be done,' Acts ii. 23, iv. 25. The crucifixion, then, of the Messiah was ordained by God, ' according to the eternal purpose which He purposed in Christ Jesus our Lord,' Eph. iii. 11, and was carried into execution by the wickedness of men, while God was not the author or actor of the sin.'

Every objection that can be made against the ordination of God respecting any wicked act, lies equally against these last two declarations. The crucifixion of Christ was by the determinate counsel and foreknowledge of God. If, then, the doctrine be chargeable with the consequences which some attribute to it, the admission of it in one case is just as impossible as in every case. It makes no difference how many evil actions are ordained, if it be admitted that one was ordained. The ordination of that one event must have been without reproach to the

---

[1] Whoever wishes to see this matter fully examined and explained, may consult Edwards *On the Will*, London edition, 1790, pp. 354-368.

holiness of God, and this shows that the ordination of all others may be equally so.

Ver. 24.—*Even us, whom He hath called, not of the Jews only, but also of the Gentiles ?*

Hitherto the Apostle had been showing that the promise of God was never made to the carnal seed of Abraham. This argument he began, ver. 6, 7, and had continued it till he comes to these words, in which he plainly states who are the true seed of Abraham and the children of the promise, even the called of God of all nations. The natural and easy manner in which, after several exemplifications, Paul here in a direct manner reverts to the main purpose of his discussion, ought not to be overlooked. Here he shows who are those vessels of mercy to whom he referred in the preceding verse. They are not only Jews but also Gentiles, and none of either Jews or Gentiles but those who are called by the Spirit and word of God. After expressing his unfeigned sorrow for the rejection of the Messiah by his countrymen in general, Paul had intimated at the 6th verse, that, notwithstanding this, the word of God had not been altogether without effect among them. He had next declared the reason why this effect had not been produced on the whole of them, namely, that all who belonged to that nation were not the true Israel of God, nor because they were descended from Abraham were they all his spiritual seed. This he had proved by the declarations of God to Abraham, and also by His dealings in regard to him, and especially respecting Isaac. In Isaac's family God had in a remarkable manner typically intimated the same truth, and displayed His sovereignty in rejecting the elder of his sons, and choosing the younger. Paul had further proved that this was according to God's usual manner of proceeding, in showing mercy to some, and hardening others. God had, notwithstanding, endured with much long-suffering that great multitude of the people of Israel who proved themselves to be vessels of wrath fitted for destruction ; and, on the other hand, had displayed the abundance of His free grace in preparing vessels of mercy both among Jews and Gentiles. The word of God had thus been effectual by His sovereign disposal to some among the people of Israel, corresponding with the examples which Paul had produced from their history ; and in the exercise of the same sovereignty God had also prepared others among the Gentiles on whom He displayed His mercy. None of the Jews or Gentiles were vessels of mercy, except those whom He had effectually called to Himself. This verse incontestibly proves, contrary to the erroneous glosses of many, that the Apostle is here speaking of the election of individuals, and not of nations.

Ver. 25.—*As He saith also in Osee, I will call them My people, which were not My people ; and her beloved, which was not beloved.*

In the preceding verse, the Apostle had spoken of those who were called among the Jews and the Gentiles, whom God had prepared unto glory. In this verse and the following, he shows that the calling of the Gentiles was not an unforeseen event, but that it was expressly foretold by the Prophets. God, by the Prophet Hosea, ii. 23, alluding to the calling of the Gentiles by the Gospel, says, *I will say to them which were not My people, Thou art my people;* that is, the Lord, at the period alluded to, would call to the knowledge of Himself, as His people, persons who were formerly living in heathenism, not having even the name of the people of God. *And her beloved, that was not beloved.*—The Jewish nation was typically the spouse of God. The Lord had betrothed Israel. But when Christ should come, He was to betroth Gentiles also, and to call her beloved that had not been beloved. Paul therefore shows, by this quotation, that the calling of these Gentiles as vessels of mercy was according to the purpose of Him who worketh all things after the counsel of His own will—according to the eternal purpose which He purposed in Christ Jesus.

Ver. 26.—*And it shall come to pass, that in the place where it was said unto them, Ye are not My people; there shall they be called the children of the living God.*

Among the nations which formerly served idols, and of whom it was usually and truly said that they were not God's people, there will be those of whom it shall be said that they are the children of the living God, Hos. i. 10. They shall be the children of the living God, in opposition to the dead idols or gods of their own imagination, which they formerly worshipped. This proves that, in their former state, they were without God in the world, Eph. ii. 12, iv. 18; and consequently that the Scriptures hold out no hope for those Gentiles who are left uncalled by the Gospel. This awful truth, though so many are unwilling to receive it, is everywhere testified in the Scriptures. It is held forth in what is said of the empire of Satan, the god of this world; and also in the character everywhere given in Scripture of heathens, who are declared not to have liked to retain God in their knowledge, and to have been ' haters of God.' It is also held forth in all the passages that affirm the final doom of idolaters; as likewise in all that is taught respecting access to God by Him who is the Way, and the Truth, and the Life; for there is no other name given among men whereby we must be saved.[1] Men may devise schemes to extend the blessings of salvation to those who never heard of Christ, but they are opposed to the plain declarations of His word. How thankful, then, ought we to be that we have lived not in the days of our heathen fathers, when God suffered them to walk in their own ways, but in the times when the Gospel has visited the Gentiles! How thankful, above all, if we have been made indeed the children of the living God! The nations of Europe are in general called Christians; but it is only in name that the great body of them bear that title. God will not recognise any as His children who are not born again of His Spirit, and conformed to the image of His Son.

Ver. 27.—*Esaias also crieth concerning Israel, Though the number of the children of Israel be as the sand of the sea, a remnant shall be saved :*

Having spoken in the 24th verse of those whom God had called, both

---

[1] All the distinguished men among the heathens, without a single exception, conformed to the idolatry of their countrymen. It is asserted by many that we have nothing to do with the state of the heathens. But we have much to do with whatever is declared in the Scriptures, for ' all Scripture is given by inspiration of God, and is profitable for doctrine, for reproof, for correction, for instruction in righteousness, that the man of God may be perfect, thoroughly furnished unto all good works.'

among Jews and Gentiles, and having referred in the two preceding verses to what had been foretold of the Gentiles, the Apostle, in the verse before us and the two that follow, introduces the predictions relative to the Jews. He quotes the Prophet Isaiah, as loudly testifying the doctrine which he is declaring. Hosea testifies with respect to God's purpose of calling the Gentiles; and Isaiah, in the passage here quoted, x. 20–22, testifies of the rejection of the great body of the Jews, and of the election of a number among them comparatively small. The Israelites looked on themselves as being all the people of God, and on the Gentiles as shut out from this relation. The Prophet here shows that out of all those vast multitudes which composed their nation, only a remnant were to be among the number of the true Israel of God. Whatever fulfilment the prophecy had in the times of the Old Testament, this is its full and proper meaning, according to the Apostle.

At first sight, it might seem that the Prophet speaks only of the return of the Jews from the captivity of Babylon; but, in regard to this, two things must be remarked. One is, that all the great events that happened to the Jews were figures and types, representing beforehand the great work of redemption by Jesus Christ. Thus the deliverance of the Israelites from Egypt, their passage through the Red Sea, and through the wilderness, the passage of Jordan, and their entrance into Canaan, were representations of what was to take place under the Gospel, as is declared, 1 Cor. x. 11, 'Now all these things happened unto them for examples (types), and they are written for our admonition, upon whom the ends of the world are come.' Hence it follows that the deliverance from the captivity of Babylon, and consequently the predictions respecting it in Scripture, are typical of the future condition of the Church of Christ. This prophecy, then, has two meanings,—the first literal, the second mystical. The other thing to be remarked is, that in the work of God in regard to His Church, there being several gradations which follow each other, it often happens that the Prophets, who viewed from a distance those future events, join together many of them, as if they related only to one and the same thing,—which is a characteristic of the spirit of prophecy. The Prophet, then, in this place joins the temporal re-establishment of the Jews with the spiritual building up of the Church of Christ, although these two things are quite distinct and separate.

These words in this prophecy, ' They shall stay upon the Lord, the Holy One of Israel, in truth,' can only have their full accomplishment in believers in Jesus Christ. The same is the case respecting the words, ' The remnant shall return ; ' for this returning or conversion denotes much more than that of the return of the Jews from Babylon—even that glorious turning to God which takes place by the Gospel. And when the Prophet says, *Though Thy people Israel be as the sand of the sea, yet a remnant of them shall return*, it is clear that this is an allusion to the promise made to Abraham, that his posterity should be as the sand of the sea, and that he means to say that whatever confidence the Jews might place in that promise, taking it in a carnal and literal sense, yet that those who were saved would be a small remnant, whom God would take to Himself in abandoning all the rest to His avenging justice. As one event, then, in Scripture prophecy is often made to shadow forth and typify another, so the events of the Jewish history are made to illustrate the spiritual things of the kingdom of God. In this way the prophecies quoted in the New Testament from the Old are to be viewed, and not to be explained in a manner which ascribes to the Apostles of Christ that false and deceitful mode of quotation called accommodation, so disparaging to their character as stewards of the mysteries of God, and so degrading to the Holy Scriptures.

Ver. 28.—*For He will finish the work, and cut it short in righteousness; because a short work will the Lord make upon the earth.*

This refers to God's judgments poured out upon the Jews for rejecting the Messiah. They were then cut off manifestly from being His people. He cut short the work in righteous judgment. The destruction determined, denotes the ruin and desolation of the whole house of Israel, with the exception of a small remnant. It was to overflow in righteous judgment, which gives the idea of an inundation. But this not having place in the re-establishment of the Jews after the Babylonish captivity, must necessarily be understood of the times of the Gospel. It was then that the consumption decreed took place; for the whole house of Israel was rejected from the covenant of God, and consumed or dispersed by the fire of His vengeance by the Roman armies, with the exception of a small remnant. Formerly God had borne with them in their sins; but now, when they had heard the Gospel and rejected it, they were destroyed or carried away into captivity as with a flood. The Lord made a short work with them at the destruction of Jerusalem. This verse and the preceding confirm what is said in the 22d verse, that although God endures the wicked for a time, He determines to punish them at last with sudden and overwhelming destruction.

Ver. 29.—*And as Esaias said before, Except the Lord of Sabaoth had left us a seed,.we had been as Sodoma, and been made like unto Gomorrha.*

This, again, verifies another prediction of Isaiah, i. 9. It was no doubt fulfilled in the events of the Jewish history; but in its proper and full sense, it extended to the times of the Messiah, and predicted the small number of Jews who were left, and the purpose for which they were left. The Jews who escaped destruction at the overthrow of their city by the Romans, were spared merely as a ' seed' from whence was to spring all the multitudes who will yet arise to Jesus Christ out of the seed of Abraham. . Had it not been for this circumstance, not one individual at that time would have been left. They would have been all cut off as Sodom and Gomorrah. 'Except those days should be shortened, there should no flesh be saved; but for the elect's sake those days shall be shortened,' Matt. xxiv. 22. Instead of remnant, the word employed by the Prophet, the Apostle substitutes the term *seed*, from the Septuagint translation, which, though the expression is varied, has a similar meaning, implying that after the whole heap besides was consumed, the remainder was reserved for sowing with a view to a future crop.

By this quotation from Isaiah, the Apostle proves that the doctrine of the unconditional election of individuals to eternal life—that doctrine against which such objections are raised by many—far from being contrary to the ideas we ought to entertain of the goodness of God, is so entirely consistent with it, that except for this election, not one of the nation of Israel would have been saved. Thus the doctrine of election, very far from being in any degree harsh or cruel, as many who misunderstand it affirm, is, as we see here, a glorious demonstration of Divine goodness and love. Had it not been for this election, through which God had before prepared vessels of mercy unto glory, neither Jew nor Gentile would have escaped, but all would have remained vessels of wrath fitted to destruction. In the case of the angels who sinned there was no election, and the whole were cast down to hell. Had there been no election among men, the whole must in like manner have perished.

Ver. 30.—*What shall we say then ?   That the Gentiles, which followed not after righteousness, have attained to righteousness, even the righteousness which is of faith :*

What shall we say then?—What is the result of all this discussion ? The conclusion from the whole is, that those Gentiles who are called by God, of whom the Apostle had spoken in the 24th verse, who were not following righteousness, but were abandoned to every kind of wickedness, obtained true righteousness, even the righteousness which is of faith. This is an astonishing instance of mercy. Men who were ' haters of God,' and guilty of all abominations, as Paul had shown in the first chapter of this Epistle, were thus made partakers of that righteousness which is commensurate to all the demands of the law.

Ver. 31.—*But Israel, which followed after the law of righteousness, hath not attained to the law of righteousness.*

Whatever objection might be made to the doctrine the Apostle was here inculcating, a clear proof was offered in the case of the Gentiles which he had adduced, of the truth he had advanced and illustrated by the examples of Jacob and Esau, namely, that the purpose of God, according to election, is unchangeable, and that salvation is not of works, but of Him that calleth. And here was a wonderful instance of Divine sovereignty. The nation of Israel were following after righteousness, yet God, instead of giving it to them, bestowed it on those who were not even looking for it. How different is this from the ways of men ! How does the proud heart of the self-righteous legalist revolt at such a view of the Divine conduct ! Man's wisdom cannot endure that God should in this sovereign way bestow His favours. But this is God's way, and whoever will not submit to it, resists the will of God. Nay, whoever finds fault with it, attempts to dethrone the Almighty, and to undeify God. The whole plan of salvation is so ordered, ' that no flesh should glory in His presence, but that, according as it is written, he that glorieth, let him glory in the Lord,' 1 Cor. i. 31.

Ver. 32.—*Wherefore ? Because they sought it not by faith, but as it were by the works of the law : for they stumbled at that stumbling-stone ;*

The Apostle here asks why the people of Israel did not attain to the righteousness they were seeking. The word ' wherefore ' has no refer-

ence to election, or a supposed objection from it, as some understand.
The question is asked to excite more attention to the answer ; and the
answer is, because they sought it in a way in which it is not to be found.
The righteousness that answers the demands of the law, is the righteousness of God, which is received only by faith. The Jews, then, did not
attain to it, because they sought it not by faith, but as of works of law.
Some commentators lay stress on the phrase, ' as it were by the works of
the law,' according to our translation, assigning as its meaning, that the
Jews did not suppose they kept the law perfectly, but expected to make
up for their deficiencies in one respect by abounding in others.   But this
is not well founded.   The Jews sought righteousness ' as by works of
law ; ' that is, as if righteousness was to be obtained by doing the works
of the law.   By the works of the law they could not obtain it, unless
they perfectly obeyed the law.   To this they could never attain.   As,
therefore, they would not submit to Christ, who alone has fulfilled the
law, they failed in obtaining righteousness.

For they stumbled at that stumbling-stone.—That is, they stumbled at
Jesus Christ.   Instead of choosing Him as the elect, precious foundation-
stone, on which to rest their hope, they rejected Him altogether.   They
looked for a Messiah of a different character, and therefore they rejected
the Christ of God.   The Apostle thus charges it upon the Jews as their
own fault that they did not attain to righteousness.   They mistook the
character of that law under which they were placed, by which, according
to the testimony of their own Prophets, no man could be justified; and
also the character of the Messiah who was promised, and so perverted
that law, and rejected Him by whom alone they could be saved.   They
thus verified the words of the Apostle,—' The natural man receiveth not
the things of the Spirit of God; for they are foolishness unto him;
neither can he know them, because they are spiritually discerned.'   Of
this Paul exhibits himself as having been an example.   In the seventh
chapter of this Epistle, he shows how entirely he once mistook the extent
of the law ; and in the beginning of the chapter before us, that he once
made it his boast that he was opposed to Christ as the Messiah.

Ver. 33.—*As it is written, Behold, I lay in Zion a stumbling-stone and rock of
offence ; and whosoever believeth on Him shall not be ashamed.*

As it is written.—The Apostle here confirms what he had just said concerning the stone of stumbling, by quoting from two places of Scripture,
Isa. viii. 14, xxviii. 16.   The stumbling, then, of the Jews at Christ,
the rock of offence, was predicted by the Prophets.   It should not, therefore, appear strange to those who lived in the times when it was accomplished.

A stumbling-stone and rock of offence.—This language of the Prophet,
applied by the Apostle to our Lord Jesus Christ, ought to be particularly
observed,—' Sanctify the Lord of Hosts Himself; and let Him be your
fear, and let Him be your dread.   And He shall be for a sanctuary ; but
for a stone of stumbling, and for a rock of offence, to both the houses of
Israel.'   As here the Prophet speaks directly of God, and the Apostle
applies what he says to Jesus Christ, it is a conclusive proof that Jesus

Christ is God, and that He is declared to be so both in the Old Testament and the New. The designations of a stone, and a rock, are given to Jesus Christ, both presenting the idea that the great work of redemption rests solely on Him. He is its author, the foundation on which it rests, the centre in which all its lines meet, and their origin from which they proceed. He is to that work what the foundation-stone and the rock on which it is erected are to the building, sustaining it, and imparting to it form and stability. In another sense, He is a stone of stumbling, occasioning His rejection by those who, not believing in Him, are cut off from communion with God.

Behold, I lay in Zion.—This stone, or rock—this 'sure foundation'—is laid by God, according to the Apostle's reference, Isa. xxviii. 16, 'Therefore, thus saith the Lord God, Behold, I lay in Zion for a foundation a stone, a tried stone, a precious corner-stone, a sure foundation.' This stone was laid in Zion, the Church of God. It was laid by God Himself. That it was 'a sure foundation,' which could not fail, is evident from all the promises of God concerning the Messiah, of upholding Him as His elect, and ensuring to Him success, dominion, and glory, in His character of Mediator, Isa. xlii. 1–8, xlix. 7–9.

All the promises to the Church of old, of the Messiah as a future Saviour, from the declaration made to our first parents in paradise, to the last prediction concerning Him delivered by the Prophet Malachi, demonstrate the impossibility that Christ, the foundation which God has laid, should fail. These promises were often renewed with great solemnity, and confirmed by the oath of God, as in Gen. xxii. 16–18. And in Ps. lxxxix. 3, 4, it is said, 'I have made a covenant with My chosen, I have sworn unto David My servant, thy seed will I establish for ever, and build up thy throne to all generations.' Nothing is more abundantly set forth in Scripture as sure and irreversible than this promise and oath to David. The Scriptures expressly speak of it as utterly impossible that the everlasting dominion of the Messiah should fail. 'In those days, and at that time, I will cause the Branch of Righteousness to grow up unto David, for thus saith the Lord, David shall never want a man to sit upon the throne of the house of Jacob.' 'If ye can break My covenant of the day, and My covenant of the night, and that there should not be day and night in their season ; then may also My covenant be broken with David My servant, that he should not have a son to reign upon his throne,' Jer. xxxiii. 15–21. David securely rested on this covenant concerning the future glorious work and kingdom of the Messiah, as all his salvation, and all his desire, and comforted himself that it was an everlasting covenant, ordered in all things and sure.

As being that foundation laid by Himself, which therefore could not fail, God proceeded to save sinners in virtue of the work of the Messiah before He appeared, as if it had been already accomplished. On this stone and rock the saints of old rested, and built their comfort. Abraham saw Christ's day and rejoiced, and all the others died in the faith of His advent. What a view does this give of the faithfulness of God, and the truth of the Scriptures; and what an inducement to rely securely upon the Rock of Ages! Its solidity is assured to us by Him whose voice shakes the heavens and the earth — by the revelation of the eternal purpose of God, which He purposed in Christ Jesus our Lord, Eph. iii. 11.

Rock of offence.—While the Messiah was indeed the sure foundation which God had laid, He was, notwithstanding, as it was written, rejected by the great body of the Jewish nation. Had they understood the language of their own Scriptures, they would have seen that, instead of receiving their Messiah when He came, the Prophets had declared that they would stumble at the lowliness of His appearance, and generally reject His claims.

And whosoever believeth on Him shall not be ashamed.—But they did not all reject Him. Some of them, referred to in verse 24th, who were called of God, acknowledged Jesus as the Messiah, sent of God, and were comforted and saved by Him. They were not ashamed to own Him before the unbelieving part of their brethren, and they shall not be put to shame before Him at His second coming. It might be supposed that the followers of the Messiah would be honoured in every country; on the contrary, they are hated and held in contempt. But when all other refuges fail, when Christ comes to judge the world, they shall not be ashamed.

A free salvation becomes an offence to men on account of their pride. They cannot bear the idea of being indebted for it to sovereign grace, which implies that in themselves they are guilty and ruined by sin. They desire to do something, were it ever so little, to merit salvation, at least in part. Salvation by a crucified Saviour was in one way opposed to the pride of the Jews, and in another to that of the Greeks. The Jews expected a mighty conqueror, who should deliver them from a foreign yoke, and render them so powerful as to triumph over all the other nations of the earth ; and in order to reconcile with these ideas what the Scriptures said of His humiliation, some among them supposed that there would be two Messiahs. The Greeks expected, in a revelation from heaven, something accordant with the systems of their vain philosophy, which might exalt their false notions of the dignity of man, and enlarge their boasted powers of understanding. All the unconverted reason in the same way. Those among them who call themselves Christians suppose that, not being perfect, they have need of Christ as a Saviour to compensate for their deficiencies, and to give weight to their good works. They do not believe that they obey the law perfectly, but suppose that what is wanting will be supplied by Jesus Christ. Thus, except a man be born again, he cannot see the kingdom of God. The doctrine of the cross is, in one way or other, misunderstood by him, and Jesus Christ is a stone of stumbling.

Many, by their forced criticisms, have in various ways perverted the meaning of this chapter. Among their other misrepresentations, they affirm that the Apostle does not speak of individual election to eternal life, but of the national election of the Jews. On the contrary, it is evident that in regard to the Jews he refers to their national rejection. The rejection of the Jewish nation, excepting a small remnant, according to the election of grace, which is again plainly declared in the beginning of the eleventh chapter, is the important subject which the Apostle illustrates by the examples and predictions he refers to, and the reasonings with which he follows them up.

The fact of a remnant of Israel being reserved by God for Himself, while the great body of the nation was abandoned to merited punishment, demonstrates that the election here spoken of is individual and not national. The Prophets everywhere speak of this small remnant chosen by God to display His mercy and goodness. ' I will also leave in the midst of thee an afflicted and poor people, and they shall trust in the name of the Lord. The remnant of Israel shall not do iniquity, nor speak lies ; neither shall a deceitful tongue be found in their mouth; for they shall feed and lie down, and none shall make them afraid,' Zeph. iii. 13.

There is nothing which more clearly manifests the natural opposition of the mind of man to the ways of God, than the rooted aversion naturally entertained to the obvious view of the doctrine of the sovereignty of God held forth in this ninth chapter of the Epistle to the Romans. Self-righteous people, as is not to be wondered at, hold this doctrine in the utmost abhorrence ; and many even of those, who are in some measure taught of God to value the great salvation, are reluctant to come to the serious study of this part of His word. Even when they are not able plausibly to pervert it, and when their conscience will not allow them directly to oppose it, with the Pharisees, they say that they do not know what to make of this chapter. But why are they at a loss on this subject? What is the difficulty which they find here ? If it be ' hard to be understood,' does this arise from anything but the innate aversion of the mind to its humbling truths ? Can anything be more palpably obvious than the meaning of the Apostle ? Is there any chapter in the Bible more plain in its grammatical meaning ? It is not in this that they find a difficulty. Their great difficulty is, that it is too obvious in its import to be perverted. Their conscience will not allow them to do violence to its language, and their own wisdom will not suffer them to submit to its dictation. Here is the solution of their difficulties. But ought not believers to renounce their own wisdom, and look up to God, in the spirit of him who said, ' Speak, Lord, for Thy servant heareth ? '

Men may attempt to explain away the example referred to in this chapter, of God's hardening Pharaoh's heart. But still the truth remains, that for the very purpose of showing His power and proclaiming His name and sovereignty, God raised him up and hardened his heart. Many will not receive this, and resort to every means they can devise to neutralize or controvert it; but God has testified it, and the Apostle illustrates it by a striking figure. God makes one vessel to honour, and another to dishonour, with the same uncontrolled right as the potter has power over the clay, and out of the same lump he makes one vessel for the noblest purpose, and another for the basest uses. Where is sovereignty, if it is not here ? Could words express it if these words do not express it ? Why, then, will men vainly struggle in so unequal a contest ? Can they hope to succeed against God ? If this doctrine be really declared in this chapter, of what avail will all their forced explanations be to deliver any of the enemies of God ? ' God is greater than man, why dost thou strive

against Him ? for He giveth not account of any of His matters.' There
are, however, too many, even of the disciples of Christ, who are disposed
to explain away the sovereignty of God, and to give a view of our fall in
Adam which considerably mitigates the extent of our ruin, and the magnitude of our guilt.   The statements contained in this chapter are to such
full of clouds and darkness.   While they cannot altogether deny the
truths it contains, they profess their inability to receive them in their
plain and obvious meaning.

'This doctrine of the sovereignty of God,' says Dr. Thomson, 'we
believe to be one of the greatest stumbling-blocks in the Gospel to the
advocates of universal redemption.   They lay down a scheme of Divine
love which they have framed only in part from the materials furnished by
the Bible, and have otherwise fashioned according to the dictates of their
own wisdom, and the sensibilities of their own hearts.   And as it is inconsistent with this, so they cannot endure to consider the Supreme Being as
communicating His benefits to men, or withholding them, according to
the pleasure and counsel of His own will.   God has said, 'I will have
mercy, and I will have compassion on whom I will have compassion, and
whom I will I harden.'   But they have settled in their own minds that
God must have compassion and mercy upon all, and that He must harden
none.   And in rebuke of this arrogance, we have only to say, Nay but,
who art thou that repliest against God ?   Shall the thing formed say to
Him that formed it, Why hast Thou made me thus ? '

The doctrine of the sovereignty of God is derogatory to the pride of
man ; it lays all his high notions of independence in the dust, and reduces
him, when acknowledged, to a sense of his utter helplessness and misery.
Happy, nevertheless, are they who have learned this lesson, for it is one
which flesh and blood cannot teach, but only our Father which is in
heaven.   In the light of this chapter these see themselves as lying
entirely in the hand of God, having nothing that distinguishes them from
others, but His sovereign will and favour in their election.   It is this
view of their situation that brings down every high imagination, and
levels to the dust every high thought.   Here Divine sovereignty reigns
in its most awful character; and nothing else, when it is fully acquiesced
in, is so much calculated to tranquillize the mind of man, and to bring it
into its proper position in relation to God.   How many bitter reflections
and how many vain regrets would be saved, were the Christian at all
times habitually and practically to recognise the sovereignty of the
Divine Disposer in all the events which happen in the world!

Whatever difficulties are found in the doctrine of the sovereignty of
God, and in the truth that He ordains for His own glory whatever comes
to pass, yet this, it is clear, is the doctrine of Scripture from beginning to
end.   Every part of it represents God as ordering and directing all
events ; and without this, and were anything left to depend or be regulated by the will of His creatures, He would cease to be the supreme
Ruler.   Many things might occur which He greatly desired might never
have taken place—an idea altogether incompatible with that which we
are taught in His word to form of the almighty Ruler of the universe.
If we lose sight of sovereignty, we lose sight of God.

CHAPTER 10
ROMANS 10:1 – 21

PAUL was fully aware that the doctrine of the sovereignty of God in the rejection of the Jews and the preaching of salvation to the Gentiles, would greatly offend his countrymen. He accordingly begins this chapter with an acknowledgment of their sincerity as actuated by a zeal of God; but before prosecuting the subject of God's sovereignty further, he more particularly reours to their unbelief, to which in the preceding chapter he had already alluded. This leads him to remark the contrast between the righteousness of the law and the righteousness of faith. He next insists on the free invitations of the Gospel, which proclaims salvation to all of every nation who believe, and from this takes occasion to point out the necessity of preaching it to the Gentiles. The Gentiles, as he had before proved, were among the children of the promise made to Abraham, and it was only by means of the Gospel that they could be brought to the knowledge of Christ, through which alone the promise to them could be fulfilled. This duty, notwithstanding the objections of the Jews, he therefore urges, and enforces it by referring to the Scriptures, while he answers the objection, that the Gospel had not been generally received. In the last place, he proves, by the testimony of the Prophets, that the rejection of Israel and the ingathering of the Gentiles had been long before predicted, and concludes the chapter by showing that the Jews had both heard and rejected the gracious and long-continued invitations to reconciliation with God. In the whole of this chapter, Paul treats in a practical way what in the preceding one he had chiefly referred to the sovereignty of God, to which he afterwards reverts.

We here see a beautiful example in Paul of the meekness and gentleness of the Lord Jesus Christ, who prayed for His murderers. The Jews considered Paul as one of their greatest enemies. They had persecuted him from city to city, again and again they had attempted his life, and had succeeded in depriving him of his liberty, yet his affection for them was not diminished. He prayed for them, he accommodated himself to their prejudices as far as his obedience to God permitted, and thus he laboured by all means to save some. He here assures those to whom he writes of his cordial good will towards Israel, and of his prayers to God that they might be saved.

Ver. 1.—*Brethren, my heart's desire and prayer to God for Israel is, that they might be saved.*

Brethren.—Those here addressed are the brethren in Christ to whom Paul wrote, and not the Jews in general, who were his brethren in the flesh. There is no doubt but by apostrophe he might address the unbelieving Jews; but there is nothing like an apostrophe here, nor is there any need of such a supposition. Whoever was addressed, the sentiment would be equally well understood by the unbelieving Jews who should read or hear the Epistle.

My heart's desire and prayer to God.—It is of great importance to remove prejudices as far as possible, and to show good will to those whom we wish to benefit by the publication of Divine truth. We see here the love of a Christian to his bitterest enemies. Paul was abused, reviled, and persecuted by his countrymen, yet he not only forgave them, but constantly prayed for their conversion. Unbelievers often accuse Christians, though very falsely, as haters of mankind, because they faithfully declare that there is no salvation but through faith in Christ.

Here we should especially remark, that while the salvation of his countrymen was the desire of Paul's heart, and while he was endeavouring in every way possible to call their attention to the Gospel, he did not neglect to offer up prayer for them to God. Other means, as we have opportunity, should not be left untried; but prayer is at all times in our power, and in this we should ever persevere. When we are shut out from access to man, we have always access to God, and with Him is the residue of the Spirit. In this duty, we learn from the Epistles that Paul was ever much engaged for his brethren in Christ, and here we see that he did not neglect it in behalf of those by whom he was hated and persecuted. He thus obeyed the injunctions, and imitated the example, of our blessed Lord. In this verse, too, standing in connection with what immediately precedes it, we learn that Paul's faithful annunciation of these doctrines, which by so many are most erroneously considered as harsh towards men, and unfavourable to the character of God, so far from being opposed to feelings of the warmest affection for others, is closely and intimately conjoined with them.

We should never cease to pray for, and to use all proper means for the conversion of, those who either oppose the Gospel with violence, or from some preconceived opinion. Secret things belong to God, and none can tell whether or not they are among the number of the elect. No one among the Jews was more opposed to the Gospel than Paul himself had been; and every Christian who knows his own heart, and who recollects the state of his mind before his conversion, should consider the repugnance he once felt to the doctrine of grace. We ought not, indeed, to treat those as Christians who do not appear to be such. This would be directly opposed to the dictates of charity, and would tend to lull them into a false security. But assuredly none can have such powerful inducements to exercise patience towards any who reject the Gospel, as they who know who it is that has made them to differ from others, and that by the grace of God they are what they are. These considerations have a direct tendency to make them humble and gentle. Those who are elected shall indeed be finally saved, but this will take place through the means which God has appointed. It is on this ground that Paul says, 'Therefore I endure all things for the elect's sake, that they may also obtain the salvation which is in Christ Jesus with eternal glory.'

Ver. 2.—*For I bear them record, that they have a zeal of God, but not according to knowledge.*

Paul acknowledged that the Jews had a zeal of God, and so far he approved of them, and was on that account the more interested in their behalf. This had formerly been the case with himself, Acts xxvi. 9; Gal. i. 14. Their zeal, however, and the sincerity of their attachment to their system, was no excuse for their unbelief. The Apostle had sorrow for their condemnation, not hope of their salvation on account of their sincerity and zeal. This is an important lesson to thousands who profess Christianity. How often is it said that if a man be sincere in his belief, his creed is of no great importance. His salvation, it is supposed, is not endangered by his ignorance or error. How far on this head does the Apostle Paul differ from those who thus judge, while his love to mankind cannot be doubted. His love to his countrymen appears to have exceeded anything to which the persons alluded to can pretend. Yet he bewails the Jews as under condemnation on account of their ignorance. We see here that men may attend to religion, and be much occupied on the subject, without being acceptable to God; and that sincerity in error is neither a means of salvation nor an excuse for any man. Nothing but the natural alienation of their minds from God prevents those who possess the Scriptures from understanding the way of salvation.

Ver. 3.—*For they, being ignorant of God's righteousness, and going about to establish their own righteousness, have not submitted themselves unto the righteousness of God.*

The ground of rejection of the Gospel by the Jews was their ignorance of God's righteousness. Had they understood this, they would have ceased to go about to establish their own righteousness; but not understanding that righteousness which God has provided in His Son, they rejected the salvation of the Gospel. Mr. Stuart translates the word rendered righteousness throughout this passage by the word *justification*, which is warranted by no authority. Dr. Macknight, who, like Mr. Stuart, denies the imputation of Christ's righteousness, says that the righteousness here spoken of is 'the righteousness which God appointed at the fall, as the righteousness of sinners,' which he explains elsewhere to mean faith, saying that God 'hath declared that He will accept and reward it as righteousness.' Dr. Campbell of Aberdeen, as has been formerly noticed, explains the righteousness here spoken of as that 'purer scheme of morality which was truly of God,' opposed to the 'system of morality or righteousness fabricated by the Jews.' In this manner do these writers, though each in a different way, make void all that is said throughout this Epistle and elsewhere in the Scriptures on that most important expression, 'the righteousness of God,' through the revelation of which the Apostle declares that the Gospel '*is the power of God unto salvation*,' Rom. i. 17.

The righteousness of God.—That is, the righteousness provided by God and revealed in the Gospel, which is received by faith, by which men are saved; and he who does not submit to this righteousness, and humbly receive it, but supposes that he can do something to give him a right to obtain or to merit it, or who attempts to add to it anything of his own, or to substitute in its place his own obedience, more or less, is equally ignorant of the corruption of his own heart, of the holiness of God, and of the perfection of the obedience which the law requires. In this verse the fatal error is clearly expressed of those who expect to be saved by any works of their own, even when, like the Pharisee who prayed in the temple, they ascribe to God all that they suppose to be good in them.

Ver. 4.—*For Christ is the end of the law for righteousness to every one that believeth.*

The Apostle here declares what he means by the righteousness of God, to which the Jews would not submit, namely, the fulfilment, object, and consummation of the law by our Lord Jesus Christ. *The end of the law.* —What the end of the law is, Paul shows, Rom. vii. 10, when he says, *It was ordained to life*, namely, that the man who doeth all that it commands, should live by it. And what is it that, in the present state of human nature, the law cannot do? It cannot justify, and so give life, because it has been broken. How then did God act? He sent His Son in the likeness of sinful flesh, and condemned sin in the flesh. And why has He done this? The answer is given, ch. viii. 4, 'that the righteousness of the law might be fulfilled in us' who are in Him. Thus it is, that Christ is the end of the law for righteousness to every one that believeth. By Him is accomplished for all such the whole purpose and object of the law—all its demands being fulfilled, and the end for which it was given attained. Christ thus redeems His people from its curse, and procures for them the blessing of life, which, under the righteous government of God, He confers on all His creatures who are conformed to His holy law. The fallen angels possessed life while they retained their obedience, and Adam, while he held fast His integrity; but this was not the full end of the law, for they apostatized. In them, therefore, the law fell short of attaining its end. But the righteousness imputed to those who believe in Christ is 'everlasting righteousness,' Dan. ix. 24, and therefore to them belongs eternal life. Their life is comprised in His life, and He is 'that eternal life;' and 'when He who is their life shall appear, they shall appear with Him in glory.' Accordingly, Jesus says, 'I am come that they might have life, and that they might have it more abundantly.'

'I have *finished*,' said our blessed Lord in His intercessory prayer to His Father, 'the work which Thou gavest Me to do;' and on the cross, just before He expired, He said, It is *finished.* In each of these passages The word rendered finished is the same as that which is here translated *end*, signifying accomplished, consummated, or perfected. In the Epistle to the Hebrews, vi. 1, the same original word is rendered 'perfection.' The Apostle there says, 'Let us go on to perfection'—to the end or finishing, meaning the consummation or completion of all that the law required, which he shows was found in the sacrifice and work of Jesus Christ. This *perfection*—this end—was not attained by the Levitical priesthood; for if '*perfection* were by the Levitical priesthood, what further need was there that another Priest should rise after the order of Melchizedek, and not be called after the order of Aaron?' Heb. vii. 11. Nor was it attained by the legal dispensation, which 'made nothing *perfect*,' ver. 19, —brought nothing to its *end* or consummation. This was found only in Christ, 'for by one offering He hath *perfected* for ever (still the same word in the original in all these places) them that are sanctified,' Heb. x. 14.

To prove that Christ was the *perfection* or the *end* of the law, is the great object of the Epistle to the Hebrews, which furnishes a complete commentary on the passage before us. That Epistle opens with declaring

Jesus Christ to be the *Son of God.* To prove and to establish this grand truth, as the foundation of all that the Apostle was afterwards to advance, was essential to his purpose. For by no one in the whole universe, excepting by Him who is infinite, could the eternal or everlasting righteousness predicted by Daniel have been brought in. It was, then, this important truth, that Christ is the end of the law for righteousness to every one that believeth, which Paul labours in that Epistle to impress on the minds of the Jewish converts, for the confirmation of their faith; and it was the ignorance of this same important truth in the great body of the nation, which in the chapter before us he laments.

The unbelieving Jews vainly went about to establish their own righteousness by their obedience to the law, instead of viewing it as a schoolmaster to lead them unto, or until, the coming of Christ, by whom alone it could be and was fulfilled, Matt. v. 18. This verifies what the Apostle says, 2 Cor. iii. 13, that 'the children of Israel could not look stedfastly to the *end*' (the same word as in the verse before us) 'of that which is abolished.' Christ, then, as is declared in this verse, is the end of the law *for righteousness to every one that believeth.* For the moment that a man believes in Him, the end of the law is attained in that man; that is, it is fulfilled in him, and he is in possession of that righteousness which the law requires, or ever can require, and consequently he *hath eternal life,* John vi. 54, to which the law was ordained, Rom. vii. 10. Christ, then, by His obedience has fulfilled the law of God in every form in which men have been under it, that His obedience or righteousness might be imputed as their righteousness to all who believe, ' He hath made Him to be sin for us, who knew no sin, that we might be made the righteousness of God in Him,' 2 Cor. v. 21.[1] 'Surely, shall one say, In the Lord have I righteousness,' Isa. xlv. 24. ' He shall be be called Jehovah our righteousness,' Jer. xxiii. 6. This is the only righteousness in which a man can stand before God in judgment, and which shall be acknowledged in the great day. They, and they only, who, by their works proceeding from that faith which unites the soul to Christ, and which receives this righteousness, are proved to possess it, shall then be pronounced ' righteous,' Matt. xxv. 37, 46. This righteousness is imputed to every one that believeth, and to such only. This makes it clear that Jesus Christ has not fulfilled the law for mankind in general, but for those in particular who should believe in His name, John

---

[1] The accuracy with which the Scriptures are written, is very observable in the passage above quoted, 2 Cor. v. 21, and in the verse preceding it. The supplement *you,* twice repeated in verse 20, is erroneous. Those whom the Apostle was addressing had been reconciled to God, therefore he could not beseech them to be what they were already. Dr. Macknight has remarked this, but he has not noticed the change from *men,* the proper supplement in verse 20, to *us* and *we* in the following verse. This change was necessary; for though Paul could declare that Christ had been made sin for him and those to whom he wrote, he could not affirm this of any man, till, like the Corinthians, there was evidence of his having received the grace of God given him in Christ Jesus, 1 Cor. i. 4. Dr. Macknight, like Mr. Stuart, by his translation, changing sin into sin-offering, destroys the contrast between sin and righteousness, and obscures, as has been remarked in a previous part of this work, one of the strongest expressions of the vicarious nature of Christ's sufferings that is to be found in the Bible, as well as the transference of the sin of His people to the Redeemer, and of His righteousness to them.

xvii. 9, 20. His atonement and intercession are of the same extent, and are presented for the same individuals. 'I pray not for the world, but for them which Thou hast given Me.'

Mr. Stuart, in his explanation of this 4th verse, introduces the following quotation from Flatt:—'Christ is the τέλος νόμου (end of the law) in respect to δικαιοσύνη (righteousness), He has brought it about, that we should not be judged after the strictness of the law. He has removed the sentence of condemnation from all those who receive the Gospel.' To this Mr. Stuart adds—'Well and truly.' That the sentence of condemnation is removed from all who receive the Gospel, although in a very different way from what Mr. Stuart supposes, is most certain. But no sentiment can be more unscriptural than that we shall not be judged after the strictness of the law. For what saith the Scripture? 'He hath appointed a day in which He will judge the world in righteousness.' In that day, instead of men not being judged *after the strictness of the law,* judgment will be laid to the line, and righteousness to the plummet, and all those in whom the righteousness of the law has not been fulfilled in all its demands, without the defalcation of one jot or tittle, will be found under its curse, and that awful sentence will be pronounced on them, 'Depart from Me, ye cursed.' The judgment, in accordance with every representation of it contained in Scripture, and with the whole plan of salvation, will be conducted in all respects, both as to those who shall be saved and those who shall be condemned, after the strictness of both law and justice. Under the righteous government of God, never was one sin committed which will not be punished either in the person of him who committed it, or in that of the Divine Surety of the new covenant.

Ver. 5.—*For Moses describeth the righteousness which is of the law, That the man which doeth those things shall live by them.*

This illustrates what the Apostle had just before said, that Christ, and Christ alone, has fulfilled the demands of the law, and therefore in vain shall life be sought by any man's personal obedience to its commandments. To live by the law requires, as Moses had declared, that the law be perfectly obeyed. But this to fallen man is impossible. The law knows no mercy; it knows no mitigation, it overlooks not even the smallest breach, or the smallest deficiency. One guilty thought or desire would condemn for ever. Whoever, then, looks for life by the law, must keep the whole law in thought, word, and deed, and not be chargeable with the smallest transgression.

Ver. 6.—*But the righteousness which is of faith speaketh on this wise, Say not in thine heart, Who shall ascend into heaven?* (*that is, to bring Christ down* from above:)

Ver. 7.—*Or, Who shall descend into the deep?* (*that is, to bring up Christ again from the dead.*)

Ver. 8.—*But what saith it? The word is nigh thee, even in thy mouth, and in thy heart; that is, the word of faith which we preach;*

We should rather expect contrast in every point of view than coincidence between the law given by Moses and the Gospel of Christ. Can there then be any illustration of the receiving of righteousness by faith, which is here the Apostle's subject, and the precepts that were given to the Israelites as a shadow of the Gospel? Doubtless, with all the difference between the law and the Gospel, there must be a point of view in which they are coincident, for in such a view it is that he chiefly makes his quotation. Paul alleges the passage to which he refers, Deut. xxx. 11-14, as in a certain respect speaking the language of the righteousness of faith. The language used by Moses described the clearness of the manner of giving the knowledge of the Divine requirements to the people of Israel. But though this was its original object, yet it had a further reference to the clearness of the manner of revealing the Gospel. For the Apostle explains it, ' *That is, to bring Christ down from above.*' The language, then, that describes the clearness of the revelation of the precepts of God to Israel, was a figure of the clearness of the revelation of the Gospel.

Moses gave the Israelites a law which was to abide with them for their constant instruction. They were not obliged to send a messenger to heaven to learn how they were to serve God, nor to search out wisdom by their own understanding. Nor had they to send over the sea to distant countries, like the heathens, for instruction. God by Moses taught them everything with respect to His worship and service in the fullest, clearest, and most practical manner. This was a shadow of the clearness of the revelation of the righteousness received by faith, which we are not left to search for by means through which it never can be obtained. Salvation is brought nigh to us, being proclaimed in the Gospel by the death and resurrection of Jesus Christ. The word is in our mouth. We receive the righteousness He has brought, not by any efforts of our own in seeking salvation, and labouring to keep the law of God, but by the belief of that word which was published at Jerusalem, announcing salvation to the guiltiest of mankind.

The Gospel is contained in figure in every part of the law. The very manner of giving the law was a shadow of the Gospel, and typified salvation through a great Mediator. And though the New Testament often contrasts the demands of the law with the voice of mercy speaking in the Gospel, yet here the Gospel also speaks through the law. The reference to what Moses observed with respect to the precepts which he delivered from God to Israel, instead of finding an opposition to the plan of salvation through Christ, finds an illustration which Divine wisdom had prepared to shadow it, in the mission of the Mediator under the law.

Wonderful is the wisdom of God manifested in the harmony of the Old and New Testaments. They who do not understand it, have laboured to show a coincidence merely by accommodation. But the Spirit of God everywhere explains the language of the Old Testament, as in its design appointed by God to be a shadow of things of Christ's kingdom.

But though there is a coincidence, there is also a contrast between the law and the Gospel. While the language of the law is, ' Do and live,' that righteousness which it demands, and which man is unable to perform, is, according to the Gospel, gratuitously communicated through faith. This righteousness is in Christ, and He is not at a distance, so that we must scale the heavens, or descend below the earth,—in one word, attempt what is impracticable, to come to Him, and derive from Him this benefit. He and this righteousness are brought near unto us, as was long before predicted. 'Hearken unto Me, ye stout-hearted, that are far from righteousness: I bring near My righteousness; it shall not be far off, and My salvation shall not tarry,' Isa. xlvi. 12. All men, till enlightened by the Spirit of God, seek salvation by doing something of which they imagine God will approve. If it is not complete, His mercy, they suppose, will still incline Him to accept of it for value; but without something of his own to present, man in his natural state never thinks of approaching God. Nothing can be more self-evidently false than that man can merit from God. Yet, notwithstanding the folly of this supposition, it is only the energy of the Holy Spirit through the truth of the Gospel that will convince him of the fallacy. Even the very Gospel of the grace of God is seen through this false medium; and while men exclaim, 'Grace, grace,' they continue to introduce a species of merit by putting Christ at a distance, and making access to Him a matter of time and difficulty. How different is the Gospel, as here exhibited by Paul!

We must not attempt in any way to merit Christ, or to bring anything like an equivalent in our hand. The language of Scripture is, 'Ho, every one that thirsteth, come ye to the waters: and he that hath no money; come ye, buy and eat; yea, come, buy wine and milk without money and without price.' 'He hath filled the hungry with good things, and the rich'—they who are worthy in their own esteem, who, that they may find acceptance, bring something of their own—'He hath sent empty away.' 'Say not,' observes Archbishop Leighton, 'unless I find some measure of sanctification, what right have I to apply Him (Christ) as my righteousness? This inverts the order, and prejudges thee of both. Thou must first, without finding, yea, or seeking anything in thyself but misery and guiltiness, lay hold on Him as thy righteousness; or else thou shalt never find sanctification by any other endeavour or pursuit.'

Ver. 9.—*That if thou shalt confess with thy mouth the Lord Jesus, and shalt believe in thine heart that God hath raised Him from the dead, thou shalt be saved.*

That if thou shalt confess with thy mouth.—The confession of Christ is salvation. But that confession which is salvation, is a confession which implies that the truth confessed with the mouth is known and received in the heart. The belief of the heart is therefore joined with the confession of the lips. Neither is genuine without the other, though it may be said that either the one or the other is salvation, because they who believe with the heart will confess with the tongue. If a man says, 'I believe in Christ,' yet denies Him when put to trial, or confesses Him with the lips, yet denies Him in His proper character, he neither confesses nor believes Christ. It should always be remembered, that if he believes anything different from the testimony of God relating to the person and work of the Saviour, he does not believe the Gospel, but something, whatever it may be, which can neither sanctify nor save. The Gospel alone is the power of God unto salvation to every one who believes it.
Hath raised Him from the dead.—Why is so much stress laid on the resurrection? Was not the work of Christ in this world finished by His

death? Most certainly it was. But His resurrection was the evidence that it was finished; and therefore the belief of His resurrection is put for that of the whole of His work.

The emphasis of the second person throughout this verse should be remarked. The Apostle does not speak indefinitely, but he says emphatically, If *thou* shalt confess with *thy* mouth, and shalt believe in *thine* heart, *thou* shalt be saved. He speaks of every one, so that all may examine themselves, for to every one believing and confessing, salvation is promised; thus teaching each one to apply the promise of salvation to himself by faith and confession. Thus the Apostle shows that every believer has as much certain assurance of his salvation as he certainly confesses Christ with his mouth, and as he believes in his heart, that the Lord Jesus was raised from the dead. Our assurance of salvation corresponds with the measure of our faith, and the boldness of our confession of Christ.

Ver. 10.—*For with the heart man believeth unto righteousness ; and with the mouth confession is made unto salvation.*

Believeth unto righteousness.—That is, unto the receiving of righteousness, namely, the righteousness of Christ. This righteousness is called ' the righteousness of faith,' Rom. iv. 13—not that it is in the faith, but it is so called as being received by faith, as it is said, Rom. iii. 22, 'the righteousness which is by faith,' and Phil. iii. 9, 'the righteousness which is of God by faith.' Faith, then, is only the appointed medium or means of our union with Christ, through which we receive this righteousness, and not the righteousness itself. ' Faith,' says the Westminster Confession, 'justifies a sinner in the sight of God, not because of those other graces which do always accompany it, or of good works that are the fruits of it; nor as if the grace of faith, or any act thereof, were imputed to him for his justification; but only as it is an instrument, by which he receiveth and applieth Christ's righteousness.' The expression, 'Faith is counted to him for righteousness,' Rom. iv. 3, is often supposed to mean, 'is counted to him instead of, or as righteousness ; ' but, as has been remarked on that text, p. 162, the literal rendering is not for righteousness, but *unto* righteousness, in conformity with the proper translation as in the verse before us.

The faith of the Gospel is not a speculation, it is not such a knowledge of religion as may be acquired like human science. This may often have the appearance of true faith ; but it is not ' the substance of things hoped for, the evidence of things not seen.' Many things connected with the Gospel may be believed by the natural man, and each of the doctrines taken separately may be in some way received by him, as notions of lights and colours are received by the blind. But the Gospel is never understood and believed, except by those who, according to the promise, are ' taught of the Lord,' Isa. liv. 13; who therefore know the Father and Him whom He hath sent, which is eternal life, John xvii. 3. In the parable of the sower, where only the fourth description of persons are represented as having truly and permanently received the word, they are characterized as *understanding* it, and they only bear fruit; the others understood it not, Matt. xiii. 19–23. ' The natural man receiveth not the things of the Spirit of God, for they are foolishness unto him; neither can he know them, because they are spiritually discerned,' 1 Cor. ii. 14. It is impossible that a man can believe that to be the word of God which he regards as foolishness. 'No man can say' (understanding and believing what he says) 'that Jesus is the Lord, but by the Holy Ghost,' 1 Cor. xii. 3. When Peter answered and said, 'Thou art the Christ, the Son of the living God,' 'Blessed,' said Jesus, 'art thou, Simon Barjona; for flesh and blood hath not revealed it unto thee, but My Father which is in heaven,' Matt. xvi. 17.

Justifying faith is the belief of the testimony of Christ, and trust in Him who is the subject of that testimony. It is believing *with the heart.* Concerning those who received a good report through faith, it is declared that they saw or understood the promises; they were persuaded of their truth, and they embraced them, taking them home personally, and resting upon them. On the passage before us, Calvin remarks, 'The seat of faith, it deserves to be observed, is not in the brain, but the heart; not that I wish to enter into any dispute concerning the part of the body which is the seat of faith, but since the word *heart* generally means a serious, sincere, ardent affection, I am desirous to show the confidence of faith to be a firm, efficacious, and operative principle in all the emotions and feelings of the soul, not a mere naked notion of the head.'

And with the mouth confession is made unto salvation.—A man becomes righteous, perfectly righteous, through believing God's record concerning His Son. But the evidence that this faith is genuine is found in the open confession of the Lord with the mouth in everything in which His will is known. Confession of Christ is as necessary as faith in Him, but necessary for a different purpose. Faith is necessary to obtain the gift of righteousness. Confession is necessary to prove that this gift is received. If a man does not confess Christ at the hazard of life, character, property, liberty, and everything dear to him, he has not the faith of Christ. In saying, then, that confession is made unto salvation, the Apostle does not mean that it is the cause of salvation, or that without it the title to salvation is incomplete. When a man believes in his heart, he is justified. But confession of Christ is the effect of faith, and will be evidence of it at the last day. Faith which interests the sinner in the righteousness of Christ is manifested by the confession of His name in the midst of enemies, or in the face of danger.

Ver. 11.—*For the Scripture saith, Whosoever believeth on Him shall not be ashamed.*

For the Scripture saith.—Here Paul shows that the Scriptures of the Prophets taught the same doctrine that he was teaching. This was not necessary in order to add authority to his own doctrine,—for he was equally inspired with the Prophets,—but in order to prove the perfect agreement of the Old and the New Testament, and to show that the Jews who denied that the Gentiles were to be fellow-heirs with them, were in error, even on their own principles. By this reference to the Scriptures, too, the Apostle in the first place confirms the truth he had been so forcibly declaring concerning the language of the righteousness by faith, namely, that it was not necessary to make some impracticable attempts—

such as to ascend into heaven, or to descend into the deep—to come to Christ, since He was brought nigh to all in the preaching of the Gospel, which proclaimed that whosoever shall call on the name of the Lord shall be saved. And, in the next place, it afforded him an opportunity of recurring to the important truth, brought into view in the preceding chapter, of the Gentiles being fellow-heirs of that righteousness, such of them as believed the promises, being part of the spiritual seed of Abraham, and equally interested in those promises with the believing remnant of the Jews. The natural and easy way in which Paul thus reverts to this subject, and connects it with his declarations concerning the perversion of the truth of God by the unbelieving part of the Jewish nation, in seeking to establish their own righteousness, and not submitting themselves to the righteousness of God, ought to be particularly remarked; as well as its opening the way for exhibiting the duty of preaching the Gospel to the Gentiles, and showing that, in respect to the manner in which they must be saved, there is no difference between them and the Jews.

Whosoever believeth on Him.—This language of the Prophet extended mercy to the Gentiles, if they believed. Here it may be remarked, that the least degree of faith embraces Christ, and unites the soul to Him. Faith does not save us by being strong or weak. It is Jesus Christ by whom we are saved, and not by our faith, which is only the instrument or hand by which we receive Him. It may be further remarked, that here, as in so many other parts of Scripture, we see a full warrant for every one of the human race to believe in Jesus Christ, with the certainty that in doing so he shall be saved. Some, however, may be disposed to say, 'We are not humbled, or at least humbled enough for our sins, and therefore we dare not place confidence in Christ for His salvation.' Such persons ought to know that true humiliation is a concomitant or a consequence of saving faith, but is not a ground of it. It gives a man no right to trust in Christ,—no title to Divine acceptance either of his person or of his performances. It is indeed, in the hand of the Spirit, a means of rendering a man willing to trust in the Lord Jesus, and the more of it he attains, he is the more willing; but it affords him no degree of warrant to trust in Him,—nor is it requisite it should; for by the invitations and calls of the Gospel he already is fully warranted, so well warranted, that nothing in himself can either diminish or increase his warrant. When any one, therefore, says that he dare not trust in the Redeemer, because he is not sufficiently humbled, he thereby shows that he is under the prevalence both of unbelief and of a legal spirit: of *unbelief,*—for he does not believe that by the calls and commands of God he is sufficiently warranted to rely on Christ, but that something *more* is requisite to afford him a sufficient warrant; of *a legal spirit,*—for he regards humiliation as that which must confer upon him a *right* to trust in Christ, since for want of it in a sufficient degree, he dare not intrust his salvation to Him. But he may be assured that he cannot obtain holy consolation till he come as he is, and place direct confidence in Jesus Christ for all his salvation; and that he cannot have true evangelical humiliation till he first trust in Christ for it, and so receive it by faith out of His fulness. The more of this humiliation he attains, the more willing will he be to come as a sinner to the Saviour; but he cannot attain an increase of it, before he trusts in Him for it as a part of his salvation.

Shall not be ashamed.—Of the word *ashamed* it has been observed, ch. v. 5, that it may import either that our hope will not be disappointed, or that it will not allow us to be ashamed of its object; and in ch. ix. 33, the same quotation as in the verse before us is expounded, of not being ashamed to own Christ before unbelievers, or of being put to shame before Him at His coming. In the last sense, it may be observed that almost all men have some hope in prospect of the bar of God. But many have hopes founded on falsehood. There is a vast variety in the opinions of men with respect to the ground of hope; and, besides the common ground, namely, a mixture of mercy and merit, every unbeliever has something peculiar to himself, which he deems an alleviation of guilt, or singularly meritorious. But in the great day all shall be ashamed of their hope, except those who have believed in Christ for salvation. Believers alone shall not be ashamed before Him at His coming. This is true, and no doubt is referred to by the Prophet from whom the quotation is here made, without, however, excluding the present effect in this life of believing in Christ, namely, that they who do so shall not be ashamed to confess their hope in Him. This last sense suits the connection in this place, and appears to be the meaning here attached to the word *ashamed.*

Ver. 12.—*For there is no difference between the Jew and the Greek; for the same Lord over all is rich unto all that call upon Him.*

For there is no difference.—So far from the Gentiles being excluded from mercy altogether, there is not, in this respect, the smallest difference between them and the Jews. *Is rich.*—That is, rich to bestow on both Jews and Gentiles all they need. Calvin is not to be followed in explaining the word rich here as meaning 'kind and beneficent.' This would sanction any abuse of words that the wildest imagination could invent. Nor is there any need of such an expedient. The meaning, as here explained, is quite obvious. *Unto all that call upon Him.*—God is able to supply the wants of all that call upon Him, and He will supply them. All of them receive out of the fulness of Jesus Christ. Here it is imported that to call on the name of the Lord is to be a believer. Let it then be understood that to call on the Lord implies to call on Him in faith as He is revealed in the Gospel. There must be the knowledge of God as a just God, and a Saviour, before any one can call on Him. To call on the Lord in this sense, amounts to the same thing as to believe in Christ for salvation, and it implies that every believer is one who calls on God. If any man professes to be a believer, and does not habitually call on God, he is not what he pretends.

Ver. 13.—*For whosoever shall call upon the name of the Lord shall be saved.*

'The context in Joel,' says Calvin, 'will fully satisfy us that his prediction applies to this passage of Paul.' But why should we need anything to convince us of this, but the authority of the Apostle himself? It is a most pernicious method of interpreting the applications of the Old Testament in the New, to make our preception of their justness the ground of acknowledging the Apostle's conclusion. It may be proper to show how far or how clearly the words of the prophecy establish the particular reference made by the Apostle. But whether we can explain the application or not, the interpretation of the Apostle is as infallible as the prophecy itself. If one will undertake to vindicate the justness of the Apostle's conclusion, another may be inclined to question it, and to allege that the prophecy has not the meaning assigned to it by the Apostle.

It is here implied, that in order to salvation it is necessary to call on the Lord, and that whoever does so shall be saved. Here, as in other places of Scripture, *the name of the Lord* signifies the Lord Himself. By calling on the name of the Lord, all the parts of religious worship which we render to God are intended. It denotes a full and entire communion with God. He who calls on the name of the Lord, profoundly humbles himself before God, recognises His power, adores His majesty, believes His promises, confides in His goodness, hopes in His mercy, honours Him as his God, and loves Him as his Saviour. It supposes that this invocation is inseparable from all the other parts of religion. To call on the name of the Lord, is to place ourselves under His protection, and to have recourse to Him for His aid.

But why does the Prophet ascribe deliverance or salvation to calling on the name of the Lord, and not merely say, ' Whoever calls on God shall be heard, shall be protected, shall receive His blessing?' The reason is, that he was treating of the new covenant, which clearly, without a veil and without a figure, announces salvation in opposition to the former covenant, which held forth temporal blessings. The Gospel speaks plainly of salvation, that is to say, of eternal happiness which we should expect after death. He uses the term *saved*, in order to remind us of the unhappy condition in which we were by nature, and to show the difference between our state and that of angels, for the angels live, but are not saved. The life of which Jesus Christ is the fountain, finds us plunged in death, lost in ourselves, children of wrath, and it is given us under the title of salvation. No one ever called upon the Lord, in the Scripture sense of this phrase, without being saved. It is here as expressly said, ' Whosoever shall call upon the name of the Lord shall be saved,' as it is, ' Whoever believeth shall be saved.' It appears that Paul, when he here speaks of calling upon the Lord, refers to the Lord Jesus Christ, whom he had named in the 9th verse. In the same way he addresses the church at Corinth, ' With all that in every place call upon the name of Jesus Christ our Lord.'

In thus calling upon the Lord, a believer, like Enoch, walks with God. It is not only that he prays to God at stated seasons; his life is a life of prayer. He prays to God ' everywhere,' and ' always.' He remembers that Jesus hath said, ' Henceforth I call you not servants; but I have called you friends.' He serves God, therefore, in newness of spirit, and goes to Him on all occasions as his covenant God, his Father, and his Friend, to whom he pours out his heart, makes known all his wants, difficulties, and desires, and consults Him on every occasion in matters great and small. From this holy and constant communion he is not at any time or in any circumstances precluded. In Nehemiah we have beautiful and encouraging examples both of stated and ejaculatory prayer in unforeseen circumstances, see ch. ii. 4; in short, of a continual appeal to God, ch. xiii. 29. Paul commands us to 'pray without ceasing.' To the exercise of this duty, so frequently enforced by the Lord in His last discourse to His disciples, believers have the highest encouragement. 'Whatsoever ye shall ask the Father in My name, He will give it you.' 'If ye abide in Me, and My words abide in you, ye shall ask what ye will, and it shall be done unto you.' We see, in the sequel, the effect of David's short prayer, 'O Lord, I pray Thee turn the counsel of Ahithophel into foolishness.' Although the Lord shows Himself at all times so ready to answer the prayers of His people, yet in the transaction with the Gibeonites, Joshua and the elders of Israel 'asked not counsel at the mouth of the Lord,' and what was the consequence? We are ready to be astonished at their conduct in this instance, yet how often is similiar negligence or unbelief exemplified in the life of every Christian! even after he has received, in innumerable instances, gracious answers to his petitions, so often reproving his little faith when he presented them; and after he has experienced so many distressing proofs of the evil of being left to his own counsels when he has neglected this duty, Josh. ix. 14.

Ver. 14,—*How then shall they call on Him in whom they have not believed? and how shall they believe in Him of whom they have not heard? and how shall they hear without a preacher?*

This and the following verse are not the objections of a Jew, as alleged by Dr. Macknight. It is all the language of the Apostle in his own character. He had said in the preceding verse, that whosoever shall call upon the name of the Lord shall be saved. From this he urges the necessity of preaching the Gospel to all men; for when it is said that whosoever calls on Him shall be saved, it is implied that none shall be saved who do not call upon Him. What, then, is the consequence to be drawn from this? Is it not that the Gospel should with all speed be published over the whole world? If the Gentiles are to be partakers of Divine mercy, it is by seeking it from Jesus Christ, who has died that mercy might be extended to Jew and Gentile. Is it not by the Holy Ghost speaking to the heart of the Gentiles without the instrumentality of the word, that they are to be converted and saved. They must hear the word and call on the Lord. Whoever is saved by Jesus Christ must call upon Him.

How then shall they call on Him in whom they have not believed?—If, in order to salvation, it be necessary to call on Christ, how can the Gentiles call on Him when they do not believe in Him? *And how shall they believe in Him of whom they have not heard?*—This is impossible. In this state were the Gentile nations before the Gospel reached them. Hence the great importance of communicating to them the glad tidings of salvation. *And how shall they hear without a preacher?*—The Gospel was not to be immediately declared by the voice of God from heaven, or by the

Holy Ghost speaking without a medium of communication, or by angels sent from heaven; it was to be carried over the world by men. How, then, according to this Divine constitution, could the nations of the earth hear the Gospel without a preacher? It is unnecessary to refute the opinion of those who hold that the Gospel cannot speak to men savingly in the Scriptures, and that it is never effectual without the living voice of a preacher. This is not the meaning of the Apostle. His doctrine is, that the Gospel must be communicated to the minds of men through the external instrumentality of the word, as well as by the internal agency of the Spirit. Men are not only saved through Christ, but they are saved through the knowledge of Christ, communicated through the Gospel.

Ver. 15.—*And how shall they preach, except they be sent? as it is written, How beautiful are the feet of them that preach the Gospel of peace, and bring glad tidings of good things!*

If the Gentiles could not believe in the Lord without hearing of Him, and if they could not hear of Him unless He was declared to them, then it follows, from the prophecy above quoted, that preachers must be sent to them. Notwithstanding, then, the violent opposition made to it by the Jews, the necessity was manifest for the Apostles, according to their Divine commission, to go forth to preach the Gospel to every creature. The accordance of this with the Old Testament Scriptures, Paul had been showing, and he now supports it by further quotation.

As it is written, etc.—This prophecy, Isa. lii. 7, which may literally respect good news of deliverance to the Jews from temporal judgments, typically refers, as the Apostle's application of it here shows, to the messengers of mercy sent forth under the Gospel. In the beginning of that chapter, Zion or Jerusalem, the Church of God, is called to arise from her degraded condition, for the Lord has prepared for her deliverance. Then follow the words here quoted. The tidings to be told are next subjoined. 'Thy God reigneth.' That the Gentiles also should partake in the blessings of His reign, is immediately intimated. 'The Lord hath made bare His holy arm in the eyes of all the nations; and all the ends of the earth shall see the salvation of our God.' Thus, beginning at Jerusalem, those commissioned by the Lord were to preach salvation in His name among all nations. In the conclusion of the chapter, the blessed effects under the reign of the Messiah are declared. ' So shall He sprinkle many nations; the kings shall shut their mouths at Him; for that which had not been told them shall they see, and that which they had not heard shall they consider.' This quotation, then, made by the Apostle, was calculated to produce the strongest conviction of the truth he was establishing, namely, the duty of preaching the Gospel to the Gentiles.

Ver. 16.—*But they have not all obeyed the Gospel: for Esaias saith, Lord, who hath believed our report?*

It is here admitted by Paul, that though the Gospel was to be preached both to Jews and Gentiles, with the assurance that whosoever believeth shall be saved, yet, as a matter of fact, all who heard did not believe it. This might seem unaccountable; or it might even appear to be an argu-

ment against the preaching of the Gospel to the Gentiles, that, notwithstanding all the blessings with which it was said to be fraught to those
who should receive it, it was still rejected by many to whom it was
preached. But this should not seem strange to any acquainted with
prophecy : it is the very testimony of Isaiah. Instead, then, of being an
objection to the preaching of the Gospel, that it was not received by the
bulk of those who heard it, it was the very thing which the Scriptures
predicted. The prophecy of Isaiah, liii. 1, is here applied to this fact, in
which a plain intimation is given of the small number who should receive
the Gospel when first preached. If, then, the Jews objected to the
preaching of the Gospel from this fact, they must object to the Prophet
Isaiah on the same ground.

Ver. 17.—*So then faith cometh by hearing, and hearing by the word of God.*

According, then, to this complaint of the Prophet, it is evident that
faith comes by hearing, which the Apostle is asserting ; and this is the
consequence to be deduced from it. The word in the preceding verse,
quoted from Isaiah, and rendered ' report,' is the same which in this verse
is rendered hearing. Faith, then, never comes but by hearing, that is,
by the word of God. The Apostles communicated their testimony by the
living voice, and by their writings. Both are comprehended in what is
called hearing. All this showed the necessity of preaching the Gospel to
the Gentiles, on which Paul had been insisting, according to which there
is no such thing as saving faith among heathens who have not heard of
Christ. *Hearing by the word of God.*—This makes the last observation
still stronger. The hearing cannot extend to Dr. Macknight's scheme of
salvation to the heathens, who supposes that they may have faith without
the knowledge of the Gospel ; for, consistently with this passage, faith
must come, not from the revelation of the works of God, but from that
of His word.

Ver. 18.—*But I say, Have they not heard ? Yes, verily, their sound went into all
the earth, and their words unto the ends of the world.*

The Gospel had now been everywhere preached, Col. i. 23. The
Apostle applies to this fact what is said in the nineteenth Psalm. That
Psalm literally refers to the preaching of the great luminaries of heaven,
the sun, moon, and stars ; but typically it refers to the preaching of the
word of God. The sun of the creation preaches to all nations the existence, the unity, the power, the wisdom, and the goodness of God. He
speaks in a language all nations may understand. All nations, indeed,
have departed from the doctrine thus preached ; but this results from
disaffection to the doctrine, and not from the obscurity of the language of
the preacher. The Apostle tells us that all nations, even the most barbarous, are without excuse in their idolatry. God is revealed in His
character as Creator in the works of His hands, and all men should know
Him as such. The sun carries the intelligence of God's perfections and
existence to every nation under heaven, which are successively informed
that there is an almighty, all-wise, and beneficent Being, the author of
all things. In like manner, the Gospel of Christ preaches to all nations,
and informs them of the glorious character of God, as manifested in the

incarnation and death of His Son Jesus Christ, while it reveals His mercy, concerning which the works of creation are silent.

Dr. Macknight supposes the question here asked, 'Have they not heard?' to be answered by the preaching of the works of creation, according to the words of the Psalm in their literal meaning. This is contrary to the whole train of the Apostle's reasoning, who is speaking of the preaching of the Gospel. Even Calvin makes the preaching spoken of in that Psalm to refer to the 'silent works of God' in ancient times, and not in any sense to the preaching of the Apostles. But it is evident that the Apostle is not referring to the former, but to the present state of the Gentile nations. The words of the Psalmist are thus spiritually, as they always have been literally, fulfilled in the preaching of the silent works of God. The description in the nineteenth Psalm, of the sun in the firmament, has, as above noticed, a strict literal and primary meaning, but it is also typical of Him who is called the Sun of Righteousness, who by His word is the spiritual light of the world. Paul therefore quotes this description in the last sense, thus taking the spiritual meaning, which was ultimately intended. This suits his object, while he drops the literal, although also a just and acknowledged sense. It is not, then, as setting aside the literal application of such passages that the Apostles quote them in their spiritual import, nor in the way of accommodation, as is so often asserted, to the great disparagement both of the Apostles and the Scriptures, but as their ultimate and most extensive signification.

Ver. 19.—*But I say, Did not Israel know ? First, Moses saith, I will provoke you to jealousy by them that are no people, and by a foolish nation I will anger you.*

Did not Israel know, that they were to be rejected as a nation, and the Gentiles called into the Divine favour? That this was communicated in their Scriptures is most clear. In the quotation here adduced, Deut. xxxii. 21, this event was foretold by Moses, who commences that prediction in a way that marks the importance of what he was about to say : ' Give ear, O ye heavens, and I will speak ; and hear, O earth, the words of my mouth.' In verse 5th, he declares the ingratitude and unbelief of Israel. ' They have corrupted themselves ; their spot is not the spot of His children ; they are a perverse and crooked generation.' He continues this complaint to the 20th verse, when he pronounces the decree of God of their rejection. ' I will hide My face from them, I will see what their end shall be ; for they are a very froward generation, children in whom is no faith.' And then immediately he adds the words from which the verse before us is taken. In these words the calling of the Gentiles is clearly predicted. The Gentiles are marked by these expressions :—1st, ' I will move them to jealousy with those which are not a people, I will provoke them to anger with a foolish nation.' 2d, Their calling is pointed out by the provocation to jealousy with which God threatens the Jews, which intimates that He will bestow His love and His covenant on those who were formerly foolish, and will withdraw them from Israel. 3d, This same calling is marked by the comparison drawn between that provocation to jealousy with which He threatens Israel, with that with which the Israelites have provoked Him. ' They have moved Me to jealousy ; '

that is, as they had given their love and their heart to others besides God, in the same way God would give His love and His heart to others besides them. This prediction, then, could only find its accomplishment in the conversion of the Gentiles by the Gospel of Jesus Christ. The word ' nation ' is here a figurative expression in reference to God's dealings with Israel. The Gentiles are called as individuals. The ' righteous nation,' Isa. xxvi. 2, is composed of believers.

Ver. 20.—*But Esaias is very bold, and saith, I was found of them that sought Me not ; I was made manifest unto them that asked not after Me.*
Ver. 21.—*But to Israel he saith, All day long I have stretched forth My hands unto a disobedient and gainsaying people.*

If Moses predicted, somewhat obscurely, the calling of the Gentiles, Isaiah had foretold it very plainly, and placed it in a light most offensive to the Jews. In this prophecy, the bringing in of the Gentiles, and their ready reception of the Gospel, and at the same time the obstinate unbelief of the Jews, notwithstanding the earnest and constant invitations of God by His servants, are plainly indicated. Nothing could more clearly describe the conduct of the Jews, and the reception they gave to the message of salvation, than this prophecy of Isaiah. In this and the preceding chapter, the Apostle has fully shown that the calling of the Gentiles, and the rejection of the great body of the Jewish nation, had been the purpose of God during the whole of that economy which separated the Jews from the rest of the world, and under which they had enjoyed such distinguished and peculiar privileges.

While in the ninth chapter the sovereignty of God in the rejection of the great body of the Jewish nation is prominently brought into view, in the chapter before us their rejection is shown to have been the immediate effect of their own unbelief. No truth is more manifest in every part of the Old Testament Scriptures, than that contained in the declaration just referred to, Isa. lxv. 2. *All day long I have stretched forth My hands unto a disobedient and gainsaying people.*—What outward means did not God employ to induce the Israelites to love and honour Him, and to lead them to submission to His authority ! ' I have hewed them by the prophets ; I have slain them by the words of My mouth,' Hos. vi. 5. ' I earnestly protested unto your fathers in the day that I brought them up out of the land of Egypt, even unto this day, rising early and protesting, saying, Obey My voice,' Jer. xi. 7. ' And now, O inhabitants of Jerusalem, and men of Judah, judge, I pray you, betwixt Me and My vineyard. What could have been done more to My vineyard that I have not done in it ? wherefore, when I looked that it should bring forth grapes, brought it forth wild grapes ? ' Isa. v. 3. Here, then, is the stretching forth of the hands of God to that people all the day long, that is, during the whole period of their dispensation ; and here the complaint is verified of their continuing, notwithstanding, disobedient and gainsaying. The fault, then, was their own, and the awful sentence that followed, Isa. v. 5, 6, was merited and just.

In this we see what is the result, when God employs only outward means to lead men to obedience, and does not accompany them with the influence of His efficacious grace. Without this, the Apostle shows in the preceding chapter, that the whole nation of Israel, without exception, would have been as Sodom and Gomorrah. Here, then, is the condition to which many in their wisdom would reduce all mankind, if they could establish their unscriptural doctrines in opposition to Divine election and efficacious grace. They are displeased at the idea that all the heathen nations were left to themselves, while so much favour was shown to Israel ; yet we see in the case of Israel, in whom so full a display is made of the character of man, what would have been the result as to the other nations of a similar dispensation of outward means. But, according to the system of such cavillers' at the clear doctrine of the Scriptures, there still remains something good in man, which may lead him, without a change of heart, to embrace the glad tidings of salvation. Many of them also affirm that man has power to resist and make void the internal operation of grace.

.In support of this last opinion, reference is made to such texts as that in Gen. vi. 3, where God says, ' My Spirit shall not always strive with man ; ' and to the words of Stephen, when he charges the Jews as stiff-necked and uncircumcised in heart and ears, who, like their fathers, always resisted the Holy Ghost, Acts vii. 51. But the answer is easy when we attend to the different aspects in which the grace of God is presented in Scripture. Besides its *existence* in the mind of God, it is spoken of either in its *manifestation* in His word, or in its *operation* in the heart. In its manifestation it may, and, unless accompanied by its internal operation, always will, be resisted. To such resistance the above passages refer, and give their attestation ; and for the truth of this we also can appeal not only to the example of the nation of Israel, but also to what we see passing before us every day. Multitudes, in the enjoyment of the full light of the revelation of grace, continually discover their resistance to its manifestation in the word. But not so with respect to grace, in its internal operation in the heart. This cannot be effectually resisted. On the contrary, so far as it proceeds, it takes away all inclination to resist, creating a new heart, and making those who are its subjects willing in the day of God's power, Ps. cx. 3. Here, then, there must be an election by God of those who shall thus be favoured, without which not one individual would be saved. If the doctrine of the fall in its proper extent be admitted, the doctrines of election aud efficacious grace must be embraced by those who do not believe that all men are to be left to perish.

In this chapter we see how highly God values His law. Though the Jews had a zeal of God, yet they were rejected, because they attempted to substitute their own obedience, which fell short of the demands of the law, which requires perfection. In order that any of the human race might be saved, it was necessary that the Son of God should fulfil the law. He alone is the end of the law for righteousness to every one that believeth. On this law of everlasting obligation, under which all mankind were placed, it may be proper to make a few general remarks, as well as on the covenant with Israel, to which there is also reference in this chapter.

God is the Legislator as well as the Creator of the world, and His law is necessarily founded on the relation in which He stands to His creatures. The law is a transcript of His character, proclaiming His holiness, His justice, and His goodness; in one word, His love, for God is love. The sum of it is, 'Thou shalt love the Lord thy God with all thy heart, and thy neighbour as thyself.' Thus love is the fulfilling of the law; the end of the commandment is love.

The love demanded from the creature is primarily for God His Creator, the great object of love. The second part of the summary of the law, far from opposing, coincides with and flows from the first, commanding us to love our neighbour as the creature of God. The love it thus requires of us for man is measured by that which we bear to ourselves, and consequently teaches that self-love is not to be condemned, unless it be excessive or exclusive. It is proper and necessary as a part of the law of our creation, which imposes on us the duty of attending to and providing for our own wants.

This law must necessarily be the law of the whole intelligent creation. According to its holiness, justice, and goodness, nothing *more* and nothing *less* can be required of any creature. 'The law of the Lord is perfect.' In nothing is it deficient; in nothing does it exceed. It requires perfect obedience, which is essential to the nature of every law; for no law can dispense with the smallest part of the obedience it demands. Any work of supererogation, then, is impossible. No creature in the universe can do more than love God with all his heart and strength.

This law is enforced by sanctions. These are indispensable in order to carry it into execution, and maintain the dignity of the Lawgiver. Both the reward of obedience and the punishment of transgression proceed from the character of God. God loves Himself and His creatures. He is love for Himself above all, being the supreme object of love, and infinitely worthy of being loved. He is also love for His creatures, as appears by the original situation in which all of them were placed. The angels at their creation were the inhabitants of heaven, where God manifests His glory. When man was created, the world was provided for him, and adapted to his nature; he enjoyed communion with God, and everything around him was pronounced to be 'very good.'

From their happy original situation, a part of the angels and all mankind have fallen by disobedience. They broke the perfect bond of love, and consequently the unhappiness which proceeds from their rebellion against God can only be attributed to themselves. God, who is infinite in every perfection, and of purer eyes than to behold iniquity, must necessarily punish sin; for sin is the violation of the law of love. It separates the creature from God, who is the source of happiness; it is rebellion against His just government; and its tendency is to produce universal confusion and misery. The love, therefore, of God for Himself and for all that is good; His holiness, which places Him in infinite opposition to sin; His regard for the honour of His law; and His justice, which requires the giving to all what is due,—demand that sin should be punished.

The evil of violating the law of God may be estimated by the punishment inflicted on the human race on account of one transgression.[1] That one transgression caused the entrance of death, spiritual, temporal, and eternal; but by the goodness of God men were immediately placed under a dispensation of mercy. Human governments, being imperfect, dispense with justice when they extend pardon to a criminal; but this cannot be so with God, who, when He shows mercy, acts consistently with justice. He remains faithful; He cannot deny Himself. He proclaims Himself to be 'a just God, and a Saviour.' In the plan, then, of mercy and salvation, the law is maintained in all its authority, and with all its sanctions. Sin is punished, while sinners are saved.

The authority, the majesty, and the sovereignty of God are evidently interested in carrying into effect His threatenings and denunciations of punishment. If human laws were not executed, it would introduce confusion and disorder into families and states; but if the law of God were left unexecuted, there would be absolute confusion and disorder throughout the universe. The object, therefore, of the law, is an object of unspeakable importance, infinitely above that of the laws of men. Its immediate end is the manifestation of the holiness and glory of God.

Besides the law of universal and eternal obligation, the observance of other laws was enjoined on the people of Israel, in subserviency to the advent of the Messiah, to prefigure that great event, and in order to keep them separate from the other nations till He should appear. The covenant with Israel consisted of three parts: the first was the moral law; the second, the ceremonial; and the third, the judicial or political law. The moral law was such as has been already described. The ceremonial law consisted of a body of worship and of services, which the Israelites were commanded to render to God; and to this belonged all the various ordinances, purifications, sacrifices, oblations, celebrations of solemn feasts, and observances of days, excepting the seventh day, Sabbath, as being a part of the moral law. The judicial law comprehended all the regulations enjoined for their social and political conduct.

Along with these laws, there was vouchsafed a manifestation of the mercy of God through the Messiah. This comprehended all the promises of grace and salvation, and of the remission of sins, which God gave to the Israelites, proclaiming Himself to them as the Lord God, merciful and gracious, together with all the exhortations to repent, and have recourse to His fatherly goodness. It likewise included all those prophecies which foretold the Messiah, and required men to believe and place in Him their confidence.

Although this manifestation of grace and of mercy did not properly belong to the legal, but to the evangelical covenant, yet, as it was connected under the same ministry with the moral, the ceremonial, and the judicial laws, the Scripture includes the whole under the term *law*; the denomination of the ministry being taken from the part that predomi-

---

[1] The malignant nature of sin, and its fatal consequences, are not only manifest in the effect of the first transgression, which brought ruin on the whole human race, but likewise in the sin committed at the renewal of the world after the flood. The bitter effects of that sin are experienced to the present day by one of the branches of the descendants of Noah, on whom the curse he pronounced still rests. 'Cursed be Canaan, a servant of servants shall he be unto his brethren.'

nated. The reason why this revelation of the Gospel was joined with the law is obvious. God purposed to save many among the Israelites, and to conduct them, as His elect and true children, to life and salvation. But this could not be effected by the legal covenant alone; for the law made nothing perfect; it was weak through the flesh, and could not justify. It was necessary, then, to connect with it a measure of the dispensation of the Spirit; and without this, the state of the Israelites would have been worse than that of the other nations.

The economy of Moses was not, however, to be permanent. The object of the ceremonial law was accomplished, when that came which is called, in the Epistle to the Hebrews, vi. 1, 'perfection,' which was the grand consummation of all the typical ordinances, by the sacrifice of Christ. From that period its use was superseded, and itself abolished. On the destruction of Jerusalem and the temple, where alone the sacrifices could be offered, and on the expulsion of the Jews from their own land, the observance both of the ceremonial and judicial laws became impracticable. The whole Mosaic economy, which had been glorious in itself, was done away, and ceased to have any glory by reason of the glory that excelleth.

The moral law, however, could never be superseded. Although it formed a part of the Mosaic economy, to that economy it did not exclusively belong. Under the moral law, as a covenant, man at the beginning had been placed, and under it, as broken, and pronouncing its curse, all unbelievers remain as one with the first man. But from this covenant, they who are united to Him by whom it has been fulfilled, are for ever freed. According to the energetic language of the Apostle, in the seventh chapter of this Epistle, they are 'dead to the law.' While dead to it, however, as a covenant, whether as to its blessing or its curse—justification by it or condemnation—it remains their rule of duty, and must for ever continue in force. And that its authority should continue, while the other parts of that first covenant were done away, as it had existed before that covenant was made, was clearly indicated at its first promulgation from Mount Sinai. On that occasion it was strikingly distinguished from the other parts of the law. These were delivered to Moses, and by him to the people. But the moral law was promulgated by the voice of God, and it is said, 'He added no more.' While the other laws were written in a book by Moses, this law of everlasting obligation was written on tables of stone by the finger of God, and it alone was deposited in the ark. 'There was nothing in the ark save the two tables of stone,' 1 Kings viii. 9. There, as inscribed on these tables, the law was placed under the mercy-seat, which was an eminent type of Him by whom it was to be fulfilled. To minister and prepare the way for His appearance was the great object in view in the calling of Abraham, in the setting apart his descendants as a people from among whom He was to spring, in the public proclamation of this law which had been transgressed, and in thus depositing it in the ark, and it alone, not even to be looked upon till He should come by whom it was fulfilled.

In the third chapter of the Second Epistle to the Corinthians, a contrast is drawn between the ministration of Moses and that of the Apostles, in order to demonstrate the superiority of the latter. The ministration committed to Moses is there denominated the 'letter,' and that committed to the Apostles, the 'spirit'—the one written and engraved in stones, the other in the fleshly tables of the heart. On the ministration of the letter or outward form, in which spiritual blessings were veiled under sensible images and carnal ordinances, a degree of obscurity remained, called the veil on Moses' face, so that Israel after the flesh could not stedfastly look to the end, or final object, of that which was to be abolished. They rested in the observance of the ordinances, without considering their grand object, and looked to their temporal deliverances, without attending to the spiritual redemption which they prefigured. In the same way, what was external to the senses in the priesthood and the sacrifices, was all that they regarded. Their services were therefore those of the *letter*, with no discernment of the *spirit*, apart from which these services were a body without a soul. The nation of Israel, in general, thus verified the declaration that the things of the Spirit of God are foolishness to the natural man ; neither can he know them, because they are spiritually discerned. Not aware of the extent of the law which is spiritual, and of the perfect conformity required to all its precepts, and relying on the sacrifices they offered for the pardon of their transgressions, they sought acceptance by their own righteousness. But neither by their obedience could they fulfil the demands of the law, nor could the sacrifices remove their guilt, while by them they could not obtain peace of conscience, or assure themselves of reconciliation with God. The covenant, then, of which Moses was the mediator, gendered to bondage. It was the ministration of 'condemnation' and 'death,' for 'the letter killeth.' The spirit only, which that letter veiled, 'giveth life,' 2 Cor. iii. 6. Paul denominates the ministration committed to him the ministration of righteousness—the righteousness of the Messiah ; and his lamentation in the chapter before us is, that Israel being ignorant of this righteousness, went about to establish their own righteousness, not submitting themselves unto the righteousness of God.

The distinction, however, between the *letter* and the *spirit* did not refer exclusively to the nation of Israel. It related formerly, and has done so at every period, to all who, professing to worship God, are still in the flesh. The moral law, as has been observed, had been in force from the beginning, as is proved in this Epistle, ch. v. 13 ; although more fully promulgated in the covenant with Israel. But as soon as Adam had committed the sin by which it was broken, and all men had thus been brought under its condemnation, in pronouncing sentence on him, a proclamation of mercy was made, and sacrifices were instituted, which indicated the *spirit* equally with those afterwards enjoined on Israel in the ceremonial law. Among the nations, therefore, the true worshippers of God—such as Abel, who offered his sacrifice in faith, Enoch, who prophesied of the coming of the Lord, Noah, who found grace in the eyes of the Lord, Melchizedek, of whom it is particularly recorded, Heb. vii. 2, that he was *first* the king of righteousness, and then, or *after* that, also king of peace,[1] and Abraham, who saw the day of Christ, with many more—

[1] No man ever enjoyed peace till *after* he possessed that righteousness.

worshipped God in the spirit. The service of all others who were ignorant of the true intent and end of the sacrifices, and of that righteousness which the Messiah was to bring in, which Noah had preached, 2 Pet. ii. 5, was the service of the letter that 'killeth.' From this the necessity of preaching the Gospel to the nations, on which the Apostle so much insists in this chapter, is manifest. The heathens have generally retained the form of sacrifice, but, having entirely lost sight of the end of that institution, like Israel after the flesh, they know nothing beyond the letter which *killeth.* Such also is the service of all professed Christians, of whatever name, who go about to establish their own righteousness, which is of the law. To all men, of every description, who are labouring under the burden of sin, our Lord by His Gospel, wherever it reaches, proclaims, as formerly to Israel, *Come unto Me, and I will give you rest;* thus extending to them the ministration, not of condemnation, but of righteousness,—not of the letter that killeth, but of the spirit that giveth life. He Himself is that Spirit; and where the Spirit of the Lord is there is liberty, 2 Cor. iii. 17. 'It is the spirit that quickeneth; the flesh profiteth nothing; the words that I speak unto you, they are spirit, and they are life.' 'If the Son, therefore, shall make you free, ye shall be free indeed.'

CHAPTER 11
ROMANS 11:1 – 36

In this chapter the Apostle first denies that the whole of the nation of Israel was indiscriminately rejected, for, as he had already intimated, there was to be a remnant saved, and of that remnant he holds himself forth as a noted example. He then brings again into view the sovereignty of God, in reserving this 'remnant according to the election of grace.' In the next place, he affirms that, though blindness in part, as had been expressly foretold, had happened to Israel, yet, seeing that the gifts and calling of God are without repentance, the period must arrive when, according to the repeated promises of Scripture, all Israel shall be saved. They shall be brought in with the fulness of the Gentiles, when the wisdom and the goodness of God, in His dealings towards both, will be finally unfolded, and the assembled universe shall with one voice acknowledge that God is all in all, and that of Him, and through Him, and to Him are all things, to whom the glory shall be ascribed through the endless ages of eternity.

Ver. 1.—*I say then, Hath God cast away His people? God forbid. For I also am an Israelite, of the seed of Abraham, of the tribe of Benjamin.*

Dr. Macknight imagines that a Jew, and Mr. Stuart that an objector, is here and in other places in this Epistle introduced as disputing with the Apostle. Such a supposition is not only unnecessary but groundless. When Paul begins with the words, *I say then,* he states in a manner familiar to the best writers, a very obvious and probable objection which he was about to remove. *Hath God cast away His people? God forbid.—* Some might conclude, from the previous declarations of the Apostle, that the whole Jewish nation was now rejected of God, and for ever excluded from the blessings of the Gospel. This inference he strongly disclaims, and shows that God designed even now to reserve for Himself a people out of the Jews as well as out of the Gentiles, while, hereafter, it is the Divine purpose to recall the whole nation to Himself. Paul therefore answers his own pointed interrogatory, by rejecting the thought with his usual energy, while, to strengthen his denial, he further exhibits himself as a signal example of one not cast away. Had his doctrine involved the total rejection of the Jews, he would have pronounced his own condemnation.

For I also am an Israelite, of the seed of Abraham, of the tribe of Benjamin.—Besides being an Israelite, Paul here states that he was of the seed of Abraham. This was implied in his being an Israelite, but it is not needless tautology. A charge is often brought of tautology when the reiteration of an important truth is made for the purpose of giving it redoubled force. Although, in declaring himself an Israelite, he virtually claimed a direct descent from Abraham, yet it was a fact of no ordinary moment, and one therefore on which he emphatically dwells. It is his object to impress on the minds of his readers a sense of its intrinsic importance, as well as to recall to their recollection the covenant of God with Abraham, which confirmed the promises made to him respecting his descendants. This was much to the Apostle's purpose, in affirming that God had not cast away the children of him who was called the friend of God. Paul likewise adds that he was of the tribe of Benjamin. It was doubtless an honour to deduce his lineage through a tribe which adhered to the true worship of God, and had not revolted from the house of David. The fact, too, of his being enabled with certainty to trace his pedigree from Benjamin was sufficient to establish the purity of his origin, and to prove that he was not merely found mingled with the nation, but was, in the expressive language which he elsewhere adopts, ' a Hebrew of the Hebrews,' an Israelite by birth, parentage, and un-broken hereditary descent. The design of the Apostle is evidently to magnify his privileges, that he may produce the conviction that he has no interest in teaching anything derogatory to the just pretensions of his countrymen.

Ver. 2.—*God hath not cast away His people which He foreknew. Wot ye not what the Scripture saith of Elias ? how he maketh intercession to God against Israel, saying,*

Ver. 3.—*Lord, they have killed Thy prophets, and digged down Thine altars ; and I am left alone, and they seek my life.*

Ver. 4.—*But what saith the answer of God unto him ? I have reserved to Myself seven thousand men, who have not bowed the knee to the image of Baal.*

In the preceding verse Paul had asked if God had cast away His people. This he had strongly denied ; and the reasons by which he supports this denial form the subject of nearly the whole of the remainder of the chapter. He first proves, from the beginning of the 2d verse to the end of the 10th, that a remnant was at present preserved, although the rest were blinded ; and, from the 11th to the 33d verse, that the whole nation shall at last be restored.

God hath not cast away His people which He foreknew.—The term people, in the preceding verse, refers to the whole of Israel as the typical people of God, but is here restricted to the elect among them who were His true people, and are distinguished as 'His people which He foreknew.' God had cast off the nation, but even then He had a people among them whom from eternity He foreknew as His people. The word foreknow, as formerly observed, signifies to know before, or it denotes a knowledge accompanied by a decree, or it imports a preconceived love, favour, and regard. Divine foreknowledge, in the first of these senses, is God's foresight of future existence and events, and His eternal prescience of whatever shall take place in all futurity. This foreknowledge is not only to be distinguished from God's decree, by which everything future comes to pass, but must be considered in the order of nature as consequent and dependent upon the determination and purpose of God. For the futurity of all things depends on the decrees of God, by which every created existence and event, with all their circumstances, are ordered, fixed, and ascertained. Being thus decreed, they are the objects of foreknowledge; for they could not be known to be future unless their futurity was established, and that by the Divine decree. God foreknew all things that were to come to pass, by knowing His own purposes and decrees. Had God determined or decreed nothing respecting future existences by creation and providence, there could have been no foreknowledge of anything whatever. Because, therefore, this foreknowledge of God necessarily implies and involves His decrees, His foreknowledge is in the inspired writings sometimes accompanied by the mention of His decrees; as, for example, 'Him, being delivered by the determinate counsel and foreknowledge of God, ye have taken, and by wicked hands have crucified and slain,' Acts ii. 23. And it is sometimes put for the decree, as in the following passage, where the word here translated foreknew is rendered fore-ordained: 'Who verily was fore-ordained before the foundation of the world,' 1 Pet. i. 20. In the third sense, as taken for a knowledge of love and approbation, it signifies, as in the verse before us, to choose and recognise as His own. God had not cast away His people whom He had before loved and chosen, for the Apostle alleges this foreknowledge as the reason why God did not cast away His people.

The people of God, whom He foreknew, were those whom He chose from all eternity, according to His sovereign pleasure; and in this sense the expression is clearly explained, when they are declared, in the 5th verse, to be a 'remnant according to the election of grace,' and when it is said, in the 4th, that God had 'reserved' to Himself His true worshippers in the time of Elijah. This proves the correctness of Calvin's observation, 'that foreknowledge does not mean a certain speculative view, by which the uncreated Cause of all effects foresaw the character of every individual of the human family, but points to the good pleasure of the decree of the Sovereign Disposer of all events, by which He hath chosen for His children those who were not yet born, and had no power to insinuate themselves into the favour of the Author of all happiness. Thus (Gal. iv. 9), Paul says, they are known of God, because He prevents by His grace and favour, and calls them to a knowledge of Christ.'

Wot ye not what the Scripture saith of Elias?—The quotation from the Old Testament Scriptures, which the Apostle here brings to bear on the point in question, fully establishes the view that has been given of the preceding passage. There was an elected remnant in the days of Elijah, when things were at the worst ; and so, at the time when the Apostle wrote, there was also an elected remnant whom God had reserved. *How he maketh intercession to God against Israel.*—'First Kings xix. 10, cited by Paul,' says Calvin, 'contains no implication, but a mere complaint. Since, however, his complaint implies a total despair of the religion of the whole Jewish nation, we may rest assured that he devoted it to destruction.' But Paul's comment may assure us that Elijah, at the time referred to, not only complained but interceded against Israel. The Apostle spoke by the Spirit that indicted the words in which Elijah's complaint is recorded, and we should not look for a voucher for such testimony. Such a mode of strengthening the Scriptures is only to weaken them. It teaches us to undervalue the inspired commentary of the New Testament, unless we can produce some other confirmation. Elijah, when solemnly interrogated by the Lord why he was in the place where he was then found, away from the proper scene of his ministry, accounted for his flight to save his life, which seems to have been without any Divine admonition, by complaining of the apostasy of the nation. As this was an exposure of their wickedness, and, had it been true in all its extent, would have led to their destruction, it was in effect intercession against Israel. But the answer of God showed that he was mistaken. God had even then reserved to Himself a goodly number, who had not apostatised from His worship.

From these words, in this answer of God, *I have reserved to Myself,* we learn that if any are preserved from false worship, if any are brought to the knowledge of God, it is by His special influence and agency, and not owing to themselves. Such favoured individuals are said to be 'reserved' by God. How different is this from the views of multitudes who profess Christianity ! It is a comfort to think that in the worst times there may be many more of the people of God than we are apt to imagine.

Bowed the knee.—This shows that any overt act of idolatry, or any compliance with the requirements of false religion, renders men unworthy of being accounted the true servants of God. So Job, in declaring the integrity of his conduct towards God and man, says, ' If I beheld the sun when it shined, or the moon walking in brightness, and my heart hath been secretly enticed, or *my mouth hath kissed my hand,* this also were an iniquity to be punished ; for I should have denied the God that is above.'

Ver. 5.—*Even so then at this present time also there is a remnant according to the election of grace.*

This is the object of the reference to the election in the times of Elijah, and renders the words at the beginning of the 2d verse quite definite. As there was a remnant then reserved by God, so there is a remnant now. Both were necessary for the preservation of the nation. The seven thousand were its salt in Elijah's time, as were the remnant here spoken of during its present blindness.

According to the election of grace.—Than this nothing can be more explicit. God had formerly reserved for Himself, by His gracious influence and special agency, a small number in Israel; and in the same way, at the time when the Apostle wrote, He had reserved, according to His sovereign choice, a remnant of that nation. And to set aside every idea that this election was the reward of an inherent good foreseen in those chosen, or of anything meritorious performed by them, the Apostle adds that it was *of grace.* It was an unconditional choice, resulting from the sovereign free favour of God.

Ver. 6.—*And if by grace, then is it no more of works; otherwise grace is no more grace. But if it be of works, then is it no more grace; otherwise work is no more work.*

The opponents of the doctrine of election maintain that men are chosen on account of their good works *foreseen.* But here it is expressly declared by the Apostle that it is not on account of works at all, whether past, present, or future. What, then, is the source of election? *Grace.*—It is an election of grace, or free favour; that is, a gratuitous election, not by the merit of works of any kind, but purely from the favour of God. Grace and works are here stated as diametrically opposite and totally irreconcilable. If, then, election is by grace, it is not of works; for this would imply a contradiction. Grace would not then be grace. Here we have the warrant of Scripture for asserting that a contradiction is necessarily untrue, and that no authority is sufficient to establish two propositions which actually contradict each other.

But if it be of works, then it is no more grace; otherwise work is no more work.—Many suppose these words are spurious, because they are wanting in some manuscripts, and because the idea is substantially included in what has been already stated. This reason, however, is not conclusive, and those who build on such a foundation show little knowledge of Scripture. It is not useless to reverse the idea, and draw the same conclusion from the converse. It is far more likely that human wisdom has in some manuscripts omitted this passage, than that it should have been transcribed from the margin into the text.

In the foregoing verses, as well as in the eighth and ninth chapters, the doctrine of election is stated in the clearest manner. This doctrine, as implying the total inability of man to recover himself from guilt and ruin, and the necessity for this end of Divine interposition, has ever been highly offensive to human pride and human wisdom. These and the preceding strong statements of it, can never be silenced; but they have often been subjected to the most violent perversions. Every artifice of human ingenuity has been employed to turn away the Apostle's words from bearing on the point; but it has been employed in vain; and nothing will ever be able to reconcile these statements to the mind of the natural man. But, after all, what does this doctrine assert that is not necessarily and obviously implied in every other doctrine of the Gospel? Are all men by nature *dead* in sin? If so, he that is made spiritually alive, must be made so by Him who alone gives life; and it is nothing short of Divine sovereignty that constitutes the difference between him and those who remain in death and enmity to God. Are Christians represented as being *born again?* Does not this refer men's spiritual existence to the sovereign choice, and mercy, and agency of their heavenly

Father ? Are Christians *saved by faith?* If faith be the gift of God, salvation by faith implies election. Why, then, should the Scriptures be wrested to avoid the admission of a doctrine which is not only essential to their consistency with themselves, but which the whole system of Christianity implies ?

The salvation of every individual of the human race who partakes of it must be wholly gratuitous on the part of God, and effected by His sovereign grace. Sinners could have no claim upon God; His justice demanded their punishment, and they could plead no *right* to mercy, which, if admitted, would make mercy justice. The sending of His Son, therefore, into the world to save sinners, was an act of free grace ; and Christ, accordingly, is spoken of as God's gift. ' He *gave* His only-begotten Son,' John iii. 16. ' Thanks be unto God for His unspeakable *gift*,' 2 Cor. ix. 15. It is no impeachment of the mercy of God, that all the fallen angels perished, and that upon the whole of them justice took its course. Could it then have been impeached, if in like manner God had left *all* men to perish ? and if not, can it be so because only a *part* of them are left under that condemnation into which they have fallen, while to another part, He, who ' hath mercy on whom He will have mercy,' has extended that mercy ? These truths, when unreservedly admitted, greatly contribute to promote in Christians, in contemplating the distinguishing goodness of God to them, joy in the Lord, and to their bringing forth all the fruits of the Spirit. It leads them to admire the mercies of God, who hath brought them from darkness to light, and hath saved and called them with an holy calling, not according to their works, but according to His own purpose and grace, which was given them in Christ Jesus before the world began, 2 Tim. i. 9 ; whereby they have the hope of eternal life, which God, that cannot lie, ' promised,' in like manner, ' before the world began,' Tit. i. 2.

The fact that the doctrines of election and of the Divine sovereignty are so clearly taught in Scripture, is a most convincing proof that they are not the invention of man. Such a view could not have suggested itself to the human mind, and, if suggested, could not have been pleasing to its author. As little would it be calculated to serve the purpose of an impostor, being universally unpalatable to those intended to be gained as converts. Nothing but the supposition of their truth and Divine origin can account for their being found in the Bible. ' It is a glorious argument,' says President Edwards, in his *Enquiry respecting the Freedom of the Will*, ' of the divinity of the Holy Scriptures, that they teach such doctrines, which in one age and another, through the blindness of men's minds, and strong prejudices of their hearts, are rejected as most absurd and unreasonable by the wise and great men of the world ; which yet, when they are most carefully and strictly examined, appear to be exactly agreeable to the most demonstrably certain and natural dictates of reason.' If the Scriptures, he observes, taught the opposite doctrines to those which are so much stumbled at, viz., the Arminian and Pelagian doctrine of free will, and other modifications of these errors, it would be the greatest of all difficulties in the way of the internal evidence of the truth of the Bible.

Ver. 7.— *What then ? Israel hath not obtained that which he seeketh for ; but the election hath obtained it, and the rest were blinded*

What then ?—What is the result of all that the Apostle had been saying ? It is this : Israel as a nation hath not obtained righteousness, of which it was in search, ch. ix. 31 ; but the election among them— the chosen remnant reserved by God, spoken of above—hath obtained it. Can anything more expressly affirm the doctrine of election ? *And the rest were blinded.*—How strong is this language ! How can it be softened by the most subtle ingenuity, so as to make it agreeable to the taste of the natural man ? The election had received the righteousness of God through Jesus Christ ; but the whole nation besides not only did not attain to the righteousness of which they were in search, but were blinded. This is a hard saying, who can hear it ? It is God's saying, and it is unsafe to reject it. It is the duty of His people, as little children, to receive it with meekness.

The election of a sinful creature is an act of the free and sovereign will of God ; while his punishment is not a sovereign or arbitrary act of Divine authority. God does not punish without an existing cause in the guilty. Condemnation supposes positive criminality. Men are in themselves sinful, and commit sin voluntarily ; and for their punishment, they are hardened, and finally perish in their sins, and their destruction is the execution of a just sentence of God against sin. Their sins, which are the cause of their destruction, are their own ; while the salvation of those whom God chooses and calls to Himself is His gift. God knows what men left to their own inclinations will do ; and as to those who are finally condemned, He determines to abandon them to their depraved inclinations, and hardens them in their rebellion against Him. But as to His determination, by grace, to cause the sinner to believe, to will, and to obey, it requires a positive interposition of Divine power—a power which creates anew, which no one merits or deserves, and which God vouchsafes or withholds according to the counsel of His own will. Conformably to this, we see through the whole of the Scriptures, that when men are saved they are saved by the sovereign grace of God, and when they perish, it is by the appointment of God, Jude 4, through their own fault.

Ver. 8.—(*According as it is written, God hath given them the spirit of slumber, eyes that they should not see, and ears that they should not hear) unto this day.*

Mr. Stuart asserts that it is not necessary to understand this as a *prediction*, in the appropriate sense of the word. But it is most undoubtedly a prediction ; and although it was adapted to describe the Jews at a preceding period, the Holy Spirit, as from Paul's application we are bound to believe, intended it to describe the people of Israel in the time of the Apostles. The same thing that in one sense is ascribed to God, in another is ascribed to man. Although, by the decree and providence of God, Israel was blinded, yet the blame was their own. The Jews, at that period, had the light of natural understanding, yet they did not see what was exhibited with the clearest evidence. This is still the case. Multitudes who are distinguished for their intellectual vigour and mental powers, are altogether blind in spiritual things. *Unto this day.*—Some join this with the words of the Prophet, and others make it the additional observation of Paul. In whatever way this is understood, they are equally the words of the Apostle, for he applies them to the case in hand.

Ver. 9.—*And David saith, Let their table be made a snare, and a trap, and a stumbling-block, and a recompense unto them ;*
Ver. 10.—*Let their eyes be darkened, that they may not see, and bow down their back alway.*

And David saith.—It is highly erroneous to suppose, with Mr. Stuart, that the Apostle quotes these passages merely to illustrate a general principle. In this sense they could be of no use. But they are eminently to the purpose as predictions. *Let their table be made a snare, and a trap, and a stumbling-block, and a recompense unto them.*—Let them experience misery and disappointment in their daily occupations and concerns, and let them find those things, of whatever description— whether sacred or common—which were calculated to be for their welfare and advantage, a snare, and a trap, and a stumbling-block, and a punishment to them. For the hope of retaining their temporal kingdom, they rejected the Lord Jesus Christ, and by this means they lost the kingdom also, with all temporal prosperity, John xi. 48, 50. Mr. Stuart observes, 'It is enough to say, at present, that the Apostle, in making this quotation, need not be supposed to design anything more than to produce an instance from the Psalms, where the same *principle* is developed as is contained in the assertions which he had made ; *i.e.,* the ancient Scriptures speak of a part of Israel as blind and deaf, as in deep distress and under heavy punishment because of their unbelief and disobedience. What happened in ancient times may take place again ; it has, in fact, happened at the present time.' How trifling would be the conduct of the Apostle, according to this representation of Mr. Stuart ? Are all these quotations made just for the purpose of showing that something in some way similar happened long ago ? Is this likeness merely accidental ? Whatever application the words might have to David and David's times, their import as a proper prediction is clear, and since they are so appropriated by the Apostle, ought never to be questioned. These words of the Old Testament Scriptures are too strong to represent anything else, in their full extent, but the fearful blindness of the Jews in the time of the Messiah, when they saw His miracles, and nevertheless did not perceive their import ; when they heard, yet did not listen to the calls of His Gospel. Then, truly, their heart was made fat, and their ears heavy, and their eyes were closed, John xii. 40 ; and then, by the issue, it appeared that God would not convert them, because He would not any more at that time do them good. The predictions concerning their spiritual blindness, as well as the denunciations contained in these verses, have been literally accomplished. Many pretend to find a difficulty in regard to the threatenings denounced against the enemies of God in the Psalms, but the difficulty arises from their own erroneous views of the subject. Does it imply a malicious or revengeful temper to utter the dictates of the Spirit of God, whoever may be the object of the Divine denunciations? This is not merely trifling, but blasphemous.

To represent this passage otherwise than as a prediction, gives a false view of the sixty-ninth Psalm, from which the quotation is taken, which contains so illustrious a prophecy of our Lord Jesus Christ. God had announced by David, in that Psalm, the maledictions it records in connection with crimes committed by the Jews. Those here quoted, in the 9th and 10th verses, immediately follow the prophetical description in the Psalm of their treatment of the Messiah. It should also be observed, that during the whole period of the former dispensation, God employed the most powerful external means to bring them back to Himself, so that they were entirely without excuse.

The sixty-ninth Psalm consists of three parts. The first respects the violent persecutions which the Lord Jesus Christ experienced from His enemies and the Jews. The second part is a prediction of the fearful judgments of the Lord, especially upon the traitor Judas. The third part regards the exaltation of Jesus Christ to glory, and the success of the Gospel. First, the prophetical characters of the Psalm are representative of the extraordinary sufferings of Him of whom it speaks, and of the reproaches against Him—sufferings and persecutions which would be both exaggerated were they limited to those persecutions which David endured at the hand of His enemies. Secondly, the cause of His sufferings is ascribed to His love of God. 'For Thy sake I have borne reproach; shame hath covered My face. I am become a stranger unto My brethren, and an alien unto My mother's children. For the zeal of Thine house hath eaten Me up; and the reproaches of them that reproached Thee are fallen upon Me.' Now, we do not read that David was ever persecuted on account of his religion, nor that he suffered because of His love to God. Thirdly, although the words, 'They gave Me also gall for My meat; and in My thirst they gave me vinegar to drink,' may be understood figuratively of David, they cannot be literally applied to him, but they apply literally to Jesus Christ.

The first division of the Psalm, which foretells the ruin of the persecutors, is too strong to be understood of the persecutors of David, as appears from what is said from the 22d to the 28th verses inclusive, which conclude with these awful words: 'Add iniquity unto their iniquity: and let them not come into Thy righteousness. Let them be blotted out of the book of the living, and not be written with the righteous.' It cannot be said that the enemies of David were absolutely cut off from the covenant of God; but these words were fully accomplished on the body of the nation of the Jews, when they did not attain, as the Apostle says, to the law of righteousness, and refused to submit themselves unto the righteousness of God. They were, therefore, blinded or hardened; the awful maledictions contained in the verses before us descended on their devoted country, and thus they were blotted out of the book of the living, and were not written with the righteous.

In the third part of the Psalm, the deliverance vouchsafed by God is declared: 'Let Thy salvation, O God, set me up on high,' which signifies the ascension of the Lord to heaven. It is afterwards said, 'I will praise the name of God with a song, and will magnify Him with thanksgiving. This also shall please the Lord better than an ox or bullock that hath horns or hoofs,' which marks the abolition of the legal sacrifices. Finally, the filling of the earth with the glory of God is declared. 'Let the heaven and earth praise Him, the seas, and everything that moveth therein.' This is too great to be applied to the temporal deliverances which God vouchsafed to David, the fame of which did not extend so far. It must, then, be ascribed to the glory which God received after the exaltation of Jesus Christ, as He Himself said, 'Father, glorify Thy Son, that Thy Son also may glorify Thee.'

The words in the beginning of the 9th verse of this Psalm, 'The zeal of Thine house hath eaten me up,' are applied to the Lord Jesus Christ, John ii. 17 ; and the concluding words, 'The reproaches of them that reproached Thee, are fallen upon Me,' by Paul, Rom. xv. 3. 'They gave Me also gall for My meat; and in My thirst they gave Me vinegar to drink,' is applied in the three Gospels, by Matthew, and Mark, and John, to what took place at His crucifixion. The words contained in the 25th verse, 'Let their habitation be desolate, and let none dwell in their tents,' are applied to Judas, Acts i. 20, who may be considered in this matter as the representative of the nation. 'Let their table become a snare before them,' verse 22, is quoted by the Apostle in the verse before us, predicting the condition of the Jewish nation when he wrote. And are all these passages to be considered as quoted by way of accommodation, and not as predictions? Such an interpretation is not only erroneous, but is degrading to the Holy Scriptures, and utterly at variance with their true meaning.

Ver. 11.—*I say then, Have they stumbled that they should fall? God forbid: but rather through their fall salvation is come unto the Gentiles, for to provoke them to jealousy.*

Having proved that God had not cast away His people, by referring to the fact that even then a remnant, according to the election of grace, was preserved, Paul supports his denial of their rejection by the consideration that in process of time the whole nation shall be restored. This restoration, as has been already remarked, forms the subject of nearly the whole remainder of the chapter.

I say then, Have they stumbled that they should fall?—This is the Apostle's own question, and does not, as Dr. Macknight and Mr. Stuart allege, proceed from an imaginary objector. It naturally springs out of the declaration made in the four preceding verses concerning the blindness of those called 'the rest,' in contradistinction to the remnant comprehended in the election. The question is, 'Has the great body of the Jewish nation stumbled, that they should fall for ever, and is this the purpose of their fall?' Paul replies by a strong negative. Nothing was further from the purpose of God with respect to His ancient people. They had stumbled, as was said, ch. ix. 32, 'at that stumbling-stone,' according to the predictions of the Prophets respecting Christ; but still it was but a temporary stumbling, from which the nation will finally recover. God had a double purpose in this. His design in their stumbling was not that they should fall for ever, but rather that through their fall

salvation should come to the Gentiles, and that, through this, the nation
of Israel might ultimately receive the Messiah.

To provoke them to jealousy.—It is probable from this, that the Jews
will be excited, by seeing God's favour to the Gentiles, to reflect on their
own fallen condition, and to desire to possess the same advantages. When
the Jews can no longer hide from themselves that the God of their fathers
is with the nations whom they abhor, they will be led to consider their
ways, and brought again into the fold of Israel. This is according to the
prophecy already quoted by the Apostle in the 19th verse of the preceding chapter.

It was in this manner, then, that God purposed to bring the Jewish
nation finally to submit to Him, in order that they might receive His
blessing; and thus in His sovereignty He overrules the fall and ruin of
some for the salvation of others. His awful judgments against the
audacious transgressors of His laws, warn the beholders to flee from the
wrath to come; and, on the other hand, the conversion of men who have
been notorious sinners, excites others to seek the salvation of Christ.
Who can calculate what extensive, permanent, and glorious effects may
result throughout the whole creation, and in eternal ages, from the fall
of angels and men—from the redemption of God's people in Christ—from
His dispensations towards the Church and the world? Eph. iii. 9–11. We
ought to remember that the Lord may have infinitely wise and gracious
motives for His most severe and terrible judgments. Thus did the fall
of the Jews become the occasion of the Gentiles being enriched with the
inexhaustible treasures that are in Christ, so that the justice, the wisdom,
and the faithfulness of God were glorified in this awful visitation.

Ver. 12.—*Now, if the fall of them be the riches of the world, and the diminishing
of them the riches of the Gentiles; how much more their fulness?*

In the foregoing verse, the Apostle had said that through the fall of
the Jews salvation was come to the Gentiles; he had also intimated that
they should be recovered from their fall. This might lead the Gentiles
to apprehend that, in the restoration of the Jews, they might in like
manner be cast off. To this Paul now answers, that, on the contrary, if
the fall of the Jews be the riches of the Gentiles, much more so will be
their restoration.

The temporary fall of the Jews was fraught with the richest blessings
to the rest of the world. Their rejection of the Messiah was the occasion
of the offering of the great sacrifice for sin, and of the Gospel being
preached to all nations. In consequence of their rejecting the testimony
of the Apostles, the remnant who believed fled from the persecution of
their countrymen, and, being scattered abroad, went everywhere preaching the word. Besides, the Jewish nation, which had been constituted
the witnesses of God, Isa. xliii. 10, and to whom the oracles of God had
been committed, have firmly preserved their sacred trust, even amidst all
their unbelief and consequent sufferings. In this we discern an illustrious proof of the Divine origin of the Old Testament Scriptures which
testify of the Messiah; while the preservation of the Jews as a distinct
people, amidst all the changes and revolutions of ages, stands forth a last-

ing miracle, not to be explained on natural principles, furnishing incontestible evidence of the truth of the Gospel.

Thus the diminishing of the Jews was the aggrandisement of the Gentiles; for, in the inscrutable counsels of Jehovah, His gift of salvation to them was connected with the degradation and downfall of His ancient people. But here the Apostle gives the assurance that the *fulness* of the Jews—their restoration as a body, when they shall acknowledge Christ as the Messiah—will yet prove a far greater blessing to the Gentiles. It will be connected with a calling of the nations to an extent beyond anything yet witnessed, and also with a great enlargement of their knowledge of the Gospel. This was consistent with what is said in the sequel of that prediction to which Paul had just referred. In the same way, Moses, after foretelling the many evils that were to come upon his nation, and of the calamities that were to be heaped upon them, concludes the whole by predicting all that the Apostle here declares: ' Rejoice, O ye nations, with His people ; for He will avenge the blood of His servants, and will render vengeance to His adversaries, and will be merciful unto His land and to His people,' Deut. xxxii. 43.

Ver. 13.—*For I speak to you Gentiles, inasmuch as I am the Apostle of the Gentiles, I magnify mine office :*

The Apostle continues, to the beginning of the 16th verse, to amplify still further what he had just announced, in proof that the salvation of the Gentiles is closely connected with God's dealings towards the Jews. The Gentiles were largely blessed with the Gospel when it was rejected by the Jews ; but they will be blessed with it to an unspeakably greater extent when the Jews shall be recalled. Paul was the Apostle of the Gentiles, and by uttering this prediction with regard to the Gentiles, at the period of the restoration of the Jews, he says he magnifies his office. He here addresses himself particularly to those in the church at Rome, who were of the Gentiles. For as he had been appointed their Apostle, he was desirous to commend his ministry among them, to assert the honour of his commission, and to prove its great importance in imparting to them the knowledge of the Gospel. He shows, with regard to the Gentiles, that its value was enchanced in proportion as a greater number of Gentiles will be saved. In this view, it is greatly for the interest of the Gentiles that the Jews should be brought back, and this should increase their efforts for their conversion.

Ver. 14.—*If by any means I may provoke to emulation them which are my flesh, and might save some of them.*

The Apostle also desired to excite the attention of his countrymen by this view of Divine favour to the Gentiles. He endeavoured to move them to emulation, that in this way they might be directed to Christ the Saviour of sinners, and that some of them might be saved. He says *some*, not all, for he was aware that the body of the nation was at that time rejected, but he knew not who among them were of the remnant according to the election of grace, who, although still rejecting the Messiah, might, by means of the Gospel which he preached, be finally saved.

Ver. 15.—*For if the casting away of them be the reconciling of the world, what shall the receiving of them be, but life from the dead ?*

Here the Apostle further explains and illustrates the argument he had employed in the 12th verse. The Gospel was preached to the world only after Israel rejected it. This was not the result of accident; it was according to the fixed purpose of God. The middle wall of partition was then broken down. The command was given to preach the Gospel to every creature. After the great sacrifice had been offered, it was no longer to be limited to the lost sheep of the house of Israel. The world was to hear the Gospel ; and thus the Gentiles received the grace of God only through the unbelief and rejection of the Jewish nation. But if the casting away of the Jews was such a blessing to the world, their recall will be a blessing unspeakably greater. It will occasion a revival among the Gentile churches, from a dead and almost lifeless state, which will resemble a resurrection. The numbers then converted will be as if all the dead had risen out of their graves. The Divine dispensations being at that period so far developed, and the prophecies respecting the rejection and restoration of the Jews so fully accomplished, no doubt will any longer be entertained regarding the Divine origin of the Holy Scriptures. A great additional light, too, will be thrown on those parts of them which at present are most obscure, so that, in the providence of God, the result will be an unexampled blessing both to Jews and Gentiles.

Ver. 16.—*For if the first-fruit be holy, the lump is also holy ; and if the root be holy, so are the branches.*

The whole of the Apostle's argument goes to establish the restoration of Israel. He shows that they were not cast off,—first, by his own example ; and, secondly, by referring to the remnant among them according to the election of grace, which proved that they were not devoted to destruction like Sodom and Gomorrah, ch. ix. 29. It was true that the predictions of which he had spoken were fulfilled ; but although, consistently with these, they had stumbled, it was not that they should irrevocably fall ; but this was the way in which God had appointed salvation to come to the Gentiles. Even in this, however, God had their restoration in view ; for the kindness shown to the Gentiles would be the means of provoking their jealousy, and great as were the benefits which accrued to the world from their fall, those of their restoration would be still greater. The verse before us contains a third argument to prove the future conversion of the Jewish nation.

The Apostle here employs two similitudes, one taken from the law, respecting the first-fruits, by which the whole of the harvest was sanctified ; and the other from nature, by which, under the figure of a tree, he evidences the truth he is exhibiting respecting the final restoration of the whole nation of Israel. By the first-fruit some understand the first Jewish converts ; but it rather appears that both the first-fruit and the root refer to Abraham, as the first-fruit to God, and the root of the Jewish nation. As Abraham was separated to the service of God, so, in the sense of a relative holiness, all his descendants in the line of Isaac were holy, standing in an external relation to God in which no other nation ever stood. But Abraham was also personally holy; and so, in every age, had been many of his descendants through the heir of promise; and so, also, shall be an innumerable multitude of them hereafter. For, according to the figure here employed, they shall as branches be graffed in again, and so all Israel shall be saved.

It is therefore here shown that the future conversion of Israel is guaranteed by the peculiar covenant relation in which they stand to Abraham. Although the whole nation had never been internally holy, they had all along been in a peculiar manner separated or consecrated to God, in the same way as, according to the law, the first-fruits of the harvest were consecrated; for when the corn was kneaded, a cake of the first of the dough was to be given to the Lord, Num. xv. 19–21; and thus the whole of the harvest was set apart or sanctified, 1 Tim. iv. 5. On this ground, Moses, even when reminding the Israelites of their un-hallowed rebellion against God in the wilderness, declared, 'Thou art a holy people unto the Lord thy God: the Lord thy God hath chosen thee to be a special people unto Himself,' Deut. vii. 6. And a little after, when rehearsing to them their several rebellions, and informing them that the Lord had pronounced them to be 'a stiff-necked people,' and when he claims the heavens and the earth, and all that they contain, as the property of Jehovah, he says to Israel, 'The Lord had a delight in thy fathers to love them, and He chose their seed after them, even you, above all people,' Deut. x. 15, and Deut. iv. 37, xiv. 2, xxvi. 19, and xxxii. 8, 9. 'God,' it is also said, 'heard their groanings, and God remembered His covenant with Abraham, with Isaac, and with Jacob. And God looked upon the children of Israel, and God had respect unto them,' Ex. ii. 24. Moses assured the people, the Lord 'will not forsake thee, neither destroy thee, nor forget the covenant of thy fathers which He sware unto them,' Deut. iv. 31. And it is said by the Prophet Isaiah, xliii. 21, 'This people have I formed for Myself.' In like manner, when Samuel was in the strongest terms reproaching Israel for their rebellion, in forsaking the Lord and choosing a king, he still exhorts them to serve the Lord, notwithstanding their past wickedness. 'For,' he adds, 'the Lord will not forsake His people for His great name's sake; because it hath pleased the Lord to make you His people,' 1 Sam. xii. 22. Innumerable declarations to the same effect are interspersed throughout the Old Testament. The Apostle's argument then is, that as the lump is holy through the offering of the first-fruit, and as the tree derives its character from the root, so the descendants of Abraham, Isaac, and Jacob, whom the Lord chose, were set apart by solemn covenant for His service and glory.

In consequence of God's love to the fathers, He delivered them from Egypt, and separated them by the Sinai covenant from all other nations as His peculiar people. But while that transaction announced the most important purposes, it was not faultless, Heb. viii. 7. It pointed out their duty, but did not communicate those dispositions which are essential to obedience. It was therefore only a figure for the time then present, imposed on them for a season, Heb. ix. 9, 10, and intended to be introductory to a better covenant, established upon better promises, by which the law was to be put in their inward parts, and God was to be a God to them in a higher sense than He was by that first covenant. This was taught them in the land of Moab, where God promised to circumcise their heart and the heart of their seed, and is repeated by Isaiah, lix. 21, Jeremiah, xxxi. 31, and referred to by the Apostle in the 26th and 27th verses of the chapter before us. Thus Israel has been set apart as a holy people, devoted to the service of God, since the call of Abraham. Their unbelief has not made the faithfulness of God of none effect. Their rebellions have all been subservient to His eternal purpose. The tree was of the Lord's right-hand planting, a noble vine; many of the branches have been broken off, but still the root remains, bound round, as it were, ' with a band of iron and brass;' and the branches shall be graffed in again, by their partaking of the faith of Abraham. And as they were God's witnesses when enjoying His blessing in the land of Canaan, Isa. xliii. 10, 12, xliv. 8, and are His witnesses in their rejection, and in being ' left as a beacon upon the top of a mountain, and as an ensign on a hill,' Isa. xxx. 17, so shall they be His witnesses in their restoration. In God's treatment of them we see His abhorrence of sin. In them we behold a memorial of the severity of God, Rom. xi. 22; but in them shall also be witnessed a nobler monument of His goodness.

The Apostle's argument, then, amounts to this—that as the lump is holy, through the offering of the first-fruits, so this is a pledge that the lump, or body of the nation, will yet be made holy. The restoration of Israel is not only plainly asserted by the Apostle here, but it is essential to the fulfilment of the parable exhibited in God's dealings with the nation of Israel. That nation was a type of the true Israel, and in God's dealings with them all the great doctrines of the Gospel are exhibited. It was therefore necessary that Israel should be restored, otherwise the parable which shadows forth the final preservation of the people of God, declared in Rom. viii. 35, would have been incomplete. We see the sovereignty of God in choosing Israel, in bestowing on them so many advantages, in punishing them so severely, and making the whole to redound to His own glory and the salvation of all who are ordained to eternal life. They have been the chosen instruments employed for the salvation of the world; and their last end, after all their wanderings, and all their rebellions, and all their unbelief, shall exhibit them as the true circumcision, who rejoice in Christ Jesus. When, therefore, the calling of the Gentiles and the rebellion of Israel are announced in the strongest terms, it is immediately added, ' Thus saith the Lord, As the new wine is found in the cluster, and one saith, destroy it not, for a blessing is in it; so will I do for My servants' sakes, that I may not destroy them all. And I will bring forth a seed out of Jacob, and out of Judah an inheritor of My mountains; and Mine elect shall inherit it, and My servants shall dwell there,' Isa. lxv. 8. ' As a teil tree, and as an oak, whose substance is in them, when they cast their leaves, so the holy seed shall be the substance thereof,' Isa. vi. 13. All this accords with those repeated declarations of Scripture already referred to, in which it is said that the Lord will never forsake His people, for His great name's sake. It likewise accords with the numerous and peculiar privileges conferred on

Israel as a nation, as enumerated in the ninth chapter of this Epistle, and summed up in these words, 'Whose are the fathers, and of whom, as concerning the flesh, Christ came.' And consistently with the whole, it is declared in the sequel of the chapter before us, that the time is coming when all Israel shall be saved, and the natural branches, or descendants of Abraham, shall be graffed in again into their own olive tree. On these grounds it is evident that, while those whom the Apostle calls the 'rest' of Israel, had in the meantime fallen, and although successive generations should behold Jerusalem forsaken, and Israel wandering without a home through the world, yet the restoration of the nation shall hereafter testify the unchangeable faithfulness of that God who, in dividing to the nations their inheritance, 'set the bounds of the people, according to the number of the children of Israel.'

Such is the method by which the Apostle in this verse continues to substantiate his declaration that God had not cast away His people. He had shown that their destruction could not have been intended, since a remnant was preserved; and he is now proving that, as a body, they shall finally be restored to God's favour. In declaring the peculiar privileges of Israel, derived from their first progenitors, the Apostle, by exhibiting their distinguished superiority over all other nations, lays a foundation for the forcible warnings which, down to the 23d verse, he proceeds to deliver to the Gentiles who had been received into the covenant of God. Mr. Stuart remarks of this 16th verse, that it is *illustration* rather than argument; but it is an illustration which has been adopted by the Spirit of God as a pledge of the event. If it be not argument, it is evidence, and is recorded as a revelation of the Divine purpose, that the lump, or body of the nation of Israel, shall yet be holy.

Ver. 17.—*And if some of the branches be broken off, and thou, being a wild olive tree, were graffed in among them, and with them partakest of the root and fatness of the olive tree;*

Before alleging anything further to prove the future conversion of the Jews, Paul here, and onwards to the 25th verse, continues to employ the figure of a tree and its branches. In doing so, he takes occasion to administer a salutary caution to the Gentile believers. In this and the following verses, down to the 25th, he warns them to beware of self-preference, or of being puffed up against the Jews, on account of the blessings with which they themselves were now favoured. The Jewish nation was God's olive tree. They were all the people of God in a typical sense, and the greater part of God's true people had been chosen out of them; but now, by their unbelief, some of the branches were broken off from the tree. By the term 'some,' as has been observed, verse 14, is meant not all, Heb. iii. 16; for it implies that others, as the Apostle had shown, verses 2–5, remained. And among, or rather instead of, those that were broken off, the Gentiles, who were a wild olive, having had no place in the good olive tree, are now made the children of Abraham by faith in Christ Jesus, Gal. iii. 26–29. They were graffed into the good olive tree, whose root Abraham was, and were made partakers of his distinguished privileges. It has sometimes been remarked that there is no graffing in the olive tree. But this makes no difference.

The illustration from the process of graffing is the same, whether the operation be performed in the particular tree mentioned or not. Mr. Stuart says that the wild olive 'was often graffed into the fruitful one when it began to decay, and thus not only brought fruit, but caused the decaying olive to revive and flourish.' This, however, whether it be fact or not, is not to the purpose of the Apostle, for he is beating down the arrogance of the Gentile believers, and not pointing out the advantages they occasioned to Jews. Nor is the stock of the olive here supposed to be decayed, but to be full of sap and fatness, to partake of which, and not to benefit the fruitful olive, is the wild olive graffed into the tree.

Ver. 18.—*Boast not against the branches: but if thou boast, thou bearest not the root, but the root thee.*

It is probable, from what is here said, that even in the Apostle's time the Gentile believers were beginning to exhibit an overbearing disposition towards the Jews, and a complacent feeling of self-preference. At all events, the sin against which they are thus warned well describes the spirit that has long prevailed among the Gentiles who profess Christianity. What marvellous ignorance, folly, and vanity, are often displayed even in God's people! Nothing but the constant lessons of the Spirit of God will teach them that all spiritual difference among men is by God's grace.

But if thou boast.—Whenever Gentile Christians feel a disposition to boast with respect to the Jews, let them remember not only that the Jews were first the people of God, but that the first Christians were also Jews. The Jews received no advantage from the Gentiles; but, on the contrary, the Gentiles have received much from the Jews, from whom the Gospel sounded out—its first preachers being Jews, and of whom even Christ Himself, as concerning the flesh, came. The Gentile believers become the children of Abraham, and all the blessings they enjoy are in virtue of that relation. Hence the covenant, Jer. xxxi. 31, includes all believers; yet it is said only to be made with the house of Israel and Judah.

Ver. 19.—*Thou wilt say then, The branches were broken off, that I might be graffed in.*

Ver. 20.—*Well; because of unbelief they were broken off, and thou standest by faith. Be not high-minded, but fear.*

The Gentile believers might reply, that the branches were broken off to give place to them, and in a certain sense this is admitted by the Apostle. But unbelief was the cause of the fall of the Jews, while it is by faith only that the Gentiles stand. It was not, then, on account of their superior merits that they were graffed into the good olive tree, since faith is the gift of God, bestowed on whom He will, and therefore leaves no room for boasting or self-preference. Among the Gentiles who professed the faith, there was soon a great falling away, and 'the man of sin,' though he boasts of being exclusively the good olive tree—the only true church —is broken off altogether, and doomed to inevitable destruction. It becomes all Christians to be humble, and to fear lest they also fall by error of the same kind. It is very usual, when they perceive the errors of other Christians, to glory over them. This is highly unbecoming. If a Christian understands any part of the will of God of which his brethren are still ignorant, it is God that has made the difference. A haughty spirit goeth before a fall ; and if arrogance be indulged by any one, it is likely that God will give him up to some error as pernicious as that into which others whom he despises have fallen.

Ver. 21.—*For if God spared not the natural branches, take heed lest He also spare not thee.*

This verse contains another argument by which the Apostle urges the Gentile believers to humility and watchfulness. If the natural branches were not spared, this was an additional reason why those whom He addressed should be on their guard lest they also should fall through unbelief. It appears also to be a prophetical intimation of the apostasy of the great body of the professors of Christianity under the mystery of iniquity.

Ver. 22.—*Behold therefore the goodness and severity of God : on them which fell, severity ; but towards thee, goodness, if thou continue in His goodness ; otherwise thou also shalt be cut off.*

The Apostle lastly enforces his warning to the Gentile believers by four concluding arguments : First, he calls on them to behold the severity of God's strict justice in cutting off and casting out the unbelieving Jews. Second, to consider His goodness in conferring unmerited favour on the Gentiles, who had attained that righteousness after which they were not following. Third, to remark the necessity of continuing in that goodness, by abiding in the faith of the Gospel ; and, Fourth, to observe the assurance that if they abide not in the faith, they should be themselves cut off.

Men generally form in their imagination the character of God according to their own inclination. It is the duty of the Christian to take God's character as it is given by Himself. His goodness is no evidence that He will not punish the guilty ; and the most dreadful punishment of the guilty is consistent with the existence of supreme goodness in the Divine character. That God will yet lay righteousness to the line, and judgment to the plummet, is now seen in His treatment of Israel, whom He had so long spared after they had sinned against Him. Let none imagine, then, that He will spare them if guilty, because they have the name of being His people. Rather let them dread the more terrible vengeance on that account. The evidence that we are the true objects of the goodness of God here mentioned, is, that we continue in it, by continuing in the faith of the Gospel. Continuing in goodness is not to be understood here to mean, our continuing in a state of integrity, according to Mr. Stuart. There is no real difficulty in the expression, continuing in God's goodness. We continue in God's goodness, by continuing in the faith.

Ver. 23.—*And they also, if they abide not still in unbelief, shall be graffed in : for God is able to graff them in again.*

The Apostle having, from the beginning of the 17th verse, pressed upon the believing Gentiles the necessity of humility, now reverts to the subject of the future conversion of the Jews. In order to furnish a new proof of this great event, he introduces a fourth argument (see exposition of verse 16), taken from the power of God. *God is able to graff them in again.*—According to the figure which the Apostle had been employing respecting the casting off and the restoration of that part of the Jewish nation that was blinded, comparing them to branches broken off, there might seem to be no probability that they could be restored. When branches are severed from a tree, they wither and cannot be replaced. Paul, therefore, here refers to the power of God. What is not done in nature, and cannot be effected by the power of man, will be done by God, with whom all things are possible. He is able to make the dry bones live, and to restore the severed branches of the Jewish nation. Some argue that, because the graffing of the Jews into the olive tree here spoken of is conditional, it is not promised. But the Apostle's design is evidently, even in this verse, to excite hopes by showing its possibility. There is no other ground of exclusion with respect to them but unbelief. If that sin were subdued, they would be received. God is able to graff them in if they believe, and He is able also to give them faith.

Ver. 24.—*For if thou wert cut out of the olive tree which is wild by nature, and wert graffed contrary to nature into a good olive tree ; how much more shall these, which be the natural branches, be graffed into their own olive tree ?*

The former argument, drawn from God's power, is here further insisted on. The Jews were so obstinately prejudiced against the Gospel, that it seemed very improbable that they should ever embrace the truth. But the Apostle had declared the possibility of this being accomplished by the mighty power of God. He now shows its probability. If the Gentiles, he says, who were strangers to the covenants of promise, have been graffed into the good olive tree, how much more is it to be expected that the descendants of the patriarchs, to whom the promises were made, and who are therefore the natural branches, shall be graffed into their own olive tree ?

Ver. 25.—*For I would not, brethren, that ye should be ignorant of this mystery, (lest ye should be wise in your own conceits,) that blindness in part is happened to Israel, until the fulness of the Gentiles be come in.*

Having in the two preceding verses exhibited first the *possibility*, and next the *probability*, of the restoration of the Jews, according to the order of God's providence, the Apostle, in this and the following verses, down to the 28th, goes on to prove the *certainty* of the future conversion and restoration of Israel. He here addresses the Gentiles as his brethren, thus expressing his affection for them, and stimulates their attention, by declaring that he was about to reveal to them a mystery—a thing hitherto hidden or unknown. The restoration of the Jews is called a mystery, for though declared in the Scriptures, it was not understood. And in this mystery there were two parts, both of which are here unfolded,—first, that blindness is happened to Israel in part only ; and, secondly, that this blindness should continue till the fulness of the Gentiles be come in. This mystery was opened to prevent the Gentiles from being *wise in their own conceits*, that is, from being puffed up on account of the preference they now enjoyed. Ignorance of the Scriptures is the cause of high-mindedness in Christians. They are often arrogant and contemptuous through want of knowledge. In the absence

of real knowledge, they often suppose that they have a true understanding of things with which they are still unacquainted, and are thus
vain and conceited.

Blindness in part is happened to Israel.—This does not mean that their
blindness was only partial, and limited in degree, for it was total and
complete; but that it did not extend to all Israel, but only to a part,
though indeed the far greater part. It is a consolation that the Jews are
under no exclusion that forbids the preaching of the Gospel to them, and
using every effort for their conversion. Though the national rejection
will continue till the appointed time, yet individuals from among them
may at any period be brought to the knowledge of God. This fact is of
great importance. They are excluded only through unbelief, and this
unbelief is not affirmed of all, but only of a part.

Until the fulness of the Gentiles be come in.—Here is the clearest attestation that the blindness of the Jews will yet cease, not only as to
individuals, but as to the body. It is not stated at what time this will
happen, but it is connected with the fulness of the Gentiles. The fulness
of the Gentiles is the accession of the Gentiles to the body of Christ.
Here we have another glorious truth presented for our consolation. The
world has hitherto groaned under heathen and antichristian idolatry, but
the time will come when the kingdoms of this world shall become the
kingdoms of our Lord and of His Christ; and this will be closely connected
with the recovery of the Jews from their unbelief. This declaration of the
Apostle coincides with that remarkable prediction of our blessed Lord:
'Jerusalem shall be trodden down of the Gentiles, until the times of the
Gentiles be fulfilled.'

Ver. 26.—*And so all Israel shall be saved: as it is written, There shall come out
of Sion the Deliverer, and shall turn away ungodliness from Jacob:*

Here the Apostle further unfolds the mystery of which he would not
have his brethren to be ignorant. In the foregoing verse he had
declared that blindness had come upon Israel—that blindness which
he had before shown was inflicted on part of the Jewish nation by the
judgment of God, verses 8–10, which would continue till a certain
period was accomplished. He now declares that at that period all Israel
shall be saved. The rejection of Israel has been general, but at no period
universal. This rejection is to continue till the fulness of the Gentiles
shall come in. Then the people of Israel, as a body, shall be brought to
the faith of the Gospel. Such expressions as that 'all Israel shall be
saved,' are no doubt, in certain situations, capable of limitation; but as
no Scripture demands any limitation of this expression, and as the
opposition here stated is between a *part* and *all*, there is no warrant to
make any exception, and with God this, like all other things, is possible.

As it is written.—'Whether Isaiah, in lix. 20,' says Mr. Stuart, 'had
respect to the salvation of Gospel times, has been called in question.
But the context seems to me very clearly to indicate this.' But why are
we to rest our conviction on this point on our view of the connection?
The Apostle's quotation of the words is ground sufficient to bear the
conclusion. This method of treating the Apostle's quotations of prophecy

should be most strenuously opposed. That it is prophecy ought to be rested on the ground of its being quoted as prophecy. 'And even if he had respect to temporal deliverance,' Mr. Stuart continues, 'there can be no difficulty in the Apostle's using his words as the vehicle of conveying his own thoughts with regard to spiritual deliverance.' There is indeed no difficulty in supposing that the same prophecy may, in its primary sense, refer to a temporal deliverance, and in its secondary, to a spiritual deliverance. But there is a very great difficulty in supposing that the Apostle would cite a prophecy respecting a temporal deliverance, which had no reference to the deliverance of which he was speaking. This would be very puerile. It would be worse than puerile—it would be a perversion of Scripture. It would be employing a false argument.

There shall come out of Sion the Deliverer, and shall turn away ungodliness from Jacob.—Mount Zion was the special residence of the God of Israel; and out of Zion was to go forth the law, and the word of the Lord from Jerusalem, Isa. ii. 3. And though Israel has for a long time departed from Him, yet thither at length will the Redeemer return, and make His word and law powerful to restore them unto Himself. 'He shall set up an ensign for the nations, and shall assemble the outcasts of Israel, and gather together the dispersed of Judah from the four corners of the earth,' Isa. xi. 12.

The Deliverer, etc.—These words are quoted from Isa. lix. 20, 'And the Redeemer shall come to Zion, and unto them that turn from transgression in Jacob.' Here it is said that the Redeemer or Deliverer shall come to Zion; but if He come out of Zion He must have come to it previously ; as it is said, Ps. xiv. 7, ' Oh, that the salvation of Israel were come out of Zion.' Besides, it is added, He shall come, namely, out of Zion, to them who turn from transgression in Jacob ; and such must have thus been turned by Him. We may be assured that the Apostle, speaking by the same Spirit as the Prophet, and directed by the Spirit to quote him, has substantially given the meaning of his words. If Jacob be turned away from transgression, it is this Deliverer who will accomplish the object.

In this prophecy, in the fifty-ninth chapter of Isaiah, God is represented as doing two things. One is, to reproach the Jews with the multitude and enormity of their transgressions ; and the other, to promise to them the redemption of the Messiah, and by Him an everlasting covenant. When, therefore, all nations shall be given to the Messiah, and submit to His authority, the prophecies concerning Him will be fulfilled in their utmost extent, and His reign over all the earth will be established. After having subdued to Himself the whole of the Gentiles, He will not forget the family of Abraham, His friend, in whom, according to His promise, all the families of the earth were to be blessed. Jews and Gentiles shall be all united in Christ, and the whole earth shall be filled with the glory of the Lord. Then what is predicted by the Prophet Hosea, iii. 4, both concerning the present and future condition of the Jews, will all have been strikingly accomplished: 'For the children of Israel shall abide many days without a king, and without a prince, and without a sacrifice, and without an image, and without an ephod, and without teraphim. Afterwards shall the children of Israel return, and seek the Lord their God, and David their king; and shall fear the Lord and His goodness in the latter days.' ' Oh, that the salvation of the Lord were come out of Zion! When the Lord bringeth back the captivity of His people, Jacob shall rejoice, and Israel shall be glad,' Ps. xiv. 7.

The coming of the Deliverer to Zion is not to be understood of any personal appearance. Jesus Christ has personally appeared once on earth, and He will appear the second time when He comes without sin unto salvation. The Scriptures, however, speak in different ways of His coming, though not in person; as of His coming to set up His kingdom, John xxi. 22 ; His coming at death and for judgment, Matt. xxiv. 44–50 ; His coming for chastisement, Rev. ii. 5 ; His coming in grace and love, John xiv. 23 ; Rev. iii. 20. And at the appointed time He will come to Zion in His power by His Spirit.

Ver. 27.—*For this is My covenant unto them, when I shall take away their sins.*

This refers to the verse which follows the one above quoted, Isa. lix. 21. ' As for Me, this is My covenant with them, saith the Lord : My Spirit that is upon thee, and My words which I have put in thy mouth, shall not depart out of thy mouth, nor out of the mouth of thy seed, nor out of the mouth of thy seed's seed, saith the Lord, from henceforth and for ever.' These words are addressed to the Redeemer, the Restorer of Israel, when God shall take away their sins. This gracious covenant is fully developed, Jer. xxxi. 31–34 ; and again, xxxii. 37–40, where the declaration referred to in the foregoing verse, of turning away ungodliness from Jacob, is more fully expressed. The Apostle grounds his conclusion from the prophecy on the fact that God in these words speaks of a time when He would take away the sins of Israel as a body, and so all Israel shall be saved.

The first characteristic of this covenant to Israel, as declared by Jeremiah, is, that it will be eternal, in opposition to the former covenant, which was temporary and was disannulled. ' Not according to the covenant that I made with their fathers, in the day that I took them by the hand, to bring them out of the land of Egypt : which My covenant they brake, although I was an husband unto them, saith the Lord.' But why shall it be eternal ? Why shall it not be broken as the first covenant was ? The reason is, 'I will put My law in their inward parts, and write it in their hearts, and will be their God, and they shall be My people.' Here is a manifest distinction between this and the former covenant, in which the law was written outwardly in tables of stone ; and therefore violated, as not being put in the hearts of the people. Under this covenant, too, it is said that they shall all know the Lord. He will fill their minds with the knowledge of Himself, by His Spirit communicated to them, which formerly He had not done. God, it is added, will also forgive their iniquity, and will remember their sin no more. This is peculiar to the evangelical covenant, which provides a real atonement for sin, which could not be removed by the sacrifices under the law. In these respects the covenant here referred to is distinguished from the former covenant, and will prove effectual for the salvation of all Israel. Immediately after the annunciation of this prophecy, it is solemnly and repeatedly averred that it shall be an unchangeable covenant; and that, sooner than Israel shall again be cut off, the most inviolable laws of God's providence in the government of nature shall be revoked. 'Thus saith the Lord, which giveth the sun for a light by day, and the ordinances of the moon and of the stars for a light by night, which divideth the sea when the waves thereof roar; The Lord of Hosts is His name: If those ordinances depart from before Me, saith the Lord, then the seed of Israel also shall cease from being a nation before Me for ever. Thus saith the Lord: If heaven above can be measured, and the foundations of the earth searched out beneath, I will also cast off all the seed of Israel, for all that they have done, saith the Lord.'

Israel, then, shall be restored to their own land, which God gave to Abraham for an everlasting possession. God hath said that He will make a full end of all the nations whither He had driven them, but He will not make a full end of them, Jer. xlvi. 28. 'Thus saith the Lord God, Behold, I will take the children of Israel from among the heathen, whither they be gone, and will gather them on every side, and bring them into their own land: and I will make them one nation in the land upon the mountains of Israel, and one king shall be king to them all: and they shall be no more two nations, neither shall they be divided into two kingdoms any more at all: and David My servant shall be king over them; and they shall have one shepherd: they shall also walk in My judgments, and observe My statutes and do them. And they shall dwell in the land that I have given unto Jacob My servant, wherein your fathers have dwelt, and they shall dwell therein, even they and their children for ever,' Ezek. xxxvii. 21, 25. 'And I will plant them upon their land, and they shall no more be pulled up out of their land which I have given them, saith the Lord thy God,' Amos ix. 15.

Ver. 28.—*As concerning the Gospel, they are enemies for your sakes; but as touching the election, they are beloved for the fathers' sakes.*

The Apostle next obviates an objection that might be brought against the future recall of the Jews. The great body of the nation—all whom the Apostle declared to be judicially blinded—were now the enemies of God with respect to the Gospel. They had rejected God's message by His Son, and thus proved themselves His enemies while they called Him their God. The Gentiles, then, might object, How can the Jewish nation ever be graffed in again, seeing they have thus refused to listen to God's message of reconciliation? This the Apostle answers: first, he grants that they were indeed enemies to God, and were dealt with as enemies for their contempt and disbelief of the Gospel. In the next place, he says that this was for the sake of the Gentiles, or on their account. The rejection of the Jews was, in the inscrutable counsels of Jehovah, connected with and overruled for the salvation of the Gentiles. Some understand the words, 'for your sakes,' as importing that the Jews were enemies to God because of His sending the Gospel to the Gentiles. This no doubt gave the Jews great offence; but it was before this event that they rejected and crucified Christ.

But as touching the election.—The election here spoken of is not the election to eternal life, as that of the remnant according to the election of grace, verse 5. The Apostle is now speaking of the great body of the nation, called the 'rest,' verse 7, namely, those that were blinded, and the branches broken off, who, in respect of the Gospel, 'were enemies' to God. This election is of the nation of Israel to be the people of God, in that sense in which no other nation ever was; according to which they are so often called His people, 2 Sam. vii. 23, 24, etc. The election of Israel 'after the flesh' was typical of the election of the true Israel of God—even all believers, contrasted with those who, although of Israel, were not Israel, ch. ix. 6. God had chosen the Jews to be a special people unto Himself, Deut. vii. 6, 'Thou art a holy people unto the Lord thy God: the Lord thy God hath chosen thee to be a special people unto Himself.' Yet they had not a heart to fear the Lord, Deut. v. 29; and they belonged only to that covenant which made nothing perfect, according to which the law was given to them externally, and not written in their hearts, which consequently they brake, Jer. xxxi. 32.

On the ground of this national election of Israel, the Apostle Peter, when he called them to repentance, addressed them in these words: 'Repent, and be baptized every one of you in the name of Jesus Christ for the remission of sins, and ye shall receive the gift of the Holy Ghost. For the promise is unto you, and to your children,' Acts ii. 38. And again, 'Repent ye, therefore, and be converted, that your sins may be blotted out. Ye are the children of the prophets, and of the covenant which God made with our fathers, saying unto Abraham, And in thy seed shall all the kindreds of the earth be blessed. Unto you first God, having raised up His Son Jesus, sent Him to bless you, in turning away every one of you from his iniquities,' Acts iii. 19, 25, 26.

Beloved for the fathers' sakes.—The election of the nation of Israel was made on account of their fathers, 'Because He loved thy fathers, therefore He chose their seed after them.' And again, 'Only the Lord had a delight in thy fathers to love them, and chose their seed after them, even you, above all people, as it is this day,' Deut. iv. 37, x. 15. It is immediately added, 'Circumcise therefore the foreskin of your heart, and be no more stiff-necked;' which proves that they were not Jews inwardly, Rom. ii. 28, 29. Compared as they were to a woman beloved of her friend, yet an adulteress, their election as a nation was only external, as is verified throughout their whole history.

Ver. 29.—*For the gifts and calling of God are without repentance.*

The Apostle here announces a general truth applicable to the case before him. The purposes of God are unchangeable, and His gifts and callings irrevocable, so that the nation of Israel cannot be deprived of what He engaged to do for them. What He has given them He will not withdraw, and His choice of them as His special people never can be altered. Calling is in this verse equivalent to election in the preceding. This election or calling as a nation cannot be revoked, and that national election was connected with and subservient to the election to eternal life of multitudes of their descendants, at the period when all Israel shall be saved. For this purpose it was, that at the destruction of Jerusalem the whole Jewish nation was not exterminated: ' Except,' said our blessed Lord, ' those days should be shortened, there should no flesh be saved : but for the elect's sake those days shall be shortened,' Matt. xxiv. 22. The term elect here cannot be applicable to those Jews who had then embraced the Gospel, for the tribulations of those days, even had they not been shortened, would not have caused their destruction, scattered as they were through many countries. It must refer to the elect of God in that future age, when all Israel shall be saved. It was for their sakes, who were to descend from the Jewish people, that the destruction of that people was limited, and for which God was pleased to preserve a part of them, and continues to preserve them to this day. The same reason, then, for this miraculous preservation, had likewise been given by the Prophet Isaiah, ' Thus saith the Lord, as the new wine is found in the cluster, and one saith, Destroy it not; for a blessing is in it : so will I do for My servants' sakes, that I may not destroy them all. And I will bring forth a seed out of Jacob, and out of Judah an inheritor of My mountains : and Mine elect shall inherit it, and My servants shall dwell there, Isa. lxv. 8.

Ver. 30.—*For as ye in times past have not believed God, yet have now obtained mercy through their unbelief;*

Here, and in the following verse, the Apostle produces the last con- firmation of his assertion that God had not cast away His people, which is further referred to in the 32d verse, and is to this effect: as the Gen- tiles have experienced mercy after a long period of alienation from God, in like manner the Jews will at last receive mercy. Whether the original be translated *have not obeyed* or *have not believed*, it comes to the same thing. The unbelief or disobedience of the Gentiles in former times, after they lost the knowledge of *the righteousness of God*, preached to the world by Noah, 2 Pet. ii. 5, respected not His word, but the knowledge of God as revealed in His works. This unbelief or disobedience, during their heathenish state, although not so aggravated, is as properly a ground of their condemnation as the rejection of the Gospel by the Jews. It is on this account that the Apostle says, ch. i. 20, that they were *without excuse;* and, in ch. ii. 12, that as many as have sinned without law (the written law) shall *perish;* and in the 14th and 15th verses, he assumes as the reason, that they had the work of the law—what it teaches—which they transgressed, written in their hearts.

Yet have now obtained mercy.—The calling of the Gentiles out of the darkness and pollution of Paganism, was the result of the pure mercy of God. How different is the language of many on this subject! They seem to think that, as the heathens have not enjoyed the benefit of the revelation of grace, it would be unjust to condemn them for their trans- gressions.

Through their unbelief.—Nothing can be plainer than that in God's plan it was necessary that the Jews should reject the Gospel, in order that it should be given to the Gentiles; yet why this was necessary we cannot tell. As far as appears to us, God might from the very first have made both Jews and Gentiles, to any extent, equally partakers of His grace, as He has promised He will do at last. Let us be satisfied that God has told us that a contrary mode of proceeding was necessary, without any vain attempts to develope the grounds of this necessity, which He Himself has not revealed. The belief of many in the word of God appears not to go further than what they imagine they can account for. To anything beyond this they refuse to hearken. This is not faith.

Ver. 31.—*Even so have these also now not believed, that through your mercy they also may obtain mercy.*

God abandoned the Jews to unbelief, in order that their restoration might prove as signal an exhibition of mercy as the grace now bestowed on the idolatrous heathens. Had the Jews all received the Gospel at first, both they and the world at large would have been inclined to believe that they did not need the same conversion or the same grace as the Gentiles. This would have confirmed the view which they hold of themselves, as by hereditary descent from Abraham entitled to heaven, and the privileges of Messiah's kingdom. But when they have crucified the Son of God, and continued in the most blasphemous rebellion against Him for so many hundred years, their conversion will display mercy as distinguished as the mercy that called the Gentiles, which followed not after righteousness, and were not seeking God. If the unbelief of the Jews was the occasion of showing mercy to the Gentiles, so the mercy shown to the Gentiles shall be the occasion of showing mercy to the Jews. *Your mercy.*—The same mercy that saved the believing heathens, without any mixture of merit, shall save the Jews ; and through the effect of that mercy shown to the Gentiles the Jews shall obtain mercy.

Ver. 32.—*For God hath concluded them all in unbelief, that He might have mercy upon all.*

As the conclusion of the foregoing discussion respecting the restoration of the Jews, and the calling of the Gentiles, the Apostle here refers to the present state of the Jews, and the past state of the Gentiles. He declares the perversity and unbelief of all who have been saved, without exception, and shows that their salvation is solely the effect of the mercy of God. God has shut them up in unbelief under the guilt and power of sin, like condemned criminals in prison, without any possibility of escaping, except by means of that salvation which, in His good pleasure, is provided for their deliverance. The Gentiles who believed had been formerly in this condition ; now it was the case with the great body of the nation of the Jews.

God having thus been pleased alternately to shut up Jews and Gentiles in unbelief, it will thus appear that both the one and the other are called to the knowledge of Himself out of pure mercy. He had left men to walk in their own ways, having abandoned the nations of the earth to that state of blindness and misery in which they were plunged. During that period He only manifested Himself to the family of Abraham, and to a small nation, by which He clearly testified that the communication which He chose still to hold with men proceeded solely from grace and His own good pleasure. For if it had been in any manner due, why was it not granted to all? Or if not granted to all, at least to the greater number, and not limited to so small a portion? Israel, however, forgot this distinguishing favour of God, and regarded it as a privilege necessarily attached to their descent from Abraham, not remembering that Abraham himself had been chosen from the mass of idolaters, and that they had been slaves in Egypt, addicted to the superstitions of that country. God was now pleased to shut up them also in unbelief, and to turn to those nations which neither knew Him nor were inquiring after Him. By doing so, His gratuitous mercy was revealed anew, and exhibited to men and angels. Besides this reason for the restriction of His peculiar revelation of grace at the beginning to the Israelites alone, it would seem that God purposed to allow the empire of Satan to attain all the power and extent of which it was capable, that, on the one hand, the greatness of human depravity might appear in all its direful effects, so that in the example of the miserable state of men thus abandoned to themselves, those whom God hath chosen may see, as in a faithful mirror, the hideousness of sin, as well as the necessity for the grace of God. On the other hand, by this means the work of the redemption of the Messiah is exalted, and its glory fully exhibited. At first God showed 'His word unto Jacob, His statutes and His judgments unto Israel.' And it is added, 'He hath not dealt so with any nation; and as for His judgments, they have not known them,' Ps. cxlvii. 19, 20.

The Jews were thus preserved from idolatry, into which the other nations had fallen; and although the covenant under which they had been placed was abolished, they still continued under its bondage, Gal. iv. 25. God Himself hardened their hearts, and abandoned them to their deep-rooted prejudices, since they had rejected the Messiah. In this condition they have continued attached to that covenant, shut up in their adherence to it in unbelief, and thus separated from all other nations. But though this be a punishment, it is overruled in the wisdom of God, so that in the end He may show mercy to the whole nation. Their house has been left unto them desolate; they have rejected Him who would have gathered them to Himself as a hen gathereth her chickens under her wings. But even in the moment of this rejection, Jesus announced that the day will arrive when they shall say, 'Blessed is He that cometh in the name of the Lord.' God then shut up both Jews and Gentiles together in unbelief, that He might in saving them manifest to both the same mercy. Had not the Jews rejected the Gospel at first, their ultimate salvation would not have so eminently appeared to be the glorious result of the exercise of God's sovereign mercy.

Ver. 33.—*O the depth of the riches both of the wisdom and knowledge of God! how unsearchable are His judgments, and His ways past finding out!*

Ver. 34.—*For who hath known the mind of the Lord? or who hath been His counsellor?*

Ver. 35.—*Or who hath first given to Him, and it shall be recompensed unto him again?*

Ver. 36.—*For of Him, and through Him, and to Him, are all things: to whom be glory for ever. Amen.*

Before passing onward to the practical conclusions which flow from the grand and peculiar doctrines of the Gospel, the Apostle pauses to contemplate the ground which he had traversed; and, looking back upon the whole, he exclaims with astonishment and admiration, '*O the depth of the riches both of the wisdom and knowledge of God! how unsearchable are His judgments, and His ways past finding out!*' In thus concluding the discussion of those deep and awful subjects which, in the former part of this Epistle, had successively engaged his attention, Paul most emphatically intimates the impossibility of comprehending the infinitude of the Divine attributes. But far from judging, like many, that we have nothing to do with such mysteries as the sovereignty of God in justifying 'the ungodly,' and choosing or rejecting sinners according to His own good pleasure, he had delighted to expatiate on the glorious perfections of Jehovah as displayed in these doctrines. And as they bear most directly upon the state and security of Christians, he designates them in the beginning of the next chapter the 'mercies of God,' involving all the blessings in store for Jews and Gentiles, and constituting the foundation and support of all his exhortations to practical duty. He thus teaches that these doctrines are conducive in the highest degree to the advancement of holiness, and that in no respect do they interfere with the responsibility of man.

Paul, however, by no means denies that these great truths are 'hard to be understood' by men who, accounting themselves 'wise and prudent,' refuse to receive the kingdom of God as 'little children.' On the contrary, he intimates the absolute impossibility of giving utterance to the boundless and unfathomable incomprehensibility of the Divine attributes as manifested in God's dealings with the children of men. How often does the profane ingenuity of man pretend to fathom, and sometimes even dares to arraign, the inscrutable ways of Jehovah! But what a contrast does the Apostle's language, in these concluding verses of this chapter, present to the vain and presumptuous speculations of some interpreters of Scripture! Multitudes receive the testimony of God only so far as they can satisfactorily account for all the reasons and grounds of His conduct, when measured according to the petty scale of their limited capacity. How unbecoming in such a creature as man! Shall he who is but 'of yesterday,' and 'knows nothing,' who is born 'like a wild ass's colt,' pretend to penetrate the counsels of the Omniscient!

If this great Apostle, enjoying as he did such unexampled privileges, favoured as he was with such 'abundance of revelations,' and writing under the dictation of the Holy Ghost, was thus compelled to confess that the riches of the wisdom and knowledge of God were unsearchable, how vain and idle are all the speculations and conjectures on the subject of this world's wisdom! It is not difficult for one man to judge of the plans and designs of another. But the judgments of the Lord must, like their Author, be infinite, and consequently can neither be measured by a finite capacity, nor ascertained further than they are revealed from the fountain of light. The Lord knows the hearts of His creatures; but the combined intellect of men and angels would be alike insufficient to penetrate the secrets of Deity. The wisest of men need counsel from others. The angels, we are told, 'desire to look into' the works of their Creator, in order to make new acquisitions of knowledge. But the majesty of

God stands alone in the universe. He needs no counsellor; and neither in the work of creation, nor in the still more astonishing scheme of redemption, does He take counsel. From the various ways in which men explain the revelation of God's salvation of sinners, we see what advice they would have given had they been permitted to assist in devising a plan for the operation of Divine mercy. God's plan of redemption is so deep and peculiar to Himself, that man does not comprehend it, even when it is presented to his view, unless the eyes of his understanding are enlightened by the Holy Spirit of God. Well, then, may the Apostle exclaim, in the contemplation of the majesty of God, and the unsearchable riches of His wisdom and knowledge, *Who hath known the mind of the Lord? or who hath been His counsellor?*

The same question substantially was put to Job, when the Lord answered him out of the whirlwind, and all the proud imaginations which he had conceived, in the agitation of his spirit, were in a moment humbled in the dust. 'I know that Thou canst do everything, and that no thought can be withholden from Thee. Who is he that hideth counsel without knowledge? therefore I have uttered that I understood not; things too wonderful for me, which I knew not.' To the same effect also, the Psalmist David, in the 131st Psalm, appeals to the Lord that he received the kingdom of God as a little child, and was not proudly attempting to scan the secret counsels of Jehovah. 'Lord,' he exclaims, 'my heart is not haughty, nor mine eyes lofty: neither do I exercise myself in great matters, or in things too high for me. Surely I have behaved and quieted myself as a child that is weaned of his mother: my soul is even as a weaned child. Let Israel hope in the Lord from henceforth and for ever.' The Apostle, in addition to what he had declared of the unsearchableness of the Lord's judgments, adds, as another reason why man should cease proudly to challenge the proceedings of his Maker, *Who hath first given to Him, and it shall be recompensed unto him again?* He thus at once declares the spring of all our knowledge, and consequently our inability to pursue our inquiries beyond the bounds of revelation; while at the same time he again reminds us how utterly impossible it is for a creature to bring his Creator under obligations. How absurd, how impious, must it then be to speak of the merit of our good works!

The conclusion to which the Apostle is conducted by all these considerations, is expressed in the last verse of the chapter. *For of Him, and through Him, and to Him, are all things: to whom be glory for ever.*— Here we have the grand truth which lies at the foundation of all religion. All things are *of God*, for He is the Author of all; His will is the origin of all existence. All things are *through Him*, for all things are created by Him as the grand agent. All things are likewise *to Him*, for all things tend to His glory as their final end.

Philosophers represent the communication of happiness as the chief end of man and of creation. But the Scriptures uniformly declare the glory of the Creator as the paramount object of all that takes place throughout the vast limits of the universe. To this the entrance of sin among angels and men is no exception. In itself sin is an affront to the majesty of God. But there can be no doubt that the results of sin, as well as of all the evil we behold in the world, shall signally enhance the glory of the Divine character. It was necessary in order to show God to be what He is. Had sin never existed, there would have been no opportunity of manifesting the righteous displeasure of God against it, and His justice in punishing it; nor of displaying His wonderful power in turning to His glory that which in itself is a dishonour to Him. This is the very reason given by the Apostle for God's suffering the vessels of wrath. 'What if God, willing to show His wrath, and make His power known, endured with much long-suffering the vessels of wrath fitted to destruction.'

That God not only permitted, but willed the entrance of sin among men, is clear from the very creation of the world, and its adaptation to illustrate the work of redemption. From the nineteenth Psalm, there can be no doubt that the sun of the firmament was, from his first dawn, a glorious type of the Sun of Righteousness; and in his manner of enlightening the earth, a figure of Him who is the light of the world, as well as of the course and progress of the Gospel. The resting from the work of creation, and the first Sabbath, were calculated to shadow the rest of the Lord Jesus from the more important work of redemption, and the glorious and everlasting rest which remaineth for the people of God. The formation of Adam and Eve, and the relation of marriage, most evidently were regulated with reference to the future relation of Christ and His Church, Eph. v. 32. Redemption, then, was in the view of God in the creation of man. From all eternity it was purposed by Him ' who created all things by Jesus Christ: to the intent that now unto the principalities and powers in heavenly places might be known by (means of) the Church the manifold wisdom of God, according to the eternal purpose which He purposed in Christ Jesus our Lord,' Eph. iii. 9. Grace was given to His people in Christ Jesus, and eternal life was promised by God that cannot lie, before the world began, 2 Tim. i. 9 ; Tit. i. 2.

It is not possible that God would have purposed the entrance of sin, had He not been able to turn it to His glory. No man would act in the way in which many consider God in this matter to have acted. Could any man foresee that what he was about to do would turn to his dishonour and injury, and would he not avoid it? And shall God will and foresee that sin should enter, and shall He permit its entrance, if it is ultimately to prove dishonourable to His character? To suppose that there were innumerable plans of creation present to the mind of the Creator, that each of them had advantages and disadvantages, and that God chose that which upon the whole was best, is nothing but disguised Atheism. This supposes that the Creator is neither all-wise nor all-powerful.

The universal apostasy of the nations of the earth from the worship of God, and the present apostasy of the Jews, are things apparently dishonourable to God, and which man with God's power would not have permitted. But both are according to the counsel of God, and will redound to His glory. We cannot understand how this can be so. It is to us a depth unfathomable ; but it is a truth which no Christian should find difficult to believe, because it is plainly testified in the word of God. The Apostle wonders at it, but does not pretend to explain it. His language in closing this subject is a recognition that the ways of Jevhovah are beyond the grasp of the human intellect. ' O the depth of the riches both of the wisdom and knowledge of God! how unsearchable are His judgments, and His ways past finding out! '

Though Satan, then, is the god of this world, yet God is glorified in all the evil that Satan has introduced. In every part of Scripture, Jehovah is seen to be glorified: in His judgments as well as in His grace, in His wrath as well as in His mercy, in those who are lost as well as in those who are saved. However disagreeable this may be to the mind of the natural man, it is truly reasonable. Can there be a higher end than the glory of the Divine character? And can man, who is a fallen and lost creature, share with His offended Sovereign in the glory of his recovery? Such a thought is as incongruous as it is unscriptural. If there be hope for the guilty, if there be recovery to any from the ruin of the fall, it is the voice of reason, properly exercised, as well as of the Divine word, that it must come from God Himself.

The practical influence of the truth contained in these concluding verses is illustrated by the following extract from the Author's 'Letter, addressed, in 1824, to Mr. Cheneviere, the well-known Socinian, and yet Pastor and Professor of Divinity at Geneva.' 'There was nothing brought under the consideration of the students of divinity who attended me at Geneva, which appeared to contribute so effectually to overthrow their false system of religion, founded on philosophy and vain deceit, as the sublime view of the majesty of God presented in the four concluding verses of this part of the Epistle. Of Him, and through Him, and to Him, are all things. Here God is described as His own last end in everything that He does. Judging of God as such an one as themselves, they were at first startled at the idea that He must love Himself supremely, infinitely more than the whole universe, and consequently must prefer His own glory to everything besides. But when they were reminded that God in reality is infinitely more amiable and more valuable than the whole creation, and that consequently, if He views things as they really are, He must regard Himself as infinitely worthy of being more valued and loved, they saw that this truth was incontrovertible. Their attention was at the same time directed to numerous passages of Scripture, which assert that the manifestation of the glory of God is the great end of creation that He has Himself chiefly in view in all His works and dispensations, and that it is a purpose in which He requires that all His intelligent creatures should acquiesce, and seek and promote it as their first and paramount duty. Passages to this effect, both in the Old and New Testament, far exceed in number what any one who has not examined the subject is at all aware of.'

CHAPTER 12
ROMANS 12:1 – 21

HERE we enter on the second division of this Epistle, where Paul, according to his accustomed method, enforces the duties of believers, by arguments dependent on his previous exhibition of the grand and influential doctrines of the Gospel. These doctrines, as well as all the commandments of God, may be summed up in one word, namely, in LOVE. By the view which they present of the goodness, the forbearance, and the long-suffering of God, believers are daily led to repentance, while the contemplation of the Divine compassion and philanthropy is calculated to beget reciprocal confidence and child-like affection. ‘We have known and believed,’ says the Apostle John, ‘the love that God hath to us.’ ‘We love Him because He first loved us.’ This love of God does not exclude reverential fear and filial devotion ; of which, on the contrary, it is the principle and the foundation—while both together unite in the spirit of adoption to inspire the cry, ‘Abba, Father.’

Ver. 1.—*I beseech you therefore, brethren, by the mercies of God, that ye present your bodies a living sacrifice, holy, acceptable unto God, which is your reasonable service.*

Brethren.—The Apostle addresses the believers at Rome as his brethren, as standing on the same level with himself regarding acceptance with God. *I beseech you.*—We may here remark the difference between the endearing manner of address often used by inspired Apostles, and the haughty, overbearing tone of Popish antichristian tyranny. Those whose authority was avouched by mighty signs and wonders, whose very word was command, strive frequently to express commands as entreaties. *Therefore.*—This may have reference to what had been said in the foregoing chapter respecting the Gentiles and the Jewish nation in general, to whom, as being part of the elect remnants, some of those addressed belonged ; or rather, as he now enters on the second division of the Epistle, Paul here refers to those grand doctrines of the Gospel which, in the preceding part of it, he had been unfolding, denominating the whole of them, as forming together the great plan of salvation, the *mercies* of God.

By the mercies of God.—The word mercies or compassions is here used in the plural number, because it refers to the different instances before enumerated of Divine compassion. In the foregoing chapter, the Apostle had been declaring the mercies of God in the calling and restoration both of the Gentiles and the Jews, verse 31. But the whole of his preceding discourse contained a most striking and encouraging display of the mercies of God to all believers, in their election and predestination to eternal life, their calling, their deliverance from condemnation, their justification, their union with the Lord Jesus Christ, and communion with God, with the enjoyment of all the unspeakable blessings of the new covenant. Christians are here urged to devote themselves to the service of God by the consideration of these mercies, because they present the

strongest motives to obedience.   How different is the mind of the Apostle
from the mind of the world on this subject!   The wisdom of this world
rejects the grace of the Gospel, because it is thought to lead to licentiousness.   The interests of morality are supposed to be better secured when
salvation is suspended on men's good works, than when it is represented
as flowing from the Divine compassion.   But Paul presents the mercies
of God to the mind of believers, as the most powerful incitement to devote
themselves to His service.   In the remainder of the Epistle, we find him
as strenuous in pressing the duty of holiness and personal obedience, as
in the previous part of it, in insisting on those truths on which obedience
is founded.   This ought to convince of their error those who, misunderstanding the doctrine which the Apostle teaches, imagine that it is inconsistent with attention to the peculiar duties of Christianity.   It will,
however, be seen that the persons who seem to fear that his doctrine
tends to licentiousness, are equally opposed to the strictness of his precepts, the observance of which they speak of as impracticable.

That ye present your bodies.—There is no necessity, with Mr. Stuart
and the majority of commentators, to understand the term 'bodies' as
denoting both soul and body.   It is of the body that the Apostle here
speaks, and it is not proper to extract out of his language more than it
contains.   The expression evidently makes a distinction between themselves and their bodies.   Those addressed are entreated to present their
bodies, and the body is here considered as the sacrifice.   This, indeed,
cannot be done without the soul, yet this is not the thing expressed.
This shows the importance of serving God with the body as well as with
the soul.   Every member of the body is to be employed in the service of
God.   Many, when they use their members sinfully, attempt to excuse
themselves, and found a plea for pardon, by alleging that they have a
good heart.   But we see from this passage that God requires the service
of the body as well as that of the mind.   Besides, an exclusive reference
to the body comports better with the figure of offering a sacrifice.   The
Apostle seems to summon attention peculiarly to our actions or outward
deportment, which are of so great importance to the Christian life.   But,
in addition to this, if we extend the expression further, and include in it
the whole man, we lose the beauty of the connection in the 2d verse,
which relates particularly, and likewise exclusively, to the state and frame
of the mind.

Sacrifice.—This term is used figuratively.   It intimates that there are
now no proper sacrifices.   The sacrifice of Jesus on the cross has put an
end to sacrifices.   The sacrifice of the mass, then, is an invention of man,
and an abomination to God.   It is also observable that even figuratively
it is not the Lord's Supper, but the service of the body, that is here called
a sacrifice.   The phraseology that afterward prevailed, by which the table
whereon the bread and wine were placed was called the altar, has no
countenance in the word of God, even as a figure of speech.   *Living*
sacrifice.—This is called a living sacrifice, in distinction from the sacrifices of the law, in which the animal offered was put to death.   The
phraseology is quite similar to the phrases *living bread* and *living way.*
Dr. Macknight, then, entirely errs when he explains the phrase as signi-

fying 'an excellent sacrifice,' from the circumstance that animals were brought alive to the altar. Formerly those believers thus called on to offer their bodies a living sacrifice were dead in trespasses and sins, and had yielded their members as servants to iniquity; but now they were quickened, and risen with Christ, to walk in newness of life. And as the sacrifices were wholly devoted to God, so believers ought to be wholly consecrated to His service, preserving their bodies pure as temples of the Holy Ghost, and remembering that they themselves are living stones, built up a spiritual house, an holy priesthood, to offer up spiritual sacrifices, acceptable to God by Jesus Christ. *Holy.*—It was necessary that the sacrifices of the law should be holy, or free from everything that would render them ceremonially unclean. In like manner, the bodies of the saints must be holy as well as their souls. They must not be employed in the service of sin, else they cannot be fit to be presented to the Lord. *Acceptable unto God.*—The Jewish sacrifices, even if offered according to the law, now ceased to be acceptable to God, since they were abolished by the coming of their antitype, the Lamb of God. But the preparation of the bodies of believers is a service that is always well-pleasing to God. This and other such things as are obviously appointed are the only sacrifices acceptable to God. The sacrifice of the mass not being appointed by God, and actually subversive of the sacrifice of the cross, instead of being agreeable to God, must be odious in His sight.

Your reasonable service.—This evidently refers to the distinction between the service of the Jews by sacrifices and ceremonial worship, and the service of Christians. Sacrificial worship, and, in general, the whole ceremonial ritual of the Jews, were not worship according to reason. It is, indeed, reasonable to worship God in whatever way He prescribes; but had not man fallen, he would not have been required to worship by such ceremonies as the Jewish law enjoined. Sacrificial worship is not in itself rational, and was appointed by God not for its own excellence, but from its adaptation to prefigure the good things to come. Many commentators appear to have mistaken the true meaning of this phrase, from an ill-grounded fear that it is disrespectful to the Divine appointments to suppose that they are not in themselves rational. This, however, is an important and obvious truth. Sacrificial service was appointed only as a shadow, and when abolished, is classed by the Apostle among 'the weak and beggarly elements.' But to worship God with our bodies is as rational as to worship Him with our souls. Such worship, then, is called reasonable worship or service, as distinguished from the Jewish ritual. Mr. Locke imagines that it is opposed to the irrational worship of the heathen. But to this the contrast is not exclusively confined; for it is evident that the sacrifices of the pagans were of the same kind as those of the Jews. If the nature of the one kind of sacrifices was irrational, so also must be the other. The difference between the heathen sacrifices and those of the Jews did not consist in the things offered, but in the object of the offerings. The one was appointed of God, and was accepted of God: the other was not only not appointed by God, but was an act of homage to devils. Agreeably to this view, it may be asserted with the utmost confidence, that sacrifices are of Divine appointment, and not an invention of men. They are not in themselves rational, and no abuse of reason would have led to such a practice.

Ver. 2.—*And be not conformed to this world ; but be ye transformed by the renewing of your mind, that ye may prove what is that good, and acceptable, and perfect will of God.*

And be not conformed to this world.—' World ' here denotes the people or inhabitants of the world. But there is no allusion, as Dr. Macknight supposes, to the heathen world. The same exhortation is as applicable to men in every age, even since so large a portion of the world has assumed the name of Christian, as it was to the pagan Roman empire. The wicked are called *the world*, not, as Dr. Macknight imagines, as the whole is put for a part, but on the principle that the righteous are comparatively so few. As the nation of Israel was so small in number as not to be counted among the nations, so are the people of God among the inhabitants of the earth. They are not counted in the world. ' We know,' says the Apostle John, ' that we are of God, and *the whole world* lieth in wickedness.' By conformity to the world is meant assimilation to the people of the world ; or the sentiments, conduct, and customs by which they are distinguished. It is the character of those who are dead in trespasses and sins, that they walk ' according to the course of this world,' acting conformably to those maxims which regard only the present life ; and they ' who mind earthly things ' are described as the enemies of the cross of Christ; but the conversation of believers, as being pilgrims and strangers, is in heaven. This prohibition, however, respects those things only that are sinful, and does not require singularity in the Christian in anything that is not contrary to the law of Christ. Pride may be indulged in the singularities of austerity, as well as in the imitation of fashionable folly. A sound Christian mind will have no difficulty in making the necessary discrimination on this subject.

Transformed.—This word signifies the change of the appearance of one thing into that of another. It is used by the fabulous writers to signify the change or metempsychosis of animals into trees, or of men into the appearance of other animals. This term denotes the entire change that passes on a man when he becomes a Christian. He is as different from what he was before, as one species of animal is from another. Let not men be so far the dupes of self-deception as to reckon themselves Christians, while they are unchanged in heart and life. ' If any man be in Christ, he is a new creature (or creation); old things are passed away, behold, all things are become new.' If there be not a radical difference between their present state and that in which they were by nature, they have no title to the character of Christians. This shows that, in general, it is not difficult to discriminate Christians from the world. If the change be as great as the word of God here teaches, what difficulty can there be, in most cases, in judging of the character of those who profess Christianity ? It is not the heart we are called to judge. If the person be metamorphosed, as the word originally implies, from a state of nature to a conformity with Christ, it will certainly appear, and the state of the heart will be evident from the life. As there are degrees in this transformation, although all Christians are transformed when they are born again, yet they ought to be urged, as here, to a further degree of this transformation.

Renewing of your mind.—It is not the conduct merely, but the heart itself, of the Christian that is changed; and it is from the renewal of the mind that the conduct is also renewed. The transformation or change that passes on the man who becomes a believer of the Gospel, is not one produced by enthusiastical imaginations, monkish austerity, or a spirit of legalism, endeavouring to attain salvation by good works. It is produced by the renewing of the mind, and by that only. Many persons become for a time changed in conduct from various motives, who are not changed in heart by the Spirit of God, and the truth believed respecting the person and work of the Lord Jesus Christ. But such changes are generally temporary, and though they should continue for life, they are of no value in the sight of God. That change of life which the Lord will approve, is a change produced by the renovation of the mind, in the understanding, the affections, and the will.

That ye may prove.—The word in the original signifies both to *prove* and to *approve*, but we cannot so properly say approve what is the will of God. The passage seems to assert that to find out and discriminate the will of God with respect to those things that He requires and forbids, it is necessary to be renewed in the mind. Calvin well remarks, ' If the renewal of our mind is necessary for the purpose of proving what the will of the Most High is, we may hence see how much this mind is opposed to God.' Indeed, nothing can be more true than that the renewal of the mind is necessary for a successful inquiry into every part of the will of God. The natural man is in everything opposed to the mind of God.

Good.—The will of God is here distinguished as good; because, however much the mind may be opposed to it, and how much soever we may think that it curtails our pleasures, and mars our enjoyments, obedience to God conduces to our happiness. To follow His law is even in this world calculated to promote happiness. *Acceptable.*—That which the Lord enjoins is acceptable to Him, and surely this is the strongest motive to practise it. Nothing else is acceptable to Him, however specious it may appear to human wisdom. All injunctions that proceed merely from men in Divine things are unacceptable to God. He approves of nothing but obedience to His own commands. All the injunctions, then, that men submit to, in obedience to the mandates of the Church of Rome, are unacceptable to God. They are abomination in His sight. *Perfect will of God.*—The will of God as exhibited in His word is perfect. Nothing can be added to it, nothing can be taken from it; yet that monstrous system of Antichristianity which has so long, in the name of Christ, lorded it over the world, has added innumerable commands to those of Christ, and even taken away many of His laws.

Ver. 3.—*For I say, through the grace given unto me, to every man that is among you, not to think of himself more highly than he ought to think ; but to think soberly, according as God hath dealt to every man the measure of faith.*

For appears to indicate the reason why those who were addressed should

in all things ascertain the will of God. By introducing a particular
instance of the importance of this duty, Paul enjoins the necessity of
giving heed to his exhortation. It is the will of God that His people
should make a just estimate of their own gifts, and not from ignorance
overvalue themselves and despise others. *I say, by the grace given unto
me.*—Although Paul sometimes addresses believers, as in the beginning
of this chapter, in the humblest and most affectionate style, yet at
other times, as in these words, he employs that tone of authority which
was the prerogative of an Apostle. He calls on them to attend to his
words, as remembering that he did not speak of himself; but, as he
elsewhere expresses it, 'as of God, in the sight of God, speak we in
Christ.' *The grace given unto me.*—This grace or favour bestowed upon
Paul, is the office of an Apostle. But it is not correct to say that grace
in this place signifies apostleship. The apostleship was a grace or favour;
but favour or grace is not apostleship. Grace or favour includes, but by
no means signifies, that office, although it is one of the innumerable gifts
conferred by grace. To explain grace as signifying office, as is often
done, is an instance of that unsound criticism that makes a word specifically designate whatever its general meaning includes, which, though in
this instance it may be harmless, is productive of much false interpretation. *To every man that is among you.*—The Epistle was addressed to all
in the church at Rome, and consequently they were all included in the
exhortation that follows. When, therefore, the Apostle addresses them
here individually, it shows that the dissuasive refers to a thing to which
all of them were naturally much inclined. With this, fact corresponds.
All men are prone to overvalue themselves; and therefore to each of
them Paul thus pointedly brings home the exhortation.

Not to think of himself more highly than he ought to think.—In the two
foregoing verses the Apostle had been enjoining the duty of entire
devotedness to God, both in body and soul. Nothing could tend more
powerfully to render his exhortation ineffectual, or stand more in the
way of the performance of those duties on which, in the following part
of the Epistle, he was about to expatiate, than high-mindedness in those
whom he addressed. According, therefore, to the example of our Lord,
both in His Sermon on the Mount, and when inviting sinners to come to
Him, Paul begins here by inculcating humility. He warns each of them
not to form a higher opinion of himself than his faith in God warranted.
To this all are naturally prone ; but there is an opposite error, assuming
the semblance of obedience to this exhortation, which ought equally to
be avoided. This is an affectation of humility by speaking of one's self
contemptuously. This species of hypocrisy ought to be avoided. When
an author speaks of his poor abilities, and tells us he is the most unfit
man for the work he has undertaken, he is generally insincere ; but if
not insincere, he must be unwise ; for God never requires us to exercise
a talent which He has not bestowed on us. *Think soberly.*—Christians
are here directed to make a sound and moderate estimate of their own
gifts, which will preserve them from both extremes,—on the one hand,
from overrating, and, on the other, from unduly depreciating, their
attainments or talents.

According as God hath dealt to every man the measure of faith.—God hath given us here, by the Apostle, a standard by which we may measure ourselves. Of the term 'faith' in this place, various explanations are given; but that it simply means faith in its usual acceptation throughout the Scriptures, as this is the most obvious, so it appears to be its true import. By faith we are united to the Saviour, and by faith is received out of His fulness all that is imparted to us by God. The measure, then, of faith, with which each believer is blessed, whether strong faith or weak, great faith or little, indicates with certainty both his real character before God, and his relative standing among other believers. According, therefore, to his faith, as evidenced by his works, every Christian ought to estimate himself. The man who has the greatest faith is the highest in the school of Christ. We here also learn that not only faith, but every degree of it, is the gift of God; for men believe according as God hath dealt to each of them the measure of faith; and ' unto every one of us is given grace, according to the measure of the gift of Christ.' By the consideration of the manner in which the Apostle thus enforces his admonition, the believer will both be moderated in his own esteem, and also in his desire for the esteem of others. He will consequently be much less exposed to encounter what may inflame his pride, or tend to his discouragement.

Ver. 4.—*For as we have many members in one body, and all members have not the same office;*

The Apostle here illustrates the union and connection of believers, by the figure of the wonderful structure of the human body. Every member has its proper place in the body, and its proper function to perform, and every member is valuable according as it is useful in the body. But no member is useless. For the smallest and least honourable is useful. But this does not imply, as Mr. Stuart understands it, that there is no superiority of value among the members. This is contrary to obvious fact, and contrary to the nature of the figure here employed. One member of the human body is more useful, and, as Paul says to the Corinthians, more honourable than another; but the least honourable is useful, and to be treated with respect. 'To show,' says Mr. Stuart, ' that no one has any reason to set up himself as superior to others, the Apostle now introduces the admirable comparison of the *body of Christ,* i.e., the Church, with the human body.' Surely it is not to teach us that all the members of the body of Christ are equally valuable, that the Apostle introduces the comparison. Such a comparison would be very ill chosen; for among the members of the body there is a great variety in their relative scale of importance. Who would not rather lose a joint of his finger than his eye? But while one member is more important than another in the human body, as well as in the body of Christ, every member is important; every member has its peculiar function, which contributes to the good of the whole, and which the most honourable members are not adapted to perform. The eye is a more important member than the foot, but the eye could not perform for the good of the body that function which the foot performs. The eye, therefore, as well as every other member of the body, ought to honour the foot, according to the value of the services it is adapted to perform. *Office.*—This does not mean office in a restricted sense, because every member of the body has such an office. It means office in its general sense of function.

Ver. 5.—*So we, being many, are one body in Christ, and every one members one of another.*

So we, being many, are one body.—This is not to be restricted to one church, as to the church at Rome, to which it was written, but refers to the Church of Christ, which embraces His people of all ages, and of all countries. The feeblest disciple, even he who of the whole number is least instructed in his Master's will, has still his place in the body, and his use in that place. Whatever church, then, refuses to receive any Christian for want of knowledge of any part of the will of Christ, acts against the spirit of this passage. It is wrong either to refuse admission to Christ's known people, or to admit His known enemies. *In Christ.*— Not, as Dr. Macknight understands it, 'under Christ.' It is not by our being under Christ that our union is effected with one another, but by being *in* Christ.

Members one of another.—By being united in Christ, believers become members of one another, that is, they are united to each other, as all the members of the body are united. The most remote members are united by their union with the body. The hands and the feet have fellowship through the intervening members. Hence Christians ought to love one another as parts of themselves. As the Apostle says, no man ever hated his own body ; and he that loveth his wife loveth himself. For a like reason, a Christian, when loving his fellow-Christians, is loving himself. It is thus that Christians, in the Church of Christ, taken individually, are many, and are together one body in Christ, having the Spirit of Christ, and all of them are members one of another. This consideration ought to operate powerfully to unite them. There is a sectarian partiality, distinct from this, too often found among the professors of Christianity. But as the union of Christians, here represented by that of the members of the human body, respects none but real Christians, and as it respects all such, whether they be externally united in Christian fellowship with us or not, we ought to cultivate love to them as to the disciples of Christ, of whatever name, and cherish this love to them, on the ground of their union with Christ. We ought to unite with the Apostle in praying, ' Grace be with all them that love our Lord Jesus Christ in sincerity.'

Ver. 6.—*Having then gifts differing according to the grace that is given to us, whether prophecy, let us prophesy according to the proportion of faith ;*

Having then gifts differing according to the grace that is given to us.— Upon this Dr. Macknight observes :—' As the *grace of apostleship* signifies the *office of an apostle* graciously conferred, so the *grace* here said to be given to the Romans may mean the particular *station and office in the Church* assigned to individuals by Christ.' But the word grace has neither the one signification nor the other. It is that favour by which Christ confers His gifts on the members of His body. Office in the Church belongs to few of them, but they all possess gifts or talents by which

they may be useful to the body.   Many of the gifts possessed when the
Apostle wrote, were gifts miraculously bestowed; but even at that time
they were not all such.   And the word *gifts* includes those gifts that are
given in providence, or conferred by constitution, talent, birth, education,
and other circumstances, as well as the extraordinary gifts immediately
conferred by the Holy Spirit.   Riches and natural eloquence are gifts,
as well as the miraculous ability to speak in languages not previously
learned.   Christians, then, should consider everything they possess as a
gift bestowed by God, which they should cultivate and use to His glory,
and for which they are accountable.   If a Christian misspend his money,
his time, his abilities, his influence, or any talent which God has conferred on him, he is not misspending his own, but is misspending what is
intrusted to him by God.   He is unfaithful in his trust.

Whether prophecy.—Prophecy strictly signifies the foretelling of future
events.   But it seems also to be extended to denote any message from
God, whether relating to things present or to come, and, in the New Testament, to refer to the exposition of Scripture.   Calvin, after remarking
that ' some mean by *prophecy* the power of prediction which flourished
in the Church at its commencement,' afterwards observes, ' I prefer the
opinion of those commentators who take the word in a more extended
sense, and apply it to the peculiar gift of explaining revelation, according
as any one executes with skill and dexterity the office of an interpreter
in declaring the will of God.   Prophecy, therefore, at this period, is
nothing else in the Christian Church than the proper understanding of
Scripture, and a peculiar faculty of explaining the same; since all the
ancient prophecies, and all the oracles of God, were contained in Christ
and His Gospel.   For Paul understood it in this sense, 1 Cor. xiv. 5,
when he said, ' I would that ye all spake with tongues, but rather that
you prophesied.'   ' We know in part, and we prophesy in part,' 1 Cor.
xiii. 9.   For it does not appear that Paul was only desirous in this
passage to recount those admirable graces by which Christ ennobled His
Gospel at the beginning, but rather gives a statement of ordinary gifts,
which certainly remain in the Church.

Proportion of faith.—They were to speak according to the extent of
their information or measure of faith.   This passage does not appear to
relate to that principle of interpretation which is called *the analogy of
faith.*   This is a canon of Scripture interpretation which has no doubt
been abused; but when rightly applied, as the word of God must be
consistent with itself, it seems both reasonable and useful.   Since the
time of Dr. Campbell of Aberdeen, who keenly opposed this principle, it
has been generally renounced by expositors of Scripture; yet, when
viewed in a proper light, it is by no means liable to the exceptions made
to it.   The objections which Dr. Campbell brings against it are fully
obviated in Dr. Carson's late work, entitled, *Examination of the Principles of Biblical Interpretation of Ernesti, Ammon, Stuart, and other
Philologists*, pp. 103–108.[1]

---

[1] That work should be carefully perused by those who have been accustomed to
admire Mr. Moses Stuart as a sound biblical critic, or who are in danger of being
misled by the works of German Neologians.

Ver. 7.—*Or ministry, let us wait on our ministering ; or he that teacheth, on teaching.*

Or ministry.—The word in the original is that which appropriately designates the office of the deacon. If it refers to office, it must refer to this officer. For though ministry equally applies to Apostles, and all who serve in the Gospel, yet appropriately it refers to one office ; and when it is applied to others, it is with circumstances that make the reference obvious. Indeed, what is here said applies to all offices as well as to that of the deacon ; but this should not influence us so as to prevent our ascertaining its immediate reference. There is no necessity here to restrict the word to an official meaning, for it will apply to every one who devotes himself to the interests of the body of Christ. As Howard, the philanthropist, was to humanity, so may many Christians be to the Church of Christ,—at least, to that part of it with which they are more immediately connected. *He that teacheth, on teaching.*—Fitness to teach is a gift of the Head of the Church, which all who teach ought to possess, and without which no appointment of any one can make him a minister of Christ. They who possess the gift of teaching ought to employ it diligently.

Ver. 8.—*Or he that exhorteth, on exhortation : he that giveth, let him do it with simplicity ; he that ruleth, with diligence ; he that showeth mercy, with cheerfulness.*

He that exhorteth.—This means to excite to duty and dissuade from sin, and requires a peculiar talent. Mr. Stuart supposes that the teacher and exhorter were different officers ; but it is quite obvious that the Apostle is not distinguishing offices, but gifts. Every gift does not require a different office. Many of the gifts required no office at all. No opinion can be more groundless, than that the gifts imply each a separate office in the Church.

He that giveth.—This is usually supposed to refer to the deacon ; but as the Apostle is not speaking of the distinction or number of offices, and as the word used is not so restricted, there is no just ground thus to limit the passage. It includes the deacon, but is not confined to him. Mr. Stuart, however, is not justified in saying that the word ' properly means to *impart among others what belongs to one's self; to give of one's own to others.*' It is not essential to the word whether the gift proceeds from the giver as the owner, or merely as the steward. The gifts conferred by the Apostles were not *their own;* yet Paul applies the word (Rom. i. 11) to the communication of a spiritual gift through his hands to the Church. But to prove that the word here extends to those who gave of their own substance, it is not required that the word cannot apply to official or vicarious alms. It is enough that the word is one of a general meaning, and applies to the giving of one's own. Why should it be confined to official giving, when there is nothing restrictive in the word or in the circumstances ? Why should it be confined to the deacon, when the Apostle is not at all treating of office, but of gifts possessed by unofficial as well as official persons. *With simplicity.*—This means singleness of view. It guards against ostentation or love of praise, on account of which the Pharisees gave their alms. The word is sometimes used to signify liberality, and is so understood here by Mr. Stuart. This meaning is not unsuitable, but still the other is more appropriate. In all cases Christians need the caution to give with simplicity, but it would not be possible for some to give with what is generally understood by liberality.

He that ruleth.—Mr. Stuart labours hard, but unsuccessfully, to make it appear that this word does not here apply to presiding or ruling in the Church, but to assisting the poor by hospitality, like Phebe. The word is usually applied to presiding in the church ; and when it is used without a regimen, the most obvious meaning must be supplied to fill up the ellipsis. That this will confine it to ruling in the church admits of no question. Presiding or ruling in the church is here considered, not with a view to its distinction from other offices, but with respect to the gift that fits for it. 'Some are of opinion,' says Dr. Macknight, 'that the *president* was one appointed to superintend those who were employed in distributing the church's alms.' There can be no doubt that the word would apply to a president of any kind. But to believe that it signifies here such presidents, when it is appropriated to other presidents in the church, and when there is no evidence that there were any presidents of the kind supposed, is building without a foundation.

With diligence.—The ruler is to attend to his office with earnestness and diligence. It is the duty of all to spend and to be spent in the service of their Lord.

Showeth mercy.—This signifies the giving of money, or anything, for the support of poor brethren ; or applies to every instance in which mercy was to be shown to the afflicted, whether the affliction arose from poverty, sickness, or any other calamity. *With cheerfulness.*—Mercy must be shown, not only so as to indicate that it is voluntary, but also with cheerfulness, which shows that is a pleasure. This spares the feelings and soothes the sorrows of the afflicted.

Ver. 9.—*Let love be without dissimulation. Abhor that which is evil, cleave to that which is good.*

Let love be without dissimulation.—There seems to be here an indirect allusion to those hollow pretensions of love so generally manifested in society. Men pretend to have the greatest love to each other, when they not only have no love at all, but when they may really be under the influence of a contrary disposition. Calvin well observes on this passage. 'It is difficult to give a view of the ingenuity with which a large portion of mankind assume the appearance of that love which they really do not possess. For they not only deceive others, but impose upon themselves, while they endeavour to believe that they entertain a very considerable share of love, even for those whom they not only treat with neglect, but in reality renounce and despise. Paul therefore declares that only to be genuine love which is free from all dissimulation and guile ; and every person can best judge for himself whether he entertains any feeling in the innermost recesses of his heart opposed to this noble and lasting affection.' Christians ought to be careful that, while they use to each other the endearing language of brethren, they feel the sentiments and perform the actions which this language imports. 'Above all things,' says the Apostle Peter, ' have fervent charity (love) among yourselves: for charity shall cover the multitude of sins.' Believers ought to throw the mantle of love over the numerous faults into which their brethren may fall, in their conduct towards them, and thus to hide them from their eyes, forgiving their faults, even as God, for Christ's sake, hath forgiven them, Eph. iv. 32.

Abhor that which is evil; cleave to that which is good.—With respect to this, Calvin observes, ' The words following in the context, *good* and *evil*, have not a general meaning; but by *evil* is intended that malicious iniquity which injures any person ; and by *good*, that kindness by which are afforded to others aid and assistance.' But it rather appears that the words in this place are to be viewed as to what is *bad* and *good* in general. We ought not only to avoid doing what is evil, but to accustom ourselves to abhor it, as the vilest and most offensive of things are abhorred. To that which is good we ought to cling with all our hearts. Christians are not to be satisfied with abstaining from what is evil, and practising what is good. The affections of their minds should be in unison with their duty ; they should hate as well as avoid what is sinful, and love as well as practise what is good. We thus learn that we are accountable to God for the state of our minds, as well as for our external conduct. We should not only not practise, but not love evil.

Ver. 10.—*Be kindly affectioned one to another with brotherly love ; in honour preferring one another ;*

Be kindly affectioned one to another with brotherly love.—This appears to indicate that in brotherly love believers ought to have that affection for one another which nature displays among those who are brothers in the flesh. Brotherhood in Christians ought not to be a mere name, but a reality, evinced by the affections of a relationship of kindred. All Christians are brethren ; they are born of one Father, who hath taught them to say, ' Our Father, who art in heaven.' He who loves the Father, loves the brethren. ' Whosoever believeth that Jesus is the Christ, is born of God ; and every one that loveth Him that begat, loveth Him also that is begotten of Him.' *In honour preferring one another.*— Among those who derive the same meaning from these words, there is a great variety in their method of expressing it. Calvin, with many others, understood it as our translators, that each in honour prefer his brother to himself, agreeably to other texts of Scripture. But the word signifies, in general, to lead before, and has a great variety of applications. The meaning here seems to be, that in showing mutual respect, they ought each to strive to take the lead. This is a thing in which they may lawfully strive with one another. While the men of the world are striving to outstrip each other in everything that respects ambition, Christians are to refrain from following their example; but they are permitted and enjoined to strive with one another in the indication of mutual respect. Dr. Macknight understands the passage to mean, ' *In every honourable action go before, and lead on one another.*' But it seems forced to understand ' honour' as signifying every honourable action. The word appears to have a limited reference to the honour to be shown to one another by the brethren. ' In lowliness of mind, let each esteem other better than himself,' Phil. ii. 3.

Ver. 11.—*Not slothful in business ; fervent in spirit; serving the Lord;*

Not slothful in business.—It does not appear that the word in the original can bear to be translated *business.* It denotes eagerness, earnestness, zeal, urgency, etc. The meaning appears to be, that in doing everything with respect to things both temporal and spiritual, believers are not to be slothful or indulge in indolence ; but in every duty to use exertion and manifest earnestness. *Fervent in spirit.*—A fervent spirit is the reverse of sloth, and always prompts to diligence and vigour of action. Christians ought to possess such a spirit in doing all their business, especially in the things of the Lord. Earnestness in doing good, says Calvin, requires a zeal and ardour, lighted up in our breasts by the Spirit of God, Acts xviii. 25. *Serving the Lord.*—Christians are here exhorted to consider themselves as the servants or slaves of the Lord Jesus Christ. They are so in the fullest sense of the word as concerns Christ's right to them, and authority over them, and the duty of their being solely devoted to Him. They have none of the disagreeable feelings of slavery, because Christ's service is their delight, their honour, and their interest. Though the precept applies generally, yet it appears to have a particular reference, from the connection, to the duty of fervency of spirit which precedes it.

Christians should consider themselves as wholly and at all times the servants of the Lord, and, remembering that His eye is ever upon them, do all things as in His presence. It is not merely in acts of worship, or on particular occasions, that they are to be considered as serving Him, but in all their lives and all their actions. They are in their worldly employments and engagements to do all with a view to the authority of their Master. Even in eating and drinking, they are exhorted by the Apostle to act for the glory of God. If Christians would keep this at all times before their minds, how much would their happiness be increased! For we may be assured that an increase in our obedience to our heavenly Master will always be accompanied with an increase of true happiness.

Ver. 12.—*Rejoicing in hope ; patient in tribulation ; continuing instant in prayer ;*

Again and again it is enjoined on believers to *rejoice* in the Lord—in the contemplation of His person, His offices, His power, His love, and in their union with Him. Here, in the midst of exhortations to attend to various duties, they are commanded to *rejoice in hope.* Hope is founded on faith, and faith on the Divine testimony. Hope, then, respects what God has declared in His word. We are here exhorted to exercise hope with respect to future glory, and to rejoice in the contemplation of the objects of hope. What can be better calculated to promote joy than the hope of obtaining blessings so glorious in a future world? Were this hope kept in lively exercise, it would raise believers above the fear of man and a concern for the honours of this world. It would also enable them to despise the shame of the cross.

The objects, then, of the believer's hope are the spiritual and celestial blessings which are yet future, to which his eyes should constantly be directed, and which are calculated to fill him with the greatest joy. It is not the prospect of terrestrial possessions in which he is to rejoice, but of a house eternal in the heavens. ' In Thy presence is fulness of joy; at Thy right hand there are pleasures for evermore.' It is that glorious communion with Jesus Christ of which the Apostle speaks, when he says, ' Having a desire to depart, and to be with Christ; which is far better.' It is that state in which believers shall be like Him, for they shall see Him as He is. 'As for me, I will behold Thy face in righteousness; I shall be satisfied when I awake with Thy likeness.' It is the hope of righteousness for which, through the Spirit, believers wait, Gal. v. 5. This hope is founded on the unchangeable promise of God—on His promise accompanied by His oath—on the blood of Christ with which He has sealed His promise—on Him who was not only dead, but is risen again, who is even at the right hand of God, who also maketh intercession for His people. This hope, then, is both sure and stedfast, and entereth into that within the vail, whither the forerunner, even Jesus, is for us entered.

This description of hope, as an anchor both sure and stedfast, confutes the erroneous doctrine of Roman Catholics, who maintain, as has been formerly observed, that the hope of the Gospel is a doubtful conjecture, instead of a firm expectation of future blessedness. They insist that the believer ought to be always in doubt as to his salvation; that he cannot know whether God loves or hates him; and that all the assurance he can have of his salvation can never go beyond conjecture. Is this, then, the anchor both sure and stedfast which enables the believer to remain firm amidst the storms and agitations of this unsettled world? Can he rejoice in a hope so uncertain and unstable? That Roman Catholics should thus reduce to doubt and uncertainty that hope which the believer is commanded to maintain perfectly (1 Pet. i. 13), is not to be wondered at, since it is partly on their own merits, and on the satisfaction and sufferings of their saints, that their hope is founded, and not exclusively on the blood of Christ. The believer is here commanded to rejoice in hope; and if he consider that he is bound to apply to himself the other injunctions contained in this portion of the word of God, and to act upon them, he ought equally to regard it as his duty to obey this injunction, and to remember that, if he is not obeying it, it is an indication that all is not right with him. The same conclusion may also be drawn, if he is not walking according to that other express command in chapter sixth, to reckon himself to be *dead indeed unto sin*, but alive unto God through Jesus Christ our Lord.

The hope of the glory of God, in which the Apostle here affirms that Christians ought to rejoice, is provided as an important part of the believer's armour,—an helmet to cover his head, to defend him against the attacks of his spiritual enemies, 1 Thess. v. 8. It supports him when ready to be cast down. ' Why art thou cast down, O my soul? and why art thou disquieted within me? Hope thou in God, for I shall yet praise Him who is the health of my countenance and my God.' It soothes the bitterness of affliction when the believer is resting on the promises of God. In prosperity it elevates his affections, and, fixing his expectation on the glory that shall be revealed, disengages him from the love of this world. ' My soul thirsteth for God, for the living God; when shall I come and appear before God?' It comforts him in the prospect of death; and he says, with his Saviour, ' My heart is glad, and my glory rejoiceth, my flesh also shall rest in hope.' His spirit at death ascends to mingle with the spirits of just men made perfect, while his body enters the grave as a place of rest, waiting for its glorious resurrection, and the day when he shall sing that song of triumph. ' O death! where is thy sting? O grave! where is thy victory?' It is the prayer of the Apostle, ch. xv. 13, that the God of hope would fill His people with all joy and peace in believing, that they may abound in hope, through the power of the Holy Ghost.

Patient in tribulation.—Since Christians have such a good hope through grace, they ought to be patient under their afflictions. Nothing is better calculated to enable us to bear calamities than the hope of a happy result. And what can equal the prospects of the Christian when he has passed through the furnace and been tried as gold? His afflictions are not only necessary for his trial, and honourable to God, but they are for his own eternal advantage. The light afflictions of the righteous, which are but for a moment, work out for them a far more exceeding and eternal weight of glory. The trial of their faith is much more precious than that of gold, though it be tried with fire, and shall be found unto praise and honour and glory in the day of Christ. Afflictions are sent by God to His people to increase their patience. On account of remaining sin, they are their portion while in the body. ' In the world ye shall have tribulation; but be of good cheer, I have overcome the world.'

Continuing instant in prayer.—The Christian is to ' pray without ceasing.' No duty can be well performed without this. It is especially necessary in the time of affliction. ' Paul also,' says Calvin, ' not only excites us to prayer, but expressly requires performance; because our warfare is unceasing, and we are daily attacked by various assaults, which champions even of the greatest bravery are unable to support without an occasional supply of new vigour. Unceasing continuance in prayer is the best remedy against fatigue.' It is impossible that believers can discharge the various duties which are here enforced, without having their eyes constantly directed to their heavenly Father, and without receiving from Him the will and the capacity necessary for their discharge Our Lord's parable of the unjust judge, Luke xviii. 1, contains the strongest encouragement to perseverance and importunity in prayer. The Lord commands His disciples to pray always, on account of the power of their spiritual enemies, who are constantly seeking their destruction. The Apostle also exhorts believers to pray always with all prayer and supplication in the Spirit, and to watch thereunto with all perseverance; to continue in prayer, and watch in the same with thanksgiving; in everything giving thanks, for this is the will of God in Christ Jesus; and to be careful for nothing, but in everything, by prayer and supplication, with thanksgiving, to let their requests be made known unto God. If a Christian undertakes anything whatever without prayer, he is neglecting his duty, and not acting up to his privileges. In that matter he is not walking with God, whose ears are open to the prayers of the righteous. On occasions, even, when there is not a moment to deliberate, and when an immediate decision is indispensable, there is still time for prayer and for receiving an answer, Neh. ii. 4, 8.

The believer, too, should ever address his heavenly Father with full confidence that his prayers will be heard, not perhaps according to his wishes, but in a way that in the issue will be more advantageous. 'This is the confidence that we have in Him, that if we ask anything according to His will, He heareth us. And if we know that He hear us whatsoever we ask, we know that we have the petitions that we desired of Him.' 'Whatsoever ye shall ask in My name, that will I do, that the Father may be glorified in the Son. If ye shall ask anything in My name, I will do it.' 'Ask and ye shall receive, that your joy may be full.' 'And all things whatsoever ye shall ask in prayer, believing, ye shall receive.' If the believer asks and does not receive, it is because he asks amiss : he does not ask in faith, he asks for things that are not proper, he asks while he is indulging in sin. 'The sacrifice of the wicked is an abomination to the Lord; but the prayer of the upright is His delight.' If I regard iniquity in my heart, the Lord will not hear me,' Ps. lxvi. 18. Here, however, it is proper to remark that there is a great difference between iniquity *prevailing* in the heart, and iniquity *regarded* in the heart. In the last case we cannot draw near with acceptance. God will not accept our prayers, because in that case we cannot draw near with 'a true heart.' But in the former case, of iniquity prevailing in the heart, we may draw near in the full assurance of faith, of which we see an example in the case of David. 'Iniquities,' he says, 'prevail against me ;' but he immediately adds, 'As for our transgressions, Thou shalt purge them away,' Ps. lxv. 3.

Ver. 13.—*Distributing to the necessity of saints ; given to hospitality.*

Distributing to the necessity of saints.—Rather ' communicating to the necessities of the saints.' The poor brethren are thus made joint partakers of the substance of their richer brethren ; the rich make their poor brethren participators with them in their substance, by giving them what is necessary to supply their wants. 'Observe,' says Calvin, ' the propriety of the expression. The Apostle thus intimates that we ought to supply the wants of our brethren with as much care as if we were assisting ourselves.' It may here be observed that this precept proves most clearly that there was no general custom among the first Christians of a community of goods. Had this been the case, the rich would not have been commanded to communicate to the necessities of the saints. It ought also to be noted that it is to the *necessities* of the saints that communication is to be made, not to their indolence. 'This we commanded you, that if any would not work neither should he eat.' So far from its being the duty of Christians to support the idle, it would be a breach of one of the laws of Christ's kingdom.

Saints.—It may also be observed that, while we are to do good unto all men, the poor saints are the peculiar care of a church of Christ. These are to be fed as children of the family who are unable to support themselves. Here, also, we may see the character of the members of the first churches. They were such only as appeared to be saints and godly in Christ Jesus. The term *saints* signify those who are separated for the service of God—sanctified in Christ Jesus. This appellation belongs to all the people of God without distinction, and not to a particular class or part of them exclusively, such as to the Apostles. The Apostles were indeed saints, and so were Noah, Abraham, Moses, and all the Prophets. If this title were indiscriminately applied to all who are sanctified in Christ Jesus,—that is, to every Christian,—as in the apostolical Epistles, it could not be misunderstood; but its exclusive application to Apostles and some others besides, leads to the supposition that all Christians are not saints. This application is one of the engines of the Man of Sin, by which he deceives. If any plead for it as a proper distinction, it is sufficient to advert to the saying of Paul, ' We have no such custom, neither the churches of God,' 1 Cor. xi. 16. Here the reference is to the approved customs of the churches acting under the immediate guidance of the Apostles, which consequently are equivalent to direct precept. We find no such custom in the Scriptures, in which Prophets and Apostles name themselves, and each other, without this distinction.

Given to hospitality.—This does not mean, as it is generally now applied, social intercourse and conviviality among neighbours, but it means the receiving and entertaining of strangers at a distance from their own habitations. This was a duty of peculiar necessity in the primitive times, when inns and places of entertainment were unusual. But it is a duty still; and the change of times and customs cannot set aside any of the precepts of our Lord Jesus Christ. Christians ought hospitably to receive their brethren coming from a distance, and to assist them in their business. We are here directed not only to practise hospitality, but, according to the import of the original, to follow or pursue it. Christians are to seek opportunities of thus manifesting love to their brethren. In another place the Apostle enforces the same duty : ' Be not forgetful to entertain strangers; for thereby some have entertained angels unawares.'

Ver. 14.—*Bless them which persecute you ; bless, and curse not.*

Bless them which persecute you.—Calvin justly cautions us against endeavouring to find a certain order in these precepts. It is their import, and not their connection with each other, that we ought to ascertain. Sometimes there may be a relation ; at other times there is entire independence. The precept here given cannot be obeyed in its genuine sense by any who are not born again of the incorruptible seed of the word ; and even to such it is a difficult duty. In proportion to their progress in the Divine life, will there be in them a difference with respect to their attainments in that heavenly spirit which enables them to comply with this injunction. But none can justly be looked on as Christians, who do not in some measure possess this spirit, and practise this precept. If this be so, how few are the genuine disciples of Christ ! ' None,' says Calvin, ' can boast himself to be a son of God, or glory in the name of a Christian, who has not in part put on this mind, which was in the Lord Jesus, and does not daily wrestle against and oppose the feeling of enmity and hatred. The law of God is in all respects a law of love, and the precept here enjoined contains a peculiar characteristic of Christianity, in the exhibition of which Christians are imitators of their heavenly Father. Our Lord Jesus Christ gave a signal example of obedience to this rule, when on the cross He prayed to his Father for the pardon of those by whom He was crucified. And Stephen, the first martyr, in imitation of his Divine Master, died in calling on His name, and praying for his murderers. This precept teaches Christians in what manner, when reviled or persecuted, they ought to act to their persecutors. 'Being defamed,' says the Apostle, 'we entreat.' The repetition of the precept in the following clause adds to the energy of the expression.

Bless, and curse not.—Paul repeats the precept to bless, on account of its importance, and its applicability to men in general, in connection with a command to curse no man. How does this condemn the Church of Rome, which so frequently manifests its antichristian character by cursing its enemies, and allowing its priests to curse from the altar those who give them offence. How many are there, who, calling themselves Christians, openly and without shame utter maledictions on those who irritate them! How few abstain from imprecations of every kind and degree![1]

Ver. 15.—*Rejoice with them that do rejoice, and weep with them that weep.*

This precept has no doubt a peculiar importance with respect to the brethren, but it is applicable in general. We ought to sympathize with our fellow-creatures in their happiness and afflictions. The meaning of the precept is quite obvious. The prosperity of others ought to inspire us with joy. Their affliction ought to affect us with sorrow. Even the very semblance of this duty among the people of the world has a beneficial influence on society, heightening the joy of prosperity, and lessening the pain of adversity.

Ver. 16.—*Be of the same mind one toward another. Mind not high things, but condescend to men of low estate. Be not wise in your own conceits.*

Be of the same mind one toward another.—This precept refers rather to unanimity, cordiality, and harmony in transacting all the business of the Church, than to oneness of mind as to the truth. With respect to faith, it is the word of God with which believers are to be in accordance, and not with the opinions of each other. Besides, this often-repeated precept is always introduced with others of a practical nature. Oneness of belief in everything, even the least part of the revelation of God, is of importance. This, however, cannot be effected but by a full knowledge of the Divine word. The injunction is most important, and cautions against a captious spirit respecting the affairs of the church with which we are connected, or our intercourse one with another. Dr. Macknight has

---

[1] Little attention is paid by many Christians entirely to abstain from improper expletives. Some are in the habit of pledging their word or honour, as 'Upon my word,' in common discourse, expressly contrary to these solemn injunctions in Matt. v. 33-37, and Jas. v. 12 ; and of even irreverently pronouncing the name of God, as 'Gracious God!' 'God knows!' 'My God!' as in France, where there is almost in every sentence, '*Mon Dieu!*'

entirely mistaken the import of this passage, making it refer to what precedes. '*Be of the same* hospitable, forgiving, sympathizing *disposition towards one another* as towards strangers and persecutors.'

Mind not high things.—Men in general are aspiring to things above them. The great efforts of life are to obtain high rank or commanding station in the world. Christians are here cautioned against setting their minds on high things. Nothing can be more opposed to progress in the Divine life, than the evil against which we are here warned. In proportion as Christians indulge it, they make their bed among thorns, turning away their eyes from the glory of their future inheritance. *Condescend to men of low estate.*—The word here translated *condescend* signifies to be led away with; and that which is rendered *men of low estate* may with equal propriety be rendered *low* or *humble things;* and in this way the clause is an antithesis to the one preceding. '*Not thinking of high things,*' says Calvin, 'by which he means that a Christian ought not to aspire, in an ambitious manner, after those things by which he may surpass others, nor indulge in haughty feelings, but meditate rather upon modesty and meekness; for our excellence, in the presence of God, consists in these virtues, not in pride or the contempt of our brethren. This precept is properly added to the former; for nothing breaks the unity mentioned by the Apostle more completely than the exalting of ourselves, and our aspiring to something still more elevated, with a view to attain a higher situation. I take the word *humble* in the neuter gender, that the antithesis may be more complete.' *Be not wise in your own conceits.*—'This sentence,' says Calvin, 'connects with the preceding part of the context; for nothing inflates the mind more than a high opinion of our own wisdom and prudence.' Self-conceit is an evidence of weakness of mind and of ignorance. So far as it manifests itself among Christians, it evidences low attainments in the knowledge of the things of God, and is most destructive to the harmony of a church, and the improvement of the individual under its influence.

Ver. 17.—*Recompense to no man evil for evil. Provide things honest in the sight of all men.*

Recompense to no man evil for evil.—It is natural to every man to return evil for evil. Those of the most indolent and passive dispositions are not without feelings of revenge. Nothing but the faith of Christ will enable any man to overcome this disposition. But faith will overcome it; and every man who believes in Christ must labour to overcome it in his heart, as well as in his practice. If Christians are tried by this test, the pretentions of the great bulk of those who usurp the name will be found groundless. *Provide things honest in the sight of all men.*—We are not to do our work to be seen of men, but we are to be careful that all our works are done so as to avoid anything that would bring a reproach upon the Gospel. We ought not only to abstain from what we know to be wrong, but we ought sedulously to avoid just suspicion, 1 Thess. v. 22. Sometimes Christians say that if they have a good conscience, they care not what any one thinks of them. But this is contrary to this precept. If we are falsely charged, we may commit ourselves to Him who judgeth righteously. But, so far as in our power, we are not only to avoid what is improper, but to avoid the blame or suspicion of what is improper. In Paul himself we see an example of solicitude in this respect. 'Providing for honest things, not only in the sight of the Lord, but also in the sight of men,' 2 Cor. viii. 21.

Ver. 18.—*If it be possible, as much as lieth in you, live peaceably with all men.*

Such is the state of human nature, that offences must needs come, and here the Apostle, in his exhortation, proceeds on the fact of the difficulty of living at peace with all. The believer is, notwithstanding, constantly to aim at this, and to pursue it even when it seems to fly from him. He ought particularly to guard against giving occasion to any just subject of complaint against him. To live at peace with all men, as far as is attainable, without sacrificing duty, is not only duty, but for his happiness. To pursue peace, then, is to fly from misery. It is impossible to be happy in disturbance, and broils, and enmities; but it may sometimes be impossible for Christians to obtain peace. When this is the case, they must submit to it as one of the greatest afflictions ; but we ought to recollect that it is God who giveth us peace with men, and to seek it from Him with ardent prayer, as well as from men, by unremitting endeavours after it. When deprived of it, we ought also to inquire whether there be not a cause of this in ourselves ; for when a man's ways please the Lord, He maketh even his enemies to be at peace with him. Calvin justly cautions us 'not so to affect the security of the favour and esteem of men, as to refuse to incur, for the sake of Christ, the hatred of any human being, when necessary.' As some Christians may be naturally of a contentious disposition, so others may, from a selfish desire of having the favour and good opinion and praise of men, be inclined to keep out of view whatever is most offensive in the religion of Christ. Such persons may congratulate themselves on the possession of a spirit of peace, but it is only a spirit of cowardice and selfishness, a spirit of worldly indifference to the glory of God and the salvation of men. We are never to seek to maintain peace, either with the world or with Christians, by the sacrifice of any part of Divine truth. A Christian must be willing to be unpopular, that he may be useful and faithful. To whatever obloquy or opposition it may expose him, he ought earnestly to contend for the faith which was once delivered unto the saints.

Ver. 19.—*Dearly beloved, avenge not yourselves, but rather give place unto wrath : for it is written, Vengeance is mine ; I will repay, saith the Lord.*

Dearly beloved, avenge not yourselves.—As by the law in the members we are most strongly urged to take revenge on those who injure us, the Apostle introduces this dissuasive against indulging this corrupt principle, with the most endearing address. Christians will constantly have opportunities of exercising themselves in obedience to this exhortation. There are innumerable occurrences calculated to provoke and excite them to retaliation. But they will find that to abstain from avenging their own cause will essentially promote their happiness. It it a painful thing to think of injuries, and it is most for our peace and happiness to forget them, and commit ourselves to the Lord. How opposite is this from the principles of the men of the world, and what are called the laws of honour, in obedience to which a man will, in cold blood, hazard his own life and that of his neighbour on account of some contemptuous expression or trivial injury! What gross ignorance does it manifest to consider any man a Christian, who is always prepared to act in this manner, and who would regard it as an affront if the contrary were supposed!

Give place unto wrath.—Calvin, Dr. Macknight, and Mr. Stuart understand this of the wrath of God; but notwithstanding what the latter has alleged in confirmation of this, the common view of the passage is unquestionably the just one. No principle of language will justify the ellipsis that makes wrath in this connection designate *the wrath of God* or *the Divine wrath*. Among the various applications of the phrase 'Give place,' one of them is, to retire from the place, that it may be occupied by another, Luke xiv. 9. The person here referred to gives the place that he occupied to another, and retires to another place. This meaning, then, is quite in accordance with that of the common explanation of this passage. Give place to wrath, that is, leave the place, and let wrath occupy it; or give place, as a man would do if attacked by a wild beast, stepping aside to let it rush by. Mr. Stuart, indeed, alleges that the other interpretation 'is rendered nearly certain by the quotation which immediately follows,' which he supposes would be wholly inapposite if wrath be understood as referring to the wrath of the enemy. This argument, however, is without force. The meaning objected to is quite consistent with the quotation. 'Take not revenge yourselves, my brethren, but retire from the contest, for it is not you but God who has a right to take vengeance.' It is a good reason why we should not take vengeance, that it is God's prerogative to take vengeance. *For it is written, Vengeance is Mine; I will repay, saith the Lord.*—It belongs to God, and He will repay it. Those threatenings of the vengeance of God which we find in the writings of the Prophets, and especially in the Book of Psalms, are not to be viewed as proceeding from the angry spirit of the writers, but from the Holy Ghost who dictated them, who hates, and will come out of His place to punish, all workers of iniquity. If any man dare to take into his own hands the vengeance which belongeth to God, it will recoil upon himself.

From this it is evident that God will avenge the injuries done to His people. What, then, shall be the punishment of those who employ themselves in persecuting, injuring, reproaching, and slandering the disciples of Christ. We are not, however, to understand this precept as prohibiting Christians from appealing to the magistrate in case of injuries. Calvin, indeed, justly observes, that it prohibits us from applying to the magistrate from a principle of revenge. It is quite true that to appeal to the magistrate out of a principle of revenge is indulging revenge as much as if we took revenge with our own hands. But it is often right to appeal to the laws of our country in order to secure the peace of society, and defend ourselves and others from similar injuries. To act on the principle avowed by some, that it is wrong to apply to the power of the civil magistrate, is not only mistaking this precept, but is contrary to the fundamental principle on which society rests. In many cases it would be highly sinful not to punish evil-doers. If the magistrate ought not to bear the sword in vain, the subject ought to assist him in executing vengeance.

Ver. 20.—*Therefore, if thine enemy hunger, feed him ; if he thirst, give him drink : for in so doing thou shalt heap coals of fire on his head.*

If thine enemy hunger, feed him.—A Christian must be an enemy to no man, but he cannot prevent others from being enemies to him; but instead of revenging their injuries, he is bound to do good to them. Conduct so opposite to nature can never be genuinely effected by the natural man. It is only to be effected by the power of God through faith. It is the fruit of the new birth only. We are not to understand this precept as always to be fulfilled by the giving of meat and drink; but meat and drink are taken as an indication that in every possible instance good will is to be manifested.

Shalt heap coals of fire.—Dr. Macknight, with many others, makes this refer to the custom of fusing metals, and supposes that it recommends this line of conduct as the most effectual way to soften or melt the enemy to repentance. This, however, is a meaning made for the words, instead of being extracted from them. Mr. Stuart makes it imply pain, but thinks that it is not the pain of punishment, but of shame or contrition. This is equally remote from the obvious meaning of the expression. Besides, it is equally unwarrantable to do anything with a view to occasion the pain of contrition, as to occasion the pain of punishment. We should desire the contrition of our enemy for his good, and not that he may endure suffering. It is vain to force the words of the Holy Spirit. They evidently assert that the conduct recommended will have the effect of increasing the punishment of the enemies of God's people; and though they should not rejoice in this effect as causing misery, yet they should hereby be led to adore the manifestation of Divine justice. Besides, this ought to be a warning to their enemies to abandon their wicked conduct, and finally to escape the fearful consequences which they cannot avoid if they persevere in their enmity. They ought to be informed of this part of the Divine pleasure. There can be no doubt that such conduct from the Lord's people, if it does not overcome their enemies, will eventually add to their guilt and punishment. We should beware not to explain away the words of Scripture.

Ver. 21.—*Be not overcome of evil, but overcome evil with good.*

Be not overcome of evil.—Christians are here exhorted not to suffer themselves to indulge a spirit of wrath or resentment from the provocations of their enemies. In the world they will experience evil on the part of others, but they ought never to allow themselves to be drawn into the commission of evil and to be overcome by it. To yield to anger is to be conquered by an enemy. Men in general suppose that to resent an injury is only to show a proper spirit. But in the estimation of God it is the opposite, and manifests defeat. He acts as the Christian, who yields not to anger, but remains without wrath under insult and ill-treatment. When the Lord commanded the disciples to forgive their offending brethren, perceiving the difficulty of acting in this manner, they immediately prayed, 'Lord, increase our faith.' No prayer could be more suitable, and nothing more necessary for the performance of this duty.

Overcome evil with good.—This implies that the injurious person may, by repeated acts of kindness, be won over from his enmity. This, indeed, frequently happens, and there is hardly a case in which it will not have some effect. But whatever may be the success, we ought always to make the trial. If our efforts shall be lost on our enemy, they will not be lost with respect to ourselves. Our Christian character will be more perfected, our happiness will be increased, our ways will be pleasing to the Lord, and our reward will be sure. Persons who cannot be overcome with good must be in the most awful state of hardened wickedness, and their punishment will be dreadful.

In the above remarkable portion of Scripture, we learn the true tendency of the doctrine of salvation wholly by grace, established in a manner so powerful in the preceding part of this Epistle, by which men are created in Christ Jesus unto good works. How beautiful is it, and how sublime when displayed in all its practical effects in the duties which flow from it, as here described! We may search all the works of the most admired writers, and, so far as they have not borrowed from the fountain of inspired truth, we shall find in them nothing comparable to the elevated maxims contained in this chapter. Especially we shall not discover the faintest shadow of resemblance to the motives by which these duties are here inculcated. If the heavens declare the glory of God, and the firmanent showeth forth His handiworks,—if the invisible things of Him from the creation of the world are clearly seen by the things that are made, even His eternal power and Godhead, so that the heathen are *without excuse,*—how much more clearly do the Scriptures proclaim their Divine origin, and the majesty of their Author! God hath magnified His word above all His name, Ps. cxxxviii. 2.

CHAPTER 13
ROMANS 13:1 – 14

CHRISTIANS having become the subjects of a kingdom which is not of this world, might be led to suppose that they were released from the ties of obedience to human authorities, especially such as were not Christians. Far different is the doctrine here taught by the Apostle. He commands ' every soul,' both Jew and Gentile, to be subject to the existing powers. He makes no exception as to the nature or constitution of any government. He speaks neither of monarchies, nor of republics, nor of mixed constitutions. But he applies all his precepts to every form that government may assume. As there is nothing from which political partisans in the present day more widely differ than from the apostolic doctrine laid down in this chapter, Christians ought to give to it the more earnest heed, lest they be led away on this subject by the opinions of the world, or of those who ' despise government.' They ought to examine carefully what is here taught by the Apostle, without attempting to accommodate it to their preconceived views of civil liberty. This is the more necessary, as many have lately embarked in politics with a keenness that will be of no service to their spiritual life, and will rather tend to make them cleave more closely to the dust.

In considering the duties enjoined in the apostolic Epistles, it is constantly to be kept in view that, while written on particular occasions, and addressed to particular churches, they are equally adapted, in the wisdom of God, to all times and circumstances. They are intended for the instruction and guidance of Christians in every country and every age, just as the Decalogue, though delivered to only one nation, and that only once, is binding on every nation under heaven, in every period, till the end of time. Christians learn at present from this passage the will of God respecting their duty to civil government, just as those to whom this Epistle was addressed. It is true that there is an innumerable variety of differences in circumstances; but this is nothing to the purpose. The things taught in these Epistles are in all circumstances duty. The Roman Christians were under a despotism, and those who read this Epistle may live under a free government. But the duty of obedience is in both cases the same. The powers are under both equally to be obeyed.

It is of the utmost moment that Christians, under all forms of government, should have a rule concerning their duty to civil government clear and precise. Such a rule we have here laid down. No practical subject is more fully or more explicitly treated in the word of God. The weakest Christian cannot be at a loss to discover the will of his Lord with respect to obedience to civil government. It is presented to us in the Scriptures in two different aspects,—the one as the ordinance of God, the other as the ordinance of man; and in both these characters obedience is enjoined by the same authority.

Connected with a warning to believers to act in such a manner as not to be spoken against, the Holy Ghost, by the instrumentality of the Apostle Peter, utters this command, ' Submit yourselves to every ordinance of man for the Lord's sake: whether it be to the king, as supreme; or unto governors, as unto them that are sent by Him for the punishment of evil-doers, and for the praise of them that do well. For so is the will of God, that with well-doing ye may put to silence the ignorance of foolish men. As free, and not using your liberty for a cloak of maliciousness, but as the servants of God. Honour all men. Love the brotherhood. Fear God. Honour the king,' 1 Pet. ii. 13–17. Paul writes to Titus, iii. 1, ' Put them in mind to be subject to principalities and powers, to obey magistrates.' By the same authority, and with more extension, the Apostle enforces this duty in the passage before us.

In the most solemn manner, subjection to the existing powers is here enjoined. This is contrary to the wisdom of the world, which takes offence at such subjection, and contrary to the proud heart of man, that would make religion a pretence to cover its secret reluctance to submit to disagreeable restraints. How natural the opposite doctrine is to the carnal heart, may be seen from the general sentiments entertained on the subject by rulers and ruled—by infidels and professed Christians—by statesmen and people of all ranks. With one consent, the generality of men, even in this country, which is comparatively so much enlightened by the Scriptures, proclaim that subjection to rulers is, even in things civil, limited and conditional—that in case of the breach of the supposed compact between the rulers and the ruled, rebellion is lawful, and resistance a duty. Even in the houses of Parliament is this doctrine boldly maintained. It is much to be desired that among those who thus trample on the commandments of God, and set aside the Scripture doctrine on this subject, there were no real Christians. It is lamentable to reflect that, to justify resistance to the civil powers, many of the people of God have resorted to the same false rules of interpretation which Neologians and other perverters of the Divine word have invented to banish the doctrines of grace from the Bible. No expedients to explain away the meaning of any part of Scripture were ever more forced than those adopted to make this chapter accord with the right of resisting the powers that be.

Ver. 1.—*Let every soul be subject unto the higher powers. For there is no power but of God ; the powers that be are ordained of God.*

In this verse the Apostle first states the duty he enjoins on Christians towards civil rulers. Next he states the ground on which the command rests as the reason why he gives the injunction : every government is to be obeyed, because there is no government but of God. Lastly, he brings it home to the existing government under which the servants of God are placed.

Let every soul.—This most comprehensive expression shows that to every Christian, in every country, in all variety of situations, and on all occasions, the doctrine which the Apostle is about to teach is applicable. *Be subject unto the higher powers.*—By this expression is meant the persons who possess the supreme authority, who are in the 3d verse denominated *rulers.* Government, in our language, is a term of similar import. No phrase could more clearly and definitely express the duty of subjection to the civil rulers whom God has placed over us, than that which the Apostle here employs. This passage *expressly* enjoins obedience to all governments equally. The word rendered ' powers ' wants the article, and has not an exclusive reference to the Roman government. It comprehends governments universally. Had any of the Roman Christians gone beyond the bounds of the empire, their duty of obedience to the government of the country is here as expressly enjoined as it is to the powers of the empire itself. And the foreigners who may have belonged to countries beyond the limits of the empire, are here taught obedience to the powers of Rome while in the country, and obedience to the powers of their own country when they should have returned home. The Apostle speaks of ' powers ' without peculiar reference. Every one, without exception, is, by the command of God, to be subject to the *existing* powers, whatever were the means by which they became possessed of the situation in which they stand. Cæsar subverted the laws of his country, Jeroboam established idolatry, and Nebuchadnezzar carried Judah captive. Yet the successors of Cæsar were recognised by Jesus, and were the rulers of the Roman empire when the Apostle wrote ; Jeroboam was expressly appointed by God as king over the ten tribes; and the oppressed Jews were commanded to pray for the peace of Babylon.

For there is no power but of God.—The meaning of the first clause, ' Let every soul be subject unto the higher powers,' is clear as noonday ; this second gives the reason why subjection is demanded,—for there is no power but of God; not ' by Divine permission,' according to Mr. Stuart, but by Divine appointment. The expression *of* or *from God*, cannot mean Divine permission. What we permit is not in any sense *of us.* There is no power but of God ; because it is God in His providence who confers power on every man who holds it. No tyrant ever seized power till God gave it him. The words ' no power ' referred neither to kinds of powers nor order in government, but necessarily apply to every civil ruler under heaven. Were there any doubt with respect to the sense in which the power is *of God,* it would be entirely removed by the next clause of the verse, in which the existing powers are said to be ordained of God. The power, then, is ' of God,' in the sense, as is there declared, of being ' ordained of God.' The 4th verse also decides this to be the meaning of the phrase, where the ruler is twice said to *be the minister of God.* Civil rulers, then, are the ministers of God ; if so, they must be of God's own appointment. The worst government in any country is of God, and is calculated to effect His purposes and promote His glory. Wicked rulers are necessary in God's plans to punish wicked nations. It is not merely the form of civil government that is from God, but the governors. Dr. Macknight says that God ' has left it to the people to choose what form is most agreeable to themselves, and to commit the exercise of the supreme power to what persons they think fit. And, therefore, whatever form of government hath been chosen, or is established in any country, hath the Divine sanction.' This is neither consonant to fact nor to Scripture. In most countries the people have had nothing to do with the choice of their governors. The powers are of God not on this account, but they are of God because they are of His setting up. Whatever may have been the means of their exaltation, it is God who has exalted them either for a blessing or a curse to the people. They who enjoin obedience to civil government on the supposition of implied compacts or conventions, overturn the ground on which it is rested by the word of God.

The powers that be are ordained of God.—Here every evasion is taken away from the ingenuity of sophistry. It will not be of any avail to attempt to limit allegiance according to the conduct of rulers, or the means by which they have acquired their authority. The existing powers in every country, and in every age, are *ordained*[1] of God. Nero was as truly a ruler ordained of God as Titus or Antoninus. The Divine ap-

---

[1] That *ordained*, or *appointed*, is here the proper rendering of the original word, that a more faithful translation could not possibly be given, and that all the attempts which have been made to impose on it a different sense are unfounded, is fully established by Dr. Carson in his *Review of Dr. John Brown on the Law of Christ respecting Civil Obedience, especially on the Duty of paying Tribute,* 1838. That review contains also a full and critical discussion on the whole of Romans xiii. 1-7. Whoever wishes thoroughly to investigate the subject of which it treats, would do well to read this very able review, printed at Edinburgh by William Whyte & Co.

pointment of the government that is over us, is the ground on which the duty of our submission rests; and the powers that be—that exist in any country—are appointed by God. 'The Most High ruleth in the kingdom of men, and giveth it to whomsoever He will, and setteth up over it the basest of men,' Dan. iv. 17. 'I have made the earth, the man and the beast that are upon the ground, by My great power, and by My out-stretched arm, and have given it unto whom it seemed meet unto Me,' Jer. xxvii. 5. Here we see how God disposes of kingdoms, and appoints their rulers according to His sovereign pleasure. It was God who set up Pharaoh, the cruel and tyrannical oppressor of Israel. 'And in very deed for this cause have I raised thee up, for to show in thee My power; and that My name may be declared throughout all the earth,' Ex. ix. 16. 'He putteth down one, and setteth up another,' Ps. lxxv. 7.

Ver. 2.—*Whosoever therefore resisteth the power, resisteth the ordinance of God: and they that resist shall receive to themselves damnation.*

Whosoever therefore resisteth the power, resisteth the ordinance of God.— Literally, 'So that he that setteth himself in opposition to the power, resisteth the ordinance of God.' Resistance to the government, then, is resistance to God; because government is God's ordinance or appointment. If God has appointed every government that exists in the world, His people are bound to submit to every government under which their lot has been cast. There is but one exception, and that is when anything is required contrary to the law of God. Then duty is plain. We are to obey God rather than men. The people of God, then, ought to consider resistance to the government under which they live as a very awful crime—even as resistance to God Himself. They are bound to obey, not good rulers only, as Dr. Macknight unwarrantably limits the words, but oppressive rulers also, if they do not command what God forbids.

And they that resist shall receive unto themselves damnation.—Here is declared the fearful consequence of resisting the ordinance of God. It is of no importance whether we understand the original word translated *damnation* to mean condemnation or punishment, because the former im-plies the latter as its consequence. If, however, we understand it of punishment, we must keep in mind that it is punishment proceeding from condemnation. And the condemnation here is not, as Mr. Stuart seems to understand it, of punishment exclusively from the hand of man. The punishment meant, whoever may be the executioner, is a judgment from God, as in 1 Cor. xi. 29, where the same word refers to those punishments with which God visited His people for the abuse of His ordinance. 'We ought, therefore,' says Calvin, 'to act with great caution, that we may not rush upon this Divine threatening. Nor do I confine this meaning of the word *damnation* to that punishment only which is inflicted by magistrates, as if the design of the Apostle was to show that rebels against authority will be punished according to law, but every kind of Divine vengeance, in whatever manner it may be exacted; for he, in general, teaches us what end awaits those who enter into a contest with God.' When the ignorance of God's people is punished for any offence against the government of their country, their chastisement should be looked on as a chastisement from God.

It ought to be observed, that God's people may be in ignorance on this subject as well as on any other, and that we are not to suppose that all who have resisted the governments under which they were placed are enemies to God. Like Peter, when he drew his sword to defend his Master, they may sometimes be ignorant of their duty. But their ignorance is sinful. If they mistake their duty on this subject, they are more inexcusable than when they are ignorant on almost any other subject, for it is taught with a plainness that nothing but strong prejudice can resist.

Ver. 3.—*For rulers are not a terror to good works, but to the evil. Wilt thou then not be afraid of the power? do that which is good, and thou shalt have praise of the same.*

For rulers are not a terror to good works, but to the evil.—This is not a mere illustration of the last clause of the second verse. It extends to more than the punishment of resistance or disobedience. The negative assertion, that rulers are not a terror to good works, is different from the positive one, that they are a terror to evil works, and an assertion equally important; and the assertion that they who do good shall have praise is still different from both the others. This verse is often supposed to limit the obedience inculcated in the preceding verses to rulers who are of a proper character, and actuated by right motives. Nothing can be more unfounded. It is not introduced as the ground of obedience to civil government. The ground of obedience is stated in the first verse, immediately subjoined to the command. The higher powers are to be obeyed, because there is not one amongst them, not even the worst on earth, which is not of God. When the government is wicked, cruel, and oppressive, in the inscrutable ways of His sovereign providence, it is overruled by God so as to forward the object He has in view. Without exception, it is true in every age, and in every country, that the existing civil powers are ordained of God. It follows, then, that whosoever resisteth the powers, resisteth the ordinance of God. This verse, as has just been remarked, does not state the reason of submission according to the first ground, but it assigns the reason why God has appointed civil government, and is another reason for the subjection before inculcated. Here there is no limitation of anything previously spoken. It is a characteristic of civil government which is universally applicable. It is true of the worst government, that it is not a terror to good works, but to the evil. Good works and bad works are not here spoken of with reference to Christianity. The reference is to the works generally accounted good or bad in society, and the worst government will not punish such good works. No man was ever punished because he would not injure his neighbours. It is a general declaration with respect to all governments. The very worst of them is a blessing. The conduct of Christians with respect to obedience to Christ, as it is offensive to civil rulers, and has often been punished by them, is not here in the Apostle's view. The persecutions they have endured on account of their religion, have arisen from the enmity of the carnal mind against God, which is not more characteristic of every government than of every individual. *Wilt thou then not be afraid of the power? do that which is good, and thou shalt have praise of the same.*—This is a truth which experience will prove to every Christian.   If he obeys the laws of the country, and does the things that are good, he will have no reason to be afraid of the government.   If called to suffer for Christ's sake, he has no need to fear.

Ver. 4.—*For he is the minister of God to thee for good.   But if thou do that which is evil, be afraid ; for he beareth not the sword in vain : for he is the minister of God, a revenger to execute wrath upon him that doeth evil.*

For he is the minister of God to thee for good.—In this verse the civil ruler is twice denominated 'the minister of God,' first for good to His people, and next for the punishment of evil-doers.   Civil rulers, then, as the ministers of God, ought not only to be obeyed without resistance, but with alacrity.   They are not only ministers of God, but ministers for good.   This is the characteristic of magistracy in all countries.   In spite of all the evils that derogate from its proper character, it promotes the good of society.   But none are so much indebted to it as Christians, to each of whom it may indeed be emphatically said, it is the minister to *thee* for good.   Were the restraints of government removed, Christians would be attacked, persecuted, or destroyed in any country.   Even the persecution of the worst government would not be so bad as the persecution of the world, if freed from the restraint of law.   Notwithstanding the numerous persecutions endured by Christians under the Roman emperors, they were still to them the ministers of God for good, without whose government they would probably have been exterminated.   'The Christians to the lions!' was the common cry of the multitude among the pagans.   The Roman government afforded protection to Paul for a long period, and saved him on different occasions from suffering death by his countrymen.   Let Christians, then, in every country, instead of joining with the enemies of its established order, be thankful for the Divine ordinance of civil government, and exert themselves to maintain obedience and peace.   It is of the utmost importance for them in every country to understand their duty to civil government.   In this way they will most effectually commend the Gospel to the world, and remove some of the most powerful obstacles to its progress.   While they show that they fear not man, where he ordains what is contrary to the commandments of God, they ought likewise to show that obedience to God, and gratitude to Him who appoints civil government for their protection, obliges them to submit to the rulers in all things temporal.

The institution of civil government is a dispensation of mercy, and its existence is so indispensable, that the moment it ceases under one form it re-establishes itself in another.   The world, ever since the fall, when the dominion of one part of the human race over another was immediately introduced, Gen. iii. 16, has been in such a state of corruption and depravity, that without the powerful obstacle presented by civil government to the selfish and malignant passions of men, it would be better to live among the beasts of the forest than in human society.   As soon as its restraints are removed, man shows himself in his real character.   When there was no king in Israel, and every man did that which was right in his own eyes, we see in the last three chapters of the Book of Judges what were the dreadful consequences.

Some have inferred from this passage that the Apostle's injunctions refer solely to such governors as are truly good and altogether what they ought to be. Nothing can be further from the truth. From this it would follow that the Apostle, while professing to furnish an explicit rule of conduct in this matter for those whom he addressed, in reality gave them none, and that he has here laid down no clear and precise direction which could apply to Christians from that time to the present. Human governments, like everything administered by men, must always be imperfect; and as it is easy to form exaggerated ideas on this subject, no administration of any form that has ever existed would appear to come up to the imaginary standard. It would, besides, be impossible for the great body of Christians to arrive at a satisfactory conclusion as to their duty in this respect. This is one of those traditions by which the Scriptures are as completely made void, as by the Pharisees of old, or by modern Neologians. The rule which is here given is clear to all. It was dictated to Paul by God under one of the worst governments that ever existed, and under which the blood of the Apostle himself was shed, as if he had been a malefactor.

When the Jews were carried captive to Babylon, God by His Prophet commanded them to seek and to pray for the peace of the city. ' Seek the peace of the city whither I have caused you to be carried away captives, and pray unto the Lord for it; for in the peace thereof shall ye have peace,' Jer. xxix. 7. The most awful maledictions were pronounced against Babylon by the same Prophet on account of her manner of treating the Jews ; but it was God Himself who, in the course of His wise and holy providence, was to execute them, by means of those instruments which He should choose. ' Vengeance is mine ; I will repay, saith the Lord.' In the meantime, God made the tyrannical rulers of Babylon, whom He purposed to punish for their wickedness, His ministers for the good of His people.

But if thou do that which is evil, be afraid.—If men will transgress the laws under which they are placed, they have reason to be afraid ; and God here warns His own people, that, in such a case, they must not count upon His protection or interference to deliver them from the punishment due to those who rise up against His institution. This ought to caution Christians against indentifying themselves with political associations to oppose or subvert the government of their country. When they do so they are likely to suffer for it,—even more likely to suffer than the wicked themselves. God may in the meantime pass over the sin of the latter, while He visits that of His people with chastisement.

For he beareth not the sword in vain.—This implies that civil government is not a mere pageant arrayed with all the ensigns of power and vengeance against the opposer, but it also shows that the providence of God so orders it that rulers will in general be successful against the disturbers of the peace, so that evil-doers will be discovered and their plots defeated. The most secret and solemnly sanctioned conspiracies are generally defeated and frustrated. Indeed, were not civil government an ordinance of God, it would be impossible for it to answer the end of its appointment.

This passage sanctions the use of the sword, or punishment by death,

with respect to the transgressors of the fundamental laws of society. The
sword is put for punishment by death of any kind. This refutes the
opinion of those who think that it is sinful, nay, that it is murder, to put
criminals to death. God here sanctions the practice. And if it is right
in the civil magistrate to punish with death the violators of the fundamental laws of society, it is right in Christians to countenance and
co-operate with the magistrate in effecting such punishments. The same
truth is taught by our Lord when He says, ' My kingdom is not of this
world. If My kingdom were of this world, then would My servants fight
that I should not be delivered to the Jews.' This intimates that worldly
power may be maintained by arms, and that it is lawful to use them for
this purpose. 'If I have been an offender,' said Paul, 'or have committed
anything worthy of death, I refuse not to die,' Acts xxv. 11. Would
the Apostle have in this way sanctioned this punishment, allowing its
justice, if it had been contrary to the law of God?

*For he is the minister of God, a revenger to execute wrath upon him that
doeth evil.*—Vengeance belongeth to God. He hath, however, delegated
this right, so far as concerns the affairs of this world, to the civil magistrate, who ought to punish evil-doers. For this purpose God has put
the sword into his hand, and has armed him with legal authority. To
suffer crime, therefore, to pass unpunished, is a dereliction of duty in
the magistrate. Instead of being a duty, it is a sin to neglect avenging
the laws when they are transgressed. The magistrate is here called a
revenger, and is said to execute wrath. This refutes the notion that the
infliction of punishment by the civil power is only for example ; yet this
false maxim is now very generally adopted. The Apostle here considers
the sufferings inflicted as punishments, and brings not example into the
account. Example is no doubt one object of punishment, but instead
of being the sole, it is not its primary object.

Dr. Carson, in his review of Dr. John Brown, gives the following
division of the above four verses. 'The first clause of the first verse
contains the law of Christ, enjoining obedience to civil rulers. The rest
of the verse, in two clauses, gives the ground of this injunction, or shows
why God enjoins obedience. He enjoins obedience to rulers because
rulers are His own appointment. An observation naturally resulting
from this follows. If rulers are God's appointment, to oppose them is
to oppose the appointment of God. This enforces the duty by the guilt
of disobedience. He that opposes civil rulers, not only opposes them,
but also opposes God's ordinance. Another observation appended to
this shows the consequence of disobeying this ordinance of God. They
who resist shall receive to themselves damnation. The third verse commences with an observation, exhibiting a fact that proves that rulers are
of God, and which anticipates an objection that was likely to occur:
Rulers are not a terror to good works, but to the evil. The assertion that
civil rulers, without any exception, are appointed by God, would appear
strange, when it was considered that they were heathens, and tyrants,
and persecutors. But heathens, and tyrants, and persecutors as they
were, they are proved to be of God, by their being a terror not to good
works, but to the evil. With all their wickedness, they uphold the great

principles on which society is founded, and on which only it can subsist. The Christian, then, has no reason to dread them; for he does not practise the evil works which they punish, and he does the good works which they approve. This verse shows the reasonableness of the command of submission to government. As if the Apostle had said, "Do not think this command a hard saying; *for rulers are not a terror to good works, but to the evil.* If you wish to avoid incurring the displeasure of rulers, do that which is good, and then, instead of being punished, you will have commendation from them."

'The fourth verse gives an additional reason why Christians should not think civil government a grievance, but a blessing: *To the Christian he is the minister of God for good.* Instead, then, of submitting with reluctance, he ought to submit with pleasure and gratitude. Indeed, civil government is more for the advantage of Christians than for that of others. They need its protection more than any other class of men. Were it not for the protection of government, Christians could not live even in the countries where there are the proudest boasts of enlargement of mind with respect to civil liberty.

'The remainder of this verse warns the Christian what he may expect from civil rulers if he does what is evil: *The minister of God bears not the sword in vain.* Not only have rulers power to punish what is evil, but the providence of God takes care to make this power effectual. It is wonderful to consider how the providence of God defeats the best concerted plans of rebellion; and brings the disturbers of society under the grasp of the magistrate. Were it not that civil government is an ordinance of God, it is not possible that it could subsist.'

Ver. 5.— *Wherefore ye must needs be subject, not only for wrath, but also for conscience' sake.*

Men in general obey the laws from fear of the punishment of transgression; and if there was no punishment, they would transgress every law which thwarted their inclinations. But this must not be the case with Christians. They must respect the laws of the countries in which they live, not merely from dread of the punishment of transgression to be inflicted by the magistrate, in exercise of the power with which God has armed him, but also from a higher motive. Even were they assured of impunity from the magistrate, they must not violate the law, for conscience' sake. Here a necessity far more imperative than the former is added. Christians are to obey from a conscientious regard to the authority of God thus interposed. This is the motive which, above every other, ought to actuate them; and it is exhibited by the Apostle as the grand consideration by which he terminates his injunctions of obedience to civil government. This is the foundation of true loyalty. If in operation, it will not only insure the obedience of the Christian to the government under which he is placed, but prevent him from defrauding it by smuggling, evasion of taxes, or any illegal transaction. 'I have set the Lord always before me,' ought to be the motto of every Christian.

'To carnal wisdom,' says Dr. Carson, 'the doctrine of unlimited submission to civil government in temporal things appears a hard saying.

Who can hear it? If this sentiment prevails, it may be said, rulers may tyrannize as they please. They who speak thus do greatly err, not knowing the Scriptures, neither the power of God in the ruling of the world. It would be a hard thing indeed if God did not rule the rulers. But the Christian has nothing to fear, when he considers that every plan and proceeding of government is overruled and directed by his God. If He puts His children into the hands of men, He retains these men in His own hand, and they can injure them in nothing without His permission. 'The king's heart is in the hand of the Lord, as the rivers of water: He turneth it whithersoever He will,' Prov. xxi. 1. So far, then, from being a doctrine that fills the mind with discomfort, it is the only view that gives peace. Have not Christians more security for their safety in the care of their Almighty Father, than in a permission given by Him to defend themselves against the oppression of rulers? They have peace whatever party gets into power, because they know that in everything God fulfils His purposes by them. God rules on earth, even in the councils of His enemies, as completely as He rules in heaven. When God chooses to overturn the empire of tyrants, He is at no loss for instruments. He is not obliged to employ the heirs of glory in such scenes of blood: He uses the wicked to overturn the wicked.'

In the preceding five verses the Apostle makes no provision, in matters of civil submission, for any case of resistance or rebellion, under any circumstances. He makes no exceptions, no modifications; he discusses no hazardous cases of conscience upon emergencies not existing; but in language which none can mistake, and with an authority the commanding solemnity of which defies opposition, he proclaims to the Greek and to the Roman, to the barbarian and the civilised, *Let every soul be subject to the higher powers. The powers that be are ordained of God.*[1]

Ver. 6.—*For for this cause pay ye tribute also: for they are God's ministers, attending continually upon this very thing.*

For this cause pay ye tribute also.—Some, instead of 'pay ye,' translate the words 'ye pay.' But it cannot be supposed that the Apostle first alleges, as a reason for rendering personal obedience, that they were already in the habit of conscientiously paying tribute, when, in the subsequent verse, he enjoins the duty of tribute as specifically as he did the duty of obedience. Besides, 'for this cause ye pay tribute also,' takes it for granted that they were already in the habit of rendering both tribute and obedience for the same reason, instead of urging obedience on the foundation that they already for that reason pay tribute. If *even* is chosen as the translation of the Greek particle instead of *also*, this supposes that tribute is much worse as a grievance than is personal

---

[1] Some feel it difficult to admit the plain and obvious doctrine contained in the preceding verses of this chapter, lest it should condemn what took place in bringing about the Revolution of 1688. But whatever may be thought of the manner in which that Revolution was produced, and however beneficial its effects have been, no such considerations ought to be allowed to interfere with, or in the smallest degree to modify or contravene, the authority of God, which is here so plainly expressed. In that Revolution there may have been much evil, and though God has in His holy providence overruled it so as to bring out of it much good, yet, like everything else, it must be judged of by the Scriptures, and not the Scriptures by it, or anything connected with it.

obedience, the contrary of which is quite obvious. *For this cause*, or on this account.—For what cause? Is it on account of conscience or on account of civil government being an appointment of God? The latter is the true answer. The reason why the thing is a matter of conscience is, because government is a Divine appointment. Taxes are to be paid to government for its support, because God has appointed government for the good of society; and this is the argument that is immediately added. *For they are God's ministers.*—They are public officers whom God Himself, as the ruler of the world, has appointed to this business. Here, in order to impress the truth that 'the powers that be are *ordained* of God,' and that they are 'of God,' it is for the third time repeated that they are *God's ministers attending continually upon this very thing;*' that is, civil governors are devoted to the affairs of the public. They give their time to the public, and they should be adequately remunerated. It is necessary that what is requisite for the support of the government and its dignity should be supplied. God, then, has enjoined on His people to acquiesce in this reasonable appointment of His providence. 'This very thing,' then, does not refer to the gathering of taxes. The 'ministers of God' are the 'powers' of whom the Apostle was treating. The 'very thing' to which they constantly attend, is not the collection of the taxes, but the ministry of God in the things of government. 'The very thing' must be something either mentioned or necessarily implied in the text. But this can be no other than the ministry of the ministers mentioned. The collection of taxes, then, is not the very thing to which civil rulers attend. They are called the ministers of God, and after this they are said to be attending continually on this very thing.[1] The thing to which they attend is their duty as ministers of God in civil things.

Ver. 7.—*Render therefore to all their dues: tribute to whom tribute is due; custom to whom custom; fear to whom fear; honour to whom honour.*

Render therefore to all their dues.—Here the Apostle enjoins a general precept, applying not only to the particular instances which he had mentioned, but to everything due by equity or love from one man to another. Here, also, it ought to be particularly remarked that he calls taxes and customs 'dues' or *debts.* A tax is a debt in the true sense of the word. The Apostle here says, Render to all their dues, and in exemplification adds, 'tribute to whom tribute, custom to whom custom.'[2] Men sometimes act on the principle that taxes are not debts, and that they may evade their payment, although clearly liable by law. Such persons are condemned by the Apostle. It is here explicitly taught that taxes stand by the law of God on the same footing as private debts, which every man is therefore under an equal obligation to discharge. The same truth is taught by our Lord, when, on the tribute-money, bearing the image of Cæsar, being presented to Him, He said, 'Render therefore unto Cæsar the things which are Cæsar's.' The produce of taxes is here determined by the Lord to be the property of the government. By the laws, too, of every country, taxes are debts, to be paid as such to

---

[1] The antecedent to which the words rendered, 'this very thing,' refers, is ministry of God taken out of 'ministers of God.'

[2] *Dues.* The same word in the original, as in Matt. xviii. 32, rendered *debt.*

the government, and even preferable in order of payment to private debts. Christians have much reason to be thankful that they are thus, by the authority of God, freed from all responsibility respecting the application of every tax, and that this responsibility rests entirely with the government. Were it otherwise, they would be in constant perplexity on the subject, and almost in every case unable to determine whether it was their duty to pay or to withhold payment. They would thus be exposed every moment to be placed in opposition to the rulers, while at all times it would be actually impossible for them to live in a heathen or a Mohammedan country.

Some persons make a distinction between general and particular taxes, and refuse to pay taxes levied for particular purposes, when these purposes are believed to be bad. But there is nothing that will render it unlawful to pay a particular or specific tax, that will not equally apply to a general tax, any part of which it is believed is to be applied to a bad use. Why are we not accountable for the application of every part of a general tax? Because we have no control over it, and our approbation of it when we pay it is not implied. The same consideration exempts us from any share of responsibility respecting the sinful application of a specific tax. If taxes are debts, then the payment of them no more implies approbation of their object, than the payment of any other debt involves approbation of the purpose to which it is applied.

Tribute to whom tribute, custom to whom custom.—Tribute refers to what are now called taxes, and custom to revenue raised from merchandise. These are particular instances of the dues or debts included in the previous precept. *Fear to whom fear.*—The Christian is not to brave the authorities whom God has set over him, nor to set them at defiance, on pretence that he is a servant of God. On the contrary, he is to fear them as God's institution for the good of society. *Honour to whom honour.*—Not only are all pecuniary exactions of government to be paid, but all customary civil honour and respect are to be cheerfully given to those in power. Christians are not to decline paying the customary respect to the civil powers, on pretence that they are Christ's servants, or that all men are naturally on a level. Difference of rank in society is God's appointment for the ordinary government of men in society. That stubborn spirit which refuses to uncover to the king, or give the customary mark of respect to men in power, is pride and rebellion against God's appointment.

On this verse, Dr. Carson, in his *Review of Dr. Brown*, observes, 'The substantive to *all* is evidently *men*. Render then to all men their dues.' After this, he gives a specification of such dues as would be least likely to be considered as dues, or to be conscientiously paid as such, namely, taxes, fear, honour. Many Christians, to this hour, who would put away with abhorrence the thought of evading an ordinary debt, think it no evil to evade the taxes, and to withhold that honour and fear that is due to men in authority. 'To him to whom you owe tribute give tribute: to him to whom you owe custom give custom: to him to whom you owe fear give fear: to him to whom you owe honour give honour.' As if he had said, 'Not only pay your ordinary debts, but

those debts also that in general are not conscientiously paid as debts.'
This is the only view that can give meaning to the particle *then* or *therefore.* The spirit of the passage is to this purpose. Obedience and taxes
are due to civil rulers : pay these dues, *then,* as well as others. It is
quite obvious that the Apostle specifies only such debts as would be most
likely to be overlooked.

Ver. 8.—*Owe no man anything, but to love one another : for he that loveth another
hath fulfilled the law.*

Owe no man anything.—In the beginning of the former verse the
Apostle commands Christians to render to all their dues, which includes
debts of money as well as of respect. Here he forbids them to owe any
man anything, that is, to withhold from any man what is his due. This
duty is imperative, and requires to be particularly specified ; and in this
way the Apostle follows out the precept he had given in the preceding
verse. Christians ought to attend most scrupulously to this injunction.
It is a great injury to men, and a reproach to Christianity, when the
servants of God neglect this duty. It is a virtual breach of the eighth
commandment, although it may not bring on them the same obloquy.

But to love one another.—Love is here beautifully represented as a debt
that is never paid. It is a debt that ever remains due. Christians ought
not only to love one another continually, but to abound in love more
and more. The more they pay of this debt, the richer will they be in
the thing that is paid. *For he that loveth another hath fulfilled the law.*
—Here love is urged, on the ground that it is fulfilment of the law in
all its precepts. The whole law is grounded on love to God and love to
man. This cannot be violated without the breach of law ; and if there
is love, it will influence to the observance of all God's commandments.
If there were perfect love, there would be a perfect observance of the
law. But no man loveth another in the perfection that the law requires ;
therefore no man perfectly keeps the law. Love, then, is the fulfilment
of the law, being the thing which it demands, and all that it demands in
respect to both God and man.

Ver. 9.—*For this, Thou shalt not commit adultery, Thou shalt not kill, Thou
shalt not steal, Thou shalt not bear false witness, · Thou shalt not covet ; and if there
be any other commandment, it is briefly comprehended in this saying, namely, Thou
shalt love thy neighbour as thyself.*

Paul here cites several of the precepts of the second table of the law,
and observes with respect to each of them, that they are comprehended
in the law that enjoins us to love our neighbour as ourselves. Nothing
can be more evident than that if we loved our neighbour perfectly,
we would commit none of the things here specified. The law of the
Lord is admirable, both in its simplicity and comprehensiveness. It is
also most reasonable and just. It requires nothing but what is implied
in love. Its prohibitions, then, are not unreasonable restraints upon our
liberty, but the just requirements of love.

Ver. 10.—*Love worketh no ill to his neighbour ; therefore love is the fulfilling of
the law.*

Love worketh no ill to his neighbour.—Love never injures our neighbour
in any respect, but, on the contrary, as far as in its power, does him

service. All disputes, then, among neighbours and among nations proceed from a want of love. What, then, shall we say of the morality of men in general, who live in strife and contention, as often as their interests in the smallest degree interfere? What is the origin of all the disputes in the world but a want of love?

Therefore love is the fulfilling of the law.—As love will prevent everything which the law forbids, love must consequently be what fulfils the law. Love, for instance, will prevent murder, and even the smallest degree of hatred to another. Love, then, will keep the sixth commandment; and so of each of the commandments of the second table of the law.

Ver. 11.—*And that, knowing the time, that now it is high time to awake out of sleep ; for now is our salvation nearer than when we believed.*

The most appropriate meaning that can be given to the word translated *that* in this occurrence seems to be *especially.* The duties recommended were the rather to be attended to, from the alleged consideration that follows. Dr. Macknight translates by supplying the phrase, ' I command,' by ellipsis, ' Also this I command.' And Mr. Stuart supplies the words, ' Do this.' There is no need for these supplements, and the above gives the most appropriate meaning. *Knowing the time.*—The time is understood by Dr. Macknight and Mr. Stuart as referring to the season of the Gospel. But the ground of the observation, which is subjoined by the Apostle, shows that it refers to the present time, in distinction from the time when those whom he addressed first believed. Why is it time to awake out of sleep? The reason alleged is, *for now is our salvation nearer than when we believed.* It is plain, then, that the times contrasted are the time of their first believing, and the time then present.

Salvation is here understood by Dr. Macknight as signifying the glad tidings of salvation in the Gospel. This meaning is so forced and unnatural, that it deserves no consideration. In the Scriptures, believers are considered as saved from the moment they are partakers of a Divine life, by the belief of the truth. Salvation is also sometimes used with respect to the complete deliverance from the pollution of sin at death, when believers enter into heavenly happiness. And sometimes it refers to the day of judgment, when their happiness will be more complete, and when the body as well as the soul shall enter into glory. It is obviously in the second acceptation that the word *salvation* is here used. It was now a considerable time since the church at Rome had been gathered, and the brethren who were first called to the knowledge of the truth were now approaching the period of their entrance into the land of promise. The near prospect of leaving this world, and entering into a state of glory, ought to have a great effect upon Christians, in making them think less of this world, and more of that of which they are about to become the inhabitants.

Ver. 12.—*The night is far spent, the day is at hand : let us therefore cast off the works of darkness, and let us put on the armour of light.*

The night is far spent, the day is at hand.—Dr. Macknight understands this of ' the night of heathenish ignorance,' which he says ' is drawing to a conclusion ; ' and to the same purpose Mr. Stuart says that it ' is the time of ignorance and darkness in which they had once been.' But with respect to the time in which the persons here addressed were in ignorance and darkness, if he means heathen ignorance and darkness, this time was already at an end to them; and the day, as contrasted with this, was already present, and could not be represented as near. And as to' the night of heathenish ignorance being nearly at an end, this is far from past. Nearly eighteen centuries have passed since this Epistle was written, and the night of heathenism, so far from being at an end, still broods over the greater part of the world. *The night* here must be the time of the believer's being on earth; for his earthly state, with all its comparative light, is but night with respect to the light of heaven. The day which was at hand was not the day of judgment, but the day of death, with respect to those addressed. Mr. Stuart notices, and satisfactorily refutes, the opinion of Mr. Tholuck and the Germans, which represents the Apostles as believing the near approach of the day of judgment.

Let us therefore cast off the works of darkness, and let us put on the armour of light.—In place of the clothing of sin, Christians are to cover themselves with the armour of light. The Christian is a soldier, and as such he is furnished with a complete suit of armour, to fit him for the encounter with his enemies. It consists of *faith*, and *love*, and *hope*. 'Let us who are of the day be sober, putting on the breastplate of faith and love; and for a helmet, the hope of salvation.'

Ver. 13.—*Let us walk honestly, as in the day ; not in rioting and drunkenness, not in chambering and wantonness, not in strife and envying.*

Let us walk honestly, as in the day.—According to the present use of the language, ' honestly ' does not adequately represent the original. The word signifies decently, becomingly. We are by this precept required to conduct ourselves before the world in a modest, decent, and becoming manner. The allusion is to persons walking from place to place in transacting their daily business. The conduct of persons thus employed shows, even in people the most immoral, some regard to appearances; and they who riot in the night will place a restraint on their conduct in the day. Christians, then, as in the light of day, ought to conduct themselves in a manner suitable to the day, and not like those who riot in the night. It may be observed that the same figure is here still continued, but varied in its application. When it is said that the night is far spent, and the day is at hand, it is implied that it was still night, and that the day was future. But here the day is present. In one point of view it is night to the Christian, and in another it is day.

Not in rioting.—The word applies to all meetings for intemperance and debauchery. It denounces all amusements that minister to the impure passions of human nature, whatever may be their name. The fashionable follies of high life, and those practised by persons in inferior stations, are alike inconsistent with the Christian character and with this precept. It is vain to allege with respect to them that they are not expressly condemned in Scripture. The Scripture does not give out law with a verbose phraseology, like the laws of men, but condemns all the particular and ever-varying follies of mankind in every age and nation on general principles.

Drunkenness.—This sin is one of the greatest destroyers of mankind. Even were there no hereafter, a wise man would shun it as a pestilence. No other evil has so great a share in bringing ruin on individuals and families. Every approach to it ought to be most carefully avoided. Too much caution cannot be used in order to guard against the formation of habits of intemperance. Many a promising professor of Christianity makes shipwreck of the faith by giving way to this vice. It is a mistaken hospitality that tempts to any approach to intemperance. If we are to eat and drink to the glory of God, we ought to drink no more than is really useful for the health.

Chambering.—The meaning of this is plain, as well as of *wantonness*, which refers to all licentiousness, in its most extensive import. *Strife and envy.*—The former applies to every kind of contention; and the latter designates that principle which, more than any other, excites to strife or contention, and tends to make a man an enemy to his kind.

Ver. 14.—*But put ye on the Lord Jesus Christ, and make not provision for the flesh, to fulfil the lusts thereof.*

Put ye on the Lord Jesus.—Having given a specimen of the things that are unbecoming the Christian who walks in the day, the Apostle now shows, summarily, what the conduct is which he enjoins on us to exemplify. Believers were in themselves wretched, and miserable, and poor, and blind, and naked; like Joshua, clothed with filthy garments; but when they come to Christ, He says, ' Take away the filthy garments from him : behold, I have caused thine iniquity to pass from thee, and I will clothe thee with change of raiment.' They are then clothed with the garments of salvation, and covered with the robe of righteousness, Isa. lxi. 10 ; and being thus justified, those whom the Apostle addressed had put on Christ. But here it is their progress in sanctification he has in view. In the twelfth verse he had exhorted them to put on the armour of light; now he is enjoining the duty of perfect conformity to His holy image, bringing into captivity every thought to the obedience of Christ ; who gave us an example that we should follow His steps, who did no sin, neither was guile found in His mouth. Thus we are to cleave to Him with purpose of heart, and, as the Apostle elsewhere exhorts, that as we have received Christ Jesus the Lord, so we should walk in Him. ' To put on Christ,' says Calvin, ' means our being surrounded and protected in every part by the virtue of His Spirit, and thus rendered fit for the performance of every duty of holiness. For the image of God, which is the only ornament of the soul, is thus renewed in us.'

Provision for the flesh, to fulfil the lusts thereof.—*Flesh* here means the sinful principles of our nature. We are to make provision for the wants of the body, but we are to make no provision for its lusts. Whatever, then, tends to excite our corrupt propensities ought to be avoided.

Beautiful are the reflections of Archbishop Leighton, in his sermon on the four last verses of this chapter, from which what follows is extracted: —' These words are as an alarm, or morning watch-bell, of singular use, not only awakening a Christian to his day work, but withal minding him what he is. The former verses, 11, 12, tell us it is time to rise, and call us to put on our clothes, and, being soldiers, our arms. Verse 13th directeth our behaviour and employment throughout the day. The last verse doth shortly and clearly fold up both together.

' All the days of sinful nature are dark night, in which there is no right discerning of spiritual things : Some light there is of reason to direct natural and civil actions, but no daylight till the sun arise. 'Tis night still, for all the stars, and the moon to help them : Notwithstanding natural speculation that are more remote, and all prudence and policy for affairs, that come somewhat nearer to actions, yet we are still in the night; and men sleep on in it, and their heads are still full of new dreams that keep them sleeping. They are constantly drunk with cares or desires of sense, and so their sleep continues. Now sleep is brother of death, and so by it not unfitly is the same state resembled.

' It is time to awake, *salvation is nearer than when ye believed.* The bright day you look for is posting forward ; it is nearer than when you began to believe : the night is far spent, the gross darkness is already past, some daylight it is, and is every moment growing, and the perfect full morning light of it is very near. O blessed Gospel ! revealing God in Christ, and calling up sinners to communion with Him, dispelling that black night of ignorance and accursed darkness that otherwise had never ended, but passed on to a night of eternal misery.

' *Put on the Lord Jesus.*—Here we have the proper beauty and orna- ment of Christians. Him we put on by faith, and are clothed with Him as our righteousness. We come unto our Father, in our Elder Brother's perfumed garment, and so obtain the blessing, which He, in a manner, was stripped of, and did undergo the curse, and was made a curse for our sakes. So the Apostle speaks of Him. We put Him on as *the Lord our righteousness*, and are made *the righteousness of God in Him.* This in- vesture is first, when our persons are made acceptable, and we come into court. But there is another putting of Him on, in the conformity of holiness, which always accompanies the former, and that is it which is here meant. And this I declare unto you, that whosoever does not thus *put Him on*, shall find themselves deceived in the other, if they imagine it belongs to them. He is the *armour of light* before spoken of ; all our ornament and safety is in Him.

' Now follows, *and make no provision for the flesh, to fulfil the lusts thereof;* and it will follow necessarily. O ! to have the heart touched by the *Spirit* with such a word as is here—it would untie it from all these things. These are the words the very reading of which wrought so with Augustine, that, of a licentious young man, he turned a holy, faithful servant of Jesus Christ. While you were without Christ, you had no higher nor other business to do but to attend and serve the flesh ; but once having put Him on, you are other men, and other manners do become you. There is a transcendent sweetness in Christ, that puts the flesh out of credit. *Put on Christ*, thy royal robe, and make no provision for the flesh. A soul clothed with Christ, stooping to any sinful delight, or an ardent pursuit of anything earthly, though lawful, doth wonder- fully indignify itself.

'Oh! raise up your spirits, you that pretend to anything in Christ; delight in Him, and let His love satisfy you at all times. What need you go a-begging elsewhere? All you would add makes you the poorer, abates so much of your enjoyment of Him; and what can compensate that? *Put on the Lord Jesus*, and then view yourselves, and see if you be fit to be slaves to flesh and earth.

'These two, *put on the Lord Jesus*, and *make no provision for the flesh*, are directly the representation of the Church—a woman clothed with the sun, and the moon under her feet, needed borrow no beauty from it, or anything under it.'

CHAPTER 14
ROMANS 14:1 – 21

Ver. 1.—*Him that is weak in the faith receive ye, but not to doubtful disputations.*

Him that is weak in the faith receive ye.—In this verse, and onwards to the 13th of the following chapter, the Apostle, as in the 8th and 10th chapters of First Corinthians, establishes the duty of mutual forbearance among Christians. The subjects of dispute often vary, but the principles here laid down are always the same. The discussion in this chapter regards things in themselves indifferent, as the observance of certain days, and the abstinence from certain kinds of food; the errors, however, into which we may fall respecting them, are represented as springing from weakness of faith, to which every evil that appears among Christians may be traced. We may here remark that, though faith is the gift of God, yet it is on that account no less a duty. Repentance and every good work are also gifts of God, Acts v. 31; 2 Tim. ii. 25; Eph. ii. 10. All men, notwithstanding, are bound to believe, to repent, and to obey, under pain of God's most awful displeasure.

Calvin, Dr. Macknight, and Mr. Stuart, and others, with almost general consent, take it for granted that the weak are the Jewish, and the strong the Gentile, believers. There is no ground in the text for this opinion. Many of the Jews might be fully instructed in the points which are here treated, and many of the Gentiles might be weak with respect to the defilement of meats offered in sacrifice to idols. Why should it be thought that the Jewish believers in general should be uninstructed, and that every Gentile believer should be fully acquainted with his duty respecting meats? Some of them might in this easily adopt the prejudices of the Jews, and others might have prejudices of their own. To confine what is left general by the Apostle, must be useless, and in some cases very hurtful.

Faith.—Faith here regards the doctrine of the Gospel as a whole. Improper views of any part of it always imply something defective with respect to its nature. But partial ignorance may be consistent with so much knowledge as is connected with salvation. Dr. Macknight paraphrases this as referring to the Jewish Christian, who is weak in the faith concerning meats and days. But how does this consist with the 2d verse, which represents the weakness as confining itself to eating herbs? This was no injunction of the Mosaic law. The weakness referred to is weakness of any kind, and will apply to anything in which it is discovered. The meats and days are particular instances adduced as illustrations of the general truth; but that truth applies as directly to weakness of any kind now, as to a weakness of a particular kind at that time. *Receive ye.* —That is, into the Church, to the fellowship of the brethren, in all the ordinances of Christ's house.

Doubtful disputations.—The phrase in the original is variously rendered and explained. The meaning seems to be, that when they should receive a weak brother, they should not press him to receive their views by harassing discussions on the points on which he is ignorant. Such conduct would either tend to wound his mind, or induce him to acquiesce without enlightened conviction. Disputation seldom begets unanimity. If a statement of the will of Christ from the Scriptures has not the effect of producing conviction, lengthened discussions are more likely to increase prejudice than to resolve doubts. While, therefore, it is greatly important that believers, who have inadequate views of any part of Divine truth, should be taught more fully the way of the Lord, it is also true that the most likely way to effect this is to avoid disputations with them on the points in which they are weak. This observation is founded on experience, and it is warranted by the command of God. To push them forward faster than they are taught by the word and Spirit of God, will stumble and injure instead of making them strong. Christians seldom argue one another into their views, and more frequently each is more confirmed in his own opinion. When it is necessary to show the weak brother his errors, it is best to exhibit the truth in its evidences, to leave him to the general use of the means of edification, and to give him affectionate instructions, for the purpose of his becoming stronger in the faith, and riper in his judgment, by the internal influences and teaching of the Holy Spirit. The principles on which the Apostle proceeds are not, that the views of those who differ among themselves are equally well founded, but that they are all brethren, having in view the glory of God and obedience to His will, and that, as their heavenly Father is so indulgent to His children, that, notwithstanding their defects in knowledge, and the consequent difference in their conduct, they ought not to be less forbearing to one another.

Ver. 2.—*For one believeth that he may eat all things ; another, who is weak, eateth herbs.*

For one believeth that he may eat all things.—'The Gentile Christian,' says Dr. Macknight, 'believeth that he may eat every kind of meat.' But why the Gentile? The Jewish Christian might believe this as well as the Gentile, when the distinction of meats was now totally abolished. And doubtless many Jewish believers already understood this matter. This shows that the Jewish law, in its ritual ordinances, was abolished before this time, for otherwise neither Jew nor Gentile had ground for such belief. This seems also to imply that the prohibition of blood, in Acts xv., was only as a law of forbearance to spare the prejudices of the

Jews. When the Mosaic law was at an end, there appears to have been no reason for abstaining from blood more than from flesh. Here the strong in faith believed that they might eat all things; why, then, should blood be excepted? If there had been an exception, doubtless it would have been given here. How could the *strong* in faith believe that they might eat all things, if one thing was forbidden on its own account?

Another, who is weak, eateth herbs.—Why should this be confined to the Jewish Christians? It is not in evidence that all Jewish Christians were so ignorant. Besides, this does not apply to their law. The law of Moses did not restrict the Jews to herbs. If it be replied that they abstained from all meat, lest it should have been offered in sacrifice to idols previously to bringing it to market, it is answered that this applies to the Gentile as well as to the Jew? This, besides, does not refer to the distinction of meats by the law, but to the pollution of meats by being offered to idols. It affected the meats allowed by the law as well as the meats prohibited. The opinion, then, of the pollution of meats, by the mere circumstance of having been offered to idols as a sacrifice, before it was sold in the shambles, might as readily be entertained by the Gentiles as by the Jews. The thing that they are thus represented as guarding against, is not the breach of the law with respect to the distinction of meats, but against the pollution of meats by idolatry. This concerned the Gentile equally with the Jew; and weakness in this point might be found in the former as well as in the latter.

Ver. 3.—*Let not him that eateth despise him that eateth not ; and let not him which eateth not judge him that eateth : for God hath received him.*

Here the peculiar sin to which each of the two characters is respectively liable, is pointed out. The pride of knowledge is prone to hold the ignorant in contempt. The weakness of ignorance is prone to condemn those who, from more enlightened views of Divine truth, are not affected by their scruples. They who could eat everything, without exception, were strong, because they had just views on the subject in question. Their temptation was to despise their brethren for their weakness. This they are forbidden to do. They who thought it unlawful to eat certain things were weak, because they had inadequate views of the subject. They, therefore, were, under a temptation to judge unfavourably of the motives of their brethren. Let us observe, it is the brethren they are forbidden to condemn, and not the thing which they did. They could not but condemn the thing as wrong which they thought unlawful. But they were not permitted to condemn those who did the thing, as if they did it from improper motives, as from the desire of gratifying the appetite, from unwillingness to practise self-denial, or from a wish to conform to the world and avoid reproach. Weak Christians are often troublesome, by ascribing the conduct of their brethren to improper motives. The weak, then, are as liable to judge improperly as the strong are to despise them. They ought both to attend to the apostolical injunctions which are respectively given to them in this place.

For God hath received him.—God had no doubt received both of them as righteous in His sight, through the righteousness of His Son. But receiving here being asserted of the one and not mentioned with respect to the other, must respect the thing in which he is condemned by the weak brother. This implies that the distinction of meats, with the whole of the law of Moses, in all its ritual ordinances, was abolished; for the conduct of Christians could not be received or accepted by God, as far as it was in violation of His law. *Receiving*, then, here does not, as is generally, if not universally, explained, refer to receiving their persons through Jesus Christ, but to the particular conduct in question. The strong were received in their using things prohibited by the law, because the law was abolished. Had not the word *receiving* this reference, it would be as applicable to the weak as to the strong, whereas it is here affirmed only of the strong. But though the weak are accepted with God through the righteousness of Christ, this weakness is not acceptable to Him. It is an error, and cannot be pleasing to God. And accordingly the strong, and not the weak, are here said to be accepted.

Ver. 4.—*Who art thou that judgest another man's servant? to his own master he standeth or falleth. Yea, he shall be holden up : for God is able to make him stand.*

Who art thou that judgest another man's servant?—It is generally supposed that the person who condemns here is the strong believer, and the person who is condemned is the weak. But this is altogether without foundation. They were the weak who condemned the strong, and not the strong who condemned the weak, in the 3d verse. The strong did not condemn, but despised the weak. When, therefore, in this 4th verse, the Apostle indignantly asks, Who art thou that condemnest another man's servant? it must apply to him who was previously represented as having condemned the strong. Had it referred to the strong, it would not have been said, Who art thou that condemnest? but 'Who art thou that despisest?' The weak condemned the strong, as if they were not at all believers. In this they were accordingly to blame. They assumed the prerogative of God, who alone is the Judge of His own servants.

To his own master he standeth or falleth.—Dr. Macknight, and after him Mr. Stuart, translate this, '*by* his own master,' and understand the words as asserting that the person stood or fell by his Master's sentence. But as the standing in the end of the verse appears to refer to the standing in the profession of Christianity, and not in the day of judgment, the common translation is to be preferred. The servant is said to stand or fall to his master, because it is to his master that he is accountable.

Yea, he shall be holden up.—This man, who is condemned as an unbeliever, or one who would soon fall from the faith, would be held up or made to stand. It was the almighty power of God that would hold him up, and not the observance of the precepts of the Mosaic law. *For God is able to make him stand.*—Here the certainty of his standing is rested on God's ability to hold him up—not on his own ability to stand. The strong are as liable to fall as the weak. Nothing can hold up either but the power of God. This is important, as showing that a man's standing is not in himself. It is also important, as it secures the standing of the true disciple. This standing is as sure as God's power; for it is rested on God's ability to make him stand. To say, then, that any of God's children shall finally fall, is to say that God is unable to hold them up.

Ver. 5.—*One man esteemeth one day above another ; another esteemeth every day alike. Let every man be fully persuaded in his own mind.*

One man esteemeth one day above another ; another esteemeth every day. —Here what had been said respecting meats is equally applied to the observance of certain days. The Apostle takes for granted that on this subject likewise different Christians held different views. For it is of believers only he is speaking. This is a clear point, but it is one of much practical importance. It recognises the Christianity of those who may be very inadequately acquainted with the will of Christ. It is proper, however, to remark that the Lord's Day cannot (which shall afterwards be shown) be included in what is here said, as the Apostle is speaking of those meats and days that were peculiar to the Jewish dispensation; as when, in writing to the Galatians, he censures their observing days, and months, and times, and years, to which they desired to be in bondage, which he terms weak and beggarly elements, Gal. iv. 9, 10.

Ver. 6.—*He that regardeth the day, regardeth it unto the Lord ; and he that regardeth not the day, to the Lord he doth not regard it. He that eateth, eateth to the Lord, for he giveth God thanks ; and he that eateth not, to the Lord he eateth not, and giveth God thanks.*

He that regardeth the day, regardeth it unto the Lord.—This regard of days, though contrary to what had been already revealed, was, from ignorance of this fact, intended as obedience to the Lord. The persons who made this distinction, believed that the Lord required it. Therefore, though they were wrong in this, and on that account were guilty, yet they acted from a view of serving the Lord. The thing performed may be wrong, while the intention of performing it may be right. In like manner, the thing performed may be right, while the motive of performing it may be wrong. *He that regardeth not the day, to the Lord he doth not regard it.*— In the same manner, the believer who did not regard the day, acted from a view of honouring the Lord, and not from thinking the observance of the day a restraint. When he gave up the day, which under the Mosaic dispensation was holy, because he believed that the Lord had made an end of that dispensation, it was honourable to the Lord.

He that eateth, eateth to the Lord.—The same thing is asserted with respect to meats as was asserted with respect to days. He that eateth the thing that formerly had been forbidden, eateth to the Lord, because he believes that the Lord hath abolished the distinction. He also who would eat what he bought in the shambles, without any respect to its having been previously offered in sacrifice to idols, because he knew that the meat was the Lord's, and could not be defiled by such an occurrence, did so out of regard to the honour of the Lord. That he acted from this view, is proved by his giving God thanks for what he did eat. Had he considered that the thing was prohibited by the Lord, he would not have ventured to give *God thanks* for permitting him the use of it.

And he that eateth not, to the Lord he eateth not.—In like manner, the weak brother, who not only abstained from the things formerly forbidden, but even from everything that he considered as polluted, by being offered to idols, acted from a desire of honouring the Lord, because he thought such things were forbidden by God. *And giveth God thanks.*—Mr. Stuart understands this of thankfulness 'for the light which is imparted to him,' as he supposes, 'with respect to making such a distinction in food.' But the meaning undoubtedly is, that he gives God thanks for what he is allowed to eat. He shows that he eats from a view of honouring God, because, instead of looking on what he supposes to be forbidden as a restraint hard to be submitted to, he gives God thanks for what he considers to be granted to him by the Lord. There are óther places in which the sacred writers exhort believers to grow in knowledge, and where they charge them as culpable if ignorant of any part of the will of the Lord. But here the Apostle's object is to show that those who have a reverential regard for the authority of Christ, and a true knowledge of His character, and thus call Him their Lord, ought to be received and recognised as His disciples.

Ver. 7.—*For none of us liveth to himself, and no man dieth to himself.*

For none of us liveth to himself.—Having stated that both parties referred to acted with a view to serve the Lord, the Apostle now extends this duty so as to embrace all Christians in all their actions. No Christian liveth to himself. As far as he lives to himself, he acts inconsistently with his character. We ought to consider ourselves as under law to God in every action of our lives. Even in temporal things, yea, even in eating and drinking, we should have in view the glory of God. To live to the Lord supposes that in all things we regard His will as the sole rule of our conduct, and His approbation as our great aim in all that we do, and that in all things we seek His glory. It supposes that we are entirely resigned to His disposal, blessing Him whether in adversity or prosperity; that we submit to His dispensations in what He gives or takes away; and, finally, that we only live to serve Him, and show forth His praise. Whether, then, the Christian lives or dies, he belongs to the Lord, desiring that He may dispose of him as He sees best; confident that, as being the object of the Saviour's love, whatever may befall him, he is safe in His hands. There is no danger, then, however great,—there is no difficulty, however arduous,—that ought to prevent us from obeying the will of the Lord. Property, character, life itself, ought to be at His service. But is it not obvious that most people have no conception of living but to themselves? Do not the mass of mankind follow their own interest to the neglect of the authority of God? Even among those who make a profession of religion, how few are there who follow the Lord at the expense of any great temporal sacrifice? Nay, are not many induced to act inconsistently with the character of a Christian for every trifle?

And no man dieth to himself.—A Christian is not to die to himself more than he is to live to himself. He has no right to yield his life as a sacrifice to his pride. This cuts off the pretensions to Christianity of all persons who, to comply with the laws of honour, risk their life, or that of their opponents, in duelling. So also is suicide here condemned. The man who dies in these ways, dies to himself, which no man has a right to do, and which no Christian will do. This shows, also, that if obedience to Christ requires it, a Christian must not decline to die to His honour. He is to risk his life rather than break any known commandment of God. He is to die rather than decline obedience to any command or institution of Christ. When he so dies, he does not throw away his life. He devotes it for a sufficient purpose. He gives it to the honour of the Lord. He yields it back to Him who gave it, and who has a right to it. He shows also that a Christian should not only be willing to die, when God wills his death, but that he should be willing to live as long as God pleases. Christians may transgress by being unwilling to die, and they may also transgress in wishing to die. They ought to be willing to live or die as it is for God's glory From this it also appears that the death of any Christian is precious in the sight of God, as well as his life. Every Christian, when he dies, dies to the glory of God. This accords with what is said with respect to Peter, ' by what death he was to glorify God.'

Ver. 8.—*For whether we live, we live unto the Lord ; and whether we die, we die unto the Lord : whether we live, therefore, or die, we are the Lord's.*

For whether we live, we live unto the Lord.—The former verse denies that we live or die to ourselves ; by inference, therefore, we live or die to Christ. But this verse makes the assertion directly which was implied in the other. Both in life and death we ought to serve God, and endeavour to promote His glory. The end of the verse draws the conclusion. *Whether we live, therefore, or die, we are the Lord's.*—Not only are we the Lord's in giving our life at His command, but we are the Lord's in the state of separation between soul and body. Our bodies are the Lord's, and will be preserved by Him till the resurrection, when in glory they shall be given back to us ; and our souls, in the presence of God, will have happiness and glory till that period shall arrive.

Ver. 9.—*For to this end Christ both died, and rose, and revived, that He might be Lord both of the dead and living.*

For to this end Christ both died, and rose, and revived.—It was the end of the death and resurrection of the Lord, that to Him, as Mediator, all power might be committed. He has received the keys of the invisible state and of death, and governs all His people both during their life and after their death, ordering all things for His own glory and their good. Christ, then, is the Lord of the living ; He is also the Lord of the dead. He must then be God. This shows, also, that the dead are alive in their souls, while their bodies are dead. It is in this way that Christ reigns over them. It would be absurd to suppose that He reigns over them as mere insensible matter. ' God is not the God of the dead, but of the living,' Matt. xxii. 32.

Ver. 10.—*But why dost thou judge thy brother ? or why dost thou set at nought thy brother ? for we shall all stand at the judgment-seat of Christ.*

But why dost thou judge thy brother ? or why dost thou set at nought thy brother ?—This shows, evidently, that the word judge in the 4th verse refers to the weak brother who condemned those who did eat things prohibited by the law, and not to the strong brother, for he is reproved for despising and not for judging. Here both the one and the other are brought distinctly forward, and each separately asked a question suitable to himself. The brother who thinks that it is wrong to eat things pro-

hibited by the law is asked why he dares to take upon himself to condemn his brother who in this differed from him; and the brother who is
better informed upon this matter is asked how he dares set at nought his
brother who was ill instructed on this point. Mr. Stuart is certainly
wrong in making both these questions refer to the strong brother. There
could be no ground for asking the first question with respect to the strong
brother. He is charged as despising. He might despise without condemning his weak brother as acting from improper motives. The Apostle
most evidently asks the two questions with respect to different characters,
and the questions are most appropriate and suitable respectively to the
two characters brought into view.

For we shall all stand before the judgment-seat of Christ.—The Apostle
gives here another reason to prevent believers from judging or despising
each other. Not only are they all the servants of Christ, and brethren,
but they must all appear at His judgment-seat, each to give an account
of himself. This is a good reason why they should neither condemn nor
despise one another. To judge one another in this manner is to invade
the prerogative of Christ; and to despise one another evidences pride and
ignorance of the source of all our knowledge. This most clearly shows
that Christians have no authority over one another's faith or Christian
practice in this world. Both as to faith and Christian practice Christians
may endeavour to enlighten one another; but when they fail, they have
no authority to force others to change their views. Each Christian, however, is bound to follow the Lord fully so far as his own knowledge
extends, and not to be stopped by the ignorance of his brother. He is
not to do what he knows to be wrong, in order to walk with his weak
brother; nor is he to avoid doing anything that he judges to be the will
of his Master, in order to retain fellowship with other Christians.

Ver. 11.—*For it is written, As I live, saith the Lord, every knee shall bow to Me,
and every tongue shall confess to God.*

For it is written.—This passage from the Old Testament, Isa. xlv. 23,
the Apostle adduces as importing that all shall stand before the judgment-
seat of Christ. It is remarkable that the Apostle so frequently quotes
from the Old Testament in support of what he teaches, though in reality
his own authority was equal to that of any writer of the Old Testament.
But this proves that the Old Testament and the New are given by one
Spirit, and harmonize in all their parts. It is also an example for us in
proving and teaching any truth contained in the word of God. If the
Apostle confirmed what he taught by the authority of the Scriptures, shall
any man now, or body of men, presume to make the authority of their
office stand in the place of the word of God ?

As I live.—The Apostle does not take the words literally; but as the
Holy Ghost spoke by him, we are assured that he gives the true meaning.
I have sworn by myself, is substantially the same with *as I live.* Uninspired
translators must not be indulged with a like liberty, for it is only when
they translate exactly that there is an assurance that they translate correctly. *Saith the Lord.*—The Apostle, by the addition of these words,
shows that in the passage he quotes it was the Messiah who, in the pre-

ceding verse, said, 'Look unto Me, and be ye saved, all the ends of the earth ; for I am God, and there is none else,' Isa. xlv. 22. *Every knee shall bow to Me.*—As in Phil. ii. 10 the same thing is asserted with respect to Christ personally, this is also applicable to Christ personally and directly. In judgment all will bow to God, seeing they will bow to Christ. *Every tongue shall confess to God.*—This is substantially the same with ' unto Me every tongue shall swear.'

In the Epistle to the Hebrews we learn that God swears by Himself, ' because He could swear by no greater ; ' and thus Jesus Christ, in here swearing by His life, or by Himself, gives, according to that declaration of the Apostle, a proof of His divinity. In the preceding verses of this chapter it is always to Jesus Christ that Paul refers when he says *the Lord.* It is by Him that we shall be judged at the last day ; it is to Him that Christians are entirely devoted, which, were He merely a creature, would evidently be a violation of the law of Him who says, ' I am a jealous God,' and ' My glory I will not give to another.' ' The Father judgeth no man ; but hath committed all judgment unto the Son: that all men should honour the Son, even as they honour the Father. He that honoureth not the Son, honoureth not the Father which hath sent Him.'

Ver. 12.—*So then every one of us shall give account of himself to God.*

So then.—Consequently then, or by consequence then. This is an inference which the Apostle draws from the passage quoted from the Old Testament. Every individual of the human race must give account of himself to God. This applies to believers as well as to others. And though all their sins are blotted out through the blood of atonement, they should not indulge themselves in sin. The fact of a future judgment ought to have a constant influence on our conduct. Standing before the judgment-seat of Christ, of which the Apostle had just before spoken, is here represented as giving an account to God.

Ver. 13.—*Let us not therefore judge one another any more ; but judge this rather, that no man put a stumblingblock, or an occasion to fall, in his brother's way.*

Let us not therefore judge one another any more.—This dissuasive appears to be now addressed to both the parties. The Apostle having declared what was peculiarly adapted to each, now declares what is equally applicable to both. Judging or condemning was in a peculiar sense the fault of the one ; but both of them in a more extended sense of the word might be said to judge or condemn one another. The strong brother who despised the weak virtually judged him or condemned him. Paul now takes them both together, and addresses them with the same caution. He extends the exhortation to himself, and to the whole body of Christians. They are not to usurp authority over one another, nor to usurp the right to judge for one another in any matter.

But judge this rather, that no man put a stumblingblock, or an occasion to fall, in his brother's way.—The word *judge* is here used in an allusive sense, and not in its proper or literal sense. Instead of judging, we ought to do another thing, which is not properly judging, but called

judging, in allusion to the word immediately going before. This is similar
to the expression, 'This is the work of God, that ye believe on Him whom
He hath sent.' The Scriptures abound with instances of this figurative
way of speaking. Instead of judging one another, Christians are to avoid
doing anything that will have a tendency to stumble one another, or
cause any to fall into sin. This is peculiarly applicable to the strong,
who, by an improper use of their liberty, might ensnare their weak
brethren.

Ver. 14.—*I know, and am persuaded by the Lord Jesus, that there is nothing unclean of itself: but to him that esteemeth anything to be unclean, to him it is unclean.*

I know, and am persuaded.—This clearly refutes the opinion of those
who argue that at the time of writing this Epistle the law was not
abolished, and that it was not in this state that the different parties were
to forbear with respect to one another, but that the Jew was still to
keep the law till its abolition should be explicitly announced. But that
it was abolished, is perfectly clear from this chapter. The Apostle knew
himself, and here he teaches others, that the Mosaic dispensation was
abolished, yet enjoins the strong and the weak to forbear mutually with
each other.

By the Lord Jesus.—That is, Paul knew this by the teaching of the
Lord Jesus. Calvin is unquestionably mistaken in applying this, not to
the teaching of the Lord Jesus, but to the cleansing of meats by the Lord
Jesus. He says, 'The Apostle adds, *in the Lord Jesus*, because His kindness and grace is the cause why all creatures are blessed to us by the
Lord, which were otherwise cursed in Adam.' This is no doubt a fact,
but it is not the thing here taught. Paul is here asserting that his
knowledge of the abolition of the distinction of meats was not obtained
by his own searching into the nature of things, but was a revelation
from the Lord Jesus. This doctrine was not a private opinion of his own,
but the revealed will of his Master.

Nothing unclean of itself.—This undoubtedly shows that there is
nothing unclean in blood more than in anything else. The Apostle here
asserts of everything that could be used for food, that there is nothing
unclean in itself. When blood and other meats were prohibited by the
law, it was not because there was anything in themselves that rendered
them unclean. It was the will of God, because they were of a typical
nature, and therefore all their uncleanness ended when Christ came.
Why, then, it may be asked, was blood prohibited in Acts xv.? Evidently as a law of forbearance, because of the prejudices of the Jews.
This is expressed in the very passage. 'For Moses of old time hath in
every city them that preach Him, being read in the synagogues every
Sabbath-day.' It would still be a duty to avoid these things, if we were
in such situations that it would give offence to the Jews. That such is
the true view of the matter, is evident from this, that though the Jews
were prohibited from eating things strangled, they were not prohibited
to give them or sell them to strangers. Had the thing been unlawful in
itself, they would not have been permitted to give to strangers that which
it was unlawful for themselves to eat. Dr. Macknight justly remarks,
'It is observable that in this discourse, which is intended to show that

under the Gospel all sorts of food may be used without sin, there is no exception of blood and things strangled.' But he is wrong in his inference from this fact. 'May we not from this infer,' he says, 'that the prohibition of these things to the Gentile converts, mentioned Acts xv. 29, is to be understood of such Gentiles only as had been proselytes?' This is forced and unnatural.

But to him that esteemeth anything to be unclean, to him it is unclean.— This is self-evident truth, which has no exception. For if a person does what he thinks God forbids, he is guilty with respect to God as really as if the thing had been actually prohibited by God. Persons in ignorance ought to be instructed, but they ought never to be encouraged to do what they themselves judge to be contrary to the will of God.

Ver. 15.—*But if thy brother be grieved with thy meat, now walkest thou not charitably. Destroy not him with thy meat for whom Christ died.*

But if thy brother be grieved with thy meat, now walkest thou not charitably.—The weak brother would be grieved in his mind when he should see the strong eating meat which he considered unclean. Now it is not love that will prompt us to do anything to afflict another. If, then, the strong loves the weak brother, would he, for the sake of his appetite, eat anything that would grieve him? Self-denial in such matters is the result of love, and when any one will not abstain from gratifying his appetite to avoid hurting his brother, it shows that he is deficient in love. *Destroy not him with thy meat.*—This supposes that the weak brother may, by the example of the strong, be induced to do what he is not persuaded is lawful; and thus, though the thing be in itself lawful, it is sin in him, and consequently its tendency is to bring him into condemnation. It is not, indeed, possible that this can ultimately be the case with any one for whom Christ died; but this is a warning to avoid doing anything that in itself tends to destroy him. *For whom Christ died.*—If Christ died for the weak brother, how unlike Christ is this strong believer, who will do what he knows will destroy his brother, if he follow his example without having his knowledge! The love of Christ in giving His life for this brother, and the indifference with respect to him which is manifested by the person who should thus abuse his liberty, are here set in strong contrast.

Ver. 16.—*Let not then your good be evil spoken of:*

Let not then your good.—Their *good* appears to be their liberty of disregarding the distinction of meats, and the law in general. This was a good thing to them, because the law was in itself a yoke and a grievous burden. They were doing what was good and right in itself in using this liberty, but they should be careful to use it in such a way as not to be the occasion of being represented as if in what they did they were regardless of the authority of God. This is a decisive distinction between the dispensation of Christ and that of Moses. It was an advantage to be delivered from the peculiar restraints of the ceremonial law, but it would be no advantage to be delivered from any part of the dispensation of Christ. This shows the sovereignty of God, in subjecting His people in one dispensation to burdens which He removes in another.

Be evil spoken of.—Their good would be evil spoken of, when their neglect of the distinctions of the law should be ascribed to the indulgence of appetite, and when their conduct should embolden the weak to do what was contrary to their conscience. *Then.*—That is, since some of the brethren were so weak as to judge those who did eat certain meats to be influenced by improper motives, then, in order to avoid this, they ought to decline the use of their liberty.

Ver. 17.—*For the kingdom of God is not meat and drink ; but righteousness, and peace, and joy in the Holy Ghost.*

For the kingdom of God is not meat and drink.—This imports that the service which belongs to the kingdom of God, and which He requires from all His subjects, does not consist in abstaining from, or in using, any kind of meats. The typical dispensation of the Old Testament enjoined a distinction of meats. Men are peculiarly prone to cling to externals in religious worship. It is, then, of great importance to attend to this decision of the Holy Ghost by the Apostle Paul. The distinction of meats has nothing to do in the service of God under the New Testament. This settles the question as to blood. If the eating of blood is still prohibited, it cannot be said that the kingdom of God is not meat and drink.

But righteousness.—This is not the righteousness of God which is imputed to the believer, as is evident from the following verse, but the righteousness of which he is the subject. Righteousness sometimes refers especially to the duties which we owe to men, but in its most comprehensive sense it includes equally our duty to God ; and there is no reason why it should not here have its most comprehensive meaning. *Peace.*—This is a criterion of a true servant in the kingdom of God. Having peace with God, he endeavours to have peace with the brethren and with all men. Nothing is more unlike the spirit of genuine Christianity than a contentious disposition. *Joy in the Holy Ghost.*—The joy of a Christian communicated by the Holy Ghost cannot be comprehended by any other. He rejoices even in the midst of trouble, and is often most happy when the world thinks him most miserable. Joy is the immediate effect of receiving the Gospel, which is glad tidings of great joy, as announced to the shepherds on the birth of our Saviour. It springs from a sense of reconciliation with God. We see it exemplified in the three thousand converted on the day of Pentecost, in the eunuch, and in the jailor at Philippi, as soon as they received the truth. Joy is enjoined again and again as the duty of believers. ' Rejoice in the Lord alway, and again I say rejoice.' 'Rejoice evermore.' 'These things write we unto you, that your joy may be full.' Our Lord dwells much upon it in His last discourse with His disciples, which contains everything calculated to impart joy to their minds, and in which He so often promises to send them the Comforter. 'These things have I spoken unto you, that My joy in you might remain, and that your joy might be full.' He had spoken to them that their joy might be *full*, but He makes no such addition when He refers to His joy in them, for it was already full. This joy in His people is an everlasting joy, neither capable of increase nor diminution ; but their joy is variable according as they are exercising faith in Him, and walking in the fear of the Lord, and in the comfort of the Holy Ghost. Joy is one of the great blessings of His kingdom. In this passage peace is placed before joy, while joy is elsewhere put before peace, as in the following chapter, ver. 13th, and especially in enumerating the fruits of the Spirit, Gal. v. 22. The first feeling on receiving the knowledge of the Gospel of salvation will be joy, and peace or tranquillity of mind will immediately succeed the agitations of the troubled conscience. However, where the one exists, there will the other be found, and in an equal proportion. Peace and righteousness are here traced up to joy in the Holy Ghost, which shows, as in other places, that it is in effect before the others.

Ver. 18.—*For he that in these things serveth Christ is acceptable to God, and approved of men.*

For he that in these things serveth Christ.—Here the Christian is said to serve Christ by righteousness, and peace, and joy in the Holy Ghost. Christ, then, must be God. Is any but God to be served? Are we servants or slaves to any but God? Here we are represented as the slaves of Christ. What is the service of God? Is it not righteousness, and peace, and joy in the Holy Ghost? And here this service is considered the service of Christ. Can there be any doubt, then, that Christ is God?

Acceptable to God.—Every righteous man is pleasing to God. But without faith it is impossible to please Him. Then without faith it is impossible to live righteously, to live in true peace, and in the joy of the Holy Ghost. These are the things in which God is honoured. What a contrast between this account, as given by Paul, and the religion of the Church of Rome at the present time! If men abstain from meats, and observe the laws of the Church, they are acknowledged as members of that Church, though they should live unrighteously, though they should be agitators or disturbers of society, though they should have no joy in believing. How unlike, then, is the Church of Rome now to that of Rome addressed by the Apostle! *Approved of men.*—When Christians live as becometh the Gospel, they have a testimony from their very enemies. The conduct here recommended is eminently useful to society, and cannot but command the approbation even of the most ungodly.

Ver. 19.—*Let us therefore follow after the things which make for peace, and things wherewith one may edify another.*

Let us therefore follow after the things which make for peace.—Since, then, meats have nothing to do in the religion of Christ; for 'meat commendeth us not to God: for neither, if we eat, are we the better: neither, if we eat not, are we the worse,' 1 Cor. viii. 8; and since He is served by righteousness, and peace, and joy in the Holy Ghost, let us pursue the things of peace. We are not only to live peaceably with all men, and especially with the brethren, but we are to pursue peace. Even should it fly from us, we should follow it. *The things of peace.*—That is, we should follow all things that tend to produce peace, and avoid everything, as far as our duty to God permits, of a contrary tendency.

And things wherewith one may edify another,—the things of edification.—
That is, such things as will have a tendency to increase the faith and
establishment of each other. We are not to have an eye merely to our
own growth and stability, but also to the growth and stability of the
whole body. Christians in general are not sufficiently aware of this
duty.

Ver. 20.—*For meat destroy not the work of God. All things indeed are pure ;
but it is evil for that man who eateth with offence.*

For meat destroy not the work of God.—The believer is here called the
work of God, in a like sense as believers are elsewhere called the building
of God. Dr. Macknight understands it of ' that which God is working
in the heart of our brother, namely, *faith and holiness.*' The other sense
seems to be the true one. The reason which he gives for not applying
the word to persons, is not to be sustained: ' For if,' says he, ' the Apostle
had been speaking of *persons* who, on account of their regeneration, are
called the *work of God,* he would have used the word ποίημα, as he does
Eph. ii. 10.' Why should he be confined to this word? The other
word is equally applicable. Mr. Stuart alleges that, as referring to the
internal work of faith, it is a possible meaning, though he prefers the
other. His observation, however, that faith is called the work of God,
John vi. 29, has no weight in confirming Dr. Macknight's opinion.
Work of God in that passage signifies not the work which God works,
but the work which God enjoins. The question was, ' What shall we do
that we might work the works of God? ' This surely is the work which
God *enjoins,* not the work which God *works.* When, therefore, in answer
to this question, Jesus replies, ' This is the work of God, that ye believe
on Him whom He hath sent,' the work of God must also refer to the
work which God *requires.* But it may be asked, How can this be, seeing
faith is not a work ? The reply is quite obvious : it is in an allusive sense
only, as has been already observed, that faith is here called a work. The
word is used merely in reference to the word in the question. It is not
a work, but it is the thing that God enjoins in order to salvation. The
Scriptures abound with examples of this manner of speaking. Dr.
Macknight observes ' that the Apostle's words, so interpreted, imply
that the truly regenerated may be destroyed.' But as it is contrary to
the whole current of Scripture that the truly regenerated can eternally
perish—for who shall separate them from the love of Christ?—it must
be understood in the sense already explained, of tending in itself to his
destruction.

All things indeed are pure.—Every kind of meat is here declared to be
pure. This at once shows that the abolition of the law had already taken
place, and that blood is not in itself unclean. *But it is evil for that man
who eateth with offence.*—Some understand the offence as referring to the
man who causes another to stumble, and some to the man who stumbles
through offence. Calvin appears to understand it in the former sense.
But the other meaning appears to be the right one. The meaning of
' with offence ' seems to be, that the eating by the person referred to is
occasioned by the stumblingblock which was laid before him.

Ver. 21.—*It is good neither to eat flesh, nor to drink wine, nor anything whereby thy brother stumbleth, or is offended, or is made weak.*

It is good.—The Apostle here extends the duty not only to the things that were prohibited by the Mosaic law, but to every kind of flesh, and even wine, and every other thing that might be the occasion of causing a weak brother to stumble.   *Nor anything.*—The expression in the original is elliptical; and this elliptical translation is preferable to that of Dr. Macknight and Mr. Stuart, who supply the phrase *to do.*   Without doubt, the words to be supplied, as left out by ellipsis, are *to eat or to drink.* This is the very way in which Mr. Stuart himself, in his Commentary, supplies the ellipsis.   Why, then, does he translate on another principle? The Apostle declares that it is wrong to eat or to drink anything that would be the occasion of bringing sin upon our brother.

Whereby thy brother stumbleth, or is offended, or is made weak.—The first of these words may refer to stumbling without falling; the second, to falling by a stumblingblock; and the third, to the effect of this upon the person who is stumbling—he becomes weak.

Ver. 22.—*Hast thou faith? have it to thyself before God.   Happy is he that condemneth not himself in that thing which he alloweth.*

Hast thou faith? have it to thyself before God.—It is of no importance whether we read this as a question, with our version, or as a declaration of a known fact.   The meaning is substantially the same.   Dr. Macknight does not seem justifiable in representing the word translated *have* as a command to hold fast this faith.   The man who has faith should not disturb his weak brother with an unseasonable declaration of his faith in this matter.   His belief in this point is correct; and let him rejoice before God in his privilege; but let him not wound the mind of his weak brother by an injudicious exercise of his privileges.   He is accountable to God for his faith in this matter as well as in all others.   But he is not to intrude it upon his weak brother.   Calvin well observes, ' This passage is evidently perverted and misunderstood when it is adduced to support the opinion that a person may observe foolish and superstitious ceremonies without danger, provided his conscience is pure and undisturbed before God. The context clearly confutes such a misconstruction.'   A Christian may forego his liberty with respect to meats and drinks, but he has no right to practise what God has not enjoined, nor to avoid practising what God has instituted.

Happy is he that condemneth not himself in that thing which he alloweth.— That man is happy, and he only can enjoy peace in his conscience, who acts according to the persuasion which he has of the lawfulness of his conduct.   And happy is it for the Christian when his just views are not acted on in such a manner as to stumble others.

Ver. 23.—*And he that doubteth is damned if he eat, because he eateth not of faith : for whatsoever is not of faith is sin.*

And he that doubteth is damned if he eat.—That is, he that doubteth whether it be right to eat the meats forbidden by the law, is in this condemned, although the thing itself is lawful.   The reason is obvious.   The person does not fully believe that the thing is right, and consequently by eating he thinks he may be offending God. This shows us that in the things of God we ought not to do anything concerning which we are in doubt. To observe any ordinance of God with doubts as to its being an ordinance of God, is to commit sin. To obey God acceptably, we must have a conviction that we are doing the thing which He has enjoined. Calvin observes on this passage, 'For if we are not allowed to take a single mouthful of bread with a doubting conscience, how much greater caution ought to be used in transactions of the highest importance?'

For whatsoever is not of faith is sin.—That is, whatsoever is not done with a conviction that it is agreeable to the will of God, is sinful in the doer, although it should be right in itself. This is the generalization of the preceding doctrine. It applies not merely to meats, but to everything. If any person be convinced that a thing is contrary to God's law, and yet practises it, he is guilty before God, although it should be found that the thing was lawful.

CHAPTER 15
ROMANS 15:1 – 33

Ver. 1.—*We then that are strong ought to bear the infirmities of the weak, and not to please ourselves.*

We then that are strong.—The Apostle continues here to treat of the subject of mutual forbearance among Christians, ranking himself with those who are strong in the faith, and who know that under the new covenant there is no longer any distinction in the sight of God between different kinds of meat, or any sanctity in the feast days enjoined to be observed under the Jewish dispensation.

To know the mind of God, as revealed in the Scriptures, is to be strong; to be ignorant of it, is to be weak. It is not the man of the greatest intellectual vigour who is strong, nor the imbecile in understanding who is weak. Many of those who possess the greatest talents, and are most distinguished for mental acquirements, even although Christians, may be weak in respect to the things of God. And many who are of feeble intellect, may be strong in the knowledge of Divine things.

Ought to bear the infirmities of the weak.—Mr. Stuart explains the word here used as signifying '*to bear with, to endure patiently, to tolerate.*' The word, indeed, denotes both to bear and to bear with ; but here it is evidently to be taken in the former signification. The allusion is to travellers assisting a weak companion, by taking a part of his burden and carrying it for him. The strong believer is to carry the weak believer's burden, by acting as if he had the same weakness, and abstaining from whatever would cause the weak brother to sin. Strictly speaking, it is improper to speak of one believer *bearing with, enduring,* or *tolerating* the opinions of another, for over these he has no control. God only is the Lord of the conscience. The man who speaks of tolerating the belief of another speaks improperly. *And not to please ourselves.*—If there be not a spirit of love, there will be a proneness in men to bring forward, and to urge with vehemence anything in which they have received more light than their brethren. This is not for the good of their weak brethren, but to please themselves, and discover their own superior acquirements.

Ver. 2.—*Let every one of us please his neighbour for his good to edification.*

Let every one of us please his neighbour.—Though no part of the truth of God is to be sacrificed to peace, yet everything consistent with truth ought to be done to avoid giving offence, or stumbling weak brethren. Some persons seem to value themselves on their setting at nought the opinion of their brethren ; but this we see is far from the doctrine of the Apostle. We are not to gratify our own humour, but to do everything in our power, consistent with our duty, to please our brother. *For his good.*—Mr. Stuart renders this 'in respect to that which is good,' or ' so far as we may do so and do what is good.' The common version is preferable, and conveys the true meaning. We are to please our brethren only *for their good.* It is for their good not to be urged to do what they cannot do with a good conscience ; but it is not for their good to have any part of the will of God concealed from them. Besides, to abstain from meats is not a good in itself. *To edification.*—This is the way in which it is for their good to treat them in the manner recommended. It is for their edification. Such treatment will convince them of the love of those by whom they are so treated, and will be the surest way to lead them forward to clearer views in the points in which they are ignorant. To urge them forward with dictatorial zeal, would shut their eyes closer, and prevent them from perceiving the truth.

Ver. 3.—*For even Christ pleased not Himself ; but, as it is written, The reproaches of them that reproached Thee fell on Me.*

For even Christ pleased not Himself.—The Apostle confirms his injunctions by the example of Christ. He did not please Himself, or look for the favour of men ; but instead of this, voluntarily acted in such a way as to subject Himself to every inconvenience and evil for the good of His people. If, then, our Lord Himself acted in this manner, how does it condemn a contrary practice in His people, if they indulge their own humour at the expense of those for whom Christ died !

But, as it is written.—Instead of directly referring to the history of the life of Christ, the Apostle refers to the Old Testament, which testified of Him. The chief facts in the life of Christ were in one way or other predicted, and foreshown in the law and the Prophets. The manner in which they are quoted by the Apostle at once shows their bearing, and attests their application to the great Antitype. The actions of our Lord were ordered in such a manner as to fulfil what was written concerning Him.

The reproaches of them that reproached Thee fell on Me.—The reproaches of those who reproached His Father fell upon His only-begotten Son when He was in the world. This imports that all the reproaches cast upon God's people, on account of their obedience to God, are really directed against God Himself. It imports that all the opposition made to Christ was really opposition to His Father. The reason why Christ was so much hated and opposed was, because He revealed or manifested the

Father. Had He avoided this, He would have been applauded by the world. Men, even the most wicked, approve of morality and acts of kindness to the human race. They hate Christ and Christians only because of their holding forth the character of God, which they dislike. Had Christ sought to please Himself, He would have avoided whatever excited the enmity of the multitude. When, therefore, the people reproached Him, because He pleased His Father and declared His will, it was His Father whom they reproached. The great aim of the intercourse of Jesus Christ with men, as it referred to them, was their good, and not His own pleasure. He bore the infirmities of the weak, accommodating His instructions to the capacities of those whom He addressed. But because of this condescension He was reproached by others. When He was found in company with the ignorant, to teach them, He was reproached as ' a friend of publicans and sinners.' This appears to be the meaning and application of this quotation, which at first sight does not seem clear.

Ver. 4.—*For whatsoever things were written aforetime were written for our learning ; that we, through patience and comfort of the Scriptures, might have hope.*

For whatsoever things were written aforetime were written for our learning.—This observation appears to refer to the Apostle's reason for making the preceding quotation. He might have referred, as already remarked, immediately to the history of the life of Christ ; but instead of this, he quotes from a passage in the Psalms. Here he justifies his doing this, and makes an observation which applies generally to the Old Testament, and shows us in what manner we ought to use it. Some persons have blasphemously said that the Old Testament is now out of date. But the writers of the New Testament give no such view of the Old. Instead of this, they refer to it as proof, and treat it as of constant use to the people of God. All that is therein written, whether history, types, prophecies, precepts, or examples, although under another dispensation, is intended for the instruction of believers, to train them to patience, and to impart the consolation which the Scriptures provide for those that have hope in God. ' Take, my brethren,' says James, ' the prophets, who have spoken in the name of the Lord, for an example of suffering affliction, and of patience.'

The passage quoted in the preceding verse is not only useful to us, as applicable to Christ, but it is, as the Apostle shows, useful as an example. If the reproaches of those who reproached God fell upon Christ, the people of God ought to live and act in such a manner as the Apostle elsewhere enjoins, when he says, ' Let us go forth, therefore, unto Him without the camp, bearing His reproach.' If Christ did not please Himself, neither ought His people to please themselves, but to please Him and His people for their edification.

That we through patience and comfort of the Scriptures.—Mr. Stuart understands this of our patience, and translates the second word by *admonition* or *exhortation :* ' That through patience, and by the exhortation of the Scriptures, we might obtain hope. But it is through the patience exhibited in example in the Scriptures that we are to have hope. And though the original word signifies exhortation as well as comfort, yet here the latter is to be preferred. In the next verse, with reference to this declaration, God is called the God of patience. Now God is the God of consolation, that is, the God who is the author of consolation to His people. But to call God the God of exhortation, would be an uncouth expression. *Might have hope.*—We ought to read the Scriptures with a view not to gratify our curiosity, but to increase and nourish our hope of future glory. This passage teaches that we should encourage ourselves by the example of those who, amidst similar temptations, have overcome. For this purpose, the conduct of those who obtained a good report through faith is set before us, that we may not be slothful, but followers of them who, through faith and patience, inherit the promises.

Ver. 5.—*Now the God of patience and consolation grant you to be like-minded one toward another, according to Christ Jesus.*

Now the God of patience and consolation.—The Apostle having in the preceding verse spoken of the patience and consolation which the Scriptures communicate, here designates God as the God of patience and consolation, and prays to Him, who is infinitely patient, and the source of all consolation, to grant that the believers at Rome might be like-minded. God is called the God of patience and consolation, because He is the author of patience and consolation to His people. Patience is essential to a Christian, and so is consolation; but neither in himself nor from any other source, but from God, has he these graces. We cannot bear the evils of the cross without Divine support. The virtues, then, of the Christian character are as much the fruit of the Spirit of God as faith is His gift. Everything good in the man of God is of God: all his sins are his own. When, therefore, we are in straits, difficulties, or troubles, we ought to look to God for patience to bear what He may see good to lay upon us, and for consolation under the burden. The form of the expression, *God of patience*, shows not only that God gives patience to His people, but that He gives it abundantly, and that there is no other source of this gift.

Grant you to be like-minded.—Mr. Stuart understands the expression translated *like-minded* to relate to matters of belief. It is true that it has this signification, but it is equally true that it refers to the will and affections, and in this place, in accordance with the common version, it is to be so understood. There may be unity of sentiment in error, as well as in truth. Christians should labour to effect union of belief in all matters, because it is their duty to endeavour to know whatever God has revealed, and not merely for the purpose of union of sentiment, in order to walk together in church fellowship. It is true that union of belief in all things tends much to harmony; but it is likewise true that difference of sentiment in some things tends more to manifest the degree of advancement in the things of God. There may be harmony from perfect agreement in belief, when there is not only error, but little of the true principle of harmony; for the true principle of harmony is love to Christ's people for Christ's sake. It is also true that, if we look to the New Testament, we do not always find perfect agreement in sentiment among the brethren. Although, therefore, the thing is desirable, it is not always to be expected, and much less is it to be made a term of communion. Christians are to walk together in the things in which they are agreed, and to differ without condemning each other. This is quite consistent with every degree of zeal for the interest of every truth about which they may differ, Phil. iii. 15, 16. If there be any who think that union of sentiment among Christians is not highly desirable, they are certainly far mistaken, and not of the same mind with the Apostle, who shows such earnestness on that subject. For surely it is desirable that Christians should know all that God has revealed ; and if they know this, they will have this unity. But a thing may be very desirable which is not essential to their fellowship, and, as a matter of fact, no two Christians have such an union of sentiment. There are among them babes, young men, and fathers, and they are of the same mind about Divine things, just as far as they are respectively taught by the Spirit. The faith of Christ is required absolutely in all who have a right to fellowship in a church of Christ ; but fellowship is not to be refused to him whom we acknowledge that Christ has received.

According to Christ Jesus.—Mr. Stuart understands this as meaning 'in accordance with the Spirit of Christ, or agreeably to what Christ or the Christian religion requires.' It undoubtedly means, according to the example of Christ Jesus, and accords with the expression, ' Let this mind be in you which was also in Christ Jesus,' Phil. ii. 5. Dr. Macknight understands it of the example of Christ, but he also includes the will of Christ. But these two meanings the phrase cannot have in the same place.

Ver. 6.—*That ye may with one mind and one mouth glorify God, even the Father of our Lord Jesus Christ.*

That ye may with one mind and one mouth.—With one mind means accordance in affection and heart. Union of affection is much more necessary to harmony in worship than perfect harmony in sentiment. There may be harmony in the service of God among Christians who differ upon many things. But if any two of them are disaffected to one another, there is no harmony, though they should both have perfectly the same judgment in all matters. It is in this view that the Apostle charges Euodias and Syntyche that they should be of the same mind. Disaffection towards each other was the evil under which they laboured, and not difference about any matter of belief. *One mouth.*—That is, this harmony should be as complete as if they all uttered their voice through one mouth. It is delightful to see a body of Christians all uniting in prayer and praise with one heart, while there may be a great variety in their attainments in the knowledge of Christ. On the other hand, there may be a professed union in everything, without having the mind that Christ here requires. The union of Christians in professed faith will not compensate for their want of union in Him.

Glorify God.—God is glorified in the prayers and praises of His people. This object, then, they should never forget. They should acknowledge Him and praise Him in every part of His character, however offensive it may be to the world. He is glorified by them literally with one mouth in prayer. He who prays is to be considered as uttering the prayer of the whole multitude of disciples, and each of them should follow in spirit, praying with him as he utters the words. *Even the Father of our Lord Jesus Christ.*—God is the God and Father of our Lord Jesus Christ. He is the God of Christ as man, and He is the Father of Christ as God. The titles Father and Son, as applied to Christ and His heavenly Father, most evidently apply to relation in Godhead. Great efforts have been made by some to overturn this view; but their efforts have been without success, and they have been most mischievous in taking away one of the strongest proofs of the deity of Christ and one which the Scriptures most frequently use. The dignity of the character of Christ is most frequently asserted in calling Him the Son of God. But if He be the Son of God in a lower sense, or one corresponding with that in which it is applicable to every good man, no definite view of His character is given when He is called the *Son of God.*

Ver. 7.—*Wherefore receive ye one another, as Christ also received us to the glory of God.*

Wherefore.—That is, since Christians ought not to please themselves, but to act in everything for the edification of each other, they ought to receive one another, notwithstanding differences of sentiment among them. *Receive.*—Mr. Stuart understands this as signifying to *show kindness.* But the word means only receive. It expresses nothing of kindness. It refers to the reception of each other as Christians to the fellowship of the Church. They ought, indeed, to manifest kindness with respect to all who are thus received, but the word does not express this. This method of giving, as is thought, a more emphatic meaning to words than usually belongs to them, is attended with the worst effects. Here it conceals a most important part of the will of God respecting the grounds on which Christians should receive each other to church fellowship. The command to receive into fellowship is turned into a command to show kindness.

As Christ also received us.—The manner in which Christians are to receive one another to church fellowship is as Christ has received them. *As,* or according as.—Now Christ has received, and does receive, all who believe the truth even in the feeblest manner. He accepts those who have the lowest degree of faith in Him. Thus He received the afflicted father, who said, 'Lord, I believe, help Thou mine unbelief.' Christ receives those who are ignorant of many things—indeed of everything but faith in Himself. The most ungodly is saved by Him the moment he believes; and Christians are received by Him, and live upon Him by faith, while they are in error as to many parts of His will. If Christ receives His people, notwithstanding their ignorance of many parts of His will, ought they to reject those whom He hath received?

To the glory of God.—Some understand this of the glory which God shall bestow upon His people. But this cannot be the meaning here, as we are not yet received to His glory; whereas the glory here spoken of is already manifested. The glory which God will confer upon His people is future. 'By whom, also, we have access by faith into this grace wherein we stand, and rejoice in hope of the glory of God,' Rom. v. 2. We have present access into the favour and grace of God, but we have now only the glory of God in hope. The glory of God, then, here means the glory that belongs to God's character. It is to the glory of God that Christians are received and saved by His Son.

Ver. 8.—*Now I say that Jesus Christ was a minister of the circumcision for the truth of God, to confirm the promises made unto the fathers :*

Now I say.—The Apostle proceeds to reconcile the Jews and Gentiles to each other, by showing them the reason why Jesus Christ, who was equally the Lord of the Jews and the Gentiles, was born a Jew, as a *minister of the circumcision.* Jesus Christ was made under the law, and ministered among the Jews; and though He gave some examples of His purpose of mercy to the Gentiles, yet He did not go out to preach to the nations. But this exclusive service among the Jews is not to be understood as indicating an exclusion of His mercy from the nations. It was *for the truth of God.* It was to fulfil the predictions and promises of Scripture, *to confirm the promises made to the fathers.* His ministry was the fulfilment of the promises that God had made to His ancient servants.

Ver. 9.—*And that the Gentiles might glorify God for His mercy ; as it is written, For this cause I will confess to Thee among the Gentiles, and sing unto Thy name.*

And that the Gentiles might glorify God for His mercy.—Though Christ's personal ministry was limited to the Jews, yet the efficacy of His work was not confined to them. The Old Testament itself contains evidence that the Gentiles were to be interested in His redemption. It was the purpose of Christ's work that Gentiles as well as Jews might glorify God on account of His mercy. The glory of God is therefore exhibited as the reason of Christ's work. This is the highest object of all God's works. Salvation is also represented as *mercy.* There is nothing here or anywhere else in Scripture to encourage the presumption of men who suppose that they can merit salvation by their own works. Salvation is of mercy. In the preceding verse, Paul had spoken of the truth of God: here he speaks of His mercy. That which was *truth* to the Jews, having been promised to their fathers, was *mercy* to the Gentiles, who were admitted to participate in the blessings promised. This the Apostle proves by the different passages he quotes, which declare that the mercy of God was to be extended to all nations. Consequently both Jews and Gentiles had the strongest reasons thus presented to them neither to condemn nor to despise one another, but, on the contrary, to regard themselves as united in Christ Jesus, as well as by the common sentiment of their obligations to Him, and the love He had shown them. 'He is our peace, who hath made both one, and hath broken down the middle wall of partition between us.'[1] *As it is written.* —Paul quotes a passage from the Old Testament to show that Christ was to be the Saviour of the Gentiles as well as of the Jews.

For this cause, etc.—In the passage referred to, Christ is represented as confessing or acknowledging God among the Gentiles, and singing to the praise of His name. Christ did not appear personally among the

---

[1] The same distinction between these expressions, *truth* and *mercy*, is made respecting Abraham and Jacob. What was truth to the one, was mercy to the other. 'Thou wilt perform the truth to Jacob, and the mercy to Abraham, which Thou hast sworn unto our fathers from the days of old,' Mic. vii. 20.

Gentile nations. This prediction, then, must be fulfilled of Him in His people, as one with Him. Than this nothing more clearly proves the unity of Christ and His people. What He does for them, they do, as they are one with Him. It is thus that believers are saved in righteousness as well as in mercy. Christ's righteousness is their righteousness, because they are one with Him. Those who repudiate the doctrine of imputation of Christ's righteousness, as both Dr. Macknight and Mr. Stuart have done, and that in a manner the most explicit and unreserved, not merely corrupt, but utterly overthrow the Gospel, and entirely remove the grounds of the justice of the Divine procedure in the plan of redemption. Grace reigns *through righteousness* unto eternal life, by Jesus Christ our Lord. In the eighteenth Psalm David speaks of himself, and the things spoken are applicable to him; yet the Apostle here quotes the words as applicable to Christ. This shows most incontrovertibly that David was a type of Christ, and that what is spoken of the type is in its ultimate sense spoken of the Antitype.

Ver. 10.—*And again He saith, Rejoice, ye Gentiles, with His people.*

And again He saith.—That is, God saith this, but it was Moses that said it, therefore what Moses here said was dictated by God. The words are the words both of God and of Moses. *Rejoice, ye Gentiles, with His people.*—This quotation is from Deut. xxxii. 43. The Gentiles are there called upon to rejoice in fellowship with the people of God. This implies that they were to be converted by the Gospel, and united with the Jews in the Church of Christ. Calvin says, ' I do not agree with those who consider this quotation to be taken from the song of Moses ; for the Jewish lawgiver intends, in that part of his writings, rather to strike terror into the adversaries of Israel, than to invite them to the participation of one common joy. I take it, therefore, from Ps. lxvii. 3, 4.' But this is a very unsafe and presumptuous mode of reasoning. We must rest on Paul's authority, rather than on the authority of Calvin, as to what was the intention of Moses in the passage quoted. Though Moses intended to strike terror into the enemies of Israel, there is no reason why Gentile believers should be terrified with this, or should not rejoice with the Jewish people of God in the victories of the Messiah over His enemies. The perfect applicability of the quotation is clearly obvious. Besides, the passage alleged by Calvin as the quotation, namely, Ps. lxvii. 3, 4, cannot without violence be made to correspond with the words of Paul. Why desert a passage where the words are easily found, and have recourse to a passage where the words are not found ? Is this to be done on the strength of our own views of the words of Moses ? Surely we ought implicitly to bow to the authority of Paul as a commentator on Moses. In fact, the quotation is as applicable to the Gentiles as to the Jews. In the typical sense of the passage, are not the Gentiles as much interested in the extension of salvation to the nations as the Jews ? Are they not much more so ? Is it not to them a matter of much greater joy ? The Jews ought, indeed, to rejoice in the glory of God and the happiness of men in the extension of the Gospel. But the Gentiles, in addition to this, rejoice in it as their own salvation.

Even in the literal sense, as applicable to the victories of Israel over their enemies, ought not believing Gentiles to have rejoiced in them? Did not Rahab rejoice in the victories of Israel over their enemies?

Ver. 11.—*And again, Praise the Lord, all ye Gentiles, and laud Him, all ye people.*

This quotation is from Ps. cxvii. 1. It calls upon all the nations to praise God. This implies that salvation was to extend to all nations, for none can praise God without the knowledge of God. Such addresses to the Gentiles are very numerous in the Book of Psalms, and refute the opinion of those who think it wrong to call on sinners to praise God. It is true that none but believers can praise God. But sinners may be called on to perform every duty incumbent on men, and charged with guilt for neglecting it. They ought to praise God. But this praise ought to be in faith, as well as every other duty. To suppose that sinners are not bound to praise God, is to suppose that their neglect of this and any other duty is not criminal. There is no danger in calling on sinners to observe the whole law of God, if it be also kept in view that no obedience in any degree can be given to God except through faith in His Son. This is quite a different thing from making prayer and praise a preparatory process to conversion. 'The original word,' says Dr. Macknight, 'signifies to praise by singing,' Luke ii. 13. This is unsound criticism, and proceeds on a false canon, namely, that a word designates everything to which it is applicable. Words may apply to many things which are not designed by them. This word applies to praise by signing, but it does not express *singing*, because it also applies to praise in any manner.

Ver. 12.—*And again, Esaias saith, There shall be a root of Jesse, and He that shall rise to reign over the Gentiles ; in Him shall the Gentiles trust.*

And again, Esaias saith.—The Apostle has in this place given multiplied quotations from the Old Testament to prove the point in hand. One proof from Scripture, if applicable, is sufficient to prove anything, yet the Apostle gives us many. This shows that Divine truth ought to be exhibited to gainsayers in all its strength, with a display of all its evidence. In proportion as prejudice is opposed to any truth, it is necessary to fortify it with multiplied evidence. The Jews were greatly prejudiced against that part of the will of God which the Apostle now teaches, and he heaps scripture upon scripture to overcome their prejudices, although his own authority and his own declaration were as valid as those of the inspired writers whom he quoted.

There shall be a root of Jesse.—Rather, there shall be *the* root of Jesse. It is a definite allusion to one particular person of the family of Jesse. Christ is called a branch in the same chapter, Isa. xi. ; but He appears here to be called the root, or a particular shoot from the root, as He is elsewhere called a root out of a dry ground. This limits the origin of the human nature of the Messiah to the family of Jesse. *And He that shall rise to reign over the Gentiles.*—This determines the Messiah to be the King of the Gentiles as well as of the Jews. The passage quoted speaks of Him as a *banner* to the Gentiles. This the Apostle interprets as a *ruler*, because soldiers follow the banner of their captain. *In Him shall the*

Gentiles trust.—This strictly asserts that the Gentiles would trust in the Messiah descended from Jesse.

Ver. 13.—*Now the God of hope fill you with all joy and peace in believing, that ye may abound in hope, through the power of the Holy Ghost.*

Now the God of hope.—God is called the God of hope, because He is the author of all the well-grounded hope of His people. All hope of which He is not the author, in the heart of men, is false and delusive. The world in general may have hope, but it is false hope. All true hope with respect to the Divine favour is effected in the human heart by God Himself. Not only is God the author of all true hope, but He can create this hope out of the midst of despair. The most desponding are often raised by Him to a good hope through grace; and the most guilty are in a moment relieved, and made to hope in His mercy. How remarkably was this the case with the thief on the cross, and with the three thousand on the day of Pentecost!

Fill you with all joy and peace.—The inward joy and peace of the Christian are the gifts of God, and not the natural effects of anything in the mind of man. All the promises and declarations of Scripture would fail in producing joy and peace in the mind of a sinner, were it not for the agency of the Spirit of God. If the Christian possesses joy and peace, he ought to ascribe it altogether to God. He ought to reflect that these blessings must be produced and continually maintained by Divine power, and not by any power of his own mind. It should always be kept in view that these fruits of the Spirit, first of joy, and next of peace, Gal. v. 22, cannot be produced except in connection with the other fruits of the Spirit, and in the way of obedience, and in carefully abstaining from grieving the Spirit. David, when he had sinned, having lost his joy in God, utters this prayer: ' Restore unto me the joy of Thy salvation, and uphold me with Thy free Spirit: then will I teach transgressors Thy ways,' Ps. li. 12. Here we may also observe that they who seek to teach transgressors the ways of God should first themselves have the experience of these ways.

Fill you.—This implies that there are degrees of joy and peace in the minds of Christians. Some may have a measure of these graces who do not abound in them. It is a great blessing to be *filled* with them; and for this blessing the Apostle prays with respect to the Christians at Rome. If there be different degrees of joy and peace, how important is it to look earnestly to God for the fullest communication of these blessings! The Psalmist had more joy in his heart, bestowed by God, than worldly men have when their corn and wine most abound. *In believing.*—Joy and peace, as well as all other spiritual blessings, are communicated by God through faith, and through faith only, and in proportion to faith. Faith, when spoken of without peculiar reference, means faith in Christ, and not, as Dr. Macknight understands it, faith in any particular promise.

That ye may abound in hope.—The above blessings the Apostle prayed for to be bestowed on those whom he addressed, in order that they might abound in hope; and the more believers are filled with joy and peace, the greater will be their hope. The people of God have high hopes, and it is their privilege to seek from their Lord an increase and abundance of hope—not that faint and common hope of possibility or probability, but a certain hope.　Such a hope springs from faith,—in effect, is one with it.　Faith rests upon the goodness and truth of Him who hath promised; and hope, raising itself upon faith so established, stands up and looks out to the future accomplishment of the promise.　*Through the power of the Holy Ghost.*—Hope is produced in the mind by the agency and power of the Spirit of God.　Here two persons of the Godhead are brought into view as each being the bestower of this gift.　The Father gives hope —He is the God of hope; but He gives it through the Holy Ghost.　In the economy of redemption, this is the province of the Holy Ghost.　Hope is natural to the mind of man; and, in general, men have hope in the worst of times.　But as to Divine things, hope is not natural to man: it is the fruit of the Spirit of God through faith in His Son.

The prayer contained in this verse reminds us that there is no blessing which does not come to us from God, Jas. i. 17.　He is called the God of love, of peace, of patience, of consolation, of hope, who fills His people with joy and peace.　If, then, we desire to be filled with joy and peace, we must look to God.　If we desire to *abound* in hope by the power of the Holy Ghost, we must with confidence pray to obtain His sacred influences and Divine teaching.　We must be careful not to grieve Him by our evil conduct and evil desires.

Ver. 14.—*And I myself also am persuaded of you, my brethren, that ye also are full of goodness, filled with all knowledge, able also to admonish one another.*

And I myself also am persuaded of you, my brethren.—The Apostle here intimates that the reason of his writing to the believers as he had done was, not that he considered them deficient in the Christian character, or uninstructed in the doctrines and duties of their profession; on the contrary, even he himself was persuaded concerning them that they were *full of goodness.*　Mr. Stuart confines this to kindness.　There is no reason why it should not be extended to goodness in general, of which *kindness* is a part.　As we ought continually and prominently to maintain that there is naturally nothing good in men, we ought likewise to give equal prominence to the fact that all believers, being born of God and made new creatures, work the works of God, and in their minds possess those dispositions which are produced by the Spirit through the truth.　In our flesh there is nothing good; but from the work of the Spirit on our hearts we may be full of goodness.　The honour of this redounds to God as much as that of our faith.　If faith is the gift of God, so 'we are His workmanship, created in Christ Jesus unto good works,' to the praise of the glory of God.

Filled with all knowledge.—Paul acknowledges that those to whom he wrote excelled in the knowledge of Divine things, though he wrote to them with respect both to truth and duty.　The commendations bestowed by the Apostle on the attainments of this church show that there are comparative degrees in the knowledge of the Lord's people, and also that it is proper, on fit occasions, to confer approbation and praise on those who excel in knowledge.　It is mere worldly wisdom, not countenanced by Scripture doctrine and example, to withhold commendation when due, lest it should serve to puff up.　*Able also to admonish one another.*—The word in the original signifies to put in mind of duty, especially when it is transgressed.   The Apostle undertook to admonish them; but this did not imply that he considered them as unfit to admonish one another.

Ver. 15.—*Nevertheless, brethren, I have written the more boldly unto you in some sort, as putting you in mind, because of the grace that is given to me of God.*

Nevertheless.—Though the Roman Christians were eminent in their attainments, yet the Apostle thought it necessary to write to them as he had done with respect to some things, as to which he trusted they were previously acquainted.   Such things he judged it right to bring again to their remembrance.   It is proper, then, in the pastors of a church to bring forward the truths and duties with which the brethren are already acquainted, as well as those with respect to which they may either be ignorant or deficient in knowledge.   *Because of the grace that is given to me of God.*—This was the ground of his boldness.   He spoke as an Apostle, and in all things advanced by him he was only the mouth of the Holy Ghost.

Ver. 16.—*That I should be the minister of Jesus Christ to the Gentiles, ministering the Gospel of God, that the offering up of the Gentiles might be acceptable, being sanctified by the Holy Ghost.*

That I should be the minister of Jesus Christ.—The grace of the apostleship was given to Paul in order to his being a minister of Christ to the Gentiles.   *Ministering the Gospel of God.*—The original word for ministry signifies to labour in a sacred office.   Our term ministry sufficiently represents it.   Calvin blames Erasmus for at first translating it in this way, and prefers to translate it ' consecrating the Gospel.'   But this is evidently an improper translation, for Paul did not consecrate the Gospel.   The Gospel is God's word, and needs no consecration.   Erasmus afterwards translated it, ' sacrificing the Gospel,' which is still worse.   It is not the Gospel which is hére represented as a figurative sacrifice, but the Gentiles.   Believers are a sacrifice presented by the Apostle to God through the Gospel.   The Gospel is the means by which the Gentiles are made a sacrifice.   Mr. Stuart translates it, ' performing the office of a priest in respect to the Gospel of God.'   But this is liable to the same objection.   It is not *in respect* to the Gospel that Paul considers himself figuratively a priest.   It is with respect to the sacrifice, namely, the believing Gentiles, who are fitted for presentation as a sacrifice by the Gospel.   *That the offering up of the Gentiles.*—The Gentiles are the thing presented to God in this sacrifice.   This, it is obvious, is a sacrifice only figuratively, just as prayer and praise are called sacrifices.   There is now no sacrifice in the proper sense of the word, and the Apostles were not priests, except as all believers are priests.

Many of the errors of the Man of Sin arise from considering teachers under the New Testament as successors of the priests under the law. But there is now no priesthood, except in Christ, who abides a Priest for ever after the order of Melchisedec.   The priests under the law of Moses were His types.   As He is come, and has engrossed the whole duties of the office to Himself, He alone possesses priesthood.   There is no longer any need of a typical priesthood ; and the great sacrifice has been already offered.   When the Apostles are spoken of as doing any part of the

priest's office, it is in a figurative sense. It is in the same sense that
the altar is spoken of. As there is no sacrifice now to be offered, there
is now no altar. To give the Lord's table the name of an altar is very
erroneous. It is wonderful to consider how, from the figurative use of a
few words in the New Testament and in early Church history, a number
of the grossest and most superstitious doctrines and practices, as has been
already observed, arose in the Church. The bread of the Lord's table at
length became the body of Christ in a literal sense; the table on which
it lay became the altar; the teachers became the priests who offered the
sacrifice of the mass; and the contributions of Christians became offerings. In all these things, and innumerable others, the figurative sense
has been, by a gross imagination and the artifice of Satan, turned into a
literal sense, to the utter subversion of truth.

Might be acceptable.—The Gentiles became an acceptable sacrifice to
God only through the faith of the Gospel. It is only by the blood of
Christ that sinners can be washed from sin, and only through faith in
Christ that any sinner obtains an interest in Christ's blood, and only
through the Gospel that faith in Christ is produced. All those who
attempt to come to God in any other way are unacceptable to Him. This
cuts off the hope of all self-righteous persons, and of all unbelievers. It
takes away, also, the foundation from the doctrine of those who teach
that Christ may be the Saviour of what they call pious heathens who
have not heard of Him. According to the Apostle Paul, the offering of
the Gentiles is acceptable only through the Gospel. *Sanctified by the
Holy Ghost.*—As the sacrifices under the law were sanctified externally
and typically, this figurative sacrifice is sanctified truly by the Holy Ghost.
No person, then, can be acceptable to God who is not sanctified by His
Spirit.

Ver. 17.—*I have therefore whereof I may glory through Jesus Christ in those things
which pertain to God.*

I have therefore whereof I may glory.—Paul says on another occasion,
'God forbid that I should glory, save in the cross of our Lord Jesus
Christ.' Is it not a contradiction, then, to say here, 'I have whereof I
may glory?' There is no contradiction: The glorying which he disclaims
respects his acceptance with God. The glorying which he here acknowledges respects his success in the preaching of the Gospel; and even this
is not a glorying in himself, but a glorying in Christ Jesus. It was the
signal favour of his Lord that gave him his office of apostleship, qualified him for its discharge, and made him successful. From all the
Apostle's writings, we learn that of this he had the most firm conviction.
He gives thanks to the Lord, who had counted him faithful, putting him
into the ministry. But elsewhere he declares that he had 'obtained
mercy of the Lord *to be faithful.*' In like manner all that he did in His
service is ascribed to God. 'Whereunto I also labour, striving according to His working, which worketh in me mightily.' He had whereof to
glory in the abundant and unmerited favour of God; but he always carefully avoids speaking of anything done by him that was not the work of
Christ. *In things that pertain to God.*—That is, things that respect the
service of God.

Ver. 18.—*For I will not dare to speak of any of those things which Christ hath not wrought by me, to make the Gentiles obedient, by word and deed.*

For I will not dare.—Paul would not take to himself any portion of praise on account of the labours and success of others. He spoke only of the success which Christ had given him in his own work. This shows that although all success is of God, yet that it is an honour and a ground of praise to be successful in Christ's work. Many have supposed that it is wrong to give any praise to the Lord's servants on account of their labours, diligence, and success in His service. They have judged that this encourages a spirit of self-righteousness and of pride. But this wisdom is not from God. It is human wisdom, and tends to damp exertion in the service of Jesus Christ. All our success is in Christ Jesus, as well as our ability and disposition to labour. Yet God has given praise to His servants for their diligence and success in His work. It is a sinful refinement to blame what God approves. The Apostle speaks here of what Christ wrought by him. In other places he also speaks of what God wrought by him, Acts xiv. 27, xv. 12.

To make the Gentiles obedient.—The obedience of the Gentiles is their belief of the Gospel. To obey the Gospel is to receive it, for it commands belief. Now this obedience of the Gentiles to the Gospel was Christ's work. *Christ wrought it.*—Faith is the gift of God. It is not to be ascribed either to him that preaches or to him that hears, but to Christ, who by His Spirit opens the heart to believe the truth. But the preacher is employed as an agent. Christ *wrought* this *through* the Apostle. No man is made a Christian by any power less than God's, and by no other means than God's word. Christ wrought the obedience of the Gentiles through Paul, but the instrumentality belongs to God's word, as well as the agency to Himself. Some connect this with the word immediately preceding, and understand it of the profession and practice of the believing Gentiles. Others understand it of the preaching, labours, and miracles of the Apostles. The next verse seems to determine for the latter sense.

Ver. 19.—*Through mighty signs and wonders, by the power of the Spirit of God ; so that from Jerusalem, and round about unto Illyricum, I have fully preached the Gospel of Christ.*

Through mighty signs and wonders.—Rather through, or by the power of, signs and miracles. These are the deeds through which, as well as by Paul's preaching, the Lord made the Gentiles obedient. This includes all the miraculous works of the Apostle for the confirmation of the Gospel. *By the power of the Spirit of God.*—Some understand this of the power by which the signs and wonders were performed ; others, of the gifts of the Holy Spirit, or the gift of tongues, prophecy, etc. The latter opinion appears to be the true meaning.

So that from Jerusalem.—Some suppose that, as there is no mention in the Acts of the Apostles of Paul's preaching in Illyricum, and as it is only said that he preached as far as Illyricum, he did not enter that country. But the silence of the Acts of the Apostles is no evidence of this, and verse 23d seems to prove that he did preach in Illyricum, as well as in the intermediate countries between that province and Jerusalem. If there was no place in those parts for him to extend his labours on unoccupied ground, he must have preached in Illyricum also. Besides, that the Gospel had been preached, and that there were churches in Illyricum, appears from Titus going into Dalmatia. *I have fully preached the Gospel of Christ*, or fulfilled the Gospel.—The Gospel was to be preached to all nations. He filled all the countries with the glad tidings of salvation through Jesus Christ. Thus was it given to Paul, who was before a blasphemer, and a persecutor, and injurious, to preach the unsearchable riches of Christ.

Ver. 20.—*Yea, so have I strived to preach the Gospel, not where Christ was named, lest I should build upon another man's foundation.*

Yea, so have I strived to preach the Gospel.—The word translated *strived* literally signifies to *love honour;* and as the love of honour stimulates to earnest exertions, the word came to signify, in a secondary sense, to endeavour earnestly, to strive. In this place, however, the primary sense appears to be that of the Apostle. He is speaking of the honour which God had conferred on him in the labour and success of the Gospel ; and consistently with this, he speaks of his ambition to occupy ground that had not been taken possession of by others. This is not indeed worldly ambition, but it is ambition which is lawful and commendable in Christians. *Not where Christ was named.*—That is, in places that had not previously even heard of Christ. Similar ambition has often stimulated modern missionaries, and by their labours the Gospel has been carried to countries that were previously strangers to the very name of Christ. This appears to show that when any are strongly inclined to have the honour of being the means of subjecting new countries to the authority of Christ, they ought to endeavour to accomplish their desire. It is through this means that God excites men to fulfil His purposes of mercy to the different nations of the earth.

Lest I should build upon another man's foundation.—This determines the meaning of the word translated *to strive* in this place. The Apostle was desirous of laying the foundation of the building in as many countries as possible. This is more honourable than to go into countries where others have been successful. Dr. Macknight understands this reason to indicate reluctance to perform the office of a subordinate teacher. But he evidently mistakes Paul's meaning. To teach believers converted by others is not necessarily to perform the office of a subordinate teacher. With respect to those of the church at Rome itself, Paul was not the first who taught them, and he doubtless preached in many places where Christ had been named. This he did not avoid, though he was ambitious, as far as possible, to break up new ground, and have the honour of preaching to men who had not previously heard of Christ. Calvin well observes, ' There is no foundation for perverting this passage by applying it to the pastoral office ; for we know that the name of Christ must always continue to be preached in well-regulated and properly constituted churches, when the truth of the Gospel has been for a long period felt and acknowledged.' He that lays the foundation has more honour than he that builds on it in the Christian's edification, but the latter is not without his reward. All cannot have the honour, and therefore have not the ambition, to go as missionaries to heathen countries. He that waters shall have his own reward, as well as he that plants.

Ver. 21.—*But as it is written, To whom He was not spoken of, they shall see ; and they that have not heard shall understand.*

But as it is written.—This ambition of the Apostle was the means of fulfilling a prophecy with respect to the spread of the Gospel in heathen countries. Thus it is that God fulfils His predictions and His purposes. He gives His people an earnest desire to be the means of accomplishing them at the moment when He designs their accomplishment. It will be thus that the Gospel will at last be effectually carried to every country under heaven. It is thus that modern missionaries have, in some measure, carried the Gospel to the heathen. And although the slothfulness of the people of God in former ages is not without blame, it is because the time to fulfil God's predictions to the nations was not come, that a like ambition to that of Paul was not found more generally to animate Christians. Whenever the Lord has work to do, He raises up men with a heart to perform it. This, however, is no excuse at any particular time for indifference or want of effort to spread the Gospel. *To whom He was not spoken of,* Isa. lii. 15.—This intimates the preaching of the Gospel to the heathens, and it proves also that the Messiah was spoken of to the Jews. The law and the Prophets spoke of Him.

Ver. 22.—*For which cause also I have been much hindered from coming to you.*

Paul's ambition to carry the Gospel into countries where it had not been previously preached, had long prevented him from visiting Rome, where the Gospel had been preached by others. It is important to teach believers all things, whatsoever Jesus has commanded. But doubtless it is more important to convert sinners from the thraldom of Satan. The peculiar business of an Apostle and of missionaries is the latter, the former that of the pastor ; though neither object is to be neglected by the one or the other.

Ver. 23.—*But now having no more place in these parts, and having a great desire these many years to come unto you ;*

But now having no more place in these parts.—Paul could not advance farther in that direction. This seems to prove, as already asserted, that the Apostle had preached in Illyricum as well as in the intermediate places. Had he not done so, there would still have been place for him in these parts. When an opportunity of serving Christ in one direction is shut up, we ought to turn to another. When there is no opportunity of preaching Christ to those who have not heard of Him, we ought to occupy ourselves in labouring among those by whom He is already known. Paul diligently employed his time to the greatest advantage. He was always in some way occupied in the service of his Master. *Having a great desire these many years to come unto you.*—This shows that the Lord's servants, with respect to the field of their labours, may lawfully be influenced by their desires. Paul was no doubt always sent by God to the place where He would have him to be ; but sometimes He sent him not by direct command, but by his own desire or providential circumstances, or the persecution of his enemies.

Ver. 24.—*Whensoever I take my journey into Spain, I will come to you : for I trust to see you in my journey, and to be brought on my way thitherward by you, if first I be somewhat filled with your company.*

Whensoever I take my journey into Spain, I will come to you.—The commission of the Apostles extended to all countries, but they were not always immediately directed with respect to the scene of their labours. Sometimes they proposed what they were unable to accomplish. This no doubt was always overruled by God for the fulfilment of His own purposes, and His sending them to the places in which He designed them to labour. Sometimes, however, they were immediately directed, and either enjoined to go to a certain place, or restrained from going. The intention of Jesus in allowing them in general to direct their own course, while He overruled it in every instance, was no doubt for an example to us, that in directing our labours we are to judge according to our own views and desires, and that we are not to expect miraculous or immediate directions. Missionaries sometimes err on this point, and seem to look for miraculous interposition to direct them in going or not going to certain places. This is what the Apostles themselves had not at all times, and which is by no means necessary. The Gospel is to be preached to every creature; and if nothing in God's providence prevent our going according to our views and desires, yet we ought to look for the Divine direction. This, however, should be sought by prayer, through the influence of the Holy Spirit on our minds, and in the providence of God, and not through any immediate impression or supernatural communication. The providence of Jesus, whose is the command to preach the Gospel, and who directs the course of all things, will either open the door or shut it according as it suits His sovereign pleasure.

It has been made a question whether Paul was ever in Spain. On the one side, some argue that, from his inspiration in writing this passage, he must have gone to that country, and others, for want of evidence that he was in Spain, argue that in writing these words he was not inspired. Both these opinions are wrong. Paul's inspiration in announcing his purposes does not imply the necessity of his always fulfilling these purposes. He had fully determined to visit Spain, and this the Holy Spirit inspired him to declare. But he did not pledge the Divine power to accomplish this resolution. It was useful to declare the resolution, whether it was to be accomplished or not. His inspiration, then, is no evidence of his having visited Spain. But much less is the want of evidence of his being in Spain a proof that he was not inspired; for if the inspiration of this passage necessarily imported that he must have been in Spain, want of positive information that he was there, so far from furnishing contrary evidence, is not even an objection. There are thousands of facts of which there are no records. Dr. Macknight, then, reasons without attending to first principles, when he says, ' This, among other instances, is a proof that in speaking of what he meant to do afterwards, the Apostle did not make known any determinations of God revealed to him by the Spirit, but his own resolutions and opinions only. For there is no evidence that he ever went to Spain.' The want of such evidence is no proof that he did not fulfil his purpose. The writer proceeds upon a false first principle, namely, that a prediction or declaration cannot be accounted as being really fulfilled unless there are records of its fulfilment. There are, indeed, other instances which show that Paul was sometimes disappointed in his expectations and purposes; but this is not such an instance. The only reason why we should hesitate in believing that Paul was in Spain is, that this is not necessarily required by the inspiration of the passage. It is possible that he might not be able to fulfil the purpose which he was inspired to declare. If the inspiration of the passage required that Paul must visit Spain, then we have the fullest warrant to believe that he was there. Tradition affirms that Paul was in Spain; but this is not evidence.

For I trust to see you in my journey.—This shows that Paul's resolution was his own, and that its fulfilment was a matter of uncertain hope, not of absolute prediction. He planned, it would appear, his visits in such a manner as not unnecessarily to consume time. He purposed to visit Rome on his way to Spain. *And to be brought on my way thitherward by you.*—The original word translated 'to be brought on my way,' signifies to conduct, escort, or send forward. In the latter sense, as implying the defraying all the expenses of the journey, the word seems to be used here, and on some other occasions in the New Testament. The Lord could have miraculously provided a supply for the Apostles while they preached the Gospel, or He could have commanded for this purpose the treasures of the Roman empire; but He chose to do this by the contributions of His people.

Filled with your company.—This shows the great delight that the Apostle had in the society of believers. Ought not Christians to delight in meeting one another from the remotest parts of the earth? What a hindrance to the cultivation of this principle are the divisions of Christians into sects and parties! *Somewhat filled.*—By this the Apostle intimates that, though their society for a short time would be highly gratifying to him, yet his delight in it could never be satiated. This is true Christian love. An introduction to the emperor and the great men of his council would not have gratified the Apostle so much as the society of the despised believers in Rome. Nothing should separate the mutual affection of those who are united in Christ. If the ignorance of the most ignorant of them does not shut the bowels of Christ with respect to them, should it do so with us? We all know but in part.

Ver. 25.—*But now I go unto Jerusalem to minister unto the saints.*

The Apostle had proposed to visit Rome, the capital of the world, and to carry the Gospel into Spain, where it had not yet been preached. He had long been prevented from visiting the Roman Christians, and yet, instead of going thither now, he chooses to go to Jerusalem, carrying money for the relief of the poor. But was not the preaching of the Gospel a greater matter than serving tables? Could not others have been found to carry this money without burdening Paul? If Paul, in order to save time for the preaching of the Gospel, seldom baptized believers, why did he spend it in carrying this gift of the Gentiles to the Jewish brethren? The object must assuredly have been very important ; and doubtless it was that he might improve the opportunity of overcoming the prejudice of the Jews towards the Gentiles, by this evidence of their liberality and love. This would tend to knit the Jews and Gentiles more closely together. And it was for this purpose, no doubt, that the dearth was occasioned in Jerusalem. For a similar purpose, it appears that God, in all ages, places some of His people in circumstances where they require to be assisted, while He renders others able to assist, because this mutually attaches them to each other, as well as tries them. We here also see that it is not merely to the wants of the brethren in the same church that His people should attend, but where it is necessary, they ought to contribute assistance to the wants of the brethren in the remotest parts of the earth. This contribution was sent from one quarter of the globe to another. Nothing can more clearly show the importance of this matter than that, in order to attend to it, Paul postponed the most important engagements.

Ver. 26.—*For it hath pleased them of Macedonia and Achaia to make a certain contribution for the poor saints which are at Jerusalem.*

For it hath pleased them of Macedonia and Achaia.—Or, Macedonia and Achaia have been pleased, or have thought good. The words Macedonia and Achaia are here used for the brethren or churches of Macedonia and Achaia. The places are put for those who live in them. Not, however, all the inhabitants of those places, but the churches of Christ only. This shows that the Scriptures employ the same figurative language that is familiar to other writings. This phraseology also justifies the manner in which we speak of the Epistles of the Apostles—the Epistle to the Romans, to the Corinthians, etc. By this we do not mean that the Epistles were addressed to the inhabitants of those cities universally—as Dr. Macknight, with an ignorance of Scripture seldom exceeded, and of the character of the apostolic Epistles, has asserted in his note, ch. i. 7, respecting this Epistle—but to the believers who resided in them. *It hath pleased.*—This contribution was not absolutely prescribed to them by the Apostle, but was a free-will offering of their own. The support of the Lord's poor is to proceed from the love of their brethren for Christ's sake. *To make a certain contribution.*—It was a collection in which they shared individually. Each contributed his part. *Poor saints,* or the poor of the saints. The word saints is not only as proper a name for all the disciples of Christ as the word Christian itself, but it is one much more frequently used in the New Testament. Yet in after times the designation of Christian was extended to whole nations, while that of saints, as has been formerly remarked, was limited to a few exalted to that rank on account of supposititious piety, by the act of the Man of Sin.

Ver. 27.—*It hath pleased them verily ; and their debtors they are. For if the Gentiles have been made partakers of their spiritual things, their duty is also to minister unto them in carnal things.*

It hath pleased them verily.—Paul repeats this expression, in order to show the grounds on which he used it. They thought it good to act so, and good reason they had for it. It was, indeed, a matter of their own free will; yet it was one to which they were called by the voice of duty. They were debtors to the Jews for the Gospel. Not only did the kingdom of God first originate with the Jews, but it was through the instrumentality of Jews that the Gentiles received it. They carried it to their doors, and besought them to receive the blessing. From this we may learn the extent of the obligation, and the unity of the body of Christ. The services of any one of the Lord's people lays those who receive them under obligations to the whole family to which they belong. If the Gentiles were under obligation to the Jewish brethren on account of being made partakers of the Gospel through their means, how much more are converts under obligation to those who are personally the means of their conversion. *Spiritual things.*—This phrase denotes the blessings of the Gospel, and communion with God, and everything that concerns the soul and body in their future state, as distinguished from those things that concern the wants of the body, and relate only to this world, which are called carnal things.

Ver. 28.—*When, therefore, I have performed this, and have sealed to them this fruit, I will come by you into Spain.*

When, therefore, I have performed this.—That is, when I shall have finished what I have commenced as to the matter of the contribution. This would be when the poor of the saints at Jerusalem had received the gift of their brethren. *And have sealed to them this fruit.*—Several different interpretations are given of this expression. The meaning appears to be this: fruit means *fruit of the faith of the Gospel.* The contribution of the Gentile churches was a fruit of their faith in Christ. As to the sealing of this fruit, it is to be remarked that a seal was used to stamp anything as genuine, and to distinguish it from a counterfeit. Now this fruit was a convincing evidence that their faith was real, and that the Gentiles had received the Gospel, not in name only, but in truth. The Apostle sealed this fruit, when he exhibited this evidence to the Jewish believers of the faith of their Gentile brethren. Dr. Macknight and Mr. Stuart, with others, understand this sealing as indicating the security, or making sure the contribution to those for whom it was destined. But this gives an unworthy view both of Paul and the Gentile churches. It represents him as personally undertaking the charge or conveyance of this contribution, in order that it might be more securely carried. But surely there were confidential persons in the churches who could have carried the money with as much security as the Apostle himself; and Paul would not indulge such an injurious jealousy with respect to the brethren. He had a higher object in conducting this mission of mercy to the Jewish brethren. By this means he would remove the doubts and disarm the jealousy of the Jews with respect to the Gentiles. No other object could be of sufficient importance to detain Paul from visiting Rome and Spain, but that paramount object of uniting the Jews and Gentiles. Union among Christians we here see even placed before the carrying of the Gospel to new countries.

I will come by you into Spain.—What Paul had stated formerly as a matter of hope, he here states absolutely. An absolute statement, how-

ever, does not necessarily bind by promise, but is only a declaration of
the full intention of the present moment. Men speak absolutely of their
purposes when they are fully resolved to perform them. But sometimes
these purposes it may not be possible to fulfil. A promise is a very
different thing from an absolute declaration. Some persons act like mere
cavilling casuists in explaining duty with respect to this point. If a
person once refuses the thing asked, it is looked on as a breach of truth
if he afterwards yield. But there may be just reason to change his
mind, and his absolute declaration in the negative was only the expression of his mind at the time of utterance. Some speculatists have
held that if a thing be matter of duty, gratitude is not due to the benefactor from him who receives the benefit, nor praise from others on
account of it. This is false morality. To make this contribution was a
duty as to the Gentiles, but it was the duty of the Jews to receive it
with gratitude; and Paul, 2 Cor. ix. 2, praises the performance. ' I
boast of you to them of Macedonia, that Achaia was ready a year ago.'
Some persons would be afraid to bestow a word of commendation on the
most disinterested Christian conduct; but the Apostle does not scruple
to boast of the conduct of Christians. We may here also notice the
condemnation of the false morality of some casuists. They hold it unscriptural, and contrary to the simplicity of the Gospel, to urge people to
duty by any other motive than the love of God. But the Apostle urges
forward the disciples by the zeal of other Christians. In fact, in Scripture, every motive belonging to human nature, as it is the work of God,
is freely employed to urge to duty and deter from sin. The refinement
which refuses any of the weapons that God has employed, is calculated
not to promote but to injure the service of God.

Ver. 29.—*And I am sure that, when I come unto you, I shall come in the fulness*
of the blessing of the Gospel of Christ.

And I am sure.—Dr. Macknight limits this knowledge to the Apostle's
experience. But this limitation is improper. If he knew this, he could
know it only from God. *Fulness of the blessing of the Gospel.*—Paul was
sure that God would give success to the Gospel, and that he would come
in the fulness of this blessing—that is, with the richest measure of this
success. This visit, then, would be fraught with the happiest results to
the Romans. How ought Christian churches to go about all their affairs,
and undertake all their work for the spreading of the kingdom and
truth of Christ, with the most earnest prayers for this blessing! And all
who preach the Gospel ought to look for this as essentially necessary to
their success. Dr. Macknight expounds this, ' I shall come empowered
to bestow on you abundantly the gifts of the Spirit.' This no doubt
was included in the blessing, but it is far from exhausting it. Calvin's
view of the passage, which he mentions as the general one, cannot be
approved. He prefers the intrepretation that makes Paul express the
conviction that he will find the Christians at Rome abounding in good
works. The words have no appearance of expressing such a meaning.
It is the Apostle himself who was to come in the fulness of this blessing.
It is not said that when he should come he would find among them this
blessing.

Ver. 30.—*Now I beseech you, brethren, for the Lord Jesus Christ's sake, and for the love of the Spirit, that ye strive together with me in your prayers to God for me ;*

Now I beseech you, brethren, for the Lord Jesus Christ's sake.—To do everything for the sake of Christ, implies that the thing is agreeable to Christ. It must show love or obedience to Him. We could not be properly required to do anything for Christ's sake which was contrary, or rather which we did not know to be agreeable, to the will of Christ. To pray for one another in our mutual difficulties, is a thing most pleasing and honourable to Christ. But when we are called upon for Christ's sake to assist in the promotion or maintenance of superstition or false religion, or in any way to support or countenance it, we ought to resist and not comply. The votaries of the Romish apostasy have the love of God or of Christ in their mouth continually when they call for assistance in their superstitious works. But the disciples of Christ ought to testify loudly against them, instead of bidding them God speed with their aid. For Christ's sake implies also that those addressed are the people of Christ. They who are not such can do nothing for His sake.

Love of the Spirit.—Some understand this of the love which the Spirit has for Christ's people, and others of the love to one another which the Spirit works in them. The expression is capable in itself of either sense ; and other considerations must determine the preference. Some unite both opinions, which is the most mischievous of all methods of interpretation, as it tends to encourage us in slothfulness with respect to the meaning of Scripture, and to a prostitution of Scripture as implying a sense which it does not truly bear. No passage unites two different senses at once. Yet those who, in interpreting Scripture, attach to it only one meaning, when, according to the best of their judgment, it is the true one, are often loudly accused of dogmatism.

The love of God may be either God's love to us, or our love to God ; and accordingly, in Scripture, it is sometimes used in the one sense, and sometimes in the other. But it never at the same time signifies both. It is always the connection and other circumstances that must determine the meaning. The love of the Spirit here is most probably the love which the Spirit works in His people, which disposes them to love one another. Now, from this principle of pure love, Paul entreats their prayers for himself. Love is not the fruit of the natural heart of man. Men are by nature hateful and hating one another. When sinners believe in Christ, the Holy Spirit produces in their hearts love to one another. This phrase, also, whether it refers to the love which the Spirit produces in believers, or which He has for them, clearly implies His Godhead.

That ye strive together with me in your prayers.—The word here employed signifies the strongest exertion, alluding to the struggle of wrestlers in the games. Prayer, then, is not a formal exercise. This shows the great importance at all times, to the Lord's people, of an ardent spirit of prayer. It is through prayer that the Lord is usually pleased to bestow His favours. He requires to be asked, and asked repeatedly and earnestly, for the things which He has promised to bestow. 'Thus saith the Lord God,'—in promising to confer the greatest blessings,—' I will yet for this be inquired of by the house of Israel to do it for them,' Ezek. xxxvi. 37. *To God*, namely, the Father.—This verse refers to the whole Godhead—the Father, the Son, and the Holy Ghost; and here the distinct personality of the Holy Ghost, His power and influence, are referred to, as in verses 13, 16, and 19. *For me.*—This shows the propriety and importance of prayer for one another. Even the Apostle Paul, with all his distinguishing privileges, deems it a matter of the greatest importance to himself. If Paul needed the prayers of his brethren, who were so far behind him, can they be unimportant to Christ's people in general?

Ver. 31.—*That I may be delivered from them that do not believe in Judea; and that my service which I have for Jerusalem may be accepted of the saints;*

That I may be delivered.—What was the thing for which the Apostle requested the prayers of his fellow-Christians? It was to be delivered from death and danger in the discharge of his work. This shows that, how willing soever we ought to be to sacrifice our lives for Christ's sake, yet that, as far as possible, we ought to desire to preserve life. The Apostle is not ashamed to call on his brethren to unite in the most fervent supplications for his preservation from death, and from the hand of his enemies. How different is this from the language of Ignatius, who seemed rather to call for the prayers of his brethren that he might be honoured with a crown of martyrdom, than to be preserved from his enemies. Christians ought to be willing to give their lives for Christ rather than deny Him or refuse to do any part of His known will. But it is not only lawful but dutiful to take every proper means for their deliverance out of danger. If even an Apostle, in the cause of Christ, was so desirous of preserving life, what shall we think of those who profess a spirit of indifference respecting it, which would wantonly throw it away?

Them that do not believe in Judea.—Paul knew the danger of the visit to his countrymen. He was in greater danger in Jerusalem than in any of the most barbarous heathen countries; yet he did not decline his duty. This is true Christian courage. We ought to take every precaution to preserve our lives, but we ought not to decline duty to save them. We should go forward, and look to God to deliver us out of the hand of them who do not believe. Those who reject the Gospel will always be its enemies, and from such, therefore, the Apostle prays to be delivered. The Gospel declares not only salvation to those who believe, but damnation to all who reject it. It must then be an object of hatred to all who do not believe. And it is remarkable that, while the most debasing superstitions are looked upon with indifference by the wise men of the world, the coolest and most philosophic of their number kindle into wrath against the Gospel. If, then, the Apostle foresaw the danger of this visit to Jerusalem, and if he so strongly desired to be delivered from it, his object of visiting his countrymen must have been exceedingly important.

My service.—Paul was in the highest dignity of the Church of Christ on earth, yet he willingly undertook an office of the most dangerous service for the supply of the temporal wants of his brethren. *For Jerusalem.*—This is another instance of figurative language employed by inspiration. Jerusalem is put for the saints in Jerusalem—the city for the inhabitants, and not all the inhabitants, but certain inhabitants well known to the reader. *May be accepted.*—This seems at first sight very strange. What fear could there be that the supply of the wants of the distressed would not be acceptable to them? Yet Paul makes it a matter of the most earnest prayer for himself and his brethren to whom he writes, that the saints at Jerusalem might be disposed to receive the gift cordially. This, beyond all contradiction, shows how averse the Jews were to the Gentiles, and the reason why the Apostle urged this collection so strongly, and conducted the mission in his own person. Why shall we now expect perfection in knowledge or attainments among the people of God? In the apostolic churches we indeed see none recognised as members but such as were judged to be believers, but they were believers with every degree of weakness, both in knowledge and in character. Calvin understands Paul's doubts with respect to the acceptableness of the gift of the Gentiles, to have reference to prejudice against himself on the part of the believing Jews. But this has no just foundation; and, had this been the fear, the danger could have been easily prevented without exposing Paul to the persecution of the unbelievers. Could not Paul have sent the money by the hands of others? This would have guarded against the supposed prejudice of the brethren in Jerusalem, and have prevented the danger of death with respect to Paul from the hands of unbelieving Jews.

Ver. 32.—*That I may come unto you with joy by the will of God, and may with you be refreshed.*

That I may come unto you with joy.—Dr. Macknight, as well as Calvin, understands this as the result of the prayer, and not as one of the things prayed for. The result of the acceptable reception of the gift would be Paul's joyful visit to Rome. But, most evidently, the words referred to are not the supposed result of the prayer, but are a part of the prayer itself, along with the other things before mentioned. The Apostle besought them not only to pray that the saints at Jerusalem might accept the gift, but, in addition to this, they were desired to pray that he might, after delivering the gift, come to them with joy. It would no doubt be a matter of joy for the Apostle that the gift of which he was the bearer might be well received. But it is not to this solely that he refers, but to joy in general. Dr. Macknight seems to be greatly mistaken when he says, ' How much the Apostle was disappointed in his generous design, and in what disadvantageous circumstances he came to Rome, the history of the Acts informs us.' There is every reason to believe that the gift was well received. He was indeed disappointed with respect to the manner of his coming to Rome, but he might not be disappointed in his joy when he arrived.

From this we may learn that if even on God's errand we have need of prayer for success in our journey, how much more do we need prayer in our own daily business! So much does God encourage the exercise of prayer, that He wills us to pray for success when we do His own work. The whole passage, also, is the strongest refutation of the theory of those who suppose that prayer is useless, because of the unchangeable purposes of God. The express command of the Spirit of inspiration annihilates all the subtle speculations of men on this subject. We here see that it is not only lawful and proper to pray to the unchangeable God, but that it is our duty to pray to Him to prosper us even in His own work. How unlike is God's book to human wisdom!—on every page there shines the evidence of its Divine origin.

By the will of God.—This shows us that all events depend on God's will. Nothing happens without His appointment. All the efforts of his enemies, as well as all the exertions of His servants, only fulfil His irresistible purposes. Without His will, nothing takes place on earth more than in heaven. God not only permits everything that takes place on earth, as some are inclined in this way to soften down His sovereignty, but He wills and appoints it. Calvin well observes on this passage, 'The sentence, *By the will of God*, instructs us in the necessity of devoting ourselves to prayer, since God alone directs all our paths and all our steps by His gracious and unerring providence.'

And may with you be refreshed.—The word literally signifies to recline together in order to mutual rest, and, in a secondary sense, to be refreshed together after fatigue. Here it beautifully expresses that mutual comfort and refreshment which believers, amidst their toils, and dangers, and troubles in the world, enjoy in speaking together of the things of Christ. To reflect on the word of God gives great refreshment, but to reflect on this in company with other Christians is the most heavenly exercise. Dr. Macknight confines the refreshment to the subject of the reconciliation of the Jews with the Gentiles. But it refers to every consolation that might be the object of their conversation about the things of Christ. From this we see that the Apostle had, like other believers, the same need of refreshment from reflection on the word of God, and from intercourse with the brethren. Paul is not ashamed to speak of the refreshment which he expected from the company of the Roman Christians, as well as of that which they should receive from his company.

Ver. 33.—*Now the God of peace be with you all. Amen.*

Now the God of peace be with you all.—In this manner the Apostle concludes this part of his Epistle to the believers at Rome, wishing them the presence and the blessing of *the God of peace.* This expression is used only by Paul in his Epistles, in which he employs it frequently. Peace, in Scripture, signifies generally all kinds of good and prosperity ; as it is said, Isa. xlv. 7, 'I form the light, and create darkness : I make peace, and create evil.' To say, then, that God is the God of peace, is to say that He is the author of every blessing. The Spirit of God calls the good state of the conscience of the believer peace and prosperity, whatever may be his case regarding things external. This peace Jesus promised to His disciples: 'Peace I leave with you, My peace I give unto you : not as the world giveth, give I unto you.' But peace may be taken particularly for the love through which God has reconciled His people to Himself by Jesus Christ, thus expressing the goodness of God revealed in the Gospel. In the Old Testament, God is called *the Lord of Hosts;* but in the New Testament, having made peace by the blood of the cross of His Son, He is pleased to call Himself *the God of peace.* It is this peace which the angel, with the heavenly host, celebrated in saying, ' Glory to God in the highest, and on earth peace, good will toward men.' The Apostles usually express this in their salutations, saying, ' Grace and peace be with you, from God our Father and the Lord Jesus Christ,' uniformly, however, placing grace first, without which they could not have peace. Paul, in here employing this title, *the God of peace,* indicates the free access which His people have to God, and the assurance that their petitions shall be heard ; for what shall they not obtain from Him who has laid aside all His wrath, and breathes towards them only grace and peace ? We see, then, the efficacy of the peace of God, and what consolation believers should experience, and what confidence towards God in their prayers, when they consider that God is the God of peace.

CHAPTER 16
ROMANS 16:1 – 27

Ver. 1.—*I commend unto you Phebe our sister, which is a servant of the church which is at Cenchrea :*

I commend unto you Phebe.—Paul here introduces Phebe to the brethren at Rome. Letters of recommendation were unnecessary for those who derived their credentials specially from the Lord, and who were officially well known to the churches. Paul disclaims the necessity of such letters for himself to the church at Corinth, though at his first visit he needed the introduction of Barnabas to the brethren at Jerusalem. There might be doubts respecting Phebe at Rome, as there were doubts at Jerusalem with respect to Paul, and these could not be removed by mere profession, unsupported by sufficient evidence, whether of her faith, or of his apostleship.

Phebe.—This was the name of the moon, one of the objects of the worship of the heathens. The moon was reverenced by females in honour of the goddess Diana. This person retaining that name shows that there is no necessity to renounce names that have been adopted under heathenism in honour of false gods. There is no necessity to give other names, as Christian names. *Sister.*—The terms brother and sister, taken from human relations, are given to express the new and spiritual relationship which subsists among believers, who by a new nature have become the sons of God and the brethren of Christ. This shows how nearly Christians are related, and how affectionately they ought to love one another. If Christians be all really brethren and sisters, nothing should disunite them in affection. *Which is a servant,* or *deaconess.*—As deacons were appointed to attend to the poor, so deaconesses were specially set apart in the churches in order to attend to the wants of their own sex.

Ver. 2.—*That ye receive her in the Lord, as becometh saints, and that ye assist her in whatsoever business she hath need of you : for she hath been a succourer of many, and of myself also.*

That ye receive her.—The purpose of Paul's recommendation was, that Phebe should be received by the church. *In the Lord.*—That is, that they would receive her as a member of the body of Christ. This shows that none ought to be received into communion by a church but those who are considered as being in the Lord. It shows also that all who are in the Lord ought to be received. The ground of Christian fellowship is union with Christ.

As becometh saints.—Literally, worthily of the saints ; that is, in a manner worthy of the saints. This is usually understood as respecting the receivers,—'in a manner that becomes saints to receive such persons.' But it may respect the received, and signify, ' in a manner worthy of those who are received, viz., the saints.' The latter appears to be the meaning. The word *worthily* applies best to this reference. The saints may be poor and despised, but they belong to the family in heaven ; they are the brethren of the Lord Jesus Christ, and the sons of God. They are therefore worthy of honourable reception by their brethren. *And that ye assist her.*—The saints are not only to receive one another into fellowship and to hospitality, but also they are to pay attention to strangers thus received, assisting them in the business which may have brought them to their place of residence.

For she hath been a succourer of many.—In addition to the general claim, the Apostle enhances the particular claims of Phebe by a reference to her own character. She was a most devoted person, and had exerted herself in assisting the brethren in distress. *Myself also.*—In what way Phebe had ministered to the assistance of the Apostle we are not informed. But she might have many opportunities of relieving him, either by contributing to his support or ministering personally to his comfort. Here we see that, while the Apostle often shows the obligation of the churches and individuals to himself, yet he acknowledges with gratitude the services of all who contributed to his relief.

Ver. 3.—*Greet Priscilla and Aquila my helpers in Christ Jesus.*

Greet Priscilla and Aquila.—The sending of salutations to particular persons or bodies was an indication of peculiar esteem and love. This shows us, in the first place, that in all things not sinful we may comply with the customs of mankind. There is no good, but much evil, in singularity with respect to anything, except such things as God has either forbidden or required. It is only when the authority of Jesus interposes that we are bound to depart from the world. There will be sufficient opportunities of doing this without creating them for ourselves. Singularity in dress or in phraseology has no countenance from the word of God. Christians are to show sobriety in their language and in their dress, but in neither are they to form a fashion of their own. In the second place, we may learn from these salutations that it is not contrary to the universal love which we ought to entertain for the whole household of God, to have a peculiar regard for individuals. Paul singles out individuals from the body in general as peculiar objects of his attentions and remembrance.

My helpers.—Paul is not ashamed to mention those persons, one of whom was a woman, who is here first named, as his helpers in the Gospel. He shows no jealousy about the invasion of his office in their labours to spread the Gospel. To fill any office in a church of Christ belongs only to those whom God has appointed to it ; but to labour in the Gospel, either publicly or privately, is not peculiar to any office—not even to the office of an Apostle, but belongs to every Christian, according to the ability conferred on him by the Head of the Church. Christians are in general to blame for labouring so little in the Lord's service, but they can never be charged with labouring too much. Priscilla and Aquila are styled by the Apostle *fellow-labourers in Christ Jesus.* And there is no doubt that Jesus will acknowledge all those persons as such, whether male or female, whether in office or out of office in his churches, who have laboured to make sinners acquainted with the Gospel of salvation.

Ver. 4.—*Who have for my life laid down their own necks : unto whom not only I give thanks, but also all the churches of the Gentiles.*

Who have for my life laid down their own necks.—We also speak of venturing the neck, or laying down the head ; and both idioms are proverbial expressions, denoting to expose to death in whatever manner it may take place. This expression is proverbial, and is grounded on the manner of taking away the life of criminals on the block. Priscilla and Aquila are said to have laid down their necks, not because they had done so literally, but because they acted in such a manner as to expose their lives to jeopardy. A Christian is not required to substitute himself in the room of another Christian who is condemned to death. For this would be to go beyond the requirement of the law—it would be to love our neighbours better than ourselves. But there may be occasions when it is duty to act in such a manner for the benefit of the brethren, as to hazard life, This we are not to decline. This is what is meant by the Apostle John when he says that ' we ought to lay down our lives for the brethren.'

Unto whom not only I give thanks.—The devoted conduct of this disciple and his wife was nothing but their duty ; yet Paul returns them thanks before all the churches, and all the world. The speculations of some on this subject would banish gratitude as a Christian virtue. To do good to the brethren is duty in all Christians, but to be thankful for good done is equally duty. *But also all the churches of the Gentiles.*— Though the particular instance of exemplary benevolence shown by Priscilla and Aquila towards the Apostle is not recorded, yet no doubt it was well known at the time in all the churches ; and the whole Gentile brethren considered themselves under obligations for the conduct of these two devoted Christians.

Ver. 5.—*Likewise greet the church that is in their house. Salute my well-beloved Epenetus, who is the first-fruits of Achaia unto Christ.*

Likewise greet the church that is in their house.—Besides saluting Priscilla and Aquila, the Apostle sends his salutation to the church which assembled in their house. The same expression respecting the church in the house of Aquila and Priscilla occurs in 1 Cor. xvi. 19. On this passage Calvin remarks : ' It is worthy of observation, that Paul could not confer a more distinguished honour and ornament on this family, than by making mention of the church in their house. I am not satisfied with Erasmus' translation *congregation;* for Paul undoubtedly made an honourable mention of the *church* in this passage.' *Salute my well-beloved* (rather, my beloved) *Epenetus.*—Paul here calls Epenetus his beloved. He loved all Christians; but when he styles any of them his beloved, it imports that they were peculiarly objects of his affection. But to show this, there is no need, with our version, to translate the word *well-beloved,* because the English word *beloved* is as capable as the Greek of expressing such a meaning. This is a distinguished honour to Epenetus. If he was the beloved of Paul, he must have been eminent as a servant of Christ.

First-fruits.—That is, the first converted in the place mentioned. Such persons are called the first-fruits of the place, in allusion to the first-fruits under the law. The first-fruits were offered unto God before any of the harvest was used, which was a setting apart of the rest to the service of man, and a pledge of the harvest. It is here implied to be a peculiar honour to be the first to believe the Gospel in any country or district. This honour is conferred by God in a sovereign way. This shows that, though all believers are equally the purchase of Christ, and that they are all equally washed from sin in His blood, yet that they are not all partakers of equal honours. Here we see, also, that Paul, instead of refusing to give praise to the saints on account of any distinction, avails himself of every opportunity to bring into notice whatever may be creditable to those whom he mentions. *Of Achaia.*—Some, on the authority of certain manuscripts and versions, have substituted Asia for Achaia. The authority, however, does not seem sufficient. The objection, namely, that the household of Stephanas is elsewhere said to be the first-fruits of Achaia, is not applicable, for Epenetus may have been one of that household, and in that case the passages are quite consistent. Besides, the change to Asia may have been adopted in the manuscripts and versions in order to avoid a contradiction which was apprehended from the common reading. *Unto Christ.*—That is, Epenetus was the first-fruits offered or presented to Christ, as the first-fruits under the law were presented unto God. This is a proof of the deity of Christ. If believers are presented as an offering to Christ, He must be God.

Ver. 6.—*Greet Mary, who bestowed much labour on us.*

That is, laboured much in serving us, not, according to Dr. Macknight, who 'laboured *with us,*' in the work of the Gospel. Many women laboured in the Gospel with the Apostle, but that is no reason for forcing this phrase to refer to such. Works of kindness to the Apostle were worthy of approbation as well as the peculiar work of disseminating the Gospel. This shows that every one has a talent, and ought to exercise it in the service of Christ. All are not missionaries or preachers of the Gospel, but all may in some way assist in it.

Ver. 7.—*Salute Andronicus and Junia, my kinsmen, and my fellow-prisoners, who are of note among the Apostles, who also were in Christ before me.*

It is true, indeed, as Dr. Macknight observes, that the Apostle (Rom. ix. 3) calls all the Jews his kinsmen; but as he here distinguishes individuals by this character, it is necessary to understand him as speaking of kindred in a more limited sense. Though every Jew was, in a certain sense, related to Paul, and he calls the whole nation his kinsmen in the sense to which he there refers, yet there would be no propriety in singling out individuals of the nation as related to him who were not so actually. Here, then, we see how desirous the Apostle is to express his consideration of the brethren individually, so far as was in his power. This also recognises the propriety of attachment to kindred. Though all Christians are brethren, yet this does not interfere with the attachment peculiar to the relations which God Himself has established among men. This is of great importance, as it sets aside the speculations of persons who would have us believe that all relations in life must be absorbed by the union of believers in Christ.

My fellow-prisoners.—When, where, or by whom this imprisonment took place, we have no account; yet it is not the less certain. How absurd, then, is it to reason, as many do, as if research were necessary, in order to prove what the Scriptures allege in general terms. It is a distinguished honour to be imprisoned for the cause of Christ. As that which is highly esteemed among men is abomination with God, so this, which is disgraceful in the eyes of men, is the highest honour before God. *Who are of note*, or distinguished.—This is another proof that, though all Christians are equally pardoned and equally justified, God acts as a sovereign in this as in everything else. *Among the Apostles.*—Those persons, from their active co-operation with the Apostles, were well known to them and distinguished among them.

Were in Christ.—To be in Christ is to be a Christian, to be a member of the spiritual body of Christ. This takes place by faith, and in the first moment of believing in Him. *Before me.*—Here priority of conversion to God is reckoned an honour; and Paul, instead of claiming all honours to himself, is solicitous to exhibit what is honourable in every man's situation, and to give the preference to others whenever that preference is due. The Fathers, as they are called, were pious men, but often lamentably deficient in judgment, and generally bad reasoners. From the fact that these persons, Andronicus and Junia, were Christians before Paul, and that they were distinguished among the Apostles, Origen infers that they were of the number of the seventy disciples. This is a conclusion without premises. Such conjectural reasoning imposes on many, as it has the appearance of giving us additional information, and containing nothing contrary to the Scriptures. But it affords a most mischievous precedent for perverting the word of God, and in no instance can it be of any service.

Ver. 8.—*Greet Amplias, my beloved in the Lord.*

This person is another of those distinguished objects of the Apostle's love. Paul loved all the brethren, but for some he had a peculiar affection. Amplias was beloved of Paul in the Lord, as a Christian, or one who was a member of the spiritual body of Christ. Amplias, then, as he was one of the peculiar objects of Paul's love in Christ, must have been distinguished for his devotedness to Christ.

Ver. 9.—*Salute Urbane, our helper in Christ, and Stachys my beloved.*

Paul, as we have before seen, felt no jealousy of others labouring in the Lord, but distinguishes all of them as peculiar objects of his regard. They who endeavour to check the efforts of any of the disciples of Christ, in aiming to save sinners by communicating to them the knowledge of the Gospel, have a spirit very opposite to that of Paul, and are counteracting what he commands. It is worthy of observation, also, that though Paul was an inspired teacher, yet he freely distinguishes the humblest of those who were in any manner engaged in the work of the Gospel as his fellow-labourers. Stachys is one of those whom Paul honours with an expression of peculiar love for Christ's sake. How unlike is the spirit of this Apostle from that of men who, under mistaken notions, regard with coldness, dislike, or jealousy the labours of those who are not called to office in the Church of Christ!

Ver. 10.—*Salute Apelles approved in Christ. Salute them which are of Aristobulus' household.*

Apelles is here distinguished as a tried disciple. It is mentioned to his honour that he was tried and *approved in Christ.* The Lord's people have various and widely diversified characteristics as Christians. The Apostle selects that peculiar trait in the characters of those of whom he writes for which they are severally distinguished. Some of them are tried with peculiar afflictions, and their obedience to their Lord is put to the severest test. When they stand this fiery trial, it is the most distinguished honour, and their trials in the service of Christ ought to be held up to notice. This is due to them from their brethren, and it is a great encouragement to others who are similarly tried. All the Lord's people are not exposed to trials equally severe; and when the Lord calls any of them to glorify His name by suffering peculiarly for His sake, we are here taught to treat them with peculiar honour. How very unfounded, then, and unscriptural, are the views of those who would fear the encouragement of a proud legal spirit, were they to utter a word of praise with respect to the characters of any of the Lord's servants. From perceiving an extreme on one hand, they plunge into the opposite. But they confound things entirely distinct. That praise which a worldly spirit is accustomed to seek or to give, is quite different from that which the Apostle confers. The latter excites to greater devotedness; but the former puffs up, and is quite opposed to the spirit of the Gospel. ' How can ye believe,' says Christ, ' who receive honour one of another? ' Such persons love the praise of men more than the praise of God. But the honour which is given by the Lord's servants, after the example of Paul, is to the honour of the Lord, and for the interest of His cause.

Aristobulus' household.—Aristobulus was evidently a personage of great distinction, who had many domestics, of whom there were some who had believed the Gospel. When the head of the family believed, he was usually saluted, and his household with him. When, therefore, salutations are sent to some of his family or slaves, and not to himself, there is no reason to conclude that Aristobulus was a believer. It is true, as Dr. Macknight suggests, he might have been abroad or dead, but there is no need of such suppositions where no part of the statement implies that he was a believer.

From this we see the sovereignty of God, in calling some of a family and leaving others in unbelief. And we may see the peculiarity of this sovereignty, in calling the slaves and overlooking the master. God does not judge as man judges. It would have been as easy for the Lord Jesus to have called Aristobulus as the meanest of his domestics ; and human wisdom would have given the preference to the master. We see this exemplified in a thousand instances in our own day. Religious parties, in order to advance their interests, often select as their chief patrons and officers the greatest personages who will consent to give them their names, and even though they should be manifest enemies to the Gospel by wicked works. When the Lord has need of the talents of the great, the rich, or the learned, He can convert them, and when He does convert them, they are a blessing for which God ought to be praised ; but some persons choose those whom Christ has not chosen, even the enemies of Christ, for which they will have no praise from their Master.

Ver. 11.—*Salute Herodion my kinsman. Greet them that be of the household of Narcissus, which are in the Lord.*

Salute Herodion my kinsman.—This is another person that Paul acknowledges as a relation, thereby recognising the affection becoming the natural ties of kindred. The household of Narcissus is saluted like that of Aristobulus. Whether this Narcissus was the distinguished favourite of the Emperor Claudius, the Scriptures do not determine, and it, therefore, can be of no importance to be ascertained. It might minister a question to curiosity, and thereby lead away from profitably considering what the Scriptures contain, in order to discover what they do not contain. This is a vain as well as an unprofitable way of spending time. Persons who indulge in it may fancy that they are studying and throwing light upon Scripture, but they are only covering God's word with a heap of rubbish, gratifying an idle curiosity, and tending to draw away attention from the truths of eternal importance which the Scriptures reveal.

Which are in the Lord.—This shows us what sort of persons were recognised in the first churches. They were such only as were believed to be in the Lord, that is, members of the spiritual body of Christ. It shows, also, that persons who at the time appeared to be Christians were considered as such without any distrust with respect to the reality of their faith, though with respect to some the fact might afterwards manifest the contrary. Man judges by evidence, and is warranted to proceed with confidence upon that evidence, though the Searcher of hearts may see the profession to be without the true knowledge of God, or change of heart. This explains the passage in Ezekiel with respect to the righteous turning away from his righteousness ; and the passage in Hebrews, ' If any man draw back, My soul shall have no pleasure in him.'

Ver. 12.—*Salute Tryphena and Tryphosa, who labour in the Lord. Salute the beloved Persis, which laboured much in the Lord.*

Salute Tryphena and Tryphosa, who labour in the Lord.—These were women who laboured in the Gospel. This shows that, while women are excluded from speaking in the church, they are not excluded from labouring in the Gospel. The Lord has not only permitted women to labour in the Gospel, but He has, both in the apostolic and in the present time, singularly blessed their labours. *Beloved Persis.*—She was another woman who employed herself in the service of the Gospel, and is peculiarly distinguished as labouring much in the Lord. Even among the faithful servants of the Lord there is a difference of activity in His service, and the servant who labours much is peculiarly noticed by Paul. As, however, all the good deeds of the Lord's people are done only by the influence of His spirit, none have in themselves ground of boasting.

Ver. 13.—*Salute Rufus chosen in the Lord, and his mother and mine.*

All believers are chosen of God. When Rufus is distinguished as *the chosen*, he must have furnished distinguished evidence of his election. He was *chosen in the Lord*, for none are elected but in Christ. Their election is without regard to merit in themselves : they are chosen in Christ. *His mother and mine.*—The word mother seems to be used in its proper signification in respect to Rufus, and figuratively in its application to Paul. This is a high honour to be so distinguished by the Apostle. This person, it appears, had behaved to the Apostle with the kindness, affection, and tenderness of a mother. This inculcates kindness and attention on the part of Christians towards those who are devotedly labouring in the service of Christ. It may, indeed, be a matter of lamentation that there are few like this woman ; but it is equally a matter of lamentation that there are so few believers who manifest that devotedness which was constantly exhibited by Paul. When the labourers in Christ's vineyard make no sacrifice, they should not expect what is due only to signal devotedness and disinterestedness.

Ver. 14.—*Salute Asyncritus, Phlegon, Hermas, Patrobas, Hermes, and the brethren which are with them.*
Ver. 15.—*Salute Philologus, and Julia, Nereus, and his sister, and Olympas, and all the saints which are with them.*

Here a number of brethren are selected without distinction. This mark of brotherly attention would gratify those whom the Apostle here names, besides the *brethren* who were with them. The Lord's people are not equally distinguished, but they are all brethren equally related to Him who is the Elder Brother of His people. Some of them are eminent, and others are without peculiar distinction. They are all, however, worthy of love. A church is not to consist of the most eminent believers, but of believers, though some be of the lowest attainments. A church of Christ is a school in which their education is to be perfected. *And all the saints which are with them.*—That is, the believers in their families and neighbourhood. These might not be personally known to the Apostle, but as believers they were worthy of his notice.

It might at first sight appear strange that in an inspired letter, which was to be preserved to the end of the world for the edification and instruction of the churches, there should be so much of it taken up with what many might consider as useless ceremony. But as the Apostle was inspired by the Spirit of God in this, as well as in the highest matters, it is evident that we ought to look for instruction from this peculiarity of his writings. This shows the value of inspiration; for were these writings merely human, we should not look for instruction from such things. It shows us that every attention that expresses and promotes love ought to be exhibited among Christians, who should employ the forms and courtesies of social life that manifest respect, in order to show their esteem and affection for one another.

Ver. 16.—*Salute one another with an holy kiss. The churches of Christ salute you.*

From the salutations sent to the brethren, Paul passes to the injunction of a form of salutation to be used among those to whom he wrote. He enjoins them to salute one another with a *holy kiss.* He calls it a holy kiss as distinguished not only from that which is sinful, but also from the kiss that merely expresses common affection. The latter was proper in itself as an expression of kindness among relations or friends; but this is grounded on the love that Christians should have for one another, and is a holy kiss. Much ridicule has been cast on this practice. But it was enjoined on the churches by the Apostles. It is again and again repeated, and was practised by all the primitive churches. Peter calls it a kiss of love. Justin Martyr, in giving an account of the weekly assemblies of the Christians of the second century, says, 'We mutually salute one another by a kiss, and then we bring forward the bread and the cup.' And the form is still maintained by the Church of Rome in what they call the osculum pacis. *The churches of Christ salute you.*—Not only did individuals send salutations to churches or individuals with whom they had a personal acquaintance, but whole churches sent salutations to one another in consideration of their common union in the Lord.

Ver. 17.—*Now I beseech you, brethren, mark them which cause divisions and offences contrary to the doctrine which ye have learned; and avoid them.*

Now I beseech you, brethren.—The churches of Christ have here the most solemn injunction given, in the most earnest manner, with respect to a thing to which at one time or other they will all be found obnoxious. They are warned against the artful attempts of dangerous hypocrites, who, for sinister and interested purposes, endeavour to make divisions in the churches with which they are united. The injunction does not respect the conscientious errors of good men, but the plausible efforts of men who, under the mask of religion, are serving themselves. There is no essential difference, whether the divisions are internal or external—whether they are merely calculated to distract the body to which they belong—or whether they tend to schism or separation in fellowship. Indeed, the most dangerous and mischievous divisions are those which do not call for separation. They eat like a gangrene; and their authors should not be tolerated. Every Christian may profess and follow his own views of the will of his Master without exciting any division in the body of Christ; and even when he is called to separate, to maintain his fidelity to his Lord, this is not dividing the body of Christ, but the most effectual way to promote its union. The motive is not self-interest, or pride, but obedience to the will of God.

Contrary to the doctrine which ye have learned.—The force of the passage lies in this sentence. The factious persons, against whom the Apostle here warns the church to which he writes, are to be watched and guarded against. Their motives are bad, and their efforts are contrary to the Gospel and the doctrine which the Church had already learned; for the Gospel teaches unity among all who believe in the Saviour. They are all one, as united in Christ, the head of the body. Such persons are to be avoided. Men who, from a view of exalting themselves, endeavour to sow division in the Church, are more to be shunned than if they were infected with pestilence; and the brethren who are connected with them ought not, from their confidence in their own stedfastness, to expose themselves to their conversation on such subjects. Such persons are in the service of Satan, who will prevail to deceive the strongest of the people of God, if he obtains permission.

Ver. 18.—*For they that are such serve not our Lord Jesus Christ, but their own belly ; and by good words and fair speeches deceive the hearts of the simple.*

Persons of this description *serve not our Lord Jesus Christ.*—To serve Christ is their profession ; and this profession they may render plausible, but with all its plausibility it is a false profession. They are not doing the Lord's work, for they are disuniting those whom Jesus has united. Instead of serving the Lord, they have a design of making gain by this conduct, which is equally to be condemned, whether they are led by vanity or ambition, or any other selfish motive not sanctioned by the word of God.

No injunction ought to be attended to with more vigilance than this. The evil that is here condemned in the persons denounced by the Apostle is more dangerous than the open profligacy of those who turn away from the truth. No one could be deceived by the openly profane ; but the hypocritical professions of such factious persons is calculated to injure or to destroy the Church of Christ, under the cloak of religion. *And by good words and fair speeches.*—Here the Apostle points out the means which those wicked persons employ to give them success. They use good words and fair speeches. Their soothing address is the bait by which Satan teaches them to ensnare the brethren. Accordingly, the Apostle says that in this manner they *deceive the hearts of the simple.* The authors of heresies have, in general, been remarkable for a winning manner and seductive address ; and thus some of the Lord's people may at least for a time be entangled in their snares. It is quite obvious that the injunction here given is not designed to discountenance Christians from denouncing any error or corruption that may have obtained place among His people. The persons against whom the Apostle warns us are those who, for their own interest or selfish purposes, excite divisions among the brethren. Calvin observes, ' To separate such as agree in the truth of Christ is an impious and sacrilegious divorce; but to defend a conspiracy for promoting lies and impious doctrines, under the pretext of peace and unity, is a shameless calumny. The Papists have no foundation for exciting, by artful guile, an unfavourable impression and low opinion of us believers from this passage, for we do not attack and confute the Gospel of Christ, but the falsehoods of the devil, by which it has hitherto been obscured.'

Ver. 19.—*For your obedience is come abroad unto all men. I am glad therefore on your behalf : but yet I would have you wise unto that which is good, and simple concerning evil.*

For your obedience is come abroad unto all men.—The Apostle intimates here that he gave the believers at Rome these warnings, not from any peculiar jealousy with respect to their liability to err ; on the contrary, he praises them for their ready obedience to the will of God as delineated by his Epistles. Obedience here may indeed respect their reception of the Gospel, which was a matter much spoken of, but it is not to be confined to this. It will apply to their readiness in receiving everything taught by the authority of God. The same authority that requires obedience to the Gospel, requires also obedience to every ordinance and precept. It is the greatest praise to any church or individual to obey cheerfully, with a childlike disposition, whatever the word of God teaches. Many Christians are not teachable, and while they have obeyed the Gospel to salvation, yet use their own wisdom in many other things respecting the institutions of God. They employ subtle and plausible reasonings, by which they impose on themselves and deceive others. This in the end will procure them neither honour nor profit. It will at last be found that he who submits most unreservedly to every tittle of the Divine injunctions, has been the wisest man. Blessed shall that servant be, who, when his Lord comes, shall be found doing His will fully.

The obedience of the Roman Christians had been published most extensively ; and this notice of the fact shows that it is important that the disciples should publicly make a profession of the Gospel, and of every commandment of the Lord. They should not be ashamed either of Him or of His word. They should boldly profess faith in His revealed character in every part of it, and of His ordinances and precepts even in the things most offensive to the world. This is to the honour of their Lord, and is designed as a testimony to men. Christians are not at liberty to decline obedience to anything that the Lord has appointed, out of fear of the reproach of the world. On the contrary, they are to hold forth before all men everything that God hath commanded. This is different from ostentation. To attend to any religious appointment to be seen of men, is the vilest hypocrisy. But to hold forth the will of God in things that the world hates, is true Christian obedience.

I am glad therefore on your behalf.—So far from suspecting the obedience of the brethren at Rome, the Apostle rejoiced concerning them. It was the greatest pleasure to him to hear of their obedience so extensively published. All Christians should imitate the Apostle in this joy. It should be matter of rejoicing to them to hear of believers in every part of the world fully obeying Christ. The disposition which the Apostle here manifests, and of which alone the Lord will approve, is a joy in hearing of Christ being honoured, and the people of Christ advanced in devotedness to His will. We ought to be zealous for every part of our belief with respect to the will of God. But we should be on our guard lest this should arise from any selfish motive, and not solely from love to Christ and Christ's people. Christ cannot be honoured, and His people cannot be profited, when they practise the inventions of men as the appointments of God. And it is hurtful to believers, as well as injurious to the honour of Christ, when His people decline conformity to to any part of His will, either from disaffection to it, or from a desire to avoid the offence of the cross.

But yet I would have you wise unto that which is good.—This is the reason why he warned them against the authors of division. The Apostle wished them to be wise with respect to that which is good. They ought not only to understand the doctrines and ordinances of Christ, but also to be aware of the fact that even in the churches of Christ there would from time to time arise deceivers to lead away the simple. Had they not been warned of this, they might be ready to think that no evil person could ever be found among the disciples, who would thereby be liable to be ensnared by crafty men. *Simple concerning evil.*—Simple here appears to mean not merely *pure*, as Dr. Macknight translates it, but *simple* as opposed to wise. The two words are here evidently contrasted. As to evil, the Apostle wishes the Christians to be without cunning, or dexterity, or skill. In this, it was his desire that they should be quite unknowing and unpractised in the ways of sin.

Ver. 20.—*And the God of peace shall bruise Satan under your feet shortly. The grace of our Lord Jesus Christ be with you. Amen.*

And the God of peace.—After the exhortation which the Apostle had just given to the saints at Rome to maintain peace among themselves, he here designates their heavenly Father, as in the conclusion of the preceding chapter, the God of peace. God is the God of peace, because He it is that is the author of all the peace that His people enjoy. Were it not for the overruling power of the Lord, His people would have no rest at any time in this world. But the Lord Jesus rules in the midst of His enemies, and He gives His people peace in the midst of their enemies. This shows us that we ought constantly to look to God for this peace. If we seek it not, but grow self-confident and secure, dangers and troubles may arise from every quarter. Our only security is God, and our duty is constantly to ask peace of Him in the midst of a world of trouble. God gives His people different gifts; but peace is a blessing which they all need, and without which they can have no happiness. We ought, therefore, constantly to pray for peace to God's people all over the world. We ought to pray for the peace of Jerusalem as our chief joy. Instead of thinking it strange that unbelievers should disturb us, or that Satan should stir up confusion even among Christians, it is owing to almighty power that His people have any peace on earth.

Even in the churches there would be no peace, were it not for God's presence. Such is the cunning of Satan, and the remaining ignorance and corruption of the Lord's people, that Satan would keep them in continual broils, if God did not powerfully counteract him. God is here called the God of peace, with a peculiar reference to the factious persons against whom the believers were warned in the preceding connection. The emissaries of Satan strive to distract the churches; but God—the

God of peace—counteracts their wicked designs. When it is considered that there is so much remaining evil in the best of the children of God, it is amazing that they ever have peace. But it is the presence of God that gives them any degree of peace. Were it not for this, no church could continue one day in peace.

Shall bruise Satan under your feet.—Christ, the seed of the woman, bruised the head of the serpent, and His people will, through Christ, bruise Satan likewise. The word *Satan* signifies adversary. The term *Devil* means calumniator or accuser. He accuses the brethren before God day and night. He is called *Leviathan*, the *Serpent*, the *great Dragon*, the old *Serpent*, the *Tempter*, *Beelzebub*, a *Murderer*, a *Liar*, *Prince of this world*, *Ruler of darkness*, *God of this world*, *Prince of the power of the air*, *Belial*, the *Angel of the bottomless pit*, whose name in the Hebrew tongue is *Abaddon*, but in Greek hath his name *Apollyon*, that is, a destroyer.

The Apostle here encourages the believers to sustain the combat against Satan, their mortal enemy, who does everything in his power to disturb their peace, and to tempt them to all evil. There were two victories to be obtained over Satan. By the first, his head was to be bruised under the feet of Jesus Christ; and by the second, the rest of his body will be bruised under the feet of believers. Of the second of these victories, Paul here speaks. In the first prediction, God speaks as the *Lord of Hosts*, the God of war—' I will put enmity.' The war continues till the bruising of Satan's head has taken place, and his empire is overthrown; and when it is subverted, peace is made, and God is the *God of peace*. As, then, the seed of the woman has bruised the head of the serpent, so His people will, through Christ, likewise bruise Satan. The Apostle says not *we* shall bruise him under our feet, but God shall do it; yet he says not He shall bruise him under His *own* feet, but under *yours*. The victory shall be ours, though wrought by Him; and He shall do it *shortly*. The God of peace shall subdue that grand disturber of our peace, and shall give us perfect victory, and after it endless peace; He shall free us of this trouble and molestation. It is not, then, in our own power that we must encounter this adversary; it is God who bruises him under our feet. ' We wrestle not against flesh and blood, but against principalities, against powers, against the rulers of the darkness of this world, against spiritual wickedness in high places;' and it is only when covered with the armour of God and by His power, that we can overcome enemies so formidable. Dr. Macknight says of the word Satan, that ' Here it is given to the unbelieving Jews, and also to the Judaizing teachers and their adherents, who, for selfish purposes, bred divisions at Rome, ver. 17, and in every church where they could obtain a footing; they are therefore called *ministers of Satan*,' 2 Cor. xi. 15, etc. But it is of Satan himself that the Apostle speaks. Though Satan works by his instruments, yet he truly works; and when his instruments are crushed, he is crushed. Paul wrote this Epistle, and Tertius wrote it,— the one as dictating, the other as amanuensis. But when Paul is said to write the Epistle, we are not to say that Paul means Tertius. Satan works personally in disturbing the churches, though his work is carried on through the instrumentality of men. He excites his emissaries and suggests his devices to them, and they are successful through his artifices.

Shortly.—Some understand this of the final victory that all the Lord's people will obtain at last over Satan and all his emissaries. But though they will not be free from the attacks of this subtle adversary as long as they are in the body, yet from the phrase ' speedily,' or 'shortly,' as well as from the immediate reference to the power of God in the Church, it appears rather to refer to a present victory. The meaning, then, is, that all the churches of Christ are to be hurt by factious people rising up among them, emissaries of Satan, under the cover of religion; and if the Church is not led away by the error of Satan, God, as the God of peace, will shortly deliver them from the malignant influence of this apostate spirit. Satan will not be permitted to harass them continually. It is consistent with God's wisdom to permit Satan to try His people; but when they are sufficiently tried, they are delivered from the temptation. So it was with the Son of God Himself. Satan was for a time permitted to harass Him, but at last he was dismissed. In like manner, churches and individual Christians are all to be tried in various ways; but if they abide the trial, they shall be delivered from the temptation, and, in the most emphatic and extensive sense, they shall all at last bruise Satan under their feet. They shall obtain a complete victory over him in the day of the appearing of their almighty Lord, who will then finally consign him to his awful punishment, and cast him into the lake of fire and brimstone. On that day the full import of this expression will be seen.

The grace of our Lord Jesus Christ be with you.—This form of expression has always been understood to import the deity of Jesus Christ, and justly it has been so understood. It is essentially and necessarily a prayer to our Lord Jesus Christ; and if He is not God, what grace has He to bestow on His people? 'My grace,' said He to Paul when praying to Him, 'is sufficient for thee; for My strength is made perfect in weakness.' It implies that there is a constant supply of grace to be communicated from Christ to His people; and if Christ so communicates His holy influences to His people in all ages, in all countries, to every individual of them, at every instant of time, what can He be but the almighty God? This implies that they who have been bought by the blood of Christ are to be supplied with grace by Him continually, in order to their standing in the truth. All their perseverance is in virtue of this. Of His Church it is said, ' I, the Lord, do keep it; I will water it every moment; lest any hurt it, I will keep it night and day.'

Ver. 21.—*Timotheus my work-fellow, and Lucius, and Jason, and Sosipater, my kinsmen, salute you.*

Timothy was a most devoted servant of the Lord Jesus, more of the same spirit with Paul than any of his other fellow-labourers. The Apostle, instead of designating himself by the superiority of his office with reference to that of Timothy, calls him his work-fellow. How different is this from the conduct of those who seek earthly honours and distinctions as the servants of Christ! All Christians are not alike obedient, and therefore not all equally honoured before God ; but their honour will be revealed in another world, though not in this. The other persons mentioned in this salutation were the kinsmen of the Apostle, whom he thus honourably recognises as his relations.

Ver. 22.—*I Tertius, who wrote this Epistle, salute you in the Lord.*

The Apostle generally employed an amanuensis to write what he dictated. Tertius wrote the Epistle, but it was in all things communicated by Paul, as what Paul communicated was dictated to him by the Holy Ghost. Tertius likewise salutes the brethren. *In the Lord.*—These salutations were not those of mere worldly acquaintance or friendship, but in the Lord, that is, as a member of the body of Christ of which they were members. He might have no acquaintance with any individual among them, yet he was full of affection to them as a Christian brother. That conformity to the world which the Scriptures condemn, is a conformity to things contrary to the law of God. All the innocent customs of society may be imitated by Christ's people without any sin. As the people of the world are accustomed to express good will by their salutations, so the Lord's people ought likewise to show their love by similar expressions. Love ought not only to exist in the heart, but also ought, on proper occasions, to be outwardly expressed. Without this it cannot edify or console those who are its objects. The people of the Lord, then, ought to recognise one another, and express their mutual love in all those ways usual among men.

Ver. 23.—*Gaius mine host, and of the whole church, saluteth you. Erastus the chamberlain of the city saluteth you, and Quartus a brother.*

Gaius was distinguished for Christian hospitality. The Apostle abode in his house at the time of writing this Epistle ; but his hospitality was of the most liberal and extensive kind. He is praised by the Apostle as the host of the whole church. Gaius also sent his salutations to the church at Rome. While Christianity does not destroy the different orders in society, all Christians are brethren, and recognise each other as such, though of different nations and of different ranks.

Erastus the chamberlain of the city.—This is another personage of distinction who sends his salutation to the brethren at Rome. He held an important office in the city where he lived. The Apostle designates him as chamberlain, which might correspond in a good measure to treasurer. But in such cases in most instances no word in one language can be found to correspond perfectly to that of another, because no two countries may have the same modification of offices. The notice of the office of Erastus, although in itself it may appear trifling, is in reality of great importance. It shows us that Christians may hold offices even under heathen governments, and that to serve Christ we are not to be abstracted from worldly business.

Quartus a brother.—The Apostle having no peculiar distinction to notice in this person, calls him a *brother.* This was a common name for all believers, because they are all brethren in Christ. It may at first sight appear superfluous to designate this person by a characteristic belonging to all Christians. But though it belongs to all Christians, yet it is not needlessly expressed. The Apostle directs attention to this circumstance that they are brethren, and that it is a real and important relation. We may know that all Christians are *brethren*, but it is nevertheless useful to be reminded of this, as we may be prone to act towards them in an un-brotherly manner.

Ver. 24.—*The grace of our Lord Jesus Christ be with you all. Amen.*

This important prayer is repeated from ver. 20, which shows us that all repetition is not vain repetition, but that it may mark a thing of peculiar importance. Three times did our Lord employ the same words in His prayer in Gethsemane. And the Apostle, from the abundance of his heart, and his great concern for the Christians at Rome, here within a short compass twice prays that the grace of the Lord Jesus Christ might be with them. Indeed, there is great need of such earnest petitions, for without the constant supply of the grace of Christ we could not abide in Him. Dr. Macknight observes that in the Syriac version this benediction is omitted at the 24th verse, and added at the end of the Epistle. But this has the appearance of human wisdom correcting the language of the Holy Ghost.

Ver. 25.—*Now to Him that is of power to stablish you according to my Gospel, and the preaching of Jesus Christ, according to the revelation of the mystery, which was kept secret since the world began.*

Now to Him that is of power to stablish you.—From this we learn that establishment in the faith is not of ourselves, but of God. It requires the power of Jehovah to establish His people in the truth. So far from being able to bring themselves into the faith of the Gospel, they are not able to continue in it without God. What blindness, then, is it to boast of the power of man to believe and to keep himself in the truth! Power to do anything in the service of God must be communicated from above.

According to my Gospel.—Here we see in what a Christian is to be established, namely, in the faith according to the Gospel. Men may be established in error, they may die for human traditions, and have a zeal of God, but not according to knowledge; but this is of no value. Paul calls the Gospel his Gospel, to intimate that different doctrines would be preached by false teachers as the Gospel. But all other gospels, except that of Paul and the other Apostles, are false. Believers must be established in Paul's Gospel. How many other gospels are now preached as the Gospel of Christ! yet none of them can avail for the salvation of the soul. *And the preaching of Jesus Christ.*—This phrase is not the mere repetition of the same thing. It is indeed the same truth, but in a different point of view. In the one it is considered as the Gospel or good news, and this according to the doctrine of Paul. In the other it is considered as the publication of the truth about Jesus Christ. We are to be stablished according to what the Apostles preached concerning Jesus Christ. Believers have nothing to do with the vain speculations and opinions of men about the way of salvation. They must believe, and ought to be confirmed, in the truth, according as it was originally preached by the Apostles. The preaching of the Gospel is called preaching Jesus Christ, Acts v. 42, who is the subject of the Gospel.

According to the revelation of the mystery.—This is another view of the same truth, but not a mere synonymous expression. The Gospel is here considered as the revelation of a mystery. It was couched in dark figures under the Old Testament dispensation, but is now developed by the Apostles of the Lord. It is first considered as the Gospel, or good news, characterized as the Gospel of Paul; secondly, as the doctrine preached concerning Jesus Christ by those whom He had inspired to reveal and publish it; and, lastly, it is considered as a mystery revealed. In this there is no tautology. It is designed to present the same thing in several different aspects. The word mystery here refers, not, as Dr. Macknight and many others suppose, to the calling of the Gentiles, but to the Gospel itself, which was obscurely revealed in the Old Testament. Calvin, without sufficient ground, states this as a difficulty, but in reality there is no difficulty in it. 'In what sense,' he says, 'Paul calls the Gospel a hidden mystery in this passage, in Eph. iii. 9, and Col. i. 26, is not fully determined even among the learned. The opinion of those who refer it to the calling in of the Gentiles, is the most forcible, to which Paul himself expressly alludes in his Epistle to the Colossians. I grant this to be one, but not the sole cause; for I think there is a greater probability in supposing Paul to have regarded other points of difference between the Old and New Testament.' All these passages use the word mystery with the same reference: none of them represent the calling of the Gentiles to be the mystery, or the reason why the Gospel was called a mystery. It is the Gospel itself which is called a mystery in Eph. iii. 9. The thing hid in God from the beginning of the world, was the plan of salvation through the death of His Son; and the revelation of it by Christ and His Apostles, was making known the manifold wisdom of God in the redemption of His people. In Col. i. 26, it is the Gospel as the word of God that is the mystery. In ver. 27, this mystery is said, by the preaching of the Gospel, to be made known among the Gentiles, just as in the verse before us. The calling of the Gentiles is not called a mystery.

Kept secret since the world began, or, in eternal times; that is, in all preceding eternity.—The common version very well expresses the meaning. The translation of Dr. Macknight, 'the times of the ages,' is an uncouth expression, and founded on views which, as stated by him, are quite fanciful. The mystery kept secret was the hidden sense of the Old Testament dispensation, which all pointed to the kingdom of God, but still left it concealed under various historical, prophetical, and typical representations. The whole of the Old Testament, indicating the truth which is revealed in the New, may properly be termed a parable, the meaning of which is, that it conveys information embodied in an action designed to represent some truth called the moral, or mystery. This method of parabolical instruction, Jesus Christ Himself, as had been predicted, Ps. lxxviii. 2, Matt. xiii. 35, adopted towards the multitude, concealing under it the mysteries to which He referred. When ' His disciples asked Him, saying, What might this parable be?' 'He said, Unto you it is given to know the mysteries of the kingdom of God, but to others in parables, that seeing they might not see, and hearing they

might not understand.' Thus the mystery, or concealed sense of what
He said, was kept secret from them. It is to the Old Testament, taken
as a whole, that our Lord seems to refer when He says, 'Know ye not
this parable, and how then will ye know *all parables?*'

Ver. 26.—*But now is made manifest, and by the scriptures of the Prophets, according to the commandment of the everlasting God, made known to all nations for the
obedience of faith.*

But now is made manifest.—Mr. Stuart construes the words translated
'the scriptures of the Prophets' with 'made manifest,' and translates
thus: 'But is now revealed by the scriptures of the Prophets, according
to the commandment of the eternal God.' But these words, 'the scriptures of the Prophets,' are evidently to be construed with 'made known.'
He observes that 'the Apostle refers to the most ancient times, before
any revelation was given, as the χρονοι αἰώνιοι next to the Messianic
prophecies contained in the Old Testament.' But this is a forced view.
In the text there is no appearance of dividing the times of the Old
Testament dispensation from ancient times. All the times preceding
Christ are included in the words translated in our version, 'since the
world began,' and by Mr. Stuart, 'ancient ages.' The revelation of the
Messiah in the Old Testament could not be spoken of as now revealed.
There was now a new revelation. In the time of the Old Testament, the
mystery of the Messiah was couched in figure and in prophecy. The
Messiah, indeed, was in a certain degree discovered by Moses and the
Prophets, but He was not made manifest. This was done when He Himself appeared. The mystery of Christ and of the Gospel is always spoken
of in the New Testament as being manifested *then*, and not in the former
dispensation. In the same manner, although the bringing in of the
'everlasting righteousness,' namely, the righteousness of God, Rom. i. 17,
was predicted by the Prophet Daniel, ix. 24, and so often made mention
of by Isaiah, yet Isaiah speaks of it as not yet revealed or made manifest,
but as shortly to be so. 'Thus saith the Lord, Keep ye judgment, and
do justice: for My salvation is near to come, and My righteousness to be
revealed,' Isa. lvi. 1. And in accordance with this, Paul, in this Epistle,
ch. i. 17, and iii. 21, declares that *now it is revealed.* 'But now the
righteousness of God without the law is manifested, being witnessed by
the law and the Prophets.' This corresponds with what the Apostle here
announces respecting the manifestation of the mystery of the Gospel.
Until the *Sun of Righteousness* arose, all the testimonies of the Prophets
were as 'a light that shineth in a dark place,' 2 Pet. i. 19; but they
came to be plainly confirmed by the appearing of our Saviour Jesus
Christ, who hath abolished death, and brought life and immortality to
light through the Gospel.

And by the scriptures of the Prophets made known to all nations.—Dr.
Macknight justly construes these words, not with the words 'made manifest,' like Mr. Stuart, but with 'made known.' But as, probably, it did
not appear to him obvious how the mystery was now made known by the
scriptures of the Prophets, he uses violence to evade this sense of the expression. He makes a transposition in translating the words which is
not justifiable, and renders the passage thus: 'But is now made mani-

fest, and by the command of the eternal God, in the prophetic writings, is made known to all the Gentiles, in order to the obedience of faith.' This not only deranges the order of the Apostle's words, but also gives a translation that is not warrantable. He renders the phrase not *through* or *by* the Scriptures, but 'in the Scriptures.' This bends the words of the Apostle to a supposed meaning. But whatever difficulty may appear in the affirmation that the mystery is now made known by the writings of the Prophets, yet as this is what the Apostle has said, our duty is to search for its signification, and not arbitrarily to force on the words a translation which is unnatural. The meaning appears to be, that by the fulfilment of the prophetical writings which had now taken place, such a light was thrown on these writings, that by them the mystery, which was in perfect consistency with their representations, was made known. In the same way the Apostle Peter, besides referring to the voice from heaven, which was heard by him and the other Apostles on the holy mount, appeals to the word of prophecy, not as 'more sure,'—a sense which would be degrading to the apostolic testimony, than which nothing can be more sure,—but as made more firm, or confirmed by its accomplishment. The revelation now made of the mystery of Christ and of the Gospel, by the Apostle, was through the prophetical writings, inasmuch as, though he was as fully inspired as the Prophets themselves, he proved his doctrines by the Scriptures, and pointed to them as containing in prediction what was now accomplished. This is a characteristic feature in the teaching of the Apostles—a feature which to many has appeared strange. In the same way as Paul here declares that the mystery was made known by the scriptures of the Prophets, Peter affirms that the Prophets prophesied of the grace that should come to us.

According to the commandment.—The publication of the Gospel was by God's special command, and by the injunction of God it was to be made known to all nations. Thus the interest of the Gentiles in the salvation of the Gospel is made to rest on the direct authority of God. The Jews were prone to consider the blessings of the Messiah as confined to themselves ; but they had no warrant, or even plausible pretext, for this error, in their own Scriptures. *Of the everlasting God,* or eternal God.—God is distinguished from all besides as eternal. All other objects that have been worshipped, and all other beings, had a beginning. God is without beginning as well as without end. *For the obedience of faith.*—That is, to be believed ; for to believe is to obey the Gospel. The command of the Gospel is to believe in the Lord Jesus Christ. Every one who believes in Him obeys the Gospel.

Ver. 27.—*To God only wise, be glory through Jesus Christ for ever. Amen.*

To God only wise.—There are three different ways in which the words in the original are translated. *God only wise,* according to our version ; or, *the only wise God;* or, *the wise God alone.* Between the first and the second there is only this difference, that the one represents God as the only wise being, and the other as the only wise God. Dr. Macknight's objections to the common version, and his reasons for the adoption of the third translation, do not seem convincing. When God is called the only wise God, it may not imply, as he alleges, that there are some gods who are not wise, but that the character of God, as exhibited in the Scriptures, is the only character that ascribes wisdom in proportion to God. The gods of the heathen are not wise. The god of the Deist is not wise. The god of the Arian is not wise. No view ever given of the Divine character exhibits the infinite wisdom of God in redemption, but that which is found in the Gospel. The expression, ' God only wise,' does not imply, as Dr. Macknight again alleges, that God possesses no perfection but wisdom. It means that God is the only wise being. Yet John, xvii. 3, where the word rendered *God* is similarly situated, seems to favour the second mode of translating the words, as in 1 Tim. i. 17; Jude 25.

Be glory through Jesus Christ for ever. Amen.—All the glory that will redound to God through the ages of eternity, from the salvation of sinners, proceeds through Jesus Christ. Through Him it is manifested. It is through Jesus Christ that we ought to ascribe to God the glory. In Jesus Christ all things are united which are in heaven and which are on earth,—not only saints, but angels. Christ is ' the power of God, and the wisdom of God.' ' God hath shined in our hearts, to give the light of the knowledge of the glory of God in the face of Jesus Christ.' All this shows that Jesus Christ is God, for Christ's work is the glory of the Father, because He is one with Him. In the same way Jude concludes his Epistle—' To the only wise God, our Saviour, be glory and majesty, dominion and power, both now and ever. Amen.'

CONCLUSION

WE are now arrived at the conclusion of this most instructive Epistle, in which our attention is so forcibly drawn to the consideration of 'the deep things of God.' On the one hand, the unbending justice of the infinitely holy God is awfully displayed, appearing like the flaming cherubim which guarded the way to the tree of life, and barred every avenue of hope to man as a transgressor. On the other hand, we behold the Divine compassion abounding in all wisdom and prudence, to the praise of the glory of God's grace, providing the glorious plan of redemption, in which mercy and truth meet together, righteousness and peace embrace each other. The righteousness of God, like the rainbow that was round about the throne, reveals all the glorious attributes of Jehovah, blended, but not confounded, in one harmonious exhibition of unrivalled majesty.

The doctrine of justification by faith in the righteousness of our Lord Jesus Christ, is established by the Apostle in the former part of this Epistle. But it is a doctrine which has in all ages been offensive to the carnal heart. It is equally obnoxious to the profligate and the virtuous, to the fanatic and the rationalist, to the devotee and the philosopher. It lays the pride of man in the dust, pouring contempt upon his boasted strength, and casting down all the lofty imaginations of his own excellence and good works. Therefore it is that with one voice they all cry out, 'This doctrine leads to licentiousness, and makes no sufficient provision for the security of morality and practical religion.' Far different from this was the judgment of the Apostle Paul, guided by the Holy Spirit, whose language he uttered. In this Epistle, the grace of the Gospel is reckoned the only safe and sure foundation for every practical virtue ; and from a view of the love of GOD in the gift of His SON, and of the work of Christ in redemption, believers are urged to every duty. 'I beseech you, therefore, brethren, by the mercies of God,' is the language of Paul at the beginning of the twelfth chapter, 'that ye present your bodies a living sacrifice, holy, acceptable unto God, which is your reasonable service.' Here he does not for a moment entertain the idea that the mercies of God, displayed in the grand doctrines of the Gospel which he had been exhibiting and unfolding, could in any way tend to encourage a continuance in sin. On the contrary, they are the very grounds on which he urges the believing Romans to surrender themselves wholly to the Lord. Paul is often ignorantly accused of teaching principles subversive of morality ; but in the latter part of this Epistle he is as fervent in establishing the necessity of holiness of life and conduct as he had previously been earnest in establishing the great doctrine of justification by faith.

The attributes of God, especially His holiness and justice, when viewed through any other medium than that of the Gospel, strike terror into the heart of man, and lead him, like Adam, to hide himself among the trees of the garden. But these attributes, in themselves so terrible to the guilty, are, through the merciful appointment of the mediation of our heavenly Surety, pledged for the deliverance of the Christian, and for his eternal salvation.

According to the acknowledged constitution of man, love and gratitude are much more effective principles of obedience than the servile spirit of self-righteousness, craving the wages of merit. It consequently happens that all who receive the grace of God in truth are found careful to maintain good works, while the advocates of salvation by works notoriously fail in practice, and frequently indulge the lusts of the flesh. They boast much of practical as opposed to doctrinal religion, and talk of morality and virtue ; but their conduct and pursuits for the most part declare them to be men of this world, living to themselves and not to Christ, delighting in the follies of the world, and actuated by its motives. But the grace of God that bringeth salvation teaches believers to deny ungodliness and worldly lusts, and to live soberly, righteously, and godly in this present world ; looking for that blessed hope, and the glorious appearing of the great God and our Saviour Jesus Christ, who gave Himself for us, that He might redeem us from all iniquity, and purify unto Himself a peculiar people, zealous of good works.

Even among the people of God many are prejudiced against some of the doctrines exhibited in the preceding part of this Epistle. But their prejudices are to be traced to the remains of ignorance and alienation from God, which, through the power of indwelling sin and the busy suggestions of the prince of darkness, still continue to obscure the views of those in whose heart the Spirit of truth has begun to shine. If, however, we appeal to the experience of believers in every age and in every country, it will be found that the more unreservedly and the more simply the Apostle's doctrines are received in all their fulness, the more will they produce of self-abasement, of trust in God, and resignation to His will. What can be more calculated to humble the believer under a sense of his own unworthiness, than the awful picture of the depravity and ruined condition of man presented in the first three chapters ; and what more productive of joy and peace, than the way of recovery disclosed in the fourth, and the contrast presented in the fifth, between the entrance of sin, condemnation, and death, and the free gifts of righteousness, justification, and life ? What more suited to allay fear and distrust, as well as to kindle the liveliest gratitude to God, than the assurance held out in the sixth chapter, that the believer, by union with Christ, is ' dead to sin,'—for ever freed from *guilt* by the death of his Saviour, and with Him made partaker of a new and immortal life, and that sin shall not have dominion over him ? The same encouragement he derives from the seventh chapter. There the grand truth taught in the sixth, of his being *dead to sin*, is illustrated and enforced by the declaration that by the sacrifice of Christ he has ' become dead to the law.' By the law, consequently, he can no longer be condemned ; and the period will shortly arrive, when, from the *pollution* of sin, under which he still groans, the Lord will deliver him.

What can be more fitted to beget confidence in God than the accumulated and ineffable mercies to His people, exhibited in the eighth chapter, in the opening of which, as a corollary from all that had gone before, is announced the assurance that there is 'now *no condemnation* to them which are in Christ Jesus ;' that *in them* the righteousness which the law demands has been, by the Son of God Himself, *fulfilled ;* that they are not in the flesh, but in the spirit, if the Spirit of God dwells in them ; and that, although their bodies, because of sin, of which they have been the instruments, must *die,* their souls, because of the righteousness of their Saviour, now made theirs, are *life,*—not merely alive, but secured in immortal life, to which even their now mortal bodies shall be raised. The spirit of bondage they have exchanged for the spirit of adoption, calling God their Father, while the Spirit Himself beareth witness with their spirits that they are heirs of God and joint-heirs with Jesus Christ. If they now suffer with Him, they shall also be glorified together, while the sufferings they are called to endure are not worthy to be compared with the glory that shall be revealed in them. They groan, indeed, at present, waiting for the redemption of their bodies, for as yet they are only saved in hope ; but they wait with patience for the full enjoyment of their salvation, the Holy Spirit Himself helping their infirmities, and making intercession in their hearts, which, being conformable to the will of God, must always prevail. Having been called according to God's purpose, all things are working together for their good. By Him they were foreknown as the objects of His everlasting love, and predestinated to be conformed to the image of His Son ; and being thus predestinated, they were called by Him and justified, and finally shall be glorified. For them God spared not His own Son, having delivered Him up for them all ; and with Him He will also freely give them all things. Who, then, shall lay anything to the charge of those who are God's elect ? If it is God that justifies, who shall condemn ? If Christ *died,* if He be *risen* again, if He is *seated* at the right hand of God, and if He makes *intercession* for them, no power in heaven, or earth, or hell, shall ever separate them from the love of God, which is in Christ Jesus their Lord.

The unspeakable value of these mercies, is, in the ninth chapter, enhanced by a solemn and practical view of the sovereignty of God in bestowing them, connected with incontrovertible proof that His promises to His people had never failed in their accomplishment. The Divine sovereignty in the choice of the subjects of salvation, is strikingly illustrated in the case of Jacob, whom God loved before he was born. And, on the other hand, His just judgment in punishing those whom He leaves in that sinful state into which all men have fallen, is with equal clearness displayed in His hating Esau before his birth. God, it is asserted, hath mercy on whom He will have mercy, and whom He will He hardeneth. All men are in His hand as clay in the hand of the potter ; and while He endureth with much long-suffering the vessels of wrath fitted to destruction, He makes known the riches of His glory on the vessels of mercy, which He had afore prepared unto glory. The conduct of Israel, and God's particular dealings with His ancient people, are in the tenth chapter next described, while the freeness of salvation by Jesus Christ, who is the end of the law for righteousness to every one that believeth, together with God's purpose that the Gospel shall be preached to the Gentiles, is fully brought into view. In the eleventh chapter, it is proved, in consistency with what had been said in the ninth, that a remnant of Israel, according to the election of grace, were saved, while the rest were blinded. But still, as a nation, Israel is not cast off. As the root was holy, so are the branches, although some were broken off; and the time is approaching when all Israel with the fulness of the Gentiles shall together abundantly experience the mercy of God.

In what prominence and strength of expression is the sovereignty of God exhibited in the above ninth chapter? Is the Apostle ashamed of this view of God? Does he cover it with a veil in treating of the rejection of the Jews? No; in the strongest terms that could be selected, he conspicuously displays it, while both there and in the eleventh chapter he represents the glory of God as the principal object in all things that exist, 'For of Him, and through Him, and to Him, are all things: to whom be glory for ever. Amen.' The wisdom of this world finds the chief end of the existence of all created beings to be the benevolent design of communicating happiness. But the Apostle gives another view of the subject. He declares the glory of God—that is, the manifestation of His perfections—to be the end of creation. Let Christians, then, not be ashamed of this display of the Divine character. Let them rather be ashamed of modifying their views of God by the systems of human science. Let them return to the strong and scriptural statements of the Reformers on the subject, and as little children believe God's account of Himself.

The attentive reader of the preceding part of this Epistle, who is willing to submit to receive in all things the true and obvious meaning of Scripture, cannot fail to perceive that all the doctrines which are there brought before us ascribe the whole glory of everything to God. Jehovah is seen to be glorified in His judgments as well as in His grace, in His wrath as well as in His mercy, in those who are lost as well as in those who are saved. However disagreeable this may be to the natural mind of man, it is truly reasonable. Can there be a higher end than the glory of the Divine character? And can man, who is a fallen and lost creature, share with his offended Sovereign in the glory of his recovery? Such a thought is as incongruous as it is palpably unscriptural. If there be hope for the guilty, if there be recovery to any from the ruins of the fall, it is the voice of reason properly exercised, as well as of the Divine word, that it must come from God Himself.

How astonishing, then, is it that men should be so averse to the doctrines of the Scripture which hold forth this view! So offensive are they to the mind of man, that every effort of ingenuity has been employed by those who understand not the Gospel, to eject them from the Scriptures; and many even of the people of God themselves labour to modify and bring them to a nearer conformity to the wisdom of the world, or, at least, to make them less offensive to human prejudices. This wisdom is foolishness, and is highly dishonourable to God, as well as pernicious to themselves. When God has brought salvation nigh as entirely His gift, and has exhibited Christ as a Saviour, through faith, to the chief of sinners, how injurious is it to the honour of His truth, and to the interests of sinners, to put the salvation of the Gospel at a distance, and, as it were in defiance of the Apostle, to send men to heaven to bring Christ down from above, or to the deep to bring Him up from the grave! What folly appears in that wisdom that sees greater security for the believer's final happiness in making him the author of his own destiny, than in resting the security of his salvation on the power and love of his almighty Saviour! How vain is that wisdom which considers the performance of good works to be better secured by resting them on the resolutions.and faithfulness of the believer himself, than on the fact of his *oneness* with Christ in His death and resurrection!

All who acknowledge regeneration by the Spirit of God, virtually concede the things which they are unwilling to confess in plain and direct statement. If men are by nature dead in sin, surely their new life is not in any sense produced by themselves. If their change from sin to holiness be a new birth, how contradictory to suppose that they have any share in this great change! Yet how many will acknowledge that everything good in us is of God, who will yet labour to show that still there is some remaining moral ability in man to turn himself to God! Is not this to sacrifice to their own wisdom? Will they proudly refuse submission to the declarations of God's word, till they are able to fathom the depths of the Divine counsels?

Many Christians, who admit the truth of all those doctrines which are most offensive to the world, act on the principle that it is wise to conceal their views on these points, or at least to keep them as much as possible in the background. They think in this way to be more useful to the world. But is it wisdom, is it duty, is it consistent with our allegiance to Christ, to keep in abeyance doctrines which so much glorify God, and are so prominently held forth in the Scriptures? Christians should recollect that, although the avoiding of certain offensive doctrines may lessen the prejudice of the world against the professors of Christianity, yet that to turn a sinner to God is in all cases the work of God Himself. How can we then expect a blessing on our efforts if we seek to conceal what He exhibits in a blaze of light? Better, much better in all things, to exhibit the truths of the Divine word just as that word itself exhibits them, and leave the success of our efforts to Him who alone can make them effectual. We cannot by all we can do bring one soul to Christ. We cannot make one sinner alive by the Gospel, more than we can raise the dead out of their graves. Let us then renounce our own wisdom, and our own plans, and let us teach Divine truth as it is taught in the Scriptures.

All religions but that of the Bible divide the glory of recovering men to happiness between God and the sinner. All false views of the Gospel do the same. The Bible alone makes the salvation of guilty men to originate solely with God, and to terminate in His glory as its chief end. This doctrine is peculiar to right views of the Christian religion. Can there, then, be more convincing evidence that the Bible is from God? If such a feature is peculiar to the Christian religion, yet offensive to most who bear the Christian name, it is the most demonstrative evidence that this revelation is not from man. How solid, then, are the foundations of the Christian religion, when the very things belonging to it most offensive to the world afford the most satisfactory evidence that it is from God!

If it be objected that the doctrines which are taught in the first part of this Epistle, while they display God's mercies in those who are saved, also exhibit His severity in condemning those who perish, this, it must be affirmed, cannot derogate from the mercy extended to those on whom He will have mercy. On the contrary, it is enhanced by the consideration of the just punishment which all men would have suffered but for the intervention of that mercy. Thus, in the 136th Psalm, where the mercy of God is so highly celebrated, it is held forth in striking contrast with the destruction of the objects of God's displeasure. ' God delighteth in mercy.' ' His mercy is on them that fear Him, from generation to generation.' ' All the paths of the Lord are mercy and truth unto such as keep His covenant and His testimonies.' And when these ineffable blessings, freely bestowed on believers, are surveyed by them, in connection with Jehovah's awful displeasure against sin, as manifested in His unalterable determination to punish with everlasting destruction from His presence those who were not more guilty than themselves, but to whom, in His unsearchable counsels, He never purposed to extend that sovereign grace which has snatched them like brands from the burning, what a foundation do they lay for their love and gratitude to God! They demonstrate, too, their entire dependence upon God, and constrain them, in the utter abandonment of self-confidence, to embrace Him as their covenant God. But if it be inquired, Why has such a distinction been made, involving consequences of such unspeakable and eternal moment? the only proper answer that can be given is that of our Lord Himself,— ' Even so, Father, for so it seemed good in Thy sight.' Believers, then, are called, in the contemplation of the goodness and severity of God, humbly and thankfully to acknowledge His goodness to themselves. As to others, the answer given to Peter when he asked, What shall this man do? is to them equally apposite,—' What is that to thee? follow thou Me.' Let them be content with the assurance that the Judge of all the earth will do right.

On the mercies of God to His people, displayed in the doctrines taught in the preceding part of the Epistle, the Apostle grounds his exhortations to holiness in the remaining chapters. The intense and burning zeal which Paul there exhibits for the manifestation of holiness in the character and conduct of believers, when viewed in connection with his great doctrine of justification by faith in the atonement of the Son of God, furnishes the strongest evidence of the truth of revelation. No man ever forged this Epistle. It carries its own credentials on the face of it, and shows the broad seal of heaven stamped upon it, as clearly as the heavens and the earth declare that creation is the work of God, and not of an impostor. Who could have forged such a work as this Epistle? For what end could it have been forged? If Antinomians could be supposed to forge the doctrine of justification through the sacrifice of Christ, who was then to forge the precepts which so urgently inculcate all good works? No man could be suspected of writing this Epistle with a view to please the bulk of mankind, or indeed any one considerable class of men. It is as much opposed to the spirit of the multitude, as it is to the pride of the enlightened few. It pleases nobody, and therefore can never be justly suspected of having been originally written in order to please, or in order to effect any sinister purpose.

It is peremptory in its doctrine of obedience to the civil magistrates, and enjoins submission to the higher powers on a footing to which the world was previously a stranger. Yet this cannot be suspected of being a contrivance of magistrates. For while it urges subjection in civil matters to those authorities whom God in His providence has appointed, it condemns as without excuse that idolatry which the existing rulers, at the time when it was written, professed, and for the support of which they persecuted Christians to the death. This can no more be a forgery of the rulers than of the subjects.

There is another peculiarity in the latter part of this Epistle, which evinces admirable wisdom, but a wisdom far removed from the wisdom of man. It contains, in the short compass of a few chapters, an amazing variety of precepts, expressed perspicuously, yet briefly, respecting conduct in domestic life, in society, and in church fellowship. Had uninspired men been discoursing on these various subjects, they would have produced a series of distinct treatises, formally handled, and largely illustrated. In the writings of the Apostle, a single sentence embraces a volume, while this peculiarity differs so widely from any procedure of human wisdom, that it proclaims itself to be the wisdom of God. It is thus that the Scriptures are contained in a comparatively short book, which is addressed to the great body of mankind, and whose contents are inexhaustible.

Yet amidst such careful parsimony of words, amidst such a condensation of matter, the Apostle closes the Epistle with what might seem a most prodigal waste, by sending so many salutations, and expressing, in such a variety of terms, ceremonious attentions to his fellow-Christians at Rome. Here, however, as in other cases, wisdom is justified of her children; for this, also, is one of those characteristics by which God stamps His image on all His productions. The Christian will be at no loss to discover, on reflection, that this part of the Epistle is not without its use; and, in the exposition of the last chapter, it has been a peculiar object to point out how we may reap instruction, from what human wisdom, in its folly, will scarcely admit to be reckoned as a part of that Book, which is nothing less than THE WORD OF GOD.

The doctrines unfolded in this Epistle reveal to us the mighty plan of redemption, by which our powerful spiritual enemies are overcome, and all the strong and deeply-rooted evils lodged within our bosoms shall finally be subdued. The whole leads believers to exclaim,—'The Lord reigneth; let the earth rejoice; let the multitude of isles be glad thereof. Clouds and darkness are round about Him: righteousness and judgment are the habitation of His throne. A fire goeth before Him, and burneth up His enemies round about. The heavens declare His righteousness, and all the people see His glory. Ye that love the Lord, hate evil; He preserveth the souls of His saints; He delivereth them out of the hand of the wicked. Light is sown for the righteous, and gladness for the upright in heart. Rejoice in the Lord, ye righteous; and give thanks at the remembrance of His holiness.' These emphatic words of the Psalmist, though recorded more than a thousand years before the age of the Apostle, most graphically delineate the leading features of Paul's Epistle to the Romans, and portray in vivid colours those emotions in the minds of believers which the consideration of them is so well fitted to produce. And those who have never perused this astonishing portion of the Divine word with a holy relish, and have not entered into its meaning, have never experienced the fulness of that joy and peace which it is calculated to produce in the heart of every true worshipper of the God and Father of our Lord Jesus Christ.

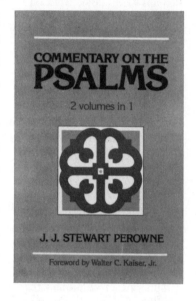